**WELLWARTH, George E.   Themes of drama: an anthology.   T. Y.
   Crowell, 1973. 647p 72-83135. 6.95 pa.   ISBN 0-690-81311-2**
An anthology of drama is hardly a new thing. However, this collection
by Wellwarth has several features that make it out of the ordinary. Organized into six thematic categories (politics, religion, alienation, etc.),
it contains a good mixture of the standard great works of Western
drama and the newer, less universally known plays. Its particular virtue
lies in this second category. Two African plays, Fugard's *The blood
knot* and Nkosi's *The rhythm of violence,* are fine inclusions. Two
Spanish plays, Ballesteros' *The best of all possible worlds* and Ruibal's
The man and the fly, represent another country whose modern drama is
often not recognized. Other choices from such playwrights as Jarry,
Adamov, Richardson, Hochwalder contribute to making this an exciting anthology containing many excellent works that are difficu't to
obtain in an inexpensive form. A good library purchase.

THEMES OF DRAMA

THEMES OF DRAMA:

An Anthology

George E. Wellwarth

State University of New York at Binghamton

Thomas Y. Crowell Company

New York Established 1834

L. C. Card 72-83135
ISBN 0-690-81311-2

MANUFACTURED IN THE UNITED STATES OF AMERICA

A C K N O W L E D G M E N T S

LYSISTRATA. New English Version by Dudley Fitts, copyright, 1954, by Harcourt Brace Jovanovich, Inc., and reprinted with their permission. CAUTION: All rights, including professional, amateur, motion picture, recitation, lecturing, public reading, radio broadcasting, and television are strictly reserved. Inquiries on all rights should be addressed to Harcourt Brace Jovanovich, Inc., 757 Third Avenue, New York, N.Y. 10017.

THE BEST OF ALL POSSIBLE WORLDS, by Antonio Martínez Ballesteros. Translated by Henry Salerno and Sevilla Gross. Reprinted by permission of Kurt Hellmer, Author's Representative, 52 Vanderbilt Ave., N.Y., N.Y. 10017.

THE RHYTHM OF VIOLENCE. Copyright © 1964, Oxford University Press. Reprinted by permission of Lewis Nkosi, c/o IFA.

THE WOULD-BE GENTLEMAN, translated by John Wood. Reprinted by permission of Penguin Books Ltd.

GALLOWS HUMOR, by Jack C. Richardson. Copyright, © 1960 by Jack C. Richardson. Dutton Paperback Edition. Reprinted in its entirety by permission of E. P. Dutton & Co., Inc.

INCIDENT AT TWILIGHT, by Friedrich Dürrenmatt. Translated by George E. Wellwarth. Reprinted by permission of Verlag der Arche, Rosenbuhlstrasse 37, Zurich, Switzerland.

THE BACCHAE. Translated by Philip Vellacott. Reprinted by permission of Penguin Books Ltd.

EVERYMAN. From An Anthology of English Drama before Shakespeare edited with an Introduction by Robert B. Heilman. Introduction copyright 1952 by Robert B. Heilman. Reprinted by permission of Holt, Rinehart and Winston, Inc.

THE HOLY EXPERIMENT, by Fritz Hochwälder. Translated by George E. Wellwarth. Reprinted by permission of Kurt Hellmer, Author's Representative, 52 Vanderbilt Avenue, New York, N.Y.

ANTONY AND CLEOPATRA. Text and notes reprinted from Antony and Cleopatra edited by C. J. Gianakaris. Copyright © 1969 by William C. Brown Company Publishers, and reprinted by permission of the publisher.

ROUND DANCE, by Arthur Schnitzler. Translated by Eric Bentley. Reprinted by permission of Eric Bentley.

MRS WARREN'S PROFESSION. Reprinted by permission of the Society of Authors, as Agent for the Bernard Shaw Estate, 84 Drayton Gardens, London S.W. 10, England.

HENRY IV, translated by Edward Storer. From the Book Naked Masks: Five Plays by Luigi Pirandello, Edited by Eric Bentley. Copyright, 1922, by E. P. Dutton & Co., Inc. Renewal, 1950, in the names of Stefano, Fausto and Lietta Pirandello. Reprinted by permission of publishers.

CARDS OF IDENTITY, by Nigel Dennis. Reprinted by permission of the publisher, The Vanguard Press, from "Two Plays and a Preface" by Nigel Dennis. © 1958, by Nigel Dennis; and by permission of George Weidenfeld & Nicolson Ltd.

THE MAN AND THE FLY, by José Ruibal. Translated by Jean Zelonis. Reprinted by permission of Kurt Hellmer, Author's Representative, 52 Vanderbilt Ave., New York, N.Y.

THE BLOOD KNOT, by Athol Fugard. Copyright © 1963, 1964 by Athol Fugard. Reprinted by permission of The Viking Press, Inc.

KING UBU, Alfred Jarry. Translated by Michael Benedikt and George E. Wellwarth. Reprinted by permission of Michael Benedikt.

ALL AGAINST ALL, by Arthur Adamov. Translated by Donna Kennedy Gildea, © 1953, by Edition Gallimard. Reprinted by permission of the author, Editions Gallimard, and Calder & Boyars Ltd.

OPEN TWENTY-FOUR HOURS. Copyright © 1966, under the title "The Laundromat," by Roger N. Cornish; copyright © 1969, revised and rewritten, by Roger N. Cornish. Reprinted by permission of the author and Samuel French, Inc., 25 W. 45th St., N.Y., N.Y. 10036. CAUTION: Professionals and amateurs are hereby warned that Open Twenty-Four Hours, being fully protected under the copyright laws of the United States of America, the British Empire, including the Dominion of Canada, and all other countries of the Copyright Union, is subject to a royalty. All rights, including professional, amateur, motion pictures, recitation, public reading, radio and television broadcasting, and the rights of translation in foreign languages are strictly reserved. Amateurs may give stage production of this play upon payment of a royalty of $10.00 Dollars for each performance one week before the play is to be given to Samuel French, Inc., at 25 West 45th St., New York, N.Y. 10036, or 7623 Sunset Blvd., Hollywood, Calif., or if in Canada to Samuel French (Canada) Lts., at 27 Grenville St., Toronto, Ont.

PREFACE

In this anthology I have tried to give the reader, as far as possible, new plays for analysis—to avoid the eternal duplication the market abounds with. A certain amount of duplication is, of course, unavoidable since the search for new plays to teach cannot be permitted to become such an obsession that the standard works of dramatic literature are eliminated entirely. But even among the so-called standard playwrights, a degree of leeway is possible. There would be no point in eliminating Shakespeare, Molière, Shaw, and Pirandello from a text anthology of world drama—indeed, doing so would destroy the book's usefulness. But there is no need, either, for offering the same selections from their works. Most teachers should be relieved to find an anthology that does not include *Hamlet*, *Tartuffe*, *Major Barbara*, and *Six Characters in Search of an Author*.

The plays are divided into what I believe to be the six chief thematic categories of drama. That drama reflects society is a truism. It is quite another thing to prove it. The purpose of this book is to demonstrate how some of the principal themes of drama have changed as the social surroundings in which they were written have changed. In each case, the student should be able to see that the form and content of a play is directly attributable to, and is an index of, the social conditions under which the play was written. This should greatly enhance the book's pedagogic value.

In preparing this book, I have been assisted by several people, none of whom should bear the blame for any of the book's eccentricities. I particularly wish to thank Lloyd Scott, my editor; Emanuel Jacquart, my liaison man in France; Robin Hirsch, who, although my student, is quite capable of speaking on equal terms with his teacher; Professor Josef Strelka; and above all Professor Leo Hamalian, my former teacher and now my friend.

G. E. W.

CONTENTS

I. POLITICS

II. SOCIETY

III. RELIGION

IV. LOVE

V. IDENTITY

VI. ALIENATION

I

Politics

THE three plays in this section deal directly with political matters. They are all plays that quite clearly would never have been written but as a response to or a reflection of a specific set of political conditions. In a very indirect sense, though one that is plainly discernible if we look closely enough, all plays are ultimately political: they reflect the society in which they are written. If we stop to think for a moment, it should be evident that the chronicle plays of Shakespeare, which are his directly political plays, could not conceivably have been written in any other place and time, and that this fact has nothing to do with Shakespeare's superiority as either poet or playwright. Had he lived in any other time and place, his poetic genius and his skill as a playwright might have been as great, but the form and tone and content of his plays would have been entirely different.

Since the nature of the society is of such paramount importance, we must ask ourselves what, precisely, causes a society to be the way it is. There are, of course, numerous theories on this subject, most of them in conflict with each other. Most theorists like to talk about a complexity of factors causing the nature of society. Although it is true enough that few things in life lack complexity ("the truth," as Oscar Wilde has advised us, "is rarely pure and never simple"), the complexity of most theories on the nature of society is largely a matter of hedging one's bets: criticisms of the theory can always be answered by pointing to its complexity. Most theories take the social structure as primary, with the political system as an outgrowth of the society, which is itself an organic development of microcosmic forms such as the tribe and family. I should like to suggest here that the political system is primary, and that the nature of society changes at the whim of the rulers.

Man as a species (with some notable though few exceptions, such as artists) tends to be slavish. Slavishness is an outgrowth of laziness, itself a manifestation of the inertia that all matter is subject to. To be active is to swim against the current, and it is an effort that few are willing and fewer still are able to make. The majority simply follow, and are molded into the form desired by their strong men. We should remember that in virtually all societies, present and past, men have had their political systems—and, consequently, their norms of behavior—imposed upon them. Even the so-called democracies of ancient Greece and the twentieth-century Western world have, as a rule, been manipulated from above—to the total satisfaction, for

1

the most part, of the mass: universal suffrage remains an attractive concept that becomes a burden in practice. Men are always happier with the appearance than with the reality, with the theory than with the practice, with the abstract platitudes than with the concrete responsibilities.

In all the plays in this section we can see the process of artists pressing against this inertia. Aristophanes has survived largely because his plays are justly celebrated as extraordinarily witty, ribald farces. In our appreciation of his brilliant humor we often tend to forget that his plays are satires, and the laughter engendered by satire is hollow and bitter. Like all satirists, Aristophanes was an angry man, a fact that in no way detracts from the purity of his humor. His plays are hilariously funny, but we lose much of the point if we forget that they are not only funny in themselves but funny at someone's expense as well. Aristophanes' particular *bête noire* was Cleon, the ruler of Athens in his day. Cleon is a prototypical example of a demagogue, a man whose skill at manipulating the emotions of the masses made him one of the first representatives of that paradoxical being, the democratic dictator. Aristophanes had no use for democracy; he believed in an oligarchy of the intellectual elite. His particular complaint against Cleon, as we can see in *Lysistrata* (411 B.C.), was that he was destroying Athens by leading it into a ruinous war against Sparta. Aristophanes was right of course, as we now know. Perhaps nothing illustrates so well the distance between his society and ours as the fact that Aristophanes was a reactionary peace advocate. His use of the sexual impulse in his plea for peace is a double stroke of genius, for it enables him not only to write a play in the superbly humorous style that later came to be known as Rabelaisian, but also to juxtapose the basic symbols of life (sex) and death (war). If being a nonviolent reactionary shows how far Aristophanes is from us, his dictum "Make love, not war" shows how close he is to us as well.

The straightforward simplicity of Aristophanes' solution is no longer possible in the complex world of today, as we can see in *The Best of All Possible Worlds* (1962) by Antonio Martínez Ballesteros, a contemporary Spanish writer. In this play we see, in broadly and savagely caricatured form, the effect on society and on individual psychology of the modern totalitarian state. It is as well to remember in reading this play that the number of countries in the world today existing either permanently or intermittently under a totalitarian political system far exceeds the number that live under a free— or comparatively free—system. What Ballesteros shows us so sharply here is how life under a totalitarian system degrades the individual and how useless, on the other hand, the alternative to self-degradation (or selling out) is. John Poor's high-minded idealism gets him nowhere and has no effect on anyone. It ruins his life and impoverishes his family, for the world belongs to the maniacal dictators who insanely pin medals on each other in a frenzy of self-gratification.

Lewis Nkosi's depiction of the South African political system and the way its perverted qualities are reflected in the society is one of the best plays to come out of contemporary Africa. Only the Nigerian Wole Soyinka (imprisoned for his artistic activities) equals Nkosi's skill in *The Rhythm of Violence* (1964). That skill consists in keeping a sharp rein on his inevitable partiality. The writer who lets his partiality get out of control writes propaganda, that is, melodrama. Nkosi has the strength to make a distinction between the groups of whites and to imply that peace is possible only through an elimination of color consciousness. At the same time that he shows a hope for the future in his depiction of the interracial relationships of the younger generation, he realistically shows the inevitable result of brutal repression in the explosion at the end. With this he shows that the frustration produced by the bland assumption of superiority on the part of the ruling class has to burst out in violence, as we have often enough seen in real life.

LYSISTRATA

Aristophanes

TRANSLATED BY
Dudley Fitts

CHARACTERS

LYSISTRATA
KALONIKE
MYRRHINE
LAMPITO
CHORUS
MAGISTRATE
KINESIAS
SPARTAN HERALD
SPARTAN AMBASSADOR
A SENTRY
ATHENIAN DRUNKARD

Scene: Athens. First, a public square; later, beneath the walls of the Akropolis; later, a courtyard within the Akropolis. Time: early in 411 B.C.

Until the *éxodos,* the CHORUS is divided into two hemichori: the first, of Old Men; the second, of Old Women. Each of these has its CHORAGOS. In the *éxodos,* the hemichori return as Athenians and Spartans.

The supernumeraries include the BABY SON of Kinesias; STRATYLLIS, a member of the hemichorus of Old Women; various individual speakers, both Spartan and Athenian.

PROLOGUE

Athens; a public square; early morning; LYSISTRATA *sola*

LYSISTRATA: If someone had invited them to a festival—
  Bacchos's, say, or Pan's, or Aphroditê's, or
  that Genetyllis business—, you couldn't get through the streets,
  what with the drums and the dancing. But now,
  not a woman in sight!
                              Except—oh, yes!

Enter KALONIKE

  Here's one, at last. Good
  morning, Kalonikê.
KALONIKE: Good morning, Lysistrata.
                                        Darling,
  don't frown so! You'll ruin your face!
LYSISTRATA: Never mind my face.
  Kalonikê,
  the way we women behave! Really, I don't blame the men
  for what they say about us.
KALONIKE: No; I imagine they're right.
LYSISTRATA: For example: I call a meeting
  to think out a most important matter—and what happens?
  The women all stay in bed!
KALONIKE: Oh, they'll be along.
  It's hard to get away, you know: a husband, a cook,
  a child . . . Home life can be *so* demanding!
LYSISTRATA: What I have in mind is even more demanding.
KALONIKE: Tell me: what is it?
LYSISTRATA: Something big.
KALONIKE: Goodness! *How* big?
LYSISTRATA: Big enough for all of us.
KALONIKE: But we're not all here!
LYSISTRATA: We would be, if *that's* what was up!
                              No, Kalonikê,
  this is something I've been turning over for nights;
  and, I may say, sleepless nights.
KALONIKE: Can't be so hard, then,
  if you've spent so much time on it.
LYSISTRATA: Hard or not,
  it comes to this: Only we women can save Greece!
KALONIKE: Only we women? Poor Greece!
LYSISTRATA: Just the same,
  it's up to us. First, we must liquidate
  the Peloponnesians—
KALONIKE: Fun, fun!
LYSISTRATA: —and then the Boiotians.
KALONIKE: Oh! But not those heavenly eels!
LYSISTRATA: You needn't worry.
  Athens shall have her sea food. —But here's the point:
  If we can get the women from those places
  to join us women here, why, we can save
  all Greece!

KALONIKE: But dearest Lysistrata!
How can women do a thing so austere, so
political? We belong at home. Our only armor's
our transparent saffron dresses and
our pretty little shoes!
LYSISTRATA: That's it exactly.
Those transparent saffron dresses, those little shoes—
well, there we are!
KALONIKE: Oh?
LYSISTRATA: Not a single man would lift
his spear—
KALONIKE: I'll get my dress from the dyer's tomorrow!
LYSISTRATA: —or need a shield—
KALONIKE: The sweetest little negligée—
LYSISTRATA: —or bring out his sword.
KALONIKE: I know where I can buy
the dreamiest sandals!
LYSISTRATA: Well, so you see. Now, shouldn't
the women have come?
KALONIKE: Come? They should have *flown!*
LYSISTRATA: Athenians are always late.
                                    But imagine!
There's no one here from the South Shore.
KALONIKE: They go to work early,
I can swear to that.
LYSISTRATA: And nobody from Acharnai.
They should have been here hours ago!
KALONIKE: Well, you'll get
that awful Theagenês woman: she's been having
her fortune told at Hekatê's shrine.
                              But look!
Someone at last! Can you see who they are?

Enter MYRRHINE *and other women*

LYSISTRATA: People from the suburbs.
KALONIKE: Yes! The entire
membership of the Suburban League!
MYRRHINE: Sorry to be late, Lysistrata.
                              Oh come,
don't scowl so! Say something!
LYSISTRATA: My dear Myrrhinê,
what is there to say? After all,
you've been pretty casual about the whole thing.
MYRRHINE: Couldn't find
my girdle in the dark, that's all.
                              But what *is*
'the whole thing'?
LYSISTRATA: Wait for the rest of them.
KALONIKE: I suppose so. But, look!
Here's Lampitô!

Enter LAMPITO *with women from Sparta*

LYSISTRATA: Darling Lampitô,
  how pretty you are today! What a nice color!
  Goodness, you look as though you could strangle a bull!
LAMPITO: Ah think Ah could! It's the work-out
  in the gym every day; and, of co'se that dance of ahs
  where y' kick yo' own tail.
LYSISTRATA: What lovely breasts!
LAMPITO: Lawdy, when y' touch me lahk that,
  Ah feel lahk a heifer at the altar!
LYSISTRATA: And this young lady?
  Where is she from?
LAMPITO: Boiotia. Social-Register type.
LYSISTRATA: Good morning, Boiotian. You're as pretty as green grass.
KALONIKE: And if you look,
  you'll find that the lawn has just been cut.
LYSISTRATA: And this lady?
LAMPITO: From Korinth. But a good woman.
LYSISTRATA: Well, in Korinth
  anything's possible.
LAMPITO: But let's get to work. Which one of you
  called this meeting, and why?
LYSISTRATA: *I* did.
LAMPITO: Well, then:
  what's up?
MYRRHINE: Yes, what *is* 'the whole thing,' after all?
LYSISTRATA: I'll tell you. —But first, one question.
MYRRHINE: Ask away!
LYSISTRATA: It's your husbands. Fathers of your children. Doesn't it bother
        you
  that they're always off with the Army? I'll stake my life,
  not one of you has a man in the house this minute!
KALONIKE: Mine's been in Thrace the last five months, keeping an eye
  on that General.
MYRRHINE: Mine's been in Pylos for seven.
LAMPITO: And mahn,
  whenever he gets a *dis*charge, he goes raht back
  with that li'l ole speah of his, and enlists again!
LYSISTRATA: And not the ghost of a lover to be found!
  From the very day the war began—
                              those Milesians!
  I could skin them alive!
                    —I've not seen so much, even,
  as one of those devices they call Widow's Delight.
  But there! What's important is: If I've found a way
  to end the war, are you with me?
MYRRHINE: I should *say* so!
  Even if I have to pawn my best dress and
  drink up the proceeds.
KALONIKE: Me, too! Even if they split me
  right up the middle, like a flounder.
LAMPITO: Ah'm shorely with you.
  Ah'd crawl up Taÿgetos on mah knees
  if that'd bring peace.

LYSISTRATA: Then here it is.
  Women! Sisters!
  If we really want our men to make an armistice,
  we must be ready to give up—
MYRRHINE: Give up what?
  Quick, tell us!
LYSISTRATA: But *will* you?
MYRRHINE: We will, even if it kills us.
LYSISTRATA: Then we must give up sleeping with our men. (*Long silence*)
  Oh? So now you're sorry? Won't look at me?
  Doubtful? Pale? All teary-eyed?
                                    But come: be frank with me,
  as I've certainly been with you. Will you do it?
MYRRHINE: I couldn't. No.
  Let the war go on.
KALONIKE: Nor I. Let the war go on.
LYSISTRATA: You, you little flounder,
  ready to be split up the middle?
KALONIKE: Lysistrata, no!
  I'd walk through fire for you—you *know* I would!—but don't
  ask us to give up *that!* Why, there's nothing like it!
LYSISTRATA: And you?
BOIOTIAN: No. I must say *I'd* rather walk through fire.
LYSISTRATA: You little salamanders!
  No wonder poets write tragedies about women.
  All we want's a quick tumble!
                          But you from Sparta:
  if you stand by me, we may win yet! Will you?
  It means so much!
LAMPITO: Ah sweah, it means *too* much!
  By the Two Goddesses, it does! Asking a girl
  to sleep—Heaven knows how long!—in a great big bed
  with nobody there but herself! But Ah'll stay with you!
  Peace comes first!
LYSISTRATA: Spoken like a true Spartan!
KALONIKE: But if—
              oh dear!
                          —if we give up what you tell us to,
  will there *be* any peace?
LYSISTRATA: Why, mercy, of course there will!
  We'll just sit snug in our very thinnest gowns,
  perfumed and powdered from top to bottom, and those men
  simply won't stand still! And when we say No,
  they'll go out of their minds! And there's your peace.
  You can take my word for it.
LAMPITO: Ah seem to remember
  that Colonel Menelaos threw his sword away
  when he saw Helen's breast all bare.
KALONIKE: But, goodness me!
  What if they just get up and leave us?
LYSISTRATA: Well,
  we'd have to fall back on ourselves, of course.
  But they won't.
KALONIKE: What if they drag us into the bedroom?

LYSISTRATA: Hang on to the door.
KALONIKE: What if they slap us?
LYSISTRATA: If they do, you'd better give in.
  But be sulky about it. Do I have to teach you how?
  You know there's no fun for men when they have to force you.
  There are millions of ways of getting them to see reason.
  Don't you worry: a man
  doesn't like it unless the girl co-operates.
KALONIKE: I suppose so. Oh, all right! We'll go along!
LAMPITO: Ah imagine us Spahtans can arrange a peace. But you
  Athenians! Why, you're just war-mongerers!
LYSISTRATA: Leave that to me.
  I know how to make them listen.
LAMPITO: Ah don't see how.
  After all, they've got their boats; and there's lots of money
  piled up in the Akropolis.
LYSISTRATA: The Akropolis? Darling,
  we're taking over the Akropolis today!
  That's the older women's job. All the rest of us
  are going to the Citadel to sacrifice—you understand me?
  And once there, we're in for good!
LAMPITO: Whee! Up the rebels!
  Ah can see you're a good strat*ee*gist.
LYSISTRATA: Well, then, Lampitô,
  let's take the oath.
LAMPITO: Say it. We'll sweah.
LYSISTRATA: This is it.
  —But Lord! Where's our Inner Guard? Never mind. —You see this
  shield? Put it down there. Now bring me the victim's entrails.
KALONIKE: But the oath?
LYSISTRATA: You remember how in Aischylos' *Seven*
  they killed a sheep and swore on a shield? Well, then?
KALONIKE: But I don't see how you can swear for peace on a shield.
LYSISTRATA: What else do you suggest?
KALONIKE: Why not a white horse?
  We could swear by that.
LYSISTRATA: And where will you get a white horse?
KALONIKE: I never thought of that. W*hat* can we do?
MYRRHINE: I have it!
  Let's set this big black wine-bowl on the ground
  and pour in a gallon or so of Thasian, and swear
  not to add one drop of water.
LAMPITO: Ah lahk *that* oath!
LYSISTRATA: Bring the bowl and the wine-jug.
KALONIKE: Oh, what a simply *huge* one!
LYSISTRATA: Set it down; and, women, place your hands on the gift-offering.
  O Goddess of Persuasion! And thou, O Loving-cup!
  Look upon this our sacrifice, and
  be gracious!
KALONIKE: It spills out like blood. How red and pretty it is!
LAMPITO: And Ah must say it smells good.
MYRRHINE: Let me swear first.
KALONIKE: No, by Aphroditê, let's toss for it!

LYSISTRATA: Lampitô: all of you women: come, touch the bowl,
> and repeat after me:
> I WILL HAVE NOTHING TO DO WITH MY HUSBAND OR MY
> LOVER

KALONIKE: *I will have nothing to do with my husband or my lover*

LYSISTRATA: THOUGH HE COME TO ME IN PITIABLE CONDITION

KALONIKE: *Though he come to me in pitiable condition*
> (Oh Lysistrata! This is killing me!)

LYSISTRATA: I WILL STAY IN MY HOUSE UNTOUCHABLE

KALONIKE: I *will stay in my house untouchable*

LYSISTRATA: IN MY THINNEST SAFFRON SILK

KALONIKE: *In my thinnest saffron silk*

LYSISTRATA: AND MAKE HIM LONG FOR ME.

KALONIKE: *And make him long for me.*

LYSISTRATA: I WILL NOT GIVE MYSELF

KALONIKE: *I will not give myself*

LYSISTRATA: AND IF HE CONSTRAINS ME

KALONIKE: *And if he constrains me*

LYSISTRATA: I WILL BE AS COLD AS ICE AND NEVER MOVE

KALONIKE: *I will be as cold as ice and never move*

LYSISTRATA: I WILL NOT LIFT MY SLIPPERS TOWARD THE
> CEILING

KALONIKE: *I will not lift my slippers toward the ceiling*

LYSISTRATA: OR CROUCH ON ALL FOURS LIKE THE LIONESS IN
> THE CARVING

KALONIKE: *Or crouch on all fours like the lioness in the carving*

LYSISTRATA: AND IF I KEEP THIS OATH LET ME DRINK FROM
> THIS BOWL

KALONIKE: *And if I keep this oath let me drink from this bowl*

LYSISTRATA: IF NOT, LET MY OWN BOWL BE FILLED WITH
> WATER.

KALONIKE: *If not, let my own bowl be filled with water.*

LYSISTRATA: You have all sworn?

MYRRHINE: We have.

LYSISTRATA: Then thus
> I sacrifice the victim. (*Drinks largely*)

KALONIKE: Save some for us!
> Here's to you, darling, and to you, and to you! It's all
> for us women. (*Loud cries off-stage*)

LAMPITO: What's all *that* whoozy-goozy?

LYSISTRATA: Just what I told you.
> The older women have taken the Akropolis. Now you, Lampitô,
> rush back to Sparta. We'll take care of things here. And
> be sure you get organized!
>   The rest of you girls,
> up to the Citadel: and mind you push in the bolts.

KALONIKE: But the men? Won't they be after us?

LYSISTRATA: Just you leave
> the men to me. There's not fire enough in the world
> to make me open *my* door.

KALONIKE: I hope so, by Aphroditê!
> At any rate,
> let's remember the League's reputation for hanging on! (*Exeunt*)

PÁRODOS: CHORAL EPISODE

The hillside just under the Akropolis. Enter CHORUS OF OLD MEN
with burning torches and braziers; much puffing and coughing

CHORAGOS ᵐ: Easy, Drakês, old friend! Don't skin your shoulders
with those damnable big olive-branches. What a job!

CHORUS ᵐ: Forward, forward, comrades! Whew!   [STROPHE 1
    The things that old age does to you!
    Neighbor Strymodoros, would you have thought it?
      We've caught it—
              And from women, too!
    Women that used to board with us, bed with us—
    Now, by the gods, they've got ahead of us,
    Taken the Akropolis (Heaven knows why!),
    Profanèd the sacred statuar-y,
          And barred the doors,
         The aggravating whores!

CHORAGOS ᵐ: Come, Philourgos, quick, pile your brushwood
next to the wall there.
         These traitors to Athens and to us,
we'll fry each last one of them! And the very first
will be old Lykôn's wife.

CHORUS ᵐ: By Deméter I swear it—(ouch!),   [ANTISTROPHE 1
    I'll not perform the Kleomenês-crouch!
    How he looked—and a good soldier, too—
      When out he flew,
            that filthy pouch
    Of a body of his all stinking and shaggy,
    Bare as an eel, except for the bag he
    Covered his rear with. Lord, what a mess!
    Never a bath in six years, I'd guess!
         Unhappy Sparta,
        With such a martyr!

CHORAGOS ᵐ: What a siege, friends! Seventeen ranks strong
we stood at the Gate, and never a chance for a nap.
And all because of women, whom the gods hate
(and so does Euripidês).
         It's enough to make a veteran
turn in his medals from Marathon!

CHORUS ᵐ: Forward, men! Just up the hillside,   [STROPHE 2
    And we're there!
    Keep to the path! A yoke of oxen
      Wouldn't care
        To haul this lumber. Mind the fire,
        Or it'll die before we're higher!
         Puff! Puff!
    This smoke will strangle me, sure enough!

    Holy Heraklês, I'm blinded,   [ANTISTROPHE 2
      Sure as fate!
    It's Lemnos-fire we've been toting;
      And isn't it great
        To be singed by this infernal flame?

(Lachês, remember the Goddess: for shame!)
                    Woof! Woof!
         A few steps more, and we're under the roof!
CHORAGOS ᵐ: It catches! It's blazing!
   Down with your loads!
   We'll sizzle 'em now,
   By all the gods!
   Vine-branches here, quick!
   Light 'em up,
   And in through the gate with 'em!
   If that doesn't stop
   Their nonsense—well,
   We'll smoke 'em to Hell.
   Ker*shoo!*
   (What we really need
   Is a grad-u-ate,
   Top of his class,
   From Samos Military State.
   Achoo!)
   Come, do
   Your duty, you!
   Pour out your braziers,
   Embers ablaze!
   But first, Gentlemen, allow me to raise
   The paian:
                    Lady
Victory, now
Assist thine adherents
Here below!
   Down with women!
   Up with men!
   Iô triumphe!
CHORUS ᵐ: Amen!

   Enter CHORUS OF OLD WOMEN *on the walls of the Akropolis, carrying*
   jars of water to extinguish the fire set by the CHORUS OF OLD MEN

CHORAGOS ʷ: Fire, fire!
   Quickly, quickly, women, if we're to save ourselves!
CHORUS ʷ: Nikodikê, run!   [STROPHE
         Or Kalykê's done
         To a turn, and poor Kratylla's
         Smoked like a ham.
                    Damn
         These men and their wars,
         Their hateful ways!
         I nearly died before I got to the place
         Where we fill our jars:
               Slaves pushing and jostling—
               Such a hustling
         I never saw in all my days!

         But here's water as last.   [ANTISTROPHE
         Sisters, make haste
         And slosh it down on them,

The silly old wrecks!
Sex
Almighty! What they want's
A hot bath? Send it down!
And thou, Athenê of Athens town,
Assist us in drowning their wheezy taunts!
O Trito-born! Helmet of Gold!
Help us to cripple their backs, the old
Fools with their semi-incendiary brawn!

The OLD MEN *capture a woman,* STRATYLLIS

STRATYLLIS: Let me go! Let me go!
CHORAGOS ^w: You walking corpses,
have you no shame?
CHORAGOS ^m: I wouldn't have believed it!
An army of women in the Akropolis!
CHORAGOS ^w: So we scare you, do we? Grandpa, you've seen
only our pickets yet!
CHORAGOS ^m: Hey, Phaidrias!
Help me with the necks of these jabbering hens!
CHORAGOS ^w: Down with your pots, girls! We'll need both hands
if these antiques attack us.
CHORAGOS ^m: Want your face kicked in?
CHORAGOS ^w: Want to try my teeth?
CHORAGOS ^m: Look out! I've got a stick!
CHORAGOS ^w: You lay a half-inch of your stick on Stratyllis,
and you'll never stick again!
CHORAGOS ^m: Fall apart!
CHORAGOS ^w: I'll chew your guts!
CHORAGOS ^m: Euripidês! Master!
How well you knew women!
CHORAGOS ^w: Listen to him! Rhodippê,
up with the pots!
CHORAGOS ^m: Demolition of God,
what good are your pots?
CHORAGOS ^w: You refugee from the tomb,
what good is your fire?
CHORAGOS ^m: Good enough to make a pyre
to barbecue you!
CHORAGOS ^w: We'll squizzle your kindling!
CHORAGOS ^m: You think so?
CHORAGOS ^w: Yah! Just hang around a while!
CHORAGOS ^m: Want a touch of my torch?
CHORAGOS ^w: Your torch needs a bath.
CHORAGOS ^m: How about you?
CHORAGOS ^w: Soap for a senile bridegroom!
CHORAGOS ^m: Senile? Hold your trap!
CHORAGOS ^w: Just *you* try to hold it!
CHORAGOS ^m: The yammer of women!
CHORAGOS ^w: The yatter of men!
But you'll never sit in the jury-box again.
CHORAGOS ^m: Gentlemen, I beg you, burn off that woman's hair!
CHORAGOS ^w: Let it come down! (*They empty their pots on the men*)
CHORAGOS ^m: What a way to drown!

CHORAGOS ^w: Hot, hey?
CHORAGOS ^m: Say,
  enough!
CHORAGOS ^w: Dandruff
  needs watering. I'll make you
  nice and fresh.
CHORAGOS ^m: For God's sake, you
  sluts, hold off!

SCENE 1

Enter a MAGISTRATE *accompanied by four constables*

MAGISTRATE: These degenerate women! What a racket of little drums,
  what a yapping for Adonis on every house-top!
  It's like the time in the Assembly when I was listening
  to a speech—out of order, as usual—by that fool
  Demostratos, all about troops for Sicily,
  that kind of nonsense—
                        and there was his wife
  trotting around in circles howling
  Alas for Adonis!—
                        and Demostratos insisting
  we must draft every last Zakynthian that can walk—
  and his wife up there on the roof,
  drunk as an owl, yowling
  Oh weep for Adonis!—
                        and that damned ox Demostratos
  mooing away through the rumpus. That's what we get
  for putting up with this wretched woman-business!
CHORAGOS ^m: Sir, you haven't heard the half of it. They laughed at us!
  Insulted us! They took pitchers of water
  and nearly drowned us! We're still wringing out our clothes,
  for all the world like unhousebroken brats.
MAGISTRATE: And a good thing, by Poseidon!
  Whose fault is it if these women-folk of ours
  get out of hand? We coddle them,
  we teach them to be wasteful and loose. You'll see a husband
  go into a jeweler's. 'Look,' he'll say,
  'jeweler,' he'll say, 'you remember that gold choker
  'you made for my wife? Well, she went to a dance last night
  'and broke the clasp. Now, I've got to go to Salamis,
  'and can't be bothered. Run over to my house tonight,
  'will you, and see if you can put it together for her.'
  Or another one
  goes to a cobbler—a good strong workman, too,
  with an awl that was never meant for child's play. 'Here,'
  he'll tell him, 'one of my wife's shoes is pinching
  'her little toe. Could you come up about noon
  'and stretch it out for her?'
                        Well, what do you expect?

Look at me, for example. I'm a Public Officer,
and it's one of my duties to pay off the sailors.
And where's the money? Up there in the Akropolis!
And those blasted women slam the door in my face!
But what are we waiting for?
                              —Look here, constable,
stop sniffing around for a tavern, and get us
some crowbars. We'll force their gates! As a matter of fact,
I'll do a little forcing myself.

Enter LYSISTRATA, *above, with* MYRRHINE, KALONIKE, *and the* BOIOTIAN

LYSISTRATA: No need of forcing.
Here I am, of my own accord. And all this talk
about locked doors—! We don't need locked doors,
but just the least bit of common sense.
MAGISTRATE: Is that so, ma'am!·
                              —Where's my constable?·
                                        —Constable,
arrest that woman, and tie her hands behind her.
LYSISTRATA: If he touches me, I swear by Artemis
there'll be one scamp dropped from the public pay-roll tomorrow!
MAGISTRATE: Well, constable? You're not afraid, I suppose? Grab her,
two of you, around the middle!
KALONIKE: No, by Pándrosos!
Lay a hand on her, and I'll jump on you so hard
your guts will come out the back door!
MAGISTRATE: That's what *you* think!
Where's the sergeant?—Here, you: tie up that trollop first,
the one with the pretty talk!
MYRRHINE: By the Moon-Goddess!
Just you try it, and you'd better call a surgeon!
MAGISTRATE: Another one!
                    Officer, seize that woman!
                                        I swear
I'll put an end to this riot!
BOIOTIAN: By the Taurian,
one inch closer and you won't have a hair on your head!
MAGISTRATE: Lord, what a mess! And my constables seem to have left me.
But—women get the best of us? By God, no!
                              —Skythians!
Close ranks and forward march!
LYSISTRATA: 'Forward,' indeed!
By the Two Goddesses, what's the sense in *that?*
They're up against four companies of women
armed from top to bottom.
MAGISTRATE: Forward, my Skythians!
LYSISTRATA: Forward, yourselves, dear comrades!
You grainlettucebeanseedmarket girls!
You garlicandonionbreadbakery girls!
Give it to 'em! Knock 'em down! Scratch 'em!
Tell 'em what you think of 'em! (*General mêlée; the Skythians yield*)
                              —Ah, that's enough!
Sound a retreat: good soldiers don't rob the dead!

MAGISTRATE: A nice day *this* has been for the police!
LYSISTRATA: Well, there you are.—Did you really think we women
  would be driven like slaves? Maybe now you'll admit
  that a woman knows something about glory.
MAGISTRATE: Glory enough,
  especially glory in bottles! Dear Lord Apollo!
CHORAGOS ᵐ: Your Honor, there's no use talking to them. Words
  mean nothing whatever to wild animals like these.
  Think of the sousing they gave us! and the water
  was not, I believe, of the purest.
CHORAGOS ʷ: You shouldn't have come after us. And if you try it again,
  you'll be one eye short!—Although, as a matter of fact,
  what I like best is just to stay at home and read,
  like a sweet little bride: never hurting a soul, no,
  never going out. But if you *must* shake hornets' nests,
  look out for the hornets!
CHORUS ᵐ: Good God, what can we do?   [STROPHE
           What are we coming to?
  These women! Who could bear it? But, for that matter, who
             Will find
             What they had in mind
             When they seized Kranaos' city
             And held it (more's the pity!)
  Against us men of Athens, and our police force, too?
CHORAGOS ᵐ: We might question them, I suppose. But I warn you, sir,
  don't believe anything you hear! It would be un-Athenian
  not to get to the bottom of this plot.
MAGISTRATE: Very well.
  My first question is this: Why, so help you God,
  did you bar the gates of the Akropolis?
LYSISTRATA: Why?
  To keep the money, of course. No money, no war.
MAGISTRATE: You think that money's the cause of war?
LYSISTRATA: I do.
  Money brought about that Peisandros business
  and all the other attacks on the State. Well and good!
  They'll not get another cent here!
MAGISTRATE: And what will you do?
LYSISTRATA: What a question! From now on, we intend
  to control the Treasury.
MAGISTRATE: Control the Treasury!
LYSISTRATA: Why not? Does that seem strange? After all,
  we control our household budgets.
MAGISTRATE: But that's different!
LYSISTRATA: 'Different'? What do you mean?
MAGISTRATE: I mean simply this:
  it's the Treasury that pays for National Defense.
LYSISTRATA: Unnecessary. We propose to abolish war!
MAGISTRATE: Good God.—And National Security?
LYSISTRATA: Leave that to us.
MAGISTRATE: You?
LYSISTRATA: Us.
MAGISTRATE: We're done for, then!

LYSISTRATA: Never mind.
We women will save you in spite of yourselves.
MAGISTRATE: What nonsense!
LYSISTRATA: If you like. But you must accept it, like it or not.
MAGISTRATE: Why, this is downright subversion!
LYSISTRATA: Maybe it is.
But we're going to save you, Judge.
MAGISTRATE: I don't *want* to be saved!
LYSISTRATA: Tut. The death-wish. All the more reason.
MAGISTRATE: But the idea
of women bothering themselves about peace and war!
LYSISTRATA: Will you listen to me?
MAGISTRATE: Yes. But be brief, or I'll—
LYSISTRATA: This is no time for stupid threats.
MAGISTRATE: By the gods,
I'm losing my mind!
AN OLD WOMAN: That's nice. If you do, remember
you've less to lose than *we* have.
MAGISTRATE: Quiet, you old buzzard!
Now, Lysistrata: tell me what you're thinking.
LYSISTRATA: Glad to.
                              Ever since this war began
we women have been watching you men, agreeing with you,
keeping our thoughts to ourselves. That doesn't mean
we were happy: we weren't, for we saw how things were going;
but we'd listen to you at dinner
arguing this way and that.
                              —Oh you, and your big
Top Secrets!—
                      And then we'd grin like little patriots
(though goodness knows we didn't feel like grinning) and ask
     you:
'Dear, did the Armistice come up in Assembly today?'
And you'd say, 'None of your business! Pipe down!', you'd say.
And so we would.
AN OLD WOMAN: *I* wouldn't have, by God!
MAGISTRATE: You'd have taken a beating, then!
                                                      —Please go on.
LYSISTRATA: Well, we'd be quiet. But then, you know, all at once
you men would think up something worse than ever.
Even *I* could see it was fatal. And, 'Darling,' I'd say,
'have you gone completely mad?' And my husband would look at me
and say, 'Wife, you've got your weaving to attend to.
'Mind your tongue, if you don't want a slap. "War's
' "a man's affair!" '
MAGISTRATE: Good words, and well pronounced!
LYSISTRATA: You're a fool if you think so.
                                              It was hard enough
to put up with all this banquet-hall strategy.
But then we'd hear you out in the public square:
'Nobody left for the draft-quota here in Athens?'
you'd say; and, 'No,' someone else would say, 'not a man!'
And so we women decided to rescue Greece.
You might as well listen to us now: you'll have to, later.

MAGISTRATE: *You* rescue Greece? Absurd!

LYSISTRATA: You're the absurd one!

MAGISTRATE: You expect me to take orders from a woman?

LYSISTRATA: Heavens, if that's what's bothering you, take my veil,
    here, and my girdle, and my market-basket. Go home
    to your weaving and your cooking! I tell you, 'War's
    a woman's affair!'

CHORAGOS ᵂ: Down with your pitchers, comrades,
    but keep them close at hand. It's time for a rally!

CHORUS ᵂ: Dance, girls, dance for peace!   [ANTISTROPHE
            Who cares if our knees
  Wobble and creak? Shall we not dance for such allies as these?
          Their wit! their grace! their beauty!
          It's a municipal duty
  To dance them luck and happiness who risk their all for Greece!

CHORAGOS ᵂ: Women, remember your grandmothers! Remember, you were
    born
  among brambles and nettles! Dance for victory!

LYSISTRATA: O Erôs, god of delight! O Aphroditê! Kyprian!
  Drench us now with the savor of love!
  Let these men, getting wind of us, dream such joy
  that they'll tail us through all the provinces of Hellas!

MAGISTRATE: And if we do?

LYSISTRATA: Well, for one thing, we shan't have to watch
  you
  going to market, a spear in one hand, and heaven knows
  what in the other.

CHORAGOS ᵂ: Nicely said, by Aphroditê!

LYSISTRATA: As things stand now, you're neither men nor women.
  Armor clanking with kitchen pans and pots—
  you sound like a pack of Korybantês!

MAGISTRATE: A man must do what a man must do.

LYSISTRATA: So I'm told.
  But to see a General, complete with Gorgon-shield,
  jingling along the dock to buy a couple of herrings!

CHORAGOS ᵂ: I saw a Captain the other day—lovely fellow he was,
  nice curly hair—sitting on his horse; and—can you believe it?—
  he'd just bought some soup, and was pouring it into his helmet!
  And there was a soldier from Thrace
  swishing his lance like something out of Euripidês,
  and the poor fruit-store woman got so scared
  that she ran away and let him have his figs free!

MAGISTRATE: All this is beside the point.
                         Will you be so kind
  as to tell me how you mean to save Greece?

LYSISTRATA: Of course!
  Nothing could be simpler.

MAGISTRATE: I assure you, I'm all ears.

LYSISTRATA: Do you know anything about weaving?
  Say the yarn gets tangled: we thread it
  this way and that through the skein, up and down,
  until it's free. And it's like that with war.

We'll send our envoys
up and down, 'this way and that, all over Greece,
until it's finished.

MAGISTRATE: Yarn? Thread? Skein?
Are you out of your mind? I tell you,
war is a serious business.

LYSISTRATA: So serious
that I'd like to go on talking about weaving.

MAGISTRATE: All right. Go ahead.

LYSISTRATA: The first thing we have to do
is to wash our yarn, get the dirt out of it.
You see? Isn't there too much dirt here in Athens?
You must wash those men away.

                    Then our spoiled wool—
that's like your job-hunters, out for a life
of no work and big pay. Back to the basket,
citizens or not, allies or not,
or friendly immigrants!

                         And your colonies?
Hanks of wool lost in various places. Pull them
together, weave them into one great whole,
and our voters are clothed for ever.

MAGISTRATE: It would take a woman
to reduce state questions to a matter of carding and weaving!

LYSISTRATA: You fool! Who were the mothers whose sons sailed off
to fight for Athens in Sicily?

MAGISTRATE: Enough!
I beg you, do not call back those memories.

LYSISTRATA: And then,
instead of the love that every woman needs,
we have only our single beds, where we can dream
of our husbands off with the Army.

                         Bad enough for wives!
But what about our girls, getting older every day,
and older, and no kisses?

MAGISTRATE: Men get older, too.

LYSISTRATA: Not in the same sense.
                         A soldier's discharged,
and he may be bald and toothless, yet he'll find
a pretty young thing to go to bed with.

                         But a woman!
Her beauty is gone with the first grey hair.
She can spend her time
consulting the oracles and the fortune-tellers,
but they'll never send her a husband.

MAGISTRATE: Still, if a man can rise to the occasion—

LYSISTRATA: Rise? Rise, yourself! (*Furiously*)
Go invest in a coffin!
                    You've money enough.
                              I'll bake you
a cake for the Underworld.
                    And here's your funeral
wreath! (*She pours water upon him*)

MYRRHINE: And here's another! (*More water*)
KALONIKE: And here's
my contribution! (*More water*)
LYSISTRATA: What are you waiting for?
All aboard Styx Ferry!
                 Charôn's calling for you!
It's sailing-time: don't disrupt the schedule!
MAGISTRATE: The insolence of women! And to me!
No, by God, I'll go back to court and show
the rest of the Bench the things that might happen to them!

Exit MAGISTRATE

LYSISTRATA: Really, I suppose we should have laid out his corpse
on the doorstep, in the usual way.
                 But never mind!
We'll give him the rites of the dead tomorrow morning!

Exit LYSISTRATA *with* MYRRHINE *and* KALONIKE

CHORAL EPISODE

CHORUS ᵐ: Sons of Liberty, strip off your clothes for action!   [STROPHE 1
Men, arise!
Shall we stand here limp and useless while old Kleisthenês' allies
Prod a herd of furious grandmas to attempt to bring to pass
A female restoration of the Reign of Hippias?
             Forbid it, gods misogynist!
             Return our Treasury, at least!
We must clothe ourselves and feed ourselves to face these civic rages,
And who can do a single thing if they cut off our wages?
CHORAGOS ᵐ: Gentlemen, we are disgraced forever if we allow
these madwomen to jabber about spears and shields
and make friends with the Spartans. What's a Spartan? a wild
wolf's a safer companion any day! No; their plan's
to bring back Dictatorship; and we won't stand for that!
From now on, let's go armed, each one of us
a new Aristogeiton!
             And to begin with,
I propose to poke a number of teeth
down the gullet of that harridan over there.
CHORUS ʷ: Hold your tongues, you senile bravoes, or, I   [ANTISTROPHE 1
swear, when you get home
Your own mothers wouldn't know you! Strip for action, ladies, come!
I bore the holy vessels in my eighth year, and at ten
I was pounding out the barley for Athenê Goddess; then
             They elected me Little Bear
             For Artemis at Brauron Fair;
I'd been made a Basket-Carrier by the time I came of age:
So trust me to advise you in this feminist rampage!
CHORAGOS ʷ: As a woman, I pay my taxes to the State,
though I pay them in baby boys. What do you contribute,
you impotent horrors? Nothing but waste:
our treasury, the so-called Glory of the Persian Wars,

gone! rifled! parceled out for privilege! And you
have the insolence to control public policy,
leading us all to disaster!
                              No, don't answer back
unless you want the heel of my slipper
slap against that ugly jaw of yours!

CHORUS ^m: What impudence!   [STROPHE 2
                              What malevolence!
                              Comrades, make haste,
          All those of you who still are sensitive below the waist!
                              Off with your clothes, men!
                              Nobody knows when
                                   We'll put them back on.
                                   Remember Leipsydrion!
                              We may be old,
                              But let's be bold!

CHORAGOS ^m: Give them an inch, and we're done for! We'll have them
     launching boats next and planning naval strategy.
     Or perhaps they fancy themselves as cavalry!
     That's fair enough: women know how to ride,
     they're good in the saddle. Just think of Mikòn's paintings,
     all those Amazons wrestling with men! No, it's time
     to bridle these wild mares!

CHORUS ^w: Hold on, or   [ANTISTROPHE 2
          You *are* done for,
               By the Two Goddesses above!
     Strip, strip, my women: we've got the veterans on the move!
               Tangle with me, Gramps,
               And you'll have cramps
                    For the rest of your days!
                    No more beans! No more cheese!
               My two legs
               Will scramble your eggs!

CHORAGOS ^w: If Lampitô stands by me, and that elegant
     Theban girl, Ismenia—what good are *you*?
                              Pass your laws!
     Laws upon laws, you decrepit legislators!
     At the worst you're just a nuisance, rationing Boiotian eels
     on the Feast of Hekatê, making our girls go without!
     That was statesmanship! And we'll have to put up with it
     until some patriot slits your silly old gizzards! (*Exeunt omnes*)

SCENE 2

The scene shifts to a court within the Akropolis.
Re-enter LYSISTRATA

CHORAGOS ^w: But Lysistrata! Leader! Why such a grim face?

LYSISTRATA: Oh the behavior of these idiotic women!
     There's something about the female temperament
     that I can't bear!

CHORAGOS ^w: What in the world do you mean?

LYSISTRATA: Exactly what I say.

CHORAGOS ^w: What dreadful thing has happened?
Come, tell us: we're all your friends.
LYSISTRATA: It isn't easy
to say it; yet, God knows, we can't hush it up.
CHORAGOS ^w: Well, then? Out with it!
LYSISTRATA: To put it bluntly,
we're desperate for men.
CHORAGOS ^w: Almighty God!
LYSISTRATA: Why bring God into it?—No, it's just as I say.
I can't manage them any longer: they've gone man-crazy,
they're all trying to get out.
Why, look:
one of them was sneaking out the back door
over there by Pan's cave; another
was sliding down the walls with rope and tackle;
another was climbing aboard a sparrow, ready to take off
for the nearest brothel—I dragged *her* back by the hair!
They're all finding some reason to leave.
Look there!
There goes another one.
—Just a minute, you!
Where are you off to so fast?
FIRST WOMAN: I've got to get home!
I've a lot of Milesian wool, and the worms are spoiling it.
LYSISTRATA: Oh bother you and your worms! Get back inside!
FIRST WOMAN: I'll be back right away, I swear I will!
I just want to get it stretched out on my bed.
LYSISTRATA: You'll do no such thing. You'll stay right here.
FIRST WOMAN: And my wool?
You want it ruined?
LYSISTRATA: Yes, for all I care.
SECOND WOMAN: Oh dear! My lovely new flax from Amorgos—
I left it at home, all uncarded!
LYSISTRATA: Another one!
And all she wants is someone to card her flax.
Get back in there!
SECOND WOMAN: But I swear by the Moon-Goddess,
the minute I get it done, I'll be back!
LYSISTRATA: I say No!
If you, why not all the other women as well?
THIRD WOMAN: O Lady Eileithyia! Radiant goddess! Thou
intercessor for women in childbirth! Stay, I pray thee,
oh stay this parturition! Shall I pollute
a sacred spot?
LYSISTRATA: And what's the matter with *you?*
THIRD WOMAN: I'm having a baby—any minute now!
LYSISTRATA: But you weren't pregnant yesterday.
THIRD WOMAN: Well, I am today!
Let me go home for a midwife, Lysistrata:
there's not much time.
LYSISTRATA: I never heard such nonsense.
What's that bulging under your cloak?
THIRD WOMAN: A little baby boy.

LYSISTRATA: It certainly isn't. But it's something hollow,
  like a basin or— Why, it's the helmet of Athenê!
  And you said you were having a baby!
THIRD WOMAN: Well, I am! So there!
LYSISTRATA: Then why the helmet?
THIRD WOMAN: I was afraid that my pains
  might begin here in the Akropolis; and I wanted
  to drop my chick into it, just as the dear doves do.
LYSISTRATA: Lies! Evasions!—But at least one thing's clear:
  you can't leave the place before your purification.
THIRD WOMAN: But I can't stay here in the Akropolis! Last night I dreamed
  of a snake.
FIRST WOMAN: And those horrible owls, the noise they make!
  I can't get a bit of sleep; I'm just about dead.
LYSISTRATA: You useless girls, that's enough: Let's have no more lying.
  Of course you want your men. But don't you imagine
  that they want you just as much? I'll give you my word,
  their nights must be pretty hard.
                                Just stick it out!
  A little patience, that's all, and our battle's won.
  I have heard an Oracle. Should you like to hear it?
FIRST WOMAN: An Oracle? Yes, tell us!
LYSISTRATA: Quiet, then.—Here
  is what it said:
  IF EVER THE SWALLOWS, ESCHEWING HOOPOE-BIRDS,
  SHALL CONSPIRE TOGETHER TO DENY THEM ALL ACCESS,
  THEIR GRIEF IS FOREVER OVER.
                                These are the words
  from the Shrine itself.   AYE, AND ZEUS WILL REDRESS
  THEIR WRONGS, AND SET THE LOWER ABOVE THE
    HIGHER.
FIRST WOMAN: Does that mean we'll be on top?
LYSISTRATA: BUT IF THEY RETIRE,
  EACH SWALLOW HER OWN WAY, FROM THIS HOLY PLACE,
  LET THE WORLD PROCLAIM NO BIRD OF SORRIER GRACE
  THAN THE SWALLOW.
FIRST WOMAN: I swear, *that* Oracle makes sense!
LYSISTRATA: Now, then, by all the gods,
  let's show that we're bigger than these annoyances.
  Back to your places! Let's not disgrace the Oracle.

> *Exeunt* LYSISTRATA *and the dissident women; the*
> CHORUSES *renew their conflict*

CHORAL EPISODE

CHORUS ᵐ: I know a little story that I learned way back in   [STROPHE
    school
  Goes like this:
  Once upon a time there was a young man—and no fool—
  Named Melanion; and his
  One aversi-on was marriage. He loathed the very thought!

So he ran off to the hills, and in a special grot
Raised a dog, and spent his days
Hunting rabbits. And it says
That he never never never did come home.
It might be called a refuge *from* the womb.
All right,
      all right,
            all right!
We're as pure as young Melanion, and we hate the very sight
Of you sluts!
A MAN: How about a kiss, old woman?
A WOMAN: Here's an onion in your eye!
A MAN: A kick in the guts, then?
A WOMAN: Try, old bristle-tail, just try!
A MAN: Yet they say Myronidês
On hands and knees
Looked just as shaggy fore and aft as I!
CHORUS ᵂ: Well, *I* know a little story, and it's just as   [ANTISTROPHE
   good as yours.
Goes like this:
Once there was a man named Timon—a rough diamond, of course,
And that whiskery face of his
Looked like murder in the shrubbery. By God, he was a son
Of the Furies, let me tell you! And what did he do but run
From the world and all its ways,
Cursing mankind! And it says
That his choicest execrations as of then
Were leveled almost wholly at *old* men.
All right,
      all right,
            all right!
But there's one thing about Timon: he could always stand the sight
Of us 'sluts'!
A WOMAN: How about a crack in the jaw, Pop?
A MAN: I can take it, Ma—no fear!
A WOMAN: How about a kick in the face?
A MAN: You'd show your venerable rear.
A WOMAN: I may be old;
But I've been told
That I've nothing to worry about down there!

SCENE 3

Re-enter LYSISTRATA

LYSISTRATA: Oh, quick, girls, quick! Come here!
CHORAGOS ᵂ: What is it?
LYSISTRATA: A man!
  A man simply bulging with love!
                         O Kyprian Queen,
  O Paphian, O Kythereian! Hear us and aid us!
CHORAGOS ᵂ: Where is this enemy?
LYSISTRATA: Over there, by Deméter's shrine.

CHORAGOS ^w: Damned if he isn't. But who *is* he?
MYRRHINE: My husband.
   Kinesias.
LYSISTRATA: Oh then, get busy! Tease him! Undermine him!
   Wreck him! Give him everything—kissing, tickling, nudging,
   whatever you generally torture him with—: give him everything
   except what we swore on the wine we would not give.
MYRRHINE: Trust me!
LYSISTRATA: I do. But I'll help you get him started.
   The rest of you women, stay back.

Enter KINESIAS

KINESIAS: Oh God! Oh my God!
   I'm stiff for lack of exercise. All I can do to stand up!
LYSISTRATA: Halt! Who are you, approaching our lines?
KINESIAS: Me? I.
LYSISTRATA: A man?
KINESIAS: You have eyes, haven't you?
LYSISTRATA: Go away.
KINESIAS: Who says so?
LYSISTRATA: Officer of the Day.
KINESIAS: Officer, I beg you,
   by all the gods at once, bring Myrrhinê out!
LYSISTRATA: Myrrhinê? And who, my good sir, are you?
KINESIAS: Kinesias. Last name's Pennison. Her husband.
LYSISTRATA: Oh, of course. I beg your pardon. We're glad to see you.
   We've heard so much about you. Dearest Myrrhinê
   is always talking about 'Kinesias'—never nibbles an egg
   or an apple without saying
   'Here's to Kinesias!'
KINESIAS: Do you really mean it?
LYSISTRATA: I do.
   When we're discussing men, she always says,
   'Well, after all, there's nobody like Kinesias!'
KINESIAS: Good God.—Well, then, please send her down here.
LYSISTRATA: And what do *I* get out of it?
KINESIAS: A standing promise.
LYSISTRATA: I'll take it up with her. (*Exit* LYSISTRATA)
KINESIAS: But be quick about it!
   Lord, what's life without a wife? Can't eat. Can't sleep.
   Every time I go home, the place is so empty, so
   insufferably sad! Love's killing me! Oh,
   hurry!

Enter MANES, *a slave, with* KINESIAS' *baby; the voice
of* MYRRHINE *is heard off-stage*

MYRRHINE: But of course I love him! Adore him!—But no,
   he hates love. No. I won't go down.

Enter MYRRHINE, *above*

KINESIAS: Myrrhinê!
   Darlingest little Myrrhinê! Come down quick!
MYRRHINE: Certainly not.
KINESIAS: Not? But why, Myrrhinê?

MYRRHINE: Why? You don't need me.
KINESIAS: Need you? My God, *look* at me!
MYRRHINE: So long! (*Turns to go*)
KINESIAS: Myrrhinê, Myrrhinê, Myrrhinê!
   If not for my sake, for our child! (*Pinches* BABY)
                                    —All right, you: pipe up!
BABY: Mummie! Mummie! Mummie!
KINESIAS: You hear that?
   Pitiful, I call it. Six days now
   with never a bath; no food; enough to break your heart!
MYRRHINE: My darlingest child! What a father *you* acquired!
KINESIAS: At least come down for his sake!
MYRRHINE: I suppose I must.
   Oh, this mother business! (*Exit*)
KINESIAS: How pretty she is! And younger!
   She's so much nicer when she's bothered!

                         MYRRHINE *enters, below*

MYRRHINE: Dearest child,
   you're as sweet as your father's horrid. Give me a kiss.
KINESIAS: Now you see how wrong it was to get involved
   in this scheming League of women. All this agony
   for nothing!
MYRRHINE: Keep your hands to yourself!
KINESIAS: But our house
   going to rack and ruin?
MYRRHINE: I don't care.
KINESIAS: And your knitting
   all torn to pieces by the chickens? Don't you care?
MYRRHINE: Not at all.
KINESIAS: And our vows to Aphroditê?
   Oh, *won't* you come back?
MYRRHINE: No.—At least, not until you men
   make a treaty to end the war.
KINESIAS: Why, if that's all you want,
   by God, we'll make your treaty!
MYRRHINE: Oh? Very well.
   When you've done that, I'll come home. But meanwhile,
   I've sworn an oath.
KINESIAS: Don't worry.—Now, let's have fun.
MYRRHINE: No! Stop it! I said no!·
                            —Although, of course,
   I *do* love you.
KINESIAS: I know you do. Darling Myrrhinê:
   come, shall we?
MYRRHINE: Are you out of your mind? In front of the child?
KINESIAS: Take him home, Manês. (*Exit* MANES *with* BABY)
                      There. He's gone.
                                    Come on!
   There's nothing to stop us now.
MYRRHINE: You devil! But where?
KINESIAS: In Pan's cave. What could be snugger than that?
MYRRHINE: But my purification before I go back to the Citadel?
KINESIAS: There's always the Klepsydra.
MYRRHINE: And my oath?

KINESIAS: Leave the oath to me.
   After all, I'm the man.
MYRRHINE: Well . . . if you say so! I'll go find a bed.
KINESIAS: Oh, bother a bed! The ground's good enough for me!
MYRRHINE: No. You're a bad man, but you deserve something better than
   dirt. (*Exit* MYRRHINE)
KINESIAS: What a love she is! And how thoughtful!

                         Re-enter MYRRHINE

MYRRHINE: Here's your bed.
   Now let me get my clothes off.
                              But, good horrors!
   We haven't a mattress!
KINESIAS: Oh, forget the mattress!
MYRRHINE: No.
   Just lying on blankets? Too sordid!
KINESIAS: Give me a kiss.
MYRRHINE: Just a second. (*Exit* MYRRHINE)
KINESIAS: I swear, I'll explode!

                         Re-enter MYRRHINE

MYRRHINE: Here's your mattress.
   Go to bed now. I'll just take my dress off.
                                     But look—
   where's our pillow?
KINESIAS: I don't need a pillow!
MYRRHINE: Well, *I* do. (*Exit* MYRRHINE)
KINESIAS: I don't suppose even Heraklês
   would stand for this!

                         Re-enter MYRRHINE

MYRRHINE: There we are. Ups-a-daisy!
KINESIAS: So we are. Well, come to bed.
MYRRHINE: But I wonder:
   is everything ready now?
KINESIAS: I can swear to that. Come, darling!
MYRRHINE: Just getting out of my girdle.
                                 But remember, now,
   what you promised about the treaty!
KINESIAS: I'll remember.
MYRRHINE: But no coverlet!
KINESIAS: Damn it, I'll be
   your coverlet!
MYRRHINE: Be right back. (*Exit* MYRRHINE)
KINESIAS: This girl and her coverlets
   will be the death of me.

                         Re-enter MYRRHINE

MYRRHINE: Here we are. Up you go!
KINESIAS: Up? I've been up for ages!
MYRRHINE: Some perfume?
KINESIAS: No, by Apollo!
MYRRHINE: Yes, by Aphroditê!
   I don't care whether you want it or not. (*Exit* MYRRHINE)
KINESIAS: For love's sake, hurry!

Re-enter MYRRHINE

MYRRHINE: Here, in your hand. Rub it right in.
KINESIAS: Never cared for perfume.
   And this is particularly strong. Still, here goes!
MYRRHINE: What a nitwit I am! I brought you the Rhodian bottle!
KINESIAS: Forget it.
MYRRHINE: No trouble at all. You just wait here. (*Exit* MYRRHINE)
KINESIAS: God damn the man who invented perfume!

Re-enter MYRRHINE

MYRRHINE: At last! The right bottle!
KINESIAS: I've got the rightest
   bottle of all, and it's right here waiting for you.
   Darling, forget everything else. Do come to bed!
MYRRHINE: Just let me get my shoes off.
                                      —And, by the way,
   you'll vote for the treaty?
KINESIAS: I'll think about it.

MYRRHINE *runs away*

   There! That's done it! Off she runs,
   with never a thought for the way I'm feeling. I must
   have *some*one, or I'll go mad! Myrrhinê
   has just about ruined me.
                                 And you, strutting little soldier:
   what about you? There's nothing for it, I guess,
   but an expedition to old Dog-fox's bordello.
CHORUS ᵐ: She's left you in a sorry state:
                  You have my sympathy.
            What upright citizen could bear
                  Your pain? I swear, not I!
   Just the look of you, with never a woman
   To come to your aid! It isn't human!
KINESIAS: The agony!
CHORAGOS ᵐ: Well, why not?
            She has you on the spot!
CHORAGOS ʷ: A lovelier girl never breathed, you old sot!
KINESIAS: A lovelier girl? Zeus! Zeus!
            Produce a hurricane
         To hoist these lovely girls aloft
            And drop them down again
         Bump on our lances! Then they'd know
   What they do that makes men suffer so. (*Exit* KINESIAS)

SCENE 4

Enter a SPARTAN HERALD

HERALD: Gentlemen, Ah beg you will be so kind
   as to direct me to the Central Committee.
   Ah have a communication.

Re-enter MAGISTRATE

MAGISTRATE: Are you a man,
  or a fertility symbol?
HERALD: Ah refuse to answer that question!
  Ah'm a certified herald from Spahta, and Ah've come
  to talk about an ahmistice.
MAGISTRATE: Then why
  that spear under your cloak?
HERALD: Ah have no speah!
MAGISTRATE: You don't walk naturally, with your tunic
  poked out so. You have a tumor, maybe,
  or a hernia?
HERALD: No, by Kastor!
MAGISTRATE: Well,
  something's wrong, I can see that. And I don't like it.
HERALD: Colonel, Ah resent this.
MAGISTRATE: So I see. But what *is* it?
HERALD: A scroll
  with a message from Spahta.
MAGISTRATE: Oh. I've heard about these scrolls.
  Well, then, man, speak out: How are things in Sparta?
HERALD: Hard, Colonel, hard! We're at a standstill.
  Can't seem to think of anything but women.
MAGISTRATE: How curious! Tell me, do you Spartans think
  that maybe Pan's to blame?
HERALD: Pan? No. Lampitô and her little naked friends.
  They won't let a man come near them.
MAGISTRATE: How are you handling it?
HERALD: Losing our minds,
  if you want to know, and walking around hunched over
  like men carrying candles in a gale.
  The women have sworn they'll have nothing to do with us
  until we get a treaty.
MAGISTRATE: Yes. I know.
  It's a general uprising, sir, in all parts of Greece.
  But as for the answer—
                Sir: go back to Sparta
  and have them send us your Armistice Commission.
  I'll arrange things in Athens.
                    And I may say
  that my standing is good enough to make them listen.
HERALD: A man after mah own heart! Sir, Ah thank you! (*Exit* HERALD)

CHORAL EPISODE

CHORUS ᵐ: Oh these women! Where will you find   [STROPHE
            A slavering beast that's more unkind?
              Where a hotter fire?
            Give me a panther, any day!
            He's not so merciless as they,
              And panthers don't conspire!
CHORUS ʷ: We may be hard, you silly old ass,   [ANTISTROPHE
            But who brought you to this stupid pass?
              You're the ones to blame.

          Fighting with us, your oldest friends,
          Simply to serve your selfish ends—
            Really, you have no shame!

CHORAGOS ᵐ: No, I'm through with women for ever!

CHORAGOS ʷ: If you say so.
  Still, you might put some clothes on. You look too absurd
  standing around naked. Come, get into this cloak.

CHORAGOS ᵐ: Thank you; you're right. I merely took it off
  because I was in such a temper.

CHORAGOS ʷ: That's much better

  Now you resemble a man again.
                           Why have you been so horrid?
  And look: there's some sort of insect in your eye!
  Shall I take it out?

CHORAGOS ᵐ: An insect, is it? So that's
  what's been bothering me! Lord, yes: take it out!

CHORAGOS ʷ: You might be more polite.
                               —But, heavens!
  What an enormous gnat!

CHORAGOS ᵐ: You've saved my life.
  That gnat was drilling an artesian well
  in my left eye.

CHORAGOS ʷ: Let me wipe
  those tears away!—And now: one little kiss?

CHORAGOS ᵐ: Over my dead body!

CHORAGOS ʷ: You're so difficult!

CHORAGOS ᵐ: These impossible women! How they do get around us!
  The poet was right: Can't live with them, or without them!
  But let's be friends.
  And to celebrate, you might lead off with an Ode.

CHORUS ʷ: Let it never be said   [STROPHE
          That my tongue is malicious:
          Both by word and by deed
  I would set an example that's noble and gracious.
          We've had sorrow and care
          Till we're sick of the tune.
          Is there anyone here
          Who would like a small loan?
            My purse is crammed,
            As you'll soon find;
  And you needn't pay me back if the Peace gets signed!
          I've invited to lunch
          Some Karystian rips—
          An esurient bunch,
  But I've ordered a menu to water their lips!
          I can still make soup
          And slaughter a pig.
          You're all coming, I hope?
          But a bath first, I beg!
           Walk right up
           As though you owned the place,
  And you'll get the front door slammed to in your face!

SCENE 5

Enter SPARTAN AMBASSADOR, *with entourage*

CHORAGOS ^m: The Commission has arrived from Sparta.
                                                 How oddly
   they're walking!
                    Gentlemen, welcome to Athens!
   How is life in Lakonia?
AMBASSADOR: Need we discuss that?
   Simply use your eyes.
CHORUS ^m: The poor man's right:
                        W*hat* a sight!
AMBASSADOR: Words fail me.
   But come, gentlemen, call in your Commissioners,
   and let's get down to a Peace.
CHORAGOS ^m: The state we're in! Can't bear
   a stitch below the waist. It's a kind of pelvic
   paralysis.
AN ATHENIAN: Won't somebody call Lysistrata?
   She has the answer.
A SPARTAN: Yes, there, look at him.
   Same thing.
            Seh, do y'all feel a certain strain
   early in the morning?
ATHENIAN: I do, sir. It's worse than a strain.
   A few more days, and there's nothing for us but Kleisthenês,
   that broken blossom!
CHORAGOS ^m: But you'd better get dressed again.
   You know these prudes who go around Athens with chisels,
   looking for prominent statues.
ATHENIAN: Sir, you are right.
SPARTAN: He certainly is! Ah'll put mah own clothes back on.

Enter ATHENIAN COMMISSIONERS

AN ATHENIAN: They're no better off than we are!·
                                    —Greetings, Lakonians!
SPARTAN: (*To one of his own group:*) Colonel, we got dressed just in time.
   Ah sweah,
   if they'd seen us the way we were, there'd have been a new war
   between the states.
ATHENIAN: Call the meeting to order.
                              Now, Lakonians,
   what's your proposal?
AMBASSADOR: We'd lahk to consider peace.
ATHENIAN: Good. That's on our minds, too.
                              —Summon Lysistrata.
   We'll never get anywhere without her.   Lysistrata?
AMBASSADOR:
   Summon Lysis-*any*body! Only, summon!
CHORAGOS ^m: No need to summon:
   here she is, herself.

Enter LYSISTRATA

Lysistrata! Lion of women!
This is your hour to be
hard and yielding, outspoken and sly, austere and
gentle. You see here
the best brains of Hellas (confused, I admit,
by your devious charming) met as one man
to turn the future over to you.

LYSISTRATA: That's fair enough,
unless you men take it into your heads
to turn to each other instead of to me. But I'd know
soon enough if you did!
                    —Where is that goddess of Peace?
Go, some of you: bring her here. (*Exeunt two* SERVANTS)
                    And now,
summon the Spartan Commission. Treat them courteously:
our husbands have been lax in that respect.
Take them by the hand, women,
or by anything else, if they seem unwilling.
                              —Spartans:
you stand here. Athenians: on this side. Now listen to me.

> *Re-enter* SERVANTS, *staggering under the weight of a more
> than life-size statue of a naked woman: this is* PEACE.

I'm only a woman, I know; but I've a mind,
and I can distinguish between sense and foolishness.
I owe the first to my father; the rest
to the local politicians. So much for that.
Now, then.
What I have to say concerns both sides in this war.
We are all Greeks.
Must I remind you of Thermopylai? of Olympia?
of Delphoi? names deep in all our hearts?
And yet you men go raiding through the country,
Greek killing Greek, storming down Greek cities—
and all the time the Barbarian across the sea
is waiting for his chance.—That's my first point.

AN ATHENIAN: Lord! I can hardly contain myself!
LYSISTRATA: And you Spartans:
Was it so long ago that Perikleidès
came here to beg our help? I can see him still,
his white face, his sombre gown. And what did he want?
An army from Athens! Messenia
was at your heels, and the sea-god splitting your shores.
Well, Kimôn and his men,
four thousand infantry, marched out of here to save you.
What thanks do we get? You come back to murder us.

ATHENIAN: Can't trust a Spartan, Lysistrata!
A SPARTAN: Ah admit it.
When Ah look at those legs, Ah sweah Ah can't trust mahself!
LYSISTRATA: And you, men of Athens:
you might remember that bad time when we were down,
and an army came from Sparta
and sent Hippias and the Thessalians
whimpering back to the hills. That was Sparta,

and only Sparta; without Sparta, we'd now be
cringing helots, not walking about like free men!

> *From this point, the male responses are less to*
> LYSISTRATA *than to the statue of* PEACE.

A SPARTAN: An eloquent speech!
AN ATHENIAN: An elegant construction!
LYSISTRATA: Why are we fighting each other? Why not make peace?
AMBASSADOR: Spahta is ready, ma'am,
  so long as we get that place back.
LYSISTRATA: Place? What place?
AMBASSADOR: Ah refer to Pylos.
MAGISTRATE: Not while I'm alive, by God!
LYSISTRATA: You'd better give in.
MAGISTRATE: But—what were we fighting about?
LYSISTRATA: Lots of places left.
MAGISTRATE: All right. Well, then:
  Hog Island first, and that gulf behind there, and the land between
  the Legs of Megara.
AMBASSADOR: Mah government objects.
LYSISTRATA: Over-ruled. Why fuss about a pair of legs?

> *General assent; the statue of* PEACE *is removed*

AN ATHENIAN: Let's take off our clothes and plow our fields.
A SPARTAN: Ah'll fertilize mahn first, by the Heavenly Twins!
LYSISTRATA: And so you shall,
  once we have peace. If you are serious,
  go, both of you, and talk with your allies.
ATHENIAN: Too much talk already. We'll stand together!
  We've only one end in view. All that we want
  is our women: and I speak for our allies.
AMBASSADOR: Mah government concurs.
ATHENIAN: So does Karystos.
LYSISTRATA: Good.—But before you come inside
  to join your wives at supper, you must perform
  the usual lustration. Then we'll open
  our baskets for you, and all that we have is yours.
  But you must promise upright good behavior
  from this day on. Then each man home with his woman!
ATHENIAN: Let's get it over with!
SPARTAN: Lead on: Ah follow!
ATHENIAN: Quick as a cat can wink! (*Exeunt all but the* CHORUSES)
CHORUS ᵂ: Embroideries ánd   [ANTISTROPHE
        Twinkling ornaments ánd
        Pretty dresses—I hand
Them all over to you, and with never a qualm.
        They'll be nice for your daughters
        On festival days
        When the girls bring the Goddess
        The ritual prize.
            Come in, one and all:
            Take what you will.
I've nothing here so tightly corked that you can't make it spill!

You may search my house,
But you'll not find
The least thing of use,
Unless your two eyes are keener than mine.
Your numberless brats
Are half starved? and your slaves?
Courage, grandpa! I've lots
Of grain left, and big loaves.
I'll fill your guts,
I'll go the whole hog;
But if you come too close to me, remember: 'ware the dog!

Exeunt CHORUSES

EXODOS

An ATHENIAN DRUNKARD *approaches the gate and is halted by a* SENTRY

DRUNKARD: Open. The. Door.
SENTRY: Now, friend, just shove along!
So you want to sit down! If it weren't such an old joke,
I'd tickle your tail with this torch. Just the sort of thing
that this kind of audience appreciates.
DRUNKARD: I. Stay. Right. Here.
SENTRY: Oh, all right. But you'll see some funny sights!
DRUNKARD: Bring. Them. On.
SENTRY: No, what am I thinking of?
The gentlemen from Sparta are just coming back from supper.
Get out of here, or I'll scalp you!

Exit DRUNKARD; *the general company re-enters; the two*
CHORUSES *now represent* SPARTANS *and* ATHENIANS

MAGISTRATE: I must say,
I've never tasted a better meal. And those Lakonians!
They're gentlemen, by the Lord! Just goes to show:
a drink to the wise is sufficient. And why not?
A sober man's an ass.
Men of Athens, mark my words: the only efficient
Ambassador's a drunk Ambassador. Is that clear?
Look: we go to Sparta,
and when we get there we're dead sober. The result?
Everyone cackling at everyone else. They make speeches;
and even if we understand, we get it all wrong
when we file our reports in Athens. But today—!
Everybody's happy. Couldn't tell the difference
between *Drink to Me Only* and
the *Star Spangled Athens.*
What's a few lies,
washed down in good strong drink?

Re-enter DRUNKARD

SENTRY: God almighty,
he's back again!
DRUNKARD: I. Resume. My. Place.

A SPARTAN (*To an* ATHENIAN): I beg you, seh,
take your instrument in your hand and play for us.
Ah'm told
you understand the intricacies of the floot?
Ah'd lahk to execute a song and dance
in honor of Athens,
                    and, of course, of Spahta.

The following song is a solo—an aria—accompanied by
flute. The CHORUS OF SPARTANS *begins a slow dance.*

DRUNKARD: Toot. On. Your. Flute.
CHORAGOS [s]: Mnemosynê,
        Inspire once more the Grecian Muse
        To sing of glory glory glory without end.
        Sing Artemesion's shore,
        Where Athens fluttered the Persian fleet—
        Alalaí, that great
        Victory! Sing Leonidas and his men,
        Those wild boars, sweat and blood
        Down in a red drench. Then, then
        The barbarians broke, though they had stood
        A myriad strong before!
                    O Artemis,
        Virgin Goddess, whose darts
        Flash in our forests: approve
        This pact of peace, and join our hearts,
        From this day on, in love.
        Huntress, descend!
LYSISTRATA: All that will come in time.
                    But now, Lakonians,
take home your wives. Athenians, take yours.
Each man be kind to his woman; and you, women,
be equally kind. Never again, pray God,
shall we lose our way in such madness.
                    —And now
let's dance our joy! (*From this point the dance becomes general*)
CHORUS OF ATHENIANS: Dance!
                    Dance!
                            Dance, you Graces!
        Artemis, dance!
                            Dance, Phoibos, Lord of dancing!
        Dance, Dionysos, in a scurry of Maenads!
                            Dance, Zeus Thunderer!
                    Dance! Lady Herê,
        Queen of the Sky!
                            Dance, dance, all you gods!
        Dance for the dearest, the bringer of peace,
        Deathless Aphroditê!
LYSISTRATA: Now let us have another song from Sparta.
CHORUS OF SPARTANS: From Taÿgetos' skyey summit,
        Lakonian Muse, come down!
        Sing the glories of Apollo,
        Regent of Amyklai Town.

Sing of Leda's Twins,
Those gallant sons,
On the banks of Eurotas—
    Alalaí Evohé!
Here's to our girls
  With their tangling curls,
    Legs a-wriggle,
    Bellies a-jiggle,
            A riot of hair,
      A fury of feet,
Evohé! Evohaí! Evohé!
                        as they pass
    Dancing,
              dancing,
                  dancing,
                        to greet
Athenê of the House of Brass!

THE BEST OF ALL POSSIBLE WORLDS

Antonio Martínez Ballesteros

TRANSLATED BY
Henry Salerno and Sevilla Gross

"Oh the people! They are betrayed by those to whom they give their souls; they are tricked by the very leaders who present honest faces, who mouth platitudes of unshakable loyalty and pocket the abundant gold of bribery."

Leonidas Andreyev

CHARACTERS

JOHN POOR
MR. CHAMELEON
THE POLICE CHIEF
THE MINISTER OF REPRESSION
MARIA
LOUISE
MINISTER'S WIFE
THE CHIEF OF PERSONNEL
A WAITER
FIRST GUARD
SECOND GUARD
GENERAL WHITE
GENERAL BLACK
THE COLONEL
THE CAPTAIN
THE DICTATOR
FIRST JAILER
SECOND JAILER
GENERAL BELLIGERENT
THE CHIEF JAILER
THE CHIEF OF STATE OF SHOW-HOW

Also guards, policemen, passers-by, and representatives of Show-How, and a prostitute.

The action takes place in Know-How, an imaginary country.

Present time . . . or any other.

ACT I

Scene 1

A city street. In the background is a building, a sign on the door reads "Police Station." To the right, an awning and outdoor tables of a cafe. At one of the tables, JOHN POOR, *a man about thirty-five, drinks coffee. Suddenly, the door of the Police Station flies open and two policemen fling the* REVOLUTIONARY *roughly into the street, first one, then the other beating him. The police wipe their hands and shout at him:*

FIRST POLICEMAN: That ought to hold you for a while!

SECOND POLICEMAN: The next time we lock you up! (*They go inside the Police Station and the door closes behind them. The* REVOLUTIONARY, *who lies sprawled on the ground, gets up immediately and begins to shout:*)

REVOLUTIONARY (*furiously*): You sons of . . . . You can't get away with this! You'll never shut me up! You'll have to kill me to keep me from having my say! (JOHN POOR *watches him with curiosity. Some people passing by stop, also curious.*) Our country bleeds from dictatorship and now we're fed up. The people's democracy! Ha! What a joke! Dictatorship and nothing but dictatorship! You can't hoodwink anybody! The people of Know-How are miserable! The people are dying of hunger! The people are worse off than ever. The people are— (*pause*)—screwed! (*He makes a violent, obscene gesture. He pauses to take another breath. Then he addresses himself to the curious spectators:*) Citizens of Know-How! They try to tell us we're better off than ever. You don't believe that, do you? Living in Know-How is no joke! They force us to live without freedom, without the right to speak our minds, they deny us the right to be human beings. And they've succeeded in trampling on every human decency because there are no men among you! Why do you keep silent? Why don't you shout your protest with me?

But a heavy blow suddenly cuts him off— from policemen who come piling out of the Police Station. Three policemen surround him. The REVOLUTIONARY *resists, struggles,* but it is futile. Another three policemen prepare to clear off the street, taking out billy clubs and swinging them.

A POLICEMAN (*swinging his club right and left*): Break it up! Move along! There's nothing to see here!

ANOTHER POLICEMAN: Didn't you hear him? Move along! It's only some lunatic!

The curious spectators, terror-stricken, leave quickly. In the doorway of the Police Station the POLICE CHIEF *appears. He signals the Police to take the* REVOLUTIONARY *inside.*

REVOLUTIONARY (*who hasn't stopped shouting and resisting*): I won't be silenced! You can't stop me from shouting the truth! (*making a futile effort to free himself*) People of Know-How, they're sucking our blood! They bleed us with taxes, starvation wages, and violence! They declare our strikes illegal and still we have strikes!

POLICE CHIEF (*shouting at the police*): Hurry! Can't you take care of him?

Now there are six policemen occupied with restraining the REVOLUTIONARY. *On the right, the* MINISTER OF REPRESSION *appears. He always carries a strange staff of office. At the lower end is a wooden cross so made that when he raises the staff in a menacing gesture, it becomes a threatening cross. As he observes the scene, his face darkens with anger.*

REVOLUTIONARY (*bobbing up from among the surrounding police*): This is a country of weaklings—cowards! (*He continues struggling as he is dragged to the doorway of the Police Station.*)

POLICE CHIEF (*who has seen the* MINISTER OF REPRESSION): Inside with him! Hurry! The Minister of Repression is coming! (*He goes off to meet the* MINISTER *while the police drag the* REVOLUTIONARY *inside.*)

MINISTER: What's going on here?

POLICE CHIEF (*fearfully*): It's only . . . only a revolutionary, my dear cousin. . . .

MINISTER (*angrily*): Only a revolutionary! Lock him up! (*He raises his staff in the direction of the Police Station, making a menacing gesture.*)

POLICE CHIEF: Precisely what I thought of doing with him. (*turning to the police*) To jail! Lock him up! (*The police have already disappeared with the* REVOLUTIONARY, *who can still be heard shouting.*)

REVOLUTIONARY (*within*): A lot of free-loading bloodsucking, official swine! All at the expense of the people! (*A heavy jail door slams shut and his voice is cut off.*)

MINISTER (*severely, raising his staff at the* POLICE CHIEF): How could you permit such a public scandal in the streets? What are the police in Know-How for?

POLICE CHIEF (*solicitously*): I don't know, dear cousin. I mean to say. . . . Well, he's . . . not all there. Every country has lunatics. If not, there would be no revolutionaries. . . .

MINISTER: Every country has lunatics! Then why are there lunatic asylums? (*He threatens him with his staff.*)

POLICE CHIEF (*nervously*): Of course, you're right. Absolutely right. Lunatic asylums. . . . But. . . . Don't you think we might discuss this better inside there? (*He points to the Police Station.*)

MINISTER (*furiously*): Inside there? No! Here! (*He gestures with his staff toward the tables.*)

POLICE CHIEF (*bewildered*): Yes, yes, as you wish, dear cousin. Then I invite you to have a cup of coffee. . . . Would you like to sit here?

MINISTER (*pointing with his staff*): No, there! Further in!

POLICE CHIEF (*aside*): Well, that's the limit! (*to the* MINISTER) Wherever you wish, dear cousin. (*In making his way to the table indicated by the* MINISTER, *he stumbles—he's so nervous and upset—over* JOHN POOR.) Oh, I beg your pardon! (*Then, looking at him closely, he says with surprise:*) But. . . . I know you. . . .

JOHN: Do you mean to say you remember my name? We were never friends, of course, but we were classmates.

POLICE CHIEF: Oh, yes, I remember now. You are John . . . John . . . I don't remember your last name. . . .

JOHN: Poor.

POLICE CHIEF: Yes, of course; John Poor. (*bragging*) I am the Chief of Police now.

MINISTER (*in an ugly tone*): You may not be for much longer.

POLICE CHIEF (*turning his attention back to the* MINISTER, *newly solicitous*): Forgive me, dear cousin. But this is John Poor. (*to* JOHN) My dear cousin is the. . . .

MINISTER (*cutting him off*): We will sit here! (*With his staff, he points to the other side.*)

POLICE CHIEF: Of course, of course! As you say. I am always at your service, dear cousin. (*He pulls out a chair for the* MINISTER. *The* MINISTER *sits down. The* POLICE CHIEF *turns to* JOHN POOR.) We'll talk some other time. For now. . . . (*indicating the* MINISTER) I am occupied. . . .

JOHN: I don't think we have anything to talk about. But I would like to take this opportunity to tell you that your methods are wrong.

POLICE CHIEF (*shocked*): What's that? Wrong? Are you referring to. . . .

JOHN: To what we have just witnessed. You know very well what I mean. (*The* POLICE CHIEF *doesn't know what to do, whether to answer him sternly, snub him or attend to the* MINISTER, *who is watching everything seriously.*)

MINISTER: Sit down at once!

POLICE CHIEF: Yes, yes, dear cousin. Right this minute. . . . I'll do it right this minute. . . . (*turning to* JOHN) You can't possibly comprehend . . . that it is absolutely necessary to handle these things in this manner. Absolutely.

JOHN (*ironically*): Really?

POLICE CHIEF: But of course. And even more so now . . . now that the Premier of Show-How is visiting our country. We must avoid all scandal so that he will get a good impression of our fair land. Soon he will pass down this very street. Haven't you seen the banners strung across the street? (JOHN *nods.*) Well, then, what I have done is the only method of maintaining order . . . the only method of protecting the power of. . . .

JOHN (*still ironical*): By force? Eliminating the opposition in one blow?

POLICE CHIEF (*not knowing what to say and crossing looks with the* MINISTER): But . . . aren't you on the side of the opposition?

JOHN: Me? You can relax.

POLICE CHIEF: Then . . . are you on our side?

JOHN: Neither.

MINISTER (*without turning*): How do you explain that?

POLICE CHIEF: Then, that is. . . . May I know *what* you are?

JOHN: I believe that . . . I'm a scoundrel.

POLICE CHIEF (*mystified*): A scoundrel?

JOHN: A bourgeois with a sleeping conscience: a neutral.

MINISTER (*relieved*): Bah! No threat! On our side after all.

JOHN (*pointing to the Police Station where the* REVOLUTIONARY *has begun to shout again*): Don't think I want to complicate my life . . . like him.

MINISTER (*turning to listen to the screams of the* REVOLUTIONARY): The truth is he has a good pair of lungs.

JOHN: That man is nothing but a lunatic.

POLICE CHIEF (*protesting*): He's a revolutionary!

JOHN: Call him what you will. But he's a crazy fanatic, like you. But on the other side, of course.

POLICE CHIEF (*offended*): What's this . . . "like you" business?

JOHN: Like you and like those who follow you.

POLICE CHIEF (*affected dignity*): Are you taking the liberty of speaking freely to me just because we were classmates?

JOHN: Of course. We're speaking confidentially, aren't we?

POLICE CHIEF (*containing himself with great difficulty*): Confidentially?

JOHN (*completely self-possessed*): Naturally. And for that reason I tell you that your method is wrong. (*gesturing toward the Police Station*)

POLICE CHIEF (*rising from his chair*): I warn you. You are going too far. . . .

MINISTER (*gripping his arm and forcing him down into his seat*): Sit down. And leave him to me. (*The* POLICE CHIEF *sits down. The* MINISTER *turns to* JOHN.) Tell me. . . . What would you have done with that man?

JOHN (*hesitating*): Well . . . (*then decisively*) I've already told you he's a fanatic and he has an empty stomach. That's the serious thing. Answer me this question: What is it governs a man's life? His stomach! Do you understand?

MINISTER (*pensively*): Not entirely. You mean that. . . .

JOHN: That by force nobody will succeed in shutting him up unless they kill him. And until that moment, he can contaminate others with his lunacy. So, then, the best method of keeping him quiet is . . . (*pause*) to fill up his stomach.

MINISTER (*pensively, stroking his chin*): I understand. I understand. . . . It is . . . a great idea . . . only. . . . (*suddenly, as if he has made his decision*) No, I said it: a great idea. You deserve a position in the Ministry.

JOHN (*with surprise*): In the Ministry?

POLICE CHIEF (*boastfully*): My dear cousin is the Minister of Repression!

JOHN (*rises, frightened*): The Minister of Repression?

MINISTER: But you have nothing to worry about. In fact, the very opposite. I can see that you are intelligent . . . and I believe I could find an important job for you in our Ministry.

JOHN (*not knowing what to say*): But I. . . .

MINISTER: No buts. Tell me, you accept or don't accept the job offer.

JOHN (*bewildered*): What job? (*a little brusquely*) I beg your pardon, but . . . I don't need it. And now . . . I have to leave . . . I beg you to excuse me.

POLICE CHIEF: But man, his excellency the Chief of State will be passing by here in a few minutes. Won't you stay to see the procession?

JOHN (*nervously*): No, that's for you two—forgive me—for you gentlemen. . . . Excuse me. . . . (*He exits rapidly. The* POLICE CHIEF *and the* MINISTER *look amazed at his sudden departure.*)

MINISTER: Is he always like that?

POLICE CHIEF: Yes, he's always been a bit strange. He opposes on principle what everyone else believes.

MINISTER: On principle? He didn't seem that stupid. He knows how to present his case, doesn't he? And convincingly?

POLICE CHIEF (*not knowing what to say*): Has he convinced you?

MINISTER: Hasn't he you?

POLICE CHIEF: Well. . . .

MINISTER: Of course. You have always been something of a blockhead.

POLICE CHIEF: Dear cousin, I. . . .

MINISTER: Shhhh. Shut up! (*He remains lis-*

tening to the REVOLUTIONARY *who can be heard again.*)

REVOLUTIONARY (*inside*): Citizens of Know-How! Don't you want your freedom? How long will you endure the executioners who oppress us?

It is obvious that they have quieted him by sheer force. The sounds of breaking furniture are heard. The POLICE CHIEF *and the* MINISTER *listen anxiously. Finally there is a silence. Pause.*

POLICE CHIEF: I'm sure of this method.

MINISTER: I'm not. He's a lunatic. He'll begin all over again as soon as he regains consciousness.

POLICE CHIEF: Then we'll give him more of the same. We'll see who lasts longer!

MINISTER (*unconvinced*): But can't you understand we have to adopt another method?

POLICE CHIEF: Another method?

MINISTER: Yes, a more practical one. (*pause*) Now, I want you to do everything I tell you.

POLICE CHIEF: Always at your command, dear cousin.

MINISTER: I want you to take that man over to the Hotel Kilton.

POLICE CHIEF (*bewildered*): To the Hotel Kilton?

MINISTER: Get him a good room. And afterwards, a good meal.

POLICE CHIEF (*more and more bewildered*): A good meal?

MINISTER: That's right. Hors d'oeuvres, pheasant, steak. All the best.

POLICE CHIEF (*believing that the other has gone mad*): All the best?

MINISTER (*getting up*): But do it quickly! The bill will be charged to the Ministry of Repression.

POLICE CHIEF (*also rises*): And afterwards . . . what do we do with him?

MINISTER: The same thing every day. The man is to remain free and his bills charged to the State. (*As the* POLICE CHIEF *appears to be dazed, the* MINISTER *threatens him with his staff:*) And right away! That's an order!

POLICE CHIEF: Yes, dear cousin. Right this minute. . . . (*He begins to make his exit through the door of the Police Station, under the threat of the* MINISTER's *staff. And the stage becomes dark.*)

The home of JOHN POOR. *A table, a dresser with a radio on it. A doorway leads to the bedroom.* MARIA, JOHN's *wife, sets dishes on the table. Then she calls toward the bedroom.*

MARIA: John . . . John. . . .

JOHN (*from the bedroom*): What?

MARIA: Whenever you're ready. The table's set. (*She turns on the radio and leaves. In the doorway she and* JOHN *pass each other. He enters and sits at the table. He waits as the radio crackles and then comes on.*)

ANNOUNCER: The visit of the Premier of Show-How to our country will serve to consolidate with strong and indestructible bonds the unity of Know-How and Show-How, the few remaining countries who can face with courage and the assurance of victory the dangers of the so-called democratic doctrines. This was declared, among other things, by our Chief of State. To continue, the Premier of Show-How offered high praise to the progress of the people of Know-How under the present administration. He added that he was astonished at the high standard of living attained by our people and that, as our excellent Chief of State has affirmed in one of his latest speeches, the foreign attacks can only be the result of the envy of other countries for the glorious resurgence of Know-How. Directly afterwards, his excellency the Chief of State of Know-How honored his excellency the Premier of Show-How with a typical glorious dinner of our country. The menu consisted of, among other delicacies, various hors d'oeuvres of Know-How, roasted pheasant à la Know-How, venison from the forests of Know-How. The dinner was served with the exquisite wines of our country. . . .

JOHN: Bah! Always the same thing! (*He turns off the radio with an angry gesture.* MARIA *has already entered and served the meal. Now both are seated at the table. They begin to eat in silence. It is quiet except for the rhythmic slurping of soup by both.*)

JOHN (*breaking the silence*): What is this?

MARIA: Can't you see? It is clam soup.

JOHN: But it doesn't have any clams in it.

MARIA: Clams! Since when do we put clams in clam soup. Clams are a luxury!

JOHN (*grumbling*): Meanwhile others eat pheasant every day and here we have the typical dinner of Know-How. (*silence*) When I think that this morning they asked me what I was and I answered a bourgeois. . . . But how could I be a bourgeois with a diet like this? (*as if speaking to himself*) Of course, there are many different ways of being a bourgeois . . . many different ways. . . .

MARIA: What are you grumbling about?

JOHN: Don't pay any attention to me. It's nothing. (*They continue eating in silence. JOHN pours something from a bottle into his glass. He drinks and makes a face.*) What the devil is this? (*holding up the bottle*)

MARIA: Wine.

JOHN: Wine! But it tastes nothing like wine.

MARIA: It's that . . . look. . . . It's so expensive that either we do without it completely or we have to mix it with water. . . .

JOHN: But they already do that at the wine store.

MARIA (*sadly*): Yes, I know. But if you want to drink it with dinner, it has to be this way. It's half and half—half wine, half water. But you see it still looks the same. That's because I take some wine coloring they sell in the drugstore and the color remains. . . .

JOHN: But damned if the flavor remains!

MARIA: Well, if you don't like it, we'll do without it . . . like dessert.

JOHN: Ah, no dessert either!

MARIA: Only on Sundays. Don't you agree that we should do that to make your paycheck last?

JOHN: All right. But today *is* Sunday.

MARIA: But since we had dessert yesterday for your birthday, today we have to do without it. We can't have it every day.

JOHN: What luxury!

MARIA: Oh, if only you had heard what I heard the other day at the butcher shop! (*JOHN looks at her in a strange manner.*) Yes, a few days ago I went to the butchers to buy a soup bone. Well, there was a woman there buying—I won't tell you what she was buying because it would make your mouth water—but she said . . .

(*hesitates*) . . . Do you know what she said? That now they're eating better than ever! (*JOHN gets up angrily from the table.*) Now I see it was a mistake to tell you. But there are things that I can't bear to suffer alone and. . . .

JOHN (*bursting out*): How right he was. . . .

MARIA (*bewildered*): Who?

JOHN: That man. . . .

MARIA: What man?

JOHN: Bah! What's the use! It's better not to think about it. Because if you do. . . . (*He sits down again.*)

MARIA: Don't get angry. Your dinner will disagree with you.

JOHN (*snorting*): My dinner!

MARIA: John, there are days when I can't say anything to you. Eat. Your soup is getting cold.

JOHN (*between his teeth*): My clam soup without clams is getting cold! (*He continues eating. Silence. Then the doorbell rings.*)

MARIA: Who could it be at this hour? (*She gets up and goes out. JOHN continues eating. LOUISE enters, distraught. Behind her MARIA returns. LOUISE is a woman about thirty-two.*)

LOUISE (*going straight to JOHN*): John! John! You have to do something! You have to do something!

JOHN (*getting up*): Louise! What's happened?

LOUISE (*bursting into tears*): They've arrested your brother! They've arrested your brother!

JOHN: What are you saying? What did he do?

LOUISE (*crying*): Do? He hasn't done anything! What do you think he could do? He couldn't hurt a fly!

MARIA: John wants to know what happened . . . why did they arrest him?

LOUISE: Because he was discussing politics with a friend . . . in a bar. . . . They were defending the men arrested in the strikes. There was a man sitting beside them . . . (*pause*) He turned and told them that in front of him nobody could speak against the government of the Chief of State. . . . And that man. . . . (*She burst into tears.*) Aaay! Can't a man speak his mind? (*She weeps without restraint.*)

JOHN: But . . . tell me . . . who was the man?

LOUISE: He turned out to be from the police. He arrested him!

JOHN: Arrested! I always told my brother to be careful whom he talked to.

LOUISE (*whining*): You must help us! What can we do?

JOHN (*recklessly*): Nothing! We can't do anything if they arrested him for criticizing the Chief of State! In this country that's worse than murder!

LOUISE: But if my husband hasn't hurt anybody. . . . All he said was that since the new regime we live worse and. . . .

JOHN (*breaking in*): That it was unjust to arrest the men who participated in the strikes!

LOUISE: But wasn't it?

MARIA: Yes, Louise. But John means you can't say that.

JOHN: Of course not. By saying that he's given them enough excuse to put him away for years!

LOUISE: But that can't be! If there's any justice. . . .

JOHN (*scornfully*): Justice! You mean you still don't know the world you live in, Louise?

LOUISE: Is it just to arrest him for that?

JOHN: Let's not discuss what's just and unjust. Leave this to me. I'll see if I can do something. (*He leaves. The two women remain, looking hopefully at each other. The stage darkens.*)

SCENE 3

The home of the MINISTER OF REPRESSION. *A small table, a sofa and a pair of armchairs. On the table is a small radio set. All the furniture is coquettish and vulgar, apparently chosen by the* MINISTER'S WIFE. *As the stage lights up, the* MINISTER, *his* WIFE, *and the* CHIEF OF PERSONNEL *of the Ministry are seated around the table.*

MINISTER (*to the* CHIEF OF PERSONNEL): You, as Chief of Personnel in the Ministry, should be able to find good positions for these three new officials my wife has spoken about.

CHIEF OF PERSONNEL: Yes, my dear Mr. Minister. (*consulting some papers he holds in his hands*) This concerns Mr. Able, Mr. Easy and Mr. Able-Easy. . . .

MINISTER'S WIFE: Precisely.

CHIEF OF PERSONNEL: And . . . in what positions do they enter the Ministry?

MINISTER'S WIFE: As department heads, naturally.

MINISTER: Naturally. As my wife has said.

CHIEF OF PERSONNEL: Very good. Now, the next step. What qualifications do these gentlemen have for these positions?

MINISTER: Qualifications?

MINISTER'S WIFE: What are qualifications?

CHIEF OF PERSONNEL: Well, qualifications, my dear lady, are based on the scores received in the civil service exams. Of course . . . in this case . . . since they haven't taken any exams. . . . (*He begins to laugh as if he had said something clever.*) He, he, he, he!

MINISTER (*after staring at him severely for a moment*): Precisely. They have not taken the exams because these three gentlemen in question are already sufficiently qualified.

CHIEF OF PERSONNEL: Oh, yes, of course! Then . . . let's see. . . . (*consulting his papers*) Mr. Able, what qualifications can we list?

MINISTER (*not knowing what to say*): Mr. Able?

MINISTER'S WIFE (*rapidly*): Mr. Able is a nephew of the Minister.

CHIEF OF PERSONNEL: Nephew? Oh, yes, of course! And Mr. Easy?

MINISTER: Mr. Easy is my wife's first cousin.

CHIEF OF PERSONNEL (*taking notes*): First cousin. . . . And Mr. Able-Easy? He's a relative on both sides?

MINISTER: No, he's no one's relative. It's merely coincidence.

CHIEF OF PERSONNEL (*fawning, wanting to be witty*): Then, more precisely he should be called Mr. Unable and Uneasy. Don't you think, my dear Mr. Minister? Hee, hee, hee, hee. . . . (*But no one joins in his laughter. The* MINISTER *and his* WIFE *remain glaring at him severely.*)

MINISTER'S WIFE: The joke is in poor taste, and you are not especially clever.

CHIEF OF PERSONNEL (*attempting to recover himself*): Forgive me, dear lady. . . . It's only that . . . I shouldn't have . . . (*very nervously*) Well, we were dealing with the qualifications of Mr. Unable-Uneasy. . . . (*The two glare at him as before.*) Forgive me . . . I don't know what I'm saying. . . . Of Mr. Able-Easy.

MINISTER: Mr. Able-Easy was recommended by the company that gave us the commission on the sale of the. . . .

MINISTER'S WIFE (*interrupting*): But how can this possibly concern you?

MINISTER: Precisely what I say. Why pay attention to this nonsense? (*rising and picking up his staff of office*) You install these new men in their offices tomorrow and as for this business of qualifications. . . . Forget it!

MINISTER'S WIFE: And there is no need to speak further on the subject.

CHIEF OF PERSONNEL: Excuse me, dear lady. . . . Excuse me, dear Mr. Minister. I won't detain you any longer. It will be as you've said. A thousand pardons, if I have inconvenienced you. (*He leaves, bowing all the way out.*)

MINISTER'S WIFE: I didn't think he would ever leave. How tiresome!

MINISTER: These are the burdens of responsibility, my dear. At times, it is necessary to sacrifice oneself.

MINISTER'S WIFE: He is totally lacking in social grace, the wretch! He hardly left us time to hear the news on the National Radio of Know-How.

MINISTER (*turning on the radio*): Perhaps we can still catch part of the program.

MINISTER'S WIFE: At this hour I don't like being interrupted by anybody. One misses the most interesting programs. (*The radio crackles and comes on.*)

COMMENTATOR: The following guests attended the banquet: His Excellency, the Chief of State of Know-How and the First Lady; His Excellency, the Premier of Show-How and the First Lady; the Honorable Minister of the Interior and his wife; the Honorable Minister of Repression and his wife. . . .

MINISTER'S WIFE (*breathing a sigh of satisfaction and vanity, like her husband*): Ah, we caught it just in time.

COMMENTATOR: The Honorable Minister of Finance and his wife; the Honorable Ambassador of Show-How and his wife; the Honorable. . . . (*The doorbell sounds.*)

MINISTER'S WIFE: Who can be interrupting us at this time? (*Outside a man's voice is heard.*)

VOICE: No, you needn't announce me. I'm a family friend and I know the way. (*The MINISTER turns the radio down. The POLICE CHIEF enters, followed by JOHN POOR.*)

POLICE CHIEF (*to the MINISTER*): My dear cousin . . . (*to the MINISTER'S WIFE*) My dear cousin. . . . But I see that you are listening to the radio. I can return at a more convenient time . . . if I am interrupting.

MINISTER'S WIFE: No, come in. You may listen with us.

POLICE CHIEF: Well . . . (*alluding to JOHN*) I came with. . . . (*to the MINISTER*) You remember him, don't you? It's John Poor.

MINISTER: Yes, yes, of course I remember him. (*to his WIFE*) This . . . is John Poor.

JOHN (*uneasy*): How do you do, Madame. (*The MINISTER'S WIFE gives him a brief courteous smile, but false and a little brittle.*)

POLICE CHIEF: John, here, came to see me a few days ago to discuss a certain matter. . . . I told him that I . . . I couldn't do anything without your approval and he . . . Well, he insists on speaking to you. I don't want to bother you with trivia, but. . . .

JOHN: Pardon me. This is not trivial.

MINISTER: Naturally not, if you say so. I will be glad to attend to this—with pleasure. I told you that you seemed to me an intelligent man, and I would like to show you that I . . . know how to appreciate intelligence when I see it.

JOHN: Please, Mr. Minister, don't deliver these eulogies for me. In the first place, you don't know me very well and. . . .

POLICE CHIEF (*to the MINISTER'S WIFE*): Dear cousin, perhaps it would be better if we left them alone. Don't you agree?

MINISTER'S WIFE: Yes, let's go into the next room. That way they will not bore us.

MINISTER: You can listen to the latest speeches of the Chief of State. (*to the POLICE CHIEF*) I have recorded them on magnetic tape so we can listen to them whenever we want.

MINISTER'S WIFE: On special occasions we invite a few friends over for luncheon and we listen to them together. We have spent some thrilling moments together. I suppose you would like to hear them also?

POLICE CHIEF: I would be delighted. (*He leaves with the* MINISTER'S WIFE.)

MINISTER (*after a silence, to* JOHN): Now what can I do for you? The other day you gave me a brilliant idea and I still want to show you my appreciation. Some favor, perhaps?

JOHN: No, thank you. Not for me, but for my brother.

MINISTER: For your brother? Whatever it is, granted.

JOHN: You won't change your mind when I tell you what it is?

MINISTER: You must believe that . . . in the end, a Minister keeps his word. What is it your brother wants?

JOHN: His freedom.

MINISTER (*a little shocked*): His freedom?

JOHN: They arrested him three days ago. He's in the People's jail.

MINISTER: All right. I don't think it will be difficult to do something for him. A little phone call to my friend, the Minister of Justice, and if it's not a serious matter. . . . What happened to your brother? He got mixed up in a business deal? A question of money, perhaps?

JOHN: None of that. I don't think it would do any good to call the Minister of Justice. Only you could arrange this.

MINISTER: Only me?

JOHN: You are the Minister of Repression.

MINISTER (*becoming serious*): Ah, I understand. Your brother has been arrested for a political crime. May I know for what? (*Now his attitude toward* JOHN *changes completely.*)

JOHN: For declaring in public that it was unjust to arrest the men who participated in the strikes.

MINISTER: Then your brother is a fanatic.

JOHN: He's a sensible man.

MINISTER: What stupidity! He must learn not to meddle in such matters! Without a doubt he'll be given a jail sentence.

JOHN (*stupefied*): But my brother hasn't done anything to land him in jail. He's not a criminal. He's a man of honor.

MINISTER (*ironically*): A man of honor! (*then, changing his tone*) Look, you: don't come to me with stories about men of honor. In the years I've been in politics I've learned that there are no men of honor, that everybody's out for himself. So tell me, what's your brother out to get by meddling in this affair?

JOHN: I don't understand. . . . My brother isn't out for anything. Certainly not for himself. He only wanted a little more justice for those men—the men arrested in the strikes.

MINISTER (*raising his staff*): Justice! Don't think they won't get it. As for him. . . . (*He pauses, smiling ironically.*)

JOHN: You mean you won't have him released?

MINISTER: Can you guarantee me that your brother's views will change once he owes his liberty to the Minister of Repression?

JOHN (*spiritlessly*): Well . . . I don't think so. Only puppets can be bought. My brother is. . . .

MINISTER: . . . a man! That's what I'm afraid of.

JOHN: But . . . I don't understand. What do you mean to do?

MINISTER: Look, I have to leave now. I must accompany his Excellency the Chief of State when he leaves for his estate, Wolf Haven, for a hunt tomorrow in honor of His Excellency the Premier of Show-How. (*sadly*) The day after tomorrow he leaves to return to his country. How quickly the time has gone! (*returning to the matter at hand*) Well, as I said. I don't have time now. Therefore, it will be better if you speak with my secretary.

JOHN: But. . . .

MINISTER: At this hour you'll find him eating, no doubt. (*gives him a card*) Go to this address and say I sent you.

JOHN: But, what shall I tell him?

MINISTER: Nothing. Don't tell him anything. I'll give him instructions over the telephone.

JOHN: Pardon, but what will you tell him?

MINISTER: Leave that to me. Don't worry.

JOHN: Yes, sir. And thank you for everything. Forgive me, if I've bothered you.

MINISTER: Go on, go on. Don't waste time.

JOHN: Yes, sir. Yes, sir. Good night. (*He exits. The* MINISTER *remains pensive for a moment. He turns on the radio. Then he dials a telephone number.*)

MINISTER (*into the telephone*): I want to

speak with Mr. Chameleon. (*While he waits, the radio comes on.*)

COMMENTATOR (*continuing as before*): . . . The Honorable Minister of Agriculture and his wife; the Honorable General of the First Military Regiment and his wife; the Honorable. . . . (*And as the radio continues announcing personalities and celebrities, the stage darkens.*)

SCENE 4

MR. CHAMELEON's *room in the Kilton Hotel. On a table sits a dinner lavishly served. Hunched over it, his back to the audience,* CHAMELEON *eats voraciously. He eats with extraordinary speed, seizing dishes from one side and the other of the table, and inclining his body over the plates to facilitate his "work." The telephone rings. But he pays no attention and continues eating without a pause. As the ringing becomes insistent, he picks up the telephone in one hand and continues eating with the other.*

CHAMELEON: Yes, yes, Mr. Minister. (*He listens without pausing in his eating.*) He's coming? Here? (*He listens.*) I understand, Mr. Minister. I'll take care of it. (*He listens.*) Yeah, yeah, one of those malcontents you find everywhere, unfortunately. (*He listens.*) Yes, yes, Mr. Minister. Don't worry. It will be taken care of. You have me always at your service, Mr. Minister. (*He hangs up. He continues eating with both hands. He sucks his fingers, drinks and claps his hands. He continues eating as a* WAITER *appears.*)

CHAMELEON: On the double. Coffee and cream.

WAITER: Right away, sir. (*And, as he has already come with the order, he serves him immediately while he speaks:*) There is a man outside who asked for you. His name is John Poor.

CHAMELEON (*gulping down several pastries*): John Poor? I don't know him.

WAITER: He says that he comes from the Minister of Repression.

CHAMELEON: He hasn't wasted any time! Can't I even eat my dinner in peace?

WAITER: Shall I tell him to wait, sir?

CHAMELEON: No, no. I'll see him while I have my coffee. I can't waste time. I'll be late for the banquet. Have him come in.

WAITER: Very well, sir. (*He begins to leave but* CHAMELEON *recovers the coffee service.*)

CHAMELEON: Leave that here. I always like to have seconds. (*The* WAITER *leaves.* CHAMELEON *finishes eating the pastries and he licks his fingers. In this attitude he is seen by* JOHN POOR *as he enters.*)

JOHN (*from the doorway*): Mr. Chameleon?

CHAMELEON (*gulping coffee, without turning*): Come in.

JOHN (*hesitating briefly*): I come from the Minister of Repression.

CHAMELEON (*stirring his coffee*): I already know that, I already know that. I've spoken to him on the telephone. . . . (*He interrupts himself to drink, in one gulp, the whole cup of coffee.*) And believe me, my friend, I don't understand what your little game is. (*He serves himself more coffee and continues speaking while he adds spoonfuls of sugar, stirs the coffee without turning around.*) Frankly, my friend. . . . (*He serves himself a cognac and drinks it.*) Do you think a crime like the one your brother committed can be overlooked? You should be ashamed to intercede for him. (*JOHN is about to defend himself against these charges, but the other, always giving him his back, leaves him no opening.*) Tell me, tell me sincerely! Do you believe that a man like your brother, a man who defends these saboteurs of the State, these strikers, these criminals against the State, should be let loose?

JOHN: But these men aren't criminals. They only wanted a raise in wages.

CHAMELEON (*between gulps of coffee*): Raise in wages! Raise in wages! As if this were possible. To earn more you have to work more. And these men went on strike to work less! (*Finishing his coffee, he turns to face* JOHN *for the first time.*) Don't you understand that? (*When he turns, we can see that he is the* REVOLUTIONARY *from the first scene, now cleaner, rounder and shinier.* JOHN *is stunned by this discovery.*)

JOHN (*unable to believe what he sees*): But . . . I know you!

CHAMELEON: Me? And what's strange about that. Lots of people know me. But . . .

do you think this is going to change things? The very opposite, my friend. I have always been a just man, and no one can sway me easily from principle. (*These words provoke from* JOHN *a nervous laugh, a little hysterical.*) Eh? What are you laughing at? (*The laugh, nearly silent to begin with, becomes more intense, shocking, convulsive, making* JOHN *seem like a jerky wind-up doll.*)

CHAMELEON (*offended, trying to be very serious*): What are you laughing at?

JOHN (*laughter still bursting out of him no matter how hard he tries to stop*): Excuse me. It's. . . . Now I remember . . . I knew someone like you. . . . (*He's obliged to pause because he can't stop laughing.* CHAMELEON *glares at him, shocked.*) He said he'd never change unless they killed him. You understand? Unless they killed him! And now. . . . (*He abandons himself completely to laughter.*)

CHAMELEON (*unable to preserve his dignity in the face of* JOHN's *laughter*): I confess I don't see the joke. . . . I don't understand you. . . . But if you wish only to annoy me. . . . (*He claps his hands.*)

JOHN (*now raving*): But don't you understand? I can't help laughing at you. You're a very funny character. With that pig's face. . . . What a specimen you are! And that gut . . . so well developed! (*The* WAITER *enters and is astonished at the scene.*)

CHAMELEON (*to the* WAITER, *authoritatively, pointing to* JOHN): Throw this man out! I think he's gone crazy!

JOHN (*scarcely offering resistance and unable to stop laughing*): Your guts . . . that's what really kills me! You are a man of prodigious guts—of big . . . fat . . . guts!

The last few words are heard offstage. His voice fades out. CHAMELEON *remains perplexed. He shrugs his shoulders and heaves a sigh of relief. He takes an enormous cigar out of his coat pocket and sits down. He sits pensively a few moments and with an absent-minded look he lights his enormous cigar. He takes a few puffs and blows out the smoke with apparent pleasure. Then, shrugging his shoulders again, he says, as if trying to reassure himself:*

CHAMELEON: Bah! He's a nut! (*He continues smoking and enjoying his cigar.*)

ACT II

SCENE 1

An open, level stretch of countryside where two roads end. Center stage is a gate and a sign over it, "Wolf Haven." Beyond the gate can be seen the front of the house and a door. The scene is empty. From the right two guards enter for guard duty, heavily armed.

FIRST GUARD: Just our rotten luck to get stuck with guard duty!

SECOND GUARD: Yeah, yeah. (*wiping his face with his handkerchief*) It's always hotter than blazes when they stick us with guard duty!

FIRST GUARD: Damned beautiful weather our beloved chief chooses for his hunt!

SECOND GUARD: They can shove it, for all of me! Why the hell do they need so damned many guards just to patrol the highways and fields of his highness' estate? Half as many would be too much!

FIRST GUARD: Listen, my friend: an order's an order. Complaining about it will get you exactly nowhere. Listen, I wouldn't mind free-loading with the best of them—hunting and then sitting down at the great banquet table for dinner. There are a lot of people coming, but did you get a look at all that food being unloaded from the trucks? I counted eight trucks!

SECOND GUARD: For all of me . . . ! Why do they bring in all that food if they're going hunting? They could easily slaughter enough. There's plenty of game here!

FIRST GUARD: Don't you see, man? It figures. They can't eat the raw game they just killed. So meanwhile, the big banquet is being prepared. (*From the left* GENERAL WHITE *appears. He is the Provost Marshal.*)

GENERAL WHITE (*entering hurriedly, to the* GUARDS, *who haven't noticed him*): Where's the Colonel?

FIRST GUARD (*coming to immediate attention and giving a brisk salute like his companion*): Right inside, General, sir. (*The* GENERAL *disappears into the estate.*)

SECOND GUARD (*looking after the exiting* GEN-ERAL): What's bugging General White? He's foaming at the mouth.

FIRST GUARD (*also looking in the direction of the* GENERAL'*s exit*): And how! I wouldn't care to be in the Colonel's shoes right now!

SECOND GUARD: Then let's clear out. It'll be our hides if the General's mad. When the General's through eating him out, the Colonel's. . . . (GENERAL BLACK *enters hurriedly, unseen by the* GUARDS. GENERAL BLACK, *the Directing General of the Guards of Highways and Roads, like the other General, is in a terrible temper.*)

GENERAL BLACK (*to the* GUARDS): Where's the Colonel? (*He continues walking and snorting without waiting for an answer. The two* GUARDS, *once aware of his presence, snap to attention, terrified.*)

SECOND GUARD: Yes, sir, General, sir. At your command, General, sir.

FIRST GUARD: Ah, shut up. Don't you see he can't hear you? (*The* GENERAL *has disappeared into the estate.*)

FIRST GUARD: Let's get out of here. The garbage is about to hit the fan. (*The two go off left. The scene remains empty a moment. Then, from the estate,* GENERAL BLACK *and the* COLONEL *appear. The latter is suffering a good dressing down.*)

GENERAL BLACK: This cannot go on. You're never around when I need you!

COLONEL: Excuse me, sir. I was. . . .

GENERAL BLACK (*interrupting him*): I will not tolerate excuses! Don't you understand what has happened?

COLONEL: Yes, General, sir. In fact I was just now informed by Commander Easy. I didn't know anything until the Commander. . . .

GENERAL BLACK: You didn't know anything! You've always got your head up. . . . I'll have to have a serious talk with you. Because on the entire highway, I saw *only one* guard. Don't you realize that it was his Excellency, the Chief of State himself, who passed down that highway? Can't you understand that we must step up security measures under such circumstances?

COLONEL: Yes, General. But I. . . .

GENERAL BLACK: I have said I will not tolerate excuses!

COLONEL: But. . . . (*He is suddenly startled to hear another voice behind him. It is* GENERAL WHITE *who is coming out of the house.*)

GENERAL WHITE: Ah, Colonel! I've caught up with you at last! Where have you been hiding yourself? (*noticing the other* GENERAL) Pardon me, General Black. I hadn't realized it was you.

COLONEL (*very frightened, coming to attention before* GENERAL WHITE): General, sir!

GENERAL BLACK (*to* GENERAL WHITE): Hello, General White. I was just reprimanding the Colonel here. I told him that on the entire highway I saw *only one guard.* And it is our Chief of State—no less than our beloved Chief of State—who is traveling down that highway. And under such circumstances we must redouble the guard.

GENERAL WHITE: You're absolutely right, General: we must redouble the guard! The smallest negligence might cost the life of his Excellency. In fact, it very nearly did cost his life this very morning—But, continue . . . continue with your reprimand. I can wait until you finish with him. (GENERAL BLACK *makes a gesture of thanks.* GENERAL WHITE *moves off to a discreet distance.*)

GENERAL BLACK (*hoarsely, as he directs himself to the* COLONEL): I suppose you have finally realized the gravity of your negligence. This concerns the Chief of State himself! Must I be forced to warn you about it again?

COLONEL: No, sir, General, sir. But I. . . .

GENERAL BLACK: I will not tolerate excuses! Do you dare justify your conduct? *Only one single solitary guard!* Will you tell me what you've been doing all this time? (*The* COLONEL *is about to speak.*) No! Don't say a word! You'll try to excuse your idiocy with some piece of nonsense. I will only accept excuses with some foundation.

COLONEL: But, General. . . .

GENERAL BLACK: I told you I will not tolerate excuses! Do you suppose I am dumb enough to believe some stupid story you've concocted to get yourself off the hook? No, sir, not on your life! This had better not happen again!

COLONEL: But I. . . .

GENERAL BLACK: I warn you! I will not tolerate excuses! I am speaking now! And when I speak, nobody answers me! Is that clearly understood?

COLONEL (*weary*): Yes, General. . . .

GENERAL BLACK: And now, if you promise me that this will not happen again. . . .

COLONEL: Yes, General. I promise anything, anything you want. . . .

GENERAL BLACK: Then we'll overlook it this time. But the next time! Beware! This is the final warning!

COLONEL: Yes, General. Thank you, General.

GENERAL BLACK (*to* GENERAL WHITE): I surrender the field to you, General White. (*He exits left.*)

GENERAL WHITE (*without moving from the spot*): Colonel! Come here!

COLONEL (*approaching him stiff with fear*): At your command, General.

GENERAL WHITE (*turning and looking at him sternly*): Colonel! (*The* COLONEL *snaps to attention before him.*) I don't like to argue with anyone. By nature, I'm a peaceful man. (*a very short pause to take a breath*) Haven't I told you that whenever his Excellency the Chief of State comes, you must keep the guards well camouflaged? And what do I find? The highway swarming with guards!

COLONEL (*bewildered and on the verge of tears*): But. . . .

GENERAL WHITE: Silence! I don't want your excuses. I want only your obedience! Discipline!

COLONEL: Yes, General, but I. . . .

GENERAL WHITE: I told you to shut up! Nothing annoys me more than to be interrupted while I'm talking! Especially by an inferior!

COLONEL (*weakened, he now gives up all defense*): As you ordered, General. . . .

GENERAL WHITE: I don't like to argue with anybody! I'm a peaceable man. But when I give an order and am not obeyed . . . ! The guards must be hidden, invisible. *Not a single one must be seen!* And I've seen more guards on the highway than at a parade.

COLONEL: But, General. . . .

GENERAL WHITE: Shut up! How many times must I repeat myself? I'm doing the talking now! *I* am! (*There is a silence. The* GENERAL, *upon silencing the* COLONEL, *can't find a way to continue the argument. This infuriates him even more. So he begins to shout.*) But, look here! Why are you just standing there? Why don't you say something?

COLONEL: Because you ordered me to be quiet, General.

GENERAL WHITE: I ordered you! (*making an effort to calm himself*) All right. Then it's all right. I don't like to argue with anybody! But this matter of the guards had better not happen again! Is that understood? It had better not happen again!

COLONEL (*snapping to attention*): Yes, sir, General. (*The two remain face to face, in silence. The* COLONEL, *at attention, maintains without blinking, a military salute. His superior looks him over from top to bottom. Then, after emitting a snort, decides to retire left. As he is on the point of leaving, the* COLONEL, *with fearful timidity, says:*) General . . . sir. . . .

GENERAL WHITE (*stopping*): Now, what nonsense. . . .

COLONEL: May I ask a question, General?

GENERAL WHITE: A question?

COLONEL: Yes, General. Only a little, tiny question. From what direction . . . on what highway will his Excellency, our Chief of State, return after the hunt?

GENERAL WHITE: What's that to you?

COLONEL: It's to station the guards, my General. I ought to know if they will return by the east or the west so that I can station the guards on the right highway. . . . (*Feeling the* GENERAL'S *glance, he adds, in order to ingratiate himself:*) Well camouflaged, of course.

GENERAL WHITE: That's for you to figure out!

COLONEL: But, General. . . .

GENERAL WHITE: Well, station guards in both places. But have those guards *well hidden!* Because if they are not! Do you think I have nothing better to do than waste time on you? Don't let it happen again! (*He begins to exit.*)

COLONEL (*thinking he is alone, he begins to tear his hair*): Ohhh! And all this because of the attempt on the Chief's life! But it didn't even happen on the highway! It happened in town!

GENERAL WHITE (*returning*): Colonel!

COLONEL (*straightening up, frightened*): At your command, General.

GENERAL WHITE: Be very careful what you say. Our beloved Chief lives. That is because there was not one single attempt made *here!* All we need is for the enemies of the State to know about the attempt on the Chief's life. Then they can claim that the people of Know-How have no respect for their Chief of State! You know that they are always looking for ways to slander us! Do you understand?

COLONEL: Yes, General.

GENERAL WHITE: I don't like to argue with anybody! But . . . careful what you say!

COLONEL: Yes, General. (*The* GENERAL *finally leaves and the* COLONEL, *exasperated almost to the point of madness, begins again to tear his hair, while he says:*) I have to arrest somebody! I have to arrest somebody! (*shouting*) Captain! . . . (*then returning to his worries*) I'm fed up with it! If there are not enough guards on the highway! If there is so much as one single guard on the highway! This could drive me to blow my brains out! (*The* CAPTAIN *of the Guard of Highways and Roads appears out of the house.*)

CAPTAIN: At your command, Colonel.

COLONEL (*still nervous*): At my command? Oh, yes, of course. You are at my command. Who called you?

CAPTAIN: Didn't you call me, Colonel?

COLONEL: Oh, yes. . . . (*aside*) I don't even know what I'm doing anymore. (*adopting a solemn attitude*) I called you because. . . . (*now overcome*) I have tremendous responsibility since the Chief of State has decided to come here!

CAPTAIN: I realize that, Colonel.

COLONEL: What do *you* realize? Don't be an idiot, Captain.

CAPTAIN: But, Colonel. . . .

COLONEL: I have to arrest somebody! Are you aware of that? That's why I'm a colonel. Do you understand?

CAPTAIN (*cowed*): Yes, Colonel. . . .

COLONEL: Let's see. Have you arrested any guards today?

CAPTAIN: No, Colonel.

COLONEL: Why not?

CAPTAIN: Because . . . they didn't give me any reason to, Colonel.

COLONEL: But you must have seen someone. . . . (*aside*) Don't I know! . . . with some impropriety in uniform . . . something . . . anything that would give you a motive for arresting him.

CAPTAIN: I have seen no one in improper uniform, Colonel.

COLONEL (*furious*): Do you see this? I'm unbuttoning my jacket because I'm hot. It's against regulations, but I'm hot! Aren't any of the guards hot?

CAPTAIN: I suppose so, Colonel, but I've seen them all properly buttoned, sir.

COLONEL (*getting more furious and snorting*): Well, we must arrest somebody! We must maintain discipline!

CAPTAIN: Yes, Colonel . . . (*But this meek submission only makes the* COLONEL *more frantic since he has no motive for unleashing his fury. He snorts, and with a gesture of strained patience, he instructs the* CAPTAIN.)

COLONEL: So that you realize what discipline is, I'm going to tell you what happened to me once when I inspected a man's uniform. First, he gave me a military salute, without blinking. I saw immediately that he was impeccable: well-shaven, not a single flaw in his uniform, shoes brilliantly shined . . . in a word, perfect, not a thing wrong that you could put your finger on! But I arrested him! Do you understand why I arrested him?

CAPTAIN: No, Colonel. . . .

COLONEL: Because I didn't like his looks! That's why. (*poking him with his finger*) Do you get the point?

CAPTAIN (*dumbfounded*): Yes, Colonel.

COLONEL: Well, this had better not happen again! (*He makes his exit with great dignity, with the air of a dynamic man. The* CAPTAIN *remains stunned.*)

CAPTAIN (*having recovered from his astonishment, in a harsh voice*): Sergeant! (*He leaves right. The stage remains empty for a moment. Then* GENERAL WHITE *and* GENERAL BLACK *enter. They display great activity, giving orders in a loud voice. Behind them comes the* COLONEL.)

GENERAL WHITE: Hurry! Hurry! Take the prisoner to jail! Don't let him escape.

GENERAL BLACK: Right away! We have to interrogate him! We have to make him sing! (*Led by four guards,* JOHN POOR *enters. He comes in with his hands tied behind him, and we see at once that he has received a severe beating. He can scarcely walk. Nonetheless, the guards keep poking him with their rifle butts. Propelled by them,* JOHN *crosses the stage and passes in front of* GENERAL WHITE, *whom he glares at fiercely. The* COLONEL *notices it, and warns the guards:*)

COLONEL: Careful with him! Don't let him bite the General! (*The guards take* JOHN *away and the stage darkens.*)

SCENE 2

The DICTATOR's *study. He is discovered seated comfortably in an armchair, listening to the radio with immense satisfaction, for the commentator merely heaps praises on the* DICTATOR *and his government.*

COMMENTATOR: They demand democracy for our people, but they do not understand that each country needs its own system of government. They do not understand that it is a very serious mistake to suppose that what is good for one is good for all. The enemies of Know-How do not understand that our government is constantly evolving and that the sacred traditions of our forefathers will not yield to the vicious conspiracy of the traitors. They do not try to understand that, for many years, Know-How did not enjoy a period of peace and prosperity as rich and lasting as that of the present. All these political regimes, under the guise of so-called democratic doctrines, continue, one after another, attacking our country. Fortunately, that heroic figure, our Chief of State, has taken a firm grasp on the reins of the nation and now leads her down the good road. To him, and only to him, in defiance of our political enemies, we owe the reestablishment of order in Know-How, the pursuit of justice, and the respect for human rights. . . . (*knocking at the door*)

DICTATOR: Come in. (*The* MINISTER OF REPRESSION *enters.*)

DICTATOR: Shhhhh! (*He indicates an armchair. The* MINISTER *sits down to listen.*)

COMMENTATOR (*continuing his eulogies*): And as all good citizens of Know-How understand, we cannot tolerate having our prosperity and peace disturbed by these isolated acts of barbarism that are committed against Know-How abroad, these hooligans organized by political trouble-makers who have failed their country and by traitors of no account. And, at the same time, we are reassured to know that every civilized individual must be stirred to anger by these stupid, secret intrigues. Only the barbaric and the irresponsible, the foolish lackeys who serve only to support by their imbecilic attitude, the enemies of the State of Know-How, only these, your commentator concludes, can go along with such traitorous acts. (*A chime sounds and the voice of another commentator is heard.*)

OTHER COMMENTATOR: You have just heard an analysis of the present political scene by our collaborator XYZ. (*The* DICTATOR *turns off the radio.*)

MINISTER (*flatteringly*): The commentary of XYZ seems particularly astute tonight.

DICTATOR: Imbecile! Only you and the Minister of Information know that XYZ is me! And you needn't tell me that the commentary is astute! I already know that!

MINISTER: Pardon me, Excellency. It is merely a way of praising your speech and, at the same time, guarding the identity of XYZ. It's imperative that no one, besides ourselves, must know.

DICTATOR: In that case, you show good judgment. But I didn't call you here to praise me, but for something more serious. What happened to that prisoner? Has he been thoroughly interrogated?

MINISTER: He's being interrogated at this very moment, your Excellency.

DICTATOR: I want you to take personal charge of the interrogation, by God! Let's not count on others to do the job.

MINISTER: Yes, Excellency. I'll take personal charge.

DICTATOR (*in a terrible temper*): I cannot understand how such a thing could happen! I pay the police well, I pay the army well, I pay everybody responsible for my security and yet this happens! I overpay the army and the police just to make sure they *do* protect me! I will not stand for such irresponsibility!

MINISTER: Yes, Excellency. I'll give orders to double the guard from now on.

DICTATOR: Double it, triple it, if necessary! But do it with responsible people! I still don't understand how this man could break through a crowd of so many police and soldiers!

MINISTER: Nor me, either, Excellency.

DICTATOR: Must a man always live in fear of his life? If this goes on, I'm pulling out! And I'll leave you with the whole mess!

MINISTER (*supplicating*): No, Excellency, please don't do that! What would become of us if your Excellency deserted us? What would become of Know-How? Our safety depends on your safety—or, rather, our heads.

DICTATOR: I have enough to do to take care of myself. For precisely that reason, I have transferred my funds to foreign banks. . . .

MINISTER: But, your Excellency. . . .

DICTATOR (*dynamically*): If I am to remain in Know-How, I must be obeyed in everything—always!

MINISTER: Yes, Excellency, that's what we are doing.

DICTATOR: Then we must have more efficiency.

MINISTER: Yes, Excellency. What happened will never happen again.

DICTATOR: Now go and interrogate the prisoner. No matter what, he must be forced to name his accomplices!

MINISTER: We'll make him talk, Excellency. (*He begins to leave.*)

DICTATOR: Joe!

MINISTER (*returning*): Your Excellency . . . ?

DICTATOR: Take a message to the Minister of Information. I have to dictate more news commentaries to be read on the National Radio of Know-How for tomorrow.

MINISTER: Yes, Excellency. (*He leaves.*)

DICTATOR (*grunting*): You have to keep your finger in everything! (*The stage darkens.*)

SCENE 3

A basement that serves as a prison. The cells are situated to the right and to the left. JOHN POOR *is fastened to a wooden construction which, though very antiquated, unfortunately serves its function. The* FIRST JAILER, *manipulating the rack of the wooden construction, is intent on forcing* JOHN *to speak, but* JOHN, *bruised and bloodied, cannot talk because he has fainted.*

FIRST JAILER (*forcing him again, brutally*): You'll confess right now! Who are your accomplices? Who's giving you orders? Who? Who? Who? (*The* SECOND JAILER *enters.*)

SECOND JAILER: Look, man, don't be stupid. You want to kill him?

FIRST JAILER: I want him to talk. (*getting ready to begin again*) Let's see who will last!

SECOND JAILER: But can't you see he's out cold? Don't kill him before he talks.

FIRST JAILER (*looking at* JOHN, *very frightened*): Hey, is he dead already?

SECOND JAILER: If he is, I'm going to tell the chief that it's all your fault.

FIRST JAILER (*threatening him with an enormous mallet*): If you say anything to the Chief, I'll smash you!

SECOND JAILER: Don't be stupid! Can't you see that he's alive? Let's get him off that. (*He begins to unfasten* JOHN. *The* FIRST JAILER *helps him.*)

FIRST JAILER: What happened to the Chief?

SECOND JAILER: He's got a broken wrist. (JOHN, *now free of the ropes, falls heavily to the ground, without recovering consciousness.*)

FIRST JAILER: All because of this pig. What are we going to do now?

SECOND JAILER: I don't believe we'll accomplish anything with this method.

FIRST JAILER (*brutally*): Leave him to me! You'll see that we'll win the reward the Minister promised us when we make him talk!

SECOND JAILER: In this case we must be very shrewd. (*He holds him.*) And you are very ignorant.

FIRST JAILER (*turning toward him and wielding the mallet*): I'm not going to let you insult me! Take back that "ignorant"!

SECOND JAILER: Don't be stupid, man! It's just the way I talk.

FIRST JAILER (*still menacing*): Take back the "stupid" too or I'll smash you!

SECOND JAILER (*with complete tranquility, nonchalantly*): Taken back.

FIRST JAILER (*doubtfully*): And you take back the "ignorant" too?

SECOND JAILER (*same as before*): Taken back too. But let's get to work.

FIRST JAILER (*sprightly*): What should we do?

SECOND JAILER: I have an idea. Since we haven't accomplished anything by force, let's try another method.

FIRST JAILER: What method?

SECOND JAILER: We'll get him drunk.

FIRST JAILER (*without comprehending*): Get him drunk?

SECOND JAILER: You heard me. And when he's drunk, he'll tell everything without even realizing it.

FIRST JAILER (*scratches his head and remains pensive for a moment, then phlegmatically*): Good! Real good! That never occurred to me.

SECOND JAILER: Nothing ever occurs to you. You're very stupid. (*The* FIRST JAILER *brandishes the mallet, threatening. Without moving, the* SECOND JAILER *says:*) Taken back. (*And the* FIRST JAILER, *pacified, puts down the mallet.*)

SECOND JAILER (*examining* JOHN): He still hasn't come to. You really gave him a going over.

FIRST JAILER: Probably he's faking.

SECOND JAILER: Let's find out right now. (*points to a bottle on top of a box*) Bring me that bottle.

FIRST JAILER: Which bottle?

SECOND JAILER: The cognac.

FIRST JAILER: You're not going to waste it on him?

SECOND JAILER: We already agreed on getting him drunk. It will all be for the glory of Know-How.

FIRST JAILER (*standing straight with his arm saluting high and with solemnity*): For the glory of Know-How.

SECOND JAILER: Amen. (*The* FIRST JAILER *brings the bottle. The two bend over* JOHN. *The* SECOND JAILER *is intent on making him swallow from the bottle.*) He can't swallow this way. Is there a funnel around here?

FIRST JAILER (*looking around*): Unless you want the one I use for putting gasoline in the truck. . . .

SECOND JAILER: It'll do. (*The* FIRST JAILER *gets up to get the funnel and gives it to his companion who puts it in* JOHN's *mouth.*) Hold the funnel. (*The* FIRST JAILER *obeys him. The* SECOND JAILER *begins to pour cognac into the funnel.*) Is he swallowing it?

FIRST JAILER: No. It's all running out of his mouth.

SECOND JAILER (*arriving at a conclusion*): I would say then that, in truth, he hasn't recovered consciousness. (*Getting to his feet, he carries* JOHN *outside the scene to the cell on the left. From within, he orders his companion.*) Bring a bucket of water. (*The* FIRST JAILER *brings him the bucket from the corner of the room. The* SECOND JAILER, *who has come again onto the stage, remains in the doorway of the cell, takes the bucket and throws the water inside, as if he were emptying it on* JOHN.) Now, let's put our shoulders to the grindstone and get down to work. He's come to. It's your turn.

FIRST JAILER (*dully*): What do I have to do?

SECOND JAILER: You'll make him drink. When you get him a little happy, I'll make him talk. (*He gives him a bottle.*)

FIRST JAILER (*preparing to disappear with the bottle*): I keep thinking that it's a shame to waste cognac, but . . . (*standing at attention, arm raised on high*) For the glory of Know-How!

SECOND JAILER: Amen. (*The* FIRST JAILER *has almost disappeared.*) Hey! (*The* FIRST JAILER *returns.*) Take this. In case he offers resistance. (*He gives him another bottle.*) And this. (*He gives him the mallet. The* FIRST JAILER *leaves with the two bottles and the mallet. Knocking is heard at the door to the entrance.*) Who is it?

VOICE (*outside*): Another prisoner! . . .

SECOND JAILER (*opens the door and speaks with the man outside*): What is he in for?

VOICE (*outside*): Embezzlement of state funds. Besides, he killed the man who denounced him. (*lowers his voice*) It's General Belligerent.

SECOND JAILER (*opening the door, inviting him to enter, respectfully*): Come in, General, sir. Make yourself comfortable. (GENERAL BELLIGERENT *enters and the* JAILER *closes the door, then with curiosity:*) It is true that you robbed the state? And killed the man who denounced you?

GENERAL (*saluting and raising his arm on high*): For the glory of Know-How!

SECOND JAILER: Amen.

GENERAL (*exacting*): Where are my quarters?

SECOND JAILER (*looking at him as if he were crazy*): Your quarters? Don't you mean your cell?

GENERAL (*stubbornly*): My quarters! I am not a political prisoner, but an honorable delinquent for the people's cause.

SECOND JAILER: Yes, General, sir. But this is no more than a provisional prison underneath "Wolf Haven" and these are only cells. Nevertheless, you will be separated from the other political prisoner, but in . . .

GENERAL: Immediately! My quarters! I don't wish to discuss the matter with insubordinates.

SECOND JAILER: Yes, General, sir. This way. (*And the* GENERAL, *very dignified, disappears in the indicated direction. The* SECOND JAILER *returns in a moment. A key is heard in the door to the entrance. It opens, and the* MINISTER *appears with his familiar staff.*)

MINISTER (*to someone outside*): Never mind, I'm already in. Stay there.

SECOND JAILER (*upon seeing the* MINISTER, *prostrates himself before him*): At your service, Your Excellency, Mr. Minister.

MINISTER (*seriously*): Has the prisoner talked yet?

SECOND JAILER: No, Mr. Minister. . . .

MINISTER (*raising his staff*): How can that be? Haven't you made use of our efficient methods?

SECOND JAILER: Yes, Mr. Minister. But. . . .

MINISTER: Stupidity! This is all due to your stupidity! Must I show you how these things should be handled?

SECOND JAILER: Pardon me, Mr. Minister, but. . . .

MINISTER: Where's the Chief Jailer?

SECOND JAILER: In the infirmary.

MINISTER (*astonished*): In the infirmary?

SECOND JAILER: Yes, Mr. Minister. What happened is . . . he broke his wrist.

MINISTER (*without understanding, but indignant*): How did he break his wrist?

SECOND JAILER: Well . . . it's an occupational hazard. (*The* MINISTER *continues to stare at him, like a fiend.*) You see, Mr. Minister. . . . The prisoner refused to speak. The Chief Jailer, wanting to oblige him, got ready to hit him. The prisoner ducked his head and . . . the Chief Jailer hit the wall. . . .

MINISTER (*jocular and ill-disposed*): And he broke his wrist!

SECOND JAILER: That's right, Mr. Minister. Like I said: an occupational hazard.

MINISTER: Must you be so stupid! Where is the prisoner?

SECOND JAILER: Do you want to see him, Mr. Minister?

MINISTER: I want to interrogate him myself!

SECOND JAILER: Yes, sir. At once. (*calling into the doorway of the cell*) Flint, bring the prisoner! (*a pause*) Flint! Hurry up! His Excellency the Minister wants to interrogate him personally. (*a pause*) Flint, don't you hear me? Flint! (*The* SECOND JAILER *enters the cell and disappears. The* MINISTER *waits impatiently with his arms crossed. Immediately the* SECOND JAILER *returns almost dragging the* FIRST JAILER *who is completely drunk.*)

FIRST JAILER (*singing, drunkenly*): For the glory of Know-How! . . . (*He salutes and assumes a serious air.*) Amen! Long live Know-How! (*same gestures*) Amen! Yes, sir! We must say "amen" to everything! Amen!

MINISTER (*without coming out of his astonishment*): Is this . . . the prisoner?

SECOND JAILER (*gesturing frantically to his companion to restrain himself; it's futile*): No, sir. The prisoner is inside there. . . .

FIRST JAILER (*showing the bottle to his companion*): I told you that it was a shame to waste good cognac. . . . I haven't wasted even the tiniest drop. (*seeing the* MINISTER) My friend, would you join me in a toast to the glory of Know-How?

SECOND JAILER (*hurriedly*): Restrain yourself. It's his Excellency, the Minister. (*But the* FIRST JAILER *is too drunk to be aware of this fact.*)

MINISTER (*overcome, indicating the drunkard with his staff*): Who is this idiot?

FIRST JAILER (*hiccuping*): Amen!

SECOND JAILER: He's Flint, my fellow worker, Mr. Minister. . . .

MINISTER (*raising his staff*): Get him out of my sight!

SECOND JAILER (*dragging his companion to the exit*): Yes, sir.

MINISTER: And you know what to do with him! The ammonia treatment and three days in the cell!

SECOND JAILER: Yes, sir.

MINISTER: And you get back here at once and station yourself by the door. I can interrogate the prisoner by myself.

SECOND JAILER: Yes, Mr. Minister. (*He leaves with his companion.*)

The MINISTER, *upon remaining alone, takes up one of the* JAILER'S *guns, assures himself that it is loaded, and, pointing it in the direction of the cell door, he kicks the door open and shouts:*

MINISTER: Come out of there! (*Handcuffed and badly beaten,* JOHN *comes out. The* MINISTER *is astonished.*) You!! How did you get here?

JOHN: You dragged me here. Don't you think you owe me an explanation for all this?

MINISTER (*very surprised*): I must remind you that you are a political prisoner. Be careful with these impertinences.

JOHN: If you like, you can call those gorillas back and have them continue torturing me.

MINISTER: I don't believe that will be necessary. (*He signals him to turn his back, and with a key he unlocks the handcuffs.*) You'll tell me everything.

JOHN: Are you sure?

MINISTER: I trust in your common sense.

JOHN: And what do you want from me? The truth . . . or a confession of guilt that will serve your ends?

MINISTER: (*containing himself*): I want you to tell the truth.

JOHN: Well, you are suffering under a delusion. Because you have made a mistake with me. A brutal error! I'm innocent of what you're accusing me!

MINISTER: I understand perfectly. If I were in your place, I would also try to deny my guilt.

JOHN: (*protesting energetically*): But I'm telling the truth! It never even entered my mind to attempt to assassinate the Chief of State! (*Then, in another tone, more serene.*) Although I believe now that there will come a time when someone will try it, to free us all from this dictatorship.

MINISTER (*the exalted politician rising in him*): Repent those words! Because, even if what you said were true, you have just committed a crime: defamation against the Chief of State!!

JOHN (*indignant*): You mean I can't say that the Chief of State is a dictator?

MINISTER (*also indignant*): It's prohibited in Know-How!

JOHN: And no one is allowed to speak his mind?

MINISTER: It's prohibited!

JOHN: And you can't say what's the truth?

MINISTER: It's prohibited!

JOHN: Then, *why*, only a minute ago, did you ask me to tell you the truth?

MINISTER (*intimidated*): Because . . . all right, this has gone far enough. I don't have to discuss it with you. Besides, I'm the Minister of Repression and I have a perfect right to interrogate a criminal against the State!

JOHN (*cocky*): And I also have a perfect right not to tell the truth!

MINISTER: Why?

JOHN: Because the truth is prohibited in Know-How!

MINISTER (*beside himself*): That's enough! Do you want to force me to employ other methods which are more persuasive?

JOHN: You've already employed your paid assassins, and, allow me to correct you, those methods are not persuasive, but brutal. They . . . are inhuman! (*The* MINISTER *is speechless.*) Call them! Call your gorillas! When you don't have good reason to convince someone, it's handy to use force.

The MINISTER *attempts to control himself. One can tell that these last questions of* JOHN'S, *although they've nearly pushed him to the breaking point, have reached him, almost making him reflect. The fact is that it seems to humanize him. And, after a pause, he says:*

MINISTER: Why do you become so aggressive? I didn't have you arrested. It was a disagreeable surprise for me to find you here. Because, really, I would like to be able to help you—to show you that. . . .

JOHN: I didn't ask you to show me anything.

MINISTER: You see? Each time you work yourself in deeper. Why don't you tell me exactly what happened?

JOHN (*ironically*): You already know: I fired a shot at the Chief of State. Only it didn't go off.

MINISTER: You didn't fire any shot. Where have you hidden the weapon with which . . . ?

JOHN (*indignant again*): Weapon, shmeapon! Do you think I'm so stupid as to risk my life for something with such little chance of success? It never even occurred to me to attempt it. And for all that happened to me—you're entirely to blame.

MINISTER (*openmouthed*): Me?

JOHN: Damned right! Because you made me almost crazy with anger when I discovered your methods. When I went to you to intervene for my brother, you sent me for an interview with your secretary.

MINISTER: You already knew him. He was the one whose stomach you told me to fill. All right, then, isn't that what I did? I followed your advice to the letter. And with good results, certainly. Because that man is now the most faithful of secretaries!

JOHN (*indignant*): You understand only what's most convenient for you. I didn't mean filling one more or less dangerous stomach! You have to fill every stomach in the country! Then there would never be complaints from any side!

MINISTER: But what you suggest is Utopian, impossible. Don't you understand that? There aren't sufficient funds to do that.

JOHN: It wouldn't be impossible if you people would give up those privileges, those luxuries you've unjustly acquired!

MINISTER (*on guard*): Now you're getting off the track again. Let's stick to what happened!

JOHN: I already told you: you're the one who's responsible. Yes, because I left there so furious, so nauseated by everything. And then, on my way home I find all the traffic stopped because. . . . All right, it seems to me a crime to stop all traffic just because the Chief of State is passing through. So I tried to cross the street, ignoring the guards. Why should I wait until the whole procession goes by?

MINISTER (*severely*): Lack of respect to the person of the Chief of State!

JOHN: Sure, whatever you want to call it! But I didn't make an attempt on his life! Why are you accusing me of that then?

MINISTER (*stubbornly*): You mean you had no accomplices?

JOHN (*losing his patience*): I mean that. . . . Look, I've already told you everything. Now you can believe whatever you like. (*There is a pause.*)

MINISTER (*pensively*): Yes. There's room for that possibility. On the other hand, no trace of a weapon has been found and . . . (*reacting*) But you've committed the crime of disrespect and defamation of character against the Chief of State!

JOHN (*ironically*): I already know it. Two very serious crimes.

MINISTER: Man, I'll tell you. They're very common crimes nowadays in Know-How. The bad thing is in committing them. When they hear of someone. . . .

JOHN: Then they put him in jail for a while.

MINISTER (*very offended*): But what do you think goes on in Know-How? In Know-How justice exists. Justice and benevolence like we've never known before, thanks to the generosity of our beloved Chief of State.

JOHN (*surprised and joking*): Generosity?

MINISTER: Yes, my friend: generosity. Our Chief of State is a very benevolent man—the loving father of all Know-Howians. You people, since you haven't any personal contact with him, pay attention to the gossip that circulates. But I'm going to demonstrate to you . . . yes, I'm going to show you! You'll be able to judge for yourself when you see with what benevolence you'll be treated. Once that it's proved that you had no intention of assassinating him, you will be treated fairly and justly. I'll take responsibility for that. I'll show you . . . you'll see, you'll see. . . . Our beloved Chief of State is a very compassionate man; he knows how to put himself in the place of others because he has a good heart. I myself will tell him the truth about what happened. (*calling*) Jailer! (SECOND JAILER *enters in a moment.*)

SECOND JAILER: Mr. Minister. . . .

MINISTER: Return the prisoner to his cell. And show him every consideration which he deserves as a political prisoner.

SECOND JAILER: Yes, Mr. Minister. (*The* MINISTER *leaves and the* SECOND JAILER *accompanies him to the door.*)

JOHN (*pensively, in an attitude of incredulity*): He has a good heart! . . . Could it be possible? (*But he is brought out of his thoughts rudely by the kick of the* SECOND JAILER, *administered automatically and swiftly.*)

SECOND JAILER: Come on, pig! To your pigsty! (*The curtain falls rapidly.*)

ACT III

SCENE 1

The bedroom of the DICTATOR. *A bed and little table with a phone. In the corner, a little chair. When the curtain rises, the stage is empty. We hear the* DICTATOR *off stage; he is noisily rinsing his mouth with water. The sound of his gargling—"Gla, gla, gla"—can be heard. Then he enters. He is wearing a long nightshirt and a little sleeping cap. His pants can be seen under the nightshirt. He goes directly to the telephone.*

DICTATOR: Who commands the guards tonight? All right, Colonel. Why wasn't I informed at once? But look, didn't you hear me when I spoke on the radio? Less excuses and more efficiency. I only want you to be more careful. That's right: I want to get a peaceful night's sleep, especially after what happened this morning. In short, if it's necessary, double the guard. What I want is a good night's sleep. You know how I suffer from insomnia.

He hangs up. And afterward he lifts his nightshirt a little and takes off his pants. With infinite care he folds them, being careful to keep the crease, and puts them at the foot of the bed. From the little table he takes a bottle of pills, takes one out and puts it in his mouth. He takes a glass of water and swallows with some difficulty. He goes to the bed and kneels down, his hands stiffly clasped. He bows his head and begins to pray:

DICTATOR: Now I lay me down to sleep. . . .

The rest is not heard since he speaks in a low voice. He rises and slides into bed, curling up under the covers and turning off the light. The stage is silent for a few seconds. Then, from the side, carefully making no noise, JOHN *enters. He approaches the bed where the* DICTATOR *snores. He lifts his hand in which a knife flashes, but at the moment of executing the blow, the telephone rings.* JOHN *looks terror-stricken. The* DICTATOR, *who has his back to* JOHN, *turns toward him, and* JOHN *remains petrified. Nevertheless, the* DICTATOR *doesn't wake up, and once he becomes accustomed to his new position, he begins snoring again.* JOHN *relaxes, although, to completely dispel his terror, he passes his hand over his eyes. Coolly appraising the scene, since the telephone hasn't stopped ringing,* JOHN *hides himself under the bed. The*

DICTATOR *begins to move around again, but he still doesn't waken. As the sound of the phone finally begins to intrude upon his consciousness, he opens his eyes. He turns on the light; he scratches, yawns, and sits on the bed, rubbing his eyes. Feeling around the top of the table, he picks up the telephone.*

DICTATOR: Yes . . . Ah, it's you, darling. (*still half asleep*) Now is it daytime or nighttime? Nighttime? What day is it? Then. . . . But I'm really in a daze. Yes, dear, you woke me up when I'd just fallen asleep. Yes . . . yes, honey . . . (*yawning*) Ahhhhh! Yes, dear. Yes, my sweet, of course I'm listening. Yes, yes, tell me, honey, how did your day go? Yes, dear, tell me where you've been. (*He yawns.*) At a fund-raising festival for . . . what? Ah, housing for the needy! Yes, my love, I can already imagine it: the place packed. The most influential ladies of society attending. Tomorrow I'll cover it on the radio. How much did you say you raised at the festival? Three hundred dollars and thirteen cents? But that's not enough to build a one-room bungalow, don't you see? No, I don't know what you can use the money for. Why don't you use it to fix the leaks in the last housing development you built? It needs it. Okay, do with it what you want, but I'm going back to bed now. Where did you say you're going tomorrow? Now, honey, don't fly off the handle. No, no, dear, of course not; I didn't mean to annoy you. (*getting off the bed*) But, darling, forgive me. I swear that wasn't my intention. I just don't know what I'm saying, honey. I'm almost falling asleep. (*very worried*) But, dear . . . Honey, listen to me . . . sweetie-pie? (*And now he is wide awake, very upset. He belches. And he says to himself:*)

DICTATOR: I think I'm going to have indigestion tonight.

He returns to bed and prepares to retire. But he remembers something and gets out of bed again. He squats and reaches his hand under the bed, producing a chamberpot. But, suddenly, he thinks he's seen something strange and he squats to have another look. His fear increases and he begins to cry for help, but he is so frightened that his voice is gone.

DICTATOR: He . . . he . . . helppp! (*We can hardly hear him.* JOHN *leaves his hiding place.*)

JOHN (*threatening him with a knife*): Shut up or I'll kill you!

DICTATOR (*in tearful supplication*): No, please, don't do that! (*backing toward the center of the stage*) Tell me what you want and I'll give it to you but . . . don't kill me! Think what would happen to Know-How if I died!

JOHN (*pursuing him everywhere, mocking*): Is it possible that you actually believe you're indispensable to Know-How?

DICTATOR (*always retreating*): Look, I'll tell you: it's not what I believe, but the newspapers and the radio keep insisting so much, that I . . .

JOHN: The newspapers and the radio are completely controlled by you. More precisely, they're the loudspeakers of your government. (*The* DICTATOR *wants to say something.*) No, don't bother, because you won't succeed in convincing me of anything. (*They are now on the other side of the stage, next to the little table.*) Besides, I have this knife.

DICTATOR (*still terror-stricken*): I've already . . . I've already seen. . . .

JOHN: And the two of us are alone. (*anticipating a move from the* DICTATOR) Careful! Don't try to call for help! (*He approaches him, menacingly.*) Now I dominate the situation. It's good for you to get used to not being the one who dominates. Everything in this world comes to its end. Haven't you ever thought of that?

DICTATOR: Well. . . .

JOHN: Your brain can't stop turning, thinking who I could be. You'd like to know that, wouldn't you?

DICTATOR (*timidly*): Well . . . If it wouldn't inconvenience you. . . .

JOHN: Well, I'm John Poor. Doesn't that name mean anything to you?

DICTATOR (*even more frightened*): John . . . Poor? You're the one who . . . this morning. . . .

JOHN: The one who this morning, what? Finish it!

DICTATOR (*dead with fear*): The one who this morning . . . tried to assassinate me. . . .

JOHN (*threatening him with the knife*): That's a lie!

DICTATOR (*still frightened*): Yes, yes, as you say, but move the knife away, if you please.

JOHN: I'll move it when you take back what you said.

DICTATOR (*stupefied*): Taken back. You're *not* the one from this morning. . . .

JOHN (*threatening him again*): Are you trying to drive me crazy? I am the one from this morning!

DICTATOR (*intimidated*): Yes, yes, of course . . . You are. . . .

JOHN: But I didn't try to kill you!

DICTATOR (*finding a way out*): Right! What I was going to say . . . Is that . . . That's exactly what the Minister of Repression has told me. . . .

JOHN: Then, you already know everything?

DICTATOR (*wanting to be complacent*): Oh, everything! I know that you were only trying to cross the street.

JOHN: But if you know everything, if you know that I'm innocent, why haven't you given orders to set me free?

DICTATOR: That's the first thing I thought I'd do when I got up tomorrow morning.

JOHN: Tomorrow? You should have done it today, right away!

DICTATOR (*excusing himself*): But . . . I'm so sleepy. But, if you wish, I'll do it right this minute. (*He sits down at the table and searches through the pocket of his coat, which is hanging on the back of the chair.*) Would you allow me a blow?

JOHN: What?

DICTATOR (*showing him the handkerchief he's taken from his pocket*): My nose. I'm catching a little cold. (*He blows his nose loudly.* JOHN, *watching him, begins to laugh.*) Why are you laughing?

JOHN: "They expected a king, and were presented with a buffoon. They awaited a dragon, and a bourgeois appeared, big-nosed, with a snotty handkerchief."

DICTATOR (*mystified*): What's that?

JOHN: I'm sure you haven't heard the name of what he wrote. His name is Andreyev.

DICTATOR: Andreyev? That name sounds a little suspicious to me.

JOHN: You're still accustomed to speaking nonsense. Naturally—because that's the way you deceive the people.

DICTATOR: You're mistaken. I couldn't deceive the people, because I love them. I love Know-How and I sacrifice myself for Know-How.

JOHN (*joking*): Really? (*He begins to laugh in bursts.*)

DICTATOR (*disconcerted*): Frankly, I don't understand you. I'm not sure if you're all there.

JOHN (*still laughing*): You believe that?

DICTATOR: But what I can least understand, frankly, is why you've come to interrupt my sleep.

JOHN (*laughing even harder*): I already told you before. . . . (*taking pleasure in frightening him*) I've come to kill you! Yes! To kill you! . . . (*He makes a growling noise.*) Buuf! . . .

DICTATOR (*stepping back*): Noooo!

JOHN: But now I don't feel like it. You can relax. (*The* DICTATOR *watches him strangely, unsure and very frightened.*) You don't trust me, do you? You're wondering why I changed my mind? Well, I'm going to tell you the reasons that saved your neck. The first. . . . You can't imagine why, can you? (*The* DICTATOR, *cornered, doesn't say a word.*) Hasn't it ever occurred to you that the life of a man—although he doesn't think like you, although he isn't continually doing harm—is the thing most worthy of respect? (*scornfully*) No! You only think about yourself! But there's another reason besides. And that is—I pity you!

DICTATOR (*protesting*): Pity?

JOHN: Yes, I feel compassion for you. Don't you know what it's like to feel compassion for a man either? When you see him defenseless, like a cast-a-way with nothing to hold on to? Of course you don't! If you did, you wouldn't have been so bloodthirsty toward your enemies!

DICTATOR (*making excuses for himself*): You *must* be merciless toward your enemies. They threaten your power.

JOHN (*scornfully*): That's why I pity you most of all: for not knowing how to pity. For not knowing how to understand other people's reasons, the anguish that those people go through who suffer your tyranny. For not knowing how to understand the men who struggle for their freedom.

DICTATOR (*skeptically*): Freedom? And what, finally, is freedom?

JOHN: I don't know how to explain it to you. But I do know that for a man the most beautiful thing is his fight for freedom.

DICTATOR: I would have said his fight for his country.

JOHN: And what is the country? Can you conceive of it as something outside yourself?

DICTATOR: Outside myself? I don't know what you mean. But before you talked about tyranny. Do you believe that I'm a tyrant?

JOHN: It's a strong word, isn't it? Would it be less offensive to you if I said—a dictator?

DICTATOR (*indignant, in a high voice*): I don't like either of the two! And I won't tolerate your speaking to me in this manner!

JOHN: Easy, easy! . . . Did you forget that I just gave you your life? (*He shows him the knife.*)

DICTATOR (*cowardly*): But . . . you offended me. . . .

JOHN: With the truth!

DICTATOR (*ready to defend his position, growing stronger each time*): That isn't the truth! My government is an organic democracy that has made Know-How the vanguard of civilization. And we'll never allow the return to those feeble systems so sadly remembered, socially and politically, years of progress over the other countries. And that's why, because they envy our progress and our country, they never cease slandering us or conspiring against us. But now the enemy is revealed! The enemy is no other than he who left our soil defeated, who plunged Know-How into chaos, and who has been overcome thanks only to the policy of my government!

JOHN (*who's been listening with his arms folded, in a mocking attitude*): Bravo! Bravissimo! That was as fine as your radio commentaries. (*in a tone ironically intimate*) But . . . do you actually believe that nonsense?

DICTATOR: It's the truth! And the proof you have is that the country is now more content than ever: satisfied and peaceful.

JOHN: A peace efficiently maintained by the force of your oppression. But, in spite of that, what about the latest strikers who wanted a higher salary and more freedom? Was that satisfaction? Was that peace?

DICTATOR: And what about the reception that Know-How-City gave me a few days ago when I went to visit?

JOHN: They came from all over the state, of course.

DICTATOR (*proudly*): Well there you have proof of the love the people feel for me.

JOHN: But all of that was organized! And your hirelings who came in shifts to applaud you were all paid for by your government! (*Playing with the knife, he has pressed it against the* DICTATOR's *throat.*) Isn't that true?

DICTATOR (*frightened again*): Take the knife away, will you? And I'll tell you . . . something I've never told anyone before.

JOHN (*removing it*): Talk.

DICTATOR: I . . . I'm not free either, you know? If I could, I'd leave all this and . . . ! But they won't let me. "You stay here," they tell me. "We've got to keep up the pretense." And me, okay, what do you want me to do?

JOHN: You should always do what your conscience dictates.

DICTATOR: But there are times when we confuse the voice of our conscience with the voices around us. I don't know what's right or wrong, you understand? I'm full of confusion! I don't know when I'm doing something if I'm myself or if I'm someone outside of me. You heard that little speech I let out a minute ago? The same thing as on the radio, you told me. But it's because I don't know if I'm the "I" from the speeches or the "I" who's talking to you confidentially right now. Everybody knows me: I'm the Chief of State of Know-How. But sometimes when I'm alone, I wonder: Who are you?—Do you believe that?

JOHN: What do you expect me to say? I don't know you well enough to. . . .

DICTATOR: Well, I would like it if you would keep trying to, because I'm in a dilemma too. And of course, *they* take advantage of it.

JOHN: They?

DICTATOR: The ones who are always following me. Because they can do whatever they want and afterward—they throw the blame on me.

JOHN: I always thought that you were surrounded by scoundrels.

DICTATOR: Isn't that right? Listen . . . You're so determined and courageous, what do you advise me to do?

JOHN: Me? Why do you ask my advice?

DICTATOR: Because you're different from the rest I know. You say what you think, you feel respect for human life, you feel compassion for others. . . . Finally, you're like a good person would be—if there were any in the world.

JOHN (*smiling*): You know that's a funny thing?

DICTATOR: What's a funny thing?

JOHN: I'm beginning to find you pleasant.

DICTATOR (*contentedly*): Really? I'm really glad! And . . . trading one secret for another, do you know something else?

JOHN: What?

DICTATOR: I envy you!

JOHN: Me? Why?

DICTATOR: Because I'd like to live a life free of responsibility. Like you.

JOHN: I have mine too. Everybody has them.

DICTATOR: Yes, but . . . you understand me. . . . Still, a simple life has its attractions. What do you do when you leave work?

JOHN: I go to my part-time job. I can't earn enough on only one job. You don't know how life is!

DICTATOR (*sincerely*): That's not right! You should be able to earn enough money to live decently! (*pensively*) Of course. . . . Am I to blame for this?

JOHN: No, you're not to blame alone. But, between one thing and another, we get by all right. Like always you tell us that you can't raise salaries and we've got to produce more . . . But . . . Bah! We live! . . .

DICTATOR: And happy, in spite of everything. You're worthy of admiration. The man of Know-How is famous for always staying happy despite adversity.

JOHN: What do you want? If on top of all we've got to put up with, we went around whining. . . . We try to amuse ourselves.

DICTATOR: And you . . . Okay, you'll think that I'm a numbskull. But, what do you do in your spare time? On holidays.

JOHN: Well . . . I go for a walk with my wife.

DICTATOR (*making a sour face*): Uf! I'm about fed up to here with that. Mine doesn't leave me alone in sun or rain.

JOHN: I get together with some friends to play cards.

DICTATOR: Poker?

JOHN: Sure, poker!

DICTATOR: Exactly what I like to do best. (*making him sit down at the table*) You want to play a short game?

JOHN: Do you have a deck?

DICTATOR: Right here. Who deals?

JOHN: You.

DICTATOR: Stupendous! (*beginning to deal the cards*) Out. (JOHN *stays. The* DICTATOR *passes out the cards.*) Draw your cards.

JOHN: I warn you it's hard to beat me at poker.

DICTATOR (*beginning to play*): We'll see. I might not know how to govern, but in poker I have no rival. Eh, careful! (*He clears away the cards he dealt.*) I won. Then, I draw first.

JOHN: Hey, that doesn't count. I won't let you cheat! The ace always takes the Jack.

DICTATOR: Shut up and deal!

JOHN: But. . . .

DICTATOR (*continuing the game*): Shut up and deal! Shut up and deal! (*The stage darkens.*)

SCENE 2

A *corner of the stage is illuminated: it is* JOHN's *cell. He is discovered sleeping on a prison cot with his hands behind his back, handcuffed. A moment before the stage lightens, in the darkness and without breaking the continuity of Scene One,* JOHN's *voice is heard in a tone of protest:*

JOHN'S VOICE: You shut up and deal! You shut up and deal! I don't want to play! I don't like cheaters! (*And the stage lightens at the moment when the* SECOND JAILER *gives* JOHN *a kick in the kidneys.*)

SECOND JAILER: Get up, imbecile! You think you're in a fancy hotel? Around here you have to get up early! (JOHN *sits up, with a moan. He sees the* SECOND JAILER *and, in the doorway of the cell, the* CHIEF JAILER. *He has a cast on his wrist and a sinister look on his face.*)

SECOND JAILER: Here he is, Chief.

CHIEF JAILER (*authoritatively*): Get up! (*The* SECOND JAILER *grabs* JOHN *by the lapel.* JOHN *resists and the* JAILER *strikes him.*)

SECOND JAILER: On your feet, pig! (*He corners him against the wall, still beating him. He consults the other.*) What shall I do with him, Chief?

CHIEF JAILER: You know what you have to do with him. (*The* SECOND JAILER *grabs* JOHN *by the shirt, pulls him toward him, and punches him on the jaw with such force that* JOHN *falls to the ground.* JOHN *suffers the beating without a complaint.*)

SECOND JAILER: Even, Chief.

CHIEF JAILER (*with a sinister air, advancing toward* JOHN): No, we're not even yet! I have a broken wrist. (*facing* JOHN) And meanwhile, you have all your bones in one piece, you stupid swine! (*He kicks* JOHN *in the head, and* JOHN *can't hold back a groan. The* CHIEF JAILER *tries to kick him again but,* JOHN, *from the ground, defends himself with his feet, and nearly knocks the* CHIEF JAILER *over. Only by bracing his shoulder against the wall does the* CHIEF *maintain his balance.*) Damn you! . . .

SECOND JAILER (*grabbing a small stool and coming to the defense of his* CHIEF): You want to fight, do you? (*He attempts to break the stool over* JOHN's *head, but* JOHN *twists away and receives the blow on his shoulders. A low bellow of pain escapes his lips. The* CHIEF JAILER, *pulling himself together, prepares to beat the prisoner, with the help of the* SECOND JAILER.)

JOHN (*terror-stricken, as he sees the two men approach*): What are you going to do to me? (*The stage becomes completely black. But in the darkness we hear the sounds of the struggle and* JOHN's *shouts.*)

JOHN (*in the darkness*): You bastards! Leave me alone just once! . . . Is this what they pay you for, you cowards? I'll report you! . . . I'll demand justice! Justice! Is there any justice in Know-How? Please! . . . No! (*A stronger blow cuts short* JOHN's *scream. Then a silence which lasts several seconds and seems interminable until, little by little, the light begins to return but in the center of the stage.)*

SCENE 3

The same scene as before. The CHIEF JAILER *and the* SECOND JAILER *leave* JOHN'S *cell.*

SECOND JAILER: Now the score's even, Chief. I think he has a broken leg.

CHIEF JAILER: The account's closed. Now let's set the General free. The order. (*The* SECOND JAILER *hands him a scroll.*) Quick! Get the drum! (*The* SECOND JAILER *gets a drum from the corner, hangs it around his neck, and accompanies the* CHIEF JAILER *to the* GENERAL's *cell. The* CHIEF JAILER *opens the cell and, without entering, salutes the man inside.*) General, sir! (*The* SECOND JAILER *very solemnly gives a drum roll.*)

CHIEF JAILER (*unrolling the scroll which the* SECOND JAILER *gave him and reading solemnly*): "Sentence of his Excellency the Chief of State against General Belligerent." (*He clears his throat and reads, carefully stressing the adverbs.*) "Reviewed by my Excellency the following case against General Belligerent, and keeping in mind that he himself, *voluntarily* and without any coercion, has confessed *nobly* his crime of robbery and murder, in which is *clearly* seen his sincere repentance, apart from the extenuating circumstances in which the deeds occurred, I order that, *immediately*, the aforementioned General be placed at liberty, *principally* bearing in mind the invaluable services rendered to the country by said person, in war and in peace. At the same time, I order the immediate transfer of General Belligerent to Regiment 13 on the front, in which he will remain for a term of at least two years. Signed in Know-How, March 19. . . . etc. (*The* SECOND JAILER *provides another roll of the drum. The* CHIEF JAILER, *rolling the document:*) Your finest hour, eh, General?

GENERAL (*leaving in a bad humor, yawning*): You might have waited to communicate this to me. I was at the best part of my dream.

CHIEF JAILER: Forgive me, General. But I thought it would make you happy to hear that. . . .

GENERAL (*angrily*): Happy? When they arrest a General with a brilliant service record like mine? I see nothing in that to make me happy! (*He leaves the stage.*)

CHIEF JAILER: Forgive me, General, sir, but . . . (*He follows him.*)

SECOND JAILER: Chief. . . . Chief. . . .

CHIEF JAILER: What's the matter?

SECOND JAILER: The other one's sentence. (*indicating* JOHN's *cell*)

CHIEF JAILER: You take care of it. I've got to take care of the General.

SECOND JAILER: But . . . who'll play the drum for me?

CHIEF JAILER: Forget the drum and the rest. Just read him the sentence—and hurry up!

He exits. The SECOND JAILER *takes off the drum and goes toward* JOHN's *cell. The cell becomes illuminated. In it, lying on the floor, is* JOHN, *terribly mistreated. The* SECOND JAILER *opens the door and, without entering, shouts.*

SECOND JAILER: The prisoner will stand! (JOHN *looks at him with eyes full of hate but makes no move to rise.*) Stand up, I tell you! You have to stand to hear your sentence! It's the rule! (*threatening him with the drum stick*) Do you want me to help you up? (JOHN, *in the face of the threat, tries laboriously to get up, leaning against the wall. It is obvious, by his manner of moving and by his painful gestures, that something is wrong with his leg, and he has very little luck trying to stand. When he falls to the floor again, he muffles a cry and clasps his hand over the break in his leg.*)

SECOND JAILER (*who has followed, impassively, the futile attempts of* JOHN): What's the matter with your leg? (JOHN, *from the floor, gives him a look of hate.*) Well, no matter. I'll read this to you anyway. (*unrolling the scroll he carries in his hand*) "Sentence of his Excellency the Chief of State of Know-How against John Poor." (*He clears his throat and reads.*) "Reviewed by my Excellency the following case against John Poor, and bearing in mind the innocence of the accused in the crime which he was accused of attempting against me, the chief representative of the country; I must, however, consider also his guilt in showing disrespect, insults, and insubordination toward my government and my person, which crimes reduce him to a third class citizen, an individual with little gratitude for our regime, legally recognized by God and by men, I order that the accused complete the sentence of twelve years and one day, in one of the state penitentiaries of Know-How. Signed in Know-How, March 19. . . . (*looking scornfully at* JOHN) Well, that's finished now. (*He leaves the cell and begins to close the door when the stage completely darkens.*)

SCENE 4

The sound of military marches is heard in the darkness. As the stage lightens, a colorful procession crosses the stage. Above the procession and sitting on a decorated platform sit the CHIEF OF STATE *of Know-How and the* CHIEF OF STATE *of Show-How, both elaborately decorated with medals and ribbons. They acknowledge the invisible multitude whose applause can be heard. In a strategic position to the side, on a smaller and lower platform,* CHAMELEON *is stationed. At apparently fixed times, he shouts above the multitude.*

CHAMELEON: Long live the Chief of State of Know-How! (CHAMELEON *holds up a large placard.*)
CROWD: Hurrah!
CHAMELEON: Long live the Chief of State of Show-How! (*Again he raises the placard.*)
CROWD: Hurrah!
CHAMELEON: Long live Know-How and Show-How! (*Again the placard goes up.*)
CROWD: Hurrrrrrrrrrrrraaaahhhhhhhhh!

Thunderous applause. The two CHIEFS OF STATE *get to their feet, acknowledging the "hurrahs." They disappear toward the back. The music has been diminishing as if the procession were moving off. Now scattered applause can be heard, then silence. The stage darkens.*

SCENE 5

Four areas are to be distinguished when the lights come up: Above stage level, a large living room in the center and well toward the back. At stage level, on the right, a room in JOHN's *house that appeared earlier in Act I, Scene 2. In the foreground, in a corner on the left,* JOHN's *cell. Also in the foreground, in the corner on the right, the apartment of* CHAMELEON.

At first, only the living room in the background is visible. In it, in a row, maintaining a parallel with the file of armchairs, the CAPTAIN, *the* COLONEL, GENERAL WHITE, GENERAL BLACK, *the* MINISTER OF REPRESSION, *the* CHIEF OF STATE *of Know-How, the* CHIEF OF STATE *of Show-How, and other representatives of Show-How in a descending order of hierarchy. The two* DICTATORS, *who remain in the center, are mounted on pedestals.*

DICTATOR OF KNOW-HOW (*addressing the* DICTATOR *of Show-How*): Now I have the honor, in accordance with the quality of such an illustrious guest, of decorating you with the highest and most meritorious distinction of my country, the medal of Good Will in Observation of Social and Political Problems. . . . (*There is a nudge to the* MINISTER OF REPRESSION, *followed by one from him to* GENERAL BLACK, *who in turn nudges the next person, and so on down the line to the* CAPTAIN. *The* CAPTAIN *takes out a jewel case and follows, in the reverse order, the same series of nudges. The* DICTATOR, *in order to stall for time, continues his speech while the medal is on its way.*) With this decoration we distinguish outstanding personalities for those extraordinary accomplishments that are open only to those few privileged ones who have attained a true knowledge of the unquestionable superiority of our regime. I award you the medal of Good Will in the Observation of Social and Political Problems. . . . (*The other* DICTATOR, *very tense and serious, allows him to pin on the medal. The* DICTATOR *of Know-How is having difficulty finding a space for the medal on the overdecorated chest. Suddenly, the* DICTATOR *of Show-How makes a grimace of pain, trying hard to repress it. He was stuck by* the pin. Then both DICTATORS *exchange a noisy embrace. The rest applaud.*)

DICTATOR OF SHOW-HOW (*after disengaging himself from the other, clears his throat and prepares to speak*): In reciprocation of such a high honor, I am going to award you the medal of Promoter of Football and Other Sports as diversion from the anarchistic politics against the State, an honor that in my country has been awarded only to those few persons whose political astuteness has permitted them to see clearly the great efficiency of our system. (*nudges and the same game as before, only this time among the representatives of Show-How*) With this honor, I give proof that my country regards you and your country in the very highest estimation, an esteem that corresponds to the solidarity which has sprung up between our two countries who, forever united, fight heroically against the cunning and corrupt infiltration of those fatal theories—theories which our enemies again and again have falsely called "democratic." (*now with the medal*) I award you, then, the distinction of Promoter of Football and Other Sports. (*The* DICTATOR *of Know-How, very seriously, receives the medal. They embrace and the others applaud.*)

DICTATOR OF KNOW-HOW: I will now award you the medal of Sincere Informer in Radio of Press. . . .

DICTATOR OF SHOW-HOW: And I award you the decoration for Fair Taxation of the People. . . .

Very loud music—perhaps a Sousa march? —and a rapid rhythm drown out both men's speeches. Nudges. The same game on both sides. The two DICTATORS *shout and gesticulate but the music makes it impossible to hear them. The apartment of* CHAMELEON *is illuminated. He is seated at the table with a scantily clad prostitute. The two, sitting at a luxurious feast, are obsessed with eating. They eat with a ferocity that keeps time with the music. Meanwhile, as the music continues,* JOHN's *cell and house are illuminated.* JOHN *is sitting pensively on his cot and* MARIA, *on the other side of the stage, is seated at the table, reading a letter, undoubtedly from* JOHN. JOHN *remains in his abstract state, not a muscle moving.* MARIA *finishes her letter and buries her face in her arms on the table.*

Meanwhile, the DICTATORS *and their parties, with a rhythm that becomes more and more insane, continue pinning medals on each other. Everyone is given over to the rhythm of the music. The scene and the music rise to an insane climax, then gradually die away as the stage darkens, leaving only* JOHN *and* MARIA *visible. Curtain.*

THE RHYTHM OF VIOLENCE

Lewis Nkosi

CHARACTERS

JAN
JIMMY ("WHITE BOY")
JOJOZI
KITTY
PIET
CHRIS
TULA
JULIE
LILI
GAMA ("AFRICAN BOY")
SLOWFOOT
MARY
SARIE

"AFRICAN BOY" and "WHITE BOY" are the same characters as GAMA and JIMMY before they are referred to by name.

NOTE: For those unfamiliar with Afrikaans, the approximate phonetic sound for the letter *g* in the Afrikaans expletive *Ag* corresponds to the German guttural *ch*.

ACT I

SCENE 1

The city of Johannesburg in the early 60's. It is just before sunset and the sky is an explosion of orange colours. The city has burst into a savage jungle of multicoloured neon lights, fluorescing nervously with a come-hither bitchiness of a city at sundown.

The foreground of the stage comprises the waiting room of the Johannesburg City Hall. What we see of the city shows through the huge glass windows which open to the city square. Through the windows we can see the silhouette shape of an African standing on a raised platform and gesticulating wildly, as though he were addressing a meeting. From left, near the back of the stage, is a door with a flight of steps leading to other chambers on the top floors of the municipal building. A door on the extreme right of the stage provides an exit to the street.

In the waiting room there are benches and a table piled high with magazines for visitors who wish to browse. On the right, a few paces back from the door, is a public telephone. The waiting room has been temporarily turned into the headquarters of the South African police who are mobilized to watch the African meeting in progress. The first clue we have of this is a police hat, a machine-gun, and a revolver in a waist-strap, all lying on the bench in the empty room.

The action begins with the sound of jazz rhythms, curiously nervous, and at times decidedly neurotic; even when subtly controlled and easygoing, the beat suggests a tenuous quality of insanity and nightmares. Jazz sounds will be used throughout wherever possible, interpolated between dialogues whenever it seems dramatically necessary.

When the play opens, the neon and the traffic lights, seen through the high windows, are going on and off to the rhythm of jazz music, also helping to emphasize the hysterical quality of the scene.

Finally, the music softens into a subtly controlled, provocative beat and then subsides completely as the roar of the offstage crowd, holding a meeting in the city square, mounts to a crescendo. There are shouts of the slogans "AFRICA!" "FREEDOM IN OUR LIFETIME," etc.

Presently, a young policeman in khaki uniform sallies from left, down the flight of steps, to the anteroom. He is weighted down by a heavy machine-gun which he carries menacingly with one hand while with the other he holds a big bone from which he is nibbling a piece of meat. He rushes to the door on right; but as he grabs the door knob, another policeman, somewhat older than he, emerges from the left and shouts nervously at him.

PIET: Jan! Jan! Wait!

The young policeman turns. He has a handsome, florid face suffused with a passionate zeal of youth. From time to time the scene is acted with a dreamlike unreality, a constant effort on the part of the people involved to detach themselves from the reality that engages them.

JAN (facing the older policeman): What is it, Piet?

PIET: Where are you running to, man! (They speak in heavy German-like accents peculiar to South African Boers.)

JAN: Ag, man, I thought these Natives was starting trouble already!

PIET: Now, take it easy, Jan! You heard what the Major said. As long as they don't start anything, stay out of sight!

JAN (dubiously): Yah, I know. (Furiously.) They drive me out of my mind! Yelling "Freedom!" "Freedom!" "Freedom!"

PIET (pacing the floor): Me, too!

JAN places the machine-gun on the bench and sits down next to it, giving his entire attention to the bone at which he nibbles. His back is against the window and the city square. A voice from the square is heard enunciating clearly.

VOICE: Sons and daughters of Africa!
Everywhere on this continent black men are stirring!
From Cape to Cairo, from Morocco to Mozambique,
Africans are shouting "Freedom!"

That one word, friends, strikes fear in the hearts of the white people of this country. At its mention they clutch their guns! (JAN, *who had quickly clutched the machine-gun when the voice was first heard, grins sheepishly and replaces the machine-gun on the bench and returns to his bone.*)

JAN: Ag, they're just talking. What can they do without the guns!

PIET (*with less conviction*): Natives love talking. It's their habit!

JAN (*nervously*): How many of us are here?

PIET: Two hundred men at the ready to shoot down any bloody-son-of-a-bitchin' kaffir who starts trouble! (*He takes the revolver which has been lying on the bench and straps it around his waist, then sits next to* JAN *on the bench with back to the window and facing the audience.*)

JAN: You think that number is enough?

PIET: We are armed and the kaffirs haven't got guns!

JAN: That's right, they haven't got guns!

PIET (*stands up and points at the silhouette in the square*): That's Gama up there shooting his bloody filthy mouth off! Thinks he's something, black bastard!

JAN: We ought to be out there at the square just to show them we won't stand no nonsense!

PIET: No, that's no good! They like showing off when they see the police!

JAN: Piet, what do you think they would do if . . . (*He abruptly drops the question.*)

PIET: If what happened?

JAN: Ag, better not talk about it! They'll never do anything!

VOICE (*enunciating again*): Friends, I ask you: What do these stubborn men trust when they flout the whole world, when they continue to keep you in subjection against all reason and advice? I'll tell you what they trust: guns! They think they can handle trouble! But can they rule by the gun forever? (*There is a resounding "NO" from the crowd.*) That's right, friends, the answer is: NO! They can only keep you slaves so long as you want to remain slaves.

JAN (*has grabbed the machine-gun and is walking about nervously*): Bloody bastard!

PIET: It's all talk! Talk! Talk!

JAN (*sitting down and nibbling at his bone again*): Yah, what can they do without guns! (*Longer pause.*)

PIET: Black Sams! Why don't they do somethin' so we can handle this once and for all! They're wearing me down, man, wearing me down! (*The telephone rings and both men grab their guns nervously, then rush to the telephone.* PIET *talks.*)

PIET: Yes, Major. No! No! It's all quiet. Yah, they're just talking, making sound and fury! No, I beg your pardon, Major, I didn't mean to make a joke! Yes, sir. Yes, sir. We'll keep an eye on them, sir. Yes, sir. Good-bye, sir. (*Turning savagely to* JAN.) Well, how do you like that! We can't even make a joke about it anymore! No time for jokes, he says! Everybody behaves as though the Natives was just about to take over the country!

JAN: Was that Major Ludorf?

PIET: I'll kiss my arse if it wasn't! (*Looking across the square.*) How long are they goin' to keep this up anyway?

JAN: Till somebody has guts to stop these demonstrations, goddammit! Natives start talking like this and before you know it they are in control!

PIET: It's the blerry English and their City Council! If this was a Boer town, nothing like this would ever happen! We'd stop those blinkin' bastards before they'd even have time to open their traps!

JAN: The English don't know nothing about handling Natives! Look what happened in Kenya! Look what happens in Rhodesia now! That's what they get for mollycoddling the Natives!

PIET (*sitting down*): Hey, Janie, give me a bit there, man! Never had anything to eat since this morning. (*Wearily.*) They are sure keeping us busy!

JAN: And give it back. (*Gives him the bone.*)

PIET (*munching*): Hey, Janie, you ever shot a Native before? (*Makes panning movement with the bone.*) Ta-ta-ta-ta-ta-ta-ta!

JAN (*grinning*): Yah, it's kind-a funny, you know, like shooting wild duck!

PIET: The first time is not easy though!

JAN: Telling me! The first time I shot a Native dead I got sick! Just stood there and threw up! His skull was ripped apart by the machine-gun! I stood over him and got sick all over his body!

PIET: Ugh, man! Got sick over him! It's not enough you rip open a kaffir's skull! You must get sick over him too!

JAN (*pacing the floor*): When I got home, I still got sick!

PIET (*walks over to him*): Hey, you look as if you want to get sick again! Now, remember, I'm eating! It's not nice!

JAN (*angrily snatching the bone away*): And who said eat all of it?

PIET: Ag, man, don't be like that! What's the matter with you?

JAN: What's the matter with you?

PIET: Okay, don't shout! You're nervous!

JAN: Who's nervous? Here, have all of it if you must. Pig!

PIET: For Christ's sake, Janie! Shoot all the damn Natives if you want, but leave me alone! I was only eating a bone and you start talking about shooting Natives an' looking as if you want to get sick. Then I ask you nicely, Don't get sick! Now, what's wrong with that!

JAN: I'm not goin' to get sick! That's what's wrong with it!

PIET: All right! All right! You aren't goin' to get sick! You were only telling a story! Don't jump on me!

JAN: You are always making a fool of me!

PIET: You're just a sensitive son-of-a-bitch!

JAN: I'm a human being! And I'm just as tough as you are!

PIET: You're nervous, man; calm down!

JAN: Who's nervous!

PIET: I meant you're sensitive; now don't go an' jump on me again.

JAN: That's right. I'm a sensitive human being. That's what my grandma always said I was. Sensitive.

PIET: I'm not. I'm academic.

JAN: What does that mean?

PIET: Means a bloke who is a realist. No emotion. I can shoot any number of Natives without getting sick. No emotions! I shoot them academically.

JAN: Nice word . . . academically.

PIET: I got it from a sergeant down at Marshall Square. He used to say, when you get into a fight with Natives, don't let your feelings run away with you. Be academic. Shoot them down academically.

VOICE (*enunciating from the square*): For years we have been waiting for action from the Congress leadership. For years we have heard nothing but speeches and rhetoric. Friends, today the young people are seizing the reins, and we promise you plenty ac-

tion! (JAN *and* PIET *seize their guns and stand attentively at the window.*) Whether the struggle will turn into a violent one or not, we say that depends on the South African police. In any case, the issue is an *academic* one. (JAN *looks at* PIET *and grins. That seems to relax them; they sit down.*) Today, here and now, we pledge ourselves to act! Before you all we resolve to strike a blow against apartheid! From now on, we are serving notice on these arrogant men that we can no longer tolerate white domination, subjugation, and repression at their hands. When the blow will be struck, I don't know. It may be sooner than they think. Tonight! Tomorrow, or the following day, but the blow shall be struck! (JAN *jumps up.*)

JAN: That is incitement! He can go to jail for that!

PIET: Take it easy, man! The Secret Police are taking notes! They know what they are doing.

JAN: They're always twiddling their thumbs until it's too late to act. Then we have to do the dirty job!

PIET: Gama is just a fool student! Going to a white man's university has gone to his head. Now he thinks of himself as bloody Lumumba or Nkrumah!

JAN: Just an ape with a big mouth. There won't be no bloody Nkrumahs here! We can take care of them.

PIET (*played with dreamlike detachment*): The sun is going down.

JAN: I don't like to see the sun setting.

PIET: I don't mind the sunset. . . . It's the sunrise I hate. The beginning of a new day.

JAN: What's wrong with the beginning of a new day?

PIET (*pacing the floor*): "What's wrong with the beginning of a new day?" he asks! I don't know! Why should I know!

JAN: What's the matter with you? You're getting jumpy!

PIET: I don't know what I'm shouting for! Forget it.

JAN: Okay.

PIET (*reflectively*): A new day . . . it's always uncertain. Sunset is all right. . . . May get a bit cold after, but it's all right!

JAN: My son loves sunrise. He loves to get up and catch the rays of the sun on his small hands and play with it. My old man used to say, "That kid is playing with his future." Funny thing to say to a child! (PIET *moves to the window to catch the pale rays of the setting sun with his hand. He plays with them for a while. As he plays absentmindedly, we hear the sad strains of jazz.* PIET *turns to* JAN *finally.*)

PIET: It's so beautiful on the hands and yet you can't hold it.

JAN: What is it you can't hold?

PIET: The rays of the setting sun.

JAN (*stubbornly*): I hate sunset!

PIET: Why? Sunset is pretty.

JAN: Pretty? . . . Sun goes down! Gets damp and cold, and some of your future goes too.

PIET: Nothing lasts forever. If the sun never set, the day would be unbearable.

JAN: But there would be no future to worry about.

PIET (*as an idea strikes him*): Hey, that's funny! That's a funny idea! And maybe we wouldn't grow old either.

JAN: We'd just go on ruling this land and the Natives would do like they're told! Forever!

PIET (*grinning happily*): And we wouldn't worry about tomorrow.

JAN: That's right! It would be a long, long day. Time just standing still!

PIET: And we'd go to work maybe and come back and eat and make love and just go on working.

JAN: Ag, it's just a dream, man.

PIET: Yah, I suppose so.

JAN: Even if there was no future, some damn fool would invent a future.

PIET: That's right! Some damn stupid professor or Communist fool would invent Time. And sooner or later you would have a call for lesser working hours and cries of more wages from the bloody Natives . . . and then riots. (*Blackout.*)

SCENE 2

Same as Scene 1. PIET *and* JAN *are occupying the waiting room. There is a knock at the door, which interrupts their conversation. A young African, looking shy and uncertain, makes his appearance. He carries a pile of signed petitions in his hand. At* the sight of the two policemen he comes to a stop near the door. The police stare at him open-mouthed.*

JAN: Good God! Piet, do you see what I see?

PIET (*staring at* TULA): No, Jan, I don't. What do you see?

JAN: Look closely, Piet. You think it's just my eyes?

PIET (*straining his eyes*): I think it's your eyes, Jan.

JAN: I could swear I saw a kaffir standing by the door. Now, I'm not so sure. Look closely, Piet. Don't you see some kind of animal standing by the doorway?

PIET (*long pause*): Now that you say so, Jan, I can see something.

JAN: What does it look like to you, Piet?

PIET: You really want to know, Jan?

JAN: I really want to know, Piet.

PIET: It looks like an ape to me. (TULA *stands there, not daring to move any further.*)

JAN: Thanks, Piet, that's all I wanted to know because that's exactly what it looks like to me. A goddam ape! (TULA *gathers enough courage to approach the two policemen.* JAN *waves him to a standstill.*) Don't come any closer, kaffir. There's already an awful stink in here! What do you want?

TULA: I am a representative of the Left Student Association, and I've been delegated to submit these petitions personally to the Mayor's office.

JAN: Piet!

PIET: Yes, Jan.

JAN: You hear that?

PIET: No, I didn't hear it, Jan.

JAN: Kaffir, say that again so the baas can hear you.

TULA: I represent the Left Student Association, and I've been asked to deliver these petitions to the Mayor's office.

JAN: Piet!

PIET: Yes, Jan.

JAN: Are you listening?

PIET: I'm listening, Jan.

JAN: This Native boy here says he's come to deliver petitions.

From here the scene is played with affected boredom, which conceals a streak of potential violence.

PIET: I heard him, Jan. Maybe he don't mean any harm, Jan. Ask him again if he's sure he wants to deliver anything.

JAN: Boy, are you sure you want to deliver these petitions?

TULA: That's what I came for, sir.

JAN (*jumping up*): Watch your tongue, kaffir, when you talk to me! You hear? Don't provoke me!

TULA: No, sir, I didn't mean to, sir!

JAN: You better not, kaffir! I'm baas to you! Don't "sir" me! I'm no bloody English!

TULA: Yes, baas!

JAN: Okay, let's start from the beginning. You came here to present the petitions. Is that right?

TULA: Yes, baas.

JAN: Your organization got complaints to make. Is that right?

TULA: Yes, baas. We've decided to register protests about the colour-bar in the major social and cultural institutions of the city of Johannesburg.

JAN: Piet, did you hear that?

PIET: No, Jan, I didn't hear that.

JAN: This boy here says his organization got a complaint.

PIET: I don't think he would say such a thing, Jan. Are you sure this boy said that? Ask him again, Jan. This boy looks reasonable to me. He almost looks too smart for a Native. I'm sure he would never say such a thing. Ask him again.

JAN: Boy, you said that, didn't you? You came here to protest against something.

TULA: Yes, baas, on behalf of my organization.

JAN: That's right. (*To* PIET.) This boy, Piet, has come to protest. What's the fancy word you used, boy? To *register* protest?

TULA: Yes, baas.

JAN: That's right. This boy, Piet, has come to "register" protest.

PIET: To register protest about what?

JAN: I don't know. About the colour-bar! (*Scornfully.*) . . . "in the major social and cultural institutions of the city of Johannesburg." Am I quoting you right, boy?

TULA: Yes, sir. (JAN *stares evilly at him.*) Yes, baas.

JAN: I thought you were forgetting, boy. I told you not to "sir" me!

TULA: I'm sorry, baas!

JAN: So I *am* quoting you right. Piet, I'm quoting this boy right. This boy has come to register protest about the colour-bar in the major social and cultural institutions in the city of Johannesburg.

PIET: Doesn't he like the colour-bar? Jan, doesn't this boy like the colour-bar?

JAN: I don't know, Piet. Maybe he doesn't. Maybe he was led astray by other student Communists.

PIET: Ask him, Jan, just to make sure. Ask him if he doesn't like the colour-bar or something.

JAN: Boy, don't you like the colour-bar? Take your time. Don't say anything you don't mean. Maybe you don't like the colour-bar?

TULA: No, baas, I don't like the colour-bar. My organization is hostile to any kind of colour-bar.

JAN (*suspicious*): "Hostile"? What's hostile?

TULA: It means my organization is violently opposed to apartheid or the colour-bar.

JAN: Opposed! Why the hell don't you say so? You like the fancy words, don't you?

TULA: No, baas.

JAN: Okay, I'm not against the fancy words myself. So we'll use your big word. Your organization is "hostile" to the colour-bar?

TULA: Yes, baas.

JAN: Piet, this boy here is hostile to the colour-bar.

PIET: That's very unfortunate. Very unfortunate! (*He stands up and walks to where* TULA *is standing.*) Boy, you don't like the colour-bar?

TULA: No, baas.

PIET: Would you like to marry a white girl? (TULA *is caught unexpectedly by the question. His honesty prevents him from giving a simple answer.* PIET *flares up suddenly.*) Yes or no? Boy, can't you answer a simple question?

TULA: That would depend on many things, baas.

PIET: Like what?

TULA: Well, sir, like whether she is the right girl to marry. Whether she is intelligent or—

PIET (*interrupting*): Look, boy! You think you're smart, eh? You think you're clever?

TULA: No, sir!

PIET: Well, you're not! You're a damn stupid Native if ever I saw one! Stupid! (*He holds* TULA *by the lapels of his coat and is shaking him against the wall.*) All Natives are bloody stupid! You hear that? You can go back and tell that to your organization. (*He seizes the petitions from* TULA *and scatters them on the floor.* TULA *moves toward the door.*) Wait a minute! Where do you think you're going? (*He takes out his police logbook, which he holds ostentatiously in front of him.*) What is your name?

TULA: Tula.

PIET: Tula? Your second name, kaffir!

TULA: Tula Zulu.

PIET (PIET'*s jaw slackens*): Ah, I see. Is Gama your brother? The fool who's always shooting his mouth off at meetings? Speak, boy! Is that damn fool out there your precious brother?

TULA: Yes, that's my brother.

PIET: Well, get the hell out of here! And you can tell your brother he won't get away with anything! Tell him we're watching him! Tell him that! And get the hell out of here! (TULA *gets out.*) Bloody kaffirs! They're all Communists before they even learn to say ah! Janie, you keep a look out while I go and get some coffee for us.

JAN: Okay, Piet.

PIET (*going out through left*): It will soon be cold.

JAN *sits alone. We hear a weird jazz melody accompanied by strong drums, evocative of death ceremonies.* JAN *moves about uneasily. The setting sun is playing on his face, since it is coming directly through the window out of which he is sometimes peering. Blackout.*

SCENE 3

Same as before. JAN *and* PIET *are sitting on the bench, drinking coffee from big mugs.*

JAN: Ah, twilight!

PIET: And soon it will be night.

JAN: It's hateful!

PIET: A man needs some sleep! Damn it!

JAN: And that's the danger! . . . Sleep . . . Anybody can go to sleep on this bloody continent but the white man. Always he must stand guard!

PIET: We're standing guard over the future.

JAN: I know, but whose future? Ours or theirs?

PIET: Ours! Why do you say that? So long as we stand guard, there is no danger.

JAN: I don't know, Piet! All I know is this is wearin' me down, goddammit! While we stand guard, we cannot sleep! It's wearin' me down, I tell you.

PIET: Look, Jan, this is US or THEM!

JAN: Yah, I know, but it's still wearin' me down.

PIET: Always the white man must be on the alert. There's nothing else we can do!

JAN (*speaks softly to himself*): Sometimes I wish all this was over somehow. . . . To walk in the sun once more! To walk in the shadows of the trees and under the moon at night . . . goddammit, to relax. Just to relax!

PIET (*agitated*): Will you stop shouting!

JAN (*aroused from his reverie*): Who is shouting? I didn't shout.

PIET: You didn't? Ag, maybe it's just my ears. Hell, I don't know what's wrong with me today.

JAN: It's nerves, man, nerves!

PIET: Are you implying that I'm frightened of THEM?

JAN: I'm not implying anything.

PIET: Maybe you are! Maybe you are not! But if you think I'm frightened, you are fumbling around in the dark, because I'm not! I can handle any number of Natives! Any number! Ten! Twenty! Fifty! Hundred! You think you know me! I'm a terror to Natives!

JAN: Hey, what's the matter with you all of a sudden?

PIET: I just don't want you to imply anything! Maybe you are nervous; I'm not! (*A glint in his eye.*) Once when we were on patrol in Sophiatown, THEY came! I tell you THEY came! It was night. Dark. And their shadows were darker than the dark itself. I was separated from the others! Alone! You understand that? Alone! You ever been alone with Death staring you in the eye? Well, I was! I started firing from my̆ sten-gun. But those Natives kept on coming! It was like eternity, and the dark shadows kept coming like the waves of eternal night. . . . Ah, but a sten-gun spits death much stronger than a thousand Natives! When it was all over, I couldn't stop shooting. I was no longer in control of my fingers. The sten-gun kept barking in the dark . . . against shadows . . . anything that moved. I began to think that even if my son had appeared there, I would have kept shooting away. . . . (*He calms down at the thought.*) I don't know what I am saying.

JAN: I know. (*Pause.*)

VOICE (*in the square*): Tonight! Maybe to-morrow!

MOB (*yells back*): Why not tonight?

VOICE: Who knows, maybe tonight! Maybe tomorrow! Or the next day!

MOB: Tonight, why not tonight?

VOICE: We must learn to use their language. Say neither this nor that. Keep them guessing! That is why I say to you, "maybe"!

JAN: What does he mean? These Natives are playing with fire.

PIET: It's Gama. . . . He is all mouth and nothing much else.

JAN: He talks dangerous words.

PIET: He learned to talk like that at the big university up there on top of the hill. But he's all talk.

JAN: I hear the Government is going to stop them from going to the white universities.

PIET: High time too.

JAN: Think of that! I never even went to a university.

PIET: A white man does not need to go. Whatever that fool up there says, he's still a Native. He can't change the colour of his skin.

JAN: Yah! (*Laughs.*) God, he can't! Some even use face creams to try to look lighter than they are.

PIET: And straighten their hair! Honestly, it's disgusting! Don't they have pride?

JAN: No, whatever they say, they all want to be white. They all want to marry white girls. You know, sometimes I lie awake at night and try to imagine what it would be like to be born black, and I start having nightmares. 'Stru's God, I'm glad I was born white!

PIET: To be black! A curse, I tell you, it's a curse! Honest, Janie, what would you do if you woke up with a black skin?

JAN (*they have shifted into a playful mood*): Ugh! Then I would start moving from my neighbourhood.

PIET: You'd have to move very early in the morning before the neighbours get up. . . . Which black township would you go to? Alexandra?

JAN: Too many goddam thugs there. Every day some black bastard is murdered there.

PIET: Western Native Township? It's not bad.

JAN: Ag, it stinks. You can't walk down a street without getting a mouthful of dust. No, not Western, for Chrissakes. Native townships stink.

PIET: If you turned black, you would have to live somewhere. Orlando, maybe. Or Meadowlands!

JAN: Hey, better not joke about this. I get pimples just thinking about it. (*Pause.*) I'll tell you what, though. Natives don't mind these places. Natives can live anywhere! No joke, Natives are a marvel to me!

PIET: That's right, but you would be a Native too, and therefore, you wouldn't mind!

JAN: And suppose Natives go on strike?

PIET: Hey, suppose that? Would you join in, Janie, just like a goddam troublemaker?

JAN: I would have no choice in the matter. . . . Hey, an' you know what? I would be the leader! I'm a born leader, so I would be a Native leader, right there in the fore-front, fightin' for rights! Christ! Can you see me wearing a black face and leading all the damn Natives down to City Hall, shaking my fists and speechifying like hell. I would be a terror to all the goddam whites in this city!

PIET: And I would be a police major, Janie. I would stand there with my men armed to the teeth an' say, who is the leader of this procession? (*They slowly submerge themselves in the roles they are playing.*)

JAN: I, Tom Lundula, am the leader of the procession. . . . Hey, that would be a good name for a trusted Native leader! A militant Native leader! (*Savouring the name.*) Tom Lundula!

PIET: Well, Tom Lundula, step forward and let me have a look at you. (JAN *steps forward stiffly.*) You look an intelligent Native to me, Tom Lundula. Maybe I'm wrong, but you look like a well-mannered Native who knows his responsibilities.

JAN: I'm flattered that you think so, sir. Under different circumstances you and I would be good friends, but this is hardly the time!

PIET: As I was saying, you look like a moderate Native who knows the laws of the land. And you know that leading thousands of Natives into the city like this without a written permission from the Chief of Police is a punishable offence.

JAN: We know the laws of the white man, Major Ludorf. We've made a career out of studying the laws of the white man.

PIET: I thought you were a clever Native, Lundula. I thought so. Also I knew that even a clever man can be misguided at times. You know, wrong advice can be given to him, which leads him into the ways of folly.

JAN: Sir, you mistake our mission. We come not to get advice from the Chief of Police. We come here—I and my people—come here to present demands to the City Hall, and unless those demands are met, not one of my men is going back to work.

PIET: Be careful about your tongue, Lundula. A clever man like you should not let his tongue get out of hand. . . . Last year you led a demonstration and the Mayor's flowers got trampled down by thousands of your men, but we understood the nature of your desperation. This year there will be no understanding if you lead your men any further than where you are.

JAN: You will not let us proceed to the City Hall, sir, to present our grievances?

PIET: It is my duty to prevent trouble in the city. There are riots all over Africa these days. A tiny thing can grow into a conflagration. Do you understand that word: CONFLAGRATION? It means big trouble. And things like riots are like a disease in Africa. They sort of spread. We are here to see to it that the disease should not spread to these parts, Lundula. In South Africa Natives are happy with things as they are so long as the likes of you leave them alone. And my job is to see to it that you leave them alone.

JAN: Sir, we intend to proceed to the City Hall. My men will be peaceful and orderly. We are peaceful and non-violent people, sir. We don't believe in shedding blood. We don't like the sight of blood, sir. It makes us sick. If you will let us proceed, sir, we will present our demands and then go home in a peaceful, non-violent fashion.

PIET: You will advance no further than where you are, Lundula. Those are orders!

JAN: You realize the gravity of the situation, sir?

PIET: Up to now I've been talking to you like an equal, Tom Lundula, but I'm running out of patience.

JAN: If there is violence, sir, you will assume every responsibility for it.

PIET: If you go home, there will be no violence!

JAN: I and my people don't like violence, sir. As you see we are unarmed. Your men are armed. That is because we don't like the sight of blood; it makes us sick to look at blood.

PIET: Tom Lundula, I give you and your men three minutes to get the hell out of here. Three minutes! If you haven't dispersed by then, it will be my painful duty to order my men to clear the streets!

JAN: Three minutes, sir! How can twenty thousand people disperse in three minutes?

PIET: That is your problem to solve! You brought them here. Now you can take them back!

JAN (*in a pompous manner, as he imagines an African leader would do; he faces an imaginary African crowd*): Sons and daughters of Africa! As always when we try to present our grievances to the oppressors, to these fascists, we always meet with arrogance, stupidity, and plain brute force! Today as before they will not let us proceed to the City Hall; they will not let your foul breaths defile the Mayor's parlour; they will not let you, and they are threatening to shoot if you will proceed any further.

But, I will tell you this, friends: there will be a day soon when they will want to listen to you, when they will want to talk to you, but that will be too late! I know they will say I'm inciting you and put me in jail for it; but when a man says that someday it's going to rain, is he inciting it to rain or is he merely saying what will come to pass? No! . . . That is why I say to you someday you're going to raise your fists against your dictators, against these fascists, against your children's and your oppressors!

PIET (*shocked*): Jan, you were carried away, man! You spoke just like a Native Communist. (JAN *grins shyly; he is embarrassed to find that he is no longer acting but has* completely identified himself with the African cause.)

JAN: Ag, man, that comes out of listening to them speak for too long. (*Pause. Jazz music again.* JAN *moves to the window.*) They're still at it!

VOICE: The time, friends, has come to strike a blow against the oppressors! And the blow, I promise you, shall be struck! Maybe tonight; who knows? Maybe tomorrow, the following day, or the day after; but the blow shall be struck! There are those who accuse us of being anti-white, but lest anybody should misunderstand the nature of our struggle: our fight, we say, is not against the white man but against the evil laws, which in South Africa, unfortunately, are symbolized by the white skin. It is no longer possible to hate the whip and not the one who wields the whip!

PIET (*with the same detachment as before, but more mechanical this time*): That Native just won't stop talkin'. He's all mouth and nothing much else.

JAN: Natives love talking. It's their habit.

PIET: But what can they do? They haven't got guns!

JAN: Yah, they'ven't got guns.

PIET: Nothing will ever come out of this. It's just big talk.

JAN: They want to panic us, but they have nothing with which to back their threats.

PIET: If they ever start anything, we'll teach them a lesson they'll never forget.

JAN: What can they do without guns?

PIET: Yah, what can they do?

JAN: Just talk!

PIET (*savagely*): Damn it, I wish they would start something! Anything! So we can handle them once and for all. They are wearing me down, too, wearing me down! (*Blackout.*) They are wearing me down! (*Voice heard in the dark as the curtain falls.*) They are wearing me down, goddammit!

ACT II

SCENE 1

The same evening. A dingy basement club-room which serves as headquarters of a

group of left-wing university students. The club is divided into two sections by a waist-high panel wall, the back room being on a slightly higher level than the front. The back room is used as a kitchen with a bar on the right-hand side. Liquor and food can be served to the people in the front room through a cubbyhole. The back and the forerooms are also linked together by a single door in the middle of the panel wall.

The foreroom, where most of the action takes place, is furnished with settees, chairs with broken legs, and some with their backs missing. There is a table with a telephone on the extreme left. Near the foreground, on left, stands a big phonograph. The walls are plastered with pictures of student riots, marches, and protest slogans. The peeling walls are inscribed with huge letters shouting: VERWOERD MUST GO! FREEDOM IN OUR LIFETIME! INTER-RACIAL SEX IS A HISTORICAL FACT! etc. There are also photographs of jazz musicians, famous writers, actors, as well as avant-garde pictures which are distinguished by their strong African motifs. On either side of the stage hang big African masks. A door on the extreme right provides the main entrance.

When the curtain goes up, the stage is completely dark. First we hear the throb of cool jazz. Then a figure, recognizable only by the lighted match-stick suspended in utter darkness, moves into the foreground area through the panel door of the back room. Another light comes in the same way, and the two figures chase each other in the dark. They stumble and curse and laugh all at once.

VOICE: Gama! Gama! (*Both lights have gone out, and the stage is dark.*) Gama, stop playing the fool! Gama, what's the matter with you? Come'un!

The two dark forms can now be seen by the trickle of light which illumines them. The second figure tackles the first one, and the two roll down on the floor in a spectacular wrestling match. As more light picks out the grunting figures, we can now see that one of them is a husky, tousle-headed young man, looking more like an Oxford undergraduate than an English South African. He is grappling with a powerful African

*young man about his own age. The young
white man is wearing a round-necked
sweater, and both are wearing jeans. While
they horse around the floor, a white girl
with long dark hair hanging over her
strongly featured face comes in through the
entrance on the extreme right of the stage.
She is carrying a huge basket stuffed with
bottles of beer and other foodstuffs. At the
sight of the girl the African young man
gets up and hugs her.*

AFRICAN BOY: Mary, you sweet flower of
European womanhood! (*She smacks him
on the face.*) Hey, what kind of humour is
that?

MARY: I warned you about calling me a
European woman! You're provoking me
again!

WHITE BOY: That's right! Gama, you're provoking Mary again.

MARY: He's always provoking me!

GAMA: All right, I'm sorry!

WHITE BOY: You're always provoking Mary!

MARY (*turning savagely on the white youth*):
Why don't you shut up!

WHITE BOY: I dare say!

GAMA (*hugging her again*): My apologies,
ma'am! No offence was intended to you!

MARY (*kissing him*): You call me that again
an' I'll break a beer bottle over your head!

GAMA: All right, I'm sorry! What a horribly
sensitive little bitch!

MARY (*slaps him again*): When you call me
that, I always know you're mocking me!
(*This time she abandons herself completely
to his embrace and kisses. He rubs her behind in a vulgar manner.*)

JIMMY (*closing his eyes*): Look at that! Isn't
it horrible? The youth of our time is sunk
in vice!

MARY: Why don't you go into the other room
and help yourself until Kitty arrives.

JIMMY: No part of the world is any better!
Not even young Africa.

MARY: Would you like me to help you?

JIMMY: Young lady, watch your tongue!
You're speaking to a young man of background!

GAMA: That's right! Mary, watch your tongue
when you talk to Mr. James MacBride
here! He is a young man of distinguished
background. A young man of impeccable

background! Isn't that right, Mr. Mac-
Bride?

JIMMY: That's right.

GAMA: That's right . . . hmmmmm, what
did you get?

MARY (*smacks his hand as it reaches for the
basket*): Don't touch the basket! You two
are not to drink until the others arrive!

JIMMY: Rubbish! We have priority claims!

MARY (*taking the basket away into the
kitchen*): Soreheads! What makes you
think you have priorities over others?

GAMA: Because, my dear—

JIMMY: Because, sweetheart—

GAMA: . . . we are in the forefront of the
African struggle for freedom!

JIMMY: That's right! The frontline of battle!

GAMA: And we are catching fire! Isn't that
right, Mr. MacBride?

JIMMY: Absolutely!

MARY (*suddenly tense*): How did it go?

GAMA (*screams hysterically*): A-a-ha-ha-ha!
How did it go? How did it go? (*Grabs
JIMMY and they do a mock waltz.*) How
did it go?

MARY: Damn it, I'm serious, Gama.

GAMA: Mr. MacBride, will you enlighten the
young lady here as to the execution of our
mission?

JIMMY: I should think it hardly advisable to
enter into such details at the moment.
Suffice it to say that the job was executed
with extreme wisdom and sensitivity, qualities which have long distinguished the
characters of the two members of your
committee, madam!

MARY (*grabs JIMMY by the shoulders*): Damn
it, this is no joke! What's the matter with
you two?

JIMMY: Do that again, you bitch, and I'll
slap your big mouth for you! (*MARY makes
to strike him. GAMA moves swiftly between
them.*)

GAMA: Aw! Aw! No hostilities! Very unwise.
Now, what seems to be the matter?

MARY (*yelling*): Goddammit! I just want to
know what happened. After all, we're all
up to our necks in this thing!

GAMA: Up to the neck! (*He makes a hanging
sign.*) You heard that, Mr. MacBride? Up
to the neck!

JIMMY: Isn't that a bit unpleasant? I think
we should weigh our actions a little carefully before we—

MARY (*yelling again*): Will somebody tell me what happened? Damn it! And stop this inconsequential mumbling!

GAMA (*mocking*): In-con-se-quen-tial mumbling!

JIMMY: Once again scholarship conspires against us!

MARY (*soft, very feminine and appealing*): Please, Gama, will you tell me? Did everything go according to plan?

GAMA: Everything according to plan! Isn't that right, Mr. MacBride?

JIMMY: That's right! I dare say I'm extremely gratified with the way the job was carried out. Extremely gratified!

GAMA: We're all extremely gratified, Mr. MacBride.

MARY: So the stage is set? (*Moving away nervously.*)

GAMA (*laughs hysterically*): That's right! The stage is set! At twelve midnight, when those fools wind up the conference . . . (*Imitating a Government speaker.*) "This Government stands firm and will not give in to threats from Native agitators and Communist trouble-makers! We have enough resources to handle any mischief from these trouble-makers. . . . Long live the Prime Minister. . . ." And then, BOOM! BOOM! BOOM! The BOMB will go off! Twelve o'clock midnight! I'd like to be there when the City Hall goes up in flames!

MARY: Jimmy, did you clear up all the papers I told you to? Just in case they come around?

GAMA: They won't! Anyway they know enough about the club already, but nothing we've done yet makes us responsible for planting a bomb under the Johannesburg City Hall while the Boers are having their rally. (*Moving to the edge of the stage.*) The very idea! Such an irresponsible idea! Isn't that an irresponsible idea, Mr. MacBride?

JIMMY: Extremely irresponsible! Nobody but an exceedingly inconsiderate person would ever think of it.

GAMA: That's right! And we are very responsible young people.

JIMMY: We believe in negotiations of the kind where a spirit of give and take exists!

GAMA (*laughs hysterically*): A-ha-haa! That's right, my boy, a spirit of give and take! (*He punches* JIMMY *on the shoulder, and* JIMMY *punches him back in a sort of reflex action.*) That's it! Give and take!

MARY (*agitated*): You two stop behaving as if this was a popular joke! We can all hang for this! (GAMA *laughs hysterically and makes as though he were throwing a noose around* JIMMY's *neck. He proceeds to tighten the noose, and* JIMMY's *eyes bulge.*)

GAMA: Did you hear that, Jimmy MacBride, me boy? You can hang for this!

JIMMY (*to* MARY): Don't worry, pussycat! Everything worked according to plan.

GAMA: Everything according to plan! . . . Boom! . . . Boom! . . . And this is only the beginning!

MARY: Suppose it doesn't go off?

JIMMY: It shall go off!

GAMA: It must go off! It's got to go off! We used an expert.

JIMMY: Knows everything about bombs and dynamite!

MARY: And if it doesn't go off?

GAMA: There will always be another night! The white supremacists will not get away so easily! Oh, no!

JIMMY (*contemplating*): At a minute slightly before twelve o'clock midnight, a man will walk down to the basement and set off the detonator!

GAMA: And boom! There'll be a mighty explosion such as Johannesburg has never heard in a long time. There will be huge flames enveloping the city. The wounded and dying and the dead—God rest their souls in peace—will be taken away by ambulances! (*He pauses. We hear the jogging rhythm of jazz and the long whine of a plaintive trumpet.*) That will only be the start of the rhythm!

MARY (*suddenly, absentmindedly*): What rhythm?

GAMA: The rhythm of violence, lovey!

MARY: Gama, I wish you would be serious just for a minute. To hear you talk, you'd think this is a picnic!

GAMA: Who said it was a picnic? We are liberating Africa. What can be more serious? (*Pompously.*) Africa shall be free!

MARY: He is never serious about anything.

JIMMY: He's never serious about love, which is unforgivable.

GAMA (*comes from the direction of the kitchen, drinking beer from a bottle*): That's slander, Mr. MacBride, me boy! I'm serious about love . . . deadly in earnest!

MARY (*snatching the bottle away from him*): All you're serious about is sex as far as I can tell!

GAMA: That's academic. What's the difference? You wouldn't want me if I wasn't good at it!

MARY: Pig! You think I'd risk all the laws of this country just for that. If I want to sleep with any man, I can find a white man tomorrow!

JIMMY: Tell him, love! He doesn't know anything about love! All these Natives think it's just getting into bed!

MARY: Why don't you ever shut up? Gama, you mustn't say what you said just now. Because it hurts! Damn it, you know I didn't ask to fall in love with a buffoon like you!

GAMA: So? Fall out of love!

MARY: Gama, you're going to make me very violent in a moment.

GAMA: Threats! Blackmail! (*Moving toward the left of the stage.*) What do you want from me? Soon you'll be asking me to marry you right here in Dr. Verwoerd's country. Mary, you have shoddy dreams!

MARY: I want to hear you say, once in a while, Mary, I love you. I need you. I just want to hear you say it.

GAMA: Mary, dear, I love you! What can I do without you? (*He laughs mockingly.*)

MARY: You think it's funny? A girl wants to hear that.

GAMA: When the struggle is over, I'll tell you that over and over again. It's business first!

MARY (*drinking from the bottle she seized from* GAMA): Men are monsters!

JIMMY: Especially black men, honey. The dark and lascivious Moors!

GAMA: Black men are kind and generous beyond measure!

MARY: Not when they become pale imitations of Western men. When they become like Jimmy here!

JIMMY: That's a very unfortunate remark, my girl! You might need my shoulder to cry on when your "dark and lascivious Moor" abandons you to a cold world!

MARY: Oh, shut up! You're getting on my nerves!

GAMA: I warned you, Jimmy, never to tangle with a woman when she is in love! Especially with a black man!

JIMMY: Damn conceit!

MARY: I hate white men! My God, I hate them! (*Both* JIMMY *and* GAMA *laugh.*)

JIMMY: You want them strong and virile and dark as the night!

MARY: Jimmy, you're such an idiot! What day were you born on?

JIMMY: On the sixth day, when the Lord was lonely!

GAMA (*sitting down next to* MARY *and pushing her hair away from her face in order to kiss her*): Don't mind him, my love. (*Strokes her behind vulgarly.*) There, does that make you feel better?

MARY (*breaking loose*): Animal!

GAMA: Women! I'll never understand them. They never make up their minds which they want most: to be stroked or sung poetry to!

MARY: We want both at its proper time. . . . Jimmy, where's Kitty? You look miserable.

JIMMY: African women! They are thoroughly unreliable. She was supposed to come early. And here I am twiddling my fingers! (*Phone rings and* GAMA *takes it.*)

GAMA (*mockingly*): The Students' Club, sir! Well, no, sir! This is a friend speaking. I can call him for you if you want. (*To* JIMMY.) Jimmy, call!

JIMMY: Ask who is it.

GAMA (*into the phone*): Who's calling, sir? Mr. Philip Bonslow. I'll tell him, sir. Just a moment. (*To* JIMMY.) Some creep by the name of Philip Bonslow.

JIMMY (*crosses to left to take the phone*): Hello, Philip, my boy. . . . Fine. How are you? (*Alarmed.*) What? You're going where? To the MacPhersons' roulette party? Philip! Philip! When will you learn that life isn't just roulette parties? All right! All right, I'm not interfering with your life! What? No, what I mean is you should dirty your fingers every once in a while . . . while there's still a bit of blood in you. . . . God knows, it won't kill you! No, no, no! I had a girl lined up for you. Very nice girl. She went to Oxford. She's a bit of a leftist, but I thought you wouldn't mind. She's quite harmless really. Of course, she doesn't believe in British control and all that, but she's really nice. Very pretty! Your who? Your wife? What you mean, what about your wife? I thought

Sylvia was in London. Has she come back? So, what are you worried about? Oh, Philip, I give up! Call me when you come back from the roulette party! (*He replaces the phone and all three of them immediately break into guffaws of laughter. Blackout.*)

SCENE 2

Same as before. As the lights come on, the three young people are behind the panel door, where they are laying on the food. GAMA comes out through the panel door; jiving his way toward the left, he chooses a record from a stack on the floor and puts it on the phonograph. Immediately, swinging jazz pulsates, and GAMA moves sinuously to its sensuous rhythm.

GAMA: Mary, is Jojozi coming?

MARY (*from the back room*): Members of the Committee are supposed to be present tonight. Jojozi may or may not come. He's under no obligation.

GAMA: And Ruth?

MARY (*coming out to the front room*): Why do you ask? She's not on the Committee.

GAMA: She may come for the party.

JIMMY (*entering*): Ruth is coming. I met Ruth and Chris at the University, and they're both coming.

GAMA: Good!

MARY: Tonight you're not to flirt with Ruth! Not with anybody!

GAMA: Woman, you forget yourself.

MARY: I mean it! I'm not going to be one of the concubines in the Zulu stable!

GAMA: When did we say the marriage vows?

MARY: If you do, I'll simply disappear with Jojozi!

GAMA (*smiling*): The old lech! He would love that!

MARY: That's right!

GAMA: But you wouldn't!

MARY: Don't be so damn conceited! You're not the only man around. . . . What happened to your brother? He was supposed to come early.

GAMA: My chubby little brother! Perhaps he's having a "crisis of conscience"! He should have been a priest instead of a revolutionary!

MARY: Some priests can be pretty militant.

A damn sight more militant than some fuddy-duddies who pass as politicians!

JIMMY (*who is sitting on a chair on left, throwing away a beer can from which he has been drinking*): That's right! Have you ever heard of a man called Trevor Huddleston?

GAMA (*religiously*): God bless him! He should have been here to give his benediction to this night of violence!

JIMMY: He was a tough priest!

GAMA: Would he have turned the other cheek?

JIMMY: He would have turned his eyes away.

MARY: He was such a saint! And so handsome! (*Dreamy.*) Such a handsome man.

JIMMY: Which one do you prefer?

GAMA: The saint or the handsome man?

MARY: Both.

GAMA: Jimmy, what's happened to Kitty?

JIMMY: The old bitch! She was supposed to to be here at seven! It's now half-past eight! (*There is a violent knock on the door.*) Here she is! (*He moves swiftly and expectantly toward the door on the right.*) You can't talk about her! (*He opens the door, and a sensuous-looking African girl, small and petite, dances through it. JIMMY yells with joy and embraces her.*) Kitty, you dark Jewel of Africa!

KITTY: Hands off, you fool! I heard you calling me a bitch!

JIMMY: That's because I love you! I can't think of anything better to call you!

KITTY (*to MARY*): Mary, darling, how are you? (*JIMMY interrupts by kissing her.*) Men are such beasts!

JIMMY: Ah, I feel revivified already! There's something mysterious about the African woman. Something mysterious and splendid!

KITTY: A myth for sex-starved white men! (*Moving to kiss MARY, who is seated on the couch.*) How're you, honey?

MARY: I'm fine, Kitty; how're you?

KITTY: All right! Couldn't concentrate on a thing today. In all the lectures I kept thinking about tonight!

MARY: Same here. Somebody dropped a bottle of ink, and I jumped as if a bomb had gone off!

KITTY (*pointing to JIMMY and GAMA, who are having a conversation by themselves on the left*): Are they drunk already?

MARY: It doesn't make any difference whether they are drunk or not. They always behave like idiots!

KITTY: Gama!

GAMA: Yes, lovey!

KITTY: How did it go?

GAMA: Oh, not that again!

KITTY: I want to know, idiot!

GAMA: At twelve midnight God will speak!

KITTY (*to* MARY): Did everything go according to plan?

JIMMY: Took a bit of doing, but with talent and extremely good sense on our part, we pulled it off!

KITTY (*to* MARY): Do you think everything is all right?

MARY: Gama says they planted it in the basement.

KITTY: Will they be hurt? I mean will many people be hurt?

GAMA: What do you think we are trying to do? Tickle them!

MARY (*betraying her own nervousness*): She's nervous! We're all nervous! Everybody is nervous! Why should we pretend we are not?

GAMA (*shouting and also betraying his own nervousness*): I am not nervous!

JIMMY: Everybody stop shouting. What's done is done. *They* started the violence! The Government started violence against unarmed people!

GAMA: Did you see the bodies at Sharpeville? Did you see the shoulders of children ripped off by machine-gun fire? Did you see anything? Ask Jojozi to show you the pictures he and the press boys took of the whole show! A butchery, I tell you!

JIMMY (*seriously*): South Africa is poised between freedom and slavery! Between action and indecision. Only a readiness to act will free this country!

MARY: We just want to be sure everything is all right. After all, this is drastic action.

GAMA: Of course! . . . And this is what this action was intended to be—drastic!

KITTY: If there's a general uprising, is there a follow-up plan?

GAMA: It's for politicians to formulate plans! What we want is action.

JIMMY: To relieve the politicians of their deadly boredom!

MARY: We didn't plan this to relieve politicians of their boredom. If I had known this

was the level of your political thinking, I wouldn't have had anything to do with this.

KITTY: Look at the Congo! There can be no success without a clearly thought-out programme. There can only be prolonged butchery!

GAMA: Butchery! . . . Ah, how I hate the sight of blood! May the Lord take pity on us for doing this!

JIMMY: Amen!

MARY: Stalinists!

JIMMY: That's libellous!

GAMA: Jimmy and I don't believe in ideologies!

MARY: You ought to talk! Who was shouting nationalist slogans this afternoon?

GAMA: We believe in political necessities! When society gets this flabby, morally and politically, change is a necessity and violence can only let in a bit of air.

JIMMY: What I fear most in life is boredom! A bomb explosion! Anything but this deadly lull. The clouds keep on gathering, but the storm never breaks!

GAMA: I agree with Jimmy!

KITTY (*sarcastically*): Isn't that unusual?

GAMA (*ignores her sarcasm*): Everybody in this country speaks about imminent violence! They've talked about it for so long, nobody believes it will ever come!

JIMMY: Look at people at political meetings! Look at their faces! They are so bored with politicians and their talk of violence, they almost wish it'd break out. People want a change of pace. That doesn't mean they want to give up privilege. They only want sport once in a while!

KITTY: Father Sitwell believes a change in Governmental policies is imminent.

GAMA (*ferociously*): We don't care what Father Sitwell believes! We're giving Jesus a last chance to choose sides in South Africa.

JIMMY: Gama, my boy, you forget what a powerful name that is. That is the man who once climbed a blood-spattered cross!

GAMA: And once bitten, twice shy, eh!

KITTY: He thinks he's funny! (*To* MARY.) I'm bored with their smart-aleck talk! I'll get myself something to drink.

GAMA: African women begin to drink and that's the beginning of the disintegration of African society.

MARY: For Christ's sake, can't you shut up

for a moment! (*Moving toward the phonograph.*) My God, I'm going crazy just listening to him.

GAMA *grins. He walks toward* MARY, *who is now inspecting records. He throws his arms affectionately around* MARY *and kisses her neck. At the same time the record begins to play, and a slow hypnotic rhythm begins to fill the room.* MARY *turns toward* GAMA. *As though involuntarily, they begin to move their bodies in response to the rhythm, slowly as though in a daze, their knees touching, moving backwards, away from each other only to come back aagin, as though pulled by a magnetic force, moving, moving toward each other. Always she throws her head back, a gesture to which she has become accustomed because of wearing her hair long; the hair always seems to fall over her face.* JIMMY *and* KITTY *come in from the back room to watch, almost entranced, the dancing of the young couple. Just at this time the door opens and a seventeen-year-old quiet-faced African student walks in.*

GAMA (*sardonically*): Tula! My own kid brother! Behold the Lamb of the Lord come to slaughter!

JIMMY: Tula, my boy, I hear you had a nasty encounter with the Law this afternoon.

TULA: They had great fun at my expense. Then they wouldn't let me deliver the petitions to the Mayor's office.

KITTY: What did they do with them?

TULA: Scattered them on the floor.

GAMA: We can expect that from these brutes! Anyway, we'll show them a thing or two tonight!

MARY: Did you go to the morning lectures today? I didn't see you.

TULA: No, I didn't go. I was too nervous! I sat at home and thought about tonight.

MARY: Honey, we're all nervous! I've prepared myself for a long stretch in jail.

GAMA: My brother even had second thoughts about it. My little brother doesn't like violence. Blood makes him sick.

JIMMY (*affecting an aloofness*): Aren't we all being rather inordinately concerned about tonight? I'm not so sure there will be a great deal of damage done. This action will merely injure the Government's pride rather than anything else. Maybe a wall or two will blow off and interrupt a minister's oratory, but that's about all.

GAMA: It's only a start! There will be more violence if this Government clings insanely to its apartheid policies!

TULA: The City Hall is crawling with cops tonight.

MARY: Oh, sure! They were mobilized to watch the Congress meeting this afternoon.

KITTY: Did Gama speak at the meeting?

MARY (*proudly*): Did he speak? At one time I thought the people would get out of hand! I was thinking, my God, they're going to start rioting and give these monsters an excuse for shooting.

JIMMY: They dare not! Not so soon after Sharpeville anyway. They'll take it easy for a while until the Johannesburg Stock Exchange picks up again.

GAMA: Jimmy, you always underestimate the stupidity of the South African police! We'll see how easy they'll take it after tonight!

TULA (*musing*): This will be the first time ever that a bomb explodes in public. They're going to comb the entire country for suspects!

GAMA: Let them and see if that helps them any!

TULA: The Liberal Party issued another statement tonight condemning violence.

JIMMY: Gama and I were talking about it this afternoon. We heard they were going to issue a statement. Somebody has to go and see the Liberal Party!

GAMA: Nobody will go and see the Liberal Party. They have a right to their opinion. Since 1912 Liberals in this country have been expressing opinion. They have yet to *influence* public opinion!

JIMMY: The whole history of this country is written in blood. That's what many people forget. Should be nice to see how the Afrikaners take their own medicine.

MARY: Jimmy, I never knew you could be so bloodthirsty!

JIMMY: It's my cannibalistic tendencies! That's what comes out of associating with Africans just emerging from barbarism!

GAMA: That's right! I come from a long line of missionary eaters! Ever see the beads the Africans wear around their necks? Every one is to celebrate a missionary who was devoured in the good old days when meat was scarce!

KITTY (*nauseated*): Gama! Honestly!

GAMA: What's the matter, honey? Can't you stand the smell of flesh?

JIMMY: I bet they wouldn't have eaten Huddleston!

GAMA (*grinning*): His skin is too tough! Damn it, that Anglican priest is tough! (*Admiringly.*) No, Huddleston would have lived, God bless his fighting claws! But some of these priests wouldn't have escaped! They would have made good corn-beef. Hey, Tula, you remember the Sundays we used to go to that church in Sophiatown? What did that African priest used to say? (TULA *smiles shyly.*)

TULA (*imitating the priest*): You don't have to worry about no white folks! You don't have to worry about nuthin' 'cause when you get to heaven, the Lord Jesus is goin' to put a gleamin' robe around you and you goin' to walk on gold-paved streets! And don't let nobody push you off. (*He smiles shyly after this as a round of applause breaks out. Quite spontaneously, the group's mood shifts into a theatrical satire of a gospel meeting.*)

GAMA: Okay, brothers and sisters, if you don't get onto this train, there isn't another one to get you home in time! Come on now! (*He claps his hands, then chants.*) Come on! What's the matter with ma Jesus!

ALL (*chanting back*): He's all right!

GAMA: What's the matter with ma Jesus!

ALL: He's all right!

GAMA: I said, what's the matter with ma Jesus?

ALL: He's all right!

GAMA: Oh, ya, I'm goin' to stand right in front of this bush!

ALL: That's all right!

GAMA: He tole me to stand right in front of this bush!

ALL: That's all right!

GAMA: Oh, ya, He's all right! (*Like a high priest.*) Come on, brothers and sisters! Don't let this train leave you behind now!

Presently we get the feeling that GAMA—*like the Afrikaner policemen in a previous scene, who assumed roles of pro- and anti-white—starts off by ridiculing worship, but slips into the genuine mood of African re-ligious feeling as he chants the Gospel songs. While the young people are at it, more push in through the door on the right. First, the bearded Jewish student called* CHRIS *and a girl friend called* JULIE; *followed by a shy baby-faced Afrikaner girl called* SARIE MARAIS, *a new recruit to the New Left Student Group; an Indian girl called* LILI; *an African reporter,* JOJOZI; *and bringing up the rear, a fat, clownish African called* SLOWFOOT. *All the young people, except the young Afrikaner girl, join in the clapping. She stands out from the group because she looks gawkily shy in this new company. In spite of her earthy Boer body, there is something touchingly ethereal about her, something virginly innocent and fragile about her. She walks gingerly, rather uncertainly, into the room. And she stands apart. All the young people come in laughing raucously or horsing around, but once inside they good-naturedly join in the clapping and Gospel chanting.*

ALL: He's all right!

GAMA: Did I hear you say—

ALL: He's all right!

GAMA: What's the matter with ma Jesus?

ALL: Oh, He's all right!

GAMA: Just what's the matter with ma Jesus?

ALL: He's all right! Oh, He's all right!

GAMA: I said, I'm goin' to stand right in front of this bush!

ALL: That's all right!

GAMA: I'm goin' to stand right here till I hear Him speak!

ALL: He's all right!

GAMA: Stand right here till this bush is set on fire!

ALL: He's all right!

GAMA: Did I hear you say—

ALL: Oh, ya, He's all right! (GAMA *joins in.*) That's right, He's all right! Amen! Amen!

CHRIS: Brothers and sisters, may I have the honour of introducing a new recruit to God's own Tabernacle!

KITTY: Amen!

CHRIS: Miss Sarie Marais. She has been campaigning among Afrikaner students for our S.R.C. candidate at the university. Sarie is a social science major!

KITTY: Alleluyah! Welcome, sister! Let's have the libation!

The other young people have mingled completely with the group except the shy, gawky SARIE. GAMA *steps forward and tries to kiss her. The girl steps back, almost involuntarily, and trips over something.* GAMA *laughs.*

GAMA: Watch it, sister! That's no good. (*Contritely.*) I'm sorry; I have an incurable desire to kiss young girls with shy bodies!

MARY (*growing jealous*): Don't let him, Sarie! He's helplessly corrupt! An awful drooling lech! Stay out of his way if you want to be safe!

SLOWFOOT (*already lifting a glass of brandy*): He's a fiend with young girls!

JOJOZI: If you want your virginity to remain intact, don't stay too long with him in the shadows!

JULIE: Really, Jojozi, all of you are just making Sarie uneasy! Nobody will harm you, Sarie! Just make yourself at home! Everybody is mad around here!

SLOWFOOT (*sombrely*): Don't say I didn't warn you! (JOJOZI *slaps the hand of* SLOWFOOT, *who has tried to manoeuvre a glass from his hand.*)

JOJOZI: That's right! Your life is totally, irreversibly, and hopelessly in your own hands while you're here, Sarie!

All this time the girl stands shyly, smiling uneasily and getting out of the way every time a boy comes toward her. TULA *advances from the confusion of the crowd; they come face to face with each other. Momentarily, their eyes meet and the girl's eyes fall to her feet.* TULA *puts out his hand. The girl takes it, and they hold on to each other a bit longer than is necessary, as if they've struck quick sympathy with each other.*

TULA: Hello!
SARIE: Hello!
TULA: May I get you anything to drink?
SARIE (*shyly*): If you have gin, I'll have a gin and tonic.
TULA: Gin and tonic! (*Laughs.*) Girls seem to drink nothing but gin and tonic!

They both laugh, and TULA *goes to the back room to get her the drink. As he walks through the crowd,* GAMA, JIMMY, JOJOZI, *and* SLOWFOOT *make murmuring noises,*

peering at the boy behind hand-shielded eyes. They are obviously ribbing him for his kind attention to SARIE. *Blackout.*

SCENE 3

Same as before. The signal jazz score which began playing in the very beginning of the play is playing again in a more pulsatingly insistent manner. When the lights come on, we see all the young people behind the panel door, eating and drinking—generally raising hell. GAMA *comes out of the back door holding a huge alarm clock in his hands, which he deposits on a table on the far left to face partly the audience and partly the group of actors on stage. While he tries to put it up, the alarm suddenly goes off loudly, attracting most of the young people from the back room.* GAMA *places the clock properly and turns to the group.*

GAMA: It's a false alarm! Only ten o'clock; you shouldn't have bothered!

CHRIS: History is full of false alarms! Meanwhile, drink and be merry while history grinds on its tortuous course! (*He drinks.*) Ah, music!

GAMA *starts the record going again.* JOJOZI *grabs* MARY, CHRIS *takes* JULIE, *and they begin the favourite crawling dance, called pata-pa-ta. The rest of the young people follow suit, taking a partner nearest. Only* SLOWFOOT, *who is watching through the back window,* GAMA, *and* SARIE *are not dancing.* GAMA *spots* SARIE *standing apart from the dancers and moves slowly, menacingly, toward her, his claws stretched out theatrically in front of him. However, before he reaches the apprehensive girl,* TULA *comes out of the back room with drinks and gives one to* SARIE. GAMA *shrugs his shoulders exaggeratedly and moves off. The music stops.* TULA *and* SARIE *move toward the front part of the stage, where they sit nervously facing each other. The rest of the young people form the backdrop of couples talking, standing in corners kissing, or girls sitting on top of boys who happen to be lying on the floor. There is a general horsing around and tumbling in a form of undergraduate sexual abandon. Occasion-*

ally, drinks are fetched from the back, things are hurled against doors, chairs collapse and are fixed again.

TULA (*nodding toward his brother*): Don't mind him! He barks more than he bites.

SARIE (*shyly, almost hesitatingly*): And you bite . . . more . . . than you bark?

TULA (*laughing at the unexpected quip*): No, no! I don't bite at all. May I get you a cushion to sit on? It's more comfortable.

SARIE: No, I'm all right, thank you!

TULA: My name is Tula. Gama is my brother.

SARIE: I'm Sarie Marais. He's your brother?

TULA: Are you surprised?

SARIE: Well . . . a bit. . . . You're so unlike him!

TULA: My brother has more dash and charm. . . . He's more lively. . . . At school he was always a leader.

SARIE (*tentatively*): And the girls scratched each other's eyes for him?

TULA: You sound as if you disapprove of my brother.

SARIE: Oh, no, I hardly know him enough to disapprove of him. But somehow he seems spoiled!

TULA: That's why girls fall for him. They think they can straighten him out. He's all right really; he loves to horse around. But he's also serious.

SARIE (*looking around the place*): How did you get a place like this? I mean, where students of all races can mix.

TULA: It belongs to Mary, the girl with the dark hair.

SARIE *turns in the direction in which* TULA *is pointing.* MARY *and* GAMA *are sharing a studio couch on which they are smooching quietly, oblivious to the crowd around them. There's a shocked expression on the girl's face as she turns to* TULA.

SARIE: The police never raid this place?

TULA: They tried once, but there was nobody around. Next time they came, we were singing Gospel songs. They dispersed in confusion! (SARIE *laughs.*)

SARIE: Maybe we better start singing Gospel songs.

TULA: Don't start that again. My brother will keep us going all night. Sometimes I think he should have been a preacher instead of studying to be a lawyer.

SARIE: Really? Is he studying to be a lawyer?

TULA: He's graduating at the end of this year.

SARIE: And what are you majoring in?

TULA: Fine arts! Those are my paintings on the wall—and the photographs. (*They both stand up to inspect the pictures as well as the slogan lettering.*)

SARIE: It's beautiful. It's very gentle. Now I understand a lot of things about you.

TULA: My brother says fine arts is a profession for women! He thinks it's unmanly . . . somehow.

SARIE: Oh, I don't think so! I think it's a very commendable profession.

TULA: Thanks for saying so.

SARIE (*again looking around the room*): This is a very gay party.

TULA (*instinctively*): Have you ever been to many parties like this? I mean where there's free mixing.

SARIE: Well, no, this is the first time. (*Pause.*) Sometimes I think I don't approve of mixing of races—I don't mean just being friends and talking together. I mean the extreme sort! I mean . . . you know what I mean?

TULA: You mean like falling in love?

SARIE: Yes. Then sometimes I think I'm just confused. All this is so new to me. If you are a Boer girl, it takes time to get used to it.

TULA: I know . . . for black people too.

SARIE: The first time I ever met black people on a social level was last year when I came to the university and I had to sit next to a coloured boy. It was strange. I kept thinking something drastic would happen. But nothing happened. You know, I think that's very important. To get together and know each other. Black and white people. You know, to be friends and know how to respect each other. I think respect between people is the most important thing. Don't you think respect is the most important thing?

TULA (*spontaneously*): Yes, but I think love is more important. . . . Oh, I don't mean that kind of love! I mean real love . . . like loving your enemy. That's real love because it expects nothing in return.

SARIE: Do you believe you can truly love your enemies? Can your people, for instance, or my people ever love each other? In spite of everything?

TULA: By loving your enemy, I don't mean letting people commit crimes against others without stopping them. I mean one should never hate them or despise them. Real love brings us all to the same level.

SARIE: Would you have told the Jews to love the Germans during the rule of the Nazis?

TULA: I would have told them to hate the crimes! To fight the Germans if necessary, but I'd have never told them to despise the German people because they succumbed to evil. The whole world watched while the Jews were being roasted in ovens. People went into the war only when their own safety was being threatened. So the whole world was an accomplice to the Nazi crimes. It is only when the Jews as well as the Germans know they are both capable of those atrocities that love can be possible between them. Love is the understanding that all people are bound together in guilt and only individuals are capable of achieving personal salvation. The duty of every sensitive individual is to see to it that conditions are created in which he and others like him can become a majority. Killing for revenge is just as bad a crime as that which inspired revenge in the first place.

SARIE: That is the most difficult quality. Most loves, at bottom, are really selfish loves. (*Sitting down together.*) You know, I'm so glad I've met somebody like you tonight. I mean, somebody I can talk to. When I came, I was so shy. May I tell you something?

TULA: Please, tell me.

SARIE: I was scared that all of you wouldn't like me because . . .

TULA: Because you're Afrikaner?

SARIE: Yes. I thought you would want to humiliate me in all sorts of subtle ways. Then Chris said I should come. I'd really have a good time.

TULA: Oh, we're glad you came. Lots of people who are members of the club don't like Afrikaners until they meet individuals. Then they find they like them. When they say things against the Afrikaners, they're just thinking of them as a group.

SARIE: I know. But it still hurts if you're Afrikaner yourself. Somehow it makes you feel responsible.

TULA: Oh, don't feel like that at all. For instance, we have an Afrikaner student who comes here every now and again. I guess he tells more cruel jokes about Afrikaners than anybody here. Maybe he feels guilty about Afrikaners too, but it's better to laugh about it than to feel miserable. (*Noticing her empty glass.*) May I get you another one?

SARIE (*hesitantly*): I don't really drink much . . . (*Smiles.*) All right, I'll have another one. (*Just then* GAMA *springs up from the couch, making ferocious noises and pointing an accusing finger at* TULA *and* SARIE.)

GAMA: Well! Well! Look at those two! Just look at them! Aren't they going pretty snugly? (TULA *goes to get drinks.*)

JIMMY: Aw, come on, Gama, leave the kids alone! They aren't doing any harm.

GAMA: That's what's so wrong about it! They aren't doing any harm!

JOJOZI: Give them time! They always say that between the Bantu and the Boer there's an unnatural attraction.

MARY: What's so unnatural about it?

JIMMY: It's too concentrated! I mean for people who are political enemies.

JOJOZI: My God! Can you imagine the stories in the paper. A Boer girl and a Bantu boy found in flat under compromising circumstances. (*Intones.*) This is the South African Broadcasting Corporation. A Boer girl and a Bantu boy were found by the police under compromising circumstances last night. They were both taken into custody after making signed statements to the police. Contrary to—

CHRIS: —to previous explanations that the girl had willingly proffered herself to the Bantu male, it is now suspected by the police—

JOJOZI: —that the girl had attended a mixed party in some dingy Hillbrow flat, a haunt for an inter-racial bohemian set—

GAMA: —given to loose living, to promiscuous sex, and abandoned drinking!

CHRIS: And having gone there, the girl had been exposed to more than the usual amount of drinks—

JIMMY: Anyway, just enough to submit herself to the disgraceful demands of a dagga-crazed Bantu youth.

MARY (*takes* SARIE *by the hand*): Don't mind

them, honey! They're the sickest bunch of people you ever saw.

TULA (*coming with the drinks*): Here, Sarie. Mary, did you want something to drink?

MARY: No, that's all right, honey. You go ahead and talk to Sarie. I'll get myself something to drink.

JOJOZI and GAMA have their arms around each other's shoulders; they are doing fancy dance steps they have learned. Seeing TULA and SARIE together again, GAMA pauses and yells to the entire group in a somewhat drunken manner.

GAMA: Everybody look at them! What's the matter with those two?

TULA: Gama, will you please leave us alone for a while!

GAMA: Did you hear that? My own brother —my own kid brother—stands there and says to me, Leave us alone! Has your kid brother ever told you to leave him alone?

JOJOZI: He never lived to tell me that. He died an untimely death, poor brother! The son of a bitch had no business to die such an untimely death.

GAMA: I'm sorry about your brother! Sincerely! Well, there's mine and there's no likelihood he will die young!

JIMMY (*crawling on all fours from some dark corner*): Don't be too sure of that. We have a very efficient police force in this country, dedicated to the elimination of young life! (LILI *crosses in front of* JOJOZI. *She is a beautiful girl, with delicate Indian features.* JOJOZI *grabs her by the arm.*)

LILI: Aw, come on, Jo, let go! . . . Will you, please?

JOJOZI: Not so fast, girlie!

LILI: Aw, come on, you're hurting me! Jo, I don't want to play.

JOJOZI (*tries to kiss her*): Not even love-play?

LILI: That especially!

JOJOZI: Why don't Indians in this country ever "integrate"?

LILI: I just wouldn't like to integrate with *you*, that's all.

He lets her go. GAMA *slaps her on the bottom as she passes him.* LILI *turns and tries to pummel him with her fists, which* GAMA *catches expertly; he pulls her roughly to him. She seems to melt in his arms as he*

kisses her. *The group gathers around in sheer fascination.* JIMMY *starts counting like a referee to calculate how long the kiss is going to last. He counts up to ten, his voice rising to a crazed pitch as he nears ten. Just then* MARY *approaches the two and separates them playfully.*

MARY: That's enough.

The rest of the group applaud the performance. KITTY *and* SLOWFOOT *emerge from the back room.* KITTY *has got hold of a red garment which she is waving like a matador in the eyes of the fat* SLOWFOOT, *who stumbles after her, trying to butt her with his head. When they make their entrance, the whole group begin to clap hands. They form a circle. The excitement rises to a pitch as* SLOWFOOT *rushes the girl and finally butts her in the stomach so that she goes down. There is wild cheering. It is then the clock suddenly strikes. There is a dead stillness. As the clock stops, the group goes about carousing again as though nothing had happened. Again attention is centered on* TULA *and* SARIE.

SARIE: What is this party for?

TULA (*lying to her*): Aw, you know, we always have get-togethers! To promote a spirit of comradeship!

SARIE: Every week!

TULA: Every week! Sometimes we have lectures on things like political leadership! Revolutionary tactics!

SARIE: Are you planning a revolution then?

TULA: Well, we aren't planning one now. (*Lying down.*) But, you know, anything can happen in this country. We as students must be prepared! Students everywhere are in the vanguard of the fight against injustice, corruption, and the status quo.

SARIE: I don't think I'd be much of a revolutionary! I couldn't hurt a fly really.

TULA: It is different when you're in the middle of it. Then you have to act one way or another.

SARIE: I don't honestly know which way I would act.

TULA: Anyway, that's not important. It's enough that you're a friend, that you won't have to act against us.

SARIE: I suppose so. You know, Tula . . . (*She looks desperately at him.*)

TULA: Yes?

SARIE: I've suddenly realized how terrible it would be to have to face you across the battle lines! I mean now I know you.

TULA: I know. I don't like thinking about what would happen to my white friends in this country when it really comes to the worst! That is why it's so important for people who think alike, both black and white, to form a united front against the Government, so that the fight will not be black against white but right against wrong!

SARIE: It's very difficult. Few white people want to join hands with black people against the Government. They fear that a change will mean a loss of privilege.

TULA: The young people can do it! There are more of them, both inside and outside the university, who are prepared to join battle. For instance, I never thought I would one day be in a party with an Afrikaner girl. But here we are! (*They are kneeling down, facing each other in the foreground of the stage.*)

SARIE: You know what I like about you?

TULA: No. What?

SARIE: You seem to be very sincere about everything you're doing.

TULA: Oh, we are all sincere about what we are doing here!

SARIE: No, but I mean, one never knows the motives of people for doing certain things.

TULA: You don't know mine.

SARIE: But I can tell they are honourable. I mean you really—well, you seem to like people. I like people who care what happens to people.

TULA: Well, thanks, but I'm really not much better than anybody else.

SARIE: You know something, too? You're very gentle! I mean, a woman can tell these things very quickly. When a man is gentle, a woman can feel it immediately.

TULA: How's that?

SARIE (*laughingly*): Well, you sort of feel safe. In many ways you're like my father. He's the gentlest man I've ever known.

TULA: And your mother?

SARIE: I don't have a mother. My mother died when I was very young. I hardly have any memory of her at all. I've always had my father to look to.

TULA: Does your father know about your associations at the university?

SARIE: Well, he knows my views have changed. He knows I mix freely with non-white students at the university.

TULA: He doesn't care? I mean, does he mind?

SARIE: He says I'm about grown enough to think for myself. Sometimes I can tell he says it just because he wants to be good to me, but he's scared! He's scared that I might get too involved. It's not easy for Afrikaner people to accept a thing like that.

TULA: Your father must be very considerate toward you.

SARIE (*suddenly, and a bit sadly*): Oh, I wish you could just talk to him, I mean just as we are talking tonight. I wish it were possible to ask you home sometimes, you know, just to talk about things. He likes that. I think that there are so many things he would learn about you, about Africans. It's just that he's never met any apart from servants. My father is a very kind man . . . (*She gets up quickly.*) Sometimes everything seems so futile! (TULA *gets up too. They stand facing each other. Somebody in the background has started playing a blues record.* TULA *and* SARIE *stand for a few seconds just facing each other. Tears are standing in* SARIE's *eyes, and* TULA *tries to smile reassuringly. The other young people start dancing.*)

TULA: Would you like to dance?

SARIE: I don't know how to dance! Africans are such wonderful dancers!

TULA: We'll just shuffle around. Who's watching here?

They begin to dance, first holding each other loosely at arm's length, and then holding each other closely, tightly finally. Sometimes they seem not to be moving at all, just standing and swaying in one area. All the time SARIE's *face is raised toward* TULA's *eyes. The record stops, but they keep on shuffling, not realizing that everybody is watching them.* GAMA *is delighted to catch them at it.*

GAMA (*banging something on the floor*): The music has stopped, lovers! (*They break off self-consciously.*) Going snugly, eh!

JULIE: What is it to you!

GAMA: Something about those two offends my sense of good taste. (TULA *and* SARIE *have drifted off toward far left.*) There's something awfully independent about them. Nobody should be that independent!

JOJOZI: What's the matter? Afraid if those two kids become independent, you'll soon run out of sheep to lead?

GAMA: There'll always be people to lead! What do you know about leadership? You're just a gossip columnist on a scandal sheet! One of the worst!

JOJOZI: There aren't enough good people in the world to write for! There aren't enough good people to write about—except those two kids out there! There's a certain charm about them.

GAMA: You must be smelling a good bit of gossip for your column!

JOJOZI: Although I don't believe in people, I prefer charm to squalor! I prefer elegance to shabbiness! Those two kids have a certain elegance, however threadbare, that is touching.

GAMA: You know, Jo, what really offends me about you is your affectation of outraged cynicism about the world's problems. At heart you're a disgusting romanticist! A romanticist! That's what you are!

JOJOZI: What is a cynic but a romanticist turned sour? Still, I love those kids! All night they have been surprising each other . . . by small things . . . little gestures! . . . I like kids who are astonished by life!

CHRIS (*taking a close look at his face*): Hey, what's suddenly happened to you tonight?

GAMA: It's the winds of change!

JULIE (*walking into the back room in the company of* LILI): If I hear that Macmillan phrase again, I'm going to pass out!

JOJOZI: I'm not like Gama! He is a professional executioner! I like to get drunk, I like to pinch bottoms; he wants to change the world; such men are dangerous!

JIMMY: Oh, crap! Who let Jo take the floor? I thought he was interdicted from making public speeches! Jo, do us a favour, will you? Stick to your typewriter.

JOJOZI: That's Gama's deputy-executioner! These boys are ambitious, I tell you. When we are rid of Verwoerd, these boys will take over, and more heads will roll then than at any other time in the history of this country!

JIMMY: That's right. . . . And see that yours doesn't roll first!

JOJOZI: I have no illusions about the safety

of my neck. When people like you and Gama get into power, I'll get out of the country.

JIMMY: Oh, bosh! Not that we would miss you.

JOJOZI: You won't. Politicians are anti-life. Me? I say bottoms up both to women and to glasses! (*He raises his glass and tosses a huge drink down his throat before he staggers away.*)

JULIE (*talking to* LILI *as they emerge from the back room with glasses*): . . . So he says to me, you're a nice Jewish girl, Julie; what are you doing here? So I say to him, what business is it of yours what I'm doing here or anywhere! So he says to me—

JIMMY (*interrupting rudely*): Julie, we've heard that story a thousand times! That story is driving me out of my mind!

JULIE: Nobody is asking you to listen! . . . I wasn't even talking to you!

The clock strikes eleven thirty. It freezes the motions of those members of the group who know something about the night's plans. After this, the pace of the dialogue moves faster, is more weirdly erratic, with more than a suggestion of self-consuming nervousness.

KITTY (*emerging from somewhere in the room*): Did anybody hear the clock strike half-past eleven?

JIMMY: Where have you been, blackie? (*She nestles in his arms as though threatened.*)

KITTY: Did you hear the clock?

GAMA: We heard the clock. We've been hearing the clock strike half-past eleven for as long as we can remember.

KITTY: It was different tonight. (*Pause.*) It's a different night altogether.

GAMA: It's like any other night. Just a change in rhythm. It's like any other night.

JIMMY: Warm and pleasant.

CHRIS: Maybe a bit tense! Maybe a storm is gathering. Maybe not.

GAMA: On the whole it's an ordinary night.

JIMMY: Almost humdrum.

CHRIS: Hell, I've seen better nights. Nights full of thrilling excitement and danger. Nights of blood and passion! I've also seen worse nights.

JIMMY: This one is neither the worst nor the best!

GAMA: And yet—

JIMMY: It may surprise a lot of people—

CHRIS: Just a bit of a change in rhythm. . . . People are easily surprised!

GAMA: All together it may be a different night! A bit jumpy! Maybe somewhat painful.

MARY (*lying on the studio couch face down, her hand holding a bottle of brandy next to her; she seems a bit drunk*): Ah, pain! I understand pain! (KITTY *goes over to see after* MARY's *condition.*)

GAMA: There are many in this country who don't! It's time they too understood pain.

JIMMY (*wandering off*): What a goddam bitchy night! I wonder if it will make any difference. I'm bored with waiting!

CHRIS: I wish I could be there to see it.

GAMA: What for? You can imagine the whole thing, can't you? A man walks down to the basement of the City Hall—

JIMMY (*approaching*): And he sets off the detonator!—

CHRIS (*apocalyptically*): Then there is a wild explosion!—

GAMA: That's right! And the power plant blows up!—

CHRIS: The walls go up like a volcano! . . . The whole Pritchard Street is covered in flames! . . . Man, it's mad! Just mad! One has got to see the whole thing happen! (JULIE *emerges from the shadows with* SLOWFOOT *this time.*)

JULIE (*to* SLOWFOOT): . . . So he says to me, Julie, I love you! You are the first Jewish girl I've really loved! I mean, I could marry you tomorrow if you'd let me, he says, but why must you always be seen in the company of black students? So I say to him, if you love me, Carmine, stop—

JIMMY: Julieeeeeeeeee!

GAMA: Julie, sweetheart, we know what you told Carmine.

JULIE: Was I talking to you? Why can't you shut up until somebody talks to you? Wiseguys!

CHRIS (*taking* JULIE *in his arms*). Don't mind these clowns, love. You go on and tell your story, because it's a nice story.

JIMMY: Sure! I guess we can still listen to it, even though it's the hundredth time we are hearing it!

KITTY (*sees the figure of* JOJOZI *sprawled against the wall*): My God! Look at Jo!

GAMA (*tartly*): My God, look at Jo! God doesn't want to look at Jo. Jo stinks!

KITTY: Does anybody want coffee? I'm going to make some coffee. (*There are several responses.*) Anybody wants coffee, come and get it. (*Several young people follow* KITTY *into the back room.* CHRIS *goes over to* JOJOZI.)

CHRIS (*shaking him up*): Hey, Jo! Jo! Do you want coffee? Come on!

JOJOZI (*stirring*): What's the matter with you? Hey, take yo' hands off me, white son of a bitch!

CHRIS: Come on, Jo; the only time your racialism shows is when you're in the pots! (JULIE's *voice from the back room can be heard distinctly.*)

JULIE: So he says to me, Julie, you're a nice kid . . .

JOJOZI (*getting up*): A man can't even have some sleep without some son of a bitch coming up to muss him up!

CHRIS: Come on! Coffee will do you some good!

JOJOZI (*staggering toward the kitchen*): Have the Government forces struck? Have the forces of destruction carried out their . . . their . . . their . . . monstrous purpose?

CHRIS: The Government forces have not struck! They are biding their time.

JOJOZI: Biding their time, eh! Well, you can tell them they stink! Everybody stinks! The whole damn lot of them! I'm the only sane person! I get drunk, maybe get myself a nice soft bottom. So what's so evil about that? Okay, you tell me. You're university, aren't you? Well, tell me what's wrong with a nice bottom? What's wrong with a piece of . . . (CHRIS *shshshs him up.*) You don't bloody well know? And you are university? What do they teach you up there at the university if they don't teach you to get out and get yourself a nice bottom? Eh, what do they teach you? Teach you to go out and shoot Natives like big game! Whites don't know nothing but to shoot! Blacks don't know nothing but imitate whites! Gama and the whole son-of-a-bitchin' lot! Don't know a thing! They think they're changing the world! They are making it worse than it is already! Why can't everybody sit down and drink? Well, I asked you, didn't I? Why can't nobody just sit down and have himself a nice piece

of bottom? Why can't everybody . . .
(CHRIS *half pushes him into the back room.*
Blackout.)

SCENE 4

Same as before. This time the young people
can be seen milling around in the back
room, drinking coffee. The party is nearing
an end. Before the action begins, there is a
harsh throb of jazz, much more insistent
than previously, with jarring rude phrases
constantly being interpolated in the con-
tinuous rhythm. When the music subsides,
TULA and SARIE emerge through the panel
door from the back room, carrying their
mugs of coffee. They sit gingerly in the
foreground of the stage. There is noticeably
more warmth, a greater ease, between the
two. When the light picks out their faces,
they seem to be glowing with an innocent,
youthful gravity and concern for each other.

SARIE: Now it seems that coming here was
the most important thing I have done in a
long, long while.
TULA: You can't imagine how glad I am you
came.
SARIE: All night we seem to have done nothing but talk and talk, and yet, somehow, I
seem to have discovered something important and vital. I can't explain it to you.
TULA: I know how you feel because this is
exactly how I feel. It's like stumbling upon
something precious, something you want
to keep. I suppose the pain of discovery is
the fear of losing.
SARIE: We can't be losers, because we care,
and caring breeds regard; and now that I
know something of your affection, even the
political problem seems less heavy, less
frightful.
TULA: I'm frightened, though. Precisely because I care. There seems to be no way of
preserving the important things when history grinds on its course, and yet one wants
to preserve the things that one has affection for.
SARIE: There must be a way of redirecting
history to avoid tragedy, provided there is
enough love. I am a woman, so my optimism is boundless. I don't feel despondent.
I used to, but now that I know there must

be many people who feel like you on your
side, I think I feel more strengthened.
TULA: You know it's very important that I
see you again soon; I'm even ashamed to
admit it.
SARIE: Oh, please don't . . . because you
make me feel important. I just wish that
it were not so difficult with all the laws controlling our lives.
TULA: Maybe we can meet for lunch at the
university canteen from time to time and
talk.
SARIE: Maybe we can too!
TULA: You don't mind if we do have lunch
together sometimes?
SARIE: Why I would love to. I don't care
what they think.
TULA: It doesn't have to be often.
SARIE: We can meet as often as it is reasonable. Anyway, I always have lunch mostly
with people who don't interest me in the
least. I'd love to have lunch with you.
There's so much to talk about! May I take
your cup?
TULA: No, no. I'll take them in for you.
(*They both get up.*)
SARIE: That's all right! I'll take them in. (*She*
goes away with the cups.) I'll be right back.

TULA *paces the floor. Although his face still*
retains something of its usual gravity, it is
now touched by a dreamy quality. We hear
a few bars of soft, fragile melody. The
music is interrupted by JULIE's voice from
the back room.

JULIE: So I say to him, Carmine, if there's
one thing I can't stand, it's a boy who remains uncommitted in this country, in spite
of the grave problems. There's absolutely
no excuse for cowardice or indifference!
(SARIE *makes her appearance again imme-*
diately after this short speech. She and
TULA *move quickly toward each other, and*
spontaneously TULA *takes* SARIE's *hand.*)
TULA: Won't your father be wondering where
you are tonight?
SARIE: He won't be back until very late. He's
gone to the Party rally.
TULA: Oh, I see . . . (*Too abruptly.*) Where
did you say?
SARIE: At the National Party rally.
TULA (*manifestly agitated*): You mean at the
City Hall?

SARIE: Yes . . . (*Looking at his face, which he is trying to keep averted.*) What's the matter, Tula? I hope you don't hold that against me. Do you?

TULA: Oh, no. No! You can't understand! You can't know what it means!

SARIE (*alarmed*): What do you mean? It can't be that important to us, what my father does!

TULA: No. I don't mean that at all. (*He makes to move away.*)

SARIE: Wait! And you know what, Tula? He's gone to tender his resignation to the Party. It's a great night for him! That is something, Tula. He may be no Liberal, but at least he is making a break with the Government régime. You can't imagine what a great step it is for him. He's been nervous all day long. I could see it the way he walked about the house! I could see it the way he stared absent-mindedly at things! Twice I asked him something, and he kept saying, yes, yes, although he wasn't listening to anything I was saying. (TULA *is more agitated and wants to break away from her.*) Tula, the way your face has changed suddenly frightens me. Something must be wrong. It's not my father? (TULA *shakes his head vigorously.*) No, then what is it? You must tell me! It's very important to me! (*Rapidly he walks away into the back room, followed closely behind by* SARIE. *Immediately, he comes out from the back room followed by* GAMA, JIMMY, *and* CHRIS.)

GAMA: What's the matter with you? (*He looks at the clock and back to* TULA.) What is it?

JIMMY: What is it, Tula?

GAMA (*shakes him roughly by the shoulders*): What is it? Can't you talk?

TULA (*wiping his face with the back of his hand*): Her father! Her father! The only parent she's got too!

CHRIS: What do you mean, Tula?

JIMMY: Whose father?

GAMA: What are you talking about?

TULA: The Afrikaner girl who's here tonight! Sarie Marais!

JIMMY: What happened to her father? Just tell us slowly what the matter is.

TULA: Her father is at the City Hall right now! At the National Party rally! If anything happens tonight, he will be there too!

He'll get hurt with the lot! (*The group is stunned. They all turn to the clock; it is eleven forty-five.*)

GAMA (*in distress*): How stupid! How damn stupid! What a damn stupid thing!

TULA: We've got to put the bomb off! We can't go on with it! There's still time to run down to the City Hall and put the whole thing off!

GAMA (*recovering from shock*): No! Nothing's to be put off!

TULA (*close to hysteria*): Are you crazy? He's the only parent she's got! That girl has nobody but her father! We can't let him get hurt.

JIMMY: Damn it! Why did we have to get mixed up with her? Why did she have to come sniffing here?

TULA: We can't let the bomb go off!

GAMA: Shut up, will you! You're not giving orders to anybody here! The bomb shall go off as planned! We can't help it if her father is a National Party supporter! He's just as guilty as any other white supremacist! He must perish with the rest!

TULA: He is not a National Party supporter!

CHRIS: What's he doing at the City Hall tonight? Why didn't she tell me about this earlier?

TULA: He's gone there to tender his resignation! He's making a break with the Party! She told me so herself! (*The whole group begins pacing up and down like caged lions without any means of escape from the dilemma. Only* TULA *has made his decision and stands accusingly before them.*)

GAMA: Don't just stand there accusingly! It's not our fault her father is at the City Hall tonight!

TULA: We can still do something! Disconnect the whole thing!

GAMA: No, we can't! It's too late!

TULA: It's not too late! If we didn't argue about this, somebody would be running down already!

GAMA (*furiously shaking him and pushing him off*): Listen, stupid! We've worked hard preparing for this! We've run grave risks! We can't just put it off for one white supremacist who's suddenly suffered a "crisis of conscience." What's the matter with you anyway! Are you in love with her? That's right! You want us to risk our necks rushing down to the City Hall because of your sentimental reasons!

TULA: Don't people mean anything to you? She's alone! She has no relatives! Her father is the only one she's got in the world!

GAMA: People mean something to me. That's why I am involved in this. Because I care about people! Hundreds of black people have been shot down mercilessly by these brutes! You don't remember that. No! And you talk about caring for people! For one white man you want to put off something that's important! Something that might mean the beginning of a change in this country! You call that caring about people?

JIMMY (*trying to be reasonable about it*): Have you told her about the plans to blow up the City Hall?

TULA: No. She doesn't know it! She thinks me a friend and here am I, murdering her father in cold blood!

JIMMY: Calm down, Tula! We are all in this! We both feel sympathy for her! But we must keep our heads!

TULA: Keep our heads and her father is just about losing his!

CHRIS: Isn't there a way of removing the father from the City Hall without telling him the reason?

GAMA: When the news breaks, her father will suspect something and she will suspect us! We can't even explain this to her! We don't know her well enough to tell her we are behind the blowing up of the City Hall!

TULA (*desperately*): You can go on arguing about it! I'm going down to cut the wire off! (*He rushes toward the door.* GAMA *runs after him and grabs him by the shoulders. There is a struggle and* GAMA *hits his younger brother with a fist repeatedly in the stomach until he sags down.*)

GAMA: You're not running to any City Hall! Damn fool! You asked for this!

The girls and the boys pile out of the back room during the struggle. They are all asking what's happened. CHRIS, JIMMY, *and* GAMA *are mute. Neither does* TULA *explain what it is all about.* SARIE *rushes to* TULA, *who is still on the floor and is groaning. She lifts his face between her hands and*

tries to find out what the matter is, but TULA *keeps shaking his head.*

MARY: Gama, did you hit him?

GAMA: Yes, I hit him!

MARY: You really hit him? Your own brother? And for what?

GAMA: He was going to do something stupid! And don't ask me what!

MARY (*furiously*): Gama, I don't want to see you again! And don't ever touch me again! You're a cruel, heartless bully, and I can't stand bullies!

GAMA: Wait a minute! You don't even know what he was going to do! You don't know a thing! Why do you always have to rush to conclusions?

MARY: What conclusions are you talking about? You hit him, didn't you? Jimmy, what was the quarrel about this time?

KITTY: Jimmy, what happened?

JIMMY (*evading the questions*): Look, this is not the time to talk about it. (*The girls help* SARIE *move* TULA *to the back room to look after his condition.*)

CHRIS: What are we going to do about it?

JIMMY: There's nothing we can do about it.

GAMA: It's none of our fault!

CHRIS: Maybe we can telephone anonymously and give him the message that his daughter has been seriously hurt! Anything to get him out of there.

JIMMY: That's a good idea, Chris! That's a splendid idea! Gama, what do you think?

GAMA (*agitated*): Ya, maybe it will work! What's the City Hall phone number?

JIMMY: We can telephone the lobby, and somebody will send the message into the conference hall.

GAMA: Okay, Jimmy, you call!

GAMA, CHRIS, *and* JIMMY *move toward the telephone, where* JIMMY *dials the number of the City Hall. There is a long quiet, with only the purring of the telephone and the vague voices from the back room. The three young people stand tensely around the telephone. There is no answer.*

JIMMY (*slamming the telephone back to the cradle*): Not a damn answer! Too busy dreaming up crazy apartheid schemes to even answer the telephone! (*He paces up and down.*)

GAMA: Why do we have to bother? We can't help it if he is there! (*The others nod half-heartedly.*) I mean, I care and all that, but what can we do about it?

CHRIS: There's danger that anybody who goes down to the City Hall might be intercepted by the police. The whole City Hall is ringed by the police.

JIMMY: You're absolutely right, Chris! We might be caught in the act of cutting off wires! There's nothing more distressing than being punished for an aborted plan. (*Every pause now is marked by increased tension.*)

GAMA: Goddammit! It's not as if we asked him to be there! (*Pause.*)

CHRIS: Thank heavens she doesn't know yet!

JIMMY: She'll soon know! Chris, how the hell did you get mixed up with her?

CHRIS: Wait a minute, Jimmy! Don't try and start pushing the blame onto me now! This group is non-racial! So, we meet a Boer girl at the university who's interested in joining, and we ask her to come along! How could I have known her father was to be at the City Hall tonight?

GAMA: Okay! Okay! Nobody's blaming you! This is nobody's fault! Besides, it's almost time for the bomb to go off! (*With a deliberate attempt at levity.*) Ah, who cares? One Boer gets blown up because he happens to be in the wrong place at the wrong time! It's not the first time it's happened. Hundreds of black people have been killed by Boers! It's a pity if one good Boer gets on the rails of history and gets ground up with the rest. (*Pause. Suddenly.*) Jimmy, what do you think? You think I am right or wrong? Tell me.

JIMMY (*uncertainly*): Right. Maybe . . .

GAMA: Maybe what? Jimmy, do you think I'm right or wrong? Why do you say maybe?

JIMMY: I mean, maybe we should try that number again.

GAMA: Okay, maybe we will get an answer this time.

They move off toward the telephone, where JIMMY *tries again. There is complete stillness, during which we can almost hear the breathing of the three young men. After a while* JIMMY *replaces the receiver with an irritated bang.*

JIMMY: They're about to be blown off the face of the earth, and they can't even answer a telephone! Too busy with the damned apartheid policies to bother!

CHRIS (*slowly, dejectedly*): I suppose that's it! There's nothing more to be done!

GAMA (*agitated*): Suppose that's it? What else is there to do? We can't destroy everything we've planned for months because of one crazy Boer bastard! Why did he have to be there! Why did she have to come here!

CHRIS: Stop putting the blame on her! That girl was invited to join this group! When all of you started a non-racial organization, nobody bothered to think about Boers joining!

JIMMY: Nobody's saying Boers shouldn't join this organization! We are not racialists!

CHRIS: Well, both of you talk as if you're blaming me for having brought this girl to the party.

GAMA: No, no! We're not blaming you! It's just that she's made everything that was right seem wrong suddenly. (*The other young people who have been in the back room come out. Everybody is remarkably tense. Occasionally their eyes are riveted to the clock.*) Is there anything left to drink? Mary, is there anything left to drink? (*She doesn't answer him.*)

JULIE: Everybody's been guzzling drinks all night! Now you want a drink!

GAMA: Jimmy, give me a cigarette, will you?

JIMMY (*to* KITTY, *after searching his pockets unsuccessfully*): Blackie, what did I do with my cigarettes?

KITTY: How should I know? Did you give them to me?

GAMA: What's the matter with everybody suddenly?

MARY (*exploding*): What's the matter with you? You're stalking the room like a lion. Look at you!

GAMA: Well, what of it! Maybe I am a lion!

MARY: Stop shouting! You're going to bring all the neighbours running here! Are you all shot up or something?

GAMA: Who's shot up? I don't get shot up that easily! I'll see this through!

SARIE *and* TULA *come in from the back room. There is suddenly a dead quiet again. They stand separately. Tension mounts and*

is only broken by the drunken entrance of
SLOWFOOT, *who stumbles and falls but
manages to save the bottle of brandy he
has been hiding from everybody. He looks
around searchingly at the group, then takes
a sip from the bottle.* TULA *slips out unnoticed.*

SLOWFOOT (*grinning sardonically*): Ah, I can
see a sombre quiet rests heavily upon this
illogical conglomeration of the flotsam and
jetsam of society! (*Nobody responds to
him. He sizes up the group and tries again.*)
A dead stillness! I see. Only drunks are not
impressed by the sober solemnity of history!

JIMMY: And history is not impressed by the
solemn sogginess of a drunkard's mind!

SLOWFOOT: Ah, Jimmy, my boy! I knew you
would rise up to the occasion!

GAMA: Will that clot shut up! He's getting
on my nerves!

SLOWFOOT (*whistles drunkenly and stumbles
forward*): Hey, waita minute! Listen who's
talking now! The tough cool boy! The
wonderboy who's in truck with history!
And for the first time he's unsure like the
rest of us mortals! Gama, rise and shine;
immortality is passing you by!

GAMA: If somebody doesn't stop that drunk,
I swear I'm going to punch him on his
blabbering mouth!

SLOWFOOT: Ah, it "was the best of times, it
was the worst of times . . . it was the
time of wisdom, it was the time of foolishness!" (*He stumbles forward.*) A time of
extreme stupidity! You see, Gama, my boy,
you're not the original thing! There've been
revolutions before! (GAMA *rushes to punch
him one, but he is intercepted by* JIMMY'S
swift action.)

GAMA: Damn him! Somebody get this drunk
out of here before he gets hurt!

JIMMY: Gama, calm down, for God's sake!
Everybody's flying off the handle. What's
the matter with everybody?

SLOWFOOT: Nothing's the matter with me.
(*Pause.*) Okay, what did I say wrong? Did
I say anything wrong? If I did, I heartily
apologize—like a gentleman. (GAMA
snatches the bottle from him.) Now, waita
minute, Gama! That's a very arbitrary
measure! Even a drunk has a democratic
right to retain his bottle—I mean—for all

practical purposes. I deman' an explanation
why my bottle is being impounded. (GAMA
*takes a swig from the bottle. He raises it
against the light and discovers there is
pretty little left in it. He empties down his
throat the rest of the contents and throws
the bottle away.*) Ah, the maestro needed
a shot in the arm too!

GAMA: And you need a shot in the head!

JIMMY (*suddenly*): Where's Tula? What's
happened to Tula?

SARIE: He said he was going to get some
fresh air.

JIMMY: What? Oh, my God!

GAMA: What? When did he leave? What
happened? Where did he say he was going? Talk, can't you? Goddammit! (*He
shakes the bewildered girl.*)

SARIE: Don't! You're hurting me! (MARY
pulls GAMA *away.*) What's the matter with
all of you? What's the matter with everybody here? What are you planning? What's
going on? (JIMMY *and* GAMA *have rushed
outside to search for* TULA.) Something is
going on here that I don't know about!

LILI: Mary, what's the matter? Do you know
what the excitement's all about?

MARY: How should I know? Why ask me?
I was in there drinking coffee, and I come
out here and there's a general commotion.
I don't know what it's all about! (GAMA
and JIMMY *come in again.*) Gama, is there
something wrong?

GAMA (*moving toward the centre of the stage.
A note of hysteria*): You bet something is
wrong! Sweet brother of mine has run
down there to watch the whole thing happen! He's goin' to be the major witness!
Who knows, maybe he's even goin' to sing
to the police! Warn them! I bet he's goin'
to do that! He's goin' to rush into the hall
and tell all those people to get out before
it happens! (GAMA *begins to shout in a
deranged fashion.*) Get out all you good
people! Get out before we blow you up!
Can you hear me? Get out of the damned
City Hall! You only have five minutes to
do it! Get out now or be blown off, goddammit! Can anybody hear me? No, nobody can hear me! Not a damn single person can hear me! You're all too damn
busy cooking up your crazy apartheid policies to listen, to care! Well you can damn
well perish! All of you perish, and see if I

care! I tell you it's your damn fault if you—

We begin to hear the clock strike the hour of midnight. Suddenly there are rumblings at a distance. Loud explosions, detonations, can be heard within two miles. Then sirens begin to scream, ambulance and police cars. The lights on stage are shaken as though by an explosion; they falter as though a power plant has been affected. A wild jazz rhythm can be heard blending with the rhythmic detonations offstage. The explosions stop suddenly. The whole group rushes for the door. The lights falter and die out suddenly. Curtain.

ACT III

The charred ruins of what had been the City Hall. It is about an hour later, but the blown-up building is still smoking. There is a lot of debris over the background area of the stage. Near the ruins lies the still figure of TULA, *over which* SARIE *is kneeling, convulsed with sobbing. In the foreground area the two policemen,* JAN *and* PIET, *are conversing in a psychopathic fashion, their backs turned on* SARIE. *It is hard to tell from the way they are talking whether they are still mentally capable of drawing the line between the dream and the reality.*

PIET: A damn good it's going to do them trying to bluff us into thinking there's something they can do!

JAN: Natives need to be taught a lesson.

PIET: Talk about taking action! Who do they think they're fooling?

JAN: Natives love talking! I tell you, it's their habit! (*They walk into the lighted area so that we can see their faces, which are covered by the dust from the debris.*)

PIET: We can handle any number of Natives! Any blinkin' number of Natives!

JAN (*nervously, perhaps reclaimed by reality*): Hey, Piet, you think this was the start tonight?

PIET: What start? What do you mean, the start?

JAN: Well, this is the first time a bomb has exploded in a public place in this country!

Goddammit, this is the first time they've killed our people! I don't like this, Piet! We could've been killed if we were in there! I tell you, man, they should let us hunt those bastards down and shoot them like dogs!

PIET: This is nothing! We'll get them all right!

JAN: So you think this *is* a start?

PIET: What start? Man, talk straight when you talk to me! What start? We're in control of the situation here!

JAN: I know.

PIET: Well, don't talk about no start, because there isn't goin' to be any damn start of anything here!

JAN: I was just asking for your opinion!

PIET: I'm giving you my opinion! There isn't goin' to be any damn start for the Natives now or tomorrow!

JAN: Okay, man, you mad at me or something? I just asked.

PIET: I'm not mad at you. I'm mad at *them!* (*A pause.*)

JAN: What a night!

PIET: Anyway, we got the situation under control! Completely under control! (JAN *hears the moaning of the girl,* SARIE.)

JAN: There's somebody moaning! (*He looks around.*) They took everybody hurt?

PIET: Yah, they did. (JAN *walks toward backstage and sees* SARIE *kneeling over a body.*)

JAN: Piet, come and look at this! Man, a white girl too! Kneeling . . . over . . . a bloody kaffir! What's this! (*He yanks her off the body.*) What are you doing with the body of a damn stinking kaffir? (*The girl is convulsed with grief. She doesn't answer.*)

PIET: Shit, man, kneeling over a kaffir! Who is she? A Communist or something? Bitch! What is your name?

SARIE (*a sudden senseless explosion*): Don't you call me a bitch! Don't you call me anything dirty! (*She throws herself at the policeman, who slaps her down.*)

PIET: Do that again, you bitch, I'll teach you a lesson! Get up! (*She gets up.*)

SARIE: Brutes! All of you! A whole pack of murderers! All of you! Black and white and yellow! It doesn't make a damn bit of difference! You're all killers! Murderers!

JAN: And what are you? A goddam prostitute! Kneeling over a bloody kaffir! (*She tries to tear at them.* PIET *hits her again. She holds her mouth and begins sobbing.*)

PIET: Shut up! You'll get inside for this! Janie, get the handcuffs on her! She must know more about this business here tonight! You're going to talk, you damn slut! Crying over your lover, heh! One of the bomb-throwers!

SARIE (*torn by grief, is no longer arguing with them; it's a sort of soliloquy*): No, no, no! . . . Not that! . . . He was not a bomb-thrower.

PIET: How do you know? What was he doing here anyway when he got blown up?

SARIE (*sobbing*): He was so good! So very, very good! One of the very few who could have saved us all.

JAN: How do you know all this? You goin' with kaffirs? I can't stand a white woman who goes with Natives!

PIET: Wait a minute. What's your name?

SARIE: Sarie! Sarie Marais! (*Both* PIET *and* JAN *stand in shocked amazement that she is Afrikaner.*)

PIET: You mean you're an Afrikaner and you go with Natives!

SARIE: I wish I had. I wish I had known him better.

JAN: Wait until your parents hear about this, you little slut! My God, wait until your father hears about this!

SARIE: He won't. My father won't hear anything. (*Pointing at the ruins.*) He was at this meeting, and they picked him away already dead. (*Again another long pause.* JAN *and* PIET *are shocked at the mystery developing here.*)

JAN: What's this? Am I crazy or is she crazy? You mean your father's just been blown to pieces by a bomb and you have the nerve to weep over a Native?

SARIE: Tula, you were so good! Such a big heart and you needn't have died.

PIET: Good, she calls him! A dirty bomb-thrower!

SARIE (*again throwing herself at the surprised policeman*): Will you stop calling him names! He tried to save my father! This boy here tried to save my father! You stand

here running your mouths, and you think you know something! (*She talks calmly.*) This boy here . . . this boy who lies in the dust here . . . his only crime . . . his one crime . . . is that he tried to stop time . . . he tried to block history . . . for me . . . for my father . . . for you and for all of us! . . . so that we might have . . . time to think . . . to reconsider. . . . He never knew how late it was . . . so he tried, and trying got ground to pieces. . . . He might just as well have stayed home. . . . Look at him now. . . . They wouldn't even take him away in their whites-only ambulances. . . . I feel now a sombre darkness upon life itself.

PIET (*uneasily*): Ah, let her go, Jan.

JAN: Wait a minute, Piet! (*To* SARIE.) What did you say his name was?

SARIE: Tula.

JAN: This is getting more complicated. Remember, Piet, this afternoon? The Native boy with the petitions?

PIET: Hey, no joke? What's his second name?

SARIE: Why do you ask?

PIET: Could it be? (*He kneels down by the body and searches the pockets, from which he gets out the identity card.*) Look at his identity papers! Tula Zulu! Exactly the same Native from the photograph. Gama's own brother! So, Gama and the lot must know something about this! And you! How did you get involved with the political gangsters?

SARIE (*apprehensively*): No, it's got nothing to do with Gama!

PIET: Aha, so you know that too! You're going to do a lot of explaining, young lady! I wouldn't like to be in your shoes! This is sedition! You know that? Jan, get the handcuffs onto her. She nearly fooled us, too!

They push SARIE *out through the right side of the stage. A slow blues number can be heard gradually mounting into a harsh, violent, discordant melody. The lights go out slowly. Curtain.*

II
Society

THE plays in this group are direct reflections of society. Unlike the political plays, they are concerned more with the depiction of society than with the causes of why society is the way it is. Plays like these give us an indication of the moral tone of the times. They show us, often satirically, what society was or is like. (For more advanced study, it would be instructive to try to see in what way the political conditions shaped society into the form depicted in the plays.) Plays of this nature may, of course, be found in all periods and countries. Outstanding examples from earlier times are the plays of Menander in ancient Greece and of Plautus and Terence in classical Rome.

The first thing to remember about Molière's plays, quite apart from their significance as mirrors of society, is the fact that they were written by an actor for actors. This fact makes clearer in Molière's plays something that is true about all plays: the printed play is a scenario for performance. This frequently makes the reading of plays difficult, since what is enormously effective when animated on stage may seem tedious and pointless in the reading. It is necessary, therefore, when reading a play always to try to visualize it being performed, or to read it aloud if at all possible. *The Would-Be Gentleman,* for example, as the translator puts it, is "often regarded as consisting of three acts of comedy, among the finest Molière wrote, and two of only half-relevant buffoonery. That is a literary judgement. On the stage the music and dances which round off each act integrate the action, heighten the effect of hilarious abandon and sweep the play along to a triumphant conclusion where the reader may see only weak anticlimax, a petering out of the original theme."

The Would-Be Gentleman is one of Molière's later plays (1670), composed at a time when the mercantile class (to which Molière himself belonged) was beginning to make itself felt in national affairs. While Louis XIV remained on the throne, however, the grip of monarchical absolutism that he had created on the foundation laid for him by Richelieu during Louis XIII's reign could not be broken. In 1670 the pretensions of a man who would be a gentleman without having had the fortune of being born into that station were still matter for derision. And Molière had to follow the lead of the arbiters of society—the upper classes, who slavishly followed the often whimsical directives of the king—in pouring scorn on poor Jourdain (the part he acted himself, by the way). Not that the scorn was not deserved, of course. What was wrong with Jourdain was that he fully subscribed to the current mores and despised his own bourgeois class as much as the upper class he was trying to emulate did. (It was not until the following century, with Louis XIV dead, that the bourgeoisie was content to be itself.)

Gallows Humor (1961) and *Incident at Twilight* (1959) are two of the many plays that attempt to depict and comment upon the complexities of our own society. All too often we have less of an idea of our own society than of past societies, which we can look on with some measure of objectivity and pass some judgment on from the perspective of time. But, for the most part, we are too close to and too involved in our own society for objective judgment. This is what Richardson and Dürrenmatt have attempted to correct. Each sees our world in a cynical, jaundiced manner.

To Richardson, the world today is a place where people react to stimuli like automatons. His idea is that most people have become so deindividualized by the routine of their social existences, so unthinkingly obedient to the pre-scribed norm, so "automated," in fact, that it has become difficult to dis-tinguish the quick from the dead. Many people are just walking dead—meekly going through the motions until the day they finally stop breathing and keel over, officially dead.

Dürrenmatt's concern is with the general morality of society—or, rather, with the fact that he sees none. In Maximilian Korbes, the great and honored writer, Dürrenmatt has created a symbol of the violence in the newspapers, in popular literature, on television, and in the movies on which the vast majority of the populace feeds, sublimating—but often only temporarily—its sadomasochistic instincts. The result is that we live, as does Korbes, in a society where lawlessness is, in effect, the accepted norm. Famous people are proud to be Korbes's friends; the neighboring Archbishop is fully cognizant of his crimes. Only Feargod Hofer, the insignificant little bookkeeper, is un-aware of the conspiracy of silence around him. But Hofer, too, is rotten. He is tainted with self-interest. He wants to become a part of the evil he has uncovered, to travel with the great man and become his confidant, to par-ticipate in Korbes's thrill-murders by proxy. His punishment is the discovery that Korbes himself commits his thrill-murders by proxy, so to speak: that as a murderer Korbes acts only as a surrogate for the sublimated wishes of the whole world. Korbes and Hofer are both puppet figures in what Dürrenmatt, arguing against the suitability of traditional concepts of tragedy in the modern world, so aptly calls "the Punch and Judy show of our century":

> Tragedy emphasizes guilt, despair, moderation, an all-encompassing vision, and a sense of responsibility. In the Punch and Judy show of our century there are no longer people who are guilty or people who have responsibility. It wasn't anybody's fault, and nobody wanted it. Everything really did happen without anyone's doing anything about it. Everyone was swept along and caught some-where. We are collectively guilty, collectively enmeshed in the sins of our fathers and of our fathers' fathers. We are simply the children of other chil-dren. This is not our guilt: it is our misfortune. Guilt exists only as a result of personal effort, as a religious deed. Comedy alone is suitable for us.*

* Friedrich Dürrenmatt, *Theaterprobleme* (Zürich: Verlag der Arche, 1955), pp. 47–48.

THE WOULD-BE GENTLEMAN

Molière

TRANSLATED BY
John Wood

CHARACTERS

MR. JOURDAIN
MRS. JOURDAIN, his wife
LUCILE, their daughter
NICOLE, a maidservant
CLEONTE, in love with Lucile
COVIELLE, valet to Cléonte
DORANTE, a nobleman
DORIMENE, a lady
MUSIC MASTER
MUSIC MASTER'S PUPIL
DANCING MASTER
FENCING MASTER
PHILOSOPHER
MASTER TAILOR
TAILOR'S APPRENTICES
TWO LACKEYS

Singers and Dancers, Musicians, Cooks, the Mufti, Turks, and Dervishes.

ACT I

The overture is played by a great assem-blage of instruments and the music pupil is discovered composing the air which MR JOURDAIN *has commissioned for his concert. As the song ends the* MUSIC MASTER *and the* DANCING MASTER *enter with their at-tendant musicians, singers, and dancers.*

MUSIC MASTER (*to musicians*): Come in here and wait until he comes.

DANCING MASTER (*to dancers*): And you can stay on this side.

MUSIC MASTER (*to his pupil*): Well, is it finished?

MUSIC PUPIL: Yes.

MUSIC MASTER (*taking manuscript*): Let me see. . . . Very good!

DANCING MASTER: Is it something new?

MUSIC MASTER: It is an air for a serenade I set him to compose while we were waiting for our friend to awake.

DANCING MASTER: May one see what it is?

MUSIC MASTER: You will hear it when he comes. He can't be long now.

DANCING MASTER: We are both being kept pretty busy at present.

MUSIC MASTER: Yes. We have found here the very man we both needed. This fellow Jourdain with the fantastic notions of gen-tility and gallantry he has got into his head means quite a nice thing for us. I only wish, both for my music and your dancing, that there were more people like him.

DANCING MASTER: I can't altogether agree. For his own sake I would like him to have a little more understanding of the things we provide for him.

MUSIC MASTER: It's true that he understands little—but he pays well, and, after all, that's the great need in our line of business just now.

DANCING MASTER: Yes—though for my own part I must confess that what I long for most is applause; it is appreciation I live for. To my way of thinking there is no fate more distressing for an artist than to have to show himself off before fools, to see his work exposed to the criticism of the vulgar and ignorant. You can say what you like but there *is* no joy like that of working for people who have a feeling for the fine points of one's art, who can appreciate the beauties of a work and repay all one's trouble by praise which is really discerning. There is no reward so delightful, no plea-sure so exquisite, as having one's work known and acclaimed by those whose ap-plause confers honour.

MUSIC MASTER: I agree. My feelings exactly. There is nothing more pleasing than the recognition you speak of, but you can't live on applause. Praise alone doesn't keep a man going. One needs something more substantial than that, and, to my mind, there's no praise to beat the sort you can put in your pocket. It's true that this fel-low here has no great share of enlighten-ment: he usually gets hold of the wrong end of the stick and applauds all the wrong things, but his money makes up for his lack of discernment. His praise has cash value. Vulgar and ignorant he may be but he's more use to us, you know, than your fine cultured gentleman who put us in touch with him.

DANCING MASTER: There's something in what you say, but I still think you set too much value on money. Cultivated people should be superior to any consideration so sordid as a mercenary interest.

MUSIC MASTER: All the same you don't refuse to take our friend's pay.

DANCING MASTER: Of course not. But I don't find that it entirely contents me. I still wish that with all his great wealth he had a little more taste.

MUSIC MASTER: So do I, and isn't that just where we are both trying to help him—so far as we can? In any case, he is giving us a chance to make a name in the world and he will make up for the others by paying while they do the praising.

DANCING MASTER: Hush! Here he comes. (*Enter* MR JOURDAIN *in dressing-gown and night-cap attended by two lackeys.*)

MR JOURDAIN: Well, gentlemen, what is it to be to-day? Are you going to show me your bit of tomfoolery?

DANCING MASTER: Tomfoolery? What bit of tomfoolery?

MR JOURDAIN: You know—your what ye may call it—your prologue or dialogue or what-ever it is—your singing and dancing.

DANCING MASTER: Oh! That's what you mean!

MUSIC MASTER: You find us quite ready.

MR JOURDAIN: I had to keep you waiting a while because I'm getting dressed up to-day like one of the quality and my tailor had sent me a pair of silk stockings so tight I thought I should never get into them.

MUSIC MASTER: We are entirely at your disposal, sir.

MR JOURDAIN: I don't want you to go, either of you, until they've brought me my suit. I want you to see how I look in it.

DANCING MASTER: Whatever you please.

MR JOURDAIN: You'll see me turned out in style—head to foot, everything just as it should be.

MUSIC MASTER: We don't doubt that at all.

MR JOURDAIN (*showing his dressing-gown*): I had this Indian stuff made up for me specially.

DANCING MASTER: Very fine indeed.

MR JOURDAIN: My tailor tells me the quality wear this sort of thing on a morning.

MUSIC MASTER: It suits you splendidly.

MR JOURDAIN: Lackey! Hello there! Both my lackeys!

FIRST LACKEY: Your wishes, sir?

MR JOURDAIN: Nothing. I just wanted to be sure you could hear me. (*To the others*) What d'ye think of my liveries, eh?

DANCING MASTER: Magnificent. (MR JOURDAIN *opens his dressing-gown and shows his tight breeches of red velvet and his green velvet jacket.*)

MR JOURDAIN: This is a little rig-out to do my morning exercises in.

DANCING MASTER: Most elegant.

MR JOURDAIN: Lackey!

LACKEY: Sir!

MR JOURDAIN: T'other lackey!

SECOND LACKEY: Sir!

MR JOURDAIN: Take my dressing-gown. (*To the others*) What d'ye think of me now?

DANCING MASTER: Excellent. Nothing could be finer.

MR JOURDAIN: Right then. Let us have a look at your show.

MUSIC MASTER: I would like you to hear first an air which this young man (*indicating the pupil*) has just composed for the serenade that you asked for. He is a pupil of mine who has quite a gift for this kind of thing.

MR JOURDAIN: Very well—but it shouldn't have been left to a pupil. You shouldn't have been above doing this job yourself.

MUSIC MASTER: Ah, don't be misled, sir, by my use of the word 'pupil'. Pupils like him know as much as the great masters, and the air itself couldn't be bettered. Do but listen.

MR JOURDAIN: Here. (*As the singer is about to begin*) Give me my dressing-gown so that I can listen better. Stop—I think perhaps I shall do better without it. No—give it me back. I can do best with it on.

SINGER: I languish night and day and sad must be my lay,
    Till consenting to their sway I give your eyes their way,
    If thus you treat your friends—fair Iris,
    If thus you treat your friends,
    Alas! Alas! How will you treat,
    How will you treat your enemies?

MR JOURDAIN: It sounds a bit dismal to me. It makes me feel sleepy. Can't you liven it up a bit here and there?

MUSIC MASTER: But the tune must suit the words, sir!

MR JOURDAIN: I learned a song once—a really pretty one it was—wait a minute—la—la la—how does it go?

DANCING MASTER: I've not the remotest idea.

MR JOURDAIN: It had something about sheep in it.

DANCING MASTER: Sheep?

MR JOURDAIN: Yes—or lambs. Now I've got it!
    (*Singing*) I thought my Janey dear
    As sweet as she was pretty, oh!
    I thought my Janey dear as gentle as a baa-lamb, oh!
    Alas, alas! She is a thousand times more cruel!
    Than any savage tiger—oh!
Isn't that nice?

MUSIC MASTER: Very nice indeed.

DANCING MASTER: And you sing it very well.

MR JOURDAIN: And yet I never learned music.

MUSIC MASTER: You ought to learn, sir, just as you are learning to dance. The two arts are closely allied.

DANCING MASTER: And develop one's appreciation of beauty.

MR JOURDAIN: What do the quality do? Do they learn music as well?

MUSIC MASTER: Of course.

MR JOURDAIN: Then I'll learn it. But I don't know how I'm to find time. I already have a fencing master giving me lessons and now

I've taken on a teacher of philosophy and he's supposed to be making a start this morning.

MUSIC MASTER: Well, there is something in philosophy, but music, sir, music—

DANCING MASTER: And dancing, music and dancing, what more can one need?

MUSIC MASTER: There's nothing so valuable in the life of the nation as music.

DANCING MASTER: And nothing so necessary to mankind as dancing.

MUSIC MASTER: Without music—the country couldn't go on.

DANCING MASTER: Without dancing—one can achieve nothing at all.

MUSIC MASTER: All the disorders, all the wars, that we see in the world to-day, come from not learning music.

DANCING MASTER: All the troubles of mankind, all the miseries which make up history, the blunders of politicians, the failures of great captains—they all come from not having learned dancing.

MR JOURDAIN: How d'ye make that out?

MUSIC MASTER: What is war but discord among nations?

MR JOURDAIN: True.

MUSIC MASTER: If all men studied music wouldn't it be a means of bringing them to harmony and universal peace?

MR JOURDAIN: That seems sound enough.

DANCING MASTER: And what do we say when a man has committed some mistake in his private life or in public affairs? Don't we say he made a false step?

MR JOURDAIN: We certainly do.

DANCING MASTER: And making a false step— doesn't that come from not knowing how to dance?

MR JOURDAIN: True enough. You are both in the right.

DANCING MASTER: We want to make you realize the importance, the usefulness of music and dancing.

MR JOURDAIN: Yes. I quite see that now.

MUSIC MASTER: Would you like to see our performances?

MR JOURDAIN: Yes.

MUSIC MASTER: As I have told you already, the first is a little exercise I devised a short time ago in the expression of various emotions through music.

MR JOURDAIN: Very good.

MUSIC MASTER (*to singers*): Come forward.

(*To* MR JOURDAIN) You must imagine them dressed as shepherds.

MR JOURDAIN: But why shepherds again? It always seems to be shepherds.

MUSIC MASTER: Because, if you are to have people discoursing in song, you must for verisimilitude conform to the pastoral convention. Singing has always been associated with shepherds. It would not seem natural for princes, or ordinary folk for that matter, to be indulging their passions in song.

MR JOURDAIN: Very well. Let's hear them.

Trio

FIRST SINGER (*woman*): Who gives her heart in loving
To a thousand cares is bound;
Men speak of love and wooing
As one continual round
Of rapture.—Not for me!
No, not for me!
I keep my fancy free,
I keep my fancy free.

SECOND SINGER (*man*): Could I succeed in proving
The ardour of my heart,
Could I succeed in moving
You to that better part—
Surrender—then for me,
Oh then for me,
How happy life would be,
How happy life would be!

THIRD SINGER (*man*): If one could find in loving
But one true faithful heart,
Could one succeed in proving
Faith were the better part
Of woman's heart—alas for me!
Alas for me!
None such there be,
None such there be!

SECOND SINGER: Oh rarest rapture.

FIRST SINGER: Would I could capture!

THIRD SINGER: Deceivers ever.

SECOND SINGER: Love, leave me never.

FIRST SINGER: Happy surrender—

THIRD SINGER: Faithless pretender—

SECOND SINGER: Change, change to love that scorn disdainful!

FIRST SINGER: Behold, behold, one lover faithful!

THIRD SINGER: Alas! where can one such a lover find?

FIRST SINGER: To vindicate my sex's part
I offer you—I offer you my heart.
SECOND SINGER: Oh, shepherdess how
can I trust—
My heart you'll ne'er deceive?
FIRST SINGER: That time shall prove,
Ah, time shall prove
Who truest loves—who truest loves.
ALL THREE SINGERS: To love's tender
ardours
Our hearts then we plight,
For whate'er can compare
With love's tender delights?
With love's tender delights?
Whate'er can compare with love's tender delights?

MR JOURDAIN: Is that all?
MUSIC MASTER: It is.
MR JOURDAIN: Well I thought it was very nicely worked out and there were some quite pretty sayings in it.
DANCING MASTER: Well now, in my show you will see a small demonstration of the most beautiful movements and attitudes which the dance can exemplify.
MR JOURDAIN: They aren't going to be shepherds again?
DANCING MASTER: They are whatever you please. (*To the dancers*) Come along!

The dancers at the command of the DANCING MASTER *perform successively minuet, saraband, coranto, galliard, and canaries. The dance forms the First Interlude.*

ACT II

MR JOURDAIN, MUSIC MASTER, DANCING MASTER, LACKEYS.

MR JOURDAIN: Well that wasn't too bad. Those fellows can certainly shake a leg.
DANCING MASTER: When the dancing and music are fully co-ordinated it will be still more effective and you will find that the little ballet we have arranged for you is a very pretty thing indeed.
MR JOURDAIN: Yes, but that's for later, when the lady I am doing all this for is going to do me the honour of dining here.
DANCING MASTER: Everything is arranged.

MUSIC MASTER: There is just one other thing, sir. A gentleman like you, sir, living in style, with a taste for fine things, ought to have a little musical at-home, say every Wednesday or Thursday.
MR JOURDAIN: Is that what the quality do?
MUSIC MASTER: It is, sir.
MR JOURDAIN: Then I'll do it too. Will it be really fine?
MUSIC MASTER: Beyond question! You will need three singers, a treble, a counter tenor, and a bass accompanied by a bass viol, a theorbo, a harpsichord for the thorough-bass, and two violins for the ritornellos.
MR JOURDAIN: I'd like a marine trumpet [1] as well. It's an instrument I'm fond of. It's really harmonious.
MUSIC MASTER: Leave these things in our hands.
MR JOURDAIN: Well, don't forget to arrange for people to sing during the meal.
MUSIC MASTER: You shall have everything as it should be.
MR JOURDAIN: And above all make sure that the ballet is really fine.
MUSIC MASTER: You will be pleased with it, particularly with some of the minuets.
MR JOURDAIN: Ah! Minuets! The minuet is my dance. You must see me dance a minuet. Come along, Mr Dancing Master.
DANCING MASTER: A hat, sir, if you please. (MR JOURDAIN *takes the* LACKEY's *hat and puts it on over his night-cap. The* DANCING MASTER *takes his hand and makes him dance to the tune which he sings.*) La, la, la la la la la etc. . . . once again . . . keep time if you ple-ease . . . la-la lala— now the right leg . . . la la . . . don't move . . . your shoulders so much . . . la la la . . . la la . . . your arms . . . are hanging too limply . . . la la la . . . up with your head, point your toes outward . . . point your toes out-ward . . . la la la . . . keep your body . . . e . . . rect.
MR JOURDAIN: Phew! What about that?
MUSIC MASTER: Well done! Well done!
MR JOURDAIN: And that reminds me. Just show me how to make a bow to a countess. I shall need to know that before long.
DANCING MASTER: How to make a bow to a countess?

---

[1] Not a trumpet but a one-stringed instrument.

MR JOURDAIN: Yes. A countess called Dori-mène.

DANCING MASTER: Give me your hand.

MR JOURDAIN: No. Just do it yourself. I shall remember.

DANCING MASTER: If you wish to show great respect you must make your bow first stepping backwards and then advance towards her bowing three times, the third time going down right to the level of her knee.

MR JOURDAIN: Let me see you do it. Good!

LACKEY: Sir, your fencing master is here.

MR JOURDAIN: Tell him to come in and give me my lesson here. (*To the* MUSIC MASTER *and* DANCING MASTER) Don't go! I'd like you to see me perform. (*Enter* FENCING MASTER *with* LACKEY *carrying the foils.*)

FENCING MASTER (*after presenting a foil to* MR JOURDAIN): Come, sir, your salute! Hold yourself straight. Take the weight of your body a little on your left thigh. Legs not so far apart. Feet more in line. Wrist in line with your hip. Point of the foil level with your shoulder. Arm not quite so far extended. Left hand level with your eye. Left shoulder squared a little more. Head up. Firm glance. Advance! Keep your body steady. Engage my point in quart and lunge. One, two. As you were. Once again, repeat! Do keep your feet firm. One, two, and recover! When you make a pass, sir, it is important that the foil should be withdrawn first—so—keeping the body well covered. One, two. Come along. Engage my foil in tierce and hold it. Advance! Keep your body steady. Advance and lunge from there! One, two, and recover. As you were. Once again. One, two. Back you go. Parry, sir, parry! (*The* FENCING MASTER *scores two or three hits crying as he does so, Parry! Parry!*)

MR JOURDAIN: Phew!

MUSIC MASTER: You do splendidly.

FENCING MASTER: I have told you before that the whole art of sword-play lies in two things only—in giving and not receiving. And, as I showed you the other day by logical demonstration, it is impossible for you to receive a hit if you know how to turn your opponent's sword from the line of your body, for which all that is needed is the slightest turn of the wrist—inward or outward.

MR JOURDAIN: At that rate, then, a fellow can be sure of killing his man and not being killed himself—without need of courage.

FENCING MASTER: Exactly! Didn't you follow my demonstration?

MR JOURDAIN: Oh yes.

FENCING MASTER: Well then, you see what respect should be paid to men of my profession and how much more important is skill in arms than such futile pursuits as dancing and music—

DANCING MASTER: Go easy, Mr Scabbard Scraper. Mind what you say about dancing.

MUSIC MASTER: And try to treat music with a little more respect if you please.

FENCING MASTER: A fine lot of jokers you are, to think of comparing your professions with mine.

MUSIC MASTER: Just listen who's talking.

DANCING MASTER: The ridiculous creature, with his leather upholstered belly!

FENCING MASTER: My little dancing master, I could make you skip if I had a mind to, and as for you, Mr Music Master, I could make you sing to some tune!

DANCING MASTER: Mr Sabre-rattler, I shall have to teach you your trade.

MR JOURDAIN (*to* DANCING MASTER): You must be mad to quarrel with a man who knows all about tierce and quart and can kill a man by logical demonstration.

DANCING MASTER: I don't give a rap for his logical demonstration, his tierce, or his quart.

MR JOURDAIN (*to* DANCING MASTER): Do be careful I tell you.

FENCING MASTER (*to* DANCING MASTER): You impertinent jackanapes!

MR JOURDAIN: Oh, Mr Fencing Master!

DANCING MASTER: You great cart horse!

MR JOURDAIN: Oh, Mr Dancing Master!

FENCING MASTER: If I once set about you—

MR JOURDAIN (*to* DANCING MASTER): Gently there—gently!

DANCING MASTER: If I once get my hands on you—

MR JOURDAIN: Easy now! Easy!

FENCING MASTER: I'll let a little daylight into you.

MR JOURDAIN (*to* FENCING MASTER): Please—please—if—you please.

DANCING MASTER: I'll give you such a drubbing.

MR JOURDAIN (*to* DANCING MASTER): I ask you—I—

MUSIC MASTER: Just give us a chance and we'll teach him how to talk to—

MR JOURDAIN (*to* MUSIC MASTER): Do for goodness sake—stop! (*Enter the* PHILOSOPHER.)

MR JOURDAIN: Ah, Mr Philosopher. You've arrived in the nick of time with your philosophy. Come and make peace between these fellows.

PHILOSOPHER: What is it? What is it all about, gentlemen?

MR JOURDAIN: They've got so worked up about which of their professions is the most important that they've started slanging each other and very nearly come to blows.

PHILOSOPHER: Come, come, gentlemen! Why let yourselves be carried away like this? Have you not read Seneca *On Anger?* Believe me there is nothing so base and contemptible as a passion which reduces men to the level of animals! Surely, surely, reason should control all our actions!

DANCING MASTER: But, my good sir, he's just been blackguarding the pair of us and disparaging music, which is this gentleman's profession, and dancing which is mine.

PHILOSOPHER: A wise man is superior to any insults which can be put upon him, and the best reply to unseemly behaviour is patience and moderation.

FENCING MASTER: They had the impudence to compare their professions with mine.

PHILOSOPHER: Well, friend, why should that move you? We should never compete in vainglory or precedence. What really distinguishes men one from another is wisdom and virtue.

DANCING MASTER: I maintain that dancing is a form of skill, a science, to which sufficient honour can never be paid.

MUSIC MASTER: And I that music has been held in foremost esteem all down the ages.

FENCING MASTER: And I still stick to my point against the pair of them that skill in arms is the finest and most necessary of all the sciences.

PHILOSOPHER: In that case where does philosophy come in? I consider you are all three presumptuous to speak with such assurance before me and impudently give the title of sciences to a set of mere accomplishments which don't even deserve the name of arts and can only be adequately described under their wretched trades of gladiator, ballad singer, and mountebank!

FENCING MASTER: Oh get out! You dog of a philosopher!

MUSIC MASTER: Get out! You miserable pedant!

DANCING MASTER: Get out! You beggarly usher!

PHILOSOPHER: What! Rascals like you dare to—(*He hurls himself upon them and all three set about him.*)

MR JOURDAIN: Mr Philosopher!

PHILOSOPHER: Scoundrels, rogues, insolent—

MR JOURDAIN: Mr Philosopher!

FENCING MASTER: Confound the brute!

MR JOURDAIN: Gentlemen!

PHILOSOPHER: Insolent scoundrels!

MR JOURDAIN: Oh, Mr Philosopher!

DANCING MASTER: The devil take the ignorant blockhead!

MR JOURDAIN: Gentlemen!

PHILOSOPHER: Villains!

MR JOURDAIN: Mr Philosopher!

MUSIC MASTER: Down with him!

MR JOURDAIN: Gentlemen!

PHILOSOPHER: Rogues! Traitors! Impostors! Mountebanks!

MR JOURDAIN: Mr Philosopher, Gentlemen, Mr Philosopher, Gentlemen, Mr Philosopher, Gentlemen. (*They rush out still fighting.*)

MR JOURDAIN: Go on then! Knock yourselves about as much as you like. I can do nothing about it and I'm not going to spoil my new dressing-gown in trying to separate you! I should look a fool shoving in among them and getting knocked about myself for my pains! (PHILOSOPHER *returns, straightening his neck-band.*)

PHILOSOPHER: Let us come to our lesson.

MR JOURDAIN: Oh, Mr Philosopher, I'm sorry they've hurt you.

PHILOSOPHER: It is nothing. A philosopher learns how to take things as they come and I will get my own back on them with a satire in the manner of Juvenal. I'll fairly tear them to pieces. Let us think no more of it. What would you like to learn?

MR JOURDAIN: Whatever I can, for I want, above all things, to become a scholar. I blame my father and mother that they never made me go in for learning when I was young.

PHILOSOPHER: A very proper sentiment! *Nam sine doctrina vita est quasi mortis imago.* You know Latin I suppose?

MR JOURDAIN: Yes, but just go on as if I didn't. Tell me what it means.

PHILOSOPHER: It means that without knowledge, life is no more than the shadow of death.

MR JOURDAIN: Ay. Your Latin has hit the nail on the head there.

PHILOSOPHER: Have you not mastered the first principles, the rudiments of the Sciences?

MR JOURDAIN: Oh yes, I can read and write.

PHILOSOPHER: Well, where would you like to begin? Shall I teach you logic?

MR JOURDAIN: Yes, but what is it?

PHILOSOPHER: Logic instructs us in the three processes of reasoning.

MR JOURDAIN: And what are they, these three processes of reasoning?

PHILOSOPHER: The first, the second, and the third. The first is the comprehension of affinities, the second discrimination by means of categories, the third deduction by means of syllogisms. *Barbara, celarent, Darii, Ferio, Baralipton.*

MR JOURDAIN: No. They sound horrible words. Logic doesn't appeal to me. Let me learn something nicer.

PHILOSOPHER: Would you like to study moral philosophy?

MR JOURDAIN: Moral philosophy?

PHILOSOPHER: Yes.

MR JOURDAIN: And what's moral philosophy about?

PHILOSOPHER: It is concerned with the good life and teaches men how to moderate their passions.

MR JOURDAIN: No, we'll leave that out. I'm as hot-tempered as they make 'em and whatever moral philosophy may say I'll be as angry as I want whenever I feel like it.

PHILOSOPHER: Well, do you wish to study physics—the natural sciences?

MR JOURDAIN: The natural sciences? What have they to say for themselves?

PHILOSOPHER: Natural science explains the principles of natural phenomena, and the properties of matter; it is concerned with the nature of the elements, metals, minerals, precious stones, plants, and animals,

and teaches us the causes of meteors, rainbows, will-o'-the-wisp, comets, lightning, thunder and thunderbolts, rain, snow, hail, tempests, and whirlwinds.

MR JOURDAIN: This is too much of a hullabaloo for me, too much of a rigmarole altogether.

PHILOSOPHER: Then what am I to teach you?

MR JOURDAIN: Teach me to spell.

PHILOSOPHER: Willingly.

MR JOURDAIN: And then you can teach me the almanac so that I shall know if there's a moon or not.

PHILOSOPHER: Very well. Now, to meet your wishes and at the same time treat the matter philosophically one must begin, according to the proper order of these things, with the precise recognition of the nature of the letters of the alphabet and the different ways of pronouncing them, and, in this connexion, I must explain that the letters are divided into vowels, so called because they express the various sounds, and consonants, so named because they are pronounced 'con', or with, the vowels and serve only to differentiate the various articulations of the voice. There are five vowels, A, E, I, O, U.[2]

MR JOURDAIN: I understand all that.

PHILOSOPHER: The vowel A is pronounced with the mouth open wide. So—A, Ah, Ah.

MR JOURDAIN: Ah, Ah. Yes.

PHILOSOPHER: The vowel E is pronounced by bringing the jaws near together. So, A, E—Ah, Eh.

MR JOURDAIN: A, E. Ah, Eh, now that's fine.

PHILOSOPHER: For the vowel I, bring the jaws still nearer together and stretch the mouth corners towards the ears, so—A, E, I. Ah, Eh, EEE.

MR JOURDAIN: A, E, I. Ah, Eh, EEE—It's quite right. Oh! what a wonderful thing is knowledge!

PHILOSOPHER: To pronounce the vowel O you must open the mouth again and round the lips so—O.

MR JOURDAIN: O, O. You are right again. A, E, I, O, splendid. I, O. I, O.

PHILOSOPHER: The opening of the mouth is exactly the shape of the letter—O.

MR JOURDAIN: O, O. You are right. O. How wonderful to know such things!

2 The Philosopher's instructions refer to the French vowels.

PHILOSOPHER: The vowel U is pronounced by bringing the teeth close together but without quite meeting and pushing the lips out so—U, U, as if you were making a face—so if you happen to show that you don't think much of a person you only need say U!

MR JOURDAIN: U, U. It's perfectly true. Oh why didn't I learn all this earlier?

PHILOSOPHER: To-morrow we will take the other letters, the consonants.

MR JOURDAIN: Are they as interesting as those we have done?

PHILOSOPHER: Undoubtedly. The consonant D, for example, is pronounced by pressing the tip of the tongue against the upper teeth so—D, D. Da.

MR JOURDAIN: Da! Da! Splendid! Splendid!

PHILOSOPHER: F by bringing the upper teeth against the lower lip. Fa!

MR JOURDAIN: Fa, Fa. It's quite true. Oh, fa-father and mother, why didn't you teach me this—

PHILOSOPHER: And R by placing the tip of the tongue against the palate so that, alternately resisting and yielding to the force of the air coming out, it makes a little trilling R, R, R.

MR JOURDAIN: R, R, Ra. R, R, R, Ra. It's true. Ah what a clever man you are and how I've been wasting my time. R, R, Ra.

PHILOSOPHER: I will explain all these fascinating things for you.

MR JOURDAIN: Do please. And now I must tell you a secret. I'm in love with a lady of quality and I want you to help me to write her a little note I can let fall at her feet.

PHILOSOPHER: Very well.

MR JOURDAIN: That's the correct thing to do, isn't it?

PHILOSOPHER: Certainly. You want it in verse no doubt?

MR JOURDAIN: No. No. None of your verse for me.

PHILOSOPHER: You want it in prose then?

MR JOURDAIN: No. I don't want it in either.

PHILOSOPHER: But it must be one or the other.

MR JOURDAIN: Why?

PHILOSOPHER: Because, my dear sir, if you want to express yourself at all there's only verse or prose for it.

MR JOURDAIN: Only verse or prose for it?

PHILOSOPHER: That's all, sir. Whatever isn't prose is verse and anything that isn't verse is prose.

MR JOURDAIN: And talking, as I am now, which is that?

PHILOSOPHER: That is prose.

MR JOURDAIN: You mean to say that when I say 'Nicole, fetch me my slippers' or 'Give me my night-cap' that's prose?

PHILOSOPHER: Certainly, sir.

MR JOURDAIN: Well, my goodness! Here I've been talking prose for forty years and never known it, and mighty grateful I am to you for telling me! Now, what I want to say in the letter is, 'Fair Countess, I am dying for love of your beautiful eyes!' but I want it put elegantly, so that it sounds genteel.

PHILOSOPHER: Then say that the ardour of her glances has reduced your heart to ashes and that you endure night and day—

MR JOURDAIN: No. No. No! I don't want that at all. All I want is what I told you. 'Fair Countess, I am dying for love of your beautiful eyes.'

PHILOSOPHER: But it must surely be elaborated a little.

MR JOURDAIN: No, I tell you I don't want anything in the letter but those very words, but I want them to be stylish and properly arranged. Just tell me some of the different ways of putting them so that I can see which I want.

PHILOSOPHER: Well, you can put them as you have done, 'Fair Countess, I am dying for love of your beautiful eyes', or perhaps 'For love, fair Countess, of your beautiful eyes I am dying', or again 'For love of your beautiful eyes, fair Countess, dying I am', or yet again 'Your beautiful eyes, fair Countess, for love of, dying am I', or even 'Dying, fair Countess, for love of your beautiful eyes, I am'.

MR JOURDAIN: But which of these is the best?

PHILOSOPHER: The one you used yourself, 'Fair Countess, I am dying for love of your beautiful eyes'.

MR JOURDAIN: Although I've never done any study I get it right first time. Thank you with all my heart. Please come in good time to-morrow.

PHILOSOPHER: You may rely upon me, sir. (*He goes out.*)

MR JOURDAIN: Hasn't my suit arrived yet?

LACKEY: Not yet, sir.

MR JOURDAIN: That confounded tailor has kept me waiting a whole day, and just when I'm so busy too. I'm getting really annoyed. Confound him! I'm sick to death of him! If only I had him here now, the detestable scoundrel, the rascally dog, I'd—I'd . . . Ah, there you are! I was beginning to get quite annoyed with you. (*The* TAILOR *has come in, followed by his apprentice carrying the suit.*)

TAILOR: I couldn't get here any earlier. I've had a score of my men at work on your suit.

MR JOURDAIN: The silk stockings you sent me were so tight I could hardly get them on. I've already torn two ladders in them.

TAILOR: They'll stretch all right, by and by.

MR JOURDAIN: Yes, if I tear them enough! Then, the shoes that you made for me pinch me most dreadfully.

TAILOR: Not at all, sir.

MR JOURDAIN: How d'ye mean 'not at all'?

TAILOR: They don't pinch you at all.

MR JOURDAIN: But I tell you they do!

TAILOR: No, you imagine it.

MR JOURDAIN: I imagine it? If I imagine it, it's because I can feel it. Isn't that a good enough reason?

TAILOR: Tch! Tch! The coat I have here is as fine as any at the court, most beautifully designed. It's a work of art to have made a suit which looks dignified without using black. You won't find another anywhere to touch it.

MR JOURDAIN: But what's this? You've put the sprigs upside down.

TAILOR: You didn't say you wanted them the other way up.

MR JOURDAIN: Ought I to have told you?

TAILOR: Certainly. All gentlemen of quality wear them this way up.

MR JOURDAIN: Gentlemen of quality wear the sprigs upside down?

TAILOR: Undoubtedly.

MR JOURDAIN: Well, that's all right then.

TAILOR: You can have them the other way up if you want.

MR JOURDAIN: No. No. No.

TAILOR: You've only to say so.

MR JOURDAIN: No, you've done very well. Do you think it will fit me?

TAILOR: What a question! If I'd drawn you on paper I couldn't have got nearer your fit. I have a man who is a genius at cutting

out breeches and another who hasn't an equal at fitting a doublet.

MR JOURDAIN: Are my wig and hat all they should be?

TAILOR: Everything is excellent.

MR JOURDAIN (*looking at the* TAILOR's *suit*): Ha ha! Master Tailor! Isn't that some of the stuff I got for the last suit you made me? I am sure that I recognize it.

TAILOR: Yes, the fact is I liked the material so much I felt I must have a suit cut from it myself.

MR JOURDAIN: That's all very well but it shouldn't have come out of my stuff.

TAILOR: Are you going to try your suit on?

MR JOURDAIN: Yes, hand it here.

TAILOR: Wait a moment! That is not the way things are done. I have brought my men with me to dress you to music. Suits like these must be put on with ceremony. Hello there! Come in! (*Enter four tailor boys dancing.*) Put on the gentleman's suit in a manner befitting a gentleman of quality!

Four tailor boys dance up to MR JOURDAIN. *Two take off the breeches in which he did his exercises: the others remove his jacket, after which they dress him in his new suit.* MR JOURDAIN *struts round to be admired in time with the music.*

FIRST TAILOR BOY: Now, kind gentleman, please give something to these fellows to drink your health.

MR JOURDAIN: What did you call me?

TAILOR BOY: 'Kind gentleman.'

MR JOURDAIN: 'Kind gentleman.' What it is to be got up as one of the quality! Go on dressing as an ordinary person and nobody will ever call you a gentleman. Here! That's for your 'kind gentleman'.

TAILOR BOY: My lord! We are infinitely obliged to you.

MR JOURDAIN: 'My lord!' Oh my goodness! 'My lord.' Wait a minute, my lad. 'My lord' is worth something more. 'My lord' is something like! Here, that's what 'My lord' brings you (*gives more money*).

TAILOR BOY: My lord, we will all drink to your Grace's good health.

MR JOURDAIN: 'Your Grace!' Oh. Oh wait! Don't go away. Come here. 'Your Grace!' (*Aside*) If he goes as far as Your Highness he'll get the whole purse. Take this for your 'Your Grace'.

TAILOR BOY: My lord, we thank your Lordship for your Grace's liberality.

MR JOURDAIN: Just as well he stopped. I nearly gave him the lot.

The four tailor boys show their satisfaction by a dance which forms the Second Interlude.

ACT III

MR JOURDAIN *and* LACKEYS.

MR JOURDAIN: Follow me! I'm going out to show off my clothes in the town. Mind you keep close behind me so that people know you belong to me.

LACKEYS: Very good, sir.

MR JOURDAIN: Wait! Call Nicole for me. I want to tell her what she has to do. No, wait a minute. She's coming. (*Enter* NICOLE.)

MR JOURDAIN: Nicole!

NICOLE: Yes sir, what is it?

MR JOURDAIN: Listen.

NICOLE (*laughing*): Ha ha ha! Ha ha ha!

MR JOURDAIN: What are you laughing at?

NICOLE: Ha ha ha! Ha ha ha!

MR JOURDAIN: What's wrong with the hussy?

NICOLE: Ha ha ha! Ha ha ha! Fancy you got up like that! Ha ha ha!

MR JOURDAIN: Whatever d'ye mean?

NICOLE: Oh, my goodness! Ha ha ha! Ha ha ha!

MR JOURDAIN: Silly creature! Are you laughing at me?

NICOLE: No master. I should hate to do that. Oh ho ho! Ho ho ho! Ha ha ha! Ha ha ha!

MR JOURDAIN: I'll box your ears if you laugh any more.

NICOLE: Ha ha ha! Ha ha ha! I can't help it, master (*laughs again*).

MR JOURDAIN: Are you never going to stop?

NICOLE: I'm sorry, master, but you look so funny I just can't help laughing (*laughs again*).

MR JOURDAIN: Oh! the impudence!

NICOLE: But you look so—so funny like that (*laughs again*).

MR JOURDAIN: I'll—

NICOLE: Forgive me, I—(*laughs again*).

MR JOURDAIN: Look here! If you laugh any more I'll give you such a smack across the face as you've never had in your life.

NICOLE: All right, master, I've finished! I shan't laugh any more.

MR JOURDAIN: Well take care you don't. You must clean up the hall ready for—

NICOLE: Ha ha ha!

MR JOURDAIN: You must clean it up properly or—

NICOLE: Ha ha ha!

MR JOURDAIN: What! Again?

NICOLE: Look here, master, wallop me afterwards but let me have my laugh out first. It'll do me more good—ha ha ha!

MR JOURDAIN: I'm losing my temper—

NICOLE: Oh master, please, let me laugh—ha ha ha!

MR JOURDAIN: If I once start to—

NICOLE: I shall die if you don't let me laugh—ha ha ha!

MR JOURDAIN: Was there ever such a good-for-nothing! She laughs in my face instead of listening to what I'm telling her.

NICOLE: What—what is it you want me to do, sir?

MR JOURDAIN: What do you think, you slut? Get the house ready for the company I'm expecting here shortly.

NICOLE: My goodness. That stops my laughing. Those visitors of yours make such an upset that the very word company puts me out.

MR JOURDAIN: And am I to shut my door on my visitors to please you?

NICOLE: You ought to shut it on some of them. (*Enter* MRS JOURDAIN.)

MRS JOURDAIN: What new nonsense is it this time? What are you doing in that get-up, man? Whatever are you thinking about to get yourself rigged out like that! Do you want to have everybody laughing at you?

MR JOURDAIN: My good woman, only the fools will laugh at me.

MRS JOURDAIN: Well, it isn't as if folk have not done it before! Your goings on have long been a laughing-stock for most people.

MR JOURDAIN: What sort of people, may I ask?

MRS JOURDAIN: People with more sense than you have. I'm disgusted with the life you are leading. I can't call the house my own any more. It's like a carnival-time all day and every day with fiddling and bawling enough to rouse the whole neighbourhood.

NICOLE: The mistress is right. I can't keep the place clean because of the good-for-nothing pack you bring into the house. They pick up mud all over the town and cart it in here. Poor Frances is wearing her knees out polishing the floors for your fine gentlemen to come and muck them up again every day.

MR JOURDAIN: Now, now, our Nicole! For a country lass you've a pretty sharp tongue.

MRS JOURDAIN: Nicole is quite right. She has more sense than you have. I'd like to know what you think you want with a dancing master at your time of life.

NICOLE: Or with that great lump of a fencing master that comes stamping in, upsetting the house and loosening the very tiles in the floor.

MR JOURDAIN: Be quiet, both of you!

MRS JOURDAIN: Are you learning dancing against the time when you'll be too feeble to walk?

NICOLE: Is it because you want to murder somebody that you are learning fencing?

MR JOURDAIN: Shut up, I tell you! You are just ignorant, both of you. You don't understand the significance of these things.

MRS JOURDAIN: You'd do much better to think about getting your daughter married now that she's of an age to be provided with a husband.

MR JOURDAIN: I'll think about getting my daughter married when a suitable husband comes along. In the meantime I want to give my mind to learning and study.

NICOLE: I've just heard tell, madam, that, to crown all, he's taken on a philosophy master to-day.

MR JOURDAIN: Well, why not? I tell you I want to improve my mind and learn to hold my own among civilized people.

MRS JOURDAIN: Then why don't you go back to school one of these days and get yourself soundly whipped?

MR JOURDAIN: Why not? I wish to goodness I could be whipped here and now and never mind who saw me if it would help me to learn what they teach them in schools.

NICOLE: My goodness! A lot of good that would do you!

MR JOURDAIN: Of course it would.

MRS JOURDAIN: No doubt it's all very useful for carrying on your household affairs.

MR JOURDAIN: Of course it is. You are both talking nonsense. I'm ashamed of your ignorance. For example, do you know what you are doing—what you are talking at this very moment?

MRS JOURDAIN: I'm talking plain common sense—you ought to be mending your ways.

MR JOURDAIN: That's not what I mean. What I'm asking is what sort of speech are you using?

MRS JOURDAIN: Speech. I'm not making a speech. But what I'm saying makes sense and that's more than can be said for your goings on.

MR JOURDAIN: I'm not talking about that. I'm asking what I am talking now. The words I am using—what are they?

MRS JOURDAIN: Stuff and nonsense!

MR JOURDAIN: Not at all! The words we are both using. What are they?

MRS JOURDAIN: Well, what on earth *are* they?

MR JOURDAIN: What are they called?

MRS JOURDAIN: Call them what you like.

MR JOURDAIN: They are prose, you ignorant creature!

MRS JOURDAIN: Prose?

MR JOURDAIN: Yes, prose! Everything that's prose isn't verse and everything that isn't verse is prose. Now you see what it is to be a scholar! And you (*to* NICOLE), do you know what you have to do to say 'U'?

NICOLE: Eh?

MR JOURDAIN: What do you have to do to say 'U'?

NICOLE: What?

MR JOURDAIN: Say 'U' and see!

NICOLE: All right then—'U'.

MR JOURDAIN: Well what did you do?

NICOLE: I said 'U'.

MR JOURDAIN: Yes, but when you said 'U' what did you do?

NICOLE: I did what you told me to.

MR JOURDAIN: Oh! What it is to have to deal with stupidity! You push your lips out and bring your lower jaw up to your upper one and—'U'—you see? I make a face like this—'U-U-U'.

NICOLE: Yes, that's grand I must say!

MRS JOURDAIN: Really remarkable!

MR JOURDAIN: Yes, but that's only one thing.

You should have heard 'O' and 'Da' and 'Fa'.

MRS JOURDAIN: What on earth is all this rigmarole?

NICOLE: And what good is it going to be to anybody?

MR JOURDAIN: It exasperates me to see how ignorant women can be!

MRS JOURDAIN: Oh get off with you! You ought to send all these fellows packing with their ridiculous tomfoolery.

NICOLE: And especially that great lump of a fencing master who fills my kitchen with dust.

MR JOURDAIN: Fencing master again! You've got him on the brain. I can see I shall have to teach you your manners. (*Calls for the foils and hands one to* NICOLE.) There, take it! Now for a logical demonstration! The line of the body! When you lunge in quart you do—so, and when you lunge in tierce you do—so! If you only do like that you can be sure that you'll never be killed. It's a grand thing to know that you are safe when you are fighting. There now—have at me. Let's see what you can do.

NICOLE: Very well, what about that? (*She thrusts at him several times.*)

MR JOURDAIN: Steady on! Steady on! Confound the silly creature!

NICOLE: Well you told me to do it.

MR JOURDAIN: Yes, but you led in tierce before you led in quart and you never gave me time to parry.

MRS JOURDAIN: You are mad, my lad! All this nonsense has gone to your head. It all comes of hanging round the gentry.

MR JOURDAIN: If I hang round the gentry I show my good taste. It's better than hanging round your shopkeeping crowd.

MRS JOURDAIN: Oh yes, I've no doubt! A lot of good you'll get out of hanging round the gentry, especially this fine gentleman you are so stuck on.

MR JOURDAIN: Be quiet and mind what you say. You don't know what you are talking about. He's a much more important person than you think. He's a nobleman in high favour at court. He talks to the king just as I'm talking to you. Isn't that something to be proud of—that folks should see him coming to my house and that a man of his rank should be calling me his friend and treating me as an equal? You've no idea

how good he is to me! I am quite embarrassed by the kindness he shows me, and quite openly too.

MRS JOURDAIN: Ay, he'll show you kindness, no doubt, and then borrow your money.

MR JOURDAIN: And isn't it a privilege to lend money to a gentleman like that? Can I do less for a nobleman who calls me his dear friend?

MRS JOURDAIN: And what does he do for you, this nobleman?

MR JOURDAIN: Things that would surprise you if you only knew.

MRS JOURDAIN: Such as?

MR JOURDAIN: Never you mind. I'm not going to explain. It's enough that, if I've lent him money, he'll pay it back before long.

MRS JOURDAIN: Do you really expect him to?

MR JOURDAIN: Of course! Has he not given me his promise?

MRS JOURDAIN: Yes, and I don't doubt he'll go back on it.

MR JOURDAIN: He's given me his word as a gentleman.

MRS JOURDAIN: Oh fiddlesticks!

MR JOURDAIN: You are very obstinate, my dear. You can take it from me he will stand by his word. I'm sure of it.

MRS JOURDAIN: And I'm sure he won't, and that all his kindness is just to get round you.

MR JOURDAIN: Be quiet! Here he comes.

MRS JOURDAIN: That's the last straw. I expect he's come to borrow again. I am fed up at the very sight of him.

MR JOURDAIN: Oh be quiet, I tell you. (*Enter* DORANTE.)

DORANTE: Ah Jourdain, my friend, how do you do?

MR JOURDAIN: I am very well, sir, at your service.

DORANTE: And Mrs Jourdain, how is she?

MRS JOURDAIN: Mrs Jourdain is as well as can be expected.

DORANTE: Well, Jourdain, you look very smart.

MR JOURDAIN: Do you think so?

DORANTE: Oh yes! You look very handsome indeed in this coat. We have no young men at court better turned out than you are.

MR JOURDAIN: He he!

MRS JOURDAIN (*aside*): That's scratching him where it itches.

DORANTE: Turn around. Most elegant.

MRS JOURDAIN (*aside*): Yes, he looks as silly behind as in front.

DORANTE: Upon my word, Jourdain, I have been looking forward to seeing you. You know I have the greatest regard for you. I was talking about you only this morning in the Royal Presence.

MR JOURDAIN: You do me great honour, sir. (*Aside to* MRS JOURDAIN) In the Royal Presence!

DORANTE: Come, put on your hat!

MR JOURDAIN: Sir, I know the respect I owe to you.

DORANTE: Please, put on your hat. No ceremony between us, I beg you.

MR JOURDAIN: Sir—

DORANTE: Do put on your hat, Mr Jourdain. You are my friend.

MR JOURDAIN: Sir, I'm your very humble servant.

DORANTE: But I cannot put on my own hat unless you put on yours.

MR JOURDAIN (*putting on his hat*): I'll forgo my manners rather than be a nuisance.

DORANTE: As you know, I am your debtor.

MRS JOURDAIN (*aside*): We know that all right.

DORANTE: You have very kindly lent me money on various occasions in a most obliging and considerate fashion.

MR JOURDAIN: Sir, you don't mean it!

DORANTE: No no! I know how to repay what I owe and how to acknowledge a kindness.

MR JOURDAIN: Sir, I don't doubt it at all.

DORANTE: I would like to settle up with you. I came along so that we might reckon up our accounts together.

MR JOURDAIN (*to* MRS JOURDAIN—*aside*): You see! What have you to say now, woman?

DORANTE: I am a man who likes to meet his obligations as promptly as possible.

MR JOURDAIN (*to* MRS JOURDAIN *as before*): What did I tell you?

DORANTE: Shall we see what I owe you?

MR JOURDAIN (*again as before*): You and your silly suspicions!

DORANTE: You can recollect, I assume, all the amounts you have lent me?

MR JOURDAIN: Yes, I think so. I have kept a note of them. Here we are—the first time I let you have two hundred guineas.

DORANTE: Agreed.

MR JOURDAIN: Next time, a hundred and twenty.

DORANTE: Yes.

MR JOURDAIN: Third time, a hundred and forty.

DORANTE: Correct.

MR JOURDAIN: That makes four hundred and sixty guineas, say four hundred and eighty-three pounds.

DORANTE: Yes, the amount is correct, four hundred and eighty-three pounds.

MR JOURDAIN: Then there was a further ninety-six pounds paid to your plume-maker.

DORANTE: Right.

MR JOURDAIN: One hundred and ninety to your tailor.

DORANTE: Good.

MR JOURDAIN: Two hundred and eighteen pounds, twelve shillings and eightpence to another of your tradesmen—

DORANTE: Twelve shillings and eightpence. That's exactly right.

MR JOURDAIN: Add eighty-seven pounds, seven shillings and fourpence paid to your saddler.

DORANTE: And what does all that come to?

MR JOURDAIN: Total—one thousand and seventy-five pounds exactly.

DORANTE: Agreed. One thousand and seventy-five pounds exactly. Now—add on another two hundred and twenty-five pounds, that you are going to let me have, and that will make thirteen hundred pounds that I will repay you at the earliest possible opportunity.

MRS JOURDAIN (*to* MR JOURDAIN *aside*): Ha ha! Didn't I guess as much.

MR JOURDAIN (*aside*): Shut up!

DORANTE: Are you sure it won't inconvenience you to let me have that amount?

MR JOURDAIN: Not at all.

MRS JOURDAIN (*to* MR JOURDAIN *aside*): This fellow is making a milch cow of you!

MR JOURDAIN (*aside*): Oh! Do be quiet!

DORANTE: If it isn't convenient I can go somewhere else.

MR JOURDAIN: No, no, sir.

MRS JOURDAIN (*as before*): He'll never be satisfied until he's brought you to ruin.

MR JOURDAIN (*aside*): Be quiet, will you!

DORANTE: If it's any trouble—you've only to say so.

MR JOURDAIN: It's no trouble at all.

MRS JOURDAIN (*as before*): He's a real wheedler, he is!

MR JOURDAIN (*aside*): Be quiet, I tell you!

MRS JOURDAIN (*aside*): He'll drain your last farthing.

MR JOURDAIN (*aside*): Will you be quiet?

DORANTE: There are plenty of people who would lend me money with pleasure, but as you are my dearest friend I thought you would be offended if I asked anyone else.

MR JOURDAIN: I'm only too glad to oblige you, sir. I'll go and fetch what you want.

MRS JOURDAIN (*aside as before*): What! You aren't going to let him have more!

MR JOURDAIN (*going*): What can I do? Would you have me refuse a man of his position—a man who was talking about me only this morning in the Royal Presence!

MRS JOURDAIN (*as before*): Oh, go on with you! You are a real mug, you are! (MR JOURDAIN *goes out.*)

DORANTE: You look troubled, Mrs Jourdain. What is the matter?

MRS JOURDAIN: I've got a head on my shoulders.

DORANTE: And your daughter, where is she? I don't see her to-day.

MRS JOURDAIN: My daughter's all right where she is.

DORANTE: And how is she getting on?

MRS JOURDAIN: On her two legs, I suppose.

DORANTE: Would you care to bring her along one day to see the ballet and the plays at the court?

MRS JOURDAIN: Yes, why not? We like a good laugh, we do that!

DORANTE: I imagine, Mrs Jourdain, you must have had many admirers in your young days—charming and attractive as you no doubt were then.

MRS JOURDAIN: Really! Mrs Jourdain is as old and doddery as all that, is she?

DORANTE: Forgive me, Mrs Jourdain! I was forgetting how young you still are—I am quite absent-minded. Please pardon my foolishness. (*Re-enter* MR JOURDAIN.)

MR JOURDAIN: Here we are. Two hundred and twenty-five pounds exactly.

DORANTE: Remember, Mr Jourdain, I am entirely at your disposal. If I can render you any service at court—I shall be only too pleased.

MR JOURDAIN: You are really too kind.

DORANTE: If Mrs Jourdain would care to see one of the Royal Entertainments, I could arrange for her to have one of the very best seats.

MRS JOURDAIN: Mrs Jourdain says no, thank you very much.

DORANTE (*to* MR JOURDAIN): As I told you in my note, our fair countess will be here soon to dine with us and see the ballet. I persuaded her in the end to accept your invitation.

MR JOURDAIN (*aside to* DORANTE): Let us move a little further away. You understand the reason why.

DORANTE: It is a week since I saw you, so I haven't told you about the diamond you entrusted me to give to her. I had the very greatest difficulty in overcoming her scruples and the fact is she only agreed to accept it to-day.

MR JOURDAIN: And how did she like it?

DORANTE: Very much indeed! I shall be surprised if the diamond doesn't make her look much more kindly upon you.

MR JOURDAIN: Ah! If only it would!

MRS JOURDAIN (*to* NICOLE): Once this fellow is with him, there's no getting him away.

DORANTE: I have impressed upon her both the value of your present and the ardour of your affection for her.

MR JOURDAIN: You overwhelm me with kindness, sir. I'm only concerned that a gentleman of your rank should demean himself so on my account.

DORANTE: Don't mention it! What are things like that between friends? Wouldn't you do as much for me if you had the chance?

MR JOURDAIN: Of course! With all my heart.

MRS JOURDAIN (*aside*): I can't bear the sight of him.

DORANTE: I never spare myself if I can be of service to a friend, and when you confided in me your love for this charming lady, I happened to know her, I offered my help at once on your behalf, as you know.

MR JOURDAIN: That's true, and I can't thank you enough for your kindness.

MRS JOURDAIN (*to* NICOLE): Is he never going to go?

NICOLE (*to* MRS JOURDAIN): Thick as thieves, they are!

DORANTE: You have gone the right way to win her affection. Women love nothing so much as having money spent on them.

Your serenades and repeated presents of flowers, the superb firework display on the lake, the diamond you sent her, and the entertainment you are now preparing are bound to influence her in your favour more than anything you could say for yourself.

MR JOURDAIN: I would go to any expense if only it would open the way to her heart. I would give anything in the world to win the love of a lady of quality.

MRS JOURDAIN (to NICOLE): What on earth are they talking about for so long? Just steal up and listen.

DORANTE: You will soon enjoy the pleasure of seeing her and be able to feast your eyes on her to your heart's content.

MR JOURDAIN: To avoid any complications, I've arranged for my wife to dine at my sister's and stay there after dinner.

DORANTE: That was very prudent. Your wife might have been in the way. I have given the necessary instructions to the cook on your behalf and made all arrangements for the ballet. Everything is just what I should have chosen myself, and, provided it comes up to my hopes, I am sure that—

MR JOURDAIN (noticing that NICOLE is eavesdropping, gives her a slap): The impudence! (To DORANTE) Let us go. (They go out. NICOLE and MRS JOURDAIN come down stage.)

NICOLE: That's what I get for being inquisitive! But I'm sure there is something fishy going on, and it's something they aren't going to let you have a hand in.

MRS JOURDAIN: It's not the first time, Nicole, that I've had suspicions of my husband. Unless I'm much mistaken, he is involved in a love affair, and I'm going to get to the bottom of it. But let us think about my daughter first. You know Cléonte is in love with her. He's a man after my own heart and I mean to help him to marry Lucile if I can.

NICOLE: Well, madam, I'm delighted to hear you say so, for if you fancy the master for her, I fancy the man for myself, and I hope our marriage can be arranged along with theirs.

MRS JOURDAIN: Go and have a word with him and ask him to come along to see me. Then we can tackle my husband together. (She goes out.)

NICOLE: I'll run along at once. Nothing could

give me more pleasure. (Alone) That ought to please these fellows, I should think. (Enter CLEONTE and COVIELLE.)

NICOLE: Ah, there you are, sir! Just at the right moment! I'm the bringer of good news and . . .

CLEONTE: Get out, you deceitful hussy! Don't try to bamboozle me with your lies.

NICOLE: Is that how you receive—

CLEONTE: Go, I tell you, and let your false mistress know that she'll never again make a fool of her too trusting Cléonte.

NICOLE: Whatever can have upset him? My dear Covielle, do tell me what it all means!

COVIELLE: Your dear Covielle! You little minx! Get out of my sight and never trouble me any more!

NICOLE: So you turn on me too!

COVIELLE: Get out of my sight! Never speak to me again!

NICOLE: Well, I never! What's bitten them? I must go tell the mistress about this. (She goes out.)

CLEONTE: What a way of treating a lover! And a lover as sincere and devoted as I am—

COVIELLE: Yes, it's too bad—too bad for the pair of us.

CLEONTE: I show her every imaginable affection and tenderness. She's the only thing in the world that I care for. I haven't a thought for anyone else. I think of her, dream of her, long for her, live for her—for her and her only! And what do I get in return? I go two days without seeing her, two days that seem like two centuries. I meet her by accident. I'm overwhelmed with the joy of it. Radiant with happiness, I fly towards her and—what happens? The perfidious creature turns away from me and passes me by as if she'd never seen me before in her life!

COVIELLE: That all goes for me too.

CLEONTE: Did you ever, Covielle, see the like of this ungrateful Lucile?

COVIELLE: Or you, sir, of this wicked Nicole?

CLEONTE: After all I have done for her, the sighs—the devotion that I have paid to her charms.

COVIELLE: After all my constant attentions, all the service I've done in the kitchen.

CLEONTE. The tears I have shed at her feet.

COVIELLE: All the buckets I've drawn from the well.

CLEONTE: The ardour I have shown for her —loving her more than myself.

COVIELLE: The heat that I've suffered—turning the spit for her.

CLEONTE: And now she passes me by in disdain.

COVIELLE: And mine just turns her back on me.

CLEONTE: Such perfidy deserves to be punished severely.

COVIELLE: What mine needs is a box on the ear.

CLEONTE: Don't dare mention her name to me any more.

COVIELLE: I, sir? Heaven forbid!

CLEONTE: Never come and try to excuse her.

COVIELLE: Never fear!

CLEONTE: Try as you will to defend her—it won't make any difference.

COVIELLE: I have no such intention.

CLEONTE: I'll nurse my resentment and have no more to do with her.

COVIELLE: I'm all for that too.

CLEONTE: That nobleman who comes to the house has perhaps taken her fancy. Clearly she is letting herself be dazzled by rank and position. For my own self-respect I must break it off first and forestall her inconstancy. She shan't have the satisfaction of jilting me first.

COVIELLE: Quite right! I am with you entirely.

CLEONTE: Hold me to my resentment. Support my resolve against any last, lingering vestige of love that may plead for her. Tell me all the harsh things you can think of her. Describe her in terms that will make me despise her. Bring out all her faults so that I may come to dislike her.

COVIELLE: Well, what is she, anyhow? She's an empty-headed piece of affectation for anyone to be so much in love with! I never could see what there was in her. You could find a hundred girls more worthy of you. In the first place—her eyes are too small.

CLEONTE: Yes. They are small. But how full of fire, how sparkling, how lively, how tender!

COVIELLE: Her mouth is too large.

CLEONTE: True, but there's no other like it— so enticing—so tempting—just made for kissing.

COVIELLE: She's not very tall.

CLEONTE: No—but how slender and graceful.

COVIELLE: She affects a casual manner of speech and behaviour.

CLEONTE: But how well it suits her! Her ways are quite irresistible.

COVIELLE: As for wit—

CLEONTE: Ah, come, Covielle! She has the most delicate wit in the world—so subtle— so—

COVIELLE: Her conversation—

CLEONTE: Her conversation's delightful.

COVIELLE: She tends to be serious—

CLEONTE: Ah! You prefer jocularity, everlasting high spirits! Don't you find something tiresome in women who giggle at everything?

COVIELLE: Finally, she's the most capricious of women.

CLEONTE: Capricious. Yes. I agree, capricious she is, but then, how her caprices become her!

COVIELLE: Well, there you are! It's obvious that you are determined to love her whatever may happen.

CLEONTE: Me? I'd sooner die first! I intend to hate her now as much as I once used to love her.

COVIELLE: But how can you, when you think she's perfection?

CLEONTE: That's how I shall get my revenge and show my strength of purpose the better—by hating her, despising her, giving her up, beautiful, charming, lovable though I know her to be! Here she comes. (*Enter* LUCILE *with* NICOLE.)

NICOLE: Really shocking, I call it!

LUCILE: It can only be what I told you, Nicole. But here he is!

CLEONTE: I won't even speak to her.

COVIELLE: Neither will I.

LUCILE: Is there something wrong, Cléonte?

NICOLE: What ails you, Covielle?

LUCILE: Has something annoyed you?

NICOLE: Did you get out of bed the wrong side this morning?

LUCILE: Can you not answer, Cléonte?

NICOLE: Have you lost your tongue, Covielle?

CLEONTE: It's shameful!

COVIELLE: A regular Jezebel.

LUCILE: I suppose our meeting a little while ago has upset you.

CLEONTE: It seems they know what they've done.

NICOLE: The way we passed you this morning has got your goat, has it?

COVIELLE: They've guessed what the trouble is.

LUCILE: Is that not it, Cléonte? Is that not why you are angry?

CLEONTE: Yes, faithless creature, since we must speak, it is. And let me tell you that you shan't have the satisfaction of jilting me, as you think, for I mean to break with you first. I shall find it hard to forget my love for you. I shall grieve. I shall suffer for a while but I shall get over it eventually, and I'd die rather than be so weak as to come back to you.

COVIELLE: That goes for me too.

LUCILE: What a fuss about nothing. Do let me tell you, Cléonte, why I avoided you this morning.

CLEONTE: No, I won't listen.

NICOLE: Let me tell you, Covielle, why we were in such a hurry.

COVIELLE: No, I don't want to hear.

LUCILE: When we met you this morning—

CLEONTE: No, I say—

NICOLE: Let me tell you that—

COVIELLE: No, no! You traitress—

LUCILE: Listen—

CLEONTE: Not a word!

NICOLE: Just let me say—

COVIELLE: I'm deaf. I can't hear.

LUCILE: Cléonte!

CLEONTE: No.

NICOLE: Covielle!

COVIELLE: Never.

LUCILE: Do stay one moment—

CLEONTE: Oh! Fiddlesticks!

NICOLE: Listen to me—

COVIELLE: Nonsense!

LUCILE: One moment.

CLEONTE: Not an instant.

NICOLE: Just be patient a minute!

COVIELLE: Fiddle de dee!

LUCILE: Just one word.

CLEONTE: It's over and done with.

NICOLE: One word in your ear.

COVIELLE: Not even a syllable.

LUCILE: Very well, then, since you won't listen, you can think what you like and do as you please.

NICOLE: If that's how you behave, take it which way you choose.

CLEONTE: Well then, let us hear why you behaved so charmingly.

LUCILE: I don't feel like telling you now.

COVIELLE: Tell us what happened.

NICOLE: No! I won't tell you either!

CLEONTE: Do please say—

LUCILE: No, I don't choose to tell.

COVIELLE: Come, won't you tell me?

NICOLE: No, I won't tell you anything.

CLEONTE: Please.

LUCILE: No, I say—

COVIELLE: Oh come, have a heart!

NICOLE: No. Nothing doing.

CLEONTE: Please, I beg you—

LUCILE: Do leave me alone.

COVIELLE: I implore you.

NICOLE: Get out of here.

CLEONTE: Lucile!

LUCILE: No.

COVIELLE: Nicole.

NICOLE: Never!

CLEONTE: For heaven's sake!

LUCILE: No, I won't.

COVIELLE: Speak to me.

NICOLE: Not I!

CLEONTE: Please clear up my doubts.

LUCILE: I shall do no such thing.

COVIELLE: Put me out of my misery.

NICOLE: No, I don't want to.

CLEONTE: Very well. Since you don't care to relieve my anxiety, since you refuse to explain your heartless behaviour to me—look on me for the last time, ungrateful girl! I'm going far away to perish of grief and love.

COVIELLE: And I'm going to follow in his footsteps.

LUCILE: Cléonte!

CLEONTE: Eh?

NICOLE: Covielle!

COVIELLE: Did you say something?

LUCILE: Where are you going?

CLEONTE: Where I told you.

COVIELLE: We are going to our death.

LUCILE: *You* aren't going to die, Cléonte?

CLEONTE: Yes, cruel girl. Since that is your wish.

LUCILE: What, I wish you to die?

CLEONTE: Yes you wish me to die.

LUCILE: Who told you that?

CLEONTE: You must wish it since you won't clear up my doubts.

LUCILE: Is it my fault? If you would only have listened I would have told you that the whole trouble you complain of arose because my old aunt was with us this morning, and she firmly believes that no young girl should ever so much as let a

man come anywhere near her. She is for
ever lecturing us on the subject. According
to her, men are all devils, and we must
shun their advances.

NICOLE: And that's all there is in it.

CLEONTE: You are not deceiving me, Lucile?

COVIELLE: Nicole, you're not taking me in?

LUCILE: That is the truth, the whole truth—

NICOLE: And nothing but the truth.

COVIELLE: Is this where we give in?

CLEONTE: Ah, Lucile, how well you know the
way to allay all my troubles with one single
word from your lips. How easily one can
be reassured by those whom one loves.

COVIELLE: How easily one can be led by the
nose you mean—by these—confounded
creatures! (*Enter* MRS JOURDAIN.)

MRS JOURDAIN: Ah, I am delighted to see
you, Cléonte. You have come just at the
right moment. My husband is coming in,
so take your chance quickly and ask him
to let you marry Lucile.

CLEONTE: Ah, madam, no command could
be nearer to my desires, or more gracious,
more acceptable to me. (*Enter* MR JOUR-
DAIN.)

CLEONTE: Sir, I wanted to put to you myself,
rather than through a third person, a request I have long been considering, so,
without further preliminary, may I ask you
to accord me the honour and the privilege
of becoming your son-in-law?

MR JOURDAIN: Before giving you a reply,
sir, I must ask you to answer one question.
Are you a gentleman?

CLEONTE: Most men would have little hesitation, sir, in answering that question. Such
a matter is quickly decided. The title is
easy enough to assume, and custom to-day
appears to sanction the appropriation. I
myself am a little more scrupulous. I believe that any form of deception is unworthy of an honourable man and that it
is wrong to disguise the estate to which it
has pleased Heaven to call one, to appear
in the eyes of the world under an assumed
title, to pretend to be what one is not. I
was born, sir, of honourable parentage. I
have served for six years in the army and
with some credit, and have, I believe,
means sufficient to maintain a pretty fair
position in the world. Nevertheless, I make
no pretence to a title which others in my
place might very well consider themselves

entitled to assume. I, therefore, tell you
frankly that I am not, as you put it, a
gentleman.

MR JOURDAIN: That settles it, then. My
daughter is not for you.

CLEONTE: What!

MR JOURDAIN: If you aren't a gentleman, you
can't have my daughter.

MRS JOURDAIN: What are you talking about?
You and your gentleman! Do you reckon
we are of the blood of St Louis?

MR JOURDAIN: Be quiet! I know what you
are getting at.

MRS JOURDAIN: What are we, either of us,
but plain, decent folk?

MR JOURDAIN: What a way to be talking!

MRS JOURDAIN: Wasn't your father a tradesman, the same as mine?

MR JOURDAIN: Oh, confound the woman!
She never fails to bring that up! If your
father was a tradesman, so much the worse
for him—but as for mine, people who
make such a statement don't know what
they are talking about. And what I do say
is that I insist on having a gentleman for
my son-in-law.

MRS JOURDAIN: And I say that our daughter should marry someone of her own sort.
Far better a decent man, good-looking and
comfortably off, than a beggarly gentleman
who is neither use nor ornament.

NICOLE: The mistress is right. The squire's
son in our village is the most awkward
good-for-nothing lout you ever saw.

MR JOURDAIN: Be quiet, Miss Impertinence!
You are always putting your oar in. I can
afford to see that my daughter goes up in
the world, and I mean to make her a marchioness.

MRS JOURDAIN: A marchioness!

MR JOURDAIN: Yes! A marchioness!

MRS JOURDAIN: Heaven forbid!

MR JOURDAIN: I've made up my mind on it.

MRS JOURDAIN: Yes, and I've made up mine
too, and I'll never consent. Marrying above
one's station always brings trouble. I don't
want a son-in-law who'll look down on my
daughter because of her parentage, and I
don't want her children to be ashamed to
call me their grandmother neither, nor to
have her coming to see me in style and
perhaps forgetting to say 'How d'ye do' to
one of the neighbours. Folk wouldn't fail
to say all sorts of ill-natured things. 'See

the grand lady with her high and mighty airs,' they would say, 'it's old Jourdain's daughter. She was glad enough to play at being ladies with us when she was a child. She's gone up in the world since then, but both her grandparents sold cloth in the market by Holy Innocents' Gate: they scraped money together for their children and they must be paying pretty dear for it now in the next world, for you don't get as rich as that by remaining honest.' No, I don't want that sort of gossip. I want a man who will be grateful to me for my daughter so that I shall be able to say to him, 'Sit down and have dinner with us, lad.'

MR JOURDAIN: That all shows what a little mind you have—not to want to rise in the world. It's no use arguing. I shall make my daughter a marchioness if all the world is against me, and if you provoke me any further I'll make her a duchess! (*He goes out.*)

MRS JOURDAIN: Don't lose heart yet, Cléonte. Come with me, Lucile, and tell your father firmly that if you can't have Cléonte you won't marry anyone (*They go out.*)

COVIELLE (*to* CLEONTE): A nice mess you've made of it now with your high-sounding sentiments.

CLEONTE: What else could I do? To me it's a matter of principle.

COVIELLE: Why take the man seriously? Can't you see that he's mad? Couldn't you have humoured his fancies?

CLEONTE: You may be right, but I never thought I should need to offer proofs of nobility to become old Jourdain's son-in-law.

COVIELLE: Ha ha ha!

CLEONTE: What are you laughing at?

COVIELLE: Just an idea that occurred to me. A way we could take the old fellow in and get what you want at the same time.

CLEONTE: Well?

COVIELLE: It's quite an amusing idea.

CLEONTE: Well then, what is it?

COVIELLE: An idea I got from a play I saw some time ago. It would make a lovely practical joke to play on the old blockhead. It's really quite farcical, but I imagine we can risk almost anything with him without worrying unduly. He fits the part to perfection and he'll swallow any nonsensical story we see fit to tell him. I have actors and costumes ready. Just leave it to me.

CLEONTE: But tell me what it's about.

COVIELLE: I'll tell you all in good time. Let's be off now, for he's coming. (*Enter* MR JOURDAIN.)

MR JOURDAIN: I don't see what the deuce the fuss is about. The only thing they have to reproach me about is my respect for the quality. Yet there is nothing to compare, in my opinion, with genteel society. There's no true honour and dignity except among the nobility. I would give my right hand to have been born a count or a marquis.

LACKEY: Sir! Here is my lord and a lady with him.

JOURDAIN: Oh! Heavens! And I still have some instructions to give. Tell them I'll be here in a minute. (*He goes out. Enter* DORIMENE *and* DORANTE.)

LACKEY: The master says that he will be with you in a moment.

DORANTE: Very good.

DORIMENE: I don't know, Dorante. I feel it is very strange behaviour on my part to allow you to bring me to a house where I don't know a soul.

DORANTE: Where then, madam, would you wish me to entertain you, since, to avoid scandal, you rule out both your own house and mine?

DORIMENE: But you do not mention how I am becoming insensibly more and more committed every day to accepting these extravagant tokens of your affection. And it is no use my objecting. You wear down my resistance. Your suave insistence is reducing me gradually to doing whatever you wish. The process began with your assiduity in calling upon me, passed in due course to protestations of love, then to serenades, entertainments, and, finally, to-day's celebrations. I set my face against all these things, but you will not take no for an answer, and step by step you undermine my resolve until I can no longer answer for anything and I believe that in the end you will persuade me into a marriage contrary to all I intended.

DORANTE: Upon my word, madam, a very good thing too. You are a widow and your own mistress. I am independent and love you more than life itself. What is to prevent your making me happy this very day?

DORIMENE: Heavens, Dorante! Many good qualities are needed, on both sides, if people are to live happily together, and even the most reasonable people in the world often find it hard to make a success of it.

DORANTE: But why imagine such difficulties, madam? Your experience of one marriage proves nothing about others.

DORIMENE: Still, I come back to my point. These expenses which I see you incurring on my behalf cause me concern for two reasons: firstly, they commit me further than I would wish, and secondly I feel sure, if I may say so, that you are spending more than you can afford—and that I don't in the least want.

DORANTE: Madam, these things are mere trifles, and on that score—

DORIMENE: No. I know what I am talking about. For example, the diamond you have obliged me to accept is so valuable that—

DORANTE: Ah, madam, please don't exaggerate the value of a thing which I feel is quite unworthy of you. Allow me to—ah, here comes the master of the house. (*Enter* MR JOURDAIN *and* LACKEY.)

MR JOURDAIN (*after making two bows and finding himself too close to* DORIMENE): A bit further back, madam.

DORIMENE: Whatever—?

MR JOURDAIN: Another step more, if you please.

DORIMENE: What is all this about?

MR JOURDAIN: You must go back a bit, for the third one.

DORANTE: Mr Jourdain knows how to behave in society, madam.

MR JOURDAIN: Madam, I am greatly honoured in having the good fortune to be favoured with your condescension in deigning to accord me the favour—of your presence and if I should also have the merit to merit a merit such as yours and had heaven —envying my good fortune—accorded me the advantage of being worthy—

DORANTE: That's enough, Mr Jourdain. My lady has no liking for fine compliments. She knows very well that you are a man of the world. (*Aside to* DORIMENE) He's a worthy merchant, but, as you see, rather foolish in his ways.

DORIMENE: It is not difficult to see that.

DORANTE: Madam, Mr Jourdain is one of my dearest friends—

MR JOURDAIN: Ah, sir, you do me too much honour.

DORANTE: A gentleman of parts.

DORIMENE: I am honoured to make his acquaintance.

MR JOURDAIN: Madam, your condescension is quite undeserved.

DORANTE (*aside to* JOURDAIN): Whatever you do, be careful not to mention the diamond you gave her.

MR JOURDAIN (*aside to* DORANTE): Can't I even inquire how she likes it?

DORANTE (*as before*): Not on any account. That would be most vulgar behaviour. If you wish to act as a gentleman should, you must behave as if it were not you who gave her the present. (*To* DORIMÈNE) Mr Jourdain is just saying, madam, how delighted he is to see you in his house.

DORIMENE: I am greatly honoured.

MR JOURDAIN (*aside to* DORANTE): I am most grateful to you, sir, for putting in a word for me.

DORANTE (*aside to* MR JOURDAIN): I had the greatest trouble in the world to get her to come.

MR JOURDAIN (*aside to* DORANTE): I don't know how to thank you.

DORANTE (*to* DORIMENE): Mr Jourdain is just saying, madam, how charming he finds you.

DORIMENE: That is extremely kind of him!

MR JOURDAIN: Ah, madam, it is you who are kind—

DORANTE: Let us think about supper.

LACKEY (*to* MR JOURDAIN): Everything is ready, sir!

DORANTE: Come, then, let us take our places. Have the musicians summoned.

Six cooks dance together and bring in a table laden with viands, which forms the Third Interlude.

ACT IV

DORIMENE, DORANTE, MR JOURDAIN, SINGERS, *and* LACKEYS.

DORIMENE: Why, Dorante, this is a magnificent repast.

MR JOURDAIN: You are not serious, madam. I only wish it were more worthy of you. (*All take their seats at the table.*)

DORANTE: What Mr Jourdain has said is quite true, madam. I am indebted to him for receiving you so hospitably in his own house, but I agree with him that the meal is not worthy of you. I made the arrangements myself but I lack the inspiration of some of our friends in such matters. Thus the meal may, I fear, be found wanting if judged by the most critical standards: you may find there are gastronomic incongruities, certain crudities of taste. If Damis had had the ordering of it, everything would have been according to rule, all elegance and erudition. He would not have omitted to commend to you each dish as it came forward, and dazzle you with his knowledge of all that pertains to good eating; he would have expatiated on the virtues of newly baked bread, golden crusted, crisp and crunchy all over; on the qualities of the wine, its smoothness, its body, its precise degree of sharpness or mellowness; on saddle of mutton, garnished with parsley, loin of Normandy veal, as long as my arm, white and delicately flavoured, melting in the mouth like almond paste; partridges cooked to preserve the flavour to perfection, and his crowning masterpiece, a plump turkey in a pearly broth flanked with young pigeons and wreathed in onions and endive. For my own part, I confess I cannot aspire to such heights, so I can only join with Mr Jourdain in wishing the meal were more worthy of you.

DORIMENE: My reply to these compliments is to eat as heartily as you see I am doing.

MR JOURDAIN: Ah! And what lovely hands!

DORIMENE: The hands are but so so, Mr Jourdain, but no doubt you are referring to the diamond, which is really magnificent.

MR JOURDAIN: I, madam! Heaven forbid that I should say a word about it. That would be shockingly vulgar behaviour, unworthy of a gentleman—the diamond is a mere bagatelle.

DORIMENE: You are very fastidious.

MR JOURDAIN: You are too kind—

DORANTE: Come! Wine for Mr Jourdain and for these gentlemen who are going to be good enough to give us a song.

DORIMENE: Nothing adds to the delights of good cheer more than music. We are most admirably entertained.

MR JOURDAIN: Madam, it isn't—

DORANTE: Mr Jourdain. Let us give silence for these gentlemen. They will entertain us better than we can ourselves. (*The singers take their glasses and sing, supported by the instrumentalists.*)

First Drinking Song

A health to you, Phyllis—we begin thus
  our round.
In a glass and your eyes our best pleasures are found:
You and wine, wine and you, combine in disarming
Our care—and we ne'er
Find you other than charming!
So we swear, so we swear,
To love and to wine, ever faithful to be;
Ever faithful to wine, ever constant to
  thee!

Touch the glass with your lips and give wine a new relish
The wine in its turn doth those bright eyes embellish.
You and wine, wine and you, together combining,
For a lass and a glass set us ever repining.
So we clink, as we drink,
To love and to wine, ever faithful we'll be;
Ever faithful to wine, ever faithful to
  thee!

Second Drinking Song

Drink, let us drink, for time is fleeting!
Drink while we may, for brief our meeting!
Once love and life have passed us by,
Too long we lie.
Drink, then, to-day and while we may—
We may not drink to-morrow!

Drink, let us drink, leave fools to reason;
Short is this life and brief our season.
Wealth, fame, and glory all pass by—
Too long we lie.
Let care away, drink while we may!
We may not drink to-morrow.
Fill up the glass, let it go round,
We may not drink to-morrow!

DORIMENE: That could not have been better sung. It was really charming.

MR JOURDAIN: But I can see something here even more charming—madam.

DORIMENE: Dear me! Mr Jourdain is more gallant than I thought.

DORANTE: Why, madam, what do you take Mr Jourdain for?

MR JOURDAIN: I know what I'd like her to take me for—

DORIMENE: What again!

DORANTE: Ah, you don't know him yet.

MR JOURDAIN: She shall know me all in good time.

DORIMENE: Oh, I give it up.

DORANTE: He is a gentleman who always has an answer ready. Have you noticed, madam, that he eats the pieces you have touched and put aside?

DORIMENE: Mr Jourdain is charming!

MR JOURDAIN: If only I could really charm you I should be—(*Enter* MRS JOURDAIN.)

MRS JOURDAIN: Ah! Here's a nice company, I must say. It's easy to see I'm not expected. So this is why you were so anxious that I should dine at my sister's! There's a theatre downstairs and a feast fit for a wedding up here. This is where your money is going—in entertaining your lady friends and providing them with music and play-acting, while I'm sent off to amuse myself elsewhere!

DORANTE: Whatever are you talking about, Mrs Jourdain? Where did you get the idea that this was your husband's festivity? Let me inform you that I am entertaining this lady and that Mr Jourdain is merely permitting me the use of his house. You should take a little more care of what you say.

MR JOURDAIN: Yes, you impudent creature! My lord is providing all this for her ladyship, and she, I would have you know, is a lady of quality. My lord does me the honour of using my house and has invited me to dine with him.

MRS JOURDAIN: Fiddlesticks! I wasn't born yesterday.

DORANTE: Allow me to tell you, madam—

MRS JOURDAIN: I don't need any telling. I can see for myself. I've known for some time there was something afoot. I'm not a fool. And it's downright wicked of a fine gentleman like you to encourage my husband's tomfoolery. As for you, madam, it ill becomes a fine lady to be causing trouble in a decent family and letting my husband think he's in love with you.

DORIMENE: How dare you say such things! Come, Dorante! What are you thinking of, to expose me to the ridiculous suspicions of this outrageous creature. (*She goes out.*)

DORANTE: Stay, madam, where are you going?

MR JOURDAIN: Madam—my lord—give her my apologies and try to bring her back. (*They are gone.*) As for you and your meddling, see what a fine mess you've made now. You come and insult me before company and drive people of quality out of the house—

MRS JOURDAIN: I don't give a rap for their quality!

MR JOURDAIN: I don't know how I keep myself from smashing the pots over your head, you old hag! (*Lackeys remove the table.*)

MRS JOURDAIN (*going*): I don't care what you do. I stand for my rights, and every wife will be on my side.

MR JOURDAIN: You'd better keep out of my way, that's all! (*Alone*) She couldn't have come at a worse time. I was just in the mood for saying all sorts of pretty things. I never felt so lively in my life. But whatever's this? (*Enter* COVIELLE *disguised.*)

COVIELLE: Sir, I don't think I have the honour of being known to you.

MR JOURDAIN: No, sir.

COVIELLE: But I knew you when you were only so high (*indicating with his hand*).

MR JOURDAIN: Me?

COVIELLE: Yes. You were the prettiest child I ever saw. All the ladies were for ever picking you up and cuddling you.

MR JOURDAIN: Cuddling me?

COVIELLE: Yes. You see I was a great friend of the late gentleman, your father.

MR JOURDAIN: The late gentleman my father.

COVIELLE: Yes—a very worthy gentleman he was too.

MR JOURDAIN: What's that you say?

COVIELLE: I said a very worthy gentleman he was too.

MR JOURDAIN: My father?

COVIELLE: Of course.

MR JOURDAIN: Did you know him well?

COVIELLE: Certainly.

MR JOURDAIN: And you knew him to be a gentleman?

COVIELLE: Undoubtedly.

MR JOURDAIN: I don't understand what people mean, then.

COVIELLE: What is your trouble?

MR JOURDAIN: There are foolish people about who will have it that my father was in trade.

COVIELLE: In trade! Sheer slander! Never in his life! It was just that he was obliging, anxious to be helpful, and as he knew all about cloth he would go round and select samples, have them brought to his house and give them to his friends—for a consideration.

MR JOURDAIN: I'm delighted to know you. You'll be able to testify that my father was a gentleman.

COVIELLE: I'll maintain it before everybody.

MR JOURDAIN: I shall be eternally grateful to you. But what brings you here?

COVIELLE: Since the time when, as I was saying, I knew the late gentleman, your father, I have been travelling all round the world.

MR JOURDAIN: All round the world!

COVIELLE: Yes.

MR JOURDAIN: That must be a tidy long way.

COVIELLE: It is. I only returned from my travels four days ago and I've hurried along here because of my concern for your interests, to bring you some most exciting news.

MR JOURDAIN: And what's that?

COVIELLE: Have you heard that the Grand Turk's son is here?

MR JOURDAIN: No, I didn't know.

COVIELLE: Why! He has a splendid retinue of attendants, and everybody is running round to get a look at him. He is being received here as a personage of the greatest distinction.

MR JOURDAIN: Upon my word! I didn't know that.

COVIELLE: What is so fortunate for you is that he has fallen in love with your daughter.

MR JOURDAIN: The son of the Grand Turk?

COVIELLE: Yes, and he won't be happy until he's your son-in-law.

MR JOURDAIN: My son-in-law. The Grand Turk's son?

COVIELLE: That's it. The son of the Grand Turk—your son-in-law. I have been to see him and, knowing the language, of course, had quite a chat. In the course of the conversation he said, 'Acciam croc soler onch alla moustaph gidelum amanahem varahini oussere carbulath,' meaning, 'Have you ever come across a very beautiful young lady, the daughter of Mr Jourdain, a gentleman of Paris?'

MR JOURDAIN: The Grand Turk's son said that about me?

COVIELLE: He did. And when I told him that I knew you personally and had met your daughter, he said, 'Marababa Sahem,' which means 'Ah, how I love her!'

MR JOURDAIN: 'Marababa Sahem' means 'Ah, how I love her!'

COVIELLE: That's it.

MR JOURDAIN: My goodness, I am glad you told me. I should never have thought that 'Marababa Sahem' meant 'Ah, how I love her!' What a wonderful language Turkish is!

COVIELLE: You'd be surprised. Do you know what 'cacaracamouchen' means?

MR JOURDAIN: 'Cacaracamouchen'? No.

COVIELLE: It means 'Dear Heart!'

MR JOURDAIN: 'Cacaracamouchen' means 'Dear Heart'?

COVIELLE: Yes.

MR JOURDAIN: Well, isn't that wonderful! 'Cacaracamouchen'—'Dear Heart.' Who would ever have thought it! It's amazing.

COVIELLE: But to conclude my mission. He's on his way here to ask to marry your daughter and in order that his father-in-law may be worthy of him he wants to make you a Mamamouchi, a title of great rank in his country.

MR JOURDAIN: Mamamouchi?

COVIELLE: Mamamouchi or, as we should say, a Paladin. Paladins are the former . . . paladins. There's no higher rank anywhere in the world. You'll be on an equality with the greatest of noblemen.

MR JOURDAIN: Well, I'm very much obliged to the son of the Grand Turk. Please take me to him so that I can thank him.

COVIELLE: But I told you—he's coming here.

MR JOURDAIN: Coming here!

COVIELLE: Yes, and he's bringing everything needed for the ceremony.

MR JOURDAIN: It's all very sudden.

COVIELLE: His love brooks no delay.

MR JOURDAIN: The only thing that worries me is that my daughter is a most obstinate girl, and she's taken a fancy to a fellow called Cléonte and swears that she'll marry nobody else.

COVIELLE: You'll see she'll change her mind when she sees the Grand Turk's son. By a most remarkable coincidence he is very like Cléonte, whom I've had pointed out to me, and her love for the one can easily be transferred to the other—but I hear him coming. Here he is. (*Enter* CLEONTE *in Turkish dress. Three pages bear his train.*)

CLEONTE: Ambousahim oqui boraf, Jordina! Salamalequi!

COVIELLE (*to* MR JOURDAIN): Which is, being interpreted, Mr Jourdain, may your heart be all the year like a rose tree in flower. These are the usual forms of polite greeting in his country.

MR JOURDAIN: I am his Turkish Highness's most humble servant.

COVIELLE: Carigar camboto oustin moraf.

CLEONTE: Oustin yoc catamalequi basum base alla moran.

COVIELLE: He prays that Heaven may endow you with the strength of lions and the wisdom of serpents.

MR JOURDAIN: His Turkish Highness is too kind. Say I wish him every prosperity.

COVIELLE: Ossa binamin sadoc babally oracaf ouram.

CLEONTE: Bel men.

COVIELLE: He requests that you go with him at once to prepare for the ceremony, so that he may then meet your daughter and conclude the marriage.

MR JOURDAIN: All that in two words?

COVIELLE: Yes. That's what the Turkish language is like. You can say a great deal in few words. Follow where he wants you to go. (MR JOURDAIN *follows* CLEONTE *and his pages.*)

COVIELLE (*alone*): Oh, oh, oh! My goodness, what a lark! And what a fool! If he had learned his part by rote he couldn't play it better. (*Enter* DORANTE.)

COVIELLE: Ha ha! I hope, sir, that we can count on your help in a little affair we have in hand here.

DORANTE: Why, Covielle! Who would have known you! What a get-up!

COVIELLE: Yes, isn't it! Ha ha!

DORANTE: What are you laughing at?

COVIELLE: Something very amusing.

DORANTE: Well?

COVIELLE: You would never guess the trick we are playing on Mr Jourdain. It's in-tended to persuade him to let his daughter marry my master.

DORANTE: I don't know what the trick is, but I've no doubt it's a good one since you have a hand in it.

COVIELLE: I see that you know me, sir.

DORANTE: Tell me what it is.

COVIELLE: Be good enough to come a little further away and watch what I see coming in. You'll be able to see something of the story and I can tell you the rest.

The Turkish ceremony with dancing and music forms the Fourth Interlude. Six Turks enter gravely, two by two, to the strains of the Turkish March. They carry carpets which they wave as they dance. Enter next Turkish singers and dancers who pass beneath the carpets held on high. They are followed by four Dervishes who escort THE MUFTI. *As the music ends, the Turks lower their carpets to the ground and kneel upon them,* THE MUFTI *remaining standing in the centre. He makes a comic invocation, raising his eyes to Heaven, moving his hands like wings at each side of his head. The Turks prostrate themselves, singing 'Allah!' as they alternately rise on their knees and prostrate themselves. They rise to their feet on the words 'Allah Eckbar!' The Dervishes now carry on* MR JOURDAIN *dressed as a Turk but without wig, turban, or sabre.* THE MUFTI *sings the folowing song:*

THE MUFTI (*singing to* MR JOURDAIN): If him
   compree him say yum yum!
   If no compree him keepee mum.
   Me am Mufti what am he?
   Him no compree?

CHORUS OF TURKS: No compree! No compree! No compree!

Two Dervishes menace MR JOURDAIN, *who retreats a step on each 'No compree.'*

THE MUFTI (*chanting*): Speakee quickly, what am he? Him no heathen? Him no Jew?

CHORUS: No, no no! No, no, no!

THE MUFTI (*chanting*): Him no Buddhist? No Hindu?

CHORUS: No, no no! No, no, no!

THE MUFTI: Him no Coffite? Puritan?

CHORUS: No, no, no! No, no, no!

THE MUFTI (*as before*): Him no Hussite? Lutheran?

CHORUS: No, no, no! No, no, no!

THE MUFTI (*as before*): What am he? Mo-hametan?

CHORUS (*as before*): We swear it. We swear it.

THE MUFTI: Him called how? How him called?

CHORUS: Him called Jourdain, Jourdain, Jourdina.

THE MUFTI (*singing and dancing*): We pray for Mr Jourdain
To Mahomet night and morn'n',
Going to make a Paladina
Of Jourdina, of Jourdina.
Give him sabre, give him turban.
Give him sabre, give him turban.
Give him galley, brigantina
Him go fight for Palestina
Good Mahometan! Jourdina!

THE MUFTI: Him be good Turk Jourdina?

TURKS: Hey Valla! Hey Valla!

THE MUFTI (*singing and dancing*): Ha la ba, ba la ba, ba la da!

TURKS (*joining in dance*): Ha la ba, ba la chou, ba la ba, ba la da! (*General dance of Turks and Dervishes, during which* THE MUFTI *retires.*)

Re-enter THE MUFTI *in his great ceremonial turban, which is an outsize in turbans, decorated with lighted candles in several rows. With him enter two Dervishes bearing the Koran. Two more Dervishes bring forward* JOURDAIN, *who is quite overcome by the ceremony, and they make him go on his knees with his hands touching the ground before him. They set the Koran on his back.* THE MUFTI *makes a second invocation, pretending to read, turning the pages rapidly, finally crying in a loud voice, 'Hou!' The* TURKS *meanwhile bow and raise themselves alternately, chanting 'Hou! Hou! Hou!'*

MR JOURDAIN (*when they take the Koran off his back*): Ouf!

THE MUFTI (*chanting*): Him no scoundrel, him no knave?

TURKS: No, no, no.

THE MUFTI (*as before*): Him no coward, him be brave?

TURKS: Him be brave! Him be brave! Give him turban! Give him turban! (*Enter Turkish dancers who put the turban on* JOURDAIN's *head.*)

THE MUFTI (*giving him sabre*): No be scoundrel? No be knave?
Take then, take then scimitar. (*Dance, during which the dancers give* JOURDAIN *slaps seriatim with their scimitars.*)

THE MUFTI (*singing*): Give him, give him Bastonnade,
Thus am Jourdain Muslim made.
(*Repeat. Dance and slaps with scimitar.*)

THE MUFTI (*singing*): Be not offended! All is ended.

TURKS (*singing*): Be not offended! All is ended.

THE MUFTI *makes a last invocation, the Turks holding up his arms, after which the Turks dance and* MR JOURDAIN *and* THE MUFTI *are carried off in triumph. Thus ends the Fourth Interlude.*

ACT V

MR JOURDAIN *and* MRS JOURDAIN. MR JOURDAIN *is making obeisances and singing Turkish phrases as she enters.*

MRS JOURDAIN: Oh Lord have mercy on us! Whatever is he up to now? What a sight! Are you going mumming? Is this a time to be in fancy dress? What's it all about? Who on earth has togged you up like this?

MR JOURDAIN: The impertinence of the woman! How dare you talk like that to a Mamamouchi?

MRS JOURDAIN: A what?

MR JOURDAIN: You'll have to be more respectful now that I've been made a Mamamouchi.

MRS JOURDAIN: What on earth is the man talking about, with his Mamamouchi?

MR JOURDAIN: I tell you I am a Mamamouchi.

MRS JOURDAIN: And whatever sort of creature is that?

MR JOURDAIN: A Mamamouchi is what we should call a—Paladin.

MRS JOURDAIN: You ought to know better than go a-ballading at your age.

MR JOURDAIN: The ignorance! Paladin is a dignity that has just been conferred upon me. I come straight from the ceremony.

MRS JOURDAIN: What sort of ceremony?

MR JOURDAIN (*singing and dancing*): Good Mahometan Jourdina!

MRS JOURDAIN: And what does that mean?

MR JOURDAIN: Jourdina means Jourdain.

MRS JOURDAIN: And what about Jourdain?

MR JOURDAIN (*sings*): Going to make a Paladina—of Jourdina, of Jourdina.

MRS JOURDAIN: Eh?

MR JOURDAIN (*sings*): Give him galley, brigantina!

MRS JOURDAIN: I don't understand a word of it!

MR JOURDAIN (*sings*): Him go fight for Palestina.

MRS JOURDAIN: What on earth—

MR JOURDAIN (*as before*): Give him, give him Bastonnade!

MRS JOURDAIN: Whatever is this nonsense?

MR JOURDAIN (*as before*): Be not offended—all is ended!

MRS JOURDAIN: What on earth!

MR JOURDAIN (*dancing and clapping his hands*): Ba la ba, ba la chou, ba la ba, ba la da! (*He tumbles over.*)

MRS JOURDAIN: Oh my goodness! He's off his head.

MR JOURDAIN (*as he picks himself up and goes off*): Silence! Show more respect to a Mamamouchi! (*He goes out.*)

MRS JOURDAIN (*alone*): He's off his head! I must run and stop him going out. (*Sees* DORANTE *and* DORIMENE *coming.*) Oh, it only needed that! I can see nothing but troubles everywhere. (*She goes out.*)

DORANTE (*laughing*): Really, madam, you have never seen anything so amusing. I would not have believed anyone could be such a fool! All the same we must try to further Cléonte's affairs and keep up the masquerade. Cléonte is a good fellow and deserves our support.

DORIMENE: Yes, I esteem him highly. He deserves to be fortunate.

DORANTE: There is still a ballet for us to see, and then perhaps we may find whether a certain hope of mine is realized.

DORIMENE: Yes, I have seen how lavish the preparations are, Dorante, and I cannot permit this sort of thing any longer. I am determined to stem the flood of your extravagance on my account, and so I have decided to marry you at once. That seems to be the only solution. Marriage puts an end to such things, as you know.

DORANTE: Ah, madam, can you really have come to the decision I have so much desired?

DORIMENE: Only to prevent you from ruining yourself. I can quite see that if I didn't you would soon be without a penny to your name.

DORANTE: I am most grateful for your consideration for my fortune, but it is entirely yours, and my heart along with it, to dispose of as you wish.

DORIMENE: I shall make demands upon both. But here comes our friend, and what a wonderful sight he is! (*Enter* MR JOURDAIN *still in his Turkish costume.*)

DORANTE: We have come to celebrate your new dignity, sir, and to join in the rejoicing on the occasion of the marriage of your daughter to the son of the Grand Turk.

MR JOURDAIN (*bowing in Turkish fashion*): Sir, I wish you the strength of serpents and the wisdom of lions.

DORIMENE: I am very pleased to be among the first with my felicitations on your newly acquired honours.

MR JOURDAIN: Madam, I hope that your rose-tree may blossom all the year. I am infinitely obliged to you for coming to share in the honours which have befallen me, and I'm the more delighted to see you here because it allows me to make my humble apologies for the ill-behaviour of my wife.

DORIMENE: That was of no consequence. One can make allowance for her feelings. She must value your affections and it is not surprising that she shows concern lest she may lose any part of them.

MR JOURDAIN: My affections, madam, are entirely in your keeping.

DORANTE: You observe, madam, that Mr Jourdain is not one of those people whom good fortune makes forgetful. Even in his new-found greatness he remembers his friends.

DORIMENE: Yes, it is the mark of a truly noble mind.

DORANTE: But where is his Turkish Highness? We should like, as your friends, to pay him our respects.

MR JOURDAIN: He's coming now and I've sent for my daughter to give him her hand. (*Enter* CLEONTE *in Turkish costume.*)

DORANTE (*to* CLEONTE): We have come to

pay our respects to Your Highness and to offer our humble services to you as friends of your father-in-law to be.

MR JOURDAIN: Where is the interpreter so that I can tell him who you are and make him understand what you are saying? You'll see he'll reply to you in Turkish. He speaks it wonderfully well. Hello! Where the deuce has he gone to? Strouf, strif, strof, straf. This gentleman is a grand signor, grand signor, grand signor—and the lady is a grand dama—dama—damnation! Ah! (*To* CLEONTE *and pointing to* DORANTE) Gentleman—him French Mamamouchi—lady, she French Mamamouchess. That's as plain as I can put it. Ah, good! Here's the interpreter! (*Enter* COVIELLE.)

MR JOURDAIN: Where have you been? We can't exchange a word without you. Just tell him that they are people of great consequence who have come as my friends to pay their respects and offer their services to him. (*To* DORANTE *and* DORIMENE) You'll see how he can talk back!

COVIELLE: Alabala crociam acci borem alabamen.

CLEONTE: Catalequi tubal ourin soter amalouchen.

MR JOURDAIN: There, you see!

COVIELLE: He says that he hopes that a rain of prosperity may ever water the gardens of your family.

MR JOURDAIN: Didn't I tell you he would speak Turkish?

DORANTE: It's wonderful! (*Enter* LUCILE.)

MR JOURDAIN: Come on, my girl! Come along and give your hand to this gentleman, who has done you the honour of asking to marry you.

LUCILE: Really, father! Whatever are you dressed like that for? Is this supposed to be a play?

MR JOURDAIN: No play about it. It's a most serious matter and a mighty lucky one for you. This is the gentleman I have arranged for you to marry.

LUCILE: Me—marry him, father?

MR JOURDAIN: Yes. You marry him. Come on, give him your hand and thank Heaven for your good fortune.

LUCILE: But I don't want to marry.

MR JOURDAIN: But I do want you to, and I'm your father.

LUCILE: Well, I shan't, that's all!

MR JOURDAIN: Oh, what a fuss! Come along, I tell you. Give him your hand.

LUCILE: No, father, I've told you no power on earth will make me marry anyone but Cléonte, and I'll go to any lengths rather than—(*Recognizing* CLEONTE) But, as you say, you are my father and it is my duty to obey you, and it is for you to decide these things.

MR JOURDAIN: I'm delighted to see you remember your duty so quickly. What a pleasure it is to have an obedient daughter! (*Enter* MRS JOURDAIN.)

MRS JOURDAIN: Now, then! What's all this? They tell me you are giving your daughter to a mummer.

MR JOURDAIN: Oh, will you be quiet, you tiresome woman! You are always butting in with your silly ideas. There seems to be no teaching you sense.

MRS JOURDAIN: It's you who need teaching sense. You go from one mad idea to another. What is all this collection here for?

MR JOURDAIN: I intend to marry my daughter to the son of the Grand Turk.

MRS JOURDAIN: To the son of the Grand Turk!

MR JOURDAIN: That's right. Make your compliments to him through the interpreter here.

MRS JOURDAIN: I need no interpreter. I'll tell him to his face that he shall never have my daughter.

MR JOURDAIN: Once again, will you be quiet!

DORANTE: How can you refuse such an honour, Mrs Jourdain. Surely you don't decline to have his Turkish Highness as your son-in-law?

MRS JOURDAIN: My goodness! Why can't you look after your own affairs?

DORIMENE: You can't refuse a great honour like this.

MRS JOURDAIN: I'd be glad, madam, if you also would not meddle with things which don't concern you.

DORANTE: It's because of our friendly feeling towards you that we wish to be helpful.

MRS JOURDAIN: I can manage without your friendly feelings, thank you.

DORANTE: But your daughter herself is willing to fall in with her father's wishes.

MRS JOURDAIN: My daughter consents to marry a Turk?

DORANTE: Beyond question.

MRS JOURDAIN: She can forget Cléonte?

DORANTE: What won't a woman do to become a great lady!

MRS JOURDAIN: I'd strangle her with my own hands if she did a thing like that.

MR JOURDAIN: Enough of your cackle. I say she shall marry him.

MRS JOURDAIN: And I say she shan't! Never! Never! Never!

MR JOURDAIN: Oh, what a row!

LUCILE: Mother, dear—

MRS JOURDAIN: Go along with you, you're a hussy!

MR JOURDAIN: What! You abuse her merely because she does as I want her to!

MRS JOURDAIN: She's my daughter as well as yours.

COVIELLE (*to* MRS JOURDAIN): Mistress.

MRS JOURDAIN: What have you got to say!

COVIELLE: One word!

MRS JOURDAIN: I don't want your one word.

COVIELLE (*to* MR JOURDAIN): Master! If she'll only give me one word in private I can promise I'll get her to agree to what you want.

MRS JOURDAIN: I shall never agree.

COVIELLE: Do listen to me.

MRS JOURDAIN: No.

MR JOURDAIN: Just listen to him.

MRS JOURDAIN: I won't listen.

MR JOURDAIN: He'll tell you—

MRS JOURDAIN: He shan't tell me anything.

MR JOURDAIN: The obstinacy of women! What harm will it do you to listen?

COVIELLE: Just listen a moment; you can do as you please afterwards.

MRS JOURDAIN: Go on, then! What is it?

COVIELLE (*aside to* MRS JOURDAIN): We have been trying to tip you the wink for the past hour! Don't you realize that we are just playing up to your husband's fantastic ideas, that we are taking him in with all this paraphernalia and that the Grand Turk's son is none other than Cléonte himself?

MRS JOURDAIN (*aside to* COVIELLE): Oh!

COVIELLE (*as before*): And that the interpreter is nobody but me—Covielle?

MRS JOURDAIN (*as before*): In that case I give in.

COVIELLE (*as before*): Don't let on!

MRS JOURDAIN: Yes, that settles it, I consent to the marriage.

MR JOURDAIN: Well, now—we all see reason at last! (*To* MRS JOURDAIN) You wouldn't listen. I knew he'd explain to you all about the Grand Turk.

MRS JOURDAIN: He has explained everything very nicely and I'm entirely satisfied. Send for a notary.

DORANTE: Well said. And finally, to set your fears at rest, Mrs Jourdain, to clear your mind of any jealousy about your husband, let me say that this lady and I intend to be married at the same time.

MRS JOURDAIN: I don't object to that either.

MR JOURDAIN (*aside to* DORANTE): Is that to make her believe that—

DORANTE (*aside to* MR JOURDAIN): Yes, we must keep up the pretence to her.

MR JOURDAIN: Good! (*To the others*) Send for the notary, then.

DORANTE: While the contracts are being drawn up, let us have the ballet to entertain his Turkish Highness.

MR JOURDAIN: Excellent idea! Come, let us take our places!

MRS JOURDAIN: But what about Nicole? Isn't she to be married?

MR JOURDAIN: I give her to the interpreter— and my wife to anyone who will have her.

COVIELLE: Thank you, sir! (*Aside*) If there's a bigger fool than this anywhere, I'd like to meet him!

Enter ballet and singers to end the play.

GALLOWS HUMOR

Jack Richardson

CHARACTERS

THE WARDEN
LUCY
WALTER
PHILLIP
MARTHA

PROLOGUE

An Actor, dressed in the costume of Death, steps before the curtain.

Ladies and gentlemen—a few words please. Now, those of you who are already beginning to fidget, squirm, and grumble about costume plays, let me begin by assuring you that I do not reappear this evening once the curtain has been raised. Indeed, it is only due to my sulking, fits of temper, and slight influence with the producer that I've managed to salvage this much of your attention from the play's remaining characters, whom all concerned found more entertaining, amusing, and dramatically effective than I. For, ladies and gentlemen, you see before you a part, a character, a creation, if you will, that has been cut— snipped out of the night's diversions by the author's second thoughts and placed here as an, we hope, inoffensive bonus, to be listened to or ignored at your pleasure. And *why* was this done, when you can see the expense I've gone to with my costume, the way I turn a phrase, and my rather relaxed manner in front of you which hints no little experience on the boards? Simply because I, I was considered too obvious, too blunt, too heavy-handed for a play struggling with your modern subtleties! My theatrical days, I was told, ended with the morality play, when other personae—Good Deeds, Knowledge, Earthly Pleasure, etc.— dragged their capitalized names and single dimensions across a bare stage, and I was well known about society as the great common denominator, familiar to everyone in the pit as that undernourished wag who skulked along the streets to the sound of flute and tabor, laying hands on kings and beggars, bishops and madmen, naughty nuns and clanking cavaliers. I was, you might say, a popular hero, and no one demanded any more from my appearances than that I stand as a reminder to the uncomfortable fact that life, with all its peculiar pleasures of the palace and the alehouse, has its dark and inevitable opposite. At times, I'll admit, the humor in these works was somewhat broad, and, on occasion, I was paired with an overbusty blonde ingenue, who, waving a few shocks of wheat in the air as a fertility symbol, would chase me about the stage to the low-bred delight of some rural audience. But such excesses were rare, and, more often, a healthy rapport was set up between the spectators and me which, while by no means making me immune from a few scattered jeers and catcalls, nevertheless allowed me to, as they say, get my laughs and make my point. But now, apparently, my point needs sharpening. Death is no longer something personal, something deeply etched, something old women claim they feel slipping lasciviously into their winter beds. Indeed, in the last years, I seem both to have expanded and blurred my activities without knowing it. The grave's dimensions suddenly have grown to include those who have not yet achieved the once necessary technicality of ceasing to breathe. It appears I now infiltrate those still bouncing to music, still kissing their wives, still wiggling their forefingers in the air to emphasize those final truths by which they think their lives are lived. But are they, after all, living? And if not, where does that leave me with my black-and-white attitude in the matter? It leaves me here, ladies and gentlemen, to deliver a poor prologue while the scenery is readied, while your tardy members stumble into their places, and the search begins for programs that have already slipped beneath, behind, or between your seats. But I cannot really be too bitter. The anger of rejection having cooled, my healthy common sense tells me that I would have been truly out of place in a play designed for your tastes. For I confess that just yesterday, I—whom centuries have trained to recognize the precise moment when the eye's glaze, the hand's stiffness, and the mind's dimness announce another ghost has been given up to my charge—I made a total ass of myself by tugging away at a good dozen or so gentlemen who had no intention as yet of quitting this world. Looking at them, noticing all the old symptoms, I could have sworn they were ready, but that mistake was just one in a whole series ranging from hospitals to beauty salons that I've been making recently with my old-fashioned methods. That one-time basic distinction between the quick and the dead has become far too abstract today for one with my earthbound mind, and this fundamental confusion was, I fear, showing up in my performances. For even on the stage, in a play darkened by the shadow of a gallows, I, so perfectly at home in such a setting, now find it difficult, with my ancient eyes, to tell the hangman from the hanged. I hope, for my future and peace of mind, that you, the author's contemporaries, do not. (*Death exits, drawing the curtain as he does so.*)

PART ONE

THE WARDEN, LUCY, WALTER.

The lights come up upon a prison cell. There is a small washbasin to the right, and, standing close against the center wall, there is a razor-thin cot. Above the monkish bed is the room's sole window, barred into sections, through which one can see that it is night outside. At the room's left is the cell door, and behind it the beginning of an outside corridor. In this passageway, looking into the cell, stand a man and woman. Next to them, on a little portable tray, is a large platter decked with silver Queen Anne cover dishes, sauceboats, etc. The man, comfortably stout, seems expansively contented with himself. He is smiling broadly. The woman, attired in a bright yellow blouse and tight black skirt, has a thin face of angle and bone which is well covered with cosmetics. Her age is indeterminate, and she is beautiful in the way a carnival mask is so.

They are looking at WALTER, *who is sitting on the cell's cot. He has the jacket of his prison suit in his lap and is attending to it with needle and thread. Caught in his undershirt, he seems very pale and fragile. His face is unremarkably inoffensive, and covered with the scribbling of a fifty-year-old life. As he sews, he hums to himself.*

After several seconds, the man, the WARDEN, *and the woman,* LUCY, *begin to speak.*

WARDEN: There he is, Lucy. Let's hope this one doesn't prove too difficult for you.

LUCY: Now what could someone who looks like that do to be hanged?

WARDEN (*chuckling*): He beat his wife to death with a golf club—forty-one strokes from the temple to the chin. (*At this point* WALTER's *humming rises a bit in pitch and volume.*)

LUCY: What a nice smile he has, and how thin his arms are. They're not tattooed either.

WARDEN (*smiling, but a bit impatient*): Now, Lucy, it's romantic notions like that that get you into trouble. If you start thinking of murderers as upper-middle-class types you'll be more successful at your work.

LUCY (*indignant*): I haven't done too bad up till now. There aren't many women, even in the trade, that can take a man's mind off your gallows when he's got less than two hours to go.

WARDEN (*in an apologetic tone*): Oh, you're a professional, all right; they just don't cut them like you any more. But sometimes I wonder if you weren't better suited to those naughty houses stuffed with incense, beaded curtains, and overhead mirrors. Maybe you're just not up to making love surrounded by four gray walls.

LUCY: Listen, Warden, I've had my victories in here too.

WARDEN: Yes, but the state's gone to a great deal of trouble bringing you ladies up here to serve as little humanizing morsels for those it's going to hang. Your whole purpose is to make these poor fellows' last hours so heady, so full of pleasure that they just float up those stairs and smile into the dull, commonplace face of our hangman. Making love to you, Lucy, is supposed to accomplish this. And yet the last two you handed over to us behaved abominably: they shuffled by those sentimental journalists looking as if they were already dead. You know what the press can do with that; and then all our good intentions are forgotten.

LUCY: I couldn't get near those two. They just weren't interested.

WARDEN (*in a slightly threatening tone*): It's your job to make them interested, Lucy.

LUCY: Now what could I do? One was over seventy, after all, and the other told me he hadn't made love to anything since he saw his cat's hysterectomy scars.

WARDEN: You were picked for this official work because you seemed to have experience with difficult types. Remember where you were when we found you? Standing in a doorway with a scraggly piece of fur around your neck and runs in your stockings. Even in the city's poorest section you weren't turning customers away, were you? And if you had to go back to it . . .

LUCY: All right, Warden, you've made your point.

WARDEN: Just a little warning, Lucy. You know how I'd hate to fire you.

LUCY: All right, all right. Now, is there anything I should know about our man in there?

WARDEN: Oh, you should really find him easy to deal with. He's been most cooperative since being with us: never cried when appeals were turned down, never spat his food back at the guards, never used the walls for thumbnosing little phrases at the world—no, he's been a perfect sort up till now.

LUCY: Good, I don't like those who have an ax to grind. They never stop talking long enough for anything to really get going between us.

WARDEN: Well, Walter there's one of the better sort, all right, that's why you were assigned to him. You used to do so well with educated types. I remembered that physicist you went after a few years ago—for six months he moped about his cell, mumbling to himself. But after you were through with him he died happily explaining the theory of subatomic particles to our executioner. You'd turned a homicidal maniac back into a useful man.

LUCY: I just got his mind back on fundamentals. That seems to pep his type up.

WARDEN: Well, that's what I want you to do for Walter. (*Tapping one of the cover dishes.*) I had our chef up all night working on the fried chicken in here, but I hope he'll enjoy you even more. I sort of like this one and want him to have a little fling before he's hanged.

LUCY (*flatly*): Oh, you have a big heart under that forty-dollar suit, Warden.

WARDEN: Why, thank you, Lucy. Sometimes I think it goes unnoticed.

LUCY: Now, shall I get to work?

WARDEN: All right, we might as well start the introductions. Ah, would you wheel his dinner in to him? I think the silver trays will set you off to advantage. (*The* WARDEN *extracts a key, opens the cell door, and he and* LUCY *enter.* WALTER, *his sewing in his hands, jumps up abruptly to meet them. He then follows* LUCY *with his eyes as, smiling, she wheels the tray past him into the lower left corner of the cell.*) Hello, Walter, how's it going today?

WALTER (*still trying to keep an eye on* LUCY *who, after leaving the tray, begins walking about the cell, tapping at the walls and poking at the chairs*): Warden, nice of you to come by. Is it time already?

WARDEN: Heavens, no; you still have nearly two hours. Some insects, I'm told, live an entire life through in less time—birth, copulation, and death, all counted off in seconds.

WALTER (*pleasantly, but still with an eye on* LUCY *who is beginning to prop up the pillow on his cot*): That sounds like a very nice arrangement.

WARDEN: Right! After all, who needs years but those who have to repeat themselves?

LUCY (*stepping back from the cot and examining it*): You're talking on my time, Warden.

WARDEN: Quite so, Lucy, quite so. Walter, I'd like you to meet Lucy. She's going to stay here with you until the end—compliments of the state.

WALTER: With me? But I don't understand.

WARDEN: No effusions of gratitude, Walter. No man should eat his last meal without a little female company.

WALTER: Do you mean she's to—to . . . ?

WARDEN (*nodding*): It's an innovation in our penal program. Takes some of the sting out of anticapital punishment arguments. Sending a man out to die with a Lucy still fresh in every part of him—well, nothing cold-blooded about that, is there? Everything else about the little ceremony is, I'll admit, rather cut and dried, a bit too much so, even for my taste. That's what puts people off about it. The clack of the guard's shoes in cadence over those cobblestones, the same number of steps to be climbed, the ritual last trite phrases—no, there's not much spice in it any more. But with this new little prologue we've added—well, it seems to keep the others like you, Walter, from being swallowed up in formality. There's something touchingly human about the whole affair when Lucy and her kind deliver you back to our official hands.

LUCY (*walking back to the tray of food, she opens a cover dish*): And it keeps girls like me off the street. Hmm! This will get cold if you don't start on it, Walter.

WALTER: Oh, I'm not really hungry.

WARDEN: But that's fried chicken in there. With a heavy crust.

WALTER: I know I ordered it, but you won't mind if I just don't begin right away.

LUCY: Well, you've no complaints if I have a leg then, do you? Being up this early in the morning always gives me an (*she says the word with a seductive smile at* WALTER) appetite.

WALTER: No, no; go right ahead.

WARDEN (*watching* LUCY *as she takes a large bite*): Look at her go after that chicken, Walter. How many men would love to be in that piece of meat's place. And you're going to get the chance.

WALTER: Well, that's very nice, and I'm grateful to both of you; but I really don't . . .

WARDEN: Come now, Walter, no protests. Lucy there brings a little unpremeditated dash into the dull cubes and well-scrubbed-down corridors of our prison. You've been here so long I'll bet you've forgotten what a woman like Lucy, wrapped snugly in a yellow blouse and black skirt, can mean.

WALTER (*backing away and waving his hand in protest*): Oh, no, I haven't.

LUCY (*taking a few tentative dance steps*): Do you know, it's a pity you can't have music piped in here. It would be nice to dance a bit before settling down to work, wouldn't it, Walter?

WALTER: I can't dance, really.

WARDEN: Well, then, she could teach you. After all, there's always time to learn something new. But now, now that a festive note's been struck in the cell, I guess I'm what they call *de trop*. Well, now, enjoy each other. (*Pointing a preceptorial finger at* WALTER.) I want to see a contented face, Walter, when I return.

WALTER: Doesn't it seem contented now?

WARDEN (*studying* WALTER's *face*): It seems a little pinched and furrowed to me. Not the way one looks when Lucy's through with him.

WALTER: I can smile a bit if you want.

WARDEN: Save all that for the lady there. (*Stepping back and looking at the two of them.*) Ah, actually you make a fine-looking couple together. You know, it's moments like this that make a welfare state seem worth while after all. (*The* WARDEN *leaves.*)

LUCY (*throwing the chicken bone over her shoulder onto the floor*): God! I'd starve if he had to pimp for me.

WALTER (*quickly going over and retrieving the bone and putting it back on the tray*): Please, I'm trying to leave a tidy cell behind me.

LUCY: Well, sorry!

WALTER: I don't mean to be rude, but you'd be surprised how hard it is keeping a little place like this in order.

LUCY (*a little confused*): You give it a scrubbing once a day?

WALTER: Yes, but that won't do it. Every time a guard comes in here, some of the lint from his uniform stays behind. (*Tracing the descent of an imaginary piece of lint with his finger.*) You can see it floating down from a sleeve or a lapel, but once it hits the gray floor it's the devil to find.

LUCY (*looking down at where* WALTER's *finger last traced the lint*): I can see it could be a problem.

WALTER: But please don't let me stop you from finishing the chicken if you want to. Just be careful the crust doesn't splatter.

LUCY: But that's *your* last meal, after all, Walter.

WALTER: Oh, I'm afraid I ordered that in a fit of absence of mind. Fried foods raise the deuce with my stomach.

LUCY: Begins to ache?

WALTER: No, just snarl. It lasts for days, and, in company, believe me, it can be very embarrassing.

LUCY (*after a pause in which she watches* WALTER *continue his sewing*): Well, then, if no food, how about a cigarette before we begin?

WALTER: No, thank you. And if you're going to, be careful of the ashes. There's a little can underneath the sink you can use.

LUCY (*returning the cigarettes to her dress pocket, she turns away from* WALTER): Jesus! (*Hunching her shoulders, she shivers and takes a few halting dance steps.*) You've got to keep moving to stay warm in here.

WALTER: That blouse you're wearing must be very thin.

LUCY (*brightening*): Well, finally noticing that there's a woman in here with you?

WALTER (*dropping his eyes back to the sewing*): Tell me, do you really do this sort of work often for the prison?

LUCY: I've signed a five-year contract. And, as I'm not getting any younger, it's turned out to be a pretty good arrangement. In the last year, though, I've been kept a little too busy. It must have been the moon phases or something, but it seems as if everybody was cementing mothers up in the basement, shooting politicians, or setting fire to their friends. I hope things begin to calm down a bit now.

WALTER: But isn't it dangerous to come into a confined place with men who are going to be hanged in a matter of hours?

LUCY (*as she sits next to* WALTER *on the cot*): No more dangerous than the streets in the summer season. I'll take a cell with a man in it who's butchered an even dozen five-year-olds to a boulevard stuffed with tourists waving credit cards in one hand and pinching with the other. No, by the time a man reaches this cell, Walter, the violence he had in him has wasted away. It's been used up on his victim, the judge, his childhood, his shoes, and God knows what else. There's nothing but the lamb left when I arrive.

WALTER: The lamb?

LUCY: I don't mean that in a bad sense now. It's just that, for a woman who doesn't like to be treated roughly, I find men who use this cell have very gentle hands.

WALTER (*looking at his hands*): Mine are a bit rough from all the floor scrubbing I've done. Prison soap isn't the best.

LUCY (*taking his hands*): They look as soft as cats' paws to me.

WALTER (*pulling his hands away, he inches back from* LUCY *and takes a big stitch in his sewing*): You must excuse me, but I have to finish this little job of mending.

LUCY: I never thought I'd have to compete with a needle and thread, Walter.

WALTER: My number-patch was loose. I was afraid it might fall off during the—well, ceremonies.

LUCY: Your number-patch?

WALTER (*defensively*): It's very important that this number stays on me. This is how I'm identified in I don't know how many files and on dozens of official cards. 43556 is the key to my ending life on the proper line in the ledger, and I've grown quite fond of it.

LUCY (*humoring* WALTER): 43556—it has a nice ring to it. Better than a number packed with a lot of zeros.

WALTER: Well, actually, I would have preferred one with all even numbers, but it would have seemed fussy, I suppose, to insist on it.

LUCY (*moving closer to* WALTER *and beginning to stroke his neck*): Well, now, why don't you put your sewing away and let me show you why the prison officials chose me out of over a thousand applicants for my job.

WALTER (*jumping up from the cot*): Oh, no, Lucy, that's quite out of the question.

LUCY (*just a slight touch of impatience showing*): Now listen, Walter . . .

WALTER: Oh, it's certainly nothing personal. (*Staring firmly at* LUCY.) You do make that blouse and skirt seem wrapped around perfect treasures, and your skin is beautifully pale and, I'm sure, exciting to stroke for hours, even with my rather insensitive hands. (*Pulling himself together.*) But, no, I just don't wish to.

LUCY (*smoothing out her blouse*): Well, from the description, there isn't any doubt that you at least like women.

WALTER: Oh I do; or, rather, I did. But that's all over now.

LUCY (*getting up and moving toward* WALTER): But it doesn't have to be over. There's still a little time left. You probably have a miniature gallows dancing in front of your eyes, and you think it's numbed those important little nerves for good. But, believe me, Lucy can start them twitching again. I've done it for dozens of others far more upset about dying than you seem to be.

WALTER (*backing away from her*): But I don't want them to start twitching now.

LUCY: After they begin, then you'll want, Walter.

WALTER: No, no; I just want to remain peaceful.

LUCY: Peaceful? How can you use that word, when, in not too much more than an hour, you'll drag yourself up those thirteen steps?

WALTER (*backed against the cell's left wall, he clutches his jacket, thread and needle in front of him*): You couldn't understand, Lucy. Being peaceful would just bore you.

LUCY: Nothing bores me, Walter. That's why I'm a success in my business.

WALTER: Please! Stay back a bit. I can hear you breathing.

LUCY: It's a nice sound, isn't it? My lungs, in fact all the machinery inside me, Walter, work perfectly.

WALTER: I'm sure; but I don't want to listen to their sounds. One of the advantages of a cell is its quiet. I've grown used to silence.

LUCY (*rubbing his arm and speaking in a coaxing voice*): But my reputation's at stake, Walter. One failure leaves a permanent mark on one in my profession. I'd have to take to deeper layers of rouge, longer eyelashes, and darker stockings. My fur coat would need more padding at the shoulders and the heels on my shoes would be raised an inch at the very least. You wouldn't want to cause that, would you, Walter? You wouldn't want to start Lucy off looking for wigs and stronger perfumes?

WALTER (*pleading*): The scent you're wearing is making me dizzy enough as it is.

LUCY: There, you see, those nerves aren't dead. They're coming back to us after all.

WALTER (*trying, but not succeeding, to remove her hand*): Please, I'm just 43556; you can't expect a number to make love.

LUCY (*tripping her finger across his chest*): I'm not touching a number now, am I? No, this is the body of a man. A little out of condition, maybe, from being closed up in a cell for months, but it still reacts to my fingers, doesn't it?

WALTER (*as though suffering, he looks down at LUCY's bosom*): Oh, I've always been partial to women of your build, with your hair; and underneath that powder, I can see freckles. For me, freckles were always an irresistible aphrodisiac.

LUCY: Well, those freckles, my fingers, everything's yours, Walter. Just forget where you are, and think of trombones, bourbon bottles, and streetcars crowded with wet people starting off on a Saturday night.

WALTER (*rigid, with his eyes closed*): People forgetting who, what, or where they've been. All getting into new skins, expressions, and troubles. But wanting to laugh through it all.

LUCY: That's it, Walter. Laughing when you slip on the dance floor, find your socks don't match or that you can't make love more than twice a night.

WALTER (*now happily, but painfully, reminiscing*): And the Chinese restaurants you mistake for your house and the hands, often with gloves on them, you grab hold of.

LUCY (*whispering in WALTER's ear*): And now stop talking, Walter, and let's . . .

WALTER (*sticking her in the back with his needle*): No! Get away from me. (*He breaks loose and moves to the center of the cell.*)

LUCY (*with a loud yell*): Why, you crazy— That was a sharp needle you stuck in me!

WALTER (*keeping the needle poised for attack*): And I'll do it again if you come after me. This is my cell—ten paces wide, twenty long. Nothing, absolutely nothing unexpected happens here.

LUCY (*feeling the wounded spot on her back*): God, I think I'm bleeding.

WALTER: Oh, no; no blood, please. I've seen all the blood I ever want to see.

LUCY: Then you shouldn't go about sticking people with needles or hitting them with golf clubs.

WALTER: You know about that?

LUCY (*somewhat abstracted as she rubs her wound and examines her hand*): It's written right across your forehead. (*Examining and rubbing her fingers together.*) Well, I'm not bleeding after all.

WALTER: I'm grateful for that at least. I'm afraid I just lost my head for a moment. I felt myself slipping back into everything this cell protects me from, and I . . . Are you angry with me, Lucy?

LUCY (*dismissing the incident*): Oh, I've had worse done to me by clients with sort of Victorian tastes in love. But you *have* disappointed me, Walter. I thought we'd strike it off right away.

WALTER: Oh, you wouldn't have found me much good anyway. My wife used to make me take pills . . .

LUCY: For God's sake, no talk about the wife, especially one whose skull you split open. It's professionally insulting after being stuck with your needle.

WALTER: Well, I just thought to pass the time . . .

LUCY: Clients talk about their wives *after* making love. (*As if pondering a new discovery.*) Wives and postcoital depression seem to go together. (*Now back to lecturing* WALTER *on his brothel manners.*) But before, it's themselves they take apart and it's our job to put them back together again.

WALTER: Well, all my pieces are in their proper place and I don't want them disarranged.

LUCY (*sweetly*): No one wants to do that, Walter. Perhaps I did rush you a little bit; but, after all, you're the one counting the minutes and I thought you'd want them stuffed with all the things your clean little cell's been lacking.

WALTER: I'd already planned how to use every second of them before you arrived: there was the number-patch to be sewn on, shoes to be polished, a final stroll four times around the cell, and then I was going to wash, which, because of the soap's poor quality, would most likely have taken me up to the time the warden and his guards came for me.

LUCY: Well, it *is* asking a lot wanting you to give up all those wild plans for me.

WALTER (*nodding in agreement*): I'll already have to pass up the shoes.

LUCY: Well, give up two of your laps around the room and talk a little about yourself. At least let me show you how well I've been trained as a sympathetic listener.

WALTER: Why, there's nothing much to say about me.

LUCY (*coaxingly*): Oh, come on; start off with the kind of job you used to have.

WALTER: Well, I was a moderately successful lawyer.

LUCY (*laughing*): A lawyer?

WALTER (*a little anxiously*): Why are you laughing?

LUCY: Well, being here—that doesn't say much for your ability to sway juries, does it?

WALTER (*testily*): I didn't defend myself; and, besides, I was irrefutably guilty.

LUCY: I thought it was always easier to win defending a guilty man than an innocent one.

WALTER (*slightly outraged at this*): Now, you see, it's just that sort of over-the-shoulder attitude that's turned our laws into a fool's game today.

LUCY: You mean like the city ordinance against soliciting on the streets? I've always thought that one was woolly-headed.

WALTER (*wagging his head impatiently*): I'm not talking about your particular likes and dislikes, Lucy. It's the nature of the law that's been abused.

LUCY: The jails seem full enough to me.

WALTER (*growing a little more excited*): No, no; laws are supposed to be as solid and immovable as these walls. At least that's what I thought when I began studying them. They weren't supposed to depend upon the judge's sinus condition, a lady juror's two Caesareans, or poor air conditioning in the courtroom. They were to be hermetically sealed—untouched by human hands.

LUCY: Calm down a bit, Walter.

WALTER (*now waving his arms*): But don't you see they weren't? They were worthless little hide-and-seek rules made up to give the neighborhood's poor children something to do in the evenings. No god had bellowed them out or burned them into a mountain.

LUCY: Be careful you don't stick yourself with the needle.

WALTER (*now quite intense*): Oh, listen to me, Lucy. Can you understand what it meant to a man devoted to the law to find out it was all one big caprice? It was as if you looked up suddenly at a night sky and saw every planet and star dancing drunkenly about.

LUCY (*smiling invitingly*): That might be exciting, Walter. And sometimes, making love out of doors, when the weather permitted, I think I did see the stars wiggle a bit.

WALTER (*angry at* LUCY's *non sequitur*): Wiggle, do they? Well, that's not going to happen here! Not in this cell. (*He jumps up on the cot and points to the barred window.*) Look through this window, Lucy. See how the sky's sectioned into nine perfect squares? On a clear night each square contains exactly five stars and the center one has a planet all to itself.

LUCY: A planet? Which one?

WALTER: A sexless one; far from the sun, always cold, but giving off a dull, dependable light. (*Patting the bars.*) No, these little bars are particular about what they let into their boundaries.

LUCY (*temporarily defeated*): All right, let's skip love for a while.

WALTER (*somewhat calmer, he comes down from the cot*): The law had most of my love. I believed all one had to do was match little scraps of fact against those fine, heavily punctuated sentences in the books and, like a candy machine, the right answer would come out neatly wrapped. Oh, you don't know how snugly I fitted into everything then. With those laws standing firm, all their lesser relatives, from chemistry formulas to table manners, seemed impregnable. In those days I knew exactly what to pray for, how often a month I should have sex (four times, only with my wife), and how stern I should be when my children spilled their soup. I knew who was the villain and who the virgin on the stage; I knew my laundry would come back on time without a piece missing; and I knew that every mirror would reflect at me a recognizable, satisfied face that had aged just the right amount since last being seen. Oh, Lucy, everything from constellation to subways seemed to be moving at my rhythm. And then . . . then . . .

LUCY: And then?

WALTER (*bitterly*): And then came the Gogarty trial.

LUCY: A trial for murder?

WALTER (*beginning wistfully, then gradually growing more involved*): No, a suit for damages. Mrs. Ellen Gogarty versus The Municipal Bus Company—that was its official title. The woman's son, age thirty-five, had been run over and completely mashed by one of their vehicles. The light had been with him, and the bus driver, by eyewitness account, had been drunk and singing "Little Alice Bottom" when the accident took place. I was whistling the same tune when, these bits of evidence snapped inside my brief case, I arrived at the courthouse on a morning that seemed no different from a thousand others. I even remember exchanging a joke with one of the guards and making a date with the opposing attorney, who was putting up only a token defense, for dinner that evening. Then the trial began: the judge smiled at me, the jury nodded in solemn agreement as I turned phrases and probed witnesses. With every second our case was strengthened, and, throughout the examinations, Mrs. Gogarty, wearing a new but inexpensive summer hat and asking only to be recompensed for the loss of her only son, sat soaking up sympathetic stares from everyone in the court. The case, as they say, was open and shut. Open and shut.

LUCY (*who has been sitting on the cot, listening intently*): And what happened?

WALTER (*now incensed over the memory*): Hiccups! Hiccups! Just before the jury was about to file out, Mrs. Gogarty began to hiccup. Oh, at first, it was hardly noticeable; but then they became louder and more frequent. I waved a warning finger at her to be silent, but she blinked back that she couldn't help herself; and while the jury stood stunned in their places, the gulping sounds went on jerking her frail little body this way and that. Finally, they actually came to be syncopated—two short, one long; one long, three short; two long. (*He puts his hands to his ears.*) And with the occasional change in pitch there was almost a little tune coming out of her. Sometimes I can still hear it, sounding like a street calliope; and then comes the laughter: first from the spectators in the court, then from the members of the jury, and, finally, from the judge himself. I try to speak, to read a few apposite remarks on courtroom behavior from the law book on my desk, but I'm literally drowned out with laughter. And through it all, like some devilish timpani in an orchestra, Mrs. Gogarty's hiccups, keeping up their erratic beat and brutal melody—(*He raises and drops his voice so the outline of a tune can be heard.*) One long, one short; two long, one short . . . (*Here he pauses and collects himself.*) Snorting, slapping each other's backs and nudging one another's ribs, the jury files out of the room. The wait is a very short one, and from behind the jury-chamber door come the sounds of still more snickers with an occasional imitation of my client's disorder. Finally, as if they'd been off on a party—collars open, ties askew, hair undone—the men and women who are to decide our case return and, while Mrs. Gogarty goes on with those loud little spasms, they announce a verdict against her. I can't believe it and, throwing protocol to the winds, ask why. "How can she be suffering grief worth any compensation at all when she hiccups?" so says the jury foreman. "Madness," I answer and turn to the judge. "My good sir," he says, chuckling like an idiot, "she really did hiccup out a little tune." "The law!" I cry. "Hiccups!" he answers, and the laughter starts all around again. (*Slowly now, as if looking in the narration of simple fact for a solution.*) I went to the governor himself, Lucy. I showed him there was nothing in the pertinent judicial paragraphs about this involuntary closure of the glottis and the noise produced therefrom, and *he* answered that those paragraphs were to be amended to include the peculiar Gogarty phenomenon. I knew then that it was all over, and that a sneeze, hiccup, or crooked nose could twist those impressive sentences into gibberish.

There is silence for a moment, and then LUCY *rises from the cot and makes an attempt at consolation.*

LUCY: Maybe it's better that way. After all, that's what makes a day interesting. It's the little unexpected matters of taste, like a man going wild over a mole on your chin, that keeps the beauty contest also-rans like me in business.

WALTER (*sadly*): I knew you'd think that, Lucy; but, for me, Mrs. Gogarty's hiccups were the end of everything. I no longer knew what clubs to join, what tie to choose, what toothpaste to use, what church to go to. At home, where I always thought things went smoothly and orderly, I suddenly found my children snipping off our dog's tail an inch a day with a pair of scissors, writing obscene couplets on my shirt collars, biting my leg whenever I passed by, and singing marching songs from the War of 1812. And my wife's birthmark, a little red triangle that had always been tucked inconspicuously behind her left ear, began turning up in the center of her forehead, in the middle of her stomach, and on the soles of her feet . . .

LUCY (*now a little impatient with him*): Are we going back to the wife again?

WALTER (*growing excited again*): My life was formless, a tiny piece of chaos. What was left to me that couldn't be hiccuped out of existence? Right and left, buy and sell, love and hate—these now meant nothing to me. I found myself on the wrong trains, in the wrong beds, with the wrong people. And my neighborhood, my neighborhood that I had helped zone to perfection, became a carnival of the lowest sort, and my neighbors, whom I knew inside and out, danced about beneath layer on layer of holiday masks until I couldn't tell one from the other. And then, God knows when or where it happened, I found a mirror sending back at me a face that I had never seen before—a face with wild eyes, bristling hair, and a heavy growth of stubble—a face I would have crossed the street to avoid had I seen it coming at me in happier times. Oh, I'd been cheated, Lucy, and gradually I began to grow angry—mad, in fact—until one morning, with everything spinning about me in complete disorder, I struck back. My poor wife happened to be closest at hand, and for all I know I might have thought I was on the golf course until I felt the club make contact with her skull. I remember it sounding as if it were a good shot, and then I looked up to follow the ball's flight and found . . .

LUCY: That's enough, Walter! I'm beginning to shiver.

WALTER (*recalled from his memories*): But now comes the pleasant part.

LUCY (*shaking her head as if to clear it*): No, for me, the goodies in your story are over.

WALTER: No, no; don't you see? The law came back to me. Everything began falling in line again. I have my number, a room that never changes, meals that arrive punctually to the moment, and guards whose manners are perfectly predictable. (*With weak joy.*) The world has boundaries again and I know my place in it.

LUCY (*almost threateningly*): In one hour your place will be at the end of a rope.

WALTER (*with military stiffness*): But my death will take place according to a rigid schedule and then be *officially* recorded. What more could I want?

LUCY (*with desperate hope*): A little sex?

WALTER (*vexed at this*): Good God! have you understood nothing? That belongs to the dizziness on the other side of those walls. Here, in my prison, the laws hold, and I won't have them disturbed by perfume and overpowdered flesh.

LUCY (*now angry*): Oh, won't you? Do you know, if they came in this minute with a rope ready, it'd be my overpowdered flesh they'd hang? Yes, they'd be looking for something live to string up, Walter, and you certainly don't pass the test.

WALTER: I know what being alive means to you.

LUCY (*beginning to unwrap the belt from around her waist*): Oh, between Mrs. Gogarty's lost case and your wife's murder you had a taste of it, all right; but it frightened you right into this cell.

WALTER (*showing apprehension*): What on earth are you doing? You're not going to undress? I promise you it won't do any good.

LUCY: I'm not understanding you, Walter. And, as a client, you have a right to that from me. I'm going to try to shorten the distance between us. (*She steps upon the cot, loops one end of the belt, and fastens the other to one of the bars across the window.*)

WALTER: You'll leave footprints on the pillow!

LUCY: You won't be using it again, Walter. I just want to see how it'd feel with a noose around my neck. Who knows? Maybe you're right; maybe the only thing I'd worry about is that they got my name and number right on the morgue card. (*She slips the belt over her head.*) There, it's in place; the hangman's taken his hands from my shoulders, the sack's dropped over my eyes; my shoes, just polished, are shining in the morning light . . .

WALTER: Stop it! Stop it! You're just pretending anyway.

LUCY (*in the tones of a spoiled little girl*): I'm in a cell with a murderer. How do I know you won't push the cot out from under me?

WALTER: I might do just that.

LUCY (*with her eyes shut and her head tilted back*): I will drop down, happy that the sky I leave behind has nice equal sections, each with so many numbers of stars. I'll be content that my dying has an alphabetical standing, that my last meal came to me on time, that my cell is immaculate, that the prison day which I'll never see will be like all the others I've lived through, and that I didn't sweat, sing, throw up, or make love to a woman. So then, let the trap doors fly open underneath me. With no regrets about this life, I'll die happily. (*Pause.*) The hell I will!

WALTER (*walking up to cot and threatening to kick one of its legs*): If you don't come down, I swear I'll kick the cot out from under you, Lucy.

LUCY (*removing the belt from around her neck*): You bet I'll come down. Dying with your point of view really makes me sick to my stomach. (*She steps down and walks as far away from* WALTER *as the confines of the cell permit.*)

WALTER (*somewhat meek and apologetic*): I'm not trying to convert you to anything, after all.

LUCY: No, you're not. You're too happy curled up in your little womb to want company.

WALTER: Please, no coarse talk, Lucy.

LUCY: Oh, of course not. You'd like to have a conversation in algebra equations, I'll bet. Well, I'm not going to let you get away with it.

WALTER (*puzzled and on the defensive*): Why are you attacking me?

LUCY: Because you remind me of a *happy* "still-life" whore, Walter. Do you know what that is? It's the last step for all of us in this business. When even the streets won't have you and you've lost your nerve for the river, then it's a twenty-four-hour-in-bed house for you. You don't own anything to wear except a grease-stained kimono the madam gives you; there's no make-up on the little table next to you, no mirror, the room's always dark, and the only sounds are the footsteps in the corridor that shuffle, with sometimes just a little hesitation, past your door that's been locked from the outside. You just lie there, Walter, waiting for the lock to click open, letting another client in at you. Oh, and there's no worry about these men like there

is when you're on your own. You don't
fret over whether or not he's a handsome
one or if he can pay up or not. You don't
have to worry about his whims or his
cracking you on the jaw or his inflamed
genital tract. Nothing that happens will
ever move you from the room, the bed,
the darkness, and the sound of footsteps.
The customers will keep coming and you'll
keep being fed no matter what your hair
looks like or what lies you think up to tell
those wheezing over you, those without
faces you can ever really see. It's peaceful,
all right, in a "still-life" house; and sometimes I wake up laughing at night thinking
about it.

WALTER: I'll bet there were times, on a December night, when business was slow on
your corner, you felt such a place wouldn't
be too bad.

LUCY: No. I liked the cold nights. Only the
really interesting ones were out when the
weather was mean. The ones who must
have been like you were after your Gogarty
trial.

WALTER: Can't you leave me out of it?

LUCY (*menacingly*): Oh, you'd like to be left
out of everything, wouldn't you? Everything but the Warden's filing cabinet.

WALTER: If you keep on this way, I'm going
to have to ask you to leave.

LUCY (*moving toward him again*): No chance
of that, Walter. Too much depends on
this for me. It's your world against mine.
There'll be no "still-life" house for Lucy
because of you!

WALTER: Must we go through this again?
I was through with everything you represent when the police took the blood-stained
seven-iron out of my hand.

LUCY (*speaking evenly, with a smile, and still
advancing*): I don't believe you, Walter.
All the talk about your little battle to keep
the laws from crumbling after the Gogarty
trial, I don't believe a word of it.

WALTER: Well, that's really beside the point.

LUCY (*reaching into her pocket, she brings
out the packet of cigarettes and extracts
several*): Do you know what I believe,
Walter? (*As she speaks, she begins throwing the cigarettes about the cell.*)

WALTER: Here, what are you doing?

LUCY (*flipping several over her shoulder*):

I'm setting up the atmosphere you really
like.

WALTER (*dropping to his hands and knees to
gather up the debris*): Stop it! Stop it! I
may not be able to find them all before
they come for me.

LUCY (*walking now to the tray of food*):
Leave them, Walter. You don't mind a
messy cell any more than you did finding
yourself on the wrong trains. (*She opens
the dish and extracts the chicken leg she'd
already bitten into.*)

WALTER: What are you saying? It made me
sick. It made me kill my wife. And put
down that chicken bone!

LUCY: I think it would go well in the center
of the floor. A little savage bone in the
center of the cell. (*She throws the bone in
the air and it lands with a clatter in the
cell's center.*) And maybe a wing in the
corner. (*The piece of chicken bounces off
the wall and drops in the cell's corner by
the washbasin.*)

WALTER: I'm going to be hanged in an hour.
How can you treat me this way?

LUCY: Yes, Walter, you were frightened of
what those hiccups touched off, all right,
but it was because you were starting to
enjoy that dizzy world outside. That's why
your wife had her head mashed, wasn't it?
You just wanted to remove yourself from
temptation.

WALTER (*no longer crawling about, but still
on his hands and knees*): That's not true!
That's not true!

LUCY: Oh, come on, Walter. Weren't you
beginning to look forward to those strange
beds you turned up in?

WALTER (*protesting too much*): No, they
terrified me. I swear it!

LUCY (*seeing she has made a breach, she
pushes on, speeding up her accusations*):
And your wife's birthmark—how many
times did you bet with yourself where it
would pop up next?

WALTER (*now breaking a bit*): Once or twice
only. But that doesn't mean . . .

LUCY: And how many snips at the dog's tail
did you take?

WALTER: It was cruel, I know. But nothing
seemed to matter in those days . . .

LUCY: And you enjoyed its howls.

WALTER: All my life I had an urge to torture a dog or cat. And it was just one snip. Just one!

LUCY: And when you went out at night, not knowing what tie you were wearing, what streets you were walking, what name you were using, admit you were twitching with excitement.

WALTER (*feebly*): I won't; I wasn't.

LUCY (*going to the cot and picking up* WALTER's *shirt*): Admit it, or the number goes.

WALTER: I didn't, I swear I didn't.

LUCY *rips the number-patch off in one short movement and* WALTER *cries as if he's been wounded. Then she holds the piece of cloth obtrusively in front of her and lets it drop slowly to the floor. Now totally defeated,* WALTER *watches it descend.*

LUCY: Now the laws are falling apart again, Walter. You're just a numberless name about to be hanged. There's a not-so-bad-looking woman in your cell. What's there to lose? Do you remember having thoughts like these?

WALTER: Yes, yes, I had them. I thought for a time that all the springs, levers, and wheels of the world had broken down and I was free!

LUCY (*softening now*): And so you were, Walter.

WALTER: No, there was too great a price. There were always those gray mornings when the mind took over, when you saw your crumpled clothes and cigarette pack from the night before, when your head pounded and you nibbled your lip in fear. Then you panicked for a world that made sense.

LUCY: No matter how much fun you got from the world that didn't?

WALTER: Oh, leave me alone.

LUCY (*helping* WALTER *to his feet*): I'm going to bring that world back to you. After all, it's the only one there is.

WALTER (*weakly*): There's my cell.

LUCY (*drawing him toward the cot*): With the cigarettes on the floor? With the number torn from your shirt? With my perfume settling over you?

WALTER: Please, don't make me start again. What I found on those mornings was death; and it's only minutes away.

LUCY: Make love to me, Walter, and you won't mind the hangover of the gallows. You'll be living again when you strangle.

WALTER: That's no consolation! Oh, everything was so perfect here before you came. I was just like one of the Warden's insects, living out my days unconsciously, letting the fixed rhythms of the prison carry me along.

LUCY: It's too late to go back now. Look at the sky. How many stars are in your sections now?

WALTER: Why, they're all bunched in two or three of them, and the planet's gone entirely.

LUCY: And the cell, isn't it beginning to push in upon you?

WALTER: I loved it for so long.

LUCY: It's not big enough to hold a live man, Walter.

WALTER: Oh, why wasn't there a glass of water next to Mrs. Gogarty in the courtroom? You would never have gotten to me then. I would have died somewhere in bed of a bad heart, thinking that a special chair had been set aside for me at an eternal dinner party where everything was properly served.

LUCY: No one's lucky enough to fool himself that way forever.

WALTER: But how can there ever be a contented expression on my face now when they come for me?

LUCY (*pulling him down onto the cot*): Trust Lucy for that, Walter. All those nights, beds, marching songs, toothpaste containers, and howling dogs packed into thirty minutes.

WALTER: I hope so. Otherwise I think I'll break down and cry when I start up those steps.

LUCY: Shall we begin, Walter?

WALTER: All right, I've paid the price now. There'd better be twenty years of living in your mouth, fingertips, and breasts.

LUCY: I'll lead you, Walter. You just follow.

WALTER (*bending over her*): And who knows? Maybe the rope will break? Or the hangman come down with a bad cold?

LUCY: That's the way to reason, Walter. On this cot, with Lucy on it, anything and everything's now possible. (*She draws* WALTER *to her and the cell's single light is extinguished. Curtain.*)

PART TWO

THE WARDEN, PHILLIP, MARTHA.

The curtain rises on the early-morning confusion of a suburban kitchen-dining room. PHILLIP, *the prison's executioner, and* MARTHA, *his wife, are standing at the kitchen table.* PHILLIP *is a small, erect man. He is dressed in the trousers, shirt, and tie of his official uniform. The hat and coat are placed on one of the kitchen chairs. His wife, her hair in curlers and dowdily attractive in a morning housecoat, begins busying herself at the stove. A large red pepper mill is the only conspicuous object on the table. As the lights come up fully, the* WARDEN *is seen pacing back and forth across the table from* PHILLIP.

WARDEN (*with rhetorical self-pity*): When I think how I stayed up nights as a boy learning the penal code by heart so someday I would be a prison warden!

PHILLIP: What I asked for isn't going to prove you wasted your youth. It seems quite reasonable to me.

WARDEN: Reasonable? How can you, the last and most important link in society's chain of punishment, how can you think it reasonable to want to dress up like a headsman from the Middle Ages?

PHILLIP: I just want to wear a black hood over my head. I think it would lend me a little more—well, personality out there.

MARTHA (*setting a pot of coffee on the kitchen table*): Well, if you ask me, the idea of a hood, especially a black one, strikes me as a little morbid.

WARDEN: There you are; from your own wife. Can you imagine what others will have to say about it? Why, it smacks of thumb-screws, iron maidens, and unsanitary dungeons.

MARTHA (*to* PHILLIP): I wish you'd come sit down and finish your oatmeal. (*Looking into one of the bowls set on the table.*) It's getting crusty and beginning to stick to the edges of the bowl.

PHILLIP (*a look of exasperation at* MARTHA): I don't want any oatmeal now. I simply want, as an employee with some twenty years' service behind him, to have a request granted. (*With a little petulance.*)

I want to wear a black hood at today's execution!

WARDEN: But think of what it will do to your reputation! Instead of being a finely edged instrument in a clinical, detached operation, you become a villain—a strangler—a black knight.

MARTHA (*vigorously buttering a piece of toast*): I can just imagine the treatment I'd get then from the girls in my bridge club.

PHILLIP: Let them jeer and hiss at me; it's better than not being noticed or thought of at all.

WARDEN: But behind a hood your face won't even be seen.

PHILLIP (*slightly angry*): My face? Don't you think I know what this collection of scribbles, bumps, and creases looks like? Any real expression I call on it to take looks ridiculous on me. But with this hood, this mask, it comes alive. My eyes, outlined by slanting black slits, crackle with perception; my mouth grows full and moist; and my chin, as if obeying a command from these other features, squares itself and, just a little arrogantly, juts forward.

MARTHA (*now beginning to pour out three cups of coffee*): It sounds as if you'd look like you were in a bad accident, Phillip.

WARDEN: I think you'd frighten the men to death before you had a chance to hang them.

PHILLIP: Then I would at least have some contact. (*A sigh.*) Oh, I didn't mind being your instrument when those condemned arrived like patients drowned in ether. But things have changed now. You yourself know that they come up those steps trembling, warm, talkative—exuding a scent so full of living that *my* head sometimes starts spinning because of it.

WARDEN: There are rules and regulations governing these things. An executioner's uniform can be blue, black, or gray; the buttons can be bone or brass; and the cap is optional. But by no stretch of interpretation is there any mention of a black hood.

PHILLIP: Hang the regulations! I'm trying to get a little color into things. (*Pleading.*) Don't you understand? I need a change.

WARDEN: You have your vacation coming up in a few months. Get in some fishing, and you'll feel better. I've always found that just dangling your line in a mountain stream relaxes the muscles, improves the digestion . . .

PHILLIP: I don't want to fish, Warden. For twenty years I've gone to little mountain streams on my vacation and caught nothing more interesting than a trout with one eye last summer.

WARDEN: A one-eyed trout? What kind of bait were you using?

PHILLIP: Don't change the subject. Now, do I or do I not wear my hood today?

WARDEN: I've already given you an answer on that.

PHILLIP: Just look at me in it, that's all. Just one glance.

WARDEN: I couldn't be less interested.

PHILLIP: All you have to say is yes or no. Just yes or no.

WARDEN (*giving in with a long sigh*): It's a waste of time; but, if you want to, go ahead.

PHILLIP: Fine; it's just upstairs. (*Starting to leave.*) Oh, I may be a little time adjusting it, though. It has to sit just right, otherwise it droops a bit and I find it difficult to breathe.

MARTHA: If you're just going to leave the oatmeal, should I have some scrambled eggs ready for you when you come down?

PHILLIP: Forget about breakfast, Martha. (*To the* WARDEN.) I hope, once I'm in my hood, that I won't have to take it off until the ceremony's over with. I wouldn't want any food stains to get on it. (PHILLIP *exits.*)

MARTHA: He used to eat such a big breakfast on special days like this. Why, I can remember when six eggs and a quarter-pound of ham were just enough for him.

WARDEN: Well, I must say I find his behavior this morning a little peculiar. The whole thing just isn't like Phillip. He's always been someone you could count on, someone who knew the importance of a good shine on his buttons and a sharp crease in his trousers.

MARTHA (*sitting down dejectedly and absently stirring her coffee*): Well, something's definitely been happening to him in the last months. If you'd been living with him every day, this business with the hood wouldn't surprise you in the least.

WARDEN: I haven't noticed anything until now.

MARTHA: Oh, he's kept these changes fairly well hidden, even from me. But you can't eat, sleep, and take out a joint bank account with a man without noticing the slightest change in him.

WARDEN: Now that you mention it, he hasn't come to any club meetings in the last months and his weekly reports have been dotted with erasure smudges—very unlike him.

MARTHA (*putting the coffee down and nervously smoothing her hair*): It's beginning to show on the outside too? Oh, I'd hoped to keep it confined to the rooms in this house.

WARDEN (*reaching down and taking* MARTHA's *hand*): Is it something you can tell me, a very old friend? Is there another woman involved in all this?

MARTHA (*hitting the kitchen table with her free hand so that the* WARDEN *turns the other loose*): Oh, how I wish there was! How I'd love to be able to sink my nails into the flesh-and-blood reason for the way things are beginning to wobble on their legs around here! Just to see a larger bosom or a firmer behind leading Phillip down a street would let me spit at him with a clear conscience. If I just knew where the weakness was, I could make life miserable for him and then forget it!

WARDEN: But you don't?

MARTHA (*rising from the kitchen table like a prosecutor at a trial*): About four months ago, after Phillip had left for work, I got up from bed and, like I do every morning the first thing, reached down for his slippers to take them to the closet. For twenty years he's always left them on his side of the bed, neatly placed next to one another, toes pointed to the wall.

WARDEN: And that morning?

MARTHA: One was underneath the bed and the other, after being used for an ash tray, was tucked beneath his pillow.

WARDEN (*shaking his head*): A bad sign!

MARTHA: Only the first, though. In the next weeks I began making all sorts of discoveries: in his bureau drawer, tucked among his underwear, I found a book of Swedish lessons; in the hall closet, squeezed behind the Christmas decorations, I uncovered a banjo with two of its strings missing; and under one of the sofa cushions, I turned up a pair of red socks with "World's Fair—1939" stitched down their sides. Red socks! I can't decide what to do with them, and just knowing they're sitting in the house drives me half out of my mind.

WARDEN (*approaching* MARTHA, *he puts his hands on her shoulders and speaks as the comforting male*): Go on, Martha. My home's not a happy one, either.

MARTHA: Well, after that, Phillip himself began upsetting things. Since we were married, he's always slept on his stomach, one hand folded beneath his chin; but a month ago I woke up to find him snoring on his back. Then his favorite chair, that he always settled in after dinner, began being neglected; and, the dishes done, I'd come in and find him pouting in a corner or sitting cross-legged like an Arab on the floor.

WARDEN (*oozing sympathy*): And you've been suffering through all this, Martha, without a word to anyone?

MARTHA: I kept hoping it would all pass over; but I see now it won't. Last night, behind a stack of bathroom towels, I discovered a box of very expensive cigars with an unpronounceable name—and then this morning the hood. (*She utters a long sigh and turns to put her head on the* WARDEN's *chest.*) Oh, Warden!

WARDEN (*a smile hinting now a little more than sympathy*): There, there. Please call me Harry.

MARTHA (*a brief smile as she pronounces the name*): Harry! (*Now the defenseless little girl.*) Oh, I just don't know what to do any longer.

WARDEN: I really can't stand thinking of you being unhappy.

MARTHA: Just last week Phillip refused to renew our country club membership or donate to the Red Cross.

WARDEN: You need help, Martha. Can Harry, an old, old, *old* friend do anything for you?

MARTHA: Don't let him wear that hood today. No matter how he coaxes, put your foot down.

WARDEN (*a vigorous nod*): You can depend on it. I'll simply tell him his pension won't be raised if he does.

MARTHA: Oh, Harry, you've always been so kind. Just having you here this morning makes everything seem much easier.

WARDEN (*lifting up her chin*): We're cut from the same timber, Martha. Perhaps we can help each other. (*He starts to kiss her.*)

MARTHA (*pulling away*): No, Harry! Even if Phillip has taken to collecting red socks and turning nasty remarks about my friends, I couldn't deceive him. It would be playing his game.

WARDEN: He does nothing but hurt you, Martha; and I've loved you ever since the day you came to my office to try to get a raise in salary out of me for Phillip.

MARTHA (*now enjoying being pursued*): Really? I remember coming out feeling you hadn't noticed me at all. And Phillip didn't get the raise.

WARDEN: You were wearing an orange-and-blue print dress, white gloves and, as it was right after lunch, there was a little drop of mayonnaise on the left side of your chin.

MARTHA: Harry! And you didn't tell me.

WARDEN (*walking up to her and speaking in a hoarse voice*): I found it terribly exciting. All the time you were going on about those extra five dollars a month, I was trying to imagine just what you could have eaten to put that tiny white mark there.

MARTHA (*pretending embarrassment*): You shouldn't talk that way. What a woman eats for lunch is an intimate matter.

WARDEN: And you? Did you notice me at all?

MARTHA: I'd only been married six months at the time. I wasn't noticing anyone but Phillip, such that he was.

WARDEN (*somewhat hurt*): You mean I made no impression at all?

MARTHA: Well, I do recall you had on a tie with a palm tree painted on it.

WARDEN (*nostalgically*): In the dark it lit up and formed a pair of woman's legs.

MARTHA (*almost warmly*): And I noticed how bloodshot your eyes were, and I thought how hard you must work to have popped so many of those little vessels.

WARDEN: Twenty years ago! Twenty years ago! If we could only have spoken frankly to each other then.

MARTHA: And why didn't you?

WARDEN: I thought of doing so, Martha. That very night I paced about in the dark of our five-room house, trying to decide just how bold I should be.

MARTHA: And then you saw your wife asleep, her head placed at just the right angle on the pillow, and you were ashamed of your thoughts. A good wife holds on even when she's unconscious.

WARDEN: Heavens no! It wasn't my wife. She'd already begun sampling the line of manual laborers that began with a teen-age elevator operator and just last week was kept going with a streetcar motorman. No, Martha, it was the twins, aged one, I think, at the time, who kept me from sending you a warm note about the stain on your chin. I wandered into their room, heard them breathing, in unison, and something made me switch on the light. I saw them: their eyes opened simultaneously, blinked once in disbelief at the questions written across my face, and gave me such a stare of clear-sighted respectability that I backed, shamefaced, from the crib. Oh, if you could have seen those accusing blue pupils daring me to jeopardize their owners' position. Martha, their plump faces were as solid as the walls of my prison, and they left me no choice but to forget your lunches and start saving for their college education.

MARTHA (*with a sigh of genuine understanding*): Well, I don't blame you for that.

WARDEN: Oh, it was the right thing then when I thought you were happy with our hangman. But now . . .

MARTHA: Now, now it's too late. I can't put mayonnaise on my sandwiches any longer and fit into last year's dress.

WARDEN: And I wouldn't dare wear a tie with a palm tree painted on it. (*Suddenly throwing off the gloom that has settled over him and tumbling out his words.*) But my sons are almost chemical engineers and my wife never stops riding streetcars and my house is empty and no matter what size dress you wear, I love you! (*He kisses* MARTHA *enthusiastically, and, for a moment, she returns in kind. Then, however, she pushes him away.*)

MARTHA: Oh, no, Harry. No, no, no. (*She walks back to the kitchen table and steadies herself with it.*) Let me reheat your coffee or make you some toast.

WARDEN (*again advancing*): Please, don't drop back behind breakfast. We're both beyond that now.

MARTHA (*again escaping*): No, not here. Phillip may come down any minute.

WARDEN: Then we must have a meeting, a rendezvous as soon as possible. Twenty years, Martha. Twenty years!

MARTHA (*after a brief pause*): All right: tomorrow, three o'clock, in front of the supermarket steps.

WARDEN: Tomorrow? (*A pause and a frown, as he consults a small black engagement book.*) No, I'm afraid tomorrow's out for me. A government inspection team is coming down for the day. (*Brightening.*) But Saturday, in the afternoon, I know a little bar . . .

MARTHA: But I've promised myself as a fourth in three card games that afternoon.

WARDEN: Cards, Martha?

MARTHA (*with just a little less enthusiasm*): We could try Monday morning. No one suspects you of anything on a Monday.

WARDEN (*a little impatient*): That's because everyone's too busy to get into mischief. If I went away from my desk for five minutes after a weekend, it'd take me a month to catch up.

MARTHA: Well, I could slip away Tuesday night and say I'm seeing a movie.

WARDEN (*dejectedly*): That's the night the twins call from school to ask for money. (*With now but faint hope.*) But Wednesday?

MARTHA (*flatly, as she checks a calendar on the kitchen wall*): Cancer Fund meeting. Thursday?

WARDEN (*in equally funereal tones*): Parole Board all day, and I visit my mother at night. (MARTHA *turns and goes to the kitchen table where she pours a fresh cup of coffee. The* WARDEN *continues as though trying to explain something to himself rather than to her.*) I've visited Mother every Thursday night since leaving her to get married. Every Thursday night, and I don't think she really enjoys seeing me at all.

MARTHA (*after a pause*): Would you like cream in your coffee, Harry?

WARDEN: Black; make it as black as you can.

MARTHA (*making conversation*): Do you suppose it will rain? I always think hangings should take place in bad weather, even if it does make Phillip's back stiffen up a bit.

WARDEN (*taking up the coffee cup and staring moodily into it*): Are we back to hangings, your husband, and another official day?

MARTHA: Your twins' eyes are still following us.

WARDEN (*putting down the cup*): Ah, but for a moment, for a moment . . .

MARTHA (*sharply*): We were being fools. Now drink your coffee.

WARDEN (*slinking around the table to her*): At least one more kiss, Martha. The second and last one in twenty years.

MARTHA (*dryly*): It would just be a wet sound to me now, Harry.

WARDEN: But not to me.

MARTHA: Your kiss would mean nothing but that I had to breathe through my nose for its duration.

WARDEN: And if I don't, I'll never breathe properly again. I feel as if I'm being sealed away forever in a very small hall closet.

MARTHA: And no matter what you do, I'll always be on the other side of the door. You won't even be near me, Harry.

WARDEN (*like a painful prayer*): Oh, just this once let those damned chemical engineers look the other way! (*He begins kissing* MARTHA's *neck passionately while she remains immobile. After a second,* PHILLIP, *his black hood over his head, enters. His voice, because of the mask, is somewhat muffled.*)

PHILLIP: And just what is this going on? (MARTHA *utters a cry and jumps back from the* WARDEN. *He turns around and is equally upset by what he sees.*)

WARDEN: Good God!

PHILLIP (*moving toward them*): I'll ask again: what were you two doing?

WARDEN (*catching his breath and paying no attention to the question*): Do you know how ridiculously ferocious you look? Your creeping in like that's sent a chill through me all the way down to my feet.

PHILLIP: Your feet? What do I care about your feet? You were kissing my wife.

WARDEN: What? That thing's covering your mouth and making it very hard to follow what you're excited about.

PHILLIP (*taking off the hood*): I *say* you were kissing my wife!

WARDEN: It's not very well-mannered to come right out and say it that way, but I suppose I was.

PHILLIP: While I was upstairs, trying to adjust this hood so you'd see it to its best advantage, you were making love to my wife. You, the Warden of the prison, who, in less than half an hour will be raising a solemn forefinger and signaling me to hang a man—you were making love to my wife in my own kitchen.

WARDEN (*really confused by all the fuss*): Man to man, Phillip, I apologize. These things happen all the time—a little slip that sets one in the bushes alongside somebody you've no business being in the bushes with. Yes, it's an unfortunate, uh, occurrence, and, as I said, I *do* apologize for it.

PHILLIP (*somewhat stunned*): Apologize? Oh, no, please don't do that. I—I couldn't accept. I don't *want* to accept.

WARDEN: Now, Phillip, I understand how you feel. I've found my wife in much more than an embrace with a plumber. He was covered with grease, too, and had . . .

PHILLIP: Oh, no, it's not that at all. I was a little shocked just now and perhaps I did sound like a predictable husband. It just seemed that, under the circumstances, bellowing was expected of me.

WARDEN: I'm not following.

PHILLIP: It's simply that, while I was in my room, I was thinking what a failure I'd be in the hood. I was thinking, Harry, that the only thing that would save me would be to turn tail on this house, this uniform, this prison—everything that keeps me jogging along in step with the rest of you. So, Harry, friend and lover of my wife, I almost opened the window, slithered down the drainpipe and slipped out of your sight forever. I was going to run away—are you listening too, Martha?—run away and find out just where those men I've been dropping through gallows' doors come from.

WARDEN: Phillip, call me names, knock me down if you want to, but don't psychoanalyze yourself in public this way. At least not while you're in uniform.

PHILLIP: Let me just say that it was my old, well-trained conscience that kept me off the drainpipe. I thought of you two, standing firm on this dreary morning, washing your misery down with coffee, keeping to the rules of the game, and I bowed my head, covered it with the hood, and came downstairs ready to go on as Phillip, the old executioner. But now, now that you two have kicked up your heels a little bit, I see no reason why I shouldn't follow suit. You don't know how long I've waited to find a crack in the wall that being Martha's husband has built around me. But now that I see it's there, I'm going through it and down the drainpipe without a regret.

WARDEN: Phillip, this is all impossible, you know that, don't you?

PHILLIP: No more so than my finding you wrapped around my wife is impossible. If you two, at breakfast time, can stomach each other to the point of embracing, then I don't see how the line of impossibility can be drawn anywhere.

WARDEN: And just who, in all honesty, is responsible for this embrace?

PHILLIP (*looking at* MARTHA, *who, during the foregoing, has folded her arms and kept her back to both of her champions*): Who, indeed?

WARDEN: You, yourself. You with your black hood, your Swedish lessons, your scattered slippers, and your brooding in the corner. You sent her into my arms, Phillip.

PHILLIP (*smiling at* MARTHA *who doesn't respond*): So you did notice these things.

WARDEN: Of course she has; and that's why what happened happened. It explains . . .

PHILLIP: At five-thirty in the morning it doesn't explain . . .

WARDEN (*raising his arm for silence*): No! No! I am now speaking in my official capacity and I don't want to be interrupted by subordinates. (*The* WARDEN *takes the deep breath of one preparing for platitudes.*) Life, Phillip, is like a long sea voyage—the comparison's an old but apt one. We begin by deciding whether we favor temperate, tropic, or arctic waters. We decide what ports to put into with proper ceremony and what savage islands to sell trinkets and contract diseases on. We select the style of ship and the type of crew that suits us; and if one turns out to have a few leaks hidden in its bottom and the other to be bad-breathed and mutinous, we don't let that force us to drift off course. For, Phillip, staying within the latitudes and longitudes we've marked out for ourselves is all that matters. There can be no floating about to take closer looks at a curvaceous coast line or a sensual horizon. There can be no seeking out restful doldrums when your nerves get a bit frayed

or poking about for a good typhoon when calm seas prove somewhat tedious. No, we keep to the prescribed path, and when other ships plow past us, flaunting well-laundered sails—well, we scrub ours up too, send everyone with scurvy out of sight, keep a good mile of sea water between us and our short-lived neighbors, and leave them with the impression of nothing but that we're occupying the exact bit of ocean marked out for us. But you, Phillip, you just weren't sticking to the chart. You were sailing into harbors that weren't even marked on the maps of your second-in-command; you were tossing sensible and costly cargo overboard to make room for unmarketable baubles; you were tilting the compass to suit yourself. Now, is there any wonder, as you were approaching the dangerous waters of middle age, that Martha should lower a dinghy over the side and paddle her way to a vessel that looked, at least from a distance, to be completely shipshape? And, of course, having a good set of sea manners and seeing your wife bobbing next to me, I took her aboard, gave her, so to speak, a change of dry clothes and am now ready to return her to your schooner which, I'm sure, will be polished up and made ready for inspection. And if you don't want her to think she has to abandon ship again, tighten the hatches, throw out your World's Fair socks; secure the rigging, don't use slippers for ash trays; scrub the decks, go to club dances; check your compass hourly, burn that revolting black hood; and, finally, appear at today's execution as if you knew what your coordinates as the state's official hangman were. For remember, Phillip, no matter how attractive you find the mermaids or the rocks they wrap their appealing green tails around, the important thing is to keep sailing on course. Take that as an old captain's advice—just keep sailing on course. (*The* WARDEN, *who during the speech has edged his way to the door, exits through it.*)

PHILLIP (*running to the door after him*): That's the same speech you gave at the club's Christmas dinner last year and the summer picnic the year before! Well, you old pirate, you'd better get your ship's lifeboats ready because there isn't going to be a hanging today. Do you hear? The person you thought you temporarily rescued is now your permanent passenger. I resign! From everything! I resign! (PHILLIP *pauses for a moment, comes back into the center of the kitchen, looks at his hood, then at* MARTHA, *and laughs softly.*) I'll have to admit you surprised me, Martha. It was pleasant, but a surprise nevertheless. (*Silence.*) Well, don't you have anything to say? After all, I just said I was leaving you.

MARTHA (*disinterested*): If you're not going to touch breakfast, I'll put the dishes away.

PHILLIP (*relieved*): Oh, I thought after twenty years of marriage that a little piece of flesh had begun to sprout, connecting us together like Siamese twins. You don't know how upset I was by the idea. And now, Martha, you've shown me that it's nothing but a flimsy band-aid—nothing more.

MARTHA (*beginning to remove the dishes and wash them*): A band-aid?

PHILLIP (*with real admiration in his eyes*): One that you had the courage to tear off. Oh, if I'd only known how simple it would be. There I was, trying to sneak into a black hood and leave little hints about the house.

MARTHA: Hints at what?

PHILLIP: Hints that I was unhappy; that I thought I'd become little more than the brass and flannel of my uniform; that I wanted to run away from everything that I was and had been. It never occurred to me that you might feel the same way. But then, seeing you pressed up against the Warden—well, Martha, I confess I underestimated you.

MARTHA: And are you planning now to go out and make love to the Warden's wife?

PHILLIP: Oh, no. I'm going to leave you and this little piece of the world forever. I'm going to become—to become . . .

MARTHA (*sharply*): What?

PHILLIP (*a visionary smile*): To become—to become something like those fellows I've been hanging in the last few months. Do you know, Martha, there's a light in their eyes, a pulse behind their ear that beats faster than mine, and an interest in the weather that makes me envy them. Oh, they're frightened all right, but it's a healthy fear—something I don't think I would ever have had.

MARTHA: As the Warden said, they've just left those official ladies. Maybe if you didn't read all night in bed we could . . .

PHILLIP: Oh, no, Martha. I need a complete and total break.

MARTHA: And when do you plan to start breaking?

PHILLIP: In the past a step like this would have meant travel folders, reservations, exact calculations down to the dollar. But now, Martha, I'm not even going to bother to pack. I'm walking straight out the door without a glance over my shoulder.

MARTHA (*holding out a plate to him*): Will you help dry first?

PHILLIP (*abstracted but pleasant*): What? Oh, certainly. (*Towel and plate in hand, he goes back to his vision.*) First, I'm going to a tailor. I'm going to have him make me something for every mood I'm going to try —silk vests, lace collars, green tweeds for reflective moments . . .

MARTHA (*handing him another dish*): Tweeds always make you break out in a rash.

PHILLIP (*thinking for a moment, he takes the new plate and stacks the old one*): That's true. Well, perhaps, I'll give up reflection —there won't be much time for it, I hope, anyway.

MARTHA: And after the tailor, then what?

PHILLIP: Ah, I want to go where the climate's very hot; where it steams, as a matter of fact; where oversized plants seem to couple with one another before your eyes and produce offspring so colorful that they look indecent.

MARTHA (*now a cup in her hand*): You never liked me to wear loud clothes: always gray, black, and brown.

PHILLIP (*taking the cup*): No offense, but you're just not a tropical plant, Martha.

MARTHA: It wasn't me who had to have an air-conditioner last summer. Put the cup face down, Phillip.

PHILLIP (*he does so and receives a bowl in its place*): Now I want the heat to prevent anything from taking on too solid and sensible a shape. I want everything about me to shimmer, sway, and change in a second's time as if it were all one big sleight-of-hand trick. People, too, should melt and harden in front of you. (*He starts to put the bowl away.*)

MARTHA: That still looks wet to me.

PHILLIP (*retrieving the bowl*): And, Martha, there might be mirages. Can you imagine, scenes floating about purely for your own amusement. Do you know, I think I've wanted to see a mirage for the last ten years.

MARTHA: You're getting water on your trousers, Phillip. (*She opens a cupboard and takes out an apron.*) Here, put this on.

PHILLIP (*getting into the apron*): I used to try to force a mirage on myself. On days like today, when I'd see the man I was to hang being escorted toward me, I used to widen my eyes, clench my fists, and try to make my brain turn the entire scene into something else. It never worked, though: my eyes would begin to water and soon I was receiving reprimands from my superiors for what they took to be my emotional attitude while on duty.

MARTHA (*handing PHILLIP the last dish*): All you want, then, is to see mirages?

PHILLIP: I want my pores to open and let out of me all the bubbling perspiration that's been stopped up by the civil service code. Think of it, Martha! Me, in the middle of a jungle, where everything's raw and fresh, where only the hungry and alive do the executing, where . . .

MARTHA: I think some grounds are still in the coffee pot.

PHILLIP (*giving the pot another rinse*): And then, Martha, once I've filled my lungs with that wild air—well, then I'll be ready to— to . . .

MARTHA: To what, Phillip?

PHILLIP (*modestly, with some embarrassment*): Oh, grow a beard perhaps.

MARTHA: All this trouble just to avoid shaving?

PHILLIP: No, what I mean is, once .I've finally shed this old skin, I'll be ready to— to take up my old profession again with a fresh hand.

MARTHA: You mean after all that sweating in the tropics you'd still want to be an executioner?

PHILLIP (*soberly*): That is my profession, my trade, the only thing I can do passably well. (*Brightening.*) But, Martha, I won't be an official piece of cloth and brass, tying the knot around living necks because someone, somewhere, has underlined their names in red ink.

MARTHA (*as if humoring someone not too sound of mind*): You're going to do free-lance work?

PHILLIP (*slowly winding the dishtowel into a strangling cord*): I'm going to have an eye peeled for all the dead branches that need pruning—for all those who want to measure away the few wild patches of weeds left to us and turn the ground, teeming with savage centipedes, into a middle-income housing development.

MARTHA (*still indulging him*): And just how do you go about determining when a branch is dead?

PHILLIP (*moving about the kitchen table, towel in hand and eyes agleam*): Oh, that won't be hard, Martha. (*He begins circling the table, his eyes on the pepper mill as if stalking it.*) Just suppose I'm standing on a busy corner at lunchtime. Oh, there'll be a lot of dead wood about, but I'll find the one beyond the help of insecticides. I'll know him: perhaps I'll notice that his tie, socks, and handkerchief match; or perhaps I'll see he doesn't cross the street until the exact moment the light blinks in his favor. Oh, I'll know him as one of those who'll spend what energy he has trying to make tomorrow a line-for-line copy of yesterday; one of those who has a favorite chair, who sees no difference but age between the woman he married and the woman he keeps. (PHILLIP *pauses, narrows his eyes, and moves in on the pepper mill.*) He won't notice me, but I'll be behind him all the time. I'll watch him stuff himself with just the right calorie count; I'll smile as he leaves the proper tip and takes the long way back to his office to get in a little exercise; I'll peek around a corner as he tells an off-color joke to his secretary and pats her knee. And then, when he's alone in his office, about to balance another day's equation, I'll just tiptoe up behind him, hold the loop for a moment over his head, and then—snap! (*He catches the pepper mill in the towel's knot and lifts it up level with his eyes.*) There won't be any struggle or sound. He might have just enough curiosity to turn and see just who's doing him in, but the only thing I'd find in his eyes would be the gleam of one whose funeral arrangements were planned down to the last flower, tear, and comma in his epitaph. Already dead,

Martha, he'd be only too happy to lie down. (PHILLIP *lets the pepper mill drop to the floor*.)

MARTHA (*getting down to retrieve it*): That pepper mill was your birthday gift from my mother!

PHILLIP (*as if suddenly startled awake*): What?

MARTHA (*putting the object back on the kitchen table*): It must have cost twenty-five dollars. (*Sharply*.) Find something less expensive to play games with, Phillip.

PHILLIP (*hurt*): Games? Martha, I was trying to share a secret with you. For the first time in our marriage, I was telling you something I really felt.

MARTHA: Don't be open-hearted and frank with me, Phillip.

PHILLIP: But aren't you at least interested in what I'm really like?

MARTHA: If I was interested in what you were really like, I don't think I'd have stayed married to you for twenty years.

PHILLIP: But you might find me—well, exciting.

MARTHA (*coldly*): I've grown used to the lies, Phillip. They make up the comfortable husband I know.

PHILLIP (*realizing he's made a mistake in confiding in her*): Oh, I see. All right, then, you keep the comfortable husband! The new one, Martha, won't bother you any longer. No, he's simply going to close his eyes, turn around, and head straight through the door. (*As he speaks,* PHILLIP *performs the above gestures. As he is half-way to the door, however,* MARTHA *speaks up*.)

MARTHA: You'd better take off my apron first.

PHILLIP (*angry with himself for not having noticed it*): Oh, yes. How did I get into it in the first place?

MARTHA (*as if she were discussing a shopping list*): And another thing: I don't see how you can pick up and leave today, Phillip.

PHILLIP (*repeating the above gestures*): And why not, Martha? Why shouldn't I just close my eyes, turn around, and . . .

MARTHA: Because you have a dentist appointment first thing tomorrow morning.

PHILLIP (*turning about in confusion*): Dentist? Dentist?

MARTHA (*innocently*): You remember. The molar in the back has to come out? It's infecting the gum? Because of it you can't eat sweets?

PHILLIP: I don't want to eat sweets. I just . . .

MARTHA: We've been invited to my sister's for dinner Friday, and you know how partial you are to her chocolate mousse.

PHILLIP (*at last rather angry*): Damn the chocolate mousse! I'm not going to your sister's for dinner anyway.

MARTHA: I've already accepted. And with the weekend whirl coming up, I don't see how you can plan to leave before next Wednesday.

PHILLIP: Plan? Something like this can't be planned and put on schedule. I'm giving up knowing where and what I'll be a week, a day, or even an hour ahead. I'm going to be . . .

MARTHA (*again sharp and bitter*): A man-eating jungle plant—I know. Well, you'll have to wait until *after* my sister's dinner to start blooming. And by that time, there'll be other things popping up to detain you.

PHILLIP (*a little unnerved*): Martha, maybe you didn't understand or listen to what I was saying. I'm sweeping all the old laws, manners, and invitations under the rug. There's nothing here that can hold me now.

MARTHA: Oh, yes, there is—me.

PHILLIP: You? Martha, I don't want to be brutal, but if nothing else were pushing me through that door, you, in your breakfast face, would be all the reason I'd need.

MARTHA (*now in full attack*): Maybe my face won't charm you into bed, but you're going to look at it, speak to it, and—yes, even kiss it in a businesslike way every day of your life. Because, Phillip, covered with cold-cream or skin oil, it's the face of your wife. And "wife," Phillip, means a thousand obstacles for you to get over before you're free to start chopping down dead branches.

PHILLIP (*in the tones of family argument*): Wife? Hah! And were you my wife with the Warden pawing over you?

MARTHA: More than ever, Phillip. That little moment with him only reminded me how snug I was with you—even with your red socks under the sofa seat. My life depends on all the little functions you perform. You're like the telephone, electricity, or underground plumbing. My life takes you for granted, but would be lost without you. Maybe we're not held together by a little piece of flesh, but there is something there even harder to snip apart. It's the word "and" in "man _and_ wife." It's official and keeps us together through mistresses, dreams, bills, and burned toast. "Man _and_ wife"—that's our world, Phillip; and everything in it has long ago been discovered, named, and placed in its proper corner.

PHILLIP: No three-letter word's going to drag me after it. Not when I finally have the chance . . .

MARTHA: You _had_ the chance, Phillip. For the briefest second, when you caught the Warden and me, you had the chance. But no; you stayed and helped me with the dishes.

PHILLIP: That was just habit.

MARTHA: No, dear, that was the law of gravity yanking you right back to earth.

PHILLIP: Well, I'm breaking the law of gravity, Martha. From now on you'll have to find someone else to eat off and dry your dishes. The first day of creation is waiting for me on the other side of the kitchen door, and all the rules of marriage or physics aren't going to keep me from it. (_He starts for the door._)

MARTHA: Touch that door and you'll find out how unpleasant the truth about yourself can be.

PHILLIP: I have all the truth I need, Martha. Goodby. And if we ever meet again be careful I don't mistake you for a dead branch. (PHILLIP _makes to open the door, but finds it refuses to budge. He begins tugging at the knob._) It must be the dampness has made the wood swell.

MARTHA (_taunting_): You'll never get it open, Phillip. You know too well what's on the other side.

PHILLIP (_increasing his efforts_): It's not locked. There's no reason for it to be this stubborn.

MARTHA: You don't want to strain yourself, Phillip. Remember that awful rubber girdle you had to wear after cleaning out the attic last year.

PHILLIP (_more and more effort_): Shut up, Martha!

MARTHA: Ha! Don't yell at _me!_ You, I, and the door know on which side of it you belong.

PHILLIP (_losing all control_): I'll tear the damned thing off its hinges.

MARTHA: That door's the speed of light—a permanent boundary fence. It can't be broken.

PHILLIP (_now pounding on the door_): Open, damn you! Open!

MARTHA: It won't because you don't want it to. You know that all your jungle will give you is athlete's foot, diarrhea, and swollen joints.

PHILLIP (_turning from the door to_ MARTHA, _he pleads with desperation in his voice_): I'm going to tear down every kitchen door in the world. I'm going to strangle, murder . . .

MARTHA: You, murder? Hah! Come on, Phillip, the game's over. You're an official executioner, a little paunchy through the middle, with thinning hair and an obedient attitude. That's as close as you'll ever be to a murderer.

PHILLIP (_menacingly_): If that door doesn't open you'll be the first to know how wrong you are.

MARTHA (_with an incredulous smile_): Are you threatening me?

PHILLIP: If you're keeping me in this kitchen —yes!

MARTHA: Oh, poor, poor Phillip. Look at you: out of breath already and not even one step away from the house yet.

PHILLIP: I won't stand you laughing at me!

MARTHA: Then don't make jokes about doing me in. You're not on your gallows now; no twenty-five forms have been filled out in triplicate authorizing you to snap my neck. (_Shouting._) You're my husband! And that makes you the most harmless person in the world as far as _I'm_ concerned!

PHILLIP (_picking up the black hood from the kitchen table and beginning to knot it ominously_): For the last time: make the door open!

MARTHA: How can I, Phillip? You're the one who's keeping it shut. If you really wanted to leave, it would spring open like a hungry mouth.

PHILLIP (_stepping toward her_): Then I'll have to prove I'm in earnest, Martha.

MARTHA: Don't be an ass. One of the things that will make the rest of our life together tolerable is that you can keep your mind buzzing with plans to murder me. Don't try it now and find out you can't. It'll make you sour, bitter, and even more difficult to get new hats and dresses out of than you are now. (PHILLIP *begins testing the hood's strength and continues his advance.*)

MARTHA (*quite earnestly*): I'm warning you. With as much love as I can squeeze out of me after twenty years, I'm warning you not to do this to yourself.

PHILLIP: As the books say: there's no good reasoning with a murderer.

MARTHA (*throwing back the challenge*): All right, murderer, if you won't listen—(*She picks up one of the kitchen table chairs, places it downstage, facing the audience, and sits in it with her neck thrust out as if for a sacrifice.*) All right then, go ahead. Try and squeeze the air out of my windpipe. Just try it! Well, what are you waiting for, Bluebeard? Come on, let me feel some of your jungle sweat dripping down the back of my neck.

PHILLIP (*a little startled by MARTHA's action*): Are you just going to sit there as if you were having your hair done?

MARTHA: You'll have to supply the noise and screams, Phillip. I'm just going to sit here and talk.

PHILLIP: Talk? Then that's just the last bit of incentive I need. (*He knots the hood around MARTHA's neck and begins tightening.*)

MARTHA (*not affected at all by PHILLIP's attack*): Oh, you'll have to pull harder than that. I'm still getting in more than enough air to tell you that the ivy plants over our bed are all the jungle you'll ever know. (PHILLIP *gives an extra hard tug, and* MARTHA *starts, as if tickled.*) And it's your turn to water them next week. You'll take care of them every other week for as long as you're on this planet.

PHILLIP (*hopefully*): Is the blood beginning to pound in your head? Do you find it difficult to focus your eyes?

MARTHA: Hah! I've never felt better. This is the closest we've come to sex in years.

PHILLIP (*increasing his efforts*): And now, Martha, is your past popping up in front of you?

MARTHA: Only my future. And you, Phillip, growing stooped, absent-minded, and a little sloppy at the table, are in every minute of it.

PHILLIP (*becoming frustrated*): You should at least be gagging now, damn it!

MARTHA (*sweetly*): I don't know how to gag. But I could cough a little if it would make things easier for you.

PHILLIP (*pleading*): Please stop breathing, Martha. Please, my arms are getting tired— please stop breathing.

MARTHA: At this rate, you'll stop before I will. Oh, what a story this will make at cards Saturday!

PHILLIP (*makes one last supreme effort, and then, with a groan, drops his hands*): I just can't do it. My wrists and fingers just aren't strong enough. (*He sits in one of the kitchen chairs.*) I can't even get out of the kitchen.

MARTHA (*rubbing her neck and rising from the chair*): I told you, Phillip, but you wouldn't listen, would you? Now look at you—panting and overheated. (*She takes the hood and begins mopping his brow.*) And you have to go out right away. I'm sure this will mean a cold by tomorrow.

PHILLIP (*docilely*): Go out?

MARTHA: There's not fifteen minutes till the execution begins. There now, that's the best I can do. (*She takes PHILLIP's coat and holds it out for him.*) All right, come on, get into this. If you keep all the buttons closed there's still a chance I won't have to spend a fortune on nose drops and cough syrup.

PHILLIP: So the execution's going to take place after all?

MARTHA (*buttoning up the coat*): Of course it is; and you're going to be on those gallows, stiff and tall, the way I, the Warden, and the man you're going to hang expect you to be. The whole thing will go very smoothly now, won't it?

PHILLIP: I suppose it will.

MARTHA (*finishing the buttoning, she steps back to admire her work*): There! Now you look like my husband and the state's official executioner. You can tell at a glance that you're a fish in the right waters now.

PHILLIP: I guess you can.

MARTHA (*picking up PHILLIP's cap*): Now,

don't be so gloomy. Look on the bright side of everything to come. Think of the certificate of merit and pension bonus you'll receive when you successfully hang your thousandth man. Think of the speeches you'll be asked to give to college students on the fine prose in the penal code. Think of the jokes you'll tell at your retirement dinner and the little cottage our insurance policy's going to give us. Think how peaceful things will be when you're certain that there's only one world and one way to live in it.

PHILLIP: Will that come with the retirement policy too?

MARTHA (*putting the cap on his head*): It just might, Phillip. It just might. And now, you're complete; not a wrinkle in you. (*She takes his arm and starts to lead him toward the door.*)

PHILLIP: My hood? Can I at least have that?

MARTHA: I'll put it under the sofa with your socks. And, on holidays, you can take them, your banjo, and the other things out to look at for a while. And on New Year's Eve, you can even sit on the floor and flip ashes into your slippers if you want to.

PHILLIP: I think I'll go back to my chair. The floor's very hard.

MARTHA: That *is* more sensible, I suppose.

(*They reach the door.*) Well, come on now. Out you go.

PHILLIP: But it won't open.

MARTHA (*she touches the door knob ever so lightly with the tips of her fingers and it springs open*): There's nothing holding it shut now.

PHILLIP (*taking a step toward the opening*): It is very cold this morning.

MARTHA: Do you have a handkerchief with you?

PHILLIP (*feeling his pocket*): Yes.

MARTHA: Well, then, you'd better be off.

PHILLIP (*turning toward* MARTHA): Martha, I just wanted to be . . .

MARTHA: But you couldn't, Phillip. Some things just can't be broken. So you'd better just try to keep warm out there and forget all about it. Now, kiss me goodby.

PHILLIP: But isn't there any chance for me at all?

MARTHA (*in a command voice and pointing to her cheek*): Kiss! (PHILLIP *does so, and then slowly turns and leaves.* MARTHA *waits for a moment and then calls out to him.*) Keep bundled up, dear. Don't work too hard. And tonight—tonight we'll have something very special for dinner. Something you really like, dear, something you really, really like. (**Curtain.**)

INCIDENT AT TWILIGHT

Friedrich Dürrenmatt

TRANSLATED BY
George E. Wellwarth

CHARACTERS

THE AUTHOR
A VISITOR
THE SECRETARY
YOUNG WOMAN
SECOND YOUNG WOMAN
THE HOTEL MANAGER

THE AUTHOR [this speech can be treated simply as a stage direction, or it can be read as a series of marginal comments]: Ladies and gentlemen, I consider it my duty, at the very outset, to describe to you the setting of this possibly somewhat peculiar but, I assure you, entirely true story. To be sure, there is a considerable element of danger in telling true stories—someone from the police or possibly even the district attorney might be among those present, even though they might not be here in their official capacity. Nonetheless I can allow myself to take the risk because I know perfectly well they won't believe my true story—at least not in their official capacity. In reality— that is to say, *un*officially—all of you of course, including the district attorney or policeman who may or may not be among us, know very well that I *only* tell true stories—scout's honor! Well then: might I ask you to concentrate for a moment? Imagine yourselves in the drawing room of a Grand Hotel suite—the kind where the bill will look as if it had been added up by highwaymen. Modern furnishings. Looks as if it's meant to be lived in. Get the picture? On your left (just close your eyes and you'll see the room distinctly—don't get discouraged, now; you've got imagination just like everyone else, even if you don't think so), on your left you can see a number of assorted tables, all pushed together every which way. Are you interested in taking a look at an author's study? Very well then, step up a little closer. Disappointing, isn't it? But believe me, it's true—even studies where *minor* authors work can look something like this. Piles of papers, a typewriter, manuscripts covered with closely written corrections in various colors, pencils, ballpoint pens, erasers, a large pair of scissors. Glue. A dagger—hmm. Oh well, that got there by mistake. . . . (*He clears his throat.*) Back of this mess there's a small improvised bar—brandy, whisky, absinthe, red wine, and so forth. That doesn't tell us anything about the quality, the genius, or the greatness of the author we're dealing with here either. Doesn't tell us anything to his advantage, but then, on the other hand, it doesn't tell us anything to his disadvantage either. However, you can reassure yourselves, ladies and gentlemen: on the right side of the room you'll find everything neatly in place. Well, almost everything anyway—I'll just get rid of this—er—well, this piece of female clothing—just throw it in the corner here and—oh, yes!—might as well put this revolver away in the desk drawer. Large, soft, comfortable sofas made to the latest designs, books scattered all over the place; on the walls you can see photographs and paintings of—well, I'm sure you'll be able to figure that out for yourselves. The nicest thing, though, is the background to the whole thing. A large, open door, a balcony, an enchanting view (quite in accordance with the price charged), a sunlit lake which was covered only a few weeks ago with red and white sails but is smooth as deep blue glass now. Behind that, hills, woods, and the foothills of the mountains. Twilight, the lake shore deserted—all in all, a late autumn orgy of red and yellow. Ah, there's still a little life on the tennis courts, and you can hear the tick-tock of the ping-pong players. Do you hear it? All right, let's come back into the room and take a look at the two leading characters of our play. Let's start with me— oh yes, you heard right: *me. I'm* one of the leading characters. I'm sorry about it, really, but that's the way it is. All the same, I'll try not to startle you by appearing to you too suddenly. I'll just saunter unobtrusively into the room from the right—I'll be coming from the bedroom, where I've obviously been—oh well, never mind, it's nobody's business really what I've been up to in there. It'll all be written up in certain newspapers, anyway; in the evening paper or in the tabloids—after all, what is there about me that you *can't* read in certain newspapers? My life is a mess—confused, crazy, full of one scandal after another. There's no point in denying it—all I have to tell you is my name and you'll have it in a nutshell: Korbes. Yes, indeed, you heard right once again! I am Maximilian Frederick Korbes, novelist, Nobel Prize-winner, etc., etc.— portly, suntanned, and unshaven—all topped off with a big bald head. As far as my personal characteristics are concerned, I'm brutal, I get what I want, and I'm a hard drinker. You see I'm honest with you, even if I'm just summing up the general impression everyone has of me anyway.

Maybe it's true, that general impression; and maybe I really am the way I've described myself to you—exactly the way, ladies and gentlemen, you know me through the picture papers and the newsreels. The Queen of Sweden, at any rate (on the occasion of the presentation of the aforementioned Nobel Prize) was of the opinion that I fitted the description exactly. Rather strange, too, because I was all dressed up in white tie and tails at the time. To be sure, though, I did manage to spill a glass of Bordeaux on the royal evening gown—quite by mistake, of course. Still, who knows anyone, least of all himself? There's no point in kidding oneself. I, at any rate, know myself only fleetingly. And no wonder. The opportunities for getting to know oneself are few and far between. In my case, for instance, one of them occurred while I was zooming down a sheet of ice on Mount Kilimanjaro, another at the moment I was being cracked over the head by the well-known, er—oh well, you know whom I mean—a real "Gothic Madonna"!—no, not the one in the bedroom next door—some other one. Hmm, well, that's something you can imagine for yourselves, and pleasant dreams to you while you're at it, too! And now a word about my clothes. Here, too, I must apologize, above all to the ladies in the audience. I've got pajama bottoms on and an open dressing gown, through which my chest, covered with white hair, is dimly visible. None of this can be concealed, I'm afraid. In my hand: an empty glass. I'm on my way to the bar, but I stop short when I observe that a visitor seems to have found his way into my study. The fellow is soon described. Small, thin, very middle class, carries a brief case under his arm, looks a bit like an old traveling insurance salesman. There's really no need to describe him more closely in view of the fact that he will be removed from the scene of action in a perfectly natural manner once our story has run its course—and consequently will then be of no more interest. But that's enough for now. The visitor begins to speak. We're ready to start.

THE VISITOR (*nervously*): I feel honored to find myself in the presence of the world-famous writer Maximilian Frederick Korbes. . . .

AUTHOR (*roughly*): What the devil are you doing in my study?

VISITOR: Your secretary let me in. I've been waiting over an hour.

AUTHOR (*after a short pause, somewhat more mildly*): Who are you?

VISITOR: My name is Hofer. Feargod Hofer.

AUTHOR (*suspiciously*): That sounds vaguely familiar. (*Remembers suddenly.*) Oh, you're the fellow who's been bombarding me with letters!

VISITOR: Quite correct. Ever since you've been taking the baths here. Besides that, I've had a chat with the doorman every morning. Not that that did me any good! Finally I managed to ambush your secretary. A very severe young man.

AUTHOR: Theology student. Poor as a church mouse. Working his way through seminary.

VISITOR: It was only my unwavering persistence that convinced him finally this meeting would be of the greatest significance for *both* of us, honored master.

AUTHOR: Korbes is the name. You can skip that "honored master" stuff.

VISITOR: Honored Mr. Korbes.

AUTHOR: Since you're nearer the bar, you might just pass me the whisky bottle—it's the one on the far left.

VISITOR: Certainly.

AUTHOR: Thank you. (*He pours.*) Care for one yourself?

VISITOR: I'd rather not, thank you.

AUTHOR: Absinthe? Campari? Something else?

VISITOR: No, thanks.

AUTHOR (*distrustfully*): You a teetotaler?

VISITOR: No, just careful. I am, after all, in the presence of a mental giant. I feel a little like St. George just before his fight with the dragon.

AUTHOR: Catholic?

VISITOR: Evangelical.

AUTHOR: I need another drink.

VISITOR: You ought to take care of yourself.

AUTHOR (*harshly*): You can keep your advice to yourself.

VISITOR: I'm from Switzerland, Mr. Korbes. May I take a closer look at the room in which the poet creates his works?

AUTHOR: Writer.

VISITOR: In which the writer creates his

works? Ah, books and manuscripts everywhere. May I take a look at the photographs on the wall? Faulkner. Personally inscribed: To my dear Korbes. Thomas Mann: To Korbes, with admiration and respect—Thomas. Hemingway: To Korbes, my best friend—as ever, Ernest. Henry Miller: To my soul mate, Korbes. It's only in love and in murder that we still remain sincere. And now the view. What a superb sight—the lake with the mountains behind it and the ever-changing clouds above it! And the sun just going down. Glowing red. Impressive.

AUTHOR (*suspiciously*): You write too, eh?

VISITOR: I read. Know your complete works by heart.

AUTHOR: Teacher?

VISITOR: Bookkeeper. Retired. Used to work for Oechsli, Trost, and Co. in Ennetwyl, near Horck.

AUTHOR: Have a seat.

VISITOR: Thanks very much. I'm a little scared of these ultramodern chairs. A very luxurious apartment.

AUTHOR: They charge enough for it.

VISITOR: I can imagine. This is an expensive spa. Absolutely catastrophic for my means, even though I live in the cheapest possible manner at the Seaview Rooming House. (*He sighs.*) It was cheaper in Adelboden.

AUTHOR: In Adelboden?

VISITOR: In Adelboden.

AUTHOR: I was in Adelboden too.

VISITOR: You were at the Grand Hotel Wildstrubel there; I was in the Pro Senectute Rest Home. Our paths have crossed several times. For example, at the ski lift in St. Moritz and on the Promenade in Baden-Baden.

AUTHOR: You were in Baden-Baden too?

VISITOR: I was.

AUTHOR: At the same time I was there?

VISITOR: At the Siloah Home for Christian Men.

AUTHOR (*impatiently*): I have to schedule my time pretty closely. I have to keep working like a slave, Mr. . . . ?

VISITOR: Feargod Hofer.

AUTHOR: Mr. Feargod Hofer. I have to deal with hundreds of thousands of people in my lifetime, and so I can only spare a quarter of an hour for you. Tell me what you want, and make it short.

VISITOR: I've come with a very definite purpose in mind.

AUTHOR (*getting up*): You want money, eh? I have none to spare for just anybody that comes along. There's such an enormous number of people who are not writers and who are perfectly easy marks, that I wish people would leave members of my profession in peace. Besides, the amount of the Nobel Prize is greatly exaggerated, anyway. And now, if you please, we'll say good-by.

VISITOR (*getting up*): Honored master . . .

AUTHOR: Korbes is the name.

VISITOR: Honored Mr. Korbes . . .

AUTHOR: Get out of here!

VISITOR (*in despair*): You misunderstand me. I didn't come to you because I need money, but because—(*determinedly*)—because ever since I retired I have been employed in detective work.

AUTHOR (*with a sigh of relief*): Oh, I see. That's a different matter altogether. Let's take a seat again. This is a great relief for me. Well then, so you're employed by the police now?

VISITOR: No, honored . . .

AUTHOR: Korbes is the name.

VISITOR: Honored Mr. Korbes. I'm a private detective. Even when I was still a bookkeeper there were all sorts of things that I uncovered. I was honorary auditor for several companies. Yes, indeed!—I even succeeded in having the town treasurer of Ennetwyl sent to jail for embezzling the orphanage funds. And so, when I had retired and the savings of a lifetime were at my disposal, my wife having died childless, I made up my mind, under the influence of your books, to devote myself entirely to my hobby.

AUTHOR: My books?

VISITOR: Your immortal books! They kindled my imagination. I read them with feverish suspense, absolutely overcome by the magnificence of the crimes you wrote about. I became a detective somewhat the way a person in the religious field, inspired by the masterful way in which the devil does his work, might become a priest, even though everything he might do calls forth an equally powerful reaction. And now, Good Heavens!—here I am sitting next to a Nobel Prize-winner, the sun going down behind the mountains, and you drinking whisky. . . .

AUTHOR: You have poetic inclinations, my dear Feargod Hofer.

VISITOR: Entirely due to reading your books.

AUTHOR: I'm sorry to hear it. You're wearing rather cheap clothes. Your new profession doesn't seem to have turned out very well for you.

VISITOR: It's true that life isn't exactly a bed of roses.

AUTHOR: The local district attorney is a friend of mine. I'll put in a good word for you with him. What particular branch of criminology are you specializing in? Espionage? Divorce? Narcotics? The white-slave traffic?

VISITOR: Literature!

AUTHOR (*getting up*): In that case, I must ask you for the second time to leave this room at once!

VISITOR (*getting up*): Honored sir!

AUTHOR: You have become a critic!

VISITOR: If you would only permit me to explain . . .

AUTHOR: Get out!

VISITOR (*in despair*): But I've only analyzed your works with respect to their *criminological* aspect.

AUTHOR (*calming down*): Oh, I see. In that case you can stay. Be seated.

VISITOR: Thank you.

AUTHOR: I have been interpreted from psychoanalytic, Catholic, Protestant, existential, Buddhist, and Marxist viewpoints, but never from the viewpoint which you have adopted.

VISITOR: I owe you an explanation, honored master . . .

AUTHOR: Korbes is the name.

VISITOR: Honored Mr. Korbes. I read your works because of a certain theory which I had formed. Whatever exists in the world of fiction—in your novels—must also exist in reality, because it seems to me impossible to invent something which does not exist somewhere in reality.

AUTHOR (*hesitantly*): A fairly reasonable conclusion.

VISITOR: As a result of this conclusion I began to look *in real life* for the murders described in your novels.

AUTHOR (*electrified*): You assumed that there was some sort of connection between my novels and reality?

VISITOR: Exactly. I proceeded to use razor-sharp logic. First I subjected your work to a searching analysis. You are not only the most notorious and newsworthy writer of our time, a man whose divorces, love affairs, alcoholic excesses, and tiger hunts are written up in all the newspapers and scandal sheets—you are also known as the creator of the most beautiful murder scenes in world literature.

AUTHOR: I have never glorified murder *per se*. I have always tried to show man as a whole. Part of that whole, of course, is the fact that he is capable of committing murder.

VISITOR: Speaking as a detective, I was not interested so much in what you tried to do as in what in fact you did do. Before you, murder was universally considered something horrible, but you have managed to bring magnificence and beauty even to this dark side of life—or, rather, of death. You are universally known as "Old Sudden Death and Homicide."

AUTHOR: That's just a mark of my popularity.

VISITOR: And of your skill in creating genuine master murderers whose identity no one can even guess at.

AUTHOR (*curiously*): You're referring to my—idiosyncrasy—of letting the criminal escape unmasked?

VISITOR: Exactly!

AUTHOR: Hmm! In other words, you read my novels as if they were police reports.

VISITOR: As if they were homicide reports. Your heroes murder neither for profit nor because of thwarted passion. They murder for psychological gratification, for pleasure, to display their skill, or to increase their range of experience—all of them motives not recognized by traditional criminological theory. You are quite literally too deep, too subtle for the police or the district attorney. Consequently they don't even suspect that a murder has been committed since as far as they are concerned, where there is no motive there is no crime. If one assumes, then, that the murders which you describe *really* took place, it follows that they must have appeared to the public to be suicides, accidents, or even natural deaths.

AUTHOR: Yes, that follows—logically speaking.

VISITOR: Exactly what they appear to be to the people in your novels.

AUTHOR: Exactly.

VISITOR: At this point in my investigations I seemed to myself to be somewhat like that Spanish knight—what's-his-name . . . Don—

AUTHOR: Don Quixote.

VISITOR: Don Quixote, whom you frequently mention in your novels. He sallied forth as he did because he took the knightly romances for reality; and I determined to take your novels for reality. But *I* did not let myself become frightened off by anything. My motto has always been "Forward!—even though the world be full of devils!"

AUTHOR (*enraptured*): Marvelous! What you've undertaken is absolutely marvelous! (*He rings.*) Sebastian! Sebastian!

SECRETARY (*enters*): Sir?

AUTHOR: We'll have to work all night. Offer Mr. Hofer a cigar. Surely there must be something we can give him a little pleasure with. Brazil? Havana?

VISITOR: No, no, no. I'll smoke one of my own if you don't mind.

AUTHOR: Certainly, certainly. You can go now, Sebastian, and take this dagger with you. I don't need it right now, after all.

SECRETARY: Certainly, honored master. (*Exits.*)

VISITOR: A beautiful piece! I noticed it some time ago, honored . . .

AUTHOR: Korbes is the name.

VISITOR: Honored Mr. Korbes. One push— and somebody's dead. It's extremely well honed.

AUTHOR: A light?

VISITOR: Nothing I enjoy so much as a good smoke.

AUTHOR: Enjoy it, my dear Hofer, enjoy it. But above all, do go on with your story.

VISITOR: It wasn't easy for me to arrive at a solution. I was obliged to perform some extremely detailed analysis. First I sifted through your novel *Rendezvous Abroad*.

AUTHOR: My first novel.

VISITOR: Published eleven years ago.

AUTHOR: Awarded the Bolling Prize and made into a movie by Hitchcock.

VISITOR: All I can say about it is, "What an achievement!" A French adventurer—fat, tanned, unshaven, with a big, bald head; dissipated, gifted, and a hard drinker— meets a woman, the wife of a German diplomat. Extraordinarily delicate way he has of expressing himself! He entices her to go with him to a run-down hotel in Ankara, a filthy hellhole of the worst sort, where he seduces her. Then, talking through his alcoholic haze like a Homer, a Shakespeare, he convinces her that the highest happiness is in a suicide pact. She believes in the passion that she's experiencing, hypnotized by his outbursts—and kills herself in a sexual ecstasy. But he doesn't kill himself. No, indeed!—he just lights up a cigarette and walks out. Then he takes a stroll through the slums, beats up a preacher of the Christian Mission to the Turks, robs its poor box, and makes off for Persia as the dawn comes up. There he goes prospecting for oil. Possibly the *Swiss Review of Books* is right in calling this a trivial plot. Nonetheless, it leaves Hemingway miles behind in brevity and conciseness.

AUTHOR (*amused*): Surely you're not going to tell me that you took your investigations all the way to Turkey in order to verify this story, my dear Hofer?

VISITOR: I had no alternative. I went to considerable expense to obtain the Ankara newspapers for 1954, the year in which your novel takes place, and got a Turkish exchange student at the Federal Technological Institute to go through them for me.

AUTHOR: And the result?

VISITOR: It was the wife of a Swedish diplomat rather than a German who committed suicide. A blond, somewhat reserved beauty, she was found in a hotel of the worst type. No reason for the suicide was discovered, precisely as I predicted.

AUTHOR: And the man with whom she went to this—er, hotel?

VISITOR: Unknown. The evidence of the desk clerk, however, indicates that we're dealing here with a German-speaking individual. I have also established that one of the preachers of the Christian Mission to the Turks was indeed beaten up. He was, however, injured too badly to give any evidence about his assailant. After this I examined *Mr. X Is Bored*.

AUTHOR: Churchill's favorite novel.

VISITOR: Your second book. A masterpiece.

Mr. X, formerly a good-for-nothing, but now an established and popular writer, moderator of the American Pen Club, meets a sixteen-year-old girl in St. Tropez. He is enchanted by her beauty and simplicity. The intensity of nature, the reflection of the sea, the merciless sun—all combine to bring out his primitive instincts. The result: rape and murder in the pouring rain of a tremendous thunderstorm. Surely the most beautiful and at the same time most horrible pages ever written. The dialogue seems merely sketched out but is actually as clear and precise as can be. Then there's the description of the police procedure—the motorcycles, the radio cars with their screaming sirens, the hunt for the killer, and the suspects, who seem to include everyone except the actual murderer—he's too famous and too admired to arouse the slightest suspicion. On the contrary: before he leaves for London in order to accept the Lord Byron Prize, Mr. X attends the funeral, with a description of which the book ends like an ancient Greek tragedy.

AUTHOR (*smiling*): Your powerful imagination is getting the better of you, my dear Hofer.

VISITOR (*insistently*): Ten years ago—in 1957—a sixteen-year-old English girl was raped and murdered in St. Tropez.

AUTHOR: And the murderer?

VISITOR: Unknown.

AUTHOR: Just like the Swedish woman's murderer, eh?

VISITOR: Exactly so—(*hesitating*)—despite an extremely efficient police force.

AUTHOR (*proudly*): Exactly so.

VISITOR: The authorities don't have the slightest clue.

AUTHOR: Did you make any further discoveries?

VISITOR: If you would be so good as to glance at this piece of paper—it is a list of all the people whose connection with characters in your novels I have established.

AUTHOR: There are—let me see—twenty-two names on this list.

VISITOR: Precisely the number of novels you have written.

AUTHOR: All of these people are dead?

VISITOR: Some of them committed suicide; some of them died because of unexpected accidents—with the exception of the young English girl who was raped and murdered, of course.

AUTHOR: Why is there a question mark next to the name of the Argentinian millionairess Juana?

VISITOR: She corresponds to Mercedes, who is strangled by the hero of your novel *Evil Nights*. As a matter of fact, however, the multimillionairess died in Ostend of natural causes.

AUTHOR: Hmm—this is a—very valuable list.

VISITOR: The result of ten years' criminological investigation. And that isn't all, either. Wherever these accidents and suicides occurred, you, my dear sir, were present.

AUTHOR (*somewhat like a schoolboy caught in the act*): Is that a fact?

VISITOR: You were in Ankara when the Swedish woman died, you were in St. Tropez when the English girl died, you were in all the twenty other places when the twenty other people on that list died. I need only mention the Parliamentary Secretary von Wattenwil in Davos, Countess Windischgrätz in Biarritz, Lord Liverpool in Split. . . .

AUTHOR: Everyone on this list, in other words.

VISITOR: Everyone.

AUTHOR: You've been on my track, eh, Mr. Hofer?

VISITOR: I *had* to follow your tracks if I was going to be a professional detective and not just a dilettante. From one resort to another, from one expensive spa to the next.

AUTHOR: So you were not merely in Adelboden and Baden-Baden with me?

VISITOR: Wherever you were, I was.

AUTHOR (*inquisitively*): Wasn't that extremely expensive for you?

VISITOR: Ruinously. Not to mention the fact that my means were extremely limited, my pension, considering the enormous profits of Oechsli, Trost, and Co., being laughably small. I had to economize, I had to deprive myself of things. Some of my trips, honored . . .

AUTHOR (*admonishingly*): Korbes is the name.

VISITOR: Thank you. Some of my trips literally meant starvation for me. The only one I wasn't able to swing at all was the one to South America seven years ago, and of course your annual excursions to the African or Indian jungle. . . .

AUTHOR: Quite unnecessary, my dear Hofer. I only hunt tigers and elephants there.

VISITOR: At all other times I stuck to you.

AUTHOR: That's beginning to be obvious.

VISITOR: And wherever we stayed—you in a five-star hotel, me in a shabby rooming house—an accident, which you later wrote up as a murder, occurred.

AUTHOR: My dear Hofer, you are the most remarkable man I have ever met.

VISITOR: The next question I was faced with —naturally!—concerned the manner in which this correspondence between your works and reality had come about.

AUTHOR: Naturally!

VISITOR: Two possibilities presented themselves to me after I had performed the necessary logical examination of the facts. Either you modeled your characters on people you had observed in real life, or your plots actually occurred in reality precisely the way you described them.

AUTHOR: Granted.

VISITOR (*portentously*): If we assume that this second theory is true, then your plots, which are universally admired as the products of your inexhaustible imagination, are nothing more nor less than factual accounts. I hesitated a long time before I permitted myself to subscribe to this theory, but now I know it is the only possible one. This brings up a new problem, however: if your novels are factual accounts, it follows that the murders you describe are also factual. And that brings us ineluctably to the question: who are the murderers?

AUTHOR: And what have you discovered?

VISITOR (*in a steely voice*): That we must look upon the various murderers as *one* murderer. All of your protagonists clearly possess characteristics common to *one* particular person. They are all powerful men with large bald heads, usually bare chested in the critical murder scene; larger than life in their gestures, they rush through the baroque sea of your prose in a permanent state of semi-intoxication. (*Pause.*) *You are the murderer!*

AUTHOR: In other words, you are saying that I have several times . . .

VISITOR: Twenty-one times.

AUTHOR: Twenty-two times.

VISITOR: Twenty-one times. The Argentinian multimillionairess constitutes an exception.

AUTHOR: All right, all right—you're saying, in other words, that I have murdered almost twenty-two people?

VISITOR: That is my firm and immovable conviction. I am in the presence not only of one of the foremost writers, but also of one of the foremost murderers of all time.

AUTHOR (*pensively*): Twenty-two . . .

VISITOR (*stubbornly*): Twenty-one times.

AUTHOR: Twenty-one times, then. When you hear a thing like that . . .

VISITOR: . . . it makes one think, honored master. (*Pause.*)

AUTHOR (*smiling*): Well now, what do you really want from me, my dear Feargod Hofer?

VISITOR: Now that I've told you the results of my researches, I can breathe again. I have often trembled at the thought of this moment, but I have not been disappointed. I see you calm and still amicably disposed to me, and would like to continue speaking with the same terrible frankness to you.

AUTHOR: By all means.

VISITOR: At first I only intended to hand you over to the forces of justice.

AUTHOR: And have you changed your mind?

VISITOR: I have, indeed.

AUTHOR: Why?

VISITOR: I have been observing you now for ten years. I have seen how masterfully you have pursued your passion, how carefully you have chosen your victims, and how calmly and resignedly you have approached your work.

AUTHOR: You admire me?

VISITOR: Immeasurably.

AUTHOR: As murderer or as writer?

VISITOR: *Both.* The more I have discovered about your criminal activities, the more I have learned to value your literary finesse. I am ready and willing to make a supreme sacrifice to your art.

AUTHOR: Namely?

VISITOR (*quietly and simply*): I am prepared to turn my back on the greatest thing in life: I will sacrifice the fame and glory that are due to me.

AUTHOR: So, you've decided not to turn me in?

VISITOR: I renounce the opportunity.

AUTHOR: And what do you expect me to give you in return?

VISITOR: A small token—of appreciation.

AUTHOR: In what form?

VISITOR: Well, you see—I'm bankrupt. I have sacrificed everything I own for my art. I am no longer in a position to lead the kind of life I have become accustomed to while serving the cause of criminological science. I can't afford to roam from one expensive resort to another any more. I shall be obliged to return to Ennetwyl near Horck with a cloud over my head and my life in ruins unless—unless—(*He hesitates.*) . . .

AUTHOR: Go on, go on.

VISITOR: . . . unless you see fit to supplement the pension I get from Oechsli, Trost, and Co. with a little extra pocket money— say, six or seven hundred Swiss francs per month—so that I can continue to play a part in your life—oh, quite discreetly, of course—as your admirer and confidant. (*Pause.*)

AUTHOR: My dear Feargod Hofer, I, too, would like to make a confession; I, too, would like to speak with terrible frankness, as you put it. There is absolutely no doubt in my mind that you are the greatest detective I've ever met. Your criminological talents and your razor-sharp mind have not led you astray. You are perfectly right. I confess everything. (*Pause.*)

VISITOR: You admit it?

AUTHOR: I admit it.

VISITOR: The Swedish woman?

AUTHOR: The Swedish woman.

VISITOR: The young English girl?

AUTHOR: Her too.

VISITOR: Countess Windischgrätz?

AUTHOR: Likewise. The Argentinian multi-millionairess as well.

VISITOR: I'm sorry, I cannot allow you that one.

AUTHOR: But, my dear sir . . .

VISITOR: You know perfectly well that you're trying to cheat now, honored master.

AUTHOR: All right, all right, we'll omit the multimillionairess.

VISITOR: And you did murder the twenty-one others?

AUTHOR: All twenty-one of them. I'm no piker, after all. (*Pause.*)

VISITOR (*pensively*): This is the culminating moment of my existence.

AUTHOR: Very true. This is the culminating moment of your existence. In a somewhat different sense from the one you intend, however. (*A young woman appears in the bedroom door, runs in despair across the room, and disappears again.*)

YOUNG WOMAN: I simply *must* go back to Papa, Maximilian Frederick!

VISITOR: Wasn't that the charming daughter of the English colonel in the next room flitting across here in her bare feet?

AUTHOR: To be sure.

VISITOR: Your next victim?

AUTHOR: Hardly. My next victim is going to be someone else. Despite the correctness of your conclusions, you have made one mistake, Mr. Hofer. Hasn't it occurred to you that it might be dangerous to come and tell me all about your knowledge of my—er, private life?

VISITOR: You mean—you could kill *me?*

AUTHOR: Precisely.

VISITOR: Well, naturally that occurred to me, my dear Mr. Korbes. I have examined the situation from every angle and quite quietly and calmly taken every imaginable precaution. A well-known American movie star lives in the room above yours, a colonel in the English army on your left, and a middle-class widow on your right.

AUTHOR: Excuse me—a widowed duchess.

VISITOR: Incorrect! My investigations reveal that her husband was a department-store doorman in Geneva. The room below yours is occupied by the tubercular Archbishop of Czernowitz. One cry for help from me and there'll be a scandal which will shake the world. So you'd have to kill me noiselessly—poison would be your only way.

AUTHOR: Quite so, quite so. So that's why you wouldn't take a drink.

VISITOR: Exactly. It wasn't very easy for me to refuse, either—I happen to be particularly fond of whisky.

AUTHOR: And you wouldn't smoke a cigar, either.

VISITOR: Well, after all, you got rid of the tenor Lorenz Hochsträsser with a particularly mild Havana impregnated with an Indian poison.

AUTHOR: My dear Feargod Hofer, you forget

one thing—that you come from Ennetwyl near Horck.

VISITOR: Don't underestimate the place. Ennetwyl is very much in the swing of things and has an active cultural life.

AUTHOR: That's exactly what I mean. Nowadays places that have an "active cultural life" are on the other side of the moon, so to speak—otherwise you would have been aware of the senselessness of your investigations. (*He pours himself another whisky.*) You have merely proved something that didn't need proving. (*Pause.*)

VISITOR (*dismayed*): You mean . . .

AUTHOR: Yes, indeed. The world has known what you seem to consider your secret for a long time.

VISITOR (*almost hysterical*): That's impossible. I've gone through all the serious newspapers with a fine-tooth comb and haven't found the slightest hint of it.

AUTHOR: The only place you can find the truth nowadays is in the scandal sheets, Feargod Hofer. They're full of my murders. Do you really suppose that the public would swallow my works if they didn't *know* that I only describe murders that I've committed?

VISITOR: But, honored mas . . .

AUTHOR: Korbes is the name.

VISITOR: Honored Mr. Korbes. . . . You'd have been arrested long ago if that were true!

AUTHOR (*amazed*): But why?

VISITOR (*in despair*): Because you're a murderer, of course! A mass murderer!

AUTHOR: Well, what of it? We writers have always been monsters, according to middle-class morality! Look at Goethe, Balzac, Baudelaire, Verlaine, Rimbaud, Edgar Allan Poe. But that isn't all. No matter how horrified the world was with us at first, it always wound up worshipping us more and more as time passed—*precisely because* we're monsters. We went up and up in the social scale until finally we were held in awe as superior beings. Society has not only accepted us, it has concentrated its interest almost exclusively on our private lives. As people who can permit themselves anything—who are supposed to permit themselves anything—we've become wish fulfillment figures for the millions. Our art gives us carte blanche for our vices and our adventures. Do you really suppose I'd have been given the Nobel Prize for my novel *The Murderer and the Child* if I hadn't been the murderer myself? Look at these letters scattered in heaps around my room. They're from high society women, from middle-class wives, from chambermaids—all of them offering themselves as victims for my future murders.

VISITOR: I'm dreaming.

AUTHOR: Well then, it's high time you woke up. Only critics suppose that a writer works on his literary form and on his dialogue. Real literature has nothing to do with literary matters—its purpose is to satisfy mankind. People don't long for new literary forms or for linguistic experiments, least of all for philosophical revelations: they long for a life that doesn't need hope because hope doesn't exist any more; they long for a life overflowing with fulfillment, with tension, with adventure, and with the pleasures of the moment—a life that the reality of our machine age can no longer offer them—and they have to turn to art for it. Literature has become a drug—a substitute for a way of life that is no longer possible. But in order to manufacture this drug writers must unfortunately lead the kind of life they describe—something which (believe me!) is one hell of a strain, particularly after one has passed a certain age. (*Another young woman appears in the doorway.*)

2ND YOUNG WOMAN: Maximilian Frederick!

AUTHOR: Get out of here! (*The second young woman also disappears.*) That was the American movie star. When I was young I concentrated strictly on style. A few provincial editors patted me on the back—other than that nobody gave a damn about me. Quite right, too. I gave up writing and bummed around, prospecting for oil in Persia. I failed at that too. That left me with only one thing to do—describe my life. I thought I'd be arrested. The first person to congratulate me and advance me an appreciable sum of money was the Swedish attaché whose wife I had had an affair with. The story of that affair became my first best seller. There—and now do have a glass of whisky since you're particularly fond of it. (*He pours.*)

VISITOR: Thank you . . . I'm . . . I don't know . . . thank you . . .

AUTHOR: As soon as I realized what the world wanted, I began to furnish it with the desired commodity. From then on I wrote nothing but autobiography. I stopped paying attention to my style in order to write without it and, presto! I had style. So, I became famous, but my fame forced me to lead an ever more abandoned life, because the public wanted to see me in ever more horrifying situations so that it could experience *through me* everything that was forbidden. And that's how I became a mass murderer! From then on, everything that happened only increased my fame. My books were impounded and destroyed, the Vatican put me on the Index, and the printings became bigger and bigger. And now you show up! You with your ridiculous proofs that my novels describe the truth. There isn't a judge or jury in the world that'd pay any attention to you, because the world wants me the way I am. They'd declare you insane, just as they've declared everyone else who's tried it insane! Do you really suppose you're the first? Mothers, wives, husbands, sons have gone bursting in on the lawyers, sniffing for revenge. Every single lawsuit has been put off so far. District attorneys and ministers of justice—yes, even presidents—have successfully intervened on my behalf in the name of art. Everyone who's tried to drag me to court has wound up looking like a fool so far. You are an idiot, Feargod Hofer. You have thrown your savings away and you deserve to be punished for it. Don't expect money from me. You'd do better to expect something else. Go on, call for help!

VISITOR (*fearfully*): For help?

AUTHOR: I need a new plot.

VISITOR: A new plot?

AUTHOR: You are the new plot.

VISITOR: What do you mean?

AUTHOR: High time I got to work.

VISITOR (*horrified*): Why are you drawing a revolver all of a sudden?

AUTHOR: Haven't you figured it out yet?

VISITOR: I'm going—I'm on my way already.

AUTHOR: I didn't draw this revolver to send you on your way—I drew it to kill you.

VISITOR: I swear to you by all I hold holy that I'll leave this place at once and go back to Ennetwyl.

AUTHOR: You've given me an idea for a radio play and so now you must die, for I only write down what I have experienced, because, you see, I don't have any imagination at all—because I can *only* write down what I experience. I'll make you a part of world literature, Feargod Hofer. Millions will see you standing before me the way you are now, trembling with fright, your eyes and mouth wide open—pits into which cataracts of horror are crashing, opening up before you—you, a mug of a bookkeeper who finally wakes up after endless self-delusion and sees truth tear away the veil.

VISITOR: HELP! (*Pause.*)

AUTHOR: Well? Do you see any people rushing in? Is the movie star or the English colonel or possibly the Archbishop of Czernowitz springing to the rescue?

VISITOR: You . . . you're the devil.

AUTHOR: I am an author and I need money. The radio play which I will write about your murder will be carried on all the networks. I *have* to kill you, if only for purely financial reasons. Do you think I enjoy doing this? God knows I'd a thousand times rather drink a bottle of wine with you down in the bar and then go bowling with you than spend the night writing the account of your death.

VISITOR: Mercy, honored master!

AUTHOR: Korbes is the name.

VISITOR: Honored Mr. Korbes, mercy!

AUTHOR: The practice of the literary profession does not involve mercy.

VISITOR (*staggering back on to the balcony*): Help!

AUTHOR (*in a powerful voice*): You are case Number Twenty-three!

VISITOR: No, twenty-two. . . . (*There is a loud noise; then a long-drawn-out cry, fading away.*) Heeeellllp! (*A silence.*)

AUTHOR: Such a bungler!

SECRETARY: Mr. Korbes! What's happened, for heaven's sake?

AUTHOR: My visitor jumped off the balcony, Sebastian. He seemed to panic all of a sudden. Can't imagine why. Ah, here's the manager.

MANAGER: My dear Mr. Korbes! I am desolate! Somebody has been permitted to annoy you! He's lying smashed up among the roses down there. The doorman's been noticing him going around like a crazy person for a long time now. Thank God no one was injured by his fall.

AUTHOR: Kindly see to it that I am not disturbed.

MANAGER (*retiring*): But of course, my dear Mr. Korbes, of course.

AUTHOR: All right, let's get to work, Sebastian. But first I believe I'll light up a cigar.

SEBASTIAN: A light, sir?

AUTHOR: Use it to burn that piece of paper on the table.

SEBASTIAN: What are these names?

AUTHOR: Oh, just names. Give it here. That's the best way. Thank you. We'll have to hurry. Tomorrow we'll pack. This place has served its purpose. We'll go to Majorca.

SEBASTIAN: Majorca?

AUTHOR: A little Mediterranean scenery will do us good. Ready?

SEBASTIAN: Ready, sir.

AUTHOR: Another whisky first.

SEBASTIAN: Here you are.

AUTHOR: All right, take this down: Ladies and gentlemen, I consider it my duty, at the very outset, to describe to you the setting of this possibly somewhat peculiar but, I assure you, entirely true story. To be sure, there is a considerable element of danger in telling true stories—someone from the police or possibly even the district attorney might be among those present, even though they might not be here in their official capacity. Nonetheless I can allow myself to take the risk because I know perfectly well they won't believe my true story—at least not in their official capacity. In reality—that is to say, *un*officially—all of you of course, including the district attorney or policeman who may or may not be among us, know very well that I *only* tell true stories—scout's honor! Well then: might I ask you to concentrate for a moment? Imagine yourselves in the drawing room of a Grand Hotel suite. . . .

III
Religion

THE plays dealing with man as a political and social animal have shown him in his most advanced stage of development. In this section and the following one on love, we see man in a more primitive and elemental state—a state that continues to exist, however, with his more sophisticated state.

Religion is born of fear. Primitive man, helpless in the grip of nature, felt a need to propitiate the mysterious powers that had created him and that controlled the physical elements threatening his survival. Unable to stand alone and unable to explain the reasons for and conditions of his existence, he created rituals to comfort himself. These rituals are dramatizations of his attempts to elucidate the mystery of existence.

Euripides' *The Bacchae* (c. 405 B.C.), although written when human society was already in an advanced stage of development—many think in the highest stage of development that it has yet attained—depicts religion in its most primitive form. Here religion was still an atavistic merging with the god himself. The entity that created and controlled life was propitiated by being worshiped through orgiastic rites intended to dehumanize the celebrants and make them part of the primal matter from which they had emanated. Pentheus's attempt to achieve rational comprehension of the rites brings about his downfall since, by trying to understand the rites and the god whom they are intended to propitiate, he is implying his own superiority to them. The submission to the primal force must be complete. We see this in the fact that it is Pentheus's own mother who leads the frenzied attack on him in which he is torn apart and who dances with his severed head: the bonds of blood and family are later elaborations and have no part in the atavistic urges of the worshipers. This type of theater closely approaches that advocated by the radical twentieth-century French theatrical theorist Antonin Artaud, who has had such a profound influence on the current avant-garde theater. Artaud felt that the artist's task was to do what Euripides had done in this play: to strip away the layers of artificiality and expose the core of reality that had been hidden for so long. To Artaud, this core was pure emotion; and the emotion was latent, instinctual savagery. He perceived that men are, as they always have been, basically barbaric, that the thick protective wall of urbane, civilized behavior they have acquired through centuries of hiding from psychological self-realization is easily crumbled by a forceful

appeal to irrational emotion. Another interesting, more socially oriented interpretation is that given by Philip Vellacott, the translator of this version.

> *The Bacchae* is a play written to convey a solemn warning against a real dan-
> ger; how real, the parallel of our own time, the growth of mass hysteria, the
> cult of violence, the spread of credulity, the "flight from reason," all bring home
> to us. Our own generation's experience of Nazism will illustrate the univer-
> sality of the theme; for the bands of youth under their worshipped leaders,
> revelling in the Bavarian mountains, believing racial myths, singing heroic
> songs, revering Woman and the Home, and beating up the next Jew they meet
> —they were in some essentials Dionysiac; and the disease which produced them
> is not yet dead.

By the time *Everyman* came to be written in the fifteenth century, religion
had become a formalized set of beliefs. It was now far removed from its
origins in elemental fear and had become a set of comforting maxims that
the believer could refer to at any time. The fear of death, which is at the
base of all fears, had been smothered by being covered over with an elaborate
mythology of an after-life that had the additional purely social quality of
being divided into a good and a bad form (the one as blissful, the other as
horrible as the most powerful human imaginations could make them) to serve
as reward or punishment for behavior during life. *Everyman* is essentially a
dramatized sermon on everyday ethical behavior that has the advantage of
being acceptable to believer and nonbeliever alike since it pleads for the
desirability of helping others and of behaving decently.

Fritz Hochwälder's *The Holy Experiment* (1947) is about Christianity in
eighteenth-century South America, but, since it is written by a contemporary
dramatist, it makes a commentary on Christianity and the way in which it is
practiced from our own viewpoint. The Jesuits had established what amounted
to a sovereign state within the Spanish-held territory of Paraguay. This state
acknowledged the sovereignty of the king of Spain, but maintained its own
army in order to keep out the Spanish colonists, who simply wished to
enslave the Indians. The Jesuit state in Paraguay was, in fact, a true communist state, with all sharing equally in the profits and benefits of the community.

The creation of a utopian state in the midst of a nonutopian one inevitably
creates an intolerable economic situation. The inhabitants of the utopian
communal state obviously produce goods better and more economically than
the inhabitants of the nonutopian competitive society. The latter become
jealous and start intriguing to have the utopians declared immoral, dis-
honest, illegal—whatever you please. This conflict between Christianity practiced as it ought to be and Christianity as it has come to be practiced is the
crux of Hochwälder's play. The Jesuits in the play practice true Christianity,
naïvely interpreting the teachings of Christ literally, but in a capitalistic
society the making of profit in order to share it is intolerable. The irony of
the play lies in the colonists' hypocritical dressing up of their naked greed

in the trappings of Christian morality. Hochwälder shows religion as something that has become utterly perverted by the mechanism of the state and the requirements of power politics. In effect, it has been destroyed by being used for purposes other than those it was created for. The play is Hochwälder's explanation of the modern world's loss of faith in religion, because something that is paid lip service and is used as an instrument is no longer a viable belief. The disillusioned plays of the avant-garde theater—the plays of Beckett, Ionesco, Genet, and Adamov—are the direct results of this realization.

THE BACCHAE

Euripides

TRANSLATED BY
Philip Vellacott

CHARACTERS

DIONYSUS
CHORUS of Oriental women, devotees of Dionysus
TEIRESIAS, a blind Seer
CADMUS, founder of Thebes, and formerly king
PENTHEUS, his grandson, now king of Thebes
A GUARD attending Pentheus
A HERDSMAN
A MESSENGER
AGAUË, daughter of Cadmus and mother of Pentheus

Before the palace of PENTHEUS *in Thebes. At one side of the stage is the monument of Semele; above it burns a low flame, and around it are the remains of ruined and blackened masonry.* DIONYSUS *enters on stage right. He has a crown of ivy, a thyrsus in his hand, and a fawnskin draped over his body. He has long flowing hair and a youthful, almost feminine beauty.*

DIONYSUS: I am Dionysus, son of Zeus. My mother was Semele, daughter of Cadmus; I was delivered from her womb by the fire of a lightning-flash. Today I have laid aside the appearance of a god, and have come disguised as a mortal man to this city of Thebes, where flow the two rivers, Dirce and Ismenus. Here by the palace I see the monument recording my mother's death by lightning; here are the smouldering ruins of her house, which bear the still living flame of Zeus's fire—the undying token of Hera's cruelty to my mother. Cadmus does well to keep this ground untrodden, a precinct consecrated to his daughter; and I now have decked it round with sprays of young vine-leaves.

From the fields of Lydia and Phrygia, fertile in gold, I came to the sun-beaten Persian plains, the walled towns of Bactria, harsh Media, wealthy Arabia, and the whole of that Asian seaboard where Greeks and Orientals live side by side in crowded magnificent cities; and before reaching this, the first city of Hellas I have seen, I had already, in all those regions of the East, danced my dance and established my ritual, to make my godhead manifest to mortal men.

And the reason why Thebes is the first place in Hellas where, at my command, women have raised the Bacchic shout, put on the fawnskin cloak, and taken my weapon in their hands, the thyrsus wreathed with ivy—the reason is this: my mother's sisters said—what they should have been the last to say—that I, Dionysus, was not the progeny of Zeus; but that Semele, being with child by some mortal, at her father's suggestion ascribed to Zeus the loss of her virginity; and they loudly insisted that this lie about the fatherhood of her child was the sin for which Zeus had struck her dead.

Therefore I have plagued these same sisters with madness, and driven them all frantic out of doors; now their home is the mountains, and their wits are gone. And I made them carry the emblems of my mysteries; and the whole female population of Thebes, every woman there was in the town, I drove raving from their homes; now they have joined the daughters of Cadmus, and there they are, sitting roofless on the rocks under the silver fir-trees. Thebes must learn, unwilling though she is, that my Bacchic revels are something beyond her present knowledge and understanding; and I must vindicate the honour of my mother Semele, by manifesting myself before the human race as the god whom she bore to Zeus.

Now Cadmus has handed over his kingly honours and his throne to his daughter's son Pentheus. And this Pentheus is a fighter against God—he defies me, excludes me from libations, never names me in prayer. Therefore I will demonstrate to him, and to all Thebes, that I am a god.

When I have set all in order here, I will pass on to some other place, and manifest myself. Meanwhile, if the Theban city in anger tries to bring the Bacchae home from the mountains by force, I will join that army of women possessed and lead them to battle. And this is why I have changed my divine form to human, and appear in the likeness of a man.

Come, my holy band of revellers, women I have brought from lands of the East, from the slopes of Tmolus, bastion of Lydia, to be with me and share my travels! Raise the music of your Phrygian home, the timbrels invented by Rhea the Great Mother and by me; surround the palace of Pentheus and strike up such a peal of sound as shall make Thebes turn to look! I will go to the glens of Cithaeron where my Bacchae are, and join their dances. (DIONYSUS *goes out towards the mountain; the* CHORUS *enter where* DIONYSUS *entered, from the road by which they have travelled.*)

CHORUS: From far-off lands of   (*Strophe* 1
   Asia,
From Tmolus the holy mountain,
We run with the god of laughter;

Labour is joy and weariness is sweet,
And our song resounds to Bacchus!

Beware of the inter-   (*Antistrophe* 1
  loper!
Indoors or out, who listens?
Let every lip be holy;
Stand well aloof, be silent, while we sing
The appointed hymn to Bacchus!

Blest is the happy man   (*Strophe* 2
Who knows the mysteries the gods ordain,
And sanctifies his life,
Joins soul with soul in mystic unity,
And, by due ritual made pure,
Enters the ecstasy of mountain solitudes;
Who observes the mystic rites
Made lawful by Cybele the Great Mother;
Who crowns his head with ivy,
And shakes aloft his wand in worship of
  Dionysus.

On, on! Run, dance, delirious, possessed!
Dionysus comes to his own;
Bring from the Phrygian hills to the broad
  streets of Hellas
The god, child of a god,
Spirit of revel and rapture, Dionysus!

Once, on the womb   (*Antistrophe* 2
  that held him
The fire-bolt flew from the hand of Zeus;
And pains of child-birth bound his mother
  fast,
And she cast him forth untimely,
And under the lightning's lash relinquished
  life;
And Zeus the son of Cronos
Ensconced him instantly in a secret womb
Chambered within his thigh,
And with golden pins closed him from
  Hera's sight.

So, when the Fates had made him ripe for
  birth,
Zeus bore the bull-horned god
And wreathed his head with wreaths of
  writhing snakes;
Which is why the Maenads catch
Wild snakes, nurse them and twine them
  round their hair.

O Thebes, old nurse that   (*Strophe* 3
  cradled Semele,

Be ivy-garlanded, burst into flower
With wreaths of lush bright-berried bryony,
Bring sprays of fir, green branches torn
  from oaks,
Fill soul and flesh with Bacchus' mystic
  power;
Fringe and bedeck your dappled fawnskin
  cloaks
With woolly tufts and locks of purest
  white.
There's a brute wildness in the fennel-
  wands—
Reverence it well. Soon the whole land will
  dance
  When the god with ecstatic shout
  Leads his companies out
  To the mountain's mounting height
  Swarming with riotous bands
  Of Theban women leaving
  Their spinning and their weaving
  Stung with the maddening trance
    Of Dionysus!

O secret chamber the   (*Antistrophe* 3
  Curetes knew!
O holy cavern in the Cretan glade
Where Zeus was cradled, where for our de-
  light
The triple-crested Corybantes drew
Tight the round drum-skin, till its wild beat
  made
Rapturous rhythm to the breathing sweet-
  ness
Of Phrygian flutes! Then divine Rhea
  found
The drum could give her Bacchic airs com-
  pleteness;
  From her, the Mother of all,
  The crazy Satyrs soon,
  In their dancing festival
  When the second year comes round,
  Seized on the timbrel's tune
  To play the leading part
  In feasts that delight the heart
    Of Dionysus.

O what delight is in the moun-   (*Epode*
  tains!
There the celebrant, wrapped in his sacred
  fawnskin,
Flings himself on the ground surrendered,
While the swift-footed company streams
  on;
There he hunts for blood, and rapturously

Eats the raw flesh of the slaughtered goat,
Hurrying on to the Phrygian or Lydian
mountain heights.
Possessed, ecstatic, he leads their happy
cries;
The earth flows with milk, flows with wine,
Flows with nectar of bees;
The air is thick with a scent of Syrian
myrrh.
The celebrant runs entranced, whirling the
torch
That blazes red from the fennel-wand in
his grasp,
And with shouts he rouses the scattered
bands,
Sets their feet dancing,
As he shakes his delicate locks to the wild
wind.
And amidst the frenzy of song he shouts
like thunder:
'On, on! Run, dance, delirious, possessed!
You, the beauty and grace of golden
Tmolus,
Sing to the rattle of thunderous drums,
Sing for joy,
Praise Dionysus, god of joy!
Shout like Phrygians, sing out the tunes
you know,
While the sacred pure-toned flute
Vibrates the air with holy merriment,
In time with the pulse of the feet that flock
To the mountains, to the mountains!'
And, like a foal with its mother at pasture,
Runs and leaps for joy every daughter of
Bacchus.

Enter TEIRESIAS. *Though blind, he makes
his way unaided to the door, and knocks.*

TEIRESIAS: Who keeps the gate? (*A servant
is heard answering from inside.*) Call out
Cadmus, the son of Agenor, who came
from Sidonia to build these walls of
Thebes. Go, someone, tell him Teiresias is
looking for him. He knows why I have
come—the agreement I made with him—
old as I am, and he older still—to get myself a Bacchic wand, put on the fawnskin
cloak, and wear a garland of young ivy-
shoots. (*Enter* CADMUS.)

CADMUS: O my dear friend, I knew your
voice, although I was indoors, as soon as I
heard it—the wise voice of a wise man.
Look, I am ready, I have everything the
god prescribes. Dionysus is my own daughter's son; and now he has shown himself to
the world as a god, it is right that I should
do all I can to exalt him. Where should
we go to dance, and take our stand with
the rest, tossing our old grey beards? You
must guide me in this, Teiresias—you're
nearly as old as I am, and you understand
such matters. No, it won't be too much for
me; I can beat time with my thyrsus night
and day! It's a happy thing to forget one's
age.

TEIRESIAS: Then you feel just as I do. I am
young too; I'll make an attempt at the
dance.

CADMUS: You don't think we should make
our way to the mountains in a carriage?

TEIRESIAS: No, no, that would not show the
same respect for the god.

CADMUS: I'll be your guide then—two old
men together.

TEIRESIAS: The god will guide us there, and
without weariness.

CADMUS: Shall we be the only men in Thebes
who dance to Bacchus?

TEIRESIAS: We are the only men right-
minded; the rest are perverse.

CADMUS: We are wasting time. Now, take my
hand.

TEIRESIAS: There; hold firmly, with a good
grip.

CADMUS: Mortals must not make light of the
gods—I would never do so.

TEIRESIAS: We entertain no theories or specu-
lations in divine matters. The beliefs we
have received from our ancestors—beliefs
as old as time—cannot be destroyed by any
argument, nor by any ingenuity the mind
can invent. No doubt I shall be criticized
for wearing an ivy-wreath and setting off
for the dance; they will say I have no sense
of what befits my age. They will be wrong:
the god has drawn no distinction between
young and old, which should dance and
which should not. He wishes to receive
honour alike from all; he will not have his
worship made a matter of nice calculation.

CADMUS: Teiresias, since you are blind I must
be your prophet. I see Pentheus the son of
Echion, to whom I have resigned my rule
in Thebes, hurrying towards the palace. He
looks thoroughly upset! What is he going
to tell us? (*Enter* PENTHEUS. *He addresses
the audience, without at first noticing* CAD-

MUS *and* TEIRESIAS, *who stand at the opposite side of the stage.*)

PENTHEUS: I've been away from Thebes, as it happens; but I've heard the news—this extraordinary scandal in the city. Our women, I discover, have abandoned their homes on some pretence of Bacchic worship, and go gadding about in the woods on the mountain side, dancing in honour of this upstart god Dionysus, whoever he may be. They tell me, in the midst of each group of revellers stands a bowl full of wine; and the women go creeping off this way and that to lonely places and there give themselves to lecherous men, under the excuse that they are Maenad priestesses; though in their ritual Aphrodite comes before Bacchus.

Well, those that I've caught, my guards are keeping safe; we've tied their hands, and lodged them at State expense. Those still at large on the mountain I am going to hunt out; and that includes my own mother Agaue, and her sisters Ino and Autonoe. Once I have them secure in iron chains I shall soon put a stop to this outrageous Bacchism.

I understand too that some Oriental magician or conjurer has arrived from Lydia, a fellow with golden hair flowing in scented ringlets, the flush of wine in his face and the charm of Aphrodite in his eyes; and that he entices our young girls with his Bacchic mysteries, and spends day and night in their company. Only let me get that fellow inside my walls—I'll cut his head from his shoulders; that will finish his thyrsus-waving and hair-tossing. *He* is the one—this foreigner—who has spread stories about Dionysus, that he is a god, that he was sewn up in Zeus's thigh. The truth about Dionysus is that he's dead, burnt to a cinder by lightning along with his mother, because she lied about Zeus—said that Zeus had lain with her. But whoever this man may be, does not his insufferable behaviour merit the worst of punishments, hanging? (*He turns to go, and sees* CADMUS *and* TEIRESIAS.)

Why, look! Another miracle! Here's the prophet Teiresias, and my mother's father, playing the Bacchant, in dappled fawnskin and carrying fennel-wands! Well, there's a sight for laughter! (*But he is raging, not*

laughing.*) Sir, I am ashamed to see two men of your age with so little sense of decency. Come, you are my grandfather: throw away your garland, get rid of that thyrsus. *You* persuaded him into this, Teiresias. No doubt you hope that, when you have introduced this new god to the people, you will be his appointed seer, you will collect the fees for sacrifices. Your grey hairs are your protection; otherwise you should sit with all these crazy females in prison, for encouraging such pernicious performances.

As for women, my opinion is this: when the sparkle of sweet wine appears at their feasts, no good can be expected from their ceremonies.

CHORUS: What profanity! Sir, do you not revere the gods, or Cadmus, who sowed the seed of the earth-born men? Echion your father was one of them—will you shame your own blood?

TEIRESIAS: When a clever man has a plausible theme to argue, to be eloquent is no great feat. But though you seem, by your glib tongue, to be intelligent, yet your words are foolish. Power and eloquence in a headstrong man can only lead to folly; and such a man is a danger to the state.

This new divinity whom you ridicule—no words of mine could adequately express the ascendancy he is destined to achieve through the length and breadth of Hellas. There are two powers, young man, which are supreme in human affairs: first, the goddess Demeter; she is the Earth—call her by what name you will; and she supplies mankind with solid food. Second, Dionysus the son of Semele; the blessing he provides is the counterpart to the blessing of bread; he discovered and bestowed on men the service of drink, the juice that streams from the vine-clusters; men have but to take their fill of wine, and the sufferings of an unhappy race are banished, each day's troubles are forgotten in sleep—indeed this is our only cure for the weariness of life. Dionysus, himself a god, is poured out in offering to the gods; so that through him mankind receives blessing.

Now for the legend that he was sewn up in Zeus's thigh—do you mock at it? Then I will explain to you the truth that lies in the legend. When Zeus snatched the infant

Dionysus away from the fire of the lightning, and brought him to Olympus as a god, Hera wanted to cast him out of heaven; so, to prevent her, Zeus—as you would expect—devised a plan. He broke off a piece of the sky that envelops the earth, made it into the likeness of a child, and gave it to Hera as a pledge, to soothe her jealousy. He entrusted the true Dionysus to others to bring up. Now the ancient word for a *pledge* is very similar to our word 'thigh'; and so in time the word was mistaken, and men said Dionysus was saved by Zeus's *thigh*, instead of by Zeus's *pledge*, because a pledge was given to Hera in his likeness.

And this god is a prophet; for the Bacchic ecstasy and frenzy contain a strong element of prophecy. When Dionysus enters in power into a human body, he endows the possessed person with power to foretell the future. He also in some degree shares the function of Ares, god of war. It has happened that an army, equipped and stationed for battle, has fled in panic before a spear has been raised. This too is a madness sent by Dionysus.

Ay, and the day will come when you shall see him on the very rocks of Delphi, amidst flaring torches bounding over the twin-peaked ridge, hurling and brandishing his Bacchic staff, honoured by all Hellas.

Come, Pentheus, listen to me. You rely on force; but it is not force that governs human affairs. If you think otherwise—beware of mistaking your perverse opinion for wisdom. Welcome Dionysus to Thebes; pour libations to him, garland your head and celebrate his rites. Dionysus will not compel women to control their lusts. Self-control in all things depends on our own natures. This is a fact you should consider; for a chaste-minded woman will come to no harm in the rites of Bacchus. And think of this too: when crowds stand at the city gates, and the people glorify the name of Pentheus, you are filled with pleasure; so, I think, Dionysus is glad to receive honour.

So then I, and Cadmus, whom you mock, will wear the ivy-wreath and join in the dancing—we are both old men, but this is our duty; and no words of yours shall persuade me to fight against the gods. For your mind is most pitifully diseased; and

there is no medicine that can heal you. Yet . . . there is one remedy for your madness.

CHORUS: What you have said, Teiresias, means no dishonour to Phoebus, whose prophet you are; and shows your wisdom in honouring Dionysus as a great god.

CADMUS: My son, Teiresias has advised you well. Do not venture outside the customary pieties; stay with us. Just now your wits are scattered; you think you are talking sense, but it is not sense at all. And even if you are right, and this god is not a god, at least let him have your word of acknowledgment; lie for a good purpose, so that Semele may be honoured as mother of a god, and I and our whole family may gain in dignity. Remember Actaeon—his tragic end; he boasted, out in these valleys, that he was a better hunter than Artemis, and was torn to pieces and devoured by the very hounds he had bred. Don't invite the same fate! Come, let me put this ivy-wreath on your head. Join us in worshipping Dionysus.

PENTHEUS: Keep your hands off! Go to your Bacchic rites; and don't wipe off your crazy folly on me! But I will punish this man who has taught you your lunacy. Go, one of you, immediately to the place of augury where Teiresias practices, smash it with crowbars, knock down the walls, turn everything upside down, fling out his holy fripperies to the winds. That will sting him more than anything else. The rest of you, comb the city and find this effeminate foreigner, who plagues our women with this strange disease and turns them into whores. If you catch him, bring him here in chains, and I'll have him stoned to death. He shall be sorry he ever came revelling in Thebes. (*Exit* PENTHEUS.)

TEIRESIAS: Foolhardy man, you don't know what you are saying. You were out of your mind before; now you are raving mad.

Come, Cadmus; let us go and pray both for this man, brutish as he is, and for Thebes, and entreat Dionysus to be forbearing. Come, take your thyrsus and follow. Try to support me—there, we will help each other. It would be a pity for us both to fall; but never mind that. We must pay our service to Dionysus the son of Zeus.

CADMUS: The name *Pentheus* means *grief*.
Let us hope he is not going to bring grief
on your house. I am not speaking by inspiration; I judge by his conduct. The
things he has said reveal the depth of his
folly. (*Exeunt* TEIRESIAS *and* CADMUS.)

CHORUS: Holiness, Queen of   (*Strophe* 1
        heaven,
    Holiness, golden-winged ranging the
        earth,
    Do you hear his blasphemy?
    Pentheus dares—do you hear?—to revile
        the god of joy,
    The son of Semele, who when the gay-
        crowned feast is set
    Is named among gods the chief;
    Whose gifts are joy and union of soul in
        dancing,
    Joy in music of flutes,
    Joy when sparkling wine at feasts of the
        gods
    Soothes the sore regret,
    Banishes every grief,
    When the reveller rests, enfolded deep
    In the cool shade of ivy-shoots,
    On wine's soft pillow of sleep.

    The brash, unbridled   (*Antistrophe* 1
        tongue,
    The lawless folly of fools, will end in
        pain.
    But the life of wise content
    Is blest with quietness, escapes the storm
    And keeps its house secure.
    Though blessed gods dwell in the distant
        skies,
    They watch the ways of men.
    To know much is not to be wise.
    Pride more than mortal hastens life to its
        end;
    And they who in pride pretend
    Beyond man's limit, will lose what lay
    Close to their hand and sure.
    I count it madness, and know no cure
        can mend
    The evil man and his evil way.

    O to set foot on Aphrodite's   (*Strophe* 2
        island,
    On Cyprus, haunted by the Loves, who en-
        chant
    Brief life with sweetness; or in that strange
        land

    Whose fertile river carves a hundred chan-
        nels
    To enrich her rainless sand;
    Or where the sacred pastures of Olympus
        slant
    Down to Pieria, where the Muses dwell—
    Take me, O Bromius, take me and inspire
    Laughter and worship! There our holy spell
    And ecstasy are welcome; there the gentle
        band
    Of Graces have their home, and sweet De-
        sire.

    Dionysus, son of Zeus,   (*Antistrophe* 2
        delights in banquets;
    And his dear love is Peace, giver of wealth,
    Saviour of young men's lives—a goddess
        rare!
    In wine, his gift that charms all griefs
        away,
    Alike both rich and poor may have their
        part.
    His enemy is the man who has no care
    To pass his years in happiness and health,
    His days in quiet and his nights in joy,
    Watchful to keep aloof both mind and
        heart
    From men whose pride claims more than
        mortals may.
    The life that wins the poor man's common
        voice,
    His creed, his practice—this shall be my
        choice.

Some of the guards whom PENTHEUS *sent
to arrest* DIONYSUS *now enter with their
prisoner.* PENTHEUS *enters from the palace.*

GUARD: Well, sir, we went after this lion you
told us to hunt, and we have been successful. But—we found the lion was tame! He
made no attempt to escape, but freely held
out his hands to be bound. He didn't even
turn pale, but kept the fresh colour you see
in his face now, smiling, and telling us to
tie him up and run him in; waited for me,
in fact—gave us no trouble at all. Naturally
I felt a bit awkward. 'You'll excuse me,
sir,' I said, 'I don't want to arrest you, but
it's the king's orders.'
    And there's another thing, sir. Those
women you rounded up and put in fetters
and in prison, those religious maniacs—
why, they're all gone, let loose to the glens;
and there they are, dancing and calling on

Bacchus. The fetters simply fell from their limbs, the bolts flew back without the touch of any mortal hand, and let the doors open. Master, this man has come to our city of Thebes with a load of miracles. What is going to happen next is your concern, not mine.

PENTHEUS: Untie his hands. (*The guard does so.*) He is in the trap, and he's not nimble enough to escape me now.

Well, my man: you have a not unhandsome figure—for attracting women, which is your object in coming to Thebes. Those long curls of yours show that you're no wrestler—cascading close over your cheeks, most seductively. Your complexion, too, shows a carefully preserved whiteness; you keep out of the sun and walk in the shade, to use your lovely face for courting Aphrodite. . . .

Ah, well; tell me first what country you were born in.

DIONYSUS: That is easily told without boasting. Doubtless you have heard of the flowery mountain, Tmolus.

PENTHEUS: Yes, the range that curves round the city of Sardis.

DIONYSUS: That was my home; I am a Lydian.

PENTHEUS: And why do you bring these rituals to Hellas?

DIONYSUS: Dionysus the son of Zeus instructed me.

PENTHEUS: Is there a Lydian Zeus, then, who begets new gods?

DIONYSUS: No; I speak of your Zeus, who made Semele his bride here in Thebes.

PENTHEUS: And when Dionysus took possession of you, did he appear in a dream by night, or visible before your eyes?

DIONYSUS: I saw him face to face; and he entrusted to me these mysteries.

PENTHEUS: What form do these mysteries of yours take?

DIONYSUS: That cannot be told to the uninitiated.

PENTHEUS: What do the worshippers gain from it?

DIONYSUS: That is not lawful for you to hear —yet it is worth hearing.

PENTHEUS: A clever answer, baited to rouse my curiosity.

DIONYSUS: Curiosity will be useless; the rites of the god abhor an impious man.

PENTHEUS: If you say you saw Dionysus clearly—what was his appearance?

DIONYSUS: It was what he wished it to be. I had no say in that.

PENTHEUS: Another clever evasion, telling nothing.

DIONYSUS: A wise speech sleeps in a foolish ear.

PENTHEUS: Is this the first place where you have introduced Dionysus?

DIONYSUS: No; every Eastern land dances these mysteries.

PENTHEUS: I believe it. Oriental standards are altogether inferior to ours.

DIONYSUS: In this point they are superior. But their customs are different.

PENTHEUS: Do you celebrate your mysteries by night or by day?

DIONYSUS: Chiefly by night. Darkness induces religious awe.

PENTHEUS: For women darkness is treacherous and impure.

DIONYSUS: Impurity can be practiced by daylight too.

PENTHEUS: It is time you were punished for your foul, slippery tongue.

DIONYSUS: And you for your crass impieties.

PENTHEUS: How bold his Bacchic inspiration makes him! He knows how to argue too.

DIONYSUS: Tell me my sentence. What punishment are you going to inflict?

PENTHEUS: First I'll cut off your scented silky hair.

DIONYSUS: My hair I keep for the god; it is sacred to him.

PENTHEUS: Next, hand over that thyrsus.

DIONYSUS: Take it from me yourself. I carry it for Dionysus, whose it is.

PENTHEUS: And I shall keep you safe in prison.

DIONYSUS: The god himself will set me free whenever I wish.

PENTHEUS: Set you free? When you stand among those frenzied women and pray to him—no doubt!

DIONYSUS: He is here, close by me, and sees what is being done to me.

PENTHEUS: Oh, indeed? Where? To my eyes he is quite invisible.

DIONYSUS: Here at my side. You, being a blasphemer, cannot see him.

PENTHEUS (*to the guards*): Get hold of him. He is laughing at me and the whole city.

DIONYSUS (*to the guards*): I warn you not to

bind me. . . . (*To* PENTHEUS.) I am sane,
you are mad.
PENTHEUS (*to* DIONYSUS): My orders overrule
yours. (*To the guards.*) Bind him, I tell you.
DIONYSUS: You do not know what life you
live, or what you do, or who you are.
PENTHEUS: Who I am? Pentheus, son of
Echion and Agauë.
DIONYSUS: Pentheus means 'sorrow'. The
name fits you well.
PENTHEUS: Take him away. Imprison him
over there in the stables; he'll have all the
darkness he wants.—You can dance in
there! As for these women you've brought
to aid and abet you, I shall either send
them to the slave market, or retain them in
my own household to work at the looms;
that will keep their hands from drumming
on tambourines!
DIONYSUS: I will go. Nothing can happen to
me that is not my destiny. But Dionysus,
who you say is dead, will pursue you and
take his revenge for this sacrilege. You are
putting *him* in prison, when you lay hands
on me. (*Guards take* DIONYSUS *away to the
stables;* PENTHEUS *follows.*)

CHORUS: Dirce, sweet and holy   (*Strophe*
     maid,
     Acheloüs' Theban daughter,
     Once the child of Zeus was made
     Welcome in your welling water,
     When the lord of earth and sky
     Snatched him from the undying flame,
     Laid him safe within his thigh,
     Calling loud the infant's name:
     'Twice-born Dithyrambus! Come,
     Enter here your father's womb;
     Bacchic child, I now proclaim
     This in Thebes shall be your name.'
Now, divine Dirce, when my head is
     crowned
     And my feet dance in Bacchus' revelry—
Now you reject me from your holy
     ground.
Why should you fear me? By the purple
     fruit
That glows in glory on Dionysus' tree,
His dread name yet shall haunt your
     memory!

     O what anger lies be-   (*Antistrophe*
          neath
     Pentheus' voice and sullen face—

Offspring of the dragon's teeth,
And Echion's earth-born race,
Brute with bloody jaws agape,
God-defying, gross and grim,
Slander of his human shape!
Soon he'll chain us limb to limb—
Bacchus' servants! Yes, and more:
Even now our comrade lies
Deep on his dark prison floor.
Dionysus! do your eyes
See us? O son of Zeus, the oppressor's
     rod
Falls on your worshippers; come, mighty
     god,
Brandish your golden thyrsus and de-
     scend
From great Olympus; touch this mur-
     derous man,
And bring his violence to a sudden end!

Where are you, Dionysus?   (*Epode*
Leading your dancing bands
Over the mountain slopes, past many a
     wild beast's lair,
Or upon rocky crags, with the thyrsus in
     their hands?
Or in the wooded coverts, maybe, of Olym-
     pus, where
Orpheus once gathered the trees and moun-
     tain beasts,
Gathered them with his lyre, and sang an
     enchanting air.
Happy vale of Pieria! Bacchus delights in
     you;
He will cross the flood and foam of the
     Axius river, and there
He will bring his whirling Maenads, with
     dancing and with feasts,—
Cross the father of waters, Lydias, generous
     giver
Of wealth and luck, they say, to the land
     he wanders through,
Whose famous horses graze by the rich and
     lovely river.

*Suddenly a shout is heard from inside the
building—the voice of* DIONYSUS.

DIONYSUS: Io, Io! Do you know my voice, do
     you hear?
     Worshippers of Bacchus! Io, Io!
CHORUS: Who is that? Where is he? The
     voice of Dionysus calling to us!
DIONYSUS: Io, Io! Hear me again: I am the
     son of Semele, the son of Zeus!

CHORUS: Io, Io, our lord, our lord!
>   Come, then, come to our company, lord of joy!

DIONYSUS: O dreadful earthquake, shake the floor of the world!

CHORUS (*with a scream of terror*): Pentheus' palace is falling, crumbling in pieces! (*They continue severally.*)
>   Dionysus stands in the palace; bow before him!
>   We bow before him. See how the roof and pillars
>   Plunge to the ground! God from the inner prison
>   Will shout the shout of victory. (*The flame on Semele's tomb grows and brightens.*)

DIONYSUS: Fan to a blaze the flame the lightning lit;
>   Kindle the conflagration of Pentheus' palace!

CHORUS: Look, look, look!
>   Do you see, do you see the flame of Semele's tomb,
>   The flame that remained when she died of the lightning-stroke? (*A noise of crashing masonry is heard.*)
>   Down, trembling Maenads! Hurl yourselves to the ground!
>   Your god is wrecking the palace, roof to floor;
>   He heard our cry—he is coming, the son of Zeus! (*The doors open and* DIONYSUS *appears.*)

DIONYSUS: Women of Asia, why are you cowering terrified on the ground? You heard Bacchus himself shattering Pentheus' palace; come, stand up! Stop this trembling! Courage!

CHORUS: Oh, what a joy to hear your Bacchic shout! You have saved us. We were deserted and alone: how happy we are to see you!

DIONYSUS: Were you plunged in despair, when I was sent inside to be thrown into Pentheus' dark dungeon?

CHORUS: How could we help it? Who was there to protect us, if you were taken? But tell us how you escaped from the clutches of this wicked man.

DIONYSUS: I alone with effortless ease delivered myself.

CHORUS: But did he not bind your arms with knotted ropes?

DIONYSUS: Ha, ha! There I made a mockery of him. He thought he was binding me; but he fed himself on delusion—he neither took hold of me nor even touched me. Near the stall where he took me to shut me in, he found a bull; and he was tying his rope round the bull's knees and hooves, panting with rage, dripping sweat, and biting his lips; while I sat quietly by and watched him. And it was then that Bacchus came and shook the building and made the flame on his mother's tomb flare up. When Pentheus saw this, he imagined the place was on fire, and went rushing this way and that, calling to the servants to bring water, till the whole household was in commotion —all for nothing.

Then he thought I had escaped. He left throwing water, snatched up his murderous sword and darted into the palace. Thereupon Dionysus—or so it seemed to me; I tell what I thought—made a phantom figure appear in the palace courtyard; and Pentheus flew at it, and kept stabbing at the sunny air, imagining he was killing *me*.

But the god had further humiliation in store for him: he laid the stable-buildings in ruins on the ground—there they lie, a heap of rubble, to break his heart as he looks at my prison. Now he is helpless with exhaustion. He has dropped his sword. He, a mortal man, dared to take arms against a god. I walked quietly out of the palace, and here I am. Pentheus does not disturb me. But I hear his heavy tread indoors; I think he will be out here in a moment. What will he say after this? For all his rage, he shall not ruffle me. The wise man preserves a smooth-tempered self-control. (*Enter* PENTHEUS.)

PENTHEUS: This is outrageous. That foreigner was locked up and in chains a little while ago; now he has escaped me. (*He sees* DIONYSUS *and gives an excited shout.*) That's the man! What's going on? How did you get out? How dare you show yourself here before my very doors?

DIONYSUS: Stay where you are. You are angry. Now control yourself.

PENTHEUS: You were bound and locked in: how did you escape?

DIONYSUS: Did you not hear me say that I should be set free by—

PENTHEUS: By whom? Everything you say is strange.

DIONYSUS: By him who plants for mortals the rich-clustered vine.

PENTHEUS: The god who makes men fools and women mad.

DIONYSUS: A splendid insult, that, to Dionysus!

PENTHEUS (*to attendant guards*): Close the gates all round—every gate in the city wall.

DIONYSUS: And why? Cannot gods pass even over walls?

PENTHEUS: Oh, you know everything—except the things you ought to know.

DIONYSUS: The things one ought to know most of all, those things I know.

But first listen to what this man has to tell you; he comes from the mountains with news.—I will stay here; I promise not to run away. (*Enter a* HERDSMAN.)

HERDSMAN: Pentheus, ruler of Thebes! I come from Cithaeron, where the ground is never free from dazzling shafts of snow.

PENTHEUS: And what urgent news do you bring me?

HERDSMAN: I have seen the holy Bacchae, who in madness went streaming bare-limbed out of the city gates. I have come with the intention of telling you, my lord, and the city, of their strange and terrible doings—things past all wonder. But I would like to know first if I may speak freely of what is going on there, or if I should trim my words. I am afraid of your hastiness, my lord, your hot temper; you are too much like a king.

PENTHEUS: Say all that you have to say; fear nothing from me. The more terrible your story about the Bacchae, the more certainly will I execute justice upon this man, the instigator of their wickedness.

HERDSMAN: Just when the sun's rays first beamed out to warm the earth, I was pasturing my cattle and working up towards the high ground; when I saw three groups of women who had been dancing together. The leader of one group was Autonoe; your mother Agauë was at the head of the second, and Ino of the third. They were all sleeping, stretched out and quiet. Some rested on beds of pine-needles, some had pillows of oak-leaves; they lay just as they had thrown themselves down on the ground,—but with modesty in their posture; they were not drunk with wine, as you told us, or with music of flutes; nor

was there any love-making there in the loveliness of the woods.

As soon as your mother Agauë heard the lowing of the horned cattle, she stood up among the Bacchae and called loudly to them to rouse themselves from sleep. And they threw off the strong sleep from their eyes and leapt to their feet. They were a sight to marvel at for modesty and comeliness—women old and young, and girls still unmarried. First they let down their hair over their shoulders; those whose fawnskins had come loose from their fastenings tied them up; and they girdled the dappled fur with snakes which licked their cheeks. And some would have in their arms a young gazelle, or wild wolf-cubs, and give them their own white milk—those who had infants at home recently born, so that their breasts were still full. And they wreathed their heads with garlands of ivy and oak and flowering bryony.

And one of them took her thyrsus and struck it on the rock; and from the rock there gushed a spring of limpid water; another struck her wand down into the earth, and there the god made a fountain of wine spring up; and any who wanted milk had only to scratch the earth with the tip of her fingers, and there was the white stream flowing for her to drink; and from the ivy-bound thyrsus a sweet ooze of honey dripped. Oh! if you had been there and seen all this, you would have entreated with prayers this god whom you now accuse.

Well, we herdsmen and shepherds gathered and stood talking together, and arguing about these strange and extraordinary doings. And one fellow, a gadder up to town, and a good speaker, addressed the rest of us. 'You who live on the holy mountain heights,' he said, 'how if we should hunt down the king's mother, Agauë, bring her away from these orgies, and do the king a service?' We thought it was a good suggestion; so we hid ourselves among the leafy bushes and waited our chance.

When the set time came, the women began brandishing their wands and preparing to dance, calling in unison on the son of Zeus, 'Iacchus! Bromius!' And the whole mountain, and the wild beasts too, became a part of their joyful dance—there was nothing that was not roused to leap and run.

Now Agauë as she ran happened to pass close to me; so I sprang out of the ambush where we lay hidden, meaning to capture her. But she cried out, 'Oh, my swift hounds, we are being hunted by these men. Come, then, and follow; arm yourselves with the thyrsus, and follow me!'

So we fled, and escaped being torn in pieces by these possessed women. But our cattle were feeding there on the fresh grass; and the Bacchae attacked them, with their bare hands. You could see Agauë take up a bellowing young heifer with full udders, and hold it by the legs with her two arms stretched wide. Others were tearing our cows limb from limb, and you could see perhaps some ribs or a cleft hoof being tossed high and low; and pieces of bloody flesh hung dripping on the pine-branches. And bulls, which one moment were savagely looking along their horns, the next were thrown bodily to the ground, dragged down by the soft hands of girls—thousands of them; and they stripped the flesh off their bodies faster than you could wink your royal eyes.

Then, like birds, skimming the ground as they ran, they scoured the plain which stretches by the river Asopus and produces a rich harvest for Thebes; and like an enemy army they bore down on the villages of Hysiae and Erythrae, which lie on the low slopes of Cithaeron, and ransacked them. They snatched up children out of the houses; all the plunder they laid on their shoulders stayed safely there without any fastening; nothing fell to the dark earth, not bronze or iron even; they carried fire on their heads, and their hair was not burnt.

The villagers, of course, were furious at being plundered by the Bacchae, and they resisted with weapons; and then, my lord, was an astonishing sight to behold. The spears cast by the villagers drew no blood; but the women, hurling the thyrsus like a spear, dealt wounds; those women turned the men to flight. There was the power of a god in that.

Then they went back to the place they had started from, to those fountains the god had made flow for them. And they washed off the blood, and the snakes licked the stains clean from their cheeks.

So, master, whoever this god may be, receive him in our city. He has great power in many ways; but especially, as I hear, it was he who gave men the gift of the vine as a cure for sorrow. And if there were no more wine, why, there's an end of love, and of every other pleasure in life.

CHORUS: I hesitate to speak freely before the king; yet I will say it: there is no greater god than Dionysus.

PENTHEUS: This outrageous Bacchism advances on us like a spreading fire, disgracing us before all Hellas. We must waste no time. (*To the* HERDSMAN.) Go at once to the Electran gate; tell all my men who bear shields, heavy or light, all who ride fast horses or twang the bowstring, to meet me there in readiness for an assault on the Bacchae. This is past all bearing, if we are to let women so defy us.

DIONYSUS: You refuse, Pentheus, to listen to what I say or to alter your behaviour. Yet, in spite of all I have suffered at your hands, I warn you to stay where you are and not to take arms against a god. Dionysus will not stand quietly by and see you drive his Bacchae from their mountain rites.

PENTHEUS: I want no instruction from you. You have escaped from your fetters—be content; or I will punish you again.

DIONYSUS: You are a mortal, he is a god. If I were you I would control my rage and sacrifice to him, rather than kick against the pricks.

PENTHEUS: Sacrifice! I will indeed—an offering of women's blood, slaughtered as they deserve in the glens of Cithaeron.

DIONYSUS: You will all be put to flight. It would be disgraceful for the wands of Bacchic women to rout your brazen shields.

PENTHEUS: This foreigner is an impossible man to deal with; in prison or out, he will not hold his tongue.

DIONYSUS: My friend! A happy settlement may still be found.

PENTHEUS: How? By making me a slave to my own slaves?

DIONYSUS: I will bring those women here, without use of weapons.

PENTHEUS: Heaven help us, you are plotting some trick.

DIONYSUS: A trick? If I use my power to save you?

PENTHEUS: This is something you have arranged with the women, so that the revelling may continue.

DIONYSUS: This is something, certainly, that I have arranged—not with them, but with the god.

PENTHEUS: That is enough from you.—Bring out my armour, there!

DIONYSUS (*with an authoritative shout*): Wait! (*Then, quietly.*) Would you like to *see* those women, sitting together, there in the mountains?

PENTHEUS: Yes, indeed; I would give a large sum of gold to see them. (*From now on* DIONYSUS *gradually establishes a complete ascendancy over* PENTHEUS.)

DIONYSUS: And what has betrayed you into this great eagerness?

PENTHEUS: I am not eager to see them drunk; that would be a painful sight.

DIONYSUS: Yet you would be glad to see a sight that would pain you?

PENTHEUS: I would, yes; if I could sit quietly under the pine-trees and watch.

DIONYSUS: However secretly you go they will track you down.

PENTHEUS: You are quite right. I will go openly.

DIONYSUS: Shall I show you the way, then? You will venture on this?

PENTHEUS: Lead me there at once; I am impatient.

DIONYSUS: Then, first dress yourself in a fine linen gown.

PENTHEUS: Why a linen gown? Must I change my sex?

DIONYSUS: They will kill you if you are seen there dressed as a man.

PENTHEUS: You are quite right; you think of everything!

DIONYSUS: It was Dionysus who inspired me with that thought.

PENTHEUS: How can your suggestion best be carried out?

DIONYSUS: I will come indoors with you and dress you.

PENTHEUS: Dress me? Not in woman's clothes? I would be ashamed.

DIONYSUS: You have lost your enthusiasm for watching the Maenads.

PENTHEUS: What kind of dress do you say you will put on me?

DIONYSUS: I will cover your head with long, flowing hair.

PENTHEUS: And after that? What will my costume look like?

DIONYSUS: A robe falling to your feet; and a snood on your head.

PENTHEUS: Anything else?

DIONYSUS: A thyrsus in your hand, and a dappled fawnskin round you.

PENTHEUS: I could never wear woman's clothes.

DIONYSUS: If you join battle with the Bacchae there will be bloodshed.

PENTHEUS: You are right; I must first go to spy on them.

DIONYSUS: That is wiser than inviting violence by using it.

PENTHEUS: And how shall I get through the streets of Thebes without being seen?

DIONYSUS: We will go by lonely ways; I will guide you.

PENTHEUS: I must not be laughed at by the Bacchae—anything rather than that. Now I will go in, and decide how best to act.

DIONYSUS: You may. My own preparations are all made.

PENTHEUS: I will go, then; and I will either visit the mountains armed—or else I will follow your advice. (*Exit* PENTHEUS.)

DIONYSUS: Women, this man is walking into the net. He will visit the Bacchae; and there he shall be punished with death.

Dionysus (for you are not far away), all is now in your hands. Let us be revenged on him! And—first assail him with fantastic madness and drive him out of his mind; for while he is sane he will never consent to put on a woman's clothes; but once he has broken from the rein of reason he will put them on. I long to set Thebes laughing at him, as I lead him dressed like a woman through the streets; to humble him from the arrogance with which he threatened me at first.

Now I will go, to array Pentheus in the dress which he will take down with him to the world of the dead, slaughtered by his own mother's hands. And he shall know the son of Zeus, Dionysus; who, though most gentle to mankind, can prove a god of terror irresistible. (DIONYSUS *follows* PEN-THEUS *into the palace*.)

CHORUS: O for long nights of   (*Strophe*
    worship, gay
With the pale gleam of dancing feet,
With head tossed high to the dewy air—
Pleasure mysterious and sweet!
O for the joy of a fawn at play
In the fragrant meadow's green delight,
Who has leapt out free from the woven
    snare,
Away from the terror of chase and flight,
And the huntsman's shout, and the strain-
    ing pack,
And skims the sand by the river's brim
With the speed of wind in each aching
    limb,
To the blessed lonely forest where
The soil's unmarked by a human track,
And leaves hang thick and the shades are
    dim.

What prayer should we call   (*Refrain*
    wise?
What gift of Heaven should man
Count a more noble prize,
A prayer more prudent, than
To stretch a conquering arm
Over the fallen crest
Of those who wished us harm?
And what is noble every heart loves best.

Slow, yet unfailing, move   (*Antistrophe*
    the Powers
Of Heaven with the moving hours.
When mind runs mad, dishonours God,
And worships self and senseless pride,
Then Law eternal wields the rod.
Still Heaven hunts down the impious man,
Though divine subtlety may hide
Time's creeping foot. No mortal ought
To challenge Time—to overbear
Custom in act, or age in thought.
All men, at little cost, may share
The blessing of a pious creed;
Truths more than mortal, which began
In the beginning, and belong
To very nature—these indeed
Reign in our world, are fixed and strong.

What prayer should we call   (*Refrain*
    wise?

What gift of Heaven should man
Count a more noble prize,
A prayer more prudent, than
To stretch a conquering arm
Over the fallen crest
Of those who wished us harm?
And what is noble every heart loves best.

Blest is the man who cheats   (*Epode*
    the stormy sea
And safely moors beside the sheltering
    quay;
So, blest is he who triumphs over trial.
One man, by various means, in wealth or
    strength
Outdoes his neighbour; hope in a thousand
    hearts
Colours a thousand different dreams; at
    length
Some find a dear fulfillment, some denial.
    But this I say,
    That he who best
    Enjoys each passing day
Is truly blest. (*Enter* DIONYSUS. *He turns
    to call* PENTHEUS.)

DIONYSUS: Come, perverse man, greedy for
sights you should not see, impatient for
deeds you should not do—Pentheus! Come
out of the palace and show yourself to me,
wearing the garb of a frenzied Bacchic
woman, ready to spy on your mother and
all her company! (*Enter* PENTHEUS *dressed
as a Bacchic devotee. He is dazed, and entirely subservient to* DIONYSUS.) Ah! You
look exactly like one of Cadmus' daughters.
PENTHEUS: Why—I seem to see two suns; I
see a double Thebes, and the city wall with
its seven gates—double! I see you leading
me forward—you are like a bull, you have
horns growing on your head. Tell me, were
you an animal a little while ago? You have
certainly become a bull.
DIONYSUS: The god did not favour us before;
now he is with us, and we have made our
peace with him. Now you see as you ought
to see.
PENTHEUS: Well, how do I look? Do you
think I stand like Ino or like my mother
Agauë?
DIONYSUS: I think you are their very image.
Wait—this curl of hair is out of place, not
as I arranged it under your snood.

PENTHEUS: I must have shaken it loose indoors, tossing my head up and down like a Bacchic reveller.

DIONYSUS: Come, it is for me to look after you; I will set it straight. Now, lift your head.

PENTHEUS: There, *you* put it right. I depend entirely on you.

DIONYSUS: And your girdle is loose; and the folds of your gown are not hanging straight to your ankles.

PENTHEUS: I agree, they are not—at least, here by the right foot. But on the other side the gown hangs well to the heel.

DIONYSUS: I think you will reckon me the chief of your friends, when you see the Bacchae and find to your surprise how well they are behaving—will you not? (*But* PENTHEUS *is not listening.*)

PENTHEUS: Ought I to hold my thyrsus in this hand or in the right, to look more like a Bacchanal?

DIONYSUS: Hold it in your right hand, and raise it at the same time as you raise your right foot. (PENTHEUS *attempts it.*) I am glad you are so—changed in mind.

PENTHEUS: Do you think I could lift up on my shoulders the glens of Cithaeron, with all the women revelling there?

DIONYSUS: You could, if you wished. Before, your mind was diseased; now, it is as it should be.

PENTHEUS: Shall we take crowbars? Or shall I simply set my shoulder, or my arm, against the mountain peaks, and tear them up with my hands?

DIONYSUS: No, you must not destroy the homes of the Nymphs, and the haunts where Pan sits piping.

PENTHEUS: You are right. Women are not to be subdued by brute force. I will hide among the pine-trees.

DIONYSUS: Hide? Yes! You shall find the right hiding-place to hide you—coming like a crafty spy to watch the Maenads!

PENTHEUS: Yes, I can picture them—like birds in the thickets, wrapped in the sweet snare of love.

DIONYSUS: That is the very thing you are going to look for; and perhaps you will catch them—if you are not first caught yourself.

PENTHEUS: Now lead me through the central streets of Thebes. There is no one dares to do this—I am the only man among them.

DIONYSUS: You alone suffer for the whole city —you alone; and the struggle that awaits you is your destined ordeal. Come; I will see you safely there; another shall bring you home.

PENTHEUS: You mean my mother?

DIONYSUS: A sight for all to see.

PENTHEUS: It is for that I am going.

DIONYSUS: You will be carried home—

PENTHEUS: What splendour that will be!

DIONYSUS:—in your mother's arms.

PENTHEUS: Why, you make a weakling of me!

DIONYSUS: That is—one way of putting it.

PENTHEUS: Yet it is what I deserve. (*Exit* PENTHEUS.)

DIONYSUS: Pentheus, you are a man to make men fear; and fearful will be your end—an end that shall raise your fame to the height of Heaven. Stretch out your hands, Agauë, and you her sisters, daughters of Cadmus! I am bringing the young man to his battle; and I and Dionysus shall be victors. (*Then he adds quietly*) What more shall happen, the event will show. (*Exit* DIONYSUS.)

CHORUS: Hounds of Madness,   (*Strophe*
  fly to the mountain, fly
Where Cadmus' daughters are dancing in ecstasy!
Madden them like a frenzied herd stampeding,
Against the madman hiding in woman's clothes
To spy on the Maenad's rapture!
First his mother shall see him craning his neck
Down from a rounded rock or a withered trunk,
And shout to the Maenads, 'Who is the man, you Bacchae,
Who has come to the mountain, come to the mountain spying
On the swift wild mountain-dances of Cadmus' daughters?
Which of you is his mother?
No, that lad never lay in a woman's womb;
A lioness gave him suck, or a Libyan Gorgon!'

Justice, now be revealed! Now let your sword

Thrust—through and through—to sever the throat
Of the godless, lawless, shameless son of Echion,
Who sprang from the womb of Earth!

See! with contempt of   (*Antistrophe*
right, with a reckless rage
To combat your and your mother's mysteries, Bacchus,
With maniac fury out he goes, stark mad,
For a trial of strength against *your* invincible arm!
The sober and humble heart
That accords the gods their due without carp or cavil,
And knows that his days are as dust, shall live untouched.
I have no wish to grudge the wise their wisdom;
But the joys *I* seek are greater, outshine all others,
And lead our life to goodness and loveliness:
The joy of the holy heart
That night and day is bent to honour the gods
And disown all custom that breaks the bounds of right.

Justice, now be revealed! Now let your sword
Thrust—through and through—to sever the throat
Of the godless, lawless, shameless son of Echion,
Who sprang from the womb of Earth!
(*Then with growing excitement,
shouting in unison, and dancing to
the rhythm of their words.*)
Come, Dionysus!   (*Epode*
Come, and appear to us!
Come like a bull or a
Hundred-headed serpent,
Come like a lion snorting
Flame from your nostrils!
Swoop down, Bacchus, on the
Hunter of the Bacchae;
Smile at him and snare him;
Then let the stampeding
Herd of the Maenads
Throw him and throttle him,
Catch, trip, trample him to death!
(*Enter a* MESSENGER.)

MESSENGER: O house once glorious throughout Hellas, house of the old Sidonian king who sowed in this soil the dragon's earthborn crop! How I weep for you! I am a slave; but a good slave feels the blow that strikes his master.

CHORUS: What has happened? Have you news from the mountains?

MESSENGER: Pentheus, the son of Echion, is dead.

CHORUS: Dionysus, god of rapture! Your power is revealed!

MESSENGER: What? What did you say? Do you even exult at the cruel end that has overtaken my master?

CHORUS: I am no Greek; I sing for joy in a foreign tune. Now I've no need to cower in terror of prison.

MESSENGER: Do you suppose Thebes has no men left to take command?

CHORUS: Dionysus commands *me*; not Thebes, but Dionysus.

MESSENGER: Allowance must be made for you; yet, when irreparable wrong has been done, it is shameful to rejoice.

CHORUS: Tell me what happened; tell me, how did he die—this tyrant pursuing his tyranny?

MESSENGER: When we had left the houses of Thebes behind, and crossed the river Asopus, we began climbing the foothills of Cithaeron, Pentheus and I—I was attending my master—, and that foreigner who was showing us the way to what we were to see.

Well, first we sat down in a grassy glade; we kept our footsteps and our talk as quiet as possible, so as to see without being seen. We were in a valley full of streams, with cliffs on either side; and there, under the close shade of pine-trees, the Maenads were sitting, their hands busy at their happy tasks. Some of them were twining with fresh leaves a thyrsus that had lost its ivy; others, like foals let loose from the painted yokes, were singing holy songs to each other in turn.

But the ill-fated Pentheus did not see these women; and he said, 'From where we are standing, my friend, I cannot clearly make out these pretended worshippers, these Maenads; if I climbed a towering pine-tree on the cliff-side I could have a proper view of their shameful behaviour.'

And then—I saw that foreigner do an amazing thing. He took hold of the topmost skiey branch of a pine and dragged it down, down, down to the dark earth. It was bent in a circle as a bow is bent, as the curve of a wheel, drawn with peg and line, bends the running rim to its own shape; so the foreigner took that mountain-pine in his hands and bent it to the ground —a thing no mortal man could do. Then he set Pentheus on the top branches, and began letting the tree spring upright, slipping it steadily through his grip, and taking care not to unseat him; and the pine-trunk straightened itself and soared into the soaring sky with the King sitting astride; so that he was more plainly visible to the women than they were to him.

And he was just coming into view on his lofty perch,—the foreigner was nowhere to be seen—when a voice—I suppose it was Dionysus—pealed out from heaven: 'Women! I bring you the man who made a mockery of you, and of me, and of my holy rites. Now punish him.' And in the very moment the voice spoke, a flash of unearthly fire stretched between the sky and the ground.

The whole air fell silent. The wooded glade held every leaf silent. You could hear no cry of any beast. The women had not caught distinctly what the voice said; they stood up and gazed around. Then came a second word of command. As soon as Cadmus' daughters recognized the clear bidding of Bacchus, they darted forward with the speed of doves on the wing, and all the Bacchae after them. Up the valley, along by the stream, over the rocks they went leaping on, possessed with the very breath of the god. When they saw the king sitting in the tree, first they climbed the cliff where it rose up like a battlement, and with all their strength pelted him with pieces of rock, or aimed pine-branches at him like javelins. Some were hurling the thyrsus at their pitiable target; but the shots fell short—the height was too great for all their efforts; while the wretched man sat there trapped and helpless.

At last, with a force like lightning, they tore down branches of oak, and used these as levers, trying to tear out the tree's roots. All their struggles were useless. Then Agauë

spoke to them: 'Come, you Maenads, stand round the tree and grip it. We must catch this climbing beast, or he will reveal the secret dances of Dionysus.' A thousand hands grasped the tree; and they tore it from the earth. Then from his high perch plunging and crashing to the ground came Pentheus, with one incessant scream as he understood what end was near.

First his mother, as priestess, began the ritual of death, and fell upon him. He tore off the headband from his hair, that his wretched mother might recognize him and not kill him. 'Mother!' he cried, touching her cheek, 'it is I, your son, Pentheus, whom you bore to Echion. O mother, have mercy on me; I have sinned, but I am your son: do not kill me!'

Agauë was foaming at the mouth, her eyes were rolling wildly. She was not in her right mind; she was under the power of Dionysus; and she would not listen to him. She gripped his right arm between wrist and elbow; she set her foot against his ribs; and she tore his arm off by the shoulder. It was no strength of hers that did it; the god was in her fingers and made it easy. Ino was at him on the other side, tearing at his flesh; and now Autonoe joined them, and the whole pack of raving women. There was a single continuous yell—Pentheus shrieking as long as life was left in him, the women howling in triumph. One of them was carrying an arm, another had a foot with the shoe still on it; the ribs were stripped—clawed clean. Every hand was thick red with blood; and they were tossing and catching, to and fro, like a ball, the flesh of Pentheus.

His body lies scattered, some under hard rocks, some in the deep green woods; it will not be easy to find. His poor head— his mother is holding it; she has fixed it on the point of her thyrsus, and carries it openly over the mountain-side, leaving her sisters dancing with the Maenads. And she is coming here to the palace, exulting in her fearful and horrible prey, shouting to Bacchus as her fellow-hunter, calling him her partner in the kill, her comrade in victory. But Bacchus gives her tears for her reward.

I am going; I want to be far away from this horror before Agauë comes.

The noblest thing a man can have is a humble and quiet heart that reveres the gods. I think that is also the wisest thing for a man to possess, if he will but use it. (*Exit.*)

CHORUS: Let us dance a dance to Bacchus, shout and sing
For the fall of Pentheus, heir of the dragon's seed,
Who hid his beard in a woman's gown,
And sealed his death with the holy sign
Of ivy wreathing a fennel-reed,
When bull led man to the ritual slaughter-ring.
Frenzied daughters of Cadmus, what renown
Your victory wins you—such a song
As groans must stifle, tears must drown!
Emblem of conquest, brave and fine!—
A mother's hand, defiled
With blood and dripping red
Caresses the torn head
Of her own murdered child!

But look! I see Pentheus' mother, Aga[u]ë, running towards the palace, with eyes wildly rolling. Welcome the worshipping company of Dionysus!

AGAUË *appears, frenzied and panting, with* PENTHEUS' *head held in her hand. The rest of her band of devotees, whom the* CHORUS *saw approaching with her, do not enter; but a few are seen standing by the entrance, where they wait until the end of the play.*

AGAUË: Women of Asia! Worshippers of Bacchus! (AGAUË *tries to show them* PENTHEUS' *head; they shrink from it.*)
CHORUS: Why do you urge me? Oh!
AGAUË: I am bringing home from the mountains
A vine-branch freshly cut,
For the gods have blessed our hunting.
CHORUS: We see it . . . and welcome you in fellowship.
AGAUË: I caught him without a trap,
A lion-cub, young and wild.
Look, you may see him: there!
CHORUS: Where was it?
AGAUË: On Cithaeron;
The wild and empty mountain—
CHORUS: Cithaeron!

AGAUË: . . . spilt his life-blood.
CHORUS: Who shot him?
AGAUË: I was first;
All the women are singing,
'Honour to great Agaüe!'
CHORUS: And then—who next?
AGAUË: Why, Cadmus' . . .
CHORUS: What—Cadmus?
AGAUË: Yes, his daughters—
But after me, after me—
Laid their hands to the kill.
Today was a splendid hunt!
Come now, join in the feast!
CHORUS: What, wretched woman? *Feast?*
AGAUË (*tenderly stroking the head as she holds it*): This calf is young: how thickly
The new-grown hair goes crisping
Up to his delicate crest!
CHORUS: Indeed, his long hair makes him
Look like some wild creature.
AGAUË: The god is a skilled hunter;
And he poised his hunting women,
And hurled them at the quarry.
CHORUS: True, our god is a hunter.
AGAUË: Do you praise me?
CHORUS: Yes, we praise you.
AGAUË: So will the sons of Cadmus . . .
CHORUS: And Pentheus too, Agaüe?
AGAUË: Yes, he will praise his mother
For the lion-cub she killed.
CHORUS: Oh, fearful!
AGAUË: Ay, fearful!
CHORUS: You are happy?
AGAUË: I am enraptured;
Great in the eyes of the world,
Great are the deeds I've done,
And the hunt that I hunted there!

CHORUS: Then, poor Agaüe, show this triumphant spoil of yours that you've carried home—show it to the people of Thebes.
AGAUË: Come, then, all you Thebans who live in this lofty and lovely city, come and see the beast we have caught and killed—we, Cadmus' daughters; caught not with nets or thonged Thessalian javelins, but with our own white arms and fingers. After this, should huntsmen boast, who buy their paltry tools from the armourer? We with our bare hands caught this quarry, then tore it limb from limb.

Where is my father? Let him come here! And my son Pentheus, where is he? Let him get a strong ladder, and take this head, and climb up and nail it to the top of the palace wall, this lion that I hunted and brought home! (*Enter* CADMUS *with attendants bearing the body of* PENTHEUS.)

CADMUS: Come, men. Bring your sad burden that was Pentheus; bring him to his home. I found the fragments of his body scattered in a thousand places, no two together, about the glens of Cithaeron, or hidden in thick woods; and with weary search I gathered them, and have brought them here.

I had already returned with old Teiresias from the Bacchic dance, and was inside the walls of the city, when news was brought me of my daughters' terrible deed. I turned straight back to the mountain; and here I bring my son, killed by the Maenads. I saw Autonoe, who bore Acteon to Aristaeus, and her sister Ino, there among the copses, still in their unhappy frenzy; but I understand that Agaue came raving towards the palace—it is true, there she is! Oh, what a terrible sight!

AGAUË: Father! You may boast as loudly as you will, that no man living is so blest in his daughters; I mean all three, but myself especially. I have left weaving at the loom for greater things—for hunting wild beasts with my bare hands. See here what I carry in my arms; this is the prize I won; I have brought it to hang on your palace wall. Take it, Father; hold it. Be proud of my hunting, and call your friends to a banquet; let them all envy and congratulate you, for the splendour of my deed.

CADMUS: O anguish unmeasured, intolerable! O pitiful hands—your splendid deed is murder! What victim is this you would lay at the gods' feet, calling Thebes, and me, to a banquet? Your suffering is worst, but mine is next. Dionysus, god of joy, has been just, but too cruel. He was born of my blood, and he has destroyed my house.

AGAUË: How ill-humoured old age makes a man! How he scowls at me! I wish that my son were a great hunter, like his mother, pursuing wild beasts with all the young men of Thebes; but he can only fight against gods. Father, you must reason with him. Let someone call him here before me, to see my good fortune.

CADMUS: Oh, my daughters! If you come to understand what you have done, how terrible your suffering will be! But if you remain always as you are now, though you could not be called happy, at least you will not know your own misery.

AGAUË: Misery? What is wrong? Where is my cause for misery?

CADMUS: First, turn your eyes this way—look at the sky.

AGAUË: I am looking. Why do you tell me to look at it?

CADMUS: Is it still the same, or does it seem to you to have changed?

AGAUË: It is brighter than before—more luminous.

CADMUS: And this madness you suffered from —is it still with you?

AGAUË: I do not know what you mean. But I feel a change in my mind; my thoughts are somehow clearer.

CADMUS: Can you now hear and answer clearly?

AGAUË: Yes . . . I have forgotten what we said just now, Father.

CADMUS: When you were married, whose house did you come to?

AGAUË: You gave me to Echion, who was said to have been sown in the ground.

CADMUS: Then, Echion had a son born to him—who was he?

AGAUË: Pentheus—my son and his father's.

CADMUS: Yes: and whose head is that you hold in your arms?

AGAUË: A lion's—or so the women said who hunted it.

CADMUS: Now look straight at it; it is not much trouble to look. (AGAUË *looks at the head in silence; then cries out.*)

AGAUË: Oh! What am I looking at? What am I holding?

CADMUS: Look at it steadily, and understand more clearly.

AGAUË: I see—O gods, what horror! What torture!

CADMUS: Does this seem to you like a lion?

AGAUË: No, it is Pentheus' head I hold in my accursed hand.

CADMUS: Tears have been shed for him already—before you knew it was he.

AGAUË: Who killed him? How did he come into my hands?

CADMUS: O bitter truth, revealed in a cruel hour!

AGAUË: Tell me—my heart is bursting—I must know the rest.

CADMUS: You killed him—you and your sisters.

AGAUË: Where was it done? At home? Or where else?

CADMUS: Where Actaeon was torn by hounds.

AGAUË: Cithaeron? What evil fate brought Pentheus there?

CADMUS: He went in scorn of Dionysus and your frenzied worship.

AGAUË: But how was it we were all there?

CADMUS: You were mad; the whole city was possessed by Dionysus.

AGAUË: Now I understand: Dionysus has destroyed us.

CADMUS: He was insulted and abused. You did not acknowledge his godhead.

AGAUË: Where is the dear body of my son, Father?

CADMUS: It is here. I searched long for it, and brought it.

AGAUË: Is it decently composed, limb to limb?

CADMUS: Not yet; we came here as quickly as possible.

AGAUË: I will do it myself, if I may be allowed to touch him.

CADMUS: You will be allowed; your guilt is not greater than his.

AGAUË: But what part had Pentheus in my madness?

CADMUS: He was like you in not reverencing Dionysus. Therefore the god has joined all in one destruction, you and your sisters, and Pentheus, to strike down my house and me. I have no son; and now I see the child of your womb, my unhappy daughter, cut off by a shameful and horrible death. Pentheus, dear boy, my daughter's child, this house looked to you as its head; you were its bond of strength; and Thebes feared you. No man would slight your old grandfather if he saw you near; you would give him his deserts. Now I, Cadmus the Great, who sowed in the ground the seed of the Theban race, and reaped a glorious harvest, shall live, a dishonoured exile, far from my home.

O dearest son—yes, even in death you shall be held most dear to me—never again will you touch my beard, and call me Grandfather, and put your arm round me and say, 'Who has wronged you, or insulted you? Who is unkind to you or vexes you? Tell me, Grandfather, that I may punish him.' . . . Never again. Now there is only misery for me, suffering for you, tears for your mother, torment for all our family.

If there be any man who derides the unseen world, let him consider the death of Pentheus, and acknowledge the gods.

CHORUS: Cadmus, I grieve for you. Your grandson suffered justly, but you most cruelly.

AGAUË: Father, you see how one terrible hour has shattered my whole life, and turned my pride to shame, my happiness to horror. Now I long only to compose my son's body for burial, and lament for him; and then to go away and die. But I do not know if this is lawful; my hands are filthy with a pollution of their own making. When I have spilt the blood that is my own, torn the flesh that grew in my own womb, how can I, without offence to the gods, clasp him to my breast, or chant his ritual dirge? Yet I beg you, if you think it not blasphemous, let me touch my son, and say farewell to that dear body which I loved, and destroyed unknowing. It is right that you should pity, for you suffer too, although you have not sinned.

CADMUS: My daughter, you and I and our whole house are crushed and broken by the anger of Dionysus. It is not for me to keep you from your son. Only I would warn you to steel your heart against a sight that must be fearful to any eyes, but most of all to a mother's. (*To his attendants*) Lay your burden here before her, and remove the covering, that Agaüe may see her son. (*The coffin is laid on the ground before* AGAUË, *who kneels beside it.*)

AGAUË: O dearest child, how unnatural are these tears, that should have fallen from your eyes upon my dead face. Now I shall die with none to weep for me. I am justly punished; for in pride I blasphemed the god Dionysus, and did not understand the things I ought to have understood. You too are punished for the same sin; and I cannot tell whether your fate or mine is the more terrible. But since you have suffered with me, you will forgive me both for what I did, not knowing what I did, and for what I do now, touching you with unholy hands—at once your cruellest enemy and your dearest lover.

Now I place your limbs as they should lie; I kiss the flesh that my own body fed, my own care reared to manhood. Come, father, help me; lay his poor head here; as far as we can, make all exact and seemly.

O dearest face, O young fresh cheek; O kingly eyes, your light now darkened! O my son! See, with this veil I now cover your head, your torn and bloodstained limbs.

Now take him up and carry him to burial—a king lured to a shameful death by the anger of a god. (DIONYSUS *appears above the wall of the palace.*)

CHORUS: But look! What is this? It is he, our lord Dionysus himself, no longer disguised as mortal, but in the glory of his godhead!

DIONYSUS: Behold me, a god great and powerful, Dionysus, immortal son of Zeus and Semele!

I come to the City of Seven Gates, to Thebes, whose men and women mocked me, denied my divinity, and refused to receive my holy rites. Now they see clearly the result of impious folly. The royal house is overthrown; the city's streets are full of guilty fear, as every Theban repents too late for his blindness and blasphemy. First and chief in sin was this man Pentheus, who not only rejected my just claims, but put me in fetters and insulted me. Therefore death came to him in the most shameful way of all, at the hands of his own mother. This fate he has justly suffered; for no god can see his worship scorned, and hear his name profaned, and not pursue vengeance to the utmost limit; that mortal men may know that the gods are greater than they.

Now listen further, while I reveal what is destined for the people of Thebes. The day will come when they will be driven from their city to wander East and West over the earth; for Zeus will not suffer a godless city to remain.

Agaue and her sisters must leave Thebes this very day; their exile will prove a full and just penance for the foul pollution they have incurred in this bloodshed. Never again shall they see their native land; for it is an offence to piety that hands so defiled should remain to take part in the city's sacrifices.

Now, Cadmus, I will tell you what suffering you yourself are destined to fulfil. You shall change your form to a serpent; and your wife Harmonia, whom you, though mortal, received from her divine father Ares, shall likewise change to a beast of the earth, and become a snake. Thus says the oracle of Zeus: You, at the head of a barbaric army, shall with your wife drive a pair of oxen yoked to a wagon; with your innumerable host you shall destroy many cities; but when they plunder the temple of Apollo's oracle, their reward shall be sorrow at their home-coming. But you yourself and Harmonia shall be saved by Ares, who shall bestow on you immortal life among the blessed ones.

I, who tell you this, am Dionysus, son of no mortal father, but of Zeus. If you all had chosen wisdom, when you would not, you would have found the son of Zeus your friend, and you would now be happy.

CADMUS: Dionysus, have mercy on us; we have sinned.

DIONYSUS: You recognize me too late; when you should have known me, you did not.

CADMUS: All this we have realized; but your vengeance is too heavy.

DIONYSUS: I am a god; and you insulted me.

CADMUS: Gods should not be like men, keeping anger for ever.

DIONYSUS: Zeus my father ordained this from the beginning.

AGAUE: All hope is gone, father. Our sentence is passed: we are exiles.

DIONYSUS: Why then put off what is inevitable? (*Exit* DIONYSUS.)

CADMUS: O my daughter, what utter misery and horror has overtaken us all—you, and your sisters, and me your unhappy father. In my old age I must leave my home and travel to strange lands. Further than that, it is foretold that I shall lead a mixed barbarian horde against Hellas. Both I and my wife, Harmonia, child of Ares, must take the brute form of serpents, and thus I am to lead her, at the head of an armed force, to desecrate the altars and tombs of the Hellenes. And I am to find no respite from suffering; I may not even cross the deep-flowing stream of Acheron to find peace in death.

AGAUË: And I shall live in exile, separated from you, father.

CADMUS: Poor child! Why do you throw your arms round me, cherishing my white hair as a swan cares for its old and helpless ones?

AGAUË: Where am I to turn, driven from my home and country?

CADMUS: I do not know, child; your father is little help to you.

AGAUË: Farewell, my home; farewell the land I know.
Exiled, accursed and wretched, now I go
Forth from this door where first I came a bride.

CADMUS: Go, daughter; find some secret place to hide
Your shame and sorrow.

AGAUË: Father, I weep for you.

CADMUS: I for your suffering, and your sisters' too.

AGAUË: There is strange tyranny in the god who sent
Against your house this cruel punishment.

CADMUS: Not strange: our citizens despised his claim,
And you, and they, put him to open shame.

AGAUË: Father, farewell.

CADMUS: Poor child! I cannot tell
How you can *fare well*; yet I say, Farewell.

AGAUË: I go to lead my sisters by the hand
To share my wretchedness in a foreign land. (*She turns to the Theban women who have been waiting at the edge of the stage.*)
Come, see me forth.
Gods, lead me to some place
Where loath'd Cithaeron may not see my face,
Nor I Cithaeron. I have had my fill
Of mountain-ecstasy; now take who will
My holy ivy-wreath, my thyrsus-rod,
All that reminds me how I served this god! (*Exit, followed by* CADMUS.)

CHORUS: Gods manifest themselves in many forms,
Bring many matters to surprising ends;
The things we thought would happen do not happen;
The unexpected God makes possible:
And that is what has happened here to-day. (*Exeunt.*)

EVERYMAN

A Fifteenth-Century Morality Play

MESSENGER
GOD: Adonai
DEATH
EVERYMAN
FELLOWSHIP
KINDRED
COUSIN
GOODS
GOOD DEEDS
KNOWLEDGE
CONFESSION
BEAUTY
STRENGTH
DISCRETION
FIVE WITS
ANGEL
DOCTOR

Here beginneth a treatise how the High Father of Heaven sendeth Death to summon every creature to come and give account of their lives in this world, and is in manner of a moral play.

Enter MESSENGER *to speak Prologue.*

MESSENGER: I pray you all give your audience,
And hear this matter with reverence,
By figure a moral play—
The *Summoning of Everyman* called it is,
That of our lives and ending shows
How transitory we be all day.
This matter is wondrous precious,
But the intent of it is more gracious,
And sweet to bear away.
The story saith:—Man, in the beginning,
Look well, and take good heed to the ending,
Be you never so gay!
Ye think sin in the beginning full sweet,
Which in the end causeth the soul to weep,
When the body lieth in clay.
Here shall you see how Fellowship and Jollity,
Both Strength, Pleasure, and Beauty,
Will fade from thee as flower in May.
For ye shall hear how our Heaven King
Calleth Everyman to a general reckoning.
Give audience, and hear what he doth say.
(*Exit.*)

GOD *speaketh (from above).*

GOD: I perceive, here in my majesty,
How that all creatures be to me unkind,
Living without dread in worldly prosperity.
Of ghostly [1] sight the people be so blind,
Drowned in sin, they know me not for their God.
In worldly riches is all their mind,
They fear not my rightwiseness, the sharp rod;
My love that I showed when I for them died
They forget clean, and shedding of my blood red;
I hanged between two, it cannot be denied;
To get them life I suffered to be dead;
I healed their feet, with thorns hurt was my head.
I could do no more than I did, truly;

And now I see the people do clean forsake me.
They use the seven deadly sins damnable;
As pride, covetise, wrath, and lechery,
Now in the world be made commendable;
And thus they leave of angels the heavenly company.
Every man liveth so after his own pleasure,
And yet of their life they be nothing sure.
I see the more that I them forbear
The worse they be from year to year;
All that liveth appaireth [2] fast.
Therefore I will, in all the haste,
Have a reckoning of every man's person;
For, and [3] I leave the people thus alone
In their life and wicked tempests,
Verily they will become much worse than beasts;
For now one would by envy another up eat;
Charity they all do clean forget.
I hoped well that every man
In my glory should make his mansion,
And thereto I had them all elect;
But now I see, like traitors deject,
They thank me not for the pleasure that I to them meant,
Nor yet for their being that I them have lent.
I proffered the people great multitude of mercy,
And few there be that asketh it heartily;
They be so cumbered with worldly riches,
That needs on them I must do justice,
On every man living, without fear.
Where art thou, Death, thou mighty messenger?

Enter DEATH.

DEATH: Almighty God, I am here at your will,
Your commandment to fulfil.
GOD: Go thou to Everyman,
And show him, in my name,
A pilgrimage he must on him take,
Which he in no wise may escape;
And that he bring with him a sure reckoning
Without delay or any tarrying.
DEATH: Lord, I will in the world go run over all,
And cruelly out search both great and small. (GOD *withdraws.*)

[2] Is impaired.
[3] If (thus frequently throughout the play).

[1] Spiritual.

Every man will I beset that liveth beastly
Out of God's laws, and dreadeth not folly.
He that loveth riches I will strike with my
  dart,
His sight to blind, and from heaven to de-
  part,
Except that alms be his good friend,
In hell for to dwell, world without end.
Lo, yonder I see Everyman walking;
Full little he thinketh on my coming;
His mind is on fleshly lusts and his trea-
  sure;
And great pain it shall cause him to endure
Before the Lord, Heaven King.
Everyman, stand still! Whither art thou
  going
Thus gaily? Hast thou thy Maker forgot?
EVERYMAN: Why askest thou?
  Wouldst thou wete? [4]
DEATH: Yea, sir, I will show you;
  In great haste I am sent to thee
  From God out of his Majesty.
EVERYMAN: What, sent to me?
DEATH: Yea, certainly.
  Though thou have forgot him here,
  He thinketh on thee in the heavenly
    sphere,
  As, ere we depart, thou shalt know.
EVERYMAN: What desireth God of me?
DEATH: That shall I show thee;
  A reckoning he will needs have
  Without any longer respite.
EVERYMAN: To give a reckoning longer lei-
  sure I crave;
  This blind matter troubleth my wit.
DEATH: On thee thou must take a long jour-
  ney;
  Therefore thy book of count with thee thou
    bring;
  For turn again thou can not by no way.
  And look thou be sure of thy reckoning,
  For before God thou shalt answer and show
  Thy many bad deeds, and good but a few,
  How thou hast spent thy life, and in what
    wise,
  Before the Chief Lord of paradise.
  Have ado [5] that we were in that way,
  For, wete thou well, thou shalt make none
    attorney.
EVERYMAN: Full unready I am such reckon-
  ing to give.
  I know thee not. What messenger art thou?

DEATH: I am Death, that no man dreadeth.
  For every man I 'rest, and no man spareth;
  For it is God's commandment
  That all to me should be obedient.
EVERYMAN: O Death! thou comest when I
  had thee least in mind!
  In thy power it lieth me to save,
  Yet of my goods will I give thee, if thou
    will be kind;
  Yea, a thousand pound shalt thou have,
  If thou defer this matter till another day.
DEATH: Everyman, it may not be, by no way!
  I set not by gold, silver, nor riches,
  Nor by pope, emperor, king, duke, nor
    princes.
  For, and I would receive gifts great,
  All the world I might get;
  But my custom is clean contrary.
  I give thee no respite. Come hence, and
    not tarry.
EVERYMAN: Alas! shall I have no longer re-
  spite?
  I may say Death giveth no warning.
  To think on thee, it maketh my heart sick,
  For all unready is my book of reckoning.
  But twelve year and I might have abiding,
  My counting-book I would make so clear,
  That my reckoning I should not need to
    fear.
  Wherefore, Death, I pray thee, for God's
    mercy,
  Spare me till I be provided of remedy.
DEATH: Thee availeth not to cry, weep, and
    pray;
  But haste thee lightly that thou were gone
    that journey,
  And prove thy friends if thou can.
  For wete thou well the tide abideth no
    man;
  And in the world each living creature
  For Adam's sin must die of nature.
EVERYMAN: Death, if I should this pilgrimage
    take,
  And my reckoning surely make,
  Show me, for saint charity,
  Should I not come again shortly?
DEATH: No, Everyman; and thou be once
    there,
  Thou mayst never more come here,
  Trust me verily.
EVERYMAN: O gracious God, in the high seat
    celestial,
  Have mercy on me in this most need!

[4] Know.   [5] Get ready.

Shall I have no company from this vale terrestrial
Of mine acquaintance that way me to lead?
DEATH: Yea, if any be so hardy,
That would go with thee and bear thee company.
Hie thee that thou were gone to God's magnificence,
Thy reckoning to give before his presence.
What! weenest thou thy life is given thee,
And thy worldly goods also?
EVERYMAN: I had weened so, verily.
DEATH: Nay, nay; it was but lent thee;
For, as soon as thou art gone,
Another a while shall have it, and then go therefrom
Even as thou hast done.
Everyman, thou art mad! Thou hast thy wits five,
And here on earth will not amend thy life;
For suddenly I do come.
EVERYMAN: O wretched caitiff! whither shall I flee,
That I might 'scape endless sorrow?
Now, gentle Death, spare me till tomorrow,
That I may amend me
With good advisement.
DEATH: Nay, thereto I will not consent,
Nor no man will I respite,
But to the heart suddenly I shall smite
Without any advisement.
And now out of thy sight I will me hie;
See thou make thee ready shortly,
For thou mayst say this is the day
That no man living may 'scape away. (*Exit* DEATH.)
EVERYMAN: Alas! I may well weep with sighs deep.
Now have I no manner of company
To help me in my journey and me to keep;
And also my writing is full unready.
How shall I do now for to excuse me?
I would to God I had never been gete! [6]
To my soul a full great profit it had be;
For now I fear pains huge and great.
The time passeth; Lord, help, that all wrought.
For though I mourn it availeth naught.
The day passeth, and is almost a-go;
I wot not well what for to do.
To whom were I best my complaint to make?

What if I to Fellowship thereof spake,
And showed him of this sudden chance?
For in him is all mine affiance,[7]
We have in the world so many a day
Been good friends in sport and play.
I see him yonder, certainly;
I trust that he will bear me company;
Therefore to him will I speak to ease my sorrow.
Well met, good Fellowship, and good morrow! (FELLOWSHIP *speaketh.*)
FELLOWSHIP: Everyman, good morrow, by this day!
Sir, why lookest thou so piteously?
If any thing be amiss, I pray thee me say,
That I may help to remedy.
EVERYMAN: Yea, good Fellowship, yea
I am in great jeopardy.
FELLOWSHIP: My true friend, show to me your mind;
I will not forsake thee to my life's end
In the way of good company.
EVERYMAN: That was well spoken, and lovingly.
FELLOWSHIP: Sir, I must needs know your heaviness;
I have pity to see you in any distress;
If any have you wronged, ye shall revenged be,
Though I on the ground be slain for thee,
Though that I know before that I should die.
EVERYMAN: Verily, Fellowship, gramercy.
FELLOWSHIP: Tush! by thy thanks I set not a straw!
Show me your grief, and say no more.
EVERYMAN: If I my heart should to you break,
And then you to turn your mind from me,
And would not me comfort when you hear me speak,
Then should I ten times sorrier be.
FELLOWSHIP: Sir, I say as I will do, indeed.
EVERYMAN: Then be you a good friend at need;
I have found you true here before.
FELLOWSHIP: And so ye shall evermore;
For, in faith, and thou go to hell,
I will not forsake thee by the way!
EVERYMAN: Ye speak like a good friend. I believe you well;
I shall deserve it, and I may.

[6] Born.

[7] Trust.

FELLOWSHIP: I speak of no deserving, by this day!
For he that will say and nothing do
Is not worthy with good company to go;
Therefore show me the grief of your mind,
As to your friend most loving and kind.
EVERYMAN: I shall show you how it is:
Commanded I am to go a journey,
A long way, hard and dangerous,
And give a strict count without delay
Before the high judge, Adonai.
Wherefore, I pray you, bear me company,
As ye have promised, in this journey.
FELLOWSHIP: That is matter indeed! Promise is duty;
But, and I should take such a voyage on me,
I know it well, it should be to my pain.
Also it maketh me afeared, certain.
But let us take counsel here as well as we can,
For your words would fright a strong man.
EVERYMAN: Why, ye said if I had need,
Ye would me never forsake, quick nor dead,
Though it were to hell, truly.
FELLOWSHIP: So I said, certainly,
But such pleasures be set aside, the sooth to say.
And also, if we took such a journey,
When should we come again?
EVERYMAN: Nay, never again till the day of doom.
FELLOWSHIP: In faith, then will not I come there!
Who hath you these tidings brought?
EVERYMAN: Indeed, Death was with me here.
FELLOWSHIP: Now, by God that all hath bought,
If Death were the messenger,
For no man that is living today
I will not go that loath journey—
Not for the father that begat me!
EVERYMAN: Ye promised otherwise, pardie.[8]
FELLOWSHIP: I wot well I said so, truly;
And yet if thou wilt eat, and drink, and make good cheer,
Or haunt to women the lusty company,
I would not forsake you while the day is clear,
Trust me verily!
EVERYMAN: Yea, thereto ye would be ready;

To go to mirth, solace, and play,
Your mind will sooner apply
Than to bear me company in my long journey.
FELLOWSHIP: Now, in good faith, I will not that way.
But and thou wilt murder, or any man kill,
In that I will help thee with a good will!
EVERYMAN: O, that is a simple advice indeed!
Gentle fellow, help me in my necessity;
We have loved long, and now I need,
And now, gentle Fellowship, remember me!
FELLOWSHIP: Whether ye have loved me or no,
By Saint John, I will not with thee go.
EVERYMAN: Yet, I pray thee, take the labor, and do so much for me
To bring me forward, for saint charity,
And comfort me till I come without the town.
FELLOWSHIP: Nay, and thou would give me a new gown,
I will not a foot with thee go;
But, and thou had tarried, I would not have left thee so.
And as now God speed thee in thy journey,
For from thee I will depart as fast as I may.
EVERYMAN: Whither away, Fellowship? Will you forsake me?
FELLOWSHIP: Yea, by my fay, to God I betake[9] thee.
EVERYMAN: Farewell, good Fellowship! For thee my heart is sore;
Adieu for ever! I shall see thee no more.
FELLOWSHIP: In faith, Everyman, farewell now at the end!
For you I will remember that parting is mourning. (*Exit* FELLOWSHIP.)
EVERYMAN: Alack! shall we thus depart indeed
(Ah, Lady, help!) without any more comfort?
Lo, Fellowship forsaketh me in my most need.
For help in this world whither shall I resort?
Fellowship here before with me would merry make,
And now little sorrow for me doth he take.
It is said, "In prosperity men friends may find,
Which in adversity be full unkind."

8 *Par dieu;* indeed.

9 Commit.

Now whither for succor shall I flee,
Sith that Fellowship hath forsaken me?
To my kinsmen I will, truly,
Praying them to help me in my necessity;
I believe that they will do so,
For "kind will creep where it may not
go." [10]
I will go say [11], for yonder I see them go.
Where be ye now, my friends and kins-
men?

Enter KINDRED *and* COUSIN.

KINDRED: Here be we now, at your com-
mandment.
Cousin, I pray you show us your intent
In any wise, and do not spare.
COUSIN: Yea, Everyman, and to us declare
If ye be disposed to go any whither,
For, wete you well, we will live and die
together.
KINDRED: In wealth and woe we will with
you hold,
For over his kin a man may be bold.
EVERYMAN: Gramercy, my friends and kins-
men kind.
Now shall I show you the grief of my mind.
I was commanded by a messenger
That is a high king's chief officer;
He bade me go a pilgrimage, to my pain,
And I know well I shall never come again;
Also I must give a reckoning straight,
For I have a great enemy that hath me in
wait,[12]
Which intendeth me for to hinder.
KINDRED: What account is that which ye
must render?
That would I know.
EVERYMAN: Of all my works I must show
How I have lived, and my days spent;
Also of ill deeds that I have used
In my time, sith life was me lent;
And of all virtues that I have refused.
Therefore I pray you go thither with me,
To help to make mine account, for saint
charity.
COUSIN: What, to go thither? Is that the
matter?
Nay, Everyman, I had liefer fast bread and
water
All this five year and more.

EVERYMAN: Alas, that ever I was bore!
For now shall I never be merry
If that you forsake me.
KINDRED: Ah, sir, what! Ye be a merry man!
Take good heart to you, and make no
moan.
But one thing I warn you, by Saint Anne,
As for me, ye shall go alone.
EVERYMAN: My Cousin, will you not with
me go?
COUSIN: No, by our Lady! I have the cramp
in my toe.
Trust not to me; for, so God me speed,
I will deceive you in your most need.
KINDRED: It availeth not us to tice.[13]
Ye shall have my maid with all my heart;
She loveth to go to feasts, there to be
nice,[14]
And to dance, and abroad to start;
I will give her leave to help you in that
journey,
If that you and she may agree.
EVERYMAN: Now show me the very effect of
your mind.
Will you go with me, or abide behind?
KINDRED: Abide behind? Yea, that will I, and
I may!
Therefore farewell till another day. (*Exit*
KINDRED.)
EVERYMAN: How should I be merry or glad?
For fair promises men to me make,
But when I have most need, they me for-
sake.
I am deceived; that maketh me sad.
COUSIN: Cousin Everyman, farewell now,
For verily I will not go with you;
Also of mine own life an unready reckoning
I have to account; therefore I make tarry-
ing.
Now, God keep thee, for now I go. (*Exit*
COUSIN.)
EVERYMAN: Ah, Jesus! is all come hereto?
Lo, fair words maketh fools fain; [15]
They promise and nothing will do certain.
My kinsmen promised me faithfully
For to abide with me steadfastly,
And now fast away do they flee.
Even so Fellowship promised me.
What friend were best me of to provide?
I lose my time here longer to abide.
Yet in my mind a thing there is:

[10] Walk.
[11] Try.
[12] Lies in wait.

[13] Entice, coax.
[14] Wanton.
[15] Glad.

All my life I have loved riches;
If that my Goods now help me might,
He would make my heart full light.
I will speak to him in this distress.
Where art thou, my Goods and riches?
GOODS (*From within*): Who calleth me?
  Everyman? What, hast thou haste?
  I lie here in corners, trussed and piled so
    high,
  And in chests I am locked so fast,
  Also sacked in bags—thou mayst see with
    thine eye—
  I cannot stir; in packs low I lie.
  What would ye have? Lightly me say.
EVERYMAN: Come hither, Goods, in all the
    haste thou may.
  For of counsel I must desire thee.

Enter GOODS.

GOODS: Sir, and ye in the world have sorrow
    or adversity,
  That can I help you to remedy shortly.
EVERYMAN: It is another disease that griev-
    eth me;
  In this world it is not, I tell thee so.
  I am sent for another way to go,
  To give a strict count general
  Before the highest Jupiter of all;
  And all my life I have had joy and pleasure
    in thee;
  Therefore I pray thee go with me,
  For, peradventure, thou mayst before God
    Almighty
  My reckoning help to clean and purify;
  For it is said ever among,
  That "money maketh all right that is
    wrong."
GOODS: Nay, Everyman; I sing another song,
  I follow no man in such voyages;
  For, and I went with thee,
  Thou shouldst fare much the worse for me;
  For because on me thou did set thy mind,
  Thy reckoning I have made blotted and
    blind,
  That thine account thou cannot make
    truly;
  And that hast thou for the love of me.
EVERYMAN: That would grieve me full sore.
  When I should come to that fearful an-
    swer.
  Up, let us go thither together.
GOODS: Nay, not so! I am too brittle, I may
    not endure;
  I will follow no man one foot, be ye sure.

EVERYMAN: Alas! I have thee loved, and had
    great pleasure
  All my life-days on goods and treasure.
GOODS: That is to thy damnation, without
    lesing! [16]
  For my love is contrary to the love ever-
    lasting.
  But if thou had me loved moderately dur-
    ing,
  As to the poor to give part of me,
  Then shouldst thou not in this dolor be,
  Nor in this great sorrow and care.
EVERYMAN: Lo, now was I deceived ere I
    was ware,
  And all I may wyte [17] my spending of time.
GOODS: What, weenest thou that I am thine?
EVERYMAN: I had weened so.
GOODS: Nay, Everyman, I say no;
  As for a while I was lent thee,
  A season thou hast had me in prosperity.
  My condition is man's soul to kill;
  If I save one, a thousand I do spill;
  Weenest thou that I will follow thee
  From this world? Nay, verily.
EVERYMAN: I had weened otherwise.
GOODS: Therefore to thy soul Goods is a
    thief;
  For when thou art dead, this is my
    guise [18]—
  Another to deceive in the same wise
  As I have done thee, and all to his soul's
    reprief. [19]
EVERYMAN: O false Goods, cursèd thou be!
  Thou traitor to God, that hast deceived me
  And caught me in thy snare.
GOODS: Marry! thou brought thyself in care,
  Whereof I am right glad.
  I must needs laugh, I cannot be sad.
EVERYMAN: Ah, Goods, thou hast had long
    my heartly love;
  I gave thee that which should be the Lord's
    above.
  But wilt thou not go with me indeed?
  I pray thee truth to say.
GOODS: No, so God me speed!
  Therefore farewell, and have good day.
    (*Exit* GOODS.)
EVERYMAN: O, to whom shall I make my
    moan
  For to go with me in that heavy journey?

[16] Lying.
[17] Blame to.
[18] Practice, trick.
[19] Reproof.

First Fellowship said he would with me
   gone;
His words were very pleasant and gay,
But afterward he left me alone.
Then spake I to my kinsmen, all in despair,
And also they gave me words fair,
They lacked no fair speaking,
But all forsook me in the ending.
Then went I to my Goods, that I loved
   best,
In hope to have comfort, but there had I
   least;
For my Goods sharply did me tell
That he bringeth many into hell.
Then of myself I was ashamed,
And so I am worthy to be blamed;
Thus may I well myself hate.
Of whom shall I now counsel take?
I think that I shall never speed
Till that I go to my Good Deeds.
But alas! she is so weak
That she can neither go nor speak.
Yet will I venture on her now.
My Good Deeds, where be you? (GOOD
DEEDS *speaks from the ground.*)
GOOD DEEDS: Here I lie, cold in the ground.
Thy sins hath me sore bound,
   That I cannot stir.
EVERYMAN: O Good Deeds! I stand in fear;
I must you pray of counsel,
For help now should come right well.
GOOD DEEDS: Everyman, I have understand-
   ing
That ye be summoned account to make
Before Messias, of Jerusalem King;
And you do by me,[20] that journey with you
   will I take.
EVERYMAN: Therefore I come to you my
   moan to make;
I pray you that ye will go with me.
GOOD DEEDS: I would full fain, but I cannot
   stand, verily.
EVERYMAN: Why, is there anything on you
   fall?
GOOD DEEDS: Yea, sir, I may thank you of all;
If ye had perfectly cheered [21] me,
Your book of count full ready had be.
Look, the books of your works and deeds
   eke;
Ah, see how they lie under the feet,
To your soul's heaviness.

20 Act by my advice.
21 Cherished.

EVERYMAN: Our Lord Jesus help me!
For one letter here I can not see.
GOOD DEEDS: There is a blind reckoning in
   time of distress!
EVERYMAN: Good Deeds, I pray you, help
   me in this need,
Or else I am for ever damned indeed;
Therefore help me to make my reckoning
Before the Redeemer of all thing,
That King is, and was, and ever shall.
GOOD DEEDS: Everyman, I am sorry of your
   fall,
And fain would I help you, and I were able.
EVERYMAN: Good Deeds, your counsel I pray
   you give me.
GOOD DEEDS: That shall I do verily;
Though that on my feet I may not go,
I have a sister that shall with you also,
Called Knowledge, which shall with you
   abide,
To help you to make that dreadful reckon-
   ing.

Enter KNOWLEDGE.

KNOWLEDGE: Everyman, I will go with thee,
   and be thy guide
In thy most need to go by thy side.
EVERYMAN: In good condition I am now in
   every thing,
And am wholly content with this good
   thing;
Thanked be God my Creator.
GOOD DEEDS: And when he hath brought thee
   there,
Where thou shalt heal thee of thy smart,
Then go you with your reckoning and your
   Good Deeds together
For to make you joyful at heart
Before the blessèd Trinity.
EVERYMAN: My Good Deeds, gramercy!
I am well content, certainly,
   With your words sweet.
KNOWLEDGE: Now go we together lovingly
To Confession, that cleansing river
EVERYMAN: For joy I weep; I would we were
   there!
But, I pray you, give me cognition
Where dwelleth that holy man, Confes-
   sion.
KNOWLEDGE: In the house of salvation;
We shall find him in that place,
That shall us comfort, by God's grace.
(KNOWLEDGE *leads* EVERYMAN *to* CON-
FESSION.)

Lo, this is Confession. Kneel down and
ask mercy,
For he is in good conceit [22] with God al-
mighty.
EVERYMAN (*Kneeling*): O glorious fountain,
that all uncleanness doth clarify,
Wash from me the spots of vice unclean,
That on me no sin may be seen.
I come, with Knowledge, for my redemp-
tion,
Redempt with hearty and full contrition;
For I am commanded a pilgrimage to take,
And great accounts before God to make.
Now, I pray you, Shrift, mother of salva-
tion.
Help my Good Deeds for my piteous ex-
clamation.
CONFESSION: I know your sorrow well, Every-
man.
Because with Knowledge ye come to me,
I will you comfort as well as I can,
And a precious jewel I will give thee,
Called penance, voider of adversity;
Therewith shall your body chastised be,
With abstinence, and perseverance in
God's service.
Here shall you receive that scourge of me.
(*Gives* EVERYMAN *a scourge.*)
Which is penance strong, that ye must
endure
To remember thy Savior was scourged for
thee
With sharp scourges, and suffered it pa-
tiently;
So must thou ere thou 'scape that painful
pilgrimage.
Knowledge, keep him in this voyage,
And by that time Good Deeds will be with
thee.
But in any wise be seeker of mercy,
For your time draweth fast, and ye will
saved be;
Ask God mercy, and He will grant truly;
When with the scourge of penance man
doth him bind,
The oil of forgiveness then shall he find.
(*Exit* CONFESSION.)
EVERYMAN: Thanked be God for his gracious
work!
For now I will my penance begin;
This hath rejoiced and lighted my heart,
Though the knots be painful and hard
within.

[22] Esteem.

KNOWLEDGE: Everyman, look your penance
that ye fulfil,
What pain that ever it to you be,
And Knowledge shall give you counsel at
will
How your account ye shall make clearly.
(EVERYMAN *kneels.*)
EVERYMAN: O eternal God! O heavenly fig-
ure!
O way of rightwiseness! O goodly vision!
Which descended down in a virgin pure
Because he would Everyman redeem,
Which Adam forfeited by his disobedience.
O blessèd Godhead! elect and high divine,
Forgive me my grievous offence;
Here I cry thee mercy in this presence.
O ghostly treasure! O ransomer and re-
deemer!
Of all the world hope and conductor,
Mirror of joy, and founder of mercy,
Which illumineth heaven and earth
thereby,
Hear my clamorous complaint, though it
late be.
Receive my prayers; unworthy in this heavy
life.
Though I be a sinner most abominable,
Yet let my name be written in Moses'
table.
O Mary! pray to the Maker of all thing,
Me for to help at my ending,
And save me from the power of my en-
emy,
For Death assaileth me strongly.
And, Lady, that I may by means of thy
prayer
Of your Son's glory to be partner,
By the means of his passion I it crave;
I beseech you, help my soul to save. (*He
rises.*)
Knowledge, give me the scourge of pen-
ance.
My flesh therewith shall give a quittance.
I will now begin, if God give me grace.
KNOWLEDGE: Everyman, God give you time
and space.
Thus I bequeath you in the hands of our
Savior,
Now may you make your reckoning sure.
EVERYMAN: In the name of the Holy Trinity,
My body sore punished shall be. (*Scourges
himself.*)
Take this, body, for the sin of the flesh;
Also thou delightest to go gay and fresh,

And in the way of damnation thou did me bring;
Therefore suffer now strokes of punishing.
Now of penance I will wade the water clear,
To save me from purgatory, that sharp fire.
(GOOD DEEDS *rises from floor.*)
GOOD DEEDS: I thank God, now I can walk and go,
And am delivered of my sickness and woe.
Therefore with Everyman I will go, and not spare;
His good works I will help him to declare.
KNOWLEDGE: Now, Everyman, be merry and glad!
Your Good Deeds cometh now, ye may not be sad;
Now is your Good Deeds whole and sound,
Going upright upon the ground.
EVERYMAN: My heart is light, and shall be evermore.
Now will I smite faster than I did before.
GOOD DEEDS: Everyman, pilgrim, my special friend,
Blessèd be thou without end.
For thee is prepared the eternal glory.
Ye have me made whole and sound,
Therefore I will bide by thee in every stound.[23]
EVERYMAN: Welcome, my Good Deeds; now I hear thy voice,
I weep for very sweetness of love.
KNOWLEDGE: Be no more sad, but ever rejoice;
God seeth thy living in his throne above.
Put on this garment to thy behoof,
Which is wet with your tears,
Or else before God you may it miss,
When you to your journey's end come shall.
EVERYMAN: Gentle Knowledge, what do ye it call?
KNOWLEDGE: It is the garment of sorrow;
From pain it will you borrow;
Contrition it is
That getteth forgiveness;
It pleaseth God passing well.
GOOD DEEDS: Everyman, will you wear it for your heal? (EVERYMAN *puts on garment of contrition.*)
EVERYMAN: Now blessèd be Jesu, Mary's Son,
For now have I on true contrition.
And let us go now without tarrying;

Good Deeds, have we clear our reckoning?
GOOD DEEDS: Yea, indeed I have it here.
EVERYMAN: Then I trust we need not fear.
Now, friends, let us not part in twain.
KNOWLEDGE: Nay, Everyman, that will we not, certain.
GOOD DEEDS: Yet must thou lead with thee
Three persons of great might.
EVERYMAN: Who should they be?
GOOD DEEDS: Discretion and Strength they hight,[24]
And thy Beauty may not abide behind.
KNOWLEDGE: Also ye must call to mind
Your Five Wits as for your counselors.
GOOD DEEDS: You must have them ready at all hours.
EVERYMAN: How shall I get them hither?
KNOWLEDGE: You must call them all together,
And they will hear you incontinent.
EVERYMAN: My friends, come hither and be present;
Discretion, Strength, my Five Wits, and Beauty.

Enter DISCRETION, STRENGTH, FIVE WITS, *and* BEAUTY.

BEAUTY: Here at your will we be all ready.
What will ye that we should do?
GOOD DEEDS: That ye would with Everyman go,
And help him in his pilgrimage.
Advise you, will ye with him or not in that voyage?
STRENGTH: We will bring him all thither,
To his help and comfort, ye may believe me.
DISCRETION: So will we go with him all together.
EVERYMAN: Almighty God, lovèd may thou be!
I give thee laud that I have hither brought
Strength, Discretion, Beauty, and Five Wits. Lack I naught;
And my Good Deeds, with Knowledge clear,
All be in company at my will here.
I desire no more to my business.
STRENGTH: And I, Strength, will by you stand in distress,
Though thou would in battle fight on the ground.

23 Always.
24 Are called.

FIVE WITS: And though it were through the world round,
We will not depart for sweet nor sour.
BEAUTY: No more will I, unto death's hour,
Whatsoever thereof befall.
DISCRETION: Everyman, advise you first of all;
Go with a good advisement and deliberation.
We all give you virtuous monition
That all shall be well.
EVERYMAN: My friends, hearken what I will tell:
I pray God reward you in his heavenly sphere.
Now hearken, all that be here,
For I will make my testament
Here before you all present:
In alms half my goods I will give with my hands twain
In the way of charity, with good intent,
And the other half still shall remain;
I it bequeath to be returned there it ought to be.
This I do in despite of the fiend of hell,
To go quite out of his peril
Ever after and this day.
KNOWLEDGE: Everyman, hearken what I say;
Go to Priesthood, I you advise,
And receive of him in any wise
The holy sacrament and ointment together;
Then shortly see ye turn again hither;
We will all abide you here.
FIVE WITS: Yea, Everyman, hie you that ye ready were.
There is no emperor, king, duke, nor baron,
That of God hath commission
As hath the least priest in the world being;
For of the blessèd sacraments pure and benign
He beareth the keys, and thereof hath the cure
For man's redemption—it is ever sure—
Which God for our soul's medicine
Gave us out of his heart with great pain,
Here in this transitory life, for thee and me.
The blessèd sacraments seven there be:
Baptism, confirmation, with priesthood good,
And the sacrament of God's precious flesh and blood,
Marriage, the holy extreme unction, and penance.
These seven be good to have in remembrance,
Gracious sacraments of high divinity.
EVERYMAN: Fain would I receive that holy body
And meekly to my ghostly [25] father I will go.
FIVE WITS: Everyman, that is the best that ye can do.
God will you to salvation bring,
For priesthood exceedeth all other thing;
To us Holy Scripture they do teach,
And converteth man from sin, heaven to reach;
God hath to them more power given,
Than to any angel that is in heaven.
With five words he may consecrate
God's body in flesh and blood to make,
And handleth his Maker between his hands.
The priest bindeth and unbindeth all bands,
Both in earth and in heaven;
Thou ministers all the sacraments seven;
Though we kissed thy feet, thou wert worthy;
Thou art the surgeon that cureth sin deadly:
No remedy we find under God
But all only priesthood.
Everyman, God gave priests that dignity,
And setteth them in his stead among us to be;
Thus be they above angels, in degree. (*Exit* EVERYMAN.)
KNOWLEDGE: If priests be good, it is so, surely.
But when Jesus hanged on the cross with great smart,
There he gave out of his blessèd heart
The same sacrament in great torment.
He sold them not to us, that Lord omnipotent.
Therefore Saint Peter the Apostle doth say
That Jesus' curse hath all they
Which God their Savior do buy or sell,
Or they for any money do take or tell.
Sinful priests giveth the sinners example bad;
Their children sitteth by other men's fires, I have heard;
And some haunteth women's company
With unclean life, as lusts of lechery.
These be with sin made blind.

25 Spiritual.

FIVE WITS: I trust to God no such may we
  find.
  Therefore let us priesthood honor,
  And follow their doctrine for our souls'
  succor.
  We be their sheep, and they shepherds be
  By whom we all be kept in surety.
  Peace! for yonder I see Everyman come,
  Which hath made true satisfaction.
GOOD DEEDS: Methinketh it is he indeed.

Re-enter EVERYMAN.

EVERYMAN: Now Jesu be your alder speed.[26]
  I have received the sacrament for my re-
  demption,
  And then mine extreme unction.
  Blessèd be all they that counseled me to
  take it!
  And now, friends, let us go without longer
  respite.
  I thank God that ye have tarried so long.
  Now set each of you on this rod [27] your
  hand,
  And shortly follow me.
  I go before, there I would be. God be our
  guide.
STRENGTH: Everyman, we will not from you
  go,
  Till ye have done this voyage long.
DISCRETION: I, Discretion, will bide by you
  also.
KNOWLEDGE: And though this pilgrimage be
  never so strong,
  I will never part you fro.
  Everyman, I will be as sure by thee
  As ever I did by Judas Maccabee. (*They
  go together to the grave.*)
EVERYMAN: Alas! I am so faint I may not
  stand,
  My limbs under me do fold.
  Friends, let us not turn again to this land,
  Not for all the world's gold;
  For into this cave must I creep
  And turn to earth, and there to sleep.
BEAUTY: What, into this grave? Alas!
EVERYMAN: Yea, there shall you consume,
  more and less.
BEAUTY: And what, should I smother here?
EVERYMAN: Yea, by my faith, and never more
  appear.
  In this world live no more we shall,

---

26 Succor of all of you.
27 Cross.

But in heaven before the highest Lord of
  all.
BEAUTY: I cross out all this; adieu, by Saint
  John!
  I take my cap in my lap and am gone.
EVERYMAN: What, Beauty, whither will ye?
BEAUTY: Peace! I am deaf. I look not behind
  me,
  Not and thou would give me all the gold
  in thy chest. (*Exit* BEAUTY.)
EVERYMAN: Alas, whereto may I trust?
  Beauty goeth fast away from me;
  She promised with me to live and die.
STRENGTH: Everyman, I will thee also for-
  sake and deny.
  Thy game liketh me not at all.
EVERYMAN: Why, then ye will forsake me all?
  Sweet Strength, tarry a little space.
STRENGTH: Nay, sir, by the rood of grace,
  I will hie me from thee fast,
  Though thou weep till thy heart to-brast.[28]
EVERYMAN: Ye would ever bide by me, ye
  said.
STRENGTH: Yea, I have you far enough con-
  veyed.
  Ye be old enough, I understand,
  Your pilgrimage to take on hand.
  I repent me that I hither came.
EVERYMAN: Strength, you to displease I am
  to blame;
  Yet promise is debt, this ye well wot.
STRENGTH: In faith, I care not!
  Thou art but a fool to complain.
  You spend your speech and waste your
  brain;
  Go, thrust thee into the ground. (*Exit
  STRENGTH.*)
EVERYMAN: I had weened surer I should you
  have found.
  He that trusteth in his Strength
  She him deceiveth at the length.
  Both Strength and Beauty forsaketh me,
  Yet they promised me fair and lovingly.
DISCRETION: Everyman, I will after Strength
  be gone;
  As for me I will leave you alone.
EVERYMAN: Why, Discretion, will ye forsake
  me?
DISCRETION: Yea, in faith, I will go from
  thee;
  For when Strength goeth before
  I follow after evermore.

---

28 Break into pieces.

EVERYMAN: Yet, I pray thee, for the love of the Trinity,
Look in my grave once piteously.

DISCRETION: Nay, so nigh will I not come.
Farewell, every one! (*Exit* DISCRETION.)

EVERYMAN: O all thing faileth, save God alone—
Beauty, Strength, and Discretion;
For when Death bloweth his blast,
They all run from me full fast.

FIVE WITS: Everyman, my leave now of thee I take;
I will follow the other, for here I thee forsake.

EVERYMAN: Alas! then may I wail and weep,
For I took you for my best friend.

FIVE WITS: I will no longer thee keep;
Now farewell, and there an end. (*Exit* FIVE WITS.)

EVERYMAN: O Jesu, help! All hath forsaken me!

GOOD DEEDS: Nay, Everyman; I will bide with thee,
I will not forsake thee indeed;
Thou shalt find me a good friend at need.

EVERYMAN: Gramercy, Good Deeds! Now may I true friends see.
They have forsaken me, every one;
I loved them better than my Good Deeds alone.
Knowledge, will ye forsake me also?

KNOWLEDGE: Yea, Everyman, when ye to death shall go;
But not yet, for no manner of danger.

EVERYMAN: Gramercy, Knowledge, with all my heart.

KNOWLEDGE: Nay, yet I will not from hence depart
Till I see where ye shall be come.

EVERYMAN: Methink, alas, that I must be gone
To make my reckoning and my debts pay,
For I see my time is nigh spent away.
Take example, all ye that this do hear or see,
How they that I loved best do forsake me,
Except my Good Deeds that bideth truly.

GOOD DEEDS: All earthly things is but vanity.
Beauty, Strength, and Discretion do man forsake,
Foolish friends and kinsmen, that fair spake,
All fleeth save Good Deeds, and that am I.

EVERYMAN: Have mercy on me, God most mighty;
And stand by me, thou Mother and Maid, holy Mary!

GOOD DEEDS: Fear not, I will speak for thee.

EVERYMAN: Here I cry God mercy!

GOOD DEEDS: Short our end, and 'minish our pain.
Let us go and never come again.

EVERYMAN: Into thy hands, Lord, my soul I commend.
Receive it, Lord, that it be not lost.
As thou me boughtest, so me defend,
And save me from the fiend's boast,
That I may appear with that blessèd host
That shall be saved at the day of doom.
In manus tuas—of might's most
For ever—*commendo spiritum meum.*[29]
(EVERYMAN *and* GOOD DEEDS *descend into the grave.*)

KNOWLEDGE: Now hath he suffered that we all shall endure;
The Good Deeds shall make all sure.
Now hath he made ending.
Methinketh that I hear angels sing
And make great joy and melody
Where Everyman's soul received shall be.

ANGEL (*within*): Come, excellent elect spouse to Jesu!
Here above thou shalt go
Because of thy singular virtue.
Now the soul is taken the body fro,
Thy reckoning is crystal clear.
Now shalt thou into the heavenly sphere,
Unto the which all ye shall come
That liveth well before the day of doom.
(*Exit* KNOWLEDGE.)

Enter DOCTOR *for Epilogue.*

DOCTOR: This moral men may have in mind;
Ye hearers, take it of worth, old and young,
And forsake Pride, for he deceiveth you in the end,
And remember Beauty, Five Wits, Strength, and Discretion,
They all at the last do Everyman forsake,
Save his Good Deeds there doth he take.
But beware, and they be small
Before God he hath no help at all.
None excuse may be there for Everyman.

29 "Into thy hands I commend my spirit."

Alas, how shall he do then?
For, after death, amends may no man
   make,
For then mercy and pity doth him forsake.
If his reckoning be not clear when he doth
   come,
God will say, "*Ite, maledicti, in ignem
aeternum.*" 30

30 "Go, cursed ones, into eternal fire."

And he that hath his account whole and
   sound,
High in heaven he shall be crowned.
Unto which place God bring us all thither,
That we may live body and soul together.
Thereto help the Trinity!
Amen, say ye, for saint charity.

THUS ENDETH THIS MORAL PLAY OF

EVERYMAN.

THE HOLY EXPERIMENT

Fritz Hochwälder

TRANSLATED BY
George E. Wellwarth

CHARACTERS

ALFONSO FERNANDEZ, S.J., Provincial
ROCHUS HUNDERTPFUND, S.J., Superior
WILLIAM CLARKE, S.J., Procurator
LADISLAUS OROS, S.J.
DON PEDRO DE MIURA ⎤
DON ESTEBAN ARAGO ⎬ Spaniards
DON MIGUEL VILLANO ⎦
LORENZO QUERINI
ANDRE CORNELIS
CARLOS GERVAZONI, Bishop of Buenos Aires
JOSE BUSTILLOS ⎤
GARCIA QUESEDA ⎬ Landowners and merchants
ALVARO CATALDE ⎦
NAGUACU ⎤
BARRIGUA ⎬ Indian converts
CANDIA ⎦
ACATU ⎦

Time: The action takes place in the course of one day, July 16, 1767.

Place: The Jesuit Mission House in Buenos Aires.

ACT I

On the left, several windows placed later-
ally and a large globe on a heavy base. To
the rear, the door to the Father Procura-
tor's room. Upstage left, a row of portraits
depicting the former Provincials of the
Order. An enormous map of the Jesuit
state hangs on the upstage left wall. In the
upper right-hand corner of the map hangs
a picture of Francisco de Xavier holding a
flaming heart in his uplifted hands. Under
the map, a small library and in front of
this stands the Father Provincial's desk.

Upstage right, a small lobby-like passage
through which a garden can be glimpsed;
only the tops of palms and olive trees can
be seen. The passage leads into the wings
on the right, seemingly to a staircase lead-
ing down. There is a large conference table
and chairs placed on a dais at the right-
hand wall. A carved wooden crucifix stands
on the table.

SCENE 1

FATHER PROVINCIAL, HUNDERTPFUND, OROS,
the Indians CANDIA *and* NAGUACU.

HUNDERTPFUND: Father Provincial, the Indians Candia and Naguacu have come to
be baptized and to request that their tribe
be permitted to settle in our state. (CANDIA
and NAGUACU *bow deeply to the* PROVIN-
CIAL.)

PROVINCIAL: You wish to be baptized?

CANDIA & NAGUACU: We wish to be baptized,
reverend Father.

PROVINCIAL: You wish to settle in our state?

CANDIA & NAGUACU: We wish to settle in your
state.

PROVINCIAL: Do you come to us of your own
free will?

CANDIA & NAGUACU: Of our own free will we
come to you, reverend Father.

PROVINCIAL: How large is your tribe?

CANDIA & NAGUACU: We are seven thousand,
reverend Father. Seven thousand—and all
of us come to you of our own free will.
Accept us into the kingdom of your God.

PROVINCIAL: Are you willing to serve Christ
with all your strength?

CANDIA & NAGUACU: We will serve Christ with
all our strength.

PROVINCIAL: Humbly?

CANDIA & NAGUACU: Humbly.

PROVINCIAL: Without question?

CANDIA & NAGUACU: Without question.

PROVINCIAL: In the name of Christ you must
be obedient to the Fathers of our Order in
all things.

CANDIA & NAGUACU: We will be obedient to
the Fathers of your Order in all things.

PROVINCIAL: You swear to set aside all other
gods?

CANDIA & NAGUACU: We wish to pray only to
the good Lord Jesus.

PROVINCIAL: You swear that you will take
unto yourselves one woman only?

CANDIA & NAGUACU: For the love of the good
Lord Jesus we will take one woman only
unto ourselves.

PROVINCIAL: You must work in the communal fields and the fruits of your work shall
belong to all—all self-interest and all desire for possessions must be set aside.

CANDIA: Our people will not lack bread and
meat under your guidance, reverend Father.
Command us in the name of the Heavenly
God—we will obey.

NAGUACU: We will obey.

PROVINCIAL (*looking at the map*): We have
built up the kingdom of God here on the
banks of the Parana and the Uruguay.
Thirty settlements—150,000 Christian Indians. Do you wish to contribute your seven
thousand to the greatness of God, Candia
and Naguacu?

CANDIA: All the Indians in this land will come
to the good God Jesus freely—just as we
seven thousand come.

PROVINCIAL: May the mercy and love of our
Lord Jesus Christ keep you and protect
you always. (HUNDERTPFUND *makes a sign*
to them that they are dismissed. CANDIA &
NAGUACU *bow deeply to the* FATHER PRO-
VINCIAL. *Exit.*)

SCENE 2

FATHER PROVINCIAL, HUNDERTPFUND, OROS.

PROVINCIAL: The Kingdom of God increases.
"The harvest is great, but the reapers are

few"—we need more Fathers. Where will we find the shepherd for this new flock?

HUNDERTPFUND: Let Father Reinegg have the new settlement!

PROVINCIAL: That delicate musician—among people who are still practically savages? No. I'll have to have an experienced missionary.

HUNDERTPFUND: Torres—from San Miguel?

PROVINCIAL: No, I don't want a Spaniard.

HUNDERTPFUND: How about Escandon, from San Xavier?

PROVINCIAL: Too young—for a still heathen tribe of seven thousand we'll need our most experienced missionary.

HUNDERTPFUND: Briegniel from Candelaria?

PROVINCIAL: I'm thinking of Berendt—from San Tomé.

HUNDERTPFUND: Berendt won't want to leave San Tomé. He's been there all of twenty years now.

PROVINCIAL: He's our most experienced missionary. He will go to our new settlement, to the heathen tribe of Candia and Naguacu. Hundertpfund, get me a messenger for San Tomé!—Now Fathers, be seated, and give me your report!—Has the Spanish delegation arrived at the Mission?

HUNDERTPFUND: The Spaniards are at present attending the service in the Church of Our Savior—they could arrive at the Mission any moment. The Negro guards will blow some music to herald their arrival.

PROVINCIAL: Wasn't there any Jesuit on the Spanish ship?

HUNDERTPFUND (*to* OROS): Did you see any Jesuit get off the ship?

OROS: No.

PROVINCIAL: We have been promised help by the Captain-General of the Order in Rome.—How is the investigation against us going in the districts you've visited, Hundertpfund?

HUNDERTPFUND: Good. Sebastian Carvalho's plots are too obvious. According to him, we have gold mines, silver mines, thousands of Indian slaves, and I don't know what else! The Commissioners' faces are as long as Israel's exile in the desert. Here they are sitting right in the middle of the Canaan of the Jesuits—and they can't find a thing! Ask Captain Villano!

PROVINCIAL: Yes, Captain Villano—see that you talk to him a lot, Oros! Act friendly to him—you used to be a soldier—fought

against the Turks, didn't you?—he probably looks on you as a comrade.—Is he a good Catholic?

HUNDERTPFUND: Well, he goes to confession and attends services—seems to be all right in that way.

PROVINCIAL: Keep your eye on him! His evidence will be important, especially as it'll be going directly to the inspector-general, Don Pedro de Miura. Get on good terms with him—have a glass of wine with him now and then.

HUNDERTPFUND: The investigating commissions will have convinced themselves by now that the accusations against us are baseless and malicious. The inspector-general's hearing will vindicate us. He'll issue a final judgment for us, just like under Philip V.

PROVINCIAL: Our work will flourish, by God's Mercy. Without that we would be helpless. But we must not neglect anything in the realm of worldly matters which might help to support the justness of our cause.

HUNDERTPFUND: We are not neglecting anything.

PROVINCIAL: Very well then! It is time to receive the Spanish delegation, Hundertpfund.

HUNDERTPFUND: Within a very few hours we will be totally vindicated. Father Oros suffers from presentiments and apprehensions. Try and calm him, Father Provincial! (*Exits.*)

SCENE 3
FATHER PROVINCIAL, OROS.

OROS: Father Provincial—we ought to be forearmed against spite and maliciousness. I don't like these Spanish mercenaries that have been making themselves at home in our territories as members of the investigating commissions for the last six months.

PROVINCIAL: The Spanish soldiers are not conducting the proceedings against us. We are expecting the king's inspector-general—and he is a nobleman. I know Don Miura very well—his appointment to the inspector-generalship has been obtained by the Fathers of our Order in Madrid.

OROS: The bishops of Buenos Aires, Tucumán, and Asunción are against us.

PROVINCIAL: The bishops are simply protecting the interests of their parishioners—and we are protecting the interests of ours.

OROS: The landowners hate us.

PROVINCIAL: The landowners can bribe the flunkies all they want; the king's inspector-general is a nobleman.

OROS: Sebastian Carvalho managed to win out in Portugal with his lies about our state.

PROVINCIAL: Spain isn't Portugal.

OROS: Our Order is banned in France as well. And all because of Carvalho's libels.

PROVINCIAL: The real reason goes deeper than that. The new philosophy is opposed to us. Monsieur D'Alembert . . .

OROS: The secular powers are threatening our state here in Paraguay.

PROVINCIAL: The Holy Father loves it and will protect it. They won't dare to set themselves against the Pope. (*Enter* BUSTILLOS *from the passage.*)

SCENE 4
FATHER PROVINCIAL, BUSTILLOS, OROS.

BUSTILLOS: So you're not at home to me, eh? What are you crawling into your holes for?

PROVINCIAL: Good morning, Señor Bustillos. To what do we owe this honor?

BUSTILLOS: Blast the honor! I'm here to protest in the name of the Catholic merchants and landowners!

PROVINCIAL: Try and contain your impatience for another hour or so! The king's inspector-general is expected at any moment. You can lodge your complaint with him.

BUSTILLOS: A fine inspector-general this one will turn out to be! Just like the others! We know you—you and your tricks! You like to appoint your own judges, that's what you like to do! We protest! We've had enough! Get your Indians out of town, and get them out fast! And as long as they're here see that you forbid them to have any contact with ours!

PROVINCIAL: We are obligated to hold those converts picked out by the commissions in readiness here in Buenos Aires. If it was up to us they wouldn't be here either. The bad example . . .

BUSTILLOS: The bad example is the one set by your Indians to ours! Nobody is getting any work done. There'll be uprisings yet if you don't put a stop to all this!

PROVINCIAL: What precisely is it that we should put a stop to?

BUSTILLOS: These fairy tales of your Indians about how this wonderful state of yours is flowing with milk and honey. About how lovely Christianity would only be without any slave drivers. And so on, et cetera.

PROVINCIAL: Much you care!

BUSTILLOS: We know all about *who* picked these people out. You did—not the commissions! We know all about you people, if you please! But we're not going to stand for it! You're not going to get our Indian workers away from us with your tricks! Go do your slave trading somewhere else since you have the king's patent for it, more's the pity! But see that your people get the hell out of Buenos Aires!

PROVINCIAL: I'll give orders that our people remain within the mission precincts and that none of them communicate with any of your people. Will that satisfy you?

BUSTILLOS: That would be the main thing.

PROVINCIAL: Peace be with you, Señor Bustillos! (*to* OROS) See the gentleman downstairs, Father Oros! (BUSTILLOS *remains where he is.*)

PROVINCIAL: Is there anything else you would like to say?

BUSTILLOS: Yes, there is something else. Get out—get out of Paraguay—*our* Paraguay!

PROVINCIAL: Good-bye, Señor!

BUSTILLOS: Go back where you came from!

PROVINCIAL: Don't let me keep you! Good-day, Señor!

BUSTILLOS (*calling back from the passage*): Go back to your monasteries! (*Exit, with* OROS.) (CORNELIS *storms in, left, followed closely by* CLARKE.)

SCENE 5
FATHER PROVINCIAL, CORNELIS, CLARKE.

CORNELIS: Goddam! I've had enough! This is it! I'm going home!

PROVINCIAL: Calm yourself, Mynheer Cornelis!

CORNELIS (*to* CLARKE): I don't need your tea, you hear me?

CLARKE (*approaching*): Mynheer Cornelis

says he'll buy his tea somewhere else this time. Over in San Sacramento.

CORNELIS: Damn right, I will. Over in San Sacramento. What do you want from me? I take all the risks and then you dangle your bags of tea right in front of my nose, just out of my reach. For the last time, and I'm asking you here where the Father Provincial can hear it, will you make a deal for 1200 pieces of gold?

CLARKE: I can't do it, Mynheer. We need iron in our settlements. We need lime. And the only way we can get them is to buy them from the proceeds of our trade in tea. It's as simple as that. Go to San Sacramento if you want to and see if you like their tea as well as ours!

CORNELIS: Oh—I know: your tea is the finest, the most aromatic, the unsurpassable Jesuit Herba-Maté, treasured the whole world over! Goddam!

CLARKE: Well then, I'm afraid we can't do business this time, Mynheer.

CORNELIS: My hat and stick—oh yes, they're downstairs. Father Provincial, I'm a heretic, but you know how I feel about your state! You know who puts in a good word for you everywhere and who defends you against your own Catholics—but things can't go on like this. You're trying to peel my skin off me in strips.

PROVINCIAL: Try and come to an agreement. (*To* CLARKE) You know Mynheer Cornelis is our friend.

CORNELIS: You'll never squeeze a single piece of gold out of me, you there—but since the Father Provincial puts it on a basis of friendship and so forth: 1300 pieces of gold for the shipload!

CLARKE: Not under 1500, Mynheer.

CORNELIS: 1500? Good-day, sir! (*Exit into the passage.*)

SCENE 6
FATHER PROVINCIAL, CLARKE.

PROVINCIAL: We'll lose a friend. Couldn't you have made a deal?

CLARKE: The Spaniards don't give us their iron for nothing. We have to keep to our figures or we'll run into debt. Besides, he'll be back.

PROVINCIAL: Cornelis?

CLARKE: He'll be back, you'll see.

PROVINCIAL: He felt insulted.

CLARKE: That's just an act. I learned how to do business from him. (*Enter* CORNELIS.)

SCENE 7
FATHER PROVINCIAL, CORNELIS, CLARKE.

CORNELIS: Goddam! . . . Hat and stick . . . not downstairs. Left it up here—perhaps! No—in there! Excuse me! (*Exit left.*)

CLARKE: He knows perfectly well where he left his hat and stick. He wants that tea.

CORNELIS (*comes back with hat and stick; stops before the* PROVINCIAL): And so we see each other for the last time, Father Provincial.

PROVINCIAL: I would deeply regret it, Mynheer. Try and come to an agreement with Father Clarke!

CORNELIS: Come to an agreement—with that man? (*To* CLARKE) Not that I absolutely have to have the tea, you understand—but since the Father Provincial puts it on a basis of friendship and so forth: 1400!

CLARKE: Well then, since it's for you, Mynheer—done!

CORNELIS (*slaps* CLARKE *on the shoulder*): Bravo! You know how to do business!

CLARKE: I'll have the bales loaded on board right away, Mynheer. Come with me and check them!

CORNELIS: You do it—I trust you. (*Exit* CLARKE.)

SCENE 8
FATHER PROVINCIAL, CORNELIS.

CORNELIS: Here's the money! (*Counts money on to the table*) 200—300—400— . . .

PROVINCIAL: May God be with you and protect you in the stormy seas of the North, Mynheer!

CORNELIS: Thank you, Father—600—700—800 . . .

PROVINCIAL: You look upon us justly and righteously. If only some Catholics were as understanding as you!

CORNELIS: Damn right. That's where your enemies are—among the Catholics—900—1000—and here's the rest. Count it!

PROVINCIAL: Leave it!

CORNELIS: If I can ever do anything for you, Father, if you ever need asylum—well, we Dutchmen have room for the Jesuits too.

PROVINCIAL: You're joking.

CORNELIS: Oh—it's just that it seems a pity to me. You're men, good men, the way men should be—and now you're going to be torn away from your work right when it's at the peak of success.

PROVINCIAL: Ah . . . so you think our downfall is already signed, sealed, and delivered?

CORNELIS: You are lost.

PROVINCIAL: So you too belong to those who think our downfall cannot be prevented. But believe me, we're only being persecuted because we're forging ahead. And we can't be stopped. We've been preparing ourselves for 150 years, and now the Jesuits of Paraguay are going to attack. (*Points at the map.*) The young giant is stretching himself. He's striding over the rivers and moving through the jungles and over the prairies—and soon every last Indian in this country will be won for Christ. Of course, our state will fall some day. But our experiment will have succeeded, and it will be repeated. Centuries from now. Until finally the world will be filled with that peace that men long for . . .

CORNELIS: God protect you and your state, Father!

PROVINCIAL: May you arrive safe and happy in Rotterdam, Mynheer! (*Exit* CORNELIS. *The* PROVINCIAL *takes the money into the room, left. March music, stopping after a while. Enter* DON PEDRO DE MIURA *from the passage. The* PROVINCIAL *enters, left.*)

Scene 9
FATHER PROVINCIAL, MIURA.

MIURA: Alfonso Fernandez!

PROVINCIAL: Pedro de Miura! (*They embrace.*)

MIURA (*steps back, formally*): Father Provincial!

PROVINCIAL: Inspector-General!

MIURA: Your father has asked me to transmit his best wishes.

PROVINCIAL: Thank you.

MIURA: Your two brothers are serving in the Spanish army.

PROVINCIAL: They have all parted from me. —You are welcome, Inspector-General!

MIURA: How many years is it since Salamanca, Father Provincial?

PROVINCIAL: It's two dozen years since Salamanca. Be seated, Inspector-General!

MIURA (*sits*): I remember you as a fire-eating young rascal, Father Provincial. And now: one of us in holy orders—the other a diplomat.

PROVINCIAL: Your fire has not been extinguished, Don Miura.

MIURA: No, it still burns—for Spain and for the king.

PROVINCIAL: And my fire still burns—for the future of Christ in Paraguay.

MIURA: My orders are to begin the inspection immediately.

PROVINCIAL: Excellent! I am glad to hear it.

MIURA: I shall be obliged to issue orders which I find personally unpleasant in the performance of my duties.

PROVINCIAL: Naturally, Don Miura, we understand that.

MIURA: My personal desire is to foster justice and condemn injustice, but I have been ordered to do certain things.

PROVINCIAL: Do them!

MIURA: The first order is that the inquiry is to be a closed inquiry.

PROVINCIAL: Of course.

MIURA: For the purposes of the present investigation, the whole Mission is to be considered the scene of the inquiry. During the investigation no one is to leave the house.

PROVINCIAL: We accept all your orders humbly.

MIURA: Thank you. The second order is that —(*Enter* CORNELIS.)

Scene 10
FATHER PROVINCIAL, MIURA, CORNELIS.

CORNELIS: I regret that I must impose on your hospitality, Father. The guards under this gentleman's command have taken possession of the Mission and refuse to permit anyone to leave.

PROVINCIAL: I am aware of that, Mynheer. (*To* MIURA) This is Mynheer Cornelis of Rotterdam—let him pass, I'll vouch for him.

MIURA: I cannot. It would be contrary to my instructions.

CORNELIS: I trust that you are aware that you are placing a citizen of the Netherlands Free State under arrest!

MIURA: I accept full responsibility for my actions.

PROVINCIAL: But surely you are not under arrest, Mynheer.

CORNELIS: I'm just as much under arrest as you are, Father.

PROVINCIAL: As I am?

CORNELIS: Certainly. What does it feel like to be under arrest?

PROVINCIAL (*still smiling*): I—under arrest?

CORNELIS: Yes indeed, under arrest—precisely. Haven't you realized yet that all the Jesuits are under arrest?

PROVINCIAL (*to* MIURA): Are we to consider your temporary isolation of the Mission as an arrest, Don Miura? (MIURA *does not answer*) Surely you can't arrest us without any reason! (MIURA *rises*) Are we then in fact (*he rises also*) under arrest?

MIURA (*politely*): The second order is that for the duration of the investigation the Jesuits are to be taken into protective custody by the Inspector-General! (PROVINCIAL *retreats a few steps. Standing in front of the map, he slowly raises his arms as if shielding the state. Curtain.*)

ACT II

SCENE 1
VILLANO, ARAGO.

ARAGO: I ought to have you strung up by the thumbs and flayed alive!—What do you think you've been doing with yourself the past few months? Your business was to get some incriminating evidence together! Where are the depositions about the silver mines? And the denunciations about hidden treasure, eh? And what have you done with the coins inscribed, "Nicholas, King of Paraguay"? We want witnesses who will swear unequivocally that the fathers have created their own slave state here, that they have broken off from the royal power of Spain, and that they are rebels and conspirators. In other words, we need precisely

the same kind of evidence that Sebastian Carvalho used to drive the Jesuits out of his country. Where is it?

VILLANO: It's right here—here it is! I've been underway for a month dragging this stuff—and plenty more besides this—over here. I packed it all on top of one donkey in Candelaria. By the time I got to San Miguel I needed two donkeys to get this mass, this flood—this, this mountain through. And in Loreto I had to buy a third donkey—

ARAGO: You're nothing but an enormous donkey yourself!

VILLANO: Are you trying to insult me?

ARAGO: Goes out there, stupid donkey—and listens to two thousand people—depositions from this tribe, depositions from that tribe, depositions, depositions, depositions!

VILLANO: I did my duty. I was told to go out and take down depositions. And besides I'm not a money-grubbing shyster anyway—I'm an old soldier. I figured if you really wanted to get rid of this Jesuit state you'd get rid of it with or without depositions—but if you want a real investigation, fine! I thought I'd take down the depositions anyway. Maybe they wanted them so they could say, here, look here, we've got depositions! All right then, tell me, what do you want in the depositions?

ARAGO: Are you trying to be funny?

VILLANO (*angry*): You're the only one round here who's being funny! You want this grease spot wiped off the map? Well then, just take your sentence out of your pocket! What do you need depositions, sworn statements, and transactions here and transactions there for? We can get all sorts of gold and honor for ourselves here. The Jesuit Provinces are full of tea, corn, and cotton —and for picking it 150,000 Indians who look like they've been created by the Good Lord especially to be slaves. So what do we need all this red tape for? A little war and the problem is taken care of!

ARAGO: Yes, but we can't afford to have a war—you understand? We have to make everyone think that we are in the right, so that the Jesuits can't even think of protesting. We have to have a trial so that we can show the whole world that the Jesuit State is, first of all, disloyal to the king; secondly, that Jesuits are enslaving the Indians; thirdly, that our purpose is to free the natives; and fourthly, that the Jesuits have silver mines which they have kept secret from the king.

VILLANO: We can't prove any of this since it simply isn't true.

ARAGO: I've just got through telling you—we *have* to prove it!

VILLANO: Why do we have to play around at these childish games? Why—

ARAGO (*pointing to the passage*): Hold your tongue! (*Enter from the passage,* DON MIURA, QUERINI, PROVINCIAL, *and several soldiers who remain standing in the entrance.*)

SCENE 2
VILLANO, ARAGO, MIURA, QUERINI, PROVINCIAL, SOLDIERS.

MIURA: Take a seat, if you please, Signor Querini.

QUERINI: I see, Mr. Inspector-General, that you want me to share in the proceedings against the Fathers. That is not my intention, however.

MIURA: I regret exceedingly, Signor Querini, that I am obliged to hinder your freedom of movement.

QUERINI: I am of course entirely at your disposal. On the other hand, I must say that I find this seizure of foreign travellers extremely peculiar.

MIURA: I am very sorry, Signor Querini, but I am only following orders.

QUERINI: I too am accustomed to follow orders at all times.

MIURA (*impatiently*): I am not forcing you to witness the proceedings. You can go and amuse yourself anywhere you like—within the Mission House.

QUERINI: Thank you. (*Turns to door.*)

PROVINCIAL (*addressing* QUERINI): May I ask you, Signor, in the name of my flock, to stay and hear?

QUERINI: Certain things may perhaps be said here against you which it would be better for an outsider not to hear.

PROVINCIAL: You are mistaken. We have nothing to hide.

QUERINI (*to* MIURA): Very well then, I will remain. (*He sits.*)

MIURA (*to* ARAGO): Let the investigating officer of the commission give us a brief outline of the accusations which have been made against the Fathers. Be seated, gentlemen! (*All sit.*)

ARAGO: Don Villano—what are the reasons for the charges made against the Fathers?

VILLANO (*rises*): The reasons for the charges against the Fathers? The reasons for the charges against the Fathers—here, they're written down here in the reports over and over again! I can't recall them all off-hand. I refer you to the reports. (*He sits.*)

MIURA: Father Provincial—are you aware of the reasons for the charges against you?

PROVINCIAL: We are accused of establishing a sovereign state and of rejecting our allegiance to the king. We are accused of keeping silver mines hidden in our settlements. We are accused of making excessive profits in our trades and thus injuring the position of the Spanish Empire, whose subjects we are. We are accused, finally, of enslaving the Indians who have been entrusted to us.

MIURA: We will examine these accusations one by one. Don Villano, is it true that the Jesuits have established a sovereign state here in Paraguay?

VILLANO: Yes, it is true.

MIURA: Father Provincial?

PROVINCIAL: We have not established a sovereign state.

VILLANO: The Jesuits do as they please here —ergo, they have established a sovereign state.

MIURA: They have not, however, withdrawn their allegiance from his Spanish Majesty?

VILLANO: No. They have not withdrawn their allegiance.

MIURA: They are therefore still, and always have been, the king's subjects?

VILLANO: Yes. They're subjects, all right.

MIURA: Then they are not sovereign after all!

VILLANO: You could put it that way too.

MIURA: Don Arago, kindly note down in the record that the charge of founding a sovereign state which has been made against the Jesuits has been found to be false.

ARAGO: As you please.

MIURA: The second charge, Don Villano.— Are the Jesuits in Paraguay disobedient to the king?

VILLANO (*wiping off the perspiration*): Disobedient. As far as I have been able to discover they are not exactly obedient.

MIURA: I am asking whether they are disobedient to the king.

VILLANO: Why should they be disobedient? The king has not demanded anything of them up to now, so there hasn't been anything for them to be obedient about. If, on the other hand, he should make some demands on them, we will have to reckon with the possibility that they won't be obedient.

MIURA: Father Provincial?

PROVINCIAL: The king is our protector, and we owe him unconditional obedience.

MIURA: And should the king cease to protect you?

PROVINCIAL: Even in that case he will remain our highest secular master.

MIURA: Does that mean that you will be obedient to the king no matter what he orders you to do?

PROVINCIAL: We owe His Majesty unconditional obedience so long as he does not ask us to commit a sin.

MIURA: Don Arago, take down that the second accusation also appears to be unproved.

ARAGO (writing): . . . ask us . . . to commit . . . a sin . . .

MIURA: Is it a fact, Don Villano, that there are silver mines to be found in the territory of the Jesuits?

VILLANO: The investigations of the commissions produced no results in this connection during the time I spent in the territory of the Jesuits. But I have not yet had time to study all of the reports. It is possible that we might find a valuable clue to this matter in one or other of the depositions. Besides, it is possible that some of the commissions have got on the track of one of these mines in the last few months. Possibly they only discovered it a few days ago and so we don't know anything about it yet. I think, therefore, that we may in all conscience say that it is very probable indeed that the Jesuits have one or more silver mines hidden in their territories.

MIURA: Father Provincial?

PROVINCIAL: I swear that neither silver nor gold nor any other precious metal has been discovered and exploited by us in any one of our settlements.

MIURA: Don Villano—have you any definite proofs for the presence of any silver mine in the Jesuit state?

VILLANO: No.

MIURA: Don Arago, if you please—Up to this time the charge that the Jesuits possess silver mines has not been backed up by the smallest particle of definite proof.

ARAGO (writing): . . . smallest particle of definite proof.

MIURA: The next accusation: The Jesuits have made excessive profits in their trades and thus have injured the Spanish Empire. Don Villano?

VILLANO: The Jesuits trade. Whoever trades, makes excessive profits. The Jesuit towns are built of stone. Their churches are full of gold. Where do they get the money? From the excessive profits they squeeze out of their trading ventures, obviously. The Jesuits make excessive profits from their trades and thus injure the Spanish state, to whom the traded goods belong by right.

MIURA: Father Provincial?

PROVINCIAL: We receive no profit from the sale of goods of which we possess an excess. Consequently there can be no question of trade—let alone excessive profit. Let me give you an example: Mynheer Cornelis of Rotterdam bought a shipload of tea worth 1400 pieces of gold from us today. With these 1400 pieces of gold our bailiff will instantly buy iron tools which we urgently need in the cultivation of our fields and which we are unable to manufacture ourselves since we do not have any iron ore. These tools will be delivered to whatever settlements may have need of them, whether they contributed any of the tea or not. We do everything in this way.

MIURA: In other words, you sell without making any profit at all?

PROVINCIAL: That is right.

MIURA: And where—for example—do you obtain the tax money which you pay the king?

PROVINCIAL: The tax money also comes from the sale of superfluous goods. That is no problem since, thanks to the king's mercy, our taxes are negligible.

MIURA: I'm not entirely clear about all this, but we shall see. In any case, the charge of making excessive profit seems to me . . . unproved . . . That brings us to the last point—that the Jesuits have enslaved the

Indians entrusted to them. Is that correct, Don Villano?

VILLANO: The whole state is ruled by a hundred Fathers. One hundred Jesuits ruling over 150,000 Indians. The settlement of Candelaria contains 7000 Indians. Only two Jesuits control this whole settlement. They are the only white men there.—The settlement of San Miguel has 6000 inhabitants, ruled by two Jesuits. None of the settlements, in fact, has more than two Fathers. Thirty settlements—sixty Fathers. The other forty are stationed in the Mission Houses of Córdoba, Tucumán, Asunción, and Buenos Aires. The Indians are nothing—just a herd of dumb beasts. The Fathers are everything: Officials, judges, slave drivers, teachers, commanders. The Indian has no freedom at all; and anyone who has no freedom is a slave. Therefore the Jesuits have created slavery and repression in their state. (*He sits and wipes the perspiration from his brow.*)

MIURA: Father Provincial?

PROVINCIAL: It is true that there are always only two Fathers watching over several thousand Indians. It is true that we Jesuits look after the secular as well as the sacred needs of the Indians—we have to! Our Indians have harmless but childish habits. If we did not look to the distribution of the crops they would eat everything up in a few days. If we did not look to the distribution of the meat, the Indians would have slaughtered all their cattle in a very few weeks. We have undertaken all sorts of tasks and positions—as craftsmen, as farmers, as officials, as judges—because of the absolute necessity of being everything to everyone. The people receive everything necessary to their spiritual and bodily health from our hands. It is in this that our absolute rule differs from that of many other secular governments.

MIURA: In other words you are trying to say that your accusers, rather than you, are the ones ruling over slaves.

PROVINCIAL: I didn't say that.

MIURA: No, but possibly you thought it. Don Arago, write this into the record: "According to the evidence of the Father Provincial, the Indians do not appear to be held in slavery."

ARAGO (*writing*): . . . do not appear to be held . . .

MIURA: It seems to me that all the accusations which have been brought against you so far are entirely baseless. I am not, however, disposed to bring about any injustice here or to lend myself as an instrument of injustice. Be so good, therefore, as to testify that I am conducting this hearing with justice and equity, Father Provincial.

PROVINCIAL: Your conduct of the hearing is admirable, Don Miura.

MIURA: I would not, however, be serving the ends of justice if I did not give a hearing to those who have accused you. Corporal!

SOLDIER: Sir!

MIURA: Bring the bishop and the landowners up here!

SOLDIER: Sir! (*Exit.*)

MIURA: What, precisely, is the object you hope to attain with your state, Father Provincial?

PROVINCIAL: The greater glory of God—nothing else.

MIURA: And how do you plan to increase the glory of God?

PROVINCIAL: By converting all the heathens.

MIURA: All the heathens. You mean all the heathen Indians in Paraguay?

PROVINCIAL: Certainly.

MIURA: You seek to bring more and more heathens to Christianity?

PROVINCIAL: Ever more and more.

MIURA: And thus your state grows ever more and more?

PROVINCIAL: Ever more and more

MIURA: Why do you not operate like the missionaries of the other Orders, for example the Dominicans, who go from place to place preaching and baptizing—and that's that. Why do you have to establish a state and intrude into worldly affairs?

PROVINCIAL: We do not intrude into worldly affairs. The state itself does not matter, but here in Paraguay it was the only way to win souls for Christ.

MIURA: Why was it the only way?

PROVINCIAL: Because the Indians lose their Christianity when they live together with Spanish or Portuguese Christians.

MIURA: Nobody forces the Indians to live with us! Let them stay in their fields and jungles—and be Christians there!

PROVINCIAL: They weren't permitted to remain in their fields and jungles. They were chased out, captured, and enslaved.

MIURA: By whom?

PROVINCIAL: By Christians. (*Pause.*)

MIURA: But are the Indians safe from capture by slave traders in your state—in the state the king has chartered to you?

PROVINCIAL: Slave traders, whatever their nationality may be, somehow seem to have lost the taste for practicing their profession within the borders of our territories.

MIURA: I see . . . And what would happen if you Jesuits were taken out of the settlements and replaced by Fathers from other orders? Does it make any difference if the preacher is dressed in a brown cassock or a white one?

PROVINCIAL: And who will take care of all the other things? The Indians are accustomed to having us think for them. They receive their bread from us, they receive their wages from us, and they receive their punishments from us. I don't think they would obey other priests as they obey us.

MIURA: In other words, you Jesuits are, so to speak, irreplaceable?

PROVINCIAL: Yes, in all humbleness we take it upon ourselves to say that here in Paraguay we are—to the greater glory of God be it said—irreplaceable.

MIURA: Put that into the record, Don Arago!

ARAGO (*writing*): The Jesuits . . . in Paraguay . . . irreplaceable . . . (*Enter from the passage the* BISHOP, BUSTILLOS, QUESEDA, CATALDE.)

SCENE 3

The above, BISHOP, BUSTILLOS, QUESEDA, CATALDE.

MIURA: Your Eminence! Gentlemen!—Be so good as to be seated and to answer my questions. I call to your attention that the slightest hint of perjury will be severely punished.

BUSTILLOS (*softly to* QUESEDA & CATALDE): We'll get nowhere with this one! You can smell the Jesuit on his filthy breath from here.

MIURA: Your Eminence, if you please! How long have you been in office, Your Eminence?

BISHOP: Two years.

MIURA: Your predecessor is dead?

BISHOP: No. My predecessor was called back to Spain because he paid excessive attention to the complaints and remonstrances of the old Christians of Buenos Aires.

MIURA: What are the complaints and remonstrances which have been made against the Society of Jesus in Paraguay?

BISHOP: You have the representatives of the most prominent Spaniards in Buenos Aires here—ask them.

MIURA: I shall ask them. Now then, Eminence, are you yourself opposed to the Society of Jesus?

BISHOP: I am a friend of the Jesuits and a great admirer of their campaign against the heretics in Europe. But despite the high respect in which I hold the Society, I am obliged to testify that what the Jesuits are doing here in Paraguay no longer bears any relation to the original purpose of the Order.

MIURA: What is the original purpose of the Order, Father Provincial?

PROVINCIAL: The conversion of the heathen to Christianity by the accustomed methods and the greater dissemination of the authority of the Holy Church and the Holy Father: *omnia ad majorem Dei gloriam.*

MIURA: Your Eminence.

BISHOP: The Society of Jesus has undergone a disastrous change here in Paraguay. They have misused their spiritual powers and have set up instead a secular tyranny against which the poor Indians are powerless. They are forbidden to learn Spanish or even to speak to any Spaniard, under pain of heavy penalty. Non-Jesuits are even forbidden so much as to enter the Jesuit territories, and men of ancient Spanish noble stock are treated contemptuously, like foreigners, even though it was their fathers and forefathers who conquered this land for Spain. As if this were not enough, they even go so far as to cast doubt on the spiritual competence of the bishops and other higher clergy in the area. They have managed to obtain privileges from the Crown by means of a constant influx of new father confessors—privileges which have naturally enough enraged and embittered the old Spanish Christians. We secular priests have never had such an influx of reinforcements but it is to us that the Spanish nobles and merchants and landowners come in order to complain of the arrogance and violence of the Jesuits. There is nothing I can do, however. I am unable to investigate the original causes of these complaints since the Father Provincial refuses to let me enter the Jesuit settlements.

MIURA: Father Provincial?

PROVINCIAL: We were unfortunately unable to permit His Eminence to inspect our settlements since he made conditions which we could not accept.

MIURA: What conditions?

PROVINCIAL: He insisted that one hundred nobles, merchants, and landowners would have to accompany him. It was simply a spying expedition. We were willing to permit the bishop to make an inspection trip in our territories—although we are in no way obligated to let the secular priesthood pass judgment on our work—but under these conditions, no!

MIURA: Why did Your Eminence make this condition?

BISHOP: Because I'm not out of my mind! I'd have to be crazy to go in there alone or accompanied only by priests! I see you are going to force me to be clearer. Despite the danger I run of being called back to Spain like my predecessor for it, I intend to open your eyes to the way in which our holy religion has been profaned in the Jesuit settlements. The priesthood has been abused there. It has been blamed for setting up a worldly tyranny. Under the guise of religion, the Jesuits have set up a Utopia which brings the Indians food, clothes, safety, and security. In other words, instead of making Christians out of heathen Indians, they have made grubbing materialists out of them. They are interested in Christ only so long as he gives them their bread, their meat, and their herb tea. The teachings of Christ mean nothing to the Indian when some servant of the Church other than a Jesuit preaches to them. That is what has been made of our holy religion in the course of time here in Paraguay—you may easily convince yourself, Don Miura!

MIURA: This is a matter which concerns the Church. Rome and not I must render a decision in this dispute.

BISHOP: We have appealed to the Holy Father several times. Unfortunately all that they know about Paraguay over in Europe is based on the apparently great success of the mission to the heathens . . .

MIURA: Supposing that Rome intervened to let the secular clergy have access to the settlements?

BISHOP: That would be desirable in the extreme—and would cause a lot of changes to be made.

MIURA: Many thanks for your evidence, Eminence. It was extremely enlightening. Corporal!

SOLDIER: Sir!

MIURA: See His Eminence down to the gate!

SOLDIER: Sir!

MIURA: Once again, many thanks, Your Eminence! (*The* BISHOP *bows slightly and exits.*)

SCENE 4
As above except for BISHOP.

MIURA (*to* BUSTILLOS, QUESEDA, & CATALDE): You gentlemen also have some complaints to make against the Society of Jesus?

BUSTILLOS (*rising*): Your Honor—I am José Bustillos and a Spaniard.

ARAGO (*writing*): José Bustillos.

BUSTILLOS: I am a landowner. This is Don Garcia Queseda, a merchant, and this is Don Alvaro Catalde, also a merchant. We are all three Spaniards.

ARAGO (*writing*): Garcia Queseda . . . Alvaro Catalde . . .

BUSTILLOS: Very well. And now, Your Honor, if you please, we will take our leave. Come along, gentlemen! We won't get any justice here. Come!

MIURA: Have you taken leave of your senses?

BUSTILLOS: No, Your Excellency, I have not taken leave of my senses. I merely observe that we have had inspector-generals like yourself pouring in on us here for years. We are not interested in listening to you amusing yourself with your little question-and-answer game here. While you are conducting the proceedings against the Jesuits and weighing your pros here and your cons there, while you are proposing improvements and knocking down complaints—our Indians are running away from us—to the Jesuit settlements! And the ships in the

Parana load up with goods from the Jesuit state while we sit by and twiddle our thumbs. We can pay our taxes on time—oh yes, to be sure—but nobody thinks of helping us. Our protests get blown away like feathers in the wind. But patience, Your Excellency, God helps those who help themselves. Come, gentlemen! (*He starts to leave with* QUESEDA & CATALDE.)

MIURA: Corporal! Bring that man back here!

SOLDIER: Sir! (*He brings* BUSTILLOS *to* MIURA.)

MIURA: My dear sir, you don't seem to realize with whom you have to deal. You are here to answer my questions—understand? —How this examination is conducted is my business!—Now then, answer! How many Indians do you have working on your property?

BUSTILLOS: Six hundred.

MIURA: Have they been baptized?

BUSTILLOS: They have—all of them are practicing Catholics, like myself.

MIURA: And why do they run away from you in order to go to the Jesuits, where they have to submit to an extremely strict rule?

BUSTILLOS: Because the Fathers spew out propaganda for their state! They send specially trained and selected people into all the towns and onto all the estates to persuade our Indians to flee. And then we're left without workers right in the middle of harvest time. It's time we Spaniards took the law into our own hands! But wait, just wait, you'll see, this is only the beginning. The Jesuit empire on the Parana is growing all the time. We've been pushed and pushed until we've got our backs to the sea. Just wait—you let the Fathers go on as they're going now, you keep them warned of everything—and you'll see: in a few years we wicked, tax-paying Spaniards will be lying in the sea while they will have created God's state in Paraguay—or, rather, I should say, *their* state full of happy, contented, stinking Indians. But much you care—all you care about is incense and sermons. Ask these gentlemen what the towns and provinces think of the Christian Republic on the Parana!

QUESEDA: I am a merchant, Excellency, an exporter. We work very hard to get our tea planted. The Indians are all lazy—all they want to do is stuff themselves and lie in the sun. And now that we've got it done, all we can do is sit on our bales of tea and watch the Jesuits taking our business away. If these people (*he points at the* PROVINCIAL) weren't here, we could make money and contribute more taxes to the king of Spain. What does the king of Spain get from the Jesuits? Nothing—in fact, he has to keep giving them money! I know what I'm talking about, Excellency. Two-thirds of the land in Spain belongs to the Church and its monasteries. The priests bathe themselves in fat and the people remain lean. As long as you live under cross and cassock you have it easy, but in the rest of the Spanish Empire, on which the sun never sets, all you can see is misery, poverty, and despair. That's all I wanted to say, Excellency—I trust you'll consider my words with favor and impartiality.

CATALDE: I too am a businessman, Excellency, although I haven't always been one. I used to be a soldier, and so I understand something about military matters. I suggest you interrogate the good Father here about the military resources of the Jesuit state—just lift up his cassock and you'll see the spurs. If you think the Jesuits put their faith in the Lord God alone, then you don't know them very well. They've got a trained army, weapons factories, and more arms stockpiled all over the place than they'll ever need. They've got plans too—plans for defense, of course. They'll decide when the time comes who attacked them. —These are some of things I wish, with all respect, to call to your Excellency's attention. . . .

PROVINCIAL: With your permission, Don Miura, I would like to answer these charges right away—

MIURA: Just a moment, Father Provincial!—Corporal!

SOLDIER (*approaches*): Sir!

MIURA (*to* PROVINCIAL): Would you ask the Fathers involved in these charges to come here?

PROVINCIAL: Of course. (*To* SOLDIER) Fathers Hundertpfund, Clarke, and Oros.

SOLDIER: Fathers Hundertpfund, Clarke, Oros.—Sir! (*Exit.*)

MIURA: Don Arago, have you taken everything down?

ARAGO: Not everything.

MIURA: What have you taken down?

ARAGO (*reading*): . . . Propaganda among the Indians in the towns and the provinces . . . business competition . . . arming for war . . .

MIURA: Correct.

PROVINCIAL: If you will permit me to say a few words, Don Miura—

MIURA (*politely*): Kindly remain patient, Father Provincial. We will see—we will see right away. (*To the three landowners*) You there—you can go.

BUSTILLOS: We would like to repeat our charges directly to the Fathers, Excellency.

QUESEDA: We would like to be able to meet them face to face, Excellency!

MIURA: I said you could go! Guard! (*Soldiers come from the passage.*) Take these three men down and see them safely out. (*The* SOLDIERS *surround the three men and lead them to the passage.*)

BUSTILLOS: So that's the way you treat taxpayers! (*Shouting*) You go ahead and act big, you from over there! We're just lousy colonials—you can spit on us now, but just wait, the world is turning! (*Exit with the others. Enter* HUNDERTPFUND, CLARKE, OROS.)

SCENE 5

MIURA, ARAGO, VILLANO, QUERINI, PROVINCIAL, HUNDERTPFUND, CLARKE, OROS, SOLDIERS.

MIURA: Father Procurator?

CLARKE (*coming forward*): Clarke—Procurator.

MIURA: Is it true that the goods exported by your state are sold in competition with those of the Spanish merchants?

CLARKE: It is not true.

MIURA: You do not, then, sell your goods—for example, your tea—for less than the Spanish merchants?

CLARKE: Quite the contrary—we sell it for more.

MIURA: More? Then why do people buy your tea instead of the Spaniards'?

CLARKE: Mynheer Cornelis, who bought some tea from us today, will no doubt be able to tell you that better than I.

MIURA: Corporal!

SOLDIER (*comes forward*): Sir!

MIURA: Mynheer Cornelis!

SOLDIER: Mynheer Cornelis! Sir! (*Exit.*)

MIURA (*to* ARAGO): Write down: the Jesuits charge more. (*To the Fathers*) The Father Superior!

HUNDERTPFUND (*coming forward*): Hundertpfund—Superior.

MIURA: Do you occasionally find Indians who have escaped from the Spanish landowners in your settlements?

HUNDERTPFUND: I'm afraid we find them very often, Excellency.

MIURA: Why do the Indians run away from the landowners in order to come to you?

HUNDERTPFUND: Because the landowners beat them and oppress them and keep them in slavery.

MIURA: And how do you punish them in your settlements? What penalties do you have?

HUNDERTPFUND: First we warn them. If the offense is repeated and is not too serious, we give them twenty-five strokes of the rod. In more serious cases, a few months' imprisonment.

MIURA: And the death penalty?

HUNDERTPFUND: We don't have it, and we don't need it. Nobody steals because everyone has what he needs. And nobody breaks any law for the sake of money—because we don't have any money.

MIURA: You don't have any money?

HUNDERTPFUND: Not a penny. Why should we? Everyone gets all the food and clothing he needs. It doesn't cost anything: work is the only thing on which we put any value.

MIURA: Great God in Heaven!—You certainly have created a new kind of state here . . . !

HUNDERTPFUND (*satisfied with himself*): Haven't we, though?

MIURA: What happens when somebody commits a murder anyway? All of the Indians aren't angels, after all!

HUNDERTPFUND: Of course not. Every now and then we have something like that happen. Yes. The murderer is banished.

MIURA: Banished—where to?

HUNDERTPFUND: Wherever he likes. We don't hurt a hair of his head. We just let him see how he likes his freedom, out there in the towns. And so he naturally becomes a slave of the landowners. That's all right—he's among Christians there too.

But what kind of Christians! (*Enter* COR-
NELIS.)

SCENE 6
The above, CORNELIS.

MIURA: Mynheer, you are a citizen of the
Netherlands and I cannot force you to give
evidence.

CORNELIS: I'll give it willingly. Call your
attention to the fact, though, that I'm not
here willingly. The Dutch ambassador in
Madrid will have a little work to do when
. . . (*to* ARAGO) Andre Cornelis of Rotterdam . . .

ARAGO (*writing*): Andre Cornelis of Rotterdam.

MIURA: Mynheer, why do you buy your tea
from the Jesuits when you could buy the
same tea cheaper from the Spanish merchants?

CORNELIS: Cheaper, yes—but not the same
tea. With Herba-Maté it's like this: you
only get a good crop if you pick it without
any thought of making a profit with it.
It's just that with Herba-Maté it's a matter
of the heart, goddamme! The Jesuits understand it—and the Indians seem to like
working in their state. Funny, eh? Your
Excellency?

MIURA: I'm told the Indians are lazy.

CORNELIS: Very true, they are lazy—when
they have to work under the whip as slaves.
But in the settlements nobody beats them.
They work six hours a day and then they
have music, plenty of food—and divine
service! The lazy Indians aren't so lazy
when it comes to going to divine service.
Peculiar, eh? Your Excellency?

MIURA: Have you been in the settlements,
Mynheer?

CORNELIS: Yes, they made an exception of
me. The Father Provincial gave me a safe-
conduct. Usually nobody is permitted inside the State of God, especially no Spanish Catholics. Amazing, eh? Your Excellency? (QUERINI *crosses to* MIURA.)

MIURA (*politely*): Signor Querini?

QUERINI: May I ask the witness a question,
Don Miura?

MIURA: Of course. If you please, Signor Querini!

QUERINI: Are you a Calvinist?

CORNELIS: Yes—I'm a heretic. And I praise
the Jesuits. A paradox—or? (*To* MIURA)
You know, Excellency, that (*indicating the
Jesuits*) not even a heretic's praise can hurt
these men anymore. (*To* QUERINI) Any
more questions, Signor?

QUERINI: No. Thank you.

MIURA: You have also said that you pay the
Jesuits more than the Spaniards for the
same amount of tea, Mynheer.

CORNELIS: Yes indeed—because the Jesuits'
tea is planted with love and the Spanish
slave drivers' with hate. And that comes
out in the taste of the tea—all over the
world.

MIURA: Thank you for your evidence, Mynheer. I am obliged to ask you to remain
in the Mission precincts for some time
longer.

CORNELIS: You let the bishop and the Spanish slave drivers go. Why do you force a
Dutch citizen to remain and let those go?

MIURA: Restrain your impatience a little
longer, Mynheer.

CORNELIS: There's a pretty depressing atmosphere down there. Something must have
leaked through. Strange, eh? Your Excellency? Would please me enormously if the
shoe were on the other foot! Your servant,
sir! (*Exit.*)

MIURA: The Father Procurator and the
Father Superior may go also. (*Exit* HUN-
DERTPFUND & CLARKE.)

SCENE 7
The above except CORNELIS, HUNDERT-
PFUND, CLARKE

MIURA: Father Oros?

OROS: Excellency?

MIURA: What particular task do you perform
in the settlements?

OROS: I have been entrusted with the defense of our territories against attack because of my military experience. I conduct
the military exercises. We have to be ready
at all times to supply the king with troops.

MIURA: To supply the king with troops. . . .
Have you led your Indians into battle in
defense of Spain?

OROS: Since the king extended the privilege
of bearing arms we have fought for Spain

altogether abouty forty times in small or large campaigns.

MIURA: Are your Indians good soldiers?

OROS: We Jesuits have formed disciplined regiments out of savage mobs. We are ready at any time to offer the king a powerful and experienced army.

MIURA: How is your army levied?

OROS: Each settlement contributes at least two regiments. That makes sixty regiments all together—infantry, cavalry, and artillery. An army of 30,000 men.

MIURA: Do you have cannon?

OROS: We have cannon foundries.

MIURA: Ammunition?

OROS: Several of the settlements manufacture guns and ammunition. We have enough in reserve at the moment to arm all our forces.

MIURA: Spain does not have any enemies in Paraguay at the moment. Your army ought really to be reduced in size.

OROS: The king has extended the privilege of keeping an army to us. We are using this privilege.

MIURA: The privilege is an old one—it goes back to Philip V. (*Pauses.*) Certain people seem to entertain the fear that you might attack them with your Indian army some day.

OROS: No one could seriously make such an assertion. Whom should we attack?

MIURA: I did not say that you yourself would attack anyone. But your Indians could take matters into their own hands one of these days.

OROS: Impossible. Our Indians obey us without question, just as we Fathers obey without question our holy superiors.

MIURA: Supposing you ordered them to lay their weapons down!

OROS: They would lay their weapons down immediately and without question.

MIURA: And who would have to order *you* to lay your weapons down?

OROS: The Father Provincial.

MIURA: And whom does the Father Provincial obey?

OROS: The king and the Captain-General of the Order.

MIURA: Let us suppose someone attacked you. Would your army fight?

OROS: Naturally.

MIURA: Are you in command?

OROS: I am in immediate command of the forces.

MIURA: But who gives the order to attack?

OROS: The Father Provincial.

MIURA (*to* ARAGO): Have you got that?

ARAGO: Everything.

OROS: We're not threatening anyone. It's absurd to attribute any warlike intent to us, but we stand ready to fight anyone who seeks to destroy God's State in Paraguay. Anyone.

MIURA: Father Provincial?

PROVINCIAL: It is exactly the way Father Oros has said. The days when hordes of outlaws and thieves could disrupt our peaceful works without being punished are over.

MIURA: Naturally—30,000 trained soldiers, that's something! Who would dare to meddle with you now? Anyone wanting to pick a quarrel with you would soon have some second thoughts. Yes, God's State has certainly become very worldly! (*To* OROS) Where did you serve before you entered the Order?

OROS: In Hungary with the Imperial Hussars.

MIURA: Any decorations?

OROS: Several bestowed by Prince Eugene.

MIURA: My compliments!—Thank you, Father Oros! (OROS *retreats.*) Don Arago, give me your notes. (ARAGO *hands it to him.* MIURA *glances at it.*) The public part of the hearing is completed. I wish to speak with the Father Provincial alone. My thanks to all of you. Corporal! (SOLDIER *comes forward.*) Post your men downstairs—and see that we are not interrupted.

SOLDIER: Sir! (*Exit all except* PROVINCIAL & MIURA.)

SCENE 8
PROVINCIAL, MIURA.

MIURA: One thing is obvious: the accusations against you are false!

PROVINCIAL: I never doubted that the truth would be clear to your impartial judgment.

MIURA: You are not disobedient to the king.

PROVINCIAL: We never have been!

MIURA: You are not repressing your people.

PROVINCIAL: We can say that our state is one of the few states in the world whose power is not founded on repression.

MIURA: You are also not guilty of unfair business practices.

PROVINCIAL: Even the heretic confirmed that fact for you.

MIURA: You do not have secret silver mines and you are not hoarding secret treasure.

PROVINCIAL: We have demonstrated that the true happiness of the people depends neither on money nor on gold.

MIURA: And yet these filthy accusations keep being made against you.

PROVINCIAL: You will clear us of them once and for all! You will—

MIURA (*stops with a gesture*): You have already been sentenced. These accusations have been accepted in Spain blindly and without proof. They have been incorporated, point for point, into the sentence. Here—read! (*Hands him a letter.* PROVINCIAL *takes it, reads, and then stares at* MIURA.) Read!

PROVINCIAL: "It having been proved that the Jesuits in Paraguay have become disloyal to the Crown; it having been proved that they have repressed and enslaved my Indian subjects under the guise of religious conversion; it having been proved that they have enriched themselves through secret mines; it having been proved . . ." (*To* MIURA)—it having been proved? It having been proved?

MIURA (*takes the letter and calmly reads on*): ". . . I hereby order by virtue of the power vested in me by God, that all members of the Society of Jesus shall leave the Paraguayan provinces and that their property shall be confiscated. Given at Buen Retiro, the 27th of February, 1767. I, REX." (*Hands the sentence back.*)

PROVINCIAL (*determined*): The sentence is worthless! The king has been misinformed.

MIURA (*agreeing*): The king has been misinformed.

PROVINCIAL: What are you going to do now?

MIURA: I cannot carry this sentence out.

PROVINCIAL: You will explain it all to the king! You are our savior! God has chosen you to be the savior of our state!

MIURA: I will explain it all to the king. I will show him the baseness of these accusations. But your state—your state must fall!

PROVINCIAL: What?

MIURA: Your state must fall!

PROVINCIAL: We—must fall?

MIURA: You.

PROVINCIAL: You testify that we have not committed any injustice—and then you want to destroy us?

MIURA: Injustice. Everyone of us commits injustice. There isn't a single state in the world that is not weighed down by injustices that cry out to Heaven. Injustice does not destroy any state. No, you stand accused of something far worse than that!

PROVINCIAL: Far worse?

MIURA: You are in the right!

PROVINCIAL (*triumphantly*): We are in the right!

MIURA: And precisely *because* you are in the right you must be destroyed! Destroyed—mercilessly destroyed!

PROVINCIAL: Have you taken leave of your senses?

MIURA: I would be a simple visionary if I said anything else!—(*Pauses.*) What have you built up out there (*he points at the map*) in the jungle and on the pampas, places where we would never have ventured to go? A state based on love and justice. You sow your seeds and harvest your crops without greed or jealousy—the Indians sing your praises—and run away from our landowners! Your goods are distributed over the whole world—and our businessmen become poor! You have peace and prosperity in your state—back home there is only poverty and dissatisfaction. You are building up this country which we conquered with our blood—to our detriment! There are just a few of you in your state—and we powerful ones have to shake in our boots at your example! We have to colonize by force of arms—you do it with peace. We lose people. You gain them. Tomorrow you'll have thirty-five settlements. In a few years you'll have seventy. How long before you own the whole continent?—And you expect us to stand by and watch? You expect us not to try and stop you? We'd just be stupid idiots if we didn't chase you out while there was still time! You must go! In the name of the Empire which permitted you to make this attempt! Enough of this experiment—it's becoming dangerous! Enough!

PROVINCIAL: This experiment is sacred! Whoever touches it or lifts a hand against it sins against God!

MIURA: Don't talk to me about religion when commercial interests are at stake!

PROVINCIAL: I am obliged to show you respect as the king's representative. What do you propose to do now?

MIURA: I cannot carry this sentence out since it is based on charges which have turned out to be unsupported.—You could easily demonstrate that you were in the right.

PROVINCIAL (*bitterly*): That, as you yourself have said, will hardly prevent us from being destroyed.

MIURA: No, but you would be able to put us in the wrong in the eyes of the whole world; and that would produce a whole mountain of unpleasant pamphlets. We cannot allow that.

PROVINCIAL: Well then, what do you propose to do?

MIURA: I will do nothing. You will. You will turn over your settlements to us *of your own free will.*

PROVINCIAL: No power in the world could force me to do that.

MIURA: I have more than enough power to force you to do it.

PROVINCIAL: Very well, try!

MIURA: If you refuse it will mean the destruction of your order throughout the whole Spanish Empire! Look at it this way: the Society of Jesus has already been banned in France and Portugal. But we will let you continue to exist anywhere in the Spanish Empire if you leave Paraguay of your own free will.

PROVINCIAL: This is blackmail.

MIURA: The means do not matter. I am serving my country.

PROVINCIAL: Only the Captain-General of the Order can decide the fate of one of our provinces.

MIURA: We have been appealing to the Pope and to the Captain-General of the Order for years, and for years they have been placating us with promises of an investigation. Now we will simply confront your Captain-General with the *fait accompli.*

PROVINCIAL (*very agitated*): Blackmailer!

MIURA (*coldly*): Paraguay—or the Society of Jesus, Father Provincial.

PROVINCIAL: Give me time to think!

MIURA: I cannot give you any time to think. Make up your mind quickly! (*Enter* OROS *from the passage, rapidly.*)

SCENE 9
PROVINCIAL, MIURA, OROS.

OROS: Father Provincial! There's a rumor going around and our people are beginning to panic! (*To* MIURA) They claim your soldiers said that they would destroy our state by force.

MIURA: That is not true.—Father Provincial! (PROVINCIAL *remains silent.*)

OROS: I await your orders, Father Provincial. The Spanish soldiers have been disarmed by our Indians and the Negro guard. If we don't do something we'll be accused of rebellion. (PROVINCIAL *remains silent.*)

MIURA: Answer, Father Provincial!

PROVINCIAL (*slowly*): It is true—they plan to stab us in the back.

OROS: I await your order to resist!

MIURA: Come to your senses, Alfonso Fernandez! There is only one right here—and that is the king's!

PROVINCIAL: There is only one right here—and that is God's! In the name of that right, you, Don Pedro de Miura, are our prisoner! Father Oros, you will see to the Inspector-General's safety!

OROS: Your Excellency, your sword, if you please!

MIURA (*stands undecided for a moment, then draws his sword and gives it to* OROS): And you still maintain that you are innocent? (*Curtain.*)

ACT III

Gathering of the FATHERS. PROVINCIAL *speaks from behind his desk. The* FATHERS *stand in front of the map.* QUERINI *and* CORNELIS *stand far left, listening but taking no part in the scene.*

SCENE 1
PROVINCIAL, HUNDERTPFUND, CLARKE, OROS, *and the other* FATHERS.

PROVINCIAL (*begins hesitantly, but becomes gradually more passionate*): Fathers of the Christian settlements on the Parana and Uruguay! We are all of us here His Catholic Majesty's subjects (*he lifts his biretta*),

and it is with a heavy heart that we have
set ourselves up against those who have
seized unto themselves the royal power
here by means of subterfuge and lies!—
Here in my hand I hold the edict extorted
from the king through whispered slander
and lies.—We have been accused of crimes
which have actually been committed by
our accusers: they blame things on us, who
are the only ones innocent of any crime,
for things which they have done a thousand times over. This is more than an attack against our mission—this is a crime
against His Catholic Majesty himself. Can
we suffer His Royal Majesty's last hours to
be poisoned by the horrors of self-reproach?
—Can we suffer a few ministers and officials to barter the salvation of His Royal
Majesty's soul for the sake of a marauding
expedition with which they hope to fill
their own pockets? The men who are to
carry out this sentence, which they have so
deceitfully obtained, presume on their warrant of absolute power. They are relying on
their positions and on their honors. But
whoever goes beyond the powers of his
office and sets himself up against God must
be stripped of his titles of honor so that he
may not commit immeasurable harm under the mask of his office. To resist in such
cases is to advance the cause of our holy
religion. Slanderers, liars, and criminals are
conquering people who hate slander, lies,
and crimes with the edge of the sword.—
May we lie rejected from the sight of God
if we hesitate to spur our free, unfettered
wills to resist these sins! Now at last the
time has come to recognize that God demands an open avowal of faith and loyalty
from us—we must not remain silent for the
sake of mercy from our fellow men lest we
some day hear ourselves damned for our
faithlessness by the fearful voice of Christ
himself! Let the Indians continue to keep
the peace! The fate of the Society of Jesus
will be decided by the Fathers alone! (*The*
PROVINCIAL *sits.* OROS, CLARKE, HUNDERT-
PFUND *approach him. He speaks to them in
a low voice.*)

OROS: The Father Provincial orders that the
Spaniards be examined in the assembly hall
in order that the truth may be established!
To the assembly hall! (*Exit the* FATHERS.)

CORNELIS (*hurries over to the* PROVINCIAL *and

shakes him heartily by the hand): I'd
never have believed it! That's the way to
behave—

PROVINCIAL: Well, Mynheer?

CORNELIS: My congratulations! The only
thing—it's too bad you're not a Calvinist!
(*Exit. The* PROVINCIAL *also makes as if to
go, but is stopped by* QUERINI.)

QUERINI: For the sake of the mercy and love
of Christ, Our Lord, grant me a few words
with you, Father Provincial!

SCENE 2
PROVINCIAL, QUERINI.

PROVINCIAL (*surprised*): For the sake of the
mercy and love of Christ, Our Lord . . .

QUERINI (*softly*): For the sake of the mercy
and love of Christ, Our Lord.

PROVINCIAL: But of course, Signor.—Be so
good as to take a seat. (*He indicates the
chair in front of the desk.*)

QUERINI (*gently*): Thank you, but—not here.

PROVINCIAL: Would you like to come with
me to the assembly hall?

QUERINI: I regret to say—I will soon be
obliged to leave you, so (*gesture of invitation*) if you would be so good—

PROVINCIAL (*advancing*): Certainly—

QUERINI (*offers the* PROVINCIAL *the chair in
front of the desk*)—as to sit down here.

PROVINCIAL (*shaking his head*): What?
(QUERINI *now goes behind the desk and
seats himself in the* PROVINCIAL's *chair.*
PROVINCIAL *is speechless.*)

QUERINI: Sit down, if you please!

PROVINCIAL (*remains standing*): Who are
you?

QUERINI (*remains calmly seated—humbly*):
*Minimus servus servorum in nomine so-
cietatis Jesu* . . .

PROVINCIAL: Who—are you?

QUERINI: A humble servant of the Order. As
I have just told you.

PROVINCIAL: I don't believe you. You are no
Jesuit.

QUERINI: Our venerable Father, the Captain-
General of the Order, considered it advisable to send his legate to you in this
disguise . . .

PROVINCIAL: You are the legate!—God has
sent you to help us in the hour of our peril.
Praise be to God!

QUERINI (*earnestly*): In the hour of our peril. (*He hands the* PROVINCIAL *a letter.*) Here are my credentials.

PROVINCIAL (*sits and reads—then, rising*): I humbly await your orders.

QUERINI (*rises*): You know that I stand here in place of the Captain-General!

PROVINCIAL (*softly*): Father . . .

QUERINI: And my orders are—that you instantly hand back authority to the Spanish Inspector-General!

PROVINCIAL (*crying out*): Father!

QUERINI (*very gently*): Hand back the authority to the Spanish Inspector-General— at once!

PROVINCIAL: Father—you yourself were a witness to the violence done to us—

QUERINI (*sharply*): —and I will never permit the use of violence by us in return!

PROVINCIAL: The Inspector-General met us with force.

QUERINI: I make no excuses for the Inspector-General.

PROVINCIAL: Our enemies are thieves and slave drivers!

QUERINI: I am aware of that.

PROVINCIAL: They lied to the king and deceived him.

QUERINI: That does not concern me.

PROVINCIAL (*showing the edict*): The king would never have signed this sentence had he known the true facts!

QUERINI: Had he not signed it it would have been very awkward indeed, since the royal edict is entirely in accord with our plans.

PROVINCIAL: But—are you absolutely blind to the immeasurable guilt which the Inspector-General has taken upon himself?

QUERINI: *You* are blind to the immeasurable guilt—which we ourselves have taken upon ourselves here in Paraguay . . .

PROVINCIAL (*after a pause*): I do not understand you . . .

QUERINI: Let us pray to God, Our Father, that he will not burden us with this immeasurable guilt in the hour of our death. We have taken it upon ourselves to bring about in fact as well as spirit the holy word of Christ in a world ruled by ineradicable greed and baseness. The Indians, dazzled by our preaching, now expect us to give them their national freedom. . . . These people expect to get protection from us against those in power—they look to us to set up the Kingdom of God on earth. And we—what have we done? Although we know perfectly well that we are basically powerless, we have let ourselves be caught up into the network of power for the sake of temporal success—we who should be free of all partisanship, whose only task it is to smooth the way for the despairing, oppressed, and suffering peoples of all nations to that Kingdom to which we all must come when death releases us. It is there that Christ will sit in judgment on the blasphemers and oppressors—it is there that the men of violence will be punished and the meek rewarded.—*This* world, however, is not the place for the Kingdom of God.

PROVINCIAL: With these words you place yourself on the side of force.

QUERINI: Yes, of course. That is precisely where our place is—on the side of force. Our task is to awake the Christian virtues in the hearts of the wicked and the mighty. We must recognize our limitations. Here in Paraguay we have not recognized them. But it is not yet too late. We must make a sacrifice: the Society of Jesus must abandon Paraguay!

PROVINCIAL: If we did that we would sacrifice the souls of hundreds of thousands of Christian Indians.

QUERINI: For the greater glory of God we must be prepared to make even such a sacrifice.

PROVINCIAL: If we did this the hundreds of thousands of heathen Indians who would be willing to become Christian would never be saved!

QUERINI: We don't want that kind of Christian. They take up our holy religion simply because we give them protection, nourishment, security, and a beneficial and just leadership.—But God is no politician. And politics is precisely what we are practicing here, and all it is doing is working to the detriment of the European Catholic princes whose vanguard we were.—Now they look upon us as their enemies, and their hate persecutes us. Their hate will continue until it will harm our whole Order—if we do not relinquish our state here in Paraguay.

PROVINCIAL: But think what it is we shall be destroying for ever and ever! We will be destroying the hopes of a people who were crushed by war and misfortune—hopes for a state that can grow only out of a pure belief in God!

QUERINI: Such hopes are vain. Our business is to save their souls!

PROVINCIAL: We will never be able to save their souls if we leave them defenseless against oppression. We must take up an unequivocal position on the side of the weary and oppressed.

QUERINI: We may not do that—it would not be politic. It would wreak immeasurable harm on our holy religion. We are only tools in the hand of the Holy Father.

PROVINCIAL: His Holiness is aware of our work and our success!

QUERINI: He does not welcome them.

PROVINCIAL: He knows that every day we win new souls in this land.

QUERINI: He knows that every day new complaints are made against us. He knows that our state in Paraguay is growing.

PROVINCIAL: The Pope could never surrender his state here.

QUERINI: I believe he would have preferred to see our state here in Paraguay destroyed long ago.

PROVINCIAL: That would mean the destruction of Christendom.

QUERINI: No. It would have meant the purification of Christendom. Satan has crept into our work without our noticing it. In what way does the Jesuit State still differ from the Republic of the arch-heretic, Calvin, in Geneva? It is truly lucky that we have not come into conflict with the Dominicans up to now, for by rights our errors ought to be dealt with by the Inquisition.

PROVINCIAL: I would willingly go before the Holy Inquisition. The shackles have not been forged that I would not be willing to wear for the glory of God.

QUERINI: You are the Father Provincial. I need not remind you of your vow of obedience.—You will obey my orders and carry out the royal edict.

PROVINCIAL: Do not ask me to do that—I humbly beg you to examine the case once more!—I will obey you—I stand ready to take your orders and turn them into my own convictions—I am only an instrument in your hands—but I beg you, have pity on our 150,000 Christians—don't deliver them over to the slave drivers with one single word!

QUERINI: This is a question of the survival of the Order—and you talk about 150,000 people!

PROVINCIAL: Visit our settlements—investigate our work—convince yourself—and then tell the Inspector-General who you are!

QUERINI: I have been ordered to keep my identity a secret. Not a word about my mission or my connection with the Order! No one must know!

PROVINCIAL: Relieve me of my office—I cannot do this!

QUERINI: What are you talking about? There is nothing that a Jesuit cannot do! (*Gently*) And so the Provincial of the Order in Paraguay has come to a better understanding of the matter—hand over the authority to the king's Inspector-General and ask to be punished for your rebellion!

PROVINCIAL: Don't order me to do that—I can't . . . I humbly beg you———(*kneels*)

QUERINI: Answer me: do you admit that my order is right? (PROVINCIAL *remains silent.*) Answer me: do you deliver yourself into my hands as a piece of putty to be molded at will? (PROVINCIAL *bows his head—remains silent.*) Oh—forgive me—I have made a mistake . . . I am, then, speaking to someone else . . . You are not, after all, the Provincial of Paraguay?

PROVINCIAL (*starts, gets up—rapidly*): I consider your orders just and correct. I will carry them out with all the powers at my command. I do not wish to be anything but a humble tool of the Order.

QUERINI: May the mercy and love of Christ, Our Lord, bring you salvation . . . (*Enter* OROS.) Many thanks for your kind hospitality, Father Provincial! (*Embraces him.*)

PROVINCIAL (*tonelessly*): Farewell, Signor Querini! (*Exit* QUERINI.)

SCENE 3

PROVINCIAL, OROS.

OROS: The meeting is waiting for you, Father.

PROVINCIAL: I know—the meeting is waiting for me . . .

oros: We must be prepared to defend the Mission House.

provincial: We must be—prepared.

oros: Bustillos and Queseda will have armed their mobs to attack us.

provincial: It may be—that certain aspects of the situation will have changed before they can do that.

oros: I am convinced that our resistance will be a success—on the whole.

provincial: On the whole.

oros: It is possible that we here in the Mission will have to surrender. But if we are defeated—we will be defeated honorably.

provincial: If we are defeated. We will see. —Do you think any of the Spaniards could escape from the Mission House?

oros: Impossible! Our Negro guards are in full control of all the gates.

provincial: I would like to have another interview with the Inspector-General. Alone. He will hardly try to escape.

oros: He will not escape. I'll have him sent up to you.

provincial: Certain things may have to be changed.—Do I possess the complete confidence of my subordinates, Oros?

oros: You command, Father. We obey!

provincial: You have confidence in me, don't you, Oros?

oros: "Confidence" is the wrong word. I have confidence in *myself*, of course. But I *obey* you. I would obey you even where I would refuse to obey myself.

provincial: And you have confidence in me —as a member of the Order?

oros: More than in myself, Father.

provincial: Thank you. You can go. Ask the assembled Fathers to be patient.—I want to speak with the Inspector-General—with our prisoner. (*Exit* oros. provincial *goes to his desk and writes a letter, hesitating over it frequently . . . he tears up several drafts and finally writes the last one rapidly. Enter* miura.)

SCENE 4
provincial, miura.

miura: So, you've won. We're in your hands. You can save yourself the trouble of trying us. You'll see soon enough where rebellion gets you.

provincial (*quietly*): We are not rebelling —we have thought better of it.

miura: You Jesuits will have to bear the brunt of the guilt—you took us prisoner.

provincial: I take the whole responsibility upon myself.

miura: It's easy to say that at the moment— but you'll soon see exactly what it means to take this on yourself.

provincial: I will soon see it, yes. At the moment, I'm delivering myself into your hands.

miura: Into my hands. (*Laughs*) I am your prisoner—how can you deliver yourself into my hands when . . .

provincial (*gives him the letter*): Here, take it!

miura (*reads—then*): What does this mean . . . ?

provincial: I am delivering myself into your hands. I am your prisoner. I have come to my senses. I acknowledge that we were in the wrong. I acknowledge that the king's Inspector-General was in the right. But none of this excuses our rebellion. I am ready to receive my punishment.

miura: I don't understand you.

provincial: Read the proclamation to the assembly downstairs. The Fathers and the Indian converts will understand it.

miura: If I read this proclamation to them, they'll kill me on the spot.

provincial: No. You will be reading a proclamation promulgated by the Provincial of the Order. Bring me the man who dares speak one word in protest against it! Bring him here to me! You do not understand the obedience the Order demands.

miura: But—we are in your power. A single one of your regiments can finish off all the official commissions. By the time the punitive expedition gets here you can be thoroughly armed to carry on a lengthy war.

provincial: We do not want war.

miura: Ah—you are afraid?

provincial: We are afraid.

miura: And so you would rather surrender to your own prisoners?

provincial: We surrender ourselves to our own prisoners.

miura: This is a rather sudden decision, isn't it?

PROVINCIAL: No. It is a thoroughly reasoned decision.

MIURA (*shaking his head*): You are definitely determined to stick by this proclamation?

PROVINCIAL: I have written and signed it with my own hand. I will stand by it.

MIURA: This solution suits me very well. You had better be prepared to calm your people down.

PROVINCIAL: You should be pleased. You've got what you wanted.

MIURA: You people are quite remarkable, really . . . You start out by defending yourselves in a way—well, in a way which commands respect, and then . . . this solution is, of course, entirely in accordance with our wishes. Very pleased to see it. I'm satisfied. Yes. (*Goes, but turns once again to the* PROVINCIAL.) Actually, though, —it's a pity.

PROVINCIAL: You'll be the darling of the businessmen and the landowners.

MIURA: It is a pity—actually. (*Exit quickly.*)

SCENE 5
PROVINCIAL.

PROVINCIAL (*tries to pray, supporting himself by leaning on the desk*): . . . Anima Christi, sanctifia me—Corpus Christi, inebria me—Aqua lateris Christi—lava me —(*He embraces the crucifix*) O my God! —Wherefore dost thou always forsake this world—wherefore? Wherefore? (*Curtain.*)

ACT IV

SCENE 1
PROVINCIAL, HUNDERTPFUND, CLARKE, OROS.

PROVINCIAL: Father Hundertpfund, repeat my orders!

HUNDERTPFUND: My orders are to turn over the administration of our settlements to the Spanish commissions. I am to see that the friendly relations between the occupying forces and our people are not to be de-stroyed by hotheaded or malicious elements.—Those are the orders which I am obliged in holy obedience to carry out.— And now, if you will permit me—

PROVINCIAL: Thank you, Father Hundertpfund.—Father Clarke!

CLARKE: My orders are to give the Inspector-General an inventory of our stocks in raw materials and manufactured products and to explain the economic structure of our territories to the Spaniards. My orders are to conceal nothing and to suppress nothing.—And now if you would permit me, Father Provincial—

PROVINCIAL: Thank you, Father Clarke.— Father Oros.

OROS: Before I repeat the orders you have given me, I would like to beg you humbly to reveal to us the reason for your sudden change of policy!

PROVINCIAL: Repeat my orders!

OROS: We all of us appeal to you to tell us, for Heaven's sake, the reason for these orders!

PROVINCIAL: I am asking you to repeat these orders so that forgetfulness will not make you lax in carrying them out!

OROS: Instead of carrying out these orders I will wait—until you have come to your senses.

PROVINCIAL (*smiling, to* HUNDERTPFUND & CLARKE): Take Father Oros' hand and squeeze it a bit. Go ahead! That's right. Do you feel anything, Father Oros?

OROS: Oh, I am fully in command of my senses.

PROVINCIAL (*to* HUNDERTPFUND & CLARKE): Very well. Thank you. He is in command of his senses again. (*To* OROS) I will overlook it. It is not necessary to apologize.— Now then, what are my orders?

OROS (*controlling himself*): My orders are to attend to the disarmament of our Indian army in all our settlements. All weapons, ammunition, and other fighting equipment are to be handed over to the Spaniards in good condition—(*strongly*) Father Provincial—

PROVINCIAL: Good. I see you have clearly grasped my intentions. (*Enter from the passage,* ACATU *and* BARRIGUA *with several other Indian notables.*)

SCENE 2

PROVINCIAL, HUNDERTPFUND, CLARKE, OROS,
ACATU, BARRIGUA, INDIANS.

All the INDIANS *bow deeply to the*
FATHER PROVINCIAL.

ACATU: Honored Father—we await your orders.

BARRIGUA: Once more the Spaniards hold this house, honored Father.—Lead us into battle.

ACATU: Lead us into battle—we shed our blood for you, honored Father, willingly.

INDIANS: Lead us into battle!

PROVINCIAL: Will you obey me?

INDIANS: We will obey.

PROVINCIAL: Humbly?

INDIANS: Humbly. (PROVINCIAL *raises his arms to bless them.* INDIANS *kneel.*)

PROVINCIAL: I order you to disperse! I order you to go back to your villages and serve the Spaniards, who will replace us. The Spaniards are your lords and masters from now on!—We, the Fathers of the Society of Jesus, are leaving Paraguay so that we may serve the will of our Holy Father in another land.—May God's Mercy look down upon you. May you remain steadfast under all trials, may you have the strength to bear your sufferings unflinchingly, and may you remain obedient.—In the Name of the Father, the Son, and the Holy Ghost. Amen.

INDIANS: Amen. (*They get up and look at each other helplessly. Finally* ACATU & BARRIGUA *step forward.*)

ACATU: Honored Father—we beg you, explain your words to us. We cannot understand.

PROVINCIAL: The Jesuits are leaving Paraguay.

ACATU (*turning to the* INDIANS): The Fathers are leaving us.

INDIANS (*to each other*): The Fathers are leaving us . . . The Fathers are leaving us— The Fathers are leaving us!

PROVINCIAL: From now on you must obey the Spaniards.

ACATU (*to the* INDIANS): From now on we have to obey the Spaniards.

INDIANS (*upset*): The Spaniards—obey! Obey the Spaniards! The Spaniards? The Spaniards? The slavemen? The landowners? No! No! No!

ACATU: The Spaniards will make us slaves. We all know that. You won't forsake us, honored Father.

PROVINCIAL: You must bear your cross.

ACATU: Shall we stand by and watch while the Spaniards drag our wives and children off to slavery?

BARRIGUA: Shall we fall to the landowners without resisting?

PROVINCIAL: Think of the suffering of Our Lord.

ACATU: We lose all—if you leave us! We lose our villages—we lose our fields, we lose our cattle . . .

BARRIGUA: Honored Father, order us to stab ourselves before your eyes—but do not order the destruction of our entire race!

ACATU: We will not obey the Spaniards!

FIRST INDIAN: We must think of our wives.

SECOND INDIAN: Of our children.

THIRD INDIAN: Of our beautiful cattle.

FOURTH INDIAN: Of our villages.

FIFTH INDIAN: Did we do all that so the Spaniards could have it?

ACATU: The Spaniards destroy our Christianity.

FIRST INDIAN: We will not worship the Christ of the Spaniards.

SECOND INDIAN: Their Christ is no good: he takes everything away.

THIRD INDIAN: Our Christ is good: he gives us everything.

FOURTH INDIAN: Let us protect the good Christ, honored Father!

FIFTH INDIAN: Lead us into battle against the bad Christ!

ACATU: Lead us into battle, honored Father! (*Kneels.*)

BARRIGUA: Lead us into battle, honored Father! (*Kneels.*)

INDIANS: Lead us into battle, honored Father! (*Kneel.*) (PROVINCIAL *sits clutching the arms of his chair, staring silently at the kneeling* INDIANS.)

OROS (*steps forward*): The Christian religion is in danger here in this land—You have heard it yourself now, Father Provincial! The Fathers all beg you: Lead us into battle! (*Kneels.*)

CLARKE: Lead us into battle—in the name of God! (*Kneels.*)

HUNDERTPFUND (*troubled*): Is there any other

alternative for us? Lead us into battle, in God's Name! (*Kneels.*)

PROVINCIAL: In God's Name?—In God's Name?—(*suddenly he explodes, his voice shaking with wrath*) Who told you to kneel to me? I am neither a king nor a minister of a king—I am a priest of God! Get up! (*Everyone gets up.*) Hundertpfund!

HUNDERTPFUND: Father Provincial.

PROVINCIAL: The two heathen Indians—where are they?

HUNDERTPFUND: In the cloister, with the others.

PROVINCIAL: I want to find out once and for all why they are so eager to become Christians. I want—all of you . . . you can go. You can go! (*All exit.*) You, Oros—

SCENE 3

PROVINCIAL, OROS.

PROVINCIAL: —report to Don Miura. Inform him that my orders have been carried out!

OROS: I cannot do that, Father Provincial!

PROVINCIAL: Inform him that my orders have been carried out!

OROS: You are ordering me to commit—a sin! The vow of obedience is no longer valid once the Superior leads us to sin.

PROVINCIAL: I am leading you to sin?

OROS: Is it not a mortal sin to assassinate one's own family?—And what are you ordering me to do?—It is a mortal sin!—It is a sin with which I will burden neither you nor the Order—I will not obey you.

PROVINCIAL: Oh, and what will you do instead?

OROS: I will place myself at the head of the Indian people and fight till my last breath against our enemies.

PROVINCIAL: You are no longer a Jesuit.

OROS: Perhaps none of us has been a Jesuit for quite some time now! God does not care what kind of cassock we wear—God wants to see this world changed! And we Jesuits here in Paraguay have changed it!

PROVINCIAL: You are released from your vows. You are no longer a member of the Order.

OROS: *You* have deserted the ideal! Throw me out of the Order! Bring me before the Inquisition! Drag me to the stake! It won't do any good—you still won't be able to

pretend that this (*he points at the map*) never happened. And as long as I have the strength to breathe, to call out, to fight, I shall continue to stand on the side of the poor, the weak, and the oppressed.

PROVINCIAL: I shall order your arrest.

OROS: Try! You'll find me in the cloister—with our people!

PROVINCIAL: Oros!

OROS: Father Provincial!

PROVINCIAL: For the last time, and in all seriousness: I must order your arrest—you will be sentenced by the Spaniards—I cannot do anything for you any more!

OROS: Let the Inspector-General try and get me: in the cloister. (*Exit* OROS. *Enter* CANDIA & NAGUACU.)

SCENE 4

PROVINCIAL, CANDIA, NAGUACU.

PROVINCIAL: You—Candia and Naguacu—I have had you brought up here. I want you to tell me why you want to be baptized. (CANDIA & NAGUACU *look at each other but remain silent*) What is it that has led you to our Savior, Jesus Christ?

CANDIA: Honored Father—we want to be converted to this God.

NAGUACU: Yes. We want to be converted.

PROVINCIAL: But why come to us? Go to the Bishop of Buenos Aires. He can baptize you and your whole tribe. The bishop can lead you to Christ too. Go to the bishop!

CANDIA: The bishop's Christ not the same as yours.

PROVINCIAL: Ah . . . our Christ—that's the one that is going to give this land (*he points at the map*) to you.

CANDIA (*overjoyed*): Yes, that the Christ we want.

PROVINCIAL: This Christ of course gives you everything . . .

CANDIA: He gives us food.

PROVINCIAL: Food.

NAGUACU: He gives us clothes.

PROVINCIAL: Clothes.

CANDIA: He protects us from the slave handlers.

PROVINCIAL: Ah—he gives you security.

NAGUACU: He builds us houses. He gives us weapons. He makes us strong.

CANDIA: If you honor him, he rewards you.

NAGUACU: That the Christ we want, honored Father.

PROVINCIAL: That is the Christ we have brought to you. Oh—we have deceived you. Christ does not give security, he does not feed, he does not clothe—he is poor himself and hardly . . . (*Shouts and shots from below.* PROVINCIAL *makes sign to* CANDIA & NAGUACU *to go. He goes to the head of the stairs. The* INDIANS *go downstairs.*)

SCENE 5
PROVINCIAL, VILLANO, ARAGO.

PROVINCIAL (*enters with* VILLANO & ARAGO. *He is excited*): My people obey me—you have provoked them. Who told you to attack?

VILLANO: Don Miura. He has waited long enough. You're playing a double game. We're clearing everyone out of here now—and high time, too.

PROVINCIAL: I discussed this with Don Miura—he promised me he would wait until evening.

VILLANO: It is evening. Don't trouble to make any more moves—you've caused trouble enough already.

ARAGO: You can see for yourself that your Indians are resisting.

PROVINCIAL: I will personally guarantee that my people will keep the peace within the Mission.

ARAGO: Here comes Don Miura—talk it over with him. (*Enter* MIURA.)

SCENE 6
PROVINCIAL, VILLANO, ARAGO, MIURA.

PROVINCIAL: Don Miura, order them to stop fighting!

MIURA: It's too late. Father Oros was urging your Indians to rebel. We couldn't just stand by and watch.

PROVINCIAL: But I asked you to let me have a little time.

MIURA: That was no longer possible. Order your people to lay their weapons down!

PROVINCIAL: I'll speak to the Indians. You tell your people to stop.

MIURA: Don Villano, Don Arago, go with the Provincial. If his people lay down their weapons, you will tell our people to stop for the time being.

VILLANO: Yes, sir!

ARAGO: Yes, sir! (PROVINCIAL *goes to the staircase. He is still visible.* ARAGO & VILLANO *follow him.*)

PROVINCIAL (*calling out*): For the mercy and love of Christ, Our Lord: lay your weapons down! (*Gunshots.*) Lay your weapons down: the Provincial commands you! (*Gunshots. Sounds of fighting.*) I will lead you into the cloister. Come. (*To* VILLANO & ARAGO.)

VILLANO: They just don't want to obey you any more, and that's all there is to it.

PROVINCIAL: Follow me. They didn't hear me. I'll take you to the cloister and put a stop to the fight. (VILLANO & ARAGO *hesitate.*)

MIURA: Go with the Provincial. They won't dare touch him. (*Exit* PROVINCIAL, VILLANO, & ARAGO. *Shots. Sounds of fighting. Sudden silence. The* PROVINCIAL *enters from the staircase. He is wounded and exerts all his strength to remain upright.*)

SCENE 7
PROVINCIAL, MIURA.

MIURA (*hurrying to him*): You're wounded. (PROVINCIAL *shakes his head.*) You're wounded. Who dared to attack you? (PROVINCIAL *staggers to the desk.*) Did your own people . . . ?

PROVINCIAL (*pointing at the map*): This . . . has . . . done . . . it! My . . . own . . . work . . . This state—the Antichrist! (*He staggers to the map, tears it off the wall, and throws it on the floor. He falls with it. All that remains on the wall is the corner of the map with the picture of St. Francis Xavier.* MIURA *goes to the help of the* PROVINCIAL, *who is lying unconscious on the floor. Enter* VILLANO & ARAGO.)

SCENE 8
PROVINCIAL, MIURA, ARAGO, VILLANO.

VILLANO (*wiping his brow*): Your commands —have been carried out.

MIURA: Have the rebels been disarmed?

VILLANO: They surrendered.

ARAGO: It's funny, but as soon as they saw that they had hit him (*he points to the* PROVINCIAL) they seem to have lost the will to fight—

VILLANO: We've done what we came to do!

MIURA: Yes. We've reached our goal. (*Looking up.*) The Kingdom of God has gone to the Devil! (*Curtain.*)

ACT V

Night. HUNDERTPFUND, CLARKE, REINEGG, *and a few other* FATHERS *are standing at the head of the dying* PROVINCIAL, *who has already received extreme unction. All of them are holding lighted candles.* OROS, *in fetters, is kneeling on the right of the table on which the* PROVINCIAL *is lying. Spanish guards surround* OROS. MIURA *and* CORNELIS *stand at the right of the table. The left side of the stage is barely lighted by two torches stuck in iron holders on the wall. One of the torches is right next to that part of the map that still remains on the wall, the other in the window niche on the far left, next to the globe.*

SCENE 1

PROVINCIAL, HUNDERTPFUND, CLARKE, REINEGG, OROS, MIURA, CORNELIS, FATHERS, SOLDIERS.

OROS: Father Provincial, absolve me!—I am under sentence of death—they will shoot me. They will try to frighten me, but I am not afraid. I am not afraid of death—I am afraid (*groaning*) of damnation. I was a disobedient servant—I confess!

PROVINCIAL (*after a pause*): You have broken your vow of obedience—You have raised your hand in enmity against your Provincial—You have covered the Order with blood and with shame—for all these things your Provincial condemns you!

OROS: I confess. I was wrong.

PROVINCIAL: Remember this: Repent—and your sins shall be forgiven, saith the Lord. I am your Provincial. I forgive you your sins—so that I too—may be forgiven—for I have remained—I have remained—steadfast in my heretical convictions (*suddenly screaming out*) and I repent it not! (*The* FATHERS *involuntarily step back a few paces.*) Should we place ourselves on the side of force? Never!—Should we serve the mighty of this world?—Never! Should we surrender everything without resistance? —Never! Should we renounce the Kingdom of God on earth? Never . . . Oh—I hear the rebellious voice in my breast saying, Never! Never! Never! I listened to it —but my mouth spoke otherwise. I told my voice it was right—but to my subordinates I said (*suddenly at the top of his voice*) I command you! Listen to me! I am the Provincial! I command—obey me!—and I myself obeyed! Obeyed—obeyed—the rebellious voice in my heart . . . First I cursed, in anger and in the blindness of my pain, this state—as the wound pained my flesh, I destroyed it with my own hands— I destroyed this work . . . (*broken*) and thus I leave this world still ruled everywhere by oppression—slavery—and everything was in vain . . . whispers . . . the voice . . . (*sinks back. Silence. The* PROVINCIAL *lies motionless.*)

OROS (*to* MIURA): Commandant . . . I am ready!

PROVINCIAL (*starting up*): No! Not like this! Not yet! Commandant—give me a little more time—a little time . . . let me see once more!—let me—once more . . . (*pulls himself up, and, turning suddenly to the left, half hangs over the edge of the table*) Ah . . . I knew it . . . he . . . he . . . has remained to us . . . see . . . see, see . . . (*Everyone looks in the direction of the* PROVINCIAL's *outstretched arm, which is pointing at the picture of St. Francis Xavier*) Francis Xavier—has stayed with us! The flaming heart—has stayed with us! You cannot take him away from us . . . see, Fathers, see—he wanders through India—a single, weak man—he converts the heathens, he sets the example—he shows the way . . . His right hand became lame —from baptizing so many thousands—he conquered Japan—he walked across the thousand islands, hungry and thirsty—but filled with faith, with faith that the whole world must become good! Oppression and war must be conquered everywhere! The whole world must become good! See—see him—the nobleman from Navarre—in threadbare cowl, humble, tirelessly preaching—but he is not satisfied, for the whole world must become good! He wants to go to China—and now he sits out the autumn storms on an island, waiting for his ship. He waits, falls ill, has faith, and prays. And then he had to die there on the island, for they had forgotten him—forgotten . . . No ship comes for him. No surgeon visits him. He lies on filthy straw, and no man brings him comfort. But he is joyous—for he knows that all men must be saved—everywhere! He will rise up once more—with flaming heart! See—see—with his flaming heart—he will rise again . . . (*sinks back.*)

HUNDERTPFUND *bends over him. Then he puts out his candle and covers the* PROVINCIAL'*s body. The* FATHERS *put out their candles and put them on the table. All kneel—even* MIURA & CORNELIS. *The right-hand corner of the stage is now in complete darkness.*

FATHERS (*praying*): *Per dominum nostrum, Jesum Christum, Filium tuum, qui tecum vivit et regnat in unitate—Spiritus Sancti deus, per omnia saecula saeculorum.* (*Silence.* MIURA & CORNELIS *get up.* MIURA *goes to the desk,* CORNELIS *goes left to the globe.*)

MIURA: Corporal!

SOLDIER (*stepping out of the darkness*): Yes sir!

MIURA: Take the condemned into the courtyard!—Have Don Arago bring me the sentences for signing. Don Villano is to be in charge of the execution!—The deportation of the Fathers will take place immediately following the executions.

SOLDIER: Yes sir! (*Shouting his commands to the darkness*) About face! Forward march! (*Sounds of the soldiers marching off.*)

SCENE 2
MIURA, CORNELIS, HUNDERTPFUND, CLARKE, REINEGG, FATHERS.

MIURA (*reads the names of the* FATHERS *from a list*): Father Hundertpfund!

HUNDERTPFUND (*stepping out of the darkness*): Here!

MIURA: You have been sentenced to be deported. Get ready, Father. Clarke!

CLARKE (*stepping out of the darkness*): Here!

MIURA: The same. Clausner!

FIRST FATHER (*stepping out of the darkness*): Here!

MIURA: Torres . . . Briegniel . . . Escandon . . . (*The* FATHERS *step forward.*) You have all been sentenced to be deported. (*All the* FATHERS *now stand in a group lit up by the torches. Enter* VILLANO & ARAGO.)

SCENE 3
The above, VILLANO, ARAGO.

ARAGO (*handing some papers to* MIURA): The sentences. If you would be so good . . .

MIURA: Right away.—Don Villano!

VILLANO: Yes sir!

MIURA (*indicating the group of* FATHERS): Get these here on to the ship. As unobtrusively as possible.

ARAGO: Unobtrusively—that's going to be difficult. The whole town is up and about. Things like this don't happen every day, after all. There's thousands of them right outside.

MIURA: The ringleaders of the rebellion will receive their just punishment before the Fathers are deported. You, Don Villano, will be in charge of the shootings.

VILLANO: Yes sir!

MIURA: Don Arago will bring you the signed sentences.

VILLANO: Yes sir! (*Turning to the group*) Forward march! (*Exit with* FATHERS.)

SCENE 4
MIURA, ARAGO, CORNELIS.

MIURA (*looking through the papers*): All of these—sentenced to death?

ARAGO: All of them.

MIURA: How many?

ARAGO: Thirty.

MIURA: Thirty.—Isn't that being a little excessively severe?

ARAGO: We have to.

MIURA: Have to?

ARAGO: Oros—the ringleader from the Fathers.

MIURA: Of course—he has forfeited his life.

ARAGO: And, as a warning, one Indian from each settlement.

MIURA: As a warning . . . (*looking up*) Of course, we couldn't very well do anything else.

ARAGO: We couldn't very well do anything else. Even if we wanted to be merciful—we couldn't.

MIURA: Even if we wanted to . . . Circumstances don't always agree with our feelings and intentions . . . (*He signs*) Death —death—death—death—death—death— death—death—(*he signs more hastily as he goes on. When he has finished he gathers the papers with his left hand and gives them to* ARAGO. *He looks exhausted.*) Here! Take them!

ARAGO: Yes sir! (*Exit.* MIURA *leans back exhausted.*)

SCENE 5
MIURA, CORNELIS.

CORNELIS (*slowly*): . . . Has your hand become lame—from signing too many death sentences?

MIURA: You too—can go wherever you want to now, Mynheer. I have carried out my orders . . .

CORNELIS: Congratulations . . . (*he looks out of the window*) Don't you want to come and take a look at the victors, Don Miura?

MIURA: The victors?

CORNELIS: Yes, of course, the victors. There they are down there celebrating—Bustillos, Queseda, Cataldo, and company . . . they're having a fine old time down there.

MIURA: We don't care about that mob. *We* are the victors!

CORNELIS: Oh yes, you Spaniards are always the victors. You've been the victors for centuries now. (*He gives the globe a push —it begins to spin.*) There! From the rising of the sun to the setting of the sun you've conquered—with the sword. (MIURA *goes to the globe.*) Always further—always more! Always more! The whole world— with the sword.

MIURA (*studying the spinning globe*): With the sword.

CORNELIS: You came in blood and now you're slowly stifling the way you came— in blood. . . . You conquered here by force too . . . and it will be your last conquest . . . for this continent is slipping away from you too. (*He takes the torch out of its iron ring on the wall and shines it on the spinning globe.*) Your East Indian possessions—what's happened to them? You've had to come to us Dutchmen to bail you out—to us whom you've burnt by the thousands—to us, whose country you have laid waste—like devils— we have become your heirs! (*points to various places on the globe*)—Straits of Magellan—the Philippines—Calcutta—Goa— Cape of Good Hope—the Fortunate Isles —what's happened to all of them? Where are they? And you still haven't learned anything—

MIURA (*tears the torch from his hand and stamps on it*): I don't need *you* to tell me about it! You can leave the Mission House! (*quieter*) My best wishes for a successful voyage, Mynheer . . .

CORNELIS: Oh—I too wish you the best— peace and quiet. Good night to you, Don Miura, and peaceful dreams. (*Exit.*)

SCENE 6
MIURA.

MIURA (*turns round—his glance falls on the picture of St. Francis Xavier—he looks for a long time at the picture, which is lighted by the single remaining torch.—Then he goes toward the right and speaks into the darkness*): My fire is not quenched either —Alfonso Fernandez . . . it still burns for Spain and for the king! (*He takes several steps to the right.*) And yet—there's something in my heart . . . something . . . that says (*he slowly goes out of the circle of light into the darkness*) "What does it profit me if I win the whole world—and yet injure my immortal soul . . ." (*He is now totally invisible in the darkness.*) . . . that voice is in my heart too, Alfonso Fernandez . . . (*Muffled drums of the parading platoons are heard from below.* MIURA'S *voice comes softly from the darkness*)— I confess it—I confess it—(*Curtain.*)

IV
Love

IF man's religions are his way of attempting to create a coherent place for himself in the cosmos, what he calls "love" is his way of attempting to create a coherent place for himself on a personal level. Just as he is unable to stand alone in the universe and has to postulate a system in which he becomes the central concern of the universe, so is he equally unable to stand alone on a microcosmic level. He still needs to be the central concern of his own personal world in someone else's eyes. "Love" is what is said to spring into existence when two people decide that they are the central concerns of each other's lives. In other words, "love" is religion on a microcosmic scale. It, too, is a manifestation of the human being's need to cling and to merge—to mean something in relation to someone else, whether it be to God or to lover. Very few people are capable of believing that they exist in themselves and are sufficient unto themselves. Such people are atheists or agnostics in their thoughts and hermits in the midst of society. They are usually considered to be egomaniacs by their fellows.

"Love" has been the theme most consistently used in literature. Rare indeed is the literary work that does not bring in the theme in one form or another. It is usually presented in one of two forms: either from the emotional aspect, in which case it becomes a means for psychological revelation; or from the personal aspect, in which case it is an important touchstone for the examination of social attitudes.

Shakespeare's *Antony and Cleopatra* (c. 1607) is one of the supreme examples in all literature of psychological revelation. At first reading, the play seems to be a celebration of "romantic" love, of a total, deliriously happy immersion in the ecstasy of love, an impression that Shakespeare reinforces by using as his protagonists two figures who are universal symbols of the extremes of virility and beauty. But the play turns out, on closer examination, to be anything but a paean to love between the embodiments of masculinity and femininity. Some seventy years after Shakespeare wrote his play, John Dryden was to rewrite the story with precisely this slant, as shown by his title, *All for Love; or, The World Well Lost*. Shakespeare's Antony gives all for love, but his world is not well lost. Giving all for love, especially when the love is directed at such a woman as Cleopatra, is to lose the world indeed, but it is not to lose it well. Shakespeare's mind was far too tough—and far too concerned in the early years of James I's reign with political stability—to subscribe to such self-indulgent emotional blather. The magnificence of his poetry and his fortunate inability to resist giving Cleopatra her powerful and moving death scene obscure the fact that his heroine is nothing more nor less than a vicious, selfish, hypocritical, scheming, and, by any standard, utterly despicable woman. Only her high station prevents her from being a woman of the streets. What Shakespeare depicts in this play is the psychologically destructive effect of love. He shows a man who is the perfection of his sex crumbling under the influence of his infatuation; and we see that it is only the sincerity and purity of his belief in his feeling that raises it to "love." The impressiveness and beauty of Cleopatra's death scene should not obscure the fact that it is her last and most brazen essay in hypocrisy. Her suicide is motivated by vanity only (she does not want to be dragged to Rome to figure in her conqueror's triumph) and not in the least by any sincere desire to meet her duped lover's shade again in some putative Elysian Fields.

Arthur Schnitzler's *Round Dance* (1900) takes us to late nineteenth-century Vienna, city of romance and gaiety. Schnitzler, a physician himself, was, however, writing in a world that Freud had spoken to. His Vienna, which he knew intimately, was not the Vienna peddled for tourists by the operettas, Vienna's leading product. He shows us no idealized pictures in beribboned frames with lovers waltzing in the streets while amiable psychiatrists pluck their beards as they mumble sympathetically in sidewalk cafes. Schnitzler shows us the scabrous underside of the phony romance and gaiety. Society— all classes from the highest to the lowest—is shown as being bound in an endless chain of lust. Sex, the great leveler, closes the Great Chain of Being so that there is no progression, only an eternal, treadmill-like intertwining of the links.

George Bernard Shaw's *Mrs. Warren's Profession* (1898) shows us two more aspects of love. First, it shows that sexual mores are entirely dependent on and determined by economic circumstances; and secondly it shows that neither love nor sexual attraction are of any importance beside self-respect. Vivie Warren recognizes that her mother was entirely justified in what she did, but she is revolted at her lack of self-respect in continuing to do it when it is no longer necessary. Her refusal to have anything to do with Frank is based on her recognition of her superiority to him and her desire to determine her own life instead of becoming a repressed Victorian housewife. Like *A Doll's House* by Ibsen, whom Shaw admired extravagantly, *Mrs. Warren's Profession* is a plea for female emancipation. Shaw's theme is the idiocy of the Victorian ideal of female submission and the necessity of equality between lovers.

ANTONY AND CLEOPATRA

William Shakespeare

DRAMATIS PERSONAE
(In order of appearance)

PHILO
DEMETRIUS } Friends and followers of Antony

CLEOPATRA, Queen of Egypt

ANTONY

CHARMIAN, Lady attending on Cleopatra

ALEXAS, Servant to Cleopatra

A SOOTHSAYER

ENOBARBUS, Friend and follower of Antony

IRAS, Lady attending on Cleopatra

OCTAVIUS CAESAR
LEPIDUS } Triumvirs, along with Antony

MARDIAN, a eunuch, servant to Cleopatra

SEXTUS POMPEIUS

MENECRATES
MENAS } Friends to Pompey
VARRIUS

VENTIDIUS, Friend and follower of Antony

MAECENAS
AGRIPPA } Friends to Caesar

OCTAVIA, Sister to Caesar, and wife to Antony

SILIUS, an Officer in Ventidius' army

EROS
CANIDIUS } Friends and followers of Antony

TAURUS, Lieutenant-general to Caesar

SCARUS, Friend and follower of Antony

DOLABELLA
THIDIAS } Friends to Caesar

DECRETAS, Friend and follower of Antony

DIOMEDES, Servant to Cleopatra

PROCULEIUS
GALLUS } Friends to Caesar

SELEUCUS, Servant to Cleopatra

CLOWN, a rustic figure

Ambassadors from Antony to Caesar, Captains, Soldiers, Messengers,
and other Attendants

ACT I

SCENE 1. *Alexandria. A room in* CLEOPATRA'*s palace.*

Enter DEMETRIUS *and* PHILO.

PHI. Nay, but this dotage [1] of our general's
O'erflows the measure: those his goodly eyes,
That o'er the files and musters of the war
Have glowed like plated [2] Mars—now bend, now turn,
The office and devotion of their view
Upon a tawny front: [3] his captain's heart,
Which in the scuffles of great fights hath burst
The buckles on his breast, reneges all temper,
And is become the bellows and the fan
To cool a gypsy's lust.

Flourish. Enter ANTONY, CLEOPATRA, *her ladies,
the train, with eunuchs fanning her.*

Look where they come:
Take but good note, and you shall see in him
The triple pillar of the world transformed
Into a strumpet's fool. Behold and see.
CLEO. If it be love indeed, tell me how much.
ANT. There's beggary in the love that can be reckoned.
CLEO. I'll set a bourn [4] how far to be beloved.
ANT. Then must thou needs find out new heaven, new earth.

Enter a MESSENGER.

MESS. News, my good lord, from Rome.
ANT.   Grates me! [5] The sum.
CLEO. Nay, hear them, Antony.
Fulvia perchance is angry; or, who knows
If the scarce-bearded Caesar [6] have not sent
His powerful mandate to you, 'Do this, or this;
Take in that kingdom, and enfranchise that;
Perform it, or else we damn thee.'
ANT.   How, my love?
CLEO. Perchance! nay, and most like:
You must not stay here longer, your dismission [7]
Is come from Caesar; therefore hear it, Antony.
Where's Fulvia's process? Caesar's I would say? both?
Call in the messengers. As I am Egypt's queen,
Thou blushest, Antony, and that blood of thine
Is Caesar's homager: [8] else so thy cheek pays shame
When shrill-torgued Fulvia scolds. The messengers!
ANT. Let Rome in Tiber melt and the wide arch
Of the ranged empire fall! Here is my space.

---

1 *dotage* not an allusion to Antony's age but rather to his doting on Cleopatra
2 *plated* covered with armor
3 *tawny front* Cleopatra's dark complexioned face; though she was queen of Egypt, Cleopatra was of Greek heritage, not African
4 *bourn* boundary

5 *Grates me* i.e., it annoys me—be quick
6 *scarce-bearded Caesar* barely grown up at 23 years old
7 *dismission* recall
8 *homager* i.e., reflects the authority of Caesar which you feel

Kingdoms are clay: our dungy earth alike
Feeds beast as man; the nobleness of life
Is to do thus; [9] when such a mutual pair
And such a twain can do't, in which I bind,
On pain of punishment, the world to weet [10]
We stand up peerless.

CLEO.　　　　　　　　　　Excellent falsehood!
Why did he marry Fulvia, and not love her?
I'll seem the fool I am not; Antony
Will be himself.

ANT.　　　　　　　But stirred by Cleopatra.
Now, for the love of Love and her soft hours,
Let's not confound the time with conference harsh.
There's not a minute of our lives should stretch
Without some pleasure new. What sport to-night?

CLEO. Hear the ambassadors.

ANT.　　　　　　　　　　Fie, wrangling queen!
Whom every thing becomes, to chide, to laugh,
To weep; whose every passion fully strives
To make itself, in thee, fair and admired!
No messenger but thine, and all alone
To-night we'll wander through the streets and note
The qualities of people. Come, my queen;
Last night you did desire it. Speak not to us.[11] (*Exeunt with the train.*)

DEM. Is Caesar with Antonius prized so slight?

PHI. Sir, sometimes when he is not Antony,
He comes too short of that great property [12]
Which still should go with Antony.

DEM.　　　　　　　　　　I am full sorry
That he approves the common liar, who
Thus speaks of him at Rome; but I will hope
Of better deeds to-morrow. Rest you happy! (*Exeunt.*)

SCENE 2

Enter ENOBARBUS, LAMPRIUS, *a* SOOTHSAYER, RANNIUS, LUCILLIUS,
CHARMIAN, IRAS, MARDIAN THE EUNUCH, *and* ALEXAS.

CHAR. Lord Alexas, sweet Alexas, most any thing Alexas, almost most absolute Alexas, where's the soothsayer that you praised so to the queen? O,
that I knew this husband, which, you say, must charge his horns with
garlands!

ALEX. Soothsayer!

SOOTH. Your will?

CHAR. Is this the man? Is't you, sir, that know things?

SOOTH. In Nature's infinite book of secrecy
A little I can read.

ALEX.　　　　　　　Show him your hand.

ENO. Bring in the banquet quickly; wine enough Cleopatra's health to drink.

CHAR. Good sir, give me good fortune.

---

[9] an embrace is probably indicated at this point
[10] *to weet* to acknowledge, to know
[11] *Speak not*, etc. thought to be spoken to the

attendant
[12] *property* distinction

SOOTH. I make not, but foresee.

CHAR. Pray then, foresee me one.

SOOTH. You shall be yet far fairer than you are.

CHAR. He means in flesh.

IRAS. No, you shall paint when you are old.

CHAR. Wrinkles forbid!

ALEX. Vex not his prescience, be attentive.

CHAR. Hush!

SOOTH. You shall be more beloving than beloved.

CHAR. I had rather heat my liver ¹ with drinking.

ALEX. Nay, hear him.

CHAR. Good now, some excellent fortune! Let me be married to three kings in a forenoon, and widow them all: let me have a child at fifty, to whom Herod of Jewry may do homage. Find me to marry me with Octavius Caesar, and companion me with my mistress.

SOOTH. You shall outlive the lady whom you serve.

CHAR. O excellent! I love long life better than figs.²

SOOTH. You have seen and proved a fairer former fortune
Than that which is to approach.

CHAR. Then belike my children shall have no names.³ Prithee, how many boys and wenches ⁴ must I have?

SOOTH. If every of your wishes had a womb,
And fertile every wish, a million.

CHAR. Out, fool! I forgive thee for a witch.⁵

ALEX. You think none but your sheets are privy to your wishes.

CHAR. Nay, come, tell Iras hers.

ALEX. We'll know all our fortunes.

ENO. Mine and most of our fortunes to-night shall be—drunk to bed.

IRAS. There's a palm presages chastity, if nothing else.

CHAR. E'en as the o'erflowing Nilus presageth famine.

IRAS. Go, you wild bedfellow, you cannot soothsay.

CHAR. Nay, if an oily palm be not a fruitful prognostication, I cannot scratch mine ear. Prithee, tell her but a worky-day ⁶ fortune.

SOOTH. Your fortunes are alike.

IRAS. But how, but how? Give me particulars.

SOOTH. I have said.

IRAS. Am I not an inch of fortune better than she?

CHAR. Well, if you were but an inch of fortune better than I, where would you choose it?

IRAS. Not in my husband's nose.

CHAR. Our worser thoughts heavens mend! Alexas—come, his fortune, his fortune! O, let him marry a woman that cannot go, sweet Isis, I beseech thee, and let her die too, and give him a worse, and let worse follow worse, till the worst of all follow him laughing to his grave, fifty-fold a cuckold! Good Isis, hear me this prayer, though thou deny me a matter of more weight: good Isis, I beseech thee!

IRAS. Amen, dear goddess, hear that prayer of thy people! For, as it is a heart-breaking to see a handsome man loose-wived,⁷ so it is a deadly sor-

---

1 *heat my liver* i.e., rather than in frustrated love; the liver was considered the seat of love
2 *figs* an allusion with obscene implications
3 *children . . . names* be illegitimate
4 *wenches* girls
5 *I . . . witch* i.e., if this is a sample of your prophetic powers, it is obvious you are no witch (at least, this is the most popular interpretation)
6 *worky-day* ordinary
7 *loose-wived* married to a loose woman

row to behold a foul knave uncuckolded. Therefore, dear Isis, keep decorum, and fortune him accordingly!

CHAR. Amen.

ALEX. Lo, now, if it lay in their hands to make me a cuckold, they would make themselves whores but they'ld do't.

ENO. Hush, here comes Antony.

Enter CLEOPATRA

CHAR.   Not 'he, the queen.

CLEO. Saw you my lord?

ENO.   No, lady.

CLEO.   Was he not here?

CHAR. No, madam.

CLEO. He was disposed to mirth, but on the sudden
    A Roman thought hath struck him. Enobarbus!

ENO. Madam?

CLEO. Seek him, and bring him hither. Where's Alexas?

ALEX. Here, at your service. My lord approaches.

Enter ANTONY, *with a* MESSENGER.

CLEO. We will not look upon him. Go with us. (*Exeunt.*)

MESS. Fulvia thy wife first came into the field.

ANT. Against my brother Lucius?

MESS. Ay:
    But soon that war had end, and the time's state
    Made friends of them, jointing their force 'gainst Caesar,
    Whose better issue [8] in the war from Italy
    Upon the first encounter drave [9] them.

ANT.   Well, what worst?

MESS. The nature of bad news infects the teller.

ANT. When it concerns the fool or coward. On!
    Things that are past are done with me. 'Tis thus—
    Who tells me true, though in his tale lie death,
    I hear him as he flattered.

MESS.   Labienus—
    This is stiff news—hath with his Parthian force
    Extended Asia: from Euphrates
    His conquering banner shook from Syria
    To Lydia and to Ionia,
    Whilst—

ANT.   Antony, thou wouldst say—

MESS.   O, my lord.

ANT. Speak to me home, mince not the general tongue,
    Name Cleopatra as she is called in Rome;
    Rail thou in Fulvia's phrase, and taunt my faults
    With such full license as both truth and malice
    Have power to utter. O, then we bring forth weeds
    When our quick minds lie still, and our ills told us
    Is as our earing.[10] Fare thee well awhile.

MESS. At your noble pleasure. (*Exit* MESSENGER.)

ANT. From Sicyon, how the news! Speak there!

[8] *issue*   success   [10] *earing*   ploughing
[9] *drave*   drove

1 ATT. The man from Sicyon, is there such an one?

2 ATT. He stays upon your will.

ANT.   Let him appear.
  These strong Egyptian fetters I must break,
  Or lose myself in dotage.

Enter another MESSENGER *with a letter.*

                            What are you?

2 MESS. Fulvia thy wife is dead.

ANT.   Where died she?

2 MESS. In Sicyon:
  Her length of sickness, with what else more serious
  Importeth thee to know, this bears. [*Gives a letter.*]

ANT.   Forbear me.¹¹ [*Exit* MESSENGER.]
  There's a great spirit gone! Thus did I desire it:
  What our contempts doth often hurl from us,
  We wish it ours again. The present pleasure,
  By revolution lowering, does become
  The opposite of itself: she's good, being gone;
  The hand could pluck her back that shoved her on.
  I must from this enchanting queen break off:
  Ten thousand harms, more than the ills I know,
  My idleness doth hatch.

Enter ENOBARBUS.

                    How now! Enobarbus!

ENO. What's your pleasure, sir?

ANT. I must with haste from hence.

ENO. Why, then we kill all our women. We see how mortal an unkindness
  is to them; if they suffer our departure, death's the word.

ANT. I must be gone.

ENO. Under a compelling occasion let women die. It were pity to cast them
  away for nothing, though between them and a great cause they should
  be esteemed nothing. Cleopatra, catching but the least noise of this, dies
  instantly; I have seen her die twenty times upon far poorer moment.
  I do think there is mettle in death which commits some loving act upon
  her, she hath such a celerity in dying.

ANT. She is cunning past man's thought.

ENO. Alack, sir, no; her passions are made of nothing but the finest part of
  pure love. We cannot call her winds and waters sighs and tears; they are
  greater storms and tempests than almanacs can report. This cannot be
  cunning in her; if it be, she makes a shower of rain as well as Jove.¹²

ANT. Would I had never seen her!

ENO. O, sir, you had then left unseen a wonderful piece of work, which
  not to have been blest withal would have discredited your travel.

ANT. Fulvia is dead.

ENO. Sir?

ANT. Fulvia is dead.

ENO. Fulvia?

ANT. Dead.

ENO. Why, sir, give the gods a thankful sacrifice. When it pleaseth their
  deities to take the wife of a man from him, it shows to man the tailors

---

11 *Forbear me* leave me   12 *Jove* Jupiter Pluvius, rain god of the Romans

of the earth; [13] comforting therein, that when old robes are worn out
there are members to make new. If there were no more women but Fulvia,
then had you indeed a cut, and the case to be lamented. This grief is
crowned with consolation; your old smock brings forth a new petticoat,
and indeed the tears live in an onion that should water this sorrow.

ANT. The business she hath broachèd in the state
     Cannot endure my absence.

ENO. And the business you have broached here cannot be without you;
     especially that of Cleopatra's, which wholly depends on your abode.

ANT. No more light answers. Let our officers
     Have notice what we purpose. I shall break
     The cause of our expedience to the queen,
     And get her leave to part. For not alone
     The death of Fulvia, with more urgent touches,
     Do strongly speak to us, but the letters too
     Of many our contriving friends in Rome
     Petition us at home. Sextus Pompeius [14]
     Hath given the dare to Caesar and commands
     The empire of the sea. Our slippery people,
     Whose love is never linked to the deserver
     Till his deserts are past, begin to throw
     Pompey the Great and all his dignities
     Upon his son, who, high in name and power,
     Higher than both in blood and life, stands up
     For the main soldier; whose quality, going on,
     The sides o' the world may danger. Much is breeding,
     Which, like the courser's hair, hath yet but life
     And not a serpent's poison. Say our pleasure,
     To such whose place is under us, requires
     Our quick remove from hence.

ENO. I shall do't. (*Exeunt.*)

SCENE 3

Enter CLEOPATRA, CHARMIAN, ALEXAS, *and* IRAS.

CLEO. Where is he?

CHAR.   I did not see him since.

CLEO. See where he is, who's with him, what he does:
     I did not send you. If you find him sad,
     Say I am dancing; if in mirth, report
     That I am sudden sick. Quick, and return. (*Exit* ALEXAS.)

CHAR. Madam, methinks, if you did love him dearly,
     You do not hold the method to enforce
     The like from him.

CLEO.   What should I do, I do not?

CHAR. In each thing give him way, cross him in nothing.

CLEO. Thou teachest like a fool: the way to lose him.

---

[13] *tailors of the earth*   the gods who design the
master patterns

[14] *Sextus Pompeius*   though this son of Pompey
(the Great) had been outlawed, he nonetheless held command of the Roman sea-routes by
seizing Sicily because of the friction between
Octavius Caesar and Antony

CHAR. Tempt him not so too far. I wish, forbear.
In time we hate that which we often fear.

Enter ANTONY.

But here comes Antony.
CLEO.   I am sick and sullen.
ANT. I am sorry to give breathing [1] to my purpose—
CLEO. Help me away, dear Charmian, I shall fall.
   It cannot be thus long, the sides of nature
   Will not sustain it.
ANT.   Now, my dearest queen—
CLEO. Pray you, stand farther from me.
ANT.   What's the matter?
CLEO. I know by that same eye there's some good news.
   What, says the married woman you may go?
   Would she had never given you leave to come!
   Let her not say 'tis I that keep you here.
   I have no power upon you; hers you are.
ANT. The gods best know—
CLEO.   O, never was there queen
   So mightily betrayed! yet at the first
   I saw the treasons planted.
ANT.   Cleopatra—
CLEO. Why should I think you can be mine and true
   (Though you in swearing shake the thronèd gods),
   Who have been false to Fulvia? Riotous madness,
   To be entangled with those mouth-made vows,
   Which break themselves in swearing.
ANT.   Most sweet queen—
CLEO. Nay, pray you, seek no color [2] for your going,
   But bid farewell, and go: when you sued staying,
   Then was the time for words: no going then,
   Eternity was in our lips and eyes,
   Bliss in our brows' bent; none our parts so poor
   But was a race of heaven. They are so still,
   Or thou, the greatest soldier of the world,
   Art turned the greatest liar.
ANT.   How now, lady?
CLEO. I would I had thy inches: thou shouldst know
   There were a heart in Egypt.
ANT.   Hear me, queen:
   The strong necessity of time commands
   Our services awhile, but my full heart
   Remains in use with you. Our Italy
   Shines o'er with civil swords; Sextus Pompeius
   Makes his approaches to the port of Rome;
   Equality of two domestic powers
   Breed scrupulous faction: the hated, grown to strength,
   Are newly grown to love: the condemned Pompey,
   Rich in his father's honor, creeps apace
   Into the hearts of such as have not thrived
   Upon the present state, whose numbers threaten;

1 *breathing* utterance   2 *color* pretext

And quietness, grown sick of rest, would purge
By any desperate change. My more particular,
And that which most with you should safe my going,
Is Fulvia's death.
CLEO. Though age from folly could not give me freedom,
It does from childishness. Can Fulvia die?
ANT. She's dead, my queen.
Look here, and at thy sovereign leisure read
The garboils [3] she awaked: at the last, best,
See when and where she died.
CLEO.   O most false love!
Where be the sacred vials thou shouldst fill
With sorrowful water? Now I see, I see,
In Fulvia's death, how mine received shall be.
ANT. Quarrel no more, but be prepared to know
The purposes I bear; which are, or cease,
As you shall give the advice. By the fire
That quickens Nilus' slime, I go from hence
Thy soldier, servant, making peace or war
As thou affects.
CLEO.   Cut my lace, Charmian, come;
But let it be, I am quickly ill, and well—
So Antony loves.
ANT.   My precious queen, forbear,
And give true evidence to his love, which stands
An honorable trial.
CLEO.   So Fulvia told me.
I prithee, turn aside and weep for her,
Then bid adieu to me, and say the tears
Belong to Egypt. Good now, play one scene
Of excellent dissembling, and let it look
Like perfect honor.
ANT.   You'll heat my blood: no more.
CLEO. You can do better yet; but this is meetly.
ANT. Now, by my sword—
CLEO.   And target. Still he mends.
But this is not the best. Look, prithee, Charmian,
How this Herculean Roman does become
The carriage of his chafe.
ANT. I'll leave you, lady.
CLEO.   Courteous lord, one word.
Sir, you and I must part, but that's not it:
Sir, you and I have loved, but there's not it:
That you know well. Something it is I would:
O, my oblivion is a very Antony,
And I am all forgotten.
ANT.   But that your royalty
Holds idleness your subject, I should take you
For idleness itself.
CLEO.   'Tis sweating labor
To bear such idleness so near the heart
As Cleopatra this. But, sir, forgive me,
Since my becomings kill me when they do not

---

[3] *garboils*   commotion, brawls

Eye well [4] to you. Your honor calls you hence;
Therefore be deaf to my unpitied folly,
And all the gods go with you! Upon your sword
Sit laurel victory, and smooth success
Be strewed before your feet!
ANT.　　　　　　　　　　　　Let us go. Come;
Our separation so abides and flies,
That thou, residing here, goes yet with me,
And I, hence fleeting, here remain with thee.
Away! (*Exeunt.*)

SCENE 4. *Rome. A room in* CAESAR's *house*

Enter OCTAVIUS [CAESAR], *reading a letter,* LEPIDUS, *and their train.*

CAES. You may see, Lepidus, and henceforth know,
It is not Caesar's natural vice to hate
Our great competitor. From Alexandria
This is the news: he fishes, drinks, and wastes
The lamps of night in revel; is not more manlike
Than Cleopatra, nor the queen of Ptolemy [1]
More womanly than he: hardly gave audience, or
Vouchsafed to think he had partners. You shall find there
A man who is the abstract of all faults
That all men follow.
LEP.　　　　　　　　I must not think there are
Evils enow [2] to darken all his goodness:
His faults in him seem as the spots of heaven,
More fiery by night's blackness; hereditary
Rather than purchased, what he cannot change
Than what he chooses.
CAES. You are too indulgent. Let's grant it is not
Amiss to tumble on the bed of Ptolemy,
To give a kingdom for a mirth, to sit
And keep the turn of tippling with a slave,
To reel the streets at noon and stand the buffet
With knaves that smell of sweat: say this becomes him—
(As his composure must be rare indeed
Whom these things cannot blemish)—yet must Antony
No way excuse his foils, when we do bear
So great weight in his lightness. If he filled
His vacancy with his voluptuousness,
Full surfeits and the dryness of his bones
Call on him for't. But to confound such time
That drums him from his sport and speaks as loud
As his own state and ours, 'tis to be chid
As we rate boys, who, being mature in knowledge,
Pawn their experience to their present pleasure,[3]
And so rebel to judgment.

Enter a MESSENGER.

---

[4] *eye well*　look appealing, appear well
[1] *Ptolemy*　Cleopatra's dead brother/husband
[2] *enow*　enough

[3] *Pawn their experience, etc.*　subordinate (exchange) knowledge for current gratification

LEP.   Here's more news.
MESS. Thy biddings have been done, and every hour,
    Most noble Caesar, shalt thou have report
    How 'tis abroad, Pompey is strong at sea,
    And it appears he is beloved of those
    That only have feared Caesar: to the ports
    The discontents repair, and men's reports
    Give him much wronged.
CAES.   I should have known no less.
    It hath been taught us from the primal state
    That he which is was wished until he were;
    And the ebbed man, ne'er loved till ne'er worth love,
    Comes deared 4 by being lacked. This common body,
    Like to a vagabond flag upon the stream,
    Goes to and back, lackeying the varying tide,
    To rot itself with motion.
MESS.   Caesar, I bring thee word,
    Menecrates and Menas, famous pirates,
    Make the sea serve them, which they ear and wound
    With keels of every kind. Many hot inroads
    They make in Italy; the borders maritime
    Lack blood to think on't, and flush youth revolt:
    No vessel can peep forth, but 'tis as soon
    Taken as seen; for Pompey's name strikes more
    Than could his war resisted.
CAES.   Antony,
    Leave thy lascivious wassails. When thou once
    Wast beaten from Modena, where thou slew'st
    Hirtius and Pansa, consuls, at thy heel
    Did famine follow, whom thou fought'st against
    (Though daintily brought up) with patience more
    Than savages could suffer. Thou didst drink
    The stale 5 of horses and the gilded puddle
    Which beasts would cough at: thy palate then did deign
    The roughest berry on the rudest hedge;
    Yea, like the stag when snow the pasture sheets,
    The barks of trees thou browsed. On the Alps
    It is reported thou didst eat strange flesh,
    Which some did die to look on. And all this—
    It wounds thine honor that I speak it now—
    Was borne so like a soldier that thy cheek
    So much as lanked not.6
LEP.   'Tis pity of him.
CAES. Let his shames quickly
    Drive him to Rome. 'Tis time we twain
    Did show ourselves i' the field, and to that end
    Assemble we immediate council. Pompey
    Thrives in our idleness.
LEP.   To-morrow, Caesar,
    I shall be furnished to inform you rightly
    Both what by sea and land I can be able
    To front 7 this present time.

4 *Comes deared* becomes highly valued   6 *lanked not* kept from becoming thin
5 *stale* urine   7 *front* confront

CAES.　　　　　　　　　　　Till which encounter,
It is my business too. Farewell.
LEP. Farewell, my Lord; what you shall know meantime
Of stirs abroad, I shall beseech you, sir,
To let me be partaker.
CAES.　　　　　　　　　　Doubt not, sir;
I knew it for my bond. (*Exeunt.*)

SCENE 5. *Alexandria. Cleopatra's palace*

Enter CLEOPATRA, CHARMIAN, IRAS, *and* MARDIAN.

CLEO. Charmian!
CHAR. Madam?
CLEO. Ha, ha!
Give me to drink mandragora.[1]
CHAR.　　　　　　　　　　Why, madam?
CLEO. That I might sleep out this great gap of time
My Antony is away.
CHAR.　　　　　　　　You think of him too much.
CLEO. O, 'tis treason!
CHAR.　　　　　　　Madam, I trust not so.
CLEO. Thou, eunuch Mardian!
MAR.　　　　　　　　What's your highness' pleasure?
CLEO. Not now to hear thee sing. I take no pleasure
In aught an eunuch has: 'tis well for thee,
That, being unseminared,[2] thy freer thoughts
May not fly forth of Egypt. Hast thou affections?
MAR. Yes, gracious madam.
CLEO. Indeed?
MAR. Not in deed, madam, for I can do nothing
But what indeed is honest to be done:
Yet have I fierce affections, and think
What Venus did with Mars.
CLEO.　　　　　　　　O Charmian,
Where think'st thou he is now? Stands he, or sits he?
Or does he walk? or is he on his horse?
O happy horse, to bear the weight of Antony!
Do bravely, horse, for wot'st[3] thou whom thou mov'st?
The demi-Atlas[4] of this earth, the arm
And burgonet[5] of men. He's speaking now,
Or murmuring 'Where's my serpent of old Nile?'
For so he calls me. Now I feed myself
With most delicious poison. Think on me,
That am with Phoebus' amorous pinches black
And wrinkled deep in time? Broad-fronted Caesar,[6]
When thou wast here above the ground, I was
A morsel for a monarch; and great Pompey
Would stand and make his eyes grow in my brow;

1 *mandragora*　mandrake, a narcotic
2 *unseminared*　unsexed
3 *wot'st*　knowest
4 *demi-Atlas*　i.e., Antony, together with Caesar,
　supports the world
5 *burgonet*　a Burgundian helmet
6 *Broad-fronted Caesar*　i.e., Julius Caesar,
　with the wide forehead

There would he anchor his aspect and die
With looking on his life.

Enter ALEXAS *from* ANTONY.

ALEX.   Sovereign of Egypt, hail!
CLEO. How much unlike art thou Mark Antony!
Yet, coming from him, this great med'cine [7] hath
With his tinct gilded thee.
How goes it with my brave Mark Antony?
ALEX. Last thing he did, dear queen,
He kissed—the last of many doubled kisses—
This orient pearl. His speech sticks in my heart.
CLEO. Mine ear must pluck it thence.
ALEX.   'Good friend,' quoth he,
'Say, the firm Roman to great Egypt sends
This treasure of an oyster; at whose foot,
To mend the petty present, I will piece
Her opulent throne with kingdoms. All the East,
(Say thou) shall call her mistress.' So he nodded,
And soberly did mount an arm-gaunt [8] steed,
Who neighed so high, that what I would have spoke
Was beastly dumbed [9] by him.
CLEO.   What was he, sad or merry?
ALEX. Like to the time o'the year between the extremes
Of hot and cold, he was nor sad nor merry.
CLEO. O well divided disposition! Note him,
Note him, good Charmian, 'tis the man; but note him.
He was not sad, for he would shine on those
That make their looks by his; he was not merry,
Which seemed to tell them his remembrance lay
In Egypt with his joy; but between both.
O heavenly mingle! Be'st thou sad or merry,
The violence of either thee becomes,
So does it no man else. Met'st thou my posts? [10]
ALEX. Ay, madam, twenty several messengers.
Why do you send so thick?
CLEO.   Who's born that day
When I forget to send to Antony,
Shall die a beggar. Ink and paper, Charmian.
Welcome, my good Alexas. Did I, Charmian,
Ever love Caesar so?
CHAR.   O that brave Caesar!
CLEO. Be choked [11] with such another emphasis!
Say, the brave Antony.
CHAR.   The valiant Caesar!
CLEO. By Isis,[12] I will give thee bloody teeth,
If thou with Caesar paragon [13] again
My man of men.

[7] *med'cine* Alexas' mere association with Antony has, as in alchemy, improved Alexas' bearing
[8] *arm-gaunt* not precisely understood, possibly even a defect in the MS; yet, toughened and lean from battle duty is very plausible
[9] *dumbed* silenced
[10] *posts* messengers
[11] *choked* i.e., be damned for such an insolent taunt
[12] *Isis* Egyptian mythological deity—hence she swears an oath
[13] *paragon* compare

CHAR.   By your most gracious pardon,
I sing but after you.
CLEO.   My salad days,[14]
When I was green in judgment, cold in blood,
To say as I said then. But come, away,
Get me ink and paper.
He shall have every day a several greeting,
Or I'll unpeople Egypt. (*Exeunt.*)

ACT II

SCENE 1. *Messina.* POMPEY's *house.*

Enter POMPEY, MENECRATES, *and* MENAS, *in warlike manner.*[1]

POM. If the great gods be just, they shall assist
The deeds of justest men.
MENE.   Know, worthy Pompey,
That what they do delay, they not deny.
POM. Whiles we are suitors to their throne, decays
The thing we sue for.
MENE.   We, ignorant of ourselves,
Beg often our own harms, which the wise powers
Deny us for our good; so find we profit
By losing of our prayers.
POM.   I shall do well:
The people love me, and the sea is mine;
My powers are crescent, and my auguring hope
Says it will come to the full. Mark Antony
In Egypt sits at dinner, and will make
No wars without doors. Caesar gets money where
He loses hearts: Lepidus flatters both,
Of both is flattered; but he neither loves,
Nor either cares for him.
MEN.   Caesar and Lepidus
Are in the field; a mighty strength they carry.
POM. Where have you this? 'Tis false.
MEN.   From Silvius, sir.
POM. He dreams: I know they are in Rome together,
Looking for Antony. But all the charms of love,
Salt [2] Cleopatra, soften thy waned [3] lip!
Let witchcraft join with beauty, lust with both!
Tie up the libertine in a field of feasts,
Keep his brain fuming; Epicurean cooks
Sharpen with cloyless [4] sauce his appetite,
That sleep and feeding may prorogue [5] his honor
Even till a Lethed dulness—[6]

Enter VARRIUS.

14 *salad days* green, inexperienced youthful age
1 there is confusion between "Menecrates" and "Menas" as speakers here.
2 *Salt* lustful
3 *waned* faded
4 *cloyless* insatiate
5 *prorogue* suspend (i.e., sense of honor)
6 *Lethed dulness* oblivion such as effected by imbibing from Lethe, the river in the mythological underworld

How now, Varrius!

VAR. This is most certain that I shall deliver:
Mark Antony is every hour in Rome
Expected. Since he went from Egypt 'tis
A space for farther travel.[7]

POM.   I could have given less matter
A better ear. Menas, I did not think
This amorous surfeiter would have donned his helm
For such a petty war: his soldiership
Is twice the other twain: but let us rear
The higher our opinion, that our stirring
Can from the lap of Egypt's widow [8] pluck
The ne'er-lust-wearied Antony.

MEN.   I cannot hope
Caesar and Antony shall well greet together;
His wife that's dead did trespasses to Caesar;
His brother warred upon him, although I think
Not moved by Antony.

POM.   I know not, Menas,
How lesser enmities may give way to greater.
Were't not that we stand up against them all,
'Twere pregnant [9] they should square between themselves,
For they have entertained cause enough
To draw their swords: but how the fear of us
May cement their divisions and bind up
The petty difference, we yet not know.
Be't as our gods will hav't! It only stands
Our lives upon [10] to use our strongest hands.
Come, Menas. (*Exeunt.*)

SCENE 2. *Rome. The house of* LEPIDUS.

Enter ENOBARBUS *and* LEPIDUS.

LEP. Good Enobarbus, 'tis a worthy deed,
And shall become you well, to entreat your captain
To soft and gentle speech.

ENO.   I shall entreat him
To answer like himself: if Caesar move him,
Let Antony look over Caesear's head,
And speak as loud as Mars. By Jupiter,
Were I the wearer of Antonio's beard,
I would not shave't to-day.[1]

LEP.   'Tis not a time
For private stomaching.[2]

ENO.   Every time
Serves for the matter that is then born in't.

LEP. But small to greater matters must give way.

---

[7] *space . . . travel* enough time had elapsed for a still longer journey
[8] *Egypt's widow* i.e., Cleopatra, as she was King Ptolemy's widow
[9] *pregnant* very likely
[10] *stands/ Our lives* matter of life and death
[1] *would not shave* i.e., leave the beard to grow, daring Caesar to pluck it
[2] *stomaching* resentment

ENO. Not if the small come first.

LEP.   Your speech is passion:
But, pray you, stir no embers up. Here comes
The noble Antony.

Enter ANTONY *and* VENTIDIUS.

ENO.   And yonder, Caesar.

Enter CAESAR, MAECENAS, *and* AGRIPPA.

ANT. If we compose [3] well here, to Parthia:
Hark, Ventidius.

CAES.   I do not know,
Maecenas; ask Agrippa.

LEP.   Noble friends,
That which combined us was most great, and let not
A leaner action rend us. What's amiss,
May it be gently heard. When we debate
Our trivial difference loud, we do commit
Murder in healing wounds. Then, noble partners,
The rather for I earnestly beseech,
Touch you the sourest points with sweetest terms,
Nor curstness [4] grow to the matter.

ANT.   'Tis spoken well.
Were we before our armies, and to fight,
I should do thus. [5] (*Flourish.*)

CAES. Welcome to Rome.

ANT.   Thank you.

CAES.   Sit.

ANT.   Sit, sir.

CAES.   Nay, then.

ANT. I learn you take things ill which are not so;
Or being, concern you not.

CAES.   I must be laughed at,
If, or for nothing or a little, I
Should say myself offended, and with you
Chiefly i'the world; more laughed at that I should
Once name you derogately, [6] when to sound your name
It not concerned me.

ANT.   My being in Egypt, Caesar,
What was't to you?

CAES. No more than my residing here at Rome
Might be to you in Egypt: yet, if you there
Did practice on [7] my state, your being in Egypt
Might be my question. [8]

ANT.   How intend you, practiced?

CAES. You may be pleased to catch at mine intent
By what did here befall me. Your wife and brother
Made wars upon me, and their contestation
Was theme for you; [9] you were the word of war.

---

3 *compose*   reach an agreement
4 *curstness*   ill temper
5 *I . . . thus*   Antony's words probably indi-
cate an embrace or other gesture of courtesy
6 *derogately*   insultingly

7 *practice on*   plot against
8 *question*   concern
9 *Was theme for you*   though not all scholars
concur here, it seems Shakespeare meant that
the fighting was carried on in Antony's behalf

ANT. You do mistake your business; my brother never
  Did urge me in his act. I did inquire it,
  And have my learning from some true reports [10]
  That drew their swords with you. Did he not rather
  Discredit my authority with yours,
  And make the wars alike against my stomach,[11]
  Having alike your cause? [12] Of this my letters
  Before did satisfy you. If you'll patch a quarrel,[13]
  As matter whole you have to make it with,
  It must not be with this.[14]

CAES.   You praise yourself
  By laying defects of judgment to me, but
  You patched up your excuses.

ANT.   Not so, not so;
  I know you could not lack, I am certain on't,
  Very necessity of this thought, that I,
  Your partner in the cause 'gainst which he fought,
  Could not with graceful eyes [15] attend those wars
  Which fronted mine own peace. As for my wife,
  I would you had her spirit in such another;
  The third o'the world is yours, which with a snaffle [16]
  You may pace easy, but not such a wife.

ENO. Would we had all such wives, that the men might go to wars with the
  women!

ANT. So much uncurbable, her garboils,[17] Caesar,
  Made out of her impatience (which not wanted
  Shrewdness of policy too), I grieving grant
  Did you too much disquiet: for that you must
  But say, I could not help it.

CAES.   I wrote to you.
  When rioting in Alexandria you
  Did pocket up my letters, and with taunts
  Did gibe my missive [18] out of audience.

ANT.   Sir,
  He fell upon me, ere admitted, then:
  Three kings I had newly feasted and did want
  Of what I was i' the morning; [19] but next day
  I told him of myself,[20] which was as much
  As to have asked him pardon. Let this fellow
  Be nothing of our strife; if we contend,
  Out of our question [21] wipe him.

CAES.   You have broken
  The article of your oath, which you shall never
  Have tongue to charge me with.

LEP.   Soft, Caesar.

ANT. No, Lepidus, let him speak.

---

10 *reports* informants
11 *stomach* desire
12 *Having . . . cause* i.e., to be displeased
  with him also
13 *patch a quarrel* pick a quarrel
14 *It must . . . this* i.e., an argument cannot
  be justified on the single complaint (piece) of
  Caesar, but rather on other grounds, if at all
15 *with graceful eyes* to regard approvingly

16 *snaffle* bridle bit
17 *garboils* agitations
18 *missive* messenger
19 *did want . . . morning* i.e., not in control
  of himself (as "sharp") as in the morning
20 *told . . . myself* i.e., explained my previous
  condition
21 *question* debate

The honor [22] is sacred which he talks on now,
Supposing that I lacked it. But on, Caesar,
The article of my oath—
CAES. To lend me arms and aid when I required them,
The which you both denied.
ANT.   Neglected rather;
And then when poisoned hours had bound me up
From mine own knowledge.[23] As nearly as I may,
I'll play the penitent to you. But mine honesty
Shall not make poor my greatness, nor my power
Work without it.[24] Truth is that Fulvia,
To have me out of Egypt, made wars here,
For which myself, the ignorant motive, do
So far ask pardon as befits mine honor
To stoop in such a case.
LEP.   'Tis noble spoken.
MAE. If it might please you, to enforce no further
The griefs between ye: to forget them quite
Were to remember that the present need
Speaks to atone [25] you.
LEP.   Worthily spoken, Maecenas.
ENO. Or, if you borrow one another's love for the instant, you may, when
you hear no more words of Pompey, return it again: you shall have time
to wrangle in when you have nothing else to do.
ANT. Thou art a soldier only; speak no more.
ENO. That truth should be silent I had almost forgot.
ANT. You wrong this presence; therefore speak no more.
ENO. Go to, then; your considerate stone.[26]
CAES. I do not much dislike the matter, but
The manner of his speech; for't cannot be
We shall remain in friendship, our conditions [27]
So differing in their acts. Yet, if I knew
What hoop should hold us staunch from edge to edge
O' the world, I would pursue it.
AGR.   Give me leave, Caesar.
CAES. Speak, Agrippa.
AGR. Thou hast a sister by the mother's side,
Admired Octavia: great Mark Antony
Is now a widower.
CAES.   Say not so, Agrippa:
If Cleopatra heard you, your reproof
Were well deserved of rashness.[28]
ANT.   I am not married, Caesar:
Let me hear Agrippa further speak.
AGR. To hold you in perpetual amity,
To make you brothers, and to knit your hearts
With an unslipping knot, take Antony

---

22 *honor* oath
23 *bound me . . . knowledge* kept me from being aware of what I was doing
24 *But mine honesty . . . it* i.e., but my actions, being prompted by honest intentions, in no way diminish my power

25 *atone* reconcile
26 *your considerate stone* i.e., I'll remain dumb as stone, though continuing to think
27 *conditions* temperaments
28 *rashness* i.e., rash of Agrippa to say what he does in light of Cleopatra's bond with Antony

Octavia to his wife; whose beauty claims
No worse a husband than the best of men;
Whose virtue and whose general graces speak
That which none else can utter. By this marriage
All little jealousies [29] which now seem great,
And all great fears which now import their dangers,
Would then be nothing: truths would be tales,
Where now half-tales be truths: her love to both
Would each to other and all loves to both
Draw after her. Pardon what I have spoke,
For 'tis a studied, not a present thought,
By duty ruminated.

ANT.   Will Caesar speak?

CAES. Not till he hears how Antony is touched
With what is spoke already.

ANT.   What power is in Agrippa,
If I would say, 'Agrippa, be it so,'
To make this good?

CAES.   The power of Caesar, and
His power unto Octavia.

ANT.   May I never
To this good purpose, that so fairly shows,
Dream of impediment! Let me have thy hand:
Further this act of grace; [30] and from this hour
The heart of brothers govern in our loves
And sway our great designs!

CAES.   There's my hand.
A sister I bequeath you, whom no brother
Did ever love so dearly. Let her live
To join our kingdoms and our hearts, and never
Fly off our loves again!

LEP.   Happily, amen!

ANT. I did not think to draw my sword 'gainst Pompey,
For he hath laid strange [31] courtesies and great
Of late upon me. I must thank him only,
Lest my remembrance [32] suffer ill report;
At heel of that, defy him.

LEP.   Time calls upon's.
Of us must Pompey presently [33] be sought,
Or else he seeks out us.

ANT.   Where lies he?

CAES. About the Mount Mesena. [34]

ANT. What is his strength by land?

CAES. Great and increasing: but by sea
He is an absolute master.

ANT.   So is the fame. [35]
Would we had spoke together! Haste we for it:
Yet, ere we put ourselves in arms, dispatch we
The business we have talked of.

[29] *jealousies*   suspicions, misunderstandings
[30] *grace*   reconciliation
[31] *strange*   unusual
[32] *remembrance*   courtesy in acknowledging favors
[33] *presently*   at once
[34] *Mesena*   Misenum, a port in southern Italy
[35] *fame*   rumored report

CAES.   With most gladness;
And do invite you to my sister's view,
Whither straight I'll lead you.
ANT.   Let us, Lepidus,
Not lack your company.
LEP.   Noble Antony,
Not sickness should detain me.

Flourish. Exit omnes [except] ENOBARBUS, AGRIPPA, MAECENAS.

MAE. Welcome from Egypt, sir.

ENO. Half [36] the heart of Caesar, worthy Maecenas! My honorable friend, Agrippa!

AGR. Good Enobarbus!

MAE. We have cause to be glad that matters are so well digested. You stayed well by't in Egypt.

ENO. Ay, sir, we did sleep day out of countenance, and made the night light with drinking.[37]

MAE. Eight wild-boars roasted whole at a breakfast, and but twelve persons there; is this true? [38]

ENO. This was but as a fly by [39] an eagle: we had much more monstrous matter of feast, which worthily deserved noting.

MAE. She's a most triumphant lady, if report be square [40] to her.

ENO. When she first met Mark Antony, she pursed [41] up his heart, upon the river of Cydnus.

AGR. There she appeared indeed; or my reporter devised well for her.

ENO. I will tell you.[42]
The barge she sat in, like a burnished throne
Burned on the water: the poop was beaten gold;
Purple the sails, and so perfumèd that
The winds were love-sick with them; the oars were silver,
Which to the tune of flutes kept stroke, and made
The water which they beat to follow faster,
As amorous of their strokes. For her own person,
It beggared all description: she did lie
In her pavilion, cloth-of-gold, of tissue,[43]
O'er-picturing that Venus where we see
The fancy outwork nature.[44] On each side her
Stood pretty dimpled boys, like smiling Cupids,
With divers-colored fans, whose wind did seem
To glow the delicate cheeks which they did cool,
And what they undid did.[45]

AGR.   O, rare for Antony!

ENO. Her gentlewomen, like the Nereides,[46]
So many mermaids, tended her i'the eyes,

---

36 *Half* Agrippa is the other half
37 *sleep day . . . drinking* i.e., reversed day and night by reveling all night long
38 *eight wild-boars, etc.* these are specific details passed on to Plutarch by his grandfather
39 *by* compared to
40 *square* just
41 *pursed* pocketed, but also with the association of puckering as for a kiss
42 Shakespeare here very closely approximates

North's language as taken from Plutarch
43 *cloth-of-gold, of tissue* a rich fabric interwoven with gold threads
44 *O'er-picturing . . . nature* surpassing that painting of Venus where we can see the imagination excelling nature itself in creative ability
45 *And . . . did* i.e., and seemed to produce the warm color they were cooling
46 *Nereides* sea nymphs

And made their bends adornings.⁴⁷ At the helm
A seeming mermaid steers: the silken tackle
Swell with the touches of those flower-soft hands,
That yarely frame the office.⁴⁸ From the barge
A strange invisible perfume hits the sense
Of the adjacent wharfs.⁴⁹ The city cast
Her people out upon her; and Antony,
Enthroned i'the market-place, did sit alone,
Whistling to the air; which, but for vacancy,⁵⁰
Had gone to gaze on Cleopatra too,
And made a gap in nature.

AGR.   Rare Egyptian!
ENO. Upon her landing, Antony sent to her,
Invited her to supper: she replied,
It should be better he became her guest,
Which she entreated. Our courteous Antony,
Whom ne'er the word of 'No' woman heard speak,
Being barbered ten times o'er, goes to the feast,
And for his ordinary ⁵¹ pays his heart
For what his eyes eat only.

AGR.   Royal wench!
She made great Caesar lay his sword to bed;
He ploughed her, and she cropped.⁵²
ENO.   I saw her once
Hop forty paces through the public street;
And having lost her breath, she spoke, and panted,
That she did make defect ⁵³ perfection,
And, breathless, power breathe forth.

MAE.   Now Antony
Must leave her utterly.
ENO.   Never; he will not:
Age cannot wither her, nor custom stale
Her infinite variety: other women cloy
The appetites they feed, but she makes hungry
Where most she satisfies. For vilest things
Become themselves in her, that the holy priests
Bless her when she is riggish.⁵⁴

MAE. If beauty, wisdom, modesty, can settle
The heart of Antony, Octavia is
A blessèd lottery ⁵⁵ to him.

AGR.   Let us go.
Good Enobarbus, make yourself my guest
Whilst you abide here.

ENO.   Humbly, sir, I thank you. (*Exeunt.*)

⁴⁷ *tended . . . adornings* stood before her and
waited on her, their bowing movements being
works of art in themselves
⁴⁸ *yarely frame the office* deftly perform the
task
⁴⁹ *wharfs* banks
⁵⁰ *but for vacancy* except that a vacuum would

result
⁵¹ *ordinary* meal
⁵² *she cropped* i.e., Cleopatra bore Caesar fruit,
represented by their son Caesarion
⁵³ *defect* i.e., her breathlessness
⁵⁴ *riggish* promiscuous
⁵⁵ *lottery* prize, allotment

Scene 3

Enter ANTONY, CAESAR, *and* OCTAVIA *between them.*

ANT. The world and my great office will sometimes
　　Divide me from your bosom.
OCT. 　　　　　　　　　　　All which time
　　Before the gods my knee shall bow in prayers
　　To them for you.
ANT. 　　　　　　　　Good night, sir. My Octavia,
　　Read not my blemishes in the world's report:
　　I have not kept my square,[1] but that to come
　　Shall all be done by the rule. Good night, dear lady.
OCT. Good night, sir.
CAES. Good night. [*Exeunt* CAESAR *and* OCTAVIA.]

Enter SOOTHSAYER.

ANT. Now, sirrah,[2] you do wish yourself in Egypt?
SOOTH. Would I had never come from thence, nor you thither!
ANT. If you can, your reason?
SOOTH. I see it in my motion, have it not in my tongue:
　　But yet hie you to Egypt again.
ANT. Say to me, whose fortunes shall rise higher, Caesar's or mine?
SOOTH. Caesar's.
　　Therefore, O Antony, stay not by his side.
　　Thy demon,[3] that thy spirit which keeps thee, is
　　Noble, courageous, high, unmatchable,
　　Where Caesar's is not. But near him thy angel
　　Becomes a fear, as being o'erpowered. Therefore
　　Make space enough between you.
ANT. 　　　　　　　　　　Speak this no more.
SOOTH. To none but thee; no more but when to thee.
　　If thou dost play with him at any game,
　　Thou are sure to lose; and of that natural luck,
　　He beats thee 'gainst the odds. Thy lustre thickens,[4]
　　When he shines by: I say again, thy spirit
　　Is all afraid to govern thee near him;
　　But he away, 'tis noble.
ANT. 　　　　　　　　Get thee gone:
　　Say to Ventidius I would speak with him. (*Exit* SOOTHSAYER.)
　　He shall to Parthia. Be it art or hap,[5]
　　He hath spoken true. The very dice obey him,
　　And in our sports my better cunning[6] faints
　　Under his chance: if we draw lots, he speeds;[7]
　　His cocks[8] do win the battle still of mine
　　When it is all to nought, and his quails ever

---

1 *square* i.e., remained prudent
2 *sirrah* the familiar form of "sir" which at times was spoken with contempt, while on other occasions with affection
3 *demon* here, as in Plutarch (Shakespeare's source), guardian spirit
4 *thickens* dims

5 *Be it art or hap* i.e., whether it is by magic or by coincidence
6 *better cunning* greater skill
7 *speeds* succeeds
8 *cocks* i.e., in the rooster fights, Caesar's birds always win, no matter what the odds against them

Beat mine, inhooped, at odds. I will to Egypt:
And though I make this marriage for my peace,
I'the East my pleasure lies.

Enter VENTIDIUS.

                    O, come, Ventidius,
You must to Parthia. Your commission's ready;
Follow me, and receive't. (*Exeunt.*)

SCENE 4

Enter LEPIDUS, MAECENAS, *and* AGRIPPA.

LEP. Trouble yourselves no further: pray you, hasten
    Your generals after.
AGR.   Sir, Mark Antony
    Will e'en but kiss Octavia, and we'll follow.
LEP. Till I shall see you in your soldier's dress,
    Which will become you both, farewell.
MAE.   We shall,
    As I conceive the journey, be at the Mount [1]
    Before you, Lepidus.
LEP.   Your way is shorter;
    My purposes do draw me much about: [2]
    You'll win two days upon me.
BOTH.   Sir, good success!
LEP. Farewell. (*Exeunt.*)

SCENE 5. *Alexandria.* CLEOPATRA's *palace.*

Enter CLEOPATRA, CHARMIAN, IRAS, *and* ALEXAS.

CLEO. Give me some music: music, moody [1] food
    Of us that trade in love.
ALL.   The music, ho!

Enter MARDIAN THE EUNUCH.

CLEO. Let it alone, let's to billiards: [2] come, Charmian.
CHAR. My arm is sore; best play with Mardian.
CLEO. As well a woman with an eunuch played
    As with a woman. Come, you'll play with me, sir?
MAR. As well as I can, madam.
CLEO. And when good will is showed, though't come too short,
    The actor may plead pardon. I'll none now,
    Give me mine angle,[3] we'll to the river: there,
        My music playing far off, I will betray [4]
    Tawny-finned fishes; my bended hook shall pierce

---

[1] *Mount* i.e., Mount Misemum
[2] *about* roundabout
[1] *moody* melancholy
[2] *billiards* although there was no historical evidence regarding this game as played in

ancient Egypt, a contemporary play, Chapman's *The Blind Beggar of Alexandria*, offered Shakespeare a literary precedent
[3] *angle* fishing tackle
[4] *betray* snare

Their slimy jaws; and as I draw them up,
I'll think them every one an Antony,
And say 'Ah, ha! you're caught.'
CHAR.   'Twas merry when
You wagered on your angling; when your diver
Did hang a salt-fish [5] on his hook, which he
With fervency drew up.
CLEO.   That time—O times!—
I laughed him out of patience; and that night
I laughed him into patience; and next morn,
Ere the ninth hour, I drunk him to his bed;
Then put my tires [6] and mantles on him, whilst
I wore his sword Philippan.[7]

Enter a MESSENGER.

                              O, from Italy!
Ram thou thy fruitful tidings in mine ears,
That long time have been barren.
MESS.   Madam, madam,—
CLEO. Antonio's dead! If thou say so, villain,
Thou kill'st thy mistress: but well and free,
If thou so yield him, there is gold, and here
My bluest veins to kiss, a hand that kings
Have lipped, and trembled kissing.
MESS. First, madam, he is well.[8]
CLEO.   Why, there's more gold.
But, sirrah, mark, we use
To say the dead are well: bring it to that,[9]
The gold I give thee will I melt and pour
Down thy ill-uttering throat.
MESS. Good madam, hear me.
CLEO.   Well, go to, I will;
But there's no goodness in thy face if Antony
Be free and healthful—so tart a favor [10]
To trumpet such good tidings! If not well,
Thou shouldst come like a Fury crowned with snakes,
Not like a formal [11] man.
MESS.   Will't please you hear me?
CLEO. I have a mind to strike thee ere thou speak'st:
Yet if thou say Antony lives, is well,
Or friends with Caesar, or not captive to him,
I'll set thee in a shower of gold, and hail
Rich pearls upon thee.
MESS.   Madam, he's well.
CLEO.   Well said.
MESS. And friends with Caesar.
CLEO.   Thou'rt an honest man.

---

[5] *salt-fish* dried up fish
[6] *tires* headdresses
[7] *Philippan* Antony had beaten Cassius and Brutus at Philippi with his sword, hence the name for the weapon
[8] *he is well* many editors interpret "well" here to be Cleopatra's misunderstanding that An-tony is in heaven; consider the subsequent lines, also
[9] *bring it to that* i.e., should that be your meaning
[10] *so tart a favor* such a sour face
[11] *formal* usual-shaped

MESS. Caesar and he are greater friends than ever.
CLEO. Make thee a fortune from me.
MESS.   But yet, madam,—
CLEO. I do not like 'But yet,' it does allay
    The good precedence; [12] fie upon 'But yet'!
    'But yet' is as a gaoler [13] to bring forth
    Some monstrous malefactor. Prithee, [14] friend,
    Pour out the pack of matter to mine ear,
    The good and bad together: he's friends with Caesar,
    In state of health, thou say'st, and thou say'st, free.
MESS. Free, madam! no; I made no such report:
    He's bound unto Octavia.
CLEO.   For what good turn?
MESS. For the best turn i'the bed.
CLEO.   I am pale, Charmian.
MESS. Madam, he's married to Octavia.
CLEO. The most infectious pestilence upon thee! (*Strikes him down.*)
MESS. Good madam, patience.
CLEO.   What say you? (*Strikes him.*)
                                        Hence,
    Horrible villain! or I'll spurn [15] thine eyes
    Like balls before me; I'll unhair thy head, (*She hales [16] him up and down.*)
    Thou shalt be whipped with wire, and stewed in brine,
    Smarting in ling'ring pickle.
MESS.   Gracious madam,
    I that do bring the news made not the match.
CLEO. Say 'tis not so, a province I will give thee,
    And make thy fortunes proud: the blow thou hadst
    Shall make thy peace for moving me to rage,
    And I will boot [17] thee with what gift beside
    Thy modesty can beg.
MESS.   He's married, madam.
CLEO. Rogue, thou hast lived too long. (*Draw a knife.*)
MESS.   Nay, then I'll run.
    What mean you, madam? I have made no fault. (*Exit.*)
CHAR. Good madam, keep yourself within yourself.
    The man is innocent.
CLEO. Some innocents 'scape not the thunderbolt.
    Melt Egypt into Nile! and kindly creatures
    Turn all to serpents! Call the slave again:
    Though I am mad, I will not bite him. Call!
CHAR. He is afeard to come.
CLEO.   I will not hurt him.
    These hands do lack nobility, that they strike
    A meaner than myself; since I myself
    Have given myself the cause.

Enter the MESSENGER *again*.[18]

12 *allay/ The good precedence* qualifies the earlier good report
13 *gaoler* jailer
14 *Prithee* casual, contracted form of "pray thee" frequently found in Elizabethan verse
15 *spurn* kick
16 *hales* drags
17 *boot* enrich, benefit
18 Dyce, with some later editors, inserted "*Charmian exit*" instructions. Such is not the case in the reliable Folio, however, nor is her exit needed for the sense of the scene. Charmian simply goes toward the door

Come hither, sir.
Though it be honest, it is never good
To bring bad news: give to a gracious message
An host of tongues, but let ill tidings tell
Themselves when they be felt.
MESS.   I have done my duty.
CLEO. Is he married?
I cannot hate thee worser than I do,
If thou again say 'Yes.'
MESS.   He's married, madam.
CLEO. The gods confound [19] thee! dost thou hold there still?
MESS. Should I lie, madam?
CLEO.   O, I would thou didst,
So half my Egypt were submerged and made
A cistern for scaled snakes! Go, get thee hence;
Hadst thou Narcissus in thy face,[20] to me
Thou wouldst appear most ugly. He is married?
MESS. I crave your highness' pardon.
CLEO.   He is married?
MESS. Take no offense that I would not offend you:
To punish me for what you make me do
Seems much unequal: [21] he's married to Octavia.
CLEO. O, that his fault should make a knave of thee,
That art not what thou'rt sure of! [22] Get thee hence:
The merchandise which thou hast brought from Rome
Are all too dear for me; lie they upon thy hand,
And be undone by 'em! [23] [*Exit* MESSENGER.]
CHAR.   Good your highness, patience.
CLEO. In praising Antony, I have dispraised Caesar.
CHAR. Many times, madam.
CLEO.   I am paid for't now.
Lead me from hence;
I faint, O Iras, Charmian! 'tis no matter.
Go to the fellow, good Alexas; bid him
Report the feature of Octavia: her years,
Her inclination,[24] let him not leave out
The color of her hair. Bring me word quickly. [*Exit* ALEXAS.]
Let him for ever go! let him not—Charmian—
Though he be painted one way like a Gorgon,[25]
The other way's a Mars.[26] [*To* MARDIAN.] Bid you Alexas
Bring me word how tall she is. Pity me, Charmian,
But do not speak to me. Lead me to my chamber. (*Exeunt.*)

SCENE 6. *Near Misenum.*

Flourish. Enter POMPEY *at one door with drum and trumpet: at another,*
CAESAR, LEPIDUS, ANTONY, ENOBARBUS, MAECENAS, AGRIPPA, MENAS *with*
soldiers marching.

19 *confound* destroy
20 *Hadst thou Narcissus* i.e., if you had the handsomeness of Narcissus, the youth in Greek legend who fell in love with his own image in a stream
21 *unequal* unjust
22 *That art not* i.e., your news is hateful, though you are not so
23 *lie they upon, etc.* i.e., may your goods remain unsold and you be ruined
24 *inclination* temperament
25 *Gorgon* Medusa, a glimpse of whose horrible face turned men to stone
26 *Mars* god of war

POM. Your hostages I have, so have you mine;
  And we shall talk before we fight.
CAES.   Most meet [1]
  That first we come to words; and therefore have we
  Our written purposes before us sent;
  Which, if thou hast considered, let us know
  If 'twill tie up thy discontented sword,
  And carry back to Sicily much tall [2] youth
  That else must perish here.
POM.   To you all three,
  The senators alone of this great world,
  Chief factors [3] for the gods: I do not know
  Wherefore my father should revengers want, [4]
  Having a son and friends, since Julius Caesar,
  Who at Philippi the good Brutus ghosted, [5]
  There saw you laboring for him. What was't
  That moved pale Cassius to conspire? And what
  Made the all-honored, honest Roman, Brutus,
  With the armed rest, courtiers of beauteous freedom,
  To drench [6] the Capitol, but that they would
  Have one man but a man? And that is it
  Hath made me rig my navy, at whose burthen [7]
  The angered ocean foams, with which I meant
  To scourge the ingratitude that despiteful Rome
  Cast on my noble father.
CAES.   Take your time.
ANT. Thou canst not fear [8] us, Pompey, with thy sails;
  We'll speak [9] with thee at sea. At land, thou know'st
  How much we do o'ercount [10] thee.
POM.   At land, indeed,
  Thou dost o'ercount me of my father's house: [11]
  But since the cuckoo builds not for himself, [12]
  Remain in't as thou mayst.
LEP.   Be pleased to tell us—
  For this is from the present [13]—how you take
  The offers we have sent you.
CAES.   There's the point.
ANT. Which do not be entreated to, but weigh
  What it is worth embraced. [14]
CAES.   And what may follow,
  To try a larger fortune.
POM.   You have made me offer
  Of Sicily, Sardinia; and I must
  Rid all the sea of pirates; then, to send

1 *meet* appropriate
2 *tall* bold, brave
3 *factors* agents
4 *Wherefore, etc.* i.e., why my father should
   lack revengers
5 *ghosted* came as a ghost to
6 *drench* i.e., with Caesar's blood
7 *burthen* burden
8 *fear* frighten
9 *speak* do battle, compete
10 *o'ercount* outnumber

11 *o'ercount me . . . house* cheat me of my
   father's house. Plutarch relates that Antony
   purchased Pompey's dwelling at an auction
   but later refused to pay
12 *cuckoo* this bird never built her own nest
   for laying eggs but instead used other birds'
   nests
13 *this . . . present* not part of the topic being
   considered
14 *embraced* if accepted

Measures of wheat to Rome; this 'greed upon,
To part with unhacked edges and bear back
Our targes undinted.[15]
OMNES.[16]	That's our offer.
POM.	Know then
I came before you here a man prepared
To take this offer; but Mark Antony
Put me to some impatience. Though I lose
The praise of it by telling, you must know,
When Caesar and your brother were at blows,
Your mother came to Sicily and did find
Her welcome friendly.
ANT.	I have heard it, Pompey,
And am well studied [17] for a liberal thanks
Which I do owe you.
POM.	Let me have your hand:
I did not think, sir, to have met you here.
ANT. The beds i'the east are soft; and thanks to you,
That called me timelier [18] than my purpose hither;
For I have gained by't.
CAES.	Since I saw you last,
There's a change upon you.
POM.	Well, I know not
What counts [19] harsh Fortune casts upon my face,
But in my bosom shall she never come
To make my heart her vassal.
LEP.	Well met here.
POM. I hope so, Lepidus. Thus we are agreed:
I crave our composition [20] may be written
And sealed between us.
CAES.	That's the next to do.
POM. We'll feast each other ere we part, and let's
Draw lots who shall begin.
ANT.	That will I, Pompey.
POM. No, Antony, take the lot:
But, first or last, your fine Egyptian cookery
Shall have the fame. I have heard that Julius Caesar
Grew fat with feasting there.
ANT.	You have heard much.
POM. I have fair meanings, sir. .
ANT.	And fair words to them.
POM. Then so much have I heard;
And I have heard Apollodorus carried—
ENO. No more of that: he did so.
POM.	What, I pray you?
ENO. A certain queen to Caesar in a mattress.[21]
POM. I know thee now; how far'st thou, soldier?

---

15 *To part . . . undinted* i.e., to settle the dispute without resorting to swords and shields
16 *Omnes* all, i.e., Antony, Lepidus, Caesar
17 *well studied* prepared with
18 *timelier* prior
19 *counts* reckonings
20 *composition* agreement

21 *Apollodorus carried, etc.* Pompey here alludes to Plutarch (via North's translation) who relates Cleopatra's ingenious manner of getting into Caesar's court by having herself wrapped in a mattress or rug and being carried into Caesar's presence (*Life of Caesar*)

ENO.   Well;
    And well am like to do, for I perceive
    Four feasts are toward.[22]
POM.   Let me shake thy hand.
    I never hated thee: I have seen thee fight,
    When I have envied thy behavior.
ENO.   Sir,
    I never loved you much, but I ha'praised ye
    When you have well deserved ten times as much
    As I have said you did.
POM.   Enjoy thy plainness,
    It nothing ill becomes thee.
    Aboard my galley I invite you all:
    Will you lead, lords?
ALL.   Show's the way, sir.
POM.   Come.

Exeunt [all but] ENOBARBUS *and* MENAS.

MEN. (*Aside.*) Thy father, Pompey, would ne'er have made this treaty. You
    and I have known,[23] sir.
ENO. At sea, I think.
MEN. We have, sir.
ENO. You have done well by water.
MEN. And you by land.
ENO. I will praise any man that will praise me; though it cannot be denied
    what I have done by land.
MEN. Nor what I have done by water.
ENO. Yes, something you can deny for your own safety: you have been a
    great thief by sea.
MEN. And you by land.
ENO. There I deny my land service. But give me your hand, Menas: if our
    eyes had authority, here they might take two thieves kissing.[24]
MEN. All men's faces are true, whatsome'er their hands are.
ENO. But there is never a fair woman has a true [25] face.
MEN. No slander, they steal hearts.
ENO. We came hither to fight with you.
MEN. For my part, I am sorry it is turned to a drinking. Pompey doth this
    day laugh away his fortune.
ENO. If he do, sure he cannot weep't back again.
MEN. You've said,[26] sir. We looked not for Mark Antony here: pray you,
    is he married to Cleopatra?
ENO. Caesar's sister is called Octavia.
MEN. True, sir; she was the wife of Caius Marcellus.
ENO. But she is now the wife of Marcus Antonius.
MEN. Pray ye, sir? [27]
ENO. 'Tis true.
MEN. Then is Caesar and he for ever knit together.
ENO. If I were bound to divine of this unity, I would not prophesy so.
MEN. I think the policy of that purpose made more [28] in the marriage than
    the love of the parties.

---

[22] *toward*   pending
[23] *known*   met
[24] *two thieves kissing*   i.e., fraternizing, by way
   of clasping hands

[25] *true*   honest
[26] *You've said*   i.e., you are exactly right
[27] *Pray ye*   i.e., what's that again?
[28] *made more*   had more to do with

ENO. I think so too. But you shall find the band that seems to tie their friendship together will be the very strangler of their amity: Octavia is of a holy, cold, and still conversation.[29]

MEN. Who would not have his wife so?

ENO. Not he that himself is not so; which is Mark Antony. He will to his Egyptian dish again: then shall the sighs of Octavia blow the fire up in Caesar, and, as I said before, that which is the strength of their amity shall prove the immediate author of their variance. Antony will use his affection where it is.[30] He married but his occasion [31] here.

MEN. And thus it may be. Come, sir, will you aboard? I have a health for you.

ENO. I shall take it, sir: we have used our throats in Egypt.

MEN. Come, let's away. (*Exeunt.*)

SCENE 7

Music plays. Enter two or three SERVANTS *with a banquet.*

1 SERV. Here they'll be, man. Some o'their plants [1] are ill-rooted already; the least wind i'the world will blow them down.

2 SERV. Lepidus is high-colored.

1 SERV. They have made him drink alms-drink.[2]

2 SERV. As they pinch one another by the disposition, he cries out 'No more'; reconciles them to his entreaty and himself to the drink.

1 SERV. But it raises the greater war between him and his discretion.

2 SERV. Why, this it is to have a name in great men's fellowship. I had as lief have a reed that will do me no service as a partisan [3] I could not heave.

1 SERV. To be called into a huge sphere, and not to be seen to move in't, are the holes where eyes should be, which pitifully disaster the cheeks.[4]

A sennet [5] sounded. Enter CAESAR, ANTONY, POMPEY, LEPIDUS, AGRIPPA, MAECENAS, ENOBARBUS, MENAS, *with other captains.*

ANT. Thus do they, sir: they take the flow o'the Nile
By certain scales [6] i'the pyramid; they know,
By the height, the lowness, or the mean, if dearth
Or foison [7] follow. The higher Nilus swells,
The more it promises: as it ebbs, the seedsman
Upon the slime and ooze scatters his grain,
And't shortly comes to harvest.

LEP. You've strange serpents there?

ANT. Ay, Lepidus.

---

29 *conversation* behavior, way of living one's life

30 *affection where it is* i.e., in Egypt with Cleopatra

31 *occasion* convenience

1 *plants* all editors remind readers of the obvious pun on "plants" as both vegetation (i.e., young trees) and feet

2 *alms-drink* Lepidus has been tricked into taking several return toasts (called "alms-drinks") for others too drunk to follow the amenities in such drinking

3 *partisan* spear

4 *To be called, etc.* Lepidus is scornfully alluded to as a small man unable to keep up with his noble associates—a fact here described by the servant as a heavenly body not capable of operating properly within its sphere and then as a face without eyes

5 *sennet* special series of trumpet notes (whose sequence is no longer known) sounded to announce the approach of dignitaries

6 *scales* marked gradations

7 *foison* abundance

LEP. Your serpent of Egypt is bred now of your mud by the operation of
    your sun: so is your crocodile.[8]

ANT. They are so.

POM. Sit—and some wine! A health to Lepidus!

LEP. I am not so well as I should be, but I'll ne'er out.[9]

ENO. Not till you have slept; I fear me you'll be in till then.

LEP. Nay, certainly, I have heard the Ptolemies' pyramises[10] are very
    goodly things; without contradiction, I have heard that.

MEN. Pompey, a word.

POM.   Say in mine ear, what is't?

MEN. Forsake thy seat, I do beseech thee, captain,
    And hear me speak a word. (*Whispers in's ear.*)

POM.   Forbear me till anon.—
    This wine for Lepidus!

LEP. What manner o'thing is your crocodile?

ANT. It is shaped, sir, like itself, and it is as broad as it hath breadth: it is
    just so high as it is, and moves with it own[11] organs. It lives by that
    which nourisheth it, and the elements once out of it, it transmigrates.[12]

LEP. What color is it of?

ANT. Of it own color too.

LEP. 'Tis a strange serpent.

ANT. 'Tis so, and the tears of it are wet.

CAES. Will this description satisfy him?

ANT. With the health that Pompey gives him, else he is a very epicure.[13]

POM. Go hang, sir, hang! Tell me of that? away!
    Do as I bid you. Where's this cup I called for?

MEN. If for the sake of merit thou wilt hear me,
    Rise from thy stool.

POM.   I think thou'rt mad. The matter?

MEN. I have ever held my cap off to thy fortunes.[14]

POM. Thou hast served me with much faith. What's else to say?
    Be jolly, lords.

ANT.   These quick-sands, Lepidus,
    Keep off them, for you sink.

MEN. Wilt thou be lord of all the world?

POM.   What say'st thou?

MEN. Wilt thou be lord of the whole world? That's twice.

POM. How should that be?

MEN.   But entertain it,[15]
    And though thou think me poor, I am the man
    Will give thee all the world.

POM.   Hast thou drunk well?

MEN. No, Pompey, I have kept me from the cup.
    Thou art, if thou dar'st be, the earthly Jove:
    Whate'er the ocean pales, or sky inclips,[16]
    Is thine, if thou wilt ha't.

POM.   Show me which way.

---

[8] *bred . . . mud* allusion to theory in Shakespeare's age regarding abiogenesis, whereby living matter (here, the serpents) could be generated from matter lacking life (here, mud)

[9] *ne'er out* never give up, i.e., refuse a pledge

[10] *pyramises* Lepidus' drunken plural form for pyramid

[11] *it own* blurred possessive for "its own"

[12] *transmigrates* Antony is joshing the drunken

Lepidus by continuing his tale of Egyptian crocodiles and their habits, here even including spirit moving into different bodies

[13] *epicure* in this context, a veteran drunkard

[14] *held my cap off* i.e., have been your devoted follower

[15] *But entertain it* just accept the thought for a moment

[16] *pales* encloses; *inclips* embraces

MEN. These three world-sharers, these competitors,[17]
   Are in thy vessel. Let me cut the cable;
   And when we are put off, fall to their throats:
   All then is thine.
POM.   Ah, this thou shouldst have done,
   And not have spoke on't! In me 'tis villainy;
   In thee't had been good service. Thou must know,
   'Tis not my profit that does lead mine honor;
   Mine honor, it.[18] Repent that e'er thy tongue
   Hath so betrayed thine act. Being done unknown,
   I should have found it afterwards well done,
   But must condemn it now. Desist, and drink.
MEN. [*aside*] For this
   I'll never follow thy palled [19] fortunes more.
   Who seeks, and will not take when once 'tis offered,
   Shall never find it more.
POM.   This health to Lepidus!
ANT. Bear him ashore. I'll pledge it for him, Pompey.
ENO. Here's to thee, Menas!
MEN.   Enobarbus, welcome!
POM. Fill till the cup be hid.
ENO. There's a strong fellow, Menas.

[Points to the attendant who carries off LEPIDUS.]

MEN. Why?
ENO. A' [20] bears the third part of the world, man; see'st not?
MEN. The third part then is drunk: would it were all,
   That it might go on wheels! [21]
ENO. Drink thou; increase the reels.[22]
MEN. Come.
POM. This is not yet an Alexandrian feast.
ANT. It ripens towards it. Strike the vessels, ho! [23]
   Here's to Caesar!
CAES.   I could well forbear't.
   It's monstrous labor, when I wash my brain
   And it grows fouler.
ANT.   Be a child o'the time.
CAES. Possess it,[24] I'll make answer:
   But I had rather fast from all, four days,
   Than drink so much in one.
ENO.   Ha, my brave emperor!
   Shall we dance now the Egyptian Bacchanals,
   And celebrate our drink?
POM.   Let's ha't, good soldier.
ANT. Come, let's all take hands,
   Till that the conquering wine hath steeped our sense
   In soft and delicate Lethe.[25]

17 *competitors* confederates
18 *Mine honor, it* i.e., my honor precedes my profit
19 *palled* weakened, diminished
20 *A'* He
21 *go on wheels* glide along speedily
22 *reels* spins, revolutions
23 *Strike the vessels* generally believed to mean tap the casks, though another possibility is that "vessels" referred to a type of kettle-drum, which would mean the instructions are to call for a noisy accompaniment for the toast
24 *Possess it* drink it down
25 *Lethe* here, oblivion or forgetfulness

ENO.   All take hands.
Make battery to our ears with the loud music;
The while I'll place you; then the boy shall sing;
The holding [26] every man shall bear as loud
As his strong sides can volley.

Music plays. ENOBARBUS *places them hand in hand.*

The Song

Come, thou monarch of the vine,
Plumpy Bacchus with pink eyne! [27]
In thy fats [28] our cares be drowned,
With thy grapes our hairs be crowned.
Cup us, till the world go round,
Cup us, till the world go round!

CAES. What would you more? Pompey, good night. Good brother,
Let me request you off: [29] our graver business
Frowns at this levity. Gentle lords, let's part;
You see we have burnt our cheeks. Strong Enobarb
Is weaker than the wine, and mine own tongue
Splits what it speaks: the wild disguise [30] hath almost
Anticked [31] us all. What needs more words? Good night.
Good Antony, your hand.
POM.   I'll try you on the shore.[32]
ANT. And shall, sir; give's your hand.
POM.   O Antony,
You have my father's house—But what, we are friends!
Come down into the boat.
ENO.   Take heed you fall not.

[*Exeunt all but* ENOBARBUS *and* MENAS.]

Menas, I'll not on shore.
MEN.   No, to my cabin.
These drums! these trumpets, flutes! what!
Let Neptune hear we bid a loud farewell
To these great fellows: sound and be hanged, sound out!

Sound a flourish, with drums.

ENO. Hoo! says a' There's my cap.
MEN. Hoo! Noble captain, come. (*Exeunt.*)

ACT III

Scene 1. *A plain in Syria.*

Enter VENTIDIUS *as it were in triumph, the dead body of* PACORUS *borne
before him; with* SILIUS, *and other Romans, officers, and soldiers.*

---

26 *holding* refrain
27 *pink eyne* half-closed eyes
28 *fats* vats
29 *you off* ask you to come away

30 *disguise* masqueraded reveling
31 *Anticked* made fools of
32 *try you on the shore* i.e., test you in another
     drinking spree back on land

ven. Now, darting Parthia,[1] art thou struck, and now
    Pleased fortune does of Marcus Crassus' death [2]
    Make me revenger. Bear the king's son's body
    Before our army. Thy Pacorus, Orodes,
    Pays this for Marcus Crassus.
silius.   Noble Ventidius,
    Whilst yet with Parthian blood thy sword is warm,
    The fugitive Parthians follow. Spur through Media,
    Mesopotamia, and the shelters whither
    The routed fly: so thy grand captain Antony
    Shall set thee on triumphant chariots and
    Put garlands on thy head.
ven.   O Silius, Silius,
    I have done enough. A lower [3] place, note well,
    May make too great an act; for learn this, Silius,
    Better to leave undone, than by our deed
    Acquire too high a fame when him we serve's away.
    Caesar and Antony have ever won
    More in their officer than person: Sossius,
    One of my place in Syria, his lieutenant,
    For quick accumulation of renown,
    Which he achieved by the minute, lost his favor.
    Who does i'the wars more than his captain can
    Becomes his captain's captain: and ambition,
    The soldier's virtue, rather makes choice of loss
    Than gain which darkens him.[4]
    I could do more to do Antonius good,
    But 'twould offend him; and in his offense [5]
    Should my performance perish.
silius.   Thou hast, Ventidius, that [6]
    Without the which a soldier and his sword
    Grants scarce distinction. Thou wilt write to Antony?
ven. I'll humbly signify what in his name,
    That magical word of war, we have effected;
    How, with his banners and his well-paid ranks,
    The ne'er-yet-beaten horse of Parthia
    We have jaded [7] out o'the field.
silius.   Where is he now?
ven. He purposeth to Athens; whither, with what haste
    The weight we must convey with's will permit,
    We shall appear before him. On, there; pass along! (*Exeunt.*)

Scene 2

Enter agrippa *at one door,* enobarbus *at another.*

agr. What, are the brothers parted? [1]
eno. They have dispatched with Pompey; he is gone;

---

[1] *darting Parthia* the Parthian warriors were renowned for their archery excellence
[2] *Marcus Crassus' death* Crassus was part of the first triumvirate along with Julius Caesar and the elder Pompey; but he was slain by the Parthians. When Pacorus, son of the Parthian king Orodes, is in turn killed in battle, the Roman revenge has been consummated.

The details are all set forth in Plutarch
[3] *lower* subordinate
[4] *darkens him* obscures his superior
[5] *in his offense* i.e., in my offending him
[6] *that* i.e., prudence
[7] *jaded* driven in a wearied state
[1] *parted* departed

The other three are sealing.[2] Octavia weeps
To part from Rome; Caesar is sad, and Lepidus
Since Pompey's feast, as Menas says, is troubled
With the green-sickness.[3]

AGR.   'Tis a noble Lepidus.

ENO. A very fine one. O, how he loves Caesar!

AGR. Nay, but how dearly he adores Mark Antony!

ENO. Caesar? Why, he's the Jupiter of men.

AGR. What's Antony? The god of Jupiter.

ENO. Spake you of Caesar? How! the nonpareil!

AGR. O Antony! O thou Arabian bird![4]

ENO. Would you praise Caesar, say 'Caesar': go no further.

AGR. Indeed he plied them both with excellent praises.

ENO. But he loves Caesar best; yet he loves Antony.
    Hoo![5] hearts, tongues, figures, scribes, bards, poets, cannot
    Think, speak, cast,[6] write, sing, number—hoo!—
    His love to Antony. But as for Caesar,
    Kneel down, kneel down, and wonder.

AGR.   Both he loves.

ENO. They are his shards,[7] and he their beetle. So!

[*Trumpet within.*]

    This is to horse.[8] Adieu, noble Agrippa.

AGR. Good fortune, worthy soldier, and farewell.

Enter CAESAR, ANTONY, LEPIDUS, *and* OCTAVIA.

ANT. No further, sir.

CAES. You take from me a great part of myself;
    Use me well in't. Sister, prove such a wife
    As my thoughts make thee, and as my farthest band
    Shall pass on thy approof.[9] Most noble Antony,
    Let not the piece [10] of virtue which is set
    Betwixt us as the cement of our love
    To keep it builded, be the ram to batter
    The fortress of it; for better might we
    Have loved without this mean,[11] if on both parts
    This be not cherished.

ANT.   Make me not offended
    In your distrust.

CAES.   I have said.

ANT.   You shall not find,
    Though you be therein curious,[12] the least cause
    For what you seem to fear. So, the gods keep you,
    And make the hearts of Romans serve your ends!
    We will here part.

2 *sealing* authorizing agreements by signing then sealing them
3 *the green-sickness* the illness attributed to love-sick girls—here ironically directed toward Lepidus who, Enobarbus suggests, is love-sick with Antony and Caesar
4 *Arabian bird* the unique phoenix, only one of which exists at a time
5 *Hoo!* an ecstatic exclamation, used here and elsewhere by Enobarbus in mimicking the expressions of Lepidus
6 *cast* figure, compute
7 *shards* wings
8 *This . . . horse* i.e., we're off
9 *as my farthest . . . approof* such as I would wager anything that would make me the winner
10 *piece* here, meant as masterpiece
11 *mean* understood both as "means" and as "intermediary," i.e., Octavia
12 *curious* inquire as to minute details

CAES. Farewell, my dearest sister, fare thee well:
　　The elements [13] be kind to thee, and make
　　Thy spirits all of comfort! fare thee well.
OCT. My noble brother!
ANT. The April's in her eyes: it is love's spring,
　　And these the showers to bring it on. Be cheerful.
OCT. Sir, look well to my husband's house; and—
CAES.　　　　　　　　　　　　　　　　　　What,
　　Octavia?
OCT.　　　　I'll tell you in your ear.
ANT. Her tongue will not obey her heart, nor can
　　Her heart inform her tongue—the swan's down-feather
　　That stands upon the swell at full of tide
　　And neither way inclines. [14]
ENO.　　　　　　　　　　　　　Will Caesar weep?
AGR. He has a cloud in's face. [15]
ENO. He were the worse for that, were he a horse; [16]
　　So is he, being a man.
AGR.　　　　　　　　　　　Why, Enobarbus,
　　When Antony found Julius Caesar dead,
　　He cried almost to roaring; and he wept
　　When at Philippi he found Brutus slain.
ENO. That year indeed he was troubled with a rheum; [17]
　　What willingly he did confound [18] he wailed,
　　Believe't, till I wept too.
CAES.　　　　　　　　　　　　No, sweet Octavia,
　　You shall hear from me still; the time shall not
　　Out-go [19] my thinking on you.
ANT.　　　　　　　　　　　　　Come, sir, come;
　　I'll wrestle [20] with you in my strength of love:
　　Look, here I have you; thus I let you go,
　　And give you to the gods.
CAES.　　　　　　　　　　Adieu; be happy!
LEP. Let all the number of the stars give light
　　To thy fair way!
CAES.　　　　　　　Farewell, farewell! (*Kisses* OCTAVIA.)
ANT.　　　　　　　　　　　　　　　Farewell!

　　　　　　　　　　　　Trumpets sound. Exeunt.

SCENE 3. *Alexandria.* CLEOPATRA's *palace.*

Enter CLEOPATRA, CHARMIAN, IRAS, *and* ALEXAS.

CLEO. Where is the fellow?
ALEX.　　　　　　　　Half afeard to come.
CLEO. Go to, go to.

Enter the MESSENGER *as before.*

13 *elements* at least two probable meanings seem clear: as weather on the voyage, and as bodily constitution or health
14 *swan's . . . inclines* i.e., her emotions cannot be swayed toward either her husband or her brother, so evenly matched are her affections
15 Enobarbus and Agrippa carry on their own conversation here through asides
16 *horse* dark-faced horses were thought to be ill-tempered
17 *rheum* a running at the eyes
18 *confound* destroy
19 *Out-go* i.e., outstrip, outrace
20 *wrestle* here, it signifies contend by way of embraces

                  Come hither, sir.

ALEX.   Good majesty,
  Herod of Jewry [1] dare not look upon you
  But when you are well pleased.

CLEO.   That Herod's head
  I'll have: [2] but how, when Antony is gone
  Through whom I might command it? Come thou near.

MESS. Most gracious majesty!

CLEO.   Didst thou behold Octavia?

MESS. Ay, dread queen.

CLEO.   Where?

MESS.   Madam, in Rome.
  I looked her in the face, and saw her led
  Between her brother and Mark Antony.

CLEO. Is she as tall as me?

MESS.   She is not, madam.

CLEO. Didst hear her speak? is she shrill-tongued or low?

MESS. Madam, I heard her speak; she is low-voiced.

CLEO. That's not so good.[3] He cannot like her long.

CHAR. Like her! O Isis! 'tis impossible.

CLEO. I think so, Charmian: dull of tongue and dwarfish.
  What majesty is in her gait? Remember,
  If e'er thou look'dst on majesty.

MESS.   She creeps:
  Her motion and her station [4] are as one;
  She shows a body rather than a life,
  A statue than a breather.

CLEO.   Is this certain?

MESS. Or I have no observance.

CHAR.   Three in Egypt
  Cannot make better note.

CLEO.   He's very knowing;
  I do perceive't. There's nothing in her yet.
  The fellow has good judgment.

CHAR.   Excellent.

CLEO. Guess at her years, I prithee.

MESS.   Madam,
  She was a widow—

CLEO.   Widow! Charmian, hark.

MESS. And I do think she's thirty.[5]

CLEO. Bear'st thou her face in mind? is't long or round? [6]

MESS. Round, even to faultiness.

CLEO. For the most part, too, they are foolish that are so.
  Her hair, what color?

---

1 *Herod of Jewry* i.e., even Herod, conventionally a tyrant, as in miracle plays

2 *That Herod's head . . . have* Antony had many notables beheaded, according to Plutarch's accounts

3 *That's . . . good* variously viewed as, e.g., that is less good news; or as her voice is not as good as mine. The latter suggestion appears slightly more probable

4 *station* manner of standing

5 *thirty* Plutarch gave Cleopatra's age as thirty-eight at this time, perhaps accounting for her reluctance to explore further the issue of Octavia's age

6 *long or round* treatises on physiognomy reflected a belief that round faces represented foolishness and long faces caution

MESS. Brown, madam: and her forehead
  As low as she would wish it.[7]
CLEO.   There's gold for thee.
  Thou must not take my former sharpness ill;
  I will employ thee back again; I find thee
  Most fit for business. Go make thee ready;
  Our letters are prepared. [*Exit* MESSENGER.]
CHAR.   A proper [8] man.
CLEO. Indeed, he is so: I repent me much
  That so I harried him. Why, methinks, by him,
  This creature's no such thing.[9]
CHAR.   Nothing, madam.
CLEO. The man hath seen some majesty, and should know.
CHAR. Hath he seen majesty? Isis else defend,
  And serving you so long!
CLEO. I have one thing more to ask him yet, good Charmian:
  But 'tis no matter, thou shalt bring him to me
  Where I will write. All may be well enough.
CHAR. I warrant you, madam. (*Exeunt.*)

SCENE 4. *Athens. A room in* ANTONY's *house.*

Enter ANTONY *and* OCTAVIA.

ANT. Nay, nay, Octavia, not only that,
  That were excusable, that and thousands more
  Of semblable [1] import, but he hath waged
  New wars 'gainst Pompey, made his will and read it
  To public ear,[2]
  Spoke scantly of me; when perforce he could not
  But pay me terms of honor, cold and sickly
  He vented them; most narrow measure [3] lent me,
  When the best hint was given him, he not took't,
  Or did it from his teeth.[4]
OCT.   O my good lord,
  Believe not all, or if you must believe,
  Stomach [5] not all. A more unhappy lady,
  If this division chance, ne'er stood between,
  Praying for both parts:
  The good gods will mock me presently,[6]
  When I shall pray, 'O, bless my lord and husband!'
  Undo that prayer, by crying out as loud,
  'O, bless my brother!' Husband win, win brother,
  Prays, and destroys the prayer—no midway
  'Twixt these extremes at all.
ANT.   Gentle Octavia,
  Let your best love draw to that point which seeks

[7] *Brown* not then a color associated with beauty. Similarly, a low forehead was not considered an attractive facial feature
[8] *proper* good-looking
[9] *no such thing* not much to be impressed with
[1] *semblable* similar
[2] *made his will . . . ear* like Julius Caesar before, Octavius purportedly has sought public sympathy by way of a generous will for the commoners
[3] *narrow measure* small credit
[4] *from his teeth* grudgingly
[5] *Stomach* bear resentment
[6] *presently* immediately

Best to preserve it. If I lose mine honor,
I lose myself: better I were not yours
Than yours so branchless.[7] But, as you requested,
Yourself shall go between's; the mean time, lady,
I'll raise the preparation of a war
Shall stain [8] your brother: make your soonest haste;
So your desires are yours.

OCT.   Thanks to my lord.
The Jove of power make me most weak, most weak,
Your reconciler! Wars 'twixt you twain would be
As if the world should cleave, and that slain men
Should solder up the rift.

ANT. When it appears to you where this begins,
Turn your displeasure that way; for our faults
Can never be so equal that your love
Can equally move with them. Provide your going;
Choose your own company, and command what cost
Your heart has mind to. (*Exeunt.*)

SCENE 5

Enter ENOBARBUS *and* EROS.

ENO. How now, friend Eros!

EROS. There's strange news come, sir.

ENO. What, man?

EROS. Caesar and Lepidus have made wars upon Pompey.

ENO. This is old: what is the success? [1]

EROS. Caesar, having made use of him in the wars 'gainst Pompey, presently denied him rivality,[2] would not let him partake in the glory of the action, and not resting here accuses him of letters he had formerly wrote to Pompey; upon his own appeal,[3] seizes him; so the poor third is up,[4] till death enlarge his confine.

ENO. Then, world, thou hast a pair of chaps,[5] no more;
And throw between them all the food thou hast,
They'll [6] grind the one the other. Where's Antony?

EROS. He's walking in the garden—thus, and spurns
The rush that lies before him; cries 'Fool Lepidus!'
And threats the throat of that his officer
That murdered Pompey.

ENO.   Our great navy's rigged.

EROS. For Italy and Caesar. More, Domitius;
My lord desires you presently: my news
I might have told hereafter.

ENO.   'Twill be naught;
But let it be. Bring me to Antony.

EROS. Come, sir. (*Exeunt.*)

[7] *branchless* i.e., clipped of honor
[8] *stain* i.e., belittle his preparations
[1] *success* outcome
[2] *rivality* status and rights of a partner
[3] *his own appeal* i.e., Caesar's own charges
[4] *is up* is imprisoned
[5] *pair of chaps* set of lips
[6] *They'll* i.e., Caesar and Antony will

Scene 6. *Rome.* caesar's *house.*

Enter agrippa, maecenas, *and* caesar.

caes. Contemning [1] Rome, he has done all this and more
   In Alexandria; here's the manner of't:
   I'the market-place on a tribunal [2] silvered,
   Cleopatra and himself in chairs of gold
   Were publicly enthroned; at the feet sat
   Caesarion, whom they call my father's son,[3]
   And all the unlawful issue that their lust
   Since then hath made between them. Unto her
   He gave the stablishment of Egypt; made her
   Of lower Syria, Cyprus, Lydia,[4]
   Absolute queen.
mae.   This in the public eye?
caes. I'the common show-place, where they exercise.
   His sons he there proclaimed the kings of kings:
   Great Media, Parthia, and Armenia,
   He gave to Alexander; to Ptolemy he assigned
   Syria, Cilicia, and Phoenicia: she
   In the habiliments of the goddess Isis [5]
   That day appeared, and oft before gave audience,
   As 'tis reported, so.
mae.   Let Rome be thus
   Informed.
agr.   Who, queasy with his insolence
   Already, will their good thoughts call from him.
caes. The people know it, and have now received
   His accusations.
agr.   Who does he accuse?
caes. Caesar, and that, having in Sicily
   Sextus Pompeius spoiled,[6] we had not rated [7] him
   His part o'the isle,[8] then does he say, he lent me
   Some shipping unrestored; lastly, he frets
   That Lepidus of the triumvirate
   Should be deposed; and, being, that we detain
   All his revenue.
agr.   Sir, this should be answered.
caes. 'Tis done already, and the messenger gone.
   I have told him Lepidus was grown too cruel,
   That he his high authority abused
   And did deserve his change: for what I have conquered,
   I grant him part; but then, in his Armenia
   And other of his conquered kingdoms, I
   Demand the like.
mae.   He'll never yield to that.
caes. Nor must not then be yielded to in this.

Enter octavia, *with her train.*

1 *Contemning* scorning
2 *tribunal* elevated platform
3 *Caesarion, etc.* Julius' son by Cleopatra; it also should be recalled that Octavius was Julius' adopted son

4 *Lydia* Plutarch gives the name as Libya
5 *Isis* Egyptian goddess of fertility and earth
6 *spoiled* despoiled, i.e., his lands taken
7 *rated* apportioned to
8 *isle* Sicily, as indicated two lines earlier

OCT. Hail, Caesar, and my lord! hail, most dear Caesar!
CAES. That ever I should call thee castaway!
OCT. You have not called me so, nor have you cause.
CAES. Why have you stol'n upon us thus? You come not
   Like Caesar's sister: the wife of Antony
   Should have an army for an usher, and
   The neighs of horse to tell of her approach
   Long ere she did appear. The trees by the way
   Should have borne men, and expectation fainted,
   Longing for what it had not. Nay, the dust
   Should have ascended to the roof of heaven,
   Raised by your populous troops. But you are come
   A market-maid to Rome, and have prevented
   The ostentation of our love, which, left unshown,
   Is often left unloved: [9] we should have met you
   By sea and land, supplying every stage
   With an augmented greeting.
OCT.   Good my lord,
   To come thus was I not constrained, but did it
   On my free will. My lord, Mark Antony,
   Hearing that you prepared for war, acquainted
   My grieved ear withal; whereon, I begged
   His pardon for return.
CAES.   Which soon he granted,
   Being an abstract [10] 'tween his lust and him.
OCT. Do not say so, my lord.
CAES.   I have eyes upon him,
   And his affairs come to me on the wind.
   Where is he now?
OCT.   My lord, in Athens.
CAES. No, my most wrongèd sister, Cleopatra
   Hath nodded him to her. He hath given his empire
   Up to a whore, who now are levying
   The kings o'the earth for war. He hath assembled
   Bocchus the king of Libya, Archelaus
   Of Cappadocia, Philadelphos king
   Of Paphlagonia, the Thracian king Adallas,
   King Manchus [11] of Arabia, King of Pont,
   Herod of Jewry, Mithridates king
   Of Comagene, Polemon and Amyntas
   The kings of Mede and Lycaonia,
   With a more larger list of sceptres.
OCT.   Ay me, most wretched,
   That have my heart parted betwixt two friends
   That do afflict each other!

9 *our love . . . left unloved* i.e., Caesar believes that if his love for his sister is not permitted to be openly displayed, that love would be thought not genuine

10 *abstract* this word has caused difficulty since the O.E.D. offers little help. Two strong possibilities are: first, "abstract" as a form of "obstruct" or "obstruction" wherein Octavia is a block to Antony's desires for Cleopatra; second, "abstract" as "short-cut" wherein Antony's encouragement of Octavia's decision to return to Caesar provides Antony with an expedient means for returning to Cleopatra more quickly

11 *Manchus* in Plutarch, it is "Malchus." But North gave him as "Manchus." A look at North's Plutarch also reveals that there is confusion of kings and kingdoms in Shakespeare's listing

CAES.   Welcome hither:
Your letters did withhold our breaking forth,
Till we perceived both how you were wrong led
And we in negligent danger.[12] Cheer your heart:
Be you not troubled with the time, which drives
O'er your content these strong necessities,
But let determined things to destiny
Hold unbewailed their way. Welcome to Rome,
Nothing more dear to me. You are abused
Beyond the mark [13] of thought: and the high gods,
To do you justice, make his ministers
Of us and those that love you. Best of comfort,
And ever welcome to us.
AGR.   Welcome, lady.
MAE. Welcome, dear madam.
Each heart in Rome does love and pity you:
Only the adulterous Antony, most large
In his abominations, turns you off,
And gives his potent regiment [14] to a trull,[15]
That noises it against us.
OCT.   Is it so, sir?
CAES. Most certain. Sister, welcome: pray you,
Be ever known to patience. My dear'st sister! (*Exeunt.*)

SCENE 7. *Near Actium.*

Enter CLEOPATRA *and* ENOBARBUS.

CLEO. I will be even with thee, doubt it not.
ENO. But why, why, why?
CLEO. Thou hast forspoke [1] my being in these wars,
And say'st it is not fit.
ENO.   Well, is it, is it?
CLEO. Is't not denounced [2] against us? Why should not we
Be there in person?
ENO. [*aside*]   Well, I could reply:
If we should serve with horse and mares together,
The horse were merely [3] lost; the mares would bear
A soldier and his horse.
CLEO.   What is't you say?
ENO. Your presence needs must puzzle [4] Antony;
Take from his heart, take from his brain, from's time,
What should not then be spared. He is already
Traduced for levity, and 'tis said in Rome
That Photinus, an eunuch,[5] and your maids
Manage this war.

---

12 *negligent danger* danger brought about by negligence
13 *mark* i.e., limit
14 *regiment* rule
15 *trull* harlot
1 *forspoke* spoken against
2 *denounced* proclaimed

3 *merely* completely
4 *puzzle* paralyze
5 *Photinus, an eunuch* the Folio, which omits commas around "an eunuch," is not clear in conveying the fact that Photinus is not the eunuch referred to here; rather, the referent is Mardian

CLEO.   Sink Rome, and their tongues rot
That speak against us! A charge [6] we bear i'the war,
And as the president of my kingdom will
Appear there for a man. Speak not against it,
I will not stay behind.

              Enter ANTONY *and* CANIDIUS.

ENO.   Nay, I have done.
Here comes the emperor.
ANT.   Is it not strange, Canidius,
That from Tarentum [7] and Brundusium [8]
He could so quickly cut the Ionian sea,
And take in Toryne? [9] You have heard on't, sweet?
CLEO. Celerity is never more admired
Than by the negligent.
ANT.   A good rebuke,
Which might have well becomed the best of men,
To taunt at slackness. Canidius, we
Will fight with him by sea.
CLEO.   By sea! what else?
CAN. Why will my lord do so?
ANT.   For that he dares us to't.
ENO. So hath my lord dared him to single fight.
CAN. Ay, and to wage this battle at Pharsalia,
Where Caesar fought with Pompey. But these offers,
Which serve not for his vantage, he shakes off,
And so should you.
ENO.   Your ships are not well manned,
Your mariners are muleters,[10] reapers, people
Ingrossed [11] by swift impress; [12] in Caesar's fleet
Are those that often have 'gainst Pompey fought;
Their ships are yare,[13] yours heavy: no disgrace
Shall fall you for refusing him at sea,
Being prepared for land.
ANT.   By sea, by sea.
ENO. Most worthy sir, you therein throw away
The absolute soldiership you have by land,
Distract [14] your army, which doth most consist
Of war-marked footmen, leave unexecuted
Your own renownèd knowledge, quite forgo
The way which promises assurance, and
Give up yourself merely [15] to chance and hazard
From firm security.
ANT.   I'll fight at sea.
CLEO. I have sixty sails, Caesar none better.
ANT. Our overplus of shipping will we burn;
And, with the rest full-manned, from the head [16] of Actium

---

[6] *charge*   responsibility
[7] *Tarentum*   Taranto
[8] *Brundusium*   Brindisi
[9] *take in Toryne*   occupy Toryne
[10] *muleters*   mule-drivers, i.e., peasants
[11] *Ingrossed*   collected

[12] *impress*   draft
[13] *yare*   nimble, easy to maneuver
[14] *distract*   both confuse and divide
[15] *merely*   entirely
[16] *head*   headland

Beat the approaching Caesar. But if we fail,
We then can do't at land.

Enter a MESSENGER.

                Thy business?
MESS. The news is true, my lord, he is descried;
  Caesar has taken Toryne.
ANT. Can he be there in person? 'Tis impossible;
  Strange that his power should be. Canidius,
  Our nineteen legions thou shalt hold by land,
  And our twelve thousand horse. We'll to our ship:
  Away, my Thetis! [17]

Enter a SOLDIER.

          How now, worthy soldier?
SOLD. O noble emperor, do not fight by sea;
  Trust not to rotten planks. Do you misdoubt
  This sword and these my wounds? Let the Egyptians
  And the Phoenicians go a-ducking: we
  Have used to conquer standing on the earth
  And fighting foot to foot.
ANT.   Well, well, away!

Exit ANTONY, CLEOPATRA, *and* ENOBARBUS.

SOLD. By Hercules, I think I am i'the right.
CAN. Soldier, thou art: but his whole action grows
  Not in the power on't: [18] so our leader's led,
  And we are women's men.
SOLD.   You keep by land
  The legions and the horse whole, do you not?
CAN. Marcus Octavius, Marcus Justeius,
  Publicola, and Caelius are for sea;
  But we keep whole by land. This speed of Caesar's
  Carries [19] beyond belief.
SOLD.   While he was yet in Rome,
  His power went out in such distractions [20] as
  Beguiled all spies.
CAN.   Who's his lieutenant, hear you?
SOLD. They say, one Taurus.
CAN.   Well I know the man.

Enter a MESSENGER.

MESS. The emperor calls Canidius.
CAN. With news the time's with labor and throws forth
  Each minute some.[21] (*Exeunt.*)

17 *Thetis* the sea goddess, here apparently applied to Cleopatra because of the navy she has just offered for aid
18 *action grows . . . power on't* his strategy is formulated without regard to his military advantage
19 *Carries* i.e., like an arrow
20 *distractions* detachments
21 *time's with labor, etc.* i.e., figure of time giving birth to news (as an animal "throws" in bearing its young)

SCENE 8

Enter CAESAR *and* TAURUS, *with his army, marching.*

CAES. Taurus!
TAUR. My lord?
CAES. Strike not by land, keep whole, provoke not battle
Till we have done at sea. Do not exceed
The prescript of this scroll: our fortune lies
Upon this jump.¹ [*Exeunt.*]

SCENE 9

Enter ANTONY *and* ENOBARBUS.

ANT. Set we our squadrons on yond side o'the hill,
In eye of Caesar's battle;¹ from which place
We may the number of the ships behold,
And so proceed accordingly. [*Exeunt.*]

SCENE 10

CANIDIUS *marcheth with his land army one way over the stage, and* TAURUS, *the lieutenant of* CAESAR, *the other way. After their going in, is heard the noise of a sea-fight. Alarum. Enter* ENOBARBUS.

ENO. Naught, naught, all naught!¹ I can behold no longer.
The Antoniad, the Egyptian admiral,²
With all their sixty, fly and turn the rudder:
To see't mine eyes are blasted.

Enter SCARUS.

SCAR.   Gods and goddesses,
All the whole synod³ of them!
ENO.   What's thy passion?
SCAR. The greater cantle⁴ of the world is lost
With very ignorance. We have kissed away
Kingdoms and provinces.
ENO.   How appears the fight?
SCAR. On our side like the tokened pestilence,⁵
Where death is sure. Yon ribald-rid nag⁶ of Egypt—
Whom leprosy o'ertake!—i'the midst o'the fight,
When vantage like a pair of twins appeared,
Both as the same, or rather ours the elder—⁷
The breese⁸ upon her, like a cow in June!—
Hoists sails and flies.

¹ *jump* hazard
¹ *battle* i.e., battle troops
¹ *Naught* all for naught, all lost
² *admiral* flagship
³ *synod* assembly of gods
⁴ *cantle* portion, arc
⁵ *tokened pestilence* symptoms seen anticipat-

ing the plague to follow
⁶ *ribald-rid nag* lewd woman
⁷ *elder* i.e., superior
⁸ *breese* a gadfly, here attacking a cow which flees; an obvious pun on "breeze" is to be seen as well

ENO.   That I beheld:
   Mine eyes did sicken at the sight, and could not
   Endure a further view.
SCAR.   She once being luffed,[9]
   The noble ruin of her magic, Antony,
   Claps on his sea-wing, and (like a doting mallard)
   Leaving the fight in height, flies after her:
   I never saw an action of such shame;
   Experience, manhood, honor, ne'er before
   Did violate so itself.
ENO.   Alack, alack!

Enter CANIDIUS.

CAN. Our fortune on the sea is out of breath,
   And sinks most lamentably. Had our general
   Been what he knew himself,[10] it had gone well:
   O, he has given example for our flight
   Most grossly by his own!
ENO.   Ay, are you thereabouts? [11]
   Why then good night indeed.
CAN. Toward Peloponnesus are they fled.
SCAR. 'Tis easy to't; and there I will attend
   What further comes.
CAN.   To Caesar will I render
   My legions and my horse; six kings already
   Show me the way of yielding.
ENO.   I'll yet follow
   The wounded chance [12] of Antony, though my reason
   Sits in the wind against me.[13] [*Exeunt.*]

SCENE 11

Enter ANTONY *with Attendants.*

ANT. Hark! the land bids me tread no more upon't—
   It is ashamed to bear me. Friends, come hither:
   I am so lated [1] in the world that I
   Have lost my way for ever. I have a ship
   Laden with gold, take that, divide it; fly,
   And make your peace with Caesar.
ALL.   Fly! not we.
ANT. I have fled myself, and have instructed cowards
   To run and show their shoulders.[2] Friends, be gone;
   I have myself resolved upon a course
   Which has no need of you. Be gone.
   My treasure's in the harbor. Take it. O,
   I followed that [3] I blush to look upon:

---

9 *luffed* ship turned head up into wind
10 *Been what he knew* had performed as he
  once was capable of performing
11 *thereabouts* thinking that way, i.e., about
  losing
12 *chance* fortune

13 *Sits in the wind* opposes my decision
1 *lated* belated
2 *show their shoulders* show their backs, i.e.,
  to run away from battle
3 *that* what, or that which

My very hairs do mutiny, for the white
Reprove the brown for rashness, and they them
For fear and doting. Friends, be gone; you shall
Have letters from me to some friends that will
Sweep your way for you.[4] Pray you, look not sad,
Nor make replies of loathness; take the hint
Which my despair proclaims. Let that [5] be left
Which leaves itself: to the sea-side straightway;
I will possess you of that ship and treasure.
Leave me, I pray, a little: pray you now,
Nay, do so; for indeed I have lost command,
Therefore I pray you: [6] I'll see you by and by. (*Sits down.*)

Enter CLEOPATRA *led by* CHARMIAN *and* EROS; IRAS *following.*

EROS. Nay, gentle madam, to him, comfort him.
IRAS. Do, most dear queen.
CHAR. Do! why, what else?
CLEO. Let me sit down. O Juno!
ANT. No, no, no, no, no.
EROS. See you here, sir?
ANT. O fie, fie, fie!
CHAR. Madam!
IRAS. Madam, O good empress!
EROS. Sir, sir!
ANT. Yes, my lord,[7] yes. He at Philippi kept
    His sword e'en like a dancer,[8] while I struck
    The lean and wrinkled Cassius; and 'twas I
    That the mad Brutus ended: he alone
    Dealt on lieutenantry,[9] and no practice had
    In the brave squares [10] of war: yet now—no matter.
CLEO. Ah! stand by.
EROS. The queen, my lord, the queen.
IRAS. Go to him, madam, speak to him;
    He is unqualitied [11] with very shame.
CLEO. Well then, sustain me: O!
EROS. Most noble sir, arise, the queen approaches:
    Her head's declined, and death will seize her, but [12]
    Your comfort makes the rescue.
ANT. I have offended reputation,
    A most unnoble swerving.
EROS.   Sir, the queen.
ANT. O, whither hast thou led me, Egypt? See,
    How I convey my shame out of thine eyes
    By looking back what I have left behind [13]
    Stroyed in dishonor.

---

4 *Sweep* facilitate a reconciliation (with Caesar)
5 *that* i.e., Antony himself
6 *I have lost . . . I pray you* i.e., I no longer am in command; hence I can only request you to do as I urge
7 *my lord* Antony speaks this ironically of Caesar
8 *sword* like the Elizabethan player or dancer, Caesar never drew his sword which served but as an ornament in the debacle

9 *Dealt on lieutenantry* fought by proxy through subordinates
10 *squares* squadrons
11 *unqualitied* unmanned
12 *but* unless
13 *How I convey . . . left behind* these lines are puzzling, though scholars concur generally in viewing them as "unmanned" Antony's statement of shame: he will avoid the reproach in her eyes by looking backwards at his infamous deeds

CLEO.   O my lord, my lord,
Forgive my fearful sails! I little thought
You would have followed.
ANT.   Egypt, thou knew'st too well
My heart was to thy rudder tied by the strings,
And thou shouldst tow me after. O'er my spirit
Thy full supremacy thou knew'st, and that
Thy beck might from the bidding of the gods
Command me.
CLEO.   O, my pardon!
ANT.   Now I must
To the young man send humble treaties, dodge
And palter [14] in the shifts of lowness, who
With half the bulk o'the world played as I pleased,
Making and marring fortunes. You did know
How much you were my conqueror, and that
My sword, made weak by my affection, would
Obey it on all cause.
CLEO.   Pardon, pardon!
ANT. Fall not a tear, I say; one of them rates [15]
All that is won and lost: give me a kiss;
Even this repays me.
We sent our schoolmaster; [16] is a' come back?
Love, I am full of lead.[17]
Some wine, within there, and our viands! Fortune knows
We scorn her most when most she offers blows. (*Exeunt.*)

SCENE 12. *Egypt.* CAESAR's *camp.*

Enter CAESAR, AGRIPPA,[1] DOLABELLA *and* THIDIAS, *with others.*

CAES. Let him appear that's come from Antony.
Know you him?
DOL.   Caesar, 'tis his schoolmaster:
An argument [2] that he is plucked, when hither
He sends so poor a pinion of his wing,
Which had superfluous kings for messengers
Not many moons gone by.

Enter AMBASSADOR *from* ANTONY.[3]

CAES.   Approach, and speak.
AMBAS. Such as I am, I come from Antony:
I was of late as petty to his ends
As is the morn-dew on the myrtle-leaf
To his grand sea.[4]
CAES.   Be't so. Declare thine office.
AMBAS. Lord of his fortunes he salutes thee, and
Requires [5] to live in Egypt, which not granted,

---

14 *palter*   use tricks and devices left to a man low in fortune
15 *rates*   equals
16 *schoolmaster*   Euphronius was tutor to their children
17 *lead*   here, grief is meant
1 Agrippa, though he does not speak in the scene,

yet probably was desired by Shakespeare to remain on stage throughout the episode
2 *argument*   evidence
3 the Ambassador is the schoolmaster mentioned
4 *sea*   i.e., ultimate source of dew
5 *Requires*   here, meant as "requests"

He lessens his requests, and to thee sues
To let him breathe between the heavens and earth,
A private man in Athens: this for him.
Next, Cleopatra does confess thy greatness,
Submits her to thy might, and of thee craves
The circle 6 of the Ptolemies for her heirs,
Now hazarded to 7 thy grace.

CAES.   For Antony,
I have no ears to his request. The queen
Of audience nor desire shall fail, so she
From Egypt drive her all-disgracèd friend,
Or take his life there: this if she perform,
She shall not sue unheard. So to them both.

AMBAS. Fortune pursue thee!

CAES.   Bring him through the bands.8

[*Exit* AMBASSADOR.]

(*To* THIDIAS) To try thy eloquence, now 'tis time: dispatch;
From Antony win Cleopatra; promise,
And in our name, what she requires; add more,
As thine invention offers.9 Women are not
In their best fortunes strong, but want will perjure
The ne'er-touched vestal. Try thy cunning, Thidias;
Make thine own edict for thy pains,10 which we
Will answer as a law.

THID.   Caesar, I go.

CAES. Observe how Antony becomes his flaw,11
And what thou think'st his very action speaks
In every power that moves.12

THID.   Caesar, I shall. (*Exeunt.*)

SCENE 13. *Alexandria.* CLEOPATRA'*s palace.*

Enter CLEOPATRA, ENOBARBUS, CHARMIAN, *and* IRAS.

CLEO. What shall we do, Enobarbus?

ENO.   Think, and die.

CLEO. Is Antony or we in fault for this?

ENO. Antony only, that would make his will 1
Lord of his reason. What though you fled
From that great face of war, whose several ranges 2
Frighted each other? Why should he follow?
The itch of his affection should not then
Have nicked 3 his captainship at such a point,
When half to half the world opposed, he being
The mered question.4 'Twas a shame no less
Than was his loss, to course 5 your flying flags
And leave his navy gazing.

6 *circle* crown
7 *hazarded to* dependent on
8 *bands* ranks, i.e., of troops
9 *As thine invention* since no one version of the muddled wording here is wholly accurate, I have employed Hanmer's form as a satisfactory alternative
10 *Make thine, etc.* name your price for a fee
11 *becomes his flaw* accepts his disgrace
12 *And what . . . moves* what you believe his reactions tell of his future acts
1 *will* here, desire
2 *ranges* lines of combat
3 *nicked* overcome
4 *mered question* sole cause
5 *course* pursue

CLEO.   Prithee, peace.

Enter the AMBASSADOR, *with* ANTONY.

ANT. Is that his answer?
AMBAS. Ay, my lord.
ANT. The queen shall then have courtesy, so she
    Will yield us up.
AMBAS.   He says so.
ANT.   Let her know't.
    To the boy Caesar send this grizzled head,
    And he will fill thy wishes to the brim
    With principalities.
CLEO.   That head, my lord?
ANT. To him again! tell him he wears the rose
    Of youth upon him; from which the world should note
    Something particular: ⁶ his coin, ships, legions,
    May be a coward's, whose ministers would prevail
    Under the service of a child as soon
    As i'the command of Caesar. I dare him therefore
    To lay his gay comparisons ⁷ apart
    And answer me declined,⁸ sword against sword,
    Ourselves alone. I'll write it: follow me.

                  [*Exeunt* ANTONY *and* AMBASSADOR.]

ENO. Yes, like enough, high-battled Caesar will
    Unstate his happiness and be staged to the show ⁹
    Against a sworder! I see men's judgments are
    A parcel of their fortunes, and things outward
    Do draw the inward quality after them,
    To suffer all alike.¹⁰ That he should dream,
    Knowing all measures,¹¹ the full Caesar will
    Answer his emptiness! Caesar, thou hast subdued
    His judgment too.

Enter a SERVANT.

SERV.   A messenger from Caesar.
CLEO. What, no more ceremony? See, my women,
    Against the blown rose may they stop their nose
    That kneeled unto the buds. Admit him, sir. [*Exit* SERVANT.]
ENO. Mine honesty and I begin to square.¹²
    The loyalty well held to fools does make
    Our faith mere folly: yet he that can endure
    To follow with allegiance a fall'n lord
    Does conquer him that did his master conquer,
    And earns a place i'the story.

Enter THIDIAS.

⁶ *Something particular* i.e., some specific evidence of his courage
⁷ *gay comparisons* showy trappings and armies in which Caesar excels
⁸ *declined* i.e., in fallen fortunes
⁹ *Unstate . . . show* strip himself of his advantage and take part in a stage show (i.e., duel)
¹⁰ *To suffer . . . alike* i.e., both decline equally
¹¹ *Knowing all measures* being a sound judge of men and situations
¹² *square* quarrel

CLEO.   Caesar's will?
THID. Hear it apart.
CLEO.   None but friends: say boldly.
THID. So, haply,[13] are they friends to Antony.
ENO. He needs as many, sir, as Caesar has,
  Or needs not us. If Caesar please, our master
  Will leap to be his friend: for us, you know,
  Whose he is we are, and that is Caesar's.
THID.   So.
  Thus then, thou most renowned, Caesar entreats
  Not to consider in what case thou stand'st
  Further than he is Caesar.
CLEO.   Go on: right royal.
THID. He knows that you embraced not Antony
  As you did love, but as you feared him.
CLEO.   O!
THID. The scars upon your honor therefore he
  Does pity as constrainèd blemishes,
  Not as deserved.
CLEO.   He is a god, and knows
  What is most right. Mine honor was not yielded,
  But conquered merely.
ENO.   To be sure of that,
  I will ask Antony. Sir, sir, thou art so leaky
  That we must leave thee to thy sinking, for
  Thy dearest quit thee. (*Exit* ENOBARBUS.)
THID.   Shall I say to Caesar
  What you require [14] of him? for he partly begs
  To be desired to give. It much would please him,
  That of his fortunes you should make a staff
  To lean upon. But it would warm his spirits
  To hear from me you had left Antony,
  And put yourself under his shroud,[15]
  The universal landlord.
CLEO.   What's your name?
THID. My name is Thidias.
CLEO.   Most kind messenger,
  Say to great Caesar this: in deputation [16]
  I kiss his conqu'ring hand; tell him, I am prompt
  To lay my crown at's feet, and there to kneel.
  Tell him, from his all-obeying [17] breath I hear
  The doom [18] of Egypt.
THID.   'Tis your noblest course.
  Wisdom and fortune combating together,
  If that the former dare but what it can,
  No chance may shake it. Give me grace to lay
  My duty on your hand.[19]
CLEO.   Your Caesar's father oft,
  When he hath mused of taking kingdoms in,[20]

---

13 *haply* very likely
14 *require* request
15 *shroud* protection
16 *in deputation* via his deputy
17 *all-obeying* which all obey
18 *doom* here, judgment on
19 *My duty* this line indicates that Thidias kisses Cleopatra's hand
20 *taking kingdoms in* i.e., conquering

Bestowed his lips on that unworthy place,
As it rained kisses.

Enter ANTONY *and* ENOBARBUS.

ANT.   Favors, by Jove that thunders!
What art thou, fellow?
THID.   One that but performs
The bidding of the fullest man and worthiest
To have command obeyed.
ENO.   You will be whipped.
ANT. Approach, there! Ah, you kite! Now, gods and devils!
Authority melts from me. Of late when I cried 'Ho!'
Like boys unto a muss,²¹ kings would start forth,
And cry 'Your will?' Have you no ears? I am
Antony yet. Take hence this Jack,²² and whip him.

Enter a SERVANT.

ENO. 'Tis better playing with a lion's whelp
Than with an old one dying.
ANT.   Moon and stars!
Whip him! Were't twenty of the greatest tributaries
That do acknowledge Caesar, should I find them
So saucy with the hand of she here—what's her name
Since she was Cleopatra? Whip him, fellows,
Till like a boy you see him cringe his face ²³
And whine aloud for mercy. Take him hence.
THID. Mark Antony—
ANT.   Tug him away: being whipped,
Bring him again. This Jack of Caesar's shall
Bear us an errand to him. (*Exeunt* SERVANTS *with* THIDIAS.)
You were half blasted ere I knew you: Ha!
Have I my pillow left unpressed in Rome,
Forborne the getting of a lawful race,
And by a gem of women, to be abused ²⁴
By one that looks on feeders? ²⁵
CLEO.   Good my lord —
ANT. You have been a boggler ²⁶ ever:
But when we in our viciousness grow hard—
O misery on't!—the wise gods seel ²⁷ our eyes,
In our own filth drop our clear judgments, make us
Adore our errors, laugh at's while we strut
To our confusion.
CLEO.   O, is't come to this?
ANT. I found you as a morsel cold upon
Dead Caesar's trencher; ²⁸ nay, you were a fragment
Of Gnaeus Pompey's; besides what hotter hours,
Unregistered in vulgar fame,²⁹ you have
Luxuriously ³⁰ picked out; for I am sure,

²¹ *muss* scramble
²² *Jack* impudent upstart
²³ *cringe* grimace in pain
²⁴ *abused* betrayed
²⁵ *feeders* servants, subordinates
²⁶ *boggler* waverer, shifty person

²⁷ *seel* sew up
²⁸ *trencher* plate, i.e., metaphor for Cleopatra
who is the Egyptian "dish"
²⁹ *vulgar fame* common gossip
³⁰ *Luxuriously* here, licentiously

Though you can guess what temperance should be,
You know not what it is.
CLEO.   Wherefore is this?
ANT. To let a fellow that will take rewards
And say 'God quit [31] you!' be familiar with
My playfellow, your hand, this kingly seal
And plighter of high hearts! O, that I were
Upon the hill of Basan,[32] to outroar
The hornèd herd! for I have savage cause,
And to proclaim it civilly were like
A haltered neck which does the hangman thank
For being yare [33] about him.

Enter a SERVANT *with* THIDIAS.

                             Is he whipped?
SERV. Soundly, my lord.
ANT.   Cried he? and begged a' pardon?
SERV. He did ask favor.
ANT. If that thy father live, let him repent
Thou wast not made his daughter; and be thou sorry
To follow Caesar in his triumph, since
Thou hast been whipped for following him: henceforth
The white hand of a lady fever thee,[34]
Shake thou to look on't. Get thee back to Caesar,
Tell him thy entertainment: [35] look thou say
He makes me angry with him. For he seems
Proud and disdainful, harping on what I am,
Not what he knew I was. He makes me angry,
And at this time most easy 'tis to do't,
When my good stars that were my former guides
Have empty left their orbs [36] and shot their fires
Into the abysm of hell. If he mislike
My speech and what is done, tell him he has
Hipparchus,[37] my enfranchèd bondman, whom
He may at pleasure whip, or hang, or torture,
As he shall like, to quit [38] me. Urge it thou:
Hence with thy stripes, be gone! (*Exit* THIDIAS.)
CLEO. Have you done yet?
ANT.   Alack, our terrene moon [39]
Is now eclipsed, and it portends alone
The fall of Antony.
CLEO.   I must stay his time.[40]
ANT. To flatter Caesar, would you mingle eyes
With one that ties his points? [41]
CLEO.   Not know me yet?

---

31 *quit* requite
32 *hill of Basan* an allusion to the biblical Bason with its fat bulls—meaning Antony considers himself the master cuckold of the earth
33 *yare* rapid
34 *white hand . . . fever* i.e., may the lady's hand bring a fever upon you
35 *entertainment* i.e., his reception by Antony
36 *orbs* spheres

37 *Hipparchus* he had gone over to Caesar before of his own accord
38 *quit* repay
39 *terrene moon* i.e., Cleopatra, compared to Isis the moon goddess. But here, Antony also alludes to her dimmed light which portends doom
40 *stay his time* wait till he comes to his senses
41 *one . . . points* i.e., a valet

ANT. Cold-hearted toward me?
CLEO.   Ah, dear, if I be so,
From my cold heart let heaven engender hail,
And poison it in the source, and the first stone
Drop in my neck: as it determines, so
Dissolve my life! The next Caesarion smite!
Till by degrees the memory of my womb,[42]
Together with my brave Egyptians all,
By the discandying [43] of this pelleted storm
Lie graveless, till the flies and gnats of Nile
Have buried them for prey!
ANT.   I am satisfied.
Caesar sets down in Alexandria, where
I will oppose his fate. Our force by land
Hath nobly held, our severed navy too
Have knit again, and fleet,[44] threat'ning most sea-like.
Where hast thou been, my heart? Dost thou hear, lady?
If from the field I shall return once more
To kiss these lips, I will appear in blood; [45]
I and my sword will earn our chronicle.[46]
There's hope in't yet.
CLEO.   That's my brave lord!
ANT. I will be treble-sinewed, hearted, breathed,
And fight maliciously: [47] for when mine hours
Were nice [48] and lucky, men did ransom lives
Of me for jests; but now I'll set my teeth,
And send to darkness all that stop me. Come,
Let's have one other gaudy [49] night: call to me
All my sad captains; fill our bowls once more:
Let's mock the midnight bell.
CLEO.   It is my birth-day,
I had thought t'have held it poor. But since my lord
Is Antony again, I will be Cleopatra.
ANT. We will yet do well.
CLEO. Call all his noble captains to my lord.
ANT. Do so, we'll speak to them; and to-night I'll force
The wine peep through their scars. Come on, my queen;
There's sap [50] in't yet. The next time I do fight
I'll make death love me, for I will contend
Even with his pestilent scythe. (*Exeunt all but* ENOBARBUS.)
ENO. Now he'll outstare the lightning. To be furious
Is to be frighted out of fear, and in that mood
The dove will peck the estridge; [51] and I see still
A diminution in our captain's brain
Restores his heart: when valor preys on [52] reason,
It eats the sword it fights with. I will seek
Some way to leave him. (*Exit.*)

[42] *memory . . . womb* i.e., her children
[43] *discandying* melting, as hard candy
[44] *fleet* are afloat
[45] *in blood* i.e., both blood besmeared from battle and blood in high spirits
[46] *earn our chronicle* earn a niche in history and history books
[47] *maliciously* viciously
[48] *nice* i.e., easy
[49] *gaudy* festive
[50] *sap* life juices, i.e., hope
[51] *estridge* a species of hawk, i.e., goshawk
[52] *preys on* F "prayes in"

ACT IV

SCENE 1

Enter CAESAR, AGRIPPA, *and* MAECENAS, *with his army;*
CAESAR *reading a letter.*

CAES. He calls me boy, and chides as he had power
To beat me out of Egypt. My messenger
He hath whipped with rods; dares me to personal combat,
Caesar to Antony. Let the old ruffian know
I have many other ways to die; meantime
Laugh at his challenge.
MAE.   Caesar must think,
When one so great begins to rage, he's hunted
Even to falling. Give him no breath, but now
Make boot [1] of his distraction. Never anger
Made good guard for itself.
CAES.   Let our best heads
Know that to-morrow the last of many battles
We mean to fight. Within our files [2] there are,
Of those that served Mark Antony but late,
Enough to fetch him in. [3] See it done,
And feast the army; we have store to do't,
And they have earned the waste. Poor Antony! (*Exeunt.*)

SCENE 2. *Alexandria.* CLEOPATRA's *palace.*

Enter ANTONY, CLEOPATRA, ENOBARBUS, CHARMIAN, IRAS, ALEXAS,
with others.

ANT. He will not fight with me, Domitius?
ENO.   No.
ANT. Why should he not?
ENO. He thinks, being twenty times of better fortune,
He is twenty men to one.
ANT.   To-morrow, soldier,
By sea and land I'll fight: or [1] I will live,
Or bathe my dying honor in the blood
Shall make it live again. Woo't [2] thou fight well?
ENO. I'll strike, and cry 'Take all.' [3]
ANT.   Well said. Come on;
Call forth my household servants: let's to-night
Be bounteous at our meal.

Enter three or four SERVITORS.

                Give me thy hand,
Thou hast been rightly honest, so hast thou,
Thou, and thou, and thou: you have served me well,
And kings have been your fellows.

[1] *Make boot* take advantage
[2] *files* Elizabethan term for army ranks or troops
[3] *Fetch him in* capture him

[1] *or* either
[2] *Woo't* Wilt
[3] *'Take all'* i.e., winner take all

CLEO.   What means this?
ENO. 'Tis one of those odd tricks which sorrow shoots
  Out of the mind.[4]
ANT.   And thou art honest too.
  I wish I could be made so many men,
  And all of you clapped up together in
  An Antony, that I might do you service
  So good as you have done.
ALL.   The gods forbid!
ANT. Well, my good fellows, wait on me to-night:
  Scant not my cups, and make as much of me
  As when mine empire was your fellow too
  And suffered my command.
CLEO.   What does he mean?
ENO. To make his followers weep.[4]
ANT.   Tend me to-night;
  May be it is the period [5] of your duty.
  Haply [6] you shall not see me more, or if,
  A mangled shadow. Perchance to-morrow
  You'll serve another master. I look on you
  As one that takes his leave. Mine honest friends,
  I turn you not away, but, like a master
  Married to your good service, stay till death:
  Tend me to-night two hours, I ask no more,
  And the gods yield [7] you for't!
ENO.   What mean you, sir,
  To give them this discomfort? Look, they weep,
  And I, an ass, am onion-eyed; for shame,
  Transform us not to women.
ANT.   Ho, ho, ho!
  Now the witch take me, if I meant it thus!
  Grace grow [8] where those drops fall! My hearty friends,
  You take me in too dolorous a sense,
  For I spake to you for your comfort, did desire you
  To burn this night with torches. Know, my hearts,
  I hope well of to-morrow, and will lead you
  Where rather I'll expect victorious life
  Than death and honor. Let's to supper, come,
  And drown consideration. (*Exeunt.*)

SCENE 3

Enter a company of SOLDIERS.

1 SOLD. Brother, good night: to-morrow is the day.
2 SOLD. It will determine one way: fare you well.
  Heard you of nothing strange about the streets?
1 SOLD. Nothing: what news?
2 SOLD. Belike 'tis but a rumor. Good night to you.
1 SOLD. Well, sir, good night. (*They meet other* SOLDIERS.)

4 such lines are spoken aside by Cleopatra and   6 *Haply*   quite probably
  Enobarbus to each other   7 *yield*   reward
5 *period* end   8 *Grace grow*   virtue spring

2 SOLD. Soldiers, have careful watch.

3 SOLD. And you. Good night, good night.

They place themselves in every corner of the stage.

4 SOLD. Here we: [1] and if to-morrow
Our navy thrive, I have an absolute hope
Our landmen will stand up.

3 SOLD.   'Tis a brave army,
And full of purpose. (*Music of the hautboys is under the stage.*)

4 SOLD.   Peace! what noise?

1 SOLD.   List, list!

2 SOLD. Hark!

1 SOLD.   Music i'the air.

3 SOLD.   Under the earth.

4 SOLD. It signs well,[2] does it not?

3 SOLD.   No.

1 SOLD.   Peace, I say!
What should this mean?

2 SOLD. 'Tis the god Hercules,[3] whom Antony loved,
Now leaves him.

1 SOLD.   Walk; let's see if other watchmen
Do hear what we do.

2 SOLD.   How now, masters!

ALL. (*Speak together.*)   How now!
How now! Do you hear this?

1 SOLD.   Ay, is't not strange?

3 SOLD. Do you hear, masters? do you hear?

1 SOLD. Follow the noise so far as we have quarter.[4]
Let's see how it will give off.

ALL.   Content. 'Tis strange. (*Exeunt.*)

SCENE 4. *A room in the palace.*

Enter ANTONY *and* CLEOPATRA, *with others.*

ANT. Eros! mine armor, Eros!

CLEO.   Sleep a little.

ANT. No, my chuck.[1] Eros, come; mine armor, Eros!

Enter EROS *with armor.*

Come, good fellow, put mine iron on.
If fortune be not ours to-day, it is
Because we brave her. Come.

CLEO.   Nay, I'll help too.
What's this for?

ANT.   Ah, let be, let be! thou art
The armorer of my heart: false, false;[2] this, this.

---

[1] *Here we* i.e., here we are at our post
[2] *It signs well* It augurs well
[3] *Hercules* Shakespeare changes the forsaking god from Bacchus (as given in Plutarch) to Hercules

[4] *quarter* i.e., as far as the boundaries of our post
[1] *chuck* chick
[2] *false* wrong

CLEO. Sooth,[3] la, I'll help: thus it must be.
ANT.   Well, well,
   We shall thrive now. Seest thou, my good fellow?
   Go put on thy defenses.
EROS.   Briefly, sir.
CLEO. Is not this buckled well?
ANT.   Rarely, rarely:
   He that unbuckles this, till we do please
   To daff't [4] for our repose, shall hear a storm.
   Thou fumblest, Eros; and my queen's a squire
   More tight [5] at this than thou: dispatch. O love,
   That thou couldst see my wars to-day, and knew'st
   The royal occupation, thou shouldst see
   A workman [6] in't.

                   Enter an armed SOLDIER.

                      Good morrow to thee, welcome,
   Thou look'st like him that knows a warlike charge: [7]
   To business that we love we rise betime,[8]
   And go to't with delight.
SOLD.   A thousand, sir,
   Early though't be, have on their riveted trim,[9]
   And at the port expect you. (*Shout. Trumpets flourish.*)

                   Enter CAPTAINS *and* SOLDIERS.

CAPT. The morn is fair. Good morrow, general.
ALL. Good morrow, general.
ANT.   'Tis well blown,[10] lads.
   This morning, like the spirit of a youth
   That means to be of note, begins betimes.
   So, so; come, give me that: this way—well said.[11]
   Fare thee well, dame; whate'er becomes of me,
   This is a soldier's kiss: rebukeable [*Kisses her.*]
   And worthy shameful check [12] it were, to stand
   On more mechanic compliment.[13] I'll leave thee
   Now like a man of steel. You that will fight,
   Follow me close; I'll bring you to't. Adieu.

             Exeunt ANTONY, EROS, CAPTAINS, *and* SOLDIERS.

CHAR. Please you, retire to your chamber?
CLEO.   Lead me.
   He goes forth gallantly. That he and Caesar might
   Determine this great war in single fight!
   Then Antony—but now—Well, on. (*Exeunt.*)

---

3 *Sooth* in faith, in truth
4 *daff't* doff it, take it off
5 *tight* adept
6 *workman* craftsman
7 *charge* duty
8 *betime* early
9 *riveted trim* armor

10 *well blown* i.e., day has begun well
11 *well said* well done (addressed to Cleopatra
    who is helping him get suited in his armor)
12 *check* reproof
13 *mechanic compliment* mundane, contrived
    farewell

SCENE 5

Trumpets sound. Enter ANTONY *and* EROS;
a SOLDIER *meeting them.*

SOLD. The gods make this a happy day to Antony!
ANT. Would thou and those thy scars had once prevailed
  To make me fight at land!
SOLD.   Hadst thou done so,
  The kings that have revolted and the soldier
  That has this morning left thee would have still
  Followed thy heels.
ANT.   Who's gone this morning?
SOLD.   Who!
  One ever near thee: call for Enobarbus,
  He shall not hear thee, or from Caesar's camp
  Say 'I am none of thine.'
ANT.   What sayest thou?
SOLD.   Sir,
  He is with Caesar.
EROS.   Sir, his chests and treasure
  He has not with him.
ANT.   Is he gone?
SOLD.   Most certain.
ANT. Go, Eros, send his treasure after; do it;
  Detain no jot, I charge thee: write to him—
  I will subscribe [1]—gentle adieus and greetings;
  Say that I wish he never find more cause
  To change a master. O, my fortunes have
  Corrupted honest men! Dispatch. Enobarbus! (*Exeunt.*)

SCENE 6

Flourish. Enter AGRIPPA, CAESAR, *with*
ENOBARBUS, *and* DOLABELLA.

CAES. Go forth, Agrippa, and begin the fight:
  Our will is Antony be took alive;
  Make it so known.
AGR.   Caesar, I shall. [*Exit.*]
CAES. The time of universal peace is near:
  Prove this a prosp'rous day, the three-nooked world [1]
  Shall bear the olive freely.

Enter a MESSENGER.

MESS.   Antony
  Is come into the field.
CAES.   Go charge Agrippa
  Plant those that have revolted in the vant,[2]
  That Antony may seem to spend his fury
  Upon himself.[3] (*Exeunt all but* ENOBARBUS.)

---

[1] *subscribe* sign (as a signature)
[1] *three-nooked world* i.e., three-cornered (Europe, Africa, and Asia)

[2] *vant* forefront of the lines
[3] *himself* i.e., his former soldier allies

ENO. Alexas did revolt, and went to Jewry on
  Affairs of Antony; there did dissuade [4]
  Great Herod to incline himself to Caesar,
  And leave his master Antony. For this pains
  Caesar hath hanged him. Canidius and the rest
  That fell away have entertainment,[5] but
  No honorable trust. I have done ill,
  Of which I do accuse myself so sorely
  That I will joy no more.

Enter a SOLDIER *of* CAESAR's.

SOLD.   Enobarbus, Antony
  Hath after thee sent all thy treasure, with
  His bounty overplus. The messenger
  Came on my guard,[6] and at thy tent is now
  Unloading of his mules.
ENO.   I give it you.
SOLD. Mock not, Enobarbus,
  I tell you true: best you safed the bringer [7]
  Out of the host; I must attend mine office,
  Or would have done't myself. Your emperor
  Continues still a Jove. (*Exit.*)
ENO. I am alone the villain of the earth,
  And feel I am so most. O Antony,
  Thou mine of bounty, how wouldst thou have paid
  My better service, when my turpitude
  Thou dost so crown with gold! This blows [8] my heart:
  If swift thought [9] break it not, a swifter mean
  Shall outstrike thought; but thought will do't, I feel.
  I fight against thee! No, I will go seek
  Some ditch wherein to die; the foul'st best fits
  My latter part of life. (*Exit.*)

SCENE 7

Alarum. Drums and trumpets. Enter AGRIPPA [*and others*].

AGR. Retire, we have engaged ourselves too far.[1]
  Caesar himself has work, and our oppression [2]
  Exceeds what we expected. (*Exit.*)

Alarums. Enter ANTONY, *and* SCARUS *wounded*.

SCAR. O my brave emperor, this is fought indeed!
  Had we done so at first, we had droven them home
  With clouts [3] about their heads.
ANT.   Thou bleed'st apace.
SCAR. I had a wound here that was like a T,

[4] *dissuade* i.e., away from Antony	[9] *thought* grief
[5] *entertainment* employment	[1] *too far* over-extended the lines
[6] *on my guard* while I was on guard	[2] *oppression* difficulties, or opposition
[7] *safed the bringer* gave safe passage to	[3] *clouts* cloths, that is, bandages
[8] *blows* makes heart swell in agony	

But now 'tis made an H.[4] [*Retreat sounded afar off.*]
ANT.   They do retire.
SCAR. We'll beat 'em into bench-holes.[5] I have yet
   Room for six scotches [6] more.

Enter EROS.

EROS. They are beaten, sir, and our advantage serves
   For a fair victory.
SCAR.   Let us score [7] their backs
   And snatch 'em up, as we take hares, behind:
   'Tis sport to maul a runner.
ANT.   I will reward thee
   Once for thy sprightly comfort, and ten-fold
   For thy good valor. Come thee on.
SCAR.   I'll halt [8] after. (*Exeunt.*)

SCENE 8

Alarum. Enter ANTONY *again, in a march;* SCARUS, *with others.*

ANT. We have beat him to his camp: run one before,
   And let the queen know of our gests.[1] To-morrow,
   Before the sun shall see's, we'll spill the blood
   That has to-day escaped. I thank you all,
   For doughty-handed are you, and have fought
   Not as you served the cause, but as't had been
   Each man's like mine; you have shown [2] all Hectors.
   Enter the city, clip [3] your wives, your friends,
   Tell them your feats, whilst they with joyful tears
   Wash the congealment from your wounds, and kiss
   The honored gashes whole.

Enter CLEOPATRA.

[*To* SCARUS.]   Give me thy hand;
   To this great Fairy [4] I'll commend thy acts,
   Make her thanks bless thee. O thou day o'the world,[5]
   Chain mine armed neck; leap thou, attire and all,
   Through proof of harness to my heart, and there
   Ride on the pants [6] triumphing!
CLEO.   Lord of lords!
   O infinite virtue,[7] comest thou smiling from
   The world's great snare [8] uncaught?
ANT.   My nightingale,
   We have beat them to their beds. What, girl! though gray
   Do something mingle with our younger brown, yet ha'we

[4] *H* pun on the letter "H" which in Shakespeare's time may have been pronounced like "ache"
[5] *bench-holes* privy holes
[6] *scotches* wounds
[7] *score* mark up
[8] *halt* limp
[1] *gests* deeds
[2] *shown* i.e., shown yourself to be

[3] *clip* embrace
[4] *Fairy* enchantress
[5] *thou day o' the world* i.e., Cleopatra is likened to the sun which brings daylight to the world
[6] *Ride on the pants* i.e., as though his heart panted like a steed
[7] *virtue* valor
[8] *snare* i.e., the war and its death

A brain that nourishes our nerves,[9] and can
Get goal for goal of youth.[10] Behold this man;
Commend unto his lips thy favoring hand:
Kiss it, my warrior: he hath fought to-day
As if a god in hate of mankind had
Destroyed in such a shape.
CLEO.   I'll give thee, friend,
An armor all of gold; it was a king's.
ANT. He has deserved it, were it carbuncled [11]
Like holy Phoebus' car.[12] Give me thy hand.
Through Alexandria make a jolly march;
Bear our hacked targets [13] like the men that owe them.
Had our great palace the capacity
To camp this host, we all would sup together
And drink carouses to the next day's fate,
Which promises royal peril. Trumpeters,
With brazen din blast you the city's ear;
Make mingle with our rattling tabourines,
That heaven and earth may strike their sounds together,
Applauding our approach. (*Exeunt.*)

SCENE 9

Enter a SENTRY *and his company;* ENOBARBUS *follows.*

SENT. If we be not relieved within this hour,
We must return to the court of guard: [1] the night
Is shiny, and they say we shall embattle
By the second hour i'the morn.
1 WATCH.   This last day was
A shrewd [2] one to's.
ENO.   O, bear me witness, night,—
2 WATCH. What man is this?
1 WATCH.   Stand close, and list him.
ENO. Be witness to me, O thou blessed moon,
When men revolted shall upon record
Bear hateful memory, poor Enobarbus did
Before thy face repent!
SENT.   Enobarbus!
2 WATCH.   Peace!
Hark further.
ENO. O sovereign mistress [3] of true melancholy,
The poisonous damp of night disponge [4] upon me,
That life, a very rebel to my will,
May hang no longer on me. Throw my heart
Against the flint and hardness of my fault,
Which, being dried with grief, will break to powder,

---

9 *nerves* muscles
10 *Get goal . . . youth* keep even with youth
  in scoring tallies
11 *carbuncled* jewelled
12 *holy Phoebus' car* the chariot of the sun god
13 *targets* shields

1 *court of guard* guard-room, or location used
  to muster
2 *shrewd* hard, arduous
3 *mistress* i.e., the moon
4 *disponge* squeeze out

And finish all foul thoughts. O Antony,
Nobler than my revolt is infamous,
Forgive me in thine own particular,[5]
But let the world rank me in register
A master-leaver [6] and a fugitive.
O Antony! O Antony! [*Dies.*]

1 WATCH.   Let's speak to him.

CENT. Let's hear him, for the things he speaks
    May concern Caesar.

2 WATCH.   Let's do so. But he sleeps.

CENT. Swoons rather, for so bad a prayer as his
    Was never yet for sleep.

1 WATCH.   Go we to him.

2 WATCH. Awake, sir, awake, speak to us.

1 WATCH.   Hear you, sir?

SENT. The hand of death hath raught [7] him. Hark! the drums

Drums afar off.

Demurely [8] wake the sleepers. Let's bear him
To the court of guard: he is of note. Our hour
Is fully out.

2 WATCH.   Come on, then;
He may recover yet. (*Exeunt.*)

SCENE 10

Enter ANTONY *and* SCARUS, *with their army.*

ANT. Their preparation is to-day by sea;
    We please them not by land.

SCAR.   For both, my lord.

ANT. I would they'ld fight i'the fire or i'the air;
    We'ld fight there too. But this it is, our foot
    Upon the hills adjoining to the city
    Shall stay with us—Order for sea is given;
    They have put forth the haven—
    Where their appointment [1] we may best discover
    And look on their endeavor. (*Exeunt.*)

SCENE 11

Enter CAESAR *and his army.*

CAES. But being charged,[1] we will be still [2] by land,
    Which as I take't we shall, for his best force
    Is forth to man his galleys. To the vales,
    And hold our best advantage. (*Exeunt.*)

---

5 *own particular* yourself
6 *master-leaver* runaway servant and/or notorious traitor
7 *raught* reached

8 *demurely* solemnly, softly
1 *appointment* stratagems
1 *But being charged* unless we are attacked
2 *still* undisturbed

SCENE 12

Enter ANTONY *and* SCARUS.

ANT. Yet they are not joined: where yond pine does stand,
　　I shall discover all. I'll bring thee word
　　Straight, how 'tis like to go. (*Exit.*)

Alarum afar off, as at a sea-fight.

SCAR. 　　　　　　　　　　Swallows have built
　　In Cleopatra's sails their nests.[1] The augurers
　　Say they know not, they cannot tell, look grimly,
　　And dare not speak their knowledge. Antony
　　Is valiant, and dejected, and by starts
　　His fretted [2] fortunes give him hope and fear
　　Of what he has, and has not.

Enter ANTONY.

ANT. 　　　　　　　　　　All is lost!
　　This foul Egyptian hath betrayed me:
　　My fleet hath yielded to the foe, and yonder
　　They cast their caps up and carouse together
　　Like friends long lost. Triple-turned [3] whore! 'tis thou
　　Hast sold me to this novice, and my heart
　　Makes only wars on thee. Bid them all fly:
　　For when I am revenged upon my charm,[4]
　　I have done all. Bid them all fly, begone! [*Exit* SCARUS.]
　　O sun, thy uprise shall I see no more;
　　Fortune and Antony part here, even here
　　Do we shake hands! All come to this? The hearts
　　That spanieled me at heels, to whom I gave
　　Their wishes, do discandy,[5] melt their sweets
　　On blossoming Caesar; and this pine is barked,
　　That overtopped them all. Betrayed I am.
　　O this false soul of Egypt! this grave charm,
　　Whose eye becked forth my wars, and called them home,
　　Whose bosom was my crownet, my chief end,[6]
　　Like a right gypsy hath at fast and loose [7]
　　Beguiled me to the very heart of loss.
　　What, Eros, Eros!

Enter CLEOPATRA.

　　　　　　　　Ah, thou spell! Avaunt! [8]
CLEO. Why is my lord enraged against his love?
ANT. Vanish, or I shall give thee thy deserving,
　　And blemish Caesar's triumph. Let him take thee,
　　And hoist thee up to the shouting plebeians;

---

[1] *Swallows . . . sails* as an omen, this image is taken by Shakespeare from North's Plutarch, then simplified and employed in a different time sequence from the original narrative
[2] *fretted* varied, altered
[3] *Triple-turned* mistress to Pompey, to Julius Caesar, and to Antony
[4] *charm* now an enchantress working against Antony
[5] *discandy* melt down
[6] *my crownet, etc.* my crown and aim of my every endeavor
[7] *fast and loose* a game
[8] *Avaunt* get thee hence

Follow his chariot, like the greatest spot
Of all thy sex. Most monster-like, be shown
For poor'st diminutives,[9] for dolts, and let
Patient Octavia plough thy visage up
With her preparèd nails. (*Exit* CLEOPATRA.)
                      'Tis well thou'rt gone,
If it be well to live; but better 'twere
Thou fell'st into my fury, for one death
Might have prevented many. Eros, ho!
The shirt of Nessus [10] is upon me; teach me,
Alcides,[11] thou mine ancestor, thy rage.
Let me lodge Lichas [12] on the horns o'the moon,
And with those hands that grasped the heaviest club
Subdue my worthiest self. The witch shall die.
To the young Roman boy she hath sold me, and I fall
Under this plot: she dies for't. Eros, ho! (*Exit.*)

SCENE 13

Enter CLEOPATRA, CHARMIAN, IRAS, MARDIAN.

CLEO. Help me, my women! O, he's more mad
    Than Telamon [1] for his shield; the boar of Thessaly
    Was never so embossed.[2]
CHAR.   To the monument! [3]
    There lock yourself, and send him word you are dead.
    The soul and body rive [4] not more in parting
    Than greatness going off.
CLEO.   To the monument!
    Mardian, go tell him I have slain myself;
    Say that the last I spoke was 'Antony,'
    And word it, prithee, piteously. Hence, Mardian,
    And bring me how he takes my death. To the monument! (*Exeunt.*)

SCENE 14

Enter ANTONY *and* EROS.

ANT. Eros, thou yet behold'st me?
EROS.   Ay, noble lord.
ANT. Sometime we see a cloud that's dragonish,
    A vapor sometime like a bear or lion,
    A towered citadel, a pendent rock,
    A forkèd mountain, or blue promontory

---

9 *diminutives*   small weak creatures, i.e., Roman commoners

10 *Nessus*   legendary centaur wounded by the poisoned arrows of Hercules; Nessus had given a blood-soaked shirt to Hercules' wife as a love charm which, when worn by Hercules, caused his torture and self-destruction

11 *Alcides*   Hercules

12 *Lichas*   the innocent messenger who conveyed the poisoned shirt to Hercules and who was thereupon flung into the sky by the maddened Hercules

1 *Telamon*   Ajax Telamon, who went insane when Ulysses received Achilles' shield instead of him

2 *embossed*   enraged

3 *monument*   Cleopatra's tomb, which would have been ready in advance, as was customary

4 *rive*   rend

With trees upon't, that nod unto the world
And mock our eyes with air. Thou hast seen these signs;
They are black Vesper's pageants.[1]

EROS.   Ay, my lord.

ANT. That which is now a horse, even with a thought
The rack [2] dislimns,[3] and makes it indistinct
As water is in water.

EROS.   It does, my lord.

ANT. My good knave Eros, now thy captain is
Even such a body: here I am Antony,
Yet cannot hold this visible shape, my knave.
I made these wars for Egypt, and the queen,
Whose heart I thought I had, for she had mine,
Which, whilst it was mine, had annexed unto't
A million moe,[4] now lost—she, Eros, has
Packed cards [5] with Caesar, and false-played my glory
Unto an enemy's triumph.[6]
Nay, weep not, gentle Eros, there is left us
Ourselves to end ourselves.

Enter MARDIAN.

O, thy vile lady!
She has robbed me of my sword.[7]

MAR.   No, Antony,
My mistress loved thee and her fortunes mingled
With thine entirely.

ANT.   Hence, saucy eunuch, peace!
She hath betrayed me, and shall die the death.

MAR. Death of one person can be paid but once,
And that she has discharged. What thou wouldst do
Is done unto thy hand: the last she spake
Was 'Antony! most noble Antony!'
Then in the midst a tearing groan did break
The name of Antony; it was divided
Between her heart and lips: she rendered [8] life,
Thy name so buried in her.

ANT.   Dead then?

MAR.   Dead.

ANT. Unarm, Eros, the long day's task is done,
And we must sleep. [*To* MARDIAN.] That thou depart'st hence safe,
Does pay thy labor richly; go. (*Exit* MARDIAN.) Off, pluck off!
The seven-fold [9] shield of Ajax cannot keep
This battery from my heart. O, cleave, my sides!
Heart, once be stronger than thy continent,[10]
Crack thy frail case! Apace, Eros, apace!
No more a soldier: bruisèd pieces, go;
You have been nobly borne. From me awhile. (*Exit* EROS.)

---

1 *black Vesper's pageants* announcing the night's coming, as in a pageant heralding the approach of royalty
2 *rack* floating cloud
3 *dislimns* erases
4 *moe* more

5 *Packed cards* i.e., stacked the deck
6 *triumph* secondary sense of trump here
7 *sword* manliness, i.e., tools of soldiers
8 *rendered* gave up
9 *seven-fold* seven layers of thickness
10 *continent* i.e., the case holding it

I will o'ertake thee, Cleopatra, and
Weep for my pardon. So it must be, for now
All length [11] is torture: since the torch is out,
Lie down and stray no farther. Now all labor
Mars what it does; yea, very force entangles
Itself with strength: seal [12] then, and all is done.
Eros!—I come, my queen. Eros!—Stay for me.
Where souls do couch on flowers,[13] we'll hand in hand,
And with our sprightly port [14] make the ghosts gaze:
Dido and her Aeneas shall want troops,[15]
And all the haunt be ours. Come, Eros, Eros!

Enter EROS.

EROS. What would my lord?
ANT.   Since Cleopatra died
I have lived in such dishonor that the gods
Detest my baseness. I, that with my sword
Quartered the world, and o'er green Neptune's back
With ships made cities, condemn myself to lack [16]
The courage of a woman—less noble mind
Than she which by her death our Caesar tells
'I am conqueror of myself.' Thou art sworn, Eros,
That; when the exigent [17] should come (which now
Is come indeed) when I should see behind me
The inevitable prosecution [18] of
Disgrace and horror, that, on my command,
Thou then wouldst kill me. Do't, the time is come.
Thou strik'st not me, 'tis Caesar thou defeat'st.
Put color in thy cheek.
EROS.   The gods withhold me!
Shall I do that which all the Parthian darts,
Though enemy, lost aim and could not?
ANT.   Eros,
Wouldst thou be windowed [19] in great Rome and see
Thy master thus with pleached arms, bending down
His corrigible [20] neck, his face subdued
To penetrative [21] shame; whilst the wheeled seat
Of fortunate Caesar, drawn before him, branded
His baseness that ensued? [22]
EROS.   I would not see't.
ANT. Come, then; for with a wound I must be cured.
Draw that thy honest sword, which thou hast worn
Most useful for thy country.
EROS.   O, sir, pardon me!
ANT. When I did make thee free, swor'st thou not then
To do this when I bade thee? Do it at once

---

11 *length*   i.e., extension of life
12 *seal*   close up, here through death
13 *couch on flowers*   an allusion to the Elysian fields
14 *port*   sport, antics
15 *want troops*   lack admirers, because onlookers will shift to observing Antony and Cleopatra who will become the center of attention
16 *to lack*   for lacking

17 *exigent*   exigency, need
18 *inevitable prosecution*   unavoidable pursuit
19 *windowed*   i.e., placed in a position (as at a window) to watch
20 *corrigible*   submissive
21 *penetrative*   penetrating
22 *His . . . ensued*   the baseness of the captive following behind

Or thy precedent²³ services are all
  But accidents unpurposed. Draw, and come.
EROS. Turn from me then that noble countenance,
  Wherein the worship of the whole world lies.
ANT. [*Turns from him.*] Lo thee!
EROS. My sword is drawn.
ANT.   Then let it do at once
  The thing why thou hast drawn it.
EROS.   My dear master,
  My captain, and my emperor, let me say,
  Before I strike this bloody stroke, farewell.
ANT. 'Tis said, man, and farewell.
EROS. Farewell, great chief. Shall I strike now?
ANT.   Now, Eros.
EROS. Why, there then: thus I do escape the sorrow
  Of Antony's death. (*Kills himself.*)
ANT.   Thrice-nobler than myself!
  Thou teachest me, O valiant Eros, what
  I should, and thou couldst not. My queen and Eros
  Have by their brave instruction got upon me
  A nobleness in record;²⁴ but I will be
  A bridegroom in my death, and run into't
  As to a lover's bed. Come then; and, Eros,
  Thy master dies thy scholar: to do thus [*Falling on his sword.*]
  I learned of thee. How! not dead? not dead?
  The guard, ho! O, dispatch me!

                Enter [DECRETAS *and*] *Guard.*

1 GUARD.   What's the noise?
ANT. I have done my work ill, friends. O, make an end
  Of what I have begun.
2 GUARD.   The star is fall'n.
1 GUARD. And time is at his period.²⁵
ALL.   Alas, and woe!
ANT. Let him that loves me strike me dead.
1 GUARD.   Not I.
2 GUARD. Nor I.
3 GUARD. Nor any one. (*Exeunt.*)
DEC. Thy death and fortunes bid thy followers fly.
  This sword but shown to Caesar, with this tidings,
  Shall enter me with him.

                Enter DIOMEDES.

DIO. Where's Antony?
DEC.   There, Diomed, there.
DIO.   Lives he?
  Wilt thou not answer, man? [*Exit* DECRETAS.]
ANT. Art thou there, Diomed? Draw thy sword, and give me
  Sufficing strokes for death.
DIO.   Most absolute lord,
  My mistress Cleopatra sent me to thee.

---

²³ *precedent* earlier
²⁴ *Have . . . record* i.e., have won from me a
noble place in history by their brave deeds
²⁵ *period* end

ANT. When did she send thee?
DIO.   Now, my lord.
ANT.   Where is she?
DIO. Locked in her monument. She had a prophesying fear
   Of what hath come to pass: for when she saw—
   Which never shall be found—you did suspect
   She had disposed [26] with Caesar, and that your rage
   Would not be purged,[27] she sent you word she was dead;
   But, fearing since how it might work, hath sent
   Me to proclaim the truth, and I am come,
   I dread, too late.
ANT. Too late, good Diomed. Call my guard, I prithee.
DIO. What, ho; the emperor's guard! The guard, what, ho!
   Come, your lord calls.

               Enter four or five of the GUARD *of* ANTONY.

ANT. Bear me, good friends, where Cleopatra bides;
   'Tis the last service that I shall command you.
1 GUARD. Woe, woe are we, sir, you may not live to wear
   All your true followers out.
ALL.   Most heavy day!
ANT. Nay, good my fellows, do not please sharp fate
   To grace it with your sorrows. Bid that welcome
   Which comes to punish us, and we punish it
   Seeming to bear it lightly. Take me up:
   I have led you oft, carry me now, good friends,
   And have my thanks for all. (*Exeunt, bearing* ANTONY.)

                         SCENE 15

     Enter CLEOPATRA *and her maids aloft, with* CHARMIAN *and* IRAS.

CLEO. O Charmian, I will never go from hence.
CHAR. Be comforted, dear madam.
CLEO.   No, I will not.
   All strange and terrible events are welcome,
   But comforts we despise; our size of sorrow,
   Proportioned to our cause, must be as great
   As that which makes it.

                    Enter DIOMEDES *below*.

               How now! is he dead?
DIO. His death's upon him, but not dead.
   Look out o'the other side your monument;
   His guard have brought him thither.

                    Enter ANTONY, *and the* GUARD.

CLEO.   O sun,
   Burn the great sphere thou mov'st in, darkling [1] stand
   The varying [2] shore o'the world. O Antony,

---

[26] *disposed*   made agreements   [1] *darkling*   darkened
[27] *purged*   expelled   [2] *varying*   ever shifting

Antony, Antony! Help, Charmian, help, Iras, help;
Help, friends below, let's draw him hither.
ANT.   Peace!
Not Caesar's valor hath o'erthrown Antony,
But Antony's hath triumphed on itself.
CLEO. So it should be, that none but Antony
Should conquer Antony, but woe 'tis so!
ANT. I am dying, Egypt, dying; only
I here importune [3] death awhile, until
Of many thousand kisses the poor last
I lay upon thy lips.
CLEO.   I dare not, dear,
Dear my lord, pardon: I dare not,[4]
Lest I be taken. Not the imperious show
Of the full-fortuned Caesar ever shall
Be brooched [5] with me, if knife, drugs, serpents have
Edge, sting, or operation, I am safe:
Your wife Octavia, with her modest eyes
And still conclusion,[6] shall acquire no honor
Demuring [7] upon me. But come, come, Antony—
Help me, my women—we must draw thee up;
Assist, good friends.[8]
ANT.   O, quick, or I am gone.
CLEO. Here's sport indeed! How heavy weighs my lord!
Our strength is all gone into heaviness; [9]
That makes the weight. Had I great Juno's power,
The strong-winged Mercury should fetch thee up
And set thee by Jove's side. Yet come a little,
Wishers were ever fools. O, come, come, come.

They heave ANTONY *aloft to* CLEOPATRA.

And welcome, welcome! Die where thou hast lived,
Quicken [10] with kissing: had my lips that power,
Thus would I wear them out.
ALL.   Ah, heavy sight!
ANT. I am dying, Egypt, dying.
Give me some wine, and let me speak a little.
CLEO. No, let me speak, and let me rail so high
That the false huswife [11] Fortune break her wheel,
Provoked by my offense.
ANT.   One word, sweet queen.
Of Caesar seek your honor, with your safety. O!
CLEO. They do not go together.
ANT.   Gentle, hear me:
None about Caesar trust but Proculeius.

---

3 *importune*   request a delay from
4 *I dare not,*   the meter here is interrupted and the full meaning is left unstated; probably Cleopatra means she dare not open the doors, or else that she dare not descend to Antony who is below
5 *brooched*   adorned
6 *still conclusion*   tacit disapproval
7 *Demuring*   looking on demurely or innocently
8 by means of a rope attached to Antony's shield-litter, Cleopatra's followers are attempting to pull up the dying Antony to her chambers
9 *heaviness* two meanings are evident, as "weight" and as "grief"
10 *Quicken*   revive
11 *huswife*   wanton, strumpet

CLEO. My resolution and my hands I'll trust,
  None about Caesar.
ANT. The miserable change now at my end
  Lament nor sorrow at; but please your thoughts
  In feeding them with those my former fortunes
  Wherein I lived: the greatest prince o'the world,
  The noblest: and do now not basely die,
  Not cowardly put off my helmet to
  My countryman: a Roman by a Roman
  Valiantly vanquished.[12] Now my spirit is going,
  I can no more.
CLEO.   Noblest of men, woo't [13] die?
  Hast thou no care of me? shall I abide
  In this dull world, which in thy absence is
  No better than a sty? O, see, my women, [ANTONY *dies.*]
  The crown o'the earth doth melt. My lord!
  O, withered is the garland [14] of the war,
  The soldier's pole [15] is fall'n: young boys and girls
  Are level now with men: the odds [16] is gone,
  And there is nothing left remarkable
  Beneath the visiting moon. [*Faints.*]
CHAR.   O, quietness, lady!
IRAS. She's dead too, our sovereign.
CHAR.   Lady!
IRAS.   Madam!
CHAR. O madam, madam, madam!
IRAS.   Royal Egypt,
  Empress!
CHAR. Peace, peace, Iras!
CLEO. No more but e'en a woman, and commanded
  By such poor passion as the maid that milks
  And does the meanest chares.[17] It were for me
  To throw my sceptre at the injurious gods,
  To tell them that this world did equal theirs
  Till they had stol'n our jewel. All's but naught;
  Patience is sottish, and impatience does
  Become a dog that's mad: then is it sin
  To rush into the secret house of death,
  Ere death dare come to us? How do you, women?
  What, what! good cheer! Why, how now, Charmian!
  My noble girls! Ah, women, women, look,
  Our lamp [18] is spent, it's out! Good sirs,[19] take heart:
  We'll bury him; and then, what's brave, what's noble,
  Let's do it after the high Roman fashion,
  And make death proud to take us. Come, away.
  This case of that huge spirit now is cold.

---

12 the awkward stops connoted by the colons may
  have been a method to depict the last gasps
  of dying Antony
13 *woo't* wilt thou
14 *garland* crown
15 *pole* possibly a standard measuring spot, such
  as the North Pole, or the garlanded May-pole
  which stood at the center of sporting activities

during these celebrations in the spring
16 *odds* standards of measurement
17 *chares* chores, tasks
18 *lamp* i.e., Antony, source of light for Cleopatra
19 *sirs* Cleopatra addresses her women as such
  here

Ah, women, women! Come; we have no friend
But resolution and the briefest end. (*Exeunt, bearing off* ANTONY's *body.*)

ACT V

SCENE 1

Enter CAESAR, AGRIPPA, DOLABELLA, MAECENAS, GALLUS,
PROCULEIUS, *with his council of war.*

CAES. Go to him, Dolabella, bid him yield;
Being so frustrate,[1] tell him he mocks
The pauses that he makes.[2]
DOL.   Caesar, I shall. [*Exit.*]

Enter DECRETAS, *with the sword of* ANTONY.

CAES. Wherefore is that? and what art thou that darest
Appear thus to us?
DEC.   I am called Decretas.
Mark Antony I served, who best was worthy
Best to be served: whilst he stood up and spoke,
He was my master, and I wore my life
To spend upon his haters. If thou please
To take me to thee, as I was to him
I'll be to Caesar; if thou pleasest not,
I yield thee up my life.
CAES.   What is't thou say'st?
DEC. I say, O Caesar, Antony is dead.
CAES. The breaking of so great a thing should make
A greater crack. The round world
Should have shook lions into civil streets,[3]
And citizens to their dens. The death of Antony
Is not a single doom; in that name lay
A moiety[4] of the world.
DEC.   He is dead, Caesar,
Not by a public minister of justice,
Nor by a hirèd knife; but that self[5] hand
Which writ his honor in the acts it did,
Hath, with the courage which the heart did lend it,
Splitted the heart. This is his sword;
I robbed his wound of it; behold it stained
With his most noble blood.
CAES.   Look you sad, friends?
The gods rebuke me, but it is tidings
To wash the eyes of kings.
AGR.   And strange it is
That nature must compel us to lament
Our most persisted[6] deeds.

---

1 *frustrate* stymied
2 *mocks . . . makes* makes his delaying ridiculous
3 *civil streets* city streets

4 *moiety* half
5 *self* same
6 *persisted* i.e., persistently repeated

MAE.   His taints and honors
    Waged equal [7] with him.
    AGR.   A rarer spirit never
    Did steer humanity; but you, gods, will give us
    Some faults to make us men. Caesar is touched.
    MAE. When such a spacious mirror's set before him,
    He needs must see himself.
    CAES.   O Antony!
    I have followed thee to this. But we do lance
    Diseases in our bodies. I must perforce
    Have shown to thee such a declining day,
    Or look on thine; we could not stall [8] together
    In the whole world. But yet let me lament
    With tears as sovereign as the blood of hearts,
    That thou, my brother, my competitor [9]
    In top of all design,[10] my mate in empire,
    Friend and companion in the front of war,
    The arm of mine own body, and the heart
    Where mine his thoughts did kindle, that our stars
    Unreconciliable should divide
    Our equalness to this. Hear me, good friends—

                    Enter an EGYPTIAN.

    But I will tell you at some meeter [11] season.
    The business of this man looks out of him; [12]
    We'll hear him what he says. Whence are you?
    EGYP. A poor Egyptian, yet the queen my mistress,
    Confined in all she has, her monument,
    Of thy intents desires instruction,
    That she preparèdly may frame herself
    To the way she's forced to.
    CAES.   Bid her have good heart:
    She soon shall know of us, by some of ours,
    How honorable and how kindly we
    Determine for her; for Caesar cannot live
    To be ungentle.
    EGYP.   So the gods preserve thee! (*Exit.*)
    CAES. Come hither, Proculeius. Go and say
    We purpose her no shame: give her what comforts
    The quality of her passion [13] shall require,
    Lest in her greatness by some mortal stroke
    She do defeat us. For her life in Rome
    Would be eternal in our triumph.[14] Go,
    And with your speediest bring us what she says
    And how you find of her.
    PRO.   Caesar, I shall. (*Exit* PROCULEIUS.)
    CAES. Gallus, go you along. [*Exit* GALLUS.] Where's Dolabella,
    To second Proculeius?

7 *Waged equal* were balanced evenly
8 *stall* dwell, abide
9 *competitor* partner
10 *In top . . . design* in every lofty scheme or
    enterprise
11 *meeter* more appropriate

12 *looks out of him* i.e., is evident in the looks
    in his eyes
13 *passion* grief
14 *her life . . . triumph* i.e., taking back the
    captive Cleopatra to Rome would eternalize
    the triumph and her name

ALL.   Dolabella!
CAES. Let him alone; for I remember now
    How he's employed: he shall in time be ready.
    Go with me to my tent, where you shall see
    How hardly I was drawn into this war,
    How calm and gentle I proceeded still
    In all my writings.[15] Go with me, and see
    What I can show in this. (*Exeunt.*)

SCENE 2

Enter CLEOPATRA, CHARMIAN, IRAS, *and* MARDIAN.

CLEO. My desolation does begin to make
    A better life.[1] 'Tis paltry to be Caesar;
    Not being Fortune, he's but Fortune's knave,[2]
    A minister of her will: and it is great
    To do that thing that ends all other deeds,
    Which shackles accidents and bolts up change;
    Which sleeps, and never palates more the dung,
    The beggar's nurse and Caesar's.[3]

Enter PROCULEIUS.[4]

PRO. Caesar sends greeting to the Queen of Egypt,
    And bids thee study on what fair demands
    Thou mean'st to have him grant thee.
CLEO.   What's thy name?
PRO. My name is Proculeius.
CLEO.   Antony
    Did tell me of you, bade me trust you, but
    I do not greatly care to be deceived,[5]
    That have no use for trusting. If your master
    Would have a queen his beggar, you must tell him
    That majesty, to keep decorum, must
    No less beg than a kingdom: if he please
    To give me conquered Egypt for my son,
    He gives me so much of mine own as [6] I
    Will kneel to him with thanks.
PRO.   Be of good cheer;
    You're fall'n into a princely hand, fear nothing.
    Make your full reference [7] freely to my lord,
    Who is so full of grace that it flows over
    On all that need. Let me report to him
    Your sweet dependency, and you shall find
    A conqueror that will pray in aid [8] for kindness,

---

15 *writings* dispatches to Antony
1 *better life* i.e., a life judged more accurately
   as to values
2 *knave* lackey
3 *never . . . Caesar's* i.e., never again to partake of earthly (dung-fertilized) fruit which
   sustained both beggars and Caesar alike
4 While Proculeius speaks to Cleopatra before
   the gates of the monument, other Roman

soldiers are stealthily entering the structure
   unseen
5 *to be deceived* usually taken as "whether or
   not I am deceived"
6 *as* that
7 *reference* appeal
8 *pray in aid* ask aid in listing favors to be
   done

Where he for grace is kneeled to.

CLEO.   Pray you, tell him
I am his fortune's vassal, and I send him
The greatness he has got. I hourly learn
A doctrine of obedience, and would gladly
Look him i'the face.

PRO.   This I'll report, dear lady.
Have comfort, for I know your plight is pitied
Of him that caused it.

        [Enter GALLUS *and other Roman soldier from behind suddenly.]*

GAL. You see how easily she may be surprised.
Guard her till Caesar come.

IRAS. Royal queen!

CHAR. O Cleopatra! thou art taken, queen!

CLEO. Quick, quick, good hands. *[Drawing a dagger.]*

PRO.   Hold, worthy lady, hold!

        [Seizes and disarms her.]

Do not yourself such wrong, who are in this
Relieved,[9] but not betrayed.

CLEO.   What, of death too,
That rids our dogs of languish? [10]

PRO.   Cleopatra,
Do not abuse my master's bounty by
The undoing of yourself: let the world see
His nobleness well acted,[11] which your death
Will never let come forth.

CLEO.   Where art thou, death?
Come hither, come! come, come, and take a queen
Worth many babes and beggars!

PRO.   O, temperance,[12] lady!

CLEO. Sir, I will eat no meat, I'll not drink, sir—
If idle talk will once be necessary—
I'll not sleep neither. This mortal house I'll ruin,
Do Caesar what he can. Know, sir, that I
Will not wait pinioned at your master's court,
Nor once be chastised with the sober eye
Of dull Octavia. Shall they hoist me up
And show me to the shouting varletry [13]
Of censuring Rome? Rather a ditch in Egypt
Be gentle grave unto me! rather on Nilus' mud
Lay me stark nak'd, and let the water-flies
Blow me [14] into abhorring! rather make
And hang me up in chains!
My country's high pyramides my gibbet,

PRO.   You do extend
These thoughts of horror further than you shall
Find cause in Caesar.

        Enter DOLABELLA.

---

9 *Relieved* rescued
10 *languish* suffering
11 *acted* enacted

12 *temperance* moderation
13 *varletry* rabble
14 *Blow me* swell me up

DOL.   Proculeius,
   What thou hast done thy master Caesar knows,
   And he hath sent for thee; for the queen,
   I'll take her to my guard.
PRO.   So, Dolabella,
   It shall content me best: be gentle to her.
   [*To Cleopatra.*] To Caesar I will speak what you shall please,
   If you'll employ me to him.
CLEO.   . Say, I would die. (*Exit* PROCULEIUS.)
DOL. Most noble Empress, you have heard of me?
CLEO. I cannot tell.
DOL.   Assuredly you know me.
CLEO. No matter, sir, what I have heard or known.
   You laugh when boys or women tell their dreams;
   Is't not your trick?
DOL.   I understand not, madam.
CLEO. I dreamed there was an Emperor Antony.
   O, such another sleep, that I might see
   But such another man!
DOL.   If it might please ye—
CLEO. His face was as the heavens, and therein stuck
   A sun and moon, which kept their course and lighted
   The little O, the earth.
DOL.   Most sovereign creature—
CLEO. His legs bestrid the ocean; his reared arm
   Crested the world: his voice was propertied
   As all the tunèd spheres,[15] and that to friends;
   But when he meant to quail [16] and shake the orb,[17]
   He was as rattling thunder. For his bounty,
   There was no winter in't; an autumn 'twas
   That grew the more by reaping: his delights
   Were dolphin-like, they showed his back above
   The element they lived in: [18] in his livery
   Walked crowns and crownets; [19] realms and islands were
   As plates [20] dropped from his pocket.
DOL.   Cleopatra—
CLEO. Think you there was, or might be, such a man
   As this I dreamed of?
DOL.   Gentle madam, no.
CLEO. You lie, up to the hearing of the gods.
   But if there be or ever were one such,
   It's past the size of dreaming: nature wants stuff
   To vie strange forms with Fancy, yet t'imagine
   An Antony were Nature's piece 'gainst Fancy,
   Condemning shadows quite.
DOL.   Hear me, good madam.
   Your loss is as yourself, great; and you bear it
   As answering to the weight: would I might never

---

[15] *was propertied . . . spheres* was as musical
in nature as
[16] *quail* terrorize
[17] *orb* earth
[18] *delights . . . lived in* i.e., Antony, like the
dolphin rising above the surface of the water,
rose above the pleasures in which he lived
[19] *crowns and crownets* i.e., monarchs and
princes
[20] *plates* silver coins

O'ertake pursued success,[21] but I do feel,
By the rebound of yours, a grief that smites
My very heart at root.
CLEO.   I thank you, sir.
Know you what Caesar means to do with me?
DOL. I am loath to tell you what I would you knew.
CLEO. Nay, pray you, sir,—
DOL.   Though he be honorable,—
CLEO. He'll lead me then in triumph?
DOL. Madam, he will, I know't.

Flourish. Enter PROCULEIUS, CAESAR, GALLUS, MAECENAS,
and others of his train.

ALL. Make way there! Caesar!
CAES. Which is the Queen of Egypt? [22]
DOL. It is the Emperor, madam. (CLEOPATRA *kneels.*)
CAES. Arise, you shall not kneel:
I pray you, rise, rise, Egypt.
CLEO.   Sir, the gods
Will have it thus; my master and my lord
I must obey.
CAES.   Take to you no hard thoughts;
The record of what injuries you did us,
Though written in our flesh, we shall remember
As things but done by chance.
CLEO.   Sole sir o' the world,
I cannot project mine own cause so well
To make it clear, but do confess I have
Been laden with like frailties which before
Have often shamed our sex.
CAES.   Cleopatra, know,
We will extenuate rather than enforce: [23]
If you apply yourself to our intents,
Which towards you are most gentle, you shall find
A benefit in this change; but if you seek
To lay on me a cruelty by taking
Antony's course, you shall bereave [24] yourself
Of my good purposes, and put your children
To that destruction which I'll guard them from
If thereon you rely. I'll take my leave.
CLEO. And may, through all the world: 'tis yours, and we,
Your scutcheons [25] and your signs of conquest, shall
Hang in what place you please. Here, my good lord. [*Offering a scroll.*]
CAES. You shall advise me in all for Cleopatra.
CLEO. This is the brief [26] of money, plate and jewels,
I am possessed of: 'tis exactly valued,
Not petty things admitted. Where's Seleucus?

[*Enter* SELEUCUS.]

---

21 *would I . . . success* i.e., May I never attain my goal if I do not
22 *Which is the Queen of Egypt?* an obvious
tactical opening in the verbal exchange to
follow

23 *enforce* emphasize
24 *bereave* deprive
25 *scutcheons* emblems of victory
26 *brief* listing

SEL. Here, madam.

CLEO. This is my treasurer. Let him speak, my lord,
Upon his peril, that I have reserved
To myself nothing. Speak the truth, Seleucus.

SEL. Madam,
I had rather seal my lips than to my peril
Speak that which is not.

CLEO.   What have I kept back?

SEL. Enough to purchase what you have made known.

CAES. Nay, blush not, Cleopatra; I approve
Your wisdom in the deed.

CLEO.   See, Caesar! O, behold,
How pomp is followed! mine 27 will now be yours,
And, should we shift estates, yours would be mine.
The ingratitude of this Seleucus does
Even make me wild. O slave, of no more trust
Than love that's hired! What, goest thou back? 28 thou shalt
Go back, I warrant thee; but I'll catch thine eyes,
Though they had wings. Slave, soulless villain, dog!
O rarely base! [*Striking him.*]

CAES.   Good queen, let us entreat you.

CLEO. O Caesar, what a wounding shame is this,
That thou, vouchsafing here to visit me,
Doing the honor of thy lordliness
To one so meek, that mine own servant should
Parcel 29 the sum of my disgraces by
Addition of his envy. Say, good Caesar,
That I some lady trifles have reserved,
Immoment 30 toys, things of such dignity 31
As we greet modern 32 friends withal; and say,
Some nobler token I have kept apart
For Livia and Octavia, to induce
Their mediation; must I be unfolded 33
With 34 one that I have bred? The gods! it smites me
Beneath the fall I have. [*To* SELEUCUS.] Prithee, go hence,
Or I shall show the cinders of my spirits
Through the ashes of my chance: wert thou a man,
Thou wouldst have mercy on me.

CAES.   Forbear, Seleucus. [*Exit* SELEUCUS.]

CLEO. Be it known, that we, the greatest, are misthought 35
For things that others do; and when we fall,
We answer others' merits in our name,36
Are therefore to be pitied.

CAES.   Cleopatra,
Not what you have reserved, nor what acknowledged,
Put we i'the roll of conquest: still be't yours,
Bestow it at your pleasure, and believe
Caesar's no merchant, to make price 37 with you

---

27 *mine*   i.e., my retainers
28 *What . . . back?*   Seleucus is cringing and
backing away from the menacing queen
29 *Parcel*   piece out
30 *Immoment*   of small consequence—
31 *dignity*   value

32 *modern*   ordinary
33 *unfolded*   be discovered
34 *With*   by
35 *misthought*   taken amiss
36 *merits . . . name*   errors in our name
37 *make price*   to bargain

Of things that merchants sold. Therefore be cheered,
Make not your thoughts your prisons: no, dear queen,
For we intend so to dispose you as
Yourself shall give us counsel. Feed, and sleep:
Our care and pity is so much upon you
That we remain your friend; and so, adieu.

CLEO. My master, and my lord!

CAES.   Not so. Adieu.

Flourish. Exeunt CAESAR *and his train.*

CLEO. He words me, girls, he words me,[38] that I should not
   Be noble to myself![39] But hark thee, Charmian. [*Whispers* CHARMIAN.]

IRAS. Finish, good lady, the bright day is done,
   And we are for the dark.

CLEO.   Hie thee again,
   I have spoke already, and it is provided;
   Go put it to the haste.

CHAR.   Madam, I will.

Re-enter DOLABELLA.

DOL. Where's the queen?

CHAR.   Behold, sir.

CLEO.   Dolabella!

DOL. Madam, as thereto sworn by your command
   (Which my love makes religion to obey),
   I tell you this: Caesar through Syria
   Intends his journey, and within three days
   You with your children will he send before.
   Make your best use of this. I have performed
   Your pleasure and my promise.

CLEO.   Dolabella,
   I shall remain your debtor.

DOL.   I your servant.
   Adieu, good queen; I must attend on Caesar. (*Exit.*)

CLEO. Farewell, and thanks.
                              Now, Iras, what think'st thou?
   Thou, an Egyptian puppet,[40] shalt be shown
   In Rome, as well as I: mechanic [41] slaves
   With greasy aprons, rules, and hammers shall
   Uplift us to the view; [42] in their thick breaths,
   Rank of gross diet, shall we be enclouded
   And forced to drink their vapor.

IRAS.   The gods forbid!

CLEO. Nay, 'tis most certain, Iras. Saucy lictors [43]
   Will catch at us like strumpets, and scald [44] rhymers
   Ballad us out o'tune: the quick comedians
   Extemporally will stage us, and present
   Our Alexandrian revels. Antony

---

38 *He words me*   i.e., he tries to trick me with
his smooth words
39 *Be noble*   i.e., by committing suicide
40 *Egyptian puppet*   i.e., subject tale for puppet
shows which were a very popular form of

entertainment at the time
41 *mechanic*   those who work manually
42 *to the view*   put on display
43 *lictors*   minor Roman officials
44 *scald*   scurvy

Shall be brought drunken forth, and I shall see
Some squeaking Cleopatra [45] boy my greatness
I'the posture of a whore.
IRAS.   O the good gods!
CLEO. Nay, that's certain.
IRAS. I'll never see't! for I am sure my nails
Are stronger than mine eyes.
CLEO.   Why, that's the way
To fool their preparation, and to conquer
Their most absurd intents.

Enter CHARMIAN.

                    Now, Charmian!
Show me, my women, like a queen: go fetch
My best attires. I am again for Cydnus,
To meet Mark Antony. Sirrah [46] Iras, go.
Now, noble Charmian, we'll dispatch indeed,
And when thou hast done this chare,[47] I'll give thee leave
To play till doomsday. Bring our crown and all.

                    [*Exit* IRAS.] *A noise within.*
Wherefore's this noise?

Enter a GUARDSMAN.

GUARDSM.   Here is a rural fellow
That will not be denied your highness' presence.
He brings you figs.
CLEO. Let him come in. (*Exit* GUARDSMAN.)
                    What poor an instrument
May do a noble deed! he brings me liberty.
My resolution's placed, and I have nothing
Of woman in me: now from head to foot
I am marble-constant; now the fleeting moon [48]
No planet is of mine.

Enter GUARDSMAN *with* CLOWN [49] *bringing in a basket.*

GUARDSM.   This is the man.
CLEO. Avoid,[50] and leave him. (*Exit* GUARDSMAN.)
Hast thou the pretty worm [51] of Nilus there,
That kills and pains not?
CLOWN. Truly, I have him: but I would not be the party that should de-
    sire you to touch him, for his biting is immortal; [52] those that do die of
    it do seldom or never recover.
CLEO. Remember'st thou any that have died on't?
CLOWN. Very many, men and women too. I heard of one of them no longer
    than yesterday—a very honest [53] woman, but something given to lie, as
    a woman should not do but in the way of honesty—how she died of the

45 *squeaking Cleopatra*   a boy actor would be
taking the role of Cleopatra, she realizes,
hence the squeaking voice
46 *Sirrah*   applied to women at times, also
47 *chare*   chore, task
48 *moon*   Cleopatra again compares herself in-
directly to the goddess Isis, monarch of the

moon
49 *Clown*   rustic
50 *Avoid*   go
51 *worm*   snake, asp
52 *immortal*   lethal
53 *honest*   respectable

biting of it, what pain she felt. Truly, she makes a very good report o'the worm; but he that will believe all that they say, shall never be saved by half that they do: but this is most falliable,[54] the worm's an odd worm.

CLEO. Get thee hence; farewell.

CLOWN. I wish you all joy of the worm.

CLEO. Farewell.

CLOWN. You must think this, look you, that the worm will do his kind.[55]

CLEO. Ay, ay; farewell.

CLOWN. Look you, the worm is not to be trusted but in the keeping of wise people: for indeed there is no goodness in the worm.

CLEO. Take thou no care, it shall be heeded.[56]

CLOWN. Very good: give it nothing, I pray you, for it is not worth the feeding.

CLEO. Will it eat me?

CLOWN. You must not think I am so simple but I know the devil himself will not eat a woman: I know that a woman is a dish for the gods, if the devil dress [57] her not. But, truly, these same whoreson devils do the gods great harm in their women; for in every ten that they make, the devils mar five.

CLEO. Well, get thee gone; farewell.

CLOWN. Yes, forsooth. I wish you joy o'the worm. (*Exit.*)

[*Re-enter* IRAS *with a robe, crown, etc.*]

CLEO. Give me my robe, put on my crown, I have
　　Immortal longings in me. Now no more
　　The juice of Egypt's grape shall moist this lip.
　　Yare, yare,[58] good Iras; quick. Methinks I hear
　　Antony call; I see him rouse himself
　　To praise my noble act. I hear him mock
　　The luck of Caesar, which the gods give men
　　To excuse their after wrath. Husband, I come:
　　Now to that name my courage prove my title!
　　I am fire and air; my other elements
　　I give to baser life.[59] So, have you done?
　　Come then, and take the last warmth of my lips.
　　Farewell, kind Charmian, Iras, long farewell.

[*Kisses them.* IRAS *falls and dies.*]

　　Have I the aspic [60] in my lips? Dost fall?
　　If thou and nature can so gently part,
　　The stroke of death is as a lover's pinch,
　　Which hurts, and is desired. Dost thou lie still?
　　If thus thou vanishest, thou tell'st the world
　　It is not worth leave-taking.

CHAR. Dissolve, thick cloud, and rain, that I may say
　　The gods themselves do weep!

CLEO. 　　　　　　　　　　This proves me base:
　　If she first meet the curlèd Antony,

---

[54] *falliable*　Clown's slip of the tongue for "in-fallible"

[55] *do his kind*　i.e., act according to his nature

[56] *heeded*　kept under guard

[57] *dress*　i.e., prepare for cooking in Hell, hence a pun

[58] *Yare*　quick

[59] *fire and air, etc.*　these are the lighter of the four elements; Cleopatra bequeaths the two baser (and heavier) elements, water and earth, to mortals

[60] *aspic*　asp

He'll make demand of her, and spend that kiss
Which is my heaven to have. Come, thou mortal wretch,

[*To an asp, which she applies to her breast.*]

With thy sharp teeth this knot intrinsicate [61]
Of life at once untie: poor venomous fool,
Be angry, and dispatch.[62] O, couldst thou speak,
That I might hear thee call great Caesar ass,
Unpolicied! [63]
CHAR.   O eastern star!
CLEO.   Peace, peace!
Dost thou not see my baby at my breast,
That sucks the nurse asleep?
CHAR.   O, break! O, break!
CLEO. As sweet as balm, as soft as air, as gentle—
O Antony!—Nay, I will take thee too:

[*Applying another asp to her arm.*]

What should I stay— (*Dies.*)
CHAR. In this wild world? So, fare thee well.
Now boast thee, death, in thy possession lies
A lass unparalleled. Downy windows, close;
And golden Phoebus never be beheld
Of eyes again so royal! Your crown's awry,
I'll mend it, and then play—

Enter the GUARD, *rustling in.*

1 GUARD. Where's the queen?
CHAR.   Speak softly, wake her not.
1 GUARD. Caesar hath sent—
CHAR.   Too slow a messenger. [*Applies an asp.*]
O, come apace, dispatch, I partly feel thee.
1 GUARD. Approach, ho! All's not well: Caesar's beguiled.[64]
2 GUARD. There's Dolabella sent from Caesar; call him.
1 GUARD. What work is here! Charmian, is this well done?
CHAR. It is well done, and fitting for a princess
Descended of so many royal kings.
Ah, soldier! (CHARMIAN *dies.*)

Enter DOLABELLA.

DOL. How goes it here?
2 GUARD.   All dead.
DOL.   Caesar, thy thoughts
Touch their effects in this: thyself art coming
To see performed the dreaded act which thou
So sought'st to hinder.
[*Within.* "A way there, a way for Caesar!"]

Enter CAESAR *and all his train, marching.*

DOL. O sir, you are too sure an augurer;
That you did fear is done.

61 *intrinsicate* intricate   63 *unpolicied* plans gone awry
62 *dispatch* make haste   64 *beguiled* tricked

CAES. Bravest at the last,
She levelled at [65] our purposes, and being royal
Took her own way. The manner of their deaths?
I do not see them bleed.
DOL. Who was last with them?
1 GUARD. A simple countryman, that brought her figs:
This was his basket.
CAES. Poisoned then.
1 GUARD. O Caesar,
This Charmian lived but now, she stood and spake:
I found her trimming up the diadem
On her dead mistress; tremblingly she stood,
And on the sudden dropped.
CAES. O noble weakness!
If they had swallowed poison, 'twould appear
By external swelling: but she looks like sleep,
As she would catch another Antony
In her strong toil [66] of grace.
DOL. Here, on her breast,
There is a vent of blood, and something blown;
The like is on her arm.
1 GUARD. This is an aspic's trail, and these fig-leaves
Have slime upon them, such as the aspic leaves
Upon the caves of Nile.
CAES. Most probable
That so she died; for her physician tells me
She hath pursued conclusions [67] infinite
Of easy ways to die. Take up her bed,
And bear her women from the monument.
She shall be buried by her Antony.
No grave upon the earth shall clip [68] in it
A pair so famous. High events as these
Strike [69] those that make them; and their story is
No less in pity than his glory which
Brought them to be lamented. Our army shall
In solemn show attend this funeral,
And then to Rome. Come, Dolabella, see
High order in this great solemnity. (*Exeunt omnes.*)

[65] *levelled at* figured out
[66] *toil* snare
[67] *conclusions* experiments
[68] *clip* embrace
[69] *strike* afflict, affect

ROUND DANCE

Arthur Schnitzler

TRANSLATED BY
Eric Bentley

CHARACTERS

THE PROSTITUTE
THE SOLDIER
THE HOUSEMAID
THE YOUNG GENTLEMAN
THE YOUNG WIFE
THE HUSBAND
THE LITTLE DARLING
THE POET
THE ACTRESS
THE COUNT
SERVANT

The Time: The eighteen-nineties

The Place: Vienna

THE DIALOGUES

I
THE PROSTITUTE AND
THE SOLDIER

Late evening on the Augarten Bridge. THE
SOLDIER, *whistling, on his way home.*

THE PROSTITUTE: Hello, good lookin'! (THE
SOLDIER *turns and goes on.*) What's your
hurry?

THE SOLDIER: Me, good-lookin'?

THE PROSTITUTE: Sure, who do you think?
Say, come on. My place is right around the
corner.

THE SOLDIER: I haven't got time. I got to get
back to the barracks.

THE PROSTITUTE: You've got plenty of time
to get back to your barracks. It's nicer here
with me.

THE SOLDIER (*close to her*): Yeah?

THE PROSTITUTE: Ps-st! Look out for the
cops.

THE SOLDIER: Cops! Say, I've got a night
stick, myself.

THE PROSTITUTE: Come on.

THE SOLDIER: Let me alone, I'm broke anyway.

THE PROSTITUTE: I don't want your money.

THE SOLDIER (*stopping. They are under a
street-lamp*): You don't want money?
What kind of a dame are you?

THE PROSTITUTE: Civilians pay me for it but
a guy like you doesn't have to pay for
things.

THE SOLDIER: Maybe you're the girl my
buddy told me about.

THE PROSTITUTE: I don't know any buddy of
yours.

THE SOLDIER: You're the one, all right! You
know—the cafe down the street. He went
home with you.

THE PROSTITUTE: I've taken lots of 'em home
with me from that place . . . lots of 'em!

THE SOLDIER: All right. Let's go!

THE PROSTITUTE: In a hurry now, huh?

THE SOLDIER: Well, what are you waiting
for? Say, gal, I've got to be back at the
barracks by ten.

THE PROSTITUTE: Been in the service long?

THE SOLDIER: What do you care how long
I've been in? Is it far?

THE PROSTITUTE: Make it in ten minutes.

THE SOLDIER: Too far for me. Give's a kiss.

THE PROSTITUTE (*kissing him*): That's what
I like best—when I love 'em.

THE SOLDIER: I don't. No. Can't go with you.
It's too far.

THE PROSTITUTE: Say, how about to-morrow
afternoon?

THE SOLDIER: Fine. Let's have your address.

THE PROSTITUTE: But maybe you won't come.

THE SOLDIER: Me! I will, if I say I will.

THE PROSTITUTE: Look here—if my place is
too far—over there . . . tonight. (*She
points toward the Danube.*)

THE SOLDIER: What's there?

THE PROSTITUTE: It's nice and quiet there
. . . no one around.

THE SOLDIER: Say, that's no good.

THE PROSTITUTE: It's always good with me.
Come on. Who knows? We may be dead
tomorrow.

THE SOLDIER: All right, let's go—but make
it snappy.

THE PROSTITUTE: Oh, it's so dark. Look out!
You'll fall in the river.

THE SOLDIER: Good thing if I did, I guess.

THE PROSTITUTE: Sh-h. Wait, we're coming
to a bench.

THE SOLDIER: You seem to know all about
this place.

THE PROSTITUTE: I'd like to have a guy like
you for a boy friend.

THE SOLDIER: I'd make you jealous all the
time.

THE PROSTITUTE: I'll fix that, all right.

THE SOLDIER: Is zat so?

THE PROSTITUTE: Don't make such a racket.
There's cops around. We're right in the
middle of Vienna.

THE SOLDIER: Come on. Come over here.

THE PROSTITUTE: Crazy! We'll fall in the
river.

THE SOLDIER (*has grabbed her*): Oh you—

THE PROSTITUTE: Hold me tight.

THE SOLDIER: Don't be afraid.

* * * * *

THE PROSTITUTE: It'd have been nicer on the
bench.

THE SOLDIER: It's all the same to me . . .
Well, get up.

THE PROSTITUTE: What's your hurry—?

THE SOLDIER: Got to get to the barracks.
I'm late already.

THE PROSTITUTE: Say, what's your name?

THE SOLDIER: What do you care what's my name?

THE PROSTITUTE: My name's Leocadia.

THE SOLDIER: What a name!

THE PROSTITUTE: Say!

THE SOLDIER: Well, what do you want?

THE PROSTITUTE: Give's two-bits for the janitor.

THE SOLDIER: Huh! . . . What do you think I am? A meal-ticket? Good-bye, Leocadia . . .

THE PROSTITUTE: Rat! Heel! (*He has disappeared.*)

II
THE SOLDIER AND THE HOUSEMAID

Prater Gardens. Sunday evening. A path leading away from the amusement park. Trees. Darkness. The wild medley from the amusement park can still be heard; also strains of music from the cheap dancehall, a vulgar polka, played by a brass band.
THE SOLDIER. THE HOUSEMAID.

THE HOUSEMAID: Now tell me why you wanted to leave. (THE SOLDIER *grins sheepishly.*) It was so nice, and I love to dance. (THE SOLDIER *puts his arm around her waist. She submits.*) But we aren't dancing. Why do you hold me so tight?

THE SOLDIER: What's your name? Katy?

THE HOUSEMAID: You've got a "Katy" on your brain.

THE SOLDIER: I know—I know . . . Marie.

THE HOUSEMAID: Goodness, it's dark here. I'm afraid.

THE SOLDIER: You needn't be afraid when I'm with you. I know how to run things.

THE HOUSEMAID: But where are we going? And nobody around. Come, let's go back! . . . It's so dark!

THE SOLDIER (*pulling at his Virginia cigar until it glows brightly*): There . . . it's lighter already. Ha—ha! Oh, you little treasure!

THE HOUSEMAID: Oh! What are you doing! If I had thought this was what you—

THE SOLDIER: I'll be a son-of-a-gun if there was any one around here who felt softer and rounder than you, Fräulein Marie.

THE HOUSEMAID: How do you know? Have you felt all of them?

THE SOLDIER: A guy notices things dancing. Lots of things!

THE HOUSEMAID: But you danced with that sourpuss blonde a lot more than you did with me.

THE SOLDIER: She's an old friend of my buddy's.

THE HOUSEMAID: That corporal with the turned-up mustache?

THE SOLDIER: No, I mean the civilian. You know, the one who was talking with me at the table before we started dancing. The one who talks so hoarse.

THE HOUSEMAID: Oh, I know. He's pretty fresh.

THE SOLDIER: Did he do anything to you? I'll show him! What did he do to you?

THE HOUSEMAID: Oh, nothing . . . I noticed what he did with the others.

THE SOLDIER: Say, Fräulein Marie . . .

THE HOUSEMAID: You'll burn me with your cigar.

THE SOLDIER: Pardon me! Fräulein Marie— or may I say Marie?

THE HOUSEMAID: We're not such good friends yet . . .

THE SOLDIER: Lots of people that don't like each other don't say Herr and Fräulein.

THE HOUSEMAID: Next time, if we . . . But, Franz!

THE SOLDIER: Oh, you got my name?

THE HOUSEMAID: But Franz . . .

THE SOLDIER: That's right, call me Franz, Fräulein Marie.

THE HOUSEMAID: Don't get fresh—but, sh-h, suppose some one should come!

THE SOLDIER: What if they did? They couldn't see a thing. Even a foot away.

THE HOUSEMAID: For goodness' sake, where are we going?

THE SOLDIER: Look! There's two just like us.

THE HOUSEMAID: Where? I can't see anything.

THE SOLDIER: There . . . straight ahead.

THE HOUSEMAID: Why do you say: "two like us"?

THE SOLDIER: Well, I mean, they like each other, too.

THE HOUSEMAID: Look out! What's that there? I nearly fell.

THE SOLDIER: Oh, that's the gate. There's a meadow on the other side.

THE HOUSEMAID: Don't shove me. I'll fall.

THE SOLDIER: Sh-h, not so loud.

THE HOUSEMAID: Stop! I'm going to scream
—What are you doing? But—

THE SOLDIER: There's no one around.

THE HOUSEMAID: Then, let's go back where
there's people.

THE SOLDIER: We don't want people. Why
Marie, what . . . we want . . . Ho! Ho!

THE HOUSEMAID: Herr Franz, please, for
heaven's sake! Listen to me. If I had . . .
known . . . oh . . . do . . .

* * * * *

THE SOLDIER (blissfully): Well, I'm damned
. . . Oh . . .

THE HOUSEMAID: I can't see your face . . .

THE SOLDIER: Face?—Hell!

* * * * *

THE SOLDIER: Well, Fräulein Marie, you
can't stay here all night.

THE HOUSEMAID: Please, Franz, help me.

THE SOLDIER: Oh, get up.

THE HOUSEMAID: Oh, good heavens, Franz!

THE SOLDIER: Well, what do you want?

THE HOUSEMAID: You're a wicked man,
Franz.

THE SOLDIER: Uhum . . . Say, wait a minute.

THE HOUSEMAID: Why are you leaving me?

THE SOLDIER: Can't you let me light my
cigar?

THE HOUSEMAID: It's so dark.

THE SOLDIER: It'll be light again tomorrow
morning.

THE HOUSEMAID: Tell me you love me, anyways.

THE SOLDIER: Well, you must have felt that,
Fräulein Marie—

THE HOUSEMAID: Where are we going now?

THE SOLDIER: Back, of course.

THE HOUSEMAID: Please don't walk so fast.

THE SOLDIER: Well, what's the matter? I
don't like to hang around in the dark.

THE HOUSEMAID: Tell me, Franz . . . do
you love me?

THE SOLDIER: I just told you I loved you!

THE HOUSEMAID: Won't you give me a little
kiss?

THE SOLDIER (condescendingly): There . . .
Listen . . . The music again.

THE HOUSEMAID: Do you really want to go
back and dance?

THE SOLDIER: Sure, why not?

THE HOUSEMAID: But, Franz, I have to get
home. Madame will scold me anyways,

she's cranky . . . she'd rather I never went
out at all.

THE SOLDIER: You can go home.

THE HOUSEMAID: But I thought you'd take
me home.

THE SOLDIER: Take you home? Huh!

THE HOUSEMAID: Please, it's kind of lonely
going home alone.

THE SOLDIER: Where do you live?

THE HOUSEMAID: Not very far—in Porzellan-
gasse.

THE SOLDIER: Sure enough! Then we go the
same way . . . but it's too early for me
. . . I want to dance . . . I won't have
to be back at the barracks before twelve
o'clock. I'm going to dance.

THE HOUSEMAID: Oh, I see, now it's that
sourpuss blonde's chance.

THE SOLDIER: Humph! She isn't such a sourpuss.

THE HOUSEMAID: Oh Lord, how wicked men
are! I bet you do the same to every girl.

THE SOLDIER: That'd be a big job for one
man!

THE HOUSEMAID: Please, Franz, no more tonight—but don't leave me, you see—

THE SOLDIER: Okay, okay. But I suppose
you'll let me dance.

THE HOUSEMAID: Today I'm not going to
dance with any one but you.

THE SOLDIER: There it is.

THE HOUSEMAID: What?

THE SOLDIER: The hall! How quick we got
back. They're playing the same thing . . .
that tatata-tum tatata-tum. (He hums with
the band.) . . . Well, I'll take you home,
if you'll wait for me . . . if not . . .
good-bye.

THE HOUSEMAID: Yes, I'll wait. (They enter
the dancehall.)

THE SOLDIER: Say, Fräulein Marie, get yourself a glass of beer. (Turning to a blonde
who is just dancing past with a young man.
Very formally.) May I have the next dance,
Fräulein?

III

THE HOUSEMAID AND THE
YOUNG GENTLEMAN

Sultry summer afternoon. The parents of
THE YOUNG GENTLEMAN *are away in the*
country. The cook is out. THE HOUSEMAID

is in the kitchen writing a letter to the soldier who is now her sweetheart. THE YOUNG GENTLEMAN's *bell rings. She gets up and goes to his room.* THE YOUNG GENTLE-MAN *is lying on a couch, smoking a cigarette and reading a French novel.*

THE HOUSEMAID: Sir?

THE YOUNG GENTLEMAN: Oh, yes, Marie, yes, I rang, yes . . . I only wanted . . . of course . . . Oh, yes, of course, let the blinds down, Marie . . . It's cooler with the blinds down . . . yes . . . (THE HOUSEMAID *goes to the window and pulls down the blinds.*)

THE YOUNG GENTLEMAN (*continues reading*): What are you doing, Marie? Oh, yes. But now I can't read.

THE HOUSEMAID: You always study so hard, sir.

THE YOUNG GENTLEMAN (*ignoring the remark*): There, that's better. (THE HOUSE-MAID *goes out.* THE YOUNG GENTLEMAN *tries to go on with his reading, lets the book fall, and rings again.* THE HOUSEMAID *enters.*)

THE YOUNG GENTLEMAN: I say, Marie . . . let's see, what was it I wanted to say? Oh, yes . . . Is there any cognac in the house?

THE HOUSEMAID: Yes, but it's locked up.

THE YOUNG GENTLEMAN: Who has the key?

THE HOUSEMAID: Lini has.

THE YOUNG GENTLEMAN: Who is Lini?

THE HOUSEMAID: The cook, Herr Alfred.

THE YOUNG GENTLEMAN: Ask Lini for it.

THE HOUSEMAID: Sure, but it's Lini's day out.

THE YOUNG GENTLEMAN: Oh . . .

THE HOUSEMAID: Can't I get anything for you from the cafe, sir?

THE YOUNG GENTLEMAN: Thank you, no . . . It's hot enough as it is. I don't need any cognac. Listen, Marie, bring me a glass of water. Wait, Marie—let it run, till it gets quite cold.

Exit HOUSEMAID. THE YOUNG GENTLEMAN *gazes after her. At the door the maid looks back at him and* THE YOUNG GENTLEMAN *looks into space.* THE HOUSEMAID *turns on the water and lets it run. Meanwhile she goes into her room, washes her hands, and arranges her curls before the mirror. Then she brings the glass of water to* THE YOUNG GENTLEMAN. THE YOUNG GENTLEMAN *raises himself a bit, leaning on his elbow.*

THE HOUSEMAID *gives him the glass of water and their fingers touch.*

THE YOUNG GENTLEMAN: Thank you—Why what is the matter?—Careful. Put the glass back on the tray. (*He leans back, and stretches himself.*) What time is it?

THE HOUSEMAID: Five o'clock, sir.

THE YOUNG GENTLEMAN: Ah, five o'clock. That's fine.

THE HOUSEMAID *goes. At the door she turns around.* THE YOUNG GENTLEMAN *has followed her with his eyes; she notices it, and smiles.* THE YOUNG GENTLEMAN *remains stretched out awhile; then, suddenly, he gets up. He walks to the door, back again, and lies down on the couch. He again tries to read. After a few moments, he rings once more.* THE HOUSEMAID *appears with a smile which she does not try to hide.*

THE YOUNG GENTLEMAN: Listen, Marie, there was something I wanted to ask you. Didn't Dr. Schueller call this morning?

THE HOUSEMAID: No, sir. Nobody called.

THE YOUNG GENTLEMAN: That is strange. So Dr. Schueller didn't call? Do you know Dr. Schueller by sight?

THE HOUSEMAID: Of course. He's the big gentleman with the black beard.

THE YOUNG GENTLEMAN: Yes. Perhaps he called after all?

THE HOUSEMAID: No, sir. Nobody called.

THE YOUNG GENTLEMAN (*resolutely*): Come here, Marie.

THE HOUSEMAID (*coming a little nearer*): Yes, sir.

THE YOUNG GENTLEMAN: Closer . . . so . . . ah . . . I only thought . . .

THE HOUSEMAID: Do you want anything, sir?

THE YOUNG GENTLEMAN: I thought . . . Well, I thought—only about your blouse. What kind of a blouse is it? Can't you come closer? I won't bite you.

THE HOUSEMAID (*comes close to him*): What is the matter with my blouse? Don't you like it, sir?

THE YOUNG GENTLEMAN (*takes hold of her blouse, and draws her down to him*): Blue? It is a nice blue. (*Simply.*) You are prettily dressed, Marie.

THE HOUSEMAID: But, sir . . .

THE YOUNG GENTLEMAN: Ah . . . What is the matter? . . . (*He has opened her blouse. In a matter of fact tone.*) You have a beautiful white skin, Marie.

THE HOUSEMAID: You flatter me, sir.

THE YOUNG GENTLEMAN (*kissing her on the breast*): That won't hurt you.

THE HOUSEMAID: Oh, no.

THE YOUNG GENTLEMAN: But you sigh. Why are you sighing?

THE HOUSEMAID: Oh, Herr Alfred . . .

THE YOUNG GENTLEMAN: And what charming little slippers you have . . .

THE HOUSEMAID: But . . . sir . . . if the doorbell rings—

THE YOUNG GENTLEMAN: Who would ring now?

THE HOUSEMAID: But, sir . . . look . . . it is so light . . .

THE YOUNG GENTLEMAN: You needn't feel shy with me. You needn't feel shy with anybody . . . a girl as pretty as you. Yes, really, you are, Marie . . . Do you know your hair smells sweet?

THE HOUSEMAID: Herr Alfred . . .

THE YOUNG GENTLEMAN: Don't make such a fuss, Marie . . . Anyway, I've already seen you different. When I came home the other night and went to get some water, the door to your room was open . . . and . . .

THE HOUSEMAID (*covering her face*): Oh, my, I didn't think Herr Alfred could be so naughty.

THE YOUNG GENTLEMAN: I saw lots then . . . this . . . and this . . . this . . . and—

THE HOUSEMAID: Oh, Herr Alfred!

THE YOUNG GENTLEMAN: Come, come . . . here . . . yes, like that . . .

THE HOUSEMAID: But if the doorbell rings now—

THE YOUNG GENTLEMAN: Forget it . . . We simply wouldn't open the door.

*   *   *   *   *

THE YOUNG GENTLEMAN (*the bell rings*): Damn it . . . What a racket that man makes—Perhaps he rang before, and we didn't hear.

THE HOUSEMAID: Oh, no. I was listening all the time.

THE YOUNG GENTLEMAN: Well, see what's the matter. Look through the peephole.

THE HOUSEMAID: Herr Alfred . . . you are . . . No . . . you're such a bad man.

THE YOUNG GENTLEMAN: Please go and see . . . (THE HOUSEMAID *goes.* THE YOUNG GENTLEMAN *quickly puts up the blinds.*)

THE HOUSEMAID (*returns*): He must have gone away. Anyway, no one is there now. Maybe it was Dr. Schueller.

THE YOUNG GENTLEMAN (*annoyed*): Thank you. (THE HOUSEMAID *drawing close to him.*)

THE YOUNG GENTLEMAN (*evading her*): Listen, Marie—I'm going to the cafe now.

THE HOUSEMAID (*tenderly*): So soon—Herr Alfred?

THE YOUNG GENTLEMAN (*formally*): I am going to the cafe now . . . If Dr. Schueller should call—

THE HOUSEMAID: He won't come any more today.

THE YOUNG GENTLEMAN (*severely*): If Dr. Schueller should come, I . . . I'm in the cafe. (*He goes to the adjoining room.* THE HOUSEMAID *takes a cigar from the smoking-stand, puts it in her blouse and goes out.*)

IV

THE YOUNG GENTLEMAN AND THE YOUNG WIFE

Evening—A drawing-room furnished with cheap elegance in a house in Schwind Street. THE YOUNG GENTLEMAN *has just come in and still has his hat and overcoat on. He lights the gas. Then he opens the door to a side-room and looks in. The light from the drawing-room shines across the inlaid floor as far as the Louis Quinze bed, which stands against the opposite wall. A reddish light plays from the fireplace in the corner of the bedroom upon the hangings of the bed.* THE YOUNG GENTLEMAN *now inspects the bedroom. He takes an atomizer from the dressing-table, and sprays the bed-pillows with essence of violet. Then he goes with the atomizer through both rooms, constantly pressing upon the bulb, so that soon the scent pervades the apartment. He then takes off his hat and coat. He sits down in a blue velvet armchair, lights a cigarette, and smokes. After a short pause he rises again, and makes sure that the green shutters are closed. Suddenly, he goes into the bedroom, and opens a drawer in the dressing-table. He feels around in the drawer and finds a tortoise-shell hairpin. He looks for a place to hide it, and finally puts it into a pocket of his overcoat. He opens the buffet in the drawing-room; takes a silver tray, with a bottle and two liqueur glasses, and puts them on the table. He goes back to his overcoat, and takes from it a small white package. Opening this, he places it beside the cognac. He goes to the buffet again and takes two small plates and knives and forks. He takes a marron glacé from the package and eats it. Then he pours himself a glass of cognac, and drinks it quickly. He then looks at his watch. He walks up and down the room. He stops awhile before a large mirror, combing his hair and tiny mustache with a pocket-comb. He next goes to the door of the vestibule and listens. Nothing there. Then he pulls together the blue portieres, which hang in front of the bedroom. The bell rings. He starts slightly. Then he sits down in the armchair, and does not rise until the door has been opened and* THE YOUNG WIFE *enters.* THE YOUNG WIFE, *heavily veiled, closes the door behind her, pausing a moment with her left hand over her heart, as though mastering a strong emotion.* THE YOUNG GENTLEMAN *goes toward her, takes her left hand, and presses a kiss on the white glove.*

THE YOUNG GENTLEMAN (*softly*): Thank you.

THE YOUNG WIFE: Alfred—Alfred!

THE YOUNG GENTLEMAN: Come, gnädige Frau . . . Come, Emma . . .

THE YOUNG WIFE: Let me alone for a minute —please . . . Oh, please, please, Alfred! (*She is still standing at the door.* THE YOUNG GENTLEMAN *standing before her, holding her hand.*)

THE YOUNG WIFE: Where am I, really?

THE YOUNG GENTLEMAN: With me.

THE YOUNG WIFE: This place is terrible, Alfred.

THE YOUNG GENTLEMAN: Why? It is a very proper house.

THE YOUNG WIFE: But I met two gentlemen on the stairs.

THE YOUNG GENTLEMAN: Acquaintances of yours?

THE YOUNG WIFE: I don't know. They might be.

THE YOUNG GENTLEMAN: But gnädige Frau —you surely know your friends!

THE YOUNG WIFE: I couldn't see their faces.

THE YOUNG GENTLEMAN: But even if they were your best friends—they couldn't possibly recognize you . . . I, myself . . . if I didn't know it was you . . . this veil—

THE YOUNG WIFE: I am wearing two veils.

THE YOUNG GENTLEMAN: Won't you come in? . . . And at least take off your hat?

THE YOUNG WIFE: What are you thinking of, Alfred? I promised five minutes . . . Not a second more . . . I swear, no more—

THE YOUNG GENTLEMAN: Well, your veil—

THE YOUNG WIFE: There are two of them.

THE YOUNG GENTLEMAN: All right, both . . . you will at least let me see your face.

THE YOUNG WIFE: Do you really love me, Alfred?

THE YOUNG GENTLEMAN (*deeply hurt*): Emma! Can you ask?

THE YOUNG WIFE: It's so warm here.

THE YOUNG GENTLEMAN: You've still got your coat on. Really, you will catch cold.

THE YOUNG WIFE (*finally enters the room, and throws herself into the armchair*): I'm tired, so tired.

THE YOUNG GENTLEMAN: Permit me. (*He takes off her veils, removes her hatpin, and puts hat, pin and veils aside.* THE YOUNG WIFE *permits.* THE YOUNG GENTLEMAN *stands before her, shaking his head.*)

THE YOUNG WIFE: Why, what's the matter?

THE YOUNG GENTLEMAN: You've never been so beautiful.

THE YOUNG WIFE: How is that?

THE YOUNG GENTLEMAN: Alone . . . alone with you, Emma! (*He kneels beside her chair, takes both her hands and covers them with kisses.*)

THE YOUNG WIFE: And now . . . now let me go. I have done what you asked me. (THE YOUNG GENTLEMAN *lets his head sink into her lap.*) You promised to be good.

THE YOUNG GENTLEMAN: Yes.

THE YOUNG WIFE: It is stifling in this room.

THE YOUNG GENTLEMAN (*gets up*): You still have your coat on.

THE YOUNG WIFE: Put it with my hat. (THE YOUNG GENTLEMAN *takes off her coat, and puts it on the sofa.*)

THE YOUNG WIFE: And now . . . good-bye—

THE YOUNG GENTLEMAN: Emma! Emma!

THE YOUNG WIFE: The five minutes were up long, long ago.

THE YOUNG GENTLEMAN: It isn't a minute!

THE YOUNG WIFE: Alfred, tell me truly now, what time is it?

THE YOUNG GENTLEMAN: It is exactly a quarter past six.

THE YOUNG WIFE: I should have been at my sister's long ago.

THE YOUNG GENTLEMAN: You can see your sister any time . . .

THE YOUNG WIFE: Oh, good God, Alfred, why did you lure me here?

THE YOUNG GENTLEMAN: Because . . . I adore you, Emma!

THE YOUNG WIFE: How many women have you said that to?

THE YOUNG GENTLEMAN: Not one, since I met you.

THE YOUNG WIFE: What a weak woman I am! If anybody had predicted . . . a week ago . . . or even yesterday.

THE YOUNG GENTLEMAN: But you had already promised me day before yesterday.

THE YOUNG WIFE: You kept after me so. But I didn't want to . . . God is my witness— I didn't want to . . . Yesterday, I was firmly decided . . . Do you know I wrote you a long letter last night?

THE YOUNG GENTLEMAN: I didn't receive any.

THE YOUNG WIFE: I tore it up. Oh, if only I had sent it!

THE YOUNG GENTLEMAN: It is better as it is.

THE YOUNG WIFE: Oh, no, it's awful . . . awful of me. I don't understand myself. Good-bye, Alfred, let me go. (THE YOUNG GENTLEMAN *seizes her, and covers her face with burning kisses.*) So . . . is that the way you keep your promise?

THE YOUNG GENTLEMAN: One more kiss . . . just one more.

THE YOUNG WIFE: The last. (*He kisses her, and she returns the kiss; their lips remain joined for a long time.*)

THE YOUNG GENTLEMAN: Shall I tell you something, Emma? Now for the first time I know what happiness is. (THE YOUNG WIFE *sinks back into the armchair.* THE YOUNG GENTLEMAN *sits on the arm of the chair, and puts one arm lightly about her neck.*) Rather, I know now what happiness might be. (THE YOUNG WIFE *sighs deeply.* THE YOUNG GENTLEMAN *kisses her again.*)

THE YOUNG WIFE: Alfred, Alfred, what are you doing!

THE YOUNG GENTLEMAN: Wasn't I right? It isn't so awfully uncomfortable here. And we are safe here. It's a thousand times better than those meetings in public.

THE YOUNG WIFE: Oh, don't remind me of them.

THE YOUNG GENTLEMAN: I shall always recall them with a thousand delights. Every minute you let me spend with you is a sweet memory.

THE YOUNG WIFE: Do you remember the ball at the Manufacturers' Club?

THE YOUNG GENTLEMAN: Do I remember it? . . . I sat beside you through the whole supper . . . close to you. Your husband had champagne . . . (THE YOUNG WIFE *looks at him with a hurt expression.*) Oh, I just meant to speak of the champagne. Emma, would you like a glass of cognac?

THE YOUNG WIFE: Only a drop, but first give me a glass of water.

THE YOUNG GENTLEMAN: Surely . . . but where is . . . oh, yes. I remember . . . (*He opens the portieres, and goes out into the bedroom.* THE YOUNG WIFE *follows him with her eyes.* THE YOUNG GENTLEMAN *comes back with a decanter and two glasses.*)

THE YOUNG WIFE: Where have you been?

THE YOUNG GENTLEMAN: In the . . . next room. (*Pours her a glass of water.*)

THE YOUNG WIFE: Now I'm going to ask you something, Alfred, and you must swear you will tell me the truth.

THE YOUNG GENTLEMAN: I swear—

THE YOUNG WIFE: Has there ever been any other woman in these rooms?

THE YOUNG GENTLEMAN: But, Emma, this house was built twenty years ago!

THE YOUNG WIFE: You know what I mean, Alfred . . . in these rooms, with you!

THE YOUNG GENTLEMAN: With me . . . here . . . Emma! It's mean of you even to imagine such a thing.

THE YOUNG WIFE: Then there was . . . how shall I . . . But, no, I'd rather not ask. It is better that I shouldn't ask. It's my own fault. And I must suffer for it.

THE YOUNG GENTLEMAN: But what is wrong? What's the matter with you? Why?

THE YOUNG WIFE: No, no, no, I mustn't let

myself think . . . If I did I should sink through the floor with shame.

THE YOUNG GENTLEMAN (*with the decanter in his hand. Shakes his head sadly*): Emma, if you only knew how you hurt me. (THE YOUNG WIFE *pours a glass of cognac.*) I want to tell you something, Emma. If you're ashamed, if you don't care for me, if you don't feel you are all the happiness in the world for me, then you'd better go.

THE YOUNG WIFE: Yes, I will go.

THE YOUNG GENTLEMAN (*taking hold of her hand*): But if you feel that I cannot live without you, that a kiss upon your hand means more to me than all the caresses of all the women in the whole world . . . Emma, I'm not like the other young men, who are experienced in love-making . . . perhaps, I am too naive . . . I . . .

THE YOUNG WIFE: But suppose you were like other young men?

THE YOUNG GENTLEMAN: Then you wouldn't be here tonight . . . because you are not like other women.

THE YOUNG WIFE: How do you know that?

THE YOUNG GENTLEMAN (*drawing her close beside him on the sofa*): I have thought a lot about you. I know you are unhappy.

THE YOUNG WIFE (*pleased*): Yes.

THE YOUNG GENTLEMAN: Life is so dreary, so empty, so futile, and so short, so frightfully short! There is only one happiness, to find some one who loves you. (THE YOUNG WIFE *takes a candied pear from the table, and puts it into her mouth.*) Give me half! (*She offers it to him with her lips.*)

THE YOUNG WIFE (*catches* THE YOUNG GENTLEMAN'*s hands as they threaten to stray*): What are you doing, Alfred? . . . Is this the way you keep your promise?

THE YOUNG GENTLEMAN (*swallows the pear, then, more daringly*): Life is so short.

THE YOUNG WIFE (*weakly*): But that's no reason—

THE YOUNG GENTLEMAN (*mechanically*): Oh, yes.

THE YOUNG WIFE (*still more weakly*): Alfred, you promised to be good . . . and it's so light . . .

THE YOUNG GENTLEMAN: Come, come, you only, only . . . (*He lifts her from the sofa.*)

THE YOUNG WIFE: What are you doing?

THE YOUNG GENTLEMAN: It isn't light in the other room.

THE YOUNG WIFE: Is there another room?

THE YOUNG GENTLEMAN (*drawing her with him*): A beautiful one . . . and quite dark.

THE YOUNG WIFE: We'd better stay here. (THE YOUNG GENTLEMAN *already past the bedroom portieres with her, loosening her waist.*) You are so . . . Merciful heaven, what are you doing to me? Alfred!

THE YOUNG GENTLEMAN: I adore you, Emma!

THE YOUNG WIFE: Then wait, wait a little . . . (*Weakly.*) Go . . . I'll call you.

THE YOUNG GENTLEMAN: Let you help me . . . let help. (*Confused.*) Let . . . me help you.

THE YOUNG WIFE: You'll tear everything.

THE YOUNG GENTLEMAN: You have no corset on?

THE YOUNG WIFE: I never wear a corset. Stylish women don't wear them any more. But you may unbutton my shoes. (THE YOUNG GENTLEMAN *unbuttons her shoes and kisses her feet.*)

THE YOUNG WIFE (*slips into bed*): Oh, how cold it is.

THE YOUNG GENTLEMAN: It'll be warm in a minute.

THE YOUNG WIFE (*laughing softly*): Do you think so?

THE YOUNG GENTLEMAN (*slightly hurt, to himself*): She oughtn't to have said that. (*He undresses in the dark.*)

THE YOUNG WIFE (*tenderly*): Come, quick, come!

THE YOUNG GENTLEMAN (*mollified*): Just a minute, dear—

THE YOUNG WIFE: It smells like violets here.

THE YOUNG GENTLEMAN: That's you . . . Yes. (*To her.*) You, yourself.

THE YOUNG WIFE: Alfred . . . Alfred . . .

THE YOUNG GENTLEMAN: Emma . . .

*   *   *   *   *

THE YOUNG GENTLEMAN: Apparently I love you too much . . . yes . . . I feel as if I were out of my mind.

THE YOUNG WIFE: . . . . . .

THE YOUNG GENTLEMAN: I have been crazy for you all these days. I was afraid of this.

THE YOUNG WIFE: Don't mind it.

THE YOUNG GENTLEMAN: Oh, certainly not. It's perfectly natural, if one . . .

THE YOUNG WIFE: No . . . don't . . . You are nervous. Calm yourself first.

THE YOUNG GENTLEMAN: Do you know Stendhal?

THE YOUNG WIFE: Stendhal?

THE YOUNG GENTLEMAN: His book on psychology, "De l'amour."

THE YOUNG WIFE: No. Why do you ask me?

THE YOUNG GENTLEMAN: There's a story in that book which is very much to the point.

THE YOUNG WIFE: What kind of a story?

THE YOUNG GENTLEMAN: A bunch of cavalry officers get together.

THE YOUNG WIFE: Yes.

THE YOUNG GENTLEMAN: And they tell each other about their love affairs. And every one of them relates that with the woman he loved best . . . most passionately, you know . . . that his, that he . . . well, in short, that the same thing happened that happened to me just now.

THE YOUNG WIFE: Yes.

THE YOUNG GENTLEMAN: That is very significant.

THE YOUNG WIFE: Yes.

THE YOUNG GENTLEMAN: The story isn't over. One of them claimed . . . that this thing had never happened to him, but, adds Stendhal . . . he was a notorious liar.

THE YOUNG WIFE: I see—

THE YOUNG GENTLEMAN: And, yet, it makes a man feel bad . . . that's the stupid part of it, because it really doesn't mean a thing.

THE YOUNG WIFE: Of course not. Anyway, you know . . . you promised to be good.

THE YOUNG GENTLEMAN: Oh! Don't make fun of me. That doesn't help a bit.

THE YOUNG WIFE: But, I'm not. That story of Stendhal's is really interesting. I have always thought that only older people or people who . . . you know, people who have been pretty fast.

THE YOUNG GENTLEMAN: The idea! That has nothing to do with it. By the way, I had completely forgotten the best of Stendhal's stories. One of the officers went so far as to say that he stayed for three or even six nights . . . I don't remember now—that is, he stayed with a woman he had wanted for weeks—*désiré*—you understand, and nothing happened all those nights except that they wept for happiness . . . both . . .

THE YOUNG WIFE: Both?

THE YOUNG GENTLEMAN: Yes. Does that surprise you? I can understand it very well . . . especially when two people love each other.

THE YOUNG WIFE: But surely there are a good many who don't weep.

THE YOUNG GENTLEMAN (*nervously*): Certainly . . . this is an exceptional case.

THE YOUNG WIFE: Oh, I thought Stendhal said all cavalry officers weep on such occasions.

THE YOUNG GENTLEMAN: Now you are laughing at me again.

THE YOUNG WIFE: What an idea! Don't be childish, Alfred.

THE YOUNG GENTLEMAN: Well, it makes me nervous anyway . . . Besides I have the feeling that you are thinking about it all the time. That's what really hurts.

THE YOUNG WIFE: I'm not thinking of it at all.

THE YOUNG GENTLEMAN: If I were only sure you love me.

THE YOUNG WIFE: Do you want more proofs?

THE YOUNG GENTLEMAN: Didn't I tell you . . . you are always laughing at me.

THE YOUNG WIFE: Why do you think so? Come, let me hold your sweet little head.

THE YOUNG GENTLEMAN: Oh, that feels good.

THE YOUNG WIFE: Do you love me?

THE YOUNG GENTLEMAN: Oh, I'm so happy.

THE YOUNG WIFE: And you needn't cry about it.

THE YOUNG GENTLEMAN (*moving away from her, highly irritated*): There! Again! I begged you not to . . .

THE YOUNG WIFE: To tell you that you shouldn't cry . . .

THE YOUNG GENTLEMAN: You said: "You needn't cry about it."

THE YOUNG WIFE: You are nervous, sweetheart.

THE YOUNG GENTLEMAN: I know.

THE YOUNG WIFE: But you ought not to be. I even like our being together like good comrades.

THE YOUNG GENTLEMAN: Now you are beginning again.

THE YOUNG WIFE: Don't you remember! That was one of the first things we said to each other. We wanted to be comrades, nothing more. Oh, how nice that was . . . at my sister's ball in January, during the quadrille . . . For heaven's sake, I should have gone long ago . . . My sister expects me . . . What shall I tell her . . . Good-bye, Alfred—

THE YOUNG GENTLEMAN: Emma! Can you leave me this way?

THE YOUNG WIFE: Yes, I can!

THE YOUNG GENTLEMAN: Five minutes more . . .

THE YOUNG WIFE: All right. Five minutes more. But if you promise me not to move? . . . Yes? . . . I want to give you a good-bye kiss . . . Psst . . . be still . . . don't move, I told you, or I'll get up at once, my sweetheart, you sweet . . .

THE YOUNG GENTLEMAN: Emma . . . my ador . . . . . .

* * * * *

THE YOUNG WIFE: My Alfred!

THE YOUNG GENTLEMAN: Oh, it is heaven to be with you.

THE YOUNG WIFE: But now I've really got to go.

THE YOUNG GENTLEMAN: Oh, let your sister wait.

THE YOUNG WIFE: I must go home. It is too late to see my sister. What time is it, anyway?

THE YOUNG GENTLEMAN: How should I know?

THE YOUNG WIFE: You might look at your watch.

THE YOUNG GENTLEMAN: My watch is in my vest.

THE YOUNG WIFE: Get it.

THE YOUNG GENTLEMAN (*gets up with a jump*): Eight o'clock.

THE YOUNG WIFE (*jumps up quickly*): For heaven's sake . . . Quick, Alfred, give me my stockings. What shall I say? They must be waiting for me at home . . . eight o'clock.

THE YOUNG GENTLEMAN: When shall I see you again?

THE YOUNG WIFE: Never.

THE YOUNG GENTLEMAN: Emma! Don't you love me any more?

THE YOUNG WIFE: It's because I do. Give me my shoes.

THE YOUNG GENTLEMAN: Never again? Here are your shoes.

THE YOUNG WIFE: My button-hook is in my bag. Please, be quick . . .

THE YOUNG GENTLEMAN: Here is the button-hook.

THE YOUNG WIFE: Alfred, this may cost us our lives.

THE YOUNG GENTLEMAN (*affected very unpleasantly*): How so?

THE YOUNG WIFE: What shall I say, if he asks me where I've been?

THE YOUNG GENTLEMAN: At your sister's.

THE YOUNG WIFE: If I could only lie.

THE YOUNG GENTLEMAN: You'll have to.

THE YOUNG WIFE: Anything for a man like you. Oh, come here . . . let me give you a last kiss. (*She embraces him.*) And now, leave me to myself, go in the other room. I can't dress with you around. (THE YOUNG GENTLEMAN *goes into the drawing-room, where he dresses. He eats some pastry and drinks a glass of cognac.*)

THE YOUNG WIFE (*calls after a while*): Alfred!

THE YOUNG GENTLEMAN: Yes, sweetheart.

THE YOUNG WIFE: Isn't it better that we didn't weep?

THE YOUNG GENTLEMAN (*smiling, not without pride*): How can you talk so flippantly?

THE YOUNG WIFE: How awful it will be now . . . if we should meet by chance in society.

THE YOUNG GENTLEMAN: By chance? . . . Surely you are coming to Lobheimer's tomorrow?

THE YOUNG WIFE: Yes. Are you?

THE YOUNG GENTLEMAN: Of course. May I ask for the cotillion?

THE YOUNG WIFE: Oh, I shan't go. What do you think I am? I'd certainly . . . (*She enters the drawing-room fully dressed, and takes a chocolate pastry.*) sink through the floor with shame.

THE YOUNG GENTLEMAN: Tomorrow at Lobheimer's. That's fine.

THE YOUNG WIFE: No, no . . . I shall decline . . . I'll certainly decline—

THE YOUNG GENTLEMAN: Well, the day after tomorrow . . . here.

THE YOUNG WIFE: The idea!

THE YOUNG GENTLEMAN: At six . . .

THE YOUNG WIFE: There are cabs at this corner, aren't there?

THE YOUNG GENTLEMAN: Yes, as many as you want. Well, the day after tomorrow, here at six o'clock. Please say "yes," sweetheart.

THE YOUNG WIFE: We'll discuss that tomorrow night during the cotillion.

THE YOUNG GENTLEMAN (*embracing her*): My angel.

THE YOUNG WIFE: Don't muss my hair again.

THE YOUNG GENTLEMAN: Well then, tomorrow night at Lobheimer's, and the day after tomorrow in my arms.

THE YOUNG WIFE: Good-bye . . .

THE YOUNG GENTLEMAN (*suddenly anxious again*): And what will you tell him to-night?

THE YOUNG WIFE: Don't ask me . . . don't ask me . . . it's too terrible. Why do I love you so? Good-bye. If I meet any one again on the stairway, I shall faint. Ugh! (THE YOUNG GENTLEMAN *kisses her hand for the last time.* THE YOUNG WIFE *exits.*)

THE YOUNG GENTLEMAN (*remains standing. Then he sits down on the couch. He smiles reflectively, and says to himself*): Well, so I have an affair with a respectable woman. At last.

V

THE YOUNG WIFE AND THE HUSBAND

A comfortable bedroom. Half past ten at night. THE YOUNG WIFE *is in bed, reading. Her* HUSBAND *enters the room in a dressing gown.*

THE YOUNG WIFE (*without looking up*): Through working?

THE HUSBAND: Yes. I'm tired. And besides . . .

THE YOUNG WIFE: What?

THE HUSBAND: I felt lonely at my desk all at once. I began to long for you.

THE YOUNG WIFE (*looking up*): Really?

THE HUSBAND (*sitting down on the bed beside her*): Don't read any more tonight. You'll surely ruin your eyes.

THE YOUNG WIFE (*closing the book*): What's the matter?

THE HUSBAND: Nothing, dear. I'm in love with you. You know that.

THE YOUNG WIFE: One might forget it sometimes.

THE HUSBAND: One must forget it sometimes.

THE YOUNG WIFE: Why?

THE HUSBAND: Because, if one didn't, marriage would be imperfect. It would . . .

how shall I express it? . . . it would lose its sanctity.

THE YOUNG WIFE: Oh . . .

THE HUSBAND: Believe me, it is so . . . If at times we hadn't forgotten that we were in love with each other during the five years we have been married, we might not be in love any more.

THE YOUNG WIFE: That's too deep for me.

THE HUSBAND: It's simply this: we've had about a dozen love-affairs with each other . . . Doesn't it seem so to you, too?

THE YOUNG WIFE: I haven't counted them!

THE HUSBAND: If we'd enjoyed the first one to the limit, if I had abandoned myself completely to my passion for you in the beginning, the same thing would have happened to us that has happened to millions of other lovers. We should be through with each other.

THE YOUNG WIFE: Ah . . . do you mean that?

THE HUSBAND: Believe me, Emma, in the early days of our marriage, I dreaded that that might happen.

THE YOUNG WIFE: So did I.

THE HUSBAND: See? Wasn't I right? That's why it is wise for us, now and then, to be nothing but good friends to each other.

THE YOUNG WIFE: Oh.

THE HUSBAND: That's how it's possible for us to keep on having new honeymoons. I never let our honeymoons . . .

THE YOUNG WIFE: Last too long.

THE HUSBAND: Exactly.

THE YOUNG WIFE: And now . . . another period of friendship is up.

THE HUSBAND (*pressing her tenderly to him*): It ought to be.

THE YOUNG WIFE: But if . . . it isn't up for me?

THE HUSBAND: It is up for you. You are the nicest and most sensible person in the world. I am very lucky to have found you.

THE YOUNG WIFE: It's wonderful, the way you make love. Now and then.

THE HUSBAND (*also gone to bed*): For a man who has seen something of the world—there, lay your head on my shoulder—marriage is much more mysterious than it is for you sheltered girls. You come to us innocent and to a degree, at least, ignorant, and so you really have a clearer perception of the true nature of love.

THE YOUNG WIFE (*laughing*): Oh!

THE HUSBAND: Certainly. For we get confused by all the experiences we went through before marriage. You women, of course, hear a lot of things, you know a lot of things, and of course, read too much, but you can't have any real idea of the things men experience. Actually we men become quite disgusted with what is commonly called love. Creatures who are thrown in our way are a sort of . . .

THE YOUNG WIFE: Of what? Tell me.

THE HUSBAND (*kissing her on the forehead*): You ought to be glad, dear child, that you never had occasion to learn. After all, most of the poor creatures are quite pitiful. Let's not cast any stones.

THE YOUNG WIFE: I can't see for the life of me, why we should pity them.

THE HUSBAND (*with gentle benevolence*): They deserve pity. Whereas you girls with your "good family background" . . . who wait at home under the protection of your parents for an eligible man to come courting! You don't know the poverty that drives most of these poor creatures into the arms of sin.

THE YOUNG WIFE: Are they all so poor that they have to sell themselves?

THE HUSBAND: That's not what I mean. I'm not speaking of material poverty, as much as of a moral misery. A lack of opportunity to know what is right, and, especially, what is noble.

THE YOUNG WIFE: But why pity them? They seem to get along pretty well.

THE HUSBAND: You have strange ideas, my dear. You mustn't forget that such creatures are naturally doomed to fall lower and lower. There is no stopping them.

THE YOUNG WIFE (*cuddling to him*): Apparently falling is quite pleasant.

THE HUSBAND (*hurt*): How can you say such things, Emma? I should think that to a respectable woman like you, no one could be more repulsive than those who have forfeited—

THE YOUNG WIFE: Of course, Karl, of course. I just said that to be saying something. Go on. It's so nice to hear you talk like this. Tell me something.

THE HUSBAND: What?

THE YOUNG WIFE: Why—about these creatures.

THE HUSBAND: What do you want to know?

THE YOUNG WIFE: Remember, when we were first married I was always asking you to tell me about your bachelor life.

THE HUSBAND: Why should that interest you?

THE YOUNG WIFE: Aren't you my husband? Isn't it an injustice for me to know nothing about your past?

THE HUSBAND: You surely don't think I have such bad taste, as . . . No, Emma . . . it would be sacrilege.

THE YOUNG WIFE: And yet you have held heaven knows how many other women in your arms, just as you are holding me now.

THE HUSBAND: Don't say "women." You are *the* woman.

THE YOUNG WIFE: But you positively must answer one question . . . or . . . or . . . there won't be any . . . honeymoon.

THE HUSBAND: That's a fine way to talk . . . remember you are a mother . . . our little girl is sleeping in there . . .

THE YOUNG WIFE (*snuggling against him*): But I want a boy, too.

THE HUSBAND: Emma!

THE YOUNG WIFE: Don't be silly . . . of course, I am your wife . . . but I'd like to be . . . to be your sweetheart, a little, too.

THE HUSBAND: Would you? . . .

THE YOUNG WIFE: First my question.

THE HUSBAND (*wheedled*): All right.

THE YOUNG WIFE: Was there . . . a married woman among them?

THE HUSBAND: Why? What do you mean?

THE YOUNG WIFE: You know what I mean.

THE HUSBAND (*slightly disconcerted*): What makes you think of such a thing?

THE YOUNG WIFE: I'd like to know if . . . I mean—there *are* such women. I know that. But did you? . . .

THE HUSBAND (*earnestly*): Do you know such a woman?

THE YOUNG WIFE: I don't know whether I do or not.

THE HUSBAND: Perhaps, one of your friends is such a person?

THE YOUNG WIFE: How can I make sure—one way or the other?

THE HUSBAND: Did any of your friends—women talk about a lot of things when they get together—did any of them ever confess?

THE YOUNG WIFE (*uncertain*): No.

THE HUSBAND: Do you suspect any friend of yours of . . .

THE YOUNG WIFE: Suspect . . . hummm . . . suspect . . .

THE HUSBAND: You seem to.

THE YOUNG WIFE: No, Karl, of course not. When I think it over, I wouldn't believe it of any of them.

THE HUSBAND: Not one?

THE YOUNG WIFE: Not any friend of mine.

THE HUSBAND: Promise me, Emma . . .

THE YOUNG WIFE: What?

THE HUSBAND: That you will never associate with a woman whom you suspect, ever so little, of not leading a perfectly blameless life.

THE YOUNG WIFE: Do I have to promise that?

THE HUSBAND: I know that you will not deliberately cultivate such women. But it might happen that you . . . in fact it often happens that such women, whose reputations are not of the best, cultivate good women, partly as foils, and partly because they feel . . . how shall I say it . . . because they feel homesick for virtue.

THE YOUNG WIFE: Do they?

THE HUSBAND: Yes. I believe it is quite true what I just said. Homesick for virtue. For all these women are really very unhappy; take my word for that.

THE YOUNG WIFE: Why are they unhappy?

THE HUSBAND: You ask me, Emma? How can you? Just imagine what a life these women lead! A life of lies, trickery, vulgarity, and danger.

THE YOUNG WIFE: Yes, of course. You are quite right.

THE HUSBAND: Truly . . . they pay for their little happiness . . . their little . . .

THE YOUNG WIFE: Pleasure.

THE HUSBAND: Why "pleasure"? What makes you call it "pleasure"?

THE YOUNG WIFE: Well, there must be something in it! Or they wouldn't do it.

THE HUSBAND: It's nothing . . . an intoxication.

THE YOUNG WIFE (pensively): Intoxication . . .

THE HUSBAND: It is not even intoxication. Anyway—it is dearly paid for, that much is certain.

THE YOUNG WIFE: Well . . . it has happened to you, hasn't it?

THE HUSBAND: Yes, Emma. It is the thing I most regret.

THE YOUNG WIFE: Who was she? Tell me! Do I know her?

THE HUSBAND: What can you be thinking of?

THE YOUNG WIFE: Was it long ago? Was it long before you married me?

THE HUSBAND: Don't ask me. Please, don't ask.

THE YOUNG WIFE: But, Karl!

THE HUSBAND: She is dead.

THE YOUNG WIFE: Honest?

THE HUSBAND: Yes . . . it may sound ridiculous, but I have the feeling that all these women die young.

THE YOUNG WIFE: Did you love her very much?

THE HUSBAND: One doesn't love women who lie.

THE YOUNG WIFE: Then why . . .

THE HUSBAND: Drink . . .

THE YOUNG WIFE: You see!

THE HUSBAND: Don't talk about it any more, please. It was over and done with long ago. I have loved only one woman: you. A man doesn't fall in love until he finds purity and truth.

THE YOUNG WIFE: Karl!

THE HUSBAND: How secure, how happy I feel in these arms. Why didn't I know you as a child? I am sure I wouldn't have looked at other women.

THE YOUNG WIFE: Karl!

THE HUSBAND: And how beautiful you are! . . . beautiful! Come . . . come . . . (He puts the light out.)

* * * * *

THE YOUNG WIFE: Do you know what I am thinking of tonight?

THE HUSBAND: What, sweetheart?

THE YOUNG WIFE: Of . . . of . . . Venice.

THE HUSBAND: The first night . . .

THE YOUNG WIFE: Yes . . .

THE HUSBAND: What else? Tell me!

THE YOUNG WIFE: You love me as much today?

THE HUSBAND: Yes, just as much.

THE YOUNG WIFE: Oh . . . if you always would . . .

THE HUSBAND (in her arms): Would what?

THE YOUNG WIFE: My Karl!

THE HUSBAND: What do you mean? If I always would? . . .

THE YOUNG WIFE: Mmmmm.

THE HUSBAND: But what? If I would always what?

THE YOUNG WIFE: Then I should always know you love me.

THE HUSBAND: Yes. But you must remember this. One cannot always be a lover, sometimes one has to go out into the hostile world, into the struggle for existence! Don't forget that, my dear. There is a time for everything in marriage—that is the beauty of it. There are not many who can remember their Venice after five years.

THE YOUNG WIFE: There certainly aren't.

THE HUSBAND: And . . . good-night, my dear.

THE YOUNG WIFE: Good-night!

VI
THE HUSBAND AND THE LITTLE DARLING

A chambre séparée in the Riedhof, comfortably and tastefully furnished. A lighted gasgrate is disclosed. The remains of a meal on the table, cream cakes, fruit, cheese. In the wine-glasses is a Hungarian white wine.
THE HUSBAND *and* THE LITTLE DARLING. THE HUSBAND *smoking a Havana cigar, and lolling at the end of the sofa.* THE LITTLE DARLING *sits near him in a chair at the table eating the cream out of a cake with a spoon, and smacking her lips.*

THE HUSBAND: Is it good?

THE LITTLE DARLING (*without stopping*): Mmmmm.

THE HUSBAND: Do you want another?

THE LITTLE DARLING: No. I've eaten too much already.

THE HUSBAND: Your wine is all gone. (*He fills her glass.*)

THE LITTLE DARLING: Stop. I wouldn't drink it.

THE HUSBAND: Come and sit here with me.

THE LITTLE DARLING: In a minute, I'm not through yet. (THE HUSBAND *gets up and stands behind her chair, puts his arms around her, turning her face toward him.*) What's the idea?

THE HUSBAND: I want a kiss.

THE LITTLE DARLING (*kissing him*): You sure got your nerve.

THE HUSBAND: Just finding that out?

THE LITTLE DARLING: No. I knew it when you stopped me in the street. You must think I'm a nice one.

THE HUSBAND: Why?

THE LITTLE DARLING: Because I came right along when you said "Let's go to a . . . to a *chambre séparée.*"

THE HUSBAND: You didn't rush, at that.

THE LITTLE DARLING: You got such a cute way of asking.

THE HUSBAND: Do you think so?

THE LITTLE DARLING: And, after all, what's the difference—

THE HUSBAND: Exactly.

THE LITTLE DARLING: Whether we go walking or—

THE HUSBAND: It's much too cold for walking.

THE LITTLE DARLING: Of course.

THE HUSBAND: But it's good and warm here, isn't it? (*He sits down again, puts his arms around the girl, and draws her to his side.*)

THE LITTLE DARLING (*weakly*): Please . . . don't.

THE HUSBAND: Tell me . . . You had noticed me before, hadn't you?

THE LITTLE DARLING: Yes. Several blocks before you spoke to me.

THE HUSBAND: I don't mean today. I mean yesterday and the day before, when I was following you.

THE LITTLE DARLING: A lot of men follow me.

THE HUSBAND: I should say so. But did you notice me?

THE LITTLE DARLING: Guess what happened to me not long ago. My cousin's husband followed me in the dark, and didn't know who I was.

THE HUSBAND: Did he speak to you?

THE LITTLE DARLING: What do you think? Think everybody is as fresh as you?

THE HUSBAND: But they sometimes do, don't they?

THE LITTLE DARLING: Of course they do.

THE HUSBAND: What do you do?

THE LITTLE DARLING: Nothing—I just don't answer.

THE HUSBAND: Hm-m—but you answered me.

THE LITTLE DARLING: Sorry, aren't you?

THE HUSBAND (*kisses her vehemently*): Your lips are as sweet as whipped cream.

THE LITTLE DARLING: They taste that way naturally.

THE HUSBAND: I suppose a good many men have told you that?

THE LITTLE DARLING: A good many! You sure got your imagination.

THE HUSBAND: Now, be honest. How many men have kissed this sweet mouth before?

THE LITTLE DARLING: Why do you ask? You wouldn't believe me if I told you.

THE HUSBAND: Why not?

THE LITTLE DARLING: Guess.

THE HUSBAND: All right, I'll guess—but you mustn't get mad!

THE LITTLE DARLING: Me get mad?

THE HUSBAND: Well, then, I guess . . . twenty.

THE LITTLE DARLING (*disengaging herself*): Why not a hundred?

THE HUSBAND: Come, I was just guessing.

THE LITTLE DARLING: You guessed wrong!

THE HUSBAND: Say—ten.

THE LITTLE DARLING (*offended*): Of course! A girl who lets a man talk to her on the street, and goes with him to a *chambre séparée!*

THE HUSBAND: Don't be childish. Whether we stroll around in the streets or sit in a room . . . we are in a restaurant. The waiter may come in any minute. There's nothing to this.

THE LITTLE DARLING: That's just what I thought.

THE HUSBAND: Have you ever been in a *chambre séparée* before?

THE LITTLE DARLING: To tell the truth—yes.

THE HUSBAND: I am glad you are honest with me.

THE LITTLE DARLING: But it wasn't the way you think. I was in a *chambre séparée* with my girl friend and her fiancé, last carnival.

THE HUSBAND: It wouldn't have been anything terrible, even if you had gone there with your boy friend—

THE LITTLE DARLING: Of course it wouldn't have been anything terrible. But I haven't any boy friend.

THE HUSBAND: Oh, go on!

THE LITTLE DARLING: I swear, I haven't.

THE HUSBAND: You aren't trying to tell me that I . . .

THE LITTLE DARLING: That you are what? I haven't had one—haven't had one for more than six months.

THE HUSBAND: I see . . . But before then? Who was he?

THE LITTLE DARLING: Why are you so curious?

THE HUSBAND: Because I love you.

THE LITTLE DARLING: Really?

THE HUSBAND: Of course! You must have seen it already. Tell me about him. (*Presses her tightly to him.*)

THE LITTLE DARLING: What do you want me to tell?

THE HUSBAND: Don't keep me asking! Who was he, that's what I want to know.

THE LITTLE DARLING (*laughing*): Just a man.

THE HUSBAND: Well . . . well . . . who?

THE LITTLE DARLING: He looked something like you.

THE HUSBAND: I see.

THE LITTLE DARLING: If you hadn't looked like him—

THE HUSBAND: What then?

THE LITTLE DARLING: Now, don't ask, don't you see that's . . .

THE HUSBAND (*understanding*): That's why you let me speak to you.

THE LITTLE DARLING: Yes, that's it.

THE HUSBAND: I really don't know whether I ought to be tickled or get mad.

THE LITTLE DARLING: If I were you, I'd be tickled.

THE HUSBAND: All right.

THE LITTLE DARLING: You talk like him too. And you have the same way of looking at . . . a person . . .

THE HUSBAND: What did he do for a living?

THE LITTLE DARLING: No, your eyes—

THE HUSBAND: What was his name?

THE LITTLE DARLING: Please, don't look at me that way; please don't. (THE HUSBAND *embraces her. A long, burning kiss.* THE LITTLE DARLING *shivers, tries to get up.*)

THE HUSBAND: Why do you want to leave?

THE LITTLE DARLING: It's time to go home.

THE HUSBAND: Later.

THE LITTLE DARLING: No, I really have to get home. What will mother say?

THE HUSBAND: You live with your mother?

THE LITTLE DARLING: Of course I live with my mother. What did you suppose?

THE HUSBAND: So—with your mother. You two alone?

THE LITTLE DARLING: Alone, like fun. There are five of us! Two boys and two more girls.

THE HUSBAND: Don't sit so far away from me. Are you the oldest?

THE LITTLE DARLING: No, I'm next oldest. Kitty is the oldest. She works in a flower store.

THE HUSBAND: Where do you work?

THE LITTLE DARLING: I stay at home.

THE HUSBAND: Always?

THE LITTLE DARLING: One of us has to stay home.

THE HUSBAND: Of course, and what do you tell your mother, when you come home so late?

THE LITTLE DARLING: That hardly ever happens.

THE HUSBAND: Well, tonight, for instance. Your mother will ask you, won't she?

THE LITTLE DARLING: Of course she'll ask. It doesn't matter how careful I am when I come home, she always wakes up.

THE HUSBAND: And what do you tell her?

THE LITTLE DARLING: Oh—that I've been to the theater.

THE HUSBAND: Does she believe it?

THE LITTLE DARLING: Why shouldn't she believe it? I often go to the theater. Only last Sunday I went to the opera with my girl friend and her fiancé, and my oldest brother.

THE HUSBAND: Where did you get the tickets?

THE LITTLE DARLING: My brother is a hairdresser.

THE HUSBAND: A hairdresser . . . oh, at the theater, I suppose.

THE LITTLE DARLING: Why do you ask so many questions?

THE HUSBAND: Just because I am interested. What does your other brother do?

THE LITTLE DARLING: He's still going to school. He wants to be a teacher. Imagine!

THE HUSBAND: And you have a little sister?

THE LITTLE DARLING: Yes, she is just a child, but you have to keep an eye on her all the time, already. You have no idea how girls are spoiled at school. What do you think? The other day I caught her having a date.

THE HUSBAND: Really?

THE LITTLE DARLING: Yes! She was out walking one evening at half-past seven with a boy from the school across the street. A baby like her!

THE HUSBAND: What did you do?

THE LITTLE DARLING: I gave her a spanking.

THE HUSBAND: Are you as strict as all that?

THE LITTLE DARLING: Who would be if I

wasn't? My older sister is working and mother does nothing but grumble . . . it's all up to me.

THE HUSBAND: Heavens, you're nice. (*Kisses her, and grows more tender.*) You remind me of someone, too.

THE LITTLE DARLING: Who?

THE HUSBAND: No one in particular . . . of bygone days . . . of my youth. Come on, drink, little girl.

THE LITTLE DARLING: Say, how old are you? . . . You . . . why . . . I don't even know your name.

THE HUSBAND: Karl.

THE LITTLE DARLING: Is it possible? Your name is Karl?

THE HUSBAND: Was his name Karl, too?

THE LITTLE DARLING: No, that's what's so queer . . . your . . . eyes . . . The way you look at me . . .

THE HUSBAND: What was he? You haven't told me yet.

THE LITTLE DARLING: Oh, he was a bad man . . . he must have been or he wouldn't have left me in the lurch.

THE HUSBAND: Did you love him very much?

THE LITTLE DARLING: Of course I loved him.

THE HUSBAND: I know what he was—a lieutenant.

THE LITTLE DARLING: No, he wasn't in the army. They wouldn't take him. His father owns a house in . . . but why do you have to know?

THE HUSBAND (*kisses her*): Your eyes are really grey. At first, I thought they were black.

THE LITTLE DARLING: Aren't they pretty enough for you? (THE HUSBAND *kisses her eyes.*) Don't please—I won't have it . . . O, please don't! Let me get up . . . only for a minute . . . please.

THE HUSBAND (*more tenderly still*): No, indeed.

THE LITTLE DARLING: But, please, Karl . . .

THE HUSBAND: How old are you? Eighteen, aren't you?

THE LITTLE DARLING: Just past nineteen.

THE HUSBAND: Nineteen . . . and I—

THE LITTLE DARLING: You are thirty . . .

THE HUSBAND: And a little over. Let's not talk about it.

THE LITTLE DARLING: He was thirty-two, when I first met him.

THE HUSBAND: How long ago was that?

THE LITTLE DARLING: I don't remember . . . Say, there must have been something in that wine.

THE HUSBAND: What makes you think so?

THE LITTLE DARLING: I am all . . . see,— everything going round and round.

THE HUSBAND: Then hold tight to me. Like this . . . (*He holds her close to him, and becomes more and more tender. She resists very little.*) I'll tell you something, dear. We might go on . . . go on . . .

THE LITTLE DARLING: Home . . .

THE HUSBAND: Well, not exactly home . . .

THE LITTLE DARLING: What do you mean? Oh, no—no . . . I won't go anywhere else. What do you think I am?

THE HUSBAND: But listen to me, child, the next time we meet, you know, we will arrange it so that . . . (*He has slipped to the floor with his head in her lap.*) This is so nice, so nice!

THE LITTLE DARLING: What are you doing? (*She kisses his hair.*) There must have been something in that wine . . . I'm so sleepy . . . What would happen, if I couldn't get up again? But, but, look, but Karl, if some one should come in . . . please . . . the waiter.

THE HUSBAND: No . . . waiter . . . will ever come in here . . .

*   *   *   *   *

THE LITTLE DARLING *leaning back at the end of the sofa with closed eyes.* THE HUSBAND *pacing up and down the little room, after lighting a cigarette. Long silence.*

THE HUSBAND (*looking for a long time at the girl; speaking to himself*): Who knows what sort of a person she really is? Damn it! So quick . . . This wasn't very prudent of me . . . hmm . . .

THE LITTLE DARLING (*without opening her eyes*): There must have been something in the wine.

THE HUSBAND: Why do you think so?

THE LITTLE DARLING: If there hadn't been . . .

THE HUSBAND: Why do you blame everything on the wine?

THE LITTLE DARLING: Where are you? Why are you so far away? Come here, to me. (THE HUSBAND *sits beside her.*) Now tell me if you really love me.

THE HUSBAND: But you know . . . (*He interrupts himself quickly.*) Of course.

THE LITTLE DARLING: Listen . . . There must have . . . Come, tell me the truth, what was in the wine?

THE HUSBAND: Why, do you think I would drug your wine?

THE LITTLE DARLING: Well, you see, I can't understand it. I'm really not the kind . . . We've just met . . . I swear, I'm not the kind . . . Honestly, I'm not. If you think that of me—

THE HUSBAND: Well, why worry about it? I don't think anything bad of you. I think you love me, that's all.

THE LITTLE DARLING: Hmm . . . hmm . . .

THE HUSBAND: After all, when two young people are alone in a room, and have dinner, and drink wine . . . there doesn't have to be anything in the wine.

THE LITTLE DARLING: I just said so to be saying something.

THE HUSBAND: Really, why?

THE LITTLE DARLING (*almost defiantly*): Because I was ashamed.

THE HUSBAND: How absurd! There is no reason to be ashamed. Especially, since I made you think of your first boy friend.

THE LITTLE DARLING: Yes.

THE HUSBAND: Your first boy friend.

THE LITTLE DARLING: Hmmm.

THE HUSBAND: Now I should like to know who the others were.

THE LITTLE DARLING: There weren't any others.

THE HUSBAND: That isn't true, it can't be true.

THE LITTLE DARLING: Oh, please, don't tease me.

THE HUSBAND: Would you like a cigarette?

THE LITTLE DARLING: No, thanks.

THE HUSBAND: Do you know what time it is?

THE LITTLE DARLING: What?

THE HUSBAND: Half-past eleven.

THE LITTLE DARLING: Really?

THE HUSBAND: Well . . . and your mother? She's used to this, isn't she?

THE LITTLE DARLING: Do you really want me to go home?

THE HUSBAND: Earlier in the evening you asked me yourself—

THE LITTLE DARLING: You're not the same person you were awhile ago. What have I done to make you change so?

THE HUSBAND: What *is* the matter with you, dear? What's on your mind?

THE LITTLE DARLING: And it was only your looks, believe me, or you could have talked yourself blue in the face. All sorts of men have asked me to go to a *chambre séparée* with them.

THE HUSBAND: Well, would you like . . . to come here again with me soon . . . or somewhere else—

THE LITTLE DARLING: I don't know.

THE HUSBAND: What do you mean, "I don't know"?

THE LITTLE DARLING: Oh, don't ask so many questions!

THE HUSBAND: Then when? First of all, I must explain that I don't live in Vienna. I'm only here for a few days at a time, now and then.

THE LITTLE DARLING: Oh, you're not Viennese?

THE HUSBAND: Yes, I am. But I'm living out of town now . . .

THE LITTLE DARLING: Where?

THE HUSBAND: Oh, that doesn't matter.

THE LITTLE DARLING: Don't get scared, I won't come to see you.

THE HUSBAND: If it'd be any fun for you, you can come. I live in Graz.

THE LITTLE DARLING: Honest?

THE HUSBAND: Yes, what's so wonderful about that?

THE LITTLE DARLING: You are married, aren't you?

THE HUSBAND (*very much astonished*): What makes you think so?

THE LITTLE DARLING: I just got a notion you were.

THE HUSBAND: You don't mind?

THE LITTLE DARLING: Well, I would rather you were single. So you are married!

THE HUSBAND: Come on, tell me what made you think I was married.

THE LITTLE DARLING: When a man says he doesn't live in Vienna and doesn't always have time—

THE HUSBAND: After all it's not very unlikely.

THE LITTLE DARLING: I don't believe it.

THE HUSBAND: Does it hurt your conscience to lead a married man astray?

THE LITTLE DARLING: I don't doubt your wife acts just like you.

THE HUSBAND (*very indignant*): That will do. Such remarks—

THE LITTLE DARLING: I thought you didn't have a wife.

THE HUSBAND: Whether I have or not, such remarks are not made in my presence. (*He has risen.*)

THE LITTLE DARLING: But Karl, Karl, what's the matter? Are you mad at me? Really, I didn't know you were married. I was just talking to hear myself talk. Come, don't be mad.

THE HUSBAND (*comes back to her after a few minutes*): You are strange creatures, you . . . women. (*He becomes tender again.*)

THE LITTLE DARLING: Please . . . don't . . . it's so late.

THE HUSBAND: Well, then, listen to me. Let's talk seriously. I'd like to see you again. I'd like to see you often.

THE LITTLE DARLING: Would you?

THE HUSBAND: But I've got to be absolutely sure I can depend on you. I can't be watching you.

THE LITTLE DARLING: Oh, I can take care of myself.

THE HUSBAND: You are . . . well, I can't say inexperienced . . . but, you are young, and, men in general are pretty thoughtless.

THE LITTLE DARLING: Oh, my!

THE HUSBAND: I'm talking about morals. You know what I mean—

THE LITTLE DARLING: Tell me, just what do you take me for?

THE HUSBAND: Look here. If you want me, and me only, we can easily arrange it, even if I do generally live in Graz. A place like this where some one may come in any moment is no place for us. (THE LITTLE DARLING *snuggles up to him.*) Next time . . . we'll go somewhere else, what do you say?

THE LITTLE DARLING: Yes.

THE HUSBAND: Where we can be entirely alone.

THE LITTLE DARLING: Yes.

THE HUSBAND (*embracing her passionately*): We'll talk it over on the way home. (*He rises, and opens the door.*) Waiter . . . the check!

VII
THE LITTLE DARLING AND
THE POET

A small room comfortably furnished. Window-drapes which make the room half-dark. Red curtains. A large writing-table covered with books and papers. A baby-grand piano against the wall. THE LITTLE DARLING *and* THE POET *are just entering.* THE POET *closes the door.*

THE POET (*kisses her*): My darling!

THE LITTLE DARLING (*has her hat and coat on*): Oh! It's gorgeous here! Only you can't see anything!

THE POET: Your eyes will get used to the soft twilight. Those sweet eyes. (*Kisses her eyes.*)

THE LITTLE DARLING: But these sweet eyes haven't time to do that.

THE POET: Why not?

THE LITTLE DARLING: Because I can only stay a minute.

THE POET: Don't you take off your hat though?

THE LITTLE DARLING: Just for a minute.

THE POET (*takes out the pin and puts the hat aside*): And your coat—

THE LITTLE DARLING: The idea! I have to leave right away.

THE POET: No, you must take a good rest. We've been knocking around for three hours.

THE LITTLE DARLING: We were riding.

THE POET: We rode home, but we ran around, it must have been fully three hours, at the country place. Please sit down, anywhere you like. Here at the desk —no, that wouldn't do. On the sofa— how's that. (*Forces her to sit down.*) If you're very tired, stretch out—like this. (*She lies down.*) Put your head on the cushion.

THE LITTLE DARLING (*laughing*): But I'm not tired a bit!

THE POET: You just think you're not. There, and if you are sleepy, go to sleep. I will be very quiet. And if you like I'll play you a lullaby . . . one of my own . . . (*He goes to the piano.*)

THE LITTLE DARLING: One of your own?

THE POET: Yes.

THE LITTLE DARLING: Why, Robert, I thought you were a doctor.

THE POET: How so? I told you I was a writer.

THE LITTLE DARLING: Well, all those writers are called doctor, aren't they?

THE POET: Not all of them. I'm not, for instance. Why did you think I was?

THE LITTLE DARLING: Why, you just said the piece you're playing is your own.

THE POET: Perhaps it isn't. But it doesn't matter, does it? It certainly doesn't matter who composed it, as long as it is beautiful. Don't you think so?

THE LITTLE DARLING: Of course it must be beautiful. That's the main thing.

THE POET: Do you know what I mean?

THE LITTLE DARLING: Mean—?

THE POET: By what I just said.

THE LITTLE DARLING (*sleepily*): Of course I do.

THE POET (*gets up, goes to her, and strokes her hair*): You can't understand a word.

THE LITTLE DARLING: I'm not so dumb.

THE POET: Yes, you are, but that is just why I love you. It is wonderful when girls are dumb. I mean in the way you are.

THE LITTLE DARLING: Say, you're being insulting!

THE POET: Angel! Little one! Isn't it nice to lie on this soft, Persian couch cover?

THE LITTLE DARLING: Oh, yes. Don't you want to play something else on the piano?

THE POET: No, I'd rather be with you. (*Caressing her.*)

THE LITTLE DARLING: Hadn't you better light the light?

THE POET: Oh, no . . . The dusk is so restful. We've been bathing in sunshine all day. Now we've just climbed out of the bath and slipped on . . . a bathrobe of twilight. (*Laughs.*) No—that ought to be expressed differently. Don't you think so?

THE LITTLE DARLING: I don't know.

THE POET (*moves away from her a little*): Divine stupidity! (*He takes out a notebook, and writes a few words in it.*)

THE LITTLE DARLING: What are you doing? (*She turns toward him.*) What are you writing?

THE POET (*softly*): Sun, bath, twilight, cloak . . . yes . . . (*He puts the notebook back. Aloud.*) Nothing . . . Now, tell me, sweetheart, wouldn't you like something to eat or drink?

THE LITTLE DARLING: I'm really not thirsty, but I'm hungry.

THE POET: Hmm . . . I'd rather you were thirsty. I have some cognac here, but I have to go out for food.

THE LITTLE DARLING: Can't you send somebody?

THE POET: Not very easily. The cleaning woman isn't here now—Oh well. I'll go . . . What would you like?

THE LITTLE DARLING: Really it's hardly worth while. I am going right home, anyway.

THE POET: That's out of the question. I'll tell you what—when we leave, let's go somewhere and have supper.

THE LITTLE DARLING: Oh, no. I haven't time for that. And, anyway, where can we go? Somebody we know might see us.

THE POET: Do you know so many people?

THE LITTLE DARLING: It takes only one to make trouble.

THE POET: What sort of trouble?

THE LITTLE DARLING: Well, suppose mother should hear about this . . .

THE POET: We can go where no one can see us. There are plenty of restaurants with *chambres séparées*.

THE LITTLE DARLING (*singing*): "A little cafe. A *chambre séparée* . . ."

THE POET: Have you ever been in a *chambre séparée*?

THE LITTLE DARLING: To tell the truth—yes.

THE POET: Who was the happy man?

THE LITTLE DARLING: Oh, it wasn't that way . . . I went with my girl friend and her fiancé. They took me along.

THE POET: You expect me to believe that?

THE LITTLE DARLING: You needn't believe it!

THE POET (*close to her*): Are you blushing? I can hardly see. I can't even distinguish your features. (*He touches her cheeks with his hands.*) But even so I recognize you.

THE LITTLE DARLING: Well, be careful you don't take me for some one else.

THE POET: It is strange, I can't remember how you look.

THE LITTLE DARLING: Thanks.

THE POET (*seriously*): It is uncanny. I can't visualize your features. In a certain sense I have forgotten you already—Now, if I couldn't remember even the sound of your voice either . . . what would you really be? Something near and far at the same time . . . Eerie.

THE LITTLE DARLING: What are you talking about?

THE POET: Nothing, my angel, nothing. Where are your lips? (*He kisses her.*)

THE LITTLE DARLING: Won't you please put the light on?

THE POET: No . . . (*Becomes very tender.*) Tell me, do you love me?

THE LITTLE DARLING: Very much . . . Oh, so much!

THE POET: Have you ever loved any one as much as me?

THE LITTLE DARLING: I told you already I never truly loved before.

THE POET: But . . . (*He sighs.*)

THE LITTLE DARLING: He was my fiancé.

THE POET: I'd rather you didn't mention him now.

THE LITTLE DARLING: Say . . . what are you doing . . . see here! . . .

THE POET: We might imagine we are in a palace in India.

THE LITTLE DARLING: I'm sure the people there aren't as naughty as you are.

THE POET: How idiotic! Perfectly divine— Ah, if you only could understand what you are to me . . .

THE LITTLE DARLING: What?

THE POET: Don't push me away like this all the time. I'm not doing anything—

THE LITTLE DARLING: But my corset hurts.

THE POET (*simply*): Take it off.

THE LITTLE DARLING: All right. But you mustn't think you can do anything, just because I haven't any corset on.

THE POET: Of course not. (THE LITTLE DARLING *rises, and takes off her corset in the darkness.*)

THE POET (*sitting, meanwhile, on the sofa*): Tell me, aren't you at all interested in knowing my name?

THE LITTLE DARLING: Yes, what is your name?

THE POET: I'd rather not tell you my real name, but my pseudonym is—

THE LITTLE DARLING: What's a pseudonym?

THE POET: The name I sign to the things I write.

THE LITTLE DARLING: Oh, you don't sign your real name? (THE POET *close to her.*) Please . . . Don't . . . Stop.

THE POET: What a fragrance ascends to my nostrils! Ah, how sweet! (*He kisses her breasts.*)

THE LITTLE DARLING: You are tearing my chemise.

THE POET: Off with it . . . Off with it . . . It's in the way.

THE LITTLE DARLING: Oh, Robert.

THE POET: And now let's enter our Indian palace.

THE LITTLE DARLING: Tell me first—do you really love me?

THE POET: I adore you. (*Kisses her passionately.*) I adore you, my sweetheart, my springtime . . . my . . .

THE LITTLE DARLING: Robert . . . Robert . . .

* * * * *

THE POET: That was celestial bliss . . . My pen name is . . .

THE LITTLE DARLING: Robert—oh, my Robert!

THE POET: Biebitz.

THE LITTLE DARLING: Why is your pen name Biebitz?

THE POET: That isn't my real name, my pseudonym . . . Well, don't you recognize it?

THE LITTLE DARLING: No.

THE POET: You don't know the name Biebitz? Divine! Really? You are only pretending you don't know it, aren't you?

THE LITTLE DARLING: I swear, I never heard it.

THE POET: Don't you ever go to the theater?

THE LITTLE DARLING: Oh, yes. I was at the opera only the other night with—you know, with one of my girl friends and her uncle, to hear *Cavalleria Rusticana.*

THE POET: Hm, you never go to plays.

THE LITTLE DARLING: I never get passes for them.

THE POET: I'll send you one very soon.

THE LITTLE DARLING: Oh, do! And don't forget, for something funny.

THE POET: Oh . . . something funny . . . you don't care to see anything sad?

THE LITTLE DARLING: I'd rather not.

THE POET: Not even if it is a play of mine?

THE LITTLE DARLING: A play of yours? Do you write plays?

THE POET: Excuse me, I just want to light a candle. I haven't seen you since you have become my beloved—Angel! (*He lights a candle.*)

THE LITTLE DARLING: Don't, I'm ashamed.

Give me something to cover myself, please.

THE POET: Later! (*He approaches her with the light, and looks at her a long time.*)

THE LITTLE DARLING (*covering her face with her hands*): Go away, Robert!

THE POET: You are beautiful. You're Beauty. Perhaps you are Nature. You are Holy Simplicity.

THE LITTLE DARLING: Ouch! You're dropping wax on me. Can't you be more careful?

THE POET (*puts the candle away*): You are that which I have long sought. You love me for my own sake. I might be only a clerk, but you would love me. It does my heart good. I must confess I could not help being suspicious until this moment. Tell me, honestly, you didn't think I might be Biebitz?

THE LITTLE DARLING: Gosh, I don't know him. What are you trying to get me to say? I never heard of Biebitz before.

THE POET: Such is fame! No, forget what I have told you. Forget Biebitz. I am Robert and I want to be only Robert to you. I was only joking. (*Lightly.*) I'm no writer at all. I'm a clerk and in the evening I play the piano in a night-club.

THE LITTLE DARLING: But now I'm all mixed up . . . and the way you look at a person. What's the matter with you? What do you mean?

THE POET: Very strange! It's something that has never happened to me, sweetheart; I am on the verge of tears. You move me deeply. Live with me, will you? We shall be very dear to each other.

THE LITTLE DARLING: Is it true about the night-club?

THE POET: Yes, but don't speak about it any more. If you love me, don't ask me any questions at all. Tell me, can you get away for a few weeks?

THE LITTLE DARLING: How do you mean—get away?

THE POET: I mean, leave home?

THE LITTLE DARLING: How can I! What would mother say? And if I wasn't there, the whole house would be upside down in no time.

THE POET: I had a beautiful picture of you and me together, in the solitude of a great forest, living the life of nature for a few weeks . . . Eden. And then, some day,

"Good-bye"—going our separate ways, not knowing where . . .

THE LITTLE DARLING: You are already talking about "Good-bye." And I thought you loved me so much.

THE POET: That's just the reason. (*Bends over her, and kisses her on the forehead.*) You sweet thing!

THE LITTLE DARLING: Please, hold me tight. I feel so cold.

THE POET: I suppose it's time you were getting dressed. Wait, I'll light a few more candles for you.

THE LITTLE DARLING (*rising*): Don't look.

THE POET: No. (*At the window.*) Tell me, sweet, are you happy?

THE LITTLE DARLING: How do you mean?

THE POET: I mean are you glad you're alive? Is the world a great old place?

THE LITTLE DARLING: Things could be a lot better.

THE POET: You don't get me. I know you're having a hard time at home. I know you are not a princess. All the same there's such a thing as feeling alive. Do you ever feel alive?

THE LITTLE DARLING: Got a comb?

THE POET (*goes to the dressing-table, hands her a comb, and watches her*): Heavens, how ravishing you look!

THE LITTLE DARLING: Please . . . no more!

THE POET: Please, stay here a while. I'll get something for supper, and . . .

THE LITTLE DARLING: But it is awfully late already.

THE POET: It isn't nine yet.

THE LITTLE DARLING: Gee. I must hurry. Please!

THE POET: When shall I see you again?

THE LITTLE DARLING: When do you want to see me?

THE POET: Tomorrow.

THE LITTLE DARLING: What's tomorrow?

THE POET: Saturday.

THE LITTLE DARLING: Oh, I can't. I must take my little sister to see her guardian.

THE POET: Then Sunday . . . hm . . . Sunday . . . on Sunday . . . now I'll have to explain something to you. I'm not Biebitz, but Biebitz is a friend of mine. I'll introduce you sometime. Biebitz's play will be given Sunday. I'll send you a pass, and take you home after the show. You'll tell me how you liked the play. Won't you?

THE LITTLE DARLING: Here you are talking about this Biebitz again. I don't understand what it's all about.

THE POET: I shan't know you really, until I know what the play means to you.

THE LITTLE DARLING: Well . . . I'm ready.

THE POET: Come, sweetheart. (*They go out.*)

VIII
THE POET AND THE ACTRESS

A room in a country inn. It is a spring night. Moonlight over the meadows and hills. The windows are open. THE POET *and* THE ACTRESS *enter, and as they cross the threshold, the candle* THE POET *carries is blown out.*

THE POET: Oh . . .

THE ACTRESS: What's the matter?

THE POET: The candle.—But we don't need it. Look how light it is. Wonderful! (THE ACTRESS *sinks down suddenly before the window with joined hands.*) What's the matter? (THE ACTRESS *remains silent.* THE POET *goes to her.*) What are you doing?

THE ACTRESS (*indignant*): Can't you see? I'm praying—

THE POET: Do you believe in God?

THE ACTRESS: Certainly. Do you take me for a scoundrel?

THE POET: I understand.

THE ACTRESS: Come, kneel down beside me. Really, you may pray just once. It won't take the crease out of your trousers. (THE POET *kneels beside her, and puts his arm around her waist.*) Profligate! (*Rises.*) And do you know to whom I prayed?

THE POET: To God, presumably.

THE ACTRESS (*with deep sarcasm*): Oh no, I was praying to you!

THE POET: Then why did you look out the window?

THE ACTRESS: Suppose you tell me first where you have dragged me, seducer.

THE POET: But, darling, it was your idea. You wanted to go to the country—and chose this very place.

THE ACTRESS: Well, isn't it a good place?

THE POET: Certainly. It's charming here. Just think—two hours from Vienna—perfect solitude. And what a landscape!

THE ACTRESS: Yes. You could even write something if you had talent.

THE POET: You've been here before?

THE ACTRESS: Have I been here before? I lived here for years.

THE POET: With whom?

THE ACTRESS: With Fred, of course.

THE POET: Oh!

THE ACTRESS: How I loved that man!

THE POET: You've told me all about it.

THE ACTRESS: I'm sorry. I can go away if I bore you!

THE POET: Bore me? You can't imagine what you mean to me . . . You are a whole world to me . . . You are divine, you are genius . . . You are Holy Simplicity. Yes, you are . . . But you oughtn't to talk about Fred now.

THE ACTRESS: That was a *faux pas*. Well?

THE POET: I'm glad you see it that way.

THE ACTRESS: Come, give me a kiss! (THE POET *kisses her*.) But now we had better say good-night. Good-night, darling!

THE POET: What do you mean?

THE ACTRESS: I mean, I am going to lie down and go to sleep.

THE POET: Certainly, do that very thing, but this . . . "good-night" business . . . Where do I stay?

THE ACTRESS: There are lots of other rooms here.

THE POET: The others don't appeal to me. Don't you think I'd better light a candle?

THE ACTRESS: Yes.

THE POET (*lights a candle, which stands upon the dressing-table*): What a charming room . . . and what pious people they must be. Pictures of saints everywhere. It would be interesting to spend some time among people like this . . . quite another world. How little we know of our fellow creatures.

THE ACTRESS: Quit talking nonsense, and reach me the bag from the table.

THE POET: Here, my only beloved! (THE ACTRESS *takes a small framed picture out of the hand-bag and puts it on the dressing-table*.) What's that?

THE ACTRESS: That's the Virgin.

THE POET: Do you always carry her around with you?

THE ACTRESS: She is my talisman. And now go, Robert!

THE POET: What kind of a joke is this? Don't you want me to . . .

THE ACTRESS: No, you must go.

THE POET: And when am I to come in?

THE ACTRESS: In ten minutes.

THE POET (*kisses her*): Au revoir!

THE ACTRESS: Where are you going?

THE POET: I shall walk up and down under your window. I love to stroll about in the fresh air at night. My finest inspirations come to me that way. And now, near you, enveloped in the atmosphere of your longing . . . and wafted away by your art . . .

THE ACTRESS: You talk like an idiot . . .

THE POET (*hurt*): There are women who might say . . . like a poet.

THE ACTRESS: All right, but now do go. And don't start an affair with the waitress. (THE POET *goes*. THE ACTRESS *undresses. She hears* THE POET *going downstairs, and now she hears his steps under her window. As soon as she is undressed, she goes to the window and looks down where he stands waiting. She whispers to him.*) Come! (THE POET *comes quickly upstairs and runs toward her. She, meanwhile, has gone to bed and put out the light. He locks the door.*) Now you may sit down beside me, and tell me a story.

THE POET (*sits down on the bed beside her*): Hadn't I better close the window? Isn't it too cold for you?

THE ACTRESS: Oh, no!

THE POET: Now, what shall I tell you?

THE ACTRESS: Tell me to whom you are unfaithful at this moment.

THE POET: Unfortunately, I'm not unfaithful at all yet.

THE ACTRESS: Then take comfort in knowing that I am unfaithful to some one.

THE POET: I can well imagine.

THE ACTRESS: Who do you suppose it is?

THE POET: But, my dear, how do you expect me to know?

THE ACTRESS: Guess, then.

THE POET: Let's see . . . your manager.

THE ACTRESS: My dear man, I'm not a chorus-girl.

THE POET: Well, I just thought . . .

THE ACTRESS: Guess again.

THE POET: Then it's your leading-man . . . Benno.

THE ACTRESS: Stupid! He doesn't care for

women . . . didn't you know that? He's having an affair with the postman!

THE POET: You don't say.

THE ACTRESS: Come, kiss me. (THE POET embraces her.) What are you doing?

THE POET: Don't torment me so!

THE ACTRESS: Listen, Robert, I'll make you a proposition. Come, lie down in bed with me.

THE POET: You bet I will!

THE ACTRESS: Hurry, hurry!

THE POET: Yes . . . if it had been up to me I'd have been there long ago . . . Listen . . .

THE ACTRESS: What to?

THE POET: To the crickets chirping out there.

THE ACTRESS: You are crazy, my dear, there are no crickets in these parts.

THE POET: But you can hear them.

THE ACTRESS: Will you hurry up?

THE POET (beside her): Here I am.

THE ACTRESS: Now lie quiet . . . sh-h . . . don't move . . .

THE POET: But, what's the idea?

THE ACTRESS: You'd like to have an affair with me?

THE POET: That ought to be pretty clear to you by now.

THE ACTRESS: There are a good many men who would like to . . .

THE POET: Yet it can scarcely be gainsaid that at this particular moment my chances seem to be the best.

THE ACTRESS: Then, come, my cricket! I shall call you "cricket" from now on.

THE POET: All right. . . .

THE ACTRESS: Now, tell me, who am I deceiving?

THE POET: Who? . . . Me perhaps . . .

THE ACTRESS: My dear, you have softening of the brain.

THE POET: Or some one . . . whom you have never seen . . . some one, whom you don't . . . some one—who is set apart for you but whom you will never find . . .

THE ACTRESS: Please! Don't talk extravagant nonsense.

THE POET: Isn't it strange . . . you too, and yet one would think . . . But no, that would take away the best in you. Come— my dear—come.

* * * * *

THE ACTRESS: That's better than acting in idiotic plays. Don't you think so?

THE POET: Well it's good to know that you get to act in an intelligent one occasionally.

THE ACTRESS: You conceited puppy. I suppose you're thinking of that play of yours?

THE POET: Yes, I am.

THE ACTRESS (seriously): Undoubtedly it is a masterpiece.

THE POET: Right!

THE ACTRESS: Yes, you are a genius, Robert!

THE POET: I seize the opportunity of asking why you cancelled your performance the night before last. There was absolutely nothing the matter with you.

THE ACTRESS: Well, I wanted to annoy you.

THE POET: But why? What have I done to you?

THE ACTRESS: You were arrogant.

THE POET: How so?

THE ACTRESS: Everybody at the theater thinks you are.

THE POET: Really?

THE ACTRESS: But I told them, "I guess he has a perfect right to be arrogant."

THE POET: And what did they say?

THE ACTRESS: How could they say anything? I don't talk to any of them.

THE POET: Oh, I see.

THE ACTRESS: They would like nothing better than to poison me, every one of them. But they won't get the chance.

THE POET: Don't think now of anybody else. Be glad that you are here with me, and tell me you love me.

THE ACTRESS: What more proof do you want?

THE POET: It can't be proved.

THE ACTRESS: Fine! Then what more do you want?

THE POET: How many other men have . . . had this sort of proof? Did you love them all?

THE ACTRESS: No, I have loved only one.

THE POET (embraces her): My . . .

THE ACTRESS: Fred . . .

THE POET: My name is Robert. What do I mean to you, if you are thinking of Fred, now?

THE ACTRESS: You are just a caprice.

THE POET: Thanks for letting me know.

THE ACTRESS: Well, aren't you glad?

THE POET: Glad of being a caprice?

THE ACTRESS: It seems to me that you have a very good reason to be glad.

THE POET: Oh, this—

THE ACTRESS: Yes, this, my pale cricket!— Say, what about that chirping? Are they still chirping?

THE POET: Don't you hear them?

THE ACTRESS: Of course, I hear them. But, my dear, those are frogs.

THE POET: You are mistaken. Frogs croak.

THE ACTRESS: Of course, they croak.

THE POET: Those things aren't croaking, dear, they're chirping.

THE ACTRESS: You are the most obstinate person I have ever run into. Kiss me, Froggie.

THE POET: Please don't call me that. It makes me nervous all over.

THE ACTRESS: Well, what shall I call you?

THE POET: I have a name. Robert.

THE ACTRESS: Oh, but that's too stupid.

THE POET: Please simply call me by my own name.

THE ACTRESS: Well, then, Robert, give me a kiss . . . Ah! (*She kisses him.*) Now, are you satisfied, Froggie? Ha-ha-ha.

THE POET: May I light a cigarette?

THE ACTRESS: Give me one, too. (*He takes his cigarette-case from the dressing-table; takes out two cigarettes, lights both, and gives her one.*) By the way, you haven't said a word about my performance yesterday.

THE POET: What performance?

THE ACTRESS: What performance!

THE POET: Oh, yes. I wasn't at the theater.

THE ACTRESS: You're trying to be funny.

THE POET: Why should I? Since you cancelled your performance only two days ago, I assumed you wouldn't be in full possession of your powers, yesterday, so I decided not to go.

THE ACTRESS: You missed something wonderful.

THE POET: Yes?

THE ACTRESS: It was a sensation. The people actually turned pale.

THE POET: You really could tell?

THE ACTRESS: Benno said, "Dearest, you acted divinely."

THE POET: Hm! . . . And so ill the day before.

THE ACTRESS: Indeed I was. And do you know why? Because of my longing for you.

THE POET: A little while ago you said you stayed away just to hurt me.

THE ACTRESS: What do *you* know about my love for you? You are so cold. I was delirious all night. Had high fever, a hundred and four.

THE POET: Rather a high temperature for a caprice.

THE ACTRESS: You call it a caprice! I am dying for love of you, and you call it a caprice . . .

THE POET: And Fred . . .

THE ACTRESS: Fred? . . . Don't mention that tramp to me!

IX
THE ACTRESS AND THE COUNT

The bedroom of THE ACTRESS, *luxuriously furnished. It is midday. The blinds are still down. A candle is burning on the dressing-table.* THE ACTRESS *is lying in her four-poster bed. On the cover are many newspapers.* THE COUNT, *wearing his uniform of captain in the Dragoons, enters. He stops just inside the door.*

THE ACTRESS: Ah, Count.

THE COUNT: Your mother said I might, otherwise I wouldn't—

THE ACTRESS: Please, come in.

THE COUNT: I kiss your hand. Pardon me . . . just coming in from the street . . . I can't see a thing yet. Oh, now I find the way. (*At her bedside.*) I kiss your hand.

THE ACTRESS: Please sit down, Count.

THE COUNT: Your mother said, "The young lady isn't well." . . . Nothing serious, I hope.

THE ACTRESS: Nothing serious? I was at the point of death.

THE COUNT: Dear me! Surely not.

THE ACTRESS: You are very kind to bother about me.

THE COUNT: At the point of death! And last night you were still able to give a divine performance.

THE ACTRESS: It seems to have been a great success.

THE COUNT: Tremendous! . . . The audience was carried away. To say nothing of myself.

THE ACTRESS: Thanks for the beautiful flowers.

THE COUNT: Don't mention it, Fräulein.

THE ACTRESS (*looking significantly at a large basket of flowers on a little table near the window*): You see I have them near me.

THE COUNT: You were literally overwhelmed with flowers and wreaths yesterday.

THE ACTRESS: I left them in my dressing-room. All I brought home was your basket.

THE COUNT (*kissing her hand*): That's nice of you. (THE ACTRESS *suddenly seizes his hand, and kisses it.*)Fräulein!

THE ACTRESS: Don't be frightened, Count, it doesn't bind you to anything.

THE COUNT: You are a strange being . . . enigmatic, one might almost say. (*Pause.*)

THE ACTRESS: Fräulein Birken, I suppose, is less puzzling.

THE COUNT: Little Birken is no puzzle at all. That is, of course, I really know her only very slightly.

THE ACTRESS: Oh!

THE COUNT: Believe me. But you are a puzzle. And I've always been fascinated by puzzles. I have missed a great deal of enjoyment by not seeing you act until last night.

THE ACTRESS: Oh, had you never? How did that happen?

THE COUNT: It's hard for me to go to the theater. I am used to dining late . . . then by the time I can get there, the best part of the play is over. Don't you see?

THE ACTRESS: From now on, I suppose, you will dine earlier.

THE COUNT: I've thought of that too. Or maybe I won't dine at all. There is really no pleasure in eating.

THE ACTRESS: What pleasure is there of any sort for an elderly man, even if he's as well preserved as you are?

THE COUNT: I often ask that myself. But I am not an old man. There are other reasons why I don't care for certain things.

THE ACTRESS: Do you think so?

THE COUNT: Yes. Louis, for instance, says I am a philosopher. You see he means I am much given to meditation.

THE ACTRESS: Yes . . . Thinking never made anyone happy.

THE COUNT: I have too much time on my hands, that's why. You see, I've often thought it would be better if they would transfer me to Vienna, where there is diversion, excitement. Really, though, it's not much better here than it was over there.

THE ACTRESS: Where is "over there"?

THE COUNT: Down in Hungary, in the ghastly holes where I've been stationed most of the time.

THE ACTRESS: What kept you in Hungary? In ghastly holes?

THE COUNT: The service, as I am telling you.

THE ACTRESS: But why so long in Hungary?

THE COUNT: It just happened that way.

THE ACTRESS: It must be enough to drive one mad.

THE COUNT: I don't know about that. There's a lot more to do there than here. You know, drilling recruits, breaking in mounts . . . and the country really isn't as bad as they say. The lowlands are really quite beautiful . . . and such sunsets. Too bad I'm no painter. I've often thought if I were, I would paint them. We have a young chap in our regiment, Splany, who could do it. But, dear me, what dull stories I'm telling you.

THE ACTRESS: Please go on; I am enjoying myself royally.

THE COUNT: I can just talk and talk with you. Louis said the same. It isn't often one can find a good listener.

THE ACTRESS: In Hungary, anyway.

THE COUNT: Or in Vienna either. People are the same everywhere. Where there are more of them, the crowd's bigger, that's all. Do you really like people?

THE ACTRESS: Like them? I detest them! I can't bear the sight of them. I never see any one. I'm always alone. Nobody ever comes here.

THE COUNT: You know, I sort of thought you were a misanthrope. Artists must often be like that. If one lives on a higher plane . . . Well, you are lucky. You know at least what you live for.

THE ACTRESS: What makes you think so? I haven't the slightest idea what I live for!

THE COUNT: But surely to be famous . . . to be fêted . . .

THE ACTRESS: And you think that is happiness?

THE COUNT: Pardon me. There is no happiness. And it's the same with all that people talk about most . . . For instance, love: there is no such thing.

THE ACTRESS: You are right about that!

THE COUNT: Pleasure . . . intoxication . . . we can have that, all right . . . they are definite things. When I'm having a good time I know I'm having a good time. When I'm drunk I know I'm drunk. All right. We can be sure of things like that. And when they're over, why, they're just over.

THE ACTRESS (*grandly*): Just over.

THE COUNT: But as soon as one—how shall I put it—as soon as one gets away from the present moment, I mean, if one looks ahead or back . . . well, everything is lost. Ahead —darkness. Back—confusion . . . In a word, one gets all mixed up. Am I right?

THE ACTRESS (*wide-eyed, nods*): You seem to have it all down.

THE COUNT: And, you see, my dear lady, once this is clear, it really doesn't matter whether one lives in Vienna or in ghastly Hungarian holes. You see, for instance . . . Where may I put my cap? Yes, thank you . . . What were we talking about?

THE ACTRESS: About living in ghastly holes in Hungary.

THE COUNT: Yes, yes. Well, as I said, there isn't much difference whether I spend the evening at the casino or at the club. It's all the same.

THE ACTRESS: And what has all this to do with love?

THE COUNT: If a person thinks there *is* such a thing, he'll always have somebody who'll love him.

THE ACTRESS: Fräulein Birken, for instance.

THE COUNT: I really don't see why you always have to come back to little Birken.

THE ACTRESS: But she's your mistress, isn't she?

THE COUNT: Who says so?

THE ACTRESS: Everybody knows it.

THE COUNT: Except myself, I would have you observe.

THE ACTRESS: But you fought a duel on her account!

THE COUNT: Maybe I was even killed without knowing it.

THE ACTRESS: Now, Count, you are a man of honor. Won't you sit closer to me?

THE COUNT: I will take the liberty.

THE ACTRESS: Over here. (*She draws him to her, and passes her hand through his hair.*) I knew you would come today.

THE COUNT: How did you know?

THE ACTRESS: I knew it last night in the theater.

THE COUNT: Could you see me from the stage?

THE ACTRESS: My dear sir! Didn't you notice I acted for you alone?

THE COUNT: Surely not?

THE ACTRESS: When I saw you in the first row, I felt I could fly.

THE COUNT: Could fly? Because of me? I never even suspected you noticed me!

THE ACTRESS: Your aristocratic reserve is enough to drive one to despair.

THE COUNT: Yes, Fräulein . . .

THE ACTRESS: "Yes, Fräulein"! . . . At least, take your saber off!

THE COUNT: If I may. (*Takes it off and leans it against the bed.*)

THE ACTRESS: And now do give me a kiss. (THE COUNT *kisses her. She does not release him.*) It would have been better if I had never seen you.

THE COUNT: No, it's better this way.

THE ACTRESS: Count, you are a poseur!

THE COUNT: I—how so?

THE ACTRESS: Can't you imagine how happy most men would be in your shoes?

THE COUNT: I am very happy.

THE ACTRESS: I thought there *was* no happiness? Why do you look at me that way? I believe I frightened you, Count!

THE COUNT: I told you, you are a puzzle.

THE ACTRESS: Oh, don't bother me with your philosophy . . . come closer . . . and ask me for anything at all . . . you can have whatever you want. You are so handsome.

THE COUNT: Well, then, I ask (*Kissing her hand.*) permission to call again this evening.

THE ACTRESS: This evening . . . but I have to work.

THE COUNT: After the play.

THE ACTRESS: And you ask for nothing else?

THE COUNT: I shall ask for everything else after the play.

THE ACTRESS (*hurt*): You can go right on asking, you abominable poseur.

THE COUNT: But, look, we've been perfectly frank with each other so far . . . it seems to me it would be much nicer after the play . . . much cozier than now, when . . . I have a sort of feeling the door might fly open any moment . . .

THE ACTRESS: It doesn't open from the outside.

THE COUNT: Well, you see, I have an idea one shouldn't lightly spoil in advance something which may be very beautiful.

THE ACTRESS: Which may be . . .

THE COUNT: To be frank, love in the morning seems horrible to me.

THE ACTRESS: Well, you are about the craziest I ever—

THE COUNT: I am not talking about women in general . . . because in general it doesn't make any difference anyway. But women like you . . . no, you may call me crazy as often as you want to. But women like you . . . one doesn't take them before breakfast. That way . . . you know . . . that way . . .

THE ACTRESS: Oh, you are a darling!

THE COUNT: You understand what I mean, don't you? Now that is what I am looking forward to . . .

THE ACTRESS: How do you want it to be?

THE COUNT: Like this . . . I wait for you in a carriage after the play, then we drive somewhere for supper . . .

THE ACTRESS: I am not Fräulein Birken.

THE COUNT: I didn't say you were. Only, it seems to me, one has to be in the right mood for everything. I don't get into the right mood until supper. The best part of it will be when we drive home, and then . . .

THE ACTRESS: And then?

THE COUNT: Well, that depends on circumstances.

THE ACTRESS: Do sit closer. Closer.

THE COUNT (*sitting down on the bed*): It seems to me the pillows are scented . . . Mignonette—isn't it?

THE ACTRESS: It's very warm in here, don't you think so? (THE COUNT *bends down, and kisses her neck.*) Oh, Count, this is contrary to your program.

THE COUNT: Who said anything about a "program"? I have none. (THE ACTRESS *drawing him close to her.*) It really is very warm.

THE ACTRESS: Do you think so? And so dark, just as if it were evening . . . (*Draws him toward her.*) It is evening . . . it is night . . . Close your eyes, if it's too light for you. Come! . . . Come! . . . (THE COUNT *offers no further resistance.*)

*   *   *   *   *

THE ACTRESS: And what about moods now, you poseur?

THE COUNT: You are a little devil.

THE ACTRESS: What a thing to say!

THE COUNT: Well, then, an angel.

THE ACTRESS: You should have been an actor. Really! You understand women. And do you know what I am going to do now?

THE COUNT: What?

THE ACTRESS: I am going to tell you I shall never see you again.

THE COUNT: But why?

THE ACTRESS: Never, never. You are too dangerous! You drive a woman mad. You stand in front of me, all of a sudden, as if nothing had happened.

THE COUNT: But . . .

THE ACTRESS: Please remember, Count, I have just become your mistress.

THE COUNT: I shall never forget it!

THE ACTRESS: And what about tonight?

THE COUNT: What do you mean?

THE ACTRESS: Well, you wanted to wait for me after the theater?

THE COUNT: Very well, let's make it the day after tomorrow.

THE ACTRESS: What do you mean, the day after tomorrow? We were talking about tonight.

THE COUNT: There wouldn't be much sense in that.

THE ACTRESS: You—you *are* getting old!

THE COUNT: You don't quite understand me. What I am talking about has to do rather —how shall I express myself—rather concerns the soul.

THE ACTRESS: What do I care about your soul?

THE COUNT: Believe me, the soul enters into this. I am sure it is a mistake to believe that the spiritual and the physical are separable.

THE ACTRESS: Don't bother me with your philosophy. If I want any of that, I will read books.

THE COUNT: One never learns from books.

THE ACTRESS: Quite true! And that's why you ought to wait for me tonight. We will come to some agreement regarding the soul, you villain!

THE COUNT: Well, then, if I may, I shall wait in my carriage . . .

THE ACTRESS: You shall wait for me here in my home—

THE COUNT: After the play . . .

THE ACTRESS: Naturally. (THE COUNT *buckles on his sword.*) What are you doing?

THE COUNT: I believe it is time for me to go. For a formal call I have stayed a little too long as it is.

THE ACTRESS: Well, this evening it shan't be any formal call.

THE COUNT: You think not?

THE ACTRESS: I'll take care of that. And now give me one more kiss, my darling little philosopher. Here, you seducer, you . . . sweet child, you seller of souls, you . . . skunk . . . you . . . (*After she has ardently kissed him several times, she thrusts him violently away.*) Count, you have done me a great honor.

THE COUNT: I kiss your hand, Fräulein. (*At the door.*) Au revoir.

THE ACTRESS: Good-bye, Hungarian hole!

X
THE COUNT AND THE PROSTITUTE

About six in the morning. A poorly furnished room with one window. Dirty yellow shutters closed. Tattered green curtains. On the dresser several photographs, and beside them a woman's hat, cheap and terrible. Behind the mirror cheap Japanese fans. On the table, which has a red cover, is an oil lamp with a shade of yellow paper. The lamp is burning low and makes a disagreeable odor. Beside it a pitcher with a bit of left-over beer, and a half-empty glass. On the floor beside the bed woman's clothes in disorderly heap, as if they had just been hastily flung off. THE PROSTITUTE *lies in the bed asleep, breathing quietly.* THE COUNT *is lying on the sofa fully dressed with his light overcoat on. His hat is on the floor at the head of the sofa.*

THE COUNT (*stirs, rubs his eyes, sits up suddenly, and looks around*): Where am I? Oh, yes. So I actually went home with that woman. (*He rises quickly, notices her bed.*) Oh, there she is. So it can all happen, even at my age. I haven't the least idea—did they carry me up here? No. I saw myself— coming into this room. I was still awake then or they waked me up or . . . or maybe it's only the room that reminds me of something? Yes . . . just yesterday I

saw it. (*Looks at his watch.*) What! yesterday, a couple of hours ago!—But, I knew something had to happen. I felt it in my bones. When I began to drink yesterday, I felt it . . . and what has happened? Nothing. Or did it? 'Pon my soul . . . for . . . ten years I haven't done anything like this. Well, the long and short of it is that I got good and god damn drunk. If I only knew when I began. I remember perfectly when Louis and I went into the night-club, and . . . no, no. We left together, so it must have been on the way. Yes, that's it, Louis and I were riding in my carriage. But why do I rack my brain about it? It really doesn't matter. Let's see how we get out of here. (*Rises. The lamp shakes.*) Oh! (*Looks at the sleeping girl.*) She's a good healthy sleeper. I don't remember anything, but I'll put the money on the table and then . . . good-bye. If I didn't know what she is! (*Studies her.*) I've known a good many who didn't look as virtuous even in their sleep. My word! Louis would say I'm philosophizing again, but it's true, sleep is the great leveler—like its brother death. Hm, I should like to know, whether—No, I'd certainly remember that. No, no, I just passed out on the sofa . . . and nothing happened. It is incredible how much alike all women look. Well, let's go. (*He is about to go.*) Oh, of course. (*He takes his wallet, and is about to take out a banknote.*)

THE PROSTITUTE (*awakening*): Well . . . who's there so early in the morning? (*Recognizing him.*) Hello, honey!

THE COUNT: Good morning. Have a good sleep?

THE PROSTITUTE (*stretching*): Oh, come here. Give's a little loving.

THE COUNT (*bends down to her, considers, and draws back*): I was just going . . .

THE PROSTITUTE: Going?

THE COUNT: It's really quite time.

THE PROSTITUTE: You want to go away?

THE COUNT (*slightly embarrassed*): Well . . .

THE PROSTITUTE: Well, good-bye, you'll come some other time.

THE COUNT: Yes, good-bye. But, won't you give me your hand? (THE PROSTITUTE *reaches out her hand from under the cover.* THE COUNT *takes her hand, and kisses it mechanically, and becoming aware of what he is doing, he smiles.*) Just as if she were a princess. Besides, if one only . . .

THE PROSTITUTE: Why do you look at me that way?

THE COUNT: If one sees nothing but the head, as I do now . . . anyway, they all look innocent when they first wake up . . . My word, one might imagine almost anything if there weren't such a stench of kerosene.

THE PROSTITUTE: Yes, the lamp's rotten.

THE COUNT: How old are you, really?

THE PROSTITUTE: Well, what would you guess?

THE COUNT: Twenty-four.

THE PROSTITUTE: Like hell I am!

THE COUNT: Older?

THE PROSTITUTE: I'm just going on twenty.

THE COUNT: And how long have you been . . .

THE PROSTITUTE: In this business? A year.

THE COUNT: You began early.

THE PROSTITUTE: Better early than late.

THE COUNT (*sits down upon her bed*): Tell me, are you really happy?

THE PROSTITUTE: Huh?

THE COUNT: I mean, are you getting along all right?

THE PROSTITUTE: I always get along O.K.

THE COUNT: I see . . . Well, did it never occur to you that you might do something else?

THE PROSTITUTE: What else?

THE COUNT: Well . . . You are a very pretty girl. You might take a lover, for instance.

THE PROSTITUTE: Do you think I haven't got any?

THE COUNT: Yes, I know. But I mean just one, understand? Just one, who would take care of you, so that you wouldn't have to go with everybody.

THE PROSTITUTE: I don't go with everybody. I don't have to, thank God. I can pick and choose. (THE COUNT *looks around the room.*)

THE PROSTITUTE (*noticing*): We're moving uptown next month.

THE COUNT: We? Who?

THE PROSTITUTE: Well, the Madam, and a couple of other girls that live here.

THE COUNT: There are others?

THE PROSTITUTE: Next door . . . don't you hear? . . . that's Milly. She was in the cafe too.

THE COUNT: I hear some one snoring.

THE PROSTITUTE: That's Milly. She'll snore all day long, until ten o'clock tonight. Then she'll get up, and go to the cafe.

THE COUNT: This is a terrible life.

THE PROSTITUTE: Sure is. And believe me the Madam gives her hell. I'm always on my beat by noon.

THE COUNT: What do you do on your beat?

THE PROSTITUTE: What do you suppose? I go lookin' for business.

THE COUNT: Oh, yes . . . of course . . . (*Rises, takes out his wallet, and puts a banknote on the table.*) Good-bye!

THE PROSTITUTE: Going already? . . . Good-bye . . . Call again soon. (*Turns on her side.*)

THE COUNT (*stands still*): Tell me, are you fed up with everything?

THE PROSTITUTE: Huh?

THE COUNT: I mean you don't get any fun out of it anymore?

THE PROSTITUTE (*yawning*): I wanna sleep.

THE COUNT: It's all the same to you whether a man is young or old or whether he . . .

THE PROSTITUTE: What's it to you?

THE COUNT: Well . . . (*Suddenly hitting upon a thought.*) My word, now I know who you remind me of . . .

THE PROSTITUTE: Do I look like some baby you know?

THE COUNT: Incredible, incredible. Now please, don't talk, at least not for a minute . . . (*Looking at her.*) The very same features. (*Suddenly he kisses her eyes.*) The very image.

THE PROSTITUTE: What the . . .

THE COUNT: My word, it's too bad that you . . . aren't something else. You could make your fortune!

THE PROSTITUTE: You gab just like Franz.

THE COUNT: Who is Franz?

THE PROSTITUTE: The waiter in the cafe where us girls hang out.

THE COUNT: In what way am I just like Franz?

THE PROSTITUTE: He is always telling me "You could make your fortune," and wanting me to marry him.

THE COUNT: Why don't you?

THE PROSTITUTE: No thank you . . . I don't want to marry, no, not for all the money in the world. Maybe I'll get hooked up when I get older.

THE COUNT: The eyes . . . the very same eyes . . . Louis would certainly say I was a fool.—But I must kiss your eyes once more . . . so . . . and now "Good-bye."

THE PROSTITUTE: Good-bye . . .

THE COUNT (*at the door*): Tell me . . . aren't you a bit surprised?

THE PROSTITUTE: What by?

THE COUNT: That I don't want anything else.

THE PROSTITUTE: Lots of men don't want it in the morning.

THE COUNT: I see . . . (*To himself.*) Absurd, that I expect her to be surprised . . . Well, good-bye . . . (*He is at the door.*) But really, I'm vexed. I ought to know that women like her care only about money. What am I saying . . . "like her"? It is fine, anyway, at least she doesn't pretend; I ought to be glad . . . (*Aloud.*) May I come to see you again very soon?

THE PROSTITUTE (*with closed eyes*): Sure.

THE COUNT: When are you at home?

THE PROSTITUTE: I'm always at home. Just ask for Leocadia.

THE COUNT: Leocadia . . . All right. Well, good-bye. (*At the door.*) I can still feel the wine. But after all, this is glorious. I go with a woman like her and do nothing but kiss her eyes, because she has reminded me of some one . . . (*Turns toward her.*) Tell me, Leocadia, does it often happen that a man leaves you in this way?

THE PROSTITUTE: What way?

THE COUNT: As I am doing.

THE PROSTITUTE: In the morning.

THE COUNT: No . . . have you ever had any one with you—who didn't want anything from you?

THE PROSTITUTE: No, that has never happened to me.

THE COUNT: Well, what do you think then? Do you think I didn't like you?

THE PROSTITUTE: Why shouldn't you like me? You sure liked me enough last night.

THE COUNT: I like you now, too.

THE PROSTITUTE: But last night you sure liked me.

THE COUNT: What makes you say so?

THE PROSTITUTE: Why ask foolish questions?

THE COUNT: Last night . . . well, tell me, didn't I drop right down on the sofa?

THE PROSTITUTE: Certainly . . . you and me together.

THE COUNT: Together!

THE PROSTITUTE: Sure, don't you remember?

THE COUNT: Together . . . I . . .

THE PROSTITUTE: But you passed right out.

THE COUNT: Right away . . . I see . . . that's what happened? . . .

THE PROSTITUTE: Sure thing, honey. But you must have been awfully stewed if you can't remember.

THE COUNT: So . . . And yet . . . there is a faint resemblance . . . Good-bye . . . (*Listens.*) What is the matter?

THE PROSTITUTE: The house-girl is up. Give her a tip as you go out. The outside door is open, so you won't have to give anything to the janitor.

THE COUNT (*in the anteroom*): Well . . . it would have been beautiful, if I had only kissed her eyes. It would have been almost an adventure . . . But . . . it wasn't to be . . . (*The servant opens the door.*) Ah —here . . . Good-night.

THE SERVANT: Good morning!

THE COUNT: Of course . . . good morning . . . Good morning.

MRS WARREN'S PROFESSION

George Bernard Shaw

CHARACTERS

VIVIE WARREN
MRS WARREN
PRAED
SIR GEORGE CROFTS
FRANK GARDNER
REV. SAMUEL GARDNER

ACT I

Summer afternoon in a cottage garden on the eastern slope of a hill a little south of Haslemere in Surrey. Looking up the hill, the cottage is seen in the left hand corner of the garden, with its thatched roof and porch, and a large latticed window to the left of the porch. A paling completely shuts in the garden, except for a gate on the right. The common rises uphill beyond the paling to the sky line. Some folded canvas garden chairs are leaning against the side bench in the porch. A lady's bicycle is propped against the wall, under the window. A little to the right of the porch a hammock is slung from two posts. A big canvas umbrella, stuck in the ground, keeps the sun off the hammock, in which a young lady lies reading and making notes, her head towards the cottage and her feet towards the gate. In front of the hammock, and within reach of her hand, is a common kitchen chair, with a pile of serious-looking books and a supply of writing paper on it.

A gentleman walking on the common comes into sight from behind the cottage. He is hardly past middle age, with something of the artist about him, unconventionally but carefully dressed, and clean-shaven except for a moustache, with an eager susceptible face and very amiable and considerate manners. He has silky black hair, with waves of grey and white in it. His eyebrows are white, his moustache black. He seems not certain of his way. He looks over the paling; takes stock of the place; and sees the young lady.

THE GENTLEMAN (*taking off his hat*): I beg your pardon. Can you direct me to Hind-head View—Mrs Alison's?

THE YOUNG LADY (*glancing up from her book*): This is Mrs Alison's. (*She resumes her work*).

THE GENTLEMAN: Indeed! Perhaps—may I ask are you Miss Vivie Warren?

THE YOUNG LADY (*sharply, as she turns on her elbow to get a good look at him*): Yes.

THE GENTLEMAN (*daunted and conciliatory*): I'm afraid I appear intrusive. My name is Praed. (VIVIE *at once throws her books upon the chair, and gets out of the hammock*). Oh, pray dont let me disturb you.

VIVIE (*striding to the gate and opening it for him*): Come in, Mr Praed. (*He comes in*). Glad to see you. (*She proffers her hand and takes his with a resolute and hearty grip. She is an attractive specimen of the sensible, able, highly-educated young middle-class Englishwoman. Age 22. Prompt, strong, confident, self-possessed. Plain business-like dress, but not dowdy. She wears a chatelaine at her belt, with a fountain pen and a paper knife among its pendants*).

PRAED: Very kind of you indeed, Miss Warren. (*She shuts the gate with a vigorous slam. He passes in to the middle of the garden, exercising his fingers, which are slightly numbed by her greeting*). Has your mother arrived?

VIVIE (*quickly, evidently scenting aggression*): Is she coming?

PRAED (*surprised*): Didnt you expect us?

VIVIE: No.

PRAED: Now, goodness me, I hope Ive not mistaken the day. That would be just like me, you know. Your mother arranged that she was to come down from London and that I was to come over from Horsham to be introduced to you.

VIVIE (*not at all pleased*): Did she? Hm! My mother has rather a trick of taking me by surprise—to see how I behave myself when she's away, I suppose. I fancy I shall take my mother very much by surprise one of these days, if she makes arrangements that concern me without consulting me beforehand. She hasnt come.

PRAED (*embarrassed*): I'm really very sorry.

VIVIE (*throwing off her displeasure*): It's not your fault, Mr Praed, is it? And I'm very glad youve come. You are the only one of my mother's friends I have ever asked her to bring to see me.

PRAED (*relieved and delighted*): Oh, now this is really very good of you, Miss Warren!

VIVIE: Will you come indoors; or would you rather sit out here and talk?

PRAED: It will be nicer out here, dont you think?

VIVIE: Then I'll go and get you a chair. (*She goes to the porch for a garden chair*).

PRAED (*following her*): Oh, pray, pray! Allow me. (*He lays hands on the chair*).

VIVIE (*letting him take it*): Take care of your fingers: theyre rather dodgy things, those chairs. (*She goes across to the chair with the books on it; pitches them into the hammock; and brings the chair forward with one swing).*

PRAED (*who has just unfolded his chair*): Oh, now do let me take that hard chair. I like hard chairs.

VIVIE: So do I. Sit down, Mr Praed. (*This invitation she gives with genial peremptoriness, his anxiety to please her clearly striking her as a sign of weakness of character on his part. But he does not immediately obey.*)

PRAED: By the way, though, hadnt we better go to the station to meet your mother?

VIVIE (*coolly*): Why? She knows the way.

PRAED (*disconcerted*): Er—I suppose she does (*he sits down*).

VIVIE: Do you know, you are just like what I expected. I hope you are disposed to be friends with me.

PRAED (*again beaming*): Thank you, my dear Miss Warren: thank you. Dear me! I'm so glad your mother hasnt spoilt you!

VIVIE: How?

PRAED: Well, in making you too conventional. You know, my dear Miss Warren, I am a born anarchist. I hate authority. It spoils the relations between parent and child: even between mother and daughter. Now I was always afraid that your mother would strain her authority to make you very conventional. It's such a relief to find that she hasnt.

VIVIE: Oh! have I been behaving unconventionally?

PRAED: Oh no: oh dear no. At least not conventionally unconventionally, you understand. (*She nods and sits down. He goes on, with a cordial outburst*) But it was so charming of you to say that you were disposed to be friends with me! You modern young ladies are splendid: perfectly splendid!

VIVIE (*dubiously*): Eh? (*watching him with dawning disappointment as to the quality of his brains and character*).

PRAED: When I was your age, young men and women were afraid of each other: there was no good fellowship. Nothing real. Only gallantry copied out of novels, and as vulgar and affected as it could be. Maidenly reserve! gentlemanly chivalry! always saying no when you meant yes! simple purgatory for shy and sincere souls.

VIVIE: Yes, I imagine there must have been a frightful waste of time. Especially women's time.

PRAED: Oh, waste of life, waste of everything. But things are improving. Do you know, I have been in a positive state of excitement about meeting you ever since your magnificent achievements at Cambridge: a thing unheard of in my day. It was perfectly splendid, your tieing with the third wrangler. Just the right place, you know. The first wrangler is always a dreamy, morbid fellow, in whom the thing is pushed to the length of a disease.

VIVIE: It doesnt pay. I wouldnt do it again for the same money.

PRAED (*aghast*): The same money!

VIVIE: I did it for £50.

PRAED: Fifty pounds!

VIVIE: Yes. Fifty pounds. Perhaps you dont know how it was. Mrs Latham, my tutor at Newnham, told my mother that I could distinguish myself in the mathematical tripos if I went in for it in earnest. The papers were full just then of Phillipa Summers beating the senior wrangler. You remember about it, of course.

PRAED (*shakes his head energetically*)!!!

VIVIE: Well anyhow she did; and nothing would please my mother but that I should do the same thing. I said flatly it was not worth my while to face the grind since I was not going in for teaching; but I offered to try for fourth wrangler or thereabouts for £50. She closed with me at that, after a little grumbling; and I was better than my bargain. But I wouldnt do it again for that. £200 would have been nearer the mark.

PRAED (*much damped*): Lord bless me! Thats a very practical way of looking at it.

VIVIE: Did you expect to find me an unpractical person?

PRAED: But surely it's practical to consider not only the work these honors cost, but also the culture they bring.

VIVIE: Culture! My dear Mr Praed: do you know what the mathematical tripos means? It means grind, grind, grind for six to eight hours a day at mathematics, and nothing but mathematics. I'm supposed to know something about science; but I know nothing except the mathematics it involves. I can make calculations for engineers, electricians, insurance companies, and so on; but I know next to nothing about engineering or electricity or insurance. I dont even know arithmetic well. Outside mathematics, lawn-tennis, eating, sleeping, cycling, and walking, I'm a more ignorant barbarian than any woman could possibly be who hadnt gone in for the tripos.

PRAED (*revolted*): What a monstrous, wicked, rascally system! I knew it! I felt at once that it meant destroying all that makes womanhood beautiful.

VIVIE: I dont object to it on that score in the least. I shall turn it to very good account, I assure you.

PRAED: Pooh! In what way?

VIVIE: I shall set up in chambers in the City, and work at actuarial calculations and conveyancing. Under cover of that I shall do some law, with one eye on the Stock Exchange all the time. Ive come down here by myself to read law: not for a holiday, as my mother imagines. I hate holidays.

PRAED: You make my blood run cold. Are you to have no romance, no beauty in your life?

VIVIE: I dont care for either, I assure you.

PRAED: You cant mean that.

VIVIE: Oh yes I do. I like working and getting paid for it. When I'm tired of working, I like a comfortable chair, a cigar, a little whisky, and a novel with a good detective story in it.

PRAED (*rising in a frenzy of repudiation*): I dont believe it. I am an artist; and I cant believe it; I refuse to believe it. It's only that you havnt discovered yet what a wonderful world art can open up to you.

VIVIE: Yes I have. Last May I spent six weeks in London with Honoria Fraser. Mamma thought we were doing a round of sightseeing together; but I was really at Honoria's chambers in Chancery Lane every day, working away at actuarial calculations for her, and helping her as well as a greenhorn could. In the evenings we smoked and talked, and never dreamt of going out except for exercise. And I never enjoyed myself more in my life. I cleared all my expenses, and got initiated into the business without a fee into the bargain.

PRAED: But bless my heart and soul, Miss Warren, do you call that discovering art?

VIVIE: Wait a bit. That wasnt the beginning. I went up to town on an invitation from some artistic people in Fitzjohn's Avenue: one of the girls was a Newnham chum. They took me to the National Gallery—

PRAED (*approving*): Ah!! (*He sits down, much relieved*).

VIVIE (*continuing*):—to the Opera—

PRAED (*still more pleased*): Good!

VIVIE:—and to a concert where the band played all the evening: Beethoven and Wagner and so on. I wouldnt go through that experience again for anything you could offer me. I held out for civility's sake until the third day; and then I said, plump out, that I couldnt stand any more of it, and went off to Chancery Lane. Now you know the sort of perfectly splendid modern young lady I am. How do you think I shall get on with my mother?

PRAED (*startled*): Well, I hope—er—

VIVIE: It's not so much what you hope as what you believe, that I want to know.

PRAED: Well, frankly, I am afraid your mother will be a little disappointed. Not from any shortcoming on your part, you know: I dont mean that. But you are so different from her ideal.

VIVIE: Her what?!

PRAED: Her ideal.

VIVIE: Do you mean her ideal of ME?

PRAED: Yes.

VIVIE: What on earth is it like?

PRAED: Well, you must have observed, Miss Warren, that people who are dissatisfied with their own bringing-up generally think that the world would be all right if everybody were to be brought up quite differently. Now your mother's life has been—er—I suppose you know—

VIVIE: Dont suppose anything, Mr Praed. I hardly know my mother. Since I was a child I have lived in England, at school or college, or with people paid to take charge of me. I have been boarded out all my life. My mother has lived in Brussels or Vienna and never let me go to her. I only see her when she visits England for a few days. I dont complain: it's been very pleasant; for people have been very good to me; and there has always been plenty of money to make things smooth. But dont imagine I know anything about my mother. I know far less than you do.

PRAED (*very ill at ease*): In that case—(*He stops, quite at a loss. Then, with a forced attempt at gaiety*) But what nonsense we are talking! Of course you and your mother will get on capitally. (*He rises, and looks abroad at the view*). What a charming little place you have here!

VIVIE (*unmoved*): Rather a violent change of subject, Mr Praed. Why wont my mother's life bear being talked about?

PRAED: Oh, you really mustnt say that. Isnt it natural that I should have a certain delicacy in talking to my old friend's daughter about her behind her back? You and she will have plenty of opportunity of talking about it when she comes.

VIVIE: No: she wont talk about it either. (*Rising*) However, I daresay you have good reasons for telling me nothing. Only, mind this, Mr Praed. I expect there will be a battle royal when my mother hears of my Chancery Lane project.

PRAED (*ruefully*): I'm afraid there will.

VIVIE: Well, I shall win, because I want nothing but my fare to London to start there to-morrow earning my own living by devilling for Honoria. Besides, I have no mysteries to keep up; and it seems she has. I shall use that advantage over her if necessary.

PRAED (*greatly shocked*): Oh no! No, pray. Youd not do such a thing.

VIVIE: Then tell me why not.

PRAED: I really cannot. I appeal to your good feeling. (*She smiles at his sentimentality*). Besides, you may be too bold. Your mother is not to be trifled with when she's angry.

VIVIE: You cant frighten me, Mr Praed. In that month at Chancery Lane I had opportunities of taking the measure of one or two women very like my mother. You may back me to win. But if I hit harder in my ignorance than I need, remember that it is you who refuse to enlighten me. Now, let us drop the subject. (*She takes her chair and replaces it near the hammock with the same vigorous swing as before*).

PRAED (*taking a desperate resolution*): One word, Miss Warren. I had better tell you. It's very difficult; but—

MRS WARREN *and* SIR GEORGE CROFTS *arrive at the gate.* MRS WARREN *is between 40 and 50, formerly pretty, showily dressed in a* brilliant hat and a gay blouse fitting tightly over her bust and flanked by fashionable sleeves. Rather spoilt and domineering, and decidedly vulgar, but, on the whole, a genial and fairly presentable old blackguard of a woman.

CROFTS *is a tall powerfully-built man of about 50, fashionably dressed in the style of a young man. Nasal voice, reedier than might be expected from his strong frame. Clean-shaven bulldog jaws, large flat ears, and thick neck: gentlemanly combination of the most brutal types of city man, sporting man, and man about town.*

VIVIE: Here they are. (*Coming to them as they enter the garden*) How do, mater? Mr Praed's been here this half hour waiting for you.

MRS WARREN: Well, if youve been waiting, Praddy, it's your own fault: I thought youd have had the gumption to know I was coming by the 3.10 train. Vivie: put your hat on, dear: youll get sunburnt. Oh, I forgot to introduce you. Sir George Crofts: my little Vivie. (CROFTS *advances to* VIVIE *with his most courtly manner. She nods, but makes no motion to shake hands*).

CROFTS: May I shake hands with a young lady whom I have known by reputation very long as the daughter of one of my oldest friends?

VIVIE (*who has been looking him up and down sharply*): If you like. (*She takes his tenderly proffered hand and gives it a squeeze that makes him open his eyes; then turns away, and says to her mother*) Will you come in, or shall I get a couple more chairs? (*She goes into the porch for the chairs*).

MRS WARREN: Well, George, what do you think of her?

CROFTS (*ruefully*): She has a powerful fist. Did you shake hands with her, Praed?

PRAED: Yes: it will pass off presently.

CROFTS: I hope so. (VIVIE *reappears with two more chairs. He hurries to her assistance*). Allow me.

MRS WARREN (*patronizingly*): Let Sir George help you with the chairs, dear.

VIVIE (*pitching them into his arms*): Here you are. (*She dusts her hands and turns to* MRS WARREN). Youd like some tea, wouldnt you?

MRS WARREN (*sitting in* PRAED's *chair and fanning herself*): I'm dying for a drop to drink.

VIVIE: I'll see about it. (*She goes into the cottage*).

SIR GEORGE *has by this time managed to unfold a chair and plant it beside* MRS WARREN, *on her left. He throws the other on the grass and sits down, looking dejected and rather foolish, with the handle of his stick in his mouth.* PRAED, *still very uneasy, fidgets about the garden on their right.*

MRS WARREN (*to* PRAED, *looking at* CROFTS): Just look at him, Praddy: he looks cheerful, dont he? He's been worrying my life out these three years to have that little girl of mine shewn to him; and now that Ive done it, he's quite out of countenance. (*Briskly*) Come! sit up, George; and take your stick out of your mouth. (CROFTS *sulkily obeys*).

PRAED: I think, you know—if you dont mind my saying so—that we had better get out of the habit of thinking of her as a little girl. You see she has really distinguished herself; and I'm not sure, from what I have seen of her, that she is not older than any of us.

MRS WARREN (*greatly amused*): Only listen to him, George! Older than any of us! Well, she has been stuffing you nicely with her importance.

PRAED: But young people are particularly sensitive about being treated in that way.

MRS WARREN: Yes; and young people have to get all that nonsense taken out of them, and a good deal more besides. Dont you interfere, Praddy: I know how to treat my own child as well as you do. (PRAED, *with a grave shake of his head, walks up the garden with his hands behind his back.* MRS WARREN *pretends to laugh, but looks after him with perceptible concern. Then she whispers to* CROFTS) Whats the matter with him? What does he take it like that for?

CROFTS (*morosely*): Youre afraid of Praed.

MRS WARREN: What! Me! Afraid of dear old Praddy! Why, a fly wouldn't be afraid of him.

CROFTS: Youre afraid of him.

MRS WARREN (*angry*): I'll trouble you to

mind your own business, and not try any of your sulks on me. I'm not afraid of you, anyhow. If you cant make yourself agreeable, youd better go home. (*She gets up, and, turning her back on him, finds herself face to face with* PRAED). Come, Praddy, I know it was only your tender-heartedness. Youre afraid I'll bully her.

PRAED: My dear Kitty: you think I'm offended. Dont imagine that: pray dont. But you know I often notice things that escape you; and though you never take my advice, you sometimes admit afterwards that you ought to have taken it.

MRS WARREN: Well, what do you notice now?

PRAED: Only that Vivie is a grown woman. Pray, Kitty, treat her with every respect.

MRS WARREN (*with genuine amazement*): Respect! Treat my own daughter with respect! What next, pray!

VIVIE (*appearing at the cottage door and calling to* MRS WARREN): Mother: will you come to my room before tea?

MRS WARREN: Yes, dearie. (*She laughs indulgently at* PRAED's *gravity, and pats him on the cheek as she passes him on her way to the porch*). Dont be cross, Praddy. (*She follows* VIVIE *into the cottage*).

CROFTS (*furtively*): I say, Praed.

PRAED: Yes.

CROFTS: I want to ask you a rather particular question.

PRAED: Certainly. (*He takes* MRS WARREN's *chair and sits close to* CROFTS).

CROFTS: Thats right: they might hear us from the window. Look here: did Kitty ever tell you who that girl's father is?

PRAED: Never.

CROFTS: Have you any suspicion of who it might be?

PRAED: None.

CROFTS (*not believing him*): I know, of course, that you perhaps might feel bound not to tell if she had said anything to you. But it's very awkward to be uncertain about it now that we shall be meeting the girl every day. We dont exactly know how we ought to feel towards her.

PRAED: What difference can that make? We take her on her own merits. What does it matter who her father was?

CROFTS (*suspiciously*): Then you know who he was?

PRAED (*with a touch of temper*): I said no just now. Did you not hear me?

CROFTS: Look here, Praed. I ask you as a particular favor. If you do know (*movement of protest from* PRAED)—I only say, if you know, you might at least set my mind at rest about her. The fact is, I feel attracted.

PRAED (*sternly*): What do you mean?

CROFTS: Oh, dont be alarmed: it's quite an innocent feeling. Thats what puzzles me about it. Why, for all I know, *I* might be her father.

PRAED: You! Impossible!

CROFTS (*catching him up cunningly*): You know for certain that I'm not?

PRAED: I know nothing about it, I tell you, any more than you. But really, Crofts—oh no, it's out of the question. Theres not the least resemblance.

CROFTS: As to that, theres no resemblance between her and her mother that I can see. I suppose she's not your daughter, is she?

PRAED (*rising indignantly*): Really, Crofts—!

CROFTS: No offence, Praed. Quite allowable as between two men of the world.

PRAED (*recovering himself with an effort and speaking gently and gravely*): Now listen to me, my dear Crofts. (*He sits down again*). I have nothing to do with that side of Mrs Warren's life, and never had. She has never spoken to me about it; and of course I have never spoken to her about it. Your delicacy will tell you that a handsome woman needs some friends who are not—well, not on that footing with her. The effect of her own beauty would become a torment to her if she could not escape from it occasionally. You are probably on much more confidential terms with Kitty than I am. Surely you can ask her the question yourself.

CROFTS: I have asked her, often enough. But she's so determined to keep the child all to herself that she would deny that it ever had a father if she could. (*Rising*) I'm thoroughly uncomfortable about it, Praed.

PRAED (*rising also*): Well, as you are, at all events, old enough to be her father, I dont mind agreeing that we both regard Miss Vivie in a parental way, as a young girl whom we are bound to protect and help. What do you say?

CROFTS (*aggressively*): I'm no older than you, if you come to that.

PRAED: Yes you are, my dear fellow: you were born old. I was born a boy: Ive never been able to feel the assurance of a grown-up man in my life. (*He folds his chair and carries it to the porch*).

MRS WARREN (*calling from within the cottage*): Prad-dee! George! Tea-ea-ea-ea!

CROFTS (*hastily*): She's calling us. (*He hurries in*).

PRAED *shakes his head bodingly, and is following* CROFTS *when he is hailed by a young gentleman who has just appeared on the common, and is making for the gate. He is pleasant, pretty, smartly dressed, cleverly good-for-nothing, not long turned 20, with a charming voice and agreeably disrespectful manner. He carries a light sporting magazine rifle.*

THE YOUNG GENTLEMAN: Hallo! Praed!

PRAED: Why, Frank Gardner! (FRANK *comes in and shakes hands cordially*). What on earth are you doing here?

FRANK: Staying with my father.

PRAED: The Roman father?

FRANK: He's rector here. I'm living with my people this autumn for the sake of economy. Things came to a crisis in July: the Roman father had to pay my debts. He's stony broke in consequence; and so am I. What are you up to in these parts? Do you know the people here?

PRAED: Yes: I'm spending the day with a Miss Warren.

FRANK (*enthusiastically*): What! Do you know Vivie? Isnt she a jolly girl? I'm teaching her to shoot with this (*putting down the rifle*). I'm so glad she knows you: youre just the sort of fellow she ought to know. (*He smiles, and raises the charming voice almost to a singing tone as he exclaims*) It's ever so jolly to find you here, Praed.

PRAED: I'm an old friend of her mother. Mrs Warren brought me over to make her daughter's acqaintance.

FRANK: The mother! Is she here?

PRAED: Yes: inside, at tea.

MRS WARREN (*calling from within*): Prad-dee-ee-ee-eee! The tea-cake'll be cold.

PRAED (*calling*): Yes, Mrs Warren. In a moment. Ive just met a friend here.

MRS WARREN: A what?

PRAED (*louder*): A friend.

MRS WARREN: Bring him in.

PRAED: All right. (*To* FRANK) Will you accept the invitation?

FRANK (*incredulous, but immensely amused*): Is that Vivie's mother?

PRAED: Yes.

FRANK: By Jove! What a lark! Do you think she'll like me?

PRAED: Ive no doubt youll make yourself popular, as usual. Come in and try (*moving towards the house*).

FRANK: Stop a bit. (*Seriously*) I want to take you into my confidence.

PRAED: Pray dont. It's only some fresh folly, like the barmaid at Redhill.

FRANK: It's ever so much more serious than that. You say youve only just met Vivie for the first time?

PRAED: Yes.

FRANK (*rhapsodically*): Then you can have no idea what a girl she is. Such character! Such sense! And her cleverness! Oh, my eye, Praed, but I can tell you she is clever! And—need I add?—she loves me.

CROFTS (*putting his head out of the window*): I say, Praed: what are you about? Do come along. (*He disappears*).

FRANK: Hallo! Sort of chap that would take a prize at a dog show, aint he? Who's he?

PRAED: Sir George Crofts, an old friend of Mrs Warren's. I think we had better come in. (*On their way to the porch they are interrupted by a call from the gate. Turning, they see an elderly clergyman looking over it*).

THE CLERGYMAN (*calling*): Frank!

FRANK: Hallo! (*To* PRAED) The Roman father. (*To the clergyman*) Yes, gov'nor: all right: presently. (*To* PRAED) Look here, Praed: youd better go in to tea. I'll join you directly.

PRAED: Very good. (*He goes into the cottage*).

The clergyman remains outside the gate, with his hands on the top of it. The REV. SAMUEL GARDNER, *a beneficed clergyman of the Established Church, is over 50. Externally he is pretentious, booming, noisy, important. Really he is that obsolescent social phenomenon the fool of the family dumped on the Church by his father the patron, clamorously asserting himself as* father and clergyman without being able to command respect in either capacity.

REV. S.: Well, sir. Who are your friends here, if I may ask?

FRANK: Oh, it's all right, gov'nor! Come in!

REV. S.: No, sir; not until I know whose garden I am entering.

FRANK: It's all right. It's Miss Warren's.

REV. S.: I have not seen her at church since she came.

FRANK: Of course not: she's a third wrangler. Ever so intellectual. Took a higher degree than you did; so why should she go to hear you preach?

REV. S.: Dont be disrespectful, sir.

FRANK: Oh, it dont matter: nobody hears us. Come in. (*He opens the gate, unceremoniously pulling his father with it into the garden.*) I want to introduce you to her. Do you remember the advice you gave me last July, gov'nor?

REV. S. (*severely*): Yes. I advised you to conquer your idleness and flippancy, and to work your way into an honorable profession and live on it and not upon me.

FRANK: No: thats what you thought of afterwards. What you actually said was that since I had neither brains nor money, I'd better turn my good looks to account by marrying somebody with both. Well, look here. Miss Warren has brains: you cant deny that.

REV. S.: Brains are not everything.

FRANK: No, of course not: theres the money—

REV. S. (*interrupting him austerely*): I was not thinking of money, sir. I was speaking of higher things. Social position, for instance.

FRANK: I dont care a rap about that.

REV. S.: But I do, sir.

FRANK: Well, nobody wants you to marry her. Anyhow, she has what amounts to a high Cambridge degree; and she seems to have as much money as she wants.

REV. S. (*sinking into a feeble vein of humor*): I greatly doubt whether she has as much money as you will want.

FRANK: Oh, come: I havnt been so very extravagant. I live ever so quietly; I dont drink; I dont bet much; and I never go regularly on the razzle-dazzle as you did when you were my age.

REV. S. (*booming hollowly*): Silence, sir.

FRANK: Well, you told me yourself, when I was making ever such an ass of myself about the barmaid at Redhill, that you once offered a woman £50 for the letters you wrote to her when—

REV. S. (*terrified*): Sh-sh-sh, Frank, for Heaven's sake! (*He looks round apprehensively. Seeing no one within earshot he plucks up courage to boom again, but more subduedly*). You are taking an ungentlemanly advantage of what I confided to you for your own good, to save you from an error you would have repented all your life long. Take warning by your father's follies, sir; and dont make them an excuse for your own.

FRANK: Did you ever hear the story of the Duke of Wellington and his letters?

REV. S.: No, sir; and I dont want to hear it.

FRANK: The old Iron Duke didn't throw away £50: not he. He just wrote: "Dear Jenny: publish and be damned! Yours affectionately, Wellington." Thats what you should have done.

REV. S. (*piteously*): Frank, my boy: when I wrote those letters I put myself into that woman's power. When I told you about them I put myself, to some extent, I am sorry to say, in your power. She refused my money with these words, which I shall never forget. "Knowledge is power" she said; "and I never sell power." Thats more than twenty years ago; and she has never made use of her power or caused me a moment's uneasiness. You are behaving worse to me than she did, Frank.

FRANK: Oh yes I dare say! Did you ever preach at her the way you preach at me every day?

REV. S. (*wounded almost to tears*): I leave you, sir. You are incorrigible. (*He turns towards the gate*).

FRANK (*utterly unmoved*): Tell them I shant be home to tea, will you, gov'nor, like a good fellow? (*He moves towards the cottage door and is met by* PRAED *and* VIVIE *coming out*).

VIVIE (*to* FRANK): Is that your father, Frank? I do so want to meet him.

FRANK: Certainly. (*Calling after his father*) Gov'nor. Youre wanted. (*The parson turns at the gate, fumbling nervously at his hat.* PRAED *crosses the garden to the opposite*

side, *beaming in anticipation of civilities*). My father: Miss Warren.

VIVIE (*going to the clergyman and shaking his hand*): Very glad to see you here, Mr Gardner. (*Calling to the cottage*) Mother: come along: youre wanted. (MRS WARREN *appears on the threshold, and is immediately transfixed recognizing the clergyman*).

VIVIE (*continuing*): Let me introduce—

MRS WARREN (*swooping on the* REVEREND SAMUEL): Why, it's Sam Gardner, gone into the Church! Well, I never! Dont you know us, Sam? This is George Crofts, as large as life and twice as natural. Dont you remember me?

REV. S. (*very red*): I really—er—

MRS WARREN: Of course you do. Why, I have a whole album of your letters still: I came across them only the other day.

REV. S. (*miserably confused*): Miss Vavasour, I believe.

MRS WARREN (*correcting him quickly in a loud whisper*): Tch! Nonsense! Mrs Warren: dont you see my daughter there?

ACT II

Inside the cottage after nightfall. Looking eastward from within instead of westward from without, the latticed window, with its curtains drawn, is now seen in the middle of the front wall of the cottage, with the porch door to the left of it. In the left-hand side wall is the door leading to the kitchen. Farther back against the same wall is a dresser with a candle and matches on it, and FRANK's *rifle standing beside them, with the barrel resting in the plate-rack. In the centre a table stands with a lighted lamp on it.* VIVIE's *books and writing materials are on a table to the right of the window, against the wall. The fireplace is on the right, with a settle: there is no fire. Two of the chairs are set right and left of the table.*

The cottage door opens, shewing a fine starlit night without; and MRS WARREN, *her shoulders wrapped in a shawl borrowed from* VIVIE, *enters, followed by* FRANK, *who throws his cap on the window seat. She has had enough of walking, and gives a gasp of relief as she unpins her hat; takes it off; sticks the pin through the crown; and puts it on the table.*

MRS WARREN: O Lord! I dont know which is the worst of the country, the walking or the sitting at home with nothing to do. I could do with a whisky and soda now very well, if only they had such a thing in this place.

FRANK: Perhaps Vivie's got some.

MRS WARREN: Nonsense! What would a young girl like her be doing with such things! Never mind: it dont matter. I wonder how she passes her time here! I'd a good deal rather be in Vienna.

FRANK: Let me take you there. (*He helps her take off her shawl, gallantly giving her shoulders a very perceptible squeeze as he does so*).

MRS WARREN: Ah! would you? I'm beginning to think youre a chip of the old block.

FRANK: Like the gov'nor, eh? (*He hangs the shawl on the nearest chair, and sits down*).

MRS WARREN: Never you mind. What do you know about such things? Youre only a boy. (*She goes to the hearth, to be farther from temptation*).

FRANK: Do come to Vienna with me? It'd be ever such larks.

MRS WARREN: No, thank you. Vienna is no place for you—at least not until youre a little older. (*She nods at him to emphasize this piece of advice. He makes a mock-piteous face, belied by his laughing eyes. She looks at him; then comes back to him*). Now, look here, little boy (*taking his face in her hands and turning it up to her*): I know you through and through by your likeness to your father, better than you know yourself. Dont you go taking any silly ideas into your head about me. Do you hear?

FRANK (*gallantly wooing her with his voice*): Cant help it, my dear Mrs Warren: it runs in the family. (*She pretends to box his ears; then looks at the pretty laughing up-turned face for a moment, tempted. At last she kisses him, and immediately turns away, out of patience with herself*).

MRS WARREN: There! I shouldnt have done that. I am wicked. Never you mind, my dear: it's only a motherly kiss. Go and make love to Vivie.

FRANK: So I have.

MRS WARREN (*turning on him with a sharp note of alarm in her voice*): What!

FRANK: Vivie and I are ever such chums.

MRS WARREN: What do you mean? Now see here: I wont have any young scamp tampering with my little girl. Do you hear? I wont have it.

FRANK (*quite unabashed*): My dear Mrs Warren: dont you be alarmed. My intentions are honorable: ever so honorable; and your little girl is jolly well able to take care of herself. She dont need looking after half so much as her mother. She aint so handsome, you know.

MRS WARREN (*taken aback by his assurance*): Well, you have got a nice healthy two inches thick of cheek all over you. I dont know where you got it. Not from your father, anyhow.

CROFTS (*in the garden*): The gipsies, I suppose?

REV. S. (*replying*): The broomsquires are far worse.

MRS WARREN (*to* FRANK): S-sh! Remember! youve had your warning.

CROFTS *and the* REVEREND SAMUEL *come in from the garden, the clergyman continuing his conversation as he enters.*

REV. S.: The perjury at the Winchester assizes is deplorable.

MRS WARREN: Well? what became of you two? And wheres Praddy and Vivie?

CROFTS (*putting his hat on the settle and his stick in the chimney corner*): They went up the hill. We went to the village. I wanted a drink. (*He sits down on the settle, putting his legs up along the seat*).

MRS WARREN: Well, she oughtnt to go off like that without telling me. (*To* FRANK) Get your father a chair, Frank: where are your manners? (FRANK *springs up and gracefully offers his father his chair; then takes another from the wall and sits down at the table, in the middle, with his father on his right and* MRS WARREN *on his left*). George: where are you going to stay tonight? You cant stay here. And whats Praddy going to do?

CROFTS: Gardner'll put me up.

MRS WARREN: Oh, no doubt youve taken care of yourself! But what about Praddy?

CROFTS: Dont know. I suppose he can sleep at the inn.

MRS WARREN: Havnt you room for him, Sam?

REV. S.: Well—er—you see, as rector here, I am not free to do as I like. Er—what is Mr Praed's social position?

MRS WARREN: Oh, he's all right: he's an architect. What an old stick-in-the-mud you are, Sam!

FRANK: Yes, it's all right, gov'nor. He built that place down in Wales for the Duke. Caernarvon Castle they call it. You must have heard of it. (*He winks with lightning smartness at* MRS WARREN, *and regards his father blandly*).

REV. S.: Oh, in that case, of course we shall only be too happy. I suppose he knows the Duke personally.

FRANK: Oh, ever so intimately! We can stick him in Georgina's old room.

MRS WARREN: Well, thats settled. Now if those two would only come in and let us have supper. Theyve no right to stay out after dark like this.

CROFTS (*aggressively*): What harm are they doing you?

MRS WARREN: Well, harm or not, I dont like it.

FRANK: Better not wait for them, Mrs Warren. Praed will stay out as long as possible. He has never known before what it is to stray over the heath on a summer night with my Vivie.

CROFTS (*sitting up in some consternation*): I say, you know! Come!

REV. S. (*rising, startled out of his professional manner into real force and sincerity*): Frank, once for all, it's out of the question. Mrs Warren will tell you that it's not to be thought of.

CROFTS: Of course not.

FRANK (*with enchanting placidity*): Is that so, Mrs Warren?

MRS WARREN (*reflectively*): Well, Sam, I dont know. If the girl wants to get married, no good can come of keeping her unmarried.

REV. S. (*astounded*): But married to him!—your daughter to my son! Only think: it's impossible.

CROFTS: Of course it's impossible. Dont be a fool, Kitty.

MRS WARREN (*nettled*): Why not? Isnt my daughter good enough for your son?

REV. S.: But surely, my dear Mrs Warren, you know the reasons—

MRS WARREN (*defiantly*): I know no reasons. If you know any, you can tell them to the lad, or to the girl, or to your congregation, if you like.

REV. S. (*collapsing helplessly into his chair*): You know very well that I couldn't tell anyone the reasons. But my boy will believe me when I tell him there are reasons.

FRANK: Quite right, Dad: he will. But has your boy's conduct ever been influenced by your reasons?

CROFTS: You cant marry her; and thats all about it. (*He gets up and stands on the hearth, with his back to the fireplace, frowning determinedly*).

MRS WARREN (*turning on him sharply*): What have you got to do with it, pray?

FRANK (*with his prettiest lyrical cadence*): Precisely what I was going to ask, myself, in my own graceful fashion.

CROFTS (*to* MRS WARREN): I suppose you dont want to marry the girl to a man younger than herself and without either a profession or twopence to keep her on. Ask Sam, if you dont believe me. (*To the parson*) How much more money are you going to give him?

REV. S.: Not another penny. He has had his patrimony; and he spent the last of it in July. (MRS WARREN's *face falls*).

CROFTS (*watching her*): There! I told you. (*He resumes his place on the settle and puts up his legs on the seat again, as if the matter were finally disposed of*).

FRANK (*plaintively*): This is ever so mercenary. Do you suppose Miss Warren's going to marry for money? If we love one another—

MRS WARREN: Thank you. Your love's a pretty cheap commodity, my lad. If you have no means of keeping a wife, that settles it: you cant have Vivie.

FRANK (*much amused*): What do you say, gov'nor, eh?

REV. S.: I agree with Mrs Warren.

FRANK: And good old Crofts has already expressed his opinion.

CROFTS (*turning angrily on his elbow*): Look here: I want none of your cheek.

FRANK (*pointedly*): I'm ever so sorry to surprise you, Crofts, but you allowed yourself the liberty of speaking to me like a father a moment ago. One father is enough, thank you.

CROFTS (*contemptuously*): Yah! (*He turns away again*).

FRANK (*rising*): Mrs Warren: I cannot give my Vivie up, even for your sake.

MRS WARREN (*muttering*): Young scamp!

FRANK (*continuing*): And as you no doubt intend to hold out other prospects to her, I shall lose no time in placing my case before her. (*They stare at him; and he begins to declaim gracefully*)

> He either fears his fate too much,
> Or his deserts are small,
> That dares not put it to the touch
> To gain or lose it all.

The cottage door opens whilst he is reciting; and VIVIE *and* PRAED *come in. He breaks off.* PRAED *puts his hat on the dresser. There is an immediate improvement in the company's behavior.* CROFTS *takes down his legs from the settle and pulls himself together as* PRAED *joins him at the fireplace.* MRS WARREN *loses her ease of manner and takes refuge in querulousness.*

MRS WARREN: Wherever have you been, Vivie?

VIVIE (*taking off her hat and throwing it carelessly on the table*): On the hill.

MRS WARREN: Well, you shouldnt go off like that without letting me know. How could I tell what had become of you? And night coming on too!

VIVIE (*going to the door of the kitchen and opening it, ignoring her mother*): Now, about supper? (*All rise except* MRS WARREN). We shall be rather crowded in here, I'm afraid.

MRS WARREN: Did you hear what I said, Vivie?

VIVIE (*quietly*): Yes, mother. (*Reverting to the supper difficulty*) How many are we? (*Counting*) One, two, three, four, five, six. Well, two will have to wait until the rest are done: Mrs Alison has only plates and knives for four.

PRAED: Oh, it doesn't matter about me. I—

VIVIE: You have had a long walk and are hungry, Mr Praed: you shall have your supper at once. I can wait myself. I want one person to wait with me. Frank: are you hungry?

FRANK: Not the least in the world. Completely off my peck, in fact.

MRS WARREN (*to* CROFTS): Neither are you, George. You can wait.

CROFTS: Oh, hang it, Ive eaten nothing since tea-time. Cant Sam do it?

FRANK: Would you starve my poor father?

REV. S. (*testily*): Allow me to speak for myself, sir. I am perfectly willing to wait.

VIVIE (*decisively*): Theres no need. Only two are wanted. (*She opens the door of the kitchen*). Will you take my mother in, Mr Gardner. (*The parson takes* MRS WARREN; *and they pass into the kitchen.* PRAED *and* CROFTS *follow. All except* PRAED *clearly disapprove of the arrangement, but do not know how to resist it.* VIVIE *stands at the door looking in at them*). Can you squeeze past to that corner, Mr Praed: it's rather a tight fit. Take care of your coat against the white-wash: thats right. Now, are you all comfortable?

PRAED (*within*): Quite, thank you.

MRS WARREN (*within*): Leave the door open, dearie. (VIVIE *frowns; but* FRANK *checks her with a gesture, and steals to the cottage door, which he softly sets wide open*). Oh Lor, what a draught! Youd better shut it, dear. (VIVIE *shuts it with a slam, and then, noting with disgust that her mother's hat and shawl are lying about, takes them tidily to the window seat, whilst* FRANK *noiselessly shuts the cottage door*).

FRANK (*exulting*): Aha! Got rid of em. Well, Vivvums: what do you think of my guvernor?

VIVIE (*preoccupied and serious*): Ive hardly spoken to him. He doesnt strike me as being a particularly able person.

FRANK: Well, you know, the old man is not altogether such a fool as he looks. You see, he was shoved into the Church rather; and in trying to live up to it he makes a much bigger ass of himself than he really is. I dont dislike him as much as you might expect. He means well. How do you think youll get on with him?

VIVIE (*rather grimly*): I dont think my future life will be much concerned with him, or with any of that old circle of my mother's, except perhaps Praed. (*She sits down on the settle*). What do you think of my mother?

FRANK: Really and truly?

VIVIE: Yes, really and truly.

FRANK: Well, she's ever so jolly. But she's rather a caution, isn't she? And Crofts! Oh, my eye, Crofts! (*He sits beside her*).

VIVIE: What a lot, Frank!

FRANK: What a crew!

VIVIE (*with intense contempt for them*): If I thought that *I* was like that—that I was going to be a waster, shifting along from one meal to another with no purpose, and no character, and no grit in me, I'd open an artery and bleed to death without one moment's hesitation.

FRANK: Oh no, you wouldnt. Why should they take any grind when they can afford not to? I wish I had their luck. No: what I object to is their form. It isnt the thing: it's slovenly, ever so slovenly.

VIVIE: Do you think your form will be any better when youre as old as Crofts, if you dont work?

FRANK: Of course I do. Ever so much better. Vivvums mustnt lecture: her little boy's incorrigible. (*He attempts to take her face caressingly in his hands*).

VIVIE (*striking his hands down sharply*): Off with you: Vivvums is not in a humor for petting her little boy this evening. (*She rises and comes forward to the other side of the room*).

FRANK (*following her*): How unkind!

VIVIE (*stamping at him*): Be serious. I'm serious.

FRANK: Good. Let us talk learnedly. Miss Warren: do you know that all the most advanced thinkers are agreed that half the diseases of modern civilization are due to starvation of the affections in the young. Now, I—

VIVIE (*cutting him short*): You are very tiresome. (*She opens the inner door*). Have you room for Frank there? He's complaining of starvation.

MRS WARREN (*within*): Of course there is (*clatter of knives and glasses as she moves the things on the table*). Here! theres room now beside me. Come along, Mr Frank.

FRANK: Her little boy will be ever so even with his Vivvums for this. (*He passes into the kitchen*).

MRS WARREN (*within*): Here, Vivie: come on you too, child. You must be famished. (*She enters, followed by* CROFTS, *who holds the door open for* VIVIE *with marked deference*.

She goes out without looking at him; and he shuts the door after her). Why, George, you cant be done: youve eaten nothing. Is there anything wrong with you?

CROFTS: Oh, all I wanted was a drink. (*He thrusts his hands in his pockets, and begins prowling about the room, restless and sulky*).

MRS WARREN: Well, I like enough to eat. But a little of that cold beef and cheese and lettuce goes a long way. (*With a sigh of only half repletion she sits down lazily on the settle*).

CROFTS: What do you go encouraging that young pup for?

MRS WARREN (*on the alert at once*): Now see here, George: what are you up to about that girl? Ive been watching your way of looking at her. Remember: I know you and what your looks mean.

CROFTS: Theres no harm in looking at her, is there?

MRS WARREN: I'd put you out and pack you back to London pretty soon if I saw any of your nonsense. My girl's little finger is more to me than your whole body and soul. (CROFTS *receives this with a sneering grin.* MRS WARREN, *flushing a little at her failure to impose on him in the character of a theatrically devoted mother, adds in a lower key*) Make your mind easy: the young pup has no more chance than you have.

CROFTS: Maynt a man take an interest in a girl?

MRS WARREN: Not a man like you.

CROFTS: How old is she?

MRS WARREN: Never you mind how old she is.

CROFTS: Why do you make such a secret of it?

MRS WARREN: Because I choose.

CROFTS: Well, I'm not fifty yet; and my property is as good as ever it was—

MRS WARREN (*interrupting him*): Yes; because youre as stingy as youre vicious.

CROFTS (*continuing*): And a baronet isnt to be picked up every day. No other man in my position would put up with you for a mother-in-law. Why shouldnt she marry me?

MRS WARREN: You!

CROFTS: We three could live together quite comfortably. I'd die before her and leave her a bouncing widow with plenty of money. Why not? It's been growing in my mind all the time Ive been walking with that fool inside there.

MRS WARREN (*revolted*): Yes: it's the sort of thing that *would* grow in your mind. (*He halts in his prowling; and the two look at one another, she steadfastly, with a sort of awe behind her contemptuous disgust: he stealthily, with a carnal gleam in his eye and a loose grin*).

CROFTS (*suddenly becoming anxious and urgent as he sees no sign of sympathy in her*): Look here, Kitty: youre a sensible woman: you neednt put on any moral airs. I'll ask no more questions; and you need answer none. I'll settle the whole property on her; and if you want a cheque for yourself on the wedding day, you can name any figure you like—in reason.

MRS WARREN: So it's come to that with you, George, like all the other worn-out old creatures!

CROFTS (*savagely*): Damn you! (*Before she can retort the door of the kitchen is opened; and the voices of the others are heard returning.* CROFTS, *unable to recover his presence of mind, hurries out of the cottage. The clergyman appears at the kitchen door*).

REV. S. (*looking round*): Where is Sir George?

MRS WARREN: Gone out to have a pipe. (*The clergyman takes his hat from the table, and joins* MRS WARREN *at the fireside. Meanwhile* VIVIE *comes in, followed by* FRANK, *who collapses into the nearest chair with an air of extreme exhaustion.* MRS WARREN *looks round at* VIVIE *and says, with her affectation of maternal patronage even more forced than usual*) Well, dearie: have you had a good supper?

VIVIE: You know what Mrs Alison's suppers are. (*She turns to* FRANK *and pets him*). Poor Frank! was all the beef gone? did it get nothing but bread and cheese and ginger beer? (*Seriously, as if she had done quite enough trifling for one evening*) Her butter is really awful. I must get some down from the stores.

FRANK: Do, in Heaven's name! (*VIVIE goes to the writing-table and makes a memorandum to order the butter.* PRAED *comes in from the kitchen, putting up his handkerchief, which he has been using as a napkin*).

REV. S.: Frank, my boy: it is time for us to be thinking of home. Your mother does not know yet that we have visitors.

PRAED: I'm afraid we're giving trouble.

FRANK (*rising*): Not the least in the world: my mother will be delighted to see you. She's a genuinely intellectual artistic woman; and she sees nobody here from one year's end to another except the gov'nor; so you can imagine how jolly dull it pans out for her. (*To his father*) Youre not intellectual or artistic: are you, pater? So take Praed home at once; and I'll stay here and entertain Mrs Warren. Youll pick up Crofts in the garden. He'll be excellent company for the bull-pup.

PRAED (*taking his hat from the dresser, and coming close to* FRANK): Come with us, Frank. Mrs Warren has not seen Miss Vivie for a long time; and we have prevented them from having a moment together yet.

FRANK (*quite softened, and looking at* PRAED *with romantic admiration*): Of course. I forgot. Ever so thanks for reminding me. Perfect gentleman, Praddy. Always were. My ideal through life. (*He rises to go, but pauses a moment between the two older men, and puts his hand on* PRAED's *shoulder*). Ah, if you had only been my father instead of this unworthy old man! (*He puts his other hand on his father's shoulder*).

REV. S. (*blustering*): Silence, sir, silence: you are profane.

MRS WARREN (*laughing heartily*): You should keep him in better order, Sam. Good-night. Here: take George his hat and stick with my compliments.

REV. S. (*taking them*): Good-night. (*They shake hands. As he passes* VIVIE *he shakes hands with her also and bids her good-night. Then, in booming command, to* FRANK) Come along, sir, at once. (*He goes out*).

MRS WARREN: Byebye, Praddy.

PRAED: Byebye, Kitty. (*They shake hands affectionately and go out together, she accompanying him to the garden gate*).

FRANK (*to* VIVIE): Kissums?

VIVIE (*fiercely*): No. I hate you. (*She takes a couple of books and some paper from the writing-table, and sits down with them at the middle table, at the end next the fireplace*).

FRANK (*grimacing*): Sorry. (*He goes for his cap and rifle.* MRS WARREN *returns. He takes her hand*) Good-night, dear Mrs Warren. (*He kisses her hand. She snatches it away, her lips tightening, and looks more than half disposed to box his ears. He laughs mischievously and runs off, clapping-to the door behind him*).

MRS WARREN (*resigning herself to an evening of boredom now that the men are gone*): Did you ever in your life hear anyone rattle on so? Isnt he a tease? (*She sits at the table*). Now that I think of it, dearie, dont you go encouraging him. I'm sure he's a regular good-for-nothing.

VIVIE (*rising to fetch more books*): I'm afraid so. Poor Frank! I shall have to get rid of him; but I shall feel sorry for him, though he's not worth it. That man Crofts does not seem to me to be good for much either: is he? (*She throws the books on the table rather roughly*).

MRS WARREN (*galled by* VIVIE'S *indifference*): What do you know of men, child, to talk that way about them? Youll have to make up your mind to see a good deal of Sir George Crofts, as he's a friend of mine.

VIVIE (*quite unmoved*): Why? (*She sits down and opens a book*). Do you expect that we shall be much together? You and I, I mean?

MRS WARREN (*staring at her*): Of course: until youre married. Youre not going back to college again.

VIVIE: Do you think my way of life would suit you? I doubt it.

MRS WARREN: Your way of life! What do you mean?

VIVIE (*cutting a page of her book with the paper knife on her chatelaine*): Has it really never occurred to you, mother, that I have a way of life like other people?

MRS WARREN: What nonsense is this youre trying to talk? Do you want to shew your independence, now that youre a great little person at school? Dont be a fool, child.

VIVIE (*indulgently*): Thats all you have to say on the subject, is it, mother.

MRS WARREN (*puzzled, then angry*): Dont you keep on asking me questions like that. (*Violently*) Hold your tongue. (VIVIE *works on, losing no time, and saying nothing*). You and your way of life, indeed! What next? (*She looks at* VIVIE *again. No reply*). Your way of life will be what I please, so

it will. (*Another pause*). Ive been noticing these airs in you ever since you got that tripos or whatever you call it. If you think I'm going to put up with them youre mistaken; and the sooner you find it out, the better. (*Muttering*) All I have to say on the subject, indeed! (*Again raising her voice angrily*) Do you know who youre speaking to, Miss?

VIVIE (*looking across at her without raising her head from her book*): No. Who are you? What are you?

MRS WARREN (*rising breathless*): You young imp!

VIVIE: Everybody knows my reputation, my social standing, and the profession I intend to pursue. I know nothing about you. What is that way of life which you invite me to share with you and Sir George Crofts, pray?

MRS WARREN: Take care. I shall do something I'll be sorry for after, and you too.

VIVIE (*putting aside her books with cool decision*): Well, let us drop the subject until you are better able to face it. (*Looking critically at her mother*) You want some good walks and a little lawn tennis to set you up. You are shockingly out of condition: you were not able to manage twenty yards uphill today without stopping to pant; and your wrists are mere rolls of fat. Look at mine. (*She holds out her wrists*).

MRS WARREN (*after looking at her helplessly, begins to whimper*): Vivie—

VIVIE (*springing up sharply*): Now pray dont begin to cry. Anything but that. I really cannot stand whimpering. I will go out of the room if you do.

MRS WARREN (*piteously*): Oh, my darling, how can you be so hard on me? Have I no rights over you as your mother?

VIVIE: Are you my mother?

MRS WARREN (*appalled*): Am I your mother! Oh, Vivie!

VIVIE: Then where are our relatives? my father? our family friends? You claim the rights of a mother: the right to call me fool and child; to speak to me as no woman in authority over me at college dare speak to me; to dictate my way of life; and to force on me the acquaintance of a brute whom anyone can see to be the most vicious sort of London man about town. Before I give myself the trouble to resist such claims, I may as well find out whether they have any real existence.

MRS WARREN (*distracted, throwing herself on her knees*): Oh no, no. Stop, stop. I am your mother: I swear it. Oh, you cant mean to turn on me—my own child! it's not natural. You believe me, dont you? Say you believe me.

VIVIE: Who was my father?

MRS WARREN: You dont know what youre asking. I cant tell you.

VIVIE (*determinedly*): Oh yes you can, if you like. I have a right to know; and you know very well that I have that right. You can refuse to tell me, if you please; but if you do, you will see the last of me tomorrow morning.

MRS WARREN: Oh, it's too horrible to hear you talk like that. You wouldnt—you couldnt leave me.

VIVIE (*ruthlessly*): Yes, without a moment's hesitation, if you trifle with me about this. (*Shivering with disgust*) How can I feel sure that I may not have the contaminated blood of that brutal waster in my veins?

MRS WARREN: No, no. On my oath it's not he, nor any of the rest that you have ever met. I'm certain of that, at least. (VIVIE's *eyes fasten sternly on her mother as the significance of this flashes on her*).

VIVIE (*slowly*): You are certain of that, at least. Ah! You mean that that is all you are certain of. (*Thoughtfully*) I see. (MRS WARREN *buries her face in her hands*). Dont do that, mother: you know you dont feel it a bit. (MRS WARREN *takes down her hands and looks up deplorably at* VIVIE, *who takes out her watch and says*) Well, that is enough for tonight. At what hour would you like breakfast? Is half-past eight too early for you?

MRS WARREN (*wildly*): My God, what sort of woman are you?

VIVIE (*coolly*): The sort the world is mostly made of, I should hope. Otherwise I dont understand how it gets its business done. Come (*taking her mother by the wrist, and pulling her up pretty resolutely*): pull yourself together. Thats right.

MRS WARREN (*querulously*): Youre very rough with me, Vivie.

VIVIE: Nonsense. What about bed? It's past ten.

MRS WARREN (*passionately*): Whats the use of my going to bed? Do you think I could sleep?

VIVIE: Why not? I shall.

MRS WARREN: You! youve no heart. (*She suddenly breaks out vehemently in her natural tongue—the dialect of a woman of the people—with all her affectations of maternal authority and conventional manners gone, and an overwhelming inspiration of true conviction and scorn in her*) Oh, I wont bear it: I wont put up with the injustice of it. What right have you to set yourself up above me like this? You boast of what you are to me—to me, who gave you the chance of being what you are. What chance had I? Shame on you for a bad daughter and a stuck-up prude!

VIVIE (*sitting down with a shrug, no longer confident; for her replies, which have sounded sensible and strong to her so far, now begin to ring rather woodenly and even priggishly against the new tone of her mother*): Dont think for a moment I set myself above you in any way. You attacked me with the conventional authority of a mother: I defended myself with the conventional superiority of a respectable woman. Frankly, I am not going to stand any of your nonsense; and when you drop it I shall not expect you to stand any of mine. I shall always respect your right to your own opinions and your own way of life.

MRS WARREN: My own opinions and my own way of life! Listen to her talking! Do you think I was brought up like you? able to pick and choose my own way of life? Do you think I did what I did because I liked it, or thought it right, or wouldnt rather have gone to college and been a lady if I'd had the chance?

VIVIE: Everybody has some choice, mother. The poorest girl alive may not be able to choose between being Queen of England or Principal of Newnham; but she can choose between ragpicking and flowerselling, according to her taste. People are always blaming their circumstances for what they are. I dont believe in circumstances. The people who get on in this world are the people who get up and look for the circumstances they want, and, if they cant find them, make them.

MRS WARREN: Oh, it's easy to talk, very easy,

isn't it? Here! would you like to know what my circumstances were?

VIVIE: Yes: you had better tell me. Wont you sit down?

MRS WARREN: Oh, I'll sit down: don't you be afraid. (*She plants her chair farther forward with brazen energy, and sits down.* VIVIE *is impressed in spite of herself*). D'you know what your gran'mother was?

VIVIE: No.

MRS WARREN: No you dont. I do. She called herself a widow and had a fried-fish shop down by the Mint, and kept herself and four daughters out of it. Two of us were sisters: that was me and Liz; and we were both good-looking and well made. I suppose our father was a well-fed man: mother pretended he was a gentleman; but I dont know. The other two were only half sisters: undersized, ugly, starved looking, hard working, honest poor creatures: Liz and I would have half-murdered them if mother hadnt half-murdered us to keep our hands off them. They were the respectable ones. Well, what did they get by their respectability? I'll tell you. One of them worked in a whitelead factory twelve hours a day for nine shillings a week until she died of lead poisoning. She only expected to get her hands a little paralyzed; but she died. The other was always held up to us as a model because she married a Government laborer in the Deptford victualling yard, and kept his room and the three children neat and tidy on eighteen shillings a week —until he took to drink. That was worth being respectable for, wasnt it?

VIVIE (*now thoughtfully attentive*): Did you and your sister think so?

MRS WARREN: Liz didnt, I can tell you: she had more spirit. We both went to a church school—that was part of the ladylike airs we gave ourselves to be superior to the children that knew nothing and went nowhere—and we stayed there until Liz went out one night and never came back. I know the schoolmistress thought I'd soon follow her example; for the clergyman was always warning me that Lizzie'd end by jumping off Waterloo Bridge. Poor fool: that was all he knew about it! But I was more afraid of the whitelead factory than I was of the river; and so would you have been in my place. That clergyman got me

a situation as scullery maid in a temperance restaurant where they sent out for anything you liked. Then I was waitress; and then I went to the bar at Waterloo station: fourteen hours a day serving drinks and washing glasses for four shillings a week and my board. That was considered a great promotion for me. Well, one cold, wretched night, when I was so tired I could hardly keep myself awake, who should come up for a half of Scotch but Lizzie, in a long fur cloak, elegant and comfortable, with a lot of sovereigns in her purse.

VIVIE (*grimly*): My aunt Lizzie!

MRS WARREN: Yes; and a very good aunt to have, too. She's living down at Winchester now, close to the cathedral, one of the most respectable ladies there. Chaperones girls at the county ball, if you please. No river for Liz, thank you! You remind me of Liz a little: she was a first-rate business woman —saved money from the beginning—never let herself look too like what she was— never lost her head or threw away a chance. When she saw I'd grown up good-looking she said to me across the bar "What are you doing there, you little fool? wearing out your health and your appearance for other people's profit!" Liz was saving money then to take a house for herself in Brussels; and she thought we two could save faster than one. So she lent me some money and gave me a start; and I saved steadily and first paid her back, and then went into business with her as her partner. Why shouldnt I have done it? The house in Brussels was real high class: a much better place for a woman to be in than the factory where Anne Jane got poisoned. None of our girls were ever treated as I was treated in the scullery of that temperance place, or at the Waterloo bar, or at home. Would you have had me stay in them and become a worn out old drudge before I was forty?

VIVIE (*intensely interested by this time*): No; but why did you choose that business? Saving money and good management will succeed in any business.

MRS WARREN: Yes, saving money. But where can a woman get the money to save in any other business? Could you save out of four shillings a week and keep yourself dressed as well? Not you. Of course, if youre a plain woman and cant earn anything more; or if you have a turn for music, or the stage, or newspaperwriting: thats different. But neither Liz nor I had any turn for such things: all we had was our appearance and our turn for pleasing men. Do you think we were such fools as to let other people trade in our good looks by employing us as shopgirls, or barmaids, or waitresses, when we could trade in them ourselves and get all the profits instead of starvation wages? Not likely.

VIVIE: You were certainly quite justified—from the business point of view.

MRS WARREN: Yes; or any other point of view. What is any respectable girl brought up to do but to catch some rich man's fancy and get the benefit of his money by marrying him?—as if a marriage ceremony could make any difference in the right or wrong of the thing! Oh, the hypocrisy of the world makes me sick! Liz and I had to work and save and calculate just like other people; elseways we should be as poor as any good-for-nothing drunken waster of a woman that thinks her luck will last for ever. (*With great energy*) I despise such people: theyve no character; and if theres a thing I hate in a woman, it's want of character.

VIVIE: Come now, mother: frankly! Isn't it part of what you call character in a woman that she should greatly dislike such a way of making money?

MRS WARREN: Why, of course. Everybody dislikes having to work and make money; but they have to do it all the same. I'm sure Ive often pitied a poor girl, tired out and in low spirits, having to try to please some man that she doesnt care two straws for—some half-drunken fool that thinks he's making himself agreeable when he's teasing and worrying and disgusting a woman so that hardly any money could pay her for putting up with it. But she has to bear with disagreeables and take the rough with the smooth, just like a nurse in a hospital or anyone else. It's not work that any woman would do for pleasure, goodness knows; though to hear the pious people talk you would suppose it was a bed of roses.

VIVIE: Still, you consider it worth while. It pays.

MRS WARREN: Of course it's worth while to a poor girl, if she can resist temptation and is good-looking and well conducted and sensible. It's far better than any other employment open to her. I always thought that oughtnt to be. It cant be right, Vivie, that there shouldnt be better opportunities for women. I stick to that: it's wrong. But it's so, right or wrong; and a girl must make the best of it. But of course it's not worth while for a lady. If you took to it youd be a fool; but I should have been a fool if I'd taken to anything else.

VIVIE (*more and more deeply moved*): Mother: suppose we were both as poor as you were in those wretched old days, are you quite sure that you wouldnt advise me to try the Waterloo bar, or marry a laborer, or even go into the factory?

MRS WARREN (*indignantly*): Of course not. What sort of mother do you take me for! How could you keep your self-respect in such starvation and slavery? And whats a woman worth? whats life worth? without self-respect! Why am I independent and able to give my daughter a first-rate education, when other women that had just as good opportunities are in the gutter? Because I always knew how to respect myself and control myself. Why is Liz looked up to in a cathedral town? The same reason. Where would we be now if we'd minded the clergyman's foolishness? Scrubbing floors for one and sixpence a day and nothing to look forward to but the workhouse infirmary. Dont you be led astray by people who dont know the world, my girl. The only way for a woman to provide for herself decently is for her to be good to some man that can afford to be good to her. If she's in his own station of life, let her make him marry her; but if she's far beneath him she cant expect it: why should she? it wouldnt be for her own happiness. Ask any lady in London society that has daughters; and she'll tell you the same, except that I tell you straight and she'll tell you crooked. Thats all the difference.

VIVIE (*fascinated, gazing at her*): My dear mother: you are a wonderful woman: you are stronger than all England. And are you really and truly not one wee bit doubtful—or—or—ashamed?

MRS WARREN: Well, of course, dearie, it's

only good manners to be ashamed of it: it's expected from a woman. Women have to pretend to feel a great deal that they dont feel. Liz used to be angry with me for plumping out the truth about it. She used to say that when every woman could learn enough from what was going on in the world before her eyes, there was no need to talk about it to her. But then Liz was such a perfect lady! She had the true instinct of it; while I was always a bit of a vulgarian. I used to be so pleased when you sent me your photos to see that you were growing up like Liz: youve just her ladylike, determined way. But I cant stand saying one thing when everyone knows I mean another. Whats the use in such hypocrisy? If people arrange the world that way for women, theres no good pretending it's arranged the other way. No: I never was a bit ashamed really. I consider I had a right to be proud of how we managed everything so respectably, and never had a word against us, and how the girls were so well taken care of. Some of them did very well: one of them married an ambassador. But of course now I darent talk about such things: whatever would they think of us! (*She yawns*). Oh dear! I do believe I'm getting sleepy after all. (*She stretches herself lazily, thoroughly relieved by her explosion, and placidly ready for her night's rest*).

VIVIE: I believe it is I who will not be able to sleep now. (*She goes to the dresser and lights the candle. Then she extinguishes the lamp, darkening the room a good deal*). Better let in some fresh air before locking up. (*She opens the cottage door, and finds that it is broad moonlight*). What a beautiful night! Look! (*She draws aside the curtains of the window. The landscape is seen bathed in the radiance of the harvest moon rising over Blackdown*).

MRS WARREN (*with a perfunctory glance at the scene*): Yes, dear; but take care you dont catch your death of cold from the night air.

VIVIE (*contemptuously*): Nonsense.

MRS WARREN (*querulously*): Oh yes: everything I say is nonsense, according to you.

VIVIE (*turning to her quickly*): No: really that is not so, mother. You have got completely the better of me tonight, though I intended it to be the other way. Let us be good friends now.

MRS WARREN (*shaking her head a little ruefully*): So it has been the other way. But I suppose I must give in to it. I always got the worst of it from Liz; and now I suppose it'll be the same with you.

VIVIE: Well, never mind. Come: goodnight, dear old mother. (*She takes her mother in her arms*).

MRS WARREN (*fondly*): I brought you up well, didnt I, dearie?

VIVIE: You did.

MRS WARREN: And youll be good to your poor old mother for it, wont you?

VIVIE: I will, dear. (*Kissing her*) Goodnight.

MRS WARREN (*with unction*): Blessings on my own dearie darling! a mother's blessing! (*She embraces her daughter protectingly, instinctively looking upward for divine sanction*).

ACT III

In the Rectory garden next morning, with the sun shining from a cloudless sky. The garden wall has a five-barred wooden gate, wide enough to admit a carriage, in the middle. Beside the gate hangs a bell on a coiled spring, communicating with a pull outside. The carriage drive comes down the middle of the garden and then swerves to its left, where it ends in a little gravelled circus opposite the Rectory porch. Beyond the gate is seen the dusty high road, parallel with the wall, bounded on the farther side by a strip of turf and an unfenced pine wood. On the lawn, between the house and the drive, is a clipped yew tree, with a garden bench in its shade. On the opposite side the garden is shut in by a box hedge; and there is a sundial on the turf, with an iron chair near it. A little path leads off through the box hedge, behind the sundial.

FRANK, seated on the chair near the sundial, on which he has placed the morning papers, is reading The Standard. His father comes from the house, red-eyed and shivery, and meets FRANK's eye with misgiving.

FRANK (*looking at his watch*): Half-past eleven. Nice hour for a rector to come down to breakfast!

REV. S.: Dont mock, Frank: dont mock. I am a little—er—(*Shivering*)—

FRANK: Off color?

REV. S. (*repudiating the expression*): No, sir: unwell this morning. Wheres your mother?

FRANK: Dont be alarmed: she's not here. Gone to town by the 11.13 with Bessie. She left several messages for you. Do you feel equal to receiving them now, or shall I wait til youve breakfasted?

REV. S.: I have breakfasted, sir. I am surprised at your mother going to town when we have people staying with us. Theyll think it very strange.

FRANK: Possibly she has considered that. At all events, if Crofts is going to stay here, and you are going to sit up every night with him until four, recalling the incidents of your fiery youth, it is clearly my mother's duty, as a prudent housekeeper, to go up to the stores and order a barrel of whisky and a few hundred siphons.

REV. S.: I did not observe that Sir George drank excessively.

FRANK: You were not in a condition to, gov'nor.

REV. S.: Do you mean to say that I—?

FRANK (*calmly*): I never saw a beneficed clergyman less sober. The anecdotes you told about your past career were so awful that I really dont think Praed would have passed the night under your roof if it hadnt been for the way my mother and he took to one another.

REV. S.: Nonsense, sir. I am Sir George Crofts' host. I must talk to him about something; and he has only one subject. Where is Mr Praed now?

FRANK: He is driving my mother and Bessie to the station.

REV. S.: Is Crofts up yet?

FRANK: Oh, long ago. He hasnt turned a hair: he's in much better practice than you. Has kept it up ever since, probably. He's taken himself off somewhere to smoke. (FRANK *resumes his paper. The parson turns disconsolately towards the gate; then comes back irresolutely*).

REV. S.: Er—Frank.

FRANK: Yes.

REV. S.: Do you think the Warrens will expect to be asked here after yesterday afternoon?

FRANK: Theyve been asked already.

REV. S. (*appalled*): What!!!

FRANK: Crofts informed us at breakfast that you told him to bring Mrs Warren and Vivie over here today, and to invite them to make this house their home. My mother then found she must go to town by the 11.13 train.

REV. S. (*with despairing vehemence*): I never gave any such invitation. I never thought of such a thing.

FRANK (*compassionately*): How do you know, gov'nor, what you said and thought last night?

PRAED (*coming in through the hedge*): Good morning.

REV. S.: Good morning. I must apologize for not having met you at breakfast. I have a touch of—of—

FRANK: Clergyman's sore throat, Praed. Fortunately not chronic.

PRAED (*changing the subject*): Well, I must say your house is in a charming spot here. Really most charming.

REV. S.: Yes: it is indeed. Frank will take you for a walk, Mr. Praed, if you like. I'll ask you to excuse me: I must take the opportunity to write my sermon while Mrs Gardner is away and you are all amusing yourselves. You wont mind, will you?

PRAED: Certainly not. Dont stand on the slightest ceremony with me.

REV. S.: Thank you. I'll—er—er—(*He stammers his way to the porch and vanishes into the house*).

PRAED: Curious thing it must be writing a sermon every week.

FRANK: Ever so curious, if he did it. He buys em. He's gone for some soda water.

PRAED: My dear boy: I wish you would be more respectful to your father. You know you can be so nice when you like.

FRANK: My dear Praddy: you forget that I have to live with the governor. When two people live together—it dont matter whether theyre father and son or husband and wife or brother and sister—they cant keep up the polite humbug thats so easy for ten minutes on an afternoon call. Now the governor, who unites to many admirable domestic qualities the irresoluteness of a sheep and the pompousness and aggressiveness of a jackass—

PRAED: No, pray, pray, my dear Frank, remember! He is your father.

FRANK: I give him due credit for that. (*Rising and flinging down his paper*) But just imagine his telling Crofts to bring the Warrens over here! He must have been ever so drunk. You know, my dear Praddy, my mother wouldnt stand Mrs Warren for a moment. Vivie mustnt come here until she's gone back to town.

PRAED: But your mother doesnt know anything about Mrs Warren, does she? (*He picks up the paper and sits down to read it*).

FRANK: I dont know. Her journey to town looks as if she did. Not that my mother would mind in the ordinary way: she has stuck like a brick to lots of women who had got into trouble. But they were all nice women. Thats what makes the real difference. Mrs Warren, no doubt, has her merits; but she's ever so rowdy; and my mother simply wouldnt put up with her. So—hallo! (*This exclamation is provoked by the reappearance of the clergyman, who comes out of the house in haste and dismay*).

REV. S.: Frank: Mrs Warren and her daughter are coming across the heath with Crofts: I saw them from the study windows. What am I to say about your mother?

FRANK: Stick on your hat and go out and say how delighted you are to see them; and that Frank's in the garden; and that mother and Bessie have been called to the bedside of a sick relative, and were ever so sorry they couldnt stop; and that you hope Mrs Warren slept well; and—and—say any blessed thing except the truth, and leave the rest to Providence.

REV. S.: But how are we to get rid of them afterwards?

FRANK: Theres no time to think of that now. Here! (*He bounds into the house*).

REV. S.: He's so impetuous. I dont know what to do with him, Mr. Praed.

FRANK (*returning with a clerical felt hat, which he claps on his father's head*): Now: off with you. (*Rushing him through the gate*). Praed and I'll wait here, to give the thing an unpremeditated air. (*The clergyman, dazed but obedient, hurries off*).

FRANK: We must get the old girl back to town somehow, Praed. Come! Honestly, dear Praddy, do you like seeing them together?

PRAED: Oh, why not?

FRANK (*his teeth on edge*): Dont it make your flesh creep ever so little? that wicked old devil, up to every villainy under the sun, I'll swear, and Vivie—ugh!

PRAED: Hush, pray. Theyre coming. (*The clergyman and* CROFTS *are seen coming along the road, followed by* MRS WARREN *and* VIVIE *walking affectionately together*).

FRANK: Look: she actually has her arm round the old woman's waist. It's her right arm: she began it. She's gone sentimental, by God! Ugh! ugh! Now do you feel the creeps? (*The clergyman opens the gate; and* MRS WARREN *and* VIVIE *pass him and stand in the middle of the garden looking at the house.* FRANK, *in an ecstasy of dissimulation, turns gaily to* MRS WARREN, *exclaiming*) Ever so delighted to see you, Mrs Warren. This quiet old rectory garden becomes you perfectly.

MRS WARREN: Well, I never! Did you hear that, George? He says I look well in a quiet old rectory garden.

REV. S. (*still holding the gate for* CROFTS, *who loafs through it, heavily bored*): You look well everywhere, Mrs Warren.

FRANK: Bravo, gov'nor! Now look here: lets have a treat before lunch. First lets see the church. Everyone has to do that. It's a regular old thirteenth century church, you know: the gov'nor's ever so fond of it, because he got up a restoration fund and had it completely rebuilt six years ago. Praed will be able to shew its points.

PRAED (*rising*): Certainly, if the restoration has left any to shew.

REV. S. (*mooning hospitably at them*): I shall be pleased, I'm sure, if Sir George and Mrs Warren really care about it.

MRS WARREN: Oh, come along and get it over.

CROFTS (*turning back towards the gate*): Ive no objection.

REV. S.: Not that way. We go through the fields, if you dont mind. Round here. (*He leads the way by the little path through the box hedge*).

CROFTS: Oh, all right. (*He goes with the parson.* PRAED *follows with* MRS WARREN. VIVIE *does not stir: she watches them until they have gone, with all the lines of purpose in her face marking it strongly*).

FRANK: Aint you coming?

VIVIE: No. I want to give you a warning, Frank. You were making fun of my mother just now when you said that about the rectory garden. That is barred in future. Please treat my mother with as much respect as you treat your own.

FRANK: My dear Viv: she wouldnt appreciate it: the two cases require different treatment. But what on earth has happened to you? Last night we were perfectly agreed as to your mother and her set. This morning I find you attitudinizing sentimentally with your arm round your parent's waist.

VIVIE (*flushing*): Attitudinizing!

FRANK: That was how it struck me. First time I ever saw you do a second-rate thing.

VIVIE (*controlling herself*): Yes, Frank: there has been a change; but I dont think it a change for the worse. Yesterday I was a little prig.

FRANK: And today?

VIVIE (*wincing; then looking at him steadily*): Today I know my mother better than you do.

FRANK: Heaven forbid!

VIVIE: What do you mean?

FRANK: Viv: theres a freemasonry among thoroughly immoral people that you know nothing of. Youve too much character. Thats the bond between your mother and me: thats why I know her better than youll ever know her.

VIVIE: You are wrong: you know nothing about her. If you knew the circumstances against which my mother had to struggle—

FRANK (*adroitly finishing the sentence for her*): I should know why she is what she is, shouldnt I? What difference would that make? Circumstances or no circumstances, Viv, you wont be able to stand your mother.

VIVIE (*very angrily*): Why not?

FRANK: Because she's an old wretch, Viv. If you ever put your arm round her waist in my presence again, I'll shoot myself there and then as a protest against an exhibition which revolts me.

VIVIE: Must I choose between dropping your acquaintance and dropping my mother's?

FRANK (*gracefully*): That would put the old lady at ever such a disadvantage. No, Viv: your infatuated little boy will have to stick to you in any case. But he's all the more anxious that you shouldnt make mistakes.

It's no use, Viv: your mother's impossible. She may be a good sort; but she's a bad lot, a very bad lot.

VIVIE (*hotly*): Frank—! (*He stands his ground. She turns away and sits down on the bench under the yew tree, struggling to recover her self-command. Then she says*) Is she to be deserted by all the world because she's what you call a bad lot? Has she no right to live?

FRANK: No fear of that, Viv: she wont ever be deserted. (*He sits on the bench beside her*).

VIVIE: But I am to desert her, I suppose.

FRANK (*babyishly, lulling her and making love to her with his voice*): Mustnt go live with her. Little family group of mother and daughter wouldnt be a success. Spoil our little group.

VIVIE (*falling under the spell*): What little group?

FRANK: The babes in the woods: Vivie and little Frank. (*He nestles against her like a weary child*). Lets go and get covered up with leaves.

VIVIE (*rhythmically, rocking him like a nurse*): Fast asleep, hand in hand, under the trees.

FRANK: The wise little girl with her silly little boy.

VIVIE: The dear little boy with his dowdy little girl.

FRANK: Ever so peaceful, and relieved from the imbecility of the little boy's father and the questionableness of the little girl's—

VIVIE (*smothering the word against her breast*): Sh-sh-sh-sh! little girl wants to forget all about her mother. (*They are silent for some moments, rocking one another. Then VIVIE wakes up with a shock, exclaiming*) What a pair of fools we are! Come: sit up. Gracious! your hair. (*She smooths it*). I wonder do all grown up people play in that childish way when nobody is looking. I never did it when I was a child.

FRANK: Neither did I. You are my first playmate. (*He catches her hand to kiss it, but checks himself to look round first. Very unexpectedly, he sees* CROFTS *emerging from the box hedge*). Oh damn!

VIVIE: Why damn, dear?

FRANK (*whispering*): Sh! Here's this brute Crofts. (*He sits farther away from her with an unconcerned air*).

CROFTS: Could I have a few words with you, Miss Vivie?

VIVIE: Certainly.

CROFTS (*to* FRANK): Youll excuse me, Gardner. Theyre waiting for you in the church, if you dont mind.

FRANK (*rising*): Anything to oblige you, Crofts—except church. If you should happen to want me, Vivvums, ring the gate bell. (*He goes into the house with unruffled suavity*).

CROFTS (*watching him with a crafty air as he disappears, and speaking to* VIVIE *with an assumption of being on privileged terms with her*): Pleasant young fellow that, Miss Vivie. Pity he has no money, isnt it?

VIVIE: Do you think so?

CROFTS: Well, whats he to do? No profession. No property. Whats he good for?

VIVIE: I realize his disadvantages, Sir George.

CROFTS (*a little taken aback at being so precisely interpreted*): Oh, it's not that. But while we're in this world we're in it; and money's money. (VIVIE *does not answer*). Nice day, isnt it?

VIVIE (*with scarcely veiled contempt for this effort at conversation*): Very.

CROFTS (*with brutal good humor, as if he liked her pluck*): Well, thats not what I came to say. (*Sitting down beside her*) Now listen, Miss Vivie. I'm quite aware that I'm not a young lady's man.

VIVIE: Indeed, Sir George?

CROFTS: No; and to tell you the honest truth I dont want to be either. But when I say a thing I mean it; when I feel a sentiment I feel it in earnest; and what I value I pay hard money for. Thats the sort of man I am.

VIVIE: It does you great credit, I'm sure.

CROFTS: Oh, I dont mean to praise myself. I have my faults, Heaven knows: no man is more sensible of that than I am. I know I'm not perfect: thats one of the advantages of being a middle-aged man; for I'm not a young man, and I know it. But my code is a simple one, and, I think, a good one. Honor between man and man; fidelity between man and woman; and no cant about this religion or that religion, but an honest belief that things are making for good on the whole.

VIVIE (*with biting irony*): "A power, not ourselves, that makes for righteousness," eh?

CROFTS (*taking her seriously*): Oh certainly. Not ourselves, of course. You understand what I mean. Well, now as to practical matters. You may have an idea that Ive flung my money about; but I havnt: I'm richer today than when I first came into ·the property. Ive used my knowledge of the world to invest my money in ways that other men have overlooked; and whatever else I may be, I'm a safe man from the money point of view.

VIVIE: It's very kind of you to tell me all this.

CROFTS: Oh well, come, Miss Vivie: you neednt pretend you dont see what I'm driving at. I want to settle down with a Lady Crofts. I suppose you think me very blunt, eh?

VIVIE: Not at all: I am much obliged to you for being so definite and business-like. I quite appreciate the offer: the money, the position, Lady Crofts, and so on. But I think I will say no, if you dont mind. I'd rather not. (*She rises, and strolls across to the sundial to get out of his immediate neighborhood*).

CROFTS (*not at all discouraged, and taking advantage of the additional room left him on the seat to spread himself comfortably, as if a few preliminary refusals were part of the inevitable routine of courtship*): I'm in no hurry. It was only just to let you know in case young Gardner should try to trap you. Leave the question open.

VIVIE (*sharply*): My no is final. I wont go back from it. (CROFTS *is not impressed. He grins; leans forward with his elbows on his knees to prod with his stick at some unfortunate insect in the grass; and looks cunningly at her. She turns away impatiently*).

CROFTS: I'm a good deal older than you. Twenty-five years: quarter of a century. I shant live for ever; and I'll take care that you shall be well off when I'm gone.

VIVIE: I am proof against even that inducement, Sir George. Dont you think youd better take your answer? There is not the slightest chance of my altering it.

CROFTS (*rising, after a final slash at a daisy, and coming nearer to her*): Well, no matter. I could tell you some things that would change your mind fast enough; but I wont, because I'd rather win you by honest affection. I was a good friend to your mother: ask her whether I wasnt. She'd never have made the money that paid for your education if it hadnt been for my advice and help, not to mention the money I advanced her. There are not many men would have stood by her as I have. I put not less than £40,000 into it, from first to last.

VIVIE (*staring at him*): Do you mean to say you were my mother's business partner?

CROFTS: Yes. Now just think of all the trouble and the explanations it would save if we were to keep the whole thing in the family, so to speak. Ask your mother whether she'd like to have to explain all her affairs to a perfect stranger.

VIVIE: I see no difficulty, since I understand that the business is wound up, and the money invested.

CROFTS (*stopping short, amazed*): Wound up! Wind up a business thats paying 35 per cent in the worst years! Not likely. Who told you that?

VIVIE (*her color quite gone*): Do you mean that it is still—? (*She stops abruptly, and puts her hand on the sundial to support herself. Then she gets quickly to the iron chair and sits down*). What business are you talking about?

CROFTS: Well, the fact is it's not what would be considered exactly a high-class business in my set—the county set, you know—our set it will be if you think better of my offer. Not that theres any mystery about it: dont .think that. Of course you know by your mother's being in it that it's perfectly straight and honest. Ive known her for many years; and I can say of her that she'd cut off her hands sooner than touch anything that was not what it ought to be. I'll tell you all about it if you like. I dont know whether youve found in travelling how hard it is to find a really comfortable private hotel.

VIVIE (*sickened, averting her face*): Yes, go on.

CROFTS: Well, thats all it is. Your mother has a genius for managing such things. We've got two in Brussels, one in Ostend, one in Vienna, and two in Budapest. Of course there are others besides ourselves in it; but we hold most of the capital; and your mother's indispensable as managing director. Youve noticed, I daresay, that she travels a good deal. But you see you cant mention such things in society. Once let out the word hotel and everybody says you keep a public-house. You wouldnt like people to say that of your mother, would you? Thats why we're so reserved about it. By the way, youll keep it to yourself, wont you? Since it's been a secret so long, it had better remain so.

VIVIE: And this is the business you invite me to join you in?

CROFTS: Oh no. My wife shant be troubled with business. Youll not be in it more than youve always been.

VIVIE: *I* always been! What do you mean?

CROFTS: Only that youve always lived on it. It paid for your education and the dress you have on your back. Dont turn up your nose at business, Miss Vivie: where would your Newnhams and Girtons be without it?

VIVIE (*rising, almost beside herself*): Take care. I know what this business is.

CROFTS (*starting, with a suppressed oath*): Who told you?

VIVIE: Your partner. My mother.

CROFTS (*black with rage*): The old—

VIVIE: Just so. (*He swallows the epithet and stands for a moment swearing and raging foully to himself. But he knows that his cue is to be sympathetic. He takes refuge in generous indignation*).

CROFTS: She ought to have had more consideration for you. *I'd* never have told you.

VIVIE: I think you would probably have told me when we were married: it would have been a convenient weapon to break me in with.

CROFTS (*quite sincerely*): I never intended that. On my word as a gentleman I didn't. (*VIVIE wonders at him. Her sense of the irony of his protest cools and braces her. She replies with contemptuous self-possession.*)

VIVIE: It does not matter. I suppose you understand that when we leave here today our acquaintance ceases.

CROFTS: Why? Is it for helping your mother?

VIVIE: My mother was a very poor woman who had no reasonable choice but to do as she did. You were a rich gentleman; and you did the same for the sake of 35 per cent. You are a pretty common sort of scoundrel, I think. That is my opinion of you.

CROFTS (*after a stare: not at all displeased, and much more at his ease on these frank terms than on their former ceremonious ones*): Ha! ha! ha! ha! Go it, little missie, go it: it doesnt hurt me and it amuses you. Why the devil shouldnt I invest my money that way? I take the interest on my capital like other people: I hope you dont think I dirty my own hands with the work. Come! you wouldnt refuse the acquaintance of my mother's cousin the Duke of Belgravia because some of the rents he gets are earned in queer ways. You wouldnt cut the Archbishop of Canterbury, I suppose, because the Ecclesiastical Commissioners have a few publicans and sinners among their tenants. Do you remember your Crofts scholarship at Newnham? Well, that was founded by my brother the M.P. He gets his 22 per cent out of a factory with 600 girls in it,. and not one of them getting wages enough to live on. How d'ye suppose they manage when they have no family to fall back on? Ask your mother. And do you expect me to turn my back on 35 per cent when all the rest are pocketing what they can, like sensible men? No such fool! If youre going to pick and choose your acquaintances on moral principles, youd better clear out of this country, unless you want to cut yourself out of all decent society.

VIVIE (*conscience stricken*): You might go on to point out that I myself never asked where the money I spent came from. I believe I am just as bad as you.

CROFTS (*greatly reassured*): Of course you are; and a very good thing too! What harm does it do after all? (*Rallying her jocularly*) So you dont think me such a scoundrel now you come to think it over. Eh?

VIVIE: I have shared profits with you; and I admitted you just now to the familiarity of knowing what I think of you.

CROFTS (*with serious friendliness*): To be sure you did. You wont find me a bad sort: I dont go in for being superfine intellectually; but Ive plenty of honest human feelings; and the old Crofts breed comes out in a sort of instinctive hatred of anything low, in which I'm sure youll sympathize with me. Believe me, Miss Vivie, the world isnt such a bad place as the croakers make out. As long as you dont fly openly in the face of society, society doesnt ask any inconvenient questions; and it makes precious short work of the cads who do. There are no secrets better kept than the secrets everybody guesses. In the class of people I can introduce you to, no lady or gentleman would so far forget themselves as to discuss my business affairs or your mother's. No man can offer you a safer position.

VIVIE (*studying him curiously*): I suppose you really think youre getting on famously with me.

CROFTS: Well, I hope I may flatter myself that you think better of me than you did at first.

VIVIE (*quietly*): I hardly find you worth thinking about at all now. When I think of the society that tolerates you, and the laws that protect you! when I think of how helpless nine out of ten young girls would be in the hands of you and my mother! the unmentionable woman and her capitalist bully—

CROFTS (*livid*): Damn you!

VIVIE: You need not. I feel among the damned already. (*She raises the latch of the gate to open it and go out. He follows her and puts his hand heavily on the top bar to prevent its opening*).

CROFTS (*panting with fury*): Do you think I'll put up with this from you, you young devil?

VIVIE (*unmoved*): Be quiet. Some one will answer the bell. (*Without flinching a step she strikes the bell with the back of her hand. It clangs harshly; and he starts back involuntarily. Almost immediately* FRANK *appears at the porch with his rifle*).

FRANK (*with cheerful politeness*): Will you have the rifle, Viv; or shall I operate?

VIVIE: Frank: have you been listening?

FRANK (*coming down into the garden*): Only for the bell, I assure you; so that you shouldnt have to wait. I think I shewed great insight into your character, Crofts.

CROFTS: For two pins I'd take that gun from you and break it across your head.

FRANK (*stalking him cautiously*): Pray dont. I'm ever so careless in handling firearms. Sure to be a fatal accident, with a reprimand from the coroner's jury for my negligence.

VIVIE: Put the rifle away, Frank: it's quite unnecessary.

FRANK: Quite right, Viv. Much more sportsmanlike to catch him in a trap. (CROFTS, *understanding the insult, makes a threatening movement.*) Crofts: there are fifteen cartridges in the magazine here; and I am a dead shot at the present distance and at an object of your size.

CROFTS: Oh, you neednt be afraid. I'm not going to touch you.

FRANK: Ever so magnanimous of you under the circumstances! Thank you!

CROFTS: I'll just tell you this before I go. It may interest you, since youre so fond of one another. Allow me, Mister Frank, to introduce you to your half-sister, the eldest daughter of the Reverend Samuel Gardner. Miss Vivie: your half-brother. Good morning. (*He goes out through the gate and along the road*).

FRANK (*after a pause of stupefaction, raising the rifle*): Youll testify before the coroner that it's an accident, Viv. (*He takes aim at the retreating figure of* CROFTS. VIVIE *seizes the muzzle and pulls it round against her breast*).

VIVIE: Fire now. You may.

FRANK (*dropping his end of the rifle hastily*): Stop! take care. (*She lets it go. It falls on the turf*). Oh, youve given your little boy such a turn. Suppose it had gone off! ugh! (*He sinks on the garden seat, overcome*).

VIVIE: Suppose it had: do you think it would not have been a relief to have some sharp physical pain tearing through me?

FRANK (*coaxingly*): Take it ever so easy, dear Viv. Remember: even if the rifle scared that fellow into telling the truth for the first time in his life, that only makes us the babes in the wood in earnest. (*He holds out his arms to her*). Come and be covered up with leaves again.

VIVIE (*with a cry of disgust*): Ah, not that, not that. You make all my flesh creep.

FRANK: Why, whats the matter?

VIVIE: Goodbye. (*She makes for the gate*).

FRANK (*jumping up*): Hallo! Stop! Viv! Viv! (*She turns in the gateway*) Where are you going to? Where shall we find you?

VIVIE: At Honoria Fraser's chambers, 67 Chancery Lane, for the rest of my life. (*She goes off quickly in the opposite direction to that taken by* CROFTS).

FRANK: But I say—wait—dash it! (*He runs after her*).

ACT IV

Honoria Fraser's chambers in Chancery Lane. An office at the top of New Stone Buildings, with a plate-glass window, distempered walls, electric light, and a patent stove. Saturday afternoon. The chimneys of Lincoln's Inn and the western sky beyond are seen through the window. There is a double writing-table in the middle of the room, with a cigar box, ash pans, and a portable electric reading lamp almost snowed up in heaps of papers and books. This table has knee holes and chairs right and left and is very untidy. The clerk's desk, closed and tidy, with its high stool, is against the wall, near a door communicating with the inner rooms. In the opposite wall is the door leading to the public corridor. Its upper panel is of opaque glass, lettered in black on the outside, FRASER AND WARREN. *A baize screen hides the corner between this door and the window.*

FRANK, *in a fashionable light-colored coaching suit, with his stick, gloves, and white hat in his hands, is pacing up and down the office. Somebody tries the door with a key.*

FRANK (*calling*): Come in. It's not locked. (VIVIE *comes in, in her hat and jacket. She stops and stares at him*).

VIVIE (*sternly*): What are you doing here?

FRANK: Waiting to see you. Ive been here for hours. Is this the way you attend to your business? (*He puts his hat and stick on the table, and perches himself with a vault on the clerk's stool, looking at her with every appearance of being in a specially restless, teasing, flippant mood*).

VIVIE: Ive been away exactly twenty minutes for a cup of tea. (*She takes off her hat and jacket and hangs them up behind the screen*). How did you get in?

FRANK: The staff had not left when I arrived. He's gone to play cricket on Primrose Hill. Why dont you employ a woman, and give your sex a chance?

VIVIE: What have you come for?

FRANK (*springing off the stool and coming close to her*): Viv: lets go and enjoy the Saturday half-holiday somewhere, like the staff. What do you say to Richmond, and then a music hall, and a jolly supper?

VIVIE: Cant afford it. I shall put in another six hours work before I go to bed.

FRANK: Cant afford it, cant we? Aha! Look here. (*He takes out a handful of sovereigns and makes them chink*). Gold, Viv: gold!

VIVIE: Where did you get it?

FRANK: Gambling, Viv: gambling. Poker.

VIVIE: Pah! It's meaner than stealing it. No: I'm not coming. (*She sits down to work at the table, with her back to the glass door, and begins turning over the papers*).

FRANK (*remonstrating piteously*): But, my dear Viv, I want to talk to you ever so seriously.

VIVIE: Very well: sit down in Honoria's chair and talk here. I like ten minutes chat after tea. (*He murmurs*). No use groaning: I'm inexorable. (*He takes the opposite seat disconsolately*). Pass that cigar box, will you?

FRANK (*pushing the cigar box across*): Nasty womanly habit. Nice men dont do it any longer.

VIVIE: Yes: they object to the smell in the office; and weve had to take to cigarets. See! (*She opens the box and takes out a cigaret, which she lights. She offers him one; but he shakes his head with a wry face. She settles herself comfortably in her chair, smoking*). Go ahead.

FRANK: Well, I want to know what youve done—what arrangements youve made.

VIVIE: Everything was settled twenty minutes after I arrived here. Honoria has found the business too much for her this year; and she was on the point of sending for me and proposing a partnership when I walked in and told her I hadnt a farthing in the world. So I installed myself and packed her off for a fortnight's holiday. What happened at Haslemere when I left?

FRANK: Nothing at all. I said youd gone to town on particular business.

VIVIE: Well?

FRANK: Well, either they were too flabbergasted to say anything, or else Crofts had prepared your mother. Anyhow, she didnt say anything; and Crofts didnt say anything; and Praddy only stared. After tea they got up and went; and Ive not seen them since.

VIVIE (*nodding placidly with one eye on a wreath of smoke*): Thats all right.

FRANK (*looking round disparagingly*): Do you intend to stick in this confounded place?

VIVIE (*blowing the wreath decisively away, and sitting straight up*): Yes. These two days have given me back all my strength and self-possession. I will never take a holiday again as long as I live.

FRANK (*with a very wry face*): Mps! You look quite happy. And as hard as nails.

VIVIE (*grimly*): Well for me that I am!

FRANK (*rising*): Look here, Viv: we must have an explanation. We parted the other day under a complete misunderstanding. (*He sits on the table, close to her*).

VIVIE (*putting away the cigaret*): Well: clear it up.

FRANK: You remember what Crofts said?

VIVIE: Yes.

FRANK: That revelation was supposed to bring about a complete change in the nature of our feeling for one another. It placed us on the footing of brother and sister.

VIVIE: Yes.

FRANK: Have you ever had a brother?

VIVIE: No.

FRANK: Then you dont know what being brother and sister feels like? Now I have lots of sisters; and the fraternal feeling is quite familiar to me. I assure you my feeling for you is not the least in the world like it. The girls will go their way; I will go mine; and we shant care if we never see one another again. Thats brother and sister. But as to you, I cant be easy if I have to pass a week without seeing you. Thats not brother and sister. It's exactly what I felt an hour before Crofts made his revelation. In short, dear Viv, it's love's young dream.

VIVIE (*bitingly*): The same feeling, Frank, that brought your father to my mother's feet. Is that it?

FRANK (*so revolted that he slips off the table for a moment*): I very strongly object, Viv, to have my feelings compared to any which the Reverend Samuel is capable of harboring; and I object still more to a comparison of you to your mother. (*Resuming his perch*). Besides, I dont believe the story. I have taxed my father with it, and obtained from him what I consider tantamount to a denial.

VIVIE: What did he say?

FRANK: He said he was sure there must be some mistake.

VIVIE: Do you believe him?

FRANK: I am prepared to take his word as against Crofts'.

VIVIE: Does it make any difference? I mean in your imagination or conscience; for of course it makes no real difference.

FRANK (*shaking his head*): None whatever to me.

VIVIE: Nor to me.

FRANK (*staring*): But this is ever so surprising! (*He goes back to his chair*). I thought our whole relations were altered in your imagination and conscience, as you put it, the moment those words were out of that brute's muzzle.

VIVIE: No: it was not that. I didn't believe him. I only wish I could.

FRANK: Eh?

VIVIE: I think brother and sister would be a very suitable relation for us.

FRANK: You really mean that?

VIVIE: Yes. It's the only relation I care for, even if we could afford any other. I mean that.

FRANK (*raising his eyebrows like one on whom a new light has dawned, and rising with quite an effusion of chivalrous sentiment*): My dear Viv: why didnt you say so before? I am ever so sorry for persecuting you. I understand, of course.

VIVIE (*puzzled*): Understand what?

FRANK: Oh, I'm not a fool in the ordinary sense: only in the Scriptural sense of doing all the things the wise man declared to be folly, after trying them himself on the most extensive scale. I see I am no longer Vivvums's little boy. Dont be alarmed: I shall never call you Vivvums again—at least unless you get tired of your new little boy, whoever he may be.

VIVIE: My new little boy!

FRANK (*with conviction*): Must be a new little boy. Always happens that way. No other way, in fact.

VIVIE: None that you know of, fortunately for you. (*Someone knocks at the door*).

FRANK: My curse upon yon caller, whoe'er he be!

VIVIE: It's Praed. He's going to Italy and wants to say goodbye. I asked him to call this afternoon. Go and let him in.

FRANK: We can continue our conversation after his departure for Italy. I'll stay him out. (*He goes to the door and opens it*). How are you, Praddy? Delighted to see you. Come in. (PRAED, *dressed for travelling, comes in, in high spirits*).

PRAED: How do you do, Miss Warren? (*She presses his hand cordially, though a certain sentimentality in his high spirits jars on her*). I start in an hour from Holborn Viaduct. I wish I could persuade you to try Italy.

VIVIE: What for?

PRAED: Why, to saturate yourself with beauty and romance, of course. (VIVIE, *with a shudder, turns her chair to the table, as if the work waiting for her there were a support to her.* PRAED *sits opposite to her.* FRANK *places a chair near* VIVIE, *and drops lazily and carelessly into it, talking at her over his shoulder*).

FRANK: No use, Praddy. Viv is a little Philistine. She is indifferent to my romance, and insensible to my beauty.

VIVIE: Mr Praed: once for all, there is no beauty and no romance in life for me. Life is what it is; and I am prepared to take it as it is.

PRAED (*enthusiastically*): You will not say that if you come with me to Verona and on to Venice. You will cry with delight at living in such a beautiful world.

FRANK: This is most eloquent, Praddy. Keep it up.

PRAED: Oh, I assure you *I* have cried—I shall cry again, I hope—at fifty! At your age, Miss Warren, you would not need to go so far as Verona. Your spirits would absolutely fly up at the mere sight of Ostend. You would be charmed with the gaiety, the vivacity, the happy air of Brussels.

VIVIE (*springing up with an exclamation of loathing*): Agh!

PRAED (*rising*): Whats the matter?

FRANK (*rising*): Hallo, Viv!

VIVIE (*to* PRAED, *with deep reproach*): Can you find no better example of your beauty and romance than Brussels to talk to me about?

PRAED (*puzzled*): Of course it's very different

from Verona. I dont suggest for a moment that —

VIVIE (*bitterly*): Probably the beauty and romance come to much the same in both places.

PRAED (*completely sobered and much concerned*): My dear Miss Warren: I—(*looking inquiringly at* FRANK) Is anything the matter?

FRANK: She thinks your enthusiasm frivolous, Praddy. She's had ever such a serious call.

VIVIE (*sharply*): Hold your tongue, Frank. Dont be silly.

FRANK (*sitting down*): Do you call this good manners, Praed?

PRAED (*anxious and considerate*): Shall I take him away, Miss Warren? I feel sure we have disturbed you at your work.

VIVIE: Sit down: I'm not ready to go back to work yet.. (PRAED *sits*). You both think I have an attack of nerves. Not a bit of it. But there are two subjects I want dropped, if you dont mind. One of them (*to* FRANK) is love's young dream in any shape or form: the other (*to* PRAED) is the romance and beauty of life, especially Ostend and the gaiety of Brussels. You are welcome to any illusions you may have left on these subjects: I have none. If we three are to remain friends, I must be treated as a woman of business, permanently single (*to* FRANK) and permanently unromantic (*to* PRAED).

FRANK: I also shall remain permanently single until you change your mind. Praddy: change the subject. Be eloquent about something else.

PRAED (*diffidently*): I'm afraid theres nothing else in the world that I can talk about. The Gospel of Art is the only one I can preach. I know Miss Warren is a great devotee of the Gospel of Getting On; but we cant discuss that without hurting your feelings, Frank, since you are determined not to get on.

FRANK: Oh, dont mind my feelings. Give me some improving advice by all means: it does me ever so much good. Have another try to make a successful man of me, Viv. Come: lets have it all: energy, thrift, foresight, self-respect, character. Dont you hate people who have no character, Viv?

VIVIE (*wincing*): Oh, stop, stop: let us have no more of that horrible cant. Mr Praed:

if there are really only those two gospels in the world, we had better all kill ourselves; for the same taint is in both, through and through.

FRANK (*looking critically at her*): There is a touch of poetry about you today, Viv, which has hitherto been lacking.

PRAED (*remonstrating*): My dear Frank, arnt you a little unsympathetic?

VIVIE (*merciless to herself*): No: it's good for me. It keeps me from being sentimental.

FRANK (*bantering her*): Checks your strong natural propensity that way, dont it?

VIVIE (*almost hysterical*): Oh yes: go on: dont spare me. I was sentimental for one moment in my life—beautifully sentimental—by moonlight; and now—

FRANK (*quickly*): I say, Viv: take care. Dont give yourself away.

VIVIE: Oh, do you think Mr Praed does not know all about my mother? (*Turning on* PRAED) You had better have told me that morning, Mr Praed. You are very old fashioned in your delicacies, after all.

PRAED: Surely it is you who are a little old fashioned in your prejudices, Miss Warren. I feel bound to tell you, speaking as an artist, and believing that the most intimate human relationships are far beyond and above the scope of the law, that though I know that your mother is an unmarried woman, I do not respect her the less on that account. I respect her more.

FRANK (*airily*): Hear! Hear!

VIVIE (*staring at him*): Is that all you know?

PRAED: Certainly that is all.

VIVIE: Then you neither of you know anything. Your guesses are innocence itself compared to the truth.

PRAED (*rising, startled and indignant, and preserving his politeness with an effort*): I hope not. (*More emphatically*) I hope not, Miss Warren.

FRANK (*whistles*): Whew!

VIVIE: You are not making it easy for me to tell you, Mr Praed.

PRAED (*his chivalry drooping before their conviction*): If there is anything worse—that is, anything else—are you sure you are right to tell us, Miss Warren?

VIVIE: I am sure that if I had the courage I should spend the rest of my life in telling everybody—stamping and branding it into them until they all felt their part in its abomination as I feel mine. There is nothing I despise more than the wicked convention that protects these things by forbidding a woman to mention them. And yet I cant tell you. The two infamous words that describe what my mother is are ringing in my ears and struggling on my tongue; but I cant utter them: the shame of them is too horrible for me. (*She buries her face in her hands. The two men, astonished, stare at one another and then at her. She raises her head again desperately and snatches a sheet of paper and a pen*). Here: let me draft you a prospectus.

FRANK: Oh, she's mad. Do you hear, Viv? mad. Come! pull yourself together.

VIVIE: You shall see. (*She writes*). "Paid up capital: not less than £40,000 standing in the name of Sir George Crofts, Baronet, the chief shareholder. Premises at Brussels, Ostend, Vienna and Budapest. Managing director: Mrs Warren"; and now dont let us forget her qualifications: the two words. (*She writes the words and pushes the paper to them.*) There! Oh no: dont read it: dont! (*She snatches it back and tears it to pieces; then seizes her head in her hands and hides her face on the table*).

FRANK, *who has watched the writing over her shoulder, and opened his eyes very widely at it, takes a card from his pocket; scribbles the two words on it; and silently hands it to* PRAED, *who reads it with amazement, and hides it hastily in his pocket.*

FRANK (*whispering tenderly*): Viv, dear: thats all right. I read what you wrote: so did Praddy. We understand. And we remain, as this leaves us at present, yours ever so devotedly.

PRAED: We do indeed, Miss Warren. I declare you are the most splendidly courageous woman I ever met. (*This sentimental compliment braces* VIVIE. *She throws it away from her with an impatient shake, and forces herself to stand up, though not without some support from the table*).

FRANK: Dont stir, Viv, if you dont want to. Take it easy.

VIVIE: Thank you. You can always depend on me for two things: not to cry and not to faint. (*She moves a few steps towards the door of the inner room, and stops close to* PRAED *to say*) I shall need much more courage than that when I tell my mother that we have come to the parting of the ways. Now I must go into the next room for a moment to make myself neat again, if you dont mind.

PRAED: Shall we go away?

VIVIE: No: I'll be back presently. Only for a moment. (*She goes into the other room,* PRAED *opening the door for her*).

PRAED: What an amazing revelation! I'm extremely disappointed in Crofts: I am indeed.

FRANK: I'm not in the least. I feel he's perfectly accounted for at last. But what a facer for me, Praddy! I cant marry her now.

PRAED (*sternly*): Frank! (*The two look at one another,* FRANK *unruffled,* PRAED *deeply indignant*). Let me tell you, Gardner, that if you desert her now you will behave very despicably.

FRANK: Good old Praddy! Ever chivalrous! But you mistake: it's not the moral aspect of the case: it's the money aspect. I really cant bring myself to touch the old woman's money now?

PRAED: And was that what you were going to marry on?

FRANK: What else? *I* havnt any money, nor the smallest turn for making it. If I married Viv now she would have to support me; and I should cost her more than I am worth.

PRAED: But surely a clever bright fellow like you can make something by your own brains.

FRANK: Oh yes, a little. (*He takes out his money again*). I made all that yesterday in an hour and a half. But I made it in a highly speculative business. No, dear Praddy: even if Bessie and Georgina marry millionaires and the governor dies after cutting them off with a shilling, I shall have only four hundred a year. And he wont die until he's three score and ten: he hasnt originality enough. I shall be on short allowance for the next twenty years. No short allowance for Viv, if I can help it. I withdraw gracefully and leave the field to the gilded youth of England. So thats settled. I shant worry her about it: I'll just send her a little note after we're gone. She'll understand.

PRAED (*grasping his hand*): Good fellow,

Frank! I heartily beg your pardon. But must you never see her again?

FRANK: Never see her again! Hang it all, be reasonable. I shall come along as often as possible, and be her brother. I can not understand the absurd consequences you romantic people expect from the most ordinary transactions. (*A knock at the door*). I wonder who this is. Would you mind opening the door? If it's a client it will look more respectable than if I appeared.

PRAED: Certainly. (*He goes to the door and opens it.* FRANK *sits down in* VIVIE's *chair to scribble a note*). My dear Kitty: come in: come in.

MRS WARREN *comes in, looking apprehensively round for* VIVIE. *She has done her best to make herself matronly and dignified. The brilliant hat is replaced by a sober bonnet, and the gay blouse covered by a costly black silk mantle. She is pitiably anxious and ill at ease: evidently panic-stricken.*

MRS WARREN (*to* FRANK): What! Youre here, are you?

FRANK (*turning in his chair from his writing, but not rising*): Here, and charmed to see you. You come like a breath of spring.

MRS WARREN: Oh, get out with your nonsense. (*In a low voice*) Wheres Vivie? (FRANK *points expressively to the door of the inner room, but says nothing*).

MRS WARREN (*sitting down suddenly and almost beginning to cry*): Praddy: wont she see me, dont you think?

PRAED: My dear Kitty: dont distress yourself. Why should she not?

MRS WARREN: Oh, you never can see why not: youre too innocent. Mr Frank: did she say anything to you?

FRANK (*folding his note*): She must see you, if (*very expressively*) you wait til she comes in.

MRS WARREN (*frightened*): Why shouldnt I wait? (FRANK *looks quizzically at her; puts his note carefully on the inkbottle, so that* VIVIE *cannot fail to find it when next she dips her pen; then rises and devotes his attention entirely to her*).

FRANK: My dear Mrs Warren: suppose you were a sparrow—ever so tiny and pretty a sparrow hopping in the roadway—and you saw a steam roller coming in your direction, would you wait for it?

MRS WARREN: Oh, dont bother me with your sparrows. What did she run away from Haslemere like that for?

FRANK: I'm afraid she'll tell you if you rashly await her return.

MRS WARREN: Do you want me to go away?

FRANK: No: I always want you to stay. But I advise you to go away.

MRS WARREN: What! And never see her again!

FRANK: Precisely.

MRS WARREN (*crying again*): Praddy: dont let him be cruel to me. (*She hastily checks her tears and wipes her eyes*). She'll be so angry if she sees Ive been crying.

FRANK (*with a touch of real compassion in his airy tenderness*): You know that Praddy is the soul of kindness, Mrs Warren. Praddy: what do you say? Go or stay?

PRAED (*to* MRS WARREN): I really should be very sorry to cause you unnecessary pain; but I think perhaps you had better not wait. The fact is—(VIVIE *is heard at the inner door*).

FRANK: Sh! Too late. She's coming.

MRS WARREN: Dont tell her I was crying. (VIVIE *comes in. She stops gravely on seeing* MRS WARREN, *who greets her with hysterical cheerfulness*). Well, dearie. So here you are at last.

VIVIE: I am glad you have come: I want to speak to you. You said you were going, Frank, I think.

FRANK: Yes. Will you come with me, Mrs Warren? What do you say to a trip to Richmond, and the theatre in the evening? There is safety in Richmond. No steam roller there.

VIVIE: Nonsense, Frank. My mother will stay here.

MRS WARREN (*scared*): I dont know: perhaps I'd better go. We're disturbing you at your work.

VIVIE (*with quiet decision*): Mr Praed: please take Frank away. Sit down, mother. (MRS WARREN *obeys helplessly*).

PRAED: Come, Frank. Goodbye, Miss Vivie.

VIVIE (*shaking hands*): Goodbye. A pleasant trip.

PRAED: Thank you: thank you. I hope so.

FRANK (*to* MRS WARREN): Goodbye: youd ever so much better have taken my advice. (*He shakes hands with her. Then airily to* VIVIE) Byebye, Viv.

VIVIE: Goodbye. (*He goes out gaily without shaking hands with her*).

PRAED (*sadly*): Goodbye, Kitty.

MRS WARREN (*snivelling*):—oobye! (PRAED goes. VIVIE, *composed and extremely grave, sits down in Honoria's chair, and waits for her mother to speak.* MRS WARREN, *dreading a pause, loses no time in beginning.*) Well, Vivie, what did you go away like that for without saying a word to me? How could you do such a thing! And what have you done to poor George? I wanted him to come with me; but he shuffled out of it. I could see that he was quite afraid of you. Only fancy: he wanted me not to come. As if (*trembling*) I should be afraid of you, dearie. (VIVIE's *gravity deepens*). But of course I told him it was all settled and comfortable between us, and that we were on the best of terms. (*She breaks down*). Vivie: whats the meaning of this? (*She produces a commercial envelope, and fumbles at the enclosure with trembling fingers*). I got it from the bank this morning.

VIVIE: It is my month's allowance. They sent it to me as usual the other day. I simply sent it back to be placed to your credit, and asked them to send you the lodgment receipt. In future I shall support myself.

MRS WARREN (*not daring to understand*): Wasnt it enough? Why didnt you tell me? (*With a cunning gleam in her eye*) I'll double it: I was intending to double it. Only let me know how much you want.

VIVIE: You know very well that that has nothing to do with it. From this time I go my own way in my own business and among my own friends. And you will go yours. (*She rises*). Goodbye.

MRS WARREN (*rising, appalled*): Goodbye?

VIVIE: Yes: Goodbye. Come: dont let us make a useless scene: you understand perfectly well. Sir George Crofts has told me the whole business.

MRS WARREN (*angrily*): Silly old—(*She swallows an epithet, and turns white at the narrowness of her escape from uttering it*).

VIVIE: Just so.

MRS WARREN: He ought to have his tongue cut out. But I thought it was ended: you said you didnt mind.

VIVIE (*steadfastly*): Excuse me: I do mind.

MRS WARREN: But I explained—

VIVIE: You explained how it came about. You did not tell me that it is still going on (*She sits.* MRS WARREN, *silenced for a moment, looks forlornly at* VIVIE, *who waits, secretly hoping that the combat is over. But the cunning expression comes back into* MRS WARREN's *face; and she bends across the table, sly and urgent, half whispering*).

MRS WARREN: Vivie: do you know how rich I am?

VIVIE: I have no doubt you are very rich.

MRS WARREN: But you dont know all that that means: youre too young. It means a new dress every day; it means theatres and balls every night; it means having the pick of all the gentlemen in Europe at your feet; it means a lovely house and plenty of servants; it means the choicest of eating and drinking; it means everything you like, everything you want, everything you can think of. And what are you here? A mere drudge, toiling and moiling early and late for your bare living and two cheap dresses a year. Think over it. (*Soothingly*) Youre shocked, I know. I can enter into your feelings; and I think they do you credit; but trust me, nobody will blame you: you may take my word for that. I know what young girls are; and I know youll think better of it when youve turned it over in your mind.

VIVIE: So thats how it's done, is it? You must have said all that to many a woman, mother, to have it so pat.

MRS WARREN (*passionately*): What harm am I asking you to do? (VIVIE *turns away contemptuously.* MRS WARREN *continues desperately*) Vivie: listen to me: you dont understand: youve been taught wrong on purpose: you dont know what the world is really like.

VIVIE (*arrested*): Taught wrong on purpose! What do you mean?

MRS WARREN: I mean that youre throwing away all your chances for nothing. You think that people are what they pretend to be: that the way you were taught at school and college to think right and proper is the way things really are. But it's not: it's all only a pretence, to keep the cowardly slavish common run of people quiet. Do you want to find that out, like other women, at forty, when youve thrown yourself away and lost your chances; or wont you take it in good time now from your own mother, that loves you and swears to you that it's truth: gospel truth? (*Urgently*) Vivie: the big people, the clever people, the managing people, all know it. They do as I do, and think what I think. I know plenty of them. I know them to speak to, to introduce you to, to make friends of for you. I dont mean anything wrong: thats what you dont understand: your head is full of ignorant ideas about me. What do the people that taught you know about life or about people like me? When did they ever meet me, or speak to me, or let anyone tell them about me? the fools! Would they ever have done anything for you if I hadnt paid them? Havnt I told you that I want you to be respectable? Havnt I brought you up to be respectable? And how can you keep it up without my money and my influence and Lizzie's friends? Cant you see that youre cutting your own throat as well as breaking my heart in turning your back on me?

VIVIE: I recognize the Crofts philosophy of life, mother. I heard it all from him that day at the Gardners'.

MRS WARREN: You think I want to force that played-out old sot on you! I dont, Vivie: on my oath I dont.

VIVIE: It would not matter if you did: you would not succeed. (MRS WARREN *winces, deeply hurt by the implied indifference towards her affectionate intention.* VIVIE, *neither understanding this nor concerning herself about it, goes on calmly*) Mother: you dont at all know the sort of person I am. I dont object to Crofts more than to any other coarsely built man of his class. To tell you the truth, I rather admire him for being strongminded enough to enjoy himself in his own way and make plenty of money instead of living the usual shooting, hunting, dining-out, tailoring, loafing life of his set merely because all the rest do it. And I'm perfectly aware that if I'd been in the same circumstances as my aunt Liz, I'd have done exactly what she did. I dont think I'm more prejudiced or straitlaced than you: I think I'm less. I'm certain I'm less sentimental. I know very well that fashionable morality is all a pretence, and that if I took your money and devoted the rest of my life to spending it fashionably, I might be as worthless and vicious as the

silliest woman could possibly want to be without having a word said to me about it. But I dont want to be worthless. I shouldnt enjoy trotting about the park to advertize my dressmaker and carriage builder, or being bored at the opera to shew off a shopwindowful of diamonds.

MRS WARREN (*bewildered*): But—

VIVIE: Wait a moment: Ive not done. Tell me why you continue your business now that you are independent of it. Your sister, you told me, has left all that behind her. Why dont you do the same?

MRS WARREN: Oh, it's all very easy for Liz: she likes good society, and has the air of being a lady. Imagine me in a cathedral town! Why, the very rooks in the trees would find me out even if I could stand the dulness of it. I must have work and excitement, or I should go melancholy mad. And what else is there for me to do? The life suits me: I'm fit for it and not for anything else. If I didnt do it somebody else would; so I dont do any real harm by it. And then it brings in money; and I like making money. No: it's no use: I cant give it up—not for anybody. But what need you know about it? I'll never mention it. I'll keep Crofts away. I'll not trouble you much: you see I have to be constantly running about from one place to another. Youll be quit of me altogether when I die.

VIVIE: No: I am my mother's daughter. I am like you: I must have work, and must make more money than I spend. But my work is not your work, and my way not your way. We must part. It will not make much difference to us: instead of meeting one another for perhaps a few months in twenty years, we shall never meet: thats all.

MRS WARREN (*her voice stifled in tears*): Vivie: I meant to have been more with you: I did indeed.

VIVIE: It's no use, mother: I am not to be changed by a few cheap tears and entreaties any more than you are, I daresay.

MRS WARREN (*wildly*): Oh, you call a mother's tears cheap.

VIVIE: They cost you nothing; and you ask me to give you the peace and quietness of my whole life in exchange for them. What use would my company be to you if you could get it? What have we two in common that could make either of us happy together?

MRS WARREN (*lapsing recklessly into her dialect*): We're mother and daughter. I want my daughter. Ive a right to you. Who is to care for me when I'm old? Plenty of girls have taken to me like daughters and cried at leaving me; but I let them all go because I had you to look forward to. I kept myself lonely for you. Youve no right to turn on me now and refuse to do your duty as a daughter.

VIVIE (*jarred and antagonized by the echo of the slums in her mother's voice*): My duty as a daughter! I thought we should come to that presently. Now once for all, mother, you want a daughter and Frank wants a wife. I dont want a mother; and I dont want a husband. I have spared neither Frank nor myself in sending him about his business. Do you think I will spare you?

MRS WARREN (*violently*): Oh, I know the sort you are: no mercy for yourself or anyone else. *I* know. My experience has done that for me anyhow: I can tell the pious, canting, hard, selfish woman when I meet her. Well, keep yourself to yourself: *I* dont want you. But listen to this. Do you know what I would do with you if you were a baby again? aye, as sure as there's a Heaven above us.

VIVIE: Strangle me, perhaps.

MRS WARREN: No: I'd bring you up to be a real daughter to me, and not what you are now, with your pride and your prejudices and the college education you stole from me: yes, stole: deny it if you can: what was it but stealing? I'd bring you up in my own house, I would.

VIVIE (*quietly*): In one of your own houses.

MRS WARREN (*screaming*): Listen to her! listen to how she spits on her mother's grey hairs! Oh, may you live to have your own daughter tear and trample on you as you have trampled on me. And you will: you will. No woman ever had luck with a mother's curse on her.

VIVIE: I wish you wouldnt rant, mother. It only hardens me. Come: I suppose I am the only young woman you ever had in your power that you did good to. Dont spoil it all now.

MRS WARREN: Yes, Heaven forgive me, it's true; and you are the only one that ever turned on me. Oh, the injustice of it! the injustice! the injustice! I always wanted to be a good woman. I tried honest work; and I was slave-driven until I cursed the day I ever heard of honest work. I was a good mother; and because I made my daughter a good woman she turns me out as if I was a leper. Oh, if I only had my life to live over again! I'd talk to that lying clergyman in the school. From this time forth, so help me Heaven in my last hour, I'll do wrong and nothing but wrong. And I'll prosper on it.

VIVIE: Yes: it's better to choose your line and go through with it. If I had been you, mother, I might have done as you did; but I should not have lived one life and believed in another. You are a conventional woman at heart. That is why I am bidding you goodbye now. I am right, am I not?

MRS WARREN (*taken aback*): Right to throw away all my money?

VIVIE: No: right to get rid of you? I should be a fool not to! Isnt that so?

MRS WARREN (*sulkily*): Oh well, yes, if you come to that, I suppose you are. But Lord help the world if everybody took to doing the right thing! And now I'd better go than stay where I'm not wanted. (*She turns to the door*).

VIVIE (*kindly*): Wont you shake hands?

MRS WARREN (*after looking at her fiercely for a moment with a savage impulse to strike her*): No, thank you. Goodbye.

VIVIE (*matter-of-factly*): Goodbye. (MRS WARREN *goes out, slamming the door behind her. The strain on* VIVIE's *face relaxes; her grave expression breaks up into one of joyous content; her breath goes out in a half sob, half laugh of intense relief. She goes buoyantly to her place at the writing-table; pushes the electric lamp out of the way; pulls over a great sheaf of papers; and is in the act of dipping her pen in the ink when she finds* FRANK's *note. She opens it unconcernedly and reads it quickly, giving a little laugh at some quaint turn of expression in it*). And goodbye, Frank. (*She tears the note up and tosses the pieces into the wastepaper basket without a second thought. Then she goes at her work with a plunge, and soon becomes absorbed in its figures*).

V
Identity

THE themes of identity and alienation are the modern parallels to the themes of love and religion. The latter have always been with us, and they have constituted the two leading themes of literature from the beginnings to the present. Religion has concerned itself with alleviating the pain of man's realization of his inability to stand alone in the cosmos; love, with man's inability to stand alone in the microcosmos—in society and in his personal relations. It is only in the present century that man has lost faith in his ability to construct intellectual systems to explain the mystery of the universe and his place in it. As a result largely of the tremendous destructive chaos brought about by the sudden increase of man's power over nature through technology, the ethical implications of which he has found himself powerless to handle, and a consequent reversion to atavistic barbarism in the behavior of large masses of his fellows, man has lost faith in the verities he has for centuries docilely accepted in the hope that they would lead him to peace in life and salvation hereafter. He has come unwillingly to the conclusion that he *is* alone in the cosmos. Similarly, only in the present century has man realized that not even he himself as an individual is an entity he is capable of understanding. The discoveries of Freud and others have shown man that his personality is fragmented and chaotic; that only by the most rigorous, painful, and lengthy probing can the depths of his own psyche be plumbed. A man's psyche or character is his essence. It is that by which he is defined—and he cannot know the definition. Hence the search for personal identity has become one of the chief themes of the modern drama.

This search has been a vain one since, just as man has developed a feeling of alienation by realizing that he is alone in the cosmos, he has come to realize that he is alone and helpless in the microcosmos as well. Love has come to seem an illusion, since how can man relate to and know another if he cannot know himself?

One of the earliest instances of the fragmentation of personality is to be found in Luigi Pirandello's *Henry IV* (1922). Here Pirandello deals with the tenuousness of mental stability by showing us that "insanity" is a purely subjective phenomenon. When "Henry IV" recovers from the effects of his fall after a lapse of twelve years he decides to continue the appearance of insanity. (During these twelve years he has, in effect, been dead, for, as Camus points out, premature death and insanity, that is, loss of consciousness of self, are the only two real disasters that can befall man.) Although Henry's decision is deliberate and rationally arrived at, it is an action that would conventionally be described as insane. In other words, Henry's "insanity" consists in a sane decision to take on the appearance of insanity. The line between sanity and insanity has become so blurred here as to be, for all practical purposes, invisible. No one can really know who or what Henry really is, least of all himself.

In Nigel Dennis's *Cards of Identity* (1956), the lack of self-knowledge has become institutionalized. For Dennis, the crisis of identity is not innate in man but imposed on him by psychoanalysis, which he sees as analogous to religious conversion: the Fisher for souls and the Fisher for minds are essentially one and the same. Dennis's thesis is that modern psychology, with its emphasis on making people "adjust" to the society around them, is stifling individualism. For Dennis, personal conspicuousness (which may be defined as a self-conscious sense of one's personal identity, however illusory that sense may really be) is not a sign of mental aberration, and his play is a protest against the pressing-iron technique of modern psychoanalysis. The way the psychoanalysts accomplish their end is by playing on the patient's inner life, on his memories. A man is made what he is by the experiences he has undergone. These experiences are all in the past and, consequently, exist only in the man's memory of them. It follows that if a man's memory of things is changed, the things themselves are actually changed; and the man's personality becomes re-formed in accordance with the new set of experiences he now remembers. Thus, if a man can be made to "remember" things that never really happened (through suggestion, hypnosis, persuasion, terror, and the like), and if his personality is contingent upon his memory of past experiences, then a man can be molded into any desired psychic shape. He becomes a piece of wet clay on a potter's wheel.

Dennis's thesis is that the Identity Club is comparable to all modern organizations dedicated to the standardization of personality, such as psychiatrists and psychoanalysts, totalitarian political parties, absolutist religious sects, and similar groups. Dennis is strictly for the individual's right of self-determination.

There is a certain anachronistic optimism latent in Dennis's play that we do not find in José Ruibal's *The Man and the Fly* (1968). This, too, is a play about brainwashing and the application of a pressing-iron technique to individual identity. In this play, we literally see a man being molded into becoming another and finally merging completely into him. The play can be taken several ways. First, it may be expressing the desire for immortality through an artificial symbolic identity rather than through a nonexistent personal identity, similar to Genet's *The Balcony*. Or it may be seen as a satire on political succession—the dynastic longings that are as prevalent in contemporary democracies as in totalitarian states.

Athol Fugard's *The Blood Knot* (1961) is a subtle study of life in contemporary South Africa and of the tortured mind of a man, half white and half black, who cannot decide what he is in a society that condemns him for his blackness or in a milieu that rejects him for his whiteness. His desperate attempt to find a spurious identity that he can live with, by trying to assume his half-brother's life and control his personality through a reliance on his blood relationship, is inevitably doomed.

HENRY IV

Luigi Pirandello

TRANSLATED BY
Edward Storer

CHARACTERS

HENRY IV
THE MARCHIONESS MATILDA SPINA
FRIDA, her daughter
CHARLES DI NOLLI, the young Marquis
BARON TITO BELCREDI
DOCTOR DIONYSIUS GENONI
HAROLD (FRANK)
LANDOLPH (LOLO)
ORDULPH (MOMO)
BERTHOLD (FINO)
JOHN, the old waiter
THE TWO VALETS IN COSTUME

The four private counsellors
(The names in parentheses
are nicknames)

A Solitary Villa in Italy in Our Own Time

ACT I

Salon in the villa, furnished and decorated so as to look exactly like the throne room of Henry IV in the royal residence at Goslar. Among the antique decorations there are two modern life-size portraits in oil painting. They are placed against the back wall, and mounted in a wooden stand that runs the whole length of the wall. (It is wide and protrudes, so that it is like a large bench.) One of the paintings is on the right; the other on the left of the throne, which is in the middle of the wall and divides the stand.

The Imperial chair and Baldachin.

The two portraits represent a lady and a gentleman, both young, dressed up in carnival costumes: one as "Henry IV," the other as the "Marchioness Matilda of Tuscany." Exits to right and left.

When the curtain goes up, the TWO VALETS *jump down, as if surprised, from the stand on which they have been lying, and go and take their positions, as rigid as statues, on either side below the throne with their halberds in their hands. Soon after, from the second exit, right, enter* HAROLD, LANDOLPH, ORDULPH *and* BERTHOLD, *young men employed by the* MARQUIS CHARLES DI NOLLI *to play the part of "Secret Counsellors" at the court of "Henry IV." They are, therefore, dressed like German knights of the XIth century.* BERTHOLD, *nicknamed Fino, is just entering on his duties for the first time. His companions are telling him what he has to do and amusing themselves at his expense. The scene is to be played rapidly and vivaciously.*

LANDOLPH (*to* BERTHOLD *as if explaining*): And this is the throne room.

HAROLD: At Goslar.

ORDULPH: Or at the castle in the Hartz, if you prefer.

HAROLD: Or at Wurms.

LANDOLPH: According as to what's doing it jumps about with us, now here, now there.

ORDULPH: In Saxony.

HAROLD: In Lombardy.

LANDOLPH: On the Rhine.

ONE OF THE VALETS (*without moving, just opening his lips*): I say . . .

HAROLD (*turning round*): What is it?

FIRST VALET (*like a statue*): Is he coming in or not? (*He alludes to* HENRY IV.)

ORDULPH: No, no, he's asleep. You needn't worry.

SECOND VALET (*releasing his pose, taking a long breath and going to lie down again on the stand*): You might have told us at once.

FIRST VALET (*going over to* HAROLD): Have you got a match, please?

LANDOLPH: What? You can't smoke a pipe here, you know.

FIRST VALET (*while* HAROLD *offers him a light*): No; a cigarette. (*Lights his cigarette and lies down again on the stand.*)

BERTHOLD (*who has been looking on in amazement, walking round the room, regarding the costumes of the others*): I say . . . this room . . . these costumes . . . Which Henry IV is it? I don't quite get it. Is he Henry IV of France or not? (*At this* LANDOLPH, HAROLD, *and* ORDULPH, *burst out laughing.*)

LANDOLPH (*still laughing; and pointing to* BERTHOLD *as if inviting the others to make fun of him*): Henry of France he says: ha! ha!

ORDULPH: He thought it was the king of France!

HAROLD: Henry IV of Germany, my boy: the Salian dynasty!

ORDULPH: The great and tragic Emperor!

LANDOLPH: He of Canossa. Every day we carry on here the terrible war between Church and State, by Jove.

ORDULPH: The Empire against the Papacy!

HAROLD: Antipopes against the Pope!

LANDOLPH: Kings against anti-kings!

ORDULPH: War on the Saxons!

HAROLD: And all the rebel Princes!

LANDOLPH: Against the Emperor's own sons!

BERTHOLD (*covering his head with his hands to protect himself against this avalanche of information*): I understand! I understand! Naturally, I didn't get the idea at first. I'm right then: these aren't costumes of the XVIth century?

HAROLD: XVIth century be hanged!

ORDULPH: We're somewhere between a thousand and eleven hundred.

LANDOLPH: Work it out for yourself: if we are before Canossa on the 25th of January, 1071 . . .

BERTHOLD (*more confused than ever*): Oh my God! What a mess I've made of it!

ORDULPH: Well, just slightly, if you supposed you were at the French court.

BERTHOLD: All that historical stuff I've swatted up!

LANDOLPH: My dear boy, it's four hundred years earlier.

BERTHOLD (*getting angry*): Good Heavens! You ought to have told me it was Germany and not France. I can't tell you how many books I've read in the last fifteen days.

HAROLD: But I say, surely you knew that poor Tito was Adalbert of Bremen, here?

BERTHOLD: Not a damned bit!

LANDOLPH: Well, don't you see how it is? When Tito died, the Marquis Di Nolli . . .

BERTHOLD: Oh, it was he, was it? He might have told me.

HAROLD: Perhaps he thought you knew.

LANDOLPH: He didn't want to engage anyone else in substitution. He thought the remaining three of us would do. But *he* began to cry out: "With Adalbert driven away . . .": because, you see, he didn't imagine poor Tito was dead; but that, as Bishop Adalbert, the rival bishops of Cologne and Mayence had driven him off . . .

BERTHOLD (*taking his head in his hand*): But I don't know a word of what you're talking about.

ORDULPH: So much the worse for you, my boy!

HAROLD: But the trouble is that not even we know who you are.

BERTHOLD: What? Not even you? You don't know who I'm supposed to be?

ORDULPH: Hum! "Berthold."

BERTHOLD: But which Berthold? And why Berthold?

LANDOLPH (*solemnly imitating* HENRY IV): "They've driven Adalbert away from me. Well then, I want Berthold! I want Berthold!" That's what he said.

HAROLD: We three looked one another in the eyes: who's got to be Berthold?

ORDULPH: And so here you are, "Berthold," my dear fellow!

LANDOLPH: I'm afraid you will make a bit of a mess of it.

BERTHOLD (*indignant, getting ready to go*): Ah, no! Thanks very much, but I'm off; I'm out of this!

HAROLD (*restraining him with the other two, amid laughter*): Steady now! Don't get excited!

LANDOLPH: Cheer up, my dear fellow! We don't any of us know who we are really. He's Harold; he's Ordulph; I'm Landolph! That's the way he calls us. We've got used to it. But who are we? Names of the period! Yours, too, is a name of the period: Berthold! Only one of us, poor Tito, had got a really decent part, as you can read in history: that of the Bishop of Bremen. He was just like a real bishop. Tito did it awfully well, poor chap!

HAROLD: Look at the study he put into it!

LANDOLPH: Why, he even ordered his Majesty about, opposed his views, guided and counselled him. We're "secret counsellors" —in a manner of speaking only; because it is written in history that Henry IV was hated by the upper aristocracy for surrounding himself at court with young men of the bourgeoisie.

ORDULPH: Us, that is.

LANDOLPH: Yes, small devoted vassals, a bit dissolute and very gay . . .

BERTHOLD: So I've got to be gay as well?

HAROLD: I should say so! Same as we are!

ORDULPH: And it isn't too easy, you know.

LANDOLPH: It's a pity; because the way we're got up, we could do a fine historical reconstruction. There's any amount of material in the story of Henry IV. But, as a matter of fact, we do nothing. We have the form without the content. We're worse than the real secret counsellors of Henry IV; because certainly no one had given them a part to play—at any rate, they didn't feel they had a part to play. It was their life. They looked after their own interests at the expense of others, sold investitures and—what not! We stop here in this magnificent court—for what?—Just doing nothing. We're like so many puppets hung on the wall, waiting for some one to come and move us or make us talk.

HAROLD: Ah, no, old sport, not quite that! We've got to give the proper answer, you know. There's trouble if he asks you something and you don't chip in with the cue.

LANDOLPH: Yes, that's true.

BERTHOLD: Don't rub it in too hard! How the devil am I to give him the proper answer, if I've swatted up Henry IV of France, and now he turns out to be Henry IV of Germany? (*The other three laugh.*)

HAROLD: You'd better start and prepare yourself at once.

ORDULPH: We'll help you out.

HAROLD: We've got any amount of books on the subject. A brief run through the main points will do to begin with.

ORDULPH: At any rate, you must have got some sort of general idea.

HAROLD: Look here! (*Turns him around and shows him the portrait of the Marchioness Matilda on the wall.*) Who's that?

BERTHOLD (*looking at it*): That? Well, the thing seems to me somewhat out of place, anyway: two modern paintings in the midst of all this respectable antiquity!

HAROLD: You're right! They weren't there in the beginning. There are two niches there behind the pictures. They were going to put up two statues in the style of the period. Then the places were covered with those canvases there.

LANDOLPH (*interrupting and continuing*): They would certainly be out of place if they really were paintings!

BERTHOLD: What are they, if they aren't paintings?

LANDOLPH: Go and touch them! Pictures all right . . . but for him! (*Makes a mysterious gesture to the right, alluding to* HENRY IV.) . . . who never touches them! . . .

BERTHOLD: No? What are they for him?

LANDOLPH: Well, I'm only supposing, you know; but I imagine I'm about right. They're images such as . . . well—such as a mirror might throw back. Do you understand? That one there represents himself, as he is in this throne room, which is all in the style of the period. What's there to marvel at? If we put you before a mirror, won't you see yourself, alive, but dressed up in ancient costume? Well, it's as if there were two mirrors there, which cast back living images in the midst of a world which, as you will see, when you have lived with us, comes to life too.

BERTHOLD: I say, look here . . . I've no particular desire to go mad here.

HAROLD: Go mad, be hanged! You'll have a fine time!

BERTHOLD: Tell me this: how have you all managed to become so learned?

LANDOLPH: My dear fellow, you can't go back over 800 years of history without picking up a bit of experience.

HAROLD: Come on! Come on! You'll see how quickly you get into it!

ORDULPH: You'll learn wisdom, too, at this school.

BERTHOLD: Well, for Heaven's sake, help me a bit! Give me the main lines, anyway.

HAROLD: Leave it to us. We'll do it all between us.

LANDOLPH: We'll put your wires on you and fix you up like a first-class marionette. Come along! (*They take him by the arm to lead him away.*)

BERTHOLD (*stopping and looking at the portrait on the wall*): Wait a minute! You haven't told me who that is. The Emperor's wife?

HAROLD: No! The Emperor's wife is Bertha of Susa, the sister of Amadeus II of Savoy.

ORDULPH: And the Emperor, who wants to be young with us, can't stand her, and wants to put her away.

LANDOLPH: That is his most ferocious enemy: Matilda, Marchioness of Tuscany.

BERTHOLD: Ah, I've got it: the one who gave hospitality to the Pope!

LANDOLPH: Exactly: at Canossa!

ORDULPH: Pope Gregory VII!

HAROLD: Our *bête noir*! Come on! come on! (*All four move toward the right to go out, when, from the left, the old servant* JOHN *enters in evening dress.*)

JOHN (*quickly, anxiously*): Hss! Hss! Frank! Lolo!

HAROLD (*turning round*): What is it?

BERTHOLD (*marvelling at seeing a man in modern clothes enter the throne room*): Oh! I say, this is a bit too much, this chap here!

LANDOLPH: A man of the XXth century, here! Oh, go away! (*They run over to him, pretending to menace him and throw him out.*)

ORDULPH (*heroically*): Messenger of Gregory VII, away!

HAROLD: Away! Away!

JOHN (*annoyed, defending himself*): Oh, stop it! Stop it, I tell you!

ORDULPH: No, you can't set foot here!

HAROLD: Out with him.

LANDOLPH (*to* BERTHOLD): Magic, you know! He's a demon conjured up by the Wizard of Rome! Out with your swords! (*Makes as if to draw a sword.*)

JOHN (*shouting*): Stop it, will you? Don't play the fool with me! The Marquis has arrived with some friends . . .

LANDOLPH: Good! Good! Are there ladies too?

ORDULPH: Old or young?

JOHN: There are two gentlemen.

HAROLD: But the ladies, the ladies, who are they?

JOHN: The Marchioness and her daughter.

LANDOLPH (*surprised*): What do you say?

ORDULPH: The Marchioness?

JOHN: The Marchioness! The Marchioness!

HAROLD: Who are the gentlemen?

JOHN: I don't know.

HAROLD (*to* BERTHOLD): They're coming to bring us a message from the Pope, do you see?

ORDULPH: All messengers of Gregory VII! What fun!

JOHN: Will you let me speak, or not?

HAROLD: Go on, then!

JOHN: One of the two gentlemen is a doctor, I fancy.

LANDOLPH: Oh, I see, one of the usual doctors.

HAROLD: Bravo Berthold, you'll bring us luck!

LANDOLPH: You wait and see how we'll manage this doctor!

BERTHOLD: It looks as if I were going to get into a nice mess right away.

JOHN: If the gentlemen would allow me to speak . . . they want to come here into the throne room.

LANDOLPH (*surprised*): What? She? The Marchioness here?

HAROLD: Then this is something quite different! No play-acting this time!

LANDOLPH: We'll have a real tragedy: that's what!

BERTHOLD (*curious*): Why? Why?

ORDULPH (*pointing to the portrait*): She is that person there, don't you understand?

LANDOLPH: The daughter is the fiancée of the Marquis. But what have they come for, I should like to know?

ORDULPH: If he sees her, there'll be trouble.

LANDOLPH: Perhaps he won't recognize her any more.

JOHN: You must keep him there, if he should wake up . . .

ORDULPH: Easier said than done, by Jove!

HAROLD: You know what he's like!

JOHN: —even by force, if necessary! Those are my orders. Go on! Go on!

HAROLD: Yes, because who knows if he hasn't already wakened up?

ORDULPH: Come on then!

LANDOLPH (*going towards* JOHN *with the others*): You'll tell us later what it all means.

JOHN (*shouting after them*): Close the door there, and hide the key! That other door too. (*Pointing to the other door on right.*)

JOHN (*to the* TWO VALETS): Be off, you two! There! (*Pointing to exit right.*) Close the door after you, and hide the key!

The TWO VALETS *go out by the first door on right.* JOHN *moves over to the left to show in:* DONNA MATILDA SPINA, *the young* MARCHIONESS FRIDA, DR. DIONYSIUS GENONI, *the* BARON TITO BELCREDI *and the young* MARQUIS CHARLES DI NOLLI, *who, as master of the house, enters last.*

DONNA MATILDA SPINA *is about 45, still handsome, although there are too patent signs of her attempts to remedy the ravages of time with make-up. Her head is thus rather like a Walkyrie. This facial make-up contrasts with her beautiful sad mouth. A widow for many years, she now has as her friend the* BARON TITO BELCREDI, *whom neither she nor anyone else takes seriously —at least so it would appear.*

What TITO BELCREDI *really is for her at bottom, he alone knows; and he is, therefore, entitled to laugh, if his friend feels the need of pretending not to know. He can always laugh at the jests which the beautiful Marchioness makes with the others at his expense. He is slim, prematurely gray, and younger than she is. His head is bird-like in shape. He would be a very vivacious person, if his ductile agility (which among other things makes him a redoubtable swordsman) were not enclosed in a sheath of Arab-like laziness, which is revealed in his strange, nasal drawn-out voice.*

FRIDA, *the daughter of the Marchioness, is* 19. *She is sad, because her imperious and too beautiful mother puts her in the shade, and provokes facile gossip against her daughter as well as against herself. Fortunately for her, she is engaged to the* MARQUIS CHARLES DI NOLLI.

CHARLES DI NOLLI *is a stiff young man, very indulgent towards others, but sure of himself for what he amounts to in the world. He is worried about all the responsibilities which he believes weigh on him. He is dressed in deep mourning for the recent death of his mother.*

DR. DIONYSIUS GENONI *has a bold rubicund Satyr-like face, prominent eyes, a pointed beard (which is silvery and shiny) and elegant manners. He is nearly bald. All enter in a state of perturbation, almost as if afraid, and all (except* DI NOLLI) *looking curiously about the room. At first, they speak sotto voce.*

DI NOLLI (*to* JOHN): Have you given the orders properly?

JOHN: Yes, my Lord; don't be anxious about that.

BELCREDI: Ah, magnificent! magnificent!

DOCTOR: How extremely interesting! Even in the surroundings his raving madness—is perfectly taken into account!

DONNA MATILDA (*glancing round for her portrait, discovers it, and goes up close to it*): Ah! Here it is! (*Going back to admire it, while mixed emotions stir within her.*) Yes . . . yes . . . (*Calls her daughter* FRIDA.)

FRIDA: Ah, your portrait!

DONNA MATILDA: No, no . . . look again; it's you, not I, there!

DI NOLLI: Yes, it's quite true. I told you so, I . . .

DONNA MATILDA: But I would never have believed it! (*Shaking as if with a chill.*) What a strange feeling it gives one! (*Then looking at her daughter.*) Frida, what's the matter? (*She pulls her to her side, and slips an arm round her waist.*) Come: don't you see yourself in me there?

FRIDA: Well, I really . . .

DONNA MATILDA: Don't you think so? Don't you, really? (*Turning to* BELCREDI.) Look at it, Tito! Speak up, man!

BELCREDI (*without looking*): Ah, no! I shan't look at it. For me, *a priori*, certainly not!

DONNA MATILDA: Stupid! You think you are paying me a compliment! (*Turning to* DOCTOR GENONI.) What do you say, Doctor? Do say something, please!

DOCTOR *makes a movement to go near to the picture.*

BELCREDI (*with his back turned, pretending to attract his attention secretly*): —Hss! No, Doctor! For the love of Heaven, have nothing to do with it!

DOCTOR (*getting bewildered and smiling*): And why shouldn't I?

DONNA MATILDA: Don't listen to him! Come here! He's insufferable!

FRIDA: He acts the fool by profession, didn't you know that?

BELCREDI (*to the* DOCTOR, *seeing him go over*): Look at your feet, Doctor! Mind where you're going!

DOCTOR: Why?

BELCREDI: Be careful you don't put your foot in it!

DOCTOR (*laughing feebly*): No, no. After all, it seems to me there's no reason to be astonished at the fact that a daughter should resemble her mother!

BELCREDI: Hullo! Hullo! He's done it now; he's said it.

DONNA MATILDA (*with exaggerated anger, advancing towards* BELCREDI): What's the matter? What has he said? What has he done?

DOCTOR (*candidly*): Well, isn't it so?

BELCREDI (*answering the* MARCHIONESS): I said there was nothing to be astounded at —and you are astounded! And why so, then, if the thing is so simple and natural for you now?

DONNA MATILDA (*still more angry*): Fool! fool! It's just because it is so natural! Just because it isn't my daughter who is there. (*Pointing to the canvas.*) That is my portrait; and to find my daughter there instead of me fills me with astonishment, an astonishment which, I beg you to believe, is sincere. I forbid you to cast doubts on it.

FRIDA (*slowly and wearily*): My God! It's always like this . . . rows over nothing . . .

BELCREDI (*also slowly, looking dejected, in accents of apology*): I cast no doubt on anything! I noticed from the beginning that you haven't shared your mother's astonishment; or, if something did astonish you, it was because the likeness between you and the portrait seemed so strong.

DONNA MATILDA: Naturally! She cannot recognize herself in me as I was at her age; while I, there, can very well recognize myself in her as she is now!

DOCTOR: Quite right! Because a portrait is always there fixed in the twinkling of an eye: for the young lady something far away and without memories, while, for the Marchioness, it can bring back everything: movements, gestures, looks, smiles, a whole heap of things . . .

DONNA MATILDA: Exactly!

DOCTOR (*continuing, turning towards her*): Naturally enough, you can live all these old sensations again in your daughter.

DONNA MATILDA: He always spoils every innocent pleasure for me, every touch I have of spontaneous sentiment! He does it merely to annoy me.

DOCTOR (*frightened at the disturbance he has caused, adopts a professorial tone*): Likeness, dear Baron, is often the result of imponderable things. So one explains that . . .

BELCREDI (*interrupting the discourse*): Somebody will soon be finding a likeness between you and me, my dear Professor!

DI NOLLI: Oh! let's finish with this, please! (*Points to the two doors on the right, as a warning that there is someone there who may be listening.*) We've wasted too much time as it is!

FRIDA: As one might expect when *he's* present. (*Alludes to* BELCREDI.)

DI NOLLI: Enough! The Doctor is here; and we have come for a very serious purpose which you all know is important for me.

DOCTOR: Yes, that is so! But now, first of all, let's try to get some points down exactly. Excuse me, Marchioness, will you tell me why your portrait is here? Did you present it to him then?

DONNA MATILDA: No, not at all. How could I have given it to him? I was just like Frida then—and not even engaged. I gave it to him three or four years after the accident. I gave it to him because his mother wished it so much . . . (*Points to* DI NOLLI.)

DOCTOR: She was his sister? (*Alludes to* HENRY IV.)

DI NOLLI: Yes, Doctor; and our coming here is a debt we pay to my mother who has been dead for more than a month. Instead of being here, she and I (*Indicating* FRIDA.) ought to be traveling together . . .

DOCTOR: . . . taking a cure of quite a different kind!

DI NOLLI: —Hum! Mother died in the firm conviction that her adored brother was just about to be cured.

DOCTOR: And can't you tell me, if you please, how she inferred this?

DI NOLLI: The conviction would appear to have derived from certain strange remarks which he made, a little before mother died.

DOCTOR: Oh, remarks! . . . Ah! . . . It would be extremely useful for me to have those remarks, word for word, if possible.

DI NOLLI: I can't remember them. I know that mother returned awfully upset from her last visit with him. On her death-bed, she made me promise that I would never neglect him, that I would have doctors see him, and examine him.

DOCTOR: Um! Um! Let me see! let me see! Sometimes very small reasons determine . . . and this portrait here then? . . .

DONNA MATILDA: For Heaven's sake, Doctor, don't attach excessive importance to this. It made an impression on me because I had not seen it for so many years!

DOCTOR: If you please, quietly, quietly . . .

DI NOLLI: —Well, yes, it must be about fifteen years ago.

DONNA MATILDA: More, more: eighteen!

DOCTOR: Forgive me, but you don't quite know what I'm trying to get at. I attach a very great importance to these two portraits . . . They were painted, naturally, prior to the famous—and most regrettable pageant, weren't they?

DONNA MATILDA: Of course!

DOCTOR: That is . . . when he was quite in his right mind—that's what I've been trying to say. Was it his suggestion that they should be painted?

DONNA MATILDA: Lots of the people who took part in the pageant had theirs done as a souvenir . . .

BELCREDI: I had mine done—as "Charles of Anjou!"

DONNA MATILDA: . . . as soon as the costumes were ready.

BELCREDI: As a matter of fact, it was proposed that the whole lot of us should be hung together in a gallery of the villa where the pageant took place. But in the end, everybody wanted to keep his own portrait.

DONNA MATILDA: And I gave him this portrait of me without very much regret . . . since his mother . . . (*Indicates* DI NOLLI.)

DOCTOR: You don't remember if it was he who asked for it?

DONNA MATILDA: Ah, that I don't remember . . . Maybe it was his sister, wanting to help out . . .

DOCTOR: One other thing: was it his idea, this pageant?

BELCREDI (*at once*): No, no, it was mine!

DOCTOR: If you please . . .

DONNA MATILDA: Don't listen to him! It was poor Belassi's idea.

BELCREDI: Belassi! What had he got to do with it?

DONNA MATILDA: Count Belassi, who died, poor fellow, two or three months after . . .

BELCREDI: But if Belassi wasn't there when . . .

DI NOLLI: Excuse me, Doctor; but is it really necessary to establish whose the original idea was?

DOCTOR: It would help me, certainly!

BELCREDI: I tell you the idea was mine! There's nothing to be proud of in it, seeing what the result's been. Look here, Doctor, it was like this. One evening, in the first days of November, I was looking at an illustrated German review in the club. I was merely glancing at the pictures, because I can't read German. There was a picture of the Kaiser, at some University town where he had been a student . . . I don't remember which.

DOCTOR: Bonn, Bonn!

BELCREDI: —You are right: Bonn! He was on horseback, dressed up in one of those ancient German student guild-costumes, followed by a procession of noble students, also in costume. The picture gave me the idea. Already someone at the club had spoken of a pageant for the forthcoming carnival. So I had the notion that each of us should choose for this Tower of Babel pageant to represent some character: a king, an emperor, a prince, with his queen, empress, or lady, alongside of him—and all on horseback. The suggestion was at once accepted.

DONNA MATILDA: I had my invitation from Belassi.

BELCREDI: Well, he wasn't speaking the truth! That's all I can say, if he told you the idea was his. He wasn't even at the club the evening I made the suggestion, just as he (*Meaning* HENRY IV.) wasn't there either.

DOCTOR: So he chose the character of Henry IV?

DONNA MATILDA: Because I . . . thinking of my name, and not giving the choice any importance, said I would be the Marchioness Matilda of Tuscany.

DOCTOR: I . . . don't understand the relation between the two.

DONNA MATILDA: —Neither did I, to begin with, when he said that in that case he would be at my feet like Henry IV at Canossa. I had heard of Canossa of course; but to tell the truth, I'd forgotten most of the story; and I remember I received a curious impression when I had to get up my part, and found that I was the faithful and zealous friend of Pope Gregory VII in deadly enmity with the Emperor of Germany. Then I understood why, since I had chosen to represent his implacable enemy, he wanted to be near me in the pageant as Henry IV.

DOCTOR: Ah, perhaps because . . .

BELCREDI: —Good Heavens, Doctor, because he was then paying furious court to her! (*Indicates the* MARCHIONESS.) And she, naturally . . .

DONNA MATILDA: Naturally? Not naturally at all . . .

BELCREDI (*pointing to her*): She couldn't stand him . . .

DONNA MATILDA: —No, that isn't true! I didn't dislike him. Not at all! But for me, when a man begins to want to be taken seriously, well . . .

BELCREDI (*continuing for her*): He gives you the clearest proof of his stupidity.

DONNA MATILDA: No, dear; not in this case; because he was never a fool like you.

BELCREDI: Anyway, I've never asked you to take me seriously.

DONNA MATILDA: Yes, I know. But with him one couldn't joke. (*Changing her tone and speaking to the* DOCTOR.) One of the many misfortunes which happen to us women, Doctor, is to see before us every now and again a pair of eyes glaring at us with a contained intense promise of eternal devotion. (*Bursts out laughing.*) There is nothing quite so funny. If men could only see themselves with that eternal look of fidelity in their faces! I've always thought it comic; then more even than now. But I want to make a confession—I can do so after twenty years or more. When I laughed at him then, it was partly out of fear. One might have almost believed a promise from those eyes of his. But it would have been very dangerous.

DOCTOR (*with lively interest*): Ah! ah! This is most interesting! Very dangerous, you say?

DONNA MATILDA: Yes, because he was very different from the others. And then, I am . . . well . . . what shall I say? . . . a little impatient of all that is pondered, or tedious. But I was too young then, and a woman. I had the bit between my teeth. It would have required more courage than I felt I possessed. So I laughed at him too —with remorse, to spite myself, indeed; since I saw that my own laugh mingled with those of all the others—the other fools —who made fun of him.

BELCREDI: My own case, more or less!

DONNA MATILDA: You make people laugh at you, my dear, with your trick of always humiliating yourself. It was quite a different affair with him. There's a vast difference. And you—you know—people laugh in your face!

BELCREDI: Well, that's better than behind one's back!

DOCTOR: Let's get to the facts. He was then already somewhat exalted, if I understand rightly.

BELCREDI: Yes, but in a curious fashion, Doctor.

DOCTOR: How?

BELCREDI: Well, cold-bloodedly so to speak.

DONNA MATILDA: Not at all! It was like this, Doctor! He was a bit strange, certainly; but only because he was fond of life: eccentric, there!

BELCREDI: I don't say he simulated exaltation. On the contrary, he was often genuinely exalted. But I could swear, Doctor, that he saw himself at once in his own exaltation. Moreover, I'm certain it made

him suffer. Sometimes he had the most comical fits of rage against himself.

DOCTOR: Yes?

DONNA MATILDA: That is true.

BELCREDI (*to* DONNA MATILDA): And why? (*To the* DOCTOR.) Evidently, because that immediate lucidity that comes from acting, assuming a part, at once put him out of key with his own feelings, which seemed to him not exactly false, but like something he was obliged to give the value there and then of—what shall I say—of an act of intelligence, to make up for that sincere cordial warmth he felt lacking. So he improvised, exaggerated, let himself go, so as to distract and forget himself. He appeared inconstant, fatuous, and—yes—even ridiculous, sometimes.

DOCTOR: And may we say unsociable?

BELCREDI: No, not at all. He was famous for getting up things: *tableaux vivants*, dances, theatrical performances for charity: all for the fun of the thing, of course. He was a jolly good actor, you know!

DI NOLLI: Madness has made a superb actor of him.

BELCREDI: —Why, so he was even in the old days. When the accident happened, after the horse fell . . .

DOCTOR: Hit the back of his head, didn't he?

DONNA MATILDA: Oh, it was horrible! He was beside me! I saw him between the horse's hoofs! It was rearing!

BELCREDI: None of us thought it was anything serious at first. There was a stop in the pageant, a bit of disorder. People wanted to know what had happened. But they'd already taken him off to the villa.

DONNA MATILDA: There wasn't the least sign of a wound, not a drop of blood.

BELCREDI: We thought he had merely fainted.

DONNA MATILDA: But two hours afterwards . . .

BELCREDI: He reappeared in the drawing-room of the villa . . . that is what I wanted to say . . .

DONNA MATILDA: My God! What a face he had. I saw the whole thing at once!

BELCREDI: No, no! that isn't true. Nobody saw it, Doctor, believe me!

DONNA MATILDA: Doubtless, because you were all like mad folk.

BELCREDI: Everybody was pretending to act his part for a joke. It was a regular Babel.

DONNA MATILDA: And you can imagine, Doctor, what terror struck into us when we understood that he, on the contrary, was playing his part in deadly earnest . . .

DOCTOR: Oh, he was there too, was he?

BELCREDI: Of course! He came straight into the midst of us. We thought he'd quite recovered, and was pretending, fooling, like all the rest of us . . . only doing it rather better; because, as I say, he knew how to act.

DONNA MATILDA: Some of them began to hit him with their whips and fans and sticks.

BELCREDI: And then—as a king, he was armed, of course—he drew out his sword and menaced two or three of us . . . It was a terrible moment, I can assure you!

DONNA MATILDA: I shall never forget that scene—all our masked faces hideous and terrified gazing at him, at that terrible mask of his face, which was no longer a mask, but madness, madness personified.

BELCREDI: He was Henry IV, Henry IV in person, in a moment of fury.

DONNA MATILDA: He'd got into it all the detail and minute preparation of a month's careful study. And it all burned and blazed there in the terrible obsession which lit his face.

DOCTOR: Yes, that is quite natural, of course. The momentary obsession of a dilettante became fixed, owing to the fall and the damage to the brain.

BELCREDI (to FRIDA and DI NOLLI): You see the kind of jokes life can play on us. (To DI NOLLI.) You were four or five years old. (To FRIDA.) Your mother imagines you've taken her place there in that portrait; when, at the time, she had not the remotest idea that she would bring you into the world. My hair is already grey; and he—look at him—(Points to portrait)—ha! A smack on the head, and he never moves again: Henry IV for ever!

DOCTOR (seeking to draw the attention of the others, looking learned and imposing): —Well, well, then it comes, we may say, to this . . . (Suddenly the first exit to right, the one nearest footlights, opens, and BERTHOLD enters all excited.)

BERTHOLD (rushing in): I say! I say! (Stops for a moment, arrested by the astonishment which his appearance has caused in the others.)

FRIDA (running away terrified): Oh dear! oh dear! it's he, it's . . .

DONNA MATILDA (covering her face with her hands so as not to see): Is it, is it he?

DI NOLLI: No, no, what are you talking about? Be calm!

DOCTOR: Who is it then?

BELCREDI: One of our masqueraders.

DI NOLLI: He is one of the four youths we keep here to help him out in his madness . . .

BERTHOLD: I beg your pardon, Marquis . . .

DI NOLLI: Pardon be damned! I gave orders that the doors were to be closed, and that nobody should be allowed to enter.

BERTHOLD: Yes, sir, but I can't stand it any longer, and I ask you to let me go away this very minute.

DI NOLLI: Oh, you're the new counsellor, are you? You were supposed to begin this morning, weren't you?

BERTHOLD: Yes, sir, and I can't stand it, I can't bear it.

DONNA MATILDA (to DI NOLLI excitedly): What? Then he's not so calm as you said?

BERTHOLD (quickly): —No, no, my lady, it isn't he; it's my companions. You say "help him out with his madness," Marquis; but they don't do anything of the kind. They're the real madmen. I come here for the first time, and instead of helping me . . . (LANDOLPH and HAROLD come in from the same door, but hesitate on the threshold.)

LANDOLPH: Excuse me?

HAROLD: May I come in, my Lord?

DI NOLLI: Come in! What's the matter? What are you all doing?

FRIDA: Oh God! I'm frightened! I'm going to run away. (Makes towards exit at left.)

DI NOLLI (restraining her at once): No, no, Frida!

LANDOLPH: My Lord, this fool here . . . (Indicates BERTHOLD.)

BERTHOLD (protesting): Ah, no thanks, my friends, no thanks! I'm not stopping here! I'm off!

LANDOLPH: What do you mean—you're not stopping here?

HAROLD: He's ruined everything, my Lord, running away in here!

LANDOLPH: He's made him quite mad. We can't keep him in there any longer. He's given orders that he's to be arrested! and he wants to "judge" him at once from the throne: What is to be done?

DI NOLLI: Shut the door, man! Shut the door! Go and close that door! (LANDOLPH *goes over to close it.*)

HAROLD: Ordulph, alone, won't be able to keep him there.

LANDOLPH: —My Lord, perhaps if we could announce the visitors at once, it would turn his thoughts. Have the gentlemen thought under what pretext they will present themselves to him?

DI NOLLI: —It's all been arranged! (*To the* DOCTOR.) If you, Doctor, think it well to see him at once. . . .

FRIDA: I'm not coming! I'm not coming! I'll keep out of this. You too, mother, for Heaven's sake, come away with me!

DOCTOR: —I say . . . I suppose he's not armed, is he?

DI NOLLI: —Nonsense! Of course not. (*To* FRIDA.) Frida, you know this is childish of you. You wanted to come!

FRIDA: I didn't at all. It was mother's idea.

DONNA MATILDA: And I'm quite ready to see him. What are we going to do?

BELCREDI: Must we absolutely dress up in some fashion or other?

LANDOLPH: —Absolutely essential, indispensable, sir. Alas! as you see . . . (*Shows his costume*), there'd be awful trouble if he saw you gentlemen in modern dress.

HAROLD: He would think it was some diabolical masquerade.

DI NOLLI: As these men seem to be in costume to you, so we appear to be in costume to him, in these modern clothes of ours.

LANDOLPH: It wouldn't matter so much if he wouldn't suppose it to be the work of his mortal enemy.

BELCREDI: Pope Gregory VII?

LANDOLPH: Precisely. He calls him "a pagan."

BELCREDI: The Pope a pagan? Not bad that!

LANDOLPH: —Yes, sir,—and a man who calls up the dead! He accuses him of all the diabolical arts. He's terribly afraid of him.

DOCTOR: Persecution mania!

HAROLD: He'd be simply furious.

DI NOLLI (*to* BELCREDI): But there's no need for you to be there, you know. It's sufficient for the Doctor to see him.

DOCTOR: —What do you mean? . . . I? Alone?

DI NOLLI: —But they are there. (*Indicates the three young men.*)

DOCTOR: I don't mean that . . . I mean if the Marchioness . . .

DONNA MATILDA: Of course. I mean to see him too, naturally. I want to see him again.

FRIDA: Oh, why, mother, why? Do come away with me, I implore you!

DONNA MATILDA (*imperiously*): Let me do as I wish! I came here for this purpose! (*To* LANDOLPH.) I shall be "Adelaide," the mother.

LANDOLPH: Excellent! The mother of the Empress Bertha. Good! It will be enough if her Ladyship wears the ducal crown and puts on a mantle that will hide her other clothes entirely. (*To* HAROLD.) Off you go, Harold!

HAROLD: Wait a moment! And this gentleman here? . . . (*Alludes to the* DOCTOR.)

DOCTOR: —Ah yes . . . we decided I was to be . . . the Bishop of Cluny, Hugh of Cluny!

HAROLD: The gentleman means the Abbot. Very good! Hugh of Cluny.

LANDOLPH: —He's often been here before!

DOCTOR (*amazed*): —What? Been here before?

LANDOLPH: —Don't be alarmed! I mean that it's an easily prepared disguise . . .

HAROLD: We've made use of it on other occasions, you see!

DOCTOR: But . . .

LANDOLPH: Oh, no, there's no risk of his remembering. He pays more attention to the dress than to the person.

DONNA MATILDA: That's fortunate for me too then.

DI NOLLI: Frida, you and I'll get along. Come on, Tito!

BELCREDI: Ah no. If she (*Indicates the* MARCHIONESS.) stops here, so do I!

DONNA MATILDA: But I don't need you at all.

BELCREDI: You may not need me, but I should like to see him again myself. Mayn't I?

LANDOLPH: Well, perhaps it would be better if there were three.

HAROLD: How is the gentleman to be dressed then?

BELCREDI: Oh, try and find some easy costume for me.

LANDOLPH (*to* HAROLD): Hum! Yes . . . he'd better be from Cluny too.

BELCREDI: What do you mean—from Cluny?

LANDOLPH: A Benedictine's habit of the Abbey of Cluny. He can be in attendance on Monsignor. (*To* HAROLD.) Off you go! (*To* BERTHOLD.) And you too get away and keep out of sight all today. No, wait a bit! (*To* BERTHOLD.) You bring here the costumes he will give you. (*To* HAROLD.) You go at once and announce the visit of the "Duchess Adelaide" and "Monsignor Hugh of Cluny." Do you understand? (HAROLD *and* BERTHOLD *go off by the first door on the right.*)

DI NOLLI: We'll retire now. (*Goes off with* FRIDA, *left.*)

DOCTOR: Shall I be a *persona grata* to him, as Hugh of Cluny?

LANDOLPH: Oh, rather! Don't worry about that! Monsignor has always been received here with great respect. You too, my Lady, he will be glad to see. He never forgets that it was owing to the intercession of you two that he was admitted to the Castle of Canossa and the presence of Gregory VII, who didn't want to receive him.

BELCREDI: And what do I do?

LANDOLPH: You stand a little apart, respectfully: that's all.

DONNA MATILDA (*irritated, nervous*): You would do well to go away, you know.

BELCREDI (*slowly, spitefully*): How upset you seem! . . .

DONNA MATILDA (*proudly*): I am as I am. Leave me alone! (BERTHOLD *comes in with the costumes.*)

LANDOLPH (*seeing him enter*): Ah, the costumes: here they are. This mantle is for the Marchioness . . .

DONNA MATILDA: Wait a minute! I'll take off my hat. (*Does so and gives it to* BERTHOLD.)

LANDOLPH: Put it down there! (*Then to the* MARCHIONESS, *while he offers to put the ducal crown on her head.*) Allow me!

DONNA MATILDA: Dear, dear! Isn't there a mirror here?

LANDOLPH: Yes, there's one there. (*Points to the door on the left.*) If the Marchioness would rather put it on herself . . .

DONNA MATILDA: Yes, yes, that will be better. Give it to me! (*Takes up her hat and goes off with* BERTHOLD, *who carries the cloak and the crown.*)

BELCREDI: Well, I must say, I never thought I should be a Benedictine monk! By the way, this business must cost an awful lot of money.

DOCTOR: Like any other fantasy, naturally!

BELCREDI: Well, there's a fortune to go upon.

LANDOLPH: We have got there a whole wardrobe of costumes of the period, copied to perfection from old models. This is my special job. I get them from the best theatrical costumers. They cost lots of money. (DONNA MATILDA *re-enters, wearing mantle and crown.*)

BELCREDI (*at once, in admiration*): Oh magnificent! Oh, truly regal!

DONNA MATILDA (*looking at* BELCREDI *and bursting out into laughter*): Oh no, no! Take it off! You're impossible. You look like an ostrich dressed up as a monk.

BELCREDI: Well, how about the Doctor?

DOCTOR: I don't think I look so bad, do I?

DONNA MATILDA: No; the Doctor's all right . . . but you are too funny for words.

DOCTOR: Do you have many receptions here then?

LANDOLPH: It depends. He often gives orders that such and such a person appear before him. Then we have to find someone who will take the part. Women too . . .

DONNA MATILDA (*hurt, but trying to hide the fact*): Ah, women too?

LANDOLPH: Oh, yes; many at first.

BELCREDI (*laughing*): Oh, that's great! In costume, like the Marchioness?

LANDOLPH: Oh well, you know, women of the kind that lend themselves to . . .

BELCREDI: Ah, I see! (*Perfidiously to the* MARCHIONESS.) Look out, you know he's becoming dangerous for you. (*The second door on the right opens, and* HAROLD *appears making first of all a discreet sign that all conversation should cease.*)

HAROLD: His Majesty, the Emperor!

The TWO VALETS *enter first, and go and stand on either side of the throne. Then* HENRY IV *comes in between* ORDULPH *and* HAROLD, *who keeps a little in the rear respectfully.* HENRY IV *is about 50 and very pale. The hair on the back of his head is already grey; over the temples and forehead it appears blond, owing to its having been tinted in an evident and puerile fashion. On his cheekbones he has two small, doll-like dabs of color, that stand out prominently against the rest of his tragic pallor. He is wearing a penitent's sack over his regal habit, as at Canossa. His eyes have a fixed look which is dreadful to see, and this expression is in strained contrast with the sackcloth.* ORDULPH *carries the Imperial crown;* HAROLD, *the sceptre with eagle, and the globe with the cross.*

HENRY IV (*bowing first to* DONNA MATILDA *and afterwards to the* DOCTOR): My lady . . . Monsignor . . . (*Then he looks at* BELCREDI *and seems about to greet him too; when, suddenly, he turns to* LANDOLPH, *who has approached him, and asks him sotto voce and with diffidence.*) Is that Peter Damiani?

LANDOLPH: No, Sire. He is a monk from Cluny who is accompanying the Abbot.

HENRY IV (*looks again at* BELCREDI *with increasing mistrust, and then noticing that he appears embarrassed and keeps glancing at* DONNA MATILDA *and the* DOCTOR, *stands upright and cries out*): No, it's Peter Damiani! It's no use, father, your looking at the Duchess. (*Then turning quickly to* DONNA MATILDA *and the* DOCTOR *as though to ward off a danger.*) I swear it! I swear that my heart is changed towards your daughter. I confess that if he (*Indicates* BELCREDI.) hadn't come to forbid it in the name of Pope Alexander, I'd have repudiated her. Yes, yes, there were people ready to favour the repudiation: the Bishop of Mayence would have done it for a matter of one hundred and twenty farms. (*Looks at* LANDOLPH *a little perplexed and adds.*) But I mustn't speak ill of the bishops at this moment! (*More humbly to* BELCREDI.) I am grateful to you, believe me, I am grateful to you for the hindrance you put in my way!—God knows, my life's been all made of humiliations: my mother, Adalbert, Tribur, Goslar! And now this sackcloth you see me wearing! (*Changes tone suddenly and speaks like one who goes over his part in a parenthesis of astuteness.*) It doesn't matter: clarity of ideas, perspicacity, firmness and patience under adversity that's the thing. (*Then turning to all and speaking solemnly.*) I know how to make amends for the mistakes I have made; and I can humiliate myself even before

you, Peter Damiani. (*Bows profoundly to him and remains curved. Then a suspicion is born in him which he is obliged to utter in menacing tones, almost against his will.*) Was it not perhaps you who started that obscene rumor that my holy mother had illicit relations with the Bishop of Augusta?

BELCREDI (*since* HENRY IV *has his finger pointed at him*): No, no, it wasn't I . . .

HENRY IV (*straightening up*): Not true, not true? Infamy! (*Looks at him and then adds.*) I didn't think you capable of it! (*Goes to the* DOCTOR *and plucks his sleeve, while winking at him knowingly.*) Always the same, Monsignor, those bishops, always the same!

HAROLD (*softly, whispering, as if to help out the* DOCTOR): Yes, yes, the rapacious bishops!

DOCTOR (*to* HAROLD, *trying to keep it up*): Ah, yes, those fellows . . . ah yes . . .

HENRY IV: Nothing satisfies them! I was a little boy, Monsignor . . . One passes the time, playing even, when, without knowing it, one is a king.—I was six years old; and they tore me away from my mother, and made use of me against her without my knowing anything about it . . . always profaning, always stealing, stealing! . . . One greedier than the other . . . Hanno worse than Stephen! Stephen worse than Hanno!

LANDOLPH (*sotto voce, persuasively, to call his attention*): Majesty!

HENRY IV (*turning round quickly*): Ah yes . . . this isn't the moment to speak ill of the bishops. But this infamy against my mother, Monsignor, is too much. (*Looks at the* MARCHIONESS *and grows tender.*) And I can't even weep for her, Lady . . . I appeal to you who have a mother's heart! She came here to see me from her convent a month ago . . . They had told me she was dead! (*Sustained pause full of feeling. Then smiling sadly.*) I can't weep for her; because if you are here now, and I am like this (*Shows the sackcloth he is wearing.*) it means I am twenty-six years old!

HAROLD: And that she is therefore alive, Majesty! . . .

ORDULPH: Still in her convent!

HENRY IV (*looking at them*): Ah yes! And I can postpone my grief to another time. (*Shows the* MARCHIONESS *almost with co-*

quetry the tint he has given to his hair.)
Look! I am still fair . . . (*Then slowly as
if in confidence.*) For you . . . there's no
need! But little exterior details do help! A
matter of time, Monsignor, do you understand me? (*Turns to the* MARCHIONESS *and
notices her hair.*) Ah, but I see that you
too, Duchess . . . Italian, eh? (*As much
as to say "false"; but without any indignation, indeed rather with malicious admiration.*) Heaven forbid that I should show
disgust or surprise! Nobody cares to recognize that obscure and fatal power which
sets limits to our will. But I say, if one is
born and one dies . . . Did you want to
be born, Monsignor? I didn't! And in both
cases, independently of our wills, so many
things happen we would wish didn't happen, and to which we resign ourselves as
best we can! . . .

DOCTOR (*merely to make a remark, while
studying* HENRY IV *carefully*): Alas! Yes,
alas!

HENRY IV: It's like this: When we are not
resigned, out come our desires. A woman
wants to be a man . . . an old man would
be young again. Desires, ridiculous fixed
ideas, of course—But reflect! Monsignor,
those other desires are not less ridiculous:
I mean, those desires where the will is kept
within the limits of the possible. Not one
of us can lie or pretend. We're all fixed in
good faith in a certain concept of ourselves.
However, Monsignor, while you keep yourself in order, holding on with both your
hands to your holy habit, there slips down
from your sleeves, there peels off from you
like . . . like a serpent . . . something you
don't notice: life, Monsignor! (*Turns to
the* MARCHIONESS.) Has it never happened
to you, my Lady, to find a different self in
yourself? Have you always been the same?
My God! One day . . . how was it, how
was it you were able to commit this or
that action? (*Fixes her so intently in the
eyes as almost to make her blanch.*) Yes,
that particular action, that very one: we
understand each other! But don't be afraid:
I shall reveal it to none. And you, Peter
Damiani, how could you be a friend of that
man? . . .

LANDOLPH: Majesty!

HENRY IV (*at once*): No, I won't name him!
(*Turning to* BELCREDI.) What did you

think of him? But we all of us cling tight
to our conceptions of ourselves, just as he
who is growing old dyes his hair. What
does it matter that this dyed hair of mine
isn't a reality for you, if it *is*, to some extent, for me?—you, you, my Lady, certainly don't dye your hair to deceive the
others, nor even yourself; but only to cheat
your own image a little before the looking-
glass. I do it for a joke! You do it seriously!
But I assure you that you too, Madam, are
in masquerade, though it be in all seriousness; and I am not speaking of the venerable crown on your brows or the ducal
mantle. I am speaking only of the memory
you wish to fix in yourself of your fair complexion one day when it pleased you—or
of your dark complexion, if you were dark:
the fading image of your youth! For you,
Peter Damiani, on the contrary, the memory of what you have been, of what you
have done, seems to you a recognition of
past realities that remain within you like
a dream. I'm in the same case too: with so
many inexplicable memories—like dreams!
Ah! . . . There's nothing to marvel at in
it, Peter Damiani! Tomorrow it will be the
same thing with our life of today! (*Suddenly getting excited and taking hold of
his sackcloth.*) This sackcloth here . . .
(*Beginning to take it off with a gesture of
almost ferocious joy while* HAROLD *and*
ORDULPH *run over to him, frightened, as if
to prevent his doing so.*) Ah, my God!
(*Draws back and throws off sackcloth.*) Tomorrow, at Bressanone, twenty-seven German and Lombard bishops will sign with
me the act of deposition of Gregory VII!
No Pope at all! Just a false monk!

ORDULPH (*with the other two*): Majesty!
Majesty! In God's name! . . .

HAROLD (*inviting him to put on the sackcloth
again*): Listen to what he says, Majesty!

LANDOLPH: Monsignor is here with the
Duchess to intercede in your favor. (*Makes
secret signs to the* DOCTOR *to say something
at once.*)

DOCTOR (*foolishly*): Ah yes . . . yes . . .
we are here to intercede . . .

HENRY IV (*repenting at once, almost terrified,
allowing the three to put on the sackcloth
again, and pulling it down over him with
his own hands*): Pardon . . . yes . . .
yes . . . pardon, Monsignor: forgive me,

my Lady . . . I swear to you I feel the whole weight of the anathema. (*Bends himself, takes his face between his hands, as though waiting for something to crush him. Then changing tone, but without moving, says softly to* LANDOLPH, HAROLD *and* ORDULPH.) But I don't know why I cannot be humble before that man there! (*Indicates* BELCREDI.)

LANDOLPH (*sotto voce*): But why, Majesty, do you insist on believing he is Peter Damiani, when he isn't, at all?

HENRY IV (*looking at him timorously*): He isn't Peter Damiani?

HAROLD: No, no, he is a poor monk, Majesty.

HENRY IV (*sadly with a touch of exasperation*): Ah! None of us can estimate what we do when we do it from instinct . . . You perhaps, Madam, can understand me better than the others, since you are a woman and a Duchess. This is a solemn and decisive moment. I could, you know, accept the assistance of the Lombard bishops, arrest the Pope, lock him up here in the castle, run to Rome and elect an anti-Pope; offer alliance to Robert Guiscard—and Gregory VII would be lost! I resist the temptation; and, believe me, I am wise in doing so. I feel the atmosphere of our times and the majesty of one who knows how to be what he ought to be! a Pope! Do you feel inclined to laugh at me, seeing me like this? You would be foolish to do so; for you don't understand the political wisdom which makes this penitent's sack advisable. The parts may be changed tomorrow. What would you do then? Would you laugh to see the Pope a prisoner? No! It would come to the same thing: I dressed as a penitent, today; he, as prisoner tomorrow! But woe to him who doesn't know how to wear his mask, be he king or Pope!—Perhaps he is a bit too cruel! No! Yes, yes, maybe!—You remember, my Lady, how your daughter Bertha, for whom, I repeat, my feelings have changed (*Turns to* BELCREDI *and shouts to his face as if he were being contradicted by him.*)—yes, changed on account of the affection and devotion she showed me in that terrible moment . . . (*Then once again to the* MARCHIONESS.) . . . you remember how she came with me, my Lady, followed me like a beggar and passed two nights out in the open, in the snow? You are her mother! Doesn't this touch your mother's heart? Doesn't this urge you to pity, so, that you will beg His Holiness for pardon, beg him to receive us?

DONNA MATILDA (*trembling, with feeble voice*): Yes, yes, at once . . .

DOCTOR: It shall be done!

HENRY IV: And one thing more! (*Draws them in to listen to him.*) It isn't enough that he should receive me! You know he can do *everything—everything* I tell you! He can even call up the dead. (*Touches his chest.*) Behold me! Do you see me? There is no magic art unknown to him. Well, Monsignor, my Lady, my torment is really this: that whether here or there (*Pointing to his portrait almost in fear.*) I can't free myself from this magic. I am a penitent now, you see; and I swear to you I shall remain so until he receives me. But you two, when the excommunication is taken off, must ask the Pope to do this thing he can so easily do: to take me away from that; (*Indicating the portrait again.*) and let me live wholly and freely my miserable life. A man can't always be twenty-six, my Lady. I ask this of you for your daughter's sake too; that I may love her as she deserves to be loved, well disposed as I am now, all tender towards her for her pity. There: it's all there! I am in your hands! (*Bows.*) My Lady! Monsignor! (*He goes off, bowing grandly, through the door by which he entered, leaving everyone stupefied, and the* MARCHIONESS *so profoundly touched, that no sooner has he gone than she breaks out into sobs and sits down almost fainting.*)

ACT II

Another room in the villa, adjoining the throne room. Its furniture is antique and severe. Principal exit at rear in the background. To the left, two windows looking on the garden. To the right, a door opening into the throne room.

Late afternoon of the same day.

DONNA MATILDA, *the* DOCTOR *and* BELCREDI *are on the stage engaged in conversation; but* DONNA MATILDA *stands to one side, evidently annoyed at what the other two are saying, although she cannot help listening, because, in her agitated state, everything interests her in spite of herself. The talk of the other two attracts her attention, because she instinctively feels the need for calm at the moment.*

BELCREDI: It may be as you say, Doctor, but that was my impression.

DOCTOR: I won't contradict you; but, believe me, it is only . . . an impression.

BELCREDI: Pardon me, but he even said so, and quite clearly. (*Turning to the* MARCHIONESS.) Didn't he, Marchioness?

DONNA MATILDA (*turning round*): What did he say? . . . (*Then not agreeing.*) Oh yes . . . but not for the reason you think!

DOCTOR: He was alluding to the costumes we had slipped on . . . Your cloak (*Indicating the* MARCHIONESS.) our Benedictine habits . . . But all this is childish!

DONNA MATILDA (*turning quickly, indignant*): Childish? What do you mean, Doctor?

DOCTOR: From one point of view, it is—I beg you to let me say so, Marchioness! Yet, on the other hand, it is much more complicated than you can imagine.

DONNA MATILDA: To me, on the contrary, it is perfectly clear!

DOCTOR (*with a smile of pity of the competent person towards those who do not understand*): We must take into account the peculiar psychology of madmen; which, you must know, enables us to be certain that they observe things and can, for instance, easily detect people who are disguised; can in fact recognize the disguise and yet believe in it; just as children do, for whom disguise is both play and reality. That is why I used the word childish. But the thing is extremely complicated, inasmuch as he must be perfectly aware of being an image to himself and for himself—that image there, in fact! (*Alluding to the portrait in the throne room, and pointing to the left.*)

BELCREDI: That's what he said!

DOCTOR: Very well then— An image before which other images, ours, have appeared: understand? Now he, in his acute and perfectly lucid delirium, was able to detect at once a difference between his image and ours: that is, he saw that ours were make-believes. So he suspected us; because all madmen are armed with a special diffidence. But that's all there is to it! Our make-believe, built up all round his, did not seem pitiful to him. While his seemed all the more tragic to us, in that he, as if in defiance—understand?—and induced by his suspicion, wanted to show us up merely as a joke. That was also partly the case with him, in coming before us with painted cheeks and hair, and saying he had done it on purpose for a jest.

DONNA MATILDA (*impatiently*): No, it's not that, Doctor. It's not like that! It's not like that!

DOCTOR: Why isn't it, may I ask?

DONNA MATILDA (*with decision but trembling*): I am perfectly certain he recognized me!

DOCTOR: It's not possible . . . it's not possible!

BELCREDI (*at the same time*): Of course not!

DONNA MATILDA (*more than ever determined, almost convulsively*): I tell you, he recognized me! When he came close up to speak to me—looking in my eyes, right into my eyes—he recognized me!

BELCREDI: But he was talking of your daughter!

DONNA MATILDA: That's not true! He was talking of me! Of me!

BELCREDI: Yes, perhaps, when he said . . .

DONNA MATILDA (*letting herself go*): About my dyed hair! But didn't you notice that he added at once: "or the memory of your dark hair, if you were dark"? He remembered perfectly well that I was dark—then!

BELCREDI: Nonsense! nonsense!

DONNA MATILDA (*not listening to him, turning to the* DOCTOR): My hair, Doctor, is really dark—like my daughter's! That's why he spoke of her.

BELCREDI: But he doesn't even know your daughter! He's never seen her!

DONNA MATILDA: Exactly! Oh, you never understand anything! By my daughter, stupid, he meant me—as I was then!

BELCREDI: Oh, this is catching! This is catching, this madness!

DONNA MATILDA (*softly, with contempt*): Fool!

BELCREDI: Excuse me, were you ever his wife? Your daughter is his wife—in his delirium: Bertha of Susa.

DONNA MATILDA: Exactly! Because I, no longer dark—as he remembered me—but *fair*, introduced myself as "Adelaide," the mother. My daughter doesn't exist for him: he's never seen her—you said so yourself! So how can he know whether she's fair or dark?

BELCREDI: But he said dark, speaking generally, just as anyone who wants to recall, whether fair or dark, a memory of youth in the color of the hair! And you, as usual, begin to imagine things! Doctor, you said I ought not to have come! It's she who ought not to have come!

DONNA MATILDA (*upset for a moment by* BELCREDI's *remark, recovers herself. Then with a touch of anger, because doubtful*): No, no . . . he spoke of me . . . He spoke all the time to me, with me, of me . . .

BELCREDI: That's not bad! He didn't leave me a moment's breathing space; and you say he was talking all the time to you? Unless you think he was alluding to you too, when he was talking to Peter Damiani!

DONNA MATILDA (*defiantly, almost exceeding the limits of courteous discussion*): Who knows? Can you tell me why, from the outset, he showed a strong dislike for you, for you alone? (*From the tone of the question, the expected answer must almost explicitly be: "because he understands you are my lover."* BELCREDI *feels this so well that he remains silent and can say nothing.*)

DOCTOR: The reason may also be found in the fact that only the visit of the Duchess Adelaide and the Abbot of Cluny was announced to him. Finding a third person present, who had not been announced, at once his suspicions . . .

BELCREDI: Yes, exactly! His suspicion made him see an enemy in me: Peter Damiani! But she's got it into her head, that he recognized her . . .

DONNA MATILDA: There's no doubt about it! I could see it from his eyes, Doctor. You know, there's a way of looking that leaves no doubt whatever . . . Perhaps it was only for an instant, but I am sure!

DOCTOR: It is not impossible: a lucid moment . . .

DONNA MATILDA: Yes, perhaps . . . And then his speech seemed to me full of regret for his and my youth—for the horrible thing that happened to him, that has held him in that disguise from which he has never been able to free himself, and from which he longs to be free—he said so himself!

BELCREDI: Yes, so as to be able to make love to your daughter, or you, as you believe—having been touched by your pity.

DONNA MATILDA: Which is very great, I would ask you to believe.

BELCREDI: As one can see, Marchioness; so much so that a miracle-worker might expect a miracle from it!

DOCTOR: Will you let me speak? I don't work miracles, because I am a doctor and not a miracle-worker. I listened very intently to all he said; and I repeat that that certain analogical elasticity, common to all systematized delirium, is evidently with him much . . . what shall I say?—much relaxed! The elements, that is, of his delirium no longer hold together. It seems to me he has lost the equilibrium of his second personality and sudden recollections drag him—and this is very comforting—not from a state of incipient apathy, but rather from a morbid inclination to reflective melancholy, which shows a . . . a very considerable cerebral activity. Very comforting, I repeat! Now if, by this violent trick we've planned . . .

DONNA MATILDA (*turning to the window, in the tone of a sick person complaining*): But how is it that the motor has not returned? It's three hours and a half since . . .

DOCTOR: What do you say?

DONNA MATILDA: The motor, Doctor! It's more than three hours and a half . . .

DOCTOR (*taking out his watch and looking at it*): Yes, more than four hours, by this!

DONNA MATILDA: It could have reached here an hour ago at least! But, as usual . . .

BELCREDI: Perhaps they can't find the dress . . .

DONNA MATILDA: But I explained exactly where it was! (*Impatiently.*) And Frida . . . where is Frida?

BELCREDI (*looking out the window*): Perhaps she is in the garden with Charles . . .

DOCTOR: He'll talk her out of her fright.

BELCREDI: She's not afraid, Doctor; don't you believe it: the thing bores her rather . . .

DONNA MATILDA: Just don't ask anything of her! I know what she's like.

DOCTOR: Let's wait patiently. Anyhow, it will soon be over, and it has to be in the evening . . . It will only be the matter of a moment! If we can succeed in rousing him, as I was saying, and in breaking at one go the threads—already slack—which still bind him to this fiction of his, giving him back what he himself asks for—you remember, he said: "one cannot always be twenty-six years old, madam!" if we can give him freedom from this torment, which even *he* feels is a torment, then if he is able to recover at one bound the sensation of the distance of time . . .

BELCREDI (*quickly*): He'll be cured! (*Then emphatically with irony.*) We'll pull him out of it all!

DOCTOR: Yes, we may hope to set him going again, like a watch which has stopped at a certain hour . . . just as if we had our watches in our hands and were waiting for that other watch to go again.—A shake—so—and let's hope it'll tell the time again after its long stop. (*At this point the* MARQUIS CHARLES DI NOLLI *enters from the principal entrance.*)

DONNA MATILDA: Oh, Charles! . . . And Frida? Where is she?

DI NOLLI: She'll be here in a moment.

DOCTOR: Has the motor arrived?

DI NOLLI: Yes.

DONNA MATILDA: Yes? Has the dress come?

DI NOLLI: It's been here some time.

DOCTOR: Good! Good!

DONNA MATILDA (*trembling*): Where is she? Where's Frida?

DI NOLLI (*shrugging his shoulders and smiling sadly, like one lending himself unwillingly to an untimely joke*): You'll see, you'll see! . . . (*Pointing towards the hall.*) Here she is! . . . (BERTHOLD *appears at the threshold of the hall, and announces with solemnity.*)

BERTHOLD: Her Highness the Countess Matilda of Canossa! (FRIDA *enters, magnificent and beautiful, arrayed in the robes of her mother as "Countess Matilda of Tuscany," so that she is a living copy of the portrait in the throne room.*)

FRIDA (*passing* BERTHOLD, *who is bowing, says to him with disdain*): Of Tuscany, of Tuscany! Canossa is just one of my castles!

BELCREDI (*in admiration*): Look! Look! She seems another person . . .

DONNA MATILDA: One would say it were I! Look!—Why, Frida, look! She's exactly my portrait, alive!

DOCTOR: Yes, yes . . . Perfect! Perfect! The portrait, to the life.

BELCREDI: Yes, there's no question about it. She *is* the portrait! Magnificent!

FRIDA: Don't make me laugh, or I shall burst! I say, mother, what a tiny waist you had. I had to squeeze so to get into this!

DONNA MATILDA (*arranging her dress a little*): Wait! . . . Keep still! . . . These pleats . . . is it really so tight?

FRIDA: I'm suffocating! I implore you, to be quick! . . .

DOCTOR: But we must wait till it's evening!

FRIDA: No, no, I can't hold out till evening!

DONNA MATILDA: Why did you put it on so soon?

FRIDA: The moment I saw it, the temptation was irresistible . . .

DONNA MATILDA: At least you could have called me, or have had someone help you! It's still all crumpled.

FRIDA: So I saw, mother; but they are old creases; they won't come out.

DOCTOR: It doesn't matter, Marchioness! The illusion is perfect. (*Then coming nearer and asking her to come in front of her daughter, without hiding her.*) If you please, stay there, there . . . at a certain distance . . . now a little more forward . . .

BELCREDI: For the feeling of the distance of time . . .

DONNA MATILDA (*slightly turning to him*): Twenty years after! A disaster! A tragedy!

BELCREDI: Now don't let's exaggerate!

DOCTOR (*embarrassed, trying to save the situation*): No, no! I meant the dress . . . so as to see . . . You know . . .

BELCREDI (*laughing*): Oh, as for the dress, Doctor, it isn't a matter of twenty years! It's eight hundred! An abyss! Do you really want to shove him across it (*Pointing first to* FRIDA *and then to* MARCHIONESS.) from there to here? But you'll have to pick him up in pieces with a basket! Just think now: for us it is a matter of twenty years, a couple of dresses, and a masquerade. But, if, as you say, Doctor, time has stopped for and around him: if he lives there

(*Pointing to* FRIDA.) with her, eight hundred years ago . . . I repeat: the giddiness of the jump will be such, that finding himself suddenly among us . . . (*The* DOCTOR *shakes his head in dissent.*) You don't think so?

DOCTOR: No, because life, my dear baron, can take up its rhythms. This—our life— will at once become real also to him; and will pull him up directly, wresting from him suddenly the illusion, and showing him that the eight hundred years, as you say, are only twenty! It will be like one of those tricks, such as the leap into space, for instance, of the Masonic rite, which appears to be heaven knows how far, and is only a step down the stairs.

BELCREDI: Ah! An idea! Yes! Look at Frida and the Marchioness, Doctor! Which is more advanced in time? We old people, Doctor! The young ones think they are more ahead; but it isn't true: we are more ahead, because time belongs to us more than to them.

DOCTOR: If the past didn't alienate us . . .

BELCREDI: It doesn't matter at all! How does it alienate us? They (*Pointing to* FRIDA *and* DI NOLLI.) have still to do what we have accomplished, Doctor: to grow old, doing the same foolish things, more or less, as we did . . . This is the illusion: that one comes forward through a door to life. It isn't so! As soon as one is born, one starts dying; therefore, he who started first is the most advanced of all. The youngest of us is father Adam! Look there: (*Pointing to* FRIDA.) eight hundred years younger than all of us—the Countess Matilda of Tuscany. (*He makes her a deep bow.*)

DI NOLLI: I say, Tito, don't start joking.

BELCREDI: Oh, you think I am joking? . . .

DI NOLLI: Of course, of course . . . all the time.

BELCREDI: Impossible! I've even dressed up as a Benedictine . . .

DI NOLLI: Yes, but for a serious purpose.

BELCREDI: Well, exactly. If it has been serious for the others . . . for Frida, now, for instance. (*Then turning to the* DOCTOR.) I swear, Doctor, I don't yet understand what you want to do.

DOCTOR (*annoyed*): You'll see! Let me do as I wish . . . At present you see the Marchioness still dressed as . . .

BELCREDI: Oh, she also . . . has to masquerade?

DOCTOR: Of course! of course! In another dress that's in there ready to be used when it comes into his head he sees the Countess Matilda of Canossa before him.

FRIDA (*while talking quietly to* DI NOLLI *notices the* DOCTOR's *mistake*): Of Tuscany, of Tuscany!

DOCTOR: It's all the same!

BELCREDI: Oh, I see! He'll be faced by two of them . . .

DOCTOR: Two, precisely! And then . . .

FRIDA (*calling him aside*): Come here, Doctor! Listen!

DOCTOR: Here I am! (*Goes near the two young people and pretends to give some explanations to them.*)

BELCREDI (*softly to* DONNA MATILDA): I say, this is getting rather strong, you know!

DONNA MATILDA (*looking him firmly in the face*): What?

BELCREDI: Does it really interest you as much as all that—to make you willing to take part in . . . ? For a woman this is simply enormous! . . .

DONNA MATILDA: Yes, for an ordinary woman.

BELCREDI: Oh, no, my dear, for all women, —in a question like this! It's an abnegation.

DONNA MATILDA: I owe it to him.

BELCREDI: Don't lie! You know well enough it's not hurting you!

DONNA MATILDA: Well, then, where does the abnegation come in?

BELCREDI: Just enough to prevent you losing caste in other people's eyes—and just enough to offend me! . . .

DONNA MATILDA: But who is worrying about you now?

DI NOLLI (*coming forward*): It's all right. It's all right. That's what we'll do! (*Turning towards* BERTHOLD.) Here you, go and call one of those fellows!

BERTHOLD: At once! (*Exit.*)

DONNA MATILDA: But first of all we've got to pretend that we are going away.

DI NOLLI: Exactly! I'll see to that . . . (*To* BELCREDI.) you don't mind staying here?

BELCREDI (*ironically*): Oh, no, I don't mind, I don't mind! . . .

DI NOLLI: We must look out not to make him suspicious again, you know.

BELCREDI: Oh, Lord! *He* doesn't amount to anything!

DOCTOR: He must believe absolutely that we've gone away. (LANDOLPH *followed by* BERTHOLD *enters from the right.*)

LANDOLPH: May I come in?

DI NOLLI: Come in! Come in! I say—your name's Lolo, isn't it?

LANDOLPH: Lolo, or Landolph, just as you like!

DI NOLLI: Well, look here: the Doctor and the Marchioness are leaving, at once.

LANDOLPH: Very well. All we've got to say is that they have been able to obtain the permission for the reception from His Holiness. He's in there in his own apartments repenting of all he said—and in an awful state to have the pardon! Would you mind coming a minute? . . . If you would, just for a minute . . . put on the dress again . . .

DOCTOR: Why, of course, with pleasure . . .

LANDOLPH: Might I be allowed to make a suggestion? Why not add that the Marchioness of Tuscany has interceded with the Pope that he should be received?

DONNA MATILDA: You see, he has recognized me!

LANDOLPH: Forgive me . . . I don't know my history very well. I am sure you gentlemen know it much better! But I thought it was believed that Henry IV had a secret passion for the Marchioness of Tuscany.

DONNA MATILDA (*at once*): Nothing of the kind! Nothing of the kind!

LANDOLPH: That's what I thought! But he says he's loved her . . . he's always saying it . . . And now he fears that her indignation for this secret love of his will work him harm with the Pope.

BELCREDI: We must let him understand that this aversion no longer exists.

LANDOLPH: Exactly! Of course!

DONNA MATILDA (*to* BELCREDI): History says —I don't know whether you know it or not—that the Pope gave way to the supplications of the Marchioness Matilda and the Abbot of Cluny. And I may say, my dear Belcredi, that I intended to take advantage of this fact—at the time of the pageant—to show him my feelings were not so hostile to him as he supposed.

BELCREDI: You are most faithful to history, Marchioness . . .

LANDOLPH: Well then, the Marchioness could spare herself a double disguise and present herself with Monsignor (*Indicating the* DOCTOR.) as the Marchioness of Tuscany.

DOCTOR (*quickly, energetically*): No, no! That won't do at all. It would ruin everything. The impression from the confrontation must be a sudden one, give a shock! No, no, Marchioness, you will appear again as the Duchess Adelaide, the mother of the Empress. And then we'll go away. This is most necessary: that he should know we've gone away. Come on! Don't let's waste any more time! There's a lot to prepare. (*Exeunt the* DOCTOR, DONNA MATILDA, *and* LANDOLPH, *right.*)

FRIDA: I am beginning to feel afraid again.

DI NOLLI: Again, Frida?

FRIDA: It would have been better if I had seen him before.

DI NOLLI: There's nothing to be frightened of, really.

FRIDA: He isn't furious, is he?

DI NOLLI: Of course not! he's quite calm.

BELCREDI (*with ironic sentimental affectation*): Melancholy! Didn't you hear that he loves you?

FRIDA: Thanks! That's just why I am afraid.

BELCREDI: He won't do you any harm.

DI NOLLI: It'll only last a minute . . .

FRIDA: Yes, but there in the dark with him . . .

DI NOLLI: Only for a moment; and I will be near you, and all the others behind the door ready to run in. As soon as you see your mother, your part will be finished . . .

BELCREDI: I'm afraid of a different thing: that we're wasting our time . . .

DI NOLLI: Don't begin again! The remedy seems a sound one to me.

FRIDA: I think so too! I feel it! I'm all trembling!

BELCREDI: But, mad people, my dear friends —though they don't know it, alas—have this felicity which we don't take into account . . .

DI NOLLI (*interrupting, annoyed*): What felicity? Nonsense!

BELCREDI (*forcefully*): They don't reason!

DI NOLLI: What's reasoning got to do with it, anyway?

BELCREDI: Don't you call it reasoning that he will have to do—according to us—when he sees her (*Indicates* FRIDA.) and her mother? We've reasoned it all out, surely!

DI NOLLI: Nothing of the kind: no reasoning at all! We put before him a double image of his own fantasy, or fiction, as the doctor says.

BELCREDI (*suddenly*): I say, I've never understood why they take degrees in medicine.

DI NOLLI (*amazed*): Who?

BELCREDI: The alienists!

DI NOLLI: What ought they to take degrees in, then?

FRIDA: If they are alienists, in what else should they take degrees?

BELCREDI: In law, of course! All a matter of talk! The more they talk, the more highly they are considered. "Analogous elasticity," "the sensation of distance in time!" And the first thing they tell you is that they don't work miracles—when a miracle's just what is wanted! But they know that the more they say they are not miracle-workers, the more folk believe in their seriousness!

BERTHOLD (*who has been looking through the keyhole of the door on right*): There they are! There they are! They're coming in here.

DI NOLLI: Are they?

BERTHOLD: He wants to come with them . . . Yes! . . . He's coming too!

DI NOLLI: Let's get away, then! Let's get away, at once! (*To* BERTHOLD.) You stop here!

BERTHOLD: Must I?

Without answering him, DI NOLLI, FRIDA, *and* BELCREDI *go out by the main exit, leaving* BERTHOLD *surprised. The door on the right opens, and* LANDOLPH *enters first, bowing. Then* DONNA MATILDA *comes in, with mantle and ducal crown as in the first act; also the* DOCTOR *as the* ABBOT OF CLUNY. HENRY IV *is among them in royal dress.* ORDULPH *and* HAROLD *enter last of all.*

HENRY IV (*following up what he has been saying in the other room*): And now I will ask you a question: how can I be astute, if you think me obstinate?

DOCTOR: No, no, not obstinate!

HENRY IV (*smiling, pleased*): Then you think me really astute?

DOCTOR: No, no, neither obstinate, nor astute.

HENRY IV (*with benevolent irony*): Monsignor, if obstinacy is not a vice which can go with astuteness, I hoped that in denying me the former, you would at least allow me a little of the latter. I can assure you I have great need of it. But if you want to keep it all for yourself . . .

DOCTOR: I? I? Do I seem astute to you?

HENRY IV: No. Monsignor! What do you say? Not in the least! Perhaps in this case, I may seem a little obstinate to you. (*Cutting short to speak to* DONNA MATILDA.) With your permission: a word in confidence to the Duchess. (*Leads her aside and asks her very earnestly.*) Is your daughter really dear to you?

DONNA MATILDA (*dismayed*): Why, yes, certainly . . .

HENRY IV: Do you wish me to compensate her with all my love, with all my devotion, for the grave wrongs I have done her—though you must not believe all the stories my enemies tell about my dissoluteness!

DONNA MATILDA: No, no, I don't believe them. I never have believed such stories.

HENRY IV: Well, then are you willing?

DONNA MATILDA (*confused*): What?

HENRY IV: That I return to love your daughter again? (*Looks at her and adds, in a mysterious tone of warning.*) You mustn't be a friend of the Marchioness of Tuscany!

DONNA MATILDA: I tell you again that she has begged and tried not less than ourselves to obtain your pardon . . .

HENRY IV (*softly, but excitedly*): Don't tell me that! Don't say that to me! Don't you see the effect it has on me, my Lady?

DONNA MATILDA (*looks at him; then very softly as if in confidence*): You love her still?

HENRY IV (*puzzled*): Still? Still, you say? You know, then? But nobody knows! Nobody must know!

DONNA MATILDA: But perhaps she knows, if she has begged so hard for you!

HENRY IV (*looks at her and says*): And you love your daughter? (*Brief pause. He turns to the* DOCTOR *with laughing accents.*) Ah, Monsignor, it's strange how little I think of my wife! It may be a sin, but I swear to you that I hardly feel her at all in my heart. What is stranger is that her own mother scarcely feels her in her heart. Confess, my Lady, that she amounts to very little for you. (*Turning to* DOCTOR.) She talks to me of that other woman, insistently, insistently, I don't know why! . . .

LANDOLPH (*humbly*): Maybe, Majesty, it is to disabuse you of some ideas you have had about the Marchioness of Tuscany. (*Then, dismayed at having allowed himself this observation, adds.*) I mean just now, of course . . .

HENRY IV: You too maintain that she has been friendly to me?

LANDOLPH: Yes, at the moment, Majesty.

DONNA MATILDA: Exactly! Exactly! . . .

HENRY IV: I understand. That is to say, you don't believe I love her. I see! I see! Nobody's ever believed it, nobody's ever thought it. Better so, then! But enough, enough! (*Turns to the* DOCTOR *with changed expression.*) Monsignor, you see? The reasons the Pope has had for revoking the excommunication have got nothing at all to do with the reasons for which he excommunicated me originally. Tell Pope Gregory we shall meet again at Brixen. And you, Madame, should you chance to meet your daughter in the courtyard of the castle of your friend the Marchioness, ask her to visit me. We shall see if I succeed in keeping her close beside me as wife and Empress. Many women have presented themselves here already assuring me that they were she. And I thought to have her—yes, I tried sometimes—there's no shame in it, with one's wife!—But when they said they were Bertha, and they were from Susa, all of them—I can't think why—started laughing! (*Confidentially.*) Understand?—in bed—I undressed—so did she—yes, by God, undressed—a man and a woman—it's natural, after all! Like that, we don't bother much about who we are. And one's dress is like a phantom that hovers always near one. Oh, Monsignor, phantoms in general are nothing more than trifling disorders of the spirit: images we cannot contain within the bounds of sleep. They reveal themselves even when we are awake, and they frighten us. I . . . ah . . . I am always afraid when, at night time, I see disordered images before me. Sometimes I am even afraid of my own blood pulsing loudly in my arteries in the silence of night, like the sound of a distant step in a lonely corridor! . . . But, forgive me! I have kept you standing too long already. I thank you, my Lady, I thank you, Monsignor. (DONNA MATILDA *and the* DOCTOR *go off bowing. As soon as they have gone,* HENRY IV *suddenly changes his tone.*) Buffoons, buffoons! One can play any tune on them! And that other fellow . . . Peter Damiani! . . . Caught him out perfectly! He's afraid to appear before me again. (*Moves up and down excitedly while saying this; then sees* BERTHOLD, *and points him out to the other three counsellors.*) Oh, look at this imbecile watching me with his mouth wide open! (*Shakes him.*) Don't you understand? Don't you see, idiot, how I treat them, how I play the fool with them, make them appear before me just as I wish? Miserable, frightened clowns that they are! And you (*Addressing the counsellors.*) are amazed that I tear off their ridiculous masks now, just as if it wasn't I who had made them mask themselves to satisfy this taste of mine for playing the madman!

LANDOLPH—HAROLD—ORDULPH (*bewildered, looking at one another*): What? What does he say? What?

HENRY IV (*answers them imperiously*): Enough! enough! Let's stop it. I'm tired of it. (*Then as if the thought left him no peace.*) By God! The impudence! To come here along with her lover! . . . And pretending to do it out of pity! So as not to infuriate a poor devil already out of the world, out of time, out of life! If it hadn't been supposed to be done out of pity, one can well imagine that fellow wouldn't have allowed it. Those people expect others to behave as they wish all the time. And, of course, there's nothing arrogant in that! Oh, no! Oh, no! It's merely their way of thinking, of feeling, of seeing. Everybody has his own way of thinking; you fellows, too. Yours is that of a flock of sheep—miserable, feeble, uncertain . . . But those others take advantage of this and make you accept their way of thinking; or, at least, they suppose they do; because, after all, what do they succeed in imposing on you? Words, words which anyone can interpret in his own manner! That's the way public opinion is formed! And it's a bad look out for a man who finds himself labelled one

day with one of these words which everyone repeats; for example "madman," or
"imbecile." Don't you think it is rather
hard for a man to keep quiet, when he
knows that there is a fellow going about
trying to persuade everybody that he is as
he sees him, trying to fix him in other
people's opinion as a "madman"—according to him? Now I am talking seriously!
Before I hurt my head, falling from my
horse . . . (*Stops suddenly, noticing the
dismay of the four young men.*) What's the
matter with you? (*Imitates their amazed
looks.*) What? Am I, or am I not, mad?
Oh, yes! I'm mad all right! (*He becomes
terrible.*) Well, then, by God, down on
your knees, down on your knees! (*Makes
them go down on their knees one by one.*)
I order you to go down on your knees before me! And touch the ground three times
with your foreheads! Down, down! That's
the way you've got to be before madmen!
(*Then annoyed with their facile humiliation.*) Get up, sheep! You obeyed me,
didn't you? You might have put the strait-
jacket on me! . . . Crush a man with the
weight of a word—it's nothing—a fly! all
our life is crushed by the weight of words:
the weight of the dead. Look at me here:
can you really suppose that Henry IV is
still alive? All the same, I speak, and order
you live men about! Do you think it's a
joke that the dead continue to live?—Yes,
here it's a joke! But get out into the live
world!—Ah, you say: what a beautiful sunrise—for us! All time is before us!—Dawn!
We will do what we like with this day—.
Ah, yes! To Hell with tradition, the old
conventions! Well, go on! You will do
nothing but repeat the old, old words,
while you imagine you are living! (*Goes up
to* BERTHOLD *who has now become quite
stupid.*) You don't understand a word of
this, do you? What's your name?

BERTHOLD: I? . . . What? . . . Berthold . . .

HENRY IV: Poor Berthold! What's your name
here?

BERTHOLD: I . . . I . . . my name is Fino.

HENRY IV (*feeling the warning and critical
glances of the others, turns to them to reduce them to silence*): Fino?

BERTHOLD: Fino Pagliuca, sire.

HENRY IV (*turning to* LANDOLPH): I've heard

you call each other by your nicknames often enough! Your name is Lolo, isn't it?

LANDOLPH: Yes, sire . . . (*Then with a
sense of immense joy.*) Oh Lord! Oh Lord!
Then he is not mad . . .

HENRY IV (*brusquely*): What?

LANDOLPH (*hesitating*): No . . . I said . . .

HENRY IV: Not mad, any more. No. Don't
you see? We're having a joke on those that
think I am mad! (*To* HAROLD.) I say, boy,
your name's Franco . . . (*To* ORDULPH)
And yours . . .

ORDULPH: Momo.

HENRY IV: Momo, Momo . . . A nice name
that!

LANDOLPH: So he isn't . . .

HENRY IV: What are you talking about? Of
course not! Let's have a jolly, good laugh!
. . . (*Laughs.*) Ah! . . . Ah! . . . Ah! . . .

LANDOLPH—HAROLD—ORDULPH (*looking at
each other half happy and half dismayed*): Then he's cured! . . . he's all
right! . . .

HENRY IV: Silence! Silence! . . . (*To* BER-
THOLD.) Why don't you laugh? Are you
offended? I didn't mean it especially for
you. It's convenient for everybody to insist
that certain people are mad, so they can be
shut up. Do you know why? Because it's
impossible to hear them speak! What shall
I say of these people who've just gone
away? That one is a whore, another a
libertine, another a swindler . . . don't
you think so? You can't believe a word he
says . . . don't you think so?—By the
way, they all listen to me terrified. And
why are they terrified, if what I say isn't
true? Of course, you can't believe what
madmen say—yet, at the same time, they
stand there with their eyes wide open with
terror!—Why? Tell me, tell me, why?—
You see I'm quite calm now!

BERTHOLD: But, perhaps, they think that . . .

HENRY IV: No, no, my dear fellow! Look me
well in the eyes! . . . I don't say that it's
true—nothing is true, Berthold! But . . .
look me in the eyes!

BERTHOLD: Well . . .

HENRY IV: You see? You see? . . . You have
terror in your own eyes now because I seem
mad to you! There's the proof of it!
(*Laughs.*)

LANDOLPH (*coming forward in the name of
the others, exasperated*): What proof?

HENRY IV: Your being so dismayed because now I seem again mad to you. You have thought me mad up to now, haven't you? You feel that this dismay of yours can become terror too—something to dash away the ground from under your feet and deprive you of the air you breathe! Do you know what it means to find yourselves face to face with a madman—with one who shakes the foundations of all you have built up in yourselves, your logic, the logic of all your constructions? Madmen, lucky folk! construct without logic, or rather with a logic that flies like a feather. Voluble! Voluble! Today like this and tomorrow—who knows? You say: "This cannot be"; but for them everything can be. You say: "This isn't true!" And why? Because it doesn't seem true to you, or you, or you . . . (*Indicates the three of them in succession.*) . . . and to a hundred thousand others! One must see what seems true to these hundred thousand others who are not supposed to be mad! What a magnificent spectacle they afford, when they reason! What flowers of logic they scatter! I know that when I was a child, I thought the moon in the pond was real. How many things I thought real! I believed everything I was told—and I was happy! Because it's a terrible thing if you don't hold on to that which seems true to you today—to that which will seem true to you tomorrow, even if it is the opposite of that which seemed true to you yesterday. I would never wish you to think, as I have done, on this horrible thing which really drives one mad: that if you were beside another and looking into his eyes—as I one day looked into somebody's eyes—you might as well be a beggar before a door never to be opened to you; for he who does enter there will never be you, but someone unknown to you with his own different and impenetrable world . . . (*Long pause. Darkness gathers in the room, increasing the sense of strangeness and consternation in which the four young men are involved.* HENRY IV *remains aloof, pondering on the misery which is not only his, but everybody's. Then he pulls himself up, and says in an ordinary tone.*) It's getting dark here . . .

ORDULPH: Shall I go for a lamp?

HENRY IV (*ironically*): The lamp, yes the lamp! . . . Do you suppose I don't know that as soon as I turn my back with my oil lamp to go to bed, you turn on the electric light for yourselves, here, and even there, in the throne room? I pretend not to see it!

ORDULPH: Well, then, shall I turn it on now?

HENRY IV: No, it would blind me! I want my lamp!

ORDULPH: It's ready here behind the door. (*Goes to the main exit, opens the door, goes out for a moment, and returns with an ancient lamp which is held by a ring at the top.*)

HENRY IV: Ah, a little light! Sit there around the table, no, not like that; in an elegant, easy, manner! . . . (*To* HAROLD.) Yes, you, like that! (*Poses him.*) (*Then to* BERTHOLD.) You, so! . . . and I, here! (*Sits opposite them.*) We could do with a little decorative moonlight. It's very useful for us, the moonlight. I feel a real necessity for it, and pass a lot of time looking up at the moon from my window. Who would think, to look at her that she knows that eight hundred years have passed, and that I, seated at the window, cannot really be Henry IV gazing at the moon like any poor devil? But, look, look! See what a magnificent night scene we have here: the emperor surrounded by his faithful counsellors! . . . How do you like it?

LANDOLPH (*softly to* HAROLD, *so as not to break the enchantment*): And to think it wasn't true! . . .

HENRY IV: True? What wasn't true?

LANDOLPH (*timidly as if to excuse himself*): No . . . I mean . . . I was saying this morning to him (*Indicates* BERTHOLD.)—he has just entered on service here—I was saying: what a pity that dressed like this and with so many beautiful costumes in the wardrobe . . . and with a room like that . . . (*Indicates the throne room.*)

HENRY IV: Well? what's the pity?

LANDOLPH: Well . . . that we didn't know . . .

HENRY IV: That it was all done in jest, this comedy?

LANDOLPH: Because we thought that . . .

HAROLD (*coming to his assistance*): Yes . . . that it was done seriously!

HENRY IV: What do you say? Doesn't it seem serious to you?

LANDOLPH: But if you say that . . .

HENRY IV: I say that—you are fools! You ought to have known how to create a fantasy for yourselves, not to act it for me, or anyone coming to see me; but naturally, simply, day by day, before nobody, feeling yourselves alive in the history of the eleventh century, here at the court of your emperor, Henry IV! You, Ordulph, (*Taking him by the arm.*) alive in the castle of Goslar, waking up in the morning, getting out of bed, and entering straightway into the dream, clothing yourself in the dream that would be no more a dream, because you would have lived it, felt it all alive in you. You would have drunk it in with the air you breathed; yet knowing all the time that it was a dream, so you could better enjoy the privilege afforded you of having to do nothing else but live this dream, this far off and yet actual dream! And to think that at a distance of eight centuries from this remote age of ours, so colored and so sepulchral, the men of the twentieth century are torturing themselves in ceaseless anxiety to know how their fates and fortunes will work out! Whereas you are already in history with me . . .

LANDOLPH: Yes, yes, very good!

HENRY IV: . . . Everything determined, everything settled!

ORDULPH: Yes, yes!

HENRY IV: And sad as is my lot, hideous as some of the events are, bitter the struggles and troublous the time—still all history! All history that cannot change, understand? All fixed for ever! And you could have admired at your ease how every effect followed obediently its cause with perfect logic, how every event took place precisely and coherently in each minute particular! The pleasure, the pleasure of history, in fact, which is so great, was yours.

LANDOLPH: Beautiful, beautiful!

HENRY IV: Beautiful, but it's finished! Now that you know, I could not do it any more! (*Takes his lamp to go to bed.*) Neither could you, if up to now you haven't understood the reason of it! I am sick of it now. (*Almost to himself with violent contained rage.*) By God, I'll make her sorry she came here! Dressed herself up as a mother-in-law for me . . . ! And he as an abott . . . ! And they bring a doctor with them to study me . . . ! Who knows if they don't hope to cure me? . . . Clowns . . . ! I'd like to smack one of them at least in the face: yes, that one—a famous swordsman, they say! . . . He'll kill me . . . Well, we'll see, we'll see! . . . (*A knock at the door.*) Who is it?

THE VOICE OF JOHN: Deo Gratias!

HAROLD (*very pleased at the chance for another joke*): Oh, it's John, it's old John, who comes every night to play the monk.

ORDULPH (*rubbing his hands*): Yes, yes! Let's make him do it!

HENRY IV (*at once, severely*): Fool, why? Just to play a joke on a poor old man who does it for love of me?

LANDOLPH (*to* ORDULPH): It has to be as if it were true.

HENRY IV: Exactly, as if true! Because, only so, truth is not a jest. (*Opens the door and admits* JOHN *dressed as a humble friar with a roll of parchment under his arm.*) Come in, come in, father! (*Then assuming a tone of tragic gravity and deep resentment.*) All the documents of my life and reign favorable to me were destroyed deliberately by my enemies. One only has escaped destruction, this, my life, written by a humble monk who is devoted to me. And you would laugh at him! (*Turns affectionately to* JOHN, *and invites him to sit down at the table.*) Sit down, father, sit down! Have the lamp near you! (*Puts the lamp near him.*) Write! Write!

JOHN (*opens the parchment and prepares to write from dictation*): I am ready, your Majesty!

HENRY IV (*dictating*): "The decree of peace proclaimed at Mayence helped the poor and the good, while it damaged the powerful and the bad. (*Curtain begins to fall.*) It brought wealth to the former, hunger and misery to the latter . . ." (*Curtain.*)

ACT III

The throne room so dark that the wall at the bottom is hardly seen. The canvases of the two portraits have been taken away; and, within their frames, FRIDA, *dressed as the "Marchioness of Tuscany" and* CHARLES DI NOLLI, *as "Henry IV," have taken the exact positions of the portraits.*

For a moment, after the raising of curtain, the stage is empty. Then the door on the left opens; and HENRY IV, *holding the lamp by the ring on top of it, enters. He looks back to speak to the four young men, who, with* JOHN, *are presumably in the adjoining hall, as at the end of the second act.*

HENRY IV: No, stay where you are, stay where you are. I shall manage all right by myself. Good night! (*Closes the door and walks, very sad and tired, across the hall towards the second door on the right, which leads into his apartments.*)

FRIDA (*as soon as she sees that he has just passed the throne, whispers from the niche like one who is on the point of fainting away with fright*): Henry . . .

HENRY IV (*stopping at the voice, as if someone had stabbed him traitorously in the back, turns a terror-stricken face towards the wall at the bottom of the room; raising an arm instinctively, as if to defend himself and ward off a blow*): Who is calling me? (*It is not a question, but an exclamation vibrating with terror, which does not expect a reply from the darkness and the terrible silence of the hall, which suddenly fills him with the suspicion that he is really mad.*)

FRIDA (*at his shudder of terror, is herself not less frightened at the part she is playing, and repeats a little more loudly*): Henry! . . . (*But, although she wishes to act the part as they have given it to her, she stretches her head a little out of the frame towards the other frame.*)

HENRY IV (*gives a dreadful cry; lets the lamp fall from his hands to cover his head with his arms, and makes a movement as if to run away.*)

FRIDA (*jumping from the frame on to the stand and shouting like a mad woman*): Henry! . . . Henry! . . . I'm afraid! . . . I'm terrified! . . .

And while DI NOLLI *jumps in turn on to the stand and thence to the floor and runs to* FRIDA *who, on the verge of fainting, continues to cry out, the* DOCTOR, DONNA MATILDA, *also dressed as "Matilda of Tuscany,"* TITO, BELCREDI, LANDOLPH, BERTHOLD *and* JOHN *enter the hall from the doors on the right and on the left. One of*

them turns on the light: a strange light coming from lamps hidden in the ceiling so that only the upper part of the stage is well lighted. The others without taking notice of HENRY IV, *who looks on astonished by the unexpected inrush, after the moment of terror which still causes him to tremble, run anxiously to support and comfort the still shaking* FRIDA, *who is moaning in the arms of her fiancé. All are speaking at the same time.*

DI NOLLI: No, no, Frida . . . Here I am . . . I am beside you!

DOCTOR (*coming with the others*): Enough! Enough! There's nothing more to be done! . . .

DONNA MATILDA: He is cured, Frida. Look! He is cured! Don't you see?

DI NOLLI (*astonished*): Cured?

BELCREDI: It was only for fun! Be calm!

FRIDA: No! I am afraid! I am afraid!

DONNA MATILDA: Afraid of what? Look at him! He was never mad at all! . . .

DI NOLLI: That isn't true! What are you saying? Cured?

DOCTOR: It appears so. I should say so . . .

BELCREDI: Yes, yes! They have told us so. (*Pointing to the four young men.*)

DONNA MATILDA: Yes, for a long time! He has confided in them, told them the truth!

DI NOLLI (*now more indignant than astonished*): But what does it mean? If, up to a short time ago . . . ?

BELCREDI: Hum! He was acting, to take you in and also us, who in good faith . . .

DI NOLLI: Is it possible? To deceive his sister, also, right up to the time of her death?

HENRY IV (*remains apart, peering at one and now at the other under the accusation and the mockery of what all believe to be a cruel joke of his, which is now revealed. He has shown by the flashing of his eyes that he is meditating a revenge, which his violent contempt prevents him from defining clearly, as yet. Stung to the quick and with a clear idea of accepting the fiction they have insidiously worked up as true, he bursts forth at this point*): Go on, I say! Go on!

DI NOLLI (*astonished at the cry*): Go on! What do you mean?

HENRY IV: It isn't *your* sister only that is dead!

DI NOLLI: My sister? Yours, I say, whom you compelled up to the last moment, to present herself here as your mother Agnes!

HENRY IV: And was she not *your* mother?

DI NOLLI: My mother? Certainly my mother!

HENRY IV: But your mother is dead for me, *old and far away!* You have just got down now from there. (*Pointing to the frame from which he jumped down.*) And how do you know whether I have not wept her long in secret, dressed even as I am?

DONNA MATILDA (*dismayed, looking at the others*): What does he say? (*Much impressed, observing him.*) Quietly! quietly, for Heaven's sake!

HENRY IV: What do I say? I ask all of you if Agnes was not the mother of Henry IV? (*Turns to* FRIDA *as if she were really the "Marchioness of Tuscany."*) You, Marchioness, it seems to me, ought to know.

FRIDA (*still frightened, draws closer to* DI NOLLI): No, no, I don't know. Not I!

DOCTOR: It's the madness returning. . . . Quiet now, everybody!

BELCREDI (*indignant*): Madness indeed, Doctor! He's acting again! . . .

HENRY IV (*suddenly*): I? You have emptied those two frames over there, and he stands before my eyes as Henry IV . . .

BELCREDI: We've had enough of this joke now.

HENRY IV: Who said joke?

DOCTOR (*loudly to* BELCREDI): Don't excite him, for the love of God!

BELCREDI (*without lending an ear to him, but speaking louder*): But they have said so, (*Pointing again to the four young men.*) they, they!

HENRY IV (*turning round and looking at them*): You? Did you say it was all a joke?

LANDOLPH (*timid and embarrassed*): No . . . really we said that you were cured.

BELCREDI: Look here! Enough of this! (*To* DONNA MATILDA.) Doesn't it seem to you that the sight of him, (*Pointing to* DI NOLLI.) Marchioness, and that of your daughter dressed so, is becoming an intolerable puerility?

DONNA MATILDA: Oh, be quiet! What does the dress matter, if he is cured?

HENRY IV: Cured, yes! I am cured! (*To* BELCREDI.) Ah, but not to let it end this way all at once, as you suppose! (*Attacks him.*) Do you know that for twenty years

nobody has ever dared to appear before me here like you and that gentleman? (*Pointing to the* DOCTOR.)

BELCREDI: Of course I know it. As a matter of fact, I too appeared before you this morning dressed . . .

HENRY IV: As a monk, yes!

BELCREDI: And you took me for Peter Damiani! And I didn't even laugh, believing, in fact, that . . .

HENRY IV: That I was mad! Does it make you laugh seeing her like that, now that I am cured? And yet you might have remembered that in my eyes her appearance now . . . (*Interrupts himself with a gesture of contempt.*) Ah! (*Suddenly turns to the* DOCTOR.) You are a doctor, aren't you?

DOCTOR: Yes.

HENRY IV: And you also took part in dressing her up as the Marchioness of Tuscany? To prepare a counter-joke for me here, eh?

DONNA MATILDA (*impetuously*): No, no! What do you say? It was done for you! I did it for your sake.

DOCTOR (*quickly*): To attempt, to try, not knowing . . .

HENRY IV (*cutting him short*): I understand. I say counter-joke, in his case (*Indicates* BELCREDI.) because he believes that I have been carrying on a jest . . .

BELCREDI: But excuse me, what do you mean? You say yourself you are cured.

HENRY IV: Let me speak! (*To the* DOCTOR.) Do you know, Doctor, that for a moment you ran the risk of making me mad again? By God, to make the portraits speak; to make them jump alive out of their frames . . .

DOCTOR: But you saw that all of us ran in at once, as soon as they told us . . .

HENRY IV: Certainly! (*Contemplates* FRIDA *and* DI NOLLI, *and then looks at the* MARCHIONESS, *and finally at his own costume.*) The combination is very beautiful . . . Two couples . . . Very good, very good, Doctor! For a madman, not bad! . . . (*With a slight wave of his hand to* BELCREDI.) It seems to him now to be a carnival out of season, eh? (*Turns to look at him.*) We'll get rid now of this masquerade costume of mine, so that I may come away with you. What do you say?

BELCREDI: With me? With us?

HENRY IV: Where shall we go? To the Club?

In dress coats and with white ties? Or shall both of us go to the Marchioness' house?

BELCREDI: Wherever you like! Do you want to remain here still, to continue—alone—what was nothing but the unfortunate joke of a day of carnival? It is really incredible, incredible how you have been able to do all this, freed from the disaster that befell you!

HENRY IV: Yes, you see how it was! The fact is that falling from my horse and striking my head as I did, I was really mad for I know not how long . . .

DOCTOR: Ah! Did it last long?

HENRY IV (very quickly to the DOCTOR): Yes, Doctor, a long time! I think it must have been about twelve years. (Then suddenly turning to speak to BELCREDI.) Thus I saw nothing, my dear fellow, of all that, after that day of carnival, happened for you but not for me: how things changed, how my friends deceived me, how my place was taken by another, and all the rest of it! And suppose my place had been taken in the heart of the woman I loved? . . . And how should I know who was dead or who had disappeared? . . . All this, you know, wasn't exactly a jest for me, as it seems to you . . .

BELCREDI: No, no! I don't mean that if you please. I mean after . . .

HENRY IV: Ah, yes? After? One day (Stops and addresses the DOCTOR.)—A most interesting case, Doctor! Study me well! Study me carefully! (Trembles while speaking.) All by itself, who knows how, one day the trouble here (Touches his forehead.) mended. Little by little, I open my eyes, and at first I don't know whether I am asleep or awake. Then I know I am awake. I touch this thing and that; I see clearly again . . . Ah!—then, as he says (Alludes to BELCREDI.) away, away with this masquerade, this incubus! Let's open the windows, breathe life once again! Away! Away! Let's run out! (Suddenly pulling himself up.) But where? And to do what? To show myself to all, secretly, as Henry IV, not like this, but arm in arm with you, among my dear friends?

BELCREDI: What are you saying?

DONNA MATILDA: Who could think it? It's not to be imagined. It was an accident.

HENRY IV: They all said I was mad before. (To BELCREDI.) And you know it! You were more ferocious than any one against those who tried to defend me.

BELCREDI: Oh, that was only a joke!

HENRY IV: Look at my hair! (Shows him the hair on the nape of his neck.)

BELCREDI: But mine is grey too!

HENRY IV: Yes, with this difference: that mine went grey here, as Henry IV, do you understand? And I never knew it! I perceived it all of a sudden, one day, when I opened my eyes; and I was terrified because I understood at once that not only had my hair gone grey, but that I was all grey, inside; that everything had fallen to pieces, that everything was finished; and I was going to arrive, hungry as a wolf, at a banquet which had already been cleared away . . .

BELCREDI: Yes, but, what about the others? . . .

HENRY IV (quickly): Ah, yes, I know! They couldn't wait until I was cured, not even those, who, behind my back, pricked my saddled horse till it bled. . . .

DI NOLLI (agitated): What, what?

HENRY IV: Yes, treacherously, to make it rear and cause me to fall.

DONNA MATILDA (quickly, in horror): This is the first time I knew that.

HENRY IV: That was also a joke, probably!

DONNA MATILDA: But who did it? Who was behind us, then?

HENRY IV: It doesn't matter who it was. All those that went on feasting and were ready to leave me their scrapings, Marchioness, of miserable pity, or some dirty remnant of remorse in the filthy plate! Thanks! (Turning quickly to the DOCTOR.) Now, Doctor, the case must be absolutely new in the history of madness; I preferred to remain mad—since I found everything ready and at my disposal for this new exquisite fantasy. I would live it—this madness of mine—with the most lucid consciousness; and thus revenge myself on the brutality of a stone which had dented my head. The solitude—this solitude—squalid and empty as it appeared to me when I opened my eyes again—I determined to deck it out with all the colors and splendors of that far-off day of carnival, when you (Looks at DONNA MATILDA and points FRIDA out to *her.*)—when you, Marchioness, triumphed. So I would oblige all those who were around me to follow, by God, at my orders that famous pageant which had been—for you and not for me—the jest of a day. I would make it become—forever—no more a joke but a reality, the reality of a real madness: here, all in masquerade, with throne room, and these my four secret counsellors: secret and, of course, traitors. (*He turns quickly towards them.*) I should like to know what you have gained by revealing the fact that I was cured! If I am cured, there's no longer any need of you, and you will be discharged! To give anyone one's confidence . . . that is really the act of a madman. But now I accuse you in my turn. (*Turning to the others.*) Do you know? They thought (*Alludes to the counsellors.*) they could make fun of me too with you. (*Bursts out laughing. The others laugh, but shamefacedly, except* DONNA MATILDA.)

BELCREDI (*to* DI NOLLI): Well, imagine that . . . That's not bad . . .

DI NOLLI (*to the four young men*): You?

HENRY IV: We must pardon them. This dress (*Plucking his dress.*) which is for me the evident, voluntary caricature of that other continuous, everlasting masquerade, of which we are the involuntary puppets (*Indicates* BELCREDI.) when, without knowing it, we mask ourselves with that which we appear to be . . . ah, that dress of theirs, this masquerade of theirs, of course, we must forgive it them, since they do not yet see it is identical with themselves . . . (*Turning again to* BELCREDI.) You know, it is quite easy to get accustomed to it. One walks about as a tragic character, just as if it were nothing . . . (*Imitates the tragic manner.*) in a room like this . . . Look here, doctor! I remember a priest, certainly Irish, a nice-looking priest, who was sleeping in the sun one November day, with his arm on the corner of the bench of a public garden. He was lost in the golden delight of the mild sunny air which must have seemed for him almost summery. One may be sure that in that moment he did not know any more that he was a priest, or even where he was. He was dreaming . . . A little boy passed with a flower in his hand. He touched the priest with it here

on the neck. I saw him open his laughing eyes, while all his mouth smiled with the beauty of his dream. He was forgetful of everything . . . But all at once, he pulled himself together, and stretched out his priest's cassock; and there came back to his eyes the same seriousness which you have seen in mine; because the Irish priests defend the seriousness of their Catholic faith with the same zeal with which I defend the sacred rights of hereditary monarchy! I am cured, gentlemen: because I can act the madman to perfection, here; and I do it very quietly, I'm only sorry for you that have to live your madness so agitatedly, without knowing it or seeing it.

BELCREDI: It comes to this, then, that it is we who are mad. That's what it is!

HENRY IV (*containing his irritation*): But if you weren't mad, both you and she (*Indicating the* MARCHIONESS.) would you have come here to see me?

BELCREDI: To tell the truth, I came here believing that you were the madman.

HENRY IV (*suddenly indicating the* MARCHIONESS): And she?

BELCREDI: Ah, as for her . . . I can't say. I see she is all fascinated by your words, by this *conscious* madness of yours. (*Turns to her.*) Dressed as you are, (*Speaking to her.*) you could even remain here to live it out, Marchioness.

DONNA MATILDA: You are insolent!

HENRY IV (*conciliatingly*): No, Marchioness, what he means to say is that the miracle would be complete, according to him, with you here, who—as the Marchioness of Tuscany, you well know,—could not be my friend, save, as at Canossa, to give me a little pity . . .

BELCREDI: Or even more than a little! She said so herself!

HENRY IV (*to the* MARCHIONESS, *continuing*): And even, shall we say, a little remorse! . . .

BELCREDI: Yes, that too she has admitted.

DONNA MATILDA (*angry*): Now look here . . .

HENRY IV (*quickly, to placate her*): Don't bother about him! Don't mind him! Let him go on infuriating me—though the Doctor's told him not to. (*Turns to* BELCREDI.) But do you suppose I am going to trouble myself any more about what happened between us—the share you had in

my misfortune with her (*Indicates the* MAR-
CHIONESS *to him and pointing* BELCREDI
out to her.) the part he has now in your
life? This is my life! Quite a different thing
from your life! Your life, the life in which
you have grown old—I have not lived that
life. (*To* DONNA MATILDA.) Was this what
you wanted to show me with this sacrifice
of yours, dressing yourself up like this, according to the Doctor's idea? Excellently
done, Doctor! Oh, an excellent idea:—"As
we were then, eh? and as we are now?" But
I am not a madman according to your way
of thinking, Doctor. I know very well that
that man there (*Indicates* DI NOLLI.) cannot be me; because I am Henry IV, and
have been, these twenty years, cast in this
eternal masquerade. She has lived these
years! (*Indicates the* MARCHIONESS.) She
has enjoyed them and has become—look at
her!—a woman I can no longer recognize.
It is so that I knew her! (*Points to* FRIDA
and draws near her.) This is the Marchioness I know, always this one! . . . You
seem a lot of children to be so easily
frightened by me . . . (*To* FRIDA.) And
you're frightened too, little girl, aren't you,
by the jest that they made you take part in
—though they didn't understand it
wouldn't be the jest they meant it to be,
for me? Oh miracle of miracles! Prodigy of
prodigies! The dream alive in you! More
than alive in you! It was an image that
wavered there and they've made you come
to life! Oh, mine! You're mine, mine, mine,
in my own right! (*He holds her in his
arms, laughing like a madman, while all
stand still terrified. Then as they advance
to tear* FRIDA *from his arms, he becomes
furious, terrible and cries imperiously to
his* VALETS.) Hold them! Hold them! I order you to hold them! (*The four young
men amazed, yet fascinated, move to execute his orders, automatically, and seize*
DI NOLLI, *the* DOCTOR, *and* BELCREDI.)

BELCREDI (*freeing himself*): Leave her alone!
Leave her alone! You're no madman!

HENRY IV (*in a flash draws the sword from the
side of* LANDOLPH, *who is close to him*):
I'm not mad, eh! Take that, you! . . .
(*Drives sword into him. A cry of horror
goes up. All rush over to assist* BELCREDI,
crying out together.)

DI NOLLI: Has he wounded you?

BERTHOLD: Yes, yes, seriously!

DOCTOR: I told you so!

FRIDA: Oh God, oh God!

DI NOLLI: Frida, come here!

DONNA MATILDA: He's mad, mad!

DI NOLLI: Hold him!

BELCREDI (*while they take him away by the
left exit, he protests as he is borne out*):
No, no, you're not mad! You're not mad.
He's not mad! (*They go out by the left
amid cries and excitement. After a moment, one hears a still sharper, more piercing cry from* DONNA MATILDA, *and then,
silence.*)

HENRY IV (*who has remained on the stage
between* LANDOLPH, HAROLD *and* ORDULPH,
*with his eyes almost starting out of his
head, terrified by the life of his own masquerade which has driven him to crime*):
Now, yes . . . we'll have to . . . (*Calls
his* VALETS *around him as if to protect
him.*) here we are . . . together . . . forever! (*Curtain.*)

CARDS OF IDENTITY

Nigel Dennis

CHARACTERS

BEAUFORT
MISS PARADISE (MRS PARADISE)
CAPTAIN MALLET
HENRY PARADISE (JELLICOE)
MRS MALLET
DR TOWZER
NURSE STEPHENSON (MISS TRAY)
LOLLY PARADISE (STAPLETON)
PRESIDENT
DR BITTERLING
MISS BLACK PLANORBIS
DR SCAVENGER
FATHER GOLDEN ORFE
BANK MANAGER

Dr Bitterling's Case History

YOUTH
MOTHER
VINSON
CUSTODIAN
FIRST RADIO COMMENTATOR
SECOND RADIO COMMENTATOR

ACT I

The empty breakfast room at Hyde's Mortimer. The furnishings are the bare necessities of people who have not finished moving in. Door to L. and R. and, in rear, French window opening on to raised terrace. Two windows on each side of the French window look on to a park. A huge, carved chest stands below L. window. On a large writing-desk stands an ancient telephone; from a brass hook nearby hangs what appears to be a frogman's mask attached to the hose of a vacuum cleaner: it is in fact a speaking-tube.

BEAUFORT (*off, on stairway leading to passage and door L., shouting with increasing loudness*): Father! *Father!* FATHER! An emergency! Do come, Father, for God's sake! (*gently*) Now then . . . this way . . . that's right . . . I tell you, Father will handle *everything*. If your brother *is* dead. . . .

MISS PARADISE (*off*): Dead! No! No! I won't have it!

BEAUFORT (*off*): Then we won't even suggest it . . . *Father!*

Enter from R., CAPTAIN MALLET, cool, poised and dressed for hunting. He stands just inside R. door listening to the clamour off L., looking at the ceiling, breathing on his nails and rubbing them up delicately. A cobweb near door R. catches his eye; he takes a handkerchief from his sleeve and sharply flicks the web away.

MISS P. (*off*): You said dead, you said! (*sobs*) But he was completely himself yesterday.

BEAUFORT (*off*): Dear lady, we *mustn't* harp on what he was *yesterday* . . .

MISS P. (*off*): Oh, don't, don't!

Enter BEAUFORT and MISS PARADISE through L. door, he supporting her with his arm. He deftly turns her away from the CAPTAIN and pulls a chair forward.

BEAUFORT: Fa—ther! . . . Now, you're going to sit tight while I get him. He's just come back from hunting. (*seats her*) There . . . (*runs frantically to telephone on desk, removes receiver, clatters receiver-rest violently*) Oh! Oh! Oh! (*slowly, staring at*

MISS PARADISE) I have an awful feeling that this line is . . .

MISS P.: No! No!

BEAUFORT: Disconnected. Oh, the damned, miserable . . . !

CAPTAIN (*moving forward and speaking very loudly*): Beaufort! What is this? (BEAUFORT *promptly drops the receiver on the carpet,* MISS PARADISE *screams once and then gapes at the CAPTAIN in silence. Quietly*) Pick it up.

BEAUFORT: Thank God, Father . . . ! *Up* what?

CAPTAIN (*coldly pointing, his voice very low*): That which you have dropped.

BEAUFORT (*grabbing up the receiver, replacing it and gasping*): I'm sorry. The shock is too much.

CAPTAIN (*pointing*): Is it lodged between its prongs? (BEAUFORT *desperately adjusts it.*) Thank you, Beaufort.

BEAUFORT: Something terrible has happened, Father . . . This is poor Miss Paradise. She lives in the lodge at the end of the drive. Her brother, whom she adores . . . (MISS PARADISE *bursts into tears again.*)

CAPTAIN: Beaufort! Will you leave the room?

BEAUFORT (*desperately*): But it's an *emergency!*

CAPTAIN (*suddenly*): What is under your trousers?

BEAUFORT (*sullenly*): Pyjamas.

CAPTAIN: Again? You accosted this good woman—in your pyjamas?

BEAUFORT: I can't deny it, Father. (*looking down*) The evidence is there. (*to MISS PARADISE, squeezing her hand quickly*) Everything will be all right now. Just put yourself completely in Father's hands. (*Exit. The CAPTAIN walks slowly to the sobbing MISS PARADISE and takes her pulse gently with a white hand.*)

CAPTAIN: Madam. My son is a good boy, but emotional. You have let him influence you. Were you on your way to see me?

MISS P.: He was so *healthy.* He was always so *careful!*

CAPTAIN: Mrs Paradise . . . That is your name?

MISS P.: *Miss* Paradise, yes.

CAPTAIN: Ah! Forgive me! Now, tell me, *Mrs* Paradise, exactly what has happened—and kindly shut your eyes to the nakedness of this room. We have not been here forty-eight hours. (_pulls up a chair close to her_) And no one to help us but our old butler! Ah! We would sell our souls for a house-keeper!

MISS P.: Going off through the park, and then—it was still foggy—it closed over him . . .

CAPTAIN: Mrs Paradise! Begin at the beginning, please! Many a man's life has been thrown away through the mumbling of his survivors. When did you last see your brother?

MISS P. (_casting back, still sobbing, but a shade calmer_): Yesterday morning, we . . .

CAPTAIN: _Yesterday_ morning?

MISS P.: Yes, yes!

CAPTAIN (_grimacing_): Ts! Ts! Never mind! Go on!

MISS P.: Yesterday morning, we were having breakfast . . .

CAPTAIN: In the little lodge at the end of the drive?

MISS P.: The little lodge—boo-hoo! Twenty years together . . . !

CAPTAIN: And . . . ?

MISS P.: And my brother was swallowing the last of his Nescaf'; and happening to look out of the window, across the park, he saw some smoke.

CAPTAIN: Smoke? Through all that fog?

MISS P.: There was smoke inside the fog.

CAPTAIN: Ah! The fog parted. Smoke then was visible.

MISS P.: That's right. So my brother exclaimed: 'Good Lord!' he exclaimed: 'That smoke's coming from (_sob_) from the—the chim(_sob_)ney—the chim(_sob_)ney of the breakfast room at the big house.'

CAPTAIN: _This_ room? But however did he know?

MISS P.: He knows _all_ these chimneys. But no one has lived here since the war. So when we suddenly saw _smoke_ rising up . . .

CAPTAIN: Quite. Quite.

MISS P.: . . . my brother _knew_ it was his duty to investigate. 'Who knows?' he said —those were his exact words—'Who knows who's got in there?' he said. 'Say now it's burglars, or bad characters? I'd better go,' he said, 'and have a look-see.' Poor darling! Off he trotted.

CAPTAIN: Has his horse returned?

MISS P.: He wasn't on a horse.

CAPTAIN: Then has his bicycle . . . ? Forgive me!

MISS P.: Nothing has returned. He was on foot. But he carried a riding-crop.

CAPTAIN: To use on the burglars?

MISS P.: Also because he was in his Bedford breeches. And his hacking jacket.

CAPTAIN: Ah! His name would be in them? Marking-ink or tape?

MISS P.: Both garments were gifts from old friends—only slightly worn. So, the jacket has an admiral's name and the breeches have a brigadier's. Confusing, I know.

CAPTAIN: Not at all confusing, Mrs Paradise. Your brother, who has a sense of duty and carries a riding-crop, disappears through a rift in the fog, dressed in a sailor's coat and a soldier's trousers, to investigate a plume of smoke. This does not happen every day: it may have left many clues . . . Ah . . . am I right in thinking that this house has often been occupied by horsemen?

MISS P.: Usually, yes.

CAPTAIN: Your brother has shared their interest in horses?

MISS P.: Very actively.

CAPTAIN: He has even, if requested, dug up a likely horse or two for these people?

MISS P.: Frequently.

CAPTAIN: I get the impression that your brother has, or _had_, no fixed profession—that he received small commissions for friendly acts.

MISS P.: Friendly acts—that's right. He always valued friendship.

CAPTAIN: Certainly, he set a price upon it . . . So, yesterday, seeing that this house was being lived in again, off he went, as usual, to make friends . . .

MISS P.: (_in tears again_) . . . Went by the footpath where the _bomb_ . . .

CAPTAIN: _Bomb_, Mrs Paradise? Surely this is not a target area?

MISS P.: . . . Where an old bomb left a deep crater—all full of water.

CAPTAIN (_rising sharply_): _Why didn't you say that at the very beginning? Why, this looks like an emergency!_ (Hurries to the speaking-tube on the desk, blows down the whistle-pipe, then puts the tube to his ear and waits for it to gurgle.) DRAG THE BOMB CRATER! IMMEDIATELY! Don't ask _me_ . . .

Find it . . . Between here and the lodge
. . .

MISS P.: Oh! Oh!

CAPTAIN (*returning to* MISS PARADISE): Mrs
Paradise, you astonish me! Why did you do
nothing for thirty-six hours?

MISS P. (*nervously*): It's hard to explain . . .
My brother hates—being—*interrupted*—
when he is making friends. . . . Oh, and
everything became a blur!

CAPTAIN (*going to the desk*): I see. Pull up
your chair, will you please, Mrs Paradise
. . . I will take a few notes . . . (*presses
bell*) A little tea, to calm your nerves? . . .
Now . . . Is your brother a tall man?

MISS P.: Oh, no; quite short. Not a dwarf,
of course.

CAPTAIN (*writing*): Not a dwarf . . . Any
moles, warts, birthmarks?

MISS P.: Not in places where a stranger could
see them.

CAPTAIN: We can always pursue them later,
if a question of identity arises. . . . He
sounds an unusual sort of man, I must say.
Now! You say he is very *friendly*?

MISS P.: He chooses his friends carefully; but
once he has done so, he sticks very closely.

CAPTAIN (*writing*): No visible warts and sticks
very closely. . . . Now, I am going to be
blunt, Mrs Paradise. Very blunt. Does
your brother stick closely to the other sex?

MISS P.: To the what?

CAPTAIN: To *women*, Mrs Paradise.

MISS P.: Women? Never! He has always been
a most practical man—even a little *distant*.

CAPTAIN: Women are often attracted by distant men, Mrs Paradise. They are confident of finding a short cut.

MISS P.: There was nothing of that sort in
my brother's life.

CAPTAIN (*writing*): Nothing of *that* sort . . .
Now, one more question, and we'll go out
and comb the park. . . . Was your brother
by any chance a little free with money?

MISS P.: With his own money?

CAPTAIN: Why!! I would never suggest he
was free with other people's!

MISS P.: No, he definitely wasn't. Never,
never.

CAPTAIN (*archly*): Ah! Inclined rather the
other way? A real Englishman? What people who didn't understand him might
call . . . ah . . . a bit of a screw . . . a
cadger? (MISS PARADISE *nods*.) Tell me

now, if I am not too rude, has this ten-
dency of his to thrift ever caused you to
quarrel with him? You know what we men
and women *are*, Mrs Paradise: we are prepared to forgive so much in those we love:
we forgive them their trespasses, we forgive
them their infidelities. And yet, for some
odd reason, if we have the least suspicion
that they are trying to hurt us in the *pocket*
—suddenly, the blood rushes to our heads
and we hear a hard voice in our hearts
saying 'No! That is where you stop, my
fine fellow!' Now, have *you* ever had any
such feelings towards your brother?

MISS P. (*after a long and troubled pause*): I
have . . . I can remember . . .

CAPTAIN: No! We'll change the subject, Mrs
Paradise. I only *mentioned* money just in
case. Now you will forgive me if I raise a
really painful point—suicide.

MISS P. (*flatly*): Out of the question. He was
far, far too . . .

CAPTAIN: Yes . . . ?

MISS P.: Too interested in . . . the things
he was doing . . . the things he had . . .
(*her mind is obviously still following the
money question*)

CAPTAIN: He was just a little selfish? I don't
mean greedy. Forgive me for being so personal.

MISS P.: I am finding it most helpful. What
troubles me is that I have never tried to
picture my brother before. I have always
accepted him simply as himself. Now that
I have begun to think about him, he seems
like quite another person. I don't know if
you'd even recognize the real him if you
saw the described one. Or do I mean it the
other way round?

CAPTAIN: We are trying to *discover* which is
the right way round, Mrs Paradise. (*The
speaking-tube whistles: the* CAPTAIN *lifts it
off, listens to its mumbled gurgles, then
speaks down it.*) . . . Nothing? . . . Have
you tried a pole? (*gurgle*) . . . Damn it
all . . . can't you get a *longer* pole?
(*gurgle*) And I should hurry. (*gurgle*) . . .
No, I suppose it doesn't really . . . about
thirty-six hours . . . (*gurgle*) Yes, face
down, with men . . . (*replaces tube*) Excuse me: you see we are trying our best.
Now, Mrs Paradise, I am going to ask you
a very blunt question indeed. Has your
brother, despite your deep affection for

each other, ever suggested breaking off connections with you?

MISS P.: Never, seriously. Only when we have had a little bickering—

CAPTAIN: What *sort* of bickering, Mrs Paradise?

MISS P.: He is difficult to satisfy. If one gets *no* reward for one's work, no thanks . . . He doesn't seem to realize how much more *expensive* everything is nowadays.

CAPTAIN: I think we eliminated money, Mrs Paradise, as a motive.

MISS P.: A *motive?*

CAPTAIN: For disappearing, for running off. He has never threatened anything like that, I'm sure . . . Is something worrying you, Mrs Paradise?

MISS P.: Nothing in particular.

CAPTAIN: Good. Just let me add, in passing, that another reason why we can eliminate the idea of his having run away is that he would get so little *advantage*. If he ran away, he would leave you that pretty little house, all your own, all the furniture, all your capital . . .

MISS P. (*suddenly screams*): My *capital!*

CAPTAIN: . . . Snugly tucked away in the Bank.

MISS P. (*springing to her feet*): My capital! Oh! My capital!

CAPTAIN: *That* he could never touch. However much he could tear your heart . . .

MISS P.: But he could! *We had a joint account!*

CAPTAIN: A joint account? Oh, Mrs Paradise! Sometimes I think that of all the words in the English language, those two are the most suggestive of tragedy!

MISS P.: Destitute! I am destitute!

CAPTAIN (*raising speaking-tube and awaiting gurgle*): Tell them to drop the pond. We are going to sound the Bank.

MISS P. (*making for L. door*): Bank! Police!

CAPTAIN (*dropping tube*): Mrs Paradise!

MISS P.: I am *Miss* Paradise! Would I marry a vulture?

CAPTAIN: But why should this be true?

MISS P.: It *is* true! I know! I know! Every instinct tells me!

CAPTAIN: But you said nothing to me of his being a thief?

MISS P.: Worse than thief! Sponger! Parasite! Murderer! Deep down, I have always

known! He has never really fooled me! Can't you use that telephone?

CAPTAIN: No. But my son will drive you to the Bank.

MISS P.: Get him, then; get him! . . . Oh, the criminal! I'll see him in the dock; I'll see him behind bars covered with arrows. I'll see him breaking stones—with his little traitor's beady eyes, his ferret's face . . . On Dartmoor, yes; he'll find it foggy there! (*The speaking-tube whistles and gurgles.*)

CAPTAIN (*to tube*): What . . . ?

MISS P.: I knew! I knew all the time. My woman's instinct!

CAPTAIN (*to tube*): Actually, we were onto another track. . . . (*Enter* BEAUFORT, *by L. door*.)

BEAUFORT: I'm terribly sorry, Father, but the doctor's coming.

CAPTAIN: *Doctor*, my dear boy!

MISS P.: Doctor indeed! *Police!* (*to* BEAUFORT) Get your car, young man!

BEAUFORT: Mrs Paradise! What on earth! I hardly recognize you!

MISS P.: Car! Car! Don't you know English?

CAPTAIN (*in tube*): Hurrying in *which* direction? (*to* BEAUFORT) Bring the car round, my boy.

MISS P. (*screaming*): Quickly!

BEAUFORT (*havering*): But the doctor's come for *Mother*, Father!

MISS P.: Are you all mad? He's in Scotland by now! (*The speaking-tube gurgles continuously and excitedly. Enter* JELLICOE, *né* HENRY PARADISE, *in butler's clothes, carrying tea on a silver tray. His bearing is distant and highly correct.*)

CAPTAIN (*sighing and holding the tube away*): I'm afraid you are right. Imagine that! In Scotland!

BEAUFORT: Poor Mrs Paradise! How *can* she imagine it?

MISS P.: She can imagine it very well! Scotland is exactly where he is. Aren't you going to . . . ?

CAPTAIN (*listening intently to a fresh burst of gurgles*): One second, Mrs Paradise! They have more information . . . Ah, blessed tea! Pour it, Beaufort.

MISS P. (*suddenly seeing the butler*): But . . . look! (JELLICOE *walks towards the centre of the stage.*)

BEAUFORT (*waving his arms between* MISS

PARADISE *and* JELLICOE): Don't talk too loud, Mrs Paradise. Father's just . . .

CAPTAIN (*loudly and angrily into the tube*): Took a ticket to *where*? . . . (*to* MISS PARADISE *and* BEAUFORT) Do be quiet!

MISS P.: But—I am seeing him! Henry! (*moves towards the butler*)

BEAUFORT (*getting in her way*): Please, Mrs Paradise! You are making a scene!

CAPTAIN (*in tube*): To Carlisle? First class?

MISS P. (*whipping round towards the speaking-tube*): Carlisle! Little beast! (*whipping round again to the butler*) But who's that?

BEAUFORT (*in the shocked whisper of one who hates scenes in front of servants*): That's only Jellicoe, our *butler*, Mrs Paradise.

CAPTAIN (*in tube*): No. Jellicoe is here with us now. . . . Tell him when he comes down. (JELLICOE *lays down his tray, turns and moves slowly and with dignity back towards the door.*)

MISS P. (*despairingly*): Hen . . . ! Hen . . . ! (*She presses rather feebly towards* JELLICOE, *who makes a slight but dignified detour to avoid her.*) Speak to me!

CAPTAIN (*into tube*): If and when they identify him . . . Very good. (*replaces tube— to* BEAUFORT) Brandy, Beaufort! Quickly! *Please*, Mrs Paradise. A little self-control . . .

MISS P.: Henry! Who are you?

CAPTAIN (*to* BEAUFORT): Now, what is this about a *doctor*! (*Exit* JELLICOE *closing the door in* MISS PARADISE'S *face.*)

BEAUFORT (*slopping tea hastily into a cup and producing a small bottle from his pocket*): Mother's all ready for him and going quite dotty.

MISS P. (*covering her face with her hands*): Oh, oh! Henry! You *were* Henry!

CAPTAIN: Then, she'll have to *go* dotty! Hurry, Beau! Then bring the car round.

BEAUFORT (*pouring from the bottle into the tea-cup*): Here we are. My God! My legs have gone all papery! (*nervously clatters over with cup and saucer. The* CAPTAIN *takes them from him.*)

CAPTAIN (*firmly*): Mrs Paradise! Chair, Beau! (BEAUFORT *shoves a chair behind* MISS PARADISE'S *legs.*) Mrs Paradise! (*she collapses into the chair*) Drink this, please; then we go straight to the police!

MISS P. (*sips*): Henry! Who *was* that?

CAPTAIN: Drink it down, Mrs Paradise. The station-master's description was exactly yours. (*she sips again, gasping*)

BEAUFORT: What a ghastly shock! Has her brother run off with all her money?

CAPTAIN: Every damned penny.

MISS P.: But he was *so very* like . . .

CAPTAIN: I'm sure he was, Mrs Paradise . . . Every drop now . . .

BEAUFORT (*in a stage whisper to the* CAPTAIN): Did she think Jellicoe was her brother?

CAPTAIN: Hold your tongue!

MISS P.: I did! I did! Am I going mad?

CAPTAIN: Mrs Paradise! You have lost your brother and your capital. Both will be arrested long before they reach Carlisle.

MISS P. (*faintly*): But why did I see . . . ?

CAPTAIN (*taking her pulse*): Go on. Tell me what you saw. (*quickly to* BEAUFORT) Get my Norfolk jacket. How long before the doctor arrives?

BEAUFORT: A good five minutes . . . (*hurries to the huge chest below the window*) Piebald spectacles too?

CAPTAIN: Naturally . . . Go on, Mrs Paradise.

MISS P. (*in a thin, faraway voice*): I seemed to see my Henry—my darling brother Henry . . . Oh! Thief! Thief! Will they stop the train?

CAPTAIN: They will put detectives on it. By now, he will have dyed his hair and changed his clothes. (*listens: then, to* BEAUFORT) Is that the doctor's car? (*An engine is heard.*)

MISS P.: Yes, yes, his hair wasn't . . . It wasn't . . . the same.

BEAUFORT (*looking through the window*): Yup. And a nice new one too. Oh! (*turning his face backwards*) How I should love to be a doctor! Day after day, new cars, new nurses!

CAPTAIN: Continue, dear Mrs Paradise. We should love to know the total of your capital. (*She only murmurs. The* CAPTAIN *raises one of her eyelids with his thumb and stares at the pupil.*) Larger than anyone would expect, I'm sure.

BEAUFORT (*bent through the window*): It's frightfully funny! He's pressing the bell like mad. . . .

CAPTAIN (*striking* MISS PARADISE'S *knee with*

the edge of one hand): Have you brought his nurse?

BEAUFORT: No; she's still at the surgery. I'll fetch her when you've got him under control. . . .

CAPTAIN: Shout 'Coming, doctor!' (*Enter through R. door,* MRS MALLET.) . . . Ready, my dear? All's well here.

BEAUFORT (*shouts*): Coming, doctor!

MRS MALLET (*staring at* BEAUFORT'S *behind*): Darling! Must you hang through the window like that? In front of ladies? (*indicating* MISS PARADISE) Who's to take her away?

BEAUFORT (*dances back from window, takes off the* CAPTAIN'S *scarlet coat, tugs off the hunting-boots, helps him on with a Norfolk jacket. He sings as he does so*): We'll send little Beaufort to fetch her away, Fetch her away, fetch her away . . .

CAPTAIN: We'll just run her into the next room, Beau: then I'll go down and let the doctor in. (*to* MRS MALLET) Get arranged on the sofa, will you? No hurry, of course.

MRS M. (*to* BEAUFORT): Be an angel and bring my eiderdown. I clean forgot it. (*heavy thumping below*) Impetuous man! I shouldn't like to have *him* as a doctor.

BEAUFORT: Let him enjoy his last fling!

CAPTAIN: Come on, Beau.

The CAPTAIN *and* BEAUFORT *seize the back of* MISS PARADISE'S *chair, tilt it up on the back castors and run it smartly to the door R., which* MRS MALLET *opens. They stop suddenly at the door, as* BEAUFORT *asks:*

BEAUFORT: Why is it always such fun to play hospitals?

CAPTAIN: Because, except in play, the hospitals always win. (*Exeunt* BEAUFORT, CAPTAIN MALLET, MISS PARADISE.)

MRS MALLET, *left alone, closes the door, arranges cushions on a sofa below the window; goes to the big chest, takes out medicine bottles, arranges them on a small table beside the sofa and performs any other fiddle-faddles that might cross the mind of a very good-looking woman about to be doctored. But she is wearing a suit—a sign of her confidence that the doctor won't get very far with his examining of her. She then sits down on the sofa, removes her slippers, and stretches out, looking com-fortable and relaxed. Enter* BEAUFORT *shrouded, as in a burnous, by a pink eider-down.*

BEAUFORT: Shall I tuck you up? All warm and cosy? (*He does so, fondling her intimately in the process.*)

MRS M.: No, darling; keep your hands from picking and stealing—we have *such* a busy morning.

BEAUFORT: What were you up to while we were labouring away?

MRS M.: I longed to come and help with her, but I thought I would put just a few finishing touches to Jellicoe before they met again. Experience has taught me that even when a brother has been completely re-made *and* re-named, he still tends to recognize his sister.

BEAUFORT: Instinct, I suppose.

MRS M.: It's not instinct. A dog would never do it.

BEAUFORT: Did you add anything to Jellicoe's new past?

MRS M.: I decided it could do with a little *alcohol* . . .

BEAUFORT: I quite agree. Particularly as we've made him a sailor.

MRS M.: . . . So I told him that when we picked him up in the gutter and brought him here, he had been on the booze for twenty years.

BEAUFORT: I bet that made him happy!

MRS M.: When you think that the poor wretch was actually shut up in that little lodge with that sister . . .

BEAUFORT: Why didn't you tell him that he'd murdered her?

MRS M.: There's no need to exaggerate. I've given him all the vice his conscience could want.

BEAUFORT (*raising the edge of the eiderdown*): Shall I snuggle in? I could amuse you until the doctor comes.

MRS M.: Beaufort! We are in the provinces, and I am *supposed* to be your mother.

BEAUFORT: What would you say if the doctor caught us together? (*slides under the eiderdown*)

MRS M.: What a woman always says: that we were just very close friends . . . No, Beau, be good, please . . . The doctor will be here any minute.

CAPTAIN (*off*): . . . in these great houses

. . . Only been here two days, my dear doctor, and get hopelessly lost . . .

DR TOWZER (*off*): Surely, sir, the patient would be *upstairs*, in a bedroom?

CAPTAIN (*off*): Have we not been upstairs?

TOWZER (*off*): No, sir, we have *not*.

CAPTAIN (*off*): I'm afraid it's a bit of a trudge, and if our bird has flown . . . (*Their voices die away.*)

BEAUFORT: Doesn't the doctor sound jumpy? And yet, I'm sure he's a bachelor . . . Why is your heart beating so fast?

MRS M.: I'm just a tiny bit nervous. I suppose I have transformed hundreds of people since I became a member of the Club, and yet I never quite trust my power to do it again. Until the doctor actually walks into the room I can't quite believe that he *wants* to be changed into a gardener—that he really does know what's good for him and will do his best to help.

BEAUFORT: But they always do. Always.

MRS M.: And I should simply *die* of shame if the Club arrived and found this place looking like the pigsty it is now. And the servants badly trained, or, trailing bits of their old selves after them. The President would say it didn't matter, but he would say it in a very nasty way.

BEAUFORT: As he says everything.

TOWZER (*off*): Surely, sir, we have been here before?

CAPTAIN (*off*): We have been in places very *like* this.

TOWZER (*off*): I have twelve patients to see before surgery.

CAPTAIN (*off*): I fear we have little sense of time in this old backwater. (*Voices die away.*)

BEAUFORT (*jerking his thumb in the* CAPTAIN'*s direction*): Isn't he in wonderful form! What a President!

MRS M.: Except that he is *not* our President.

BEAUFORT: But he's going to be. He knows we can't postpone it much longer.

MRS M.: You'll never say that to him, will you?

BEAUFORT: But if he *knows* . . .

MRS M.: Then don't even hint that he knows. People feel much happier if they don't *quite* know what they know . . .

BEAUFORT (*clasping her*): Am I as good at pretending to be your son as he is at pretending to be your husband?

MRS M.: Neither of you would deceive *me* for very long . . . Do I hear the gardener again? A sort of medical grunting?

BEAUFORT: Oh! I haven't told you how wonderfully you gurgled down that tube! Show me!

MRS M.: Beau, you are terribly difficult this morning! We must get this house staffed. All we have so far is one very raw butler and an unconscious housekeeper.

BEAUFORT: Just one trill of gurgles! (MRS MALLET *imitates previous gurgling, mentioning words like pond, pole, station, warts, not-a-dwarf.*) Heavenly! Again!

CAPTAIN (*off*): Milli-cent! Milli-cent! Where are you, Mil-ly? (MRS MALLET *continues to gurgle. They both burst out laughing.* BEAUFORT *kisses her passionately.*)

TOWZER (*off*): But, surely, sir, in the name of all conscience . . . you know your own wife's whereabouts?

MRS M.: You're right. He *is* a bachelor.

CAPTAIN (*off*): Millicent!

MRS M.: Off you go, darling! The gardener is getting warm.

BEAUFORT (*going to the chest and producing a violin and bow*): How long will you take to diagnose him? I have to bring his nurse on when he's been cleared away.

MRS M. (*reflecting*): A *good* twenty minutes. And, darling, promise not to be too excruciating with that fiddle.

BEAUFORT: I'll promise nothing. But I shall probably improvise on *Wozzeck*. It's in tune with the times. *Wozzeck* vile you vork. (*Exit.*)

MRS M. (*settling herself*): Ed-ward! Ed-ward!

CAPTAIN (*off—hopefully*): Mil-ly!

MRS M.: Ed-ward!

CAPTAIN (*off, but closer*): Milly! We-are-looking-for-you!

MRS M. (*liltingly*): In the breakfast room!

CAPTAIN (*very near*): Where? Did I hear you?

MRS M.: He-ere!

BEAUFORT (*off*): Fa-ther! Mother's waiting!

CAPTAIN (*slightly further off*): Where?

MRS M.: Ed-ward! Edward, I am *here*!

BEAUFORT (*off*): Fa-ther! Have you got the doc-tor? Mother says she's *downstairs*. (*The door is flung open violently and* DR TOWZER, *ravaged, enters at full speed and looks wildly round the room.*)

CAPTAIN (*off*): Do stop *shou*-ting! How can I hear her?

BEAUFORT (*off*): But she's down-stair-hairs!

CAPTAIN (*off*): Down *which* stairs?

TOWZER (*breathlessly*): Good afternoon. Are you the patient?

MRS M. (*reproachfully*): At last, doctor! I thought you were never coming.

CAPTAIN (*off*): Milly! (*He hurries in. Rather bent, in Norfolk jacket and pince-nez on ribbon with hair dishevelled, he is most unlike his previous self, giving an impression of angry, old-fashioned woolly-headedness.*) We've been looking for you everywhere! Surely you were not too weak to call?

MRS M. (*bursting into tears*): I called and called. No one came. I feel so—so *abandoned*.

CAPTAIN: Abandoned! What nonsense! The whole house in a bloody uproar!

TOWZER: A chair, please!

MRS M.: Oh, Edward, don't swear and be beastly!

CAPTAIN: But I *shall* swear and be beastly. You've run Dr Frobisher quite off his legs.

TOWZER: Chair! Chair! Chair!

CAPTAIN: What sort of chair? . . . It's really *too* selfish, Milly. At least half a dozen other patients are going to die like flies just because *you* are too well-bred to raise your voice! Now! High chair? Low chair?

MRS M.: I shan't even speak to you, tyrannical beast!

TOWZER: Sir! Any chair, chair, chair! (*He puffs out these words with exactly the sound of a locomotive leaving a station.*)

MRS M.: One hears the trains from here, doctor.

CAPTAIN: Who the devil cares what trains you hear? Tell Dr Brewster about your eternal inflammations and irrigations while I fetch him a chair. (*Exit.*)

TOWZER (*shouting*): My name, for the hundredth time, sir, is Towzer! Dr Towzer!

MRS M.: When I was a child, doctor, I could never play with other girls . . .

TOWZER (*harshly*): Madam, life is short! Let us start with your maturity!

MRS M.: But, doctor, the *symptoms* didn't. (*Enter* CAPTAIN *with the same chair that was used for* MISS PARADISE.)

CAPTAIN: Doctor! Would this be a shade too low?

TOWZER: Sir! Will you bring that seat? Madam! Will you be brief?

MRS M.: Doctor, you look exhausted!

CAPTAIN: For God's sake, Milly, forget Dr Benson's looks! He is not a film-star. (*Presses the chair against the doctor's calves.*)

TOWZER (*with a sudden attempt to be calm*): Madam. The modern doctor works under extreme pressure. . . .

MRS M.: But that is what is so wrong! Doctors aren't steam engines, Dr Frobisher.

TOWZER (*tremulously*): The whole nation is in a state of decay. From Land's End to John o' Groat's, we doctors and our nurses run from bed to bed like rabbits . . .

CAPTAIN: A gay picture, Dr Benson!

TOWZER (*furiously*): Dr *Towzer*, sir! (*From a room above come the first excruciating notes of* BEAUFORT's *improvising upon* Wozzeck.)

MRS M. (*clasping her head*): Oh, that ghastly noise! Only my son could make it.

CAPTAIN: Look! D'you want to make Frobisher what you've made me—a screaming mute?

MRS M. (*weeping*): I'll begin, Dr Williamson . . .

TOWZER (*dully*): Do, madam, do.

In what follows, the actress may please herself as to how she plays this important monologue. Her aim is to drive the doctor out of his wits by translating her feigned hysteria into his genuine one, which is just below the surface, awaiting diagnosis. She can do it wild-haired, madly, loudly, or in a low, terrible, calm way—the calmness of lunacy. But she must watch the doctor like a hawk, and whenever he shows by a twitch or grimace that she is hitting home, she must seem to take prompt advantage of his exposed weakness—gradually drawing him further and further up to hysterical heights. The CAPTAIN's *part is to act what he guesses the* DOCTOR *is feeling: he twists his face into anguished grimaces, lets out sharp hisses and groans, stares excruciatingly into the* DOCTOR's *face and winces away. Whenever* MRS MALLET *pauses in her monologue the space is filled by the agonizing sound from* BEAUFORT's *violin upstairs, and occasional heavy crashes suggesting he has dropped something. By the end of the monologue,* DR TOWZER *must be shaking like a jelly, his head turning frantically now* upwards (*in protest against the screeching violin*), *now desperately away from the grimacing, hissing* CAPTAIN, *now sideways-on to the full-blown hysteria of* MRS MALLET.

MRS M.: A sort of trembling, doctor, every morning when I wake up—as though I was somehow expecting the *worst*. At first, all snug in bed, I am puzzled—why, I ask myself dreamily, should I feel afraid? Suddenly it dawns on me—oh, God! Morning has come again and I am here again to meet it. *I am myself! I am myself!* Another morning has come, but it is I, always the same I, who has woken to it. This agonizing realization is followed by a 'Hah-hah-hah-hah' sort of asthmatic panting, like a sheep caught by its horns in a thicket.

TOWZER (*sharply but tremulously*): Omit sheep and thickets, madam, for God's sake! We are not a Bible class!

MRS M. (*continuing*): . . . Then everything suddenly becomes thicker and more tangled; my arms and legs begin to get wrapped in strands and tendrils—terrible tough tendrils that bind me and begin to squeeze my head. And at this moment, like getting a signal, everything in the room begins to revolve, at first quite slowly, so that I tell myself that if I can stop it *now* I will stop it for ever. And for just one second, I succeed. The room stops turning. Everything is still. Then, violently, abruptly, as if the world were enraged by my interference, the whirling and spinning starts again—this time at lunatic speed—crockery, furniture, walls, doors, husband, night-light—all whizzing round like a world on skates—and slowly, horribly, I feel this whirring drawing me into itself, making me a part of its hideous velocity. I scream, scream, but I am sucked into the heart of it, suffocated, dumb, the pillow now-over-now-under what once was my head. Now I am turned on my side, my toes chilled to frangible ice, my gorge rising, my hair streaming out behind me so far that it is caught in my pursuing open mouth—a terrible moment, because at once my taut head begins to strain at its trunk and, failing to break away there, rips in half with a tearing noise, and the two halves, cloven, chase each other at a distance like mad half-moons. 'Is this hysteria?' I ask myself —and though my voice cannot be heard it is none the less the only solid object within reach, so I attempt to clutch it, but cannot place its whereabouts. I try to *imagine* its sound, so that I may track it down and find some clue to myself, but all I hear is the note of a huge gong-stick beating upon my ear-drums—so, what with speed reducing everything to a blur, and sound and vision fighting to split this blur into a thousand slivers, I am simultaneously beaten and smothered into a jelly and yet fired through the centre of myself like hard machine-gun bullets. I am far beyond screaming by now; and yet questions, hard as rocks and written in black, appear like print across the middle of my split mind: *Who am I? Who are you*—you who does this to me? At which there is a chuckling, dancing mixture of sound and movement inside me, a terrible laughter followed by a burst of words: Only rend, tear, compress, slaughter, dismember, but hammer eternally compact! (*At this point,* DR TOWZER, *whose eyes have been glistening for some time, gives a loud shriek and falls with a crash against the back of the chair.*)

CAPTAIN: My dear, *what* a diagnosis! Why, you almost frightened *me*! (*He hurries forward and lays his fingers on the doctor's pulse. He puts his lips close to the doctor's ear and says in a strong, curt voice:*) Now, Towzer, we have had quite enough of your stoicism! You have driven us too far with your phlegmatic tantrums! We are exasperated. It is time for you to reform—to become quite another person! From now on, you will remember that your life is *roses, roses all the way.* Oh, Towzer, reborn Towzer, take up a new spade on behalf of the rose—that apostle of peace, that loving fire in which steeled hearts first look soft as wax and then firm afresh in the substance of naked pinkness! All your road now, Towzer, till life's very end, is beds of roses:

Polyantha, hybrid tea,
Pernetiana, pray for me!
Ah, perpetual delight!
Ah, the open, sunny site!
Nevermore will Towzer walk
Where the earnest microbes stalk;
Aphid, black-spot, now his cure,

Snowy mildew his allure.
Slide at last the sick-bed back,
Blanket down the baggèd quack.
In the gizzard of the rose
Hairy Towzer finds repose.

(*A slow, happy smile creeps over* TOWZER'*s face: he relaxes unconscious in his chair.*)

MRS M.: The poor dear! We came just in time. Did you say he ought to have a beard?

CAPTAIN: I was thinking of his nurse. Nurses do adore making nests.

MRS M.: But where'll we put him while he's growing it?

CAPTAIN: In the Paradise Lodge—with the nurse.

MRS M.: But nurses are such awful chorus-girls! They always ask whether what they are doing is respectable—and the answer is always No.

CAPTAIN: I think I can steer her round that. (*They wheel* TOWZER *to a corner, in view of the audience, but concealed from door L. The* CAPTAIN *goes to the big chest, selects a fresh change of clothes and happens to glance out of the window.*)

CAPTAIN (*to* MRS MALLET): Excuse me. (*shouts out of the window*) Who are you? What do you want? . . . Who? . . . No, certainly not. Come back another time; I'm busy. (*to* MRS MALLET) How interesting! The Paradises have a nephew. He wants to know if we've seen his uncle or aunt.

MRS M.: I don't think we want him, do we? (*looks out of window*) What a seedy-looking young man! He looks like a mechanic. (*A knock at the door L.*) Come in! (*Enter* JELLICOE.) What is it, Jellicoe?

JELLICOE: There is a suspicious character in the park, madam.

MRS M.: We were just discussing him, Jellicoe. The Captain was saying that he had seen him before. Have you?

JELLICOE: Never, madam.

MRS M.: He is certainly not the type you associate with, Jellicoe, though of course in your younger days . . .

JELLICOE: Yes, madam.

CAPTAIN: By the way, Jellicoe, you seem to be falling behind with your work.

JELLICOE: I am sorry, sir. It's moving all that furniture, sir.

CAPTAIN: When furniture arrives from the town house, Jellicoe, do you not expect to move it?

JELLICOE: I am happy to move anything, sir.

CAPTAIN: I hope you've got the drawing-room ready.

JELLICOE: Very nearly, sir. I am struggling with the carpet a little. It is fifty-eight feet long.

CAPTAIN: Jellicoe, you do realize that if you had behaved just a little more decently when you were young, you would not find a mere carpet beyond your strength in middle age?

JELLICOE: Oh, I do, sir. I never complain, sir.

CAPTAIN: You do very little else. Incidentally, after today you can stop preparing the meals. Dear old Cookie has recovered from her nervous breakdown.

JELLICOE: Thank God for that, sir!

CAPTAIN: Selfishly meant, to judge by your voice. (*There is the sound of a car driving up.*) Bring up the young woman Master Beaufort has just brought, will you? Tell her the doctor will be here in a minute.

JELLICOE: Very good, sir. (*Exit.*)

CAPTAIN: Next time Jellicoe's nephew comes, we'll ask him in, don't you think?

MRS M.: We can't use him in the house, I don't think. Butler, cook-housekeeper—we've got them now; and we've got a gardener and are about to get an under-gardener. But certainly *interview* the nephew . . . Let me help you with the gardener. (*opens door R.*)

CAPTAIN: Aren't you exhausted? (*They take the back of* TOWZER'*s chair and wheel it towards door R.*)

MRS M.: Do you suggest I see a doctor? (*Exeunt R. laughing heartily.*)

There is a pause: footsteps sound in L. corridor. L. door is opened by JELLICOE, *who ushers in* NURSE STEPHENSON, *a plump and pretty young woman.*

JELLICOE: The doctor will be here in a minute, miss.

NURSE: Pardon?

JELLICOE: The doctor will be here in a minute, miss.

NURSE: Thanks. (*Exit* JELLICOE.)

The NURSE *stands in the centre of the room, looking round vaguely, her mouth slightly open and humming a dreamy tune. She doesn't move from this position nor show any real interest in her surroundings: she is dreaming, as always. At last, foot-steps sound in the corridor, R. door swings open smartly and the* CAPTAIN *breezes in disguised as a psycho-analyst in velvet jacket, winged collar, unrimmed glasses and swinging a curved pipe between his teeth.*

CAPTAIN (*briskly*): Good morning, Miss Tray! And what can I do for you?

NURSE: Pardon?

CAPTAIN: I said: What can I do for you, Miss Tray?

NURSE: I am Nurse Stephenson from the surgery. I thought you said Tray.

CAPTAIN: *Miss* Tray, my dear, *Miss* Tray.

NURSE: Then I am not the one you want?

CAPTAIN: Let us not say that, Miss Tray. To-day's unwanted woman is tomorrow's alcoholic case.

NURSE: Oh, never mind! Where's the doctor, please?

CAPTAIN: Doctor?

NURSE: The doctor wants me. I know it's urgent. It always is.

CAPTAIN: What doctor always wants you so urgently, my dear? (*The* CAPTAIN *pulls the pipe from his mouth and squints at the* NURSE *over the looping stem*) Is something the matter with someone?

NURSE: Dr Towzer. He sent a young man to fetch me. That's Dr Towzer's car outside.

CAPTAIN: Towzer . . . Towzer. We do *have* a Towzer here. But he would be very upset if you accused him of being a doctor.

NURSE: But what else can he be?

CAPTAIN: My dear young lady, Towzer is our gardener. Are you sure we are talking of the same Towzer?

NURSE: I am talking of the one who wants me.

CAPTAIN: You have told me that twice already, Miss Tray, for some reason.

NURSE: And my name's Stephenson.

CAPTAIN: That, too, you have twice insisted on. (*takes out a pocket diary*) Yes. Four-thirty . . . Miss Blanche Tray . . . May I ask who booked your appointment?

NURSE: There's *no* appointment. I . . .

CAPTAIN: Dear lady, there *has* to be! I never *see* anybody who hasn't an appointment. You are down for four-thirty.

NURSE: I was still at surgery, when suddenly . . .

CAPTAIN (*abruptly*): Surgery! Dear me, I am an old addlepate this afternoon. Forgive me, my dear Miss Tray! I have only just realized why you are here. And who you are.

NURSE: Because Dr Towzer wants . . .

CAPTAIN: Yes, yes: I know *all* about it. So don't feel guilty, will you?

NURSE: I have nothing to feel guilty about!

CAPTAIN (*laughing*): You are not the first patient to tell me that! But may I ask just one question? Just one, just one . . . Miss Tray, do you often feel that doctors urgently want you? Or even want you in quite a leisurely way? Not that I have any right, really, to expect you to answer. It is not the patient who knows the answers. It is the psychiatrist.

NURSE (*astonished*): *Psychiatrist?* (*nervously*) I don't think I understand.

CAPTAIN (*coyly*): That is why we visit psychiatrists. No?

NURSE: But I am not visiting psychiatrists! I am the nurse from the surgery.

CAPTAIN: Of course! Do you sometimes think you are not?

NURSE: Why should I?

CAPTAIN (*smiling*): Indeed, why should you? Together, we must answer that, mustn't we? . . . By the way, *who* did you say brought you here?

NURSE: A young man in a sports car.

CAPTAIN (*smiling*): Good gracious! Something tells me he drove *very* fast. Am I right?

NURSE: Seventy-five miles an hour. I saw the speedometer.

CAPTAIN: Indeed! You *saw* the speedometer? What *did* it look like?

NURSE: Like all of them—round, covered with luminous figures, and had a red arrow.

CAPTAIN: And what did this red arrow do?

NURSE: Twirled through the luminous figures, of course.

CAPTAIN (*reflectively*): Hmm . . . ! Miss Tray! There is a *little* more to this than I thought.

NURSE (*very nervously*): May I see the doctor, please?

CAPTAIN (*taking a letter from his desk*): Now let me see . . . I do wish these physicians of yours would write clearly. But don't *you* feel guilty . . . What *is* his name—the slim one in your surgery?

NURSE: Dr Burke is slim. But so is Dr Rogers.

CAPTAIN: This is from Burke. Rogers is only a name to me. Let's see now: (*reads*) 'We should hate to lose her because all of us, myself, Rogers, and even Towzer, are confident that somehow you will steer her round this awkward corner' . . . interesting, don't you think, that Burke should speak of you as if you were a motor-car? Perhaps you told him about this famous drive of yours?

NURSE: How could I? It's only just happened.

CAPTAIN: But my dear young lady, this is not the first time you have been in a car!

NURSE: Has Dr Burke sent me here? What's this about awkward corners? Dr Towzer sent for me. Where is he? His car is outside.

CAPTAIN: Outside where, my dear?

NURSE (*crossing to window*): Here . . . Oh . . . Don't tell me he has gone? (*There is a knock on door R.*) Where is he? What is this house?

CAPTAIN: Come in! (*Enter* BEAUFORT, *wearing a doctor's white uniform.*)

BEAUFORT: Very sorry, sir, but . . . (*The* CAPTAIN *moves over to him: they exchange a few sentences in inaudible voices with a lot of nodding and frowning, after which* BEAUFORT *turns back towards door R.*)

CAPTAIN: And tell Higgins I am with a patient. He'll have to wait.

BEAUFORT: Yes, sir. I think he only wanted to know if we could take Mrs Venables for a short walk.

CAPTAIN (*reflectively*): Better not.

BEAUFORT: I'll tell him, sir. (*Exit R.*)

NURSE: Is he a doctor?

CAPTAIN: Who?

NURSE: That young man.

CAPTAIN: He is my assistant, Miss Tray. Why do you ask?

NURSE (*very upset*): Nothing.

CAPTAIN: Have you seen him before?

NURSE: Never mind.

CAPTAIN: Now, Miss Tray, let's try not to get upset! I can see by your face that you are worrying about the sort of treatment you will get here; so let me put you completely at your ease by saying that we never use shock treatment, nor do we believe in

cutting pieces of the nerves out of our patient's brains. (*he chuckles in a jolly way*) Incidentally, Dr Burke thinks that quite apart from your fantasies—which are the main thing, as you know—you are also anxious and worried. Would you agree?

NURSE (*tearfully*): Why did Dr Burke not tell me he was sending me to a psychiatrist?

CAPTAIN: I am going to answer that very bluntly, Miss Tray. Dr Burke thought you would refuse to come. Was he right?

NURSE (*guiltily*): Yes.

CAPTAIN: Don't feel guilty! Why shouldn't you have refused? As far as you knew, you were a normal, healthy, young woman. Is that right? (*Knock at the door.*) Come in! (*Enter* MRS MALLET, *re-dressed as a hospital matron. She whispers in the* CAPTAIN'S *ear.*) Yes . . . yes . . . Five grains is perfectly safe, matron—but I'll come along myself. Thank you, matron. (*Exit* MRS MALLET.) . . . Now, where were we? Oh, yes . . .

NURSE: I always thought they liked me at the surgery.

CAPTAIN: Would they have bothered to send you to me if they had *not* liked you?

NURSE: They never suggested I was a—a *case*. They never said one word about it.

CAPTAIN (*laughing kindly*): Is that not to their credit? Doctors are not usually so tactful with nurses, are they?

NURSE: I . . . I can feel that something may be . . . well . . . confused, or wrong, about me . . .

CAPTAIN: My dear Miss Tray, wrong is a word we never use! What *you* imagine, is bound to be right—*to you*. The question is: can we help you to use your mind in such a way that what you imagine is also right to *normal people*?

NURSE (*walking to the window and staring out*): I could have sworn that Dr Towzer's car . . . Oh, doctor, how much I have to learn!

CAPTAIN: But you are *willing* to learn, Miss Tray. What a difference that makes! The trouble with most of my patients is that they will *argue* about everything—in fact, I hardly ever meet a single one who realizes that nowadays all argument is absolutely useless. You see, Miss Tray, all we experts on the human personality work according to a particular theory, and though we have many different *patients*, our *theories* always remain the same. Take *my* particular theory, for instance. It contains a final answer to every argument you can possibly raise. Try and imagine an enormous room with a beautifully polished floor and furnishings created by the most ingenious craftsmen. You decide to get out of it. You see a likely door. You open it—it is the easiest thing in the world. But there, blocking your way with a friendly smile, stands a sentry. He is seven feet tall. He is armed with every conceivable modern weapon. He is infallible. He never sleeps. Miss Tray, there is a sentry like him posted at every exit from my theory. I hope you do not propose to argue with *all* of them.

NURSE: Doctor, what am I to *do*?

CAPTAIN (*laughing*): Let's see now . . . I think something of a physical nature . . . How about garden work? How would you like to help *our* Towzer (*laughing*) since your own has disappeared so abruptly? He's a grumpy old fellow with a beard. You could share the gardener's cottage with him. (*presses bell*)

NURSE: Would that be quite nice, doctor?

CAPTAIN: It would be rather *useful*. Shall I tell you why? What was the first thing you said when you came in here?

NURSE (*guiltily*): That a doctor wanted me.

CAPTAIN: Precisely. I have had many women patients, Miss Tray. Do you know: I have yet to meet one who, if she was at all attractive, didn't feel that men *wanted* her. Know what I mean?

NURSE (*ruefully*): Yes.

CAPTAIN: Take nurses, for instance. Nurses feel that doctors *want* them—just as many pretty stenographers feel that they are *wanted* by company directors. Most women, in fact, actually go about with a picture in their minds of men as something quite outside themselves, always making advances to them, wanting to descend on them—as if men were spaceships or wild bulls. And of course, sometimes you get a very interesting double illusion—as when both a stenographer and a company director feel that each is *wanted* by the other.

NURSE (*sighing*): I think it is the medical students who first give a nurse the illusion that men want her.

CAPTAIN (*waggishly*): And perhaps it is the nurses who give the students . . . (*They laugh together.*) So we'll put you with Towzer, my dear, who never wants *anything*, and get you a little more adjusted to the fact that we *can*, if we *try*, be an attractive young woman without always feeling *wanted*. And I hope you will make progress because in a few weeks something rather exciting is going to happen. The annual conference of the world's leading mental specialists is going to take place—in this house—in this very room. I want you to be in the pink of condition when they arrive. (*A knock on the door R.*) Come in! . . . Ah! Here's matron! (*Enter MRS MALLET, still in matron's uniform.*) Er, matron, this is Miss Tray, whom Dr Burke invited to stay with us for a little while.

NURSE: Pleased to meet you.

MRS M.: How do you do?

CAPTAIN: Matron will show you the cottage, Miss Tray. I think a room is ready there.

MRS M.: A very nice room, Miss Tray, because Dr Burke warned us you were coming.

NURSE: Oh, thanks!

CAPTAIN: And I think matron can give you more suitable clothes than those you have on. Miss Tray is going to help in the garden, matron, and do the boilers and clinkers and things like that. Have you anything that would fit?

MRS M. (*thoughtfully*): There is a good cord jacket and some Bedford breeches available, sir.

CAPTAIN: Perfect, matron! I should slip straight into them, Miss Tray. We'll talk again tomorrow.

NURSE: Thank you, doctor. Good-bye. (*MRS MALLET puts her arm round the NURSE and leads her off the stage.*)

The CAPTAIN, who is tired after all his efforts, yawns, stretches, pulls off his winged collar, velvet jacket and spectacles and wearily returns them to the big chest. He throws the curved pipe in after them, lights a cigarette and takes an elegant dressing-gown out of the chest. He is standing in his shirt-sleeves, pulling on the dressing-gown and smoking, when BEAUFORT comes rushing in by the door L., waving a handful of papers enthusiastically. Over his arm is his doctor's gown: his free hand clutches the violin and bow.

BEAUFORT: Would you ever believe it! Look!

CAPTAIN (*taking the papers*): From the Paradise cottage?

BEAUFORT: Yes! Look at the bank book! (*The* CAPTAIN *does so, while* BEAUFORT *lays his gown, bow and violin on top of the big chest.*)

CAPTAIN (*studying the book*): This is admirable! There is enough here to finance the whole conference!

BEAUFORT: What a pair of misers! It makes one ashamed to be in the same house with them. (*Enter* MRS MALLET, *still in matron's uniform.*)

BEAUFORT: Look, darling! Devalued pounds!! (MRS MALLET *studies the papers.*)

MRS M.: Never did I see a more avaricious monument! And just the sort of signatures one prays for.

CAPTAIN (*studying a paper*): I wouldn't say that of Jellicoe's. (*He takes a fountain-pen and makes tentative efforts to forge a signature.*)

MRS M.: Why, you dear old simpleton! Look! (*snatches the paper, studies it for a moment, takes the fountain-pen offered by the* CAPTAIN *and boldly writes*) There!

CAPTAIN (*laughing*): You are a woman in a million!

MRS M. (*studying the bank book*): Certainly in four thousand, five hundred and eighty. (MRS MALLET *switches on the light, crosses over to the windows and draws the heavy, faded curtains.*) It hurts me to think that we'll have to use a little of it to pay their wages with. I shall find that hard to forgive. (*All three laugh happily.* BEAUFORT *picks up his violin and plays 'The Lincolnshire Poacher': all three do a jaunty little dance for a few seconds.*)

CAPTAIN (*seating himself firmly*): Enough! Listen! We have worked hard. We have got our servants. We are extremely tired. But there is still work to do before we relax. Jellicoe is nicely in hand; we can leave him for the moment. But his sister has still no fresh identity at all. What is her new part to be?

BEAUFORT: I think she has worked with us in this house ever since I was a baby.

CAPTAIN: In that case, she is bound to the family by ties of loyalty and devotion. What name should such a woman have?

MRS M.: I think she should keep her old surname. But change her Christian name from Ethel to Florence.

CAPTAIN: Florence Paradise—could a devoted old servant ask for more? Now, she is to be a widow, is she not?

MRS M.: After fifty years of being a spinster, I think she would appreciate a dead husband.

BEAUFORT: Any objection to her husband having been our dear old chauffeur?

CAPTAIN: None at all. He had better take her brother's name, Henry: it means so much to her. Henry Paradise . . . and he has just died. Where?

MRS M.: In Nottingham. One's always safe with Nottingham: nobody's ever been there.

CAPTAIN: They were a devoted couple. One can tell that from the postcard he sent her from Nottingham, a few hours before his death. Can you scribble that tonight, my dear?

MRS M.: It'll be on her dressing-table when she wakes up, ready to arouse the tenderest memories.

BEAUFORT (*sulkily*): Nottingham! Now I'll have to go through my stamp collection. (*fetches a large bag from the chest and empties hundreds of used stamps on to the table*) Aren't you going to give poor Miss Tray a past?

CAPTAIN: Miss Tray is the sort of woman who likes to live entirely in the future. By dreaming of tomorrow, she will create memories of yesterday. (*to* MRS MALLET) Now! You, my dear, will keep an eye on our housekeeper in the coming weeks. I shall be responsible for Towzer and Tray. Now, Beaufort, I have a surprise for *you*. I am going to give you Jellicoe.

BEAUFORT (*delighted*): For my very own?

CAPTAIN: To use as you think best . . . No, don't thank me. You have more than earned a human being of your own. Work hard on Jellicoe, so that when the Club arrive they will see impressive evidence of your handicraft.

BEAUFORT (*sorting his stamps in a discouraged way*): I'm not sure that the Club deserves it.

CAPTAIN: My dear boy: You shock me!

MRS M. (*taking some knitting out of her bag*): Beau is just a little discouraged, today.

CAPTAIN: Discouraged! In twenty-four hours we three have totally transformed the lives and characters of no less than four persons. . . .

BEAUFORT (*angrily*): We *three*! That's the point! (*he strikes the table with his fist*)

MRS M.: Give me that a minute, darling! (*She takes the fist and measures the foot of a part-made sock round it.*)

BEAUFORT: With *you* leading, we *all* move forward. But once the old President arrives . . .

CAPTAIN (*raising his hand*): Beaufort! I am highly flattered by your esteem. . . .

Suddenly there is the hard, clear sound of rapping on the French windows. All three characters spring to their feet like lightning, transformed in the twinkling of an eye from a trio engaged in personal discussion into three alert, dangerous animals. Moving like a cat, BEAUFORT nimbly takes a small pistol from his pocket and moves towards the curtains. MRS MALLET stands coldly erect, her eyes fixed in the same direction, her fingers tight round her knitting needles. The CAPTAIN, with taut self-control, moves silently and quickly to one side of the curtains, makes a chink with two fingers and puts his eye to it. The other two wait with tense expectancy.

It's that damned, greasy mechanic—that Paradise nephew!

He steps angrily to the centre-point of the curtains and, taking one-half in each hand, sweeps both halves back simultaneously. Like a well-lit phantom, LOLLY PARADISE's figure is seen through the long glass pane, blinking in the light. His hair is untidy: he wears an old, greasy wind-cheater and soiled, unpressed trousers. The audience must see him with perfect clarity, so that they may contrast him as he is now with what he becomes in Act Two.

MRS M. (*letting out her breath sharply*): Stupid little beast! How he made me jump! (*LOLLY's mouth opens and shuts soundlessly.*)

CAPTAIN (*abruptly making up his mind*): Beaufort! Go to the front door and let him in!

BEAUFORT: What! More work?

CAPTAIN: At once! Talk to him; confuse him; leave him; come back and report! (*Shaking his head and cursing, BEAUFORT obeys immediately. The CAPTAIN addresses LOLLY through the French window.*) GO TO THE FRONT DOOR! D'YOU HEAR? FRONT DOOR! (*He points downwards. LOLLY makes a muffled response and turns away from the window. The CAPTAIN draws the curtains.*) I am sorry, my dear, but this is his second visit and I do feel that if Providence *twice* insists on sending a missionary . . .

MRS M.: It becomes the duty of cannibals to eat him. (*They both laugh.*) But how can we *use* him?

CAPTAIN: Send him to London. If he *is* a mechanic, he can drive Dr Towzer's car up to the Club. Then, the President can transform him into a new member and bring him back here for the summer session.

MRS M.: Make *him* a *member*? But has he a brain in his head?

CAPTAIN: No. But he may be quick with his *hands*.

MRS M. (*looking at him reflectively*): Ah, yes . . . a *handy* man. (*Enter BEAUFORT rapidly by R. door.*)

BEAUFORT (*talking fast*): He's still looking for his uncle and aunt . . . Cheap, low type . . . Small spiv . . . Tiny mind . . . Lazy . . . Machine-shop breed . . . Everything that makes a motorist.

CAPTAIN (*rubbing his hands*): Excellent! Excellent! Have you told him anything about himself?

BEAUFORT: I just said I was sure I'd met him in the R.A.F.

CAPTAIN: Good boy! Did you give him a name?

BEAUFORT: Stapleton.

CAPTAIN: A good, steady name . . . Ex RAF Stapleton . . . we'll tell the President and he can build on from there.

BEAUFORT: But what's he *for*?

CAPTAIN: For the Club, my dear boy! (*He opens the chest and rummages into it. He takes out and puts on a double-breasted jacket and puts a large cigar in his mouth.*)

BEAUFORT: He's going to be made into a *member*! That spotted dick?

CAPTAIN: Now, let's see . . . What should he wear? (*humming thoughtfully, he finally pulls out a fur-collared overcoat and a smart Homburg)* Just in case he takes the doctor's car through Harley Street.

MRS M.: May we ask who *you* are?

CAPTAIN *(standing erect, puffing his cigar, and playing the part)*: Do I or don't I own a large chain of garages?

MRS M.: In one of which he will find employment?

CAPTAIN *(puffing at the cigar)*: In my London depot! *(They all laugh at this. Exit* CAPTAIN R.)

MRS M. *(going to the chest and taking out a bundle of postcards)*: I must write my heart-rending postcard.

BEAUFORT *(sitting down to his stamps)*: Why is this chimpanzee coming into the Club?

MRS M. *(sitting down and selecting her postcard)*: Because a chimp is so clever with its hands. (MRS MALLET *takes up her pen, nibbles the end, then studies a page of* JELLICOE's *handwriting.)*

MRS M.: I do hate people who make ugly G's! How long after writing this postcard does he die?

BEAUFORT *(sorting busily)*: Oh, about three hours. Be sure the pubs aren't open. She mustn't suspect that his spotless life ended with a blow from a pint pot. (MRS MALLET *begins to write.)* Oh! I'll never find Nottingham in this damned mess!

MRS M. *(writing)*: You aren't methodical, darling. I hope you won't handle Jellicoe's psyche in such a disorderly way.

BEAUFORT: I'm thinking of giving his character a touch of homicide.

MRS M.: *So* like you, darling! At the age of twenty-one, you are presented with your first personality—and bingo! it *must* have a yen for murder.

BEAUFORT: Why not? Why shouldn't Jellicoe go berserk suddenly?

MRS M.: And murder the President, I suppose?

BEAUFORT: Yes. I can't deny it. That thought did cross my mind.

MRS M.: I think we'll wait and see how our new member turns out.

BEAUFORT *(impressed)*: Oh-ho! So that's the idea, is it!

MRS M.: Dear Beaufort! Will you never learn to be indirect? We members of modern Clubs do make certain *arrangements*, but we believe that it is not ourselves but what

we call *history* that—puts them into effect. If history has decided that the President is getting out of date—well, she will act as she thinks best. The most we can do is put certain materials at her disposal.

BEAUFORT: History seems very slow to make up her mind.

MRS M.: She has heavy responsibilities.

BEAUFORT: She needs me, to give her a pinch in the behind . . . *(pause)* . . . About Jellicoe's drinking. Did you tell him he was still an alcoholic? Or can I tell him that he has signed the pledge?

MRS M.: Why not both? They usually go together.

BEAUFORT: I'll tempt him with half a bottle.

MRS M. *(who is still writing)*: Tempt him, darling, that's right . . . *(studying her postcard)* Oh, what a jewel of a husband he was!

BEAUFORT: I hope you're not making it *too* gushing. You must put in the things a man really *does* worry about when he is separated from the woman he loves. You know: '*Don't forget to sift the clinkers*'; '*Open the henhouse flap if the weather gets warm.*'

MRS M. *(writing)*: Oh! Beaufort! Beaufort! Will you *never* understand the needs of the human heart? *(There is the sound of a door opening downstairs, steps on the gravel, the* CAPTAIN's *voice talking. Both of them look up in astonishment.)*

MRS M.: No! Impossible!

BEAUFORT: Prince of men! Wizard! Genius! How many minutes flat?

MRS M. *(returning to her writing)*: Certainly not more than ten.

BEAUFORT: He *must* be President! He *must!* Oh, what a Club we'd have! *(There is the sound of a car starting.)*

MRS M. *(gaily throwing down her pen)*: Fini-to!

BEAUFORT *(gently drawing the curtain slightly and opening the French windows a crack)*: Sh-sh! I must listen . . . *(The* CAPTAIN's *and* LOLLY's *voices are plainly and clearly heard.)*

CAPTAIN: Now, just a minute! You remember your instructions?

LOLLY: Yes, sir.

CAPTAIN: You remember what to say when they open the door?

LOLLY: Yes, sir.

CAPTAIN: Let me hear you say it, then.
LOLLY (*clearly and loudly*): I say: 'THE CAP-
TAIN SENT ME TO THE PRESIDENT.' (*A moment's pause, then the car roars off into
the darkness. Curtain.*)

ACT II

SCENE 1

*A part of the Great Kitchen of Hyde's
Mortimer, occupying the forestage alone.*
MRS PARADISE, *in widow's weeds, sits at
one end of a kitchen table holding the
famous Nottingham postcard.* MISS TRAY,
*attractively dressed in the famous Bedford
breeches and hacking jacket, sits listening
dreamily. This scene, in sharp contrast to
the eventfulness and urgency of Act One,
must have an air of suspended time and
hallucination. Transformed into new persons by the adroit psychologist, the characters are busily putting out new roots into
their new pasts, which they are construct-
ing out of invented memories and anecdotes. They are thus dreaming themselves
into existence and then impressing the fab-
ulous results upon one another—a spectacle
of pure nonsense portrayed with the deepest self-conviction.*

MRS P. (*gesturing with postcard*): Yes, Miss
Tray, that's how it was. I gave him twenty
years of love and care . . . and then, all
alone in Nottingham, death took him.
MISS TRAY (*sighing*): I suppose it takes us all
in the end, Mrs Paradise.
MRS P. (*firmly*): It shouldn't take us in the
middle—that's my point, Miss Tray . . .
Ah! Ah! The best husband a woman ever
had. Twenty years we worked together in
this house, and never a quarrel . . . But
I've shown you this before, haven't I? (*she
holds up the postcard*)
MISS TRAY (*tactfully*): Only once or twice,
Mrs Paradise. You remember, a few weeks
ago we laughed because he signed it 'Robin
Hood.'
MRS P.: But put 'Henry' in brackets. So there
would be no doubt.
MISS TRAY (*vaguely*): No doubt at all, Mrs
Paradise.

MRS P.: How he loved a good joke! Madam
was reminding me the other day how he
used to shock my father when we were
engaged.
MISS TRAY (*dreamily*): And they were long
engagements in those days, weren't they?
MRS P.: Of course! In those days, *everything*
just went on and on and on: it was *all*
like the Old Testament. (*Bells and hammering sounds from upstairs.*) Dear me!
The gentlemen are beginning to debate!
(*Heavy crashes and shouts upstairs.*) Do
you know, Miss Tray, this is the noisiest
house-party I can ever remember? And the
state of their *rooms*, Miss Tray! All over
their beds, books as thick as your arm; pictures of men and women called Miss X
and Mr Y . . . They must be very *brainy*
. . . So naughty of Mr Towzer! We got
the big room looking so nice and now he's
not brought the flowers . . . Such a sad
coincidence—Mr Towzer's mind going just
when my husband went. They were such
good friends. Ah, well! My Henry's happier where he is now.
MISS TRAY: You believe in an after-life, Mrs
Paradise—a next world?
MRS P.: Miss Tray! Every bone in my body
tells me that my Henry is in a lighter,
brighter place. (*As if to demonstrate this
statement, enter* JELLICOE *in shirt sleeves,
breathing on and polishing a huge silver
salver which casts brilliant reflections in all
directions.*)
JELLICOE: Good morning, all and sundry!
MISS TRAY: What do *you* think, Mr Jellicoe?
JELLICOE: About what, young lady? I think
many things.
MISS TRAY: About a future life.
JELLICOE: Thanks, Miss Tray! I am much
too haunted by my real past to waste time
on an imaginary future. (*Prolonged clap-
ping and applause upstairs.*) Still no flow-
ers? I'll get a nice wigging from the Cap-
tain!
MISS TRAY: Any minute now, Mr Jellicoe
. . . You know, when I was on the stage
. . .
JELLICOE: } On the stage, Miss Tray!
MRS P.:
MISS TRAY: Yes, when I was an actress. . . .
MRS P.: You never told us *that* before!
MISS TRAY: How could I? I didn't know it.

Of course, I did *really* know it, but I had repressed it—buried the whole theatre in my unconscious mind. It only came out two days ago, when I was talking to the doctor.

JELLICOE: I wish I could repress *my* past like that! Heaven knows! It has worse things than the stage in it!

MRS P.: Tell us more, dear!

MISS TRAY: I can't. The doctor hasn't brought any more to the surface yet. So, you see, *my* past is something I look *forward* to.

MRS P. (*puzzled*): That's too deep for me!

MISS TRAY: Oh, it's quite common, now-adays.

JELLICOE (*puzzled*): Do you often see this doctor of yours, Miss Tray?

MISS TRAY: I see him all the time. Don't you? (JELLICOE *looks more puzzled, but receives from* MRS PARADISE *a warning gesture not to press the poor girl.*)

JELLICOE: Well, I don't envy you, Miss Tray, having all your memories still ahead. I only pray they won't look like mine. As Master Beaufort said the other day: 'In your place, Jellicoe,' he said, 'I think I should feel too ashamed to go on living.'

MRS P. (*sighing*): Yes! Memories, memories —always haunting you!

JELLICOE (*sighing and polishing*): Always reminding you of who you are—that nothing can ever change you!

MISS TRAY: I don't believe that a *bit*, Mr Jellicoe! I'm sure I'm not the person I was when I was on the stage.

JELLICOE (*very tartly*): It's because you're so sure of that, Miss Tray, that you've been put under a doctor.

MRS P.: Mr Jellicoe! *What* a rude way to talk!

JELLICOE: Pardon me, Miss Tray! It was very rude. Sometimes I forget I'm not still in the navy.

Enter TOWZER *with a large bunch of roses. He never speaks: his stance and movements are shambling: but he is perfectly happy in a babyish sort of way, so long as he is not pressed or frightened. Though quite under* MISS TRAY's *thumb, he has a slave's furtive obstinacy: the complete, contented irresponsibility of his new identity is precisely the opposite of his old, medical one. He has grown a heavy beard and his*

clothes, though rough, as a gardener's should be, show that MISS TRAY *has added a pretty touch here and there.*

MISS TRAY (*advancing on* TOWZER *with a wagging finger*): Well, you are a naughty boy, aren't you? One whole hour late! Just to *vex me*, wasn't it? No! Don't try and pretend! I can see through you as clearly as the doctor can see through me.

JELLICOE (*placing a crystal bowl on the silver salver*): I don't think time means anything to him.

MISS TRAY: Nothing whatever! *We* may live in the past or in the future, but *he* lives entirely in the present.

JELLICOE (*taking the roses from* TOWZER): I wish he could be more punctual with it.

MRS P.: I must say, you've spruced him up wonderfully in the last weeks.

MISS TRAY: Not too bad, is he? Do you like his tie?

MRS P.: Very much indeed. Mauve always looks pretty with that shade of green.

JELLICOE (*arranging roses in bowl*): Is there much chance of *his* memory coming back? Or should I say, coming *forward*?

MISS TRAY: It's too early to say. The doctor's keeping his fingers crossed. (*Loud laughter and applause upstairs.*) Of course, he's terribly busy with this conference. I do most of the therapy on Mr Towzer.

MRS P.: Considering you're only a Land Girl, I think you've done wonders.

MISS TRAY: Oh, thank you, Mrs Paradise! . . . Just look at him! He knows we're talking about him!

JELLICOE: Aren't you imagining that, Miss Tray? Of course, I know that animals know. Our ship's cat always walked out if you mocked it.

MRS P.: My husband always said that horses knew. (*A bell rings loudly. Exit* TOWZER *rapidly with a terrified expression.*) What's up?

MISS TRAY: I can't *think* why, but the sound of any *bell* seems to horrify him. At some time in his life, he must have had too many bells. Excuse me, won't you? (*She hurries out in pursuit of* TOWZER.)

MRS P.: Poor girl! She's getting quite fond of him. I don't think the Captain ought to allow it. He ought to send her away.

JELLICOE: That's just the trouble. As Master

Beaufort explained to me the other day, she's only here out of kindness. She wouldn't *get* a job in any house but this.

MRS P.: An *actress* indeed! I've nothing against her, but it does change the atmosphere of a house when someone's not quite all there.

JELLICOE: As a woman, you're bound to feel that, Mrs Paradise. A man is always more detached. (*he pulls on his butler's coat*) I'll just rush these up.

MRS P.: They look simply lovely. Did Mr Towzer *really* grow them?

JELLICOE: He *believes* he did, Mrs Paradise. And in a case like his, what he believes, is the only thing that matters.

Exit JELLICOE with roses. MRS PARADISE, shaking her head in a what's-the-world-coming-to manner, follows him off. The main curtain rises immediately the fore-stage is empty, showing the Identity Club in full session, in the breakfast room.

SCENE 2

The Club in full session.

PRESIDENT (*standing before the Speaker's lectern*): . . . is the only thing that matters, ladies and gentlemen! (*Applause—long enough to accustom the audience's eye to the new scene.*) For what *makes* the world in which we live today? Well: we hear much of something called 'the individual'. We hear much of a body vaguely named 'society'. But what *are* these, ladies and gentlemen, but ghosts—verbal vestiges, mere wisps of fantasy in the brains of deluded librarians? The world of today is a world of *groups*—of hard, fanatical groups of men, too united in their aims for any one member of them to be individual; too zealous and rebellious in their fanaticism to be deemed social. (*Laughter.*)

At this very minute, ladies and gentlemen, a man is lying in a box. He believes, as do all members of his group, that the astral powers of the cosmos are shedding spiritual and electrical vibrations upon him, that in his box he is cunningly trapping the secret power of the universe. (*Laughter.*)

Not far away from this box-dweller, another man of another group is busy explaining himself to himself by reflecting on the wonderful mysteries of his *libido*. Unseen, intangible as God himself, is this *libido*, but how dear to him, who, prone upon his master's couch, believes it to be the very seat of his passions, his ego's very bottom! (*Laughter.*)

What scorn this libidinous gentleman feels for the fellow in the *next* room, who, by long study of *his* master's voice, knows infallibly that man can be explained only in terms of *capital investment*! Ah, gentlemen, modern man is accused repeatedly of having lost his religious sense—but, in fact, has this world ever seen such an age of faith? What are the miracles of the old religion, what are loaves, fishes and risen Lazaruses, compared with the miracles of the cosmic box, the libidinous couch, the charts, graphs and compost heaps which are the modern godheads?

Enter JELLICOE with the roses, which he places on the table before the PRESIDENT and exits. He is watched in silence by every eye: when he has closed the door, the PRESIDENT gestures after him.

See! A modern Lazarus—risen from an imaginary grave and carrying roses grown in the imagination of a doctor's ghost! (*shrugs*) How *commonplace!* How *everyday!* (*He bends solemnly towards his audience.*) Ladies and gentlemen! We, the members of this Club, *who know what the truth really is* . . . (*Loud applause.*) . . . we must be patient about the delusions of *other* Clubs. Fifty years have passed since our great founder, Dr Black Planorbis, first expounded the Great Theory of Identity—*the only true theory ever known to man.* (*Wild applause.*)

We know—as only we *can* know—that the day will come when all groups will become one group—one group devoted to *our* Great Theory, one group believing that identity is the answer to everything, that there is nothing that cannot be explained by means of the only primary question: Who am I? Only we, the members of the Identity Club, know how much toil, pain and ingenuity go into the making of an identity; only we can tell the misguided how and why they have blundered in their acts of self-creation. Only we can fit them out with selves better suited to their requirements. There is no sort of identity we are not able to create, no self so nonsensical that we cannot make it plausible. We can make an average man out of a Teddy Boy, a St Augustine out of a Logical Positivist, a charitable man out of an Archbishop of Canterbury. But many years must pass before the supreme truth of our Great Theory is accepted by the world—and, in the interim, it is our custom, once a year, to present case-histories on the floor of our meeting-room, case-histories enacted by groups within our group, by specialists in the many aspects of our beloved theory. Today, we are about to proceed with the first of these dramatic studies, but before we proceed, I, your President, must say one or two blunt words. I have noticed signs of discontent among you in recent months. I have overheard mutterings. I have seen sulky expressions on your highly-expressive faces. I shall not ask why. I shall only say that of all modern sins, that of treachery to the group is the greatest. On occasion, in the past, there have been members of this Club who have asserted that the Great Theory is capable of modification, that certain elements are missing from it. Today, gentlemen, we still have the Great Theory: it is only those misguided members who are . . . (*grimly*) *missing*. Let me therefore remind you that rebellion against your leader—myself—is rebellion against the Great Theory itself. Remember this, gentlemen, (*looking at* MRS MALLET) *lady* and gentlemen! Now, let us proceed! (*A murmur: 'Questions! Questions!' runs round the Club.*) Questions? Very well.

A MEMBER (*rising*): Why are none of our foreign members present? Where, for instance, is our French contingent?

PRESIDENT: For reasons I do not pretend to understand, they have written to say that at any moment they may be called on to form a *government*. In fact, we have received very curious excuses from all over the world. Our American members write to say that they are entirely preoccupied with denying their identities before some kind of Committee. One South African member says quite seriously that he cannot attend because, although he had always appeared to be perfectly white, his government have suddenly declared him to be quite black.

A MEMBER: What steps has the President taken to get round these obstacles?

PRESIDENT: None, sir. I am an octogenarian, not a centipede. (*Loud murmurings.*) What did you say, sir? (*pointing a sharp finger*) I heard the words 'our turn next'.

A MEMBER (*nervously*): I only *hinted*—scarcely even that—that if our foreign members were left in the lurch . . .

PRESIDENT: It would be our turn next . . . Thank you, sir. I shall make a note of that remark. (*takes out his notebook and makes a jotting.* STAPLETON, *an RAF type, leaning on a stick, rises.*) Yes, Mr. Stapleton?

STAPLETON: I have only just joined this wonderful Club. It seems like Heaven, after the RAF. The President is such a wonderful leader, and he has just told us not to quarrel. I do think he is right . . . and I do think . . .

MRS M. (*in a silvery voice*): We are all so happy to welcome Mr Stapleton as our new member. (*Welcoming claps.*) But I *think* he ought to be told that this is not the time to make personal *statements*—only *questions*. (*Applause.*) Though, of course, we all agree with him.

STAPLETON: I'm awfully sorry! (*hurriedly sits down*)

PRESIDENT (*grimly*): Thank you, madam! . . . Very well. Let us proceed. Dr Bitterling! Your group is to enact the first case-history?

DR BITTERLING: We are all ready, Mr President. (*rises with script*)

CAPTAIN (*gently and very politely*): May I rise to a small point of order, Mr President? I am sure that the President merely *forgot*—that he meant no *disrespect* to the memory of our great founder—when he failed to ask Miss Black Planorbis, our founder's distinguished daughter, to open the session—as she has done for thirty years. (*Applause.*)

PRESIDENT (*grumpily*): Where *is* our oldest tradition?

MISS BLACK PLANORBIS, *an ancient lady who looks like a totem pole and has a huge ear-trumpet, is pushed upright by a Member on each side of her. She has not the slight-*

est idea what's up or where she is: but her face clears when one of her supporting Members puts her wise in a sharp whisper: 'Come along now—say something!' etc.

MISS PLANORBIS (*quaveringly*): So we are all here again, are we, in this familiar room! How time does pass! How *exciting* it all is! If only the war would stop! (MEMBER *gives her a stern tug and whispers something.*) Oh, yes, *of course!* . . . I do want to say how proud my dear father would be if he could see all your distinguished faces. (*Applause.*) Who knows, perhaps he *can* see them? (MEMBER *tugs her crossly.*) Oh dear! I've said something religious! . . . And my dear mother: how *she* would love it! I was really much fonder of her than I was of Father—(MEMBER *tugs her very angrily.*) —well, not *really*, of course, because Father *was* such a wonderful man. (*Applause.*) I never understood the Great Theory, of course, because I'm not very clever, but what I did love about Father was . . . was . . . (*She stops, quite at sea. The* MEMBER *whispers encouragingly.*)—yes, how *could* I have forgotten!—what I loved about my father was his *wonderful humanity.* (*Loud applause. The* MEMBER *prompts her again.*) Father loved children and animals *so* much. (*Applause.*) He used to give me sweets and pick-a-backs. (*Applause.*) He knew that the Great Theory was purely for the service of the human race. He knew that he had to be rather ruthless in his methods, or nobody would pay any attention. (*Loud applause.*) I have never agreed with that horrible judge who said that Father was no better than a common gangster . . .

PRESIDENT: Enough, enough, Miss Planorbis! A charming speech!

MISS PLANORBIS: . . . though I must say that when dear mother died so suddenly . . . (*There are shocked exclamations.* MISS PLANORBIS *is hurriedly pulled down into her seat again.*)

PRESIDENT (*grimly*): Your escorts are not giving you the attention you deserve, Miss Planorbis.

BEAUFORT (*instantly*): Allow *me*, dear lady! (*he plants himself beside her in one quick movement*)

MRS M.: I think another *woman* would be more effective, Mr President. (*She removes the* MEMBER *on* MISS PLANORBIS's *other side with a friendly smile, and takes his place.*)

PRESIDENT (*pointing sharply*): Dr Scavenger! Did I hear you say: 'That was a wily manœuvre'?

DR SCAVENGER: Certainly not, Mr President. I said: 'It would be wise to remove her.'

CAPTAIN (*very politely*): I can endorse that, Mr President.

PRESIDENT: How kind! Scavenger! Stand up and thank Mallet for his *rubber stamp!* (*Cries of 'Shame', led by* BEAUFORT *and* MRS MALLET. *Coldly.*) Dr Bitterling's Group will now present our first case-history. It is entitled 'The Making of a Well-bred Identity, or, Old Wine in New Bottles'. Those of you who think that this is a damned dull subject should remember that of all our groups Bitterling's is the most ready to employ the latest techniques of histrionic illumination. Dr Bitterling!

Glancing first at a script in his hand, DR BITTERLING *moves right down towards the audience with seductive, beckoning arms. He has the dramatic manner of an old-fashioned actor, a rubber face that over-expresses all his feelings, and the hearty, winning voice of an old family-doctor.*

DR BITT.: Now! Come on everybody! *Let's make an identity . . . !*

PRESIDENT: Bitterling! W*here* did you get that voice?

DR BITT.: On the wireless. It's the voice of democracy.

PRESIDENT: It shall not be heard in these halls. Continue in a less odious way. (*Murmurs from the* BITTERLING *clique. One of them hands the* DOCTOR *a sheet of paper, which obviously contains an alternative opening. The* DOCTOR *looks it over sourly, but accepts it.*)

DR BITT. (*sulkily at first*): . . . Childhood, ah, happy, careless childhood! (*glares at the* PRESIDENT) Can we ever recapture you in the net of memory? Can we ever, as your form slips backward into the oblivious arms of time . . .

PRESIDENT: Very good, Bitterling! We take your drift. Omit the next pages!

DR BITT. (*furiously*): What! All my poetry?

After adolescence, there's nothing but prose!

PRESIDENT (*firmly*): On what page does the hero's voice break?

DR BITT. (*leafing angrily through the script*): Not until page forty-two! (*Sympathetic cries of 'Shame'.*)

PRESIDENT: Resume, then, on forty-five. Just to be on the safe side of poetry. (*Indignant murmurs.*) Silence, gentlemen, please! Continue, Bitterling!

DR BITT. (*very sulkily*) . . . but as I have already described these influences to you, in detail, I shall say no more about Uncle Roger, Nanny, Mrs Stokes and my fear of the dark . . . but will say simply that one question alone remained: what were my *values* to be? Well, it was left to my mother to instruct me on these points, as the following discussion of first principles will show. . . . (*A* MEMBER *dressed like a boy steps forward.*)

BOY: Mummy! Can I have some notepaper?

MOTHER (*who is a middle-aged professor, steps forward like a tragedy-queen, tears her hair in anguish, and answers in a racked, throbbing voice*): O, my God! The little beast has said it again! Do you want God to love you? Do you want *me* to love you? Then *don't* say *notepaper!*

BOY: I'm sorry, Mummy. I *meant* writing-paper.

MOTHER: He *meant* writing-paper! (*wrings her hands*) How many times have I told you, you horrid little boy, that it's not what you *mean* that matters, but the *word* you use for it? You are growing up in a world that is becoming more common every day. How will you give yourself an *un*common identity? I shall tell you . . . You must go through life remembering that it is *the little things that count*. Even if you become the cleverest person in the world, remember that nothing you may put to paper is so important as the name you call the paper by. My son, it is better to wipe your mouth with the back of your hand in a cabman's shelter, and call it a table-napkin, than stuff yourself at the Ritz and use—*a serviette!*

DR BITT.: Here's a novel identity with a vengeance! You ask: Can *any* real identity be built upon table-napkins and writing-paper? Well, many people manage to do it, you know. Our young man might have managed well enough, but for two decisive things. First, a war came along and pushed napkins and writing-paper into the background. Second: our young man met another young man, who had a stronger, more passionate understanding of *little things* and was prepared to follow them to their logical conclusions. Behold these two, discussing the state of the nation, on their return from the war . . .

PRESIDENT: After which particular war, Bitterling?

DR BITT. (*with the impatience of one who won't be stopped now*): Any damned war! They're all alike! (*Applause. The* BOY, *now a* YOUTH, *steps forward with his friend,* VINSON.)

YOUTH: Everything, everybody—all changed, Vinson. Everybody living in different houses . . .

VINSON: Nobody wearing a hat . . .

YOUTH: All talking like Americans . . .

VINSON: I know they had a rough time while we were away. But that's no excuse for saying mantelpiece.

YOUTH: For not calling pêche melba pudding . . .

DR BITT.: Here, gentlemen, is tragedy indeed! Two idealistic, well-bred, young men, their identities cut to a single pattern, come home from the wars and find that the veil of writing-paper has been rent! Below it, is the face of Ancient Britain—hard, hairy and avaricious! What will our two young men do? Will they re-mould their identities into a new pattern? Or will they struggle to re-establish the old superstitions?

VINSON: My course is fixed. No man in England will return to the world of his grandfathers more resolutely than I! My Rolls-Royce shall be a Silver Ghost, more silvery than silver itself, more ghostly than any phantom. My garden shall be filled with the ancient roses of Damascus, Lancaster and York; my hand-writing shall be of Renaissance Italy; I shall eat perch from my pools with two fishforks of France. But these things are not enough. First, I must find something to pin my faith to.

YOUTH: Something that doesn't exist any more?

VINSON: It *can* exist, but it has to be very old, quite dead, and barely usable.

YOUTH: Something like the Coronation Chair?

VINSON: Except we don't want anything to do with the Scots. Their ways of going backwards aren't the same as ours. No: whatever we take up must have an ancient English tradition behind it, be very difficult to understand but still give the impression that the country would be poorer without it.

YOUTH: I have an old cousin who is the Custodian of all the Ancient Bodies in the country.

VINSON: Now, that's just the sort of thing we're after! Let's go and see him. . . .

DR BITT.: Our young man is lucky! Like the man who lies in a box, like the man who lies upon a couch, he has found a leader— a strong-minded, uncompromising maniac who will put the last vestiges of his common sense through a hard sieve of *non sequiturs* and serve them up a purée of buttered nonsense. His barren disappointment will be developed into fruitful lunacy, for man does not live by bread alone. Man lives by what he believes, and he does *not* believe in anything that he can eat. Or even in anything that he can see. Once a thing exists he sees no reason to believe in it. Let us see what emerges from these two young men's interview with the Custodian of Ancient Bodies. . . . (*The* CUSTODIAN *steps forward.*)

CUSTODIAN (*who has a very trembly voice and a palpitating body*): Well, this *is* a pleasant surprise! If there were chairs, I should ask you to sit down . . . Now; you want some honorific, traditional occupation, do you? Let me see . . . (*he mounts an imaginary ladder and brings down a huge, imaginary folio with tremulous hands*) . . . Marshals of the Welsh Ridings . . . no . . . have to be peers for that, alas! . . . Bee-Keepers of Hampton Court . . . quite a decent salary goes with that, I'm afraid, so it's a political appointment . . . Knights of Ealing—now that's not too bad, you know—don't have to be a real Knight, don't have to go to Ealing except at Michaelmas . . . Co-Wardens of the Badgeries. . . .

VINSON: I like the sound of that.

CUSTODIAN: Not bad, not bad! You only have to pay an annual gross of peppercorns for it—to the Knights of Ealing, oddly enough —and in return you get a bushel of oats from the Yeomen of Hertford Forest.

VINSON (*coldly*): We are not interested in the *income!*

CUSTODIAN: No, no, of course! Well, the Badgeries is a most ancient institution. It dates back . . . to . . . to . . . 1136 . . . it involves the wearing of a hauberk on Lady Day . . . I'm afraid you have to supply the hauberk . . .

VINSON: Sir, our interest goes deeper than the costume!

CUSTODIAN: Let's see now . . . ah . . . you would have the rights to all faggots, windfalls, blowdowns and vestigeries on Holborn Common . . .

VINSON: What are vestigeries?

CUSTODIAN: Oh, you know, *little* things, remnants of things, little odds-and-ends, pieces of things, bits of string, small buttons.

VINSON: And where is Holborn Common?

CUSTODIAN: I'm afraid that's not there any more.

VINSON: Excellent!

CUSTODIAN: Of course, although it's not there, that doesn't mean that things like vestigeries are not still attached to it. But most of the site is now Fleet Street and I doubt if you would *find* any faggots or blowdowns on Fleet Street now (*laughs*) anyway, not within the meaning of the Act.

VINSON: Now, what about the badgers? Is there a real badger?

CUSTODIAN: Not an *actual* badger, no. Only the tradition of one.

VINSON: Good! Good! Now: are there occasions when my friend and I must show the invisible badger to the public?

CUSTODIAN: You yourselves must march in all State processions. But you only take the imaginary badger with you in the funeral procession of the Lord Royal. The Lord Royal is your titular chief, you see. That means that though he is not there, he holds the office.

YOUTH: How do we apply for the post?

CUSTODIAN: My dear boy, you have already done so! One thing about Ancient Bodies, their forms are not in triplicate! . . . You can take the oath immediately.

VINSON: But where's the Lord Royal?

CUSTODIAN: He is vested in me, my dear fellow! Now if you will just go down on your knees . . . sorry the carpet's so thin . . . The Treasury doesn't allow us very much . . . and repeat the oath after me . . . Now, where's that oath . . . (VINSON *and the* YOUTH *kneel.*) Ah! Here we are! On your marks . . . ? 'We do most solemnly swear . . .'

YOUTH: } 'We do most solemnly swear . . .'
VINSON: }

CUSTODIAN: 'In all our Lord's demesnes, boundaries and maintenance . . .'

YOUTH: } 'In all our Lord's demesnes, bound-
VINSON: } aries and maintenance . . .'

CUSTODIAN: 'To heal, succour, support and decently uphold . . .'

YOUTH: } 'To heal, succour, support and de-
VINSON: } cently uphold . . .'

CUSTODIAN: 'All badgers, badgeries and whatsoever may purport thereto . . .'

YOUTH: } 'All badgers, badgeries and whatso-
VINSON: } ever may purport thereto . . .'

CUSTODIAN: 'In token whereof we thricely do pronounce and cry . . .'

YOUTH: } 'In token whereof we thricely do
VINSON: } pronounce and cry . . .'

CUSTODIAN: 'Broc! Broc! Broc!'

YOUTH: } 'Broc! Broc! Broc!'
VINSON: }

CUSTODIAN: And there we are! Congratulations! (*Shakes their hands.*) You are now fully vested Co-Wardens of the Badgeries. I'm afraid there's a bit of stamp-duty . . .

VINSON: We'll pay that out of our gratuities.

CUSTODIAN: How very sporting!

VINSON: About the badger. When do we come into symbolic possession of him?

CUSTODIAN: You have already done so, my dear fellow, by virtue of your oath.

VINSON: We are holding him now?

CUSTODIAN: If you were not, the oath would be an empty one. (VINSON *and* YOUTH *come close together, cupping and shaping the badger's form.*) Well, you'll have to whisk him off now, I'm afraid. I have an appointment with another old Body . . . Phone me, won't you, if you get in a balls-up?

DR BITT.: The die is cast! The Co-Wardens return to their unheated flat, carrying in their arms the traditional spirit of the nation . . .

VINSON: Let's put him down now . . . (*angrily*) Easy! Easy! . . . He's not made of iron . . .

YOUTH: Would he like some water?

VINSON: Try him with a symbolic saucerful. (YOUTH *twiddles an imaginary tap.*)

YOUTH: I'll have to fill it with token water: the pipes are frozen. (*He sets an imaginary saucer, overflowing with non-existent water, before the invisible badger. Both watch with tense interest.*) . . . He's drinking it, by Jove, every drop! . . . Won't he be very cold?

VINSON: Not in his winter coat. Do try and get into your head that he's still perfectly himself. It's just that we can't see him . . . Let's put him in his kennel. (*They open the imaginary door of a non-existent cupboard, kick out a fancied mess of boots and things, and reverently place the invisible badger inside.*)

YOUTH: The whole atmosphere of this place seems different suddenly. I feel like quite another person—(*very reverently*) now I've found *him* . . .

DR BITT.: Little do these idealists know that their great moment is almost upon them! Two months later, one of them turns on the wireless in order to hear a talk on 'Forest Life in Old Britain' . . .

YOUTH (*as slow music by Elgar fills the room*): Funny! This doesn't *sound* like 'Forest Life'. It sounds like Edward Elgar.

VINSON: Try another station. (YOUTH *obeys: a deep, disembodied voice says: '. . . and leaves the world to darkness and to me.'*)

YOUTH: Why, that's Gray's *Elegy!* What's up?

VINSON: Something important must have happened! It always has, when there's only Elgar and the *Elegy* . . . Good heavens! No! Impossible!

YOUTH: You *don't* mean . . . ?

VINSON: } *The Lord Royal's dead!*
YOUTH: }

DR BITT.: Yes! The Lord Royal is dead! Ah, death, death, beloved of every Briton! Death—moment of profundity, passion and pageantry! Upon the ears falls nothing but Elgar, Elegy and eulogy—and behind the scenes the Custodian of Ancient Bodies is marshalling his men—those colourful Ancient Bodies who will march in the procession and lend to death that vital touch of old tradition. Our two young men are ready and waiting . . . happy as a pair of taxidermists. . . .

VINSON: Where's the tinsel for my hauberk?

YOUTH: Under your bag of peppercorns.

VINSON: Oh, thanks . . . Hammer up my back, will you? What's the time?

YOUTH (*hammering* VINSON): We've got three-quarters of an hour.

VINSON: O.K. We'd better wake him up and get cracking.

YOUTH ⎱ (*opening the imaginary kennel door*):
VINSON ⎰ Broc! Broc! *Bon jour!*

DR BITT.: We cannot hope to see the whole procession through the eyes of our young men. We had much better follow it with the help of two well-trained commentators, who are doing it for the wireless and making it possible for thousands of ordinary people to bring death into their living-rooms. . . . (TWO COMMENTATORS *step forward with a microphone.*)

1ST COMM. (*his voice is not adenoidal: it simply sounds as if years of pointing his head down towards a microphone had made it inevitable that his voice should seem to be obeying the law of gravity and passing through his nose*): . . . Still about two minutes before the Lord Royal's hearse emerges, followed by the Ancient Bodies. The hearse, as you probably know, has been made entirely from Commonwealth wood . . . that's correct, isn't it, Boynton?

2ND COMM.: Quite correct, Meiklejohn. Each country of the British Commonwealth has donated a plank. So the hearse is entirely a family affair.

1ST COMM.: They're off! Absolutely on the very second! . . . (*Applause.*) Those cheers you hear are for the hearse, which has just swept out in a very stately way, behind the six black horses—really very impressive, wouldn't you say, Boynton?

2ND COMM.: I would say very impressive.

1ST COMM.: And so would I. It is really very impressive—the six horses and then the long hearse, built entirely of Commonwealth wood. The wood, of course, is quite invisible below the great sable pall, which was made in the Shetlands, as I have told you, by Mrs Mackenzie and the Mackenzie girls, working day and night at the hand-loom for three days and nights on end, without a break, without any stop at all. (*Applause.*) Ah! The Ancient Bodies are now appearing and at once the whole scene on this *very* wet, *very* damp, day is completely transfigured into a marvellous blaze of colour. (*Stage lights begin to dim at this point and continue to get dimmer until the end of the scene.*) Through the drizzle come the Ancient Body of Honourable Pikemen—about a platoon of them—all six-footers dressed completely in black and carrying their pikes in rest—that is to say, with the business-end pointing downwards. I don't think I'd like to meet those gentlemen on a dark night, would you, Boynton?

2ND COMM.: No, I would not, Meiklejohn.

1ST COMM.: Meanwhile, the hearse has just passed below me, that is to say, underneath where I am standing, and has just, but only just, managed to enter the roundabout at Soho Square. It is built entirely of Commonwealth wood. The crowds are very thick here. (*Applause.*) One rather interesting point I'd like to allude to is the fact that in this magnificent funeral—quite one of the best I have ever seen—those who are marching to the grave seem to be much more *alive* than those who are staying behind . . . (*Applause, more distant.*) Ah! Now, what's this they're cheering? Let me see my programme . . . Ah, yes! Behind the pikemen, two most extraordinary figures have just loomed into view. They are the Co-Wardens of the Badgeries, and behind them they are towing a sort of flat trolley-affair, which is not actually carrying anything, but is simply a sort of symbol of what it is meant to be carrying, namely a token badger. There is really something very impressive about these two young men . . . it is as if they were reminding the crowd of what faith and death really mean, and the crowd is not resenting this at all, they are positively loving it.

2ND COMM.: Up in front again . . .

1ST COMM.: The hearse is crossing Oxford Street. It is very difficult to see clearly on this very wet day but there seems to be a spot of trouble at the top end of Rathbone Place: a man in a plastic raincoat, from the Electricity Board, I suppose, is pointing towards a large hole that has been made on one side of the street: and a policeman at the head of the road is gesturing to the grooms to lead the horses round the edge of the hole—which they are doing quite beautifully, may I say, a very tricky little twisting manœuvre with the near-side lead-horse all but grazing the wall on the front side while the off-side rear wheel of the hearse just skirts the hole on the back side. There go the chamberlains, giving the hole a very wide berth. Up come the pike-men, looking a little jumpy, their pikes held well up, I suppose to prevent the dead metal touching a live wire . . . Yes, there's a policeman in rather a frenzy! Now another: he's running towards them and pointing—it must be that hole . . . Yes, I think he is trying to draw the hole to the attention of the Co-Wardens who are just moving up. . . . Of course, they are pay-ing no attention—wonderful discipline! Good Lord! It's the badger's trolley! It's there—it's half-way round—it's on the edge—it's going in . . .

Immediately a brilliant blue light flashes across the dark stage illuminating the as-tonished faces of the Club, followed by a deafening explosion and total darkness. MISS PLANORBIS *gives a piercing shriek: then, out of nowhere, comes a tragic voice, fading slowly into silence.*

VOICE: Broc! Broc! Broc!

When the lights come on again a few sec-onds later, the curtain has been dropped on the Club and we are again on the fore-stage, in the Great Kitchen.

SCENE 3

In the Great Kitchen. MRS PARADISE *is ar-ranging numerous cups and saucers on a large tray.* JELLICOE *sits brooding beside her.*

JELLICOE: The Navy was like that, Mrs Para-dise. Explosions all the time. At night, the whole sky lit up for miles around. We used to stuff our ears with gun-cotton.

MRS P.: I do hate loud bangs! What are they *doing* upstairs? . . . Oh, Mr Jellicoe, *don't* sit dreaming of the Navy! Heat up the Ovaltine! Sort the biscuits!

JELLICOE (*moving off R.*): We were a decent lot. But when a man's been sent to the bottom of the sea three or four times, you can never trust him again with a woman.

(*Exit R.* MRS PARADISE *goes on with her cups; enter* MRS MALLET, *L.*)

MRS M.: Elevenses ready, Florence, dear?

MRS P.: Nearly, madam, nearly! Oh, madam, what *was* that loud bang?

MRS M.: Only *history*, Florence, only *history*. (*Violent outburst of angry shouts from up-stairs.*) They need a little cup of something, Florence.

MRS P.: Mr Jellicoe's warming it this minute, madam. (*she drops her voice and ap-proaches* MRS MALLET) Madam, I'm wor-ried about Mr Jellicoe. He's acting stranger every day. He talks about nothing but his past.

MRS M.: I am sorry to say, Florence, that it *was* that sort of past.

MRS P.: But, madam! He talks about his *wives*—as if he'd had *dozens*—and illegiti-mate children . . . and the other day . . . (*she goes to R. door to listen for* JELLICOE) . . . the other day, right in front of poor Miss Tray, he said he had run away to join the Navy because he was in love with his mother! He never *used* to talk like that, madam! (JELLICOE *enters from R. with a tray of cups and saucers and a jug, passes across the stage with a dignified bow to* MRS MALLET *and exits L.*) . . . And the funny thing about it, madam—the more shameful the story is, the more dignified he walks about . . . madam, am I gos-siping?

MRS M.: *Dear* Florence, when do you *ever* gossip? All you do is tell me what is hap-pening downstairs. Your husband had just the same helpful habit.

MRS P.: My poor Henry, madam! A good thing he's in his grave. If he could hear his old friend Mr Jellicoe now, it'd be the death of him. . . . All ready, madam. I bet they're dry upstairs.

MRS M.: As dry as bookworms, Florence. (*Exeunt L.,* MRS PARADISE *carrying her loaded tray.*)

Enter JELLICOE *L. He stands close to the L. exit, anxiously listening, as the women's feet die away, for the sound of footsteps coming downstairs. Soon, measured steps sound: enter* BEAUFORT *with a cold, grim look on his face.*

JELLICOE (*advancing on him with excited trembling*): Oh, Master Beaufort—you caught my wink?

BEAUFORT (*every inch the haughty master*): Why not? You used the whole left side of your body.

JELLICOE (*half-laughing, half-imploring*): Oh, Master Beau, I was desperate . . . ! I said to myself: 'I can't go another night without it—no, I can't!' Oh, Master Beau —have you brought it? (BEAUFORT, *studying him coldly, slowly draws a half-bottle of whisky from his pocket and hands it to* JELLICOE, *who seizes it with a gasp and pats it rapturously.*) Oh, Master Beau, thank you, thank you! My old Scotch friend-in-need!

BEAUFORT: Don't you start chumming-up with your old Scotch friend until the guests have gone to bed! You know what'll happen if Father smells him on you.

JELLICOE: Don't I know, Master Beau!

BEAUFORT: All those old police charges against you . . . Father wouldn't hush 'em up long, if he knew you were hitting the Great North Road again. A nice sight you'd be in the dock, wouldn't you? One look at you, and the judge would tuck his mug under his wig and throw you to the dogs!

JELLICOE (*shuddering*): Don't revive old memories, Master Beau. Oh, I am grateful!

BEAUFORT: I hope you don't get so drunk you can't remember the things I tell you.

JELLICOE: It's the other way round, Master Beau. A little drop now and then helps me to swallow them.

BEAUFORT (*taking out notebook and pencil*): I don't suppose we've reached the bottom of your trouble yet. Have you dreamt about your mother again?

JELLICOE: Ever since you mentioned her, Master Beau, I've seemed to dream about her all the time. I never used to.

BEAUFORT: Do you know *why* you never used to?

JELLICOE (*guiltily*): Yes, Master Beau. I was ashamed to admit such a filthy passion.

BEAUFORT: So what did you do?

JELLICOE: When her image tried to enter my dream, I dropped a mental block on her. If she persisted, I disguised her with blue trousers and used her like a common sailor. (*his voice drops*)

BEAUFORT (*scribbling*): That's better, Jellicoe . . . Now! What about those homicidal tendencies you used to bottle up?

JELLICOE: Flowing freely now, Master Beau, I am glad to say. I rarely wake up in the morning without a blood-stained murder on my conscience.

BEAUFORT: Then we are making *some* progress, Jellicoe.

JELLICOE: Oh, good, Master Beau! Will I ever be a normal man?

BEAUFORT (*shrugging*): In nine, ten years. Don't let's anticipate. . . . Off you go now and get your trays! (*Exit* JELLICOE, L., *tucking away his precious bottle.*)

High voices break out again upstairs. BEAUFORT *makes a few notes in his notebook, stands thoughtfully a moment and then exits L. His footsteps, still audible on the first steps of the stairs, come to a very audible halt when* MISS TRAY *enters* R., *followed by* TOWZER *carrying vegetables.*

MISS TRAY: Put them on the trolley, naughty boy! Oh, you'll be the death of me—going on repressing yourself like this! Why can't you open yourself up and be healthy, like me and others? As the doctor says: 'It's not what you *do* that's dangerous: it's what you *refuse* to do—that's what makes the social body fester.' But what do *you* know about social bodies? (*changing her tone and studying him intently*) How long have you been a gardener here? (TOWZER *mutters an inaudible reply.*) As long as you can remember? . . . Well, what did you do before that . . . ? Don't remember, eh? Show me your hands . . . Turn them up . . . No, the other way . . . Are those gardener's hands? (*He puts them deep into his pockets.*) You don't want to give yourself away, do you? You don't want to *please* me. (*she allows her face to work and gives a snivel; he puts out one hand in a worried way*) Well, if you do want to please me, will you try your best to remember who you were? (*He nods.*) If I tell you all sorts of names—like Clara, Mary, Lily, Ann, Barbara—will you tell me if one of them sounds familiar? (*He nods.*) Or if I talk about *places* and kinds of *work*—London, business, carpentry, school . . . (*He gives a slight start.*)—oh! School, eh? Teacher—teacher—teacher? . . . Nothing doing, eh? . . . Clothes—footballs—uniforms? (*He again gives a slight start.*) School and uniforms! (*she sighs*) Well, it's not much, but it's something! Why did you wait so long, you naughty boy? Just two words in two weeks! Now, stop looking miserable! I promise we won't do any more therapy today. Let's go and weed the strawberries . . . But soon, we'll surprise the doctor, won't we, you and me?

*She takes his arm and leads him to exit R. and exeunt. After they have gone there is a brief silence and then the formidable sound of footsteps (*BEAUFORT's*) continuing up stairs off L. As these footsteps climb higher and higher and grow fainter and fainter, the noise of quarrelling upstairs grows louder and louder and reaches its height as the curtain rises again on the breakfast room, with Club members shakily draining the last of their elevenses and handing their empty cups and saucers to* JELLICOE *and* MRS PARADISE. *But* DR BITTERLING *is still on his feet and using his cup to beat his saucer.*

SCENE 4

The breakfast room.

DR BITT.: A nice reward! Months of laborious work by my group! Eighteen rehearsals! Hours upon hours of group toil, group struggle, group artistry . . .

PRESIDENT: Dr Bitterling! Let their aim be the brotherhood of man itself, I shall *not* permit bombs to be thrown in this Club.

STAPLETON (*earnestly*): I do know what the President means about bombs. . . . When I was in the RAF . . .

DR BITT.: To hell with the RAF! Let me drive home my point!

PRESIDENT: It is already blunt with domesticity. (*Cries of 'Shame'.*)

DR BITT.: It was only a very small, child's bomb. Aren't we supposed to make our case-histories as lifelike as possible?

PRESIDENT: No bomb can ever fall in *that* category, Dr Bitterling. In the present instance, Miss Planorbis fainted dead away.

MISS PLANORBIS: My dear, good friend soon pulled me round again. (*She presses* MRS MALLET's *hand. Enter* BEAUFORT *from L. and resumes his seat beside* MISS PLANORBIS.)

MRS M.: You have been *so* plucky, Miss Planorbis!

MISS P.: My dear father always said that to meet life, one needed courage. (*Applause.*)

DR BITT.: We are getting out of date in this Club! Our Great Theory is for all time. But here we are, while others are paying deposits on tickets to the moon, still discussing the invention of the steam engine!

PRESIDENT: Is that a reference to my age, Dr Bitterling? (*There is a long and nervous silence.* CAPTAIN MALLET *rises slowly and dignifiedly to his feet, every inch a strong leader.*) Mallet! I am addressing Bitterling. Will you kindly resume your seat? (*There is a shocked gasp from everyone.*)

CAPTAIN (*very courteously sitting down*): Why, most certainly, Mr President, if you so order. (*He is given a round of claps.*)

PRESIDENT: Bitterling?

DR BITT. (*desperately*): It is not *my* fault if the President remembers the Siege of Mafeking! I suppose an *apology* is expected.

PRESIDENT: We stand patiently upon the platform—hoping to see one come puffing round the bend. (STAPLETON *rises, a worried look on his face.*) Sit down, Mr Stapleton! I do not need your assistance. (STAPLETON, *cut to the heart, obeys.*) I am not so old that I cannot hunt without a spaniel! (*Cries of 'Oh! Oh!' The* PRESIDENT *bares his teeth angrily.*)

MRS M. (*rising*): I am sure Miss Planorbis will confirm that it is *not* traditional, Mr President, to sink our teeth into new members. (*There are murmurs of agreement.* STAPLETON *gives her a grateful look.*)

MISS P.: I am sure my dear father was opposed to the habit. (*Cries of 'Hear, Hear'.*)

PRESIDENT (*ignoring it all*): Well, Bitterling? (*The* CAPTAIN *again slowly rises; the* PRESIDENT, *though furious, has not the nerve to order him down again.*)

CAPTAIN: May I make a small suggestion? We all know the misery that is suffered by a profound thinker when he is asked to make an apology. (*Cheers.*) For an intellectual there is no greater agony, perhaps, except, of course, feelings of insecurity, loss of faith in his group, his leadership . . . (*Cheers.*) which do not, of course, affect *us*. (*Silence.*) My little suggestion is that since the President is the only one who has objected—wisely, I am sure—to Bitterling's little firecracker, all the rest of us are, in a sense, culpable. May I therefore apologize to the President in the name of the whole Club?

DR BITT.: May I second that proposal? Words cannot describe the enthusiasm I feel for it. (*Loud cheers.*)

PRESIDENT (*rising suddenly and looking savage but very old*): Gentlemen! I declare the session closed. We will meet again tomorrow. (*Shakily, but very rapidly, he leaves the room, leaving a wild buzz of astonishment and exclamation behind.*)

The MEMBERS *collect their papers and slowly file out.* MRS MALLET *remains behind, ostensibly to tidy the room, but in fact with an eye to* STAPLETON, *who is slouched in his chair looking lonely and miserable. When all the other members are gone,* MRS MALLET *comes over to him.*

MRS M.: All alone, Mr Stapleton?

STAPLETON: I must thank you very, very much for your kind defence.

MRS M.: Don't mention it, Mr Stapleton. (*laughs*) I know what an old Tartar he can be!

STAPLETON: I have never seen him like that before. I had thought that he was like our Great Theory—something sublime, beautiful and eternally true.

MRS M.: Sublime, beautifully and eternally true—no, Mr Stapleton: I don't think the President has ever had *those* qualities; they are not found very often in leaders of modern groups. (*she sighs hypocritically*) The trouble with the President is that he no longer has the vigour and authority that give members of a Club that safe, cosy feeling. (*Enter* BEAUFORT.) Beau, poor Mr Stapleton has been rather distressed by the President's behaviour today.

BEAUFORT (*getting the idea at once*): Oh, I shouldn't bother about that, Stapleton!

STAPLETON: But I *do* bother! It seems terrible!

BEAUFORT: The old boy was only being spiteful. Just old age. *We'll* be like that, one day.

MRS M.: Mr Stapleton had the feeling that the President was not doing his best for the Great Theory.

BEAUFORT: That's a serious charge! Going a bit far, aren't you?

STAPLETON (*anguishedly*): How can I explain what I feel to two people who never knew me before I joined the Club? Oh, Mrs Mallet—if you had only caught a glimpse of me in those days! I was no better than an animal! I had a good war-record: I was a first-class mechanic—but I just went through life from day to day, never suspecting for a moment that there was any point to it. Oddly enough, I can't remember any more who it was that advised me to join the Identity Club—all I *do* remember is how wonderful it was to wake up next morning in London and realize that my old dead self had disappeared for ever—that the Great Theory had taken possession of me, that life made sense for the first time. And I owe all that to *him*, Mrs Mallet—my transformer, my teacher, my saviour!

BEAUFORT (*shrugging*): Well, that's the way life is, you know!

MRS M.: Beau, I think you could be a *little more sympathetic!* If *you* looked on someone as your saviour and he called *you* a spaniel . . .

STAPLETON: Yes—his very word!

BEAUFORT: I should fight against my feelings of revenge—but they might well prove too strong for me.

MRS M.: At least Mr Stapleton can take comfort from the fact that everyone *else* in the Club regards him with affection and respect. Only this morning, the Captain was saying how wise you were for your years, Mr Stapleton. (*Enter* CAPTAIN MALLET.)

MRS M.: We are saying nice things about you.

CAPTAIN (*assuming a burdened air*): Ah! Ah! The number of problems in this house that I have to cope with . . .

STAPLETON: Can I do anything to help you, sir?

CAPTAIN: Just to know that you are prepared to do so, is help enough, my dear boy! . . . You look upset! Anything the matter? (STAPLETON *is silent.*)

MRS M. (*confidingly to the* CAPTAIN): He is

a little downcast at the way things went this morning. Rather *disappointed.*

CAPTAIN: I see. (*he comes up to* STAPLETON *in a firm, fatherly manner*) Mr Stapleton! Try and remember that when things go wrong in a Club like ours, we are all equally to blame. Perhaps we are all dreaming too much; perhaps we are not using our efforts to the full; perhaps, if we tried harder, we could serve our Great Theory better.

MRS M. (*understandingly*): Which is always *so* difficult if we have individual loyalties that distract us from our group duties.

CAPTAIN: That would be so in the case of a weak kind of man. But not in a man like Stapleton.

BEAUFORT: I agree. There's nothing weak about Stapleton.

MRS M.: I think you men ask too much of poor Mr Stapleton.

STAPLETON: They are right to do so, Mrs Mallet. From now on, I must act for the Club—and the Club alone . . . Thank you for this talk. I shall not forget it. (*He bows ceremoniously and exits, slowly.*)

BEAUFORT (*triumphantly*): I told you history got a move on if you kicked her in the pants!

MRS M. (*warningly*): Beaufort!

CAPTAIN: History is doing precisely that—to our great disadvantage. (*he takes out a letter*) Jellicoe's bank manager has written for the third time.

MRS M.: Don't tell me Jellicoe has overdrawn? I have been scrupulously careful with his cheques.

CAPTAIN: It's the *size* of the cheques that worries the manager. He insists that if the wretched man continues to spend capital at the rate of £300 a week, he and his sister will soon have nothing left.

MRS M.: Insolence! I defy anyone to run a house-party of forty people on less!

CAPTAIN: He says he will drop in for a little chat with Jellicoe in the next day or two.

BEAUFORT: Let him! Don't we know what to do with visitors?

CAPTAIN: Beaufort! In this Club, we do *not* transform bank managers. Society never misses an occasional doctor or nurse, but it detects instantly the disappearance of a single banker. . . . How is your work going?

BEAUFORT: Jellicoe's coming along nicely.

Even his ears are becoming those of a criminal type. . . . And by the way, Miss Tray is catching up on Towzer. He's almost admitted that he went to medical school.

MRS M. (*taking out her knitting*): Time seems to be getting short. (*she puts a hand on the* CAPTAIN'*s arm*) You go about *your* duties, dear. Beaufort and I will go about ours.

CAPTAIN: A talk with you two always does me good. You always know what is best for the Club. (*Exit.*)

BEAUFORT: So? What does it all add up to?

MRS M.: (*settling into the President's high chair*): History must hurry up. (*she counts her stitches*) We must be all finished before the bank manager comes.

BEAUFORT (*astonished*): Finished with the President! In twenty-four hours! How? I can't get Jellicoe ready in *that* time!

MRS M.: If I had only been told before the elevenses went up! Never mind! There are tonight's night-caps.

BEAUFORT: Night-caps!?

MRS M.: I can drift down this evening and help dear Florence with them. (*pause*) Beau! Will you be an absolute angel?

BEAUFORT: What?

MRS M.: Find Dr Towzer's black bag—and bring it to my bedroom. (*Curtain.*)

ACT III

SCENE 1

Next morning, in the Great Kitchen, just after breakfast. An ugly heap of unwashed breakfast things is on the table: MRS PARADISE *is sorting and stacking them. Enter* JELLICOE, *suffering from a shocking hangover, but managing to carry four messy trayfuls, one of which consists of an uneaten breakfast.*

JELLICOE (*groaning through the centre of his heaped burden*): Oh, Mrs Paradise! What you see in my hands only duplicates what I feel in my head!

MRS P.: Is that the lot, Mr Jellicoe?

JELLICOE: Could you ask for more?

MRS P. (*seeing the uneaten trayful*): Somebody hasn't eaten his breakfast! Not even *touched!* Now, I call that simply *criminal!*

JELLICOE (*sitting down and burying his face in his hands*): Oh! Scotland! Scotland! God may forgive you, but *man*—never!

MRS P. (*ignoring him*): Which gentleman left all that poached egg and *good* buttered toast?

JELLICOE (*shuddering*): Must you recite the menu? (*He winces and groans.*)

MRS P.: What are we going to do with it? (*indicating the uneaten breakfast*)

JELLICOE: If I am any judge of women, Mrs Paradise, you intend to offer it to *me*.

MRS P.: Well, where else can it go?

JELLICOE: Crush it up with Spiller's Shapes and put it in Towzer's bowl. Oh! Oh! Oh!

Enter L. MRS MALLET, *calm and composed, but showing the slight nervousness that any person is bound to feel when they want to find out if they have succeeded in poisoning somebody.* JELLICOE *comes fairly smartly to attention, but not smartly enough.*

MRS M.: Whatever is the matter, Jellicoe?

JELLICOE: I was resting my legs, madam.

MRS M. (*looking at him suspiciously*): Resting your legs at nine in the morning? (*looking sceptical, but turning briskly to* MRS PARADISE) Good morning, Florence! Breakfasts all done? What a good soldier you are!

MRS P.: Good morning, madam! You're early this morning.

MRS M. (*studying the crockery carefully*): Am I? . . . Oh, dear! Has someone not been able to eat his breakfast?

MRS P.: Such a waste, madam, isn't it? It makes me feel quite bitter against whoever it is.

MRS M. (*startled*): Whoever it is? Is there any doubt about that?

MRS P.: I don't know, madam. But never mind! People *do* sometimes feel they can't face breakfast.

JELLICOE (*feelingly*): Indeed they do, madam.

MRS M. (*looking sharply at* JELLICOE): But who?

MRS P.: Madam; is something worrying you?

MRS M. (*nervously*): I only want to know whose tray that is, Florence. It is not very much to ask. (*At this moment,* JELLICOE, *overcome by his hangover, sits down abruptly on his chair.*)

MRS P.: Mr Jellicoe brought it down, madam.

MRS M.: Who is it, Jellicoe?

JELLICOE: I beg your pardon, madam? My attention suddenly escaped me.

MRS M. (*suddenly rounding on him and letting all her own nervousness appear*): Jellicoe! Whose tray is that? Tell me immediately! (*His face becomes anguished, but he says nothing.*) What is the matter with you, Jellicoe? Ah! I think I can guess! Stand up! (*He obeys.*) Step forward! (*He does so.*) Breathe! (*He holds his hands to his sides, raises his head, his mouth closed tight, and inhales deeply through his nose.*) Not *that* way! The *other* way! (*His face anguished, his eyes closed,* JELLICOE *allows a faint breath to trickle from his nostrils.*) Drunkard! So that's what it is!

JELLICOE: Madam . . . !

MRS M. (*panting with genuine alarm*): Who left that breakfast?

JELLICOE: I . . . can't say for sure, madam.

MRS M.: Can't say what room it came from?

JELLICOE: No, madam.

MRS M. (*turning on her heel angrily to go out, then suddenly halting and turning back*): Jellicoe! Were you by any chance in this fuddled condition last night—when you took up the night-caps?

JELLICOE: But, madam, you were here when I took them up.

MRS M.: You don't need to remind *me*, Jellicoe, of where I was last night. Answer me! When you took up the night-caps, had you started drinking?

JELLICOE: I *had* opened the bottle, madam, and left it short of a drop or two.

MRS M.: So everyone probably got the wrong night-caps?

JELLICOE: Oh, madam, I do hope not!

MRS M. (*very sharply*): So do I, Jellicoe! (*She turns immediately on her heel and hurries from the kitchen. Her expression of horror is not feigned.*)

MRS P.: Oh, Mr Jellicoe! You've done it now!

JELLICOE (*listening at the foot of the stairs*): Oh, Lord! (*resumes his chair*) Oh, what a thing it is to have an evil past!

MRS P.: Come along, cheer up! Don't look so miserable! *I'll* defend you. I know you're not a drinker.

JELLICOE: It's very good of you, Mrs Paradise. But I'm afraid my whole past will contradict you . . . No, don't argue, please, Mrs Paradise! Let's face the facts and not escape into an imaginary world. I know my history. My character was shaped when I was in the cradle.

MRS P.: *In the cradle?*

JELLICOE: Or even slightly before . . . (*he throws out his arms*) *I am what I was*, Mrs Paradise—*that* is the verdict of modern science.

MRS P.: But who cares what you were or what you are, Mr Jellicoe? Isn't it what you *do* that matters? Do you *want* to feel that you have committed a dreadful crime?

JELLICOE (*in agony*): Will you never understand, Mrs Paradise? (*strikes his breast*) I am the crime! (*suddenly cocks his ear*) Oh, my God! Here comes the toast of the regiment with old butter-fingers! (*Enter* MISS TRAY *and* TOWZER *with baskets of vegetables.*)

MISS TRAY (*joyously*): Guess what! (*long pause*) He's learnt to say 'Good morning'!

JELLICOE (*sneeringly*): Why, bless my soul! By tomorrow, he'll be singing the Hallelujah Chorus!

MISS TRAY: Say good morning, Tow, and show the kind lady and gentleman. (TOWZER *coyly looks the other way and says nothing.*) Isn't that like him? He said it about twenty times last night.

JELLICOE: A proper little prophet.

MISS TRAY: Do you know what I've discovered? That when I press him and press him and nag him and nag him, I'm not really acting in *his* best interests. I am satisfying something deep inside myself.

MRS P.: Oh, don't say things like that, Miss Tray! It's believing things of that sort that's doing so much harm to poor Mr Jellicoe!

JELLICOE (*rather pleased by this*): That's quite true, Miss Tray. Don't stray into my pasture. There's only dandelions, dock and sorrel in it. And bitter nettles.

MISS TRAY: All I meant to say was: I am going to cut down on his therapy.

MRS P.: Will he like that?

MISS TRAY: Of course. It's like a treat. Without therapy he can just sink back into himself. (*sighs*) Whoever that may be . . . Do you think we would have time to play some little game with him? Something that would relax his tension, but at the same time make him feel that he shared the life of the whole community?

JELLICOE (*bitterly*): We could play Happy Families with him.

MISS TRAY (*delighted*): Mr Jellicoe! What a stroke of genius!

JELLICOE: It was intended as a harsh rebuff.

MRS P.: Miss Tray! Let me warn you! Mr Jellicoe is nothing but a wet blanket this morning.

JELLICOE: How tactfully you choose your similes, Mrs Paradise! But she is quite right, Miss Tray. I am not in a playful mood. (*he turns away*)

MRS P. (*to* MISS TRAY): Come along now, dear! We'll get the washing-up done and see if we can squeeze in just half an hour. What about the cards? There are heaps in the old nursery.

MISS TRAY: Oh, you are a pet, dear Mrs Paradise!

MRS P.: Well, I like to see a woman struggle. (MISS TRAY *embraces* MRS PARADISE. *At that moment footsteps clatter down* L. *stairs and* BEAUFORT *enters at speed, crossing furiously over to* JELLICOE.)

BEAUFORT: Well! *You've done it now!* Fuddled, bungling idiot—a nice way you've repaid me! If Father sinks his teeth into your flesh, don't ask me to pull him off! (*Exit* L. *as rapidly as he came.*)

JELLICOE (*hurrying to the foot of the stairs*): Master Beau! Master Beau! What have I done?

But there is only the sound of BEAUFORT'S *footsteps clattering up the stairs and the sudden notes of a bell.* JELLICOE *now being off* L. *and the two women and* TOWZER *having moved off* R., *the curtain rises on the main stage.*

SCENE 2

The empty conference room. Enter from R. CAPTAIN *and* MRS MALLET, *talking rapidly. The* CAPTAIN *holds a hand-bell by the clapper.*

CAPTAIN: . . . No, no . . . nothing like that! Just stand by quietly and say something about a temporary indisposition. You can break the real news later.

MRS M.: When?

CAPTAIN: When I give you a sign.

MRS M.: What about the servants?

CAPTAIN: Lock the bedroom door, my dear!

MRS M.: It hasn't got a key!

CAPTAIN: Then tell the servants to leave the rooms until this afternoon. Say we won't be in for lunch. Say we're going to a picnic at a ruined abbey. (*Exit* MRS MALLET *L. as* BEAUFORT *enters.*)

BEAUFORT: I could break that Jellicoe's neck!

CAPTAIN: My dear boy, whatever you do, don't break *that!* History may have to fall back on it. (*He rings the bell loudly.*) The cars are all in good running order, I hope?

BEAUFORT: Absolutely! When do we go?

CAPTAIN (*grimly*): When it is time to go.

He rings his bell. MEMBERS *begin to pour in and take their seats—with the greatest possible criss-crossing and fuss so that the audience cannot check too easily on who's there.* MRS MALLET *is the last ordinary member to enter and take her seat. Finally, all are seated—but the* PRESIDENT'S *chair remains prominently empty. All at once, just when members are getting uneasy, and looking towards the door, the* PRESIDENT, *lively as a cricket, sweeps in from R. and mounts his dais.*

PRESIDENT (*beaming, briskly rubbing his hands*): Good morning, ladies and gentlemen! I hope you have all slept peacefully. I hope you are in better tempers. Let me say at once: this is going to be a dull, quiet day. No child's bomb will threaten to carry us from the cradle to the grave. This may be a sharp disappointment to some of you, but I am confident our dear, respected lady . . . (*Breaks off and stares round the room with a puzzled frown.*) Well, well, well! Where is our sacred grove, our rock of ages, our collective unconscious?

Only now, if possible, should the audience realize that the uneaten breakfast was that of MISS PLANORBIS.

MRS M. (*smiling, but pale and rather tense*): Miss Planorbis has asked me to convey her apologies, Mr President. She is not quite feeling her usual self. . . .

PRESIDENT: After yesterday's detonation, it is a wonder that she feels anything. Is there a doctor in the Club?

MRS M. (*hastily*): Miss Planorbis asked me particularly to say, Mr President, that she has no desire to see a doctor.

PRESIDENT: Why, at the age of eighty-five, this sudden stroke of cynicism?

MRS M.: She hopes to come down later.

PRESIDENT: We must see she does. This will be the first case-history she has missed since Cain and Abel. I don't like it . . . I don't like it at all. (*he is in a very ugly mood and his eyes dart this way and that bitterly and suspiciously*) You have changed your seat, Mr Stapleton! Why?

STAPLETON (*who is sitting behind* BEAUFORT *and* MRS MALLET): I . . . I . . . I . . .

PRESIDENT: Never mind your I, Mr Stapleton! We know who you are. Or does the change in your seat express a change in your identity?

STAPLETON (*nervously but bravely*): It is to show, sir, that I am not a spaniel.

PRESIDENT (*scornfully*): Ah! That you have become a retriever—to another game-keeper? (*The* CAPTAIN *immediately begins to rise to his feet.*) Not now, Mallet! We have business to do.

CAPTAIN: I feel it my duty to protest, sir . . . (*Applause.*)

DR BITT.: I, too, protest! (*Murmurs of agreement.*)

CAPTAIN: As today may be a *little* difficult, I think members should be warned to act as calmly as possible . . . Mr President, there is a chance that we shall have a visitor. (*Excited murmurs.*)

PRESIDENT: Ah hah! Didn't I say that would happen? When this jaunt to the country was proposed, did I not object that we should have visitors?

CAPTAIN: I still think, Mr President, that the Club is strong enough to deal with a casual guest.

PRESIDENT: Bitterling can mow him down with hand-grenades. Who is the victim?

CAPTAIN: The local bank manager, sir. He is worried about the money that is being spent on this conference. (*Hearty laughter from all the* MEMBERS.) I have no desire to excite any feelings of insecurity in the Club. . . .

PRESIDENT: I am sorry that desire was not present when you did so. (*There are murmurs from* MEMBERS, *but the* PRESIDENT *continues briskly.*) Today's history, entitled 'Multiple Confessions of a Singular Identity' is being presented by Father Golden Orfe. It will be a solo performance, with our good Father playing all his many parts himself. Personally, I am not averse to a brilliant solo. After yesterday's degrading, collective pandemonium . . .

DR BITT. (*shouting*): Mr President! I can tolerate no more! All yesterday, I was insulted! Today began with another handful of mud . . . (*Applause from his clique*.) . . . Now, a fresh flood of Billingsgate ushers in a Lambeth Conference!

CAPTAIN: I am in duty bound, Mr President, to suggest that any further attack on Bitterling will be a reflection on the Presidential Chair. (*Loud applause*.) I hope I may be allowed to add that the nervousness felt this morning by our great founder's daughter is due more to a feeling of—well, shall I say, general insecurity?—than to any shock she may have suffered.

PRESIDENT: Mallet! What are you up to? Are you trying to pin Miss P. on me?

MRS M. (*taking the* CAPTAIN's *cue immediately*): I had not wished to say so before, but during breakfast Miss Planorbis did murmur something about feeling despised and unwanted. . . .

BEAUFORT: Shame! (*Cries of 'Shame'*.)

DR SCAV.: Mallet is absolutely right! The whole Club is being swept by nervousness and instability! General bickering and alarm! Where is it going to end?

CAPTAIN (*very coldly*): If we all try, I am sure we will come to a satisfactory conclusion.

FATHER GOLDEN ORFE, *a whisky-priest wearing a robe, a biretta and dark glasses, now speaks in a clear, harsh voice.*

ORFE: As priest to this Club, I do my best not to join in quarrels. But if I am not allowed to deliver my case-history pretty soon, I am going to turn *very* ugly. (*he takes out his flask and swigs*)

PRESIDENT: I stand firmly behind the Church Militant! What of a bank manager? Can we not proceed with God, and still keep a sharp look-out for Mammon? . . . Gentlemen! When I joined this Club some forty years ago, we had two clergymen in it. They were tall, grave, reverend gentlemen, with large private incomes. Their movements were assured and stately, and once they entered a pulpit—as they often did—one could be sure that most of a long

morning would pass before they called it a day. How times have changed! Where are the incomes and the sermons now? Cut to nothing! And the modern priest—what is *he* now but a poor dirty persecuted blasphemer, desperately pursuing God through the hotter latitudes and the deeper sewers! Indeed, so incomprehensible are the ways of today's divine that he alone is able to explain them. . . . Father Golden Orfe . . . ! (*Applause. Putting his bottle away,* FATHER ORFE *moves to the centre of the stage, pauses, then suddenly cries out, loudly and dramatically.*)

ORFE: I stink: therefore, I am. (*This superb and unexpected opening causes the whole Club to break into spontaneous applause. There are cries of 'Bravo!' 'Bis! Bis!' to which* ORFE *responds with the dignified bows of a great pianist. He then starts off again.*) I stink . . .

PRESIDENT: Stop that, Orfe! No encores until the end! (*Cries of 'Shame! shame!' from* ORFE's *supporters.*)

ORFE (*bowing ceremoniously to the* PRESIDENT *and resuming*): This is my text today, dearly beloved! Is it not the most up-to-date text imaginable? Do your guilty hearts not respond to it immediately? Moreover, to talk about guilt means to talk about oneself, and I for one cannot think of any subject that lies closer to my heart. Moreover, while *I* am talking, *you* are going to have to forget yourselves and concentrate on me. How healthy for *you*! How delightful for *me*!

You see in me a great sinner. He is clinging to the Cross. Nearly all great sinners nowadays cling to the Cross. We hope that if the Cross could speak, it would say: 'This supports me more than it supports you.' But, so far, it hasn't said a word.

There was a time when people reached the Cross by behaving as decently as possible. But, nowadays, we get to Golgotha rather differently. First, we behave as *badly* as possible. Then we rush to the Cross and throw our arms round it. We call this 'making retribution'. I myself have been making retribution for many years now, but I still remember the first time I made it. 'Excuse me just a moment,' I said, 'but I *must* make retribution.' 'You can't make it here,' they said. 'You'll have to wait till we get home.' 'I'm sorry,' I said, 'but I simply have to make it now.' 'Then for Heaven's sake,' they said, 'make it as inconspicuously as possible.'

Inconspicuously indeed! Nowadays, an honest-to-God sinner has two aims. The first is to make of himself a candle that will never be put out. The second is to make retribution by confessing—by stripping himself down to the last G-string and then getting a publisher to print it. What a far cry it all is from the olden days, when a sinner compressed his sins into a few words and was told: 'Go, thou, and sin no more.' Nowadays, we don't want our shrift to be quite as short as that! Indeed, we regard absolution as rather a threat to our identities—*who would we be*, if we were to let ourselves be absolved? No, we sinners think it much better to avoid absolution and pray for God's grace instead. Dear Grace! I always think of her as an extremely patient woman, with a kind but rather tired face. (*takes a swig*) We hope her patience will never snap.

I haven't always been an alcoholic. I had a much bigger and better sin on my conscience some years ago: I was a spy, a secret agent. It's not a job you can return to, once you have confessed it, so, in order still to need grace, I took to alcohol instead. Soon I shall write my alcoholic confessions —and take up a third vice. I wonder what it will be? Already I imagine myself walking down the street with the anguish of the new vice written all over my face . . . (*does a demonstrative walk*) I can hear the whispers of the passers-by: 'What's up with Orfe?' 'Don't you know? He's become so-and-so. Goes through absolute Hell.' 'Yes, I can see that by his face. I'm told he's praying like anything for grace.'

I have laid some stress upon my face. There are two reasons for this. The first is that I am extremely attached to it. The second is that if one handles one's face properly, one can make it confess volumes. Let me tell you how I made mine.

The turning point in my life came when my father said: 'Children! I have a surprise! I'm going to take all you little bastards to the circus!' My brothers and my sisters shrieked with joy—and so did I. Or rather, I tried to shriek, but I was a greedy little boy and had just stuffed my mouth with potatoes. Only a sibilant, purring sound came from my lips—like the exhaust of an expensive car. My father was very hurt by my silence—but my mother drew her serviette across my mouth and said, 'Deep down inside, he's terribly excited!' 'So that's it?' said my father. 'He keeps his thoughts in the back of his mind, does he?' He turned his chair round and studied me very closely. How well I remember the thrill of this, my first scrutiny! It had never occurred to me until that moment that the human mind *had* a back; but once this had been pointed out to me, as the place where admiration is found, I began to stuff things into it at once.

By adolescence, I had nothing in the *front* of my mind except my face. And nobody could look at a face like mine without wondering what was going on at the *back*.

Most of you put the cart before the horse in the matter of faces. You think, for instance, that a Lord Chief Justice has that extraordinary expression on his face as the result of being a Lord Chief Justice. It's just the other way round! He made that revolting face for himself when he was quite a boy, and then slowly worked himself up into the only position that could do it justice. In the same way, *my* face was a secret agent's face long before I became one. When my friends used to say: 'Come to the Palais and shake a leg with the girls!' I used to shake my head—but in such a mysterious way as to suggest that I had some deep, secret understanding of the Palais and the girls: rather like the mysterious communion I have nowadays with God and Grace. But from time to time, to confuse them more, I would exclaim: 'To the Palais? Certainly! A whirl with the girls is just what I had—*in the back of my mind!*' Let me just show you what a young man with his mind at the back looks like, dancing at the Palais and making a profound impression of mystery upon his partner. . . . (ORFE *does an effective demonstration, followed by applause from the Club; after which he takes a long pull from his flask and slowly begins to work himself into the state of hysterical drunkenness in which his history concludes.*)

I shall not take up your time by describing my life as a secret agent. You have already read my agonized account of all the crimes I committed in that extremely long and very popular confession I published a few years ago—the book that was the Easter Week Selection of The Religious Book Club. If you missed the book, no doubt you saw the dramatized version that came to the Hippodrome a year later—or if you missed the play too, you probably saw the movie that was made from it—the one that's on the telly this week, the one on which the opera will be based. . . . Mind you, I wouldn't *mind* describing these crimes to you all over again—on the contrary, I should get a fresh gush of pleasure from it—but I'm not going to because the truth is that the exact nature of the crime isn't nearly as thrilling as the feelings of guilt and the longing for grace that *follow* the crime—if you know how to play your cards. It so happened that *I* reached the Cross by sending people to Siberia and betraying my nearest and dearest: but you can choose the way that suits your temperament best. You can work yourself up into a most ghastly state of remorse, which *everyone* will notice, simply by not loving your dog enough, or taking full responsibility for myxomatosis.

'I stink—therefore, I am!' Oh, brethren, brethren, if we could not feel ourselves to be the vilest of sinners—where would we be, *who* would we be? (*shouting*) I am the guilty shepherd! You ask me: 'How shall I find salvation?' I answer: 'Only through ignominy!' With a sin in the left hand and a prayer in the right (*mimics a two-gun man*) yee-ow—*mea culpa*; yee-ow—*mea culpa!* Is your soul tranquil? Let me mortify it! Have you a wound? Let me rub salt in it! Is the world full of sorrow? Let me make *you* responsible! Let me roll you in remorse and wrap you in anguish, until you cease to be man or woman and become a trembling skin of helpless indignity! Here is my prayer—take it as your own! (*He drops on his knees.*)

'I am a sanctimonious sot, guilty of all crimes whether I committed them or not. Pour down upon me every morning your chastising hangovers, that I may continue to earn them every night. Assure me daily

that I am of all worms the wormiest, of all slime the slimiest. Bury me not when I die, for rotting is too good for me. Nail me, still living, to a large cross in a busy, public place, and let my agony be so pronounced that I shall attract in death as much admiration as I received in life. And write in large letters above my head: (*He stands and extends himself as on a cross.*) HERE HANGS A SELF-MADE PARASITE! SELF-CONSCIOUS TO THE LAST!

Two MEMBERS *spring forward and catch the intoxicated* ORFE, *who collapses into their arms and is dragged to a back seat, where his collar is opened and he is fanned with his own script.* MEMBERS *are much too awed to applaud or even speak: they let out gasps, clear their throats, mop their brows; even the* PRESIDENT *looks nervous and upset. A clock strikes a few times; on the last note a shrill, penetrating scream comes from upstairs.* MEMBERS *spring to their feet aghast: there is the sound of feet clattering downstairs, and* MRS MALLET *enters from R.*

PRESIDENT (*in a high, cracked voice*): Well! What is it?

MRS M. (*controlled, grim and accusing*): Mr President! It is my sad duty to inform the Club . . .

PRESIDENT: Spit it out, you gloomy witch!

MRS M.: Our great founder's daughter is dead in her bed!

PRESIDENT: *What!* Under *my* presidency? (*Shouts and consternation.*)

DR BITT.: *Your* presidency! What does *your* presidency matter? Our last link with the past—smashed; our very roots—torn up! Yes! *You've* done it now!

PRESIDENT: I refuse responsibility for this!

DR SCAV.: Is there anything you accept it *for*? 'I refuse responsibility!' *Nice* words to hear from the man in authority!

CAPTAIN: Gentlemen! We must judge this matter calmly!

DR BITT.: Judge it! Yes! We'll judge it!

CAPTAIN: In an orderly way. A motion.

PRESIDENT: A motion! By our rules, gentlemen, let me remind you, all motions must be put from this chair!

DR SCAV.: Then put it! (*Shouts of 'Put it!' 'Go on! Put it!'*)

STAPLETON (*torn and anxious*): Perhaps we should all feel better if the President made an apology and resigned. . . .

PRESIDENT: Mr Stapleton, let me say, even if it is with my last breath, that death is as nothing compared with the humiliation of being defended by you!

CAPTAIN: I am afraid that Mr Stapleton cannot let *that* insult pass.

MRS M. (*taking her cue as usual*): He will not dream of doing so! It is a wicked, shameless attack on his highest ideals—his very identity.

PRESIDENT: His identity, indeed! Who made his identity? A little cat's-paw came crawling to my feet one night with a greasy coat and a fur collar! Who was he *then*? What did he *say*? (BEAUFORT *offers* STAPLETON *a pistol.* STAPLETON, *blazing with anger, snatches the pistol and points it at the* PRESIDENT, *who is looking straight at the* CAPTAIN *and mimicking* LOLLY's *old voice*) 'The Captain sent me to the President!' Now, I see *why!*

STAPLETON *pulls the trigger: the* PRESIDENT *spins and falls. Shouts and clamour from the Club.* STAPLETON *drops into his chair, letting the pistol fall:* BEAUFORT *snatches it up. The Club* MEMBERS, *overcome with panic at the sight of their dead* PRESIDENT, *begin hustling towards the exit L., squeaking and exclaiming as they go. But* BEAUFORT *has reached the door first and the hurrying* MEMBERS *are brought up short by his pistol. Instantly, their clamour stops: they stand in total silence, staring at the weapon.*

Behind them, CAPTAIN MALLET *has mounted the dais and stands in front of the Presidential chair. He utters one word in a low but penetrating voice, filling it with a tone of rising rebuke, as if amazed by the spectacle he sees.*

CAPTAIN: Gentle-men! (*With one accord, every head switches round to face the* CAPTAIN.) Is panic your reply to destiny? (*They shuffle and look ashamed.*) Is your faith in the Great Theory so weak that you cannot accept a plain fact? (*He points to the* PRESIDENT's *corpse. Then he continues in a firm, controlled voice.*) Gentlemen! History has acted! There lies the shell of yes-terday, a thing of qualms and squeamishness, unfit to breathe the air of modern bigotry! Time, place and circumstance have conspired to rub him out! His identity, chosen and fixed, was Presidential: when he could sustain it no longer, merciful time and kindly history—changed it for ever. (MRS MALLET *presses a handkerchief to her eyes: other* MEMBERS *promptly follow suit.*) Gentlemen! We weep for the past, but our eyes turn towards tomorrow. Our Great Theory stands as always, uninjured, undismayed. We have only to think of it—and our tears dry up; we face the future with a new exhilaration. (BEAUFORT *and* MRS MALLET *begin to clap; the* MEMBERS *join in, but none too happily.*) History has replaced what it has taken away. Yesterday, your Captain; today, I am your President. Follow me into the glorious dogma of tomorrow, when all the world will know but one theory, the one true theory—*The Great Theory of Identity!* (*Prolonged applause.*) Gentlemen! In one hour, we return to London. Go to your rooms, and pack! (*The* MEMBERS *begin to hurry out, but* DR SCAVENGER *halts and addresses the* CAPTAIN *in a small, fearful voice.*)

DR SCAV.: Mr President! May I ask just a small question?

CAPTAIN (*in a purring voice*): Why not, my good Scavenger?

DR SCAV.: What are we going to do with . . . ah . . . with . . . the two victims of history?

CAPTAIN: Dr Scavenger! Master-thinkers must not look back. They must leave their debris in the hands of others. We who are *up*-stairs, gentlemen, must hand over the dead past to those who are *downstairs*. I refer to our domestic staff, who are well equipped to take full responsibility for our fallen idols. I repeat, gentlemen: go to your rooms and pack: by the time we leave here, the past will be where it belongs. (*Curtain.*)

SCENE 3

The Great Kitchen, half an hour later. A game of Happy Families is in progress, all four servants participating: MISS TRAY *kibitzing for* TOWZER.

MRS P.: It isn't your past I'm quarrelling with, Mr Jellicoe—not that I would have chosen it for myself. What annoys me is the selfish way you use it . . . Miss Tray, *may* I please have Miss Drill the Dentist's Daughter?

JELLICOE: Of course it's selfish! I *am* selfish.

MISS TRAY: Sorry, not at home!

MRS P.: And it's not even *polite*.

JELLICOE: How could it be? To be polite would be not to be me. . . . May I add, Mrs Paradise, that I like you very much better when you are indignant with me? It makes me feel that I carry more weight.

MISS TRAY (*bending over* TOWZER's *cards*): Mrs Paradise, Mr Towzer says: can he have Mrs Lynch the Lawyer's Wife?

JELLICOE: It's not his turn, lovebird. It's yours.

MISS TRAY: Oh, dear: that's the trouble with psycho-therapy! You never know whether you're playing your own hand or the patient's . . . Mr Jellicoe! May *I* have Master Voice the Vicar's Son?

JELLICOE: Let me see now . . . Where is little Master *Vice* the Vicar's Son . . . ?

MRS P.: And it only spoils the game, Mr Jellicoe, to give sordid names to Happy Families.

JELLICOE: Sorry, Miss Tray, young Vice is not at home! . . . Mr Towzer! Would you kindly oblige me with Mrs Rust the Surgeon's Wife?

MISS TRAY (*bending over* TOWZER's *hand*): We know what he *really* means, don't we, Tow? We're *very, very* clever, aren't we? Now, *have* we got Mrs Drug the Doctor's Wife? No? Well, I quite agree. Mr Jellicoe, Mr Towzer says: Sorry, not at home.

JELLICOE: Miss Tray, I'm sure Mr Towzer is the soul of honesty, but can he *see*? If *he's* not holding Mrs Drug, who is?

MRS P.: He looks very pale this morning. I doubt if he can *really* tell the identities on his cards. Dear me! What *is* he doing now? (TOWZER *rises suddenly, moistening his lips, and sharply folding up his cards.*)

MISS TRAY: Oh, Lord! Don't say a word, Mrs Paradise! I can see Mrs Drug on the floor . . . she must have slipped through his fingers . . . Sit down, Tow! Nearly over, dear! (TOWZER, *trembling, is slowly reseating himself, when* MRS MALLET *enters from L., dressed in a travelling suit, with handbag, and pulling on her gloves.* JELLICOE *rises to his feet with bent head.*)

MRS M.: We're just slipping off for our picnic, Florence. . . . Jellicoe! The Captain would like a word with you.

JELLICOE (*anxiously*): Er . . . When he comes back, madam?

MRS M. (*very clearly and firmly*): No, Jellicoe. Before he goes. Now. (JELLICOE *hesitates, then exit L.*) You can do the rooms now, Florence. We won't be in your way.

MRS P.: What time will you be coming back, madam?

MRS M. (*going to the window*): If the day goes on as brightly as it has begun, Florence, we shan't be in a hurry. (*There is the sound of cars being brought to the front of the house.*) And how are *you* managing, Miss Tray? The doctor tells me that Mr Towzer is coming on very well.

MISS TRAY: The trouble is that each time he comes forward, the next moment he slips half-way back.

MRS M.: Women find that with even the healthiest men, Miss Tray. So, don't let it discourage you. He will probably surrender quite suddenly.

MRS P.: Madam! I hope the Captain won't be *too* hard on poor Mr Jellicoe. He is so ashamed.

MRS M.: He has reason to be, Florence.

MRS P.: I never saw him the worse for drink before, madam.

MRS M.: It's not the drinking so much, Florence; it's the dreadful things he *does* when he's drunk.

MRS P.: I don't know about them, madam.

MRS M.: But *we* do—upstairs. (BEAUFORT's *voice on the stairs shouts: 'Come on!' 'Ready!'*) Well, I must be off.

MRS P.: You'll ask the Captain to be lenient, won't you, madam? Just drop a word in his ear.

MRS M. (*shrugging*): He'd only think it was poison, Florence. (*Exit* MRS MALLET *by L. stair.*)

MRS P. (*sighing*): Oh! If only my husband were alive! He used to twist the Captain round his little finger. (*A silence. Then the sound of cars driving away.*) Doesn't it seem *funny* to be all alone? Listen! Silent as the grave! (MISS TRAY *suddenly begins to cry.*) Now, whatever is the matter!

MISS TRAY (*sobbing*): It's easy to say—don't

be discouraged. But I *am* discouraged! I'm not going to try *any* more. If he wants to stay like this, he can! (*to* TOWZER) I'm never going to speak to you again! You don't help. You don't *want* to help. I've *finished* with you! (*Enter* JELLICOE, *a crushed man.*)

JELLICOE: Well, my goose is cooked! (*angrily to* MRS PARADISE) Why didn't you believe me when I told you the truth?

MRS P.: Oh, Mr Jellicoe! Have you got the sack?

JELLICOE: The *sack*? Who cares about the sack? Oh, Mrs Paradise, there are times when I'd like to take a hammer and *beat* some sense into your innocent head!

MRS P. (*horrified*): Mr Jellicoe! (JELLICOE *goes to a corner and sits down, staring at his feet.* MISS TRAY *has a fresh burst of tears:* MRS PARADISE's *face begins to work: she, too, starts to sob.*) Whatever is the matter with you all? It always used to be so happy here! (TOWZER, *alarmed and distressed, lays a timid hand on* MISS TRAY's *shoulder.*)

MISS TRAY: No, go away! I don't love you *any* more!

JELLICOE: You'd better all go away—before the police come and march me off! Unless I use this. (*produces* BEAUFORT's *pistol*)

MRS P. (*screaming*): Mr Jellicoe! Who gave you that?

JELLICOE: Nobody *gave* it to me. It was just picked up where I had left it and politely returned to me.

MRS P.: But it may be loaded!

JELLICOE: Apparently it was—when I last used it.

There is an aghast silence: suddenly TOWZER *rises to his feet, takes a glass from the sink, fills it with water and presses it on* MISS TRAY *with a trembling hand. She is astonished: her mouth drops open and* TOWZER *gravely thrusts an old pencil into it, like a thermometer. Then, drawing back his right cuff, he puts his fingers delicately on her wrist and listens to her pulse with a faraway look. After a pause,* MISS TRAY *explodes, shooting the pencil across the table.*

MISS TRAY (*shouting*): A doctor! Are you a doctor? (*He turns his back.*) Are you? Are you?

Knocking is heard on an outside door. Then footsteps off L. *and suddenly a deep voice, saying 'Is anyone at home?' There is a stupefied silence. Enter* BANK MANAGER.

BANK MANAGER (*to* MRS PARADISE *and* JELLICOE): So *here* you are! . . . *What* a chase! I tried the lodge—nothing doing—then I was just despairing when I saw a plume of smoke.

MRS P. (*puzzled*): You saw a plume of smoke . . . ?

MANAGER: 'Why, that's coming from the chimneys of the big house,' I said to myself! They can't be there; but worth trying . . . (*to* MISS TRAY) Of course. You, too, Miss Stephenson! Excuse me; for a moment I didn't know who you were.

JELLICOE (*stepping forward*): You have come for me, sir. I am ready to confess.

MANAGER: Oh, come, come! All I want is just a word or two with *both* of you, in private.

JELLICOE: *She* has nothing to do with this. I acted entirely alone.

MANAGER: Oh, I do hope not! Nothing is more damaging to a joint account.

MRS P.: Joint account!

TOWZER (*in a low, strong, surly voice*): Nurse!

MISS TRAY (*in a tiny voice, bowing her head*): Yes—doctor?

TOWZER (*fingering his beard*): What is *this*?

MISS TRAY: I can't imagine, doctor!

TOWZER: Give me a mirror! (*With faltering step,* MISS TRAY *unhooks one from the wall, hands it to* TOWZER *and turns her face away in terror. Looking at himself in the glass*) Outrageous! Nurse!

MISS TRAY: Yes, Dr Towzer?

TOWZER: Who is responsible for this? Take it off immediately! (MISS TRAY *takes his beard in both hands and tries to pull it off.*) Not like that, idiot! Look and see—is it stuck on, or is it hooked? . . . Oh, go away! Such a fool! Why are you dressed for hunting?

MISS TRAY (*bursting into tears*): I can't imagine!

MRS P. (*indignantly*): Well, isn't that a nice reward! (*to* TOWZER) No one will ever give *you* therapy again!

TOWZER (*sharply*): I know you, sir. You are Stourbridge? From Pritchard's Bank?

MANAGER: I am.

TOWZER: Then will you explain *what* I am doing here, *where* I am, and *who* is responsible?

MANAGER: This is the kitchen of the big house.

TOWZER: I came here to attend the lady of the house. That is correct, nurse?

MISS TRAY (*sobbing*): You may have come, but you weren't here.

TOWZER: You are not at your cleverest, today, Miss Stephenson.

JELLICOE (*advancing and addressing the* MANAGER): May I interrupt this nonsense? Neither he nor she, sir, is right in the head. I am. I ask to be taken to the police station immediately.

MRS P.: Oh, Mr Jellicoe! At it again! Don't believe a word he says, sir! He's as innocent as a child!

JELLICOE (*furious*): Call me innocent in front of a stranger, and I'll break your insolent neck! (*pulls out pistol and waves it*)

TOWZER: Who is this howling neurotic?

JELLICOE (*with hauteur*): I was a great criminal when you, sir, were still a bearded mute.

MANAGER (*rising*): Miss Paradise! I had come to discuss your money, but I think your brother is right. This is a matter for the police. (*he looks anxiously at the pistol*)

MRS P.: My *brother*?

JELLICOE (*waving pistol*): To kill my father! For years it was only a dream! But—*I've done it now!*

TOWZER (*remorselessly*): Nurse!

MISS TRAY: Oh, Dr Towzer! Please! Please! Don't ask me questions!

TOWZER: I was at surgery this morning. I came to this house. There is a sick woman in bed upstairs.

MRS P. (*angrily to* TOWZER): How do *you* know who's in bed upstairs. You were never allowed up there!

TOWZER (*ignoring* MRS PARADISE): I sat beside her bed. There was a violin—and a crazy old man who kept dancing round me.

JELLICOE: Well, I don't know about the violin, but *I've* taken care of the dancer! (*he laughs harshly*)

TOWZER: I remember the woman saying: 'Something is being fired through the middle of me, like hard machine-gun bullets.'

JELLICOE: Rubbish! I *loved* my mother.

MANAGER (*gingerly picking up the pistol in a handkerchief*): Excuse me interrupting, but does anyone want to come with me? My car is just outside.

MISS TRAY (*hysterically*): Oh no, it isn't! You only think it is! That's how the trouble begins!

TOWZER: Nurse! Come upstairs with me at once! (*Exit R. followed by* MISS TRAY, *sobbing.*

The other three remain below for a moment, then follow them upstairs. The curtain rises to reveal the breakfast room, where the bodies of the PRESIDENT *and* MISS PLANORBIS *are laid out, their hands folded on their chests. Beside* MISS PLANORBIS, *who is on the couch where* MRS MALLET *lay in Act I, and partly covered by the same eiderdown,* DR TOWZER's *black bag stands prominently. Beside it is an empty medicine glass.* TOWZER *hurries straight to the body, feels* MISS PLANORBIS's *pulse, sniffs the glass, then stands erect, horror on his face.*

TOWZER: What is this? What have I done?

MISS TRAY: I can't *imagine!*

MRS P. (*coming to herself with growing fury*): But I can! Oh, now I remember—this is the room where it all began. (*turns furiously on* JELLICOE) You! You! Thief! Traitor! Criminal! May you hang by the neck! Oh, my capital, my capital! (*Exit L. at top speed, screaming: 'Police! Police!' 'My capital!'*)

JELLICOE (*walking towards the footlights and thankfully raising both hands to heaven*): The Lord be praised! She has come to her senses at last! (*Curtain.*)

THE MAN AND THE FLY

José Ruibal

TRANSLATED BY
Jean Zelonis

CHARACTERS
(In order of appearance)

THE MAN
THE DOUBLE
ANGELS
DEVILS
VOICES

ACT I
THE COURAGE TRANSPLANT

SCENE 1

THE MAN *and* THE DOUBLE *live in an enormous crystal dome, which has a small unfinished section. It is constructed of glass panels decorated with battle scenes; trophies of hunting, fishing, and war; apparitions; unearthly visions, painted like Gothic stained-glass windows. The dome rests on a base of skulls.*

The dome, constructed piece by piece by THE MAN, *is situated in a strategic location. It is a formidable observatory from which the surrounding territory can be scrutinized.*

Inside is a rococo desk, piled with papers, and a rococo armchair. In another part is a circus trapeze, a horse, hoops, tightropes, barbed wire, and a pile of sand. There is a powerful electronic telescope for seeing distant areas.

THE MAN *is very old, his face weathered and tough.* THE DOUBLE, *seventy years younger, is physically identical to* THE MAN, *but his pallid face reflects the fact that he has been nurtured in a greenhouse.* THE DOUBLE *is hanging by his feet from the trapeze, reading a highly technical article on warfare.* THE MAN, *seated in the armchair, throws a little water and sand at* THE DOUBLE, *whose reading is heard before the curtain rises.*

THE MAN: Enough! Don't read me any more. Those idiots say that we're a bunch of cowards and that we're hiding. They've made a game out of war. In the old days, some trotting horses and a few swords whistling through the air were enough to make a war and to fill a nation with heroes and widows. But now war costs more than a high-class mistress. Valor, the nation, and patriotic fervor aren't enough any more. You have to have huge industrial complexes. That's really the limit! Now only the enormously wealthy countries can have the pleasure of fighting. Warfare has become a sport of the powerful—like golf.

It was something else in the old days. The colonial wars, all cheaply run, served as laboratories for courage. I toughened my-

self up on them. Thanks to them, I look like a hero, besides being one, with a face like parchment fried by the sun. I am what you might call a product manufactured by the fury of the elements. You, on the other hand, are a hothouse plant. No matter how much sand I throw in your eyes, you'll have a hard time ever getting my scorched eyelashes. No matter how many whippings I give you, you'll never have my elephant skin. I was beat to a pulp by people who really hated me, but I, on the other hand, I love you. (*Whips him brutally.*) Enough of that, let's measure ourselves. (*They measure themselves against each other.*) Wonderful! You've grown sufficiently. Now we're the same height. That's one problem less. Now we must attack the face, mature that baby face.

THE DOUBLE: Sir, I don't know if I can . . .

THE MAN: You can. I want it, and that's enough. It just happens that you're seventy years younger than I am.

THE DOUBLE: Forgive me.

THE MAN: I've chosen you from among the flock of mortals to succeed me because you are somewhat younger. You were somewhat shorter than I, but we've taken care of that by stretching you.

THE DOUBLE (*almost crying*): But I don't have your wrinkles or burns in my face.

THE MAN: And you're crying about that? (*Goes toward him.*) In one way you're like me. You don't have my wrinkles, but you have room for them. We'll fix up the rest in there, in the laboratory of courage. (*Points to the gymnastics area.*) You'll be perfect as my successor. (*Shoots him in the face. It bleeds.*) Hurrah! Now your face is burned and you'll have a scar exactly like mine.

THE DOUBLE (*hugs his legs*): Oh, thank you, sir!

THE MAN: So that it's an exact copy of my scar, you should put a spider web on it. It'll stop the bleeding.

THE DOUBLE: I'll look for a really fat spider.

THE MAN: It'll be an original and a cheap cure . . . because for the present, spider webs aren't made by the Yankees . . . (THE DOUBLE *exits in search of the cure.*) I'll make him the image of myself. When I decide to die, I'll be able to do it peacefully and no one will notice the slightest change. That'll be the crowning point of my career. (*Points to the unfinished part of the dome.*) All that's needed is that top piece. And nobody will know anything. What a neat little trick I'll be playing on history! I've been very careful to keep the existence of my double a secret. At one time he was page at the Rothschild Bank, but who's going to remember a page? He doesn't exist as himself anymore, but only as the wax in which I'm molding my physical and even my spiritual self. The day when I can infuse him with my personality and when we're physically alike as two eggs, I'll be able to close my eyes in peace. He'll guarantee the perpetuation of my work. He's seventy years younger than I am. But that shouldn't be noticeable when he's substituted for me in the public eye. He'll have to act as old and sickly as I am. That's how I'll rob history of seventy years. But it will be a trick with a worthy purpose. My prolongation will fix in man's mind the idea that my work is eternal: a supernatural mandate that petrifies life.

THE DOUBLE (*his wound is covered with a spider web*): I used the treatment.

THE MAN: You've found a magnificent spider web, identical to the one I had seventy years ago.

THE DOUBLE: It was a horrible spider; it was sucking the blood of a fly.

THE MAN: Didn't you break its head?

THE DOUBLE: I got them both with one swipe of my knife.

THE MAN: A brave act of war. The spider died for being inhuman, the fly for being stupid.

THE DOUBLE: A bunch of little spiders came out of the spider's belly.

THE MAN: Those will keep us supplied with first-aid treatments. Does the wound hurt?

THE DOUBLE: A little, especially when I talk.

THE MAN: Then you should talk and talk so the pain keeps hurting inside. Come on, give a speech.

THE DOUBLE: It'll open the wound.

THE MAN: It shouldn't close completely, but should leave a line like mine. While mine was healing a horse kicked me. That's why mine is so wrinkled. Seeing that we have no horse here that knows how to do that, sometime when you're not expecting it, I'll give you a good kick.

THE DOUBLE: Your excellency is going to lower himself to being a horse?

THE MAN: It's not lowering myself; it's raising the horse to my level. Come on, let's have a speech. Talk about love; that's not compromising.

THE DOUBLE (*jumps on the horse and raises his arms in a* **V**): Love, love . . . a great topic. (*While speaking, he jumps from one piece of apparatus to another, as would a bird hopping about in his cage.*) "I speak to you on behalf of the nation . . ."

THE MAN: Who wound you up?

THE DOUBLE (*ignoring him*): "I speak to you on behalf of the nation, which is like talking to myself about me. At times like this I feel like the national belly button . . ."

THE MAN (*tries to correct him*): We haven't yet arrived at that very intimate part. Don't get ahead of yourself. For the present your belly button is still not mine.

THE DOUBLE: ". . . for the country lives in me and I live mystically in it, the one growing from the entrails of the other like a hangnail, which we must realize is also a product of the hand. And this being so, how can we help but love one another? I, as the one who administers everything, made you happy sharing nothing, the absolute nothing which, modestly speaking, always brings to mind the original matter of creation. And in the center of love, like a Buddha enamored of his own belly button . . ."

THE MAN (*picks up a fly swatter and goes to hit him*): You're back to that umbilical confusion. (*Hits him and the orator falls to the ground, dazed.*) Your voice and gestures are very good, but the concept is boring. Your belly button, I've told you plainly, is still not mine. Mine contains more history than an Egyptian pyramid. Yours, on the other hand . . . Let's have a look at it. (*Looks at it.*) Just as I thought. Soft and smooth as a novice's. We'll give it the proper treatment. Where's a firecracker? (THE DOUBLE *gets up quickly and gives him the firecracker.*) Lie down on the horse with your belly up. Uncover your navel. Everybody knows that that's where a stick of dynamite exploded on me. The firecracker will make a similar burn that'll do the trick. When I'm dead, you could become ill and my doctor, noticing that you had no burned belly button, could draw strange conclusions. He knows all the damage that's been done to my heroic body. (*The firecracker explodes.*)

THE DOUBLE: Augh!

THE MAN: Why are you complaining?

THE DOUBLE: Out of gratitude. That way I imitate your excellency better. Didn't your excellency scream?

THE MAN: History will tell. There, you're taken care of already.

THE DOUBLE: I see that your excellency loves me like a son.

THE MAN: Don't talk nonsense. How do I know how one loves children if I've never had any?

THE DOUBLE: I'm so sorry!

THE MAN: I'm not. Children today turn out any which way, the opposite of their parents. Kids today are a nightmare. You, however, are how I want you to be; you're hand-made. And so that you won't doubt our similarity, I'll show you my belly button. (*Shows it to him.*)

THE DOUBLE: Twin brothers in every respect.

THE MAN: To make us even more identical, you should toughen yourself under this barbed wire. (*Makes him go through the barbed-wire obstacles.*) Now for some sand. (*Shovels sand on him.*) You can swallow some; it'll build up your lungs. It'll also make your voice a bit scratchy, but we'll take care of that in good time. We'll be exactly alike and not even the most sharp-eyed person will be able to tell the slightest difference. Of course, if there were the slightest doubt that you weren't me, it would be a disaster. All my work would go down the drain. (*Leans on the shovel like a gravedigger.*) Now that you're covered with earth as I have been so many times, you should think spiritual thoughts. One is genuinely happy when covered with dirt, because one feels real fear. Fear makes the soul expand and reach the infinite with its fingertips. But don't go too fast. It's very dangerous. Remember that by getting carried away and seeing too much, Lazarus was struck dumb. It's just as dangerous to see nothing and thereby lose the capacity to lie. The lie should be the only truth allowed in a constructive political system. As far as this world goes, your spirit should be like a boiled egg: not so cooked that it

looks like stone nor so raw that it's repulsive. The idea of the egg cooked just right is a perfect point because it's advantageous to know a little of everything, although not too much of any one thing, so that you can avoid the temptation of being distracted by that one thing, which would be the death of your political career. Everything should be at your service, like toilet paper or a toothbrush. But if you get too interested, for example, in philosophy, you're lost: you'll only reap doubts. (*The sound of horses' hooves is heard.*) You're lucky. A cavalry regiment is going to pass over you. Don't move. (*Trots over him.*) The cavalry is pushed back by the enemy's cavalry. (*Steps on him again.*) The two enemy forces fight furiously. (*He fights and mounts* THE DOUBLE. *He falls off. Gets on again. Trots, brandishing his sword right and left. A rocket falls and both jump. Blackout.*)

SCENE 2

THE MAN *and* THE DOUBLE *are seated on the floor, looking at slides projected on a screen in the background. From the back, they are identical. The head and left hand of each are covered with spider webs, emergency treatment for identical injuries. The slides are showing the wounds received by* THE MAN. *The first slide shows the whole body, a bloody figure with numerous wounds produced by various weapons. The following slides show magnified details of the wounds, along with the weapon that produced each one, and at the same time the shot, explosion, or blow that went with it is heard. Martial music is played in the background.*

THE MAN: These images are the topographic map of my body. One big wound. You can see that the fame I've had as a hero for seventy years is well deserved and more. I planted my courage and reaped the fear of mortals, flies included. These images are part of the Universal Encyclopedia of Courage, a work that's been accumulating from the time of Charlemagne to ours, or perhaps even longer. This is the image you have to imitate and incorporate in your body, not only to be the same as I—your true progenitor—but so that when the weather's bad or trouble threatens, you'll know just what to complain about to my doctor, to whom you shouldn't go with things that have never bothered me. (*A slide shows a tremendous kick in the buttock.*) I got that seventy years ago in old Indochina.

THE DOUBLE: That's hardly a noble place to be wounded.

THE MAN: Sensitive, though!

THE DOUBLE: Do they give decorations for wounds received there?

THE MAN: For any part of the body. Now the Americans are getting it there in Vietnam.

THE DOUBLE: That goes to show that nobody learns from someone else's hind end.

THE MAN: You won't make that mistake. Like all the other parts of your body, that one will end up being mine, and I'll give it the benefit of my broad experience. And if sometime something hurts you that doesn't show up on these slides, what'll you do?

THE DOUBLE: Take care of myself in private.

THE MAN: Exactly, but don't let anyone suspect that you're making personal use of power. Power, remember, is always used against others. (*Makes a gesture of pain which* THE DOUBLE *reproduces simultaneously.*) Augh!

THE DOUBLE: Augh!

THE MAN: What are you moaning about?

THE DOUBLE: About the injuries, the same as your excellency.

THE MAN: I forbid complaining.

THE DOUBLE: But you said . . .

THE MAN: I'm the only one who can complain.

THE DOUBLE: I've received exactly the same wounds.

THE MAN: Of course. My system functions marvelously. Our identity is guaranteed, even in excesses like our present wounds. I shouldn't have them, even though I really got them. As powerful as I am, how can I justify battle wounds if it's been seventy years since there's been a reasonably priced war? There's no wound in my left knee according to my map of courage, nor in my left hand, nor on the left side of my skull. . . . Where could this leftist attack have come from?

THE DOUBLE: From the sky.

THE MAN: Have the Yankees bought it already?

THE DOUBLE: I don't know exactly, but when there's a drought, our peasants don't ask the saints for water, as their ancestors did. They look at the sky and pray to the Yankees to drop an H-bomb so that later it will rain dollars of compensation to make up for the harvests that were never planted. . . . I have an idea. We could ask them for some compensation for the wounds they caused us.

THE MAN: Those people annoy me; they've put such a high price on war that I have no choice but to live in peace.

THE DOUBLE: It's more tranquil.

THE MAN: That's what you say, you hothouse plant. If you don't copy my war scars to the letter, your valor will be a hoax. You won't even be able to kill a fly.

THE DOUBLE: But I've just received real wounds.

THE MAN: They're peace wounds.

THE DOUBLE: Peace with bombs?

THE MAN: American peace! When are you going to understand? Those wounds that we've received, as you've seen, are not marked on my map of courage.

THE DOUBLE: Well, you'll have to put them there because they hurt me as much as the ones that are there.

THE MAN: If I don't have them, how do you dare to complain? Say that they don't hurt you.

THE DOUBLE: No, they don't hurt me.

THE MAN: Get up and walk.

THE DOUBLE: I'm lame. (THE MAN *commands him with a look.* THE DOUBLE *gets up and limps.*)

THE MAN: I told you that you're not lame. You can't have those wounds since they don't agree with my *curriculum vitae*. Therefore you should still be jumping and singing. (*Jumps and hums.*)

THE DOUBLE: And your excellency . . . do . . . do your sores hurt?

THE MAN: My body has become a scar. I can't even move.

THE DOUBLE: But I'm in the same state.

THE MAN: Let's not start that again. Take off the emergency spider webs immediately and consider yourself cured. (*He takes them off and starts bleeding.*) Go let a dog lick off the blood. A dog's saliva is a phenomenal disinfectant.

THE DOUBLE: And what if it has rabies?

THE MAN: Then the cure will really be something! But keep it a secret. If the Yankees find out, within a week's time they'll have drained every canine salivary gland. They need a lot of dog saliva because there they turn out heroes on an assembly line.

THE DOUBLE: I'm going to get licked by an expert. (*Marches off.*)

THE MAN (*trying to get up*): Oh, the pain! Ay, ay, ay!

THE DOUBLE (*from off stage*): Oh, the pain! Ay, ay, ay!

THE MAN: Why are you complaining?

THE DOUBLE: Because you are.

THE MAN: That's no reason. These wounds are mine to suffer alone. They are wounds on the margin of my curriculum and therefore you have no reason to complain. Yes, I complain, but secretly. As long as I'm not completely well, I can't appear in public. I won't say anything to my doctor, because how can I justify wounds without war as such? Now go put on my suit and get back here immediately. You have an errand to do.

THE DOUBLE: Which suit, excellency?

THE MAN: The one that I've put on every Wednesday for seventy years. (*Tries to get up.*) Ay, ay, ay! (*Listens to hear if the other cries out. He hears him whistling.*) My commands are like the mantle of Saint Louis: they heal wounds. The trouble is that I can't order myself around with the same force. (*Furtively.*) I'm not afraid enough of myself.

THE DOUBLE (*enters wearing an old suit. He is afraid of tearing it. Looks at himself in the mirror*): Why, if I'm not your excellency, himself!

THE MAN: Excellency, nothing. You're only my copy. But it's amazing how much you look like me. How many years have you been with me?

THE DOUBLE: Exactly seventy years today.

THE MAN: Well then, the similarity isn't so surprising. I remember when I got my first pair of boots in the army. They were common boots that looked just like any others. I was so proud to put them on that I stamped my heels on the ground. There was such communication between my boots and me that they started taking on my features. After a year they were exactly like me. When I retired them from active service, my mother kept them as a souvenir. During my absence, nothing reminded her as much of the fruit of her womb as did those calfskin boots. The similarity shouldn't surprise you. Man, for as little talent as he has, still has more ability to imitate than a pair of boots has. Those boots were the first recipient of my personality; you will be the last.

THE DOUBLE: I'd like to kiss those boots.

THE MAN: Are you crazy?

THE DOUBLE: It's just that after what you've told me, I love those boots as if they were my twin brothers. Let me see them. When I was little, I always wished that I had brothers to fight with.

THE MAN: You can't do that. The one thing that is impossible for great men to achieve, although it doesn't seem so, is family intimacy.

THE DOUBLE: But those boots . . .

THE MAN: When I die those boots will go to the museum. . . .

THE DOUBLE: I hope I can see them soon!

THE MAN: Think about what you just said. Even in private you shouldn't reveal what you feel.

THE DOUBLE: Oh, I'm sorry. I didn't mean that I wanted you to die.

THE MAN: I'm the one who'll say when I die. Anyway, when I decide to die, you still won't be able to see those boots, because, as far as history is concerned, I will die, not when I, myself, die, but when you die.

THE DOUBLE: That's true, damn it! But enough of sentiment. I'll be as tough as the statue of a public servant: no mollycoddling.

THE MAN: If you rid yourself of that, we'll be as identical as two drops of blood inside and out. To commemorate your seventy years in my service, I'm going to give you your first assignment.

THE DOUBLE: I'm happy to hear it.

THE MAN: From now on you have my confidence. To prove this to you, you will represent me at a public function.

THE DOUBLE (*his knees buckle under him and he has to hit them so that they will hold him up*): Me?

THE MAN: You have to be of some use.

THE DOUBLE: No . . . no . . .

THE MAN: I order you.

THE DOUBLE (*his legs straighten up*): But is your excellency planning to die?

THE MAN: I want you to be well trained when I do die. That way I'll die happy. (*Mystically.*)

> I live without living in myself
> . And the death that I await is such
> That I lie when I die.

THE DOUBLE: Don't talk about death. Your excellency, to whom God grant many more years, can . . .

THE MAN: I can send you in my place. I'm not going to go, wounded as I am, dragging a leg, with a cracked skull, and a bloody hand. No one must know that I have received these wounds that aren't listed in my curriculum. (*Sees that* THE DOUBLE *limps.*) The wounds that you got today, forget them. (THE DOUBLE *stops limping.*) Get going.

THE DOUBLE: And what if they find out that I'm not your excellency?

THE MAN: No one will dare to have the slightest suspicion.

THE DOUBLE (*looking at himself in the mirror*): Looking at me, they'll believe that your excellency has been rejuvenated.

THE MAN: That will make a lot of them happy.

THE DOUBLE: But some other day, when they really see your excellency, they'll notice a sudden aging.

THE MAN: That will also make a lot of them happy. So you see, by our taking turns, we'll keep up the illusions of all of them. A people without illusions is a cadaver.

THE DOUBLE: Illusion . . .

THE MAN: If you want to maintain it, never let down your guard. Scorn everybody so they'll work hard to make themselves worthy of you, which of course nobody will ever be. Snub them and they'll respect you. They'll hate you, that's for sure, but that's better than having them love you. Things are more stable if they fear you than if they love you. If you love them, you'll be obligated to be forever giving them things, just like when you spoil children. If you hate them, as they won't be expecting anything, if you one day give them something that you don't need, they'll regard that day as miraculous and remember it forever. But don't go overboard because receiving is a dismal vice. If you get them to hate you, there'll be many advantages. Someone who hates you doesn't ask favors, but is constantly bestowing on you the fluid of his fear, which is the oxygen that you need to keep you afloat. (THE DOUBLE *laughs hysterically.*) What are you laughing about?

THE DOUBLE (*controlling himself*): Of how afraid they're going to be of me.

THE MAN: Watch out.

THE DOUBLE (*seriously*): Excellency . . .

THE MAN: I half believe that a laugh must be good at the circus, but in politics it's the most corrosive thing of all. Never laugh. You need a face to be a person, but you should use it to express no emotion whatsoever. That's something that we have to practice perfectly. If your face becomes the mirror of your soul, you're in real trouble. Above all, don't laugh. In case you have to laugh when you're alone, stick a handkerchief in your mouth and smother it.

THE DOUBLE: I'll do that gladly. (*Sticks a handkerchief in his mouth.*)

THE MAN: The Americans drop a bomb, and they smile; they trample you, and smile; they give you a loan so they can sell you arms, and smile; they demolish a country, and smile. They are the professional smilers. That's not serious. (THE MAN *sticks his fingers in* THE DOUBLE's *mouth and takes out the handkerchief. He wrings blood out of it.*) Look, the blood of your smile. It has died forever!

THE DOUBLE: Operation Smile, completed.

THE MAN: You are a strong man. (*Whips him.*)

THE DOUBLE: Thank you, thank you! (*Kisses the whip.*)

THE MAN: What's with you? I thought we agreed on no more sentiment.

THE DOUBLE: It's a long time since your excellency has whipped me.

THE MAN: That's right, and you've already become unaccustomed to it.

THE DOUBLE: Something worse. I know that it'll take many beatings to get me in shape, and since you haven't whipped me for so

long, I thought you considered me unworthy.

THE MAN: What nonsense! (*Whips him several times.*)

THE DOUBLE (*jubilant*): I'd gotten it into my head that you had laid eyes on another candidate for the succession.

THE MAN: Do you like power?

THE DOUBLE: I love it. I dream about it every night.

THE MAN: Many do, but they don't know how to progress from that stage. Most men believe themselves predestined to exercise power. Individuals who don't even have a say about anything in their own homes talk in the café or in the tavern about the things they would do if they ruled.

THE DOUBLE: I really have no competitors?

THE MAN (*hits him*): I've put too much work into that body of yours to throw you to the dogs now. All that accumulated labor has made you something of my own. Sometimes, when I beat you in order to mold you, the blows that I give you make me tremble. That's real identification.

THE DOUBLE: I'm sorry that you suffer for me.

THE MAN: It's good discipline.

THE DOUBLE: So that you won't have to continue suffering for me, I'll tell you in great detail which parts of my body are not yet yours. . . . You can hit those parts without feeling pity.

THE MAN: I already do. Forming a statesman is an unbelievably difficult task. (*Looks at his watch.*) It's time for you to go. Go to the affair and play my part. If they ask you things you don't know, don't answer foolishly: you should attack by asking, "But don't you know?"

THE DOUBLE: "But don't you know?"

THE MAN: Devastating! That's called the insecticide of the clever. Go on. (THE DOUBLE *exits.*) Hey! Come back! Don't start acting as if you were me before you leave. (THE DOUBLE *re-enters and backs out, bowing and scraping as he goes. He stumbles and makes a hole in the dome. From off stage comes the sound of falling, broken glass.*) This is what you call undermining power from within. Good grief! Has he killed himself? (*Shouts.*) Hey, don't go feeling sorry for yourself, it's getting late! (*Looks at the hole.*) Like a bull in a china shop. Let him

fix it when he returns. That way he'll learn what it is to have a tidy house. Actually, the dome is impregnable from the outside, but very fragile from the inside. In building it, I've followed not the expensive American method, but the one the hen uses in building her egg; tough on the outside and sensitive to the chick's beak on the inside. That's why no one else enters but me and my second me; that is, me two times. (*Sound of distant drums. They come closer as* THE MAN *raises his voice.*) From here I examine the whole panorama of the nation. Not even a fly moves without my seeing it. (*Looks outside.*) Everything's peaceful. The flies know me and are so afraid of me that I subdue them without ground-to-air missiles; all I have to do is look at them. My fame as a hero kills them without firing a shot. They know that my pistol is still smoking. I've planted peace and now tranquillity surrounds me. The envious claim that my concept of power is feudal (*Looks through the telescope.*), but can you call this telescope feudal? I survey the panorama with it, I examine reality, I inform myself of its problems. So if my optical apparatus is a mechanism of scientific precision, who has the right to preach against my supposed feudalism? Besides, Charlemagne was feudal, too, and no one says that because of it he's any less great than I am. Undoubtedly we're a couple of greats. They slander me out of envy. The envious would have loved to know enough to build a dome like this on top of the useless ashes of the dead, where I'm happier than a fish in water. It all comes from knowing how to take advantage of death, as death is like the fertilizer of the living. That's why I've founded my dome on a base of skulls, in that way killing two birds with one stone, for at the same time I'm memorializing those who lost their heads in my colonial expeditions. The whole dome, piece by piece, is a memorial to my glorious past: my battles against the resisters; my adventures in big-game hunting; the dates of the national holidays in my honor; my celestial hallucinations that never let me alone. . . . In a word (*Gets on the horse, opens his arms in a* V *and shouts*.), greatness, greatness, greatness! ME!!

Loud drums. He falls unconscious. THE DOUBLE *enters several seconds later. Looks at him fearfully.*

THE DOUBLE: He's dead. . . . Yes, yes, he's dead. . . .

THE MAN: Don't count on it yet.

THE DOUBLE (*attentively*): What happened, excellency?

THE MAN: One of my visions . . . I fell off the horse and I broke a leg.

THE DOUBLE: How awful!

THE MAN: I'll compensate myself for it, seeing how it happened in the line of duty. I was contemplating my greatness. The break will be included in my *curriculum vitae.* It's not wasted. It will be considered another sacrifice for the common good, a gold medal on my map of courage. I'll have to have slides made of the fracture. How was your appearance?

THE DOUBLE: Not the slightest suspicion. I gave a long speech.

THE MAN: What did you say?

THE DOUBLE: Absolutely nothing.

THE MAN: Well done. (*Points to the hole.*) You see the damage. You'll have to repair it immediately.

THE DOUBLE: O.K., tomorrow.

THE MAN: Right now.

THE DOUBLE: No flies will get in.

THE MAN: While I breathe there's no fly that would dare come near this place. But you have to repair it today. You'll be lame tomorrow.

THE DOUBLE: I already am.

THE MAN: Forget those scratches.

THE DOUBLE: I've forgotten them, but they're stubborn.

THE MAN: The stubborn have been swept away. I mean that tomorrow you'll really be lame. My broken leg belongs to you, too.

THE DOUBLE: I'm ready for that, sir. The truth is that I don't feel worthy to follow your example to the letter and yet your excellency is so good to me. Which leg shall I break?

THE MAN: That pleasure is mine.

THE DOUBLE: What an honor!

THE MAN: But first I must teach you something important: seeing with the back of your neck. If you had been a real soldier

instead of a hothouse plant, you'd have eyes everywhere. When enemies are creeping up on you, you find you have eyes that you never knew of before. Of all those eyes, the most important ones are the ones in the back of your neck because they permit you to retreat when your position becomes impossible to hold. For making war, that rear eye is as important as a bloodhound's nose.

THE DOUBLE: I never heard the Yankees talk about that eye.

THE MAN: They've had it closed down. Too much of that technical stuff makes man a brute. That doesn't mean to say that they don't retreat, but when they don't have their helicopters, they're finished. I'm glad that it happens to them. They deserve it for having put war up into the clouds.

THE DOUBLE (*walking backwards*): I feel like a crab.

THE MAN: It's more complicated than that. Let me tell you that I'm teaching you a great number of things. Most of the heads of state don't know the half of what I've taught you. Not even half! If they even knew a quarter, they wouldn't act like tourists where power is concerned. You see what happens to our beloved opposition, supposing that such a thing exists. I admire them very much for how good they are. They live with the illusion of my impending death, without the slightest suspicion of my game. But with these eyes or with these others (*Points to those of* THE DOUBLE.), I'll watch them leaving in the funeral procession of their illusions.

THE DOUBLE: Tourists don't have the right to rule.

THE MAN: You took the words right out of my mouth.

THE DOUBLE (*continues walking backwards*): Now I'm a crab! Now I'm a crab!

THE MAN: Right! Left! About face! Hit the dirt! (THE DOUBLE *obeys the commands. First he jumps over small obstacles, then bigger ones. He goes to step on* THE MAN *who is still on the floor.*) Careful! You'll trample me! (*Sits up with great difficulty and pain.*) Don't you remember that I fell off the horse when I was in a trance?

THE DOUBLE: I feel like that accident were my own.

THE MAN: It will be. (THE DOUBLE *is still on*

the floor with his back to THE MAN.) Do you see me?

THE DOUBLE: Your excellency is seated on the floor with your finger in your nose.

THE MAN (*picks up a brick to throw at him*): And now?

THE DOUBLE: Your excellency is about to throw a brick at my head. Shall I let it hit me?

THE MAN: Do what you want. (THE DOUBLE *moves and the brick falls at his side.*) Wonderful! (*Makes face at him.*) What am I doing now?

THE DOUBLE: You're making faces.

THE MAN: Don't flatter me, idiot.

THE DOUBLE: You're making fun of yourself.

THE MAN: Of myself?

THE DOUBLE: Of course, aren't I your future excellency?

THE MAN: Then I'll stop making faces. (*Shots are heard.*) Attack! Retreat! Use your rear eye or you'll break your neck. (THE DOUBLE *retreats.*) Very good! (*The shots stop.*) You're out of the line of enemy fire. Attention! (*He doesn't get up.*) Why don't you obey?

THE DOUBLE: What if they attack me with napalm?

THE MAN: Our enemies are poor.

THE DOUBLE: But the Yankees could attack us.

THE MAN: But then they'd have to pay us off. Attention! (*Then he gives him orders of left, right, and about face. He makes him avoid all the obstacles but the horse.*) To the rear, march. Step lightly. You already know how to look perfectly with the back of your neck. There's no doubt that I'm an excellent instructor. Did you know that Machiavelli was inspired by me? (THE DOUBLE *marches over* THE MAN, *who holds his breath.*) Quickly, a jump backwards. (THE DOUBLE *mounts the horse, totters, and falls off noisily.*) That's it. (THE DOUBLE *stands up and hops on one leg, the other dragging brokenly.*) What's that?

THE DOUBLE: Excellency, now we're the same! I've broken my leg!

THE MAN: My system of succession works marvelously. (*Blackout.*)

THE DOUBLE: Ay, ay, ay! I see the stars.

THE MAN: That's because it's night. (*Music with elements of an operating room. Curtain.*)

ACT II
THE CONFUSION OF THE "I"

SCENE 1

THE MAN *is dressed in formal attire to attend an important public function. He and* THE DOUBLE *look off into the distance. The number of papers on the desk is increasing.*

THE MAN: Look. It's amazing. Everything's the same as it was seventy years ago. (THE DOUBLE *looks through the telescope.*)

THE DOUBLE (*disconcerted*): Sir, I don't see anything at all.

THE MAN: What do you mean you don't see anything?

THE DOUBLE: Nothing.

THE MAN: Well, that depends on what you call nothing.

THE DOUBLE: I see a completely scorched land, nothing else.

THE MAN (*indignant*): And you call that nothing?

THE DOUBLE: Is it something?

THE MAN: Of course it is: it's my work. There, right there is where I fought my decisive battle against the enemy.

THE DOUBLE: Magnificent! Stupendous!

THE MAN: Do you see something?

THE DOUBLE: Not even a flower.

THE MAN: A fly?

THE DOUBLE: Not one.

THE MAN: And it's been that way for seventy years. Today it's completed. It has been a decisive expedition. I got most of my skulls in that burnt field.

THE DOUBLE: Why do you say yours?

THE MAN: I have a right to call them mine.

THE DOUBLE: Because you put them there?

THE MAN: You don't understand anything. They're mine because they're the skulls of my dead. (THE DOUBLE *wants to ask him something.*) I know; you're surprised because I say *my* dead. (THE DOUBLE *makes gestures of bafflement.*) What patience I have to have with you! Will you ever understand the meaning of my revolution? (THE DOUBLE *is shocked by this final word.*)

THE DOUBLE: Your revolution! Your dead!

THE MAN: Now you've got it. (THE DOUBLE *is overwhelmed.*) You've hit on it, but only by chance. My revolution and my dead are one and the same thing. That's the essential part of my political theory: ideological death.

THE DOUBLE: Ah, now I get it!

THE MAN: I'll explain the reason for my ownership of the dead. They are mine because, thanks to me, they exist. I created them. Without me, they wouldn't have become a part of history, and nobody would have stopped to count their skulls.

THE DOUBLE: Your excellency has saved them from oblivion.

THE MAN: And made them world famous. In honor of them, today we celebrate our biggest holiday: that of the immortal skulls.

THE DOUBLE (*pointing to the foundation of skulls*): What a pleasure to be surrounded by so many famous people!

THE MAN: I'm glad that you appreciate them. I love them very much. Thanks to them, here I am, in peace, and dreaming about passing my succession on to you.

THE DOUBLE: Poor little skulls!

THE MAN: Are you going to cry over them?

THE DOUBLE: They are so good!

THE MAN: They wouldn't be anything without me. Thanks to me, they will be ashes, they will be dust, more . . .

THE DOUBLE: Dust in love.

THE MAN: With death.

THE DOUBLE (*looks through the telescope*): Now I see it all perfectly.

THE MAN (*surprised*): What?

THE DOUBLE: There isn't even a fly.

THE MAN (*relaxing*): Yes, peace. That's what I'm going to talk about in my speech today. I take such pleasure in that word despite its unworthy implications. But, also thanks to me, today, that word will have a new context. Not the context of some simpleton's dream, but something you must defend with tooth and nail. Today I feel like peace itself. (*Acts like a dove.*) Cooo. Cooo.

THE DOUBLE (*applauds*): That's great!

THE MAN: Bullets are like dove's eggs when they're new. Coo! When competent soldiers put them into the nests of their machine guns, Coo! they fly out like little doves.

THE DOUBLE (*flatteringly*): I'm going to take your picture, excellency. We'll have it published in an important paper and it's sure to get the Nobel Peace Prize.

THE MAN: How disgusting! Coo!

THE DOUBLE: It would be just recognition.

THE MAN: I don't need it. I, Coo! am a natural-born pacifist.

THE DOUBLE: But that needs publicity.

THE MAN: No, it doesn't.

THE DOUBLE: Don't be so modest.

THE MAN: If it were known that I am a peace lover, the peace would end.

THE DOUBLE: With publicity, it would get across better.

THE MAN: If they saw me like this, Coo! they'd lose fear of me. And do you know what that means? A bomb on the tail of this dove, Coo!

THE DOUBLE: How bad they are!

THE MAN: That's how men are when they see a tender dove. They want to gobble it up. That's why I violently defend peace, Coo! Peace is an armored dove, Coo! Doves, little doves, with a pistol on their hip. A dove in a tank, Coo! A dove with a grenade in its beak, Coo! A dove on a torpedo. An atomic bomb that explodes and a mushroom cloud that rises in the shape of a dove, Coo! Today I feel inspired to talk about universal peace. But that's not so strange, it's my great day of war. Seventy years ago, on a day like today, I annihilated the opposition. That will be the theme of today's speech. No. Nothing to do with war. I'll say (THE DOUBLE *does and says the same things, producing a simultaneous speech*): "Today, on such a noteworthy day, I ought to talk about my great victory, but I refuse to do so. Don't think that I won't talk about my resounding victory because I don't want to stir things up. (*Looks at* THE DOUBLE, *annoyed.*) It's just that I'm not spiteful. The enemy has been wiped out and I'm not going to hold a grudge now that I have no one to hold it against. Mine is a pardoning spirit. I would tell that to the enemy themselves, if they existed. But those damned people haven't reproduced themselves. The terrible thing is that because of this incapacity, they slander and defame me. They say that my revolution was inhuman, when it was biological. What could be more stupid? (*Makes a threatening gesture at* THE DOUBLE, *who mimics it.*) Having eliminated the enemy is more worthy of the Nobel Prize than of contempt. I look through my super-modern telescope and they say I have a feudal point of view, while all the time they know that my telescope is technically the latest thing. They're afraid of me, but am I to blame for having been so brave? And I'm not saying this lightly, but with true sentiment. It is true that the enemy was afraid of me: they would die from my slightest glance, to the credit of my courage; but that fear penetrates the bones of my own friends and collaborators is something which exasperates me. I know from a reliable source that my friends and collaborators love me, but with an overpowering fear. In order to correct this corruption of sentiments today, the seventieth anniversary of my victory, I propose and decree that a monument to love be built, to that fragile word with which I would like to envelop everyone, due to the event we celebrate today. I have forced myself to talk to you without even mentioning the enemy although they hang on the tip of my tongue as ticks stick to the ears of hungry dogs." (*Looks indignantly at* THE DOUBLE.) Enough!

THE DOUBLE (*repeating*): Enough!

THE MAN: I'm telling *you* enough, not the enemy. They can't hear.

THE DOUBLE: I'm telling *you* enough, not the enemy. They can't hear.

THE MAN (*scrutinizing him*): Have you gone over to the enemy? (THE DOUBLE *starts to repeat, but he cuts him off.*) Enough of playing me! I'm still here, on my skeleton and not there, in your hide.

THE DOUBLE: Sir . . .

THE MAN: You're taking undue liberties.

THE DOUBLE (*swears, kissing the sign of the cross he makes with his fingers*): I swear that I'll never be anything but you. (*Kneels.*)

THE MAN: But if you add anything of your own or change the future in the slightest, I'll crush you like a cockroach. (*Makes a gesture of stepping on something, which makes* THE DOUBLE *shudder.*)

THE DOUBLE: I'll never have an idea of my own.

THE MAN: And if you do have one, it'll be a stupid one.

THE DOUBLE: And if I do have one, it'll be a stupid one.

THE MAN: A ridiculous one.

THE DOUBLE: And a ridiculous one.

THE MAN: Get up. (*He gets up.*) Now you're consecrated. But don't get out of line again. Because I'm still the one who's doing the instructing.

THE DOUBLE: And you'll keep instructing me. It's just that I am already so identical to you that it's amazing that your excellency goes on living.

THE MAN: Yes, yes, your mouth waters thinking that I no longer exist.

THE DOUBLE: By no means. I still don't consider myself mature enough to be by myself. My admiration of our similarity is clothed in the greatest modesty. What I admire and bless is the job that your excellency has done on me, making a simple bank employee the successor of such a supernatural being who is able to annihilate a swarm of flies with a glance. You don't even see prowess like that in the circus. Let me kiss your hands (*Does it.*), those hands that made me a perfect piece of political stock. If it seems at times that I get carried away, don't take me wrong; I'm only showing my disinterested and loyal servility.

THE MAN: Quickly, shine my boots because I have to go. (THE DOUBLE *takes shoe-shining equipment and sits down on a bench to clean them.* THE MAN *hiccoughs violently.*) What's this? At my age, hiccoughing is dangerous.

THE DOUBLE: Drink some water. (*Gives it to him and* THE MAN *gulps it down.*) Slowly, more slowly . . . and the hiccough, stubborn as it is, will be overcome.

THE MAN (*continues hiccoughing*): No, it's not dead yet.

THE DOUBLE: It's the stubbornest hiccough I've seen in my life.

THE MAN: It's just that everything of mine is immortal. But I can't go out in public like this. A great man can't hiccough in public. Can you imagine Charlemagne hiccoughing?

THE DOUBLE: I always imagine him mounted on the Holy German Empire.

THE MAN: Yes, lopping off heads. (*Refuses the water that is given him.*) You're flooding me. And to top it all I have to give a formidable speech. Have the Yankees invented something for hiccoughs?

THE DOUBLE: They have invented the war in Vietnam.

THE MAN: An exorbitant remedy! I want something cheaper.

THE DOUBLE: Give yourself a good scare.

THE MAN: The problem is that nothing frightens me.

THE DOUBLE (*jubilant to be of service*): I know a wonderful scare.

THE MAN (*furious*): Don't you know that I cannot be scared? You go in my place. I'm not about to celebrate my great day hiccoughing for everyone to see. Put on my suit. (THE DOUBLE *helps him to undress. He does the same, and both are then in long underwear.*) You already know that in my speech I don't even want to touch on the enemy.

THE DOUBLE: I have that on the tip of my tongue.

THE MAN: And try to be as sincere as you can.

THE DOUBLE: What do you mean?

THE MAN: The more sincere you are, the better you'll lie. Now go or you'll be late. (THE DOUBLE *leaves, marching backwards and saluting.*) He doesn't fall any more. He sees perfectly with the back of his neck. Not even *my* rear eye works so well. But I can be tranquil: the perpetuation of my era is guaranteed. Without the slightest social upheaval, as neat as anything, my double will slip it into history. And like an identification card that guarantees everything, he will inherit the fear that everyone has of me. (*Looks through the telescope.*) I'm sure that he will do everything better than I, if that were possible. But it wouldn't be surprising. Man excels in what his own defects create or else makes his defects the style. As soon as I give him clear vision, he'll work like a clock. It hasn't been in vain that in molding him, I've been avoiding my questionable qualities. It's not been all that easy for me. The world that I inherited was so false that I have had to lie a lot in order to straighten it out. (*Looks at the telescope.*) Really, strange things have happened to me with the truth. I take something and no matter how true it is, after passing through the still of my elocutionary system, it becomes a bunch of lies. For some reason I never believe anything I say. My faith is in what I don't talk about, behind which I barricade myself and scheme to save the country. But he won't have to lie. Why will he have to lie if his whole being is a lie? With naturalness, without blushing, he will lie clearly and smoothly, because lying is his nature. At the same time he will be astute, but in a normal way, which will give a touch of innocence to his congenital foxiness; he will be cynical, but he'll have the natural freshness of lettuce. In a word, all that is double-dealing in me, will be sincerity in him. (*Surprised that his hiccoughing is gone.*) Hey, my hiccoughs are gone! And they went without my knowing it, while I was philosophizing. Evidently, philosophy is good for hiccoughs. It had better be good for something. (THE DOUBLE *enters with a sports trophy. Slowly,* THE DOUBLE *is making the movements, gestures, tics, and hoarseness of* THE MAN.)

THE DOUBLE: Look, excellency!

THE MAN: Where has it come from?

THE DOUBLE: It's a hunting trophy they've presented me.

THE MAN: Have you ever hunted?

THE DOUBLE: Never. (*Points to the courage laboratory.*) I never see rabbits or partridges over there.

THE MAN: What do you know about hunting!

THE DOUBLE: I know those creatures. I've seen them a million times in the market, hanging by their feet.

THE MAN: That's what I've told you. And the trophy, I'm sure you were glad enough to grab that!

THE DOUBLE: Excellency! Why, I wouldn't even take anything from myself!

THE MAN: Then that trophy is mine. (*Tries to take it away.*)

THE DOUBLE: I've earned it. After the speech, we went on a hunt.

THE MAN (*very sarcastic*): You, hunting!

THE DOUBLE (*undaunted*): Yes, we went. It was all automatic. I felt in command and they told me, "Sir, press the button that says 'rabbits.'" And I pressed it hard. (*Distant shots are heard.*) "Sir," they said again, "press the button that says 'tuna fish.'" And a depth charge sounded in the water. (*Acts as though listening for the discharge which is heard in the distance.*) "Sir, press the button that says . . ."

THE MAN: Shit!

THE DOUBLE: I didn't hear anything but the discharge.

THE MAN: And you dared to kill in my name?

THE DOUBLE: I shot with my own fingers.

THE MAN: Yours? Maybe I didn't give you thousands of whacks on the knuckles?

THE DOUBLE (*shrinking*): They carried me on their shoulders.

THE MAN: It was for me.

THE DOUBLE: They cheered me like I never saw them cheer a soccer player.

THE MAN: It was for me!

THE DOUBLE: They touched me as if I were a saint.

THE MAN: It was for me!!

THE DOUBLE (*extremely enthused*): They kissed me, they threw me kisses, they took photographs, they asked for my autograph . . .

THE MAN: It was for me!!!

THE DOUBLE: And then they gave me this valuable trophy.

THE MAN (*grabbing it cunningly*): It's mine, it's mine, it's mine!

THE DOUBLE: Your hiccoughs are gone.

THE MAN: You have managed to scare me. You're a monster! Usurper!

THE DOUBLE: It was the happiest day of my life.

THE MAN: But don't you see how you're robbing me?

THE DOUBLE: I still have a pleasant taste in my mouth.

THE MAN (*lunging at* THE DOUBLE): That pleasant taste is mine too! (*Lets him go like something wrung out.*) Hurry up, get undressed. (THE DOUBLE *begins to take off his clothes, and coughs.*) And that cough?

THE DOUBLE: I caught it there. When I pressed the button that said "tuna fish," I got hit with a spray of water. (*Keeps coughing.*)

THE MAN: Well, that cough is the only thing that belongs to you. (*Coughs.*)

THE DOUBLE: I'm delighted that your excellency has gotten something of mine. (*They cough until they start to cry. They fumble around. Both in underwear, they stumble around confusedly. They make the same gestures and say the same words.*)

BOTH: Why do you leave the uniform thrown over there? It's a suit of honor. It's clear that you haven't paid the tailor bill. From a distance, it has seen many people die. It fits me as well as a lion's skin fits him. Everything has just been handed to you. I'm going to hang it up. (*Each one pulls on the suit.*) Who's who here? Are we one or are we two? We are one; me, without a doubt. Who is joined onto whom? One should die; you first. Who's the oldest? We're a damned decrepit old wretch. One or two? (*Look at their wounds.*) Here I have a wound. That's nothing, I have another exactly like it. My face has an enormous scar, it is a face tanned by heroism. Mine is no less tough than yours. In the belly button, twin explosions. A kick in the buttock. Yes, it's the same as the one that I'm touching. A wound in the left knee, another in the left hand, another on the left side of the head. Three wounds that equal zero. They can't exist, although they do exist: they're not on my map of courage. We're so alike that we can't tell who is who. And all by being dressed in nothing but underwear. But there must be something that distinguishes us. One has to die as soon as possible. I know, one day you fell on your back over there. (*Both point to the place.*) Yes, I remember it perfectly. You hurt yourself pretty badly, so you must have quite a scar. (*Touches him.*) Not a trace. Well, it's pretty far from there to the floor. Yes, enough to kill you. Then what did you do about the fall? Your excellency will remember that when I was leaving you told me (*Shouts.*), "Hey, don't go feeling sorry for yourself, it's getting late!" And that was like a parachute. I'm so sorry that you didn't break anything! Because a scratch on the buttock, no matter how small it were, would be the solution of the national dilemma. I have another idea. Let me look at your teeth. (*Each looks at the other's mouth.*) This won't fail. An animal's age can be calculated perfectly by his teeth. The same molars, the same incisors, the same eye teeth. My work is too perfect. Damn it! I did it to confuse the rest, but now I'm biting my own tail. *I* am confused! I had my continuity assured, the happiness of the country was in my grasp, and now, because we're stripped to our underwear, it's all shot to hell. Who did they applaud today? Me, of course. Whose trophy is this? Mine, mine, mine! We've fallen into subversive chaos. You're to blame, you, you, you. (*They get set to fight.*) I'm going to wring your neck. (*One*

of them begins to hiccough. They listen.)
What delicious noise is that?

THE MAN: My hiccough, my sweet hiccough!
The redeeming hiccough. (*Continues hiccoughing.*)

THE DOUBLE: The hiccough has saved the
country from catastrophe. A monument
should be built to it. We should contract
an inspired artist to do it.

THE MAN: But the hiccough is spiritual.

THE DOUBLE: Well then, in the form of an
angel. (*Strikes several poses.*) Then when
the statue is unveiled, I'll declare a national
hiccoughing day.

THE MAN: Nobody will hiccough.

THE DOUBLE: It'll be obligatory.

THE MAN: Impossible. This country will
never hiccough. Don't you remember that
they live frightened?

THE DOUBLE: But the hiccough deserves homage.

THE MAN: Put on your pants before I stop
hiccoughing and we fall back into the
babel of the undershorts. (*Blackout.*)

SCENE 2

*Music and strange sounds. The skulls,
phosphorescent, wink in the darkness. They
all laugh, except one that cries, giving a
pathetic note to the frolic. Many papers
on the desk. Phosphorescent haze.* THE
MAN *and* THE DOUBLE *have their backs
turned to each other.*

THE DOUBLE: Help! Help! We've fallen into
a tomb.

THE MAN: Shut up!

THE DOUBLE: I want to get out of here.

THE MAN: And give up succeeding me?

THE DOUBLE: I wouldn't even let go of that
under water.

THE MAN: Listen to me.

THE DOUBLE: I'm all skulls.

THE MAN (*in a cavernous voice*): Today we
have celebrated my great day.

THE DOUBLE: Yes, I've gone hunting.

THE MAN: Well, tonight we're going skulling.

THE DOUBLE: How frightening!

THE MAN: The skulls celebrate their holiday.

THE DOUBLE: Horrors!

THE MAN: It's their national night. They

celebrate the peace that they have cemented and kept afloat.

THE DOUBLE: But they could go some other
place to laugh. They make me dizzy. As if
I'm dangling over an abyss.

THE MAN: You are: over there's the other
world.

THE DOUBLE: Help!

THE MAN: Your shouts are going to wake the
foreign correspondents. They'll come here
with their cameras and tape recorders and
bury you alive.

THE DOUBLE: You mean I'm not dead?

THE MAN: Here I'm showing you the greatest of my secrets and instead of being
happy, you defecate.

THE DOUBLE: Sorry! I don't know what I'm
doing. My nose has blocked up.

THE MAN: Keep quiet.

THE DOUBLE: I'll try to contain myself.

THE MAN: This is my most solemn ritual.
These skulls, which belong to me and are
very frightening, assist me and inspire me
one night out of the year, a night that
illuminates me during the 365 days that
follow.

THE DOUBLE: One night gives that much
light?

THE MAN: Not even a whole night. Our stay
ends at 12:00 sharp. So prepare yourself to
take advantage of this visceral contact with
the people of the other world.

THE DOUBLE: I'm horribly afraid.

THE MAN: Aren't you a believer?

THE DOUBLE: I don't have any choice.

THE MAN: Thank heavens. If you were an
atheist, you wouldn't see anything in this.

THE DOUBLE: Oh, how I wish I were an
atheist!

THE MAN: What's that?

THE DOUBLE: Until 12:00 midnight.

THE MAN: Without this communion with
death, it's impossible for you to think of
succeeding me.

THE DOUBLE: I'll pluck up my courage.

THE MAN: You are experiencing your baptism with death. (THE DOUBLE *looks at the
audience. His skull, also phosphorescent,
laughs incessantly.*)

THE DOUBLE: My face tickles.

THE MAN: It's the laughing of your skull.

THE DOUBLE: Well, the last thing I want to
do is laugh!

THE MAN (*turning toward him*): Look how happy mine is. (*He also laughs.*)

THE DOUBLE: I didn't know that your excellency had it on. I thought that you kept it in those niches.

THE MAN: Those are for my dearly departed.

THE DOUBLE: So much laughter frightens me. Your excellency told me that laughter had no place in politics. I could never imagine that you were so happy.

THE MAN: Today, only today. But it's not me, it's my skull that laughs.

THE DOUBLE: The laughing of mine makes me very nervous.

THE MAN: Let it do whatever it wants. You'll see; afterwards you'll feel much better. And, what's more important, you won't feel like laughing at anything. Laughter is like poison. The Yankees use it in abundance and you see the result. When they laugh, everyone else cries. Laughter is so malignant that it should be expelled from the body. (*Confidentially.*) If we throw out the laugh and the smile, our face will gain that frozen rigidity that is so necessary.

THE DOUBLE: Now I'm getting it: an anti-American political face.

THE MAN: You see how you're learning?

THE DOUBLE: I hear a cry.

THE MAN: It's that one. (*Points to the skull that cries.*)

THE DOUBLE: And why isn't it having a good time?

THE MAN: It's stubborn.

THE DOUBLE: I believed that we were all the same after death.

THE MAN: That one doesn't believe, it's an atheist.

THE DOUBLE: Then what's it doing here?

THE MAN: That's for me to know.

THE DOUBLE: Perhaps some inexplicable tolerance.

THE MAN: If you look carefully, this skull serves a great purpose here. Its crying makes the others happy, those who died defending my cause.

THE DOUBLE: And that one dared to raise a fist against your excellency?

THE MAN: No.

THE DOUBLE: He worked with thoughts?

THE MAN: No.

THE DOUBLE: He made a bomb?

THE MAN: No. He signed a protest.

THE DOUBLE: How horrible! It makes my hair stand on end.

THE MAN: Then comb it.

THE DOUBLE: I can't explain your tolerance.

THE MAN: Well, really he didn't get to sign.

THE DOUBLE: Then he shouldn't be here.

THE MAN: Oh, yes!

THE DOUBLE: Why?

THE MAN: I pardoned his intention. But after he died, he looked for the document, and because he was illiterate, he signed it with an "X."

THE DOUBLE (*moves threateningly toward the skull*): Dirty dog! (*The skull laughs.*)

THE MAN: Look how stubborn he is.

THE DOUBLE: Impudent! Bandit! Traitor! (*The skull guffaws.*)

THE MAN: Stop insulting it. He likes it if you attack him. Treat him badly and he'll cry for us. Little skull of mine, darling! (*The skull begins to cry again.*) His crying encourages the laughter of the others. (*They go to the table. He gives him a pile of papers.*) We're going to throw these papers in the fire.

THE DOUBLE: Are we in hell? I thought we were in heaven.

THE MAN: And so we are. What happens is that in the beyond, like on earth, everything is a little mixed up. Throw in that trash. (*He opens a small door in the foundation through which can be seen the light of the flames.*)

THE DOUBLE: I never read these papers.

THE MAN: It's not necessary that you do; they're complaints.

THE DOUBLE: Look how they burn!

THE MAN: They are the firewood of hell.

THE DOUBLE: Wouldn't it be proper to leave a few pieces?

THE MAN: They come pretty often. In my last seventy years, I've burned other such piles.

THE DOUBLE: My skull doesn't tickle me anymore.

THE MAN: It's already tired of laughing. That indicates that it's almost twelve. Mine has also quieted down. (*They stop laughing.*) Don't even tell yourself what has happened here tonight. In this visceral contact with death, our face has taken on its frozen coldness for another year. Next year you'll be alone here. Are you going to be afraid?

THE DOUBLE: I've cured myself of frights.

THE MAN: That means that you already know as much as I. (*Twelve o'clock strikes. March of trumpet and drum. The skulls turn to show their profiles and keep time.*)

The March of the Skulls

I am a valiant, loyal skull
My former life is worthless.
All together, we keep the death watch:
A destiny a thousand times better.

Skull, skull,
Ex-hero, cannon fodder,
If you had no luck in life,
They tempt you with national brine.
Skulls, laugh!
Skulls, cry!

For the first time THE DOUBLE *appears seated in* THE MAN's *chair, while* THE MAN *looks at it with a great desire to sit in it. There are still some papers on the desk.* THE DOUBLE *goes about picking them up with his fingertips, smells them, sneezes, and then throws them on the desk.* THE MAN *watches the operation and assumes the same expression of displeasure and sneezes simultaneously. A paper falls.* THE DOUBLE *goes to pick it up and* THE MAN *steals his seat.* THE DOUBLE *goes around the chair. Then he takes the telescope and looks toward the outside.* THE MAN *does the same.* THE DOUBLE *scratches a leg while the other takes over the telescope. Afterwards* THE MAN *begins to pace.* THE DOUBLE *walks behind him, stepping on his heels. Sometimes slowly and other times quickly, they both want to put their feet in the same place. At the same time, they try to look through the telescope, leave through the door, or sit in the chair. They lean over the desk, sign in the same place and say in one voice, "Do it!" Shots sound offstage. Both wring their hands.*

THE MAN: Now we can have breakfast.
THE DOUBLE: That's what I say.
THE MAN: You can serve it.
THE DOUBLE: That's what I say.
THE MAN: Don't I say anything?
THE DOUBLE: That's what I say.
THE MAN: Aren't we going to have breakfast today?

THE DOUBLE: That's what I say.
THE MAN (*pushing* THE DOUBLE): Get out. Don't you know that you're in my place?
THE DOUBLE: That's what I say.
THE MAN: You owe submission and veneration to my person.
THE DOUBLE: That's what I say.
THE MAN (*bellowing*): I detest you.
THE DOUBLE: That's what I say.
THE MAN: You're being ridiculous.
THE DOUBLE: That's what I say.
THE MAN: Don't you have a sense of honor?
THE DOUBLE: Oh, yes! I have yours.
THE MAN: And don't I deserve more respect from you?
THE DOUBLE: The same that I deserve from you.
THE MAN: I hope you make a million mistakes!
THE DOUBLE: All my errors will be charged to your account. I don't exist. Believe me, with the transfer of your personality to mine, I feel like the freest thing in this world.
THE MAN (*feeling the stab*): You're killing me.
THE DOUBLE: I hope so.
THE MAN: Thankless wretch!
THE DOUBLE: I'll be the perfect successor. I'll last more than a hundred years.
THE MAN: You don't have the guts.
THE DOUBLE: Yes, I have yours. Want to see them?
THE MAN (*puts his fists in his eyes*): I don't want to see you!
THE DOUBLE: What's the matter, excellency?
THE MAN: I'm hungry. Hungry! Hungry!
THE DOUBLE: Excellency, that's how subversives talk.
THE MAN: You are a monster, but I adore you! (*Embraces him. Curtain.*)

ACT III
THE WORD WAS MADE DOUBLE

SCENE 1

Before the lights go up, the noise of work being done on the dome is heard. In the dim light, a stepladder can be seen. On top of it two blindfolded individuals are putting the finishing touches on the top of the dome. They come down, fold the ladder and stand facing the audience. THE MAN *enters on tiptoe, carrying a flashlight. He checks to see if they have finished the work and shines the light on the blindfolds of the workers. They haven't been able to see anything. He claps his hands and the workers get in line and march out to the beat of a drum. The ladder then exits in step.* THE MAN *makes expressions of self-admiration.*

THE MAN: What a great day! We're going to celebrate a great event, but absolutely no one will see it. No one! (*In a multitude of forms, colors, and types, against the walls of the dome, and on* THE MAN, *are projected slides which announce: ENTRANCE PROHIBITED TO ANYONE BUT ME/ WHOEVER ENTERS COMMITS ADULTERY/ NOT EVEN MY SHADOW IS ADMITTED*) To put the crowning touch on the dome is no trifle. And without making the slightest noise. Not even the Yankees, who are so fond of sticking their noses into everything, know anything about it. The Yankees, what a nightmare! Tonight I dreamed about them. They are my obsession. Will I have to pay for that! A dream about Yankees must be expensive. I, however, am very cheap. My succession, thanks to the miracle it contains, comes very cheaply. In total, what have I spent? They aren't even aware of his existence in the kitchen. We both have eaten from the same plate, even using the same spoon. My suits, made seventy years ago, will be his suits. No one has even suspected that two birds live in this cage.

THE DOUBLE (*enters in pajamas*): How horrible!

THE MAN: Have they seen you?

THE DOUBLE: I spent a terrible night. I thought that morning would never come. I dreamt about the Yankees.

THE MAN: Perfect! We're even the same in our dreams.

THE DOUBLE: But it was horrible. I dreamt that the Yankees didn't exist. What a nightmare!

THE MAN: Who, the Yankees?

THE DOUBLE (*still under the effects of the dream*): Yes, if they didn't exist.

THE MAN: We'd have to invent them. The Yankees are as indispensable as the Devil.

THE DOUBLE: But electronic.

THE MAN: Today is the day.

THE DOUBLE: Today?

THE MAN: I've decided.

THE DOUBLE (*looks at the top of the dome*): Is the dome finished?

THE MAN: All that's left is the unveiling.

THE DOUBLE: Excellency, you still have at least seventy years to go!

THE MAN: I'm not telling you that I don't.

THE DOUBLE: Then you'll go on living?

THE MAN: I prefer to disappear. Why should we go around stepping on each other's heels? My work is finished. Through your person . . .

THE DOUBLE: . . . your person . . .

THE MAN: . . . I will continue ruling. And that's what's important. You will continue copying me . . .

THE DOUBLE: . . . the rest of my days . . .

THE MAN: . . . if you manage that, you already know how to go about dovetailing me.

THE DOUBLE: I swear that I will dovetail. The one who succeeds me will also be your excellency.

THE MAN: Yes, it's right that the feared historical cataclysm won't be produced. My reign will bother some. They will say that they can't stand any more, that they suffer horrors, that they are desperate. But nothing will happen. And do you know why?

THE DOUBLE (*repeating something learned*): Because it will always be easier to put up with you than to throw you out.

THE MAN: I see that you repeat it to the letter. I know that I could go on living indefinitely, but the desire to receive the reward that awaits me is so great that my mouth waters.

THE DOUBLE: Mine too.

THE MAN (*alarmed*): Careful! Let's not die together. That would be the peak of our symmetry. You'd better take an aspirin immediately. If they are taken in time, the greatest catastrophes can be avoided. (THE DOUBLE *exits.*) Take two aspirins! And put on my dress suit because we're going to begin the ceremony. (*Stamps on the floor and the dome is lighted with vigil lanterns. Another stamp and they go out.*) These are

my powers! (*Stamps again and they light.*)
I'm in great form. Yes, just like when I
got rid of the last resisters. It's seventy
years today. I've done so many great things
that I go through each day as though passing through an arch of triumph. (*Prepares
himself for battle. The noises and blows of
such a battle are heard.*) Damn resister!
You thought you could fool me with your
damn cheep, cheep, cheep. I threw myself
at him, and with one blow left him one-
eyed. You're already mine! (*The resister
jumps, tries to escape, falls wounded.*) I've
got you by the neck and I'll beat you
against the ground as if you were a sack of
cats. Go on, go on with your cheep, cheep,
cheep. It seems like an innocent cry, but
it's the most destructive kind. I think that
you've had enough. Anyway, I'm going to
wring your neck (*Does it.*) so you don't
suffer idiotically. Now, now you're with
your own kind. (*Throws the victim down
as though he were trash.*) The devil bless
you! (*Fatigue overcomes* THE MAN. *He
staggers toward the chair, trips over it, then
falls into it.*) But the resisters are stupid:
they don't love death. (*Little by little he
begins to recuperate. In a little while* THE
DOUBLE *enters casting a long shadow.*)

THE DOUBLE: Excellency . . .

THE MAN (*frightened at seeing the shadow*):
How dare you enter dragging your shadow?
(*THE DOUBLE looks at it and exits quickly.*)
The shadow is prohibited. (*Enters again
without the shadow.*) Where did you leave
it?

THE DOUBLE: I tied it outside.

THE MAN: There are things that not even
shadows should see.

THE DOUBLE: The shadow is blind.

THE MAN: Don't you believe it! Let's begin.
(*Solemn music. The curtain that covers the
top of the dome is drawn, revealing something like a large coin on which is engraved
a nude man grafted to another. This legend
forms a circle:* 1 TIMES 1 EQUALS ME
—THE 70TH YEAR OF MY ERA. *Sings.*)

When I die
The present will be with me.

When I die
The past will be relived

When I die
The future will sleep in peace.

When I die
Woe to him who suspects that I'm not
   still alive!

And now I'm going to swear you in. (*They
go about doing what they say.*) Kneel
down. Put your hand on that book. Open
it and touch its pages. That way you'll be
touching its spirit.

THE DOUBLE (*reading a paper emotionally*):

   I solemnly swear
   That I'll never be me.

THE MAN (*making him repeat*):

   And even though I am
   I will refuse to be.

THE DOUBLE:

   I swear that there will always
   Be haves and have-nots.

THE MAN (*making him repeat*):

   Post data:
   And that, moreover,
   They will always be the same.

THE DOUBLE:

   I solemnly swear
   That the present state
   Will be reborn in itself.

THE MAN (*making him repeat*):

   And the one who swears is me,
   Solemnly,
   Even though I'm not me.

THE DOUBLE:

   And after me
   Will not come the deluge.

THE MAN (*making him repeat*):

   But me,
   Always, always me.

(From the socle, he takes a bunch of clothing and objects from his colonial expeditions and gives them to THE DOUBLE *or makes him put them on, converting him into a shapeless pile of things.)* I'm going to throw the weight of history upon you. It's something you shouldn't mistake for used clothing or junk. You'll feel fortified under its weight by the loot of my great deeds. You'll soon feel that the means of power are within your grasp. Look, scrolls. On these, they've called me everything from "father of the country" to "soccer player"—honorary, of course. This is a catalog you should know by heart. With its help, you'll find out how the price of a square meter of your country is quoted in America. Or how you ought to shoot your artillery against the naked underbelly of the revolution. And now I'll hang the whole lot of my five hundred medals on you. I earned them all when the soldier was the only armored thing on the battlefield; when his heart exploded like a grenade; when the Yankees didn't even exist, when, even though the price of bread rose, war was cheap. All that you wear are prizes of valor. They are legitimate medals, none is tin-plate. Finally, here is my pistol, a pistol whose charge is sacred; he who has the privilege of dying from its bullets is guaranteed resurrection. *(Looks at him, stepping back a bit.)* How pleasant to see you like that! Finally you're entirely the flesh of my flesh, heart of my heart. And seeing how you're already me, you're no longer you. Get up and walk!

THE DOUBLE *(tries to move under the weight)*: I'm suffocating!

THE MAN: What's the matter? (THE DOUBLE *moves like a pile of rags.*)

THE DOUBLE: It must be emotion.

THE MAN: Stop being so emotional. Swell up your lungs and do honor to the gifts you've received.

THE DOUBLE: That's what I want, but my strength slips away through some underground drain.

THE MAN: Well, a bad smell is not a proper guest for parties. Besides, everything that smells bad is usually subversive.

THE DOUBLE: Surely all this weakness is unleashed emotion. *(Tries to get up.)*

THE MAN: Milksop, that's enough laziness.

Kindly face up to your heritage. I'm in a hurry.

THE DOUBLE: I'm going, excellency. *(Falls.)*

THE MAN: This smells rotten. You must have done something wrong. *(Looks at the book.)* I knew it: you've sworn with your hand on the Apocalypse.

THE DOUBLE: The most sublime.

THE MAN: Too much folderol.

THE DOUBLE: I've always had a lot of faith in it.

THE MAN: What you need now is strength.

THE DOUBLE: And faith.

THE MAN: Yes, yes, faith in strength. Get up, stupid! *(Falls again.)* It seems that I'm going to have to get the whip.

THE DOUBLE: Why are you in such a hurry, excellency?

THE MAN: I have to go.

THE DOUBLE: Does it smell that bad?

THE MAN: Never mind the smells; men make me sick.

THE DOUBLE: They've always obeyed you.

THE MAN: Don't remind me! At the moment of death I want to forget all worldly pleasures. You can have them!

THE DOUBLE: Thank you, thank you.

THE MAN *(whips him)*: Take this for dessert. Get up! (THE DOUBLE *almost gets up, but falls again.)* I see that the medicine is still necessary. *(Hits him hard.)* And now, my last order: Get up and walk! (THE DOUBLE *gets up automatically, although staggering.* THE MAN *tries to show him how to take his first steps, as though he were a small child.)* A little half-step, another little half-step. That's it. Now, a little step, another little step. Wonderful. Two steps to the front. Careful! Stupendous.

THE DOUBLE *(enthused)*: I know how to walk, I know how to walk! I've taken three steps.

THE MAN: Three little steps on the road to power. That's what counts. More, walk some more. Come here. *(Stretches out his arms to catch him, at the same time as he puts his arms in front of him.)* Very good. I feel like giving you a piece of candy. Come, a little bit more. *(As he gets closer to* THE MAN, *the latter steps back.)*

THE DOUBLE *(tottering)*: No, no, excellency; it won't work that way.

THE MAN: You have to force yourself. Do you feel a new sensation?

THE DOUBLE: Yes, I feel like I've swallowed a sword.

THE MAN: You must be already digesting it. But you must walk. Walking is good for the digestion. (*He manages to walk, although haltingly.*)

THE DOUBLE (*observing his own efforts*): I'm walking by myself!

THE MAN: In a manner of speaking, you've just been born and you walk superbly. I'm a unique teacher: in two steps I've taught you to climb the road to power. From now on you rule. Tell me, I'm curious, what do you plan to do?

THE DOUBLE: Nothing, absolutely nothing.

THE MAN: Then I can die in peace.

THE DOUBLE: When?

THE MAN: Right now. I'm the one who rules over my death! (*Falls dead. Lights and funeral music.* THE DOUBLE *stands like a stone.*)

THE DOUBLE: But . . . is he really dead? He must be, he never makes a false move. I ought to take his pulse, see if he's still breathing. But if I move, I'll fall; if I kneel to see if his body is cold, I'm sure that I won't be able to get up. I can't move. However, I have to do something. And if he is dead, I suppose I'll have to cry for him. He was a great man. Do you cry for great men when they die? No. Great men don't die. At least this one hasn't died: here I am to confirm his immortality. Anyway I'll have to do something with the cadaver. Or has he died in the odor of sainthood? (*Blackout. Celestial glow. Flageolet music. Two golden angels come out of a cloud. They carry golden swords. They honor* THE MAN. *They sing.*)

ANGELS: Failure of death
    That wanted to kill you,
    As if you weren't
    A mighty warrior.

    The stars shine
    To see you walk,
    Armed and secret
    To eternity.

    The earth owes your body
    To the great beyond;
    The badge with which you buy,
    The heavenly land.

Two red DEVILS *make a hole in the floor and come out through it, armed with black and smoking pitchforks.*

DEVILS (*they speak in a vulgar manner and each keeps taking the words from the other's mouth. Pointing to the angels*): Look at those fools!

ANGELS (*reciting*): What's this?

DEVILS: You're seeing it.

ANGELS: We see it, but we don't believe it.

DEVILS: Well, you have two jobs.

ANGELS: What impudence! We'd better cover our ears.

DEVILS: Let's quit messing around and get down to brass tacks.

ANGELS: What are you going to do?

DEVILS: We're going to divide the spoils with you.

ANGELS: Have more respect. You're talking about an immortal.

DEVILS: We see that he's still kicking. Tell your story to somebody else. We know each other too well.

ANGELS: We don't know you at all.

DEVILS: Do you mean that this is the first time we've seen each other? (*They take a bottle from the socle and drink, after first fighting over the wine.*) It's been a long time since I've tasted such good wine. Do you want some?

ANGELS: We're not alcoholics. (*While the others continue drinking, the* ANGELS *try to lift the dead man.*)

DEVILS: Hey, you guys, you're going to wear yourselves out with that load!

ANGELS: Are you talking to us?

DEVILS: Why, they must be stupid. Don't you understand about sharing up there?

ANGELS: With us, it's all or nothing.

DEVILS: Well, then you'll have to leave empty-handed. (*Attack them.*)

ANGELS: Help, help! (*The* DEVILS *get hold of the dead man.*) One ambushed warrior. What insolent rascals! They're a revolutionary kind of devil. Let's behead them. Where's the man? Let's free the man!

A ferocious fight begins between the ANGELS *and the* DEVILS. *The dead man passes from one to the other. Little by little, they are pulling his body apart. At times, confused, they all hit it. At other times, while the* DEVILS *drink, the* ANGELS *fight between themselves, plucking out each other's feathers.*)

DEVILS: Peace! Peace! Let's divide the man's body at the seventeenth parallel and have an armistice.

ANGELS: Man's happiness is indivisible. Ready! Aim! Fire! We'll kill to free man. (*The battle becomes confused again. Words that sound like insults are heard: "Peace," "Assassins," "Pimps," "Armistice," "Long live liberty—but not too long," "Murderers," "Honor," "Fire." The combatants wound each other mercilessly. The battle stops only because of the exhaustion of the opponents.*) You're brutes. You've broken our wings. Now we can't fly anymore.

DEVILS: Come with us to hell, it's near here.

ANGELS: Thanks for the offer. We'll wait until we grow new wings.

DEVILS: You have the luck of lizards.

ANGELS: Of lizards?

DEVILS: When they lose a tail, they grow a new one. On the other hand, when we lose a horn, we retire from active service and things go very badly. That's why they say, "A retired devil doesn't even eat well in hell."

ANGELS: That's because you're damned.

DEVILS: But less than you.

ANGELS: Wise guys! Churls! Insolent rascals!

DEVILS: Don't go screaming like worthless women just because you fought with somebody brave.

ANGELS: We've fought to defend man.

DEVILS: Well, be content, you've already ripped him apart.

ANGELS: It was for his own good.

DEVILS: The same old story. And now, do you want peace?

ANGELS: If there's no choice.

DEVILS: We've acted very humanely: first blows, then sharing the spoils.

ANGELS: We're bleeding.

DEVILS: Put on these spider webs. You'll see how soon you'll be all right.

ANGELS: You treat us. We can't move. Besides this first aid makes us a little sick. (*They put them on.*) What relief! Aren't you bleeding?

DEVILS: Our blood's coagulated.

ANGELS: How modern! How did you get to be so advanced?

DEVILS: Thanks to the many intellectuals you send us.

ANGELS: Then you have the atomic bomb?

DEVILS: That's a lot of nonsense to us.

ANGELS: Now we're better. (*Start to put* THE MAN's *body back together so they can carry it.*) We're in a great hurry. (*The* DEVILS *block their path.*)

DEVILS: And our share?

ANGELS: This great man belongs entirely to us: he annihilated the resisters.

DEVILS: And a multitude of innocent people.

ANGELS: Do the innocent bother you so much?

DEVILS: As much as the resisters bother you.

ANGELS: They were a plague.

DEVILS: The innocent were a blessed lot. That's why this wicked one's got to roast.

ANGELS: Not even if you were the lawyers of the poor.

DEVILS: You leave us the scraps. Give us our fair share or we'll trounce you.

ANGELS: Do you think that we're afraid of you? (*The* DEVILS *pull the spider webs off them.*) Ay, ay! The International Red Cross prohibits attacking the wounded. What are you going to do?

DEVILS: Divide the prey by the seventeenth parallel.

ANGELS: That's going to cause a lot of fuss. It'd be better to share his insides.

DEVILS: We want his heart.

ANGELS: Are you going to perform a transplant? By no means! His heart belongs to us; with it he loves us and fears us. We'll swap you the brain for it.

DEVILS: You always give us the brain!

ANGELS: We don't need it. All our matters are thought out beforehand. It's an immutable reign.

DEVILS: Ha, ha! Your dominion has stopped being absolute. You can no longer kill anyone in heaven that you feel like.

ANGELS: What?

DEVILS: You're already seeing it. Who'd think a couple of years ago that you'd have to enter into negotiations with us?

ANGELS (*give them the brain in a plastic bag*): Here's the brain.

DEVILS (*smell it*): It's still fresh. What else will you give us?

ANGELS: The brain is the center of the nervous system!

DEVILS: We want his right hand.

ANGELS: Forget it! We'll give you that other one. (*Throw them another bag.*)

DEVILS (*after looking at it*): A lousy piece of flesh! (*Give it back.*)

ANGELS (*very surprised*): What! You refuse the sinner's viscera?

DEVILS: It hasn't been used. You'd better keep it.

ANGELS: That word can't enter in the celestial kingdom! (*Cats are heard fighting outside.*) That viscera naturally belongs to you. (*Return the bag to the* DEVILS.)

DEVILS: We don't have room to take it with us.

ANGELS: Well, we refuse it emphatically.

DEVILS: The cats claim their part of the booty. Let's be charitable to the animals. (*A* DEVIL *exits with the bag hanging from his hand. The noise of the cats increases. The* DEVIL *reenters. They all cover their ears. The noise stops, they uncover their ears, but the noise suddenly starts again with more fury. The cats move away, fighting.*) What a clatter!

ANGELS: Even in that detail you can see that it's the viscera of a superior sinner. (*The* ANGELS *turn around to leave with everything. The* DEVILS *attack them and grab part of the dead man.*)

DEVILS: We said by the seventeenth parallel.

ANGELS: Barbarians! That would mean cutting him at the waist.

DEVILS: That depends on your way of looking at it. You see him standing, but we always saw him on all fours. So the sharing is already done.

ANGELS: You've beaten us. How are we going to explain this upstairs?

DEVILS: Tell just what's happened.

ANGELS: If they find out the truth, they'll break our heads. A dialogue with you is something inconceivable. We'll have to say that thieves assaulted us.

DEVILS (*laughing*): This has been a very profitable encounter for us. We're going to rack up a lot of points. And it's even possible that they'll put us on the central committee.

ANGELS (*furious*): You're like witches. You thrive on sin. Go to hell!

DEVILS: That's where we come from. (*Blackout. Mixture of celestial and infernal music, lights, and noises. Voices sing from heaven and others from hell.*)

SONG OF THE DIVIDED MAN

ANGELS: Here is half a good man,
DEVILS: Here is the other half.
ANGELS: The other part was robbed
     By dark forces of evil.
DEVILS: The other we shared
     With the celestial region.
ANGELS: Take the prize, sir,
     Of half of glory.
DEVILS: We are going to give you
     All of hell.
ANGELS: Here is half a good man,
DEVILS: Here is the other half.

SCENE 2

The light of dawn returns to the dome. Birds sing. THE DOUBLE *sleeps standing up, with his head fallen to one side. He stretches and rubs his eyes. Then he goes about trying to walk.*

THE DOUBLE: I'm walking completely by myself! My teacher really was a champion prognosticator. Here I am—I mean, he is—walking with my own two feet—I mean, his. (*Passes a finger over the desk.*) How dusty! The floor is filthy. It looks like a pitched battle was celebrated here instead of a top-secret ceremony of succession. I'm going to clean it up. (*Starts to sweep.*) Yes, it's proper to give it all a good sweeping. (*Pushes the broom.*)

VOICE 1: No, don't touch me!

THE DOUBLE: Who's talking?

VOICE 1: I am.

THE DOUBLE: Who?

VOICE 1: I, the mark of history.

THE DOUBLE: How did you get in here?

VOICE 1: Riding on invisible atoms of air.

THE DOUBLE: I'm going to sweep you away.

VOICE 1: Don't be illiterate: I am the dust, that is to say, the patina of time.

THE DOUBLE: I have to clean up.

VOICE 1: You promised not to be a revolutionary.

THE DOUBLE: But not to be a pig.

VOICE 1: You'd better leave if you are. Some day you too will be dust and you won't like it if they whip you with a feather duster.

THE DOUBLE: Does it hurt much?

VOICE 1: That's not the worst of it. The bad part is that if you remove the dust, you will destroy your own person. You must know that we're only a subtle film of dust that keeps accumulating throughout time. The more dust, the more time; the more time, the more dust. That's why it's accumulated dust and not the clock that's the symbol of time. If you want to last, let the dust accumulate, untouched.

THE DOUBLE (*after a silence*): What else, what else do you have to advise me?

VOICE 1: I have spoken.

THE DOUBLE (*clutches his neck*): I'm suffocating in here. It's impossible to breathe. I'll open a window. (*He goes to open it.*)

VOICE 2: No, don't open it.

THE DOUBLE: Who's talking now?

VOICE 2: I, polluted air. I've been trapped in here seventy years and a day. If you open the window, you'll kill me.

THE DOUBLE: I want to freshen the air.

VOICE 2: You promised not to take the slightest initiative.

THE DOUBLE: Polluted air or whatever you are, you're killing me.

VOICE 2: That's the first impression. You'll see how you get used to it. The most delicate bacteria wind up accustoming themselves to the most poisoned air.

THE DOUBLE: I can't stand it.

VOICE 2: Your life will join perfectly with me, polluted air. You'll end up thanking me, because it will be wonderful for your personal defense. If anyone dares enter here, you won't have to lift a finger to liquidate him. I, polluted air, will dope him in the act.

THE DOUBLE: That interests me a great deal. (*Pauses.*) Tell me, how do you advise me?

VOICE 2: I have spoken.

THE DOUBLE: Merciful heavens! How many secrets this dome keeps! I thought that I knew it like the palm of my hand, but no indeed! Undoubtedly these elements advised my master, but I never suspected the slightest thing. Oh, I'm so tired! So many emotions leave one limp. I'll sit down awhile in the morning sun. (*Moves the armchair to sit down.*)

VOICE 3: Leave me where I was!

THE DOUBLE: Good grief! This is getting to be bothersome.

VOICE 3: I order you to put me where I was.

THE DOUBLE: If you insist, I'll do it. (*Returns the chair to its place.*)

VOICE 3: Better, that's better! (THE DOUBLE *shoves it violently.*) Don't treat me that way. Put me exactly where I was.

THE DOUBLE: Like this?

VOICE 3: No.

THE DOUBLE: And now?

VOICE 3: Stupid! Are you sleeping?

THE DOUBLE: How do I know where you were?

VOICE 3: Open your eyes and look at my marks in the dust.

THE DOUBLE: Ah! Now I get it. (*Puts it in position.*)

VOICE 3: In everything you do, follow the routine to the letter. If you're faithful to this watchword, you won't even make a false move in your sleep. You have to realize that everything you change here will be noticed in the street, and then whatever you've gained will be lost.

THE DOUBLE: Repeat it, repeat that last business to me.

VOICE 3: I have spoken.

THE DOUBLE (*sits down, satisfied*): Now I can breathe perfectly. How right the polluted air was! I'm like a fish in water. Now I'm starting to worry about going out into the street. I'd like to be a snail and carry the dome on my back. It wouldn't be a bad solution, because that way I'd carry everywhere these venerable elements that so wisely counsel me. That way I'd be as good a ruler as my master. I'm sure of it. And, who knows, maybe I'd even go him one better.

VOICE 4: Idiot!

THE DOUBLE: I'll not agree to that no matter where it comes from.

VOICE 4: Idiot!

THE DOUBLE: I'll wring your neck.

VOICE 4: Idiot!

THE DOUBLE: But where's that insult coming from?

VOICE 4: It's not an insult; it's advice.

THE DOUBLE: I won't do anything to you. I want to see you. Where are you?

VOICE 4: Here, in the desk drawer. (*Looks in the drawer and finds a small microphone.*)

THE DOUBLE: A spy! Confess what you're doing here.

VOICE 4: I'm an American counsellor.

THE DOUBLE: My master hated you.

VOICE 4: But he always took advice from the enemy.

THE DOUBLE: How, how?

VOICE 4: I have spoken.

THE DOUBLE (*he remains preoccupied. Paces in silence. His lips move, but his voice is not heard*): If I shouldn't do anything, what should I do? This is the question. Because a thing is clearer than water: in order to do nothing about nothing, you have to do something. Well, that's what I'll do. The first thing, look! (*Looks through the telescope in different directions.*) Not even a fly moves. Nothing, but nothing in the four directions. I can be at peace. But I should stop the danger of the nothingness: so much of doing nothing can lead to philosophical unhinging. I'm not going to fall in love with philosophy and believe that I'm useless. I should do whatever must be done. For right now (*Goes about doing what he says, each time faster.*), I'm yawning. I'll take an aspirin. I don't need it, but it's the ordinarily expedient thing to do. Now I'll scratch myself to avoid itching. I look up. I adjust my pants. I light the light . . . No, no! Not more light. I clean my gun. I make my medals jingle so that they don't rust. I won't give myself a moment's rest. I have to see the many things I did in a flash. Hit the dirt! Let's advance to the enemy fences; we don't have enemies, but we have to be ready for them when we do. Straighten up! Now I've got to step delicately. (*Goes about taking off things which he leaves all over. He is suffocating more each time.*) I'm so tired, but I won't rest even though resting is doing something. (*Continues undressing until he wears only the pajamas that he had on before.*) As the crowning glory of my workout, I'll practice in the laboratory of courage where I have sacrificed the flower of my youth. My youth? Well, whatever it was. (*Exercises.*) Here's where I cut my face. A firecracker exploded in my belly button. I broke a leg . . . I'm already cured of the anguish of not doing anything. Let's see, where is the patriot who has done more than I? And all in a flash. I'm sweating like crazy (*Wipes the sweat from his forehead.*), but I'm not going to rest for a second. (*Sits down at the desk.*) I'll sign some decrees even though they haven't been written yet.

I like to be ahead in my work. I should also study. They won't say that I'm a purely pragmatic politician. I'll study. (*Takes the book on which he swore.*) I'll study even though I know that nobody is going to collect my homework, even though I know that nobody is going to give me a bad grade. I'll study for studying's sake, even those things about which I know absolutely nothing. And all without loud noises, in the pneumatic silence of this dome. Besides that I'll compose verses. My muse is far from those modern muses who destroy everything. And, now, like an explosion of the spirit, I'll sing my own verses, with my own personal music. (*While he sings, a giant fly flits around and lands on the outside of the dome. An overpowering alarm is heard.*)

Sound the cannons.
Hit the dirt!
The country is doomed.
One step forward!

Shoot at close range.
A miracle has been performed:
We saved our pride.
And the ash.

(*Sees the fly. Shrinks back, livid. Pokes himself to prove that he exists and that he is awake. His mouth is dry. He can't find the words.*) I see, what do I see? . . . I hear, what do I hear? . . . a damned fly! With whose permission has she come to the dome? This hasn't happened for seventy years and a day. (*To the fly.*) Dissolve immediately. Individual gatherings are prohibited. I'm going to kill you right now. It'll be enough just to look you in the eyes for you to fall dead, as my master did. (*Stares at it. The fly polishes its wings.*) You're getting ready to die with dignity. You seem like a fly from a good family . . . But why don't you fall over dead?

VOICE 4: Idiot!

THE DOUBLE: Thank you, enemy. (*Rapidly gets dressed in all his clothes.*) In a minute, armed with all my attributes, I'll have the deadly power of my master. I'll show that brazen thing that things haven't changed in the slightest here. The strength that these rags give me is incredible. I'll sleep fully clothed. I'll do everything dressed. I'll roast, but the common good requires sacrifices. (*Now fully dressed, he advances like a leopard toward the fly.*) Look me in the eyes; they roast, they burn my sockets. Don't you dare to look me in the face? (*Moves around seeking the eyes of the fly.*) I'll look for your glance. As much as you try to divert it, I'll roast you. Now! Die! Are you deaf? Die like it's written. (*Disconcerted.*) Something's wrong here. Do I have all the necessary paraphernalia on me? (*Checks.*) And these medals, did my master take the real ones? (*Bites them to see if they're real.*) No, they're pure gold. How did I dare think that about my master? Speak to me, patina of time, polluted air, venerable chair, what should I do? Tell me. Sacred institutions, don't you see that I'm asking your advice? (*Pause.*) The institutions are quiet. It's the man who must decide. But before making the final decision, what do you say? (*Hits the desk. Takes out the microphone.*) I'm all ears. Although it cuts me to the quick, I'll take the advice of the enemy. (*Shouting.*) Speak clearly, without hairs on your tongue!

VOICE 4: I'll do that gladly. Although we are enemies. I'll give you my help. What's discussed in this watchtower of the west is all too important . . .

THE DOUBLE: Stop beating around the bush!

VOICE 4: I'm getting to it. It so happens that your master, undoubtedly impelled by his eagerness to go to a better life, forgot to pass along to you something important: the fear that the others had of him.

THE DOUBLE: Damn!

VOICE 4: Don't damn his memory.

THE DOUBLE: I said damn fear.

VOICE 4: Fear and your master were one and the same.

THE DOUBLE: Then he passed it along to me.

I'm afraid, I can feel it running through me.

VOICE 4: But fear, the reverse of wisdom, is only inspired in the rest when one doesn't have it himself.

THE DOUBLE: I have inherited everything.

VOICE 4: The fear that you need them to have for you is an untransferable gift.

THE DOUBLE: What can be done?

VOICE 4: Get your own immediately.

THE DOUBLE: How? How? Sell me the formula.

VOICE 4: I have spoken.

THE DOUBLE: Speak clearly. <u>Quickly</u>!

VOICE 4: I have spoken.

THE DOUBLE: Damn you! Speak or I'll kill you. (*Pauses.*) Dog! (*Throws the microphone on the floor and kicks it.*)

VOICE 4: Ungrateful. (*Crashing noises within the mechanism of the microphone.*)

THE DOUBLE: I'll level the earth. I'll plant the seed of fear. I'll have my own dead—mine, mine, mine! Not these borrowed skulls. I'll do what I desire and my desire, my real desire, will be the law and order that all will follow without thinking twice. Yes, I'd like to see someone contradict me so that I could wring his neck. The fear that you're going to have of me will make you crawl. But first, I'll liquidate this insolent fly. If it's necessary for me to demonstrate my unleashed fury, I'll do it. Fear has to be planted! Well, on with the planting! (*Goes violently toward the fly. Makes a brusque gesture and hits the spot where the fly is.*) Out! Get out of here! Die!

Hits the part of the dome where the fly is. The fly gets up, glides a little, then flies away. The dome begins to break apart and crumble. It keeps falling on THE DOUBLE *who continues gesticulating violently. Curtain.*

THE BLOOD KNOT

Athol Fugard

CHARACTERS

ZACHARIAH
MORRIS

SCENE 1

Lying on his bed, the one with the shelf, and staring up at the ceiling, is MORRIS. *After a few seconds he stands up on the bed, looks at the alarm clock and then lies down again in the same position. Time passes. The alarm rings and* MORRIS *jumps purposefully to his feet. He knows exactly what he is going to do. First, he winds and resets the clock, then lights the oilstove and puts on a kettle of water. Next, he places an enamel washbasin on the floor in front of the other bed and lays out a towel. He feels the kettle on the stove and then goes to the door and looks out. Nothing. He wanders aimlessly around the room, for a few more seconds pausing at the window for a long look at whatever lies beyond. Eventually he is back at the door again and, after a short wait, he sees someone coming. A second burst of activity. He places a packet of footsalts beside the basin, turns off the stove, pours hot water into the basin and finally replaces the kettle.* ZACHARIAH *comes in through the door.*

Their meeting is without words. MORRIS *nods and* ZACHARIAH *grunts on his way to the bed where he sits down, drags off his shoes and rolls up his trousers. While he does this* MORRIS *sprinkles footsalts into the basin and then sits back on his haunches and waits.* ZACHARIAH *dips his feet into the basin, sighs with satisfaction, but stops abruptly when he sees* MORRIS *smile. He frowns, pretends to think and makes a great business of testing the water with his foot.*

ZACHARIAH: Not as hot as last night, hey?

MORRIS: Last night you said it was too hot.

ZACHARIAH (*thinks about this*): That's what I mean.

MORRIS: So what is it? Too hot or too cold?

ZACHARIAH: When?

MORRIS: Now.

ZACHARIAH: Luke-ish. (*Bends forward and smells*) New stuff?

MORRIS: Yes.

ZACHARIAH: Oh! Let's see. (MORRIS *hands him the packet.* ZACHARIAH *first smells it, then takes out a pinch between thumb and forefinger.*) It's also white.

MORRIS: Yes, but it is different stuff.

ZACHARIAH: The other lot was also white but it didn't help, hey?

MORRIS: This is definitely different stuff, Zach. (*Pointing*) See. There's the name. Radium Salts. (ZACHARIAH *is not convinced.* MORRIS *fetches a second packet.*) Here's the other. Schultz's Foot Salts.

ZACHARIAH (*taking the second packet and looking inside*): They look the same, don't they? (*smells*) But they smell different. You know something? I think the old lot smells nicest. What do you say we go back to the old lot?

MORRIS: And you just said it didn't help!

ZACHARIAH: But it smells better.

MORRIS: It's not the smell, Zach. You don't go by the smell, man.

ZACHARIAH: No?

MORRIS: It's the healing properties.

ZACHARIAH: Maybe.

MORRIS (*taking back the new packet*): Listen to this . . . (*reads*) 'For all agonies of the joints: Lumbago, rheumatism, tennis elbows, housemaid's knees; also ideal for bunions, corns, callouses' . . . that's what you got . . . 'and for soothing irritated skins.' (ZACHARIAH *lets him finish, examining the old packet while* MORRIS *reads.*)

ZACHARIAH: How much that new stuff cost?

MORRIS: Why?

ZACHARIAH: Tell me, man!

MORRIS (*aware of what is coming*): Listen, Zach. It's the healing properties. Price has got nothing . . .

ZACHARIAH (*insistent*): How—much—does—that—cost?

MORRIS: Two and six.

ZACHARIAH (*with a small laugh*): You know something?

MORRIS: Yes, yes, I know what you're going to say.

ZACHARIAH: This old stuff, which isn't so good, is three bob. A sixpence more! (*He starts to laugh*)

MORRIS: So? Listen, Zach. No. Wait man! Price, Zach. . . . ZACH! Do you want to listen or don't you? (ZACHARIAH *is laughing loud in triumph.*) PRICE HAS GOT NOTHING TO DO WITH IT!!

ZACHARIAH: Then why is this more money?

MORRIS: Profit. He's making more profit on the old stuff. Satisfied?

ZACHARIAH: So?

MORRIS: So.

ZACHARIAH: Oh. (*Slowly*) So he's making more profit on the old stuff. (*The thought comes.*) But that's what you been buying, man! Ja . . . and with my money, remember! So it happens to be my profit he's making. Isn't that so? I work for the money. Not him. He's been making my profit. (ZACH. *is getting excited and now stands in the basin of water.*) Ja. I see it now. I do the bloody work . . . all day long . . . in the sun. Not him. It's my stinking feet that got the hardnesses. But he goes and makes my profit. (*Steps out of the basin.*) I want to work this out, please. How long you been buying that old stuff? Four weeks? That makes four packets, hey? So you say sixpence profit . . . which comes to . . . two bob . . . isn't that so? Whose? Mine. Who's got it? Him . . . him . . . some dirty, rotting, stinking, creeping, little . . .

MORRIS: But we are buying the cheap salts now, Zach.! (*pause*) He's not going to get the profits anymore. And what is more still, the new salts is better. (*The thread of* ZACHARIAH's *reasoning has been broken. He stares blankly at* MORRIS.)

ZACHARIAH: I still say the old smells sweeter.

MORRIS: I tell you what. I'll give you a double dose. One of the old and of the new . . . together! That way you get the healing properties and the smell. By God, that sounds like a cure! Hey? How's that Zach.? Okay?

ZACHARIAH: Okay. (*He goes to the bed, sits down and once again soaks his feet.*) You got any more warm? (MORRIS *pours the last of the hot water into the basin.* ZACH. *now settles down to enjoy the luxury of his footbath.* MORRIS *helps him off with his tie, and afterwards puts away his shoes.*)

MORRIS: How did it go today?

ZACHARIAH: He's got me standing again.

MORRIS: At the gate?

ZACHARIAH: Ja.

MORRIS: But didn't you tell him, Zach.? I told you to tell him that your feet are calloused and that you wanted to go back to pots.

ZACHARIAH: I did.

MORRIS: And then?

ZACHARIAH: He said: Go to the gate or go to hell.

MORRIS: That's an insult.

ZACHARIAH: What's the other one?

MORRIS: Injury!

ZACHARIAH: No. The long one, man.

MORRIS: Inhumanity!

ZACHARIAH: Ja. That's what I think it is. My inhumanity *from him.* 'Go to the gate or go to hell.' What do they think I am?

MORRIS: What about me?

ZACHARIAH (*anger*): Okay. What do you think I am?

MORRIS: No, Zach.! Good heavens! You got it all wrong. What do *they* think *I* am, when they think what *you* are.

ZACHARIAH: Oh.

MORRIS: Yes. I'm on your side, they're on theirs. There's always two sides to a sad story and I mean . . . I couldn't be living here and not be on yours, could I? (MORRIS *is helping* ZACHARIAH *off with his coat. When* ZACH. *is not looking he smells it.*) Zach., I think we must borrow Minnie's bath again.

ZACHARIAH: Okay.

MORRIS: What about me? Do I smell?

ZACHARIAH: No. (*pause*) Have I started again? (MORRIS *doesn't answer.* ZACHARIAH *laughs.*)

MORRIS: Yes, you do.

ZACHARIAH (*with sly amusement*): How?

MORRIS: Sweat . . .

ZACHARIAH: Go on.

MORRIS: You're still using paper the way I showed you, hey?

ZACHARIAH: Ja. What's that thing you say, Morrie? The one about smelling?

MORRIS (*quoting*): 'The rude odours of manhood.'

ZACHARIAH: 'The rude odours of manhood.' And the other one? The long one?

MORRIS: No smell? (ZACHARIAH *nods.*)
'No smell doth stink as sweet as labour.
'Tis joyous times when man and man
Do work and sweat in common toil,
When all the world's my neighbour.'

ZACHARIAH: 'When all the world's my neighbour.' (ZACHARIAH *starts drying his feet with the towel.* MORRIS *empties the basin and puts it away*.) Minnie.

MORRIS: What about Minnie?

ZACHARIAH: Our neighbour. Strange thing about Minnie. He doesn't come anymore.

MORRIS: I don't miss him.

ZACHARIAH: You don't remember. I'm talking about before you.

MORRIS: Of course I remember. Didn't he come that once when I was here? And sit all night and say nothing?

ZACHARIAH: Before that, Morrie. I'm meaning before your time, man. He came every night. Ja! (*little laugh*) Me and him use to go out . . . together you know . . . quite a bit. (*pause*) Hey!

MORRIS: What's the matter?

ZACHARIAH: How did I forget a thing like that!

MORRIS: What are you talking about?

ZACHARIAH: Me and Minnie going out! Almost every night . . . and I've forgotten. (*pause*) How long you been here?

MORRIS: Let's see. About a year.

ZACHARIAH: Only one miserable year and I forgotten just like that! Just like it might not hardly have never happened!

MORRIS: Yes, Zach. The year has flown by.

ZACHARIAH: You never want to go out, Morrie.

MORRIS: So I don't want to go out.

ZACHARIAH: That's all.

MORRIS: No. Wait. Why? Ask me why and I'll tell you. Come on.

ZACHARIAH: Why?

MORRIS: Because we got plans, remember? We're saving for a future, which is something Minnie didn't have.

ZACHARIAH: Ja. He doesn't come no more.

MORRIS: You said that already, you know. I heard you the first time.

ZACHARIAH: I was just thinking. I remembered him today. I was at the gate. It was lunchtime. I was eating my bread.

MORRIS: Did you like the peanut butter?

ZACHARIAH: I was eating my bread. All of a suddenly like, I know I'm alone, eating my bread at the gate and it's lunchtime.

MORRIS: You can have it again tomorrow.

ZACHARIAH: And then it comes, the thought: What the hell has happened to old Minnie?

MORRIS: Zach., I was asking you . . .

ZACHARIAH: Wait man! I'm remembering it now. He used to come, I thought to myself, with his guitar to this room, to me, to his friend, old Zachariah, waiting for him here. Friday nights it was, when a ou's got pay in his pocket and there's no work tomorrow and Minnie is coming. There was friend for a man! He could laugh, could Minnie, and drink! He knew the spots, I'm telling you, the places to be and the good times and . . . and what else? Ja! (*reverently*) Minnie had music! Listen, he could do a *vastrap*, that man, non-stop,

on all strings, at once. He knew the lot. Polka, tickey-draai, opskud en uitkap, ek sê . . . that was jollification for you, with Minnie. So, when I'm waiting here, and I hear that guitar in the street, at my door, I'm happy!

It's you, I shout. He stops. I know it's you, I say. He pretends he isn't there, you see. Minnie, I call. Minnie! So what does he do then? He gives me a quick chik-a-doem in G. He knows I like G. It's Friday night, Minnie, I say. Chik-a-doem-doem. Are you ready? Doem-doem, he says. And then I'm laughing. You bugger! You motherless-bastard. So I open the door, and what do I see? Minnie! And what's that he got in his hand? Golden Moments at two bob a bottle. Out there, Morrie. Standing just right on that spot out there in the street with his bottle and his music and laughing with me. Zach., he says, Ou Pellie, tonight is the night . . . (*The alarm goes off*) . . . is the night . . . tonight . . . (ZACHARIAH *loses the thread of his story. By the time the alarm stops, he has forgotten what he was saying. The moment the alarm goes off* MORRIS *springs to his feet and busies himself at the table with their supper.* ZACHARIAH *eventually goes back to the bed.*) What's for supper tonight?

MORRIS: Fish, as usual. (*Watching* ZACHARIAH *surreptitiously from the table*) I been thinking, Zach. It's time we started making some definite plans. I mean . . . we've agreed on the main idea. The thing now is to find the right place. (*pause*) Zach.? (*pause*) We have agreed, haven't we?

ZACHARIAH: About what?

MORRIS: Hell, man. The future. It is going to be a small two-man farm, just big enough for you and me; or what is it going to be?

ZACHARIAH: Ja.

MORRIS: Right. We agree. Now, I'm saying we got to find the right place. (*pause*) Zach.! What's the matter with you?

ZACHARIAH: I was trying to remember what I was saying about Minnie. There was something else.

MORRIS: Now listen, Zach.! I'm sorry, but I'll have to talk to you now. What's the matter with you? Hey? You said yourself he doesn't come no more. So what are you doing thinking about it? Here am I putting our future to you and you don't even listen.

The farm, Zach.! Remember, man? The things we're going to do. Picture it! Picking our own fruit. Chasing those damned baboons helter-skelter in the koppies. Chopping the firewood trees . . . and a cow . . . and a horse . . . and little chickens. Isn't it exciting? Well, I haven't been sitting still, Zachie. I been saying to myself: What's the problem? The right place, I replied. And that's a problem all right. It's a big world this. A big, bloody world. Korsten, my friend, is just the beginning. (MORRIS *fetches an old map from the shelf over his bed.*) Now, I want you to take a look at this. You want to know what it is? A map. Of what? . . . you might ask. Of Africa, I reply. Now, this is the point, Zach. There . . . and there . . . and there . . . and down here . . . Do you see it? Blank. Large, blank spaces. Not a town, not a road, not even those thin little red lines. And, notice, they're green. That means grass. So what you say? So this. I reckon we should be able to get a few acres in one of these blank spaces for next to nothing. I look at it this way. (ZACHARIAH, *bored, leaves the bed and goes to the window and looks out.*) You listening, Zach.?

ZACHARIAH: Ja.

MORRIS: This is not just talk, you know. It's serious. I'm not smiling. One fine day, you wait and see. We'll pack our things in something and get to hell and gone out of here.

Yes! Now that I come to think of it. You say I don't want to get out? My reply is that I do, but I want to get right out. You think I like it here more than you? You should have been here this afternoon. The wind was blowing again. Coming this way it was, right across the lake. You should have smelt it. I'm telling you that water has gone bad. Really rotten! And what about the factories there on the other side? Hey? And the lavatories all around us? They've left no room for a man to breathe.

Go out, you say. But go out where? On to the streets? Are they any better? Where do they lead? Nowhere. That's my lesson. City streets lead nowhere . . . just corners and lamp posts. And roads are no different, let me tell you . . . only longer, and no corners and no lamp posts which, in a way, is even worse. I mean . . . I've seen them,

haven't I? Leading away into the world,— the big empty world.

But when we go, Zach., together, and we got a place to go, our farm in the future . . . that will be different. (ZACHARIAH *has been at the window all the time, staring out. He now sees something which makes him laugh. Just a chuckle to begin with, but with a suggestion of lechery.*) What's so funny?

ZACHARIAH: Come here.

MORRIS: What's there?

ZACHARIAH: Two donkeys, man. You know. (MORRIS *makes no move to the window.* ZACHARIAH *stays there, laughing from time to time.*)

MORRIS: Yes. It's not just talk. When you bring your pay home tomorrow and we put away the usual, guess what we will have? Go on. Guess. Forty-five pounds. If it wasn't for me you wouldn't have nothing. Ever think about that. You talk about going out, but forty-five pounds . . .

ZACHARIAH (*breaking off in the middle of a laugh*): Hey! I remember now! By hell! About Minnie. (*His voice expresses vast disbelief.*) How did I forget? Where has it gone? It was . . . ja . . . ja . . . It was woman! That's what we had when we went out at night. Woman!! (MORRIS *doesn't move. He stares at* ZACHARIAH *blankly. When the latter pauses for a second* MORRIS *speaks again in an almost normal voice.*)

MORRIS: Supper is ready. (ZACHARIAH *loses the train of his thought, as with the alarm clock, earlier.* MORRIS *sits down.*) So . . . where were we? Yes. Our plans. When, Zach.? That's another thing we got to think about. Should we take our chance with a hundred pounds, one hundred and fifty? I mean . . . we can even wait till there is three hundred, isn't that so? (ZACHARIAH *is still standing.*) Bring that chair over there, man, and sit down and eat. (MORRIS *has already started on his supper. As if hypnotised by the sound of the other man's voice,* ZACHARIAH *fetches the chair and sits.*) So what are we going to do, you ask? This. Find out what the deposit, cash, on a small two-man farm, in one of those blank spaces, is. There are people who handle this sort of thing. So we'll find one. Have no worry about that. We'll hunt him down. Take some bread, man. (*offer-*

ing a slice) For all we know, only a couple of months more over here, and then . . .

ZACHARIAH: No! (*Hurls, into a corner, the slice of bread he took from* MORRIS.)

MORRIS: What's this? (*With even greater violence* ZACHARIAH *sweeps away the plate of food in front of him.*) What's that?

ZACHARIAH: You're not going to make me forget. I won't. I'm not going to. We had woman, I tell you. (*Pounding the table with his fists.*) Woman. Woman! Woman!

MORRIS: Do you still want the farm?

ZACHARIAH: Stop it! I won't listen! (*Jumps up from the table. Rushes across to the other side where his jacket is hanging. Begins to put it on.*) What do you think I am, hey? Guess! Two legs and trousers. I'm a man. And in this world there is also woman, and the one has got to get the other. Even donkeys know that. What I want to know now, right this very now, is why me, Zach., a man, for a whole miserable little year has had none. I was doing all right before that, wasn't I? Minnie used to come. He had a bottle, or I had a bottle, but we both had a good time, for a long time. And then you came . . . and . . . (*pause*)

MORRIS: Say it.

ZACHARIAH: . . . then you came. That's all. (ZACHARIAH's *violence is ebbing away. Perplexity takes its place.*) You knocked on the door. It was Friday night. I remember. I got a fright. A knocking on my door on Friday night? On *my* door? Who? Not Minnie. Minnie's coming all right, but not like that. A knocking on my door on a Friday night? So I had a look, and it was you standing there, and you said something, hey? What did I say? Come in. Didn't I? Come in, I said. And when we had eaten I said again, come out with me and a friend of mine, called Minnie. Then you said: Zach., let us spend tonight talking. Ja, that's it. That's all. A whole year of spending tonights talking, talking. I'm sick of talking. I'm sick of this room.

MORRIS: I know, Zach. (*He speaks quietly, soothingly.*) That's why we got plans for the future.

ZACHARIAH: But I was in here ten years without plans and never needed them!

MORRIS: Time, Zach. It passes, and a man gets sick of things. It's happened to you.

ZACHARIAH: I was in here ten years and didn't worry about my feet, or a future, or having supper on time!

MORRIS: The body, Zach. It gets old. A man feels things more.

ZACHARIAH: But I had fun and Minnie's music!

MORRIS: That's life for you. The passing of time and worthless friends.

ZACHARIAH: I want woman.

MORRIS: I see. I see that, Zach. Believe me, I do. But let me think about it. Okay? Now finish your supper and I'll think about it. (MORRIS *puts his own plate of food in front of* ZACHARIAH *and then moves around the room picking up the food that* ZACHARIAH *swept to the floor.*) You get fed up with talking, I know, but it helps, doesn't it? You find the answers to things, like we are going to find the answer to your problem. I mean . . . Look what it's done for us already. Our plans! Our future! You should be grateful, man. And remember what I said. You're not the only one who's sick of this room. It also gets me down. I say: a whole year . . . and sigh . . . but to myself. That's why you never hear. A whole year, I say, and sigh, and always the smell of the rotting waters. In between my cleaning and making the room ready when you're at work, I look at the lake. Even when I can't smell it. I just come here to the window and look. (MORRIS *is now at the window and looking at the lake.*) It's a remarkable sheet of water. Have you noticed it never changes colour? On blue days or grey days it stays the same dirty brown. And so calm, hey, Zach.! Like a face without feeling. But the mystery of my life, man, is the birds. Why, they come and settle here and fly around so white and beautiful on the water and never get dirty from it too! (*Turning to* ZACHARIAH) How you doing, chap? (*Leaving the window*) Have you noticed, Zach., the days are getting shorter again, the nights longer? Autumn is in our smelly air. It's the time I came back, hey! About a year ago! We should have remembered what day it was, though. Would have made a good birthday, don't you think? A candle on a cake for the day that Morrie came back to Zach. Yes. That's bitter. Not to have remembered what day it was. I mean . . .

so much started for both of us, and it wasn't easy, hey? I reckon it's one of the hard things in life to begin again when you're already in the middle. (ZACHARIAH *leaves the table and goes to his bed*.) You finished?

ZACHARIAH: Ja.

MORRIS: Jam or peanut butter tomorrow?

ZACHARIAH: Jam.

MORRIS: Don't you like the peanut butter?

ZACHARIAH: It's all right.

MORRIS: Shall we make it peanut butter then?

ZACHARIAH: Ja, okay.

MORRIS: I knew you'd like it. (*Pause.* MORRIS *makes the sandwiches*.) Has it helped, Zach.?

ZACHARIAH: What?

MORRIS: The talking.

ZACHARIAH: Helped what?

MORRIS: About . . . woman.

ZACHARIAH: No. It's still there. You said you was going to think about it and me.

MORRIS: I'm still busy, Zach. It takes time. Shall I talk some more?

ZACHARIAH: Let me! (*He speaks eagerly. The first sign of life since the outburst*) Let me talk about . . . woman?

MORRIS: You think it wise?

ZACHARIAH: You said it helps. I want to help.

MORRIS: Go on.

ZACHARIAH: You know what I was remembering, Morrie? As I sat here?

MORRIS: No.

ZACHARIAH: Guess.

MORRIS: I can't.

ZACHARIAH (*soft, nostalgic smile*): The first one. My very first one. You was already gone. It was in those years.

MORRIS (*looking at* ZACHARIAH *with interest*): Tell me about her.

ZACHARIAH (*visibly moved*): Hell, man! You say a thing like that! You know, about being young and not caring a damn.

MORRIS: 'So sweet did pass that summer time, Of youth and fruit upon the tree When pretty girls and laughing boys Did hop and skip and all were free.'

ZACHARIAH: 'Did skop and skip the pretty girls.' (*sigh*) Her name was Connie.

MORRIS: That's a lovely name, Zach.

ZACHARIAH: Connie Ferreira.

MORRIS: You were happy, hey?

ZACHARIAH: Ja.

MORRIS: Don't be shy. Tell me more.

ZACHARIAH: We were young.

MORRIS: Shame! That's a moving thought. Must have been a sad sight. You and Connie.

ZACHARIAH: Her mother did washing. Connie used to buy blue soap from the Chinaman on the corner.

MORRIS: Your sweetheart, hey!

ZACHARIAH: I waited for her.

MORRIS: Was it true love?

ZACHARIAH: She called me a black hotnot, the bitch, so I waited for her. She had tits like fruits. So I waited for her in the bushes.

MORRIS (*absolute loss of interest*): Yes, Zach.

ZACHARIAH: She was coming along alone. Hell! Don't I remember Connie now. Coming along alone, she was, and I was waiting in the bushes. (*laugh*) She got a fright, she did. She tried to fight, to bite . . .

MORRIS: All right, Zach.!

ZACHARIAH: She might have screamed, but when I had her . . .

MORRIS: That's enough!! (*Pause*)

ZACHARIAH: That was Connie. (*He broods*.)

MORRIS: And I was away.

ZACHARIAH: Ja. It was the years when you was away.

MORRIS: Feeling better?

ZACHARIAH: A little.

MORRIS: Talking helps, doesn't it? I said so. You find the answers to things.

ZACHARIAH (*undressing for bed*): Talking to one would help me even more.

MORRIS: Yes . . . (*pause*) You mean to a woman?

ZACHARIAH: I'm telling you, Morrie, I mean it, man. With all my heart.

MORRIS (*the idea is coming*): There's a thought there, Zach.

ZACHARIAH: There is?

MORRIS: In fact I think we got it.

ZACHARIAH: What?

MORRIS: The answer to your problem, man.

ZACHARIAH: Woman?

MORRIS: That's it! You said talking to one would help you, didn't you? So what about writing? Just as good, isn't it, if she writes back?

ZACHARIAH: Who . . . who you talking about?

MORRIS: A pen-pal, Zach.! A corresponding pen-pal of the opposite sex! Don't you know them? (ZACHARIAH'S *face is blank*.) It's people, Zach., who write letters to each other. My God! Why didn't I think of it before! It's a woman, you see! She wants a man friend, but she's in another town, so she writes to him . . . to you!

ZACHARIAH: I don't know her.

MORRIS: You will. You're her pen-pal!

ZACHARIAH: I don't write letters.

MORRIS: I will.

ZACHARIAH: Then it's your pen-pal.

MORRIS: No, Zach. You tell me what to say. I write just what you say. You see, she writes to you. She doesn't even know about me. Can't you see it, man? A letter to Mr. Zachariah Pietersen . . . you . . . from her.

ZACHARIAH: I don't read letters.

MORRIS: I'll read them to you.

ZACHARIAH: From a woman.

MORRIS: From a woman. You can take your pick.

ZACHARIAH (*now really interested*): Hey!

MORRIS: There's so many.

ZACHARIAH: Is that so!

MORRIS: Big ones, small ones.

ZACHARIAH: What do you know about that!

MORRIS: Young ones, old ones.

ZACHARIAH: No. Not the old ones, Morrie. (*excited*) The young ones, on the small side.

MORRIS (*happy*): Just take your pick.

ZACHARIAH: Okay. I will.

MORRIS: Now listen, Zach. When you get your pay tomorrow, take a tickey, go into a shop, and ask for a newspaper with pen-pals.

ZACHARIAH (*repeating*): . . . with pen-pals.

MORRIS: That's it. We'll study them and you can make your pick.

ZACHARIAH: And I can say what I like?

MORRIS (*hesitant*): Y-e-s . . . but she's a lady remember, so you must be decent.

ZACHARIAH: And she will write back?

MORRIS: That's what they're there for . . . That's pen-pals.

ZACHARIAH: Hell, Morrie!

MORRIS: Tomorrow you'll see.

ZACHARIAH: And she's going to write to me. Hey what do you know. Pen-pals!

MORRIS: That's it! (ZACHARIAH *flops back on his bed laughing.* MORRIS *drifts to the window.*)

MORRIS: Wind's coming up. You sleepy?

ZACHARIAH: It's been a long day.

MORRIS: Okay, we'll cut it short. (MORRIS *fetches a Bible from the shelf over his bed. He hands it to* ZACHARIAH *who, with his eyes tightly closed, opens it and brings his finger down on the page.*) Four? (ZACHARIAH *nods.* MORRIS *reads.*) 'And if thou bring an oblation of a meat offering baken in the oven, it shall be unleavened cakes of fine flour with oil or unleavened wafers anointed with oil: And if the oblation be a meat offering baken in a pan it shall be of fine flour, unleavened, mingled with oil: Thou shalt part it in pieces and pour oil thereon. It is a meat offering.'

ZACHARIAH: Sounds nice.

MORRIS: Yes. But we haven't got a pan. (*He replaces the Bible, finds needle and cotton and then takes* ZACHARIAH'S *coat to the table.*) I'm helping you, aren't I, Zach.?

ZACHARIAH: Ja, Morrie.

MORRIS: I want to believe that. You see . . . (*pause*) . . . there was all those years, when I was away.

ZACHARIAH: Why did you come back?

MORRIS: I was passing this way.

ZACHARIAH: Why did you stay?

MORRIS: We are brothers, remember. (*A few seconds pass in silence.* MORRIS *threads his needle and then starts working on a tear in* ZACHARIAH'S *coat.*) That's a word hey! Brothers! There's a broody sound for you if ever there was. I mean . . . Take the others. Father. What is there for us in . . . Father? We never knew him. Even Mother. Maybe a sadness in that one, though, I think, at times. Like the wind. But not much else. She died and we were young. What else is there? Sister. Sissy, they say, for short. Like something snaky in the grass, hey? But we never had one, so we can't be sure. You got to use a word a long time to know its real meaning. That's the trouble with 'Mother'. We never said it enough. (*He tries it*) Mother. Mother! Yes. Just a touch of sadness in it, and maybe a grey dress on Sundays, and soapsuds on brown hands. That's the lot. Father, Mother, and the sisters we haven't got. The rest is just the people of the world. Strangers, and a few friends. And none of them are blood.

But brothers! Try it. Brotherhood. Brother-in-arms, each other's arms. Brotherly love. Ah, it breeds, man! It's warm and feathery, like eggs in a nest. (*Pause*) I'll tell you a secret now, Zach. Of all the things there are in this world, I like most to hear you call me that. Zach.? (*He looks at* ZACHARIAH's *bed.*) Zachie? Zachariah! (*He is asleep.* MORRIS *takes the lamp, goes to the bed and looks down at the sleeping man. He returns to the table, picks up the Bible and after an inward struggle speaks in a solemn, 'Sunday' voice.*) 'And he said: What hast thou done? The voice of thy Brother's blood crieth unto me!' (MORRIS *drops his head in an admission of guilt.*) Oh Lord! Oh Lord! So he became a hobo and wandered away, a marked man, on a long road until a year later, in another dream, He spake again: Maybe he needs you He said. You better go home, man! (*Pause*) So he turned around on the road, and came back. About this time, a year ago. Could have been today. I remember turning off the road and coming this way across the veld. The sun was on my back. Yes! I left the road because it went a longer way around . . . and I was in a hurry . . . and it was autumn. I had noticed the signs on the way. Motor cars were fewer and fast. All of them were crowded and never stopped. Their dust was yellow. Telephone poles had lost all their birds . . . and I was alone . . . and getting worried.

I needed comfort. It's only a season, I said bravely. Only the beginning of the end of another year. It happens all the time! Be patient! . . . which was hard hurrying home after all those years . . . Don't dream at night! You must get by without the old dreams. Maybe a few new ones will come with time . . . and in time, please! . . . because I'm getting desperate, hey! . . . I remember praying.

Then I was off the road and coming here across the veld, and I thought: it looks the same. It was. Because when I reached the first pondokkies and the thin dogs, the wind turned and brought the stink from the lake and tears, and a clear memory of two little outjies in khaki broeks.

No-one recognised me, after all those years. I must have changed. I could see they weren't sure, and wanting to say Sir at the end of a sentence, and ask me for work and wanting to carry my bundle for a tickey. At first I was glad . . . but then came a certain sadness in being a stranger in my old home township. I asked the

time. It's not late, they said. Not really dark, don't worry. It always gets this way when the wind blows up the factory smoke. The birds are always fooled and settle down too soon to sleep . . . they assured me.

I also asked the way. Six down, they said, pointing to the water's edge. So then there was only time left for a few, short thoughts between counting the doors. Will he be home? Will I be welcome? Be remembered? Be forgiven . . . or forgotten, after all those years? Be brave, Morris! Because I had arrived at that door, here, about a year ago. I remember I reached it . . . and held my breath . . . and knocked . . . and waited . . . outside in the cold . . . hearing a move inside here . . . and then there was my heart as well, the smell of the water behind my back, his steps beyond the door, the slow terrible turning of the knob, the squeak of a rusty hinge, my sweat, until at last, at long last after a lonely road he stood before me . . . frowning. (*Pause*) You were wearing this coat. It's been a big help to me, this warm old coat . . . then . . . and in the days that followed. But specially then. It was all I saw at first! I didn't dare look up, because your eyes were there, and down below on the ground were your sad, square feet, and coming out to me, your hands . . . your empty hands. So I looked at your coat! At the buttons. At the tears, and your pockets hanging out . . . while we talked.

And that night, in the dark, when you slept, I put it on . . . because, I've got to get to know him again, I said, this brother of mine, all over again. (MORRIS *puts on* ZACHARIAH's *coat . . . It is several sizes too large.*) It was a big help. You get right inside the man when you can wrap-up in the smell of him, and imagine the sins of idle hands in empty pockets and see the sadness of snot smears on the sleeve, while having no lining, and one button had a lot to say about what it's like to be him . . . when it rains . . . and cold winds. It helped a lot. It prepared me for your flesh, Zach. Because your flesh, you see, has an effect on me. The sight of it, the feel of it . . . it . . . it feels, you see. Pain, and all those dumb dreams throbbing under the raw skin, I feel, you see . . . I saw you again after all those years . . . and it hurt.

SCENE 2

The next evening.

ZACHARIAH *sits disconsolately on the bed, his feet in the basin.* MORRIS *is studying a newspaper.*

MORRIS: Well, Zach., you ready? There's three women here. The young ladies Ethel Lange, Nellie de Wet and Betty Jones.

ZACHARIAH: So what do we do?

MORRIS: I'll get the ball rolling with this thought: they are all pretty good names.

ZACHARIAH: That's for true.

MORRIS: Ethel, Nellie and Betty. Good, simple, decent, clean, common names. About equal, I'd say.

ZACHARIAH (*hopefully*): There's no Connie, is there, Morrie?

MORRIS: No. Now, before you decide, I suppose I'd better tell you about them.

ZACHARIAH: What do you know about them?

MORRIS: It's written down here, man. That's why you bought the paper. Listen . . . (*reads*) "Ethel Lange, 10 de Villiers Street, Oudtshoorn. I am eighteen years old and well-developed and would like to correspond with a gent. of sober habits and a good outlook on life. My interests are nature, rock-and-roll, swimming and a happy future. My motto is, 'rolling stones gather no moss'. Please note: I promise to reply faithfully." How's that!

ZACHARIAH: Well developed.

MORRIS: She gives a ou a clear picture, hey! Here's the next one. (*reads*) "Nellie de Wet" . . . she's in Bloemfontein . . . "Twenty-two and no strings attached. Would like letters from men of the same age or older. My interests are beauty contests and going out. A snap with the first letter, please." (*pause*) That's all there is to her. I think I preferred Ethel. I mean . . . there was more to her, it sounds to me and . . . well . . . Nellie's greedy, isn't she?

ZACHARIAH: Ja. And what do I know how old I am?

MORRIS: Exactly, Zach.! I mean . . . it was

years ago, hey! Maybe forty or more, taking a quick look at you. Where does she think she comes from . . . my age or older.

ZACHARIAH: Bloemfontein.

MORRIS: Yes. Last one. (*reads*) "Betty Jones. Roodepoort. Young and pleasing personality. I'd like to write to gentlemen friends of maturity. No ducktails need reply. My hobby at the moment is historical films, but I'm prepared to go back to last year's, which was autograph hunting. I would appreciate a photograph." She's got a education. Anyway . . . it's up to you. Take your pick.

ZACHARIAH (*after thinking about it*): Hey, Morrie! Let's take all three.

MORRIS: No, Zach.

ZACHARIAH: Ag, come on.

MORRIS: You don't understand.

ZACHARIAH: Just for sports, man!

MORRIS: I don't think they'd allow that.

ZACHARIAH (*losing interest*): Oh.

MORRIS (*emphatic*): No, they wouldn't. (*pause*) Listen, Zach., you must take this serious.

ZACHARIAH: Okay.

MORRIS (*losing patience*): Well, it's no good saying 'Okay' like that!

ZACHARIAH: Okay!

MORRIS: Must I talk to you again? Hey! What's the use, Zach.? You ask me to help you, and when I do, you're not interested anymore. What's the matter?

ZACHARIAH: I can't get hot about a name on a piece of paper. It's not real to me.

MORRIS (*outraged*): Not real! (*reads*) "I am eighteen years old and well-developed." . . . eighteen years old and well-developed! If I called that Connie it would be real enough, wouldn't it?

ZACHARIAH (*his face lighting up*): Ja!

MORRIS: So the only difference is a name. This is Ethel and not Connie . . . which makes no difference to being eighteen years old and well-developed! Think man!

ZACHARIAH (*without hesitation*): Look Morrie, I'll take her.

MORRIS: That's better. So it's going to be Miss Ethel Lange at 10, de Villiers Street, Oudtshoorn, who is eighteen years old and well-developed and would like to correspond with a gent of sober habits and a good outlook on life. (*Putting down the paper*) Yes, she's the one for you all right.

Your outlook is quite good, Zach. You have a friendly smile—especially when you're sober, which is what she wants. And I know what we do. How about asking Ethel to take a snapshot of herself? The others done it. Nellie and Betty. We'll get one from Ethel so that you can know what *her* outlook is. Then . . . just think of it . . . you can see her, hear from her, write to her, correspond with her, post your letter off to her . . . Hell, man! What more do you want! (ZACHARIAH *smiles.*) No! don't tell me. That's something else. This is pen-pals, and you got yourself Ethel in Oudts-hoorn. Now, come and eat and we'll talk about our first letter to her. (*At the table*) I got polony and chips tonight. Variety spiced with life, as they say. (ZACHARIAH *sits down at the table and starts eating.*) You want to hear about Oudtshoorn, Zach.? I been there.

ZACHARIAH: Okay.

MORRIS: Sort of give you the picture, so that you can see it.

ZACHARIAH: What's the difference? (MORRIS *looks at him sharply*) One town, another town. This place, her place. She lives in a room in a street, like us.

MORRIS: So you're not interested in Oudts-hoorn. Is that it?

ZACHARIAH: What's it got to do with it? We're going to send a letter to this . . .

MORRIS: Her name is Ethel Lange.

ZACHARIAH: That's right. (*Continues eating.* MORRIS *waits.*)

MORRIS: Well? Finish what you were going to say.

ZACHARIAH: When?

MORRIS: You said: we're going to send a letter to this . . .

ZACHARIAH: Her name is Ethel Lange.

MORRIS: That's right. (*pause*) Okay. Fine. And I was going to tell you about Oudts-hoorn where she lives because I been there, wasn't I? Yes. Well . . . it's about four days from here with good lifts. I been along that road twice and both times it was four days. But I've met those who done it in two . . . even one! Anyway, about Oudtshoorn. I think they call it the dusty uplands of the Karroo, that part where it is behind the mountains. Dry country, man. White, white thorns and the bushes grey and broken off. They roll

about the veld when the wind blows. And, of course, there's the dust as well. Dusty as hell it is, when that wind blows. To get there, Zach., you turn your back on the sea and go north through the mountains. The sky gets big and the earth ends up flat and round like a penny. I want to say this: I'm surprised there's a pen-pal in Oudts-hoorn. It doesn't strike in my memory as a pally sort of place at all. I remember mostly yellow walls and red roofs. That's what you see when you reach there where the road bends beside a river running dry. It was summer, you see, and I was going in on a lorry. We passed people walking to town. They just stopped, and stood there in the dust, and watched us go by. They were our sort. You get them everywhere. Country folk, simple folk. They always stop and watch you go by. Now for Oudts-hoorn itself. I'll give it to you clear. Not too big, as I remember; not too small, either, because it was a long walk through to the other end where the road carried on. Houses, like I said. Red roofs, yellow walls . . . that yellow, sunny wall, you know, with fig trees on the other side, and, of course, the people. Both times I went straight through. I didn't make no friends there. (*pause*) Anything else you want to know, Zach.?

ZACHARIAH: Nothing.

MORRIS: Aren't you interested in the climate?

ZACHARIAH: Ja.

MORRIS: That's a question all right. Well, I thought I was going to die of thirst until that lorry stopped.

ZACHARIAH: Thirsty.

MORRIS: And what about the major industries?

ZACHARIAH: Them too.

MORRIS: Well, as I was saying, I didn't stop long, but I reckon you could get work there like any place else. (ZACHARIAH *leaves the table.*) You finished?

ZACHARIAH: Ja.

MORRIS: Left your chips, Zach. What's wrong?

ZACHARIAH: Not nice chips.

MORRIS: Same as always. Ferreira's.

ZACHARIAH: I-said-they-aren't-nice-chips!

MORRIS: And the bread, too?

ZACHARIAH: Ja. And the bread too.

MORRIS: Okay. (*Starts clearing the table*) But we always have polony and chips on a Friday. (ZACHARIAH *says nothing.*) I mean . . . that was an agreement, like fish on Thursday.

ZACHARIAH (*in a rage*): Well I'm telling you now! They—aren't—nice—chips! (MORRIS *looks blankly at him. This enrages* ZACHARIAH *even more.*) Look at them, will you! Look! This one! Now I just want to know one thing! Does that look like it came from a potato? Hey? And this one? Now tell me. Would you even give this to a horse?

MORRIS: Why a horse?

ZACHARIAH: Why not? Some stinking horse.

MORRIS: They don't eat . . .

ZACHARIAH: You just keep quiet, Morris, and let me finish this time, and don't think I'm going to get lost in my words again. That bloody clock of yours doesn't go off till bed-time, so I got plenty of time to talk. So just you shut up, please! Now this chip . . . and the other one I showed you . . . and the whole, rotten, stinking lot. (ZACHARIAH *is throwing them all round the room.*) If my profit is tied up in this as well, I'll go out and murder the bastard. Well? Is it?

MORRIS: I don't think so.

ZACHARIAH: So you don't think so. How much you pay for them?

MORRIS: Sixpence. Like always.

ZACHARIAH: Like always. Well, all I can say is that he's lucky, because if I ever meet that Ferreira, I'm going to ask him what he thinks I am. A hotnot! A swartgat kaffer!

MORRIS: Stop it! (MORRIS *jumps forward with his arm raised as if to hit* ZACHARIAH. *This silences* ZACHARIAH, *who looks at his brother, first with surprise, then amusement, which finally starts him laughing. His laughter becomes uproarious and he has to sit down on the bed.* MORRIS *turns away.*)

ZACHARIAH: Your face! Your poor bloody face! Hey, Morrie? Why's it you get like that?

MORRIS: I don't know what you're talking about.

ZACHARIAH: Come on, man. I was just making a joke.

MORRIS: A joke!

ZACHARIAH: This hotnot joke. But it always gets you, hey? Now come on. There's a question. To hell with Oudtshoorn, and tell me why it always gets you like that?

MORRIS: I don't like to hear it.

ZACHARIAH (*A pause, then realising his question hasn't been answered*): But why?

MORRIS: Because you're my brother! (ZACHARIAH *shakes his head and turns away.*) What's wrong?

ZACHARIAH: There is something in the way you say that word, that . . .

MORRIS: What?

ZACHARIAH: Something . . .

MORRIS: Go on.

ZACHARIAH: . . . in that word . . .

MORRIS: Brother?

ZACHARIAH: . . . and the way you say it like . . . say it.

MORRIS: Brother.

ZACHARIAH: Like a soft sound.

MORRIS (*trying it out*): Brother!

ZACHARIAH: And a dark sound, too. It's . . .

MORRIS: Brothers!

ZACHARIAH: When I heard it for the first time, I said it means something. He means something, I thought, does Morrie when he says it so often . . . ? So soft and . . . I don't know! What?

MORRIS: Why not, Zach.? It's us. Our meaning. Me and you . . . in here.

ZACHARIAH: Warm. A warm word.

MORRIS: Ah! Now you're on to it. A woolly one. Like old brown jackets a size too big. But what does that matter, as long as it keeps out the cold, and the world.

ZACHARIAH (*breaking away to the window*): Hell, it's hot tonight. You want to know something? I'd like to jump into that lake and swim away.

MORRIS: Mustn't do that. You've seen the notices.

ZACHARIAH: I don't read notices.

MORRIS: They're warnings. It's unfit for human consumption being full of goggas that begin with a B. I can never remember.

ZACHARIAH: Then it's no bloody use, is it?

MORRIS: Just a dead bit of water. They should drain it away, now that winter's coming and the birds are gone. Pull out the plug and fill up with fresh.

ZACHARIAH: You say a thing about it. The one that gives me the creeps.

MORRIS: 'No fish nor fowl,
    Did break the still hate of its face.'

ZACHARIAH: Hell!

MORRIS (*breaking the mood*): Well, what about Ethel? What about writing to her all alone in her eighteen well-developed years up Oudtshoorn way, where I've been. What do you say, Zach.? Do you still want her?

ZACHARIAH (*fervently*): Do I still want her!

MORRIS: Or Nellie?

ZACHARIAH: Nellie.

MORRIS: Or Betty? Do you still want Ethel?

ZACHARIAH: Or Betty, or Nellie. (*pause*) Bellie. (*pause*) Nelly's belly.

MORRIS (*encouragingly*): That's good, Zach.! A little game like that with a word or two.

ZACHARIAH (*sitting on his bed*): You know, Morrie, it's a long time since I called a woman's name.

MORRIS: Now you got three to pick from.

ZACHARIAH: In a woman's name, man, there is . . . (*pause, and a gesture*) When you call it out loud on a Friday night, you know, outside her door, it's like . . . (*pause, and a gesture*). When you whisper it, man, in the grass, in the wet grass, when you start to fiddle and she makes her little cries, it's . . . it's . . . (*pause, and a gesture*) Hey! It's a long time since I called a woman's name. You know, Morrie, you know the one I called with the gladdest heart?

MORRIS: Connie.

ZACHARIAH: No, man. Then I was in hiding. It was by surprise, that time, and only once. I never saw her again. No . . . no, man. The one that gave me the happiest heart was Hetty.

MORRIS: That's a new one.

ZACHARIAH: New one! (ZACHARIAH *laughs broadly*.) New one! You don't know what you mean. She was second-hand. The whole world had fingered her. Connie was new, but Hetty was second-hand . . . something old and a long time ago. It was my youth. You took your chance, you see. You went to her window and called her name and she came when the sound was right. I'm telling you, Morrie, some of them used to come back six times and try, with a dop in between to give them hope. No-one knew what the right sound was, you see. Some days she liked it soft, another day loud, or maybe with a little laugh. I was a shy boy with pimples. Old Sarah sent me to borrow a candle, because Joseph was dying and she needed the light. So I stood in the street, very shy, and called: Hetty . . . Hetty! I only wanted a candle for old Sarah to see Joseph dying, but Hetty came to the window because she liked the sound. She took me and taught me. And you know something? It always worked if I did it that way. And not just Hetty. Sannie too, and Maria . . . they always came if I spoke,—like asking for candles. I'm telling you, man, Morrie, not even Minnie . . . (*pause*) ai . . . ai . . . ai! What the hell has happened to old Minnie!

MORRIS: You said that yesterday.

ZACHARIAH: I'm thinking it again now.

MORRIS: A man can't spend his life with only one thought, Zach.

ZACHARIAH: But why doesn't he come no more?

MORRIS: Maybe he's sick.

ZACHARIAH: Never. Not a day in his long life did he caught a cold.

MORRIS: Then maybe he got old, if it was such a long life as you say. Yes. There's a thought for you.

ZACHARIAH (*horrified*): Minnie,—old?

MORRIS: It happens . . . to men . . . before their time . . . after women and too much life. Can't you see him?

ZACHARIAH: Minnie?

MORRIS: Yes. Take a good look with your mind's eye. No more dancing. No more drinking there! Gone are the vastraps and tickey-draai's.

ZACHARIAH: Why?

MORRIS: His legs are stiff with old age.

ZACHARIAH: Grey hair, too?

MORRIS: If he's got any left. It falls out, you know.

ZACHARIAH: Bald head?

MORRIS: . . . cold bones . . . and nowhere to rest them.

ZACHARIAH: No home?

MORRIS: He's all alone, man, and on the streets, drifting sadly from lamp post to lamp post.

ZACHARIAH: With his old guitar, hey, Morrie!

MORRIS: No! He sold that for food. (ZACHARIAH *has nothing left to say*.) Yes. You ever thought about that? Having to sell things for food. Having to leave this room because you couldn't pay the rent, so you sold it for food. Where would you go, hey?

With that last little loaf wrapped up in newspaper. What would you do when it was finished? You've lost your job, remember . . . and like Minnie, you're alone. Unhappy thoughts, aren't they? And they would be, if I wasn't here. As it is, I am. But only because we're brothers. So you see, you mustn't let that word frighten you. It means there won't be no cold old age for us. We're saving for the future, for the best years of a man's life, when we'll have a place to go and things to do. And, in the meantime, there is Ethel. Which is a good idea, you'll see. She'll fill those empty hours without wasting you away. Which brings us round to your letter. Ready to write it? (*pause*) Come on, Zach. Cheer up, man. Don't be so listless. (*nudging him slyly*) Eighteen years and well-developed. You still want her? (ZACHARIAH *looks up.*) That's better. (MORRIS *moves to the table where he sorts out a piece of writing paper, a pencil and an envelope.*) I've got everything ready. One day I must show you how. Maybe have a go at a letter yourself. Address in the top righthand corner. Mr. Zachariah Pietersen, Korsten, P.O. Port Elizabeth. Okay, now take aim and fire away. (*He waits for* ZACHARIAH) Well?

ZACHARIAH: What?

MORRIS: Speak to Ethel.

ZACHARIAH (*shy*): Go jump in the lake, man.

MORRIS: No, listen, Zach. I'm sitting here ready to write. You must speak up.

ZACHARIAH: What?

MORRIS: To begin with, address her.

ZACHARIAH: What!

MORRIS: Address her.

ZACHARIAH: Oudtshoorn.

MORRIS: You're not understanding. Now imagine, if there was a woman, and you want to say something to her, what would you say? Go on.

ZACHARIAH: Cookie . . . or . . . Bokkie . . .

MORRIS (*quickly*): You're getting hot, but that Zach., is what we call a personal address, but you only use it later. This time you say: Dear Ethel.

ZACHARIAH: Just like that?

MORRIS: You got her on friendly terms. Now comes the introduction. (*writes*) 'With reply to your advert for a pen-pal, I hereby write.' (*holds up the writing paper.*) Tak-

ing shape, hey! Now tell her who you are and where you are.

ZACHARIAH: How?

MORRIS: I am . . . and so on.

ZACHARIAH: I am Zach. and I . . .

MORRIS: . . . ariah Pietersen . . . go on.

ZACHARIAH: And I am at Korsten.

MORRIS: As you will see from the above.

ZACHARIAH: What's that?

MORRIS: Something you must add in letters. (*newspaper*) She says here: My interests are nature, rock-and-roll, swimming and a happy future. Well, what do you say to that?

ZACHARIAH: Shit! (*Pause. Frozen stare from* MORRIS.) Sorry, Morrie. Nature and a happy future. Ja. Good luck! How's that? Good luck, Ethel.

MORRIS: Not bad. A little short, though. How about: I notice your plans, and wish you good luck with them.

ZACHARIAH: Sure, sure. Put that there. (MORRIS *writes, then returns to the newspaper.*)

MORRIS: 'My motto is: rolling stones gather no moss.' (*pause*) That's tricky.

ZACHARIAH: I can see that.

MORRIS: What does she mean?

ZACHARIAH: I wonder.

MORRIS: Wait! I have it. How do you feel about: 'Too many cooks spoil the broth.' That's my favourite.

ZACHARIAH: Why not? Why not, I ask?

MORRIS: Then it's agreed. (*writes*) 'Experience has taught me to make my motto: Too many cooks spoil the broth.' Now let's get a bit general, Zach.

ZACHARIAH (*yawning*): Just as you say.

MORRIS (*after a pause*): Well, it's your letter.

ZACHARIAH: Just a little bit general. Not too much, hey!

MORRIS (*not fooled by the feigned interest*): No. (*pause*) I can make a suggestion.

ZACHARIAH: That's fine. Put that down there, too.

MORRIS: No, Zach. Here it is. How about: I have a brother who has seen Oudtshoorn twice.

ZACHARIAH: You.

MORRIS: Of course. (*pause*) Well?

ZACHARIAH: Maybe.

MORRIS: You mean . . . you don't like it?

ZACHARIAH: I'll tell you what. Put in there: I'd like to see Oudtshoorn. I've heard about it from someone. (MORRIS *writes.*)

MORRIS: What else?

ZACHARIAH: I'd like to see you too. Send me a photo.

MORRIS: . . . please . . . I'm near the bottom now.

ZACHARIAH: That's all.

MORRIS: Please write soon. Yours . . .

ZACHARIAH: Hers?

MORRIS: . . . faithfully. Zachariah Pietersen. (ZACHARIAH *prepares for bed.* MORRIS *addresses and seals the envelope.*) I'll get this off tomorrow. Remember, this is your letter, and what comes back is going to be your reply.

ZACHARIAH: And yours?

MORRIS: Mine?

ZACHARIAH: There's still Nellie. Or Betty. Plenty of big words there, as I remember.

MORRIS: One's enough. (ZACHARIAH *lies down on his bed and watches* MORRIS *who has taken down the Bible.*) My turn tonight. (*Opens the Bible and chooses a passage.*) Matthew. I like Matthew. (*reads*) "And Asa begat Josaphat and Josaphat begat Joram, and Joram begat Ozias, and Ozias begat Joatham, and Joatham begat Achas, and Achas begat Ezekias, and Ezekias begat Manasses, and Manasses begat Amon, and Amon begat Josias!" (*pause*) That must have been a family. (*Puts away the Bible and prepares his own bed.*) Why you looking at me like that, Zach.?

ZACHARIAH: I'm thinking.

MORRIS: Aha! Out with it.

ZACHARIAH: You ever had a woman, Morris? (MORRIS *looks at* ZACHARIAH *blankly, then pretends he hasn't heard.*) Have you?

MORRIS: What do you mean?

ZACHARIAH: You know what I mean.

MORRIS: Why?

ZACHARIAH: Have—you—ever—had—a—woman?

MORRIS: When?

ZACHARIAH: Why have I never thought of that before? You been here a long time now, and never once did you go out, or speak to me about woman. Not like Minnie did. Anything the matter with you?

MORRIS: Not like Minnie! What's that mean? Not like Minnie! Maybe it's not nice to be like Minnie. Hey? Or maybe I just don't want to be like Minnie! Ever thought about that? That there might be another way, a different way? Listen. You think I don't know there's woman in this world, or that I haven't got two legs and trousers too? That I haven't longed for beauty? Well, I do. But that's not what you're talking about, is it? That's not what Minnie means, hey! That's two bloody donkeys on a road full of stones and Connie crying in the bushes. Well, you're right about that. I am not interested. I touched the other thing once, with my life and these hands, and there was no blood, or screaming, or pain. I just touched it and felt warmth and softness and wanted it like I've never wanted anything in my whole life. Ask me what's the matter with me for not taking it when I touched it. That's the question. Do you want to know what was the matter with me? Do you? Zach.? (*Pause, then softly*) Zach.? (ZACHARIAH *is asleep.* MORRIS *takes the blanket off his own bed and covers the sleeping man. He puts out the light and goes to bed.*)

SCENE 3

A few days later.

MORRIS *is at the table counting their savings—banknotes and silver. The alarm clock rings. He sweeps the money into a tin which he then carefully hides among the pots on the kitchen-dresser. Next he resets the clock and prepares the footbath as in the first scene.* ZACHARIAH *appears, silent and sullen, goes straight to the bed, where he sits.*

MORRIS: You look tired tonight, old man. (ZACHARIAH *looks at him askance.*) Today too long? I watched you dragging your feet home along the edge of the lake. I'd say, I said, that that was a weary body. Am I right, old fellow?

ZACHARIAH: What's this 'old fellow' thing you got hold of tonight?

MORRIS: Just a figure of speaking, Zach. The shape of round shoulders, a bent back, a tired face. The Englishman would say 'old boy' . . . but we don't like that 'boy' business, hey?

ZACHARIAH: Ja. They call a man a boy. You got a word for that, Morrie?

MORRIS: Long or short?

ZACHARIAH: Squashed, like it didn't fit the mouth.

MORRIS: I know the one you mean.

ZACHARIAH: Then say it.

MORRIS: Prejudice.

ZACHARIAH: Pre-ja-dis.

MORRIS: Injustice!

ZACHARIAH: That's all out of shape as well.

MORRIS: Inhumanity!

ZACHARIAH: No. That's when he makes me stand at the gate.

MORRIS: Am I right in thinking you were there again today?

ZACHARIAH: All day long.

MORRIS: You tried to go back to pots?

ZACHARIAH: I tried to go back to pots. My feet, I said, are killing me.

MORRIS: And then?

ZACHARIAH: Go to the gate or go to hell . . . Boy!

MORRIS: He said boy as well?

ZACHARIAH: He did.

MORRIS: In one sentence?

ZACHARIAH: Prejudice and inhumanity in one sentence! (*He starts to work off one shoe with the other foot and then dips the bare foot into the basin of water. He will not get as far as taking off the other shoe.*)

ZACHARIAH: When your feet are bad, you feel it.

MORRIS: Try resting your legs.

ZACHARIAH: It's not so much in the legs.

MORRIS: Find a chair, then. Support your back.

ZACHARIAH: Chair! (*scorn and contempt*) A chair over there! What you talking about? A chair at the gate! Wake up, man! Anyway, it's not so much in my back also. It's here. (*A hand over his heart*)

MORRIS: Ah, yes. *That* weariness.

ZACHARIAH: What is it?

MORRIS: The muscles of your heart.

ZACHARIAH: Ja. Ja! That sounds like it all right. The muscles of my heart are weary. That's it, man! Inside me, just here, I'm so tired, so damn tired to the bottom of my body of . . . what?

MORRIS: Beating. That's what a heart does to a man.

ZACHARIAH (*gratitude*): By God, Morrie, you're on to it tonight. I'm tired of beating, beating, every day another beating. (*Pause*) What's all this beating for anyway?

MORRIS: Blood.

ZACHARIAH: It gets worse and worse, hey! (*Pause*) I looked at the stuff once, on my hands. It was red, so red as . . .

MORRIS: Pain.

ZACHARIAH: Ja. (*little laugh*) But it wasn't mine. So it's my heart, is it? Getting tired. Tell me about it, Morrie. (MORRIS *says nothing, but holds up his hand and rhythmically clenches and unclenches his fist.*) What's that?

MORRIS: Your heart.

ZACHARIAH: Eina! (MORRIS *continues.*) Give it a rest.

MORRIS: Doesn't rest.

ZACHARIAH: Not at all?

MORRIS: All the time.

ZACHARIAH: All the day?

MORRIS: And the night.

ZACHARIAH: Day and night?

MORRIS: In your bed.

ZACHARIAH: At the gate?

MORRIS: Until . . . (*He breaks the rhythm. Keeps his fist clenched*) Do you know what that is?

ZACHARIAH: No.

MORRIS: A failure. Dead.

ZACHARIAH (*upset*): No, man!

MORRIS: Put your hand on your chest. You can feel it.

ZACHARIAH: Oh no, oh no!

MORRIS: Like I just showed you.

ZACHARIAH: I don't want to see it.

MORRIS: Don't be scared, man. (ZACHARIAH *shakes his head.*) Then let me. (*Puts his hand over* ZACHARIAH's *heart.* ZACHARIAH *tenses.*)

ZACHARIAH: Still beating?

MORRIS: Yes. (*Pause*)

ZACHARIAH: Still there?

MORRIS: Yes. It's going: dub-dub dub-dub dub-dub . . . (*The strain is too much for* ZACHARIAH. *He pushes* MORRIS *away.*)

ZACHARIAH: That's enough.

MORRIS: Come on . . .

ZACHARIAH: I'm all right now. It's feeling fine. Tiredness gone.

MORRIS: Okay. (*Starts helping* ZACHARIAH *take off his coat.*) Funny, you know. I never thought about that before. That old heart of yours, beating away all the time, all the years when I was away. It's a sad thought. (*At this point* MORRIS *finds an envelope in the inside pocket of* ZACHARIAH's *coat. He examines it secretly.* ZACHARIAH *broods on, one foot in the basin.*) Did you stop by the Post Office on your way back?

ZACHARIAH: Ja.

MORRIS: Nothing again? (*pause*) Looks like she's not replying.

ZACHARIAH: Who?

MORRIS: Ethel.

ZACHARIAH: Ja. There was a letter.

MORRIS: I know there was. (*holding up the envelope*) I just found it.

ZACHARIAH: Good.

MORRIS: Good? What do you mean good?

ZACHARIAH: You know . . . good, like Okay.

MORRIS (*excited and annoyed*): What's the matter with you?

ZACHARIAH (*hand to his heart*): What's the matter with me?

MORRIS: Don't you realise? This is your pen-pal. This is your reply from Ethel!

ZACHARIAH: In Oudtshoorn.

MORRIS: But Zach.! You must get excited, man! Don't you want to know what she said?

ZACHARIAH: Sure.

MORRIS: Shall we open it then?

ZACHARIAH: Why not! (MORRIS *tears open the letter.*)

MORRIS: By God, she did it! She sent you a picture of herself.

ZACHARIAH (*first flicker of interest*): She did?

MORRIS: So this is Ethel!

ZACHARIAH: Morrie . . . ?

MORRIS: Eighteen years . . . and fully . . . developed.

ZACHARIAH: Let me see, man! (*He grabs the photograph. The certainty and excitement fade from* MORRIS' *face. He is obviously perplexed at something.*) Hey! Not bad. Now that's what I call a goosie. Good for old Oudtshoorn, I say. You don't get them like this over here. That I can tell you. Not with a watch! Old Hetty couldn't even tell the time. But she's got one. You see that, Morrie? Good for old Ethel, all right. Pretty smart, too. No doek. Nice hair. Just look at those locks. And how's that for a wall she's standing against? Ever seen a wall like that, as big as that, in Korsten? I mean it's made of bricks, isn't it!

MORRIS (*snatching the photograph out of* ZACHARIAH'S *hands and taking it to the window where he has a good look*): Give it to me!

ZACHARIAH: Hey! What's the matter with you! It's my pen-pal, isn't it? It is!

MORRIS: Keep quiet, Zach.!

ZACHARIAH: What's this, 'keep quiet'? It's my room, isn't it? It is!

MORRIS: Where's the letter?

ZACHARIAH: You had it.

MORRIS: Where did I put it? (*He throws the photograph down on the bed and finds the letter, which he reads feverishly.* ZACHARIAH *picks up the photograph and continues his study.*)

ZACHARIAH: You're acting like you never seen a woman in your life. Why don't you get you a pen-pal? Maybe one's not enough.

MORRIS (*having finished the letter, his agitation is now even more pronounced*): That newspaper, Zach. Where is the newspaper?

ZACHARIAH: I don't know.

MORRIS (*anguish*): Think, man!

ZACHARIAH: You had it. (MORRIS *is scratching around frantically.*) What's the matter with you tonight? Maybe you threw it away.

MORRIS: No. I was keeping it in case . . . (*finds it*) Thank God! Oh, please, God, now make it that I am wrong!

ZACHARIAH: What the hell are you talking about? (MORRIS *takes a look at the newspaper, pages through it and then drops it. He stands quite still, unnaturally calm after the frenzy of the previous few seconds.*)

MORRIS: You know what you done, don't you?

ZACHARIAH: Me?

MORRIS: Who was it then? Me?

ZACHARIAH: But what?

MORRIS: Who wanted woman?

ZACHARIAH: Me.

MORRIS: Right. Who bought the paper?

ZACHARIAH: Me.

MORRIS: Right. Who's been carrying on about Minnie, and Connie, and good times? Not me.

ZACHARIAH: Morrie! What are you talking about?

MORRIS: That photograph.

ZACHARIAH: I've seen it.

MORRIS: Well, have another look.

ZACHARIAH (*he does*): It's Ethel.

MORRIS: *Miss* Ethel Lange to you!

ZACHARIAH: Okay, I looked. Now what?

MORRIS: Can't you see, man! Ethel Lange is

a white woman! (*Pause. They look at each other in silence.*)

ZACHARIAH (*slowly*): You mean that this Ethel . . . here . . .

MORRIS: Is a white woman!

ZACHARIAH: How do you know?

MORRIS: Use your eyes. Anyway, that paper you bought, it's white. There's no news about our sort.

ZACHARIAH (*studying the photo*): You're right, Morrie. (*Delighted*) You're damn well right. And she's written to me, to a hotnot, a swartgat. This white woman thinks I'm a white man. That I like! (ZACHARIAH *bursts into laughter.* MORRIS *jumps forward and snatches the photograph out of his hand.*) Hey! What you going to do?

MORRIS: What do you think?

ZACHARIAH (*hopefully*): Read it?

MORRIS: I'm going to burn it.

ZACHARIAH: No!

MORRIS: Yes.

ZACHARIAH: I say no! (ZACHARIAH *jumps up and comes to grips with* MORRIS *who, after a short struggle, is thrown violently to the floor.* ZACHARIAH *picks up the letter and the photograph. He stands looking down at* MORRIS *for a few seconds, amazed at what he has done.*) No, Morrie. You're not going to burn it.

MORRIS: You hit me!

ZACHARIAH: I didn't mean it.

MORRIS: But you did, didn't you? Here on my chest.

ZACHARIAH: You was going to burn it.

MORRIS (*vehemently*): Yes, burn it! Destroy it!

ZACHARIAH: But it's my pen-pal, Morris. Now, isn't it? Doesn't it say here: Mr. Zachariah Pietersen? Well, that's me . . . isn't it? It is. My letter. You just don't go and burn another man's letter, Morrie.

MORRIS: But it's an error, Zach.! Can't you see? The whole thing is an error.

ZACHARIAH: You must read it to me first. I don't know. (*The alarm rings.*)

MORRIS: Supper time.

ZACHARIAH: Later.

MORRIS: Listen . . .

ZACHARIAH: Letter first.

MORRIS: Then can I burn it?

ZACHARIAH: Read the letter first, man. Let's hear it. (*Handing* MORRIS *the letter*) No funny business, hey!

MORRIS (*reading*): 'Dear Zach., many thanks for your letter. You asked me for a snap, so I'm sending you it. Do you like it? That's my brother's foot sticking in the picture behind the bench on the side . . .'

ZACHARIAH: She's right! Here it is.

MORRIS: 'Cornelius is a . . . policeman.' (*Pause*)

ZACHARIAH (*serene*): Go on.

MORRIS: 'He's got a motorbike, and I been with him to the dam, on the back. My best friend is Lucy van Tonder. Both of us hates Oudtshoorn, man. How is P.E.? There's only two bios here, so we don't know what to do on the other nights. That's why I want pen-pals. How about a . . . picture . . .' (*Pause*)

ZACHARIAH (*still serenely confident*): Go on.

MORRIS: 'How about a picture of you? You got a car? All for now. Tot siens, Ethel. P.S. Please write soon.' (MORRIS *folds the letter*) Satisfied?

ZACHARIAH (*gratefully*): Thank you, Morrie. (*Holds out his hand for the letter.*)

MORRIS: Can I burn it now?

ZACHARIAH: Burn it! It's a all right letter, man. A little bit of this and a little bit of that.

MORRIS: Like her brother being a policeman.

ZACHARIAH (*ignoring the last remark*): Supper ready yet? Let's talk after supper, man. I'm hungry. What you got, Morrie?

MORRIS: Boiled egg and chips.

ZACHARIAH: Sounds good. Hey! We never had that before.

MORRIS (*sulking*): It was meant to be a surprise.

ZACHARIAH: But that's wonderful. (ZACHARIAH *is full of vigour and life.*) No. I mean it, Morrie. Cross my heart, and hope to die. Boiled egg! I never even knew you could do it. (ZACHARIAH *takes his place at the table, and stands up the photograph in front of him. When* MORRIS *brings the food to the table, he sees it and hesitates.*)

ZACHARIAH: Just looking, Morrie. She sent it for me to look at her, didn't she? (*Eats.* MORRIS *sits down.*) What's it got here on the back?

MORRIS (*examines the back of the photograph*): 'To Zach., with love, from Ethel.' (*Another burst of laughter from* ZACHARIAH. MORRIS *leaves the table abruptly.*)

ZACHARIAH (*calmly continuing with his meal*):
What's the matter?

MORRIS: I'm not hungry.

ZACHARIAH: You mean, you don't like to hear
me laugh?

MORRIS: It's not that . . .

ZACHARIAH: It is. But it's funny, man. She
and me. Of course, it wouldn't be so funny
if it was you who was pally with her.

MORRIS: What does that suppose it means?

ZACHARIAH: Don't you know?

MORRIS: No. So will you kindly please tell
me?

ZACHARIAH: You never seen yourself, Morrie?

MORRIS (*trembling with emotion*): Be careful, Zach.! I'm warning you now. Just you
be careful of where your words are taking
you!

ZACHARIAH: Okay. Okay. (*eats in silence*)
You was telling me the other day about
Oudtshoorn. How far you say it was?

MORRIS (*viciously*): Hundreds of miles.

ZACHARIAH: So far, hey?

MORRIS: Ah! I get your game. Don't fool
yourself. It's *not* far enough for safety's
sake. Cornelius has got a motorbike, remember?

ZACHARIAH: Ja. But we don't write to him,
man.

MORRIS: Listen, Zach., if you think for one
moment that I'm going to write . . .

ZACHARIAH: Think? Who says? I been eating
my supper. It was good, Morrie. The eggs
and chips. Tasty.

MORRIS: Don't try to change the subject matter!

ZACHARIAH: Me? I like that. You mean,
what's the matter with you! You was the
one that spoke about pen-pals first. Not me.

MORRIS: So here it comes at last. I've been
waiting for it. I'm to blame, am I? All
right. I'll take the blame. I always did,
didn't I? But this is where it ends. I'm
telling you now, burn that letter, because
when they come around here and ask me,
I'll say I got nothing more to do with it.

ZACHARIAH (*bluff indignation*): Burn this letter! What's wrong with this letter?

MORRIS: Ethel Lange is a white woman!

ZACHARIAH: Wait . . . wait . . . wait . . . not
so fast. I'm a sort of slow man. We were
talking about this letter, not her. Now tell
me, what's wrong with what you did read?
Does she call me names? No. Does she

laugh at me? No. Does she swear at me?
No. Just a simple letter with a little bit of
this and a little bit of that. Now comes
the clue. What sort of chap is it that
throws away a few kind words? Hey, Morrie? Aren't they, as you say, precious things
these days? And this pretty picture of a
lovely girl? I burn it! What sort of doing
is that? Bad. Think of Ethel, man. Think!
Sitting up there in Oudtshoorn with Lucy,
waiting . . . waiting . . . for what? For
nothing. For why? Because bad Zach. Pietersen burnt it. No, Morrie. Good is good,
fair is fair and I may be a shade of black,
but I go gently as a man.

MORRIS: Are you finished? (*Pause*) I just want
to remind you, Zach., that when I was
writing to her you weren't even interested
in a single thing I said. Ja . . . Ja . . . Okay
. . . Okay . . . That's all that came from
you. But now, suddenly, now you are!
Why? Why, I ask myself . . . and a suspicious little voice answers: is it maybe because she's white? (*pause*) Well?

ZACHARIAH: Okay. Do you want to hear me
say it? (MORRIS *says nothing.*) It's because
she's white! I like this little white girl! I
like the thought of this little white girl. I'm
thinking it, now. Look at me. Ja. Can't
you see? I'm serious, but I'm also smiling.
I'm telling you I like the thought of this
little white Ethel better than our future,
or the plans, or getting away, or foot salts
or any other damned thing in here. It's a
warm thought for a man in winter. It's the
best thought I ever had and I'm keeping it.
So maybe it's a error as you say. Well that's
just too bad. We done it, and now I got
it and I'm keeping it, and don't you try
no tricks like trying to get it away from
me. Who knows? You might get to liking
it too. (MORRIS *says nothing.* ZACHARIAH
comes closer.) Ja. There's a thought there.
What about *you*, Morrie? You never had
it before? . . . that thought? A man like
you, specially you, always thinking so many
things! A man like you who's been places!
You're always telling me about the places
you been. Wasn't there ever no white
woman thereabouts? I mean . . . You
must have smelt them someplace. That
sweet, white smell, you know. They leave
it behind. (*Nudging* MORRIS) Of course,
you did. Hey? I bet you had that thought

all the time. I bet you been having it in here. Hey? You should have shared it, Morrie. I'm a man with a taste for thoughts these days. It hurts to think you didn't share a good one like that with your brother. Giving me all that shit about future and plans, and then keeping the real goosie for yourself. You weren't scared, were you? That I would tell? Come on. Confess. You were scared, hey! A little bit poopy. I've noticed that. But you needn't worry now. I'm a man for keeping a secret, and anyway, we'll play this very careful . . . very, very careful. Ethel won't never know about us, and I know how to handle that brother. Mustn't let a policeman bugger you about, man. So go get your pencil and piece of paper. (MORRIS *defeated. He sits at the table.* ZACHARIAH *paces.*) We'll go gently with this one. There'll be others . . . later. So we'll take her on friendly terms again. (*pause*) "Dear Ethel, (MORRIS *writes.*) I think you might like to know I got your letter, and the picture. I'd say Oudtshoorn seems all right. You were quite all right too. I would like to send you a picture of me, but it's this way. It's winter down here now. The light is bad, the lake is black, the birds have gone. Wait for spring, when things improve. Okay? Good. I heard you ask about my car. Yes. I have it. We pumped the tyres today. Tomorrow I think I'll put in some petrol. I'd like to take you for a drive, Ethel, and Lucy too. In fact, I'd like to drive both of you. They say over here, I'm fast. I'll tell you this. If I could drive you, I would do it so fast, Ethel, and Lucy too, both of you, so fast I would, it would hurt . . ."

MORRIS: Okay, Zach.!!

ZACHARIAH (*pulling himself together*): "Ja! But don't worry. I got brakes. (*pause*) I notice your brother got boots. All policeman got boots, I notice. Good luck to him, anyway, and Lucy too. Write soon. Zachariah Pietersen." (*pause*) Okay, Morrie. Do your business on the envelope, but I'll post it. There, you see! Nothing to it, was there? A little bit of this and a little bit of that and nothing about some things. When Ethel gets it, she'll say: He's okay. This Zachariah Pietersen is okay, Lucy! Say something, Morrie.

MORRIS: I'm okay.

ZACHARIAH: That's better. Don't you think it was a good letter? For a man who hasn't done one before?

MORRIS: I have a feeling about it Zach., about this whole business.

ZACHARIAH: A feeling about Ethel? (*laughs*) I told you!

MORRIS: Zach.! Listen to me without getting angry. (*pause*) Let me burn it.

ZACHARIAH: My letter?

MORRIS: Yes.

ZACHARIAH: The one we just done?

MORRIS: Yes.

ZACHARIAH: Ethel's letter, now my letter! (*He gets up and takes the letter in question away from* MORRIS.) You're in a burning mood, all right.

MORRIS: Please, Zach. You're going to get hurt.

ZACHARIAH (*aggression*): Such as by who?

MORRIS: Ethel. (ZACHARIAH *laughs.*) Then yourself! Yes. Do you think a man can't hurt himself? Let me tell you, he can. More than anybody else can hurt him, he can hurt him . . . self. I know. What's to stop him dreaming forbidden dreams at night and waking up too late? Hey? Or playing dangerous games with himself and forgetting where to stop? I know them, I tell you, these dreams and games a man has with himself. That. There in your hand. To Miss Ethel Lange, Oudtshoorn. You think that's a letter? I'm telling you it's a dream, and the most dangerous one. Maybe, just maybe, when the lights are out, when you lie alone in the darkest hour of the night, then, just maybe, a man can dream that one for a little while. But remember, that even then, where ever you lie, breathing fast and dreaming, God's Watching With His Secret Eye to see how far you go! You think he hasn't seen us tonight? Now, you got it on paper as well! That's what they call evidence, you know. (*pause*) God, Zach., I have a feeling about this business, man!

ZACHARIAH: Cheer up, Morrie.

MORRIS: You won't let me burn it?

ZACHARIAH: Like you said, it's just a game.

MORRIS: But you're playing with fire, Zach.!

ZACHARIAH: Maybe. But then I never had much to play with.

MORRIS: Didn't you?

ZACHARIAH: Don't you remember? You got the toys.

MORRIS: Did I?

ZACHARIAH: Ja. Like that top, Morrie. Don't you? I have always specially remembered that top. That brown stinkwood top. She gave me her old cotton reels to play with, but it wasn't the same. I wanted a top.

MORRIS: Who? Who gave me the top?

ZACHARIAH: Mother!

MORRIS: Mother!

ZACHARIAH: Ja. She said she only had one. There was always only one.

MORRIS: Zach., you're telling me a thing now!

ZACHARIAH: Did you forget her?

MORRIS: No, Zach. I meant the top. I can't, for the life of me, remember that top.

ZACHARIAH: And the marbles?

MORRIS: Was there marbles, too?

ZACHARIAH: Ja. One time. A bag of them with a big green ghoen. Such a ghoen, man! Another time there was the little soldiers.

MORRIS (*shaking his head*): No . . .

ZACHARIAH: And what about the tackies?

MORRIS: Tackies . . . ? Yes, yes I do! I remember her calling and putting them on and taking me to church. How it comes back, hey! And what about her, Zach.? There's a memory for you. I tried it out the other day. Mother, I said, Mother! A sadness, I thought.

ZACHARIAH: Ja.

MORRIS: Just a touch of sadness.

ZACHARIAH: A soft touch with sadness.

MORRIS: And soapsuds on brown hands.

ZACHARIAH: And her feet. (*Pause.* MORRIS *looks at* ZACHARIAH.)

MORRIS: What do you mean?

ZACHARIAH: There was her feet.

MORRIS: Who had feet?

ZACHARIAH: Mother, man.

MORRIS: I don't remember her feet, Zach.

ZACHARIAH (*serenely confident*): Ja, man. The toes was crooked, the nails skew and there was pain. They didn't fit the shoes.

MORRIS (*growing agitation*): Zach., are you sure that wasn't somebody else?

ZACHARIAH: It was mother's feet. She let me feel the hardnesses and then pruned them down with a razor blade.

MORRIS: No, Zach. You got me worried now! A grey dress?

ZACHARIAH: Maybe.

MORRIS (*persistent*): Going to church. She wore it going to . . .

ZACHARIAH: The butcher shop! That's it! That's where she went.

MORRIS: What for?

ZACHARIAH: Offal.

MORRIS: Offal! Stop, Zach. Stop! We must sort this out, man. I mean . . . it sounds like some other mother.

ZACHARIAH (*gently*): How can that be?

MORRIS: Listen, Zach. Do you remember the songs she sang?

ZACHARIAH: Do I! (*He laughs and then sings.*)
My skin is black,
the soap is blue,
But the washing comes out white.

I took a man
On a Friday night;
Now I'm washing a baby too.

Just a little bit black,
And a little bit white,
He's a Capie through and through.
(MORRIS *is staring at him in horror*) What's the matter?

MORRIS: That wasn't what she sang to me.

ZACHARIAH: No?

MORRIS: Lullaby-baby it was . . . '. . . you'll get to the top.'

ZACHARIAH: I don't remember that at all.

MORRIS (*anguish*): This is some sort of terrible error. What . . . wait! I've got it . . . I think. Oh, God, let it be that I've got it. (*to* ZACHARIAH) How about the games we played? Think, Zach. Think carefully! There was one special one. Just me and you. I'll give you a clue. Toot-toot. Toot-toot.

ZACHARIAH (*thinking*): Wasn't there an old car?

MORRIS: Where would it be?

ZACHARIAH: Rusting by the side of the road.

MORRIS: Could it be the ruins of an old Chevy, Zach.?

ZACHARIAH: It could.

MORRIS: And can we say without tyres and wires and things?

ZACHARIAH: We may.

MORRIS: . . . and all the glass blown away by the wind?

ZACHARIAH: Dusty.

MORRIS: Deserted.

ZACHARIAH: Sting bees on the bonnet.

MORRIS: Webs in the windscreen.

ZACHARIAH: Nothing in the boot.

MORRIS: And us?

ZACHARIAH: In it.

MORRIS: We are? How?

ZACHARIAH: Side by side.

MORRIS: Like this? (*He sits beside* ZACHARIAH.)

ZACHARIAH: That's right.

MORRIS: Doing what?

ZACHARIAH: Staring.

MORRIS: Not both of us!

ZACHARIAH: Me at the wheel, you at the window.

MORRIS: Okay. Now what?

ZACHARIAH: Now, I got this gear here and I'm going to go.

MORRIS: Where?

ZACHARIAH: To hell and gone far away, and we aren't coming back.

MORRIS: Wait! What will I do while you drive?

ZACHARIAH: You must tell me what we pass. Are you ready? Here we go! (ZACHARIAH *goes through the motions of driving a car.* MORRIS *looks eagerly out of the window.*)

MORRIS: We're slipping through the streets, passing homes and people on the pavements who are quite friendly and wave as we drive by. It's a fine, sunny sort of a day. What are we doing?

ZACHARIAH: Twenty-four.

MORRIS: Do you see that bus ahead of us? (*They lean over to one side as* ZACHARIAH *swings the wheel.* MORRIS *looks back.*) Chock-a-block with early morning workers. Shame. And what about those children over there, going to school. Shame again. On such a nice day. What are we doing?

ZACHARIAH: Thirty-four.

MORRIS: That means we're coming to open country. The white houses have given way to patches of green, and animals and not so many people anymore. But they still wave . . . with their spades.

ZACHARIAH: Fifty.

MORRIS: You're going quite fast. You've killed a cat, flattened a frog, frightened a dog . . . who jumped!

ZACHARIAH: Sixty.

MORRIS: Passing trees, and haystacks, and sunshine and the smoke from little houses drifting up . . . shooting by!

ZACHARIAH: Eighty!

MORRIS: Birds flying abreast, and bulls, billy-goats, black sheep . . .

ZACHARIAH: One hundred!

MORRIS: . . . cross a river, up a hill, to the top, coming down, down, down . . . stop! stop!

ZACHARIAH (*slamming on the brakes*): Eeeeeooooooooooaaah! (*pause*) Why?

MORRIS: Look! There's a butterfly.

ZACHARIAH: On your side?

MORRIS: Yours as well. Just look.

ZACHARIAH: All round us, hey!

MORRIS: This is rare, Zach.! We've driven into a flock of butterflies. (ZACHARIAH *smiles and then laughs.*) You remember, hey! We've found it, Zach. We've found it! This is our youth!

ZACHARIAH: And driving to hell and gone was our game.

MORRIS: Our best one.

ZACHARIAH: What about chasing donkeys in the veld? Remember that?

MORRIS: And the trees! Me and you in the trees. Tarzan and his ape.

ZACHARIAH: Teasing the girls.

MORRIS: Stealing the fruit.

ZACHARIAH: Catching the birds.

MORRIS: My God! The things a man can forget!

ZACHARIAH: Ja. Those were the days!

MORRIS: God knows!

ZACHARIAH: Goodness, hey!

MORRIS: They were that.

ZACHARIAH: And gladness, too.

MORRIS: Making hay, man, come and play, man, while the sun is sinking . . . which it did.

ZACHARIAH: What's that . . that . . . that nice thing you say, Morrie?

MORRIS: 'So sweet did pass that summer time,
Of youth and fruit upon the trees,
When laughing boys and pretty girls
Did hop and skip and all were free.'

ZACHARIAH: Did shop and skip the pretty girls. They did, too.

MORRIS: Hopscotch.

ZACHARIAH: That was it.

MORRIS: We played our games, Zach.

ZACHARIAH: We could. There was no work.

MORRIS: Or worries.

ZACHARIAH: No hurry.

MORRIS: That's true. We took our time and our chances. There were a few falls of

course. I mean . . . can a man climb without a fall?

ZACHARIAH: You got to come tumbling down
sometime, the laughing boys and pretty
girls.

MORRIS: But you picked yourself up . . .

ZACHARIAH: And the scabs off your knees
. . .

MORRIS: And carried on. A few inner hurts,
too, from time to time.

ZACHARIAH: What was those?

MORRIS: Don't you remember?
Kaffertjie, Kaffertjie, waar is jou pas?

ZACHARIAH (*taking up the jingle*): But my
old man was a white man.

MORRIS: Maar, jou ma was 'n Bantoe,
So dis nou jou ras.

ZACHARIAH (*shaking his head*): Ja. That hurt.

MORRIS: But on the whole it was fun.

ZACHARIAH: While it lasted, which wasn't
for long.

MORRIS: It had to happen, Zach. We grew
upright, mother lay down and died, so I
went away. I took the long road away.

ZACHARIAH: And me? What did I do?

MORRIS: Connie.

ZACHARIAH: That's right.

MORRIS: And Minnie.

ZACHARIAH: That was all right.

MORRIS: So then I came back.

ZACHARIAH: And now?

MORRIS: See for yourself. Here we are, later.
And now there's Ethel as well, and that
makes me frightened.

ZACHARIAH: Sounds like another game, hey?

MORRIS: Yes. But not ours . . . this time.
(*They sit together, overshadowed by the
presence in their words.*) I often wonder.

ZACHARIAH: Same here.

MORRIS: I mean . . . where do they go? The
good times in a man's life?

ZACHARIAH: And the bad ones?

MORRIS: Yes. That's a thought. Where do
they come from?

ZACHARIAH: Oudtshoorn.

SCENE 4

An evening later.

ZACHARIAH *is seated at the table, eating.
He is obviously in good spirits, radiating an*
inward satisfaction and secrecy. MORRIS *is
moving about nervously behind his back.*

MORRIS: So it has come to this. Who would
have thought it, hey! That one day, one of
us would come in here with a secret and
keep it to himself! If someone had tried to
tell me that, I would have thrown up my
hands in horror. To Morrie and Zach.!
. . . I would have cried. No! Emphatically
not! (*pause*) Which just goes to show you.
Because I was wrong, wasn't I? There is a
secret in this room, at this moment. This
is how friendships get wrecked, you know,
Zach., in secrecy. It's the hidden things
that hurt and do the harm. (*Pause.* MORRIS
watches ZACHARIAH's *back.*) So. Do you
want to tell me?

ZACHARIAH: What are you talking about,
Morrie?

MORRIS: You got a letter today, didn't you?

ZACHARIAH: Who?

MORRIS: You.

ZACHARIAH: What?

MORRIS: A letter. From Ethel. And you're
not telling me about it. (*pause*) Okay. Two
can play at this game, you know. Yes! Now
that I come to think of it, I've also got a
secret. And such a wicked secret! Hey! It's
almost a sin! But I'm not going to tell
somebody I know . . . Oh no!

ZACHARIAH (*complacently*): Good. (*He continues eating, unaffected by* MORRIS' *manoeuvre. Realising his tactics have failed,*
MORRIS *tries another approach, hiding his
impatience and curiosity behind a mask of
indifference.*)

MORRIS (*joining* ZACHARIAH *at the table*): It's
good value for a tuppenny stamp, all right.
Hey, Zach.?

ZACHARIAH (*cautiously*): What?

MORRIS: Postage. Your letters, getting safely
to Oudtshoorn, and in only a couple of days,
and finding the right person at the other
end . . . for only tuppence! Tell me that's
not a bargain. That's the really big thing
about pen-pals, I think. A man's letters
have got somewhere to go, and he gets a
couple himself from time to time . . .
like you, today. Come on now, Zach. You
did, didn't you?

ZACHARIAH (*after thought*): Ja.

MORRIS: That's all I'm saying. Some more
bread? (*He offers* ZACHARIAH *a slice. He*

takes it.) Same sort as usual? (ZACHARIAH *looks at* MORRIS.) The letter. (ZACHARIAH *puts down his bread and thinks.* MORRIS *seizes his opportunity.*) Didn't you notice? Hell, Zach.! You surprise me.

ZACHARIAH: What do you mean: the same sort?

MORRIS (*simulated shock*): Zach.!

ZACHARIAH: So I'm asking you what you mean.

MORRIS: Well, I never! To begin with there's the . . . envelope. Is it the same colour, or isn't it? I can see that somebody didn't take a good look, did he? (*Reluctantly* ZACHARIAH *takes the letter out of his inside pocket.*) She's changed her colours! They used to be blue. What about inside?

ZACHARIAH: I'm not ready for that yet.

MORRIS: Okay. All I'm saying is . . . I don't care.

ZACHARIAH (*studying the envelope*): I see they got animals on stamps nowadays.

MORRIS (*his patience wearing thin*): You mean to tell me you only see that now?

ZACHARIAH: The donkeys with stripes.

MORRIS: Zebras.

ZACHARIAH: . . . with stripes.

MORRIS: That's not the point about a letter, Zach.

ZACHARIAH: What?

MORRIS: The stamps. You're wasting your time with the stamps. It's what's inside that you got to read.

ZACHARIAH: You're in a hurry, Morrie.

MORRIS: Who?

ZACHARIAH: You.

MORRIS: Look, I told you that all I'm saying is . . . I don't care and the stamps don't count. Other than that, have your fun. Go ahead. It means nothing to me.

ZACHARIAH: And my name on the envelope. How do you like that, hey?

MORRIS: *Your* name?

ZACHARIAH: Ja. My name.

MORRIS: Oh.

ZACHARIAH: Now what do you mean, with an 'Oh' like that?

MORRIS: What makes you so sure that that is your name? (ZACHARIAH *is trapped.*) How do you spell your name, Zach.? Come on, let's hear.

ZACHARIAH (*after a long struggle*): Zach. . . . ah . . . ri . . . yah.

MORRIS: Oh, no, you don't! That's no spell-

ing. That's a pronunciation. A b c d e . . . that's the alphabet. (*After a moment's hesitation* ZACHARIAH *holds up the letter so that* MORRIS *can see the address.*)

ZACHARIAH: Is it for me, Morrie?

MORRIS: I'm not sure.

ZACHARIAH: Mr. Zachariah Pietersen.

MORRIS: I know your name. It's for one Z. Pietersen.

ZACHARIAH: Well, that's okay then.

MORRIS: Is it?

ZACHARIAH: Isn't it?

MORRIS: Since when are you the only thing that begins with a Z? And how many Pietersens didn't we know as boys, right here in this very self-same Korsten? (ZACHARIAH *keeps the letter for a few more seconds, then hands it to* MORRIS.)

ZACHARIAH: You win. Read it.

MORRIS: I win! (*laughs happily*) Good old Zach.! I win! I'll sit down to this. (*nudging* ZACHARIAH) It pays to have a brother who can read, hey? (*opens the letter*) Ready? "Dear Zach., How's things? I'm okay, to-day, again. I got your letter. Lucy had a laugh at you . . ."

ZACHARIAH: What's that?

MORRIS: "Lucy had a laugh at you . . ." I think she means a smile.

ZACHARIAH: What's funny?

MORRIS: Not that sort of smile, Zach. I'm sure she means the kind sort. (ZACHARIAH *is not convinced.*) Look at me. (*He smiles at* ZACHARIAH.) Is there anything funny? Of course not. Only you. I was feeling sympathy, not funny. (*continues his reading*) "Lucy had a laugh at you, but my brother is not so sure." (*pause*) That's something. That, I feel, means something. What does it do to you?

ZACHARIAH: Nothing.

MORRIS: Remember his boots.

ZACHARIAH: No. Nothing.

MORRIS: Not even a little bit of fear? (*He reads on*) "I'm looking forward to a ride in your car . . ." They believed it, Zach.! (ZACHARIAH *smiles.*) They believed our cock and bull about the car.

ZACHARIAH (*laughing*): I told you.

MORRIS: "I'm looking forward to a ride in your car . . . and what about Lucy? Can she come?" (*Their amusement knows no bounds.*)

ZACHARIAH: You must come too, Morrie.

You and Lucy! Hey? We'll take them at ninety.

MORRIS: To hell and gone. (*reads on through his laughter*) "We're coming down for a holiday in June, so where . . . can we . . . meet you?" (*Long pause. He reads again.*) "We're coming down for a holiday in June, so where can we meet you?"

ZACHARIAH: Ethel . . . ?

MORRIS: Is coming here. (*Puts down the letter and stands up. A false yawn and stretch before going to the window.*) I've noticed that hardly any moths . . .

ZACHARIAH: Coming here!

MORRIS: As I was saying. Hardly any moths I've noticed have . . .

ZACHARIAH: Ethel! (MORRIS *abandons his thoughts about the moths.*)

MORRIS: I warned you, didn't I? I said: I have a feeling about this business. I remember my words; and wise ones they turn out to be. Because now you've got it! I told you to leave it alone. Hands off! Don't touch! Not for you! I know these things, I said. But, oh, no, Mr. Z. Pietersen was clever. He knew how to handle it. Well, handle this, will you please?

ZACHARIAH (*dumbly*): What else does she say?

MORRIS (*brutally*): I'm not going to read it. You want to know why? Because it doesn't matter. The game's up, man. Nothing else matters now except: I'm coming down in June, so where can we meet you? That is what Mr. Z. Pietersen had better start thinking about . . . and quick!

ZACHARIAH: When's June?

MORRIS: Soon.

ZACHARIAH: How soon?

MORRIS: Look. Are you trying to make me out a liar? (*Ticking them off on his fingers*) January, February, March, April, May, June, July, August, September, October, November, December? Satisfied? (*Another long pause.* MORRIS *goes back to the window.*)

ZACHARIAH: So?

MORRIS (*to the table, where he reads further into the letter*): "I'll be staying with my uncle at Kensington." (*little laugh*) Kensington! Near enough for you? About five minutes walking from here, hey? And notice . . . with my uncle. Uncle! (*another laugh*) That's a ugly word, when you get to

know its meanings. Oom Jakob! Do you hear it? Hairy wrists in khaki sleeves with thick fingers. When they curled up, that fist was as big as my head! (*Back to the window.* ZACHARIAH *is frightened.*)

ZACHARIAH: Morrie, I know. I'll tell her I can't see her.

MORRIS: She will want to know why.

ZACHARIAH: It's because I'm sick, with my heart.

MORRIS: And if she feels sorry and comes to comfort you?

ZACHARIAH (*growing desperation*): But I'm going away.

MORRIS: When?

ZACHARIAH: Soon. June.

MORRIS: And what about where, and why and what, if she says she'll wait until you come back.

ZACHARIAH: Then I'll tell her . . . (*Pause. He can think of nothing else to say.*)

MORRIS: What? No, Zach. You can't even tell her you're dead. You see, I happen to know. There is no white-washing away a man's . . . facts. They'll speak for themselves at first sight, if you don't say it.

ZACHARIAH: Say what?

MORRIS: The truth. You know it.

ZACHARIAH: I don't. I don't know nothing.

MORRIS: Then listen, because *I* know it. "Dear Ethel, forgive me, but I was born a dark sort of boy who wanted to play with whiteness . . ."

ZACHARIAH (*rebelling*): No!

MORRIS: ". . . and that's the truth, so help me God, help me!"

ZACHARIAH: I say no!

MORRIS: Then tell me what else you can say? Come on. Let's hear it. What is there a man can say or pray that will change the colour of his skin or blind them to it.

ZACHARIAH: There must be something.

MORRIS: I'm telling you there's nothing. When it's a question of smiles, and whispers, and thoughts in strange eyes . . . there is only the truth and . . . (*he pauses*)

ZACHARIAH: And then what?

MORRIS: And then to make a run for it. Yes. They don't like these games with their whiteness. You've heard them. "How would you like your daughter to correspond with a black man?" Ethel's got a policeman brother and an uncle and *your* address.

ZACHARIAH: What have I done, hey? I done nothing.

MORRIS: What have you thought! That's the question. That's the crime. I seem to remember somebody saying: "I like the thought of this little white girl." And what about your dreams? They've kept me awake these past few nights, Zach. I've heard them, mumbling and moaning away in the darkness. They'll hear them quick enough. When they get their hands on a dark-born boy playing with a white idea, you think they don't find out what he's been dreaming at night? They have ways and means, my friend. Mean ways. Like confinement, in a cell, on bread and water, for days without end. They sit outside with their ears to the keyhole and wait . . . and wait. They got time. You'll get tired. So they wait. And soon you do, and no matter how you fight, your eyeballs start rolling round and . . . around and then, before you know it, maybe while you're still praying, before you can cry, or scream for help . . . you fall asleep and dream! All they need for evidence is a man's dreams. Not so much his hate. They say they can live with that. It's his dreams that they drag off to judgment, shouting: "Silence! He's been caught! With convictions? He's pleading! He's guilty! Take him away." (*pause*) Where? You ask, where, with your eyes I see. You know where, Zach. You've seen them, in the streets, carrying their spades and the man with his gun. Bald heads, short trousers and that ugly jersey with the red, painful red stripes around the body. (MORRIS *goes back to the window.*) I miss the moths. They made the night a friendly sort of place. (*Turning to* ZACH.) What are you going to do about it, Zach.?

ZACHARIAH: I'm thinking about it.

MORRIS: What are you thinking about it?

ZACHARIAH: What am I going to do?

MORRIS: Better be quick.

ZACHARIAH: Help me, Morrie.

MORRIS: Are you serious?

ZACHARIAH: I'm not smiling.

MORRIS: Dead serious?

ZACHARIAH: God.

MORRIS: Good. Then let's go. Begin at the beginning. Give me the first fact.

ZACHARIAH (*severe and bitter*): Ethel is white. I am black.

MORRIS: That's a very good beginning, Zach.

ZACHARIAH: If she sees me . . .

MORRIS: Keep it up.

ZACHARIAH: . . . she'll be surprised.

MORRIS: Harder, Zach.

ZACHARIAH: She'll laugh.

MORRIS: Let it hurt, man!

ZACHARIAH: She'll swear!

MORRIS: Now make it loud!

ZACHARIAH: She'll scream!

MORRIS: Good! Now for yourself. (*pause*) She's surprised, remember?

ZACHARIAH: I'm not strange.

MORRIS: And when she laughs?

ZACHARIAH: I'm not funny.

MORRIS: When she swears?

ZACHARIAH: I'm no dog.

MORRIS: She screams!

ZACHARIAH: I just wanted to smell you, lady!

MORRIS: Good, Zach. Very good. You're seeing it clearly, man. But, remember there is still the others.

ZACHARIAH: What others?

MORRIS: The uncles with fists and brothers in boots who come running when a lady screams.

ZACHARIAH: What about them?

MORRIS: They've come to ransack you.

ZACHARIAH: I'll say it wasn't me.

MORRIS: They won't believe you.

ZACHARIAH: Leave me alone!

MORRIS: They'll hit you for that.

ZACHARIAH: I'll fight.

MORRIS: There's too many for you.

ZACHARIAH: I'll call a policeman.

MORRIS: He's on their side.

ZACHARIAH: I'll run away!

MORRIS: That's better, and bitter of course. I realise that. You see, we're digging up the roots of what's the matter with you now. I know they're deep: that's why it hurts. But we must get them out. Once the roots are out, this thing will die and never grow again. I'm telling you I know. So we've got to get them out, right out. You're lucky, Zach.

ZACHARIAH: Me?

MORRIS: Yes, you. I think, for a man like you, there shouldn't be too much discomfort in pulling it right out.

ZACHARIAH: Just show me how!

MORRIS: Go back to the beginning. Give me again that first fact. (*pause*) It started with Ethel remember. Ethel . . .

ZACHARIAH: . . . is white.

MORRIS: That's it. And . . .

ZACHARIAH: . . . and I am black.

MORRIS: You've got it.

ZACHARIAH: Ethel is white and I am black.

MORRIS: Now take a good grip.

ZACHARIAH: Ethel is so . . . so . . . snow white.

MORRIS: Hold it! Grab it all!

ZACHARIAH: And I am too . . . truly . . . too black.

MORRIS: Now, this is the hard part, Zach., so be prepared, hey? Be broad in the shoulder. Be a man and brace yourself to take the strain. Some men I know couldn't, and sustained eternal injuries. Now, get ready, I'll urge you on, keep steady, I'm with you all the way remember . . . and pull! With all your might and all your woe, heave, harder, still harder, Zach.! Let it hurt, man! It has to hurt a man to do him good because once bitten twice shy, just this one cry and then never again; just this once, try to think of it as one of those bitter pills that pull a man through to better days and being himself again . . . at last and in peace, in one piece, because you'll mend you'll see, and, as they say, tomorrow is another, yet another day, and a man must carry on. Doesn't matter so much where; just on, just carry your load on somewhere and teach your lips to smile with your eyes closed, to say, lightheartedly if you can, with a laugh as if you didn't care, to say . . . let's hear it, Zach.

ZACHARIAH: I can never have her.

MORRIS: Never ever.

ZACHARIAH: She wouldn't want me anyway.

MORRIS: It's as simple as that.

ZACHARIAH: She's too white to want me anyway.

MORRIS: For better or for worse.

ZACHARIAH: So I won't want her anymore.

MORRIS: Not in this life, or that one, if death us do part, that next one, God help us! For ever and ever no more, thank you!

ZACHARIAH: Please, no more.

MORRIS: We cry enough.

ZACHARIAH: I know now.

MORRIS: We do.

ZACHARIAH: Everything.

MORRIS: Every last little thing.

ZACHARIAH: From the beginning.

MORRIS: And then on without end.

ZACHARIAH: Why it was.

MORRIS: And will be.

ZACHARIAH: The lot in fact.

MORRIS: The human one.

ZACHARIAH: The whole, rotten, stinking lot is all because I'm black!

MORRIS: Yes. That explains it, clearly. Which is something. I mean when a man can see 'why?', quite clearly, it's something. Think of those who can't.

ZACHARIAH: I'm black all right. What is there as black as me?

MORRIS: To equal you? To match you? How about a dangerous night. Try that for the size and colour of its darkness. You go with it, Zach., as with certain smells and simple sorrows too. And what about the sadness of shoes without socks, or no shoes at all!

ZACHARIAH: I take it. I take them all. Black days, black ways, black things. They're me. I'm happy. Ha Ha Ha! Do you hear my black happiness?

MORRIS: Oh yes, Zach., I hear it, I promise you.

ZACHARIAH: Can you feel it?

MORRIS: I do. I do.

ZACHARIAH: And see it?

MORRIS: Midnight, man! Like the twelve strokes of midnight you stand before my wondering eyes.

ZACHARIAH: And my thoughts! What about my thoughts?

MORRIS: Let's hear it.

ZACHARIAH: I'm on my side, they're on theirs.

MORRIS: That's what they want.

ZACHARIAH: They'll get it.

MORRIS: You heard him.

ZACHARIAH: This time it's serious.

MORRIS: We warn you.

ZACHARIAH: Because from now on, I'll be what I am. They can be what they like. I don't care. I don't want to mix. It's bad for the blood and the poor babies. So I'll keep mine clean, and theirs I'll scrub off, afterwards, off my hands, my unskilled, my stained hands and say I'm not sorry! The trembles you felt was something else. You see you were too white, so blindingly white that I couldn't see what I was doing.

MORRIS (*quietly, and with absolute sincerity*): Zach.! Oh Zach.! When I hear that certainty about whys and wherefores, about how to live and what not to love, I wish, believe me, deep down in the bottom of my heart where my blood is as red as yours, I wish that old washerwoman had bruised me too at birth. I wish . . . (*The alarm goes off.* MORRIS *looks up to find* ZACH. *staring strangely at him.* MORRIS *goes to the window to avoid* ZACHARIAH's *eyes.*) Yes. I remember now. The moths. I was on the road somewhere and it got dark again. So I stopped at a petrol station and sat up with the night boy in his little room. An elderly ou. I asked his name. Kleinbooi. But he didn't ask mine. He wasn't sure, you see. So often in my life they haven't been sure, you see. We sat there on the floor and cars came a few times in the night, but mostly it was just Kleinbooi and me, dozing . . . and, of course, the moths. Soft, dusty moths, flying in through the door to the lamp, or on the floor dragging their wings, or on their backs. I'm telling you there are millions of moths in this world, but only in summer; because where do they go when it's winter? I remember having a deep thought about moths that night, Zach. . . . (*He turns from the window to find* ZACHARIAH *still staring at him.* MORRIS *goes to the table to turn off the lamp.*)

ZACHARIAH: Morris!

MORRIS: Zachariah?

ZACHARIAH: Keep on the light.

MORRIS: Why?

ZACHARIAH: I saw something.

MORRIS: What?

ZACHARIAH: Your skin. How can I put it? It's . . . (*pause*)

MORRIS (*easily*): On the light side?

ZACHARIAH: Ja.

MORRIS (*very easily*): One of those things. (*Another move to the lamp.*)

ZACHARIAH: Wait, Morrie!

MORRIS: It's late.

ZACHARIAH: I want to have a good look at you, man.

MORRIS: It's a bit late in the day to be seeing your brother for the first time. I been here a whole year now, you know.

ZACHARIAH: Ja. But after a whole life I only seen me properly tonight. You helped me. I'm grateful.

MORRIS: It was nothing . . .

ZACHARIAH: No! I'm not a man that forgets a favour. I want to help you now.

MORRIS: I don't need any assistance, thank you.

ZACHARIAH: But you do. A man can't really see himself. Look at me. I had an odd look at me in the mirror—but so what? Did it make things clearer? No. Why? Because it's the others what does. They got sharper eyes. I want to give you the benefit of mine. Sit down. (MORRIS *sits.*) You're on the lighter side of life all right. You like that . . . all over? Your legs and things?

MORRIS: It's evenly spread.

ZACHARIAH: Not even a foot on the darker side, hey! I'd say you must be quite a bright boy with nothing on.

MORRIS: Please, Zach.!

ZACHARIAH: You're shy! Ja. You always get undressed in the dark. Always well closed up, like a woman. Like Ethel. I bet she shines.

MORRIS: Sis, Zach.!

ZACHARIAH: You know something? I bet if it was you she saw and not me she wouldn't say nothing. (MORRIS *closes his eyes and gives a light, nervous laugh.* ZACHARIAH *also laughs, but hollowly.*) I'm sure she wouldn't be surprised, or laugh, or swear or scream. Nobody would come running. I bet you she would just say: How do you do, Mr. Pietersen? (*pause*) There's a thought there, Morrie. You ever think it?

MORRIS: No.

ZACHARIAH: Not even a little bit of it? Like there, where you say: Hello, Ethel . . . and shake her hand. Then what do you do? Ah, yes! I see this thing very clear. You say: Would you like a walk with me? Ja. You'd manage all right, Morrie. One thing is for certain: you would look all right, with her, and that's the main thing, hey?

MORRIS: You're dreaming again, Zach.

ZACHARIAH: No, man! This is not my sort of dream. (*He laughs*) My dream was different. I didn't shake her hands. You're the man for shaking hands, Morrie.

MORRIS: Finished, Zach.?

ZACHARIAH: No. We're still coming to the big thought.

MORRIS: What is that?

ZACHARIAH: Why don't you meet her? (*pause*)

MORRIS: You want to know why?

ZACHARIAH: Ja.

MORRIS: You really want to know?

ZACHARIAH: I do.

MORRIS: She's not my pen-pal. (MORRIS *moves to get up.* ZACHARIAH *stops him.*)

ZACHARIAH: All right. Let's try it another way. Would you like to meet her?

MORRIS: Listen, Zach. I've told you before. Ethel is your . . .

ZACHARIAH (*pained*): Please, Morrie! Would —you—like—to—meet—her?

MORRIS: That's no sort of question.

ZACHARIAH: Why not?

MORRIS: Because all my life I've been interested in meeting people. Not just Ethel. Anybody. I'm telling you the question is meaningless.

ZACHARIAH: Okay, I'll put it this way. Would you like to see her, or hear her, or maybe touch her?

MORRIS: That still doesn't give the question any meaning! Look, you know me. Don't I like to touch . . . horses? Don't I like to hear . . . church bells? Don't I like to see anything that's nice to see? And anyway, Ethel is your pen-pal.

ZACHARIAH: Right. Wait! You can have her.

MORRIS: What's this now?

ZACHARIAH: She's yours. I'm giving her to you.

MORRIS (*angry*): This is no game, Zach.!

ZACHARIAH: But I mean it. Look. I can't use her. We seen that. She'll see it too. But why throw away a good pen-pal if somebody else can do it? You can. You're bright enough, Morrie. I don't know why I never seen it before, but you're pretty . . . a pretty white. I'm telling you now, as your brother, that when Ethel sees you all she will say is: How do you do, Mr. Pietersen? She'll never know otherwise.

MORRIS: You think so?

ZACHARIAH: You could fool me, Morrie, if I didn't know who you was.

MORRIS: You mean that, Zach.?

ZACHARIAH: Cross my heart and hope to die. And the way you can talk! She'd be impressed.

MORRIS: That's true. I like to talk.

ZACHARIAH: No harm in it, man. A couple of words, a little walk and a packet of monkey-nuts on the way.

MORRIS: Monkey-nuts?

ZACHARIAH: Tickey a packet. Something to chew.

MORRIS: Good God, Zach.! You take a lady friend to tea, man!

ZACHARIAH: To tea, hey?

MORRIS: With buns, if she's hungry. Hot-cross buns.

ZACHARIAH: Now, you see! I would have just bought monkey-nuts. She's definitely not for me.

MORRIS: Yes, to tea. A pot of afternoon tea. When she sits down, you pull out her chair . . . like this. (*He demonstrates.*)

ZACHARIAH: I think I seen that.

MORRIS: The woman pours the tea but the man butters the bun.

ZACHARIAH: Well, well, well.

MORRIS: Only two spoons of sugar, and don't drink out of the saucer.

ZACHARIAH: Very good.

MORRIS: Take it slow, chew it small and swallow before you speak.

ZACHARIAH: What else?

MORRIS: If she wants to blow her nose, offer your hanky, which you keep in a breast pocket.

ZACHARIAH: Go on.

MORRIS (*waking up to reality*): It's no good! (*bitterly*) You're wasting my time, talking like this! It's a lot of rot. I'm going to bed.

ZACHARIAH: But what's the matter, man? You were telling me everything so damn good. Come on. Tell me. (*coaxing*) Tell your brother what's the matter.

MORRIS: I haven't got a hanky.

ZACHARIAH: I think we can buy one. Couldn't we? I reckon for a meeting with Ethel we can manage a hanky all right.

MORRIS: And the breast pocket?

ZACHARIAH: What's the problem there? Let's also . . .

MORRIS: Don't be a bloody fool! You got to buy a whole suit to get the breast pocket. And that's still not all. What about socks, decent shoes, a spotty tie and a clean white shirt? How do you think a man steps out to meet a waiting lady? On his bare feet, wearing rags, and stinking because he hasn't had a bath? She'd even laugh and scream at me if I went like this. So I'm giving Ethel back to you. There's nothing I can do with her, thank you very much. (MORRIS *to his bed.* ZACHARIAH *thinks.*)

ZACHARIAH: Haven't we got enough money?

MORRIS: All I got left from the fish today is one shilling, and until you get paid . . . What am I talking about! You know what a right sort of for-a-meeting-with-the-lady type of suit costs? Pounds and pounds and pounds. Shoes? Pounds and pounds. Shirt? Pounds. And then there's still two socks and a tie.

ZACHARIAH (*patiently*): We got that sort of money.

MORRIS: Here it is. One shilling. Take it and go and buy me a suit, please.

ZACHARIAH: Thank you. (*Takes the coin and throws it away without even looking at it.*) Where's the tin?

MORRIS: Tin?

ZACHARIAH: Round sort of tin.

MORRIS (*horror*): Our tin?

ZACHARIAH: There was sweets in it at Christmas.

MORRIS: You mean, our future?

ZACHARIAH: That's the one. The future tin.

MORRIS: Our two-man farm?

ZACHARIAH: Where is it?

MORRIS: I won't tell you. (*He runs and stands spread-eagled in front of the cupboard where the tin is hidden.*)

ZACHARIAH: Ah-ha!

MORRIS: No, Zach.!

ZACHARIAH: Give it to me!

MORRIS: I won't! I won't! (*Grabs the tin and runs away.* ZACHARIAH *lurches after him.* MORRIS *is quick and elusive.*)

ZACHARIAH: I'll catch you, Morrie, and when I do . . .

MORRIS: Zach., please! Just stop! Please! Just stand still and listen to me. Everything . . . everything we got, the most precious thing a man can have, a future, is in here. You've worked hard, I've done the saving.

ZACHARIAH: We'll start again.

MORRIS: It will take too long.

ZACHARIAH: I'll work overtime.

MORRIS: It won't be the same. (ZACHARIAH *lunges suddenly, but* MORRIS *escapes.*)

ZACHARIAH: Bliksem! Wait, Morrie! Wait! Fair is fair. Now this time you stand still . . . and think. Ethel . . .

MORRIS: I won't.

ZACHARIAH: Yes you will, because Ethel is coming and you want to meet her. But like you say, not like any ou Hotnot in the street, but smartly. Now this is it. You're wearing a pretty smart for a meeting-with-the-lady type of suit. (MORRIS, *clutching the tin to his chest, closes his eyes.* ZACHARIAH *creeps closer.*) Shiny shoes, white socks, a good shirt and a spotty tie. And the people watch you go by and say: Hey! Hey! Just come and look, man. Will you please just come and look at that! . . . Who's you . . . There goes something! And Ethel says: Who's this coming? Could it be my friend, Mr. Pietersen? And you say: Good day to you, Miss Ethel. May I shake your white hands with my white hands? Of course, Mr. Pietersen. (ZACHARIAH *has reached* MORRIS. *He takes the tin.*) Thank you, Morrie. (MORRIS *doesn't move.* ZACHARIAH *opens the tin, takes out the money and then callously throws the tin away. He takes the money to the table where he counts it.*)

MORRIS: Why are you doing this to me?

ZACHARIAH: Aren't we brothers? (*Pause*)

MORRIS: Where was I? Yes. At a garage, on the floor, with Kleinbooi and there were moths. Then I had that deep thought. You see they were flying in out of the darkness, out of the black, lonely night . . . to the lamp . . . into the flame. Always to light, I thought. Everything always flying, or growing, or turning, or crying for the whiteness of light. Birds following the sun when winter comes; trees and things standing, begging for it; moths hunting it; Man wanting it. All of us, always, out of darkness and into light.

ZACHARIAH: What sort of suit? And what about the shoes.

MORRIS: Go to a good shop. Ask for the outfit, for a gentleman.

SCENE 5

The next day.

MORRIS *is lying on his bed, staring up at the ceiling. There is a knock at the door.* MORRIS *rises slowly on his bed.*

MORRIS: Who is there? (*The knock is heard again.*) Speak up. I can't hear. (*Silence.*

MORRIS's *fear is now apparent. He waits until the knock is heard a third time.*) Ethel . . . I mean, Madam . . . no, no! . . . I mean to say Miss Ethel Lange, could that be you? (*In reply there is a raucous burst of laughter, unmistakably* ZACHARIAH's.) What's this? (*silence*) What's the meaning of this? (MORRIS *rushes to his bed and looks at the alarm clock.*) This is all wrong, Zach.! It's still only the middle of the day.

ZACHARIAH (*outside*): I know.

MORRIS: Go back to work! At once!

ZACHARIAH: I can't.

MORRIS: Why not?

ZACHARIAH: I took some leave, Morris, and left. Let me in.

MORRIS: What's the matter with you? The door's not locked.

ZACHARIAH: My hands are full. (*pause*) I been shopping, Morrie. (MORRIS *rushes to the door, but collects himself before opening it.* ZACHARIAH *comes in, his arms piled high with parcels. He smiles slyly at* MORRIS *who has assumed a pose of indifference.*)

ZACHARIAH: Oh, no, you don't, this time! I heard you run. So you thought it was maybe our little Miss Ethel, and a bit scared too at that thought, I think I heard? Well, don't worry no more, Morrie, because you know what these is? Your outfit! Number one, and what do we have? A wonderful hat . . . Sir. (*Takes it out and holds it up for approval. His manner is exaggerated and suggestive of the shopkeeper who sold him the clothing.*) . . . which is guaranteed to protect the head on Sundays and rainy days. Because! Think for a moment! Who ever knows what the weather will be! It's been bad before. Number two is the shirt, and a grey tie, which is much better taste. Spots are too loud for a gentleman. Next we have—two grey socks, left and right, and a hanky to blow her nose. (*next parcel*) Aha! We've come to the suit. Now before I show you the suit, my friend, I want to ask you, what does a man really look for in a good suit? A good cloth. Isn't that so?

MORRIS: What are you talking about?

ZACHARIAH: That's what he said. The fashion might be a season old, but will you please feel the difference. It's lasted for years already. All I can say is, take it or leave it. But remember, only a fool would leave it at that price. So I took it. (*next parcel*) Here we have a real Ostrich wallet.

MORRIS: What for?

ZACHARIAH: Your inside pocket. Ja! You forgot about the inside pocket, he said. A gentleman always got a wallet for the inside pocket. (*next parcel*) And a cigarette lighter, and a cigarette case for the outside pocket. Chramonium!

MORRIS: Since when do I smoke?

ZACHARIAH: I know. But Ethel might, he said.

MORRIS (*fear*): You told him?

ZACHARIAH: Don't worry. I just said there was a lady who someone was going to meet. He winked at me and said it was a good thing, now and then, and reminded me that ladies like presents. (*holds up a scarf*) A pretty doek in case the wind blows her hair away, he said. Here we got a umbrella in case it's sopping wet. And over here . . . (*last parcel*) . . . Guess! Come on, Morrie. Guess what's in this box. I'll shake it. Listen.

MORRIS: Shoes.

ZACHARIAH: (*triumphantly*) No! It's boots! I got you boots. Ha ha! Ja. (*watching* MORRIS' *reaction*) They frighten a ou, don't they. (*happy*) Satisfied?

MORRIS (*looking at the pile of clothing*): It seems all right.

ZACHARIAH: It wasn't easy. At the first shop, when I asked for the outfit for a gentleman, they said I was a agitator and was going to call the police. I had to get out, man . . . quick! Even this fellow . . . Mr. Moses . . . "come again my friend" . . . "You're drunk," he said. But when I showed him our future he sobered up. You know what he said? Guess.

MORRIS: No.

ZACHARIAH: He said: "Are you the gentleman?" Me! He did. So I said: "Do I look like a gentleman, Mr. Moses?" He said: "My friend, it takes all sorts of different sorts to make this world." "I'm the black sort," I said. So he said: "You don't say." He also said to mention his name and the fair deal to any other gentlemen wanting reasonable outfits. Go ahead, Morrie. (*the clothing*) Let's see the gentle sort of man.

MORRIS: Okay. Okay. Don't rush me. (*Moves*

cautiously to the pile of clothing. Flicks an imaginary speck of dust off the hat. ZACHARIAH *is waiting.*) Well?

ZACHARIAH: Well, I'm waiting.

MORRIS: Give me time.

ZACHARIAH: What for? You got the clothes.

MORRIS: For God's sake, Zach.! This is deep water. I'm not just going to jump right in. Men drown that way. You must paddle around first.

ZACHARIAH: Paddle around?

MORRIS: Try it out!

ZACHARIAH (*offering him the hat*): Try it on.

MORRIS: The idea, man. I got to try it out. There's more to wearing a white skin than just putting on a hat. You've seen white men before without hats, but they're still white men, aren't they?

ZACHARIAH: Ja.

MORRIS: And without suits or socks, or shoes . . .

ZACHARIAH: No, Morrie. Never without socks and shoes. Never a barefoot white man.

MORRIS: Well, the suit then. Look, Zach., what I'm trying to say is this. The clothes will help, but only help. They don't maketh the white man. It's that white something inside you, that special meaning and manner of whiteness that I got to find. I know what I'm talking about because . . . I'll be honest with you now, Zach. . . . I've thought about it for a long time. Why do you think I really read the Bible, hey? What do you think I'm thinking about when I'm not saying something? I'm being critical of colour, and the first fruit of my thought is that this whiteness of theirs is not just in the skin, otherwise . . . well, I mean . . . I'd be one of them, wouldn't I? Because, let me tell you, I seen them that's darker than me. Yes. Really dark, man. Only they had that something I'm telling you about. That's what I got to pin down in here.

ZACHARIAH: What?

MORRIS: White living, man! Like . . . like . . . like let's take looking at things. Haven't you noticed it? They look at things differently. Haven't you seen their eyes when they look at you? (*pause*) That snapshot of Ethel. See how she stands there against that brick wall, facing the camera without fear. They're born with that sort of courage. Just suppose, when I'm taking her away to afternoon tea, a man jumps out and points a camera at me! I'm telling you, my first thought will be to run like hell, to protect my face! It's not that I'm a coward. It's what they call instinct, and I was born with it, and now I got to learn to conquer it. Because if I don't, you think that Ethel won't know what it means? I'll be done for, man! . . . again. How else did they know? Because we agree that I'm just as white as some of them. It all boils down to this different thing they got, and, let me tell you, it's even in their way of walking. Something happened to me once which proves it. It was on the road. The first time I had started going.

ZACHARIAH: Where?

MORRIS: Just places. I've got to explain something, Zach., otherwise you won't feel what I mean. A road, Zach., is not a street. It's not just that there isn't houses, or lamp posts, or it hasn't got a name. It's that it doesn't stop. The road goes on and on, passing all the time through nothing. And when a man, a city man, a man used to streets and things, walks out onto it . . . he just doesn't know what he's walking into. You see, you're used to people . . . but there's no people there! You're used to a roof . . . there there is only a sky . . . silence instead of sound. I'm telling you, man, it was nothing instead of something, some any old thing like a donkey, or a dog or children kicking an empty tin . . . there was nothing, and it was the first time. This is no place for me, I thought, this emptiness! Not even trees, Zach. Only small, dry, little, brittle bushes and flat hills in the distance. That, and the road running straight. God, that hurts the eyeball! That straight, never-stopping road! You've reached the end you think, you come to the top, and there . . . t-h-e-r-e it goes again. So the bushes and the hills and the road and nothing else . . . or maybe just a car running away in the dust . . . but only a few of them, and far between, a long way between each one. You see, they never stopped. So all of that and me, there, in the middle for the first time. It hits you when sun goes. That's when you really know why men build homes, and the meaning of that word 'home', because the veld's gone grey and cold with a blind, bad feeling about you being there. (*pause*) So there I was on the road. I'd been watching him all day.

ZACHARIAH: Who?

MORRIS: The man ahead of me.

ZACHARIAH: I thought you was alone.

MORRIS: I was feeling alone, but there was. this man ahead of me. At first it was enough just to see him there, a spot in the dusty distance. A man! Another man! There was one other man on that road with me, going my way! But, then, the time came for the sun to drop, and I found myself walking through the shadows of those white stones on the side of the way. When a man sees shadows he thinks of night, doesn't he? I did. So I began to walk a little faster. I think he began to walk a little slower. I'm sure he also saw the shadows. Now comes the point. The more I walked a little bit faster and faster each time, the more I began to worry. About what you ask? About him. There was something about him, about the way he walked, the way he went to the top when the road had a hill and stood there against the sky and looked back at me, and then walked on again. And all the time, with this worry in my heart, the loneliness was creeping across the veld and I was hurrying a bit more. In fact, I was going quite quick by then. When the sun went at last, I was trotting you might say, and worried, Zach., really worried, man, because I could see the warm glow of his fire as I ran that last little bit through the dark. When I was even nearer he saw me coming and stood up, but when he saw me clearer he picked up a stick and held it like a hitting stick, stepping back for safety and a good aim . . . so what could I do but pass peacefully. (*pause*) Because he was white, Zach. I had been right all along . . . the road . . . since midday. That's what I mean, you see. It's in the way they walk as well.

ZACHARIAH: So you must learn to walk properly then.

MORRIS: Yes.

ZACHARIAH: And to look right at things.

MORRIS: Yes.

ZACHARIAH: And to sound right.

MORRIS: Yes! There's that, as well. The sound of it.

ZACHARIAH: So go on. (*again offering the hat*) Try it. For size. Just for the sake of the size. (MORRIS *takes the hat, plays with it for a few seconds, then impulsively puts it on.*) Ha!

MORRIS: Yes?

ZACHARIAH: Aha!

MORRIS (*whipping off the hat in embarrassment*): No.

ZACHARIAH: Yes.

MORRIS (*shaking his head*): Uhuh!

ZACHARIAH: Come.

MORRIS: No, man.

ZACHARIAH: Please, man.

MORRIS: You're teasing.

ZACHARIAH: No, man. I like the look of that on your head.

MORRIS: Really?

ZACHARIAH: S'true's God.

MORRIS: It looked right?

ZACHARIAH: I'm telling you.

MORRIS: It seemed to fit.

ZACHARIAH: It did, I know.

MORRIS (*using this as an excuse to get it back on his head*): The brim was just right on the brow . . . and with plenty of room for the brain! I'll try it again, shall I? Just for size.

ZACHARIAH: Just for size. (MORRIS *puts it on.*) Ja. A good fit.

MORRIS: A very good fit, in fact. (*lifting the hat*) Good morning!

ZACHARIAH: Very good.

MORRIS: Did it look right? (*again*) Good morning . . . Miss Ethel Lange! (*Looks quickly to see* ZACHARIAH's *reaction. He betrays nothing.*)

ZACHARIAH: Maybe a little bit higher.

MORRIS (*again*): Good morning . . . (*a flourish*) and how do you do today, Miss Ethel Lange! (*laughing with delight*) How about the jacket?

ZACHARIAH: Okay. (*Hands him the jacket.* MORRIS *puts it on.*)

MORRIS (*preening*): How did you do it?

ZACHARIAH: I said: The gentleman is smaller than me, Mr. Moses.

MORRIS: It's so smug. Look, Zach., I'm going to do that little bit again. Watch me careful. (*once again lifting his hat*) Good day, Miss Ethel Lange . . . (*pleading, servile*) . . . I beg your pardon, but I do hope you wouldn't mind to take a little walk with . . .

ZACHARIAH: Stop!

MORRIS: What's wrong?

ZACHARIAH: Your voice.

MORRIS: What's wrong with it?

ZACHARIAH: Too soft. They don't never sound like that.

MORRIS: To a lady they do! I admit, if it wasn't Ethel I was addressing, it would be different.

ZACHARIAH: Okay. Try me.

MORRIS: How?

ZACHARIAH: You're walking with Ethel. I'm selling monkey-nuts.

MORRIS: So?

ZACHARIAH: So you want some monkey-nuts.

MORRIS: That's a good idea . . . (*his voice trails off*)

ZACHARIAH: Go on. I'm selling monkey-nuts.

MORRIS (*after hesitation*): I can't.

ZACHARIAH (*simulated shock*): What!

MORRIS (*frightened*): What I mean is . . . I don't want any monkey-nuts. I'm not hungry.

ZACHARIAH: Ethel wants some.

MORRIS: Ethel.

ZACHARIAH: Ja. And I'm selling them.

MORRIS: This is hard for me, Zach.

ZACHARIAH: You must learn your lesson, Morrie. You want to pass, don't you?

MORRIS (*steeling himself*): Excuse me!

ZACHARIAH: I'll never hear that.

MORRIS: Hey!

ZACHARIAH: Or that.

MORRIS: Boy!

ZACHARIAH: I'm ignoring you, man. I'm a cheeky one.

MORRIS: You're asking for it, Zach.!

ZACHARIAH: I am.

MORRIS: I warn you, I will!

ZACHARIAH: Go ahead.

MORRIS (*with brutality and coarseness*): Hey, Swartgat! (*An immediate reaction from* ZACHARIAH. *His head whips around. He stares at* MORRIS *in disbelief.* MORRIS *replies with a weak little laugh, which soon dies on his lips.*) Just a joke! (*softly*) Oh, my God! What did I do! Forgive me, Zach. Say it, please. Forgiveness. Don't look at me like that! (*a step to* ZACHARIAH *who backs away*) Say something. For God's sake, say anything! I didn't mean it now. I didn't do it then. Truly. I came back. I'm your brother.

ZACHARIAH (*disbelief*): My brother?

MORRIS: Me, Zach., Morris!

ZACHARIAH: Morris? (MORRIS *at last realises what has happened. He tears off the jacket and hat in a frenzy.*)

MORRIS: Now do you see?

ZACHARIAH: It's you.

MORRIS: Yes!

ZACHARIAH: That's funny. I thought . . .

MORRIS: I know. I saw it again.

ZACHARIAH: What?

MORRIS: The pain, man. The pity of it all and the pain in your eyes.

ZACHARIAH: I was looking, I thought, at a different sort of man.

MORRIS: But don't you see, Zach.? It was me! That different sort of man you saw was me: It's happened, man! And I'll swear, I'll take God's name in vain that I no longer wanted it. That's why I came back. I didn't want it anymore. I turned around on the road and came back here because I couldn't stand that look in your eyes anymore. Those bright, brotherly eyes in my dreams at night, always wet with love, full of pity and pain . . . God, such lonely eyes they were! . . . watching and sad and asking me, why? softly, why? sorrowfully, why? . . . Why did I do it? . . . Why try to deny it? Because . . . because . . . I'll tell you the whole truth now . . . Because I did try it! It didn't seem a sin. If a man was born with a chance at a change, why not take it, I thought . . . thinking of worms lying warm in their silk, to come out one day with wings and things! Why not a man? If his dreams are soft and keep him warm at night, why not stand up the next morning, Different . . . Beautiful! It's the natural law! The long arm of the real law frightened me—but I might have been lucky. We all know that some are not caught, so . . . so . . . so what was worrying me? You. Yes, in my dreams at night, there was you, as well. What about you? My own brother. What sort of a thing was that to do to a ou's own flesh and blood brother? Because he is, you know. There was only one mother, and she's what counts. And watch out! She will, too, up in heaven, her two little chickens down here and find one missing. She'll know what you've done! If you don't mind about hell, all right, go ahead . . . but even so there was still you, because it wasn't that next life but this old, worn out and wicked one, and I was tired because there was still you. Anywhere, anyplace or road, there was still you. So I came back. (*pause*) It's not been too hard. A little uneasy at times, but not too hard. And I've proved I'm no Judas. Gentle Jesus meek and mild, I'm no Judas! (*The alarm rings. Neither responds.*)

SCENE 6

Night.

The two men are asleep. Silence. Suddenly ZACHARIAH *sits up in bed. Without looking at* MORRIS *he gets up, goes to the corner where the new suit of clothes is hanging, and puts on the suit and hat. The final effect is an absurdity bordering on the grotesque. The hat is too small and so is the jacket, which he has buttoned up incorrectly, while the trousers are too short.* ZACHARIAH *stands barefooted, holding the umbrella, the hat pulled down low over his eyes so that his face is almost hidden.*

ZACHARIAH: Ma. Ma! Mother! Hullo. How are you, old woman? What's that? You don't recognise me? Well, well, well. Take a guess. (*shakes his head*) No. (*shakes his head*) No. Try again. (*shakes his head*) What's the matter with you, Ma? Don't you recognise your own son? (*shakes his head violently*) No, no! Not him! It's me, Zach.! (*sweeps off the hat to show his face*) Ja. Zach.! Didn't think I could do it, did you? Well, to tell you the truth, the whole truth, so help me God, I got sick of myself and made a change. Him? At home, Ma. Ja. A lonely boy, as you say. A sad story, as I will tell you. He went on the road, Ma, but strange to say, he came back quite white. No tan at all. I don't recognise him no more. (*he sits*) I'll ask you again, how are you, old woman? I see some signs of wear and tear. (*nodding his head*) That's true . . . such sorrow . . . tomorrow . . . Ja . . . it's cruel . . . it's callous . . . and your feet as well? Still a bad fit in the shoe? Ai ai ai! Me? (*Pause. He struggles*) There's something I need to know, Ma. You see, we been talking, me and him

. . . ja, I talk to him, he says it helps . . . and now we got to know. Whose mother were you really? At the bottom of your heart, where your blood is red with pain, tell me, whom did you really love? No evil feelings, Ma, but, I mean, a man's got to know. You see, he's been such a burden as a brother. (*agitation*) Don't be dumb! Don't cry! It was just a question! Look! I brought you a present, old soul. (*holds out a hand with the fingers lightly closed*) It's a butterfly. A real beauty butterfly. We were travelling fast, Ma. We hit them at ninety . . . a whole flock. But one was still alive, and made me think of . . . Mother . . . So I caught it, myself, for you, remembering what I caught from you. This, old Ma of mine, is gratitude for you, and it proves it, doesn't it? Some things are only skin deep, because I got it, here in my hand, I got beauty . . . too . . . haven't I?

SCENE 7

The next evening.

For the first time the room is untidy. The beds are not made, the table cluttered, the floor littered with the strings and wrappings of the parcels of the previous day. MORRIS *is alone. He sits lifelessly at the table, his head fallen on his chest, his arms hanging limp at his sides. On the table is a small bundle. Then* ZACHARIAH *comes in. He behaves normally, going straight to the bed and taking off his shoes. Only when this is done, does he realise something is wrong. The footbath hasn't been prepared.*

ZACHARIAH: What's this? (*looking around for the basin*) Footsalts finished? Hell, man! Couldn't you have seen? What must I do now? My feet are killing me again. I've been on them today, you know. (*touching the toes*) Eina! Eina! Forget the salts then. Just give me some hot. A soak will do them good. (MORRIS *doesn't move.*) Some hot, Morrie! Please! (*nothing happens*) What's the matter with you? Don't tell me the stove is buggered up! (*Goes to the stove and feels the kettle*) Ag, no, man! What the hell's happened? A man works all day, his feet are killing him and he comes home and finds this (*the stove*) . . . and this. (*the room*) Floor not swept! Beds not made! (*beginning to realise*) There is something wrong in here. You say nothing. (MORRIS *struggles to find a word, but fails and drops his shoulders in a gesture of defeat and resignation.*) You mean . . . (*disbelief*) . . . You mean you got nothing to say? (*a little laugh, but this quickly dies*) No! It's not funny. Try to say something, Morrie. Please. (*desperate*) Try telling me what happened. Ja! What happened?

MORRIS: I've given up.

ZACHARIAH: What?

MORRIS: I mean, I can't carry on.

ZACHARIAH: Oh, so you've just stopped.

MORRIS: Yes.

ZACHARIAH: But that won't do! Emphatically not! A man can't just stop like that, like you. That's definitely no good, because . . . You want to know why? Because a man must carry on. Most certainly. Otherwise who is going to sweep the floor? Ja. Ever think about that? If everybody just gave up, just sat down and couldn't carry on . . . me at the gate . . . you in here . . . why, nothing would happen. Isn't that so? One by one we would just topple over and nothing would happen. But we all know that *something* got to happen. So that proves it, doesn't it? We *must* carry on. Okay? Feeling better? (*Sees the bundle on the table for the first time*) What's this bundle, Morrie?

MORRIS: My belongings.

ZACHARIAH: What's that?

MORRIS: My Bible, my other shirt and my alarm clock.

ZACHARIAH: And what would they be doing in here?

MORRIS: I was leaving, Zach.

ZACHARIAH: Leaving?

MORRIS: Going away.

ZACHARIAH: Where?

MORRIS: The road. Wherever it went.

ZACHARIAH: Oh! (*pause*) And what about me?

MORRIS: I know, I know.

ZACHARIAH: But you don't care, hey?

MORRIS: I do care, Zach.!

ZACHARIAH (*ignoring the denial*): That's a fine thought for a loving brother. I'm surprised at you. In fact, I'm shocked.

MORRIS: Stop it, Zach.! I'm still here. I know

I can't go. You see, this morning when you were at work, I thought it out. It's no use anymore, I said. There's no future left for us now, in here. So I wrapped up my Bible and my clock in my shirt and wrote the farewell note. Four pages! I explained everything. I was ready to go, man . . . until I realised that you couldn't read. My God, that hurt! That cut me deep! Zach. can't read without me! (*pause*) So you see, I know I can't go . . . but I've given up.

ZACHARIAH: Come on, cheer up. It's not so bad.

MORRIS: I can't, Zach. Honestly I can't anymore.

ZACHARIAH: But I've got a surprise for you.

MORRIS: It will have to be damn good to make any difference.

ZACHARIAH: How good is a letter from Ethel?

MORRIS: No damn good! You've missed the point. Don't you see, man! She's to blame. (ZACHARIAH *takes out the letter.*) I don't want it. Take it away.

ZACHARIAH (*putting the letter down on the table so that* MORRIS *can see it*): It's not mine. I gave her to you.

MORRIS: Everything was fine until she came along.

ZACHARIAH: She hasn't yet.

MORRIS: What do you mean?

ZACHARIAH: Come along. You've missed the problem. Ethel coming along was the problem. She hasn't yet. But she might be on her way. I mean . . . It could be June, couldn't it? Where's the moths? And she did say June. That's what I'm saying. She might be on the train, on her way right now, and one fine day, you know what? Guess.

MORRIS: What?

ZACHARIAH: Another knock at the door. But it won't be me. So, you see, if I was you, just for safety's sake, of course, I'd have a quick peep at that letter. (ZACHARIAH *goes to his bed.* MORRIS *hesitates for a second, then takes the letter, opens it and reads in silence. When he has finished he puts it down and looks at* ZACHARIAH *vacantly.*)

ZACHARIAH (*unable to contain himself any longer*): She's coming! Let me guess. She's on the train, on her way, and it's June. When do you meet, man? What did she say? Tell me, Morrie.

MORRIS: No. She's not coming. Never. Prepare yourself for . . . good news. Ethel's gone and got engaged to get married, to Luckyman Stoffel.

ZACHARIAH: No.

MORRIS: Yes.

ZACHARIAH: No.

MORRIS: It's true.

ZACHARIAH: No!

MORRIS: Then listen. (*reads*) "Dear Pen-pal, it's sad news for you but good news for me. I've decided to get married. Ma says it's Okay. The lucky man is Stoffel, who plays in my brother's team, full-back. It's a long story. Lucy thought she had him, but she didn't, so now we're not on talking terms no more. Stoffel works at Boetie's Garage and doesn't like competition so he says pen-pals is out if we're going to get married to each other. He's sitting here now and he says he wants to say this: Leave my woman alone if you know what's good for you. That was Stoffel. He's a one all right. Well pal, that's all for now, for ever. Ethel." (*pause*) Down here at the bottom she says: "You can keep the snapshot for a keepsake." (MORRIS *looks vacantly at* ZACHARIAH *whose attitude has hardened with bitter disappointment.*)

ZACHARIAH: So?

MORRIS: So I think we can begin again.

ZACHARIAH: What?

MORRIS: That's a good question. (*pause*) Well, let's work it out. Where are we? Here. That's a good beginning. What is this? Our room. Me and you, Morrie and Zach. . . . live here . . . in peace. Yes. It's coming now, Zach. I feel it. I'm filling up again with thoughts and things. We're living here in peace because the problem's gone . . . and got engaged to be married . . . and I'm Morrie . . . and I was going to go, but now I'm going to stay! (*With something of his old self* MORRIE *goes to work. Opens his bundle and packs out his belongings.*) Hey, Zach.! (*holding up the clock*) It's stopped. Like me. What time shall we make it? Supper?

ZACHARIAH: I'm not hungry.

MORRIS: Bed time?

ZACHARIAH: I don't want to sleep.

MORRIS: Just after supper, then. We'll say we've eaten.

ZACHARIAH: You can say what you like!

MORRIS: What's the matter, Zach.? I don't like to see you so . . . so . . . sort of. Come on now. Tell me what it is. I've helped you before, haven't I?

ZACHARIAH (*slowly*): You aren't going to wear that suit anymore?

MORRIS: I see. Zach., look at me now. Solemnly, on this Bible, I promise you I won't.

ZACHARIAH: That's it.

MORRIS: What?

ZACHARIAH (*slyly*): You looked so damn smart in that suit, Morrie. It made me feel good.

MORRIS: You mean that!

ZACHARIAH: Cross my heart.

MORRIS: You mean you want to see me *in it?*

ZACHARIAH: I do.

MORRIS: Be honest now, Zach. Is what you are saying that you would like me to put that suit on?

ZACHARIAH (*emphatically*): Now.

MORRIS: Now! This comes as a surprise, Zach. But if as you say it makes you feel better . . . well . . . that just about makes it my duty, doesn't it? (*moving to the suit*) It was a damn good buy, Ethel or no Ethel. I really am tempted.

ZACHARIAH: Then get in.

MORRIS: You'll have to help me. It's not so easy now . . . after yesterday. Say something to help me.

ZACHARIAH: Just for size. No harm done. We're brothers. She's gone for the good. We're only playing now.

MORRIS: Only playing! Of course! That does it. (*With a laugh* MORRIS *puts on the suit. When he is dressed, he walks around the room in exaggerated style.* ZACHARIAH *encourages him.*)

ZACHARIAH: Ek sê! Just look! Hoe's dit vir 'n ding. Links draai, regs swaai . . . Aitsa! Ou pellie, you're stepping high tonight! (MORRIS *stops, turns suddenly.*)

MORRIS: Hey Swartgat! (*A second of silence, and then* ZACHARIAH *laughs hollowly*) No harm done now, hey, Zach.?

ZACHARIAH: No pain.

MORRIS: That's the way to take a joke. (*again*) Hey, Swartgat!

ZACHARIAH (*playing along*): Ja, Baas?

MORRIS: Who are you?

ZACHARIAH: I'm your boy, Zach., Baas.

MORRIS: Who am I?

ZACHARIAH: Baas Morrie, Baas.

MORRIS: Baas Morrie and his boy, Zach.! My God, you're comical! Where the hell you get that joke from, Zach.?

ZACHARIAH: At the gate.

MORRIS: So that's what it's like.

ZACHARIAH: They're all dressed up smart like you, and go walking by. Go on. Try it.

MORRIS: What?

ZACHARIAH: Walk past.

MORRIS: You want to play it?

ZACHARIAH: Why not?

MORRIS: I haven't seen the gate before, Zach. It's difficult to play something you haven't seen.

ZACHARIAH: I'll show you. Here it is. (*vague gesture*) This here is the gate.

MORRIS: What's on the other side?

ZACHARIAH: Does it matter?

MORRIS: It does if we're going to play this thing right.

ZACHARIAH (*looking back*): Trees.

MORRIS: Ah: Tall trees, with picnics in the shade.

ZACHARIAH: Grass.

MORRIS: Green, hey! We'll make it spring.

ZACHARIAH: Flowers with butterflies.

MORRIS: That's a good touch.

ZACHARIAH: And benches.

MORRIS: How thoughtful! I'll want to rest.

ZACHARIAH: And I'm squatting here.

MORRIS: Right. So you'll open the gate for me when I get there.

ZACHARIAH: No. It's open. I'll just watch your boots as you go by.

MORRIS: Then what's your job at the gate?

ZACHARIAH (*pause*): They put me there to chase the black kids away. (MORRIS *hesitates.*)

MORRIS: Are you sure we should play this?

ZACHARIAH: It's only a game. Walk past. (MORRIS *flourishes his umbrella and then saunters slowly towards* ZACHARIAH.)

MORRIS: Shame! Look at that poor old boy. John? What are you doing . . . ?

ZACHARIAH (*cutting him*): No, Morrie.

MORRIS: What's wrong?

ZACHARIAH: They never talk to me. Start again. (MORRIS *tries it again. This time he doesn't speak, but pretends to take a coin out of his pocket and tosses it to* ZACHARIAH.) How much?

MORRIS: Half a crown.

ZACHARIAH: What!

MORRIS: Shilling.

ZACHARIAH: Too much.

MORRIS: Sixpence. (ZACHARIAH *is still doubtful.*) All right then, a penny.

ZACHARIAH: That's a bit better, but . . .

MORRIS: But what?

ZACHARIAH: You think you're the soft sort of white man, hey! Giving me a penny like that.

MORRIS: What's wrong with being the soft sort? You find them.

ZACHARIAH: I know. But not you. Not with boots, Morrie. Never with boots. That sort doesn't even see me. So don't stop. Just walk past. (*The mime is repeated. This time* MORRIS *walks straight past.*)

MORRIS: Now what?

ZACHARIAH: I have a thought. I'm squatting here, watching you, and I think.

MORRIS: Okay.

ZACHARIAH: Bastard!

MORRIS (*sharply*): Who?

ZACHARIAH: Don't spoil it, man! You don't hear me. It's a thought. (*taps his forehead*)

MORRIS (*looking away, frowning*): Carry on.

ZACHARIAH: That's all.

MORRIS: Just . . . ?

ZACHARIAH: Just a bastard.

MORRIS: What happens now?

ZACHARIAH: I'm watching you, but you're looking up the trees, remember?

MORRIS: Yes, of course. It's a tall tree. I'm wondering if I've ever seen a tree as tall as this tree. There's also a great weight of birdies on the branches and . . . actually I'm finding difficulty keeping my mind up the tree with you behind my back. I feel your presence. So I think, I'll move further on. You see, you bothered me as I passed. Moments of recognition, you know, at first sight, and all that. So I'll take this road. I mean . . . I'll have to get away if I want to admire the beauty, won't I? Yes. It's a good road. It's going places, because ahead of me I see the sky. I see it through the trees . . . so I'm climbing up the hill in this road, putting miles between us; and now, at last, there ahead of me is the sky, big, blue; and I hurry on to the top where I turn against it and look back at you . . . far behind me now, in the distance, outside the gate. Can you see me?

ZACHARIAH: A little.

MORRIS: What is it you see here, in the distance, beyond the trees, upon the hill, against the sky?

ZACHARIAH: Could it be a . . . man?

MORRIS: A white man! Don't you see the way I stand? Didn't you see how I turned and looked back at you, at all that is past and forgotten? What do you think now?

ZACHARIAH: He's a bastard!

MORRIS (*reckless in his elation*): Well, I don't care. It's too far away now for me to see your eyes. In fact, I'm almost free . . . because down hill is always easier! I can run now! So I turn my back and away I go, laughing, over the green spring grass, into the flowers and among the butterflies. And what do I say? What do I shout? I've changed! Look at me, will you please! I too flew from darkness to light, but I didn't burn my wings. (*pause*) Now I'm tired. After so many years, so much beauty is a burden. I need rest. (*sits*) Ah dearie, dearie me. (ZACHARIAH *comes past, bent low, miming the picking up of litter in the park. One hand trails a sack, the other is stabbing with a stick at pieces of paper.* MORRIS *watches this with critical interest.*) What are you doing?

ZACHARIAH: Picking up rubbish. I got a stick with a nail on the end. Every afternoon, at four o'clock, I go through the trees and around the benches and pick up the papers and peels.

MORRIS: I thought I'd left you behind.

ZACHARIAH: I know.

MORRIS: The sight of you affects me, Swartgat.

ZACHARIAH (*continuing with his mime*): I can feel it does.

MORRIS: It's interesting. Just looking at you, does it. I don't need the other senses. Just sight. Not even smell. Just the sight of you crawling around like some . . . some . . . thing . . . makes me want to bring up.

ZACHARIAH: Is that so?

MORRIS (*rising*): In fact I'd like to . . . (*stops himself*)

ZACHARIAH: Carry on.

MORRIS (*walking away*): I can't.

ZACHARIAH: Try.

MORRIS: I'm telling you, I can't.

ZACHARIAH: Why?

MORRIS: Not with that old woman watching us. (ZACHARIAH *stops and looks questioningly at* MORRIS.) Over there. (*pointing*)

ZACHARIAH: Old woman?

MORRIS: Horribly old.

ZACHARIAH: Alone?

MORRIS: All by her lonely self.

ZACHARIAH: And she's watching us?

MORRIS: All the time. (*impatience*) Can't you *see*! She's wearing a grey dress on Sunday.

ZACHARIAH (*recognition dawning*): Soapsuds . . .

MORRIS: . . . on brown hands.

ZACHARIAH: And sore feet! The toes are crooked, hey!

MORRIS: With sadness. She's been following me all day, all along the road, the long, unending road . . . begging!

ZACHARIAH: Call the police.

MORRIS: No, no. Not that.

ZACHARIAH: Then what will we do?

MORRIS: Let's work it out. We can't carry on with her watching us . . . behind that bush . . . like an old spy.

ZACHARIAH: So she must go.

MORRIS: I think so, too. (*A step in the direction of the old woman*) Go away.

ZACHARIAH: Is she moving?

MORRIS: No. (*trying again*) Go away, old one! Begat and be gone! Go home! (*sigh*) It's no use.

ZACHARIAH (*trying to scare her off*): Hey!

MORRIS (*excited*): She jumped! Ha ha. She jumped!

ZACHARIAH: Voertsek!

MORRIS: Another jump. (ZACHARIAH *goes down on his hands and knees.*) What are you doing?

ZACHARIAH: Stones.

MORRIS: Hoooooo! She heard you. She's trotted off a little distance. But you're not really going to use them, are you?

ZACHARIAH: It's the only way. (*throws*)

MORRIS: Almost. (ZACHARIAH *throws again.*) She jumped!

ZACHARIAH: Voertsek!

MORRIS: Yes. Voertsek off! We don't want you!

ZACHARIAH: Bugger off!

MORRIS: You old bitch! You made life unbearable!

ZACHARIAH (*starts throwing with renewed violence*): Hamba!

MORRIS: She's running now.

ZACHARIAH: Get out!

MORRIS: Kaffermeid!

ZACHARIAH: Ou hoer!

MORRIS: Luisgat!

ZACHARIAH: Swartgat!

MORRIS: You've hit her! She's down. Look . . . Look!

ZACHARIAH: Look at those old legs sticking up!

MORRIS: She's got no broeks on! (*Their derision rises to a climax,* MORRIS *shaking his umbrella,* ZACHARIAH *his fists.*) That's the last of her, I think. By God, she ran! (*pause while they get their breath*) Where were we?

ZACHARIAH: It was four o'clock. I was collecting the rubbish. You wanted to do . . . something.

MORRIS: Yes. I remember now. I just wanted to . . . just wanted to . . . Poke you with my umbrella. He-he-he! (*He attacks* ZACHARIAH *savagely.*) Just wanted to poke you a little bit. That's all. He-he! What do you think umbrellas are for when it doesn't rain? Hey? (ZACHARIAH *tries to escape, but* MORRIS *catches him with the crook of the umbrella.*) Wait, wait! Not so fast, John. I want to have a good look at you. My God! What sort of a mistake is this! A black man! All over, my boy?

ZACHARIAH: Ja, Baas.

MORRIS: Your pits and privates?

ZACHARIAH: Ja, Baas.

MORRIS: Nothing white?

ZACHARIAH: Forgive me please, my Baas.

MORRIS: You're horrible.

ZACHARIAH: Sorry, Baas.

MORRIS: You stink.

ZACHARIAH: Please, my Baasie . . .

MORRIS: You don't use paper do you?

ZACHARIAH: . . . oh, my Baasie, my Baasie, my good little Baasie.

MORRIS: You know something? I hate you! What did you mean crawling around like that? Spoiling the view, spoiling my chances? What's your game, hey? Trying to be an embarrassment? Is that it? A two-legged embarrassment? Well, I hate you, do you hear! Hate! . . . Hate! . . . Hate! . . . (*He attacks* ZACHARIAH *savagely with the umbrella. When his fury is spent he turns away and sits down.*) It was a good day. The sun shone. The sky was blue. I was happy. (*smiling, released of all tensions*) Not the sort of day to forget in a hurry. There's a spiny chill sprung up now,

though. (*Shivering.* ZACHARIAH *is moaning softly.*) Something sighing among the trees . . . must be the wind. Yes! There were the trees as well today. The tall trees. So much to remember! Still . . . (*shivering*) . . . it has got nippy . . . and I haven't got an overcoat . . . with me.

ZACHARIAH: Ding-dong . . . ong . . . ong . . . Ding-dong . . . ong . . . ong.

MORRIS: What is that sound I hear?

ZACHARIAH: The bells. They're closing up. Ding-dong . . . ong . . . ong.

MORRIS: I'd better hurry home. (*stands*) Yes, it was a good day . . . while it lasted.

ZACHARIAH: Ding-dong . . . ong . . . ong.

MORRIS: Ah, there's the gate.

ZACHARIAH: What's the matter with you?

MORRIS: What's the matter with me?

ZACHARIAH: Can't you see the gate is locked?

MORRIS: Is it? (*tries the gate*) It is.

ZACHARIAH: I locked it before I rang the bell.

MORRIS: Heavens above! Then I'd better climb over.

ZACHARIAH: Over those sharp pieces of glass they got on the top?

MORRIS: Then the fence.

ZACHARIAH: Barbed wire . . . very high . . .

MORRIS: So what do I do?

ZACHARIAH: You might try calling.

MORRIS: Hello! Hello there! Hello, anybody there!!

ZACHARIAH: Nobody hears you, hey!

MORRIS: Now what?

ZACHARIAH: Now, you think you'll try the gate on the other side.

MORRIS (*alarm*): All the way back?

ZACHARIAH: Ja. (*moves quietly to the lamp on the table*)

MORRIS: Through the trees?

ZACHARIAH: Looks like it.

MORRIS: But it's getting dark! (ZACHARIAH *is turning down the lamp.*)

ZACHARIAH: It happens, every day.

MORRIS: And cold . . . and I never did like shadows . . . and . . . (*pause*) . . . where are you?

ZACHARIAH: Behind a tree.

MORRIS: But . . . but I thought you were the good sort of boy?

ZACHARIAH: Me?

MORRIS: The simple, trustworthy type of John-boy. Weren't you that?

ZACHARIAH: I've changed.

MORRIS: Who gave you the right?

ZACHARIAH: I took it!

MORRIS: That's illegal! They weren't yours! That's theft. 'Thou shalt not steal.' I arrest you in the name of God. That's it! God! (*looking around wildly*) My prayers . . . please! My last wish . . . is to say my prayers, please. You see . . . you might hear them. (MORRIS *goes down on his knees.* ZACHARIAH *begins to move to him.*) Our Father, which art our Father in heaven, because we never knew the other one; Forgive us this day our trespassing; I couldn't help it; The gate was open, God, your sun was too bright and blinded my eyes, so I didn't see the notice prohibiting! And 'beware of the dog' was in Bantu, so how was I to know, Oh Lord! My sins are not that black. Furthermore, just some bread for the poor, daily, and let Your Kingdom come as quick as it can, for Yours is the power and the glory, but ours is the fear and the judgment of eyes behind our back for the sins of our birth and the man behind the tree in the darkness while I wait . . . Eina! (ZACHARIAH *stands above* MORRIS *on the point of violence. The alarm clock rings.* MORRIS *crawls frantically away.*) Bedtime! (MORRIS *jumps up, rushes to the table and turns up the lamp.* ZACHARIAH *goes to his bed and sits. A long silence. They avoid each other's eyes.* MORRIS *takes off the jacket. At the window.*) Wind's turning again.

ZACHARIAH: Ja. I got the whiff coming home.

MORRIS: Not a bird left now . . . to break the still hate of its face.

ZACHARIAH (*moved to fear, as always, by these words*): Hell!

MORRIS: Yes. I know what you mean . . . what you feel. The waters are shivering, too. Always in a shiver when the wind blows. Have you noticed?

ZACHARIAH: No.

MORRIS: Yes. It's the mystery of my life that lake. I mean . . . It smells dead, doesn't it? If ever there was a piece of water that looks dead and done for, that's what I'm looking at now. And yet, who knows? Who really knows what's at the bottom?

ZACHARIAH: I knew him.

MORRIS: Who?

ZACHARIAH: At the bottom.

MORRIS (*looking out of the window with added interest*): Yes!

ZACHARIAH: Went for a swim and drowned.

MORRIS: Didn't they get him out?

ZACHARIAH: Never found him.

MORRIS: That's a hell of a way to go! And not be found in the bargain! But it proves it, doesn't it? (*leaving the window*) We'll sleep well tonight, you'll see.

ZACHARIAH: Morris?

MORRIS: Yes?

ZACHARIAH: What happened?

MORRIS: You mean . . . ?

ZACHARIAH: Ja.

MORRIS: We were carried away, as they would say, by the game . . . quite far in fact. Mustn't get worried, though . . . I don't think. I mean, it was only a game . . . as long as we play in the right spirit . . . we'll be all right. I'll keep the clock winded, don't worry. One thing I'm certain is sure, it's a good thing we got the game. It will pass the time. Because we got a lot left, you know! (*little laugh*) Almost a whole life . . . stretching ahead . . . in here . . . (*pause*) Yes. (*pause*) As I said . . . I'm not too worried at all. Not at all . . . too worried. I mean, other men get by without a future. In fact, I think there's quite a lot of people getting by without futures these days. (*Silence.* MORRIS *makes the last preparations for bed.*)

ZACHARIAH: Morris?

MORRIS: Yes?

ZACHARIAH: What is it, Morrie? The two of us . . . you know . . . in here?

MORRIS: Home.

ZACHARIAH: Is there no other way?

MORRIS: No. You see, we're tied together, Zach. It's what they call the blood knot . . . the bond between brothers. (*As* MORRIS *moves to his bed . . . Curtain.*)

VI
Alienation

Man's unwilling realization that he *is* alone in the cosmos is called alienation. We have seen, in the previous sections, the progression from religion and love to alienation and the search for personal identity. Alienation and the search for personal identity are characteristic of twentieth-century trends of thought. With the loss of faith in an omnipotent and ultimately benevolent Supreme Being who had created Humanity and was even now avuncularly watching over it, men came to realize that they themselves—their own existence, their own integrity—were all they had to fall back on and believe in. There could no longer be a falsely comforting appeal to a higher order: "Prayer," says the modern French writer Alain, "is when night descends over thought." Hence the search for the definition of the self. The same knowledge has led to the conception of alienation. Camus has called this feeling of strangeness in one's setting the absurd. The feeling of the absurd begins, Camus tells us, when we see through things, when "the stage sets collapse: Rising, streetcar, four hours in the office or the factory, meal, streetcar, four hours of work, meal, sleep, and Monday Tuesday Wednesday Thursday Friday and Saturday according to the same rhythm. . . . But one day the 'why' arises and everything begins in that weariness tinged with amazement. . . . Weariness comes at the end of the acts of a mechanical life. . . ."

The sense of frustration and helplessness coming from a mechanical life is seen poignantly in Georg Büchner's *Woyzeck*, written shortly before the author's death. Büchner died in 1837 at the age of twenty-four, totally unrecognized. It is always an injustice when a good writer is not recognized in his lifetime, but in Büchner's case there is little reason for berating his contemporaries as insensitive. Büchner was a living anachronism, so far ahead of his time that he still seems avant-garde today. In his story of the soldier who had the misfortune to be too aware and sensitive for his position, who had feelings and a sense of his own dignity as an individual in a situation admitting of no such luxuries, Büchner created a story that speaks to the modern mind. Woyzeck is the prototype of the brainwashed, downtrodden part of society, a phenomenon we are all too familiar with today. His tragedy is, ironically, that a spark of doubt and of outrage remains within him, lambent and inextinguishable. That spark, which saves him from an unthinking, robotlike existence, destroys him.

Toward the end of the nineteenth century, the feeling of alienation took shape in Alfred Jarry's curious play *King Ubu,* the play that provided the original impetus for the drama now called the "theater of the absurd." Jarry's feeling of alienation was both seminal and instinctive. The blasé audiences of today are accustomed to the most extreme forms of obscenity in everyday conversations. Consequently, obscenity as a symbol of protest against the rigidities of convention has lost all effect. To us, the famous opening line of *King Ubu* seems mildly amusing, perhaps even a little trite, and certainly innocuous. But in 1896, the public utterance of that one word *"merdre"* (slightly altered to make it Jarryesque) had a cataclysmic effect. It was a slap in the face of society. The rebellion implicit in the utterance of the word on a public stage was a rebellion against all society. It was an evocation of disgust so deep that conventional language was powerless to express it, and at the same time the very unconventionality of the word was a gesture of defiance itself. The scatological references sprinkled through the play represent rebellion on its most instinctive and elementary level—that of a child's refusal to bow to toilet training. The purpose is deeper, however. Jarry's protest against the human condition was primitive and untutored; it was protest based on blind nihilism. The cosmic malignity that hovers invisibly over the characters in present-day avant-garde dramas is tangible and personified in Jarry's plays. Instead of being a helpless pawn (like Vladimir and Estragon in *Waiting for Godot,* or the employee in Adamov's *La Parodie,* or Maurice in Genet's *Deathwatch*), Jarry's protagonist, Father Ubu, is dirty, treacherous, greedy, ungrateful, cowardly, and cruel. In other words, the grotesquely bloated but still human figure of Father Ubu has all the attributes of the cosmic malignant force that pervades the avant-garde drama.

Arthur Adamov's *All Against All* is about the instinctive enmity human beings display toward each other. The play is not so much an indictment of a social system that forces human beings to act in their habitual dog-eat-dog manner as an implication that the social system is a result of human nature. A social system, Adamov is saying, is no more than a conglomeration of individuals and their traits. The only rule the individual respects is the rule of self; therefore, the society in which he lives is an impersonal one where the law of self-preservation is the only guiding principle and treachery the accepted mode of conduct.

As in all plays of rebellion, the great enemy is death, the realization of whose inevitability alienates man from his setting by making him realize he is only a temporary intruder in it. Here, though, the inevitably futile struggle against the onslaught of death produces not the heroic protester, but a small, sneaking, sniveling, shameless schemer who tries to subvert death, to slide unnoticed away from it, to shove someone else into its jaws instead of defying it. As one reads the play, one feels only disgust and revulsion at such a picture of the human race. But it is a true picture; there is no doubt of that.

Adamov has stated that the play is an allegory of the Central European persecution of the Jews and of the attempt of many of those Jews to continue living their old lives at whatever cost to their personal dignity. The play ends with the brutal, violent, and, above all, *senseless* death of all the main characters.

Finally, in *Open Twenty-Four Hours* we see the alienation man has created within society. Unable to relate to the cosmos (religion), to himself (identity), to another (love), man has, with a masochistic intensity, set up artificial barriers within society as well. Of all the conflicts man is subject to, that caused by the alienation of the races is the only one that rises from willfulness rather than from necessity. The total lack of understanding between the races that Roger Cornish shows us in his play is as realistic today as it is pointless. Man's despair at his condition has led him to exacerbate that condition so that we have a totally unnecessary geometric progression of alienation. The black and white races are shown here as completely and hopelessly polarized, as if they were magnetic poles instinctively repelling each other. The irony, of course, is that only like magnetic poles repel each other.

WOYZECK

Georg Büchner

TRANSLATED BY
George E. Wellwarth

CHARACTERS

CAPTAIN
FRANZ WOYZECK
ANDRES
MARIE
MARGRET
DRUM MAJOR
OLD MAN
CHILD
BARKER
SERGEANT
DOCTOR
FIRST APPRENTICE
SECOND APPRENTICE
FIRST WOMAN
SECOND WOMAN
JEW
KARL, THE IDIOT
FIRST GIRL
SECOND GIRL
THIRD GIRL
GRANDMOTHER
KATIE
INNKEEPER
FIRST MAN
SECOND MAN

Soldiers, Students, Apprentices, Boys, Girls, and Children

Scene 1

At the CAPTAIN's. *The* CAPTAIN *sitting in a chair,* WOYZECK *shaving him.*

CAPTAIN: Slowly, Woyzeck, slowly; one thing at a time! You're making me quite dizzy. What am I supposed to do with the ten minutes you save me by finishing earlier today? Think, Woyzeck, think: you've still got a good thirty years to live—thirty years! That's three hundred and sixty months! And days! Hours! Minutes! What are you going to do with all that fantastic amount of time? Schedule yourself, Woyzeck, schedule yourself!

WOYZECK: Yes, sir, Captain.

CAPTAIN: When I think about eternity I get positively alarmed about the state of the world. You've got to keep busy, Woyzeck, busy! Eternal—well, that's eternal, that's eternal. You can understand that for yourself. But then again it isn't eternal, it's only a moment, yes, only a moment. Woyzeck, when I think that the world turns round completely in one day, I shudder! What a waste of time! What's it all coming to? Woyzeck, I can't even look at a mill wheel anymore without becoming melancholy.

WOYZECK: Yes, sir, Captain.

CAPTAIN: You always act like someone's after you, Woyzeck. A good man, a good man who's got a good conscience, doesn't do that. Well, speak up, Woyzeck! What's the weather like today?

WOYZECK: Bad, Captain, bad: windy!

CAPTAIN: I can feel it; it's like something rushing around outside; a wind like that reminds me of a mouse running about. (*Slyly.*) It feels like a south-north wind, doesn't it?

WOYZECK: Yes, sir, Captain.

CAPTAIN: Ha, ha, ha! South-north! Ha, ha, ha! Oh, you're stupid, really abominably stupid! (*Moved.*) You're a good man, Woyzeck, but (*Impressively.*) you're not a moral man, Woyzeck! Morality—that's when you're moral, you understand. It's a good word. You have a child without the blessing of the Church, as our honorable garrison preacher puts it—without the blessing of the Church; it's not my expression.

WOYZECK: Captain, the good God won't care whether the Amen was said over the poor little worm before he was made. The Lord said, Suffer little children to come unto me.

CAPTAIN: What's that? What kind of a peculiar answer is that? He's muddling me up completely with his answer. When I say "he" I mean you, you—

WOYZECK: We poor pepole—You see, Captain: money, money! People who don't have money—just try and find one of them that brings people into the world morally! We're flesh and blood too! People like us get the wrong end of the stick in this world and the next. They'll probably make us help with the thunder when we get to Heaven.

CAPTAIN: You have no virtue, Woyzeck! You're not a virtuous man! Flesh and blood? When I look out of the window after it's been raining and peek at the white stockings of the girls as they hop across the street—dammit, Woyzeck, that's when I feel love! I'm flesh and blood too. But virtue, virtue, Woyzeck! Virtue! How could I live without that? I always say to myself: You're a virtuous man, (*Moved.*) a good man, a good man.

WOYZECK: Yes, Captain, virtue—it isn't all that simple for me. You see, we common people, we don't have any virtue, it just comes over us and we have to do it; but if I were a gentleman and had a hat and a watch and a cloak and could talk properly, I'd want to be virtuous too. There must be something lovely about virtue, Captain. But I'm just a poor fellow!

CAPTAIN: Good, Woyzeck. You're a good man, a good man. But you think too much, and that wears you out; you always look like someone's after you. Our discourse has affected me. Go now, and don't run so much; slowly, nice and slowly down the street!

Scene 2

WOYZECK *and* ANDRES *are cutting sticks in the bushes.* ANDRES *is whistling.*

WOYZECK: Yes, this place is bewitched, Andres. You see that light-colored stripe across the grass where the toadstools are growing? That's where the head rolls along in the evenings. Somebody picked it up once thinking it was a hedgehog; three days and three nights, that's how long he lasted after that. (*Softly.*) It was the Freemasons, Andres! That's it, it was the Freemasons!

ANDRES (*sings*): Two little rabbits sat on a mound,
Eating the green, green grass . . .

WOYZECK: Quiet! D'you hear it, Andres? D'you hear it? Something's going on!

ANDRES: Eating the green, green grass
Right down to the ground.

WOYZECK: It's behind me; it's under me. (*He stamps on the ground.*) You hear—hollow! Everything's hollow under here! It's the Freemasons!

ANDRES: I'm scared.

WOYZECK: Funny, it's so quiet around here! You want to hold your breath. Andres!

ANDRES: What?

WOYZECK: Say something! (*Peers around.*) Andres! How light it is! The whole town looks like it's glowing! There's fire in the sky and a sound like trombones coming down. There's a draft from under here! Quick, let's go! Don't look back! (*Pulls him into the bushes.*)

ANDRES (*after a pause*): You still hear it, Woyzeck?

WOYZECK: Quiet—everything's quiet, just as if the world were dead.

ANDRES: D'you hear? They're drumming back there. We have to go!

SCENE 3

The town. MARIE *is at a window with her child.* MARGRET *is at another. The troops are marching by with the* DRUM MAJOR *at their head.*

MARIE (*rocking the child in her arms*): Hey, boy! Da da da da! D'you hear? Here they come!

MARGRET: What a man—like a tree!

MARIE: He stands there like a lion! (*The* DRUM MAJOR *waves.*)

MARGRET: Well, you've certainly got a friendly eye out today, neighbor! We're not used to that from you.

MARIE (*sings*): Soldiers lads are handsome young men . . .

MARGRET: Your eyes are still shining . . .

MARIE: So what! Take your own eyes to the Jew and get them polished; maybe you can still get them to shine enough so you can sell them as two buttons.

MARGRET: What's that? You! You . . . I'm an honest woman, but you—everyone knows you've got a look that could see through seven pairs of leather pants!

MARIE: Bitch! (*Slams the window.*) Come, boy! They're all against you. You're just a little whore's baby, but you make your mother happy with your shifty little face! Da da! (*Sings.*)
What're you going to do now, my girl?
You've got no man, but you've got a little child!
Oh, why do I ask and why do I care?
I'll sing the whole night long,
Heigh ho, popeio, my boy, ho hey!
You're all I need, I want no more.
(*There is a knock at the window.*) Who's there? Is that you, Franz? Come in!

WOYZECK: I can't. I have to go to roll call.

MARIE: Did you cut sticks for the Captain?

WOYZECK: Yes, Marie.

MARIE: What's the matter with you, Franz? You look worried.

WOYZECK (*mysteriously*): It happened again, Marie. There's lots that isn't written: and see, a cloud of smoke went round the land, like the smoke from an oven.

MARIE: Man!

WOYZECK: It followed me all the way to town. Something we can't imagine, something we can't understand, something that drives us mad. What's going to happen?

MARIE: Franz!

WOYZECK: I have to go. I'll see you tonight at the fair! I've saved something again. (*He leaves.*)

MARIE: That man! He's all up in the air. He didn't even look at his child! Those thoughts will drive him crazy yet! Why're you so quiet, boy? Scared? It's getting so dark; you'd think you were going blind. Usually the street lamp shines in here. I can't stand it; it scares me! (*Exits.*)

SCENE 4

Fairground booths. Lights. People. An OLD MAN *sings while a* CHILD *dances to the music of a hurdy-gurdy.*

OLD MAN: Nobody in the world knows anything
We all have to die
We all know that.

WOYZECK: Hey, hopsa! Poor old fellow! Poor little child! Worries and joys!

MARIE: Man, if even the fools are sensible, we're all fools. Funny world! Beautiful world! (*They go over to listen to the* BARKER.)

BARKER (*standing in front of a booth with a dressed-up monkey and his wife, who is wearing pants*): Ladies and gentlemen! Take a look at creation the way God made it, and what do you see? Nothing—not a thing! Now take a look at it after Art's got through with it: goes upright on two legs, wears a jacket and pants, carries a sword! The monkey as soldier! That's not much yet, of course, the lowest step of human development. Hey, there! Bow to the people! There—now you're a baron! Give me a kiss! (*The monkey blows the trumpet.*) The little brat's got talent! —— Ladies and gentlemen! Here you can see the astronomical horse and the little canary. Favorites of the crowned heads of Europe, they'll tell you everything you want to know: how old you are, how many children you've got, and what ails you. The performances are about to begin! In one little moment we'll have the beginning of the beginning.

WOYZECK: You want to go in?

MARIE: I don't care. It must be real nice to see. Look at all the tassels on that fellow! And the woman's wearing pants! (*They both go into the booth.*)

DRUM MAJOR: Squad, halt! D'you see that one? What a woman!

SERGEANT: The Devil! Just right for sowing a few dragoons in!

DRUM MAJOR: And for the breeding of drum majors!

SERGEANT: Look at the way she holds her head up! You'd think all that black hair would weigh her down. And her eyes . . .

DRUM MAJOR: Like looking into a well or down a chimney. Forward march, right behind her!

SCENE 5

The interior of the brightly lighted booth.

MARIE: What a lot of light!

WOYZECK: Yes, Marie: black cats with eyes of fire. Hey, what an evening, eh?

BARKER (*leading a horse forward*): Show them what you can do! Show them your beastly cleverness! Put human society to shame! Ladies and gentlemen, the animal you're looking at, standing on four hooves with its tail swishing around behind it, is a member of all the learned societies and is a professor at our university, where he teaches the students how to ride and how to fight. All he's shown you up to now is simple understanding. Now, think with double reasoning! What do you do when you think with double reasoning? Is there a donkey in our learned society here? (*The horse shakes its head.*) See, that's double reasoning! That's horsognomy. Yes, this here is no dumb animal, this here is a person, a man, a beastly human being—and still it's an animal, a beast. (*The horse behaves in an improper manner.*) That's it, put the learned society to shame! You see, the beast is still all nature, real nature without the trimmings! Take a lesson from it! Ask your doctor first, or it could be very harmful! What that meant was: Man, be natural! You have been created out of dust and sand and dirt. Would you be more than dust and sand and dirt? See how smart he is: he can figure even though he can't count on his fingers. How come? It's just that he can't talk, he can't explain himself because he's a transformed human being. Tell the gentlemen what time it is! Which of you ladies and gentlemen has a watch? A watch, please.

SERGEANT: A watch? (*Pulls a watch out of his pocket with a grandiose gesture.*) Here, my good man!

MARIE: I've got to see this. (*She climbs down to the first row, the* SERGEANT *helping her.*)

DRUM MAJOR: What a woman!

SCENE 6

MARIE'S *room.*

MARIE (*looking at herself in a piece of mirror, her child in her lap*): That other fellow gave him an order and he had to go! (*Looks at herself in the mirror.*) How the stones sparkle! I wonder what kind they are. What did he say? —— Go to sleep, boy! Shut your eyes tight! (*The child hides its eyes behind its hands.*) Tighter! Now you stay that way—quiet, or he'll get you! (*Sings.*)

> Close your shutters, my pretty young thing,
> There's a gypsy lad a-coming,
> He'll take you by your pretty young hand,
> And lead you away into gypsy land.

(*Looks at herself in the mirror again.*) I'm sure it's gold! I wonder how it'll look on me at the dance. People like us only have a little corner in the world and a little bit of mirror, and just the same I've got a mouth as red as the big ladies with their mirrors from head to foot and their handsome men that kiss their hands for them. I'm just a poor girl! (*The child sits up.*) Quiet, boy, shut your eyes! The sleep angel's running up and down the wall there. (*She flashes the mirror at him.*) Shut your eyes or it'll look into them so you'll become blind! (WOYZECK *enters behind her. Startled, she puts her hands to her ears.*)

WOYZECK: What have you got there?

MARIE: Nothing.

WOYZECK: There's something shining under your fingers.

MARIE: It's an earring: I found it.

WOYZECK: I've never found a thing. And two at once!

MARIE: I'm human, aren't I?

WOYZECK: It's all right, Marie. How the child sleeps! Put your hand under his arm, the chair's pressing against him there. Look how the drops stand out clear on his forehead; nothing but work under the sun, we even sweat in our sleep. We poor people! —— Here's some more money, Marie; my pay and something extra from the Captain.

MARIE: God bless you, Franz.

WOYZECK: I've got to go. I'll see you this evening, Marie! 'Bye!

MARIE (*alone, after a pause*): I really am no good! I could stab myself. Oh, what a world! Man or woman, we're all headed to the Devil!

SCENE 7

At the DOCTOR's.

DOCTOR: So I've lived to see even this, Woyzeck! A man of his word!

WOYZECK: What is it, Doctor?

DOCTOR: I saw it, Woyzeck. You took a piss in the street, right up against the wall you pissed, just like a dog! And here I am paying you three groschen a day and your board! Woyzeck, this is bad of you; the world's becoming bad, very bad!

WOYZECK: But, Doctor, when Nature calls!

DOCTOR: Nature calls, Nature calls! Nature! Haven't I demonstrated that the constrictor vesicae muscle is subject to the will? Nature! Man is free, Woyzeck; in man the personality transforms itself into freedom! So you can't hold your urine! (*He shakes his head, puts his hands behind his back, and paces up and down.*) Have you eaten your peas, Woyzeck? Nothing but peas, by Heaven, just you remember that! There's going to be a revolution in science: I'll blow them all to bits! Ten percent urea, ammonium chloride, hyperoxide. Woyzeck, don't you have to piss again? Go on in there and give it a try!

WOYZECK: I can't, Doctor.

DOCTOR (*irritated*): But you can piss against the wall, all right! I've got our agreement right here, it's all down in writing! I saw it, I saw it with my own eyes; I'm just sticking my nose out of the window and letting the sun come in so I can make observations of sneezing. (*Starts to rush at* WOYZECK.) No, Woyzeck, I'm not angry; anger is unhealthy, it's unscientific. I'm calm, quite calm; my pulse is going at its usual sixty, and I'm talking to you absolutely calmly and cold-bloodedly. God forbid anyone should get angry at another human being —a human being! . . . But you shouldn't have pissed against the wall, Woyzeck! . . .

WOYZECK: You see, Doctor, sometimes a man's got a character like this or a structure like that. But it's quite different with Nature, you see; with Nature (*He snaps his fingers.*) it's like this, how shall I put it, for example . . .

DOCTOR: Woyzeck, you're philosophizing again.

WOYZECK (*confidentially*): Doctor, have you ever come across anything about double Nature? When the sun's right above us at midday and it feels like the world's going to burn up, I heard a terrible voice speaking to me!

DOCTOR: Woyzeck, you're not all there.

WOYZECK (*putting a finger on his nose*): It's all in the toadstools, Doctor. Have you ever noticed the patterns in which toadstools grow? If we could only figure them out!

DOCTOR: Woyzeck, you've got a wonderful example of a mentalis partialis aberration of the second class. I'll give you a raise, Woyzeck! Aberration second class: *idée fixe* with all aspects perfectly normal. You do do everything just the same as usual, don't you? Do you shave the Captain?

WOYZECK: Yes, sir.

DOCTOR: Do you eat your peas?

WOYZECK: Always regularly, Doctor. My wife gets the money for the household expenses.

DOCTOR: You get all your duties done?

WOYZECK: Yes, sir.

DOCTOR: You're an interesting case. Keep up the good work, subject Woyzeck, you're getting a raise! Let me take your pulse. Yes.

SCENE 8

MARIE's *room.*

DRUM MAJOR: Marie!

MARIE (*looking at him, emotionally*): March up and down! A chest like a bull's and a beard like a lion's mane. There's nobody else like that! I've got it all over all the other women!

DRUM MAJOR: Just you wait till you see me Sunday with my white gloves and the big plume on my helmet. Goddam! The prince always says, "Man, that's some fellow!"

MARIE (*mockingly*): Ah, go on! (*Goes up to him.*) Man!

DRUM MAJOR: And you're quite a woman! Goddammit, we'll breed a whole row of drum majors, eh? (*He embraces her.*)

MARIE (*annoyed*): Let me go!

DRUM MAJOR: You wild beast, you!

MARIE (*forcefully*): Don't touch me!

DRUM MAJOR: You've got the Devil looking out through your eyes!

MARIE: Maybe! It doesn't matter!

SCENE 9

A *street. The* CAPTAIN *is coming down the street, wheezing. He stops, looks around, sees the* DOCTOR, *wheezes some more.*

CAPTAIN: Don't run like that, Doctor! And stop rowing through the air with your walking stick like that! You're chasing your own death for all you're worth. A good man with a good conscience doesn't go so fast. A good man— (*He catches the* DOCTOR *by the coat.*) Allow me to save a life, Doctor!

DOCTOR: I'm in a hurry, Captain, in a hurry!

CAPTAIN: I've been so depressed lately, Doctor, and I get so overwrought; I keep bursting into tears when I see my coat hanging on the wall . . .

DOCTOR: Hmm! Bloated, fat, thick neck: an apoplectic constitution. Yes, Captain, you could get an apoplexia cerebri any time; you might get it on one side only, though, and then be paralyzed on one side; or, better still, you might get paralysis of the brain and just vegetate from then on: those are more or less your prospects for the next four weeks! I can assure you, though, that you're really one of the most interesting cases, and if, God willing, your powers of speech become paralyzed as well, we'll conduct some really immortal experiments with you.

CAPTAIN: Stop frightening me, Doctor! People have died of fright before now—just from a sudden shock. I can see the people already with lemons in their hands, but they'll say, he was a good man, a good man —Devil take the coffin nails!

DOCTOR (*holding his hat out to the* CAPTAIN): What's that, Captain? That's a hollow head, honored Sir Drillprick!

CAPTAIN (*making a fold in his coat*): And what is this, Doctor? This is folderol, my dear Mr. Coffinnail! Hahaha! No offense! I'm a good man, but I can do it too when I want, Doctor, hahahaha, when I want to . . . (WOYZECK *comes along the street and tries to hurry past.*) Hey, Woyzeck, what are you trying to rush by us like that for? Stop a bit, Woyzeck! You rush through the world like an open straight razor—everyone cuts himself on you. You run about as if you had to shave a regiment of eunuchs and would be hung for missing a hair before you got a chance to disappear. But, speaking of long beards—what was it I wanted to say? Long beards, Woyzeck . . .

DOCTOR: Soldiers should be discouraged from

wearing long beards—you can find that as early as Pliny . . .

CAPTAIN (*picking up his train of thought*): Ah, yes! Long beards! Well, what's up with you, Woyzeck? Haven't you picked a hair from a long beard out of your dish yet? You understand what I'm talking about, don't you? A human hair, a sapper's hair, a noncommissioned officer's hair—perhaps, perhaps a drum major's? Eh, Woyzeck? But you've got a good woman there; you don't have the same kind of troubles as other people.

WOYZECK: Yes, sir! What do you mean, Captain?

CAPTAIN: What a face the fellow's pulling! . . . Well, maybe you didn't find it in the soup, but if you hurry up now and rush around the corner, maybe you'll find one on a pair of lips. A pair of lips, Woyzeck—I've felt love too, Woyzeck. Man, he's gone white as chalk!

WOYZECK: I'm just a poor devil, Captain—and that's all I've got in the world. If you're making jokes, Captain . . .

CAPTAIN: Me, joke? The joke's on you, boy!

DOCTOR: Your pulse, Woyzeck, your pulse! Weak, pounding, skipping, and uneven.

WOYZECK: The earth is hot as hell, Captain—but it's ice-cold to me, ice-cold—hell is cold, I'll bet it is.——Impossible! Man! Man! Impossible!

CAPTAIN: Look here, fellow—you want to get a couple of bullets through your head? Fellow stabs right through me with his eyes, and all I'm trying to do is be nice to him because he's a good man—yes, you are, Woyzeck—a good man.

DOCTOR: Facial muscles fixed, strained, intermittently twitching. Appearance excited, strained.

WOYZECK: I'm going. There's a great many things possible. That's the way man is! There's a great many things possible.—— It's nice weather, Captain. See, such a nice, solid, gray sky; it's enough to make one feel like ramming a piece of wood into it and hanging oneself on it—all because of that little gap between a Yes and another Yes—or a No. Both yes and no, Captain? Is the Yes the No's fault, or is the No the Yes's fault? I'll have to think about that.

(*Marches off, at first slowly, then quicker and quicker.*)

DOCTOR (*rushing after him*): Phenomenal! Woyzeck, another raise!

CAPTAIN: That fellow's making me completely dizzy. Look at the way they're running! That long beanpole strides along looking like the shadow of a daddy longlegs and the little one bounces along beside him. The tall one's the lightning and the little one's the thunder. Haha . . . grotesque! Grotesque!

SCENE 10

MARIE's *room.*

WOYZECK (*looks at her fixedly, shaking his head*): Hmm! I don't see anything, I don't see anything! You'd have to be able to see it, to grab it with your fists!

MARIE (*frightened*): What's the matter with you, Franz? You're crazy, Franz.

WOYZECK: A sin as big and thick as that—it stinks so bad, you could smoke the angels out of Heaven with it! You've got a red mouth, Marie. Aren't there any blisters on it? You're as lovely as sin, Marie—can mortal sin be so lovely?

MARIE: You're feverish, Franz!

WOYZECK: The Devil! Did he stand here? Here? Here?

MARIE: Lots of people can stand in the same place, one after the other: the day is long and the world is old.

WOYZECK: I saw him!

MARIE: There's lots of things you can see if you have two eyes and aren't blind and the sun is shining.

WOYZECK: Man! (*Rushes at her.*)

MARIE: Don't touch me, Franz! I'd rather have a knife sticking in me than your hand on mine. My father didn't dare do anything to me when I was only ten years old just because of the way I looked at him.

WOYZECK: Woman!——No, it would have to show on you somewhere! Every being is an abyss; it makes one dizzy to look. It would be as if she were going around like innocence itself. Innocence has a sign it shows, doesn't it? Do I know what it is? Do I? Who knows it? (*Exits.*)

SCENE 11

The guardroom.

ANDRES (*singing*): The inn it has a pretty
  maid,
    She sits in the garden day and night,
    She sits in her garden . . .
WOYZECK: Andres!
ANDRES: What?
WOYZECK: Nice weather.
ANDRES: It's sunny Sunday weather. There's
  a band playing outside the town. All the
  broads are out there already; people are
  steaming out there—things are really jump-
  ing!
WOYZECK (*nervously*): Dancing—they're
  dancing, Andres!
ANDRES: At the Horse and at the Star inns.
WOYZECK: Dancing, dancing!
ANDRES: If you like.
    She sits in her garden,
    Till the little clock strikes twelve,
    And watches the soldier boys pass by.
WOYZECK: I can't stand it anymore, Andres.
ANDRES: Idiot!
WOYZECK: I've got to get out of here. I feel
  dizzy. Dance, dance! Her hands'll be sweat-
  ing! Dammit, Andres!
ANDRES: What's the matter with you?
WOYZECK: I've got to get out of here; I've
  got to go and see.
ANDRES: You're just looking for trouble! Be-
  cause of that fellow?
WOYZECK: I've got to get out of here; it's so
  hot in here.

SCENE 12

*An inn. The windows are open, there are
benches outside, young men are hanging
around, some people are dancing.*

FIRST APPRENTICE: I've got a shirt on but it
  isn't mine,
    My soul stinks from drinking brandy-
    wine . . .
SECOND APPRENTICE: You want me to put a
  hole in you just out of pure friendship,
  brother? Forward march! I'm going to put
  a hole in you! You know I'm quite a fellow
  too—I'll squash every flea on your body
  flat as a pancake.

FIRST APPRENTICE: My soul, my soul stinks
  of brandywine! Even money starts rotting!
  Forget-me-not, the world's a lovely place! I
  feel so sad I'll cry a rain barrel full, brother.
  I wish our noses were two bottles and we
  could pour them down each other's throats.
OTHER APPRENTICES (*in chorus*):
    A huntsman from the royal pack
    Once rode through a green and leafy
    wood.
    Halloo, halloo for a huntsman's life,
    All over the green and grassy heath,
    Hunting's the life for me.
(WOYZECK *appears at the window.* MARIE
dances by with the DRUM MAJOR *without
noticing him.*)
WOYZECK: He! She! The Devil!
MARIE (*dancing by*): Keep it up! Keep it
  up!——
WOYZECK (*choking*): Keep it up—keep it up!
  (*Starts up violently, then sinks back onto
  the bench.*) Keep it up, keep it up! (*Pounds
  his hands together.*) Go on, spin around,
  whirl around! Why doesn't God blow the
  sun out so that everyone can whirl around
  and over everyone else without decency—
  man and woman, beast and human?! Do
  it in broad daylight! Do it on the palms
  of my hands like the fleas!——Woman!
  The woman's hot, hot! Keep it up, keep it
  up! (*Starts up.*) Look at the way the
  fellow's feeling her up! He, he's got her—
  just like me at the beginning. (*He collapses.*)
FIRST APPRENTICE (*jumps on the table and
  starts preaching*): Nonetheless, when a
  wanderer stands leaning on the stream of
  time or, on the other hand, answers the
  divine wisdom for his own part and saith,
  Wherefore is man? Wherefore is man?—
  But in truth I say to you: if God had not
  created man how would the farmer, the
  cooper, the cobbler, and the doctor have
  lived? How would the tailor have been able
  to make ends meet if he hadn't planted
  the idea of shame in man? How would the
  soldier have been able to keep body and
  soul together if he hadn't armed himself
  with a desire to kill? Therefore doubt ye
  not—yes, yes, all things are lovely and
  beautiful, but all earthly things are evil,
  and even money rots. In conclusion, my
  beloved flock, let's all piss on the cross so

that another Jew may die! (WOYZECK *wakes up while the hooting and yelling is at its height and runs away.*)

SCENE 13

An open field.

WOYZECK: Keep it up! Keep it up!—Hish! Hash! the fiddles and the horns play on.— Keep it up! Keep it up!—Stop, music! Who's talking down there? (*Stretches out on the ground.*) Ha! What? What's that you say? Louder! Louder! Shall I? Must I?—Do I hear it here too?—Does the wind whistle it too?—I hear it everywhere, always: stab, stab, stab her dead!

SCENE 14

A room in the barracks. Night. ANDRES *and* WOYZECK *are lying in the same bed.*

WOYZECK (*softly*): Andres! (ANDRES *mumbles in his sleep.* WOYZECK *shakes him.*) Hey, Andres! Andres!

ANDRES: Well, what is it?

WOYZECK: I can't sleep! I just get dizzy when I close my eyes and I keep hearing the fiddles playing all the time, all the time. And then I hear the walls talking. Don't you hear anything?

ANDRES: Yeah—let them dance! I'm tired. God have mercy on us, Amen.

WOYZECK: It keeps saying: Stab! Stab!—and it's like it was drawing a knife in front of my eyes—

ANDRES: Go to sleep, you idiot. (*He falls asleep again.*)

WOYZECK: Keep it up! Keep it up!

SCENE 15

The courtyard of the DOCTOR'S *house.* WOYZECK *and the students are below; the* DOCTOR *is looking down from the attic window.*

DOCTOR: Gentlemen, I am up here on the roof, just like David when he saw Bath-

sheba, but all I can see are the frilly underthings of the little girls from the boarding school drying in the garden. Gentlemen, today we take up the important topic of the relationship of the subject to the object. Let us just take one of the things wherein the organic self-affirmation of the divine is manifested to such high degree and examine its relationships to its surroundings, to the earth, and to the planets. Supposing I throw this cat out of the window, gentlemen: what will be its conduct towards the centrum gravitationis in accordance with its own instincts? Hey, Woyzeck, (*Yells.*) Woyzeck!

WOYZECK (*catching the cat*): It's biting me, Doctor!

DOCTOR: Stop handling that beast as tenderly as if it were your grandmother, you fool. (*He comes down.*)

WOYZECK: I'm shaking all over, Doctor.

DOCTOR (*enormously pleased*): Ah, ah, very nice, Woyzeck! (*Rubs his hands. Takes the cat.*) What's this I see, gentlemen? It's a rabbit louse, a new species—a very nice species . . . (*He takes a magnifying glass out; the cat runs away.*) That animal doesn't have any scientific instinct, gentlemen . . . I'll show you something else instead. Look here: this fellow here has eaten nothing but peas for three months now. Notice the effect, feel his pulse: very irregular. That and his eyes!

WOYZECK: Everything's getting dark, Doctor! (*He sits down.*)

DOCTOR: Courage, Woyzeck! Just a few more days and then it'll be all over. Feel him, gentlemen, feel him! (*The students feel* WOYZECK'S *forehead, pulse, and chest.*) By the way, Woyzeck, wiggle your ears for the gentlemen! I've been meaning to show you; he's got two muscles for that. Well, come on, let's go!

WOYZECK: Oh, Doctor!

DOCTOR: You want me to wiggle your ears for you, you animal? You want to act like that cat? There, gentlemen! He gets these donkey-like periods, usually the result of being raised by woman and using the German language. How many hairs did your mother rip out of you out of pure tenderness? They've got very thin in the last few days. Yes, gentlemen, peas!

SCENE 16

The barracks yard.

WOYZECK: Didn't you hear anything?
ANDRES: He's here with somebody else.
WOYZECK: Did he say anything?
ANDRES: What do you know about it? Why should I tell you? Oh well, he laughed and then he said: What a broad! Legs and thighs—and hot as hell!
WOYZECK (*coldly*): Really, is that what he said? What was it I dreamt about last night? Wasn't it something about a knife? Crazy dreams one gets!
ANDRES: Where are you going?
WOYZECK: I have to get wine for the Captain. She really was a girl you only find once, Andres.
ANDRES: Who was?
WOYZECK: Nothing, good-bye! (*Exits.*)

SCENE 17

The inn. WOYZECK, *the* DRUM MAJOR, *and others.*

DRUM MAJOR: I'm a man! (*Pounds his chest.*) I say, I'm a man. Anyone want to make something of it? Anyone who isn't drunk as a lord better keep out of my way or I'll ram his nose into his asshole for him! I'll— (*To* WOYZECK.) You, fellow, drink! I wish the world were made of brandy, brandy—man must drink! (WOYZECK *whistles.*) You want me to pull your tongue out of your mouth and wrap it round your body, fellow? (*They wrestle and* WOYZECK *is thrown.*) You want me to leave you as much breath as an old lady's fart? Eh? (WOYZECK *sits down on a bench, exhausted and shaking.*) The fellow can blow himself blue in the face for all I care.
    Brandy, brandy, that's my life,
    Brandy makes you brave!
FIRST WOMAN: He got his lumps, all right.
SECOND WOMAN: He's bleeding.
WOYZECK: One thing at a time.

SCENE 18

A junk shop.

WOYZECK: That little pistol is too much.
JEW: Well, you buying it or not—make up your mind.

WOYZECK: How much for the knife?
JEW: Straight as an arrow. You want to cut your throat with it? Well now, how much? Nobody undersells me. You got a right to a cheap death, but not a free one. How much? You deserve an economical death.
WOYZECK: You can cut more than bread with this . . .
JEW: Two groschen.
WOYZECK: Here! (*Exits.*)
JEW: Here! As if it didn't mean a thing! It's money all the same, though.——The dog!

SCENE 19

MARIE'S *room.*

IDIOT (*lying down and indicating the points of the fairy tale he is telling himself on his fingers*): The king he wears a golden crown . . . Tomorrow I'll bring the queen her child . . . Bloodsausage says, Come along, liversausage . . .
MARIE (*leafing through the Bible*): "Neither was there deceit in his mouth" . . . Oh God! Oh God! Look not on me! (*She turns some pages.*) "And the scribes and Pharisees brought unto him a woman taken in adultery; and when they had sat her in the midst . . . And Jesus said unto her, Neither do I condemn thee: go, and sin no more." (*Clasps her hands.*) Oh God! Oh God! I can't go on! Oh God, help me to pray! (*The child creeps close to her.*) The child makes my heart ache! (*To the* IDIOT.) Karl! There you are, basking in the sun again! (*The* IDIOT *takes the child and grows quiet.*) Franz didn't show up yesterday or today. It's getting hot here! (*She opens the window and starts reading again.*) "And stood at his feet behind him weeping, and began to wash his feet with tears, and did wipe them with the hairs of her head, and kissed his feet, and anointed them with the ointment." (*Beats her breast.*) All dead! Savior! Savior! I would anoint your feet!

SCENE 20

The barracks.

WOYZECK (*rummaging around in his things*): This jacket doesn't belong to the uniform, but you can use it anyway, Andres. (ANDRES *remains absolutely numb and just answers "All right" to everything.*) This cross and this little ring belong to my sister.

ANDRES: All right.

WOYZECK: I've got a holy picture here too—two hearts and real gold; it was in my mother's Bible and it had written in it:

Oh Lord! whose flesh was hurt and sore,
So let my heart be evermore!

The only thing my mother can feel anymore is the sun burning her hand—well, never mind.

ANDRES: All right.

WOYZECK (*pulling out a paper*): Friedrich Johann Franz Woyzeck, Militiaman, Fusilier in the Second Regiment, Second Batallion, Fourth Company, born Annunciation Day, July 20. I'm 30 years, 7 months and 12 days old today.

ANDRES: Listen Franz, you'd better report yourself sick. What you need is some powder dissolved in brandy—that'll bring your fever down.

WOYZECK: Andres, when the carpenter sweeps up his shavings, there's no knowing who's going to lay his head in what he's made.

SCENE 21

A street. MARIE *and the* GRANDMOTHER *are standing in front of the house with some little girls.*

GIRLS: The sun shines bright on Candlemas day,
The corn blooms in the fields.
They went far out into the fields,
They went by two and two.
The pipers marched out at the front,
The fiddlers came behind,
They had red socks upon their feet . . .

FIRST GIRL: That's not nice.

SECOND GIRL: You're always complaining!

FIRST GIRL: You sing to us, Marie!

MARIE: I can't.

FIRST GIRL: Why not?

MARIE: Just because.

SECOND GIRL: But why because?

THIRD GIRL: Tell us a story, grandmother!

GRANDMOTHER: Well, come here, dears! Once upon a time there was a poor child that had no father or mother because everyone was dead and there wasn't anyone on the earth anymore. Everyone was dead and so it went and looked night and day. And because there wasn't anyone on the earth anymore it wanted to go to heaven, and the moon looked at it in such a nice way. But when it finally got to the moon it found that the moon was just a piece of rotten wood. And so it went to the sun, but when it came to the sun it found that the sun was just a faded sunflower. And when it came to the stars it found that the stars were like little golden bugs stuck on thorns by a shrike. And when it wanted to get back to the earth, it found that the earth was a broken pot. And so it was all alone. And so it sat down and cried, and it's still sitting there and is still all alone.

WOYZECK (*appears*): Marie!

MARIE (*startled*): What is it?

WOYZECK: Let's go, Marie, it's time.

MARIE: Where to?

WOYZECK: How should I know?

SCENE 22

A lake at the edge of the forest.

MARIE: The town's back that way. It's dark.

WOYZECK: Don't go yet. Come on, sit down!

MARIE: But I have to get back.

WOYZECK: You don't want to run till your feet are sore.

MARIE: What's up with you?

WOYZECK: You know how long it's been, Marie?

MARIE: Two years, come Whitsuntide.

WOYZECK: And do you know how much longer it's going to be, Marie?

MARIE: I've got to get back and get supper ready.

WOYZECK: You getting cold, Marie? You're warm enough, though. How hot your lips are! Hot; hot whore's breath! And I'd still give up Heaven to kiss them once again. You getting cold? You don't shiver anymore when you're really cold. You won't be shivering at tomorrow's dew.

MARIE: What do you mean?

WOYZECK: Nothing. (*Pause.*)

MARIE: How red the moon is!

WOYZECK: Like iron with blood on it.

MARIE: What are you going to do? You're so pale, Franz. (*He threatens her with the knife.*) Stop, Franz! For God's sake, help, help!

WOYZECK (*stabbing her*): Take that and that! Can't you die? There! There! Ha, she's still twitching; not dead yet? Not yet? Again! (*He stabs her again.*) You dead now? Dead! Dead! (*He drops the knife and runs away.*)

SCENE 23

The inn.

WOYZECK: Everyone dance—keep it up! Stink and sweat! He'll get you all in the end anyway!

> Daughter, oh, daughter,
> What was in your mind,
> When you joined up with the coachmen
> And with the postboys behind.

(*He dances.*) There, Katie! Sit down! I'm hot, hot! (*He takes his jacket off.*) That's the way it is—the devil takes one and lets the other go. You're hot, Katie! Why? You'll be cold yet too, Katie. See that you behave yourself. Can't you sing something?

KATIE (*sings*): To Swabia I will not fare,
> And lengthy dresses I'll not wear,
> For lengthy dresses, pointed shoes,
> Is not for a servant girl to choose.

WOYZECK: No, no shoes—you can go to hell without shoes too.

KATIE (*sings*): O fie, my dear, that was not nice,
> Keep your money and sleep alone.

WOYZECK: Yes, truly, I wouldn't want to be all bloody.

KATIE: What's that you've got on your hand?

WOYZECK: Me? Me?

KATIE: Red! Blood! (*People crowd round them.*)

WOYZECK: Blood? Blood?

INNKEEPER: Ugh—blood!

WOYZECK: I think I cut myself there on the right hand.

INNKEEPER: Then why is your elbow bloody?

WOYZECK: From wiping myself.

INNKEEPER: What? You wiped yourself with your right hand on your right elbow? That's quite a trick!

IDIOT: And then the giant said: I smell, I smell the flesh of a man. Pah! What a smell!

WOYZECK: Devil take it, what do you want? What's it to do with you? Out of my way, or I'll——Devil take it! You think I've murdered someone? Am I a murderer? What are you all staring at? Take a look at yourselves instead! Out of my way! (*He runs out.*)

SCENE 24

By the lake.

WOYZECK: The knife, where's the knife? I left it here. It'll give me away! Nearer, no, it was nearer! What is this place? What's that I hear? Something's moving. Quiet. ——Right here. Marie? Hey, Marie! Quiet. Everything quiet. Why are you so pale, Marie? Why do you have a red ribbon round your neck? Where did you earn that neckband with your sins? You were black with them, black! Did I make you pale? Why is your hair hanging down like that? Didn't you braid your pigtails today? . . . The knife, the knife! Is that it? There! (*He runs to the water's edge.*) There, down there! (*He throws the knife into the water.*) It sinks into the dark water like a stone. No, that's not right, it's too close to shore —they'll find it when they go bathing. (*He walks into the water, picks up the knife, and throws it in further.*) There, that'll do it——but what if they find it in the summer when they dive for shells? Bah, it'll be rusted by that time; nobody'll know it. I should have broken the blade! Have I still got blood on me? I've got to wash. There's a stain, and there's another . . . (*Two men approach.*)

FIRST MAN: Wait!

SECOND MAN: D'you hear? Quiet! There!

FIRST MAN: Ohh! Here! What a sound!

SECOND MAN: It's the water calling: nobody's drowned here for a long time now. Let's go! It's not good to listen to things like that.

FIRST MAN: Ohh! There it is again! Like a man dying!

SECOND MAN: It's uncanny! It's so misty all around, all hazy and gray—and the buzzing of the insects like cracked bells. Let's go!

FIRST MAN: No, it's too clear and too loud! Up here! Come on!

KING UBU

Alfred Jarry

TRANSLATED BY
Michael Benedikt and George E. Wellwarth

Then Father Ubu shakes
his peare, who was afterwards
yclept SHAKESPEARE by the
Englishe, and you have from
him in his own hand manie
lovely tragedies
under this name.

CHARACTERS AND COSTUMES

FATHER UBU: Casual gray suit, a cane always stuffed in his right-hand pocket, bowler hat. A crown over his hat at the beginning of Act II, Scene 2. Bareheaded at the beginning of Act II, Scene 6. Act III, Scene 22, crown and white hood, flaring to a royal cape. Act III, Scene 4, cloak, cap pulled down over his ears; same outfit, but with bare head in Scene 7. Scene 8, hood, helmet, a sword stuck in his belt, a hook, chisels, a knife, a cane still in his right-hand pocket. A bottle bounces at his side. Act IV, Scene 5, cloak and cap but without above weapons or stick. In the sailing scene a small suitcase is in Father Ubu's hand.

MOTHER UBU: Concierge's clothes or a toiletries saleswoman's ensemble. Pink bonnet or a hat with flowers and feathers and a veil. An apron in the feasting scene. Royal cloak at the opening of Act II, Scene 6.

CAPTAIN BORDURE: Hungarian musician's costume, very close-fitting, red. Big mantle, large sword, crenelated boots, feathery hat.

KING WENCESLAS: Royal mantle and the crown Ubu wears after murdering him.

QUEEN ROSEMONDE: The mantle and crown Mother Ubu later wears.

BOLESLAS, LADISLAS (sons of King Wenceslas and Queen Rosemonde): Gray Polish costumes, heavily frogged; short pants.

BOUGRELAS (the youngest son): Dressed as a child in a little skirt and bonnet.

GENERAL LASCY: Polish costume, with an admiral's hat with white plumes, and a sword.

STANISLAS LECZINSKI: Polish costume. White beard.

JOHN SOBIESKI, NICHOLAS RENSKY: Polish costume.

THE CZAR, EMPEROR ALEXIS: Black clothing, enormous yellow sword, dagger, numerous military decorations, big boots. Huge frill at the throat. Hat in the form of a black cone.

THE PALOTINS (GIRON, PILE, COTICE): Long beards, fur-trimmed greatcoats, shitr-colored; or red or green if necessary; tights beneath.

CROWD: Polish costume.

MICHAEL FEDEROVITCH: Same. Fur hat.

NOBLES: Polish costume, with cloaks edged with fur or embroidery.

ADVISERS, FINANCIERS: Swathed in black, with astrologers' hats, eyeglasses, pointed noses.

PHYNANCIAL FLUNKIES: The Palotins.

PEASANTS: Polish costume.

THE POLISH ARMY: In gray, with frogging and fur trimmings: three men with rifles.

THE RUSSIAN ARMY: Two horsemen: uniform like that of the Poles, but green, with fur headgear. They carry cardboard horses' heads.

A RUSSIAN FOOTSOLDIER: In green, with headgear.

MOTHER UBU'S GUARDS: Polish costume, with halberds.

A CAPTAIN: General Lascy.

THE BEAR: Bordure in bearskin.

THE PHYNANCIAL HORSE: Large wooden rocking horse on casters, or else cardboard horse's head, as required.

THE CREW: Two men in sailor suits, in blue, collars turned down, and so on.

THE CAPTAIN OF THE SHIP: In a French naval officer's uniform.

JAILER *

MESSENGER *

COMPOSITION OF THE ORCHESTRA

Oboes

Pipes

Blutwurst

Large Bass

Flageolets   Transverse Flutes

Flute

Little Bassoon   Big Bassoon

Triple Bassoon   Little Black Cornets

Shrill White Cornets

Horns   Sackbuts   Trombones

Green Hunting Horns   Reeds

Bagpipes

Bombardons   Timbals

Drum   Bass Drum

Grand Organs

* Jarry did not include suggestions for the costuming of these two characters in these notes, which were published from manuscript by the Collège de 'Pataphysique in 1951.

ACT I

SCENE 1

FATHER UBU, MOTHER UBU.

FATHER UBU: Shitr!

MOTHER UBU: Well, that's a fine way to talk, Father Ubu. What a pigheaded ass you are!

FATHER UBU: I don't know what keeps me from bouncing your head off the wall, Mother Ubu!

MOTHER UBU: It's not *my* head you ought to be cracking, Father Ubu.

FATHER UBU: By my green candle, I don't know what you're talking about.

MOTHER UBU: What's this, Father Ubu, you mean to tell me you're satisfied with the way things are?

FATHER UBU: By my green candle, shitr, madam, certainly I'm satisfied with the way things are. After all, aren't I Captain of the Dragoons, confidential adviser to King Wenceslas, decorated with the order of the Red Eagle of Poland, and ex-King of Aragon—what more do you want?

MOTHER UBU: What's this! After having been King of Aragon you're satisfied with leading fifty-odd flunkies armed with cabbage-cutters to parades? When you could just as well have the crown of Poland replace the crown of Aragon on your big fat nut?

FATHER UBU: Ah! Mother Ubu, I don't know what you're talking about.

MOTHER UBU: You're so stupid!

FATHER UBU: By my green candle, King Wenceslas is still very much alive; and even if he does die he's still got hordes of children, hasn't he?

MOTHER UBU: What's stopping you from chopping up his whole family and putting yourself in their place?

FATHER UBU: Ah! Mother Ubu, you're doing me an injustice, and I'll stick you in your stewpot in a minute.

MOTHER UBU: Ha! Poor wretch, if I were stuck in the pot who'd sew up the seat of your pants?

FATHER UBU: Oh, really! And what of it? Don't I have an ass like everyone else?

MOTHER UBU: If I were you, I'd want to install that ass on a throne. You could get any amount of money, eat sausages all the time, and roll around the streets in a carriage.

FATHER UBU: If I were king I'd have them build me a big helmet just like the one I had in Aragon which those Spanish swine had the nerve to steal from me.

MOTHER UBU: You could also get yourself an umbrella and a big cape which would reach to your heels.

FATHER UBU: Ah! that does it! I succumb to temptation. That crock of shitr, that shitr of crock, if I ever run into him in a dark alley, I'll give him a bad fifteen minutes.

MOTHER UBU: Ah! Fine, Father Ubu, at last you're acting like a real man.

FATHER UBU: Oh, no! Me, the Captain of the Dragoons slaughter the King of Poland! Better far to die!

MOTHER UBU (*aside*): Oh, shitr! (*Aloud.*) So, then, you want to stay as poor as a churchmouse, Father Ubu?

FATHER UBU: Zounds, by my green candle, I'd rather be as poor as a starving, good rat than as rich as a wicked, fat cat.

MOTHER UBU: And the helmet? And the umbrella? And the big cape?

FATHER UBU: And what about them, Mother Ubu? (*He leaves, slamming the door.*)

MOTHER UBU (*alone*): Crap, shitr, it's hard to get him started, but, crap, shitr, I think I've stirred him up. With the help of God and of myself, perhaps in eight days I'll be Queen of Poland.

SCENE 2

A room in FATHER UBU's *house, with a splendidly laid table.* FATHER UBU, MOTHER UBU.

MOTHER UBU: So! Our guests are very late.

FATHER UBU: Yes, by my green candle, I'm dying of hunger. Mother Ubu, you're really ugly today. Is it because company's coming?

MOTHER UBU (*shrugging her shoulders*): Shitr!

FATHER UBU (*grabbing a roast chicken*): Gad, I'm hungry; I'm going to have a piece of this bird. It's a chicken, I think. Not bad at all.

MOTHER UBU: What are you doing, you swine? What will be left for our guests?

FATHER UBU: There will be plenty left for them. I won't touch another thing. Mother Ubu, go to the window and see if our guests are coming.

MOTHER UBU (*going*): I don't see anything. (*Meanwhile,* FATHER UBU *takes a piece of veal.*) Ah, here come Captain Bordure and his boys. What are you eating now, Father Ubu?

FATHER UBU: Nothing, a little veal.

MOTHER UBU: Oh! the veal! the veal! The ox! He's eaten the veal! Help, help!

FATHER UBU: By my green candle, I'll scratch your eyes out. (*The door opens.*)

SCENE 3

FATHER UBU, MOTHER UBU, CAPTAIN BORDURE *and his followers.*

MOTHER UBU: Good day, gentlemen; we've been anxiously awaiting you. Sit down.

CAPTAIN BORDURE: Good day, madam. Where's Father Ubu?

FATHER UBU: Here I am, here I am! Good lord, by my green candle, I'm fat enough, aren't I?

CAPTAIN BORDURE: Good day, Father Ubu. Sit down, boys. (*They all sit.*)

FATHER UBU: Oof, a little more, and I'd have bust my chair.

CAPTAIN BORDURE: Well, Mother Ubu! What have you got that's good today?

MOTHER UBU: Here's the menu.

FATHER UBU: Oh! That interests me.

MOTHER UBU: Polish soup, roast ram, veal, chicken, chopped dog's liver, turkey's ass, charlotte russe . . .

FATHER UBU: Hey, that's plenty, I should think. You mean there's more?

MOTHER UBU (*continuing*): Frozen pudding, salad, fruits, dessert, boiled beef, Jerusalem artichokes, cauliflower à la shitr.

FATHER UBU: Hey! Do you think I'm the Emperor of China, to give all that away?

MOTHER UBU: Don't listen to him, he's feeble-minded.

FATHER UBU: Ah! I'll sharpen my teeth on your shanks.

MOTHER UBU: Try this instead, Father Ubu. Here's the Polish soup.

FATHER UBU: Crap, is that lousy!

CAPTAIN BORDURE: Hmm—it isn't very good, at that.

MOTHER UBU: What do you want, you bunch of crooks!

FATHER UBU (*striking his forehead*): Wait, I've got an idea. I'll be right back. (*He leaves.*)

MOTHER UBU: Let's try the veal now, gentlemen.

CAPTAIN BORDURE: It's very good—I'm through.

MOTHER UBU: To the turkey's ass, next.

CAPTAIN BORDURE: Delicious, delicious! Long live Mother Ubu!

ALL: Long live Mother Ubu!

FATHER UBU (*returning*): And you will soon be shouting long live Father Ubu. (*He has a toilet brush in his hand, and he throws it on the festive board.*)

MOTHER UBU: Miserable creature, what are you up to now?

FATHER UBU: Try a little. (*Several try it, and fall, poisoned.*) Mother Ubu, pass me the roast ram chops, so that I can serve them.

MOTHER UBU: Here they are.

FATHER UBU: Everyone out! Captain Bordure, I want to talk to you.

THE OTHERS: But we haven't eaten yet.

FATHER UBU: What's that, you haven't eaten yet? Out, out, everyone out! Stay here, Bordure. (*Nobody moves.*) You haven't gone yet? By my green candle, I'll give you your ram chops. (*He begins to throw them.*)

ALL: Oh! Ouch! Help! Woe! Help! Misery! I'm dead!

FATHER UBU: Shitr, shitr, shitr! Outside! I want my way!

ALL: Everyone for himself! Miserable Father Ubu! Traitor! Meanie!

FATHER UBU: Ah! They've gone. I can breathe again—but I've had a rotten dinner. Come on, Bordure. (*They go out with* MOTHER UBU.)

SCENE 4

FATHER UBU, MOTHER UBU, CAPTAIN BORDURE.

FATHER UBU: Well, now, Captain, have you had a good dinner?

CAPTAIN BORDURE: Very good, sir, except for the shitr.

FATHER UBU: Oh, come now, the shitr wasn't bad at all.

MOTHER UBU: Chacun à son goût.

FATHER UBU: Captain Bordure, I've decided to make you Duke of Lithuania.

CAPTAIN BORDURE: Why, I thought you were miserably poor, Father Ubu.

FATHER UBU: If you choose, I'll be King of Poland in a few days.

CAPTAIN BORDURE: You're going to kill Wenceslas?

FATHER UBU: He's not so stupid, the idiot; he's guessed it.

CAPTAIN BORDURE: If it's a question of killing Wenceslas, I'm for it. I'm his mortal enemy, and I can answer for my men.

FATHER UBU (*throwing his arms around him*): Oh! Oh! How I love you, Bordure.

CAPTAIN BORDURE: Ugh, you stink, Father Ubu. Don't you ever wash?

FATHER UBU: Rarely.

MOTHER UBU: Never!

FATHER UBU: I'll stamp on your toes.

MOTHER UBU: Big shitr!

FATHER UBU: All right, Bordure, that's all for now; but, by my green candle, I swear on Mother Ubu to make you Duke of Lithuania.

MOTHER UBU: But . . .

FATHER UBU: Be quiet, my sweet child. . . . (*They go out.*)

SCENE 5

FATHER UBU, MOTHER UBU, A MESSENGER.

FATHER UBU: Sir, what do you want? Beat it, you're boring me.

THE MESSENGER: Sir, the king summons you. (*He leaves.*)

FATHER UBU: Oh, shitr! Great Jumping Jupiter, by my green candle, I've been discovered; they'll cut my head off, alas! alas!

MOTHER UBU: What a spineless clod! And just when time's getting short.

FATHER UBU: Oh, I've got an idea: I'll say that it was Mother Ubu and Bordure.

MOTHER UBU: You fat Ubu, if you do that . . .

FATHER UBU: I'm off right now. (*He leaves.*)

MOTHER UBU (*running after him*): Oh, Father Ubu, Father Ubu, I'll give you some sausage! (*She leaves.*)

FATHER UBU (*from the wings*): Oh, shitr! You're a prize sausage yourself.

SCENE 6

The palace. KING WENCESLAS, *surrounded by his officers;* CAPTAIN BORDURE; *the king's sons,* BOLESLAS, LADISLAS, *and* BOUGRELAS; *and* FATHER UBU.

FATHER UBU (*entering*): Oh! You know, it wasn't me, it was Mother Ubu and Bordure.

KING WENCESLAS: What's the matter with you, Father Ubu?

CAPTAIN BORDURE: He's drunk.

KING WENCESLAS: So was I, this morning.

FATHER UBU: Yes, I'm potted, because I've drunk too much French wine.

KING WENCESLAS: Father Ubu, I desire to recompense your numerous services as Captain of the Dragoons, and I'm going to make you Count of Sandomir today.

FATHER UBU: Oh, Mr. Wenceslas, I don't know how to thank you.

KING WENCESLAS: Don't thank me, Father Ubu, and don't forget to appear tomorrow morning at the big parade.

FATHER UBU: I'll be there, but be good enough to accept this toy whistle. (*He presents the king with a toy whistle.*)

KING WENCESLAS: What can I do with a toy whistle at my age? I'll give it to Bougrelas.

BOUGRELAS: What an idiot Father Ubu is!

FATHER UBU: And now I'll scram. (*He falls as he turns around.*) Oh! Ouch! Help! By my green candle, I've split my gut and bruised my butt!

KING WENCESLAS (*helping him up*): Did you hurt yourself, Father Ubu?

FATHER UBU: Yes, I certainly did, and I'll probably die soon. What will become of Mother Ubu?

KING WENCESLAS: We shall provide for her upkeep.

FATHER UBU: Your kindness is unparalleled. (*He leaves.*) But you'll be slaughtered just the same, King Wenceslas.

Scene 7

FATHER UBU's *house.* GIRON, PILE, COTICE, FATHER UBU, MOTHER UBU, CONSPIRATORS *and* SOLDIERS, CAPTAIN BORDURE.

FATHER UBU: Well, my good friends, it's about time we discussed the plan of the conspiracy. Let each one give his advice. First of all, I'll give mine, if you'll permit me.

CAPTAIN BORDURE: Speak, Father Ubu.

FATHER UBU: Very well, my friends, I'm in favor of simply poisoning the king by slipping a little arsenic in his lunch. At the first nibble he'll drop dead, and then I'll be king.

ALL: How base!

FATHER UBU: What's that? You don't like my suggestion? Let Bordure give his.

CAPTAIN BORDURE: I'm of the opinion that we should give him one good stroke of the sword and slice him in two, lengthwise.

ALL: Hooray! How noble and valiant.

FATHER UBU: And what if he kicks you? I remember now that he always puts on iron shoes, which hurt a great deal, for parades. If I had any sense I'd go off and denounce you for dragging me into this dirty mess, and I think he'd give me plenty of money.

MOTHER UBU: Oh! The traitor, the coward, the villain, and sneak.

ALL: Down with Father Ubu!

FATHER UBU: Gentlemen, keep calm, or I'll get mad. In any case, I agree to stick out my neck for you. Bordure, I put you in charge of slicing the king in half.

CAPTAIN BORDURE: Wouldn't it be better to throw ourselves on the king all together, screaming and yelling? That way we might win the troops to our side.

FATHER UBU: All right, then. I'll attempt to tread on his toes; he'll protest, and then I'll say, SHITR, and at this signal you'll all throw yourselves on him.

MOTHER UBU: Yes, and as soon as he's dead you'll take his scepter and crown.

CAPTAIN BORDURE: And I'll pursue the royal family with my men.

FATHER UBU: Yes, and be extra sure that you catch young Bougrelas. (*They go out. Running after them and bringing them back.*) Gentlemen, we have forgotten an indispensable ceremony: we must swear to fight bravely.

CAPTAIN BORDURE: How are we going to do that? We don't have a priest.

FATHER UBU: Mother Ubu will take his place.

ALL: Very well, so be it.

FATHER UBU: Then you really swear to kill the king?

ALL: Yes, we swear it. Long live Father Ubu!

ACT II

Scene 1

The palace. KING WENCESLAS, QUEEN ROSEMONDE, BOLESLAS, LADISLAS, *and* BOUGRELAS.

KING WENCESLAS: Mr. Bougrelas, you were very impertinent this morning with Mr. Ubu, knight of my orders and Count of Sandomir. That's why I'm forbidding you to appear at my parade.

QUEEN ROSEMONDE: But, Wenceslas, you need your whole family around you to protect you.

KING WENCESLAS: Madam, I never retract my commands. You weary me with your chatter.

BOUGRELAS: It shall be as you desire, my father.

QUEEN ROSEMONDE: Sire, have you definitely decided to attend this parade?

KING WENCESLAS: Why shouldn't I, madam?

QUEEN ROSEMONDE: For the last time, didn't I tell you that I dreamed that I saw you being knocked down by a mob of his men and thrown into the Vistula, and an eagle just like the one in the arms of Poland placing the crown on his head?

KING WENCESLAS: On whose?

QUEEN ROSEMONDE: On Father Ubu's.

KING WENCESLAS: What nonsense! Count de Ubu is a very fine gentleman who would let himself be torn apart by horses in my service.

QUEEN ROSEMONDE *and* BOUGRELAS: What a delusion!

KING WENCESLAS: Be quiet, you little ape. And as for you, madam, just to show you how little I fear Mr. Ubu, I'll go to the parade just as I am, without sword or armor.

QUEEN ROSEMONDE: Fatal imprudence! I shall never see you alive again.

KING WENCESLAS: Come along, Ladislas, come along, Boleslas. (*They go out.* QUEEN ROSEMONDE *and* BOUGRELAS *go to the window.*)

QUEEN ROSEMONDE *and* BOUGRELAS: May God and holy Saint Nicholas protect you!

QUEEN ROSEMONDE: Bougrelas, come to the chapel with me to pray for your father and your brothers.

SCENE 2

The parade grounds. The Polish Army, KING WENCESLAS, BOLESLAS, LADISLAS, FATHER UBU, CAPTAIN BORDURE *and his men,* GIRON, PILE, COTICE.

KING WENCESLAS: Noble Father Ubu, accompany me with your companions while I inspect the troops.

FATHER UBU (*to his men*): On your toes, boys. (*To the king.*) Coming, sir, coming. (UBU's *men surround the king.*)

KING WENCESLAS: Ah! Here is the Dantzick Horseguard Regiment. Aren't they magnificent!

FATHER UBU: You really think so? They look rotten to me. Look at this one. (*To the soldier.*) When did you last shave, varlet?

KING WENCESLAS: But this soldier is absolutely impeccable. What's the matter with you, Father Ubu?

FATHER UBU: Take that! (*He stamps on his foot.*)

KING WENCESLAS: Wretch!

FATHER UBU: Shitr! Come on, men!

CAPTAIN BORDURE: Hooray! Charge! (*They all hit the king; a Palotin explodes.*)

KING WENCESLAS: Oh! Help! Holy Mother, I'm dead.

BOLESLAS (*to* LADISLAS): What's going on? Let's draw.

FATHER UBU: Ah, I've got the crown! To the others, now.

CAPTAIN BORDURE: After the traitors! (*The princes flee, pursued by all.*)

SCENE 3

QUEEN ROSEMONDE *and* BOUGRELAS.

QUEEN ROSEMONDE: At last I can begin to relax.

BOUGRELAS: You've no reason to be afraid. (*A frightful din is heard from outside.*) Oh! What's this I see? My two brothers pursued by Father Ubu and his men.

QUEEN ROSEMONDE: Oh, my God! Holy Mother, they're losing, they're losing ground!

BOUGRELAS: The whole army is following Father Ubu. I don't see the king. Horror! Help!

QUEEN ROSEMONDE: There's Boleslas, dead! He's been shot.

BOUGRELAS: Hey! Defend yourself! Hooray, Ladislas!

QUEEN ROSEMONDE: Oh! He's surrounded.

BOUGRELAS: He's finished. Bordure's just sliced him in half like a sausage.

QUEEN ROSEMONDE: Alas! Those madmen have broken into the palace; they're coming up the stairs. (*The din grows louder.*)

QUEEN ROSEMONDE *and* BOUGRELAS (*on their knees*): Oh, God, defend us!

BOUGRELAS: Oh! That Father Ubu! The swine, the wretch, if I could get my hands on him . . .

SCENE 4

The same. The door is smashed down. FATHER UBU *and his rabble break through.*

FATHER UBU: So, Bougrelas, what's that you want to do to me?

BOUGRELAS: Great God! I'll defend my mother to the death! The first man to make a move dies.

FATHER UBU: Oh! Bordure, I'm scared. Let me out of here.

A SOLDIER (*advancing*): Give yourself up, Bougrelas!

BOUGRELAS: Here, scum, take that! (*He splits his skull.*)

QUEEN ROSEMONDE: Hold your ground, Bougrelas; hold your ground!

SEVERAL (*advancing*): Bougrelas, we promise to let you go.

BOUGRELAS: Good-for-nothings, sots, turncoats! (*He swings his sword and kills them all.*)

FATHER UBU: I'll win out in the end!

BOUGRELAS: Mother, escape by the secret staircase.

QUEEN ROSEMONDE: And what about you, my son? What about you?

BOUGRELAS: I'll follow you.

FATHER UBU: Try to catch the queen. Oh, there she goes. As for you, you little . . . (*He approaches* BOUGRELAS.)

BOUGRELAS: Great God! Here is my vengeance! (*With a terrible blow of his sword he rips open* FATHER UBU's *paunch-protector.*) Mother, I'm coming! (*He disappears down the secret staircase.*)

SCENE 5

A cave in the mountains. Young BOUGRELAS *enters, followed by* QUEEN ROSEMONDE.

BOUGRELAS: We'll be safe here.

QUEEN ROSEMONDE: Yes, I think so. Bougrelas, help me! (*She falls to the snow.*)

BOUGRELAS: What's the matter, Mother?

QUEEN ROSEMONDE: Believe me, I'm very sick, Bougrelas. I don't have more than two hours to live.

BOUGRELAS: What do you mean? Has the cold got you?

QUEEN ROSEMONDE: How can I bear up against so many blows? The king massacred, our family destroyed, and you, the representative of the most noble race that has ever worn a sword, forced to flee into the mountains like a common brigand.

BOUGRELAS: And by whom, O Lord, by whom? A vulgar fellow like Father Ubu, an adventurer coming from no one knows where, a vile blackguard, a shameless vagabond! And when I think that my father decorated him and made him a count and that the next day this low-bred dog had the nerve to raise his hand against him.

QUEEN ROSEMONDE: Oh, Bougrelas! When I remember how happy we were before this Father Ubu came! But now, alas! All is changed!

BOUGRELAS: What can we do? Let us wait in hope and never renounce our rights.

QUEEN ROSEMONDE: May your wish be granted, my dear child, but as for me, I shall never see that happy day.

BOUGRELAS: What's the matter with you? Ah, she pales, she falls. Help me! But I'm in a desert! Oh, my God! Her heart is stilled forever. She is dead? Can it be? Another victim for Father Ubu! (*He hides his face in his hands, and weeps.*) Oh, my God! How sad it is to have such a terrible vengeance to fulfill! And I'm only fourteen years old! (*He falls down in the throes of a most extravagant despair.*)

Meanwhile, the souls of WENCESLAS, BOLESLAS, LADISLAS, *and of* QUEEN ROSEMONDE *enter the cave. Their ancestors, accompanying them, fill up the cave. The oldest goes to* BOUGRELAS *and gently awakes him.*

Ah! What's this I see? My whole family, all my ancestors . . . how can this be?

THE SHADE: Know, Bougrelas, that during my life I was the Lord Mathias of Königsberg, the first king and founder of our house. I entrust our vengeance to your hands. (*He gives him a large sword.*) And may this sword which I have given you never rest until it has brought about the death of the usurper. (*All vanish, and* BOUGRELAS *remains alone, in an attitude of ecstasy.*)

SCENE 6

The palace. FATHER UBU, MOTHER UBU, CAPTAIN BORDURE.

FATHER UBU: No! Never! I don't want to! Do you want me to ruin myself for these buffoons?

CAPTAIN BORDURE: But after all, Father Ubu, don't you see that the people are waiting for the gifts to celebrate your joyous coronation?

MOTHER UBU: If you don't give out meat and gold, you'll be overthrown in two hours.

FATHER UBU: Meat, yes! Gold, no! Slaughter the three oldest horses—that'll be good enough for those apes.

MOTHER UBU: Ape, yourself! How did I ever get stuck with an animal like you?

FATHER UBU: Once and for all, I'm trying to get rich; I'm not going to let go of a cent.

MOTHER UBU: But we've got the whole Polish treasury at our disposal.

CAPTAIN BORDURE: Yes, I happen to know that there's an enormous treasure in the royal chapel; we'll distribute it.

FATHER UBU: Just you dare, you wretch!

CAPTAIN BORDURE: But, Father Ubu, if you don't distribute money to the people, they'll refuse to pay the taxes.

FATHER UBU: Is that a fact?

MOTHER UBU: Yes, of course!

FATHER UBU: Oh, well, in that case I agree to everything. Withdraw three millions, roast a hundred and fifty cattle and sheep —especially since I'll have some myself! (*They go out.*)

SCENE 7

The palace courtyard full of people. FATHER UBU *crowned,* MOTHER UBU, CAPTAIN BORDURE, *flunkies carrying meat.*

PEOPLE: There's the king! Long live the king! Hooray!

FATHER UBU (*throwing gold*): Here, that's for you. It doesn't make me very happy to give you any money; it's Mother Ubu who wanted me to. At least promise me you'll really pay the taxes.

ALL: Yes! Yes!

CAPTAIN BORDURE: Look how they're fighting over that gold, Mother Ubu. What a battle!

MOTHER UBU: It's really awful. Ugh! There's one just had his skull split open.

FATHER UBU: What a beautiful sight! Bring on more gold.

CAPTAIN BORDURE: How about making them race for it?

FATHER UBU: Good idea! (*To the people.*) My friends, take a look at this chest of gold. It contains three hundred thousand Polish coins, of the purest gold, guaranteed genuine. Let those who wish to compete for it assemble at the end of the courtyard. The race will begin when I wave my hand-kerchief, and the first one to get here wins the chest. As for those who don't win, they will share this other chest as a consolation prize.

ALL: Yes! Long live Father Ubu! What a king! We never had anything like this in the days of Wenceslas.

FATHER UBU (*to* MOTHER UBU, *with joy*): Listen to them! (*All the people line up at the end of the courtyard.*) One, two, three! Ready?

ALL: Yes! Yes!

FATHER UBU: Set! Go! (*They start, falling all over one another. Cries and tumult.*)

CAPTAIN BORDURE: They're coming! They're coming!

FATHER UBU: Look! The leader's losing ground.

MOTHER UBU: No, he's going ahead again.

CAPTAIN BORDURE: He's losing, he's losing! He's lost! The other one won.

ALL: Long live Michael Federovitch! Long live Michael Federovitch!

MICHAEL FEDEROVITCH: Sire, I don't know how to thank your Majesty. . . .

FATHER UBU: Think nothing of it, my dear friend. Take your money home with you, Michael; and you others, share the rest— each take a piece until they're all gone.

ALL: Long live Michael Federovitch! Long live Father Ubu!

FATHER UBU: And you, my friends, come and eat! I open the gates of the palace to you— may you do honor to my table!

PEOPLE: Let's go in, let's go in! Long live Father Ubu! He's the noblest monarch of them all! (*They go into the palace. The noise of the orgy is audible throughout the night. The curtain falls.*)

ACT III

SCENE 1

The palace. FATHER UBU, MOTHER UBU.

FATHER UBU: By my green candle, here I am king of this country, I've already got a fine case of indigestion, and they're going to bring me my big helmet.

MOTHER UBU: What's it made out of, Father Ubu? Even if we are sitting on the throne, we have to watch the pennies.

FATHER UBU: Madam my wife, it's made out of sheepskin with a clasp and with laces made out of dogskin.

MOTHER UBU: That's very extraordinary, but it's even more extraordinary that we're here on the throne.

FATHER UBU: How right you are, Mother Ubu.

MOTHER UBU: We owe quite a debt to the Duke of Lithuania.

FATHER UBU: Who's that?

MOTHER UBU: Why, Captain Bordure.

FATHER UBU: If you please, Mother Ubu,

don't speak to me about that buffoon. Now that I don't need him any more, he can go whistle for his dukedom.

MOTHER UBU: You're making a big mistake, Father Ubu; he's going to turn against you.

FATHER UBU: Well, now, the poor little fellow has my deepest sympathy, but I'm not going to worry about him any more than about Bougrelas.

MOTHER UBU: Ha! You think you've seen the last of Bougrelas, do you?

FATHER UBU: By my financial sword, of course I have! What do you think that fourteen-year-old midget is going to do to me?

MOTHER UBU: Father Ubu, pay attention to what I'm going to say to you. Believe me, you ought to be nice to Bougrelas to get him on your side.

FATHER UBU: Do you think I'm made of money? Well, I'm not! You've already made me waste twenty-two millions.

MOTHER UBU: Have it your own way, Father Ubu; he'll roast you alive.

FATHER UBU: Fine! You'll be in the pot with me.

MOTHER UBU: For the last time, listen to me: I'm sure that young Bougrelas will triumph, because he has right on his side.

FATHER UBU: Oh, crap! Doesn't the wrong always get you more than the right? Ah, you do me an injustice, Mother Ubu, I'll chop you into little pieces. (MOTHER UBU *runs away, pursued by* FATHER UBU.)

SCENE 2

The Great Hall of the palace. FATHER UBU, MOTHER UBU, *Officers and Soldiers;* GIRON, PILE, COTICE, NOBLES *in chains,* FINANCIERS, MAGISTRATES, CLERKS.

FATHER UBU: Bring forward the Nobles' money box and the Nobles' hook and the Nobles' knife and the Nobles' book! And then bring forward the Nobles. (NOBLES *are brutally pushed forward.*)

MOTHER UBU: For goodness' sakes, control yourself, Father Ubu.

FATHER UBU: I have the honor to announce to you that in order to enrich the kingdom I shall annihilate all the Nobles and grab their property.

NOBLES: How awful! To the rescue, people and soldiers!

FATHER UBU: Bring forward the first Noble and hand me the Nobles' hook. Those who are condemned to death, I will drop down the trapdoor. They will fall into the Pig-Pinching Cellars and the Money Vault, where they will be disembrained. (*To the* NOBLE.) Who are you, buffoon?

THE NOBLE: Count of Vitebsk.

FATHER UBU: What's your income?

THE NOBLE: Three million rixthalers.

FATHER UBU: Condemned! (*He seizes him with the hook and drops him down the trapdoor.*)

MOTHER UBU: What vile savagery!

FATHER UBU: Second Noble, who are you? (*The* NOBLE *doesn't reply.*) Answer, buffoon!

THE NOBLE: Grand Duke of Posen.

FATHER UBU: Excellent! Excellent! I'll not trouble you any longer. Down the trap. Third Noble, who are you? You're an ugly one.

THE NOBLE: Duke of Courland, and of the cities of Riga, Reval, and Mitau.

FATHER UBU: Very good! Very good! Anything else?

THE NOBLE: That's all.

FATHER UBU: Well, down the trap, then. Fourth Noble, who are you?

THE NOBLE: The Prince of Podolia.

FATHER UBU: What's your income?

THE NOBLE: I'm bankrupt.

FATHER UBU: For that nasty word, into the trap with you. Fifth Noble, who are you?

THE NOBLE: Margrave of Thorn, Palatin of Polack.

FATHER UBU: That doesn't sound like very much. Nothing else?

THE NOBLE: It was enough for me.

FATHER UBU: Half a loaf is better than no loaf at all. Down the trap. What's the matter with you, Mother Ubu?

MOTHER UBU: You're too ferocious, Father Ubu.

FATHER UBU: Please! I'm working! And now I'm going to have MY list of MY property read to me. Clerk, read MY list of MY property.

THE CLERK: County of Sandomir.

FATHER UBU: Start with the big ones.

THE CLERK: Princedom of Podolia, Grand Duchy of Posen, Duchy of Courland,

County of Sandomir, County of Vitebsk, Palatinate of Polack, Margraviate of Thorn.

FATHER UBU: Well, go on.

THE CLERK: That's all.

FATHER UBU: What do you mean, that's all! Oh, very well, then, bring the Nobles forward. Since I'm not finished enriching myself yet, I'm going to execute all the Nobles and seize all their estates at once. Let's go; stick the Nobles in the trap. (*The* NOBLES *are pushed into the trap.*) Hurry it up, let's go, I want to make some laws now.

SEVERAL: This ought to be a good one.

FATHER UBU: First I'm going to reform the laws, and then we'll proceed to matters of finance.

MAGISTRATES: We're opposed to any change.

FATHER UBU: Shitr! To begin with, Magistrates will not be paid any more.

MAGISTRATES: What are we supposed to live on? We're poor.

FATHER UBU: You shall have the fines which you will impose and the property of those you condemn to death.

A MAGISTRATE: Horrors!

A SECOND: Infamy!

A THIRD: Scandal!

A FOURTH: Indignity!

ALL: We refuse to act as judges under such conditions.

FATHER UBU: Down the trap with the Magistrates! (*They struggle in vain.*)

MOTHER UBU: What are you doing, Father Ubu? Who will dispense justice now?

FATHER UBU: Why, me! You'll see how smoothly it'll go.

MOTHER UBU: I can just imagine.

FATHER UBU: That's enough out of you, buffooness. And now, gentlemen, we will proceed to matters of finance.

FINANCIERS: No changes are needed.

FATHER UBU: I intend to change everything. First of all, I'll keep half the taxes for myself.

FINANCIERS: That's too much.

FATHER UBU: Gentlemen, we will establish a tax of 10 percent on property, another on commerce and industry, a third on marriages and a fourth on deaths—fifteen francs each.

FIRST FINANCIER: But that's idiotic, Father Ubu.

SECOND FINANCIER: It's absurd.

THIRD FINANCIER: It's impossible.

FATHER UBU: You're trying to confuse me! Down the trap with the Financiers! (*The* FINANCIERS *are pushed in.*)

MOTHER UBU: But, Father Ubu, what kind of king are you? You're murdering everybody!

FATHER UBU: Oh, shitr!

MOTHER UBU: No more justice, no more finances!

FATHER UBU: Have no fear, my sweet child; I myself will go from village to village, collecting the taxes.

SCENE 3

A peasant house in the outskirts of Warsaw. Several peasants are assembled.

A PEASANT (*entering*): Have you heard the news? The king and the dukes are all dead, and young Bougrelas has fled to the mountains with his mother. What's more, Father Ubu has seized the throne.

ANOTHER: That's nothing. I've just come from Cracow where I saw the bodies of more than three hundred nobles and five hundred magistrates, and I hear that the taxes are going to be doubled and that Father Ubu is coming to collect them himself.

ALL: Great heavens! What will become of us? Father Ubu is a horrible beast, and they say his family is abominable.

A PEASANT: Listen! Isn't somebody knocking at the door?

A VOICE (*outside*): Hornsbuggers! Open up, by my shitr, by Saint John, Saint Peter, and Saint Nicholas! Open up, by my financial sword, by my financial horns, I'm coming to collect the taxes! (*The door is smashed in, and* FATHER UBU *enters followed by hordes of tax collectors.*)

SCENE 4

FATHER UBU: Which one of you is the oldest? (*A peasant steps forward.*) What's your name?

THE PEASANT: Stanislas Leczinski.

FATHER UBU: Fine, hornsbuggers! Listen to me, since if you don't these gentlemen here will cut your ears off. Well, are you listening?

STANISLAS: But your Excellency hasn't said anything yet.

FATHER UBU: What do you mean? I've been speaking for an hour. Do you think I've come here to preach in the desert?

STANISLAS: Far be it from my thoughts.

FATHER UBU: I've come to tell you, to order you, and to intimate to you that you are to produce forthwith and exhibit promptly your finance, unless you wish to be slaughtered. Let's go, gentlemen, my financial swine, vehiculize hither the phynancial vehicle. (*The vehicle is brought in.*)

STANISLAS: Sire, we are down on the register for a hundred and fifty-two rixthalers which we paid six weeks ago come Saint Matthew's Day.

FATHER UBU: That's very possible, but I've changed the government and run an advertisement in the paper that says you have to pay all present taxes twice and all those which I will levy later on three times. With this system, I'll make my fortune quickly; then I'll kill everyone and run away.

PEASANTS: Mr. Ubu, please have pity on us; we are poor, simple citizens.

FATHER UBU: Nuts! Pay up.

PEASANTS: We can't, we've already paid.

FATHER UBU: Pay up! Or I'll stick you in my pocket with torturing and beheading of the neck and head! Hornsbuggers, I'm the king, aren't I?

ALL: Ah! So that's the way it is! To arms! Long live Bougrelas, by the grace of God King of Poland and Lithuania!

FATHER UBU: Forward, gentlemen of Finance, do your duty. (*A struggle ensues; the house is destroyed, and old* STANISLAS *flees across the plain, alone.* FATHER UBU *stays to collect the money.*)

SCENE 5

A dungeon in the Fortress of Thorn. CAPTAIN BORDURE *in chains,* FATHER UBU.

FATHER UBU: So, Citizen, that's the way it is: you wanted me to pay you what I owed you; then you rebelled because I refused; you conspired and here you are retired. Horns of finance, I've done so well you must admire it yourself.

CAPTAIN BORDURE: Take care, Father Ubu.

During the five days that you've been king, you've committed enough murders to damn all the saints in Paradise. The blood of the king and of the nobles cries for vengeance, and their cries will be heard.

FATHER UBU: Ah, my fine friend, that's quite a tongue you've got there. I have no doubt that if you escaped, it would cause all sorts of complications, but I don't think that the dungeons of Thorn have ever let even one of the honest fellows go who have been entrusted to them. Therefore I bid you a very good night and I invite you to sleep soundly, although I must say the rats dance a very pretty saraband down here. (*He leaves. The jailers come and bolt all the doors.*)

SCENE 6

The Palace at Moscow. The EMPEROR ALEXIS *and his court,* CAPTAIN BORDURE.

ALEXIS: Infamous adventurer, aren't you the one who helped kill our cousin Wenceslas?

CAPTAIN BORDURE: Sire, forgive me, I was carried away despite myself by Father Ubu.

ALEXIS: Oh, what a big liar! Well, what can I do for you?

CAPTAIN BORDURE: Father Ubu imprisoned me on charges of conspiracy; I succeeded in escaping and I have ridden five days and five nights across the steppes to come and beg your gracious forgiveness.

ALEXIS: What have you got for me as proof of your loyalty?

CAPTAIN BORDURE: My honor as a knight, and a detailed map of the town of Thorn. (*Kneels and presents his sword to* ALEXIS.)

ALEXIS: I accept your sword, but by Saint George, burn the map. I don't want to owe my victory to an act of treachery.

CAPTAIN BORDURE: One of the sons of Wenceslas, young Bougrelas, is still alive. I would do anything to restore him.

ALEXIS: What was your rank in the Polish Army?

CAPTAIN BORDURE: I commanded the fifth regiment of the Dragoons of Vilna and a company of mercenaries in the service of Father Ubu.

ALEXIS: Fine, I appoint you second in command of the tenth regiment of Cossacks, and woe to you if you betray me. If you fight well, you'll be rewarded.

CAPTAIN BORDURE: I don't lack courage, Sire.

ALEXIS: Fine, remove yourself from my sight. (*He leaves.*)

SCENE 7

UBU's *Council Chamber.* FATHER UBU, MOTHER UBU, PHYNANCIAL ADVISERS.

FATHER UBU: Gentlemen, the meeting has begun, and see that you keep your ears open and your mouths shut. First of all, we'll turn to the subject of finance; then we'll speak about a little scheme I've thought up to bring good weather and prevent rain.

AN ADVISER: Very good, Mr. Ubu.

MOTHER UBU: What a stupid fool!

FATHER UBU: Take care, madam of my shitr, I'm not going to stand for your idiocies much longer. I'd like you to know, gentlemen, that the finances are proceeding satisfactorily. The streets are mobbed every morning by a crowd of the local low-life, and my men do wonders with them. In every direction you can see only burning houses, and people bent under the weight of our finances.

THE ADVISER: And are the new taxes going well, Mr. Ubu?

MOTHER UBU: Not at all. The tax on marriages has brought in only eleven cents so far, although Father Ubu chases people everywhere to convince them to marry.

FATHER UBU: By my financial sword, hornsbuggers, Madam financieress, I've got ears to speak with and you've a mouth to listen to me with. (*Shouts of laughter.*) You're mixing me up and it's your fault that I'm making a fool of myself! But, horn of Ubu! . . . (*A messenger enters.*) Well, what do you have to say for yourself? Get out of here, you little monkey, before I pocket you with beheading and twisting of the legs.

MOTHER UBU: There he goes, but he's left a letter.

FATHER UBU: Read it. I don't feel like it, or come to think of it perhaps I can't read.

Hurry up, buffooness, it must be from Bordure.

MOTHER UBU: Right. He says that the Czar has received him very well, that he's going to invade your lands to restore Bougrelas, and that you're going to be killed.

FATHER UBU: Oh! Oh! I'm scared! I'm scared! I bet I'm going to die. Oh, poor little man that I am! What will become of me, great God? This wicked man is going to kill me. Saint Anthony and all the saints, protect me, and I'll give you some phynance and burn some candles for you. Lord, what will become of me? (*He cries and sobs.*)

MOTHER UBU: There's only one safe course to follow, Father Ubu.

FATHER UBU: What's that, my love?

MOTHER UBU: War!!!

ALL: Great heavens! What a noble idea!

FATHER UBU: Yes, and I'll be the one to get hurt, as usual.

FIRST ADVISER: Hurry, hurry, let's organize the army.

SECOND: And requisition the provisions.

THIRD: And set up the artillery and the fortresses.

FOURTH: And get up the money for the troops.

FATHER UBU: That's enough of that, now, you, or I'll kill you on the spot. I'm not going to spend any money. That's a good one, isn't it! I used to be paid to wage war, and now it's being waged at my expense. Wait—by my green candle, let's wage war, since you're so excited about it, but let's not spend a penny.

ALL: Hooray for war!

SCENE 8

The camp outside Warsaw.

SOLDIERS *and* PALOTINS: Long live Poland! Long live Father Ubu.

FATHER UBU: Ah, Mother Ubu, give me my breastplate and my little stick. I'll soon be so heavy that I won't be able to move even if I'm being chased.

MOTHER UBU: Pooh, what a coward!

FATHER UBU: Ah! Here's the sword of shitr

running away first thing and there's the financial hook which won't stay put!!! (*Drops both.*) I'll never be ready, and the Russians are coming to kill me.

A SOLDIER: Lord Ubu, here's your ear-pick, which you've dropped.

FATHER UBU: I'll kill you with my shitr hook and my gizzard-saw.

MOTHER UBU: How handsome he is with his helmet and his breastplate! He looks just like an armed pumpkin.

FATHER UBU: Now I'll get my horse. Gentlemen, bring forth the phynancial horse.

MOTHER UBU: Father Ubu, your horse can't carry you—it's had nothing to eat for five days and it's about to die.

FATHER UBU: That's a good one! I have to pay twelve cents a day for this sway-backed nag and it can't even carry me. You're making fun of me, horn of Ubu, or else perhaps you're stealing from me? (MOTHER UBU *blushes and lowers her eyes.*) Now bring me another beast, because I'm not going to go on foot, hornsbuggers! (*An enormous horse is brought out.*) I'm going to get on. Oops, better sit down before I fall off. (*The horse starts to leave.*) Stop this beast. Great God, I'm going to fall off and be killed!!!

MOTHER UBU: He's an absolute idiot. There he is up again; no, he's down again.

FATHER UBU: Horn of Physics, I'm half dead. But never mind, I'm going to the war and I'll kill everyone. Woe to him who doesn't keep up with me! I'll put him in my pocket with twisting of the nose and teeth and extraction of the tongue.

MOTHER UBU: Good luck, Mr. Ubu!

FATHER UBU: I forgot to tell you that I'm making you the regent. But I'm keeping the financial book, so you'd better not try and rob me. I'll leave you the Palotin Giron to help you. Farewell, Mother Ubu.

MOTHER UBU: Farewell, Father Ubu. Kill the Czar thoroughly.

FATHER UBU: Of course. Twisting of the nose and teeth, extraction of the tongue and insertion of the ear-pick. (*The army marches away to the sound of fanfares.*)

MOTHER UBU (*alone*): Now that that big fat booby has gone, let's look to our own affairs, kill Bougrelas, and grab the treasure.

ACT IV

SCENE 1

The Royal Crypt in the Cathedral at Warsaw.

MOTHER UBU: Where on earth is that treasure? None of these slabs sounds hollow. I've counted thirteen slabs beyond the tomb of Ladislas the Great along the length of the wall, and I've found nothing. Someone seems to have deceived me. What's this? The stone sounds hollow here. To work, Mother Ubu. Courage, we'll have it pried up in a minute. It's stuck fast. The end of this financial hook will do the trick. There! There's the gold in the middle of the royal bones. Into the sack with it. Oh! What's that noise? Can there still be someone alive in these ancient vaults? No, it's nothing; let's hurry up. Let's take everything. This money will look better in the light of day than in the middle of these graves. Back with the stone. What's that! There's that noise again! There's something not quite right about this place. I'll get the rest of this gold some other time—I'll come back tomorrow.

A VOICE (*coming from the tomb of John Sigismund*): Never, Mother Ubu! (MOTHER UBU *runs away terrified, through the secret door, carrying the stolen gold.*)

SCENE 2

The Main Square in Warsaw. BOUGRELAS *and his men, People and Soldiers.*

BOUGRELAS: Forward, my friends! Long live Wenceslas and Poland! That old blackguard Father Ubu is gone; only that old witch Mother Ubu and her Palotin are left. I'm going to march at your head and restore my father's house to the throne.

ALL: Long live Bougrelas!

BOUGRELAS: And we'll abolish all taxes imposed by that horrible Father Ubu.

ALL: Hooray! Forward! To the palace, and death to the Ubus!

BOUGRELAS: Look! There's Mother Ubu coming out on the porch with her guards!

MOTHER UBU: What can I do for you, gentlemen? Ah! It's Bougrelas. (_The crowd throws stones._)

FIRST GUARD: They've broken all the windows.

SECOND GUARD: Saint George, I'm done for.

THIRD GUARD: Hornsass, I'm dying.

BOUGRELAS: Throw some more stones, my friends.

PALOTIN GIRON: Ho! So that's the way it is! (_He draws his sword and leaps into the crowd, performing horrible slaughter._)

BOUGRELAS: Have at you! Defend yourself, you cowardly pisspot! (_They fight._)

GIRON: I die!

BOUGRELAS: Victory, my friends! Now for Mother Ubu! (_Trumpets are heard._) Ah! The Nobles are arriving. Run and catch the old hag.

ALL: She'll do until we can strangle the old bandit himself! (MOTHER UBU _runs away pursued by all the Poles. Rifle shots and a hail of stones._)

SCENE 3

The Polish Army marching in the Ukraine.

FATHER UBU: Hornsass, godslegs, cowsheads! We're about to perish, because we're dying of thirst and we're tired. Sir Soldier, be so good as to carry our financial helmet, and you, Sir Lancer, take charge of the shitr-pick and the physic-stick to unencumber our person, because, let me repeat, we are tired. (_The soldiers obey._)

PILE: Ho, my Lord! It's surprising that there are no Russians to be seen.

FATHER UBU: It's regrettable that the state of our finances does not permit us to have a vehicle commensurate to our grandeur; for, for fear of demolishing our steed, we have gone all the way on foot, leading our horse by the bridle. When we get back to Poland, we shall devise, by means of our physical science and with the aid of the wisdom of our advisers, a way of transporting our entire army by wind.

COTICE: Here comes Nicholas Rensky, in a great hurry.

FATHER UBU: What's the matter with him?

RENSKY: All is lost. Sir, the Poles have revolted, Giron has been killed, and Mother Ubu has fled to the mountains.

FATHER UBU: Bird of night, beast of misery, owl's underwear! Where did you hear this nonsense? What won't you be saying next! Who's responsible for this? Bougrelas, I'll bet. Where'd you just come from?

RENSKY: From Warsaw, noble Lord.

FATHER UBU: Child of my shitr, if I believed you I would retreat with the whole army. But, Sir Child, you've got feathers in your head instead of brains and you've been dreaming nonsense. Run off to the outposts, my child; the Russians can't be far, and we'll soon be flourishing our arms, shitr, phynancial, and physical.

GENERAL LASCY: Father Ubu, can't you see the Russians down there on the plain?

FATHER UBU: It's true, the Russians! A fine mess this is. If only there were still a way to run out, but there isn't; we're up here on a hill and we'll be exposed to attack on all sides.

THE ARMY: The Russians! The enemy!

FATHER UBU: Let's go, gentlemen, into our battle positions. We will remain on top of the hill and under no circumstances commit the idiocy of descending. I'll keep myself in the middle like a living fortress, and all you others will gravitate around me. I advise you to load your guns with as many bullets as they will hold, because eight bullets can kill eight Russians and that will be eight Russians the less. We will station the infantry at the foot of the hill to receive the Russians and kill them a little, the cavalry in back of them so that they can throw themselves into the confusion, and the artillery around this windmill here so that they can fire into the whole mess. As for us, we will take up our position inside the windmill and fire through the window with the phynancial pistol, and bar the door with the physical stick, and if anyone still tries to get in let him beware of the shitr-hook!!!

OFFICERS: Your orders, Lord Ubu, shall be executed.

FATHER UBU: Fine, we'll win, then. What time is it?

GENERAL LASCY: It's eleven o'clock in the morning.

FATHER UBU: In that case, let's have lunch, because the Russians won't attack before midday. Tell the soldiers, my lord General, to take a crap and strike up the Financial Song. (LASCY *withdraws*.)

SOLDIERS *and* PALOTINS: Long live Father Ubu, our great Financier! Ting, ting, ting; ting, ting, ting; ting, ting, ta-ting!

FATHER UBU: Oh, how noble, I adore gallantry! (*A Russian cannonball breaks one of the arms of the windmill*.) Aaaaah! I'm frightened. Lord God, I'm dead! No, no, I'm not.

SCENE 4

The same, a CAPTAIN *and the Russian Army*.

A CAPTAIN (*entering*): Lord Ubu, the Russians are attacking.

FATHER UBU: All right, all right, what do you want me to do about it? I didn't tell them to attack. Nevertheless, gentlemen of Finance, let us prepare ourselves for battle.

GENERAL LASCY: Another cannonball!

FATHER UBU: Ah! That's enough of that! It's raining lead and steel around here, and it might put a dent in our precious person. Down we go. (*They all run away. The battle has just begun. They disappear in the clouds of smoke at the foot of the hill*.)

A RUSSIAN (*thrusting*): For God and the Czar!

RENSKY: Ah! I'm dead.

FATHER UBU: Forward! As for you, sir, I'll get you because you've hurt me, do you hear? You drunken sot, with your popless little popgun.

THE RUSSIAN: Ah! I'll show you! (*He fires*.)

FATHER UBU: Ah! Oh! I'm wounded, I'm shot full of holes, I'm perforated, I'm done for, I'm buried. And now I've got you! (*He tears him to pieces*.) Just try that again.

GENERAL LASCY: Forward, charge, across the trench! Victory is ours!

FATHER UBU: Do you really think so? So far my brow has felt more lumps than laurels.

RUSSIAN KNIGHTS: Hooray! Make way for the Czar! (*Enter the* CZAR, *accompanied by* CAPTAIN BORDURE, *in disguise*.)

A POLE: Great God! Every man for himself, there's the Czar!

ANOTHER: Oh, my God, he's crossed the trench.

ANOTHER: Bing! Bang! Four more chopped up by that big ox of a lieutenant.

CAPTAIN BORDURE: So! The rest of you won't surrender, eh? All right, your time has come, John Sobiesky! (*He chops him up*.) Now for the others! (*He massacres Poles*.)

FATHER UBU: Forward, my friends! Capture that rat! Make mincemeat of the Muscovites! Victory is ours! Long live the Red Eagle!

ALL: Charge! Hooray! Godslegs! Capture the big ox.

CAPTAIN BORDURE: By Saint George, they've got me.

FATHER UBU: Ah! it's you, Bordure! How are you, my friend? I, and all the company, are very happy to welcome you again. I'm going to broil you over a slow fire. Gentlemen of the Finances, light the fire. Oh! Ah! Oh! I'm dead. I must have been hit with a cannonball at least. Oh! My God, forgive my sins. Yes, it's definitely a cannonball.

CAPTAIN BORDURE: It was a pistol with a blank cartridge.

FATHER UBU: Oh, you're making fun of me! All right, into the pocket you go! (*He flings himself upon him and tears him to pieces*.)

GENERAL LASCY: Father Ubu, we're advancing on all fronts.

FATHER UBU: I can see that. But I can't go on any more, because everyone's been stepping on my toes. I absolutely have to sit down. Oh, where's my bottle?

GENERAL LASCY: Go get the Czar's bottle, Father Ubu!

FATHER UBU: Ah! Just what I had in mind. Let's go. Sword of Shitr, do your duty, and you, financial hook, don't lag behind! As for you, physical stick, see that you work just as hard and share with the little bit of wood the honor of massacring, scooping out, and imposing upon the Muscovite Emperor. Forward, my Phynancial Horse! (*He throws himself on the* CZAR.)

A RUSSIAN OFFICER: Look out, Your Majesty!

FATHER UBU: Take that! Oh! Ow! Ah! Goodness me. Ah! Oh, sir, excuse me, leave me alone. I didn't do it on purpose! (*He runs away, pursued by the* CZAR.) Holy Mother, that madman is coming after me! Great God, what shall I do? Ah, I've got that trench ahead of me again. I've got him

behind me and the trench in front of me!
Courage! I'm going to close my eyes! (*He
jumps the trench. The* CZAR *falls in.*)

THE CZAR: God, I've fallen in!

THE POLES: Hooray! The Czar has fallen in!

FATHER UBU: I'm afraid to turn around. Ah!
He fell in. That's fine; they've jumped on
him. Let's go, you Poles; swing away; he's
a tough one, that swine! As for me, I can't
look. But our prediction has been completely fulfilled: the physical stick has performed wonders, and without doubt I would
have been about to have killed him completely, had not an inexplicable fear come
to combat and annul in us the fruits of our
courage. But we suddenly had to turn tail,
and we owe our salvation only to our skill
in the saddle as well as to the sturdy hocks
of our Phynancial Horse, whose rapidity is
only equaled by its solidity and whose levi-
tation makes its reputation, as well as the
depth of the trench which located itself so
appropriately under the enemy of us, the
presently-before-you Master of Phynances.
That was very nice, but nobody was listening. Oops, there they go again! (*The Russian dragoons charge and rescue the* CZAR.)

GENERAL LASCY: It looks like it's turning into
a rout.

FATHER UBU: Now's the time to make tracks.
Now then, gentlemen of Poland, forward!
Or rather, backward!

POLES: Every man for himself!

FATHER UBU: Come on! Let's go! What a big
crowd, what a stampede, what a mob! How
am I ever going to get out of this mess?
(*He is jostled.*) You there, watch your step,
or you will sample the boiling rage of the
Master of Phynances. Ha! There he goes.
Now let's get out of here fast, while Lascy's
looking the other way. (*He runs off; the*
CZAR *and the Russian Army go by, chasing
Poles.*)

SCENE 5

A cave in Lithuania. It is snowing. FATHER
UBU, PILE, COTICE.

FATHER UBU: Oh, what a bitch of a day! It's
cold enough to make the rocks crack open,
and the person of the Master of Phynances
finds itself severely damaged.

PILE: Ho! Mr. Ubu, have you recovered from
your fright and from your flight?

FATHER UBU: Well, I'm not frightened any
more, but, believe me, I'm still running.

COTICE (*aside*): What a turd!

FATHER UBU: Well, Sire Cotice, how's your
ear feeling?

COTICE: As well as can be expected, sir, considering how bad it is. I can't get the bullet
out, and consequently the lead is making
me tilt.

FATHER UBU: Well, serves you right! You're
always looking for a fight. As for me, I've
always demonstrated the greatest valor, and
without in any way exposing myself I massacred four enemies with my own hand,
not counting, of course, those who were
already dead and whom we dispatched.

COTICE: Do you know what happened to
little Rensky, Pile?

PILE: A bullet in his head.

FATHER UBU: As the poppy and the dande-
lion are scythed in the flower of their age
by the pitiless scythe of the pitiless scyther
who scythes pitilessly their pitiful parts—
just so little Rensky has played the poppy's
part: he fought well, but there were just
too many Russians around.

PILE *and* COTICE: Hey! Sir Ubu?

AN ECHO: Grrrrr!

PILE: What's that? On guard!

FATHER UBU: Oh, no! Not the Russians
again! I've had enough of them. And, anyway, it's very simple: if they catch me I'll
just put them all in my pocket.

SCENE 6

The same. Enter a bear.

COTICE: Ho! Master of Phynances!

FATHER UBU: Oh! What a sweet little dog-
gie! Isn't he cute?

PILE: Watch out! What a huge bear! Hand
me my gun!

FATHER UBU: A bear! What a horrible beast!
Oh, poor me, I'm going to be eaten alive.
May God protect me! He's coming this
way. No, he's got Cotice. I can breathe
again! (*The bear jumps on* COTICE. PILE
attacks him with his sword. UBU *takes
refuge on a high rock.*)

COTICE: Save me, Pile! Save me! Help, Sir Ubu!

FATHER UBU: Fat chance! Get out of it yourself, my friend; right now I'm going to recite my Paternoster. Everyone will be eaten in his turn.

PILE: I've got him, I'm holding him.

COTICE: Hold him tight, my friend, he's starting to let me go.

FATHER UBU: Sanctificetur nomen tuum.

COTICE: Cowardly lout!

PILE: Oh! It's biting me! O Lord, save us, I'm dead.

FATHER UBU: Fiat voluntas tua!

COTICE: I've wounded it!

PILE: Hooray! It's bleeding now. (*While the* PALOTINS *shout, the bear bellows with pain and* UBU *continues to mumble.*)

COTICE: Hang on, while I find my exploding brass knuckles.

FATHER UBU: Panem nostrum quotidianum da nobis hodie.

PILE: Haven't you got it yet? I can't hold on any longer.

FATHER UBU: Sicut et nos dimittimus debitoribus nostris.

COTICE: Ah! I've got it. (*A resounding explosion; the bear falls dead.*)

PILE *and* COTICE: Victory!

FATHER UBU: Sed libera nos a malo. Amen. Is he really dead? Can I come down now?

PILE (*with disgust*): Just as you like.

FATHER UBU (*coming down*): You may be assured that if you are still alive and if you tread once more the Lithuanian snow, you owe it to the lofty virtue of the Master of Phynances, who has struggled, broken his back, and shouted himself hoarse reciting Paternosters for your safety, and who has wielded the spiritual sword of prayer with just as much courage as you have wielded with dexterity the temporal one of the here-attendant Palotin Cotice's exploding brass knuckles. We have even pushed our devotion further, for we did not hesitate to climb to the top of a very high rock so that our prayers had less far to travel to reach heaven.

PILE: Disgusting pig!

FATHER UBU: Oh, you beast! Thanks to me, you've got something to eat. What a belly he has, gentlemen! The Greeks would have been more comfortable in there than in their wooden horse, and we very barely escaped, my dear friends, being able to satisfy ourselves of his interior capacity with our own eyes.

PILE: I'm dying of hunger. What can we eat?

COTICE: The bear!

FATHER UBU: My poor friends, are you going to eat it completely raw? We don't have anything to make a fire with.

PILE: What about our flintstones?

FATHER UBU: Ah, that's true. And it seems to me that not far from here there is a little wood where dry branches may be found. Sire Cotice, go and fetch some. (COTICE *runs off across the snow.*)

PILE: And now, Sir Ubu, you can go and carve up the bear.

FATHER UBU: Oh, no. It may not be completely dead yet. Since it has already half-eaten you, and chewed upon all your members, you're obviously the man to take care of that. I'll go and light the fire while we're waiting for him to bring the wood. (PILE *starts to carve up the bear.*) Oh! Watch out! It just moved.

PILE: But Sir Ubu, it's stone cold already.

FATHER UBU: That's a pity. It would have been much better to have had him hot. We're running the risk of giving the Master of Phynances an attack of indigestion.

PILE (*aside*): Disgusting fellow! (*Aloud.*) Give me a hand, Mr. Ubu; I can't do everything myself.

FATHER UBU: No, I'm sorry I can't help you. I'm really excessively fatigued.

COTICE (*re-entering*): What a lot of snow, my friends; anyone would think this was Castile or the North Pole. Night is beginning to fall. In an hour it'll be dark. Let's make haste while we can still see.

FATHER UBU: Did you hear that, Pile? Get a move on. In fact, get a move on, both of you! Skewer the beast, cook the beast, I'm hungry!

PILE: Well, that does it! You'll work or you'll get nothing, do you hear me, you big hog?

FATHER UBU: Oh! It's all the same to me; I'd just as soon eat it raw; you're the ones whose stomachs it won't agree with. Anyway, I'm sleepy.

COTICE: What can we expect from him, Pile? Let's cook dinner ourselves. We just won't give him any, that's all. Or at most we'll throw him a few bones.

PILE: Good enough. Ah, the fire's catching.

FATHER UBU: Oh, that's very nice. It's getting warm now. But I see Russians everywhere. My God, what a retreat! Ah! (*He falls asleep.*)

COTICE: I wonder if Rensky was telling the truth about Mother Ubu being dethroned. It wouldn't surprise me at all.

PILE: Let's finish cooking supper.

COTICE: No, we've got more important problems. I think it would be a good idea to inquire into the truth of the news.

PILE: You're right. Should we desert Father Ubu or stay with him?

COTICE: Let's sleep on it; we'll decide tomorrow.

PILE: No—let's sneak off under cover of darkness.

COTICE: Let's go, then. (*They go.*)

SCENE 7

FATHER UBU (*talking in his sleep*): Ah, Sir Russian Dragoon, watch out, don't shoot in this direction; there's someone here. Oh, there's Bordure; he looks mean, like a bear. And there's Bougrelas coming at me! The bear, the bear! He's right below me; he looks fierce. My God! No, I'm sorry I can't help you! Go away, Bougrelas! Don't you hear me, you clown? There's Rensky now, and the Czar. Oh, they're going to beat me up. And Mother Ubu. Where did you get all that gold? You've stolen my gold, you miserable witch; you've been ransacking my tomb in Warsaw Cathedral, under the moon. I've been dead a long time; Bougrelas has killed me and I've been buried in Warsaw next to Ladislas the Great, and also at Cracow next to John Sigismund, and also at Thorn in the dungeon with Bordure. There it is again. Get out of here, you nasty bear! You look like Bordure. Do you hear, you devilish beast? No, he can't hear me, the Salopins have cut his ears off. Disembrain them, devitalize them, cut off their ears, confiscate their money and drink yourself to death, that's the life of a Salopin, that's happiness for the Master of Phynances. (*He falls silent and sleeps.*)

ACT V

SCENE 1

It is night. FATHER UBU *is asleep. Enter* MOTHER UBU, *without seeing him. The stage is in total darkness.*

MOTHER UBU: Shelter at last. I'm alone here, which is fine, but what an awful journey: crossing all Poland in four days! And even before that, everything happened to me at once! As soon as that fat fool left, I went to the crypt to grab what I could. And right after that, I was almost stoned to death by that Bougrelas and his madmen. I lost the Palotin Giron, my knight, who was so stricken by my beauty that he swooned whenever he saw me, and even, I've been told, when he didn't see me, which is the height of passion. He would have let himself be cut in two for my sake, the poor boy. The proof is that he was cut in four, by Bougrelas. Snip, snap, snop! I thought I'd die. Right after that, I took to flight, pursued by the maddened mob. I flee the palace, reach the Vistula, and find all the bridges guarded. I swim across the river, hoping to escape my persecutors. Nobles come from every direction and chase me. I die a thousand deaths, surrounded by a ring of Poles, screaming for my blood. Finally I wriggle out of their clutches, and after four days of running across the snow of my former kingdom, I reach my refuge here. I haven't had a thing to eat or drink for four days. Bougrelas was right behind me. . . . And here I am, safe at last. Oh, I'm nearly dead of cold and exhaustion. But I'd really like to know what's become of my big buffoon—I mean my honored spouse. Have I fleeced him! Have I taken his rixthalers! Have I pulled the wool over his eyes! And his starving phynancial horse: he's not going to see any oats very soon, either, the poor devil. Oh, what a joke! But alas! My treasure is lost! It's in Warsaw, and let anybody who wants it, go and get it.

FATHER UBU (*starting to wake up*): Capture Mother Ubu! Cut off her ears!

MOTHER UBU: Oh, my God! Where am I? I'm losing my mind. Good Lord, no!

God be praised
I think I can see
Mr. Ubu
Sleeping near me.
Let's show a little sweetness. Well, my fat fellow, did you have a good sleep?

FATHER UBU: A very bad one! That was a tough bear! A fight of hunger against toughness, but hunger has completely eaten and devoured the toughness, as you will see when it gets light in here. Do you hear, my noble Palotins?

MOTHER UBU: What's he babbling about? He seems even stupider than when he left. What's the matter with him?

FATHER UBU: Cotice, Pile, answer me, by my bag of shitr! Where are you? Oh, I'm afraid. Somebody did speak. Who spoke? Not the bear, I suppose. Shitr! Where are my matches? Ah! I lost them in the battle.

MOTHER UBU (*aside*): Let's take advantage of the situation and the darkness and pretend to be a ghost. We'll make him promise to forgive us our little pilfering.

FATHER UBU: By Saint Anthony, somebody is speaking! Godslegs! I'll be damned!

MOTHER UBU (*deepening her voice*): Yes, Mr. Ubu, somebody is indeed speaking, and the trumpet of the archangel which will call the dead from dust and ashes on Judgment Day would not speak otherwise! Listen to my stern voice. It is that of Saint Gabriel who cannot help but give good advice.

FATHER UBU: To be sure!

MOTHER UBU: Don't interrupt me or I'll fall silent, and that will settle your hash!

FATHER UBU: Oh, buggers! I'll be quiet, I won't say another word. Please go on, Madam Apparition!

MOTHER UBU: We were saying, Mr. Ubu, that you are a big fat fellow.

FATHER UBU: Very fat, that's true.

MOTHER UBU: Shut up, Goddammit!

FATHER UBU: Oh my! Angels aren't supposed to curse!

MOTHER UBU (*aside*): Shitr! (*Continuing.*) You are married, Mr. Ubu?

FATHER UBU: Absolutely. To the Queen of Witches.

MOTHER UBU: What you mean to say is that she is a charming woman.

FATHER UBU: A perfect horror. She has claws all over her; you don't know where to grab her.

MOTHER UBU: You should grab her with sweetness, Sir Ubu, and if you grab her thus you will see that Venus herself couldn't be as nice.

FATHER UBU: Who did you say has lice?

MOTHER UBU: You're not listening, Mr. Ubu. Try and keep your ears open now. (*Aside.*) We'd better get a move on; it's getting light in here. Mr. Ubu, your wife is adorable and delicious; she doesn't have a single fault.

FATHER UBU: Ah, you're wrong there: there isn't a single fault that she doesn't have.

MOTHER UBU: That's enough now. Your wife is not unfaithful to you!

FATHER UBU: I'd like to see someone who could stand making her unfaithful. She's an absolute harpy!

MOTHER UBU: She doesn't drink!

FATHER UBU: Only since I've taken the key to the cellar away from her. Before that, she was drunk by seven in the morning and perfumed herself with brandy. Now that she perfumes herself with heliotrope, she doesn't smell so bad any more. Not that I care about that. But now I'm the only one that can get drunk!

MOTHER UBU: Stupid idiot! Your wife doesn't steal your gold.

FATHER UBU: No, that's peculiar.

MOTHER UBU: She doesn't pinch a cent!

FATHER UBU: As witness our noble and unfortunate Phynancial Horse, who, not having been fed for three months, has had to undergo the entire campaign being dragged by the bridle across the Ukraine. He died on the job, poor beast!

MOTHER UBU: That's all a bunch of lies— you've got a model wife, and you're a monster.

FATHER UBU: That's all a bunch of truth. My wife's a slut, and you're a sausage.

MOTHER UBU: Take care, Father Ubu!

FATHER UBU: Oh, that's right, I forgot whom I was talking to. I take it all back.

MOTHER UBU: You killed Wenceslas.

FATHER UBU: That wasn't my fault, actually. Mother Ubu wanted it.

MOTHER UBU: You had Boleslas and Ladislas killed.

FATHER UBU: Too bad for them. They wanted to do me in.

MOTHER UBU: You didn't keep your promise to Bordure, and moreover, you killed him.

FATHER UBU: I'd rather I ruled Lithuania than he. For the moment, neither of us is doing it. Certainly you can see that I'm not.

MOTHER UBU: There's only one way you can make up for all your sins.

FATHER UBU: What's that? I'm all ready to become a holy man; I'd like to be a bishop and have my name on the calendar.

MOTHER UBU: You must forgive Mother Ubu for having sidetracked some of the funds.

FATHER UBU: What do you think of this: I'll pardon her when she's given everything back, when she's been soundly thrashed, and when she's revived my phynancial horse.

MOTHER UBU: He's got that horse on the brain. Ah, I'm lost, day is breaking!

FATHER UBU: Well, I'm happy to know at last for sure that my dear wife steals from me. Now I have it on the highest authority. Omnis a Deo scientia, which is to say: omnis, all; a Deo, knowledge; scientia, comes from God. That explains this marvel. But Madam Apparition is so silent now! What can I offer her to revive her? What she said was very entertaining. But, look, it's daybreak! Ah! Good Lord, by my Phynancial Horse, it's Mother Ubu!

MOTHER UBU (*brazenly*): That's not true, and I'm going to excommunicate you.

FATHER UBU: Ah, you old slut!

MOTHER UBU: Such impiety!

FATHER UBU: That's too much! I can see very well that it's you, you half-witted hag! What the devil are you doing here?

MOTHER UBU: Giron is dead and the Poles chased me.

FATHER UBU: And the Russians chased me. So two great souls meet again.

MOTHER UBU: Say rather that a great soul has met an ass!

FATHER UBU: Fine, and now it's going to meet this little monster. (*He throws the bear at her.*)

MOTHER UBU (*falling down crushed beneath the weight of the bear*): Oh, great God! How horrible! I'm dying! I'm suffocating! It's chewing on me! It's swallowing me! I'm being digested!

FATHER UBU: He's dead, you gargoyle! Oh, wait, perhaps he's not. Lord, he's not dead, save us. (*Climbing back on his rock.*) Pater noster qui es . . .

MOTHER UBU (*disentangling herself*): Where did he go?

FATHER UBU: Oh, Lord, there she is again. Stupid creature, there's no way of getting rid of her. Is that bear dead?

MOTHER UBU: Of course, you stupid ass, he's stone cold. How did he get here?

FATHER UBU (*bewildered*): I don't know. Oh, yes, I do know. He wanted to eat Pile and Cotice, and I killed him with one swipe of a Paternoster.

MOTHER UBU: Pile, Cotice, Paternoster? What's that all about? He's out of his mind, my financé!

FATHER UBU: It happened exactly the way I said. And you're an idiot, you stinkpot!

MOTHER UBU: Describe your campaign to me, Father Ubu.

FATHER UBU: Holy Mother, no! It would take too long. All I know is that despite my incontestable valor, everybody beat me up.

MOTHER UBU: What, even the Poles?

FATHER UBU: They were shouting: Long live Wenceslas and Bougrelas! I thought they were going to chop me up. Oh, those madmen! And then they killed Rensky!

MOTHER UBU: I don't care about that! Did you know that Bougrelas killed Palotin Giron?

FATHER UBU: I don't care about that! And then they killed poor Lascy!

MOTHER UBU: I don't care about that!

FATHER UBU: Oh, well, in that case, come over here, you old slut! Get down on your knees before your master. (*He grabs her and throws her on her knees.*) You're about to suffer the extreme penalty.

MOTHER UBU: Ho, ho, Mr. Ubu!

FATHER UBU: Oh! Oh! Oh! Are you all through now? I'm just about to begin: twisting of the nose, tearing out of the hair, penetration of the little bit of wood into the ears, extraction of the brain by the heels, laceration of the posterior, partial or perhaps even total suppression of the spinal marrow (assuming that would make her character less spiny), not forgetting the puncturing of the swimming bladder and finally the grand re-enacted decollation of John the Baptist, the whole taken from the very Holy Scriptures, from the Old as well as the New Testament, as edited, corrected and perfected by the here-attendant Master of Phynances! How does that suit you, you sausage? (*He begins to tear her to pieces.*)

MOTHER UBU: Mercy, Mr. Ubu! (*A loud noise at the entrance to the cave.*)

SCENE 2

The same, and BOUGRELAS, *who rushes into the cave with his soldiers.*

BOUGRELAS: Forward, my friends. Long live Poland!

FATHER UBU: Oh! Oh! Wait a moment, Mr. Pole. Wait until I've finished with madam my other half!

BOUGRELAS (*hitting him*): Take that, coward, tramp, braggart, laggard, Mussulman!

FATHER UBU (*countering*): Take that! Polack, drunkard, bastard, hussar, tartar, pisspot, inkblot, sneak, freak, anarchist!

MOTHER UBU (*hitting out also*): Take that, prig, pig, rake, fake, snake, mistake, mercenary! (*The soldiers throw themselves on the* UBUS, *who defend themselves as best they can.*)

FATHER UBU: Gods! What a battle!

MOTHER UBU: Watch out for our feet, Gentlemen of Poland.

FATHER UBU: By my green candle, when will this endlessness be ended? Another one! Ah, if only I had my Phynancial Horse here!

BOUGRELAS: Hit them, keep hitting them!

VOICES FROM WITHOUT: Long live Father Ubu, our Great Financier!

FATHER UBU: Ah! There they are. Hooray! There are the Father Ubuists. Forward, come on, you're desperately needed, Gentlemen of Finance. (*Enter the* PALOTINS, *who throw themselves into the fight.*)

COTICE: All out, you Poles!

PILE: Ho! We meet again, my Financial sir. Forward, push as hard as you can, get to the exit; once outside, we'll run away.

FATHER UBU: Oh! He's my best man. Look the way he hits them!

BOUGRELAS: Good God! I'm wounded!

STANISLAS LECZINSKI: It's nothing, Sire.

BOUGRELAS: No, I'm just a little stunned.

JOHN SOBIESKI: Fight, keep fighting, they're getting to the door, the knaves.

COTICE: We're getting there; follow me, everybody. By conseyquence of the whiche, the sky becomes visible.

PILE: Courage, Sir Ubu!

FATHER UBU: Oh! I just crapped in my pants. Forward, hornsbuggers! Killem, bleedem, skinnem, massacrem, by Ubu's horn! Ah! It's quieting down.

COTICE: There are only two of them guarding the exit!

FATHER UBU (*knocking them down with the bear*): And one, and two! Oof! Here I am outside! Let's run now! Follow, you others, and don't stop for anything!

SCENE 3

The scene represents the Province of Livonia covered with snow. The UBUS *and their followers are in flight.*

FATHER UBU: Ah! I think they've stopped trying to catch us.

MOTHER UBU: Yes, Bougrelas has gone to get himself crowned.

FATHER UBU: I don't envy him that crown, either.

MOTHER UBU: You're quite right, Father Ubu. (*They disappear into the distance.*)

SCENE 4

The bridge of a close-hauled schooner on the Baltic. FATHER UBU *and his entire gang are on the bridge.*

THE CAPTAIN: What a lovely breeze!

FATHER UBU: We are indeed sailing with a rapidity which borders on the miraculous. We must be making at least a million knots an hour, and these knots have been tied so well that once tied they cannot be untied. It's true that we have the wind behind us.

PILE: What a pathetic imbecile! (*A squall arises, the ship rolls, the sea foams.*)

FATHER UBU: Oh! Ah! My God, we're going to be capsized. The ship is leaning over too far, it'll fall!

THE CAPTAIN: Everyone to leeward, furl the foresail!

FATHER UBU: Oh, no, don't put everybody on the same side! That's imprudent. What if the wind changed direction—everybody would sink to the bottom of the sea and the fishes would eat us.

THE CAPTAIN: Don't rush, line up and close ranks!

FATHER UBU: Yes, yes, rush! I'm in a hurry! Rush, do you hear! It's your fault that we aren't getting there, brute of a captain. We should have been there already. I'm going to take charge of this myself. Get ready to tack about. Drop anchor, tack with the wind, tack against the wind. Run up the sails, run down the sails, tiller up, tiller down, tiller to the side. You see, everything's going fine. Come broadside to the waves now and everything will be perfect. (*All are convulsed with laughter; the wind rises.*)

THE CAPTAIN: Haul over the jibsail, reef over the topsail!

FATHER UBU: That's not bad, it's even good! Swab out the steward and jump in the crow's-nest. (*Several choke with laughter. A wave is shipped.*) Oh, what a deluge! All this is the result of the maneuvers which we just ordered.

MOTHER UBU *and* PILE: What a wonderful thing navigation is! (*A second wave is shipped.*)

PILE (*drenched*): But watch out for Satan, his pomps and pumps.

FATHER UBU: Sir Boy, get us something to drink. (*They all sit down to drink.*)

MOTHER UBU: What a pleasure it will be to see our sweet France again, our old friends and our castle of Mondragon!

FATHER UBU: We'll be there soon. At the moment we've passed below the castle of Elsinore.

PILE: I feel cheerful at the thought of seeing my dear Spain again.

COTICE: Yes, and we'll amaze our countrymen with the stories of our wonderful adventures.

FATHER UBU: Oh, certainly! And I'm going to get myself appointed Minister of Finances in Paris.

MOTHER UBU: Oh, that's right! Oops, what a bump that was!

COTICE: That's nothing, we're just doubling the point of Elsinore.

PILE: And now our noble ship plows at full speed through the somber waves of the North Sea.

FATHER UBU: A fierce and inhospitable sea which bathes the shores of the land called Germany, so named because the inhabitants of this land are all cousins-german.

MOTHER UBU: That's what I call true learning. They say that this country is very beautiful.

FATHER UBU: Ah! Gentlemen! Beautiful as it may be, it cannot compare with Poland. For if there were no Poland, there would be no Poles! (*Curtain.*)

ALL AGAINST ALL

Arthur Adamov

TRANSLATED BY
Donna Kennedy Gildea

CHARACTERS

ZENNO
JEAN
DARBON
YOUNG MAN
MARIE
MOTHER
NOEMI
YOUNG WOMAN
FIRST GUARD
SECOND PARTISAN
SECOND GUARD
FIRST PARTISAN
SHOPKEEPER
MAN
WORKER
RADIO

It is important that the YOUNG MAN, *the* YOUNG WOMAN, *and* NOEMI *immediately attract the sympathy of the audience, and that they have none of the characteristics that propaganda gives to the refugees.* ZENNO *is the only one among them who corresponds to the refugee stereotype. The* MOTHER, *although not a refugee, is also a typical refugee character.*

PART I

RADIO (*before the lights go up; neuter, impersonal voice*): In the course of yesterday's events, several incidents occurred simultaneously in various sections of the suburbs. Several store windows of buildings held by the refugees have been broken. Later, some groups of strikers tried to organize a march, but they were quickly dispersed by the armed forces. There were no reported injuries. The incidents are still of undetermined origin.

Scene 1

The lights go up. Deserted street. The only scenery, a sidewalk and a section of a wall. Voices, first in the distance, then closer and closer.

MAN'S VOICE: They're all alike!
WOMAN'S VOICE: And to think that we almost had it . . .
MAN'S VOICE: It's not all that bad!
MAN'S VOICE: What did he do? Hey, you, do you know what he did?
MAN'S VOICE: I heard that he took the garage owner's wife.
WOMAN'S VOICE: Is he married?
MAN'S VOICE: They take our money, our wives . . .
SEVERAL VOICES: They take everything! (ZENNO *enters running and scared. He is frail, badly dressed, he limps. Fearfully, he glances around him, then he flattens himself against the wall and freezes. Only his head continues to move. Sounds of footsteps growing fainter. Faint whispering.*)
MAN'S VOICE: This has got to change.
MAN'S VOICE: At any rate, is that him?

WOMAN'S VOICE: Obviously, since he's limping.
MAN'S VOICE: They're all rotten!
WOMAN'S VOICE: Every last one a stinking coward!
SEVERAL VOICES: They're all alike! (JEAN *enters slowly, tired. He is wearing a work shirt. He carries a radio on his shoulder, held on by straps. Having stopped several feet away from* ZENNO, *whom he doesn't see, he lowers his load to the ground with difficulty.*)
ZENNO: You didn't see me, did you? (JEAN *sits down on the curb.*) Hey, didn't you see me? (*Pause.* ZENNO *folds his hands.* JEAN *doesn't move.*)
MAN'S VOICE: Children, this way! (*Sound of approaching footsteps.*)
WOMAN'S VOICE: What are they going to do to him? (*Laughter.*)
ZENNO (*taking a step toward* JEAN): Right . . . , huh . . . you didn't see me?
JEAN: Hide! (*A* SHOPKEEPER *enters.*)
SHOPKEEPER (*approaching* JEAN): Hey, you, we're looking for somebody. A lousy refugee. Did you see him?
JEAN: No, nobody.
SHOPKEEPER: He must have passed through here somewhere. (*Exiting.*) Another one that's got away. (*Sound of footsteps fading away. Silence.* ZENNO *goes toward* JEAN.)
ZENNO (*taking* JEAN's *hand and bringing it up to his lips*): Thank you, thank you. (JEAN *pulls his hand away abruptly and turns away.*) Pardon me. . . . But I want so much to show you . . . show you . . . my gratitude. I don't have anything much on me, I didn't know I was going to come out, but . . . (*He puts his hand in his pocket.*) Maybe this would help you . . . (*He wants to give him money, but* JEAN *pulls his hand away again, and the coins scatter all over the ground.* ZENNO *tries to watch where all the coins roll.*)
JEAN: Come on, stop fooling around. Pick them up! What are you waiting for? (ZENNO *gets down on his hands and knees and picks up the coins.* JEAN *picks up the radio and gets ready to hoist it clumsily to his shoulders.* MARIE *enters, blonde, almost a child. She is wearing a skimpy coat which is too tight and a checkered dress.* MARIE *hasn't noticed* ZENNO, *who begins to walk*

around her and JEAN, *but at a distance*.) What are you doing here?

MARIE: I was worried; I came to meet you! Shouldn't I have?

JEAN: I'm a nuisance to you, huh? You'd trade me in for somebody else, more clever, who'd get along better, who's loaded with money. No worries, no questions, and all the little dresses you want!

MARIE: Am I complaining?

JEAN: No, you know it isn't worth the trouble! Complain to a miserable bastard like me!

MARIE: Have I done anything to you, Jean?

JEAN: No, nothing, Marie. Pardon me. I'm just saying anything that comes into my head! (*Pause*.) That's funny, *I'm* cold now.

MARIE: You're tired. It's this work. Ask for a few days off, maybe they'll give it to you.

JEAN: You know darn well that if I take a few days off, I'll be at home all day long between you and your old lady. Oh! Sure I don't get in the way, I'll stay in my little corner; but even so, when you want to get away, you'll have to explain, tell me where, who with and stuff like that.

MARIE: I don't deserve that.

JEAN: Yeah, O.K., so I'm unfair, so what? What good is it to keep on saying: unfair, unfair, unfair. I am what I am, and you can't change it. And things are the way they are, too. There's no use whining and making faces. But I've had it. That's it. (*Pause*.) Anyway, I'll be able to complain today. There's enough to complain about!

MARIE (*approaching* JEAN): What's happened?

JEAN: I'm going to lose my job.

MARIE: What? Do they want to lay everybody off again?

JEAN: No, not everybody! Me! It seems that I'm not fast enough on the deliveries. It's true, I'm not cut out for this work, it disgusts me. You wouldn't think it to look at me, would you? A delivery boy, that's just exactly right for Jean Rist! He can consider himself happy! There's some who are on strike, but him, he works, the bastard!

MARIE: Did somebody complain? The people you were supposed to deliver a radio to?

JEAN: Yeah.

MARIE: Who were they?

JEAN: I don't know. Refugees, I think.

(*Pause*.) They confiscated everything from us. They thought it was Melik. *Me*, it wouldn't have even occurred to them it was me. But Melik, he knew it was me. So he gets himself up and he says to me: "You're gonna turn yourself in, or I'll bash your teeth in." I was going to tell them that it was me. He only had to give me some time . . .

MARIE: Didn't you try to see the boss and explain to him?

JEAN: Of course I tried. What do *you* think? Only there was a man in his office with him. I waited for one hour, two hours, but those bastards, it didn't make any difference to them, they just talked and laughed and slapped their bellies. (*Pause*.) I couldn't stand any more, so I left.

MARIE: You'll see the boss tomorrow, everything will work out, I'm sure of it. It's got to work out. (*Pause*.) I'll go with you if you want.

JEAN: So that's it, you think I can't talk for myself. Well, listen! You're wrong. All I need is the chance to talk to him. (*Laughing*.) The chance, just the chance!

MARIE (*embracing* JEAN): Listen to me! We won't die. Instead of making one blouse a day, I'll make two, that's all there is to it. And you register for relief. You'll find somebody to recommend you.

JEAN: Who?

MARIE: I don't know off hand, we have to look around.

JEAN (*getting up*): Thanks a lot. I'll spare you the trouble of asking your relatives.

MARIE: All right then, you try to register for relief without a recommendation.

JEAN: It's silly to go to the trouble. They don't want anything to do with me. Yeah! I know them! I'll wait for hours, everybody will go through, but me, they'll push me to the end of the line. They won't even see *me*. The others, they see them, they listen to them, but not me.

MARIE: And your little Marie, didn't she notice you? (*Pause*.) I'm here, Jean, right next to you.

JEAN: Yeah, you're there, but one day you won't be able to take it anymore, you'll feel like getting some air, and . . . you'll lose your respect for me. And me, that day . . . that day . . . (ZENNO *approaches*.)

MARIE (*pointing to* ZENNO): Who's that?

JEAN: Him? I don't know. Some miserable bastard.

ZENNO (*to* MARIE): Yeah, a miserable bastard . . . and who, if it weren't for your husband, would be worse off still. He'll tell you about it himself. *I* wouldn't know . . . (*Turning toward* JEAN, *who is tapping his foot impatiently*.) I swear to you that I had nothing to do with this . . . this thing . . . I didn't do . . . what they say. . . . It's simply a case of mistaken identity. . . . Anyway, when they see me, it's hard to . . . confuse. (*To* MARIE *and* JEAN.) Of course, I ran; what else could I do? Anybody would have done the same thing in my place. Finally, all the ones who . . . I didn't want . . . considering what I am . . .

MARIE (*to* JEAN): What's he talking about? What happened? I don't understand.

JEAN: What about me, do you think I know anything about this nonsense? (*Pause*.) Shall we go?

ZENNO: It's out of prejudice. Only out of prejudice. You really think that I don't need, to find a woman, any . . . (*Laughing*.) As if it were all that hard!

JEAN: We're not asking *you* anything. (*To* MARIE.) Are you coming, Marie?

MARIE (*supporting him*): Don't you want to rest for a few more minutes?

JEAN: No, I've got to go and deliver it. Otherwise, there'll be more bullshit; and bullshit, I've had enough of it. (*Pointing to the radio*.) After this one, let's put an end to this nonsense. (MARIE *helps* JEAN *put the radio on his shoulders*.)

ZENNO: Will you let me go with you? I'm not bothering you, I hope. I'll walk . . . a little ways behind. You understand, I'm . . . I wouldn't want to stay . . . completely out of the way. Yeah, on the street. . . . They could still. . . . You know. . . . But if there's two others, it's different. . . . Yeah, they'd recognize me from far away. . . . Because of . . . (*He points to his leg*.) You see. . . . A miserable cripple!

JEAN (*to* ZENNO): Are you going to leave us alone or not? (*To* MARIE.) Those bastards, they're always hanging around you! Always stuck to you! All alike! (JEAN *and* MARIE *exit*. ZENNO *follows them. Darkness*.)

RADIO (*in the dark*): Hoping to improve working conditions, and to arrive at a satisfactory solution to the urgent problems posed by the strike, the government has been forced to adopt a series of measures pertaining specifically to the refugee law. One law has just been passed, which states that refugees will no longer be able to be employed by public enterprises. Those who are currently employed by the said enterprises will be given notice at some as yet unspecified time in the near future.

SCENE 2

JEAN's *room. The lights go up. The room is a mess. It is poorly and sparsely furnished.* MARIE *walks about disconcertedly, then stops and combs her hair. The* RADIO *continues.*

RADIO: The law pertaining to the refugee statute applies, as far as the latest order is concerned, only to public enterprises. As a result, the heads of large private businesses, both industrial and commercial, are still authorized to recruit their personnel from any category whatsoever. (MARIE *turns the radio off and picks up her purse. Sound of footsteps. She puts down her purse.* JEAN *enters*.)

JEAN: I've just come from the welfare office.

MARIE: There's no reason to act like it's the end of the world. (*Pause*.) You're all dirty. What's happened to you now?

JEAN: They're taking away my allotment.

MARIE (*shrugging her shoulders*): Under what pretext?

JEAN: Huh! Pretexts, there's plenty of them! They either find some, or they make them up. (*Pause*.) I didn't punch in last week, so they say!

MARIE: And you didn't think of going to see the little cripple, the one who's always helped you?

JEAN: He's not there anymore. The measures were passed, and they got rid of him! This refugee business!

MARIE: Then here's your chance.

JEAN: You didn't ask me what happened.

MARIE: I'm listening.

JEAN: No, you're not listening. I know darn well you're not listening, but it doesn't make any difference. I'm gonna tell you anyway. There's no reason for me to get upset.

MARIE: All right then, don't get upset.

JEAN: I saw the new clerk. I tried to make him understand, to get his sympathy . . .

MARIE: And what did he tell you?

JEAN: I don't know, I didn't hear him. . . . All I understood was: "I can't do anything. . . . A man without family . . . too bad, just too bad . . ." And then somebody else came, he passed right by me as if I didn't even exist. The clerk leaned toward him and they started talking real low. That time, I didn't hear anything at all. To think they did it deliberately!

MARIE: You've said that a thousand times! It's always the same thing.

JEAN: Well! Get it into your head that today it wasn't the same thing. Today, I had nerve. I pounced on them, and punched one of them right in the mouth. It was crazy the way he bled. His nose bled for ages. That surprises you, doesn't it? (*Pause.*) Not much chance of getting any welfare benefits after that! (MARIE *gets ready to go out.*) What are you doing? You're going out?

MARIE: I have to go and deliver the blouse. I'm late enough as it is. If I don't leave right away, they won't give me any more work. (*She picks up the blouse, wraps it, and goes toward the door.*)

JEAN (*trembling*): You're not gonna leave, Marie. Not . . . not right now! (*The* MOTHER *enters. She is a woman of about fifty, her hair is a mess, and she is sloppily dressed.*)

MOTHER (*standing at the door*): What's going on, kids? (*She limps grotesquely.*) I see we're fighting, for a change . . . (*limping toward them*) Well, I've got some good news for you. But maybe you know what it is already.

JEAN (*facing* MARIE): What news?

MOTHER (*sitting down*): It seems that things are beginning to happen in the South. The refugees are in a pretty tight spot. In the past couple days, they've thrown out about a hundred (*laughing*) "untrainables." That made quite an impression on the others, so they took off at a fast pace, a gallop actually. What a mob on the highways! It must really be something!

MARIE: I have to go. (*She tries to get* JEAN's *attention.*)

MOTHER: When they've killed all of them, every last one of them, then maybe there'll be work for the poor people and the both of you will stop bickering. After all, work means money. And the money, that's what counts, kids! For everybody . . .

MARIE: For them just as much as for us. Then maybe they'll let them alone.

JEAN: What do you mean—let them alone? Do they ever let *me* alone? (MARIE *approaches the door again.*)

MOTHER (*getting up*): You're really in a hurry, dear. Are they waiting for you? A handsome refugee, maybe? (*Darkness.*)

ZENNO (*his voice in the dark, impersonal, almost unrecognizable, accompanied by the sound of a typewriter*): Taking into consideration the substantial decrease in the price of raw materials, a decrease recorded on all the markets and which, in light of past events, one has every reason to believe will benefit the national interest more and more . . .

SCENE 3

ZENNO's *room. The lights go up. Furniture in bad taste, neither rich nor poor.* ZENNO *walks back and forth with some papers in his hand.* MARIE, *at the right, is typing.*

ZENNO (*in a businesslike, confident voice continues his dictation*): The general interest demands . . . (MARIE *types.*) You got that? (*Pause.*) The immediate selling of all remaining stocks. (*He stops to think. Pause.*) Therefore, we are ready to buy from you, without further delay, all of the stocks which we know to be in your possession. (MARIE *types.*) If no agreement can be reached between us, we will regretfully be . . .

MARIE: (*spelling*): Regretfully . . .

ZENNO: What's the matter, my little Marie? Aren't you getting it? Tired, little Marie? (*He kisses her.*)

MARIE: Yeah.

ZENNO: A little mad about having to work with Zenno, huh? Even though Zenno does all he can to make his little Marie happy.

MARIE: Yeah.

ZENNO: I know, you've got it in for me . . . You think I hired you as a secretary so I could save money. But that wasn't the only reason, my dear, not the only reason.

MARIE: Did I say anything about it?

ZENNO: You ought to know that what counts for me is having my little darling there, right there, always nice, always happy.

MARIE: I know.

ZENNO: Don't be sad like that. We're going to get rich, both of us, and fast. You'll see! As soon as we've gotten out of this rotten hole where we're never happy. I'll have a fantastic job, a job that everybody will wish *they* had. Come on, things have gotten better lately, haven't they?

MARIE: Of course.

ZENNO: But I'm forgetting the most important thing . . . You know, I checked out . . . (*raising his voice*) certain reliable sources. (*Pause.*) The measures don't apply to just everybody. There are refugees and then there are refugees . . . Since I'm a specialist, I don't have to worry about anything. (*Pause.*) Oh, of course it's not because they feel sorry for us. If they could, they'd kill off every last one of us, right down to the last man. But the thing is, they can't, because they need specialists. Poor bastards, what would they do without us? Right? (*Pause.*) Let's finish the letter, O.K.?

MARIE: O.K.

ZENNO (*continuing to dictate*): We will regretfully be obliged to seize the aforementioned stocks immediately. (*He laughs.*) Kindly agree . . . You know the rest, I'll let you do it. (MARIE *types. Long pause.*)

MARIE: I feel completely alone . . . Tell me, do you really need me? Do you love me?

ZENNO: Very much, my love; very, very much! But do *you* love me?

MARIE (*tired*): Yes.

ZENNO: A lot?

MARIE: As much as I can. (ZENNO *goes over to* MARIE *and caresses her shoulder, balancing himself on his good foot. The* MOTHER *enters.*)

MOTHER: Forgive me for pestering you. I really hate to do it, but I said to myself that little Marie would understand.

ZENNO: What do you want here? (*Pause; then, bluntly.*) How did you get the address? Is your son playing detective these days?

MARIE: Did something happen to . . . ?

MOTHER: No, I swear to you, he doesn't know a thing. You don't have anything to be afraid of. I want . . , I've come . . . to . . . talk to my little Marie.

ZENNO: And you would have preferred to have her all to yourself.

MOTHER: No, no, of course not, just the opposite . . . I didn't have the nerve to even hope for that. Just to find you at home! To see you busy! . . .

ZENNO: Oh, really, and it's just by accident that . . . (*Pause.*) Are you sure you didn't tell anybody you were coming?

MOTHER: I swear, honestly, I swear I didn't . . . My poor Jean . . . to be scared of him! As if he had any strength . . . (*Looking around her.*) Hey, you really have a nice setup here! And nice and warm, too. Must have cost you . . . (*admiringly*) . . . a fortune.

ZENNO (*laughing*): Yeah, well, you can tell your son that Marie didn't get shortchanged in the deal. (MARIE *drums nervously on the table.*)

MOTHER: Poor Jean! I'm sure she hasn't lost anything! . . . I love him dearly, my Jean, but I know. . , I know . . . Only I don't think it's all his fault. It's his health. When you haven't got your health . . . I know what it's like, young man.

MARIE (*abruptly*): Is Jean sick?

MOTHER: Oh, just tired as usual. You know, diet, and poor blood, they all take their toll. Poor Jean!

ZENNO: Pardon me, Ma'am, but . . . (*Businesslike.*) . . . I was just dictating some letters and . . .

MOTHER: And you'd like me to leave you alone. I understand, Mr. Zenno, you don't have to make excuses. I understand perfectly, but, before I leave, I'd like, if you don't mind . . .

ZENNO: Fine, but stop wasting time. What's up?

MOTHER: It's about Jean. (ZENNO *makes a gesture of discouragement.*) Jean was sick, you know, and right after being sick, he lost his job; a job that he wasn't really cut out for. Isn't that right, my little Marie, that job tired him out so much . . . But it was better than nothing.

ZENNO: And what did you come here to tell me all this for?

MOTHER: Please don't get mad, Mr. Zenno. I'm just rambling on a little . . . I realize . . . (MARIE *gets up and paces.*) It's just that I don't have the nerve. But I'll get it, I'm coming to it. Aren't I, my little Marie, I can put it straight to Mr. Zenno, can't I?

MARIE: You can, if you want to.

MOTHER (*kneeling down almost right in front of* ZENNO): Dear Mr. Zenno, listen, please. I'm begging you. Jean . . . (MARIE *stops.*) doesn't hold anything against you . . . He's not a bad guy. (ZENNO *is growing impatient.*) We don't know what to do anymore, who to turn to, either one of us. Try to understand! He has to take care of his poor mother. It isn't easy . . . you know I'm a burden for him, Mr. Zenno, a heavy burden, but he's always carried it bravely, I'll say that much for him.

ZENNO: Do you want money?

MOTHER (*after a slight hesitation*): No, no, although . . . I came to ask you . . .

ZENNO: For work?

MOTHER: Yes, that's it. Work!

MARIE: Jean will never take it.

ZENNO: And why not?

MOTHER: Any kind, it doesn't matter where! We're not fussy, either one of us. And then, you know, he isn't stupid, my Jean. Helpless, unable to find a job, granted, but once he's got one . . . he'll do it, and he'll do a good job. A good worker, an excellent worker.

MARIE: But this is ridiculous. I don't want any part of it.

MOTHER: And why not, my little Marie? He's not mad at you, you know. He understood very well that it just couldn't possibly work out. He's not stupid, you know, not in the least. (*To* ZENNO.) Now, my good Mr. Zenno, are you willing to try to get him something? You know a lot of people. They listen to you and respect you. (MARIE, *growing increasingly nervous, goes toward* ZENNO.)

ZENNO (*drawing* MARIE *aside*): O.K. You can count on me. We're leaving on some business tomorrow; but I'll talk to one of my colleagues about him. Don't worry, you'll have an answer as soon as possible.

MOTHER: Oh thank you so much, Mr. Zenno, my dear Mr. Zenno. How can I ever really thank you? My little Marie, I always knew it. I've always said that Mr. Zenno was a good man. There're good people everywhere. What difference does it make if they're from here or somewhere else? (*Darkness.*)

SCENE 4

JEAN's *room. In the dark, one can make out* JEAN *in bed. The lights go up with the entrance of the* MOTHER.

MOTHER: Jean! I've got some good news, some really great news for you.

JEAN: What's the matter now?

MOTHER: Don't even try to figure it out, you'll never guess! (*She laughs.*)

JEAN: Not so loud. You're making me deaf.

MOTHER: What do you mean, not so loud? When you're happy, you laugh, that's no big thing. (*Pause.*) From now on, we will no longer have to tighten our belts. By this time next week everything will have changed, and thanks to whom? Thanks to your old mother.

JEAN: What the hell are you blabbering about now?

MOTHER: Just that my little Jean is going to have a job, and that he'll be happy once he's got it!

JEAN: Me, a job? Doing what? I'm being supported by my mother. A great setup. And now that I have it, I'm not going to give it up, right?

MOTHER: Always the same! I know what it is, you're still sad about Marie. But who ever told you she'd never come back? You can't predict the future, you know, Jean. The future is just totally unpredictable. Once you've got a job, that's when things change . . .

JEAN: What do you want to change? I had a job before. You might say that it straightened things out.

MOTHER: Well, don't have a fit about it. Maybe she isn't all that happy with this . . . Zenno. Sure, she has it easy, she isn't short of anything, but . . .

JEAN (*interrupting her*): Happy or unhappy, what do you know about it? You wouldn't be the one she'd confide in.

MOTHER: Maybe. Anyway, I've seen her.

JEAN (*getting up*): You saw Marie? Where? When? Was she here? (*Shaking the* MOTHER.) Are you gonna tell me?

MOTHER: Now don't get upset, Jean, I'm going to tell you all about it. Just be a little patient. Well, yes, I've seen her. I went to pay them . . . her . . . a little visit, to ask her . . . to ask them . . . (*Provokingly.*) Yeah, just imagine, I even saw Mr. Zenno. He's got a great job, this Mr. Zenno, an easy as hell job. (*She laughs lightly.*) Do you realize that he's taken over private enterprises! (*Pause.*) I thought that he could at least be of some use to you in something . . . So I asked him . . .

JEAN: You mean to say you had the nerve to . . . ? Ask him for work for me? You bitch! (*He shakes the* MOTHER *again.*)

MOTHER: Oh, so this is what you get for telling the truth. That'll teach me. I didn't have to tell you anything at all about it, my boy, not a thing. And as for your job, you never would have known where it came from. It's just that *I* don't like secrecy. (*Pause.*) You know, Mr. Zenno even offered me money, but I didn't take it . . .

JEAN: I don't give a damn about you. But how the hell could Marie do a thing like this? . . . How did she have the nerve to think for one minute . . . and him? Then what! A settlement for damages! That takes the cake! The first time, it was to save my life . . . that could have gone on like that, but now, now . . . (*He is trembling.*)

MOTHER: What's the matter, Jean? You're all covered with sweat! Come on, don't be mad at me. I did it for you, for my little baby. I thought I was doing a good thing under the circumstances. Let's just say that I was wrong. It happens to everybody. You know, it took nerve . . . You know, to talk to those people, a thing like that's never pleasant. (*JEAN has sat down, still trembling. The* MOTHER *goes over to the radio.*) Shall I turn it on for a while? That'll take our minds off things. (*She switches it on;* JEAN *doesn't move.*)

RADIO: They are officially refuting the rumors which say that the government intended to revise the law authorizing the retention of certain qualified personnel in their particular field. The refugees having dis-

played an exceptional degree of competence . . .

JEAN (*violently turning off the radio*): No, absolutely no exceptions! (*Crying.*) Everybody goes! (*Darkness.*)

SCENE 5

The square. The lights go up. DARBON *is standing up on the platform.* JEAN *is seated on his left.*

DARBON (*facing the public*): When we say that the exception laws must be maintained, we do so in complete knowledge of the facts.

We aren't challenging the actual right of public dissent, we are merely preventing the abuses of it. Certain compromises are necessary. One is completely justified in saying that the refugees who have distinguished themselves through their abilities, or through the rank which they've been able to attain, are totally capable of practicing their professions. To apply the same ruling to all of the refugees, no matter who, would condone all of the violence, approve all of the excesses, it would throw open the doors to anarchy. And once those doors have been opened, who will be able to close them? Once the country has become a prey of disorder, who will be able to maintain its valor?

I want everyone to understand my position completely. We aren't taking up the defense of a minority group whose faults we know only too well. We are only coming out in defense of several individuals who have displayed qualities of initiative and perseverance which the country has always needed, and which, today more than ever, we cannot deprive it of without the fear of doing it a great injustice. (*JEAN rises and gets ready to take the floor.* DARBON *extends his hand in his direction: he still has something to say.*) As for the others, those rotten little swindlers who are sponging off of you, leeches who are bleeding you dry, it's up to you to track them down and render them harmless. (*Lowering his voice.*) The powers that be will know how to look the other way.

JEAN (*facing the public*): My friends, I know

what's on your minds, and that you don't have the courage to speak up. But I will say it for all of you.

What is making Darbon address you today? Fear. (DARBON *makes a gesture of protest.*) It isn't wisdom that we're lacking, it's courage. Of course, if we don't make a distinction among the refugees, if we strike out at every one of them, we run the risk of turning all those whom they've succeeded in buying against us; but I think that we can avoid this risk. How? By striking out hard enough. Rich and poor, they're all alike! They're all ready to steal your livelihood, to chase after your wives. As for the poor, you know where to find them, you can make them pay up. When it comes to the rich though, what can you do? Nothing. They've got money, they can go wherever they want, take off, disappear, live in peace under an assumed name, because after all, names can be bought too. Like everything else! They've taken everything from you . . . even your honor. So if I ask that they strike down all of the refugees without making any distinctions, it's . . . , it's so I can give you back your honor. (*Enter two* GUARDS *pushing ahead of them a* YOUNG MAN *with a thin face, and almost in rags.*)

YOUNG MAN: But I've already told you that it isn't true . . .

FIRST GUARD: Yeah, we know the old song and dance.

JEAN (*to the* GUARD): What did he do?

FIRST GUARD: He's going to tell you what. (*To the* YOUNG MAN.) Well, then, aren't you coming up with any ideas, huh? (*He hits him.*)

SECOND GUARD: Supposing we give you some. (*He hits him.*)

DARBON: What's going on, anyway? You might fill us in on things.

FIRST GUARD (*stammering*): We were . . . we came for that.

YOUNG MAN: No, I won't let you . . . It's mine . . . mine. It's the opposite, exactly the opposite.

DARBON: The opposite of what? You might express yourself more clearly.

YOUNG MAN: If they'd only let me talk! I've been trying for hours on end but. . . .

FIRST GUARD: So we're upsetting you, huh?

SECOND GUARD: Oh, we're getting in your way. (*He hits the* YOUNG MAN.)

JEAN: You can beat him up later. He hasn't talked yet.

SECOND GUARD (*dumbfounded*): Huh, he hasn't talked?

DARBON: This is exactly what I can't stand. (*To the* YOUNG MAN.) You can't really tell if you're on the level. (*He laughs lightly.*)

YOUNG MAN (*to* JEAN): Look at me. Do I look like a man who . . .

FIRST GUARD: The way you look you'd be better off not even talking about it. (*Laughter.*)

DARBON: I'll admit that, if you trust in appearances . . . (*Turning towards* JEAN.) Well, what does Jean Rist think about it?

JEAN: I don't think anything, seeing as how I don't know anything. (*To the* YOUNG MAN.) Come here. What's going on? What are they accusing you of? (*The* YOUNG MAN *takes a step forward. The* GUARDS *hold him close to them.*)

FIRST GUARD: If you let . . .

JEAN: I'm not letting him.

DARBON: Yeah, but I *am* letting him.

JEAN (*to the* FIRST GUARD): All right then, quick.

FIRST GUARD: He was running like an idiot. We caught him, and then do you know what he did?

SECOND GUARD: He tried to give us money.

FIRST GUARD: No two ways about it.

SECOND GUARD: We don't even have to say that his little bribe didn't work.

FIRST GUARD: Money, money, that's all these dogs know.

SECOND GUARD: And they think we're just like them.

FIRST GUARD: I bet we'd be in for a big surprise if we searched him.

SECOND GUARD: Shall we search him?

YOUNG MAN: Go ahead, search me and you'll see for yourselves that I haven't got any money, not one red cent! I haven't even earned a cent for months . . . not even welfare . . .

FIRST GUARD: There you are: the usual complaints!

JEAN: Shut your trap! Let him talk.

DARBON (*to the* YOUNG MAN): So then, you don't have any money! No money at all! Well then, what do you live on? Your wits, no doubt. But what sort of wits?

JEAN (*to the* GUARDS): All right then. Why did you bring him in? Because he had too much dough? Or didn't he have enough?

DARBON: That's a significant enough detail.

JEAN (*to* DARBON): Who's telling you any different?

FIRST GUARD: We didn't arrest him just for that . . . He's got . . . (*Loud and stupid laughter.*)

JEAN: He's got what?

FIRST GUARD: Well, uh, he's got . . . (*He looks at the* SECOND GUARD *for advice. The* GUARD *gives him an affirmative sign.*) He's taken the wife of a . . . friend of ours.

JEAN (*going toward the* YOUNG MAN): Well now! . . .

YOUNG MAN (*to the* GUARDS): How can you say a thing like that? (*The* FIRST GUARD *strikes the* YOUNG MAN, *the* SECOND GUARD *holds him by putting his hand on his mouth.*)

SECOND GUARD: A poor bastard who's always sick and practically blind . . .

FIRST GUARD: One fine day, he finds himself all alone . . .

SECOND GUARD: And never hears anything of her again!

FIRST GUARD (*pointing to the* YOUNG MAN): She took off with that thing there.

SECOND GUARD: When the old fellow found out, he didn't know what the hell to do.

FIRST GUARD: So he asked us to help him out.

YOUNG MAN (*succeeding in freeing himself*): I swear to you . . . It isn't true. I haven't done any of the things they say. They must be taking me for somebody else. It isn't possible . . . If I was running it was because . . . You only have to look at me. (*The* GUARDS *make him keep quiet.*)

JEAN: Look at you! And what else! I've seen enough of you, my good fellow. (*The* YOUNG MAN *tries to talk, they shake him.*) Not one more word, do you hear me, you're wasting your time; I already know what you're going to tell us. (*Imitating* ZENNO's *voice.*) "If I was running, it was . . . because they were running after me . . . Anybody would have done the same thing in my place." No, not anybody. Just you people! Nobody but you people!

YOUNG MAN: You don't know . . . (*The* GUARDS *make the* YOUNG MAN *keep quiet again. The* SHOPKEEPER *enters.*)

FIRST GUARD: And he still wants to make up excuses.

SHOPKEEPER: Hey, I recognize him! Of course it's him. (*To the* GUARDS.) That woman, it's the optician's wife, the one who just went bankrupt! Poor guy! She was the only thing he had left!

JEAN (*to the* YOUNG MAN, *who wants to talk*): Huh, so he had nobody but her and not a cent to boot! So you wormed your way in, you spent some money, and she followed you. (*To the* GUARDS.) Bring that bastard over here. I think there's room in the prison camps.

FIRST GUARD (*laughing and grabbing hold of the* YOUNG MAN): If there isn't any, we'll make some.

SHOPKEEPER (*laughing*): They can move over a little! They're used to it.

YOUNG MAN (*whom the* GUARDS *are leading away*): You'll be sorry.

JEAN: That'll surprise me. (*He goes, trembling, sits down again at his place.* DARBON *laughs.*)

SECOND GUARD: Let's go!

DARBON (*putting his hand on* JEAN's *shoulder*): I always knew that our differences were of a purely theoretical type. (*Darkness.*)

RADIO (*in the darkness*): The new law which includes the measures regarding the refugee statute has just been passed by unanimous vote.

The measures previously mentioned will become effective at a date to be announced in the near future and the public will be informed of them immediately.

SCENE 6

ZENNO's *room. The lights go up. Large room, smartly furnished.* ZENNO *is bent over the radio set.*)

RADIO (*getting louder and louder*): Directors of large industrial and commercial enterprises are required to declare, within the month, the refugees that they have among their personnel. The number of refugees that they will be allowed to keep in their employ will not be able to go beyond a certain percentage, a percentage which has not yet been determined, but which will almost certainly be very small.

The directors who fail to comply with this formality will be denied all privileges and will risk being expropriated in a period which will vary from one to fourteen months. Also, the refugees who have not been declared will be sent to the camps immediately. (MARIE *enters, elegantly dressed.*)

ZENNO: Marie . . . I'm finished.

MARIE (*switching off the radio*): What are you talking about? Who's finished?

ZENNO: Me! Me!

MARIE: I don't get it.

ZENNO: Marie, my little Marie, it's terrible. What'll become of us? (*Pointing to the radio.*) If you'd heard what they said! I knew it would happen some day . . . , but I didn't want to know it. I was doing all I could . . . and now, here it is . . .

MARIE: What is it? Are they arresting all the refugees? Are they looking for you?

ZENNO: Not yet, not yet . . . , but they will be, in no time. Before we have time to turn around. Marie, they want to stop us from working, from breathing . . . They don't want anybody anymore, not even the specialists . . . nobody. Of course, they're talking about a . . . (*Despairingly.*) percentage. But I know them, they're lying. It's just to get us used to it, just to get us used to it little by little. They'll only let us in peace when they've got every little bit of our hides . . . They start out by reducing us to poverty, it's a good line. From there, it's so easy . . . When you don't have any money, you don't have anything, you aren't anything, they come and get you, and it's all over . . . Marie, my darling, what's going to happen to us?

MARIE: It's not as bad as all that. You've got some money, now, you've earned it. You can live in peace for a long time, for years and years, then . . .

ZENNO: Money! You think I've got money. I don't have all that much, my dear; I've handed you my fair share of bullshit. I had to make you feel secure, you know. (*Pause.*) At any rate, I'd never have enough to . . .

MARIE: To what?

ZENNO (*trembling*): To bribe one of them . . . , to get one on my side and not to

have to be afraid . . . never be afraid again!

MARIE: Money! That's the only word I ever hear out of your mouth. But even if you do pay somebody off, what's to keep them from turning on you later on, because the very guy who . . .

ZENNO: Yeah, you're right, I can't be sure . . . You can't tell ahead of time. Nothing . . . ahead of time . . . not a thing. (*He cries.*) Marie, my darling, say something, tell me what to do. Please.

MARIE: I already told you what I thought.

ZENNO (*tearfully*): What did you tell me? I don't know anymore what you told me . . . Are you mad? Because I've . . . , because I've admitted that I'd gladly . . . pay. . . . Is that it?

MARIE: It's not just because of that.

ZENNO: All right then, what is it?

MARIE: It's just that . . . I shouldn't ever have moved in with you.

ZENNO: And you had to wait until today to tell me?

MARIE: I know. I shouldn't have; it's not exactly the perfect moment. But it's stronger than I am. Some things are stronger than we are. What can you do? Even yesterday, and the other day in the car, you should have seen . . .

ZENNO: I only see one thing. I see that you're sorry you gave him up, your little good-for-nothing! The only thing is that you couldn't see ahead of time way back then, that he'd be able to buy you dresses and lined coats . . . , flowered silk lining, at that! And it would have lasted longer! Jean Rist, the village revolutionary: a sure thing!

MARIE: He never would have done . . . what he did if I hadn't left him. He lost his head because I wasn't there anymore. Oh, if I'd only known!

ZENNO: If you had known that . . . (*Raising his voice.*) the tables were going to turn, you wouldn't have taken off with a dog, a sick one at that. That's for sure!

MARIE: You liar! That's not what . . .

ZENNO: No, I'm not a liar. Why do you want to make yourself out to be better than you are?

MARIE: How can I make you see?

ZENNO: Make me see what? (*He walks, then*

stops abruptly.) Marie, my darling, will you help me?

MARIE: *Me*, help you? What can *I* do?

ZENNO (*walking around her*): Listen, I have an idea . . . My little Marie, since you were saying . . . seeing as how you wanted to prove to me that . . . (*kneeling down*) well then, you're going to help me. Without you, you know, your poor Zenno can't take care of himself, my little darling. Only good for the camps!

MARIE: What do you want?

ZENNO: To go away, far away. I'm scared, my little Marie, so damned scared. I know, you don't see it, can't understand it. That's because nothing can happen to you. But it isn't the same with me. For me, from one minute to the next . . .

MARIE: What can I . . . ?

ZENNO: You can do everything, darling, absolutely everything. They can't say no to you for anything! All you have to do is be there, and they'll hang around looking at you and admiring you. Don't say it isn't so, you know it as well as me . . . Just to have his little Marie near him, to keep her around, what wouldn't anybody do?

MARIE: What are you getting at?

ZENNO: You know what, you know exactly what I'm getting at. My little Marie, you know your Zenno. What could he ask you for?

MARIE (*arrogantly*): To go find Jean, why the hell not?

ZENNO: That's right!

MARIE: What, you mean you're not afraid of him anymore?

ZENNO: And be nice to him like before . . . , and explain to him . . . I'm not asking any big thing: just a pass, a simple pass! He can get one; he'd do it for you.

MARIE: So I go and see Jean, after what I've . . . what you . . . and I talk to him for you. Aren't you ashamed?

ZENNO: Yes, a little bit, a tiny bit. (*Shouting.*) But I'm not as ashamed as all that!

MARIE: I figured as much.

ZENNO: Would you like to see me reduced to nothing, your Zenno? (MARIE *gestures impatiently*.) I'm not exaggerating, you know. If I stay here like this, just waiting, they'll take everything away from me, and then, when they don't have anything more to take . . . Marie, my little Marie, you

were saying how he took it so hard, so I thought that, if he had you back . . . , that if he saw you again . . .

MARIE: That if he saw me again?

ZENNO: That, maybe, he wouldn't want you to go away anymore . . . You'd be happier with him than with me. Times have changed. You can't do anything about the time you're living in. We're all helpless. (*He kneels down in front of* MARIE.) Come on, my little Marie, will you do it? Can't you see, I'm trusting you . . . I know you'll never tell him where I am . . . no matter what happens . . . ; everything will be arranged by a middleman . . . (*Going toward* MARIE.) But I'm not just thinking of myself! Of you too. If you think for one moment that I don't know how much it costs you . . . (*Pointing to his bad leg.*) Not just because of that . . . I'm not very pretty to look at, I know, my love, not very pretty . . . and not exactly straight. (*He cries.*)

MARIE (*putting her hand on* ZENNO's *head*): You don't have to say that.

ZENNO: Then you'll do it?

MARIE: O.K., I'll go. But I don't know if he'll do it. I don't know anything anymore.

ZENNO (*hugging* MARIE's *knees; she disengages herself*): Oh, thank you, thank you, thank you, my darling! I was sure that, for poor little Zenno . . . (*Changing his voice.*) Of course he will, naturally, if you're there. I forgot . . . I wanted to tell you something else, to ask you . . . one last thing. O.K.? You'll have to . . . if you will . . . , if only you will . . . come with me to the border. (*Terrified.*) If you don't come it'll be bad for both of us, I just know it . . . You see, don't you, you're not a refugee, you'll be able to talk to them, put a word in for me. But not me! Not me! They can take my papers away from me, tear them up on me. With them, you never know. (*Pause.*) It's not a long trip. Two days at the most! (*Darkness.*)

RADIO (*in the dark*): From now on, the aiding and abetting of refugees by citizens will be liable to severe penalties. Any refugee who makes an attempt to bribe an official, or escapes from a camp, or leaves the country illegally, or for any other reason, will run the risk of death.

Any citizen who is persuaded or bribed

by a refugee will lose his civil rights and be sentenced to prison. The term of the sentence will vary proportionately with the severity of the offense.

SCENE 7

JEAN's *room. The lights go up.* JEAN *and* MARIE *are standing.*

JEAN: What's said is said. He'll get it, his little pass! Huh, don't you think I'm high enough to get him one? That's what we're gonna find out. But anyway, I can't promise you what'll happen to him after that. He hasn't gotten to the border yet, your little friend. Paper or not, with his kisser!

MARIE: That's exactly why . . . I swore to him and you promised me too . . .

JEAN: Well, after all, I hope he saves his own neck. Anyway, it'll just delay things for a while. That won't stop him from kicking off, and fast. There'll be camps everywhere. They'll never run fast enough. It's a great service you're doing him!

MARIE: Jean, tell me . . . do you forgive me . . . For everything?

JEAN: Of course I forgive you. That was no life you had with me. (MARIE *cries.*) Nothing to eat, freezing all winter long, and then my carrying on every day. Not to mention the old lady.

MARIE: What'll she say if she sees me here again? (*The* MOTHER *appears in the doorway. She watches* JEAN *and* MARIE, *who don't see her.*)

JEAN: Not a thing. (*Pause.*) You know, things have changed. Now, *I'm* the one who's boss. As far as money's concerned, I have as much as I want, whenever I need it. (*Laughing.*) I just take it every chance I get.

MARIE: Jean, I wouldn't want you to think . . .

JEAN: That you came here for my money? No, Marie, I don't think that. You came back because one fine day you saw your Zenno for what he was, and is, the dirty bastard! (MARIE *is still crying.*) Don't cry, Marie . . . it really gets to me. (*The* MOTHER, *who had remained until now immobile in the doorway, goes toward* JEAN *and* MARIE.)

MOTHER: Good morning, children! (*To* MARIE.) You know, my dear, I know about everything, Jean told me all about it.

JEAN: What? What did I tell you?

MOTHER: He doesn't keep anything from his mommy, my Jean. And anyway, his mother would have found out about it. She knows what's going on!

JEAN (*to the* MOTHER): Get out. (*Taking a threatening step toward her.*) I'm warning you.

MOTHER (*taking a step toward* MARIE, *who is tense with fear*): Well, now, we finally remembered we had a husband, we come to see him . . . to console him a bit. And then we take advantage of the occasion to show him that we did pretty good for ourselves in the meantime!

JEAN (*grabbing the* MOTHER's *arm*): Are you going to shut up and clear the hell out of here?

MOTHER (*to* MARIE): Am I wrong? Do we have better reasons? Do we want to patch things up, begin . . . (*laughing*) a new life together? (JEAN, *who had moved away, comes back toward the* MOTHER, *almost threatening. The* MOTHER *crosses her arms and looks him right in the eyes; he stops, trembling.*) One of the poor in spirit, our Jean, that's what we tell ourselves! He'd be willing to take her back. And seeing as how these poor bastard refugees are having such problems! Well, then, why not?

MARIE: You've got no right to tell me . . . (JEAN, *who is trembling more and more, drops down onto a chair.*)

MOTHER: And why don't I have the right?

MARIE: Because you . . . you . . .

MOTHER: Because I went and asked your rotten bastard for a job for Jean? But that was for Jean! Because he was hungry! Hungry, do you understand? Nothing on the table! (*She taps her fingers.*) Of course I didn't have to go around begging for crumbs! Only because it was for Jean! But as for you, it's for the other guy, the yellow-belly, that you came here! To work things out between you two! (*Pushing* MARIE.) Admit it!

MARIE: No! Not for us two! (*Shouting.*) Jean!

MOTHER (*pointing to* JEAN): If you think that Jean is going to shut me up, you must be out of your mind, my little one. (*Pause.*)

Poor Jean! Look at him. You've made a hell of a mess out of him.

MARIE: Jean, make her shut up. Please. Do it for me.

JEAN (*pushing the* MOTHER): You're gonna get the hell out of here. Do you understand?

MOTHER (*pleading, taking a step forward*): People like them, you can't get rid of them! They stick to you like glue! (*Laughing and turning toward* MARIE.) Isn't that so, little one? (*To* JEAN.) At any rate, you should know that well enough, you say it in every speech. (*To* MARIE.) At least he makes the speeches! And they applaud him! (*She applauds.*) Everybody! He makes a real uproar! (*Shouting.*) Long live Jean Rist! Death to the dogs! Every last one of them! No exceptions! And their bitches with them!

JEAN (*shouting*): That's enough!

MOTHER (*to* MARIE): Come on now, you know darn well what he'll do with his little piece of paper! (*Imitating* ZENNO's *voice.*) "Just look at it, my pass! It was Jean Rist who got it for me, Jean Rist who does all the yelling! It's thanks to him . . ." (*She puts out her hand and makes a gesture with her fingers which means money.*)

MARIE: She's a liar! He won't do a thing like that! Jean, I know him, I'm sure of it. (*Darkness.*)

SCENE 8

The country. The lights go up dimly. A winter night. A border sign with an arrow. Downstage, a large rock. ZENNO *enters, dressed in a large coat, leaning on* MARIE.

ZENNO: I can't go another step, my love, not another step. Ouuuuuu! It's dragging! My poor leg . . . (*Shivering.*) Can't we sit down for a minute?

MARIE: If you want to. (*He sits down on the rock.*)

ZENNO: What are we doing, my little Marie?

MARIE: We're doing what you wanted to do. We're going to the border.

ZENNO: I don't know, my darling Marie, I don't know anymore. Your poor Zenno doesn't know anymore. (*Shivering.*) He isn't sure about anything anymore, anything at all.

MARIE: Would you like us to turn back, maybe?

ZENNO: Yeah, maybe . . . My darling Marie, you don't have to take it out on me. How could I know that things were going to get so bad? And so fast, so darn fast!

MARIE: You have your little pass! What are you afraid of now?

ZENNO: Yeah, I have one, but . . .

MARIE: Don't whine all the time! (*Pause.*) You've already shown the pass, ten, twenty times, and they didn't stop you, did they?

ZENNO: That doesn't mean a thing, not a thing. One time they let you go, and then the next time . . . The waiter, at the inn . . . , the look he gave me!

MARIE: Is that the first time anybody's ever looked at you like that?

ZENNO: Don't make fun of your poor Zenno, Marie, this isn't the time for it, it isn't the time . . . Oh! Ouch!

MARIE: Is it hurting you?

ZENNO: Yeah, it hurts. (*Pause.*) And, that isn't all . . . It isn't . . . , I don't think it's exactly right. This paper's funny. How come it only has one stamp on it, and not a couple? Do you see?

MARIE: You don't trust it because it was Jean who got it for you, admit it.

ZENNO (*whining*): I didn't say that, Marie. What are you putting words in my mouth for?

MARIE: Let's get going, O.K.?

ZENNO: Get going where? (*Pause.*) My little Marie!

MARIE: I'm listening.

ZENNO: Do you really think it's safe? . . .

MARIE: To stay here? Absolutely not.

ZENNO (*rising*): No, not to stay here, to leave; to stick at it, in spite of the news, the way things are changing . . . What the radio says . . . It's terrible! "Immediately apprehended, shot right away." If I had only known!

MARIE: What could you have done? (*Pause.*) Think about me for a change. I didn't have to come with you, for one thing. And I did it anyway. It wasn't easy.

ZENNO: Of course, of course I'm thinking about you, about you too, of course. My darling, maybe it would be better . . .

MARIE (*angrily*): To go back? No.

ZENNO: I don't know, I'm asking you.

MARIE: You're going to get out of here, and I'm leaving you at the border. We'll do what we decided on.

ZENNO: I get it, you want to get rid of your poor Zenno. You jilt him at the border . . . maybe a little bit before the border; and then you head for home, for his home, to clap for *him*. He speaks so well, this Jean Rist! Whenever it's a question of killing one of them, one of those filthy dogs, he's right there. We can go, we're going. No risks at all!

MARIE: But it's thanks to him . . . You're just too disgusting.

ZENNO (*kneeling down quickly in front of* MARIE): Tell me, my little Marie, do you want, are you really going to . . . go back to him, be with him again? . . . Tell me, he's waiting for you, and you . . .

MARIE: I don't know, I don't know anything. (*Slight noise in the wings.*)

ZENNO (*getting up again quickly*): Do you hear that?

MARIE: No, not a thing.

ZENNO: Something moved. God! Marie, they've seen me.

MARIE: You're imagining things.

ZENNO: They saw us, I know it, I'm sure of it. They're following me. They're watching me. Oh! Why did I ever listen to you? (MARIE *bursts out laughing.*) What are we doing here? We've got to hide. Quick, Marie! Faster! (*He crouches down.* MARIE *doesn't move. Noises continue in the wings.*) Naturally, you don't give a damn. (*Shouting.*) You aren't the one who's a refugee, you're not taking any chances. (*Gunshots coming from the wings.* MARIE *screams and falls.* ZENNO *feels his own body to make sure he hasn't been shot, then kneels down in front of* MARIE. *Darkness.*)

RADIO (*in the dark*): Persons wishing to aid the Government with its public health movement are asked to contact the Bureau of Information in their neighborhood. They will be kept up to date on their progress, in their own specific category.

SCENE 9

DARBON's *office. The lights go up.* DARBON *is seated at his desk.* ZENNO *is standing in front of him.*

DARBON: I'm Darbon. (*Pause.*) You're alleging that you were using a pass given to you by Jean Rist?

ZENNO: That's not exactly what I meant, but . . .

DARBON: All right then, why did you mention this pass? And give a name?

ZENNO: Because I thought that . . . it was the only way . . . because I wanted you . . . wanted to see you, to talk to you . . . (*Almost shouting.*) in person!

DARBON: One doesn't usually ask for a pass unless one intends to . . . cross (*He laughs.*) a border, for instance.

ZENNO: I mean . . .

DARBON: Why did you want to leave us?

ZENNO: I didn't say I wanted to leave . . . All I had was a paper that would let me, in case . . .

DARBON: Maybe you wanted to leave because you felt uncomfortable in our country?

ZENNO: No, not at all uncomfortable, not a bit. But naturally, like all the . . . other refugees, I thought . . .

DARBON: That you might get hurt here one of these days? Whereas, now, you don't think that anymore. And why not?

ZENNO: Because . . .

DARBON: Because you just heard the statements on the radio?

ZENNO: Yes, it seems to me that . . . I know quite a few people in the broadcasting field . . . So, I thought that I might be able to do you some important favors, in the future!

DARBON: Let's take this in chronological order, O.K.? First tell me about the past, I'm referring to (*Insistent.*) your past.

ZENNO: I'm . . . a specialist . . . , I used to be a commercial advisor until . . .

DARBON: Until . . . ?

ZENNO: Until the measures which . . . well, you know. (DARBON *laughs lightly.*) I was earning my living quite honorably; without exploiting anybody at all.

DARBON: It would have bothered you to be an exploiter. Now that's a principle that does you great honor. (*He laughs lightly again.* ZENNO *tries to imitate him.*)

ZENNO: Of course. One manages as best as one can. And then, there's the matter . . . of intuition.

DARBON: Would you say you have intuition, generally speaking, that is?

ZENNO: I . . . I don't know.

DARBON: Do you know that it isn't such a good idea to come to see me using Jean Rist's name? That name isn't always a recommendation.

ZENNO: I . . . I know. But, as I've already said, it was only . . . I'm not a friend of Jean Rist.

DARBON: How come then? An ideological bent, or maybe some motive of a (*Laughing.*) personal nature?

ZENNO: Especially for motives . . . of the personal kind.

DARBON: You're beginning to interest me. (*Pause, then, looking at* ZENNO's *leg, which is moving.*) You limp, don't you?

ZENNO: Yes.

DARBON: If I'm not mistaken, you see a lot of his . . . girlfriend?

ZENNO: Yes, I knew her.

DARBON: Would you happen to be the . . . guy, who Jean Rist speaks of quite often, and whose head Jean Rist never stops demanding of the authorities (*Laughing very lightly.*) because he would have liked to take his girlfriend away from him? I'm just theorizing, because you limp, and it was the same thing with the other . . . guy. A resemblance which, of course, doesn't necessarily prove . . .

ZENNO: Of course, I'm not the only one . . .

DARBON: Let me go back to my line of thought. Therefore, you're the lover of our friend Jean Rist's woman. (ZENNO *trembles all over.*) Don't shake. I'm not the one who'll give you any trouble. If little Marie went with you, it was because she had her reasons, and women's reasons, well . . . (*He gets up and taps* ZENNO's *shoulder.*) in spite of our official statements . . . (*He laughs.* ZENNO *tries to imitate him, but his laugh is forced.*) To tell you the truth, I can guess the reasons that pushed Marie. Jean Rist is a bit, let us say, fervent, and fervency stems frequently, it seems, from a . . . difficulty in performing certain acts . . . which are quite commonplace . . . I think you understand what I'm getting at. (*He laughs.* ZENNO *tries to imitate him again, but does it even worse than before.*) But let's not trouble ourselves about that. (*Pause.*) You can be of some use to us, Mr. Zenno. That *is* your name, isn't it?

ZENNO: Yes.

DARBON: Well then! Mr. Zenno, we're going to set up a small file about this business. You'll give us certain insights on the thing, and, of course, your curriculum vitae.

ZENNO (*scared*): You're not going to . . . make me . . . ? I came without any ulterior motives, Mr. Darbon. That's right, no ulterior motives! (*He extends his hands, palms up.*)

DARBON: Are you afraid of exposing Jean Rist?

ZENNO: But if . . . if . . . I expose him, he . . . I . . . , I . . . ,

DARBON: You what? You'll change your name and residence, that's all there is to it . . . There's nothing to worry about. We'll arrange everything without any trouble. Everybody'll know that Jean Rist tried to save a refugee named Zenno, and you, in the meantime, you'll be somebody else, . . . You'll change your identity! Does that bother you so much, to change your identity? Are you so well off (*Laughing lightly.*) with your own?

ZENNO: No, no.

DARBON (*very coldly*): All right, then, are we agreed?

ZENNO: Of course . . . yes . . . on the contrary . . .

DARBON: Do you have the pass on you?

ZENNO: Yes.

DARBON: Please give it to me, if you don't mind. (ZENNO *pulls a piece of paper out of his pocket and, after some hesitation, gives it to* DARBON.) Thank you. (*Examining the pass.*) Before we get to the heart of the matter, I'd like to ask you a question. In your opinion, why did Jean Rist get you this pass, even though he was looking for you (*Laughing very flippantly.*) . . . and is still looking for you for . . . well, you can guess why? (*He laughs.*)

ZENNO: He isn't here, is he? They assured me that he'd left for a couple of days . . . to arrange some meetings in the . . . in the country . . . That's right, isn't it? (*He trembles.*)

DARBON: At any rate, you're under our protection here, Mr. Zenno. (*Pause.*) So then, if I understand correctly, you only came here temporarily, in the hope that we would let you take off as soon as possible; a quite justified hope, besides.

ZENNO: Yes, as soon as possible, and as far as possible.

DARBON: Another thing; how does Marie figure in all this? I intended to call her in.

Where is she at the moment? (ZENNO *lurches*.) You certainly are close-mouthed. (*Pause*.) You see, around here we don't like for our friends to be so close-mouthed.

ZENNO (*crying*): Dead! She's dead! They killed her, you killed her! Shot down like a dog! At the border!

DARBON: Oh! She was going with you and the guards fired on her. By mistake, of course? But then (*Laughing lightly*.) you tried to get away once and for all.

ZENNO: What . . . ? What do you want to do to me?

DARBON: Just some good. Haven't you already proven your attachment to our country? Believe me, you were right not to give up your citizenship. You're always better off in your own home than at your neighbors'.

ZENNO: Tell me. . . . I didn't want . . . (*Doorbell*.)

DARBON: That must be Jean Rist. (*Laughing*.) I don't suppose you want to see him, although to tell you the truth, you don't have anything to be afraid of. (*Laughing*.) Our friend has passed the stage of having personal grudges. (*He grabs* ZENNO *again who, at the name of* JEAN RIST, *has lost his head, and pushes him to the right*.) This way! (*He hits him on the shoulder*.) Now, now, I'm not forgetting you. (ZENNO *exits to the right.* JEAN *enters from the left, very upset*.) Jean Rist, I have some sad news to tell you. An accident on the border . . . (*Darkness*.)

SCENE 10

The square. The lights go up. JEAN, *his head lowered, is seated at his table on the platform. The two* GUARDS *enter pushing ahead of them a very beautiful, poorly dressed, innocent-looking young woman. Her checkered dress almost exactly like the one* MARIE *wore in Scene 1.*

YOUNG WOMAN: Fine, I did it. Did I ever say I didn't? Bring me in, it doesn't make any difference to me. But as for him, you'll never have him.

FIRST GUARD: Huh! You think so? (*He hits her*.)

SECOND GUARD (*to* JEAN): We came to ask you some advice.

FIRST GUARD: It's about that bitch there. We just caught her. She helped her boyfriend escape. What should we do about it? (JEAN *rises and remains immobile, one foot on the stool*.)

SECOND GUARD: You think your honey couldn't have managed without you?

FIRST GUARD: They always manage to get out.

SECOND GUARD: Free to kill a guard! That isn't what bothers them!

FIRST GUARD: Last week, it was a guard's wife who took off. She was coming to bring the linen, and then . . . (*Vague gesture*.)

JEAN (*going over to them*): And then, what? When you begin a story, finish it to the end. (*Pause*.) If you only messed up the guards' wives, it wouldn't be so bad. (*Pause*.) No more fooling around. What did she do?

FIRST GUARD: She helped her boyfriend escape.

SECOND GUARD: By sleeping with the guard.

FIRST GUARD: Or else by slipping him some cash.

YOUNG WOMAN: I didn't have any money, so I couldn't have given any to the guard.

FIRST GUARD: So you went to bed with him!

JEAN (*to the* YOUNG WOMAN): What do you have to say for yourself?

YOUNG WOMAN: He'd been in for two years, and for what? Nothing. He seduced me, supposedly . . . , but it didn't last. We lived together for years. That isn't hard to prove.

FIRST GUARD: Huh! You trying to say we're not doing a good job? (*He strikes the* YOUNG WOMAN.)

YOUNG WOMAN: I know the guy who turned him in, and I know why he did it: so I'd be all alone, and he could move in . . .

FIRST GUARD: There you are, she's going to give us a name!

SECOND GUARD: She thinks it works every time . . .

JEAN: Oh! so you want to squeal like all the others! Well, it doesn't work with me. This isn't the police station here, you know.

FIRST GUARD: Well, if you'd rather go to the police! (*He strikes the* YOUNG WOMAN.)

SECOND GUARD: So you got your little guard to play the game your way, huh?

FIRST GUARD: For a small bonus, huh!

SECOND GUARD: You take money wherever you can get it!

JEAN: Then he gave you money?

YOUNG WOMAN: Who? What money? I don't know what the hell you're talking about. You're all crazy.

JEAN: And now you'd like to turn him in . . . There's no risk after all. Another pay-off, why not?

SECOND GUARD (*laughing*): One inside the other.

YOUNG WOMAN: I didn't get any money, I swear to you! From anybody! I'm not asking anybody for anything! If I did it . . . it's because I loved him . . . , because I still love him . . . But obviously you don't understand!

JEAN (*shaking the* YOUNG WOMAN): Huh! You love him? He's as handsome as that? (*Yelling.*) Who knows, maybe he limps, too! (*He laughs and lets go of the* YOUNG WOMAN. *The* GUARDS *strike her.*)

YOUNG WOMAN: Go ahead, go on . . . what do you think you're gonna do to me, as long as he's free! He's doing what he wants now, he's laughing at us!

FIRST GUARD: Oh! he's doing what he wants, huh!

SECOND GUARD: And he's making fun of us!

FIRST GUARD: And so are you!

SECOND GUARD: You see—she's making fun of us! (*The* MOTHER *enters bewilderedly, she threads her way to the front and, immobile, watches the scene.*)

JEAN: Not like that! Not like that! With a gun! Like them! (*To the* GUARDS.) What are you waiting for? Go to it! Shoot her!

SECOND GUARD (*to the* FIRST GUARD): We going to?

FIRST GUARD: It's an order. We're not scared of anything. (*The* GUARDS *adjust their guns.*)

YOUNG WOMAN: You're not going . . . to shoot . . . You're saying that . . . just to scare me! Aren't you? . . . Just to scare me . . . (*The* GUARDS *shoot, she falls. Complete silence.*)

JEAN: Get it out of here! (*The* GUARDS *collect the* YOUNG WOMAN's *corpse and go away.* JEAN *doesn't move.*)

SECOND GUARD: Well, there's one who won't give us any more trouble! (*They exit.*)

MOTHER (*going toward* JEAN): Don't you think you're a bit crazy? To do a thing like that! In your situation! I know how it is, with bastards like that! It's all because of that pass, Jean. Darbon has the pass, and if he wants . . . (*Curtain.*)

PART II

SCENE 11

The square. The spotlight is on DARBON's *face only.*

DARBON: The first duty of the new government will be to establish Justice, and it means to accomplish this task without fail.

Fully aware of the heavy responsibilities which weigh on it at this critical moment, it will draw up a new constitution immediately, based on the dignity of every individual and the right to work for all men.

From this point on, refugees will benefit from the same rights as all other citizens. The only things taken into consideration will be personal merit, initiative, and services rendered to the country.

We must learn a lesson from the events of these last, bloody years. We have seen the sorrowful abuses to which a sectarian and passionate vision of the world can lead us. We no longer wish to witness the horrible scenes which have unfolded before our very eyes: respectable workers stricken and rendered worthless, prominent men summarily executed, buildings of every kind seized and burned! . . . The moral and economic life of the community are one and the same. Whosoever attacks one deals a blow to the other which could prove fatal to both.

SCENE 12

JEAN's *room. The lights go up. The* MOTHER, *bent grotesquely over the radio, is listening. Her face and posture express terror.*

DARBON (*his voice continuing on the radio*): I, Darbon, head of the bureau of Criminal Affairs and Public Information, do hereby demand, as an exemplary measure, the immediate arrest of all those who led our people to commit certain acts, acts for which they need not be ashamed, because they never actually condoned them in their own consciences, but which could very well be blamed on them in the future!

MOTHER (*crying*): Jean, where are you? (*She runs confusedly in every direction.*) Jean! (JEAN *enters from the left, defeated.*)

MOTHER (*running to meet* JEAN): Jean! We're finished! (*Pause.*)

JEAN: Yeah, it looks as though things are going to break.

MOTHER: Is that all you can say? But they want to kill us, to kill you, Jean. (*She wrings her hands.*) I knew it would end like this.

JEAN: It's ending just like it began; that's the way it goes.

MOTHER: This is no time for philosophizing! They're going to come, Jean! And take you away! Take both of us away! We have to . . . We have to . . . do something, quick, right now . . . We're not just going to sit around and wait for them, no matter what!

JEAN: Why not? Everybody gets their turn. Eventually.

MOTHER: It's not fair! Darbon's had some killed too! Just as many as you! Almost as many! Only he was a little more careful: he gauged the wind direction a little better! Speaking in the name of the . . . new Government! He must have a great job! To think that you could have done what he's doing, Jean, to be up there too, with the new Government! We wouldn't be here! But you, you just did stupid things, nothing but stupid things. (*Pause.*) Talk, say something. It's because . . . Jean, my little Jean, they're not going to separate us, are they? (*She clings to* JEAN, *who pushes her away.*) And without a trial (*Shouting.*) like dogs!

JEAN: No trials! No more blabbering! I can't stand it! I've got nothing to say. Nothing! Absolutely nothing!

MOTHER: Jean, we're going to go away. Anywhere! Right away!

JEAN (*pushing the* MOTHER *away brutally*): No, no running away! I don't want to run!

MOTHER: You're right . . . We won't run away . . . It's far too late! We'll let them take us in, that's all there is to it. (*Pause.*)

Jean . . . , you'd do better to try to . . . team up with . . . Darbon. I know what you're going to say: that he can't stand you . . . and that . . . But all the same, they know Darbon! And his father was a friend of your uncle's. They were great stamp collectors, those two! You know, those two were inseparable. They were always getting into discussions with each other! And then, you saved one of them! (JEAN *bursts out laughing.*) There's nothing to laugh about. This is perfect! Was it you, yes or no, who got Zenno his pass? And without you . . . If Darbon wanted to! He'd give you the paper! Proof! Extenuating circumstances! The paper! If only you had the paper! (*Pause.*) Jean, you don't understand! I'm not telling you to go and find Zenno. Of course that would upset you after what's happened between you . . . (*Going toward* JEAN.) Although it's already old hat . . . Finished and done with!

JEAN (*still laughing*): Done with! The way you talk!

MOTHER: But Darbon isn't Zenno, after all . . .

JEAN (*softly*): No, not finished. Dumped in the garbage! Like Marie! Jean Rist, the guard!

MOTHER: You're right, Jean. It would be a bit risky to go to Darbon . . . Yeah, we don't have to see Darbon. That wasn't good advice, that bit. (*She babbles.*) My first idea was the good one. We've got to run away, get out of here and hide, that's all there is to it. They do a good job of hiding themselves, they do. Believe me, Jean, we're going to hide, both of us, in a hole! A hole where we'll make ourselves real small. (*Reassured.*) We'll change our name, it's not hard. I know some people . . . obviously, they won't do it for nothing; they'll want money. But that's something we've got, we'll give them some. (*Pause.*) No, wait, I've got a better idea. I limp. You do too—don't you see? We'll pretend to be refugees. People always tell me I look like one, and not just because of my leg . . . well? And you, well uh, you . . . , you'll limp too. It's not hard. Don't you want to? (JEAN *laughs quite hard.*) We'll go to some city down South. There's a lot of them down there; we mustn't generalize, Jean. Generalizing, always generalizing, that's what's brought you to this. (JEAN *laughs even louder.*) Don't be an imbecile, look at me for a minute. (*She begins to toddle, convulsive movement.*) How your poor mother . . . (*She clings to* JEAN.)

JEAN (*who has stopped laughing*): Get your paws off of me! (*The* MOTHER *doesn't obey.* JEAN *pushes her, she falls.*)

MOTHER (*getting up with difficulty*): All this because Zenno limped! (*Finally on her feet again.*) All right then, let's not talk about it anymore. We're going to hide. I don't know where, but we'll look around and we'll find something. (*Pause.*) My Jean's a sensitive guy! A sweet little boy who wouldn't hurt a fly. (*Maliciously.*) But he still had some people killed! (*Crying.*) I'm scared, Jean, that's why I'm saying stupid things . . . You're right, we're going to hide, that's all there is to it, without looking for any other angles.

JEAN: No, you know, your plan isn't so bad after all. (*He starts to limp. Then in a low voice.*) Like Zenno . . . Exactly like Zenno . . . (*Darkness.*)

RADIO (*in the dark*): The new refugee statute will go into effect as of today. The refugees will benefit from the same advantages in the practicing of their professions, as the natives.

SCENE 13

The street. The lights go up. The lighting suggests a southern city. JEAN, *in shirt sleeves and wearing sandals, is carrying a radio on his shoulders with some difficulty, as in the beginning of the play. He limps. Visibly exhausted, he rests his radio on the ground and sits down. He does not see a man with a thin and repugnant face who is leaning nonchalantly against the foot of a wall, dressed in overalls, eating a piece of fruit, and throwing the seeds at his feet. The* MAN *watches* JEAN.

MAN (*to* JEAN): Tired? (*Pause.*) It doesn't take much! (*Pause.*) Hey, buddy, I'm talking to you. (*Pause.*) Yeah, man, some people got work and some don't. (*Pause.*) And who's the guys what got it? The same ones every time.

JEAN (*getting up*): What's that mean?

MAN: It means the . . . good for nothings, the freaks, the . . . cripples, man!

JEAN: What have they ever done to you! Come on, tell me what they've done to you.

MAN: Plenty! Don't think I'm gonna go into all the details! (*He laughs.*)

JEAN (*going toward the* MAN): We've all got our stories to tell. Every one of us, do you hear? You, me, everybody! (*A* WORKER *enters from the left. He stops, his hands in his pockets.*)

MAN (*shouting and gesturing*): Look at that one! It limps, it works, it grubs off the poor, and, to beat everything, it wants to make laws, too. (*He goes menacingly toward* JEAN, *who doesn't move.*)

JEAN: Go on! Only I'm warning you . . .

MAN: You gonna call the cops, is that it?

JEAN (*his voice changed, threatening*): Who me? What for? Didn't you get a good look at me? (*He approaches the* MAN, *who draws back.*) It's over with! Finished, do you hear me? We can't do anything anymore, about anybody.

WORKER (*to the* MAN): He's right, it's all over. And besides, just between us, do you think it was any better when we were on them, all the time? (*The* MAN *makes protesting gestures.*) Idiot! The ones who're hurting us are a lot better off than that guy.

MAN (*disconcerted, giving in*): Huh? What did I tell you? (JEAN *stops. The* MAN *regains his self-control.*) No, but there were times . . .

JEAN (*shouting*): Times when what? (*He sits down again.*)

MAN (*getting up his courage again and going ahead*): You don't scare me, man. *I'm* in home territory. (*He goes toward* JEAN, *but this time more cautiously.*)

WORKER (*to the* MAN): Let him alone. He's no happier than we are . . . And this business of work, even if you offered it to him . . . Go on, get out of here and stop the bullshit. (*The* MAN *lets him lead him away, still continuing to brag.* JEAN *remains seated, his head in his hands.* NOEMI, *a thin, dark, beautiful girl enters from the right. She takes in the scene at a glance, then goes toward* JEAN.)

NOEMI: Huh! He's not here anymore, he got

scared . . . (JEAN *raises his head.*) Pardon me, but I was up at the window, I came down purposely to tell him, to make him feel ashamed . . . (*Going closer to* JEAN.) It didn't really surprise me all that much. I knew darn well they still hated us. But I still didn't think they'd have that much nerve! Again! . . . It's almost as bad as before. (*Pause.*) We shouldn't have let him go, we should have . . . (JEAN *looks at her.*) To start it all over again, after everything that's happened! I can't believe . . .

JEAN (*sharply*): There's a lot of unbelievable things.

NOEMI (*sitting down near him*): I escaped with a girlfriend of mine. We'd gone a few feet, they fired, they killed her, right in front of me . . . (JEAN *shudders.*) I don't know why I'm telling you all this. (*Pause.*) Didn't you have . . . another job, before? (*She points to the radio.*)

JEAN: No, I've always done this. A vocation!

NOEMI (*very softly*): Did they keep you a long time in the camps? (*Long pause.*) I know, there are some memories so horrible that you can't even talk about them . . . I'm sorry. (JEAN *lowers his head. Darkness.*)

RADIO (*in the dark*): In view of the present labor surplus, salaried workers employed for less than a year will be laid off within the next six months. They will receive unemployment compensation. Refugees who are affected by this decision are asked to register within two weeks.

SCENE 14

JEAN's *new room. The lights go up. Furniture still poorer than in the preceding scenes.* JEAN, *barefoot, is seated;* NOEMI *is standing in front of him.*

NOEMI: You don't seem to understand that everything's going to start all over again. Not all at once, of course, but little by little. But before you know what's happening, it's already too late.

JEAN: You want the two of us to get out our luggage right this minute? Go on, say it, say it already, since that's what you want, since it's the only thing you think of from morning till night. (*Pause.*) Run away, a

lovely idea, but run away where? And how? You need money to go away.

NOEMI: Excuses, nothing but excuses! Because you don't have the nerve!

JEAN: All right, let's just say I'm a coward, and let it go at that.

NOEMI: Why a coward? It's already been established: the refugees, every one of them, are yellow; they all end up by running away. Huh! You're one of us, in spite of your airs which you get from heaven knows where, and your strange ways. (*Pause.*) You see, they're closing in on us, and we're the ones who're giving the signal. (*Pause.*) What are you scared of? That they'll shoot us at the border? They won't shoot . . . Unless, of course, we wait for days and months . . . Then, obviously . . . (*Pause.*) Have you forgotten?

JEAN (*rising, trembling all over, and shouting*): Forgotten what?

NOEMI: Jean, you're all white! You're shaking! What's the matter?

JEAN: Nothing. It'll go away. (*The* MOTHER *appears in the doorway, a shirt and an iron in her hand. Neither* JEAN *nor* NOEMI *notices her. Immobile, she watches them.*)

NOEMI: You've had it. Like me, like all of us. We can't go on living in fear, it's impossible, it gets to you in the end. (*Pause.*) You've forgotten everything, absolutely everything, completely. If not, you'd only have one thing in mind: to get out of here, no matter where, or how, anything rather than to have to hide again. Didn't you ever have to hide? Don't you know what it's like?

JEAN (*who has sat down again, in a low voice*): I know what it's like.

NOEMI: Then say something: talk, for crying out loud, just once. Try. (*Pause.*) Is it because of your mother that you don't want to leave? Noemi doesn't exist as far as you're concerned, but let's not hurt Mama. And good old Mama's quite an optimist, she wants to stay right here, to see . . . (*Imitating the* MOTHER's *voice.*) "Everything'll work out, Jean." (*Pause.*) It's because of her, isn't it?

JEAN: All right, it's because of her. Don't you see! To do a thing like that to a poor old lady (*Laughing.*), me who's her only consolation (*Laughing harder.*), her pride and joy. (*The* MOTHER *goes forward.* JEAN *and* NOEMI *just now notice her.*)

MOTHER: Am I disturbing you? Lovers don't like to be disturbed, I know how they like to have little heart-to-hearts. But I won't bother you for long; just long enough to iron this shirt. (*To* NOEMI.) There's no room for a table in there. To think that we're reduced to this, people like us! (NOEMI *goes toward the door.*) I hope I'm not chasing you away?

NOEMI: It's not just you. (*She remains near the door.*)

MOTHER (*laughing*): You'd think you two kids had a fight. Poor Jean! You've put him in a heck of a shape for me! (*Laughing.*) I see. (*To* NOEMI, *who hasn't moved.*) You wanted to get him to talk, to force him to make a decision, that's exactly what it looks like to me. He always makes that face when someone's pushing him. Some advice, my dear: you've got to take Jean like he is. (NOEMI *takes a step forward, the* MOTHER *puts the shirt down on the table.*)

JEAN: Leave it go. You can do it later. (*He throws the shirt over a chair.*)

MOTHER (*picking up the shirt again*): Later! Always the same! You've lost your job, the least you can do is get unemployment. And you can't go to the unemployment office with a shirt that's all grubby. They won't give you your check if you don't look good. Well now, what's going to become of the two of us?

NOEMI: He doesn't have to go there! Jean, do you hear, I don't want you to. It's too . . . (JEAN *doesn't move.*)

MOTHER: I know, you can always put on your scarf. That way, they won't see the color of your collar. But what about the sleeves? They're pretty obvious. (*Very loud.*) Everything's obvious!

NOEMI: Don't you understand that if they tell the refugees to register it's just so they can make up the lists again?

MOTHER: Do you really think that the situation is as bad as all that for . . . (*Laughing.*) for us? (*Advancing threateningly toward* NOEMI, *who goes to* JEAN.) You wanted to leave me here, all by myself, in this mess? (*Pause.*) I heard everything, my lambs. Your old mother isn't as deaf as all that. An invalid, maybe, but not a bit deaf. (NOEMI *gets ready to exit to the right.*)

JEAN (*weakly, straightening up*): Noemi!

NOEMI (*turning around*): No, I've had it. (JEAN *rises.* NOEMI *goes out.*)

MOTHER (*approaching* JEAN *cautiously*): Well now, so the little love-bird wanted to run away with my Jean, take a little trip abroad. That's panicking a little too fast. You really think that it's going to work out . . . (*Laughing.*) I mean: blow up? But then, it wouldn't be so bad if it blew up once and for all! (*Laughing.*) Then, at least, we'd be able . . . But I think Noemi's making a big thing out of nothing. Things aren't all that bad yet. And anyway, nothing can happen to you . . . I mean to us. After all, we've still got connections.

JEAN: Ah! Now you're getting to the point. . . . (*He pushes the* MOTHER *toward the door.*) You'll never take the prize for speed!

MOTHER (*drawing back*): All I'm asking of you is not to let your old mother down. I know I'm a burden, but I'm a burden you've carried up until now. Well, I was thinking . . . (*She cries.*)

JEAN: What were you thinking? That I'd always have you on my back? Well, I'm dropping you. (*He pushes the* MOTHER.) Oh! I wouldn't think twice about leaving, if . . .

MOTHER (*shaking*): If . . . If you weren't afraid of hurting me! Or are there more important reasons? (*Standing up.*) Do you know what I happened to find out completely by accident? (*Pause.*) Zenno has a great job now . . . His name's Zenno again, of course. But that probably won't last long.

JEAN (*upset*): What kind of nonsense is that? Who told you? . . .

MOTHER: If I had known that my little news would upset you so much, I wouldn't have told you. But I was under the impression that (*Raising her voice.*) the inquiries were all finished, over for good . . . , that Zenno, was out of the picture. And after all, there's no point in dwelling on the past. We should be thinking about more important, more interesting things. (*Darkness.*)

RADIO (*in the dark*): Over the past two weeks, certain disruptive elements have taken to acts of looting and burning. The amount of damage as a result of these acts has not yet been determined. Extremely severe measures have been passed in order to prevent a recurrence of these crimes. The majority of the offenders have been apprehended.

On the other hand, the amnesty bill initially proposed as a means of attaining a national reconciliation has been passed unanimously in the House. It is clearly specified that the amnesty in question will not apply to all offenders, but only to those who have been prematurely judged and condemned for certain excesses that they committed in order to calm the unrest of these past years.

SCENE 15

Police headquarters. DARBON, *elegantly dressed, is pacing up and down.* ZENNO *takes his dictation. Two* POLICEMEN *are seated with their backs to the audience.*

DARBON: We have granted the underprivileged classes all the support which our present economic conditions would allow. And what do we see? Gangs which have spread through the country, inciting to riot, looting and ransacking everything in their path; in a word, endangering the inalienable well-being of both individuals and their property. Will we stand by and allow these disruptions to terrify a people whose patience and kindness cannot be doubted for a moment? The Government has given enough proof of its generosity to enable it, in light of the incidents which have just taken place, to take the most severe measures. It seems to me that no one can dispute the necessity of these measures. It remains to examine the methods of punishment with which we, the responsible heads of the Police, wish to punish the offenders. After having carefully weighed the pros and cons, I came to the decision which I will impart to you at this time. I propose, as an exemplary measure, and for a length of time which has not yet been determined, the penalty of death. If someone has any objections to raise, let him speak up, I'll be glad to give him the floor. (*The two* POLICEMEN *shake their heads negatively.*) I wish to thank all the members of this Assembly who have voted in the general interest . . . (*For a moment* ZENNO *has stopped taking shorthand.* DARBON *turns toward him.*) What's the matter? Aren't you following me anymore? (ZENNO *squirms on his chair.* DARBON *takes up his orator's tone again.*) . . . For having placed the general interest above the demands of a sentiment whose harmful powers we have learned at our own expense. (*Mixed noises in the wings, and bursts of voices.*)

FIRST GUARD (*offstage*): Come on, are you crazy?

SECOND GUARD (*offstage*): Huh! Damn right he's crazy.

YOUNG MAN (*offstage, shouting*): Just 'cause I want you to kill me, to kill me!

FIRST GUARD (*offstage*): If you keep this up, we'll take care of you ourselves!

SECOND GUARD (*offstage*): No reason to bother the boss.

YOUNG MAN (*offstage*): Let me through! You'll see . . . (*The* YOUNG MAN, *his clothes a mess, enters from the left, followed immediately by the* GUARDS, *who seize him by the arms.* ZENNO, *visibly uncomfortable, lowers and turns his head away. He keeps up this attitude throughout the scene.*)

FIRST GUARD: Bastard!

DARBON (*sitting, to the* GUARDS): You certainly have a strange way of performing your duties. Do you realize that we could punish you severely for this?

FIRST GUARD: We've got our reasons, we're gonna explain to you . . .

SECOND GUARD: He came up on us . . . by surprise.

DARBON: Don't let a thing like this happen again, is that understood?

FIRST GUARD *and* SECOND GUARD: Yeah! Right! (*Again they seize the* YOUNG MAN, *whom they had let go.*)

YOUNG MAN (*struggling and shouting*): I won't go away . . . I'll stay here . . . until you've killed me. I swear, you're going to kill me. You killed her, then why not me? You hear? (*Pause.*) I'm the one she loved. Nobody but me! We lived together, and you . . . , you, just like that . . . Because we were refugees . . . Liars! (*The* GUARDS *hit him.*)

DARBON: Under what particular section would

you like us to kill you? As a refugee? (*With a light laugh.*) You're wasting time, young man. (*Pointing at the* YOUNG MAN, *to the* GUARDS.) Get that out of my sight. (*The* GUARDS *try to lead the* YOUNG MAN *out. He struggles.*)

FIRST GUARD: Cool it, you bastard!

YOUNG MAN: You're the bastards!

DARBON: You'd better watch your language. You might regret . . .

YOUNG MAN (*the* GUARDS *have not been able to force him to leave or to control him*): You don't scare me. I know you too well for that. Since I escaped, I haven't missed a single day. The riots, I was there. Yeah, I smashed those windows with rocks. And I knocked out anybody who was behind the windows! And not for their money, it was just because I saw their rotten heads. They're easy to spot, damn it, easier than ours!

DARBON: Oh! So you took part in the . . . recent incidents. Perfect. (*With a smile.*) In that case we might be able to give you some satisfaction after all. (*To the* GUARDS.) Put him in with the others, we'll have a hearing later. (*The* GUARDS *exit, leading the* YOUNG MAN. ZENNO *raises his head again.*)

YOUNG MAN (*in the wings*): Well, kill me already! What the hell are you waiting for? Cowards! What's the matter, don't you have the guts? You have to wait for orders? (*He laughs.*)

DARBON (*rising after consulting his watch*): The meeting is over. (*All rise, except* ZENNO. DARBON *goes over to the* POLICE-MEN.) Well, then, Gentlemen, that finishes our little get-together. But it has confirmed us, I think, in our resolutions. I just hope the Houses prove to be understanding. (*The officials nod and exit.* ZENNO *rises, descends from the platform, and takes several steps, embarrassed.*) No, don't leave. I have to talk to you.

ZENNO: Well . . . Uh . . .

DARBON: Well, have a seat. We can talk just as well here as any place else, don't you think?

ZENNO (*sitting*): Yes.

DARBON: First one question, Mr. Zenno. It seems to me that I've already met the . . . (*Laughing lightly.*) the man who introduced himself just before. Isn't he the guy . . . , a bit older, of course, that we locked up . . . thanks to you? I know, it's been a while.

ZENNO: No, I don't know him, you must be mistaken.

DARBON (*thoughtful*): Maybe. (*Taking up his normal voice.*) Actually, I'm confused. That's what happens when you have a lot of memories. It wasn't you, it was . . . Jean Rist (ZENNO *trembles*) who took care of it during one of those so spectacular outbursts. (*Pause.*) But it was precisely about Jean Rist that I wanted to talk to you. I just heard in the past couple of days— which proves that our agencies are sometimes a bit slow, we have to admit—I just learned that Jean Rist is hiding somewhere down South, disguised as a refugee. (*Pause.*) A funny idea, isn't it? At any rate, it wouldn't have occurred to me, what advantages such a disguise might offer, for a while, at least. (ZENNO *squirms.*) Pardon me, Mr. Zenno, I didn't mean to offend you, believe me.

ZENNO: You . . . you . . . aren't offending me. (*Very quickly, sorrowfully.*) You can't hurt me, you know that. (*Murmur in the distance,* ZENNO *listens, the noise stops.*)

DARBON (*tapping* ZENNO'*s shoulder*): I know we can rely on you. You've proved it to us on several occasions. (*Pause.*) But I'd like you to prove it to us one more time. By tracking down Jean Rist, for instance.

ZENNO: But you . . . you know all about it. I can't.

DARBON: I know . . . I know . . . Although after so many years . . . But then you don't have to see him in person. There're such things as contacts.

ZENNO: What can we do now that . . . that the amnesty has been passed?

DARBON: The reasons why I insist on contacting him are my business. (*Pause.*) You're usually more discreet, Mr. Zenno.

ZENNO: I . . .

DARBON: Well, we'll talk about this again tomorrow, when we're all rested. O.K.? (*Explosions.* ZENNO *begins to tremble.* DARBON *watches him.*) What's the matter, Mr. Zenno? You seem upset.

ZENNO: Nothing. I don't take too well to explosions.

DARBON: That's right, you were never a soldier. (*He laughs.*)

ZENNO: You know that . . . (*He points to his leg.*)

DARBON: I wasn't reproaching you. (*Pause.*) I thought that execution was slightly hasty and a bit premature. Didn't you? (*Leaning toward* ZENNO *who trembles more and more.*) Come now, pull yourself together, Mr. Zenno; what's bothering you right now? I hope you're not afraid that . . . well, for yourself. We're not out to get you, Mr. Zenno, I assure you. You've changed fields, but you're still . . . a specialist, and we don't go after specialists. We need them and their services, too much.

ZENNO: I know.

DARBON: Later, much later though, I don't know. Nobody can predict the future. There are some things that are beyond us. But for the moment anyway, you've given proof of your faithfulness. Keep it up, and you won't have anything to worry about, at least not as long as I'm here. And I'll be here for a long time to come, I hope, anyway.

ZENNO: I'm . . . I'm not worried about anything. I'm O.K.

DARBON: Yeah, I know, I was just kidding. You can fool around once in a while, you know. (*Pause.*) I'm surprised you couldn't tell that right away. What I like about you, about . . . your kind, is your great sense of humor—it's so characteristic. (*Darkness.*)

RADIO (*in the dark*): Several persons have been arrested for inciting to riot. In order to prevent a recurrence of events of this type once and for all, the House has passed a law by unanimous vote providing for the most severe penalties for all those who, in one way or another, threaten the national security. Among the offenders, who are all members of disruptive elements of the population, there is a rather large proportion of refugees, provoking a specific public sentiment which has expressed itself in several acts of violence, regrettable but nevertheless understandable.

SCENE 16

JEAN's *room. The lights go up. The* MOTHER *is alone, standing in the center.*

She rushes almost immediately to the right.

MOTHER (*shouting*): Jean!

JEAN (*appearing in the doorway*): There's no need to yell—I'm right here. What is it now?

MOTHER: It's . . . we're finished . . . and . . . (JEAN *covers his ears.*) O.K., I won't say anything more about it. (*Throwing her arms around* JEAN, *who disengages himself and goes to sit at the other end of the stage, where he remains until the arrival of* NOEMI.) Only you're gonna come with me . . . Jean, we can't put it off till tomorrow again, absolutely not. Jean, please, your poor mommy's begging you. (*She tries to kiss* JEAN's *hands but he pulls away violently.*) You won't have to say anything, I'll do all the talking . . . I'll explain to them. They'll understand. I'll say that you had . . . that they were afraid for you, and that they had you . . . that I advised you . . . , but considering the circumstances . . . the pardon . . . (*Hugging* JEAN.) Only, you've got to come with your mother, so it looks good. (*Shouting.*) Believable! (JEAN *pushes her away with a vague gesture.* NOEMI *enters left.*)

JEAN (*jumping up*): Noemi!

NOEMI (*embracing* JEAN): Yes, it's me. I stayed. I thought about you the whole time. I couldn't.

JEAN: Stayed, you stayed, for me!

NOEMI: I didn't want to come. (*She motions to the* MOTHER *with a movement of her head. The* MOTHER *watches* JEAN.) But do you know what they're saying today? There're armed troops all over the place. They go right into houses, they're looking for refugees to . . . Jean, I'm so scared! Oh! Of course, I knew well enough . . . We've got to leave. Right now! But how'll we do it, with your leg? I tried to find a car. Impossible.

JEAN (*taking* NOEMI's *arm*): The two of us are going to leave right now.

MOTHER (*rushing toward* NOEMI): Yes, he runs pretty fast, even with his leg. Right, Jean, tell Noemi that your little leg doesn't bother you so much when you've got to make a run for it.

NOEMI (*pushing the* MOTHER *away*): I'm not asking *you* anything.

MOTHER: Huh! You're not asking me for anything. (*To* JEAN, *who lets* NOEMI *go.*) Jean, don't you want to confide in your girlfriend? Are we afraid, still scared?

JEAN (*pushing the* MOTHER, *who falls*): Pig!

MOTHER (*groveling on the floor*): Oh! Well then *I'm* the one who's going to tell her, tell her everything! (*She gets up again with great effort.*)

NOEMI: What's she talking about? Jean, I don't understand.

JEAN: Listen, Noemi. For a long time now I've wanted . . . , but now, I don't . . . No, I don't have to . . . Noemi! (*Noise in the wings.*)

NOEMI: You hear? They're coming!

MOTHER (*shrinking into herself, frightened*): Jean, my baby, there they are, they're coming. (*The noises get closer. Footsteps can be heard.*)

NOEMI (*throwing herself into* JEAN'S *arms*): Jean!

MOTHER: Oh! You don't want to be bothered with me! All right, then, *I'm* going to talk to them, I'm going to tell them everything . . .

JEAN (*going toward the* MOTHER): And what if you can't talk? (*He grabs the* MOTHER'S *neck, she shouts.*)

NOEMI: Jean! (JEAN *releases the* MOTHER. *Banging on the door.* JEAN *leads* NOEMI *to the left.*)

FIRST PARTISAN (*offstage*): Anybody in there? (TWO PARTISANS *enter on the right, working-class types, poorly dressed, armed with guns. They take in the scene with one look.*)

FIRST PARTISAN: Nobody. They're watching out for us, the bastards. Can never catch them off guard.

SECOND PARTISAN: Naturally. With all their money, they don't have any trouble finding things out. (*The* MOTHER *struggles, still held back by* JEAN.)

FIRST PARTISAN: Something moved over there. (*They see* JEAN, NOEMI *and the* MOTHER. JEAN *and* NOEMI *do not move.*)

SECOND PARTISAN: Well, then, are we hiding?

MOTHER (*coming to meet the* PARTISANS): No, no, we're not hiding. (*She shouts, pointing to* JEAN.) That one there is my baby. It's Jean, Jean Rist! The revolutionary, you know . . . He's making believe he limps . . . I told him to . . . His

mother was afraid for him, you see? Under the circumstances . . . But now that . . . the nightmare's over. (JEAN *tries to grab the* MOTHER, *but the* PARTISANS *seize him. He struggles.* NOEMI *remains petrified. To* JEAN.) Oh! You don't want it to end! You want to go on this way. For her! For her! Because you love her! Ha! Ha! (*To the* PARTISANS, *pointing to* NOEMI.) He's in love with that little bitch so he wants to keep up the charade. Stupid little fool! We have to forgive him. (*Shouting.*) He's had hundreds and thousands killed! You can check on it. Everybody will tell you.

NOEMI (*going to* JEAN *in spite of the* PARTISANS): Jean, that's not true, is it? Tell me, it's not true? It's just because she's scared, . . . because she's crazy with fear!

JEAN (*in a resolute voice*): Yes, of course, it's because she's scared. (*To the* PARTISANS, *pointing to the* MOTHER.) Look at her! Just look at her! A refugee! Purebred! And she limps, to top it all. (*Shouting to the* MOTHER.) Walk! Walk a little, so they can see how you limp!

FIRST PARTISAN: Do you want to give the old lady a little run, just to see?

SECOND PARTISAN (*laughing stupidly*): That makes sense. (*The* PARTISANS *push the* MOTHER, *making her walk. In spite of all her efforts, she limps. They burst out laughing.*)

JEAN: Fake it! Go on fake it, if you can! (*He laughs.*)

MOTHER (*in the middle of the laughter*): That doesn't mean anything! Not a thing! A lot of people limp . . . It was a car accident . . . it could happen to anybody. I was sixteen . . . in the mountains! (*Pointing to* JEAN.) That's Jean Rist . . . that's him! Him! Haven't you ever heard the name?

FIRST PARTISAN (*who has stopped laughing*): We're not here to worry about names.

SECOND PARTISAN: That's right. (*He takes hold of the* MOTHER. *The* FIRST PARTISAN *goes over to the* MOTHER *and* NOEMI, *who haven't moved.*)

MOTHER: Let me go! Leave go of me! I'm telling you, you're making a mistake. You'll be sorry! (*To* NOEMI, *while the* PARTISANS *break out in a loud laugh.*) The thing he can't tell you . . . that's what it was . . . it was that! (NOEMI *looks at* JEAN.)

JEAN (*looking at* NOEMI): No. No it wasn't. It's not true.

FIRST PARTISAN: Come on now! We're gonna get to the bottom of this!

MOTHER: He's lying! He's lying, to get rid of his mommy . . . Get rid of her once and for all!

SECOND PARTISAN: And that bitch thinks she's going to get out of this by bawling. They're all the same! (ZENNO *enters.* JEAN *trembles, but does not move.*)

MOTHER: Mr. Zenno! It's you, you! What luck!

ZENNO (*who doesn't dare go forward, after having looked at each one of them*): I assure you . . . I didn't come here for anything . . . By chance . . . I came for . . . I swear to you . . . I wasn't expecting . . .

FIRST PARTISAN: What?

SECOND PARTISAN: At any rate, you're going to get something out of this. When there's enough for three, there's enough for four. (*He takes hold of* ZENNO *who struggles. The* FIRST PARTISAN *laughs.* JEAN *doesn't move.*)

ZENNO: Let go of me! You don't know who you're dealing with! (*He searches clumsily in his pocket, then takes out a paper which he hands to the* PARTISANS.) Read that. (*The* FIRST PARTISAN *takes the paper and reads; the* SECOND PARTISAN *looks over his shoulder.*)

MOTHER: My dear Mr. Zenno, I never would have thought . . . never thought that you . . . well . . . Dear Mr. Zenno, you've got pull . . . talk to them, tell them . . . tell these gentlemen that you've known us for a long time, for ages, and that Jean isn't what they think . . . , that on the contrary, on the contrary . . .

FIRST PARTISAN (*to the* SECOND): Did you make anything out of it, out of his paper?

SECOND PARTISAN: Give me it! (*He takes the paper and examines it. The* FIRST PARTISAN *begins to rummage around the room.*)

MOTHER (*falling to her knees in front of* ZENNO): Please, my good, my dear Mr. Zenno, you've always been so good to us . . . Tell them . . . have mercy, that Jean . . . I've already told them, but they don't want to believe me. I'm a poor invalid. Like you, Mr. Zenno, like you. Well, both of us, we know . . .

NOEMI (*still immobile*): Jean, who is he? Do you know him?

JEAN (*with effort*): No. (ZENNO *trembles.*)

FIRST PARTISAN (*to the* SECOND, *who is still rummaging*): It's not hard to understand. He figured out their little gag. But that isn't going to stop two good spies like us. (*Pointing to* ZENNO *and the* MOTHER.) Take those two there. (*Pointing to* NOEMI *and* JEAN.) I'll take care of the lovebirds. (*He goes toward* NOEMI *and* JEAN.)

ZENNO (*barring the way of the* FIRST PARTISAN): You're gonna let that man alone. I'm telling you for your own good!

FIRST PARTISAN (*laughing*): You didn't look at it from my angle, did you? (*He pushes him toward the door on the right.*)

ZENNO: I'm telling you because . . . (*Pointing to* JEAN.) Because he isn't . . . what you think. (*The two* PARTISANS *look upset.*)

MOTHER: It's true . . . he isn't . . . what you think!

ZENNO (*after having studied* JEAN, *who is hiding his head in his hands while* NOEMI *rubs her head on his shoulder*): Can't you see that it's Jean Rist? That's right, the revolutionary! Jean Rist in the flesh! When things started getting hot, he got scared, he tried to change his identity! Ahhh, come on now! Don't be difficult about it. Things like that happen. But now that everything's worked out, now, there's no reason to . . . Now he can show his true colors! Exactly what he really is! (*To* JEAN.) That's enough now, give yourself up!

MOTHER: Oh, thank you, Mr. Zenno, thank you so much, my good, dear, kind, Mr. Zenno. (*To the* PARTISANS.) You . . . you see now . . . a witness! An eyewitness at that!

JEAN: It isn't true!

MOTHER: Jean! How can you say that? I don't understand.

FIRST PARTISAN: Well, the only thing we understand is that we're wasting our time, and if it keeps up, we'll lose our heads. (*He goes to seize* JEAN *and motions to the* SECOND PARTISAN *to seize the* MOTHER *and* ZENNO.)

ZENNO (*grabbing hold of the* FIRST PARTISAN): Don't touch him . . . He belongs . . . to . . .

NOEMI (*taking* JEAN'S *hand*): Only to me.

FIRST PARTISAN (*to* ZENNO, *who is still hold-*

ing on): Shut up! (*He hits him, then, to the* SECOND PARTISAN.) What'll we do with this one? Take him in?

SECOND PARTISAN: Why not?

FIRST PARTISAN: All the same, he has a paper.

SECOND PARTISAN (*who goes away from* JEAN *and toward* ZENNO): Take your paper back. For what it's worth! Now, we're gonna play cops ourselves. No more papers! (*He hands him the paper.* ZENNO *doesn't take it in time. The paper falls.* ZENNO, *on all fours, picks it up again, trembling.*) Don't be scared, we're not gonna do anything to you. (*While* ZENNO *straightens up.*) Let's go. (*He gestures to the* FIRST PARTISAN, *who takes hold of the* MOTHER.)

MOTHER (*struggling*): You don't have any right! (*Pointing to* ZENNO.) He told you, he had . . . he has . . . a pass. What you're doing . . . it's illegal.

FIRST PARTISAN (*in bursts of laughter*): Illegal! That's a good one!

SECOND PARTISAN (*laughing*): Justice is just like you! Crippled . . . a damned cripple! (*He pushes the* MOTHER, *who nearly falls.*)

MOTHER: If . . . if . . . I limp . . . that doesn't mean anything . . . nothing . . . (*Crying out and pointing to* NOEMI.) Look at her, her, with her little kisser . . . she doesn't limp . . . and still, she's one of them . . . They're all over the place, here, there, and everywhere! (*Shaking her arms in every direction.*) It doesn't prove a thing. (*The* FIRST PARTISAN *leads the* MOTHER *out. They exit at right.* NOEMI *takes* JEAN's *hand.*)

SECOND PARTISAN: The executions will be right away. (*He takes hold of* JEAN *and* NOEMI, *who offer no resistance. The* FIRST PARTISAN *comes back.*)

JEAN: Listen . . .

SECOND PARTISAN: Still have something to say?

JEAN (*very quickly*): What if I were like you? What if it were true what they told you . . . Would? . . .

NOEMI (*loudly, to* JEAN): Jean, look at me.

FIRST PARTISAN: Just to cut you down to size, you "others" are the only ones there are. (*He leads* JEAN *and* NOEMI *out.*)

ZENNO (*to* JEAN *just as he leaves*): We others! You got it now, didn't you, Jean Rist? We can go together. (*Going toward the* SECOND PARTISAN.) Me too while you are at it!

SECOND PARTISAN (*seizing* ZENNO, *who struggles, and leading him out in spite of his protests*): They're all alike! (*He exits, leading* ZENNO *away.*)

The stage remains empty. After a moment, one hears three shots, then, suddenly, the MOTHER's *voice crying: "That doesn't prove anything, that doesn't prove . . ." A final shot interrupts the sentence. Curtain.*

OPEN TWENTY-FOUR HOURS

Roger N. Cornish

CHARACTERS
(In order of appearance)

A WHITE WOMAN
A BLACK WOMAN
HAROLD
NUMBER ONE
GEORGE
CUSTODIAN
POLICEMAN

Scene: A commercial laundromat.

DESCRIPTION OF CHARACTERS

WHITE WOMAN: Age thirty to fifty, physical type open. She is on welfare and should reflect this somewhat in her appearance without being dressed in rags.

BLACK WOMAN: Again there is a broad scope for age and appearance. She contrasts with the WHITE WOMAN by way of her more positive attitude toward life.

HAROLD: About thirty, pleasant looking, casually but well dressed. He is not terribly bright but his open personality and unforced friendliness should win the audience quickly.

NUMBER ONE: Early twenties, sharply dressed in either J. Press or African Heritage style. His physical type is open because his body is an afterthought. It is his brain that dominates—we can sense it tracking at a constant sprint. Whatever he may say, he never ate soul food at home.

GEORGE: Of the three principals, he is closest to a healthy, normal human being. He has the anger potential of most people and can therefore become a violent black man in the face of the black man's frustration. But unlike NUMBER ONE, he cannot constantly chew on the same grievance. And unlike HAROLD, he has no feelings of guilt—probably because he has nothing to feel guilty about—up to this point.

CUSTODIAN: Black or white, elderly but not decrepit. Role, not race, governs his attitudes.

POLICEMAN: Black or white. Like the CUSTODIAN, he has professional attitudes.

Scene: A garden variety commercial laun-dromat, none too well tended. Assets in-clude top loading washers, large driers, coke machine, change maker, soap and cigarette vending machines and a bulletin board dis-playing notices, ads and a couple of items of mislaid clothing, including a sock—all pinned up with thumb tacks. It is night: The electric clock high on the wall reads two-thirty. The clock is chained to the wall and further protected by a metal grill. Fur-niture is limited to a couple of plain benches, long, bare tables for folding clothes and a couple of trash containers. There are one or two extremely battered laundry carts. There is nothing else port-able, and nothing at all worth stealing. The walls are decorated with faded posters in-structing, directing and warning the cus-tomers. They are illustrated with simple pas-tel drawings. One prohibits dyeing clothes in the machines; another instructs custom-ers to be present when their machines go off; at least two warn the unwary that the management is not to be held responsible for stolen property. These latter are illus-trated by masked thieves tiptoeing off clutching items of lingerie. By the coin-changer is a notice that the establishment is protected by a fearless and formidable agency of private detectives who will track malefactors to the ends of the earth.

At rise: Two persons are on stage: a BLACK WOMAN *and a* WHITE WOMAN. *The former folds her laundry and the latter watches hers go round in the drier.*

WHITE WOMAN (*Picking up a small, open box of soap, the kind dispensed by the vending machines.*): How come I always got part of a box left over?

BLACK WOMAN: They're pretty smart . . . The machine takes a cup of detergent—the box gives you three quarters of a cup for a dime—so you have to buy another box and you got soap left over.

WHITE WOMAN (*Proffering the box.*): You want it?

BLACK WOMAN: No, thanks . . .

WHITE WOMAN: What am I supposed to do? Throw it away?

BLACK WOMAN: That's the idea. My husband says that's why they make the boxes that size—so you'll have to throw some away—"patriotic consumption."

WHITE WOMAN: What's that?

BLACK WOMAN: That's when you help the national economy by buying more stuff than you can use and then throw part of it away so you have to buy more the next time. That's the primary goal of the pack-aging industry.

WHITE WOMAN: Well, I can't afford to be patriotic.

BLACK WOMAN: Why don't you buy the large economy size in the store and bring what you need in a paper bag, like me? (*The* BLACK WOMAN *should be about finished with her folding and the* WHITE WOMAN *taking her clothes from the drier.*)

WHITE WOMAN: I can see you're not on wel-fare—the large economy size costs ninety-three cents.

BLACK WOMAN: But in the long run—

WHITE WOMAN: —it costs more to be poor. You should try raising five on a welfare check.

BLACK WOMAN: Try raising 'em on what my husband brings home—I could get more from welfare. After all, the city pays by the kid, but his boss doesn't.

WHITE WOMAN: Then let your old man take off, you'll get a raise.

BLACK WOMAN: No, I don't think so—I'd miss my winter sports too much.

WHITE WOMAN: Why? My old man drops in often enough to keep me from going through the ceiling.

BLACK WOMAN: Don't you get checked by your case-worker?

WHITE WOMAN: I get checked, all right. He knocks on my door at one o'clock in the morning, but he isn't looking for the man on the premises, the creep!

HAROLD, *a white man, enters, carrying a bag of laundry. He is dressed informally, but well. He sets a portable radio on a washer while he busies himself with his laundry. The* WOMEN *ignore him until he speaks.*

BLACK WOMAN: Maybe he only wants to keep you from going through the ceiling.

WHITE WOMAN: Yeah, he wants to get me pinned to the floor. But I'm not that hard up yet. (*Sees the* OTHER *is ready to go.*) Well, I'll be seeing you—

BLACK WOMAN: Oh, you live down near me, I might as well wait.

WHITE WOMAN: You don't have to—

BLACK WOMAN: I better . . . At this time of night, this neighborhood—

HAROLD (*At the vending machine.*): I beg your pardon, ladies . . . Can you tell me which kind of soap to use?

WHITE WOMAN: Do you want a white tornado or a washer ten feet tall?

HAROLD: What? Oh, ha ha ha, it doesn't make much difference, eh?

WHITE WOMAN: Not much—

BLACK WOMAN: Now me, I never use a white tornado—

HAROLD: Then neither will I. When in Rome, you know . . . but you'll have to get me a ladder to get my clothes out of the washer—ha, ha, ha. (*He receives a small box of soap for his coin.*)

WHITE WOMAN: You don't do clothes too often, eh?

HAROLD: No, but I'm game for anything once.

WHITE WOMAN: I guess you got a maid to do all that stuff for you.

HAROLD: No, but my wife says I treat her like a maid. . . . what makes you think I have a maid?

WHITE WOMAN: You live in that fancy building over on the avenue, don't you?

HAROLD: Well, yes—

WHITE WOMAN (*To* BLACK WOMAN.): You can always tell—

HAROLD: It's really not very fancy, and we only have a one-bedroom anyway—until we move into the new place . . . (*He is loading his clothes in a machine.*)

BLACK WOMAN: Hey, you better get those socks out of there.

HAROLD: Oh?

BLACK WOMAN: Unless you want to dye those white things charcoal grey—

WHITE WOMAN: Especially those brassieres . . . Your wife'll have a hernia.

HAROLD: Oh boy, she'd really let me have it, all right—it's all her stuff—nightgowns and things . . . Thanks a lot. (*He sorts out the socks and one or two other colored items as they talk. He starts the machine with the white load and puts the colored things in another.*)

BLACK WOMAN: Hey, how come you brought your laundry way over here? You got a laundromat in your own neighborhood.

HAROLD: Really?

BLACK WOMAN: Sure, a block from your building, right on this street.

HAROLD: Oh, now I get it. I *thought* she said it was only a block away—I just went in the wrong direction.

WHITE WOMAN: It couldn't have been wronger.

HAROLD: Do I put in the whole box?

BLACK WOMAN: And then some.

WHITE WOMAN: Here's some more, you can use it on them socks.

HAROLD: Why, thank you.

WHITE WOMAN: Don't mention it. My part in the war on poverty.

BLACK WOMAN: Uh oh, listen . . .

HAROLD: What is it?

BLACK WOMAN: Listen to that machine.

HAROLD: What's it doing?

BLACK WOMAN: Everything to those clothes but clean 'em. (*At the machine.*) Well, for heaven's sake . . . look what you did!

HAROLD: Don't tell me . . . what?

BLACK WOMAN: See this little tag?

HAROLD (*Reading.*): "Sorry, tired today."

BLACK WOMAN: This machine is busted. You hardly got as far as the wash cycle.

HAROLD: What do I do now?

WHITE WOMAN: Dredge it all out and put it in another machine with another quarter.

HAROLD: Oh great . . .

BLACK WOMAN: Why'd your wife ever trust you out of the house, anyway?

HAROLD (*Laughs.*): I'm that bad, eh? She's in the hospital . . . My wife . . . We had a baby yesterday.

WHITE WOMAN: Oooh, isn't that wonderful?

BLACK WOMAN: Congratulations.

HAROLD: Can I offer you a cigar? Ha, ha, ha.

BLACK WOMAN: Your first, eh?

HAROLD: Uh-huh. Anyway, she asked me to bring her nightgowns and stuff, so here I am, washing them up.

WHITE WOMAN: Get used to it, it'll be three nights a week with diapers from now on. But use the launderette in your own neighborhood—it's healthier.

HAROLD: Why, there's nothing wrong with this place—not when I have two such charming ladies to help me. But, of course, we'll be getting diaper service. That's more sensible, don't you think?

WHITE WOMAN: Oh, sure— Well, I'm ready to go . . . (HAROLD *begins to remove the clothes from the broken machine—a messy, sudsy business.*)

BLACK WOMAN: Well, friend, here's where the rats desert the sinking ship. Good luck.

WHITE WOMAN: We'd give you a hand, but it's awful late—

HAROLD: Thanks, no point in sharing the misery. (*Young black man,* NUMBER ONE, *enters, looks around, goes to cigarette machine.*)

WHITE WOMAN (*From the door.*): Hey, was it a boy or a girl?

HAROLD (*Arms full of sudsy clothes.*): A boy, the little—beggar.

BLACK WOMAN (*As they leave.*): You ain't seen nothing yet! (*Exits with a little laugh. Alone,* HAROLD *goes about his business. He looks to put the sudsy clothes in another washer. All tops are down, so he puts clothes atop one; blows a cloud of suds off his arms, opens washer, picks up clothes and dumps them in, reaches into pocket and comes out with wet change.*)

HAROLD: Dimes, for God's sake! (*He goes to the change machine and reads the instructions.*) "Two dimes and a nickel or one dime and three nickels." (*In despair, he bangs the change machine with his fist.* NUMBER ONE, *having found right change and his brand, buys a pack, and turns to go. Roused,* HAROLD *jumps at the chance of aid.*) Excuse me, friend, would you happen to have a quarter? I'm all screwed up here with a load of wet-wash.

NUMBER ONE: I might. Let me take a look . . . (*He fishes out his change.*) Yeah, here you go— (*Offers quarter.*)

HAROLD: Thanks a lot, you saved my life! (*Starts to take coin.*) Oh, excuse me, wet hands.

NUMBER ONE: That's okay. Don't worry about it . . .

HAROLD (*Wiping his hands under his arms.*) There . . . (*Takes quarter.*) Listen, you saved my life . . . (*Fishing out his own change.*) I could just see myself wallowing home with a load of sudsy underwear. Dammit, I don't have the exact change— as you might imagine . . . Well, here's three dimes, okay?

NUMBER ONE: Just give me two and we'll call it even. You might need the other for the drier.

HAROLD: Oh no, I couldn't—I mean, why should you pay for my stupidity?

NUMBER ONE: It's only a nickel—

HAROLD: Well, you know—the principle of the thing and all that . . .

NUMBER ONE: You don't want to be—in my debt, huh, man?

HAROLD: No, no, it's not that—but fair is fair, why should you have to pay?

NUMBER ONE: That's mighty white of you—

HAROLD: I insist! Come on, take my dime or I won't take your quarter. Blame it on my foolish pride. Ha, ha, ha.

NUMBER ONE (*Taking dime.*): Okay, man, have it your own way—I guess you've got me beat for pride—

HAROLD: My stubborn Yankee stock. Well, thanks for helping me out—

NUMBER ONE: Any time, man. (*He extends his hand to* HAROLD *who starts to respond. But* NUMBER ONE *draws his hand back before* HAROLD *can grasp it.*) Whoops, I forgot—wet hands. (*Exits with a skip and a little wave.*)

HAROLD: Thanks again. (*He goes to the new washer, checks his laundry and inserts his quarter, starting the machine. He takes out a dime and gets another box of soap from the vending machine. He opens the box, dumps the soap in the washer and throws the box away. He starts to turn on his radio but, seeing that his hands are covered with soap particles, stops. He looks about and spies the sock on the bulletin board, takes it down, wipes his hands and starts to throw it away. Then, thinking better of it, he tacks it up again. He sits on a bench and turns on the radio. He tunes in loud classical music. After a moment, he notices that the machine with his socks in it has stopped. He removes the socks and puts them in a drier. Meanwhile, unnoticed by* HAROLD, NUMBER ONE *and* GEORGE *enter. The latter carries a tiny bag of laundry over his shoulder.*)

NUMBER ONE: Here's a first-class machine, George.

GEORGE: Hey, we really gonna fool aroun' with this washin' business?

NUMBER ONE: You betray a lack of understanding, George. (HAROLD *has not heard them because of the loud music on his radio.* NUMBER ONE *now raises his voice to carry over it.*) Remember, child, cleanliness is not only next to Godliness, but is the key to upward mobility in the society of rising expectations.

HAROLD: Oh! It's you. Hi—

NUMBER ONE: Whaddya say, man?

HAROLD: I didn't expect to see you again—so soon—

NUMBER ONE: Dump it in, George. (GEORGE *sets about doing the small load of clothes.*) Well, I'll tell you what brought me back—besides my underwear—that entire load is underwear—all skivvies, you know—

HAROLD: Well, we all have to wear underwear, don't we? Ha, ha, ha—if we didn't, our outerwear would be our underwear.

NUMBER ONE: Ha, ha, ha. That's right, and if there's one thing I like, it's clean underwear, right, George?

GEORGE: You're Mister Clean with hair, Number One.

NUMBER ONE: I don't care what I got on outside, black, brown or beige, but underneath I gotta be lily-white . . . How about that, George?

GEORGE: Yeah, that's good, ha, ha, ha.

HAROLD: Ha, ha, ha—

NUMBER ONE: You don't have to laugh, man. George is one of those idiots who laughs at everything about color—you know, he's hipped on the subject. Say, you're not hipped on it too, are you?

HAROLD: Oh, no—but I wouldn't say I was unaware—

NUMBER ONE: Groovy, man. Hey, I'll tell you why I came back . . . (*He proffers* HAROLD *a nickel.*)

HAROLD: The nickel?

NUMBER ONE: I know, baby, it's only five cents. But then I got to thinking about Abraham Lincoln walking twenty miles in a blizzard to return a penny—what was that anyway, a library fine? I forget—and I said to myself, "That's what's wrong with my people, not enough of that Yankee pride." Isn't that right?

HAROLD: No, I don't think so. I'd say a Negro has about as much pride as anybody else—

NUMBER ONE: Negroes! Who's talking about Negroes? I'm talking about Unitarians. I'm a Unitarian and George there is one of my co-religionists—

HAROLD: Oh, I'm sorry, I misunderstood—

NUMBER ONE: Say, man, you didn't think we were some of those Black Muslims or something, did you? Not us. Say something in Unitarian, George.

GEORGE: I can't get any soap out of this machine.

NUMBER ONE: You did put in a dime—

GEORGE: Come on, Number One—

NUMBER ONE: Okay. What's the standard procedure when The Man tries to screw us?

GEORGE: Lean on him.

NUMBER ONE: Right. (GEORGE *deals the soap vendor a terrific blow with the side of his fist and a box of soap falls out. He holds it up for* NUMBER ONE *to see.*) The first lesson. You're learning, baby.

HAROLD: The first lesson—

NUMBER ONE: I'm instructing George in the Unitarian creed. George, recite the first lesson of the creed.

GEORGE: Oh, now—

NUMBER ONE: We mustn't be ashamed to bear witness for the faith, brother!

GEORGE: The first lesson: And the Leader spake, saying, "If ye go unto The Man, go unto him with thy fist."

HAROLD: That's Unitarianism?

NUMBER ONE: Eastern rite, man. That's from the apocryphal portions of The Sermon on the Mount.

HAROLD: That's a helluva gospel for the meek.

NUMBER ONE: Well, man, among us Unitarians, there's a doctrinal schism going on—the orthodox church versus the reform movement. There's Pope Innocent Abernathy the Second and Cardinal Wilkins on the one side, and on the other there's us reformers, the meek who are tired of inheriting the earth—we have proclaimed the New Gospel.

HAROLD: Actually, I think Roy Wilkins is a pretty good man—one of the few statesmen in America today.

NUMBER ONE: And we all love him . . . Why, he's the Bernard Baruch of us Unitarians, but he hasn't got the new revelation—

HAROLD: Like Rap Brown, I suppose—

NUMBER ONE: Well, baby, Rap's all right—for a middle-of-the-roader—

HAROLD: Middle-of-the-road!

NUMBER ONE: But hear the new Gospel!

Blessed are they that lean on The Man, for they shall see Westchester County—

HAROLD: You keep saying "lean on the man."

NUMBER ONE: Look, that machine belongs to a white man, right?

HAROLD: Wrong! You don't *know* that. Anyone might own this business—

NUMBER ONE: No 'fense, Charlie . . . Let's just say it belongs to the Establishment then—I mean, if you own anything, you're in the Establishment by definition. Well now, if the disestablished—that's us Unitarians—want anything from the Established, even after we've sweat for it and paid for it, we have to lean on 'em, bounce 'em around a little. That's the first law of progress in these here United States.

HAROLD: Come now, you're too intelligent to believe that.

NUMBER ONE: Do I believe it, George?

GEORGE: You wrote the book, Number One.

HAROLD: But that's crazy—

NUMBER ONE: Yeah . . .

HAROLD: After all, there are only a handful of—Unitarians compared to everyone else. Even putting ethics aside—it's a matter of practicality. You can't win with blood, only with brains. You have to get people on your side—along with the ones that are already there. After all, most of us want the same thing, don't we? Excuse me, I think my socks are dry.

NUMBER ONE: How are your palms? (HAROLD *is busy with his laundry.*) How are my scanties doing, brother?

GEORGE: Forget the laundry. What are we waiting for?

NUMBER ONE: The light of realization—

GEORGE: Huh?

NUMBER ONE: Without which there is no beneficence in harsh medicine.

GEORGE: Don't put me down, Number One.

NUMBER ONE: Never, baby. I'm going to pull you way up high.

GEORGE: Then talk so I can understand you.

NUMBER ONE: Georgie, your Leader isn't to be understood. If things were that simple, what would be the point? (*To* HAROLD.) Hey, man, do something with that box, all right? You're playing the racket so loud, I'm about to lose my natural rhythm.

HAROLD: I'm sorry. You don't care for classical music?

NUMBER ONE: Care for it? Why lawdy, Rastus yere an' me, we jus' *loves* symphony music, don' we, Rastus? Except it hasn't got any balls. Can it.

HAROLD: All right. There's no need for unpleasantness. (*Turns off radio.*)

NUMBER ONE: You're absolutely correct. We certainly don't want any undue unpleasantness disturbing the status which—or do we, George?

GEORGE: The second lesson: And the Leader saith, "The Man heareth the slave in the soft voice; therefore speak unto him with harshness and discord."

NUMBER ONE: You get another gold star. (*To* HAROLD.) Pay no attention to him, he's under the influence of one of those cockamamy, radical philosophies—yesterday, he burned his library card.

HAROLD: Yes, well I'd better get my clothes out of the washer—

NUMBER ONE: Aren't you going to play any music at all?

HAROLD: I thought you wanted it off—

NUMBER ONE: That's your second mistake, thinking—not off, man, different.

HAROLD (*Turns radio on.*): Oh, sure . . . Say, I think Jazzbo's on now—

NUMBER ONE: No, man, I don't want jazz either. Nor do I want some disc jockey who tries to make up like a Unitarian when he can't even get his hair to kink.

HAROLD: I just assumed you meant jazz—

NUMBER ONE: You dig it, right, man? Miles, Max, Milt—you dig 'em, right?

HAROLD: As a matter of fact, I have everything Miles Davis ever cut—

NUMBER ONE: Not quite, but let it pass . . . And learn something, aficionado of Africa's great contribution to our national heritage, jazz is just one more way of putting us Unitarians down, man—classical thirty-threes played at seventy-eight.

HAROLD: Well, what kind of music do you want?

NUMBER ONE: Haven't you heard the Dominoes?

HAROLD: Well—

NUMBER ONE: What about the Chevelles, The Impalas, The Corvettes?

HAROLD: They're okay if you like them, I'm sure—

NUMBER ONE: How about the Kaiser Frazers?

HAROLD: Well, you're entitled to your own

taste, and I'm sure you wouldn't deny me mine.

NUMBER ONE (*Dialing in a group.*): Listen! Are you gonna stand there and tell me that's not art? What are you, some kind of bigot?

HAROLD: Now, hold on a minute—

NUMBER ONE: *Listen!* That's the black-ass, black mass culture; don't you like it? *Ain't it art?*

HAROLD: As a matter of fact, I can't truthfully say I like it at all. But it's a free country and there's as much room for that kind of music as any other kind, I suppose.

NUMBER ONE: Nice try, Charlie. What's the matter, haven't you got the nerve to say it turns your stomach to think that noise is the national culture? That's the urban sound, baby—the black monkey, the brown banana, the beige mashed potato—

HAROLD: All right, I don't like it. If that makes me a bigot, I'm sorry. (*He heads back to the washer.*)

NUMBER ONE: Hey, man, I was just kidding. I don't dig that stuff either. George does though, don't you, George? (*Turns radio off.*)

GEORGE: It's okay, you didn't have to turn it off.

NUMBER ONE: George is part of the mass culture, aren't you, George? A regular soul brother, aren't you, George?

GEORGE: Cut it out, Number One—

NUMBER ONE: In fact, George is the archetype of the primitive, uninhibited swinger, aren't you, George?

GEORGE: I said cut it out, Number One—

NUMBER ONE: Say, (*To* HAROLD.) can you do the Monkey?

HAROLD: I'm afraid not—

NUMBER ONE: But you've got a girl, or a wife, haven't you?

HAROLD: Yes—I'm married.

NUMBER ONE: Then you gotta be able to do the Monkey, man—it's very pre-coital—

HAROLD: So is the fox-trot if you've got the right posture.

NUMBER ONE: Say, that's good, that's very good. Take that man's name, George—what is your name, by the way?

HAROLD: Uh—Harold.

NUMBER ONE: George, this is Harold; Harold, this is George. George, teach Harold to do the Monkey.

HAROLD: I'd really just as soon—

NUMBER ONE: Don't miss this chance, Harold. Dancing with George is a real experience. He's light as a feather, aren't you, George?

GEORGE: Aw, cut out that fairy stuff—

NUMBER ONE: That's middle-class hypocrisy talking, George . . . Dance with Harold.

GEORGE: You wanna do the Monkey?

HAROLD: No thank you, George—

NUMBER ONE: Aw, is your card all filled up?

HAROLD: Look, I just want to get my laundry into the drier.

NUMBER ONE: Ah'll take keer o' that, boss. (*He makes a grotesque dive at the washer.*) You jes joy yaself at the play party—

HAROLD: Please, I'd rather do it myself!

NUMBER ONE: You sound like a headache commercial, Harold. What's the matter with you anyway, are you prejudiced? You won't dance with George because he's a Unitarian and you won't let me finger your wife's panties because I bite my nails—

HAROLD: Look! I just don't want to Monkey with another man in a laundromat!

NUMBER ONE: Oh, would you rather go up to his apartment?

HAROLD: No, and I won't reconsider for the mashed potato either.

NUMBER ONE: Well, as long as you put it that way . . . Your feelings aren't hurt, are they, George?

GEORGE: Shoot, you know I don't go for that fairy stuff—

NUMBER ONE: And you don't dance very well, either. (*To* HAROLD.) All kidding aside, Harold, I knew you were a right-thinking liberal all along—you have a real sincere look about you.

HAROLD (*As he puts his laundry in drier.*): What makes you think you can just look at me and know anything about me?

NUMBER ONE: You can't tell a book by its cover—that's a nice liberal sentiment, Harold.

HAROLD: All right, it's a cliché, but that doesn't mean it's untrue . . . Well, does it?

NUMBER ONE: Absolutely not! Don't you agree, George?

GEORGE: Whatever you say, Number One.

HAROLD: Excuse me, but why does he call you *Number One?*

NUMBER ONE: It's okay, he can speak without an interpreter. Tell him, George.

GEORGE: He's my leader.

NUMBER ONE: He's my follower.

HAROLD: That's a pretty small—what do you call it—club, lodge, party?

NUMBER ONE: A mass movement, a practical revolutionary organization.

HAROLD: Where do you hold your convention, in a phone booth?

NUMBER ONE: Laugh while you can, baby. No real politician ever laughed at a man with a follower, not one who'll do what his leader tells him—and you will, won't you, George?

GEORGE: You say shit, I squat and strain—

NUMBER ONE: Suppose I say spit on the floor . . . (GEORGE *obliges*.) Suppose I say wipe it up with your sleeve? (GEORGE *does so*.) Suppose I say—I'm not saying it—kill this ofay bastard?

GEORGE: He's dead.

NUMBER ONE: Lean on that cancer dispenser. (GEORGE *punches in the glass front of the machine. To* HAROLD.) You can't laugh off a movement with discipline like that, baby.

HAROLD (*To* GEORGE.): Did you cut yourself?

NUMBER ONE: He doesn't care. If it hurts, he'll enjoy it.

GEORGE: Yeah, we're breaking things up.

HAROLD: This is all crazy—I can't understand your attitude. You're not deprived—

NUMBER ONE: You mean how can I be such a goddam nut when The Man, he let me go to school and I'm invited to dinner every year on Brotherhood Week and pink-toe babies are scrambling to beat each other into the sack with me just to prove whose behind is the most liberal, not to mention the fact that there are now two black-ass heroes on television—all this and the skirmish on poverty too? How can I be such an ingrate?

HAROLD: Well, before there were two heroes, there were none, right? What the hell do you want if you don't want progress?

NUMBER ONE: Well of course, and you have a right to be proud. You're a right-thinking liberal—some of your best friends eat watermelon.

HAROLD: I never mentioned pride and I certainly try not to be smug.

NUMBER ONE: Smug—you? Never! You have sensitivity; why, you're probably even ashamed to live in that high-price, tangerine flake, elevator shafted, mocha-maid-tended, antiseptic tower right next to the cockroach barracks—aren't you?

HAROLD: You're in love with the sound of your own voice, aren't you?

NUMBER ONE: Maybe I just think you ought to hear a black voice now and then—

HAROLD: I hear plenty. And for your information, I live in an integrated building—we have plenty of Negro tenants.

NUMBER ONE: Sure—a doctor, a lawyer and an African chief . . . And I bet you treat them just like people.

HAROLD: As a matter of fact, I don't treat them any way at all—just like any other neighbor—I don't curry them and I don't cut them . . . I think I do have a little sensitivity, enough to put myself in someone else's place—

NUMBER ONE: I have it, by Jove! You're one of those fellows James Baldwin's always talking about—you're one of those white Negroes—hey, maybe you're really Norman Mailer . . . We can all sit around and make kissy-face together, the White Negro and the Black Ofay . . . It's a party—

GEORGE: Number One, what the hell are you talking about?

NUMBER ONE: Don't strain yourself, George. Norman knows, don't you, Norman?

HAROLD: If you mean me, no I don't. It doesn't make any sense to me that you should attack the very people who want to help you. That wouldn't fit any man's definition of reasonable behavior—

NUMBER ONE: Well now, Harold, it's this helping business—

HAROLD: I know all about that . . . Certainly, our help seems patronizing—but what can we do? If we can't understand your life, it's not our unwillingness, we just haven't lived it—

NUMBER ONE: Harold, you're the greatest—really, I mean, you *would* let your daughter marry Arthur Ashe.

HAROLD: I don't have a daughter—

NUMBER ONE: Oh, what a shame, what a loss to the movement—

HAROLD: I have a son—he was born yesterday.

NUMBER ONE: Say, you hear that, George?

GEORGE: Yeah, where's my cigar?

NUMBER ONE: Why, George, we should give cigars to Harold, the friend of the race.

HAROLD: I don't smoke anymore, doctor's orders.

NUMBER ONE: Well, it's the spirit that counts. Say, I bet you wouldn't mind if he brought home a nice colored girl some time, would you?

HAROLD: Of course not, he'll be free to do as he pleases.

NUMBER ONE: Right! And some day, when he's teaching you all about the birds and the bees, you'll poke him in the ribs and ask him about that black poontang, huh? . . . I mean all them sex fears go right out the window when it comes to our women; now, don't they?

HAROLD: As a matter of fact, I don't think I have any sex fears at all—

NUMBER ONE: Not even a teensy one?

HAROLD: Well, I certainly don't subscribe to superstitions about Negro sexuality—

NUMBER ONE: You mean you don't envy our superior male potency, our jumpin' jungle juices? Look at yourself, white-eyes—have you got the nerve to stand there and say you're our sexual equal?

HAROLD (Trying for right answer.): Well, I don't know. . . . Envy? There's spontaneity of course, I mean—but I'm not jealous—

NUMBER ONE: That's right, Harold, we're all rompin', stompin' studs . . . Look at George there—stand up straight, George—doesn't he look like a regular love machine?

GEORGE: That's me, two hundred and ten pounds of solid royal jelly.

HAROLD: Yes, I suppose I'd have to give you cards and . . .

NUMBER ONE: And? . . . Go on, Harold, say it . . . You're among friends, say it . . . Say it.

HAROLD: Spades.

NUMBER ONE: What delicacy. Well, I'm gonna let you in on a little secret. I'm gonna flush all those racial sex fears right out of your little psyche. Is your wife nice?

HAROLD: Is that part of the routine laundry interrogation?

NUMBER ONE: Come on, baby, you certainly aren't ashamed of her, are you—?

HAROLD: Of course not—

NUMBER ONE: Has she got a nice ass—a hot little body?

HAROLD: Well, I don't see that it's any of your damn . . . Well, she's certainly attractive; yes, as a matter of fact, she's very nice—

NUMBER ONE: Lucky man! Well listen, baby, you slip your lady fair and Big George there between the same sheets and she couldn't be safer. You see, big stud is a faggot!

GEORGE: Aw, cut it out, Number One—

NUMBER ONE: In fact, he's just about the whole bundle of sticks. Why, he isn't a fairy, he's a regular g-nome, a pixie, a two hundred and ten pound elf!

HAROLD: He certainly doesn't look it—

NUMBER ONE: What a diplomat—enlist that man for the foreign service!

GEORGE: You're puttin' me down, Number One—

HAROLD: Really, you look quite masculine to me—

NUMBER ONE: There's only one way to settle this disagreement . . . George, soul sister, give Harold a nice big kiss.

GEORGE: Aw, come on—

NUMBER ONE: Yeah, show Harold what he's been missing . . .

HAROLD: Wait a minute, this has gone far enough . . .

NUMBER ONE: In the pursuit of truth, there's no such thing as far enough.

HAROLD: Look . . .

NUMBER ONE: Move, Georgie Girl, pleasure that dude!

GEORGE: Shit man, this is stupid . . .

NUMBER ONE (Serious.): This is the big quiz, Georgie, move.

GEORGE: All right. (He starts lumbering toward HAROLD, who backs off.)

HAROLD: Please, this is ridiculous . . .

NUMBER ONE: He's being coy, Georgie—romance him, talk to him, he wants to be coaxed!

GEORGE (Woodenly, as he moves toward HAROLD, arms wide.): Kiss me, I love you.

HAROLD (Cornered, pointing at GEORGE.): For God's sake, will you turn him off!

NUMBER ONE (Laughing.): Okay, okay. (To GEORGE.) Simmer down, lover boy. Ha, ha, ha. Okay. (To HAROLD.) The party's over . . . but I had you goin' for a minute, eh?

HAROLD: Oh, no—no. Why, George, anyone could just look at you and tell you're not—that way.

NUMBER ONE: "You can't judge a book by its cover."

GEORGE: Come on, Number One, let's get it over with . . .

NUMBER ONE: What do you say, Harold, shall we get it over with?

GEORGE: Oh, Jesus, be decent—

HAROLD: Get what over with—?

NUMBER ONE: Maybe you're right, George. I don't see much hope for enlightenment— no apocalyptic vision—

HAROLD: Are you talking about me? (*The* NIGHT CUSTODIAN *enters to make a routine check, clean out the garbage, etc. He is elderly and not very prosperous looking.*)

CUSTODIAN: Good evening, gentlemen . . . Found out how to beat the crowd, eh?

NUMBER ONE (*To* HAROLD.): No, man, we're talking about something else completely, not you. (*To* CUSTODIAN.) Yeah, Pops, we jus' 'bout got the whole place to ourselves.

CUSTODIAN (*To* HAROLD.): Our machines doing a good job on your clothes, sir?

HAROLD: Oh, fine . . . I did have a little trouble with a broken washer—I didn't notice the little sign saying it was out of order.

CUSTODIAN: Don't you worry about that . . . You just fill out one of our complaint forms . . . (*Pointing to pad and pencil stub on bulletin board.*) You'll get your quarter right back.

HAROLD: Thank you, that's very kind.

CUSTODIAN: It's just good business, sir—we want you to come back. (*He is collecting trash which he will later consolidate and lug out the back way.*)

NUMBER ONE: Hey, Pops, I got a complaint—

CUSTODIAN: Fill out a complaint form and you'll get your quarter back.

NUMBER ONE: Old man, I can overlook your lack of warmth, but a quarter will hardly assuage my anguish—

CUSTODIAN: Now, young fella, I live around here and I know your kind—now, what's the trouble?

NUMBER ONE: Well now, when we got here —George will back me up on this, won't you, George?

GEORGE: It's the absolute truth—

NUMBER ONE: I put a large bundle of black underwear in that washer, and it came out white, *white*. Now what I want to know is what is the meaning of that? Are you in league with the N.A.A.C.P. or what?

CUSTODIAN: Now don't you try your stuff on me, Mister, I know you and I won't stand for it—

NUMBER ONE: I forgot myself—

CUSTODIAN: You just finish your laundry and move on—the police don't like to see loitering in here . . . (*To* HAROLD.) Have these men been bothering you, sir?

NUMBER ONE: Oh man, is that crazy talk. What are you going to do with people like that, Harold? You can't even have a friendly discussion without some John Bircher starting an investigation.

HAROLD: It's all right. We've just been chatting, a friendly discussion, as he says.

CUSTODIAN: Yes, sir . . . (*Dragging barrel off to rear.*) But don't let them get fresh, sir; it doesn't pay . . . (*He is off.*)

NUMBER ONE: Man, hardening of the arteries really makes you nutty!

HAROLD: Well, sometimes imagination does improve with age—

NUMBER ONE: Long wear hasn't improved his brain any . . . Say, if we were troublemakers, George would have leaned on that old man, right, George, flapping his mouth like that?

GEORGE: Medicare time—

HAROLD: Well, let's face it, you did provoke him.

NUMBER ONE: You're right, Harold, and I feel sorry about that. (*The* CUSTODIAN *enters rear to exit front.*) Hey, Pops, no hard feelin's—we was just spoofin'.

CUSTODIAN: No, no hard feelings . . . (*Passing cigarette machine, notices broken glass for first time.*) Hey, what happened here?

NUMBER ONE: My guess is that someone broke the front of the machine.

CUSTODIAN: I can see that! Now what?

NUMBER ONE: Why don't you fill out a complaint form—maybe they'll send you a quarter?

CUSTODIAN: Don't you fool with me, Mister Smart Guy, I know you . . . hey, did you have anything to do with this?

NUMBER ONE: Not I . . . George?

GEORGE: I think it was like that when we come, Number One.

NUMBER ONE: That's right, I remember now . . . (*To* HAROLD.) Harold . . . remem-

ber, when we came in you said to watch
out for the broken glass?

HAROLD: Uh—yes, that's right—it was like
that when I arrived.

CUSTODIAN: (*Piling shards together with his
foot.*) If you say so, sir. I'll just have to report this for an unknown cause . . . (*He
starts out.*) Well, good night.

HAROLD: Good night.

GEORGE: See ya, Dick Tracy.

NUMBER ONE: George! Good night, old timer,
take care of yourself. (*The* CUSTODIAN *is
gone.*) Harold, you really saved our lives,
didn't he, George?

GEORGE: Yeah . . . Uh, look, your stuff is
done, let's get out of here—

HAROLD: It wasn't anything. I mean, what's
the point of making trouble?

NUMBER ONE: You're right, it wasn't anything—so your conscience is clear. George,
we don't have to change our plans.

GEORGE: Okay. Let's get it over with then, all
right?

NUMBER ONE: All right! Turn on the radio,
George.

HAROLD: Why did you do that? . . . What
are you . . . What is it you have to get
over with?

NUMBER ONE: Come on, Harold, you *know*
. . .

HAROLD: No I *don't* know . . . For God's
sake, will you stop talking in riddles? (*By
this time,* GEORGE *and* NUMBER ONE *should
be in such positions as to cut off* HAROLD's
escape.)

NUMBER ONE: Harold, you don't *want* to understand . . . but down at the tip of your
little pink toe, you know what's going to
happen.

HAROLD: No—

NUMBER ONE: You knew before the old family retainer blew in to lug out the garbage—
but you muffed your big chance because
you won't harbor evil thoughts about Unitarians in your liberal heart. It wouldn't be
cricket to suspect two nice colored boys
like us of being troublemakers . . . (*Mimics* HAROLD's *speech to the* CUSTODIAN.)
"We've just been chatting, three stock
brokers chewin' the fat while our drawers
go round together." Come on, Harold!

HAROLD: Well, it *was* just talk—

NUMBER ONE: Sure it was and you really believed I came back here just to dabble my

dainties, didn't you? That's because you
fine, open-minded, unprejudiced friends of
black folk figure we just move ass down to
the laundromat every night and do our
delicate things—we just can't stand for our
undies to get moldy in the laundry basket,
even though you can.

HAROLD: Are you trying to frighten me?

NUMBER ONE: Nothing could be further from
my mind.

HAROLD: George, you'll give me a straight
answer . . . Why did you come here?

GEORGE: I got nothin' to tell you.

HAROLD: You have to tell me.

GEORGE: Like hell I do. Ask *him!*

NUMBER ONE: Two of a kind! Well, there
you are, Harold. You're just going to have
to say it for yourself.

HAROLD: Say what?

NUMBER ONE: You already know that,
Harold.

HAROLD: No, I don't know anything . . .

NUMBER ONE: Just say it, Harold, for the
good of your soul . . .

HAROLD: George, please . . .

GEORGE: Get off me, mother.

NUMBER ONE: Say it, Harold . . .

HAROLD: Oh, my God . . .

NUMBER ONE: Like you could have said it the
minute we walked in . . .

HAROLD: No, that's not right . . .

NUMBER ONE: Come on, Harold, *say it.*

HAROLD: I can't . . .

NUMBER ONE: But you know it.

HAROLD: But why?

NUMBER ONE: There!

HAROLD: Why?

GEORGE: Because he says so.

NUMBER ONE: And see, Harold, you weren't
the least bit surprised, you knew all along
—of course, you kept pushing all those
nasty thoughts about poor old black folk
to the back of your mind . . . (*He bends
at the knees and does a pattycake routine
on his hands and thighs, ending palms out-
ward with a big minstrel show grin.*) Dat's
me, Mistuh Bones, dey ain't a mean
thought in mah poh ol' black body . . .
It would never occur to you, Harold, to
give me credit for being as mean a son of
a bitch as an Alabama sheriff—it pains me
to say so, Harold, but you really are a bigot.

HAROLD: All because I thought well of you?

NUMBER ONE: It's bigotry, isn't it, Georgie?

GEORGE: That's right, it is, man, pure white bigotry.

NUMBER ONE: So you won't have to feel guilty, Georgie. Does it make sense now, Harold—that it's for your prejudice—I mean, who gave you the *right* to think well of us?

HAROLD: But what do you want from me?

NUMBER ONE: The same cold neutrality you give everybody else, Harold, to look right through me without even noticing what I am—forget I'm black and lump me together with the rest of the garbage.

HAROLD: Not a word of that is true! If I saw right through you, you'd hate me even more—you want what you can never have, you want us to help you and see right through you at the same time—it's childish!

NUMBER ONE: Why, Harold, you are a gritty little fellow after all, isn't he, George?

HAROLD: And it isn't possible anyway. If you live here today—you have to choose a side—

NUMBER ONE: You suffocating, patronizing Negro-lover, don't choose my side. Where do you get off treating me as if I were a black African and you were a one-man Marshall plan—be against me or ignore, but don't degrade me!

HAROLD: But your life is part of my life—nobody's innocent. I have to be aware of blackness.

NUMBER ONE: Now you are in a quandary, Harold. But then, that's your problem, not mine.

HAROLD: Mine only?

NUMBER ONE: Rule Number Six, George . . .

GEORGE: And the Leader speaketh, saying: Let the sins of the father be the sins of the child and let the generation of sin be his children's children.

NUMBER ONE: The Man invented the problem, fed the problem and cuddled the problem—so it's his problem.

GEORGE: And all the problem's babies are your babies—

HAROLD: You don't really believe that, you're just spouting lessons—

NUMBER ONE: He can act on it—

HAROLD: How can you possibly blame me for three hundred years of history? I'm nobody—

GEORGE: You're The Man.

HAROLD: If I have to stand for something bigger than myself, it's for the other white man, the one who wants wrongs righted, the one who's ashamed—

NUMBER ONE: If you're not at fault, how come you're ashamed, baby?

HAROLD: I can't explain . . . I'm not ashamed of *myself* exactly—

NUMBER ONE: Not even now that you know you're a bigot?

HAROLD: I'm *not!* You're the only bigot here—

NUMBER ONE: Are you so thick you still don't get it? The day you can look at George there and think to yourself he might not *have* a big prick but might *be* one—*then* you won't be a bigot any more.

HAROLD: I can't understand you people—

NUMBER ONE: Stop trying! That's the final kernel of white superiority that drives us wild—you keep thinking you can understand—

HAROLD: All right! I can't understand what it's like to be black—ever! Then how do you think you can understand me? Is your suffering so complex and my guilt so simple?

NUMBER ONE: Let's just say our suffering is so concrete and your guilt so theoretical—

HAROLD: Theoretical! Do you think guilt doesn't hurt? Do you know how it feels to enjoy your happiness at the expense of others?

NUMBER ONE: We're willing to learn.

HAROLD: Can't you believe that some of us are troubled and confused to the depths of our souls by this—?

NUMBER ONE: There may be something to that, Harold . . . In fact, that's why we're still talking, haven't opened you up so all your confusion could run out on the floor and then shoveled it into one of the driers —cause we's good colored folk, mind, and we don' wanna make no mess hyar on Massa Charlie's nice, clean flo'.

GEORGE: Come on, let's get it done with—

NUMBER ONE: You're missing the point, George . . . Harold has to understand why we erase him . . . I don't know where George gets his puritan strain, Harold—he can throttle a chicken, but he doesn't like to talk about it.

HAROLD: George, this isn't your idea at all, is it?

GEORGE: Ideas aren't my job—

NUMBER ONE: You're riding a dead horse, Harold. George has made the leap to faith, haven't you, Georgie?

GEORGE: Don't call me Georgie, Number One . . .

NUMBER ONE: *George* understands the principles of revolution— I taught him: One mind, one body, no hesitation . . . No, you better try me . . . who knows, maybe you'll convince me you're more valuable alive than dead.

HAROLD: Now I see—that's it, this is just a game—you want to *give* me my life. That's it, isn't it? You're making *me* the slave and you the masters—then you'll let me beg my way free—

NUMBER ONE: That displays a certain imagination, Harold, but you haven't got it quite right. I'm going to let you talk until you realize you *deserve* to be put away, and then I'll let Georgie lean on you. You'll shuffle off like a Greek hero, with a new self-knowledge—the modern salvation, see yourself and die.

HAROLD: But you have nothing to gain from my death.

NUMBER ONE: Your death will frighten the Establishment, and the Establishment only changes when it's frightened.

HAROLD: You talk like a tract! Like a textbook—

NUMBER ONE: That's what I am, baby, the New Primer of Social Progress.

HAROLD: But people can act out of sheer decency, if you only teach them what's right.

NUMBER ONE: The difference between good people and bad people: Neither gets off his behind until he's pushed—when the pushing gets too rough, the good does good, the bad does bad.

HAROLD: But you've just admitted you don't know what effect pressure will have . . . Maybe if you—hurt me, the result will harm your cause, not help it.

NUMBER ONE: Good thinking! And you're right, Harold, sufficient irritation will bring on the apocalypse, the two ends of infinity. We push and we push and we push until one day The Man either gives us everything we want or he rises up and . . . The final solution to the Jewish question . . . Twenty million sweaty blacks bound

back to Bechuanaland, or forty million sides of black beef—canned like Spam . . . Yes, I think that would be most efficient. After all, we run two and a half million cars through these car crushers every year, and they come out nice cubes of corrugated steel, ready to use as bridge and building foundation blocks . . . You put four of us into each car just before it's driven into the crusher, and in two years—you've solved the problem! Not only that, but when those five million blocks of meat and metal are shoring up hospitals and whorehouses, temples and tenements—you'll be right back to the *status quo*—America the Beautiful standing tall and straight on the bodies of black people.

HAROLD: Your mind is impossible—not even science fiction could match that . . .

NUMBER ONE: What about history? The new marching song could be "We did it before and we can do it again . . ." (*Sung.*)

HAROLD: Horror like that could never happen here.

NUMBER ONE: Then we're not taking any chances by erasing you—it can only result in another step toward brotherly love.

HAROLD (*Tries to laugh.*): This is all wild theorizing. You wouldn't kill me without some immediate gain—

NUMBER ONE: I'd get my nickel back—

HAROLD: If you were caught it would be for nothing.

NUMBER ONE: You're wrong, Harold, it's for everything, here, now, tonight—you, especially you . . .

HAROLD: George, you're sane—why should anyone have to kill me? Why me?

GEORGE: I'm not the one to ask—

HAROLD: But I'm asking you anyway—this game has *some* rules evidently—and one is that you have to answer me . . . Why me?

GEORGE: So we can have—the movement—because he *has* to.

NUMBER ONE: George knows, but he isn't very articulate. Are you, George?

GEORGE: Am I what?

NUMBER ONE: Articulate.

GEORGE: No—

NUMBER ONE (*Taking off* GEORGE.): An ah doesn't talk much nuther, Marse Boss—

GEORGE: Come on, cut it out—

NUMBER ONE: Harold, we need you for the

baby to grow. Right now, my movement is two bricks, Georgie and me, with no cement—you're the cement.

HAROLD: I think you must be a poet—I can't make sense of anything you say . . .

NUMBER ONE: My deah, that's the nicest compliment I've had since my draft board called me a misfit . . . Try to understand, Harold . . . a mass movement takes blood. Once we shed it, we can never turn back . . . See, you're the cement, you'll bind us together . . . Why, you'll be famous, like Charles the First, or Louis the Fifteenth—you'll be Harold—the Clean, ha, ha, ha—

HAROLD: But I'm not famous, I'm nobody, I won't be noticed—

NUMBER ONE: We'll notice you, Harold.

HAROLD: But why me? Anyone would do—is it just dumb chance?

NUMBER ONE: Not a bit—in fact, you more or less volunteered, baby. Here were George and I just cruising down the street, see, talking about our movement, and I say to him, "Kimosabe, for five cents, I'd knock off the next paleface we see." Well, then I come in here for a pack of weeds, and you give me a nickel—it's fate! I went out to the car and told Georgie there's a round-shouldered Ivy-league square volunteering for duty. I said, "We're in business," right, George?

GEORGE: "Now or never," you said.

NUMBER ONE: So it's all settled, Harold—"Now or never." I can't renege now—Georgie would lose faith in me, I'd be a leader without a follower; Georgie would be a lost black sheep; and you'd be confused again.

HAROLD: George—

NUMBER ONE: Here comes the big pitch, Georgie—

GEORGE: Don't call me *Georgie*—

NUMBER ONE: Sorry, Soul Brother.

HAROLD: George, if this is all for your benefit, then you have to decide . . . Do you really want to kill a man?

GEORGE: I—just want to follow orders—

HAROLD: You can't get off that easy—if you do it, it's because *you* make the decision to do it—it's all on you.

NUMBER ONE: Listen close, Georgie, now you're gonna learn everything I told you about The Man—

GEORGE: Why don't both of you shut up and leave me be?

HAROLD: George, it's not me who won't leave you be, is it? I don't need anything from you except to be alone myself, but *he* needs something from you—

NUMBER ONE: And away we go! Charlie White-eyes strikes again with the devastating power of his superior intellect. He's putting you down, baby—

HAROLD: I'm not the one who puts you down, George—I don't treat you like a fool; I don't call you "Georgie"; I don't need your unquestioning obedience to make me feel like a big man—

NUMBER ONE: And you'll never have it, man—those days are gone!

HAROLD: He's getting worried, George—hear him? I'm getting close—

NUMBER ONE: Worried. One word, baby, one word from me and George lowers the boom.

HAROLD: Hear that, George? . . . You're in his pocket, that's what he's saying—he *owns* you.

NUMBER ONE: This game has gone far enough—

GEORGE: Shut up a minute—

HAROLD: What is this great "Movement"? It's a two-man plantation, one master and one slave, and you know which one you are. He bought you with a lot of talk about the "Movement," but what did you buy?

NUMBER ONE: See, Georgie, The Man has got a thousand tricks and this is one of the best—divide and conquer—you should listen to me, baby.

HAROLD: Yes, listen to him, after all he owns your mind as well as your body—

NUMBER ONE: Only The Man ever owned people, baby—

HAROLD: And after you do what he wants you to do with me—

NUMBER ONE: We fooled around long enough, George—

HAROLD: He'll own you *forever!*

NUMBER ONE (*Moving toward* HAROLD.): The party's over, Harold—

GEORGE (*Without actually stepping between.*): Let him finish his say, Number One—

NUMBER ONE: You big jerk, he's turning you to a first class Uncle Tom—

HAROLD: Black or white, what's the difference, George?

NUMBER ONE: Come on, George, we can't waste any more time—

HAROLD: When someone *owns* you, you're a slave no matter what color he is—

NUMBER ONE: Let's do it now!

GEORGE: Shut up!

NUMBER ONE: Do it now!

HAROLD: Where's Number Three?

GEORGE: What?

HAROLD: He's Number One, you're Number Two, where's Number Three, the one who takes orders from you?

GEORGE: What do you mean—?

NUMBER ONE: You dumb idiot, what are you listening to?

HAROLD: Or are you only good for taking orders—for memorizing *lessons* and winning gold stars like a school kid—where's Number Three?

GEORGE: Where is he, Number One?

NUMBER ONE: You're nuts, Georgie—

HAROLD: You certainly are if you think there's ever going to be anyone but you and him, slave and master —

NUMBER ONE: Stomp him now!

GEORGE: *Why*, just to make you feel big?

NUMBER ONE: *I'm your Leader! Do it!* (GEORGE *doesn't make a move.*) Do it! (*To* HAROLD.) You ofay bastard . . . (*We can't be sure if* NUMBER ONE *would attack* HAROLD *by himself, because during the pause after his words, a* POLICEMAN *enters the laundromat. The three* PRINCIPALS *immediately relax into casual postures, even* HAROLD *somehow joining in a conspiratorial mood.*)

POLICEMAN: What's happening, fellas?

NUMBER ONE: Well, we're doing laundry, sir —what else would be going on?

POLICEMAN: Nobody in this neighborhood has that much laundry, boy.

NUMBER ONE: My friend and I have only been here a few minutes—

POLICEMAN: Don't give me that crap, friend. The old man told me to keep an eye on you half an hour ago. Now, what's the party all about? (NUMBER ONE *starts to speak.*) Not you. What's the matter with you two? (HAROLD *and* GEORGE.) You— (GEORGE.) you're big enough to talk.

GEORGE: I— (*Referring to* NUMBER ONE.) it's like he says, man.

POLICEMAN: Sure . . . What about you— (HAROLD.) You're the odd man here . . .

HAROLD: I beg your pardon—

POLICEMAN: You don't live in this neighborhood, do you?

HAROLD: As a matter of fact—

POLICEMAN: What's so irresistible about this laundromat?

HAROLD: Actually, I ended up here by mistake.

POLICEMAN: I'll say . . . Well, the three of you finish your wetwash and move out. If you want to have a party, hire a hall. Okay?

NUMBER ONE: Yes, sir, we'll be done in a minute.

POLICEMAN (*Calling out to his partner.*): Okay. Let's go, Frank, there's nothing happening here. (*He is gone.*)

GEORGE: Let's get out of here while we got the chance.

NUMBER ONE: What's the hurry, baby? They're gone—

HAROLD (*Gathering up his things.*): Well, I'd better be on my way—

NUMBER ONE: Exit the conquering hero—

GEORGE: Hey, man, thanks for cooling it—

NUMBER ONE: That was a real surprise, wasn't it, Georgie?

GEORGE: Cut it out. Hey, man, how come you didn't say anything?

HAROLD: I—uh—

NUMBER ONE: In fact, I think Harold was as surprised as we were, weren't you, Harold?

HAROLD: Frankly, I wouldn't want to see George have trouble over this—

NUMBER ONE: The man is a prince—thank him again, Georgie—

HAROLD: You don't have to—

NUMBER ONE: You're damn right you don't have to! Don't get it, baby? You've been had—

HAROLD: My God, you don't think you can start all over—

NUMBER ONE: It never got stopped, Harold— I told you, George, I told you The Man had a thousand weapons—how do you think he's whipped us for three hundred years? We knew what we came for, but he found a way to make you forget—what they've always done, baby, divide and conquer—

HAROLD (*To* GEORGE.): I freed you—

NUMBER ONE: Who the hell do you think you are, Abraham Lincoln? He made you a house Negro, baby, and then he stuck it in deep—don't you feel it? Why didn't he spill his guts to that cop?

HAROLD: I told you—

NUMBER ONE: Because he had you sewn up, baby, because you were faithful old George, just like one of the family— (*To* HAROLD.) Who gave you the right to trust him? (*To* GEORGE.) He knew he had you licked with his superior white brain, that's why . . . (*To* HAROLD.) But you blew it, man— you're never going to climb into that saddle again—especially you—

HAROLD: You turn everything I say inside out—

GEORGE: Like you turned me inside out—

HAROLD: I could have turned you in—

NUMBER ONE: But you figured you didn't need help with two simple children of the jungle—

HAROLD: I'm wasting my breath—

NUMBER ONE: You have a point, Harold, we're wasting time. Now, George, it's cement time—nobody'll be able to pry us apart again—

HAROLD: Please—

NUMBER ONE: Sorry, Harold, no time for last requests— Unless you'd like to finish folding your clothes first—there's no time for a last meal or anything, but if you really want to fold those undies— (*They are very close to* HAROLD *now, pressing in.*)

HAROLD: My wife's in the hospital . . . it was caesarean . . . how will she know?

NUMBER ONE: Don't worry, Harold, we'll put a note in her dainties.

HAROLD (*A little quiet.*): Not knives . . . I'm afraid of knives—

NUMBER ONE: Weapons! We don't carry weapons . . . do we look like hoodlums, Harold?

GEORGE: Come on, let's get it done—

HAROLD: Then what—?

NUMBER ONE: Tonight we improvise . . . We'll just have to stomp you, I guess—

HAROLD (*Almost ready to vomit—crosses hands over his chest—his heart is beating wildly.*): Oh, my God— (*He has backed against the washer or table where most of his laundry is piled.*)

NUMBER ONE: Oh, it won't be so bad, it'll be quick—look at those gunboats on George . . . All right, George. . . . (*They start to move in.* HAROLD, *his knees already*

starting to buckle, feels desperately behind him for some kind of a weapon. Absurdly, he grabs a bra and brings it forward in one hand without realizing what he's doing.) Sorry, Harold, that's about a thirty-six and you need at least a forty-five . . . (*They are almost upon him and* HAROLD *sinks to his knees, certain he is about to die, and hides his face in the bra, sobbing, completely dissolved.*)

GEORGE (*Taken aback by* HAROLD's *abject posture.*): Aw, come on . . . Hey, Number One—

NUMBER ONE: Defend yourself, Harold— you're letting George down—come on, a vicious adversary to the end . . . where are your balls, man?

GEORGE: You said man to man—

NUMBER ONE: Get up, for Christ's sake—act like a man, you bastard—

GEORGE: Shoot, I can't lean on a man with his face in a brassiere—

NUMBER ONE (*To* HAROLD.): You think you're pretty smart—

GEORGE: Come on, Number One, he ain't The Man—

NUMBER ONE: Yes, he is, the smart son-of-a-bitch! He's ofay Charlie with one more trick up his sleeve, just like always—

GEORGE: Just piss on him an' let's get out of here—

NUMBER ONE: You'd like that, wouldn't you, you pasty-face? You'd like to get off like a fag in the Penn Station john—and just run home to your fancy tile shower . . . Get up and fight! (*Screaming in frustration.*) Get up! (NUMBER ONE *reaches down and tears the bra away from* HAROLD, *who, his last vestige of protection gone, is more terrified than ever.* NUMBER ONE *seizes one of the bra cups in his teeth, tears away a piece and flings the bra in* HAROLD's *face, spitting the bitten out piece after it.* HAROLD *is petrified.*) Get up, you motherless sucker, or I'll stomp you where you sit!

HAROLD: I can't—

GEORGE: *Fight*, man? What can you lose?

HAROLD (*With shame as well as fear.*): I can't fight— I never could—

GEORGE: Damn, what a letdown—

HAROLD: I'm sorry—

NUMBER ONE: You're sorry! Listen, Harold. . . . Baby, you're The Man—you're on top of it all and we're trying to take it all away from you—get it? That's what it's all about. We're trying to take it away and you're fighting to keep it—that's how it works, goddamit—

HAROLD: Not with me, I'm not your man . . . If you got down on the floor with a brassiere over your face and I had George—I still couldn't fight you—I never could—

NUMBER ONE: Man, you have to fight. How else did you get that fancy apartment, that clean shirt, that cushy job? By putting us down, that's how, by being The Man, the top dog—

HAROLD: No—no, those things just happened to me—like . . .

NUMBER ONE: Like what?

HAROLD: Like you're happening to me.

NUMBER ONE: What about that sexy, butter-bottom wife, what about her? How did you get her?

HAROLD: I don't know—I think she got me—

GEORGE: Well she sure didn't want much . . . Come on, Number One, he ain't worth the shoe leather . . .

NUMBER ONE: No! He doesn't get off so easy. There's just two kinds of people, outs and ins—and you're an in—

HAROLD: But I belong to no secret order, have no ruling power. My life just happened to me—

NUMBER ONE: A poor innocent lamb—

HAROLD: All I ever did was say, "I don't mind . . ." My parents told me I was going to college and I said, "I don't mind." Someone offered me a job and I said, "I don't mind."

GEORGE: How about your wife—she say, "Do you mind?"

NUMBER ONE (*Mimicking*.): No, I don't mind.

HAROLD: I guess the effect was the same—

GEORGE: Dumb luck—

NUMBER ONE: Is that all it is, Harold?

HAROLD: I guess so.

NUMBER ONE: You could just as well have been poor.

HAROLD: Yes.

NUMBER ONE: Or ignorant.

HAROLD: Of course. I had nothing to do with it.

NUMBER ONE: In fact, in short, you could just as well have been black.

HAROLD: Certainly—

GEORGE: Only nobody asked him, so he couldn't say, "I don't mind." Ha, ha, ha.

NUMBER ONE: Shut up! Harold, you're a mindless, gutless bug that's been blown into a warm place—aren't you?

HAROLD: I can't argue—

NUMBER ONE: But what if you had been born black—how would gutless, mindless, *black* Harold have turned out?

GEORGE: Kiss that duplex by-by, baby!

NUMBER ONE: Harold, the college man?

HAROLD: Probably not.

NUMBER ONE: Harold, the frat man? Harold, the assimilated, middle class, white collar, grey flannel black man . . . ?

HAROLD: No—

NUMBER ONE: Harold, the drunken, down-trodden *nigger*, right, George?

GEORGE: You couldn't hack it, baby, being black—

NUMBER ONE: Could you hack it, Harold?

HAROLD: I don't know—

NUMBER ONE: You don't have George's muscle—you don't have my brains or imagination—have you? You haven't anything—have you? . . . *Have you?*

HAROLD: No . . . nothing—none of those things—

NUMBER ONE: Why, Harold, do you know what that makes you? The real factory reject—get it, George? Under that pasty, lucky skin, he's a junkie, alkie, illiterate welfare case—

GEORGE: You could never cut it, man—

NUMBER ONE: Norman Mailer may be the white Negro, baby, but you, you, Harold, are the white *nigger*. Do you follow me, *nigger*?

HAROLD: Yes—

NUMBER ONE: Yes, *sir*, nigger!

HAROLD: Yes, sir . . .

GEORGE: Hey, Number One, he's a fine nigger—

NUMBER ONE: Well, he has potential. Hey, boy—boy!

HAROLD: Yes, sir?

NUMBER ONE: That's right, Harold, boy, play the game sharp and we might let you hang around 'til sundown . . . You *do* want to play the game?

HAROLD: Yes, sir.

NUMBER ONE: You haven't got that just right, boy—it's *yassuh*.

HAROLD: Yassuh.

NUMBER ONE (*Laying on a tremendous Stepin Fetchit accent.*): Yassuh.

HAROLD (*Equally thick.*): Yassuh.

GEORGE: Hey, that boy has talent—

NUMBER ONE: George, who's teachin' this nigger?

GEORGE: You don't have to teach 'em, it's in their blood.

NUMBER ONE (*Laughing.*): Shut up, George. Listen, Harold, boy, I want you to say yassuh again, but this time, I want you to put a *smile* in it.

HAROLD: Yassuh—

NUMBER ONE: More!

HAROLD (*Practically singing, a broad rictus and rolling eyes.*): Yassuh!

NUMBER ONE: More!

HAROLD: YASSUH!!

NUMBER ONE: That's better. We like happy niggers around here, don't we, George?

GEORGE: Full of grits and goobers—

NUMBER ONE: And remember, Harold, boy, happy niggers are healthy niggers.

HAROLD: Yassuh.

NUMBER ONE: How's life treatin' you, boy?

HAROLD: Yassuh.

NUMBER ONE: What kind of a dumb answer is that, boy? If you're too stupid to play right, we can go back to the other game, dig?

HAROLD: Yassuh!

NUMBER ONE: That's better, boy. Now, the question was, "How's life been treatin' you?"

HAROLD: Jes fahn—Mistuh Boss—

GEORGE (*Laughing.*): He certainly is a *good* nigger, he could live to eighty-five in Biloxi.

NUMBER ONE: How do you like slobbering on your knees in a laundromat, boy?

HAROLD: Ah likes it fahn, yassuh.

NUMBER ONE: You don't have any desire to stand up, do you, boy?

HAROLD: Oh, no, suh.

NUMBER ONE: And if some agitatin' red bastard walked in and told you to stand on your own two feet and tell us where to get off, what would you say, boy?

HAROLD: No thank you, suh.

NUMBER ONE: Shoot, nigger, where's your loyalty? Tell that agitatin' red bastard that your masters love you and know what's best for you. Tell him.

HAROLD: Marse Boss, he know wha's bes' fo me . . .

NUMBER ONE: Go on.

HAROLD: He say I'm happier on my knees, so I's gwine to stay hyar . . .

NUMBER ONE: Harold, you're a good boy. Stand up and wipe yourself off. (*Taking a pair of underpants from* HAROLD'*s laundry.*) Here, wipe your face.

HAROLD (*Doing so after only a slight hesitation.*): Thank you, Marse Boss.

NUMBER ONE (*Arm around* HAROLD'*s shoulder.*): Don't mention it, boy. Why, I got a soft spot in my heart for a white nigger who knows his place.

HAROLD: Can I go home now?

NUMBER ONE: How's that?

HAROLD: Kin ah go home now, boss?

NUMBER ONE: George, Harold is tired of our new game . . .

GEORGE: Would you like to go back to the old game, Harold?

NUMBER ONE: We could finish it.

HAROLD: Please, no . . .

NUMBER ONE: Turn up the boy's radio, George. (GEORGE *obliges.*)

HAROLD: Please—

NUMBER ONE: And we'll play with a will—hey, we'll have a party—c'mon, boy, now's your chance to shine for the boss—dance—dance, Harold—

HAROLD: I can't—

NUMBER ONE: Who is that, George?

GEORGE: The Bananas.

NUMBER ONE: That's first class music, nigger. C'mon, dance—

HAROLD: I can't dance, I don't know how—

NUMBER ONE: You puttin' us on, boy, but you can't get away with it. We know you're all born with it—it's in your jumpin', jivin' blood. Dance, nigger!

HAROLD: Yassuh . . . (*The music is hard rock*—HAROLD *tries to dance. At first, he merely shuffles his feet, but as* NUMBER ONE *prods him, he gradually brings everything, hips, hands, elbows, eyes and teeth, into play. He taps, soft shoes and bops, at each of which he is completely inept and graceless. By the climax of the dance, he is completely involved, putting one hundred percent of his energy and concentration into it. After that point, when his chest is paining, he becomes more and more exhausted until we feel, at his exit, that he could not possibly dance another step.*)

NUMBER ONE: I said, dance, boy—you're a nigger, aren't you?

HAROLD: Yassuh.

NUMBER ONE: Up on stage, Stepin Fetchit. (*They force* HAROLD *onto the folding table where he does his dance.*)

HAROLD: Yassuh.

NUMBER ONE: Now dance, wild child of nature, swing! George, I don't think he hears the beat—

GEORGE (*Clapping time.*): One an' two an' one an' two an' one—

NUMBER ONE: You're dogging it, boy . . . Use those hands, those hips . . . Shake your ass . . . That's a little better, now enjoy yourself . . . Look like you havin' a good time, dammit . . . C'mon, nigger, if we wasn't makin' you dance, you'd do it all night just for fun . . . more, *more* . . . MORE . . . FASTER . . . Yay, now you're swingin'! (*During this speech,* NUMBER ONE *jumps in a laundry cart and* GEORGE *pushes him in a circle around the dancing* HAROLD. NUMBER ONE *takes pennies from his pocket and starts to toss them at* HAROLD. GEORGE *follows suit. They toss the coins, not hard, but around* HAROLD's *face, just swiftly enough to terrorize him further.*)

HAROLD: Stop, I can't dance any more—

NUMBER ONE: Sure you can, you just hittin' the big money now—

GEORGE: Shoot, nigger, you can dance all night and pick ten bags tomorrow—

HAROLD (*Breathing very hard.*): No more— no more—

NUMBER ONE: No more? (*Tossing a sheet to* GEORGE *and donning one himself.* GEORGE *follows suit.*) Why this is a party, boy, a dress-up play party—we'll all dance. (*With a whoop, he and* GEORGE, *covered with sheets, start to dance a circle around the stumbling, dancing* HAROLD. *The* ACTORS *support the lines with improvised sounds scattered between the lines. For example,* GEORGE *launches into a complicated jazz scat.* HAROLD, *attempting to please, tries to imitate* GEORGE's *scatting but can only produce a ludicrous parody.*)

HAROLD: Please, boss, ah's a good nigger—

GEORGE (*Screaming under the sheet.*): The best, the best of the niggers!

NUMBER ONE (*Also sheeted.*): Dance, love-child, dance—

HAROLD: Ah's a good nigger—

NUMBER ONE: We love our pickaninny sweet-heart—

HAROLD: Ah's a mite tired . . .

GEORGE (*Under* NUMBER ONE.): Dance, dance, dance, mother, dance, mother, dance! (*Etc.*)

NUMBER ONE (*Screaming under his sheet.*): Dance me, kiss me, hug me— (*He and* GEORGE *lurch together, meeting around* HAROLD, *and bear him off the table, his head protruding over their white-sheeted mass.*) Squeeze me, hold me, choke me . . . (*They dance* HAROLD *round the table and finally cast him to the floor. Breathless,* GEORGE *and* NUMBER ONE *step back. Then* NUMBER ONE *speaks.*) Hey, white nigger, are you fallin' down on the job?

HAROLD: Can't I rest a minute, boss?

NUMBER ONE: Dance, nigger! (HAROLD *struggles up and continues dancing.*) You can rest tomorrow—

HAROLD (*Dancing.*): Tomorrow?

NUMBER ONE: I know that seems far away to your primitive heart, but it'll come—if you keeps us entertained—

HAROLD (*Dancing harder.*): You won't do anything—else?

NUMBER ONE: Now, Harold, you don't think George and I would harm a nigger, do you? There are so few left—and you're so authentic—

HAROLD: Yassuh . . .

GEORGE: One of nature's noblemen, but he doesn't dance very well—

NUMBER ONE: Well, there's always the freak that ain't born with it—

HAROLD: God bless you, boss.

NUMBER ONE: George, I think we've taught this nigger a lesson. Should we let him dance his way home?

HAROLD: Kin ah go now, boss?

NUMBER ONE: "If he hollers, let him go."

GEORGE: Sure, back to his soft pad, to laugh us off—

NUMBER ONE: You gonna laugh, dancin' boy?

HAROLD: Please, let me stop—my chest—

NUMBER ONE: Are you gonna dance over to the maternity ward and tell your groovy wife all about it? Man, she'll laugh so hard she'll strain her milk—especially over what a good dancin' nigger you turned out to be—

HAROLD: She wouldn't laugh—

NUMBER ONE: And she'd think you were much man, too, wouldn't she?

HAROLD: No, suh—

NUMBER ONE: No, Harold boy will keep this all to himself—after all, if he told people he was a secret nigger, they might break his lease. You won't be laughing, will you, nigger?

HAROLD: No, suh.

NUMBER ONE: Okay, *dance* over and pick up your laundry—oh, don't forget that tasty little brassiere. (HAROLD *obeys*.) If little mother asks about the hole in the cup—just say you got awful lonely while she was gone. (HAROLD *dances toward the door with his laundry. He looks to* NUMBER ONE *for final permission*.) Dance right out, boy—it's a free country. George, open the door for Harold—show him you're no bigot.

GEORGE (*Opening door*.): Sure. There's nothing I like better than helping a white nigger who knows his place. (HAROLD *starts to dance out*.)

NUMBER ONE: Oh, Harold . . . (HAROLD *freezes—there is no physical restraint preventing his escape*.) Aren't you going to say goodbye?

HAROLD: Goodbye.

NUMBER ONE: That's not a very warm farewell, Harold. Come on, one little farewell performance for your friends—you do still like us, don't you?

HAROLD: Like you?

NUMBER ONE: Us—us noble savages—us poor, downtrodden, Negro Americans—to the bottom of your dancing feet, you still love us, don't you?

HAROLD: I think Negroes are very—please let me go—my chest—

NUMBER ONE: Are very?

HAROLD: I respect Negroes—I sympathize with their goals—

NUMBER ONE: Harold, you play kiss-my-foot like you been playing it all your life. Ain't he a joy, George?

GEORGE: Yeah, he's an honor student— We can graduate him. (HAROLD *is about to collapse against the door frame. He could exit before they could stop him, but does not do so*.)

NUMBER ONE: Uh-unh, Harold, you can't sit this one out yet. (HAROLD *continues dancing*.) You've told us what you thought we

wanted to hear—that's nigger survival training . . . Now tell us the truth.

HAROLD: Please let me stop.

NUMBER ONE: Not till you've told the truth, Harold—for the sake of your white-nigger soul.

HAROLD: WHICH TRUTH DO YOU WANT?

NUMBER ONE: The truth about *inside* Harold Nigger—inside your gut—

GEORGE: How you wish *you* could lean on *us*—

HAROLD: I don't wish that—

GEORGE: How you wish you was eight feet tall, with steel-toe stompin' boots and nut-cracker fingers—how you'd like to crack some black nuts—

HAROLD: I wouldn't do that . . . Please—let me go—

NUMBER ONE: You couldn't *do*, boy, but how you can *wish* . . . wish you could cut us up, burn us down, tear us apart and scatter our seed—boy, you'd like to cut off our balls with a rusty beer can—but you know you'll never do it, because we beat you to the punch. Isn't that right—isn't it? The truth now, boy—you'd like to kill us, *right?*

HAROLD (*Stops dancing—rigid, shaking*.): Yes!

GEORGE: Halleluia, brother!

HAROLD: Yes, do to you what you've done to me! I'd like to rip your belly open with a razor blade—I'd like to cut your—

NUMBER ONE: Congratulations, Harold. You are now a classic, one-hundred-percent, pure-blooded nigger! Yes, you're one of the few perfect specimens left—a low-down, spineless nigger—all gut-hate on the inside and shuffling lick-spit on the outside—

GEORGE: The last of the red-hot niggers!

HAROLD (*Quivering, speaking with difficulty*.): I'd like to—

NUMBER ONE: To what, *nigger?*

HAROLD: To—to—I'd like to—

GEORGE: You got something to say, boy?

HAROLD: Nothing. Please—let me go home.

NUMBER ONE (*With a threatening step*.): Then move your ass out of here—

GEORGE (*With a step*.): Yeah, drag-ass—

NUMBER ONE: Back where you belong, nigger! (HAROLD *staggers out and is gone*. NUMBER ONE *shouting after him*.) And don't show your face around here again. (*A pause.*

GEORGE *and* NUMBER ONE *look at each other.* GEORGE *goes to the washer and removes* NUMBER ONE'*s things with the intention of putting them in the drier.*) Man, I'll bet he's really burning up the sidewalk —if he's got any wind left. What's the matter with you?

GEORGE: Let's cut, man.

NUMBER ONE: Hey, George, I'm still Number One, aren't I?

GEORGE (*Pause.*): Yeah . . .

NUMBER ONE: You don't sound too sure—

GEORGE: What we did—wasn't what we came for—

NUMBER ONE: Why, Georgie, I didn't know you were so bloodthirsty—

GEORGE: Don't shit me, Number One, we came to do a job but we just been playin' games.

NUMBER ONE: You think I let you down, is that it?

GEORGE: You said we were gonna get The Man. We didn't get him . . . and he wasn't The Man anyway.

NUMBER ONE: You've been thinkin' very hard . . .

GEORGE: He's just a sad-ass ofay loser.

NUMBER ONE: . . . and you're gonna strain your head if you don't stop it. (GEORGE *turns away peevishly and jams more laundry into the bag.*)

NUMBER ONE: That's the whole point, don't you dig? The Man *is* a loser. We opened him up and got inside him and there was nothing there—zero! We *got* him . . .

GEORGE: And let him off . . .

NUMBER ONE: No, he's gonna stay got—we're inside for good.

GEORGE: What if he was puttin' us on?

NUMBER ONE: Man, he couldn't be . . .

GEORGE: But if he was, he beat us one more time . . .

NUMBER ONE: George, you *saw* him—you can believe me . . .

GEORGE: You can talk, but you can't ever prove it was real.

NUMBER ONE: No one is that good an actor! Nobody . . . (*At this point, we become conscious of the flashing blue light of a police cruiser in the street.* GEORGE *and* NUMBER ONE *freeze, look at each other, move to the window and look down the street.*)

GEORGE: What are they doin'?

NUMBER ONE: I can't tell. Pick up the laundry quick. (*He steps out the front door as* GEORGE *moves swiftly to collect their things. In a moment,* NUMBER ONE *returns.*)

GEORGE: What's happenin'?

NUMBER ONE: Your worries are over, brother. He really *couldn't* hack it.

GEORGE: Who?

NUMBER ONE: Harold the Clean—he's out there on the sidewalk—they just pulled a sheet over his face.

GEORGE: You're kiddin' me . . .

NUMBER ONE: Right! I'm kiddin' you. Why don't you go ask the pig to pull the sheet back so you can see his face.

GEORGE: . . . Hey, did we do that, Number One?

NUMBER ONE (*Pointing where* HAROLD *would be.*): That?

GEORGE: Yeah . . .

NUMBER ONE: Yes, George, I think maybe we killed us a nigger.

GEORGE: . . . You know, he wasn't such a bad cat . . .

NUMBER ONE: Didn't I tell you? Lots of them aren't such bad cats—but that doesn't cut any ice, baby, does it?

GEORGE: Don't it?

NUMBER ONE: George, you're getting too complicated—you can't get your mind together. (GEORGE *has moved toward the window.*)

GEORGE: Hey, man, they're lookin' around. Let's make it outta here.

NUMBER ONE (*Revelation.*): I know what you need!

GEORGE: Let's go, man!

NUMBER ONE: But with dignity, George, with dignity. Get the stuff. (GEORGE *gets the laundry.* NUMBER ONE *puts the "Sorry, Tired Today" sign back on the washer.*)

NUMBER ONE: Yeah, I know what you need. (*They are moving toward the rear exit.*)

GEORGE: What?

NUMBER ONE: Let's you and I go out and find us a Number Three.

GEORGE: Yeah? (*They are exiting.*)

NUMBER ONE: Yeah. And a Number Four, and a Number Five, and a . . . (*They are off. Lights fade until only the blue flasher alternately reveals and hides the legend, "Sorry, Tired Today."*)

Notes on the Authors

ARTHUR ADAMOV (1908–1970) is of Armenian extraction but has lived in France most of his life and writes in French. His early plays, of which *All Against All* is an example, belong to the absurdist school; in his later work he has concentrated more on left-wing political polemics.

ARISTOPHANES (*c.* 445 B.C.–*c.* 385 B.C.) is possibly the only exception to Jean-Paul Sartre's dictum that no reactionary can be a great writer. Passionately opposed to the democratic and expansionist trend in Athenian politics, he wrote a series of brilliant, witty, and raucous comedies, satirizing what he considered the demagoguery and warmongering of the Athenian progressives. *Lysistrata* is his most famous and frequently revived play.

GEORG BÜCHNER (1813–1837) wrote two extremely significant plays in his short career: *Woyzeck* and *Danton's Death*. Both are so far ahead of their time that they still seem avant-garde today. Büchner is the most perfect example of a literary anachronism. He was, of course, not taken seriously in his own day.

ROGER CORNISH won the first prize in the Fifteenth Annual Playwriting Contest sponsored by Samuel French, Inc., with *Open Twenty-four Hours*.

NIGEL DENNIS (b. 1912) is known principally as one of England's outstanding drama critics. Nevertheless, he has written one other superb play besides the one included here. This is *The Making of Moo*, a satire on religion, the tone of which can be judged from one of Dennis's remarks in its preface: "When Garibaldi drew his teeth, the Pope awarded himself Infallible dentures as a consolation prize and began to gnash them bitterly."

FRIEDRICH DÜRRENMATT (b. 1921), together with Max Frisch, makes Switzerland the leading producer of outstanding playwrights in the world today. If we count Fritz Hochwälder, an Austrian permanently based there, as well, Switzerland is far ahead of her nearest competition. Dürrenmatt's work is marked by a detached, sardonic quality that is perfectly demonstrated in *Incident at Twilight*, which was originally written as a radio play.

EURIPIDES (480 B.C.–406 B.C.) was the maverick among the ancient Greek playwrights. In a sense he was the first playwright, since he was the first to write with the tastes of a majority of his audience in mind. As a result, he won very few prizes in the priest-controlled dramatic competitions, but his plays survived in greater numbers than those of any of his contemporaries.

ATHOL FUGARD lives and writes in South Africa, one of the few men in that country who has been able to speak intelligently on the race problem. He has written several other plays, one of which, *Boesman and Lena,* has been produced off-Broadway.

FRITZ HOCHWÄLDER (b. 1911) was born in Vienna but fled Austria with the coming of the Nazis. He is now a permanent resident of Switzerland, although he travels a great deal and was recently writer-in-residence at Oberlin College. *The Holy Experiment* was his first play and is still his most frequently revived one.

ALFRED JARRY (1873–1907) was an eccentric personality famous in the Bohemian circles of turn-of-the-century Paris. He was the founder of 'Pataphysics, the science of imaginary solutions, and is generally recognized as the founding father of the absurdist drama.

ANTONIO MARTÍNEZ BALLESTEROS (b. 1929) was born in Toledo, Spain, and still lives there. Almost entirely self-educated, he is a civil-service clerk writing plays in his very limited spare time, under conditions that would discourage most other men. To write plays in Spain today is to exhibit that quality that Hemingway so much admired in the Spaniards: grace under pressure.

MOLIÈRE (Jean Baptiste Poquelin, 1622–1673) ranks as one of the supreme geniuses of the comic art, along with Aristophanes, Shakespeare, and Jonson. A favorite of Louis XIV's, he was able to satirize a great many things with impunity in a society where there was little freedom of expression.

LEWIS NKOSI (b. 1936) was born in Durban, South Africa. He worked for a time on the Zulu-English weekly *Ilanga lase Natal* (*The Natal Sun*) and later as chief reporter on *The Golden City Post* in Johannesburg. He was awarded a Neiman Fellowship in Journalism at Harvard, and as a result, has been barred from returning to his homeland. This play is reputed to be the first since 1936 to be written in English by a black South African.

LUIGI PIRANDELLO (1867–1936) has been one of the most influential of modern dramatists as a result of his investigations into the nature of theatrical reality. His principal themes are the subjectivism of truth (there are as many truths as there are perceivers of it) and of identity (a man's nature is relative to time, place, and perceiver). For Pirandello, there is a myriad of realities, each equally important and valid.

JACK RICHARDSON (b. 1935) is perhaps America's most underrated young playwright. His *The Prodigal* is the finest modern version of the Orestes story, and his *Gallows Humor* is a clever and mordant adaptation of the morality-play form for contemporary purposes. He is also the author of *Lorenzo* and *Xmas in Las Vegas*, both of which failed on Broadway, though neither deserved to.

JOSÉ RUIBAL (b. 1925) is one of Spain's two or three best contemporary dramatists. Ironically, he is known in Spain only to a comparatively small circle of enthusiastic admirers as a result of his country's censorship policies. This situation is fortunately being slowly remedied, and he is gradually achieving the recognition he deserves. Several of his plays have been published in English in *Modern International Drama Magazine* and *The New Wave Spanish Drama*.

ARTHUR SCHNITZLER (1862–1931), like Freud, whose theories influenced him deeply, started his career as a physician. In his plays, he deals both with the pathology of character and with the decadence of Vienna, the city that has almost become a universal symbol for neurosis. *Round Dance* is still the most explicit statement in drama of sexual determinism.

WILLIAM SHAKESPEARE (1564–1616) was an English playwright who wrote tragedies, comedies, and chronicle plays. His plays are still frequently revived and there are annual festivals commemorating him in his native Stratford-on-Avon, in other towns named Stratford around the world, and in towns not named Stratford.

GEORGE BERNARD SHAW (1856–1950) holds an extremely high reputation as a playwright among those who feel that drama is not an art form to be enjoyed in a vacuum, but rather as a representation of the moral life of the community. Shaw saw the theater as a glorified lecture-hall and the drama as an art form whose purpose was to entertain in order to teach painlessly. Although his reputation is now undergoing the inevitable eclipse that always comes in the years immediately after a writer's death, at least one prominent critic has recently called him the greatest writer ever to put pen to paper in the English language.

9835

Wellwarth, George E   1932–   comp.
        Themes of drama; an anthology [by] George E. Well-
warth. New York, Crowell [1973]
        vii, 647 p. 24 cm.
        CONTENTS: Politics: Aristophanes. Lysistrata. Ballesteros,
A. M. The best of all possible worlds. Nkosi, L. The rhythm of
violence.—Society: Molière. The would-be gentleman. Richardson.
J. Gallows humor. Dürrenmatt, F. Incident at twilight.—Religion:
Euripides. The Bacchae. Everyman. Hochwälder, F. The holy
experiment.—Love: Shakespeare, W. Antony and Cleopatra.
Schnitzler, A. Round dance. Shaw, G. B. Mrs. Warren's profession.—Identity: Pirandello, L. Henry IV. Dennis, N. Cards of
identity. Ruibal J. The man and the fly. Fugard, A. The blood
knot.—Alienation: Büchner, G. Woyzeck. Jarry, A. King Ubu.
Adamov, A. All against all. Cornish, R. Open twenty-four hours.
        1. Drama—Collec-   tions.   I. Title.